RON SHANDLER's
Baseball Forecaster
2007
Legal in Every State Edition

Shandler Enterprises, LLC
Roanoke, VA

Copyright © 2006, Shandler Enterprises LLC

Shandler Enterprises LLC
P.O. Box 20303
Roanoke, VA 24018

Offices	540-772-6315
Fax	540-772-1969
Customer service	800-422-7820
E-mail	comments@baseballforecaster.com
Internet	http://www.baseballforecaster.com
	http://www.baseballhq.com
	http://www.rotohq.com
	http://www.firstpitchforums.com

Ron Shandler's Baseball Forecaster is intended for entertainment purposes only. Neither the author nor publisher assume any liability beyond the purchase price for any reason.

Shandler Enterprises LLC ("Publisher") creates the content of this book through extensive work. Financially, the Publisher can publish this book only if all users purchase a copy. Accordingly, by purchasing this book, you agree that you may not reproduce, resell, distribute, transmit, or display this book or any part of it for any commercial purpose, such as selling any part of the materials in this book or incorporating them into a Web site. You may not create derivative works based upon this book. The limitations in this paragraph apply not only to the Publisher's Intellectual Property, but also to any non-copyrightable information provided by this book. If you disagree, please return this book to the point of purchase for a refund.

Also, this Service contains material that is the copyright, trademark, service mark and trade dress property of the Publisher or of third parties who have licensed material to the Publisher (collectively, "Publisher's Intellectual Property"). The Publisher's Intellectual Property includes the following: logos, trademarks, service marks, photographs and other images, articles and columns, other text, graphics and illustrations, other artwork, unique names for statistical categories, formulas used for creating unique statistical categories, opinions expressed as to the meaning of statistical performance levels (e.g. benchmark analytical levels), the selection of statistics and information included within the Service (and the structure and sequence of it), and software. You may use this book for your personal use only, and the limitations in the first paragraph apply to Publisher's Intellectual Property.

Rotisserie League Baseball is a registered trademark of the Rotisserie League Baseball Association, Inc.

Statistics provided by Baseball Info Solutions.

Cover design by Jon Resh@Go-Undaunted.com
Front cover photograph courtesy of Corbis
Author photograph by Kevin Hurley

ISBN 1-891566-07-5
Printed in the United States of America

Acknowledgments

It goes something like this… Immediately following the last pitch of the regular season, we begin a 10-day period of intense number-crunching. Following this is three days of computer model fine-tuning and the official "spitting out" of the preliminary set of player pages. For the next two weeks, 10 of baseball's finest analysts pore over 900 player boxes, each containing 225 data points (that's 202,500 data points, for those scoring at home), and create pithy 40-word commentaries that capture the sum total of life, the universe and everything. (42.) Then there's another week of fine-tuning, page design and finally... much joy and merrymaking.

And that's just for the 100 pages of player boxes. Don't ask how the other 172 pages get done. I really don't know.

But I do know that none of this would happen without all the following amazing people…

First, the *Forecaster's* two editors Ray Murphy and Rod Truesdell. As this effort has grown over the years, it has gotten more and more difficult to keep everything moving forward while maintaining our high quality. This duo anchored the writing effort this year, and even went so far as to reject the Introduction — "Shandler, this stinks. Try again." (Thank goodness.)

Paul Petera once again led the number crunchers, and along with Mike Shears, Matt Dodge and Peter Sheridan, deftly handled far more than 202,500 pieces of data. (I lost count after half a million.)

Deric McKamey is now slumming in *Forecaster*-land now that he has his own book. But his contributions are vital for those of us who need to know who Troy Tulowitzki is. And how to spell his name.

Rick Wilton has also been branching out lately, first with BaseballInjuryReport.com and now, with his own book this winter. Injury analysis with a fantasy spin – where else can you get that?

John Burnson, Patrick Davitt, Doug Dennis and Brandon Kruse have been advancing the fanalytic discussion, and thankfully sharing their fine work with *Forecaster* and Baseball HQ readers.

Dave Adler, Harold Nichols, Stephen Nickrand, Tom Todaro and Jeffrey Tomich — the player analysts whose incredible work constitutes the foundation of this book.

Andy Andres, Neil Bonner, Hal Cohen, Jeremy Deloney, Rob Gordon, Brent Hershey, Phil Hertz, Gerald Holmes, Craig Kronzer, Scott Monroe, Frank Noto, Doug Ohlandt, Mark Padden, Josh Paley, Jay Pobis, Joshua Randall, Michael Sanderson, Skip Snow and Jock Thompson – the brain trust that makes BaseballHQ.com® the industry's #1 site for fantasy baseball analysis, bar none.

Matt Yonkovit, Mike Krebs and Rob Rosenfeld, our tech team, currently creating features on Baseball HQ that we never could have imagined just a few short years ago.

Lynda Knezovich, who keeps everything running so smoothly behind the scenes. Thanks soooo much!

Greg Ambrosius, Jeff Barton, Matthew Berry, Jim Callis, Don Drooker, Jeff Erickson, Brian Feldman, Jason Grey, Peter Kreutzer, Gene McCaffrey, John Menna, Lawr Michaels, Steve Moyer, Rob Neyer, Alex Patton, Peter Schoenke, Joe Sheehan, John Sickels, Perry Van Hook, Sam Walker, Brian Walton, Jeff Winick, Trace Wood and Todd Zola – These are baseball's top analysts and toughest fantasy players. And for me, valued colleagues and friends.

A special thanks to Carlos Beltran, whose called third strike bought me five additional evenings of work time.

"Behind every great man is a great woman." Though I'd never consider myself great, I *am* blessed to have three great women who support me. High school sophomore Darielle looks to be following in her old man's footsteps as she landed a writing gig this fall with the local newspaper. Justina staged an impressive campaign in winning the election for student government president to put the icing on her middle school career. And Sue has shown the epitome of "character" this year, racking up mega-frequent flier miles providing support to her extended family.

And as always, I am eternally grateful to every one of you who've purchased this book over the past 21 years. Though I still get rattled when strangers refer to me as "that fantasy baseball guy," I wouldn't have it any other way.

CONTENTS

I	**WATCH**	1
II	**FANALYTICS**	
	Foundation Principles	7
	Forecaster's Toolbox	9
	Research Abstracts	23
III	**GAMING**	
	Advanced Strategies	38
	New Gaming Formats	39
	Gaming Abstracts	41
IV	**MAJOR LEAGUES**	
	The Teams	55
	The Batters	60
	The Pitchers	113
	PQS Pitching Logs	162
	Bullpen Indicators	170
	Health Conditions	175
V	**MINOR LEAGUES**	
	Top Prospects for 2007	181
	Major League Equivalents	184
VI	**RATINGS, RANKINGS, CHEAT SHEETS**	227
VII	**SABERMETRIC TOOLS**	
	One Glossary	247
	The Other Glossary	249
	Cheaters Bookmark	253
VIII	**Blatant Advertisements for Our Other Products**	259

"Life is a battle between faith and reason in which each feeds upon the other, drawing sustenance from it and destroying it."
— Reinhold Niebuhr

WATCH

We often make decisions based on incomplete information. Most of them are inconsequential, like grabbing the first open parking spot even though there may be another one much closer to the store. On a more relevant level, we might grab Jason Bay at a buck or two over value without knowing that Matt Holliday would go for $5 under in the next round.

Life's tough that way. But we aren't always privy to the best possible information when we need to make these decisions. Sometimes the effort to get that information is not worth the cost of potential opportunities lost. The time spent searching for a closer parking spot — which might not exist — could mean we get to the store after it closes. Had we waited for Holliday and stayed in the bidding, his eventual owner might have stayed in as well, pushing the price above what we paid for Bay.

There are some things you simply do not know, cannot prove and sometimes have to take on faith. Often, that is all we have to go on when there is a need to make a decision or form an opinion. However, if you have at least a little bit of fact and a bunch of observation, sometimes that is enough.

Oftentimes, that has to be enough. There are decisions that have to be made. Jason Bay at $2 over value or the unknown of Matt Holliday? Decide!

* * *

There is a new tool in my personal fanalytic arsenal.

I call it the **W**ide **A**ccess **T**otal **C**ognizance **H**elmet. *(There is another model called the Baseball Insider Total Cognizance Helmet, but it costs much more and provides very annoying results.)* The WATCH is a piece of bright yellow headgear with built-in, fog-coated, impact-resistant amber goggles for the ultimate in perfectly colored viewing. This new tool provides a revolutionary take on reality.

When you strap on the WATCH, it gives you three perspectives on everything you look at: face value, decomposition and truth.

Face value is what things appear to be, sans analysis or speculation; just what is seen by the naked eye.

Decomposition breaks down face value into component observations and then reassembles them into a variety of configurations. This allows us to analyze and speculate, though it does not judge the merits of any conclusions drawn. Some may see this as an opportunity for cynicism to seep in. As a devout cynic, I don't have a problem with that. We need to be able to see all alternate realities.

Truth is truth, though it is the one view where the lens is the thickest. As such, it is the most difficult to see.

While you never really know which perspective is real — and on very rare occasion, all views are the same — the WATCH is the only tool that allows you to open your eyes to all three possibilities. Then it's up to you to choose.

The bottom line is that you have to form your own opinions and make your own decisions. The WATCH is just another tool to help you.

How does it work? Helmets and goggles in place? Good.

WATCH: Quack
Face value: It looks like a duck.
Decomposition: We could conduct DNA testing to determine beyond a shadow of a doubt that this small waterfowl with a flat bill and webbed feet is a duck. However, if it looks like a duck and quacks like a duck, then odds are it is a duck.
Truth: It's a freakin' duck.

WATCH: Who Needs Facts?
Face value: Dear Mr. Shandler: "Steroid use is a serious accusation. If you want to titter about what anonymous know-nothings are whispering, knock yourself out — it's your prerogative. However, if your facts consist of nothing more than otherwise explainable statistical trends and rumor-mongering, you're going to find your credibility severely strained."
Decomposition: Accusation, speculation, call it whatever you want. It impacts how I do my job of projecting player performance, so it is important to me. However, I am willing to poll my readers for their opinion. When I did this last February, I expected that the results would look something like this:

50% - There's not enough info to draw conclusions. Do nothing.
10% - Educated speculation is okay. Make some adjustments.
10% - Give me names. I'll decide what to do with them.
30% - I am sick of the steroids hysteria. Stop writing about it.

Truth: The actual results looked like this:

17% - There's not enough info to draw conclusions. Do nothing.
40% - Educated speculation is okay. Make some adjustments.
32% - Give me names. I'll decide what to do with them.
11% - I am sick of the steroids hysteria. Stop writing about it.

Nearly three quarters of you are content to pass judgment at some level based on appearance and audible quackery of baseball's bulked-up waterfowls.

Well, all-righty then. Some of my reluctance to embrace this in the past was a fixation on providing firm data. How many players are using? Who in particular? What has been the impact on these players' statistics? But apparently we don't need to know beyond a shadow of a doubt. It is not important how much impact performance enhancing drugs may or may not have had. All that is important is enough information for us to suspect some aquatic tendencies. This is gonna be fun!

WATCH: Drug Busts
Face value: There is only good news to report. After a difficult 2005 season where a dozen major league players were suspended for illegal steroid use, a stricter drug policy was enacted. In 2006, only three "Major League" players failed a drug test — Mets pitchers Yusaku Iriki and Guillermo Mota, and Arizona dealer Jason Grimsley.

Whether the new policy served as an effective deterrent, or the ballplayers decided to clean up on their own, the bottom line is that fewer players failed drug testing. You might say that Bud Selig has effectively cleaned up the sport by 75% in one short year. The lack of comment or action by MLB or the media seems to point to the fact that illegal performance enhancing drugs (PED's), including amphetamines, are no longer a problem. Nothing to the contrary has come out of the media, right?

Decomposition: Where *is* the media? Grimsely was nailed for using and supplying human growth hormones and the most we got was a page 37 note that his salary had been donated to charity. Why were the high profile names that might have been connected, like Albert Pujols and Roger Clemens, mentioned briefly and then never again? Why was Mota conveniently outed *after* the post-season? And who the heck is Yusaku Iriki?

There are too many disconnected events and no attempt to put the pieces together. With the lack of transparency in the testing policy, we never know what's really going on. Is MLB waiting for the Mitchell report? Is the underlying directive to protect any threat to the integrity of the game, even at the expense of truth? Or is the public too distracted by non-stories like the Fall of A-Rod to care any more?

Truth: There is no truth yet; there is only noise.

WATCH: Greenies

Face value: From the *Washington Post*... "There has been little measurable evidence of amphetamine testing having a quantifiable effect on the game." *(August 28, 2006)*

Decomposition: How's this? Is it possible that relief pitchers who rack mega-IP in one year might not be as resilient without an extra boost in year #2? There were 13 that resided in the upper marshes in 2005. Their numbers:

	2005			2006		
	IP	ERA	BPV	IP	ERA	BPV
Rafael Betancourt	67	2.81	138	57	3.86	95
Jesse Crain	79	2.73	27	76	3.77	93
Tom Gordon	80	2.58	83	58	3.09	105
Bob Howry	73	2.47	100	76	3.24	101
Ryan Madson	87	4.14	85	132	5.84	41
Gary Majewski	86	2.93	59	71	4.61	44
Chad Qualls	79	3.30	78	86	4.03	42
Juan Rincon	77	2.45	121	72	3.01	105
Duaner Sanchez	82	3.73	68	54	2.65	67
Scot Shields	91	2.76	113	87	3.07	99
Mike Timlin	80	2.25	95	64	4.26	35
Salomon Torres	94	2.77	54	91	3.38	60
Todd Williams	76	3.31	45	58	4.77	12

Of the 13 pitchers...
- Nine (69%) saw a decline in their BPV.
- Ten (77%) pitched fewer innings.
- Twelve (92%) saw a rise in their ERA.

But we are not branding all these pitchers as being web-footed (well, maybe a *few* proven quackers). These are just a group of players who we suspected *could* have been impacted by discontinuing the use of amphetamines.

Pitchers who fit the profile for 2007? Scott Proctor, Hector Carrasco, Brad Hennessey, Julian Tavarez, Jeremy Affeldt, Fernando Nieve, Brad Halsey, Salomon Torres, Oscar Villarreal, Jon Rauch, Geoff Geary and Chad Qualls.

Truth: Normal regression to the mean, the gravity principle and a host of other typical statistical processes could easily explain away this group.

But so could removing amphetamines from the equation.

WATCH: Sammy Speaks

Face value: From ESPN... Sammy Sosa, contemplating a return to baseball in 2007, would like to end the speculation that steroid use played a part in his impressive career slugging statistics. Sosa told the *Chicago Tribune*: "I am clean, and I always have been clean. There has been a lot of speculation, but they don't have no evidence. So you take it from there."

Decomposition: If it wasn't the steroids, then maybe it was the corked bats? The precedent has already been set for his propensity to cheat. As for "they don't have no evidence," doesn't that mean they *do* have evidence?

Truth: This 39-year-old is already taking the Steve Carlton Path to Retirement. If he comes back and surpasses 2005's sub-par 14-HR, .221 performance, PED use will be suspected. If he falls short of those levels, he'll be seen more as pitiable than vindicated. This is a no-win situation.

WATCH: Brown Hand Disease

Face value: Kenny Rogers had some type of foreign, brown, pine-tarish substance on his hand during Game 2 of the World Series. And during an earlier playoff series. And in games during the summer.

Rule 8.02 of the Official Baseball Rules: The pitcher shall not
(a) (1) bring his pitching hand in contact with his mouth or lips while in the 18 foot circle surrounding the pitching rubber. EXCEPTION: Provided it is agreed to by both managers, the umpire prior to the start of a game played in cold weather, may permit the pitcher to blow on his hand. PENALTY: For violation of this part of this rule the umpires shall immediately call a ball. However, if the pitch is made and a batter reaches first base on a hit, an error, a hit batsman or otherwise, and no other runner is put out before advancing at least one base, the play shall proceed without reference to the violation. Repeated offenders shall be subject to a fine by the league president.
(2) expectorate on the ball, either hand or his glove;
(3) rub the ball on his glove, person or clothing;
(4) apply a foreign substance of any kind to the ball;
(5) deface the ball in any manner; or

According to the penalties set forth in the Official Baseball Rules, "For violation of any part of Rules 8.02(a)(2) through (5): The pitcher shall be ejected immediately from the game and shall be suspended automatically for 10 games."

However, at the bottom of the 'penalties' section is the following disclaimer:

If a pitcher violates either Rule 8.02(a)(2) or Rule 8.02(a)(3) and, in the judgment of the umpire, the pitcher did not intend, by his act, to alter the characteristics of a pitched ball, then the umpire may, in his discretion, warn the pitcher in lieu of applying the penalty.

Decomposition: Well, it *seems* like Rogers cheated but got a pass. Tony LaRussa didn't want to press the issue because of his friendship with Jim Leyland and the possibility that his own pitchers might have something to hide. MLB didn't want to take anything away from a World Series match-up with already low TV ratings. Of course, the rules disclaimer essentially makes this a non-issue... but then you have to question the credibility of an umpire that would allow this seemingly clear violation to slide.

The bigger question for fantasy leaguers is, will there be

any more mulligans for Rogers in 2007? He's been exceeding our BPIs for awhile now. If the Pine Tar Police crack down on him, will he experience the massive regression we've been expecting? Or will we just start seeing an outbreak of Brown Hand Disease on pitching mounds all across ballparks this summer?

Truth: According to the articulate Jim Leyland: "Let's not chew yesterday's breakfast."

I don't own a Leyland-to-English dictionary, but I think it means one of the following:
- The pancakes are cold and no longer edible.
- All past infractions have already been digested.
- It's okay to break the rules once they start serving lunch.
- The only way to fix the problem is to eat the sausage whole.

WATCH: The New Coors Effect

Face value: For five months out of Coors Field's 12 year history (April-August 2006), this stadium played as a veritable pitcher's park. For the other 67 months, it was the most extreme hitter's park in the history of the sport.

Decomposition: Okay, it was the humidor, at least until they ran out of all the pre-treated balls at the end of August. But this entire humidor issue is unsettling. It sets two dangerous precedents:

1. Teams can play by different rules. This is not entirely a precedent. After all, 14 out of baseball's 30 teams use a designated hitter. Each team plays their home games in ballparks of varying dimensions. But the humidor puts an isolated variable into the hands of a single team. *That's* unsettling. What's next — orange baseballs in Oakland?

2. Altering the baseball is okay. Ahhh... Suddenly Kenny Rogers doesn't seem like such a villain anymore. Perhaps Rule 8.02 doesn't apply directly, but they are sure walking a very thin line here, aren't they?

There have been recent murmurs that MLB might be willing to level the playing field and allow any team to treat their baseballs in a humidor. But would that really be leveling the field?

Let's say I owned a team that played in an extreme pitcher's park — say, San Diego — and I "humidored" all my balls. I might be tempted to trade off every one of my power bats for groundball pitchers and speedy singles hitters. While we'd "small ball" the opposition into submission, all of *their* sluggers would be lofting easy fly outs. It would be a real-life application of Rotisserie's Sweeney Plan!

Truth: Frankly, I'm getting tired of trying to find the truth in all this. There are two schools of thought when it comes to how Coors will play in 2007. The first school says that it will revert to pre-2006 levels. The other school disagrees and has challenged the first school to a rumble in the parking lot after seventh period.

WATCH: Just Another Maris Run

Face value: The beginning of baseball's "post-steroid" era started with...
- Chris Shelton hitting 9 HRs in his first 13 games.
- Albert Pujols on pace for 79 HRs on June 1
- Ryan Howard making a late run at 61 HRs.

Decomposition: What better way to turn around the public's perception of baseball's credibility than with some good, old-fashioned home run chases? In 1998, MLB discovered that such a media event could cure all its ills. If nothing else, it takes the focus off Barry Bonds and reinforces the fact that professional ballplayers don't need artificial substances in order to hit home runs.

However, if Rogers' crime can be ignored and humidored baseballs are all the rave, perhaps there is no real sanctity to "the ball." MLB has retooled the manufacturing process before; who's to say that some tightly wound numbers didn't find their way to Philly this summer? Perhaps the real PED problem is not one of biology but of engineering!

Truth: The beginning of baseball's "post-steroid" era ended with...
- Chris Shelton hitting 7 HRs in his next 119 games.
- Albert Pujols missing a month and hitting *only* 49 HRs
- Ryan Howard getting pitched around to 58 HRs

...and the public generally losing interest in Barry Bonds. That was the intent all along, wasn't it?

WATCH: A New Truth

Face value: No player in the history of Major League Baseball has ever posted the type of performance numbers that Barry Bonds has at his age. The same can be said for Roger Clemens. Neither has ever failed a drug test. Yet, grand jury leaks, circumstantial evidence and best-selling books have already convicted Bonds in the court of public opinion. Apparently, Clemens holds more iconic status so nobody would dare investigate *him*. But his performance at age 44 is no less remarkable or worthy of question.

Decomposition: While the percentage of players using PED's has been cited at anywhere from 0% to 85%, most analysts believe that the true percentage is probably somewhere under 30%. *That's still as many as 360 players.*

If we were to speculate as to which ones are most likely taking these undetectable PEDs, the first place we'd *naturally* look is to those players who are doing things that are... um, *unnatural*. That's why we went through last year's exercise of correlating sudden weight gain with sudden performance spikes. It was not scientific; weight data is sketchy; correlations were not perfect. Still, it provided another data point to evaluate, and some of the specimens continue to support the assertions.

Could Roger Clemens be swimming with the waterfowl? If he is, he's been doing a good job of it and will likely keep on paddling. If he's not, we'll just have to relent to being in awe. In either case, *the numbers don't change*.

Truth: MLB has successfully filtered out the careless 0.75% of players who would get caught by drug testing. What's left are those players who either aren't using or are successfully beating the system. Those who are beating the system will likely continue to beat the system.

What this means is that every player now resides in his own personal reality. Each set of natural or unnatural stats represents what we have to consider to be a new truth.

Still, as long as we are living in wetlands that have become huge breeding grounds for Anas Platyrhynchos, it's not a bad idea to keep your guard up. And your helmet on.

Welcome to the 21st Edition of the *Baseball Forecaster*. We are now officially "of age" and can legally partake in alcoholic beverages in every major league ballpark.

As it is with all great inventions, this book was an accident; a well-timed collision of sabermetrics and fantasy. It is equally embraced and shunned by the two schools. Neither wants to be seen slumming with the other; we accommodate both groups by shipping the book in a plain unmarked envelope.

If you purchased the *Forecaster* in a bookstore, out in public where people could see you, I am in awe of your courage. I could never do that. Sabermetricians would laugh at me ("Is that Shandler, the *fantasy guy?*"). Fantasy leaguers are no less virulent ("Is that Shandler, the *stat geek?*"). Thank goodness for anonymous chat rooms.

The unique, hybrid brand of analysis that we perpetrate here is what we call **fanalytics**. Fanalytics is a measured, deliberate approach to evaluating and projecting player performance within the context of fantasy baseball. It takes from both schools and provides deeper insight than any other analytical process. Sabermetrics becomes more than just a bunch of incomprehensible formulas, and fantasy becomes more than just blindly picking a bunch of players and praying.

But we're still perceived as radicals because we tout courses of action that are counter-intuitive. There are very thin lines that separate genius from eccentricity and even dementia. For us, perhaps the only difference is that our recommendations are too often on target.

New Readers – Welcome!

The *Baseball Forecaster* was the first book to approach prognostication by breaking performance down into its component parts. Rather than predicting batting average, for instance, we look at the elements of skill that make up that stat — a batter's ability to distinguish between balls and strikes, his propensity to make contact with the ball, and what happens after he makes contact — and reverse-engineer those skills back into batting average. This process has proven itself as being a better predictor than any quantitative model using the actual gauges themselves.

In all, we call this "component skills analysis."

You should know that there is some rudimentary math involved and there is a bit of a learning curve. The nice thing about the math, though, is that most of it is logical and intuitive. For instance, when we talk about "contact rate," that's just the percentage of time a batter makes contact with the ball. It is calculated simply as $((AB - K) / AB)$. As you would expect, the more contact a batter makes, the higher his batting average tends to be. We have benchmarks at the upper and lower ends of the scale — 70% and 90% — and we can project a player's batting average off of that.

And the pieces all fit together very neatly in the end.

Naturally, I think this approach is the best way to evaluate and project performance, but I'll let you decide for yourself. I do ask, however, that you keep an open mind. These tools do work, but you may have to toss away some of your preconceptions in order to embrace the possibilities.

How to Use This Book

The place to start your journey is in the next section, **Fanalytics**. It is here that you will discover our foundation principles as well as all the research results we use to draw conclusions about player performance. It contains the core concepts for this book.

Then take a quick scan through the two **Sabermetric Glossaries** in the back of the book. One is for beginners, the other contains more advanced concepts. You don't need to memorize anything, but you should know where to go in case you run across something unfamiliar.

The meat of the book is the **Batter** and **Pitcher** sections. Here, there is a brief commentary for each player that provides an overall evaluation of performance and likely future direction. These are written by humans, just like you. Your greatest value will be to use them as a springboard to your own analysis of the data. Odds are, if you take the time, you'll find hidden indicators that we might have missed. *Forecaster* veterans say that this self-guided excursion is the best part of owning the book.

Some people buy this book for the projected statistics alone, and then live and die by them. That's a mistake. It's like going to a ballgame, being given a choice of any seat in the park, and deliberately choosing the last row in the right field corner with an obstructed view. The projections are there, you can look at them, but there are so many better places to sit. We have to publish those numbers, but performance is highly variable. Best to treat them as general expectations, not as gospel.

The rest of the book provides invaluable support information, from pitcher logs and bullpen indicators to the extensive minor league coverage and gaming sections. We've got major league equivalent statistics, fantasy cheat sheets, a closer volatility analysis and much more.

There's a ton of information here. At first glance, it will seem overwhelming. But you don't have to take it in all at once. Start slow; take as much time as you need.

What's New?

1. Expected home runs: John Burnson did some research that allows us to better approximate how many home runs a batter should hit based on the distribution of his extra base hits. These estimates appear in each batter box.

2. League base performance indicators: Last year, we added team pages but neglected to provide the baselines on a league level. Those have been added this year.

3. Gaming research: The past few years, we tucked the gaming content in the back of the book, a subconscious acquiescence to sabermetricians. This year, it's up front and beefed up with more gaming strategy insights, including a comprehensive look at the trends that shape our games.

4. Updated formulas: There has been some fine-tuning of formulas like xBA and XERA. The current versions appear in the advanced glossary. Note that all data have been updated so these values may not tie out with what appears in previous editions of this book.

5. More rankings: There are lots of new goodies in this section. I'll let you discover them on your own.

Important Notes
Notes and clarifications that may come in handy…

1. We continue to tinker with the formula for Reliability Scores. This year's version goes further than any of the previous iterations in separating the "haves" from the "have-nots." This will be most evident with pitchers; there is a much steeper drop-off in reliability and many more single-digit scores than we've ever had.

2. Our statistical database at Baseball HQ has grown tremendously in the past year. Although we do not have room in this book to include all the new cuts, our analysts will occasionally add tidbits to the player commentaries that do not appear in the boxes. You may see things like monthly BPI splits, OPS handedness splits, etc. All of this, and more, will be available at Baseball HQ in 2007.

3. You'll note that there is an increased focus on in-season analysis. While I know you use the *Forecaster* primarily as a draft tool, we have done a good amount of recent research on running your teams *during* the season and thought it appropriate to share some of that in this edition.

4. In the week before we went to press, there was some important player news not included in the book. Most notable was the posting of several Japanese players. We decided to remove three player boxes and replace them with Daisuke Matsuzaka, Akinori Iwamura and Kei Igawa. The players we removed were D'Angelo Jimenez, Sun Woo Kim and Phil Hughes, although their projections were retained for the ranking lists in the back of the book.

5. Finally, we also went to press with the expectation that Jeff Bagwell and Sammy Sosa would not be factors in 2007; apparently, that may not be the case. If necessary, we'll add them to the projections for the free March update.

Updates

Content Update page: If there are any corrections or clarifications on the information in this book, they will be posted at www.baseballforecaster.com/bfupdates.shtml.

Free Projections Update: As a buyer of this book, you get one free 2007 projections update, available online only, at BaseballForecaster.com. These are text and spreadsheet data files, to be posted on or about March 1, 2007.

Electronic book: The complete PDF version of the *Forecaster* – plus MS Excel versions of most key charts – is available free to those who bought the book directly through Shandler Enterprises. These files will be available in February 2007; contact us if you do not receive information via e-mail about accessing them. If you purchased the *Forecaster* through an online vendor or bookstore, you can purchase these files from us for $8.95. Call 1-800-422-7820 for more information.

Beyond the *Forecaster*

The *Forecaster* is just the beginning, The following companion products and services are described in more detail in the back of the book.

BaseballHQ.com is our primary website. It provides regular updates to everything in this book, plus a ton more. In 2007, we'll have *daily* updated projections all season long and robust new tools for managing your teams.

First Pitch Forums are a series of conferences we run all over the country, where you can meet some of the top industry analysts and network with fellow fantasy leaguers. In 2007, we'll be back in Chicago and Milwaukee, we'll be making our annual East Coast swing from DC to Boston, and are currently working out the logistics to make stops in SoCal and the Bay area for the first time.

RotoHQ.com is the largest library of fantasy strategy essays and tools known to man. And woman.

Graphical Player, the fourth edition of John Burnson's book, provides Forecaster-style data and more, in a series of insightful graphs and charts. *Available now.*

Minor League Baseball Analyst, the second edition of Deric McKamey's book, is a minor league version of the Forecaster, with stat boxes for over 1000 prospects, and more. *Available in January.*

Baseball Injury Report is a new book from injury analyst Rick Wilton. It includes complete injury histories for hundreds of players, 5-year disabled list stats, medical primer, 2007 prognoses and more. *Available in February.*

How to Value Players for Rotisserie Baseball, Art McGee's ground-breaking book on valuation theory is being expanded and updated for this 10th anniversary reprint. *Available in January.*

RotoLab is the best draft software on the market, and not just because it comes bundled with our player projections. It's a terrific tool for those who use laptops on Draft Day.

Fantasyland, by Sam Walker, is a fun read about the bizarre world in which I live. The book tracks a Rotisserie neophyte's quest to win Tout Wars. The paperback edition hits bookstores in February.

Most folks will find one or more of these supplemental products of interest to them, whether they are a fantasy leaguer, sabermetrician or general fan. But more important is that you already own the 272-page tome that's currently in your hands. It's time to turn the page. I've often been told that once you turn this page, the baseball season officially begins.

Good luck to your teams in 2007!

— *Ron Shandler*

II.
FANALYTICS

Read "The Great Myths of Projective Accuracy"
http://www.baseballforecaster.com/myths.shtml

Foundation Principles

Forecasting is the systematic process of determining likely end results. Baseball, as in most disciplines, uses some type of quantitative analysis in this process.

Baseball performance forecasting is inherently a high-risk exercise with a very modest accuracy rate. This is because the process involves not only statistics, but also unscientific elements, from random chance to human volatility. And even from within the statistical aspect there are multiple elements that need to be evaluated, from skill to playing time to a host of external variables.

Projections of playing time can be an exercise in futility. Beyond the small group of players who have guaranteed jobs each year, there are hundreds of others whose roles change frequently. Injuries, ill-timed slumps and managerial whim can all impact a player's chances to put up AB and IP. This book does not attempt to tackle playing time. Rather than making arbitrary decisions about how roles will shake out, we focus on performance. The playing time projections presented here are merely to help you better evaluate each player's talent. Our online pre-season projections update provides more current AB/IP expectations based on how roles are being assigned.

Due to the abundance of all these variables, **baseball projections are prone to excessive noise.** For instance, projecting pitching wins requires the analysis and projection of not only the pitcher's skill, but the skills of his team's offense, defense, bullpen and the tendencies of his manager. *All* those variables must be projected.

Forecasting is not an isolated exercise that produces a single set of numbers. **Baseball forecasting is dynamic, cyclical and ongoing.** Conditions are constantly changing and we must react to those changes by adjusting our expectations. A pre-season projection is just a snapshot in time. Once the first batter steps to the plate on Opening Day, that projection has become obsolete. Its value to fantasy leaguers is merely to provide a starting point, a baseline for what is about to occur.

During the season, if a projection appears to have been invalidated by current performance, the process continues. It is then that we need to ask... What went wrong? What conditions have changed? In fact, has *anything* changed? We need to analyze the situation and revise our expectation, if necessary. This process must be ongoing.

Finally, the outcomes of forecasted events should not be confused with the process itself. Outcomes may be the components that are the most closely scrutinized, but as long as the process is sound, the forecast has done its job.

In the end, our brand of forecasting is more about finding logical journeys than shouting about blind destinations.

Component Skills Analysis

Familiar gauges like HR and ERA have long been used to measure skill. In fact, these gauges only measure the outcome of an individual event, or series of events. They represent statistical output. They are "surface stats."

Raw skill is the talent beneath the stats, the individual elements of a player's makeup. For batters, skill includes the ability to see and follow pitches, the ability to make contact with the ball and the ability to hit with authority. For pitchers, skill includes the ability to get the ball over the plate, the ability to fool or dominate hitters and the ability to prevent batted balls from being hit with authority. In order for us to get a better read on raw skill, we use formulas that contain relevant raw statistical categories.

Players use these skills to create the individual events that we record using measures like HR and ERA. Why are these events not skills unto themselves? In tracking a batter's home run trend, for instance, what we are really trying to track is his *power* skills. And power is comprised of not only HRs, but *every* event that displays a batter's power — doubles, triples, fly outs, and even long foul balls. Taking it a step further, power has really nothing to do with these *outcomes* at all but with the *distance* a batter hits the ball. Current research is working toward better analysis here.

Statistical output also includes the element of *random chance.* From the perspective of a round bat meeting a round ball, it may be only a fraction of an inch at the point of contact that makes the difference between a HR or a long foul ball. When a ball is hit safely, often it is only a few inches that separate a HR from a double. Yet we tend to neglect these facts in our analyses, although the outcomes — the doubles, triples, long fly balls — may be no less a measure of that batter's raw skill.

Random chance also includes those elements that are not intrinsically skills-based, but do affect a player's statistical output. These gauges measure elements beyond the control of the player and can include defense, bullpen or managerial decision, as well as the random bounce of the ball. In order for us to get a better read on random chance, we use formulas that capture the external variability of a player's numbers.

Why is all this important? Analysts complain about the lack of predictability of many traditional statistical gauges. The reason they find it difficult is that they are trying to project performance using gauges that are loaded with external noise. Raw skills gauges are more pure and follow better defined trends during a player's career. And as we get a better handle on random chance, we can construct a complete picture of what a player's statistics really mean.

The next step is to assemble these evaluators in such a way that they can provide a more accurate view of performance. By creating a structure, sequence and organization to these gauges, we can paint a picture that can be used to validate our observations, analyze their relevance and project a likely future direction.

The beauty of this process is it allows us to identify variances between statistical output and raw skill gauges, and from that, project changes in performance within a season or from one season to another. How it works...

In a perfect world, if a player's raw skills improve, then so should his statistical output. If his skills decline, then his stats should follow as well. But, sometimes a player's skill may increase while his surface stats may decline. These variances may be due to a variety of factors, from the performances of other players to random chance.

Component Skills Analysis is based on the philosophy that events tend to move towards universal order. This has been proven in other areas of baseball analysis... Players' performance tends to move towards their career averages, team W/L records tend to move towards their statistical levels. In stat-head circles, it's called "regression to the mean." These variances will correct themselves over time. Surface stats will eventually approach their raw skill levels. Gauges that measure random chance regress to the mean as well. And from this, we can identify players whose performance, as a whole, may change.

This process provides an important starting point for any forecasting analysis. For most of us, that analysis begins with the previous season's numbers. Last season provides us with a point of reference, so it's a natural way to begin the process of looking at the future.

Component skills analysis allows us to validate last year's numbers. A batter with few HRs but a high linear weighted power level has a good probability of improving his future HR output. A pitcher whose ERA was solid while his command ratio was poor is a good bet for an ERA spike.

Of course, these leading indicators do not always follow the rules. There are more shades of greys than blacks and whites in baseball analysis. When indicators are in conflict – for instance, a pitcher who is displaying both a rising strikeout rate and a rising walk rate – then we have to find ways to sort out what these indicators might be saying.

It is often helpful to look at leading indicators in a hierarchy, of sorts. In fact, a hierarchy of the most important pitching BPIs might look like this: command (k/bb), control (bb/9), dominance (k/9), GB/FB rate and opposition BA. For batters, contact rate might top the list, followed by power, walk rate and speed.

Assimilating Additional Research

Once we've painted the statistical picture of a player's potential, we then use additional criteria and research results to help us add some more color. These other criteria include the player's health, age, changes in role, ballpark, and a variety of other factors. We also use our *Forecaster's Toolbox* research results, which are described in the next section. These analyses look at things like traditional periods of peak performance and breakout profiles.

The final element of the process is assimilating the news into the forecast. This is the element that many fantasy leaguers tend to rely on most since it is the most accessible. However, it is also the element that provides the most noise.

Players, management and the media have absolute control over what we are allowed to know. Factors such as hidden injuries, messy divorces and clubhouse unrest are routinely kept from us, while we are fed red herrings and media spam. *We will never know the entire truth.*

And so... As long as we do not know all the facts, we cannot dismiss the possibility that any one fact is true. No matter how often the media assures it, deplores it, or ignores it. Don't believe everything you read; use your own judgment. If your observations conflict with what is being reported, that's powerful insight that should not be ignored.

Quite often, all you are reading is just other people's opinions... a manager who believes that a player has what it takes to be a regular, a team physician whose diagnosis is that a player is healthy enough to play. These words from experts have some element of truth, but cannot be wholly relied upon to provide an accurate expectation of future events. As such, it is often helpful to develop an appropriate cynicism for what you read.

For instance, if a player is struggling for no apparent reason, and there are denials about health issues, don't dismiss the possibility that an injury does exist. There are often motives for such news to be withheld from the public.

Also remember that nothing lasts forever in major league baseball. *Reality is fluid.* One decision begets a series of events that lead to other decisions. Any reported action can easily be reversed based on subsequent events. My favorite examples are announcements of a team's new bullpen closer. Those are about the shortest realities known to man.

We need the media to provide us with context for our analyses, and the *real* news they provide is valuable intelligence. But separating the news from the noise is difficult. In most cases, the only thing you can trust is how that player actually performs.

Embracing Imprecision

Precision and accuracy in baseball prognosticating is a fool's quest. There are far too many unexpected variables and noise that can render our projections useless. The truth is, the best we can ever hope for is to accurately forecast general tendencies and percentage plays.

However, even when you follow an 80% percentage play, for instance, you will still lose 20% of the time. Those 20% worth of outlying players are what skeptics like to use as proof that all prognosticators are frauds. HQ writer John Burnson once wrote: "The issue is not the success rate for one player, but the success rate for all players. No system is 100% reliable, and in trying to capture the outliers, you weaken the middle and thereby lose more predictive pull than you gain. At some level, everyone is an exception!"

The paradox, of course, is that fantasy league titles are often won or lost by those exceptions. Still, long-term success dictates that you always chase the 80% and accept the fact that you will be wrong 20% of the time. Or, whatever that percentage play happens to be.

For fantasy league purposes, playing the percentages can take on an even less precise spin. The best projections are often the ones that are just far enough away from the field of expectation to alter decision-making. In other words, it doesn't matter if I project Player X to bat .320 and he only bats .295 as long as everyone else projected .280.

Or, perhaps we should evaluate projections based upon their intrinsic value. For instance, coming into 2006, would it have been more important for me to tell you that Johan Santana was going to post a 3.00 ERA or that Bronson Arroyo was going to have a career-best sub-4.00 ERA? By season's end, the Santana projection would have been more accurate, but the Arroyo projection would have been more *valuable.*

And that should be enough. Actually, it *has* to be enough. Any tout who exactly projects any player's statistics dead-on will have just been lucky with his dart throws that day.

Forecaster's Toolbox

The following tools, rules and research findings represent the work of many authors. Much of our own research is here. There are works of other baseball analysts, including Baseball HQ writers. And of course, Bill James, who was the founding father of this type of research.

There are two types of information here. There are analytical tools, which are methods to put events and performances into context. And there are actual research results. Generally, we only include the results of each particular piece of research, rather than take up space with all the methodologies and minutia. The back-up data have appeared in our other publications and on Baseball HQ in the past. Our purpose here is to give you the tools you need to make evaluations, and quickly. So pardon the lack of support data. Rest assured we're not making this stuff up.

Be aware that these research findings represent tendencies, not absolutes. If we tell you that 96% of batters with eye ratios over 1.50 will hit over .250, don't send us hate mail if the former batting champion you drafted in the second round falls into the other 4%. It happens. It's not our fault. Consider this a universal disclaimer.

But beyond that, there is great value here. Consider this your own personal fanalytic arsenal.

Validating Overall Performance

Performance Validation Criteria

The following list of criteria helps us validate that a player's performance is "for real." When a player puts up numbers that vary from expectation, we can assemble a set of support variables that can help us determine whether his statistical output is an accurate reflection of his skills, or if other variables have come into play that have skewed the stats. Essentially, we're asking, is this performance a "fact or fluke?"

1. The player's age... Is he at the stage of development when we might expect a change in performance?

2. Health status... Is he coming off an injury, reconditioned and healthy for the first time in years, or a habitual resident of the disabled list?

3. Minor league performance... Has he ever shown the potential for greater things at some level of the minors? Or does his minor league history show a poor skill set that might indicate a lower skills ceiling?

4. Historical trends... Have his raw skill levels been on an upswing or downswing?

5. Hidden indicators behind traditional stats... Looking beyond batting averages and ERAs, what do his support ratios look like?

6. Change in ballpark, team, league... Pitchers going to Texas will see their ERA spike. Pitchers going to Petco Field will see their ERA improve. Stuff like that.

7. Change in team performance... Has a player's performance been affected by overall team chemistry or the environment fostered by a winning or losing club?

8. Change in batting stance, pitching style... Has a change in performance been due to an adjustment made during the off-season?

9. Change in usage, lineup position, etc.... Has a change in RBI opportunities been a result of moving further up or down in the batting order? Has pitching effectiveness been impacted by moving from the bullpen to the rotation?

10. Change in managerial strategy (opportunity)... Does his sudden change in performance have less to do with ability than with playing time, or perhaps not having a well-defined role?

11. Coaching effects... Has the coaching staff changed the way a player approaches his conditioning, or how he approaches the game itself?

12. Off-season activity... Has a player spent the winter frequenting workout rooms or banquet tables?

13. Personal factors... Has the player undergone a family crisis? Experienced spiritual rebirth? Given up red meat?

Skills Ownership

Once a player displays a skill, he owns it. That display could occur at any time – earlier in his career, back in the minors, or even in winter ball play. And while that skill may lie dormant after its initial display, the potential is always there for him to tap back into that skill at some point, barring injury or age. That dormant skill can reappear at any time given the right set of circumstances.

Caveat... The initial display of skill must have occurred over an extended period of time. An isolated 1-hit shut-out in Single-A ball amidst a 5.00 ERA season is not enough. The shorter the display of skill in the past, the more likely it can be attributed to random chance. The longer the display, the more likely that any re-emergence of that skill is for real. Typically, you'd want to see a consistent level of performance over at least a several month period.

Corollaries:

1. Once a player displays a vulnerability or skills deficiency, he owns that as well. That vulnerability could be an old injury problem, an inability to hit breaking pitches, or just a tendency to go into prolonged slumps.

2. The probability of a player addressing and correcting a skills deficiency declines with each year he allows that deficiency to continue to exist.

Categories of Surprises

When a player has an uncharacteristically good or bad season, it is helpful to characterize that performance to determine its likelihood of being repeated. By answering a question such as, "Was Bronson Arroyo's 2006 breakout a career year, maturation, or aberration?" we can start the process of projecting what he is likely to do in 2007.

Career year: These are players who have established a certain level of performance over several years, then suddenly put up exceptional numbers. Career years may be explained from the list of validation criteria, but are usually one-shot deals.

Maturation: These players have also established a certain level of performance over time, but the performance spike is truly indicative of their potential and will likely be maintained.

Off year: These are players who have established a certain level of performance over several years, then suddenly drop off. This could be a performance blip, an adjustment period or an injury-induced decline. These players have the potential to bounce back.

Comedown: These players have also established a certain level of performance over time, but their performance drop is indicative of a new level at which they will likely plateau. The typical 30something syndrome.

Opportunity: Sometimes a surprise isn't a change in performance at all but the effect a change in playing time has on performance. Often, a role player gets thrust into a full-time job and suddenly puts up extraordinary numbers. This can work both ways — a player may rise to the occasion, or find that the regular day-to-day grind has an adverse effect on his numbers. Opportunity surprises are created by events like injuries or changes in managerial strategy and can last as long as the opportunity lasts.

No surprise: We sometimes form unrealistic expectations about players due to media hype or short-term performance levels. Rookies fall into this category, for instance, but the success or failure of unproven commodities should not be unexpected. In addition, frequently injured players who've lowered our expectations, then bounce back to previous productivity levels when healthy, should not be surprises either (except, perhaps, that they managed to stay healthy).

Aberration: These are the performances that simply cannot be adequately explained by the validation criteria. Chance occurrences do happen, and sometimes in bunches. There are stretches in a player's career when a spray hitter might see a few week's worth of fat, juicy homer balls, or a pitcher might face a string of wiffle bats. It just happens, then it stops. Most times, it will never happen again.

Risk Management and Reliability Scores

Forecasts are constructed with the best data available, but there are factors that can impact the variability around that projection. One way we manage this risk is to assign each player a Reliability Score (Rel). The more certainty we see in a data set, the higher the potential reliability of the forecast. The following variables are evaluated:

Experience: The greater the pool of major league history to draw from, the greater our ability to construct a viable forecast. Length of service is important, as is length of consistent service. So players who bounce up and down from the majors to the minors are higher risk players. And rookies are all high risk.

Consistency: Consistent performers are easier to project and garner higher reliability scores. Players that mix mediocrity, or worse, with occasional flashes of brilliance generate higher risk projections.

Health: Players with an injury history — whether or not they are healthy now — will generate lower Rel scores.

Age: Players' skills develop and erode as they age. During the rise of that skills curve, as well as during their late career descent, their performance will be more prone to fluctuation, and hence, higher risk.

Burnout potential: For a pitcher, workload levels need to be monitored, especially in the formative years of his career. Exceeding those levels elevates the risk of injury, burnout, or breakdown.

The reliability scores are expressed on a scale of 0-100. A score of 100 would represent the following:

Batters
- Between 27 and 30 years of age
- Average min. 550 PA in MLB each of the past three years
- Spent no time on the DL over the past three years
- RC/G over the past three years was perfectly consistent

Starting Pitchers
- Between 28 and 31 years of age
- Averaged at least 200 MLB innings each of the past 3 years
- Spent no time on the DL over the past three years
- For pitchers currently 29 years or younger, did not pitch an excessive number of innings prior to age 25
- xERA over the past three years was perfectly consistent

Relief pitchers
Same criteria as starting pitchers with one exception:
- The total of IP plus (saves x 5) over the past three years averaged at least 200

The benchmark for acceptability is a score of 50. Any levels above this represent gradually increasing reliability (or gradually decreasing risk). Players with levels under 25 should generally be avoided, especially by the risk averse.

You'll note that relief pitchers have very low scores. This is by design since playing time is one of the elements that drive these scores. Just one bad outing can completely skew a stat line. Those with the higher scores are typically closers who've been consistent in that role over time.

Remember that these levels have nothing to do with *quality* of performance; they strictly refer to consistency and confidence in our expectations. So a Rel of 82 for Josh Fogg, for instance, only means that there is a high probability he will perform as poorly as we've projected.

April Performance as a Leading Indicator

We isolated all 2005 players who earned at least $10 more or $10 less than we had projected in March. Then we looked at the April stats of these players to see if we could have picked out the $10 outliers after just one month.

	No.	Identifiable in April	Pct.
Earned $10+ more than proj			
BATTERS	41	16	39%
PITCHERS	32	14	44%
Earned -$10 less than proj			
BATTERS	43	24	56%
PITCHERS	54	40	74%

Nearly three out of every four pitchers who earned at least $10 less than projected also struggled in April. For all the other 2005 surprises — batters or pitchers — April was not a strong leading indicator. Another look:

	April	Year	Pct.
Batters who finished +$25	44	20	45%
Pitchers who finished +$20	34	15	44%
Batters who finished under $0	42	25	60%
Pitchers who finished under -$5	60	47	78%

April surgers are less than a 50/50 proposition to maintain that level all season. Those who finished April at the bottom of the roto rankings were more likely to continue struggling, especially pitchers. In fact, if we selected only those pitchers who finished April with a roto value *under -$10,* an overwhelming 21 of 23 (91%) finished the season in the red. Holes are tough to dig out of.

Courtship Period

Any time a player is put into a new situation, he enters into what we might call a *courtship period*. This period might occur when a player switches leagues, or switches teams. It could be the first few games when a minor leaguer is called up to the majors. It could occur when a reliever moves into the rotation, or when a lead-off hitter is moved to another spot in the lineup. There is a team-wide courtship period when a manager is replaced. Any external situation that could have an effect on a player's performance sets off a new decision point in evaluating that performance.

During this courtship period, it is difficult to get a true read on how a player is going to ultimately perform. He is adjusting to the new situation. His teammates, or opponents, are adjusting to him. And things could be volatile during this time. For instance, a role change that doesn't work during this period could spur other moves. A rookie hurler might buy himself a few extra starts with a solid outing in his debut, even if he has questionable skills.

So... it is probably best not to make a decision on a player who is going through a courtship period. Wait until his statistics stabilize. Don't cut a struggling pitcher in his first few starts after a managerial change. Don't pick up a hitter who has just smacked a pair of home runs in his first game after having been traded.

Unless, of course, talent and track record say otherwise.

We play a tactical game, and it is important to take all variables into consideration before making moves.

Half-Season Fallacies

A popular exercise at the midpoint of each season is to analyze those players who are *consistent* first half to second half surgers or faders. There are several fallacies with this analytical approach.

1. Half-season consistency is rare. There are very few players who show consistent changes in performance from one half of the season to the other.

Research results from a three-year study conducted in the late-1990s: The total of all batters who compiled a minimum of 300 full season ABs, and a minimum of 150 first half ABs in this study was 98. Of that group, 40% demonstrated a consistent first half to second half trend in at least one statistical category for all three years. Only 18% demonstrated any half-season tendency in more than one category. And only 3% demonstrated consistent tendencies in more than two categories over the three-year period.

The total of all pitchers who compiled a minimum of 100 full season IPs, and a minimum of 50 first half IPs in this study was only 42. Of that group, 57% demonstrated a consistent first half to second half trend in at least one stat category for all three years. Only 21% demonstrated any half-season tendency in more than one category. And only 5% had consistent tendencies in more than two categories.

When the analysis was stretched to a fourth year, only 1% of all players showed consistency in even one category.

2. Analysts often use false indicators. Situational statistics provide us with tools that are often misused. Several sources offer up three and 5-year statistics intended to paint a picture of a long-term performance. Some analysts look at a player's half-season batting average swing over that multi-year period and conclude that he is demonstrating consistent performance.

The fallacy is that those multi-year scans may not show any consistency at all. They are not individual season performances but *aggregate* performances. A player whose 5-year batting average shows a 15-point rise in the 2nd half, for instance, may actually have experienced a BA *decline* in several of those years, a fact that might have been offset by a huge BA rise in one of the years.

3. It's arbitrary. The season's midpoint is really an arbitrary delineator of performance swings. Some players are slow starters and might be more appropriately evaluated as pre-May 1 and post-May 1. Others bring their game up a notch with a pennant chase and might see a performance swing with August 15 as the cut-off. Each player has his own individual tendency, if, in fact, one exists at all. There's nothing magical about mid-season as the break point, and certainly not over a multi-year period.

Contract Year Performance

There is anecdotal evidence that players tend to step up their game when they are playing for a new contract. Recent research looked at players in the last year of their contract, their performance during that year (as compared to their career levels) and whether they reverted to form in the first year of their new contract. Of the batters and pitchers studied, 53% of the batters performed as if they were on a salary drive, while only 15% of the pitchers managed to exhibit some level of contract year behavior.

Batting Toolbox

Batting Eye as a Leading Indicator

The raw ability to distinguish between balls and strikes — strike zone judgment — is a good descriptor of a batter's potential batting average, and in some cases, can be used as a rough predictor of future performance. Research findings:

There is a high correlation between a batter's eye ratio and his batting average:

Batting Eye	Batting Average				
	2002	2003	2004	2005	2006
0.00 - 0.25	.251	.247	.235	.244	.251
0.26 - 0.50	.254	.261	.262	.261	.267
0.51 - 0.75	.266	.270	.276	.274	.279
0.76 - 1.00	.282	.281	.279	.279	.286
1.01 and over	.293	.294	.300	.290	.287

We can create percentage plays for the different levels:

For Eye Levels of	Pct who bat .300+	.250-
0.00 - 0.25	7%	39%
0.26 - 0.50	14%	26%
0.51 - 0.75	18%	17%
0.76 - 1.00	32%	14%
1.01 - 1.50	51%	9%
1.51 +	59%	4%

Any batter with an eye ratio over 1.50 has about a 4% chance of hitting under .250 over 500 at bats.

Of all .300 hitters, those with ratios of at least 1.00 have a 65% chance of repeating as .300 hitters. Those with ratios under 1.00 have less than a 50% chance of repeating.

Sub-.250 batters with eye ratios under 1.00 are not likely to mature into .300 hitters the following year. Only 12% of those with ratios between 0.50 and 0.99, and only 4% of those with ratios under 0.50 will hit .300 in year #2.

Batters with eye ratios under 0.50 are a high risk group. They may hit over .300 at some point in their careers (some batters can hack their way to anything), but pitchers eventually figure out that they do not have to give these free-swingers anything good to hit. At that point, it takes a large scale adjustment on the part of the batter to return to the .300 plateau.

In a study covering 1995-2000, there were only 37 batters that had hit .300 or better with an eye ratio of 0.50 or less over at least 300 AB in a single season. Of this group, 30% exhibited the unique ability to accomplish this feat on a consistent basis. For the other 70%, a .300-plus BA and sub-0.50 eye ratio was a short-term aberration.

Contact Rate as a Leading Indicator

It follows intuitively that the more often a batter makes contact with the ball, the higher the likelihood that he will hit safely. Not rocket science here, but good to see that the numbers do bear this out.

Contact Rate	Batting Average				
	2002	2003	2004	2005	2006
0% - 60%	.185	.161	.187	.207	.181
61% - 65%	.233	.201	.186	.221	.220
66% - 70%	.242	.240	.242	.244	.251
71% - 75%	.247	.247	.249	.252	.256
76% - 80%	.261	.264	.265	.266	.270
81% - 85%	.268	.271	.273	.270	.274
86% - 90%	.279	.280	.283	.279	.287
Over 90%	.272	.284	.298	.282	.295

Contact Rate & Walk Rate as Leading Indicators

A matrix of contact rates and walk rates can provide us with expectation benchmarks for a player's batting average:

		bb%			
		0-5	6-10	11-15	16+
ct%	65-	.179	.195	.229	.237
	66-75	.190	.248	.254	.272
	76-85	.265	.267	.276	.283
	86+	.269	.279	.301	.309

A contact rate of 65% or lower offers virtually no chance for a player to hit even .250, no matter how high a walk rate he has. The .300 hitters will most often come from the group with a minimum 86% contact rate and 11% walk rate.

Hit Rate as a Leading Indicator *(Patrick Davitt)*

Every hitter establishes his own individual hit rate (percentage of balls-in-play that fall for hits) that stabilizes over time. A batter whose seasonal hit rate (H%) varies significantly from the H% he has established over the preceding three seasons is likely to improve or regress to his individual H% mean (with over-performer declines both more likely and sharper than under-performer recoveries). H% levels for a three-year period strongly predict a player's H% in the succeeding year.

Batting Eye and Power

We often ignore the batting eye ratio when evaluating power because so many batters achieve their lofty HR numbers by opening up their swing, thereby increasing their strikeout totals and depressing their eye ratio. However, this path to power success is a riskier one.

During the four-year study period, any batter who slammed 30 HRs in a season had less than a 3 in 10 chance of improving his power skills in the following year. But by adding in the eye ratios of each batter, the power decline can be better defined...

	YEAR 2	
Batting eye	PX increased	PX declined
Less than 0.50	13%	87%
0.50 - 0.99	24%	76%
1.00 and over	31%	69%

Batters with lower ratios were more likely to experience a power drop-off in the year following a 30-HR campaign.

Power Breakouts

It is not an easy task to predict which batters are going to put up an extraordinary power season. What we can do is categorize power breakouts in order to determine the likelihood of a player taking a step up or of a surprise performer repeating his feat.

1. Increase in playing time. An unexpected HR increase might not be a product of any change in skills but just the result of an increase in playing time.

2. History of power skills. A player may have displayed power skills sometime in the past, be it in his early major league career or prior.

3. Distribution of extra base hits. There is not much difference in skill between a double and a HR. A HR breakout may merely be a random redistribution of already demonstrated extra base hit power.

4. Normal skills growth. The power spike may be a normal occurrence along a batter's growth curve. A batter's breakout year may have been easily predicted from a review of his power index (PX) trend.

5. Situational breakouts. No matter how impressive the HR-hitting feats of Vinny Castilla were in the past, the fact that he played half his games in Coors Field discounted any true spike in skills. Similar for any player moving into a more power-conducive venue.

6. Fly ball tendency. See Olkin research below.

7. Steroids. A power spike might be the result of a player using illegal performance-enhancing substances.

8. The unexplained. Sometimes, a power spike makes no logical sense and cannot be explained by any of the previous criteria. These power surges hold the lowest probability for a comparable follow-up performance.

Fly Ball Tendency and Power *(Mat Olkin)*

There is a proven connection between a hitter's ground ball-fly ball tendencies and his power production.

1. Extreme ground ball hitters generally do not hit for much power. It's almost impossible for a hitter with a ground/fly ratio over 1.80 to hit enough fly balls to produce even 25 HRs in a season. However, this does not mean that a low G/F ratio necessarily guarantees power production. Some players have no problem getting the ball into the air, but simply lack the strength to reach the fences consistently.

2. Most batters' ground/fly ratios stay pretty steady over time. Most year-to-year changes are small and random, as they are in any other statistical category. A large, sudden change in G/F, on the other hand, can signal a conscious change in plate approach. And so...

3. If a player posts high G/F ratios in his first few years, he probably isn't ever going to hit for all that much power.

4. When a batter's power suddenly jumps, his G/F ratio often drops at the same time.

5. Every once in a while, a hitter's ratio will drop significantly even as his power production remains level. In these rare cases, impending power development is likely, since the two factors almost always follow each other.

Handedness Notes

1. While pure southpaws account for about 27% of total ABs (RHers about 55% and switch-hitters about 18%), they hit 31% of the triples and take 30% of the walks.

2. The average lefty posts a batting average about 10 points higher than the average RHer. The on base averages of pure LHers are nearly 20 points higher than RHers, but only 10 points higher than switch-hitters.

3. LHers tend to have a better batting eye ratio than RHers, but about the same as switch-hitters.

4. Pure righties and lefties have virtually identical power skills. Switch-hitters tend to have less power, on average.

5. Switch-hitters tend to have the best speed, followed by LHers, and then RHers.

6. On an overall production basis, LHers have about an 8% advantage over RHers and about a 14% edge over switch-hitters.

Batting Average Perception

Early season batting average strugglers who surge later in the year get no respect because they have to live with the weight of their early numbers all season long. Conversely, quick starters who fade late get far more accolades than they deserve.

For instance, take Rafael Furcal's 2006 month-by-month batting averages. Perception, which is typically based solely on a player's cumulative season stat line, was that he struggled in batting average for most of the year until a late surge boosted him up to .300. Reality is different. He had one truly off-month, and it happened to occur in April. How many people knew he batted .317 from May 1 on and over .310 in four of the six months of 2006?

Month	BA	Cum BA
April	.198	.198
May	.311	.260
June	.257	.259
July	.333	.278
August	.313	.285
September	.369	.300

Optimal Ages

Players develop at different paces, but in general terms, age can be helpful to determine where they should be along the developmental curve. Bill James' original research showed that batters tended to peak at about age 27. More recent research suggests that a variety of factors have pushed that average up closer to 30. More tendencies:

"26 With Experience" *(John Benson)*: While batters may peak at about age 27, the players most likely to exhibit the most dramatic spike in performance are those aged 26 who have several years of major league experience.

Power: Batting power skills tend to grow consistently between ages 24 and 29. Many batters experience a power peak at about age 30-31. Catchers often experience a power spike in the mid-30's.

Speed: Base-running and speed are skills of the young. When given the choice of two speedsters of fairly equivalent abilities and opportunity, always go after the younger one. A sharp drop-off in speed skills typically occurs at age 34.

Batting eye: For batters who continue to play into their 30's, this is a skill that can develop and grow throughout their career. A decline in this level, which can occur at any age, often indicates a decline in overall skills.

Thirtysomethings *(Ed Spaulding)*: Batters tend to lose points on their batting average, steal fewer bases (and with a lower success rate) and draw more walks. While players on the outside of the defensive spectrum (1B, 3B, LF, RF, DH) often have their best seasons in their 30's, players in the middle (2B, SS, CF) tend to fade. Many former stars move to new positions (Ripken, Molitor, Banks, etc.).

Catchers *(Ed Spaulding)*: Many catchers — particularly second line catchers — have their best seasons late in their careers. Some possible reasons why:

1. Catchers, like shortstops, often get to the big leagues for defensive reasons and not their offensive skills. These skills take longer to develop.

2. The heavy emphasis on learning the catching/defense/pitching side of the game detracts from their time to learn about, and practice, hitting.

3. Injuries often curtail their ability to show offensive skills, though these injuries (typically jammed fingers, bruises on the arms, rib injuries from collisions) often don't lead to time on the disabled list.

4. The time spent behind the plate has to impact the ability to recognize, and eventually hit, all kinds of pitches.

Spring Training Leading Indicator *(John Dewan)*

A hitter with a positive difference between his spring training slugging percentage and his lifetime slugging percentage of .200 or more correlates to a better than normal season.

Projecting In-Season RBI *(Patrick Davitt)*

Evaluating players in-season for RBI potential is a function of the interplay among four factors:
- Teammates' ability to reach base ahead of him and to run the bases efficiently;
- His own ability to drive them around by hitting, especially for extra bases
- Number of Games Played
- Place in the batting order

3-4-5 Hitters:
(0.69 x GP x TOB) + (0.30 x ITB) + (0.275 x HR) – (.191 x GP)

6-7-8 Hitters:
(0.63 x GP x TOB) + (0.27 x ITB) + (0.250 x HR) – (.191 x GP)

9-1-2 Hitters:
(0.57 x GP x TOB) + (0.24 x ITB) + (0.225 x HR) – (.191 x GP)

...where GP = games played, TOB = team on-base pct. and ITB = individual total bases (ITB).

Apply this pRBI formula after 70 games played or so (to reduce the variation from small sample size) to find players more than 9 RBI's over or under their projected RBI. There could be a correction coming.

You should also consider other factors, like injury or trade (involving the player or a top-of-the-order speedster) or team SB philosophy and success rate.

As well, remember that the player himself has an impact on his TOB. When we first did this study, we excluded the player from his TOB and got slightly better results. The formula overestimates projected RBI for players like Barry Bonds, whose high OBP skews his teams' OBP upwards but who can't benefit in RBI from that effect.

September Performance Declines *(Harold Brooks)*

Overall, batting average (-.002), on base average (-.002) and slugging average (-.006) decline after the end of August. Those who play every day of the season are more prone to decline. Throwing infielders (2B, 3B, SS) appear to suffer more than outfielders. As little as five days off during the season alleviates any of the problems in September, and with 10 days off, the chances of a September fade are very small.

Pitching Toolbox
Fundamental Skills

"There's no way to project pitchers accurately from year to year." — Bill James.

"Your most valuable commodity is a starting pitcher you can count on. The only problem is, you can't count on any of them." — Peter Golenbock

"Where else in the realm of fantasy sports can you have worse odds on success than from the wonderful world of the pitcher?" — Rod Beaton

"Starting pitchers are the most unreliable, unpredictable, unpleasant group of people in the world, statistically speaking that is." — John Benson

"No one, not the most astute major league scout nor the world's top number cruncher, can correctly project the statistical output of more than a couple a dozen of the game's 400 hurlers." — Steve Mann

While it's difficult to argue with the collective wisdom of these top baseball writers, their perception is tainted. Unreliable pitching performance is a fallacy driven by the practice of attempting to project pitching stats using gauges that are poor evaluators of skill.

How can we better evaluate pitching skill? We can start with the two statistical categories that are generally unaffected by external factors. These two stats capture the outcome of an individual pitcher versus batter match-up without regard to supporting offense, defense or bullpen:

Walks Allowed and Strikeouts

Even with only two stats to observe, there is a wealth of insight that these measures can provide. In fact, these two stats alone can measure several fundamental pitching skills:

Control (bb/9), the ability to get the ball over the plate.
Dominance (k/9), the ability to dominate hitters.
Command (k/bb), the overall ability to control the plate.

We used to include HR allowed as a third fundamental skill. However, research has shown that, while a pitcher has some ability to influence BIP hit on the ground or in the air, the percent of fly balls that go yard is not under his control.

Command Ratio as a Leading Indicator

The ability to get the ball over the plate — command of the strike zone — is one of the best leading indicators for future performance. Command ratio (K/BB) can be used to project potential in ERA as well as other skills gauges.

1. Research indicates that there is a high correlation between a pitcher's Cmd ratio and his ERA.

	Earned Run Average				
Command	**2002**	**2003**	**2004**	**2005**	**2006**
0.0 - 1.0	6.05	5.85	6.24	6.22	6.42
1.1 - 1.5	4.79	5.05	5.16	4.93	5.06
1.6 - 2.0	4.59	4.51	4.63	4.41	4.65
2.1 - 2.5	3.98	4.22	4.30	4.28	4.48
2.6 - 3.0	3.60	3.80	3.80	3.60	4.15
3.1 and over	3.15	3.30	3.30	3.45	3.49

We can create percentage plays for the different levels:

For Cmd	Pct who post	
Levels of	3.50-	4.50+
0.0 - 1.0	0%	87%
1.1 - 1.5	7%	67%
1.6 - 2.0	7%	57%
2.1 - 2.5	19%	35%
2.6 - 3.0	26%	25%
3.1 +	53%	5%

Any pitcher with a command ratio over 3.0 has only about a 5% chance of posting an ERA of 4.50 or higher. In general, pitchers who maintain a command ratio of over 2.5 have a high probability of long-term success. For fantasy drafting purposes, it is best to avoid pitchers with ratios of less than 2.0. Bullpen closers should be avoided if they have a command ratio under 2.5.

2. A pitcher's command in tandem with dominance (strikeout rate) provides even greater predictive abilities.

	Earned Run Average	
Command	-5.6 Dom	5.6+ Dom
0.0-0.9	5.36	5.99
1.0-1.4	4.94	5.03
1.5-1.9	4.67	4.47
2.0-2.4	4.32	4.08
2.5-2.9	4.21	3.88
3.0-3.9	4.04	3.46
4.0+	4.12	2.96

This helps to highlight the limited upside potential of soft-tossers with pinpoint control. The extra dominance makes a huge difference.

3. Research also suggests that there is a strong correlation between a pitcher's command ratio and his propensity to win ballgames. Over three quarters of those with ratios over 3.0 post winning records, and the collective W/L record of those command artists is nearly .600.

The command/winning correlation holds up in both leagues, although the effect was much more pronounced in the NL. Over four times more NL hurlers than AL hurlers have command ratios over 3.0, and it appears that higher command ratios are required in the NL to maintain good winning percentages. While a ratio between 2.0 and 2.9 might be good enough for a winning record for over 70% of AL pitchers, that level of command in the NL will generate an above-.500 mark only slightly more than half the time.

In short, in order to have at least a 70% chance of drafting a pitcher with a winning record, you must target NL pitchers with at least a 3.0 command ratio. To achieve the same odds in the AL, a 2.0 command ratio will suffice.

Strand Rate as a Leading Indicator

Strand Rate finds great utility in explaining variances between a pitcher's ERA and his performance indicators.

Pitchers with strand rates over 80% almost always have exemplary ERAs. Starters and middle relievers who post this level in a given season have an 80% likelihood of watching their ERA rise in the following year. The percentage drops to 50% for short relievers.

Pitchers with strand rates under 65% almost always have inflated ERAs, but have an 89% likelihood of watching their ERA improve in the following year. In addition, 83% will improve their ERA by more than one run.

Hit Rate as a Leading Indicator *(Voros McCracken)*

In 2000, Voros McCracken published a study that concluded that "there is little if any difference among major league pitchers in their ability to prevent hits on balls hit in the field of play."

His assertion was that, while a Johan Santana would have a better ability to prevent a batter from getting wood on a ball, or perhaps keeping the ball in the park, once that ball was hit in the field of play, the probability of it falling for a hit was virtually no different than for any other pitcher.

Among the findings in his study were:
- There is little correlation between what a pitcher does one year in the stat and what he will do the next. This is not true with other significant stats (BB, K, HR).
- You can better predict a pitcher's hits per balls in play from the rate of the rest of the pitcher's team than from the pitcher's own rate.

This last point brings a team's defense into the picture. It begs the question, when a batter gets a hit, is it because the pitcher made a bad pitch, the batter took a good swing, or the defense was not positioned correctly to field it? McCracken's findings take the onus away from the pitcher and puts it on the shoulders of the batter and defense.

Pitchers will often post hit rates per balls-in-play that are far off from the league average, but then revert to the mean the following year. As such, we can use that mean – approximately 30% – in much the same way we use strand rate to project the direction of a pitcher's ERA.

Subsequent research has shown that a pitcher's ground ball or fly ball propensity may have a small impact on his hit rate.

HR/FB Rate as a Leading Indicator *(John Burnson)*

McCracken's work focused on "balls in play," omitting home runs from the study. However, pitchers also do not have much control over the percentage of fly balls that turn into HR. Research shows that there is an underlying rate of HR as a percentage of fly balls of 10%. A pitcher's HR/FB rate will vary each year but always tends to regress to that 10%. The element that pitchers *do* have control over is the number of fly balls they allow. That is the underlying skill or deficiency that controls their HR rate.

Those pitchers who tend to keep the ball out of the air more often, via ground balls or strikeouts, correlate well with Rotisserie value. The formula *(K + 0.3GB) / Batters Faced* provides a strong gauge for "air superiority."

Line Drive Pct. as a Leading Indicator *(Seth Samuels)*

Another statistic shown to be beyond a pitcher's control is the percentage of balls-in-play that are line drives. Line drives do the most damage; from 1994-2003, here are the expected hit rates and number of total bases per type of BIP.

	|—— Type of BIP ——|	
	GB	FB	LD
H%	26%	23%	56%
Total bases	0.29	0.57	0.80

Despite the damage done by LDs, pitchers do not have any innate skill to avoid them. There is little relationship between a pitcher's LD% one year and his rate the next year. All rates tend to regress towards a mean of 22.6%.

However, ground ball pitchers do have a slight ability to prevent line drives (21.7%) and extreme ground ball hurlers even moreso (18.5%). Extreme fly ball pitchers have a slight ability to prevent LDs (21.1%) as well.

Ground Ball Tendency as a Leading Indicator
(John Burnson)

Ground ball pitchers tend to give up fewer HRs than do fly ball pitchers. There is also evidence that GB pitchers have higher hit rates. In other words, a ground ball has a higher chance of being a hit than does a fly ball that is not out of the park.

GB pitchers have lower strikeout rates. We should be more forgiving of a low strikeout rate (under 5.5 K/9) if it belongs to an extreme ground ball pitcher.

GB pitchers have a lower ERA than do fly ball pitchers but a higher WHIP. On balance, GB pitchers come out ahead, even when considering strikeouts, because a lower ERA also leads to more wins.

Ground Ball and Strikeout Tendencies as Indicators
(Mike Dranchak)

Pitchers were assembled into 9 groups based on the following profiles (minimum 23 starts in 2005):

Profile	Ground Ball Rate
Ground Ball	higher than 47%
Neutral	42% to 47%
Fly Ball	less than 42%

Profile	Strikeout Rate (k/9)
Strikeout	higher than 6.6 k/9
Average	5.4 to 6.6 k/9
Soft-Tosser	less than 5.4 k/9

Findings: Pitchers with higher strikeout rates had better ERA's and WHIPs than pitchers with lower strikeout rates, regardless of ground ball profile. However, for pitchers with similar strikeout rates, those with higher ground ball rates had better ERA's and WHIPs than those with lower ground ball rates.

Pitchers with higher strikeout rates tended to strand more baserunners than those with lower K rates. Fly ball pitchers tended to strand fewer runners than their GB or neutral counterparts within their strikeout profile.

Ground ball pitchers (especially those who lacked high-dominance) yielded more home runs per fly ball than did fly ball pitchers. However, the ERA risk was mitigated by the fact that ground ball pitchers (by definition) gave up fewer fly balls to begin with.

Projecting Wins

Using regression analyses, we can rank the importance of the variables that impact pitching win totals. In order:
1. Team offense (run support)
2. Pitching Effectiveness (base performance value)
3. Run Prevention (strand rate)
4. Bullpen support (inherited runners stranded %)
5. Managerial Tendencies (quick hooks/slow hooks)
6. Team Defense (fielding percentage)

When a fantasy leaguer needs to draft or beef up the Wins category, the most prudent approach is to target pitchers on teams with good offensive support.

Projecting Breakout Performances

Research has provided us with a set of criteria that can be used to identify candidates with the potential to experience large-scale ERA improvement. For pitchers that have consistently posted ERAs at or above the league average, target those that...

- will be between 24 and 28 years of age (and eliminate anyone over 29)
- have a minimum of two full years of major league experience
- have a history of command ratios over 2.0 (although the most recent year may be below 2.0)
- have had consistent strikeout rates of 6.0 or above
- have had consistent opposition OBA under .350
- have had strand rates of 70% or less and the promise of improved bullpen support in the next season.
- have had BPVs that showed potential for 50-plus levels, either via rising trends or minor league success.

Very few pitchers will meet all seven criteria; target those who meet the most, with a minimum of five.

Projecting Saves: Origin of Closers

History has long maintained that ace closers are not easily recognizable early on in their careers, so that every season does see its share of the unexpected. J.J. Putz, Jonathan Papelbon, Akinori Otsuka, Takashi Saito... who would have thought it a year ago?

Some accepted facts...
- You cannot find major league closers from pitchers who were closers in the minors.
- Closers begin their careers as starters.
- Closers are converted set-up men.
- Closers are pitchers who were unable to develop a third effective pitch.

All four statements are true. But the reality is a lot more simple... closers are a product of circumstance.

Are the minor leagues a place to look at all?

From 1990-2004, there were 280 twenty-save performances in Double-A and Triple-A, accomplished by 254 different pitchers.

Of those 254, only 46 ever made it to the majors.

Of those 46, only 13 ever saved 20 games in a season.

Of those 13, only 5 ever posted more than one 20-save season in the majors: John Wetteland, Mark Wohlers, Ricky Bottalico, Braden Looper and Francisco Cordero.

Five out of 254 pitchers over 15 years, a rate of 2%.

One of the reasons that minor league closers rarely become major league closers is because, in general, they do not get enough innings in the minors to sufficiently develop their arms into big-league caliber.

And in fact, organizations do not look at minor league closing performance seriously, assigning that role to pitchers who they do not see as legitimate prospects. In 2006, the average age of all Double-A and Triple-A pitchers who posted 20-plus saves was 27. In 2005, it was 28.

Projecting Saves

The task of finding future closing potential comes down to looking at two elements:

Talent: The raw skills to mow down hitters for short periods of time. Optimal BPVs over 100, but not under 75.

Opportunity: The more important element, yet the one that pitchers have no control over.

There are pitchers that have *Talent, but not Opportunity.* These pitchers are not given a chance to close for a variety of reasons (e.g. being blocked by a solid front-liner in the pen, being left-handed, etc.), but are good to own because they will not likely hurt your pitching staff. You just can't count on them for saves, at least not in the near term.

There are pitchers that have *Opportunity, but not Talent.* MLB managers decide who to give the ball to in the 9th inning based on their own perceptions about what skills are required to succeed, even if those perceived "skills" don't translate into acceptable BPI levels. Those pitchers without the BPIs may have some initial short-term success, but their long-term prognosis is poor and they are high risks to your roster. Classic examples of the short life span of these types of pitchers include Matt Karchner, Heath Slocumb, Ryan Kohlmeier, Dan Miceli and Danny Kolb.

Projecting Holds *(Doug Dennis)*

Here are some general rules of thumb for identifying pitchers who might be in line to accumulate Holds. The percentages represent the portion of 2003's top Holds leaders who fell into the category noted.

1. Left-handed set-up men with excellent BPIs. (43%)
2. A "go-to" right-handed set-up man with excellent BPIs. This is the one set-up RHer that a manager turns to with a small lead in the 7th or 8th innings. These pitchers also tend to vulture wins. (43%, but 6 of the top 9)
3. Excellent BPIs, but not a firm role as the main LHed or RHed set-up man. Roles change during the season; cream rises to the top. Relievers projected to post great BPIs often overtake lesser set-up men during the season. (14%)

Skill versus Consistency

Two pitchers have identical 4.50 ERAs and identical 3.0 PQS averages. Their PQS logs look like this:

PITCHER A:	3	3	3	3	3
PITCHER B:	5	0	5	0	5

Which pitcher would you rather have on your team? The risk-averse manager would choose Pitcher A as he represents the perfectly known commodity. Many fantasy leaguers might opt for Pitcher B because his occasional dominating starts show that there is an upside. His Achilles Heel is inconsistency. Is there any hope for Pitcher B?

- If a pitcher's inconsistency is characterized by more poor starts than good starts, his upside is limited.
- Pitchers with extreme inconsistency rarely get a full season of starts.
- However, inconsistency is neither chronic nor fatal.

The outlook for Pitcher A is actually worse. Disaster avoidance might buy these pitchers more starts, but history shows that the lack of dominating outings is more telling of future potential. In short, consistent mediocrity is bad.

Pitching Streaks

It is possible to find predictive value in strings of DOMinating or DISaster starts:

Once a pitcher enters into a DOM streak of any length, the probability for his subsequent start is going to be a better-than-average outing. The further a player is into a DOM streak, the higher the likelihood that the subsequent performance will be of high quality. In fact, once a pitcher has posted six DOM starts in a row, there is greater than a 70% probability that the streak will continue. When it does end, there is less than a 10% probability that the streak-breaker is going to be a DISaster.

Once a pitcher enters into a DIS streak of any length, the probability is that his next start is going to be a below average outing, even if that outing breaks the streak. However, DIS streaks erode quickly. Once a pitcher hits the skids, there is little potential for him to start posting productive numbers in the short term, even though the duration of the plummet itself should be brief.

Optimal Ages

As with batters, pitchers develop at different rates, but in general terms, a look at their age can be helpful to determine where they should be along the developmental curve. Here are some tendencies...

While peaks vary, most all pitchers (who are still around) tend to experience a sharp drop-off in their skills at age 38.

Starting pitchers *(Rick Wilton)*: Their first productive season in the majors (10 wins, 150 IP, sub-4.00 ERA) is at age 25 or 26. Starters who experience a career year after age 31 are far less likely to repeat that performance than those who achieve their career year at a younger age.

Relief aces *(Rick Wilton)*: Their first 20-save season arrives at about age 26. About three of every four relievers who begin a run of 20-save seasons in their 20's will likely sustain that level for about four years, with their value beginning to decline at the beginning of the third year.

Many aces achieve a certain level of maturity in their 30's and can experience a run of 20-save seasons between ages 33 and 36. For some, this may be their first time in the role of bullpen closer. However, those who achieve their first 20-save season after age 34 are unlikely to repeat.

Thirtysomethings *(Ed Spaulding)*: Older pitchers, as they lose velocity and movement on the ball, must rely on more variety and better location. Thus, if strikeouts are a priority, you don't want many pitchers over 30. The over-30 set that tends to be surprising includes finesse types, career minor leaguers who break through for 2-3 seasons often in relief, and knuckleballers (a young knuckleballer is 31).

Career Year Drop-off *(Rick Wilton)*

Research shows that a pitcher's post-career year drop-off, on average, looks like this...

- ERA increases by 1.00
- WHIP increases by 0.14.
- Nearly 6 fewer wins

Usage Warning Flags

Research suggests that there is a finite number of innings in a pitcher's arm. This number varies by pitcher, by development cycle, and by pitching style and repertoire. We can measure a pitcher's potential for future arm problems and/or reduced effectiveness:

- *Sharp increases in usage from one year to the next...* Any pitcher who increases his workload by 50 IP or more from year #1 to year #2 is a candidate to experience symptoms of burnout in year #3.
- *Starters' overuse...* Consistent "batters faced per game" (BF/G) levels of 28.0 or higher, combined with consistent seasonal IP totals of 200 or more may indicate burnout potential. Within a season, a BF/G of over 30.0 with a projected IP total of 200 may indicate a late season fade.
- *Relievers' overuse...* Warning flags should be up for relievers who post in excess of 100 IP in a season, while averaging fewer than 2 IP per outing.

When focusing solely on minor league pitchers, research results are striking:

Stamina: Virtually every minor league pitcher who has had a BF/G of 28.5 or more in one season will experience a drop-off in BF/G the following year. Many will be unable to ever duplicate that previous level of durability.

Performance: Most pitchers experience an associated drop-off in their BPVs in the years following the 28.5 BF/G season. Some are able to salvage their effectiveness later on by moving to the bullpen.

Protecting Young Pitchers *(Craig Wright)*

There is a link between some degree of eventual arm trouble and a history of heavy workloads in a pitcher's formative years. Some recommendations from this research:

Teenagers (A-ball): No 200 IP seasons and no BF/G over 28.5 in any 150 IP span. No starts on three days rest.

Ages 20-22: Average no more than 105 pitches per start with a single game ceiling of 130 pitches.

Ages 23-24: Average no more than 110 pitches per start with a single game ceiling of 140 pitches.

When possible, a young rookie starter should be introduced to the major leagues in a long relief role before he goes into the rotation.

Catchers' Effect on Pitching *(Thomas Hanrahan)*

A typical catcher handles a pitching staff better after having been with a club for a few years. Research has shown that there is an improvement in team ERA of approximately 0.37 runs from a catcher's rookie season to his prime years with a club. For fanalytic purposes, you should expect a pitcher's ERA to be higher than expected if he is throwing to a rookie backstop.

Handedness Notes

1. LHers tend to peak about a year after RHers.
2. LH post only 15% of the total saves. Typically, LHers are reserved for specialist roles so few are frontline closers.
3. RHers have slightly better Cmd, slightly better HR rate.
4. There is no significant variance in ERA.
5. On an overall basis, RHers have about a 6% advantage.

Minor League Toolbox

Minor League Information Management
(Terry Linhart)

The increased attention that the minor leagues are getting has created some dangerous analytical by-products.

Hype. With the minor leagues still largely uncovered by the media, one reporter's short-term observations can make their way into the mainstream as fact. This growing subjective information base is often not rooted in fact at all, yet drives perception about prospects.

There is a **rush** to scour the lower minors statistically for the next great phenom before anyone else does. But statistics alone do not tell the whole story. Often, there is an exaggerated emphasis on short-term performance in an environment (major league player development) that is supposed to focus on the long-term. Two poor outings don't mean a 21-year-old pitcher is washed up.

Other common factors that affect statistics:

League variances: Some leagues favor hitters or pitchers.

Ballpark variances: Dimensions and altitude create hitters parks and pitchers parks, but a factor rarely mentioned is that many ballparks in the lower minors are inconsistent in their field quality. Minor league clubs have limited resources to maintain their field conditions, and this can artificially depress defensive statistics while inflating gauges like batting average.

Widely variant skills: Some players' skills are so superior to the caliber of competition at their level that you can't truly get a picture of what they're going to do from their statistics alone.

Player development assignments: Many pitchers are told to work on secondary pitches while moving through the minors, throwing curveballs and change-ups on 3-2 or 2-2 counts to gain confidence in the pitch. The result is an increased number of walks affecting their command ratio. Again, the bigger picture is the long-term development for a major league club. They may be able to get hitters out with a sharp, moving fastball, but are trying to work on keeping hitters off-stride.

Pitching rotations: The #3, #4, and #5 pitchers in the lower minors are truly longshots to make the majors. They often possess only two pitches and can barely go five innings. The most obvious weakness is the inability to disguise the off-speed pitches with their delivery and arm speed. Hitters can see inflated statistics in these leagues.

Minor League Level versus Age

When evaluating minor league talent, you must look at the age of the prospect in relation to the median age of the league he is in:

Low level A	Between 19-20
Upper level A	Around 20
Double-A	21
Triple-A	22

These are the ideal ages for prospects at the particular level. If a prospect is younger than most and he holds his own against older and more experienced players, elevate his status. If a prospect is older than the median, reduce his status. These adjustments are taken into account in the Major League Equivalents section.

Call-up Success Rates I

The overall probability that a promoted minor leaguer will immediately succeed at the major league level can vary depending upon the level of Triple-A experience that player has amassed at the time of call-up. Research conclusions:

	BATTERS		PITCHERS	
	≤1 Yr	Full	≤1 Yr	Full
Performed well	57%	56%	16%	56%
Performed poorly	21%	38%	77%	33%
2nd half drop-off	21%	7%	6%	10%

The odds of a batter achieving immediate major league success, no matter what his minor league experience, remains slightly more than 50-50. However, over 80% of all minor league pitchers promoted with less than a full year at Triple-A will struggle in their first year in the majors. Those pitchers who do have a full year in Triple-A increase their success rate to a level equal to that of batters (about 50-50).

Call-up Success Rates II

Historical BPIs have some value in determining which minor league pitching call-ups fare well.

Based on a recent study, the percentage of hurlers that were good investments in the year that they were called up varied by the level of their historical BPIs *prior* to that year.

Pitchers who had:	Fared well	Fared poorly
Good indicators	79%	21%
Marginal or poor indicators	18%	82%

The minor league data used to classify these pitchers were MLE levels from the previous two years, not the season in which they were called up. What is the significance of this? Typically, it is solid current year performance that merits the call-up in the first place, but those numbers had little bearing on who fared well. Early season performance in the minors is not a good indicator of short-term major league success, for two reasons:

1. The performance data set is too small, typically just a few month's worth of statistics. For pitchers, this is not nearly enough data to draw any reasonable conclusions.

2. For those pitchers putting up those stats at a new minor league level, there has not been enough time for the scouting reports to make their rounds, so we do not know if they have truly mastered that level yet.

Minor League BPV as a Leading Indicator *(Al Melchior)*

There is a link between minor league skill and how a pitching prospect will fare in his first 5 starts upon call-up.

	MLE BPV		
PQS Avg	≤ 50	50-99	100+
0.0-1.9	60%	28%	19%
2.0-2.9	32%	40%	29%
3.0-5.0	8%	33%	52%
TOTAL	100%	100%	100%

Pitchers who demonstrate sub-par skills in the minors, as indicated by a sub-50 BPV, tend to fare poorly in their first big league starts. Three-fifths of these pitchers register a PQS average below 2.0, while only 8% average over 3.0.

At the other end of the spectrum, fewer than one out of five minor leaguers with a 100+ MLE BPV go on to post a sub-2.0 PQS average in their initial major league starts, but more than half average 3.0 or better.

Projecting Second Year Success

One of the most accurate indicators of a rookie's future potential is his performance during the second half of his debut season in the majors. First year players often get off to particularly fast or slow starts. During their second tour of the league is when we get to see whether the slow starters have adjusted to the level of play or whether the rest of the league has figured out the fast starters. That second half "adjustment" performance level is the one you want to look at when projecting the sophomore campaign and beyond.

Adjusting to the Competition

The phenomenon of "adjusting to the competition" occurs at every level of professional play. When a player gets promoted to, say Triple-A, he is, in fact, a "rookie" during his first year at that level. An analysis of his second half Triple-A performance gives us a better indication of his true ability there. And... premature major league call-ups often negate the ability for us to evaluate a player's true potential.

E.g. A hotshot Double-A player opens the new season in Triple-A. After putting up solid numbers for a month, he gets a call to the bigs... and then struggles. We wonder why. The fact is, at the point of call-up, we do not have enough evidence that the player has mastered the Triple-A level. We don't know whether the rest of the league would have caught up to him during his second tour of the league. But now he's labeled as an underperformer in the bigs when in fact he has never truly proven his skills at the lower levels.

Older Prospects

There is some longshot potential talent in older prospects — age 26, 27 or higher — who, for whatever reason (untimely injury, circumstance, bad luck, etc.), don't reach the majors until they've lost their Official Prospect Status. Downgrading potential with age is an economic reality for Major League clubs, but not necessarily a skills reality.

Most clubs approach the calling up of a minor leaguer in the same way as they approach all their investments. They are more likely to take a chance on a 23-year-old who might return long-term dividends than a 29-year-old whose return is likely far lower.

But skills growth and decline is universal, whether it occurs at the major league level or in the minors. So a high skills journeyman in Triple-A is just as likely to peak at age 27 as a major leaguer of the same age. The question becomes one of opportunity — will the parent club see fit to reap the benefits of that peak performance?

Prospecting these players for your fantasy team is, admittedly, a high risk endeavor, though there are some criteria you can use. Look for a player who is/has:

- Optimally, age 27-28 for overall peak skills, age 30-31 for power skills, or age 28-31 for pitchers.
- At least two seasons of experience at Triple-A. Career Double-A players are generally not good picks.
- Solid base skills levels.
- Shallow organizational depth at their position.
- Notable winter league or spring training performance.

Players who meet these conditions are not typically draftable players, but worthwhile reserve or FAAB picks.

Team Toolbox

Johnson Effect *(Bryan Johnson)*: Teams whose actual won/loss record exceeds or falls short of their statistically projected record in one season will tend to revert to the level of their projection in the following season.

Law of Competitive Balance *(Bill James)*: The level at which a team (or player) will address its problems is inversely related to its current level of success. Losing teams/low performing players will tend to make changes to improve; winning teams/high performing players will not. This law is the explanation for the existence of the Plexiglass Principle and the Whirlpool Principle.

Plexiglass Principle *(Bill James)*: If a player or team improves markedly in one season, it will likely decline in the next. The opposite is also true but with a slightly lower frequency (because a poorer performing player will get fewer opportunities to rebound).

Whirlpool Principle *(Bill James)*: All team and player performances are forcefully drawn to the center. For teams, that center is a .500 record. For players, it represents their career average level of performance.

Japanese Baseball Toolbox

Japan's Pacific and Central Leagues are generally considered to be equivalent to very good Triple-A level ball, and the pitching may be even better.

As good as this league is, Japanese statistics are difficult to convert to a major league equivalent due to a variety of differences in the way the game is played there:

1. Japanese baseball's guiding philosophy centers on risk avoidance. Mistakes are not tolerated. Since fewer risks are taken, runners rarely take extra bases, batters focus on making contact rather than driving the ball, and managers play for one run at a time, rather than going for a big inning. As a result, offenses score fewer runs than they should given the number of hits produced. And pitching stats tend to look better than the talent behind them.

2. Stadiums in Japan have much shorter fences. Normally this would mean more HRs, but given #1 above, it is the American players who make up the majority of Japan's power elite. This skews offensive statistics.

3. There are more artificial turf fields, which increases the number of ground ball singles.

4. The quality of umpiring is questionable. Far fewer errors are called (again, the cultural philosophy of low tolerance for mistakes).

5. Teams have smaller pitching staffs, often no more than about seven deep. Three-man pitching rotations are common, there is no relief specialization, and the best starters often work out of the pen between starts. Despite superior conditioning, Japanese pitchers tend to burn out early, often before age 30.

Other Diamonds

The Fanalytic Fundamentals

1. This is not a game of precision. It is a game of human beings and tendencies.
2. This is not a game of projections. It is a game of market value versus real value.
3. Draft skills, not stats.
4. Eventually, a player's ability to post acceptable stats despite lousy BPIs will run out.
5. Once you display a skill, you own it.
6. Virtually every player is vulnerable to a month of aberrant performance. Or a year.
7. Exercise excruciating patience.

Aging Axioms

1. The aging process slows down for those players who maintain a firm grasp on the strike zone. Plate patience and pitching command can help preserve whatever waning skill they have left.
2. Negatives tend to snowball as you age.

Age 26 Paradox: 26 is when a player begins to reach his peak skill, no matter what his address is. If circumstances have him celebrating that birthday in the majors, he is a breakout candidate. If circumstances have him celebrating that birthday in the minors, he is washed up.

A-Rod 10-Step Path to Stardom: Not all well-hyped prospects hit the ground running. More often they follow an alternative path...

1. Prospect puts up phenomenal minor league numbers.
2. The media machine gets oiled up.
3. Prospect gets called up, but struggles, Year 1.
4. Prospect gets demoted.
5. Prospect tears it up in Triple-A, Year 2.
6. Prospect gets called up, but struggles, Year 2.
7. Prospect gets demoted.
8. The media turns their backs and fantasy leaguers reduce their expectations.
9. Prospect tears it up in Triple-A, Year 3. The public shrugs its collective shoulders.
10. Prospect is promoted in Year 3 and explodes. Some lucky fantasy leaguer lands a franchise player for under $5.

Some players that are currently stuck at one of the interim steps, and may or may not ever reach Step 10, include Edwin Jackson, Andy Marte, Dan Johnson, Hee Seop Choi.

Ashley-Perry Statistical Axioms:

1. Numbers are tools, not rules.
2. Numbers are symbols for things; the number and the thing are not the same.
3. Skill in manipulating numbers is a talent, not evidence of divine guidance.
4. Like other occult techniques of divination, the statistical method has a private jargon deliberately contrived to obscure its methods from non-practitioners.
5. The product of an arithmetical computation is the answer to an equation; it is not the solution to a problem.
6. Arithmetical proofs of theorems that do not have arithmetical bases prove nothing.

Steve Avery List: Players who hang onto major league rosters for six years searching for a skill level they only had for three.

Bylaws of Badness
1. Some players are better than an open roster spot, but not by much.
2. Some players have bad years because they are unlucky. Others have *many* bad years because they are bad... and lucky.

Challenge to Core Belief Systems: For those who believe in astrology, how do you explain that Tom Seaver, Lorne Michaels and Danny DeVito were all born on November 17, 1944?

Geronimo Berroa List: Older minor leaguers who sneak onto major league rosters and shine for brief periods, showing what a mistake it is to pigeon-hole talented players just because they are not 24 and beautiful.

Rickey Bones List: Pitchers with BPIs so incredibly horrible that you have to wonder how they can possibly draw a major league paycheck year after year.

George Brett Path to Retirement: Get out while you're still putting up good numbers and the public perception of you is favorable. *(See Steve Carlton Path to Retirement.)*

Steve Carlton Path to Retirement: Hang around the major leagues long enough for your numbers to become so wretched that people begin to forget your past successes. *(See George Brett Path to Retirement.)*

Among the many players who have taken this path include Roberto Alomar, Bobby Bonilla, Kevin Brown, David Cone, Eric Davis, Doc Gooden, Hideo Nomo, Tim Raines, Al Leiter and of course, Steve Carlton. Current players who look to be on the same course include Steve Finley and perhaps Randy Johnson.

Chaconian: Having the ability to post many saves despite sub-Mendoza BPIs and an ERA in the stratosphere.

Chicken and Egg Problem: Did irregular playing time take its toll on the player's performance or did poor performance force a reduction in his playing time?

Chronology of the Classic Free-Swinger with Pop
1. Gets off to a good start.
2. Thinks he's in a groove.
3. Gets lax, careless.
4. Pitchers begin to catch on.
5. Fades down the stretch.

Crickets: The sound heard when someone's opening draft bid on a player is also the only bid.

Developmental Dogmata
1. Defense is what gets a minor league prospect to the majors; offense is what keeps him there. *(Deric McKamey)*
2. The reason why minor leaguers who are promoted rapidly often fail is that they are never given the opportunity to master the skill of "adjusting to the competition."
3. Rookies who are promoted in-season often perform better than those that make the club out of spring training. Inferior March competition can inflate the latter group's perceived talent level.
4. Young players rarely lose their inherent skills. Pitchers may uncover weaknesses and the players may have difficulty adjusting. These are bumps along the growth curve, but they do not reflect a loss off skill.
5. Late bloomers have smaller windows of opportunity and much less chance for forgiveness.
6. The greatest risk in this game is to pay for performance that a player has never achieved.
7. Some outwardly talented prospects simply have a ceiling that's spelled AAA.

Edwhitsonitis: A dreaded malady marked by the sudden and unexplained loss of pitching ability upon a trade to the New York Yankees.

Employment Standards
1. If you are right-brain dominant, own a catcher's mitt and are under 40, you will always be gainfully employed.
2. Some teams believe that it is better to gainfully employ a pitcher with *any* experience because it has to be better than the devil they don't know.
3. It's not so good to go pffft in a contract year.

FAAB Forewarnings
1. Spend early and often.
2. Emptying your budget for one prime league-crosser is a tactic that should be reserved for the desperate.
3. If you chase two rabbits, you will lose them both.

Fantasy Economics 101: The market value for a player is generally based on the aura of past performance, not the promise of future potential. Your greatest advantage is to leverage the variance between market value and real value.

Fantasy Economics 102: The variance between market value and real value is far more important than the absolute accuracy of any individual player projection.

Fantasy Experts: The Truth
1. People use the word "guru" because nobody can spell "charlatan." *(Peter Drucker)*
2. No amount of genius can overcome a preoccupation with detail. *(Levy's Eighth Law)*
3. An expert is one who knows more and more about less and less until he knows absolutely everything about nothing. *(Weber's Definition)*

Frankie Frisch Fact: "Baseball is like this. Have one good year and you can fool them for five more, because for five more years they expect you to have another good one."

Doug Glanville List: Players with excellent speed and sub-.300 on base averages who get a lot of practice running down the line to first base, and then back to the dugout.

The Gravity Principles
1. It is easier to be crappy than it is to be good.
2. All performance starts at zero, ends at zero and can drop to zero at any time.
3. The odds of a good performer slumping are far greater than the odds of a poor performer surging.
4. Once they're in a slump, it takes several 3 for 5 days to get out of it. Once they're on a streak, it takes a single 0 for 4 day to begin the downward spiral.
Corollary: Once they're in a slump, not only does it take several 3 for 5 days to get out of it, but they also have to get their name back on the lineup card.
5. Eventually all performance comes down to earth. It may take a week, or a month, or may not happen until they're 45, but eventually it's going to happen.

Health Homilies
1. A $40 player can get hurt just as easily as a $5 player but is eight times tougher to replace.
2. Chronically injured players never suddenly get healthy.
3. There are two kinds of pitchers: those that are hurt and those that are not hurt... yet.

4. Players with back problems are always worth $10 less.

5. "Opting out of surgery" usually means it's coming anyway, just later.

Luke Hudson (1/3 inning, 10 ER) Rationalization: Occasional nightmares are just a part of the game.

Kamin's Sixth Law (fantasy baseball variation): When attempting to predict and forecast player performance, never be misled by what a player says; instead watch what he does.

Matt Kinney List: Players you drop out on when the bidding reaches $1.

The Knuckleballers Rule: Knuckleballers don't follow any of the rules.

Lance Painter Lesson: Six months of solid performance can be screwed up by one bad outing. (In 2000, Painter finished with an ERA of 4.76. However, prior to his final appearance of the year — in which he pitched 1 inning and gave up 8 earned runs — his ERA was 3.70.)

The Pitching Postulates

1. Never sign a soft-tosser to a long-term contract.
2. Right-brain dominance has a very long shelf life.
3. A fly ball pitcher who gives up a lot of HRs is expected. A ground ball pitcher who gives up a lot of HRs is making mistakes.
4. Never draft a contact fly ball pitcher who plays in a hitter's park.
5. Only bad teams ever have a need for an inning-eater.
6. Never chase wins.

Reclamation Conundrum: The problem with stockpiling bench players in the hope that one pans out is that you end up evaluating performance using data sets that are far too small to be reliable.

Rule 5 Reminder: Don't ignore the Rule 5 draft lest you ignore the 1% possibility of a Johan Santana.

The Five Saves Certainties:

1. On every team, there *will* be save opportunities and *someone* will get them. In fact, at a bare minimum, there will be at least 30 saves to go around, and not unlikely that there could be over 45.

2. *Any* pitcher could end up being the chief beneficiary. Bullpen management is a fickle endeavor.

3. Relief pitchers are often the ones that require the most time at the start of the season to find a groove. The weather is cold, the schedule is sparse and their usage is erratic.

4. Despite the talk about "bullpens by committee," managers prefer a go-to guy. It makes their job easier.

5. As many as 50% of the available saves in any given year will come from pitchers who are in the free agent pool at the end of Draft Day.

Position Perspectives

First Place: It's lonely at the top, but it's comforting to look down upon everyone else.

Last Place: If you can't learn to do something well, learn to enjoy doing it badly.

Tenets of Optimal Timing

1. If a second half fader had put up his second half stats in the first half and his first half stats in the second half, then he probably wouldn't even have had a second half.
2. Fast starters can often buy six months of playing time out of one month of productivity.
3. Poor 2nd halves don't get recognized until it's too late.

Mike Timlin List: Players who you are unable to resist drafting even though they have burned you multiple times in the past.

Walbeckian: Possessing below replacement level stats, as in "Guzman's season was downright Walbeckian." *Alternate usage:* "Guzman's stats were so bad that I might as well have had Walbeck in there."

Mark Wohlers Lament: When a closer posts a 65% strand rate, he has nobody to blame but himself.

Seasonal Assessment Standard: If you still have reason to be reading the boxscores during the last weekend of the season, then your year has to be considered a success.

The Three Cardinal Rules for Winners: If you cherish this hobby, you will live by them or die by them…

1. Revel in your success; fame is fleeting.
2. Exercise excruciating humility.
3. 100% of winnings must be spent on significant others.

Research Abstracts

STATISTICAL INSIGHTS
Reliability and experience

A few years before the turn of the century, at a time when I was trying out all sorts of wacky draft strategies, I stumbled upon something that yielded a fantasy baseball championship. But it wasn't the LIMA Plan.

We were running a Scoresheet Baseball Exhibition at Baseball HQ, experimenting with different draft and roster management strategies. There was one owner who stocked up on offense to the exclusion of pitchers, another who drafted a '85 Cardinals all-speed-and batting-average team, and yet another who drafted a team composed of nothing but the league's top defenders. The fact that I won that league is forgotten news and pretty much irrelevant today. The interesting aspect, though, was the strategy that I had chosen and the fact that there has never been a follow-up to see whether or not my success was a single-season fluke.

I drafted a team of all players over the age of 30.

The concept was simple. Older players tended to be more stable, and thus more projectable. If a player had reached 30, he had ascended past prospect/suspect status and likely had a firm role in the majors. The only downside of drafting older players was the increased incidence of injury.

A statistical scan of our BPIs by age *(right)* reveals much that we know already. It shows that some of the highest skills seasons do occur at age 30 and after. These results cover the period 1996-2005, and update the research that appears in the *Baseball Forecaster's* Toolbox.

Given that these tables just represent the pool of statistics at each age, they do not show trends of skills progression (because there are different players in each group). Doing age studies like this is inherently problematic. Rob Neyer described it well in a recent ESPN.com column:

> *"One thing that complicates studies of aging is that if you look at a group of 28-year-old pitchers and a group of 38-year-old pitchers, they'll be equally effective (roughly speaking), though of course there will be more 28-year-olds than 38-year-olds. Why? Because there's a bar you have to clear if you want to keep pitching, and that bar's roughly the same no matter how old you are."*

However, our goal here is largely to observe the general skills levels from among those players that make up each particular age pool. If we are to filter our draft lists by age, what might we be getting? This exercise does provide a general sense of that.

Most of the data is intuitive; some of it perhaps not. We'd expect to see skills spikes at the youngest and oldest limits of these charts; only the best players are going to debut under 22 or still be playing into their late thirties. The morass of mediocrity in the middle is also not surprising as that represents the largest population of all players — good and bad — fighting to claim their place in the bigs.

But the high-level talent in the mid-30s makes a statement. While more and more poor performers drop off at each subsequent age, the remaining talent far surpasses anything we see at earlier levels. It almost begs us to limit our draft targets to those previously thought of as "past their prime." Does this open up an opportunity for fantasy leaguers to grab the best players from a group we tend to shy away from?

The last piece of the puzzle is to see if older players are more risky. They may be more productive on a per-AB or per-IP basis, but if they are not regularly on their teams' lineup cards, we may still have to dip into the youth pool to replace the lost playing time.

We can use reliability scores as a gauge since playing time and injury history are at its core. Beyond playing time, the inclusion of performance consistency in these scores is important to know as well. Unfortunately, we've only been doing these scores for two years, so the sample may be too small to draw firm conclusions from. Still, the results are intriguing *(see next page)*.

BATTERS

Age	BA	OB	Slg	OPS	bb%	ct%	Eye	PX
21-	277	337	455	792	8%	80%	0.46	105
22	281	333	436	769	7%	83%	0.45	89
23	276	333	446	779	8%	82%	0.48	99
24	278	337	445	782	8%	83%	0.52	96
25	278	340	451	791	9%	82%	0.52	101
26	278	342	451	793	9%	82%	0.54	100
27	278	342	449	791	9%	82%	0.55	100
28	277	343	447	790	9%	82%	0.57	99
29	279	346	451	797	9%	83%	0.59	99
30	278	347	451	798	10%	83%	0.62	99
31	276	347	447	794	10%	83%	0.62	99
32	277	349	452	801	10%	82%	0.63	101
33	276	351	451	802	10%	83%	0.67	100
34	275	351	450	801	10%	82%	0.66	101
35	278	355	459	814	11%	82%	0.68	104
36	280	358	460	819	11%	83%	0.74	103
37	279	359	463	822	11%	84%	0.76	104
38	277	361	445	806	12%	84%	0.83	96
39	293	370	490	860	11%	85%	0.85	108
40+	275	369	443	812	13%	84%	0.94	95

PITCHERS

Age	ERA	WHIP	OBA	Ctl	Dom	Cmd	hr/9	BPV
21-	4.20	1.39	237	4.6	9.1	2.0	0.9	76
22	4.28	1.37	254	3.7	7.1	1.9	1.0	58
23	4.09	1.37	259	3.4	7.1	2.1	1.0	60
24	4.29	1.38	261	3.4	6.7	1.9	1.1	52
25	4.17	1.35	258	3.3	6.9	2.1	1.0	58
26	4.14	1.35	262	3.2	6.7	2.1	1.0	56
27	4.22	1.36	262	3.3	6.7	2.1	1.0	56
28	4.09	1.36	262	3.2	6.7	2.1	1.0	57
29	4.18	1.35	262	3.1	6.6	2.1	1.0	55
30	4.19	1.37	263	3.3	6.7	2.0	1.0	55
31	4.17	1.36	262	3.3	6.6	2.0	1.0	54
32	4.05	1.34	259	3.1	6.6	2.1	1.0	56
33	4.17	1.36	263	3.2	6.7	2.1	1.0	55
34	4.05	1.33	259	3.1	6.8	2.2	1.0	60
35	3.87	1.30	257	2.9	7.0	2.4	1.0	66
36	3.68	1.29	252	3.0	7.3	2.4	0.9	71
37	3.95	1.32	262	2.9	6.9	2.4	1.0	65
38	4.17	1.33	263	2.9	6.9	2.4	1.0	63
39	3.98	1.32	262	2.9	6.4	2.2	1.1	57
40+	4.18	1.32	268	2.6	6.3	2.4	1.0	59

Batters

Common wisdom states that batters' skills take their largest step up at age 26. Given that a performance spike would impact consistency, it's not surprising to see average reliability scores stall at age 26.

Peak batting reliability occurs at ages 29 and 30, followed by a minor decline for four years. So, to draft the most reliable batters — and by extension, to maximize the odds of returning at least par value on your investments — you would need to target the age range of 28-34.

Age	RELIABILITY SCORE Batters	Pitchers
22-	10	8
23	19	10
24	23	12
25	33	16
26	31	19
27	39	28
28	44	30
29	50	32
30	50	36
31	48	48
32	47	46
33	46	38
34	46	34
35	30	25
36	35	19
37	38	15
38	35	23
39	32	29
40+	28	40

There is an odd drop in reliability at 35, after which there is a small secondary spike and decline. This is likely due to the filtering out of all but the best older players, plus the small sample sizes at the far end of the scale. But 35 seems to be an important aging break point.

By combining this information with the earlier tables, we can target the best age range for both skills and reliability. Ages 29-34 would seem to be that range. Despite the terrific skills upswings in the mid-to-late 30s, the drop in reliability makes those targets too risky.

Pitchers

The most fascinating part of this table is what happens to pitchers at ages 31 and 32, the peak years. Despite the fact that reliability scores for pitchers generally run, on average, much lower than for batters, during those two years, the batter and pitcher scores are virtually identical. One could even draw the conclusion that 31- and 32-year-old pitchers are *more reliable* than same-aged batters.

Pitchers also see a sharp drop in reliability at age 35, which continues to age 37. As the dead wood filters out, the remaining Golden Oldies actually display *increased* reliability as they pass 40. Thank you, Roger Clemens, David Wells, Jamie Moyer and friends.

The most reliable age range seems to be about 29-34. The skills table does not reveal a single peak range, but several smaller pockets. The only range where high skills and high reliability cross is at about 32-34.

Conclusions, maybe

To maximize your upside from both a skills and reliability standpoint, you might consider limiting the pool of draftable players to 29-34 year-old batters and 32-34 year-old pitchers.

While we are forever looking for "sleepers" and upwardly mobile prospects, these charts seem to indicate that it does not make sense to draft anyone under the age of 27. Or over the age of 35.

So, going with this line of analysis, it's entirely possible that my Scoresheet championship was not a fluke at all.

Reliability revisited
by Patrick Davitt

In last year's *Forecaster*, we measured the 2005 pre-season dollar projections and Reliability Scores (RELs) against actual outcomes. Time for a follow-up.

Method

The REL metric combines experience, consistency, health and injury history, age and burnout potential (for pitchers, based on workload and pitch-count).

We used our last pre-season projection, on March 31, and kept 329 hitters and 225 pitchers who projected greater than $0 value in 5x5 scoring.

Last year, we sorted players into three REL tiers. This year we broke them into eight:

TIER	Hitter REL	Pitcher REL
A	80-99 (40)	80-99 (29)
B	69-79 (41)	65-79 (29)
C	51-68 (47)	50-64 (27)
D	41-50 (42)	31-47 (29)
E	28-40 (41)	19-30 (31)
F	20-27 (38)	6-18 (24)
G	10-19 (34)	0*-5 (28)
H	0-9 (46)	0** (28)

* 0-REL pitchers projected >$8
** 0-REL pitchers projected <$8

We then compared players' 2006 projected $5x5 values with performance. Because the projections were uniformly slightly high (the median performance was about $1.30 short of projected $5x5), we measured using roughly one standard deviation to set these thresholds:

- **Killing:** More than $3 over projection.
- **Gain:** Between even with projection and $3 over
- **Par:** Between even with projection and $2.50 short
- **Loss:** Between $2.50 and $5 short of projection
- **Bust:** More than $5 short of projection

RESULTS

About 55% players returned Par or better, with the 'D' tier of midrange REL doing the worst, and the 'A' tier of highest REL doing better than average — advantageous considering the number of higher-projected players there.

REL Tier	KILL	GAIN	PAR	LOSS	BUST	PAR+
A	19	10	11	5	24	**58%**
B	12	12	10	15	21	**49%**
C	19	12	7	4	32	**51%**
D	9	12	10	12	28	**44%**
E	23	15	7	9	18	**63%**
F	19	13	9	6	15	**66%**
G	16	10	7	10	19	**53%**
H	20	10	13	8	23	**58%**
TOTAL	137	94	74	69	180	**55%**
	25%	17%	13%	12%	32%	

The seeming opportunity seen at first glance in the lower 'E' and 'F' tiers is blunted by lower projected 5x5 values — the median $5x5 just $7.90 in the 'E' tier and $6.60 in the 'F'. And consider this: It's pretty hard to come up $5.00 short on a $7.00 projection, but an uncomfortable number of these 'E' and 'F' players managed it.

Still, these are not results that led to any firm conclusions — especially with the large number of Busts in all tiers.

So we checked for "sweet spots" where projected 5x5 value and REL worked in tandem to give us risk-management advantage.

Hitters

It worked. Among hitters, we found high-REL (A, B, C) hitters with $10-$20 value pushed the Par-or-better percentage to 59%, notably better than results for $20+ hitters, where more than half of high-REL players failed to deliver to Par or better.

There was also some bargain-hunting potential in the $0-$9 range, where almost two-thirds of the high-REL hitters made profits (although there weren't many high-REL hitters in that lower price category):

Tier A-C	KILL	GAIN	PAR	LOSS	BUST	PAR+
$21+	8	10	4	6	18	48%
$10-$20	16	6	10	6	16	59%
$0-$9	13	5	1	3	8	63%

Pitchers

Among pitchers, especially starters, the decision to combine REL with projected $5x5 paid off handsomely. Basically, pitchers overall were coin-tosses, with the higher value pitchers faring worse than others:

Proj 5x5	KILL	GAIN	PAR	LOSS	BUST	PAR+
$26+	1	3	2	0	6	50%
$21-$25	1	2	3	2	7	40%
$16-$20	4	5	2	2	15	39%
$11-$15	10	6	6	2	18	52%
$6-$10	13	9	6	4	17	57%
$0-$5	20	12	11	13	23	54%
TOTAL	49	37	30	23	81	53%

Almost all the Killings in the $15 or higher categories were made by closers or relievers who became closers. Among $15+ starters, only Brandon Webb made a Killing, while four (Roy Halladay, John Lackey, Curt Schilling and Danny Haren) made Gains and four others (Johan Santana, Chris Carpenter, Chris Young and Scott Kazmir) were Par.

The table suggested looking instead in the $6-$15 $5x5 range. Sure enough, of the 46 SPs in that range, 34 (74%) were Par or better, with 26 (57%) making a Gain or a Killing. Within that subset, *all 34 profitable pitchers had RELs of A, B or C!* Nine of 16 Killings, 8 of 10 Gains and 7 of 8 Pars were by these High-REL starters.

Conclusion

Rostering lower-price players spreads your risk while absolving you of the difficult task of landing that productive $1 or $2 player to offset a $40 bid. This research supports the thesis that you're better off taking three $15 regulars than one $40 stud with a $3 and $2 benchwarmer gamble.

Lower-priced pitchers in particular offer another advantage. Since pitching is a more fungible commodity than hitting, underperformers are more easily replaced. The savvy manager can load up on relatively cheap pitching, knowing it's more easily replaced (in leagues with reasonably liberal free-agent policies).

So if your league allows you to drop and add free-agents, a sound strategy is to minimize pitching risk by grabbing low-price/high-REL SPs to compete in Ks and meet the IP minimum, rounding out with LIMA relievers and a closer, and filling the offense with high-REL hitters in that dependable high-REL $10-$20 range.

It's not a guarantee, of course, but it is a way to go into a season with a method to contain your risks and be reasonably confident that you will field a competitive team.

New xBA
by John Burnson

Every year, we like to unpack our microscope and peer again at Expected Batting Average (xBA). This season, we had ideas about hit rate (H%). Recall the form of xH%:

$$xH\% = GB\%*(aPX + bSX + c)$$
$$+ FB\%*(dPX + eSX + f)$$
$$+ LD\%*(gPX + hSX + i)$$

We split hit rate into the three types of hits and then identify the influence of power (PX) and speed (SX) on each. For 2007, we first want to split H% into rates for home run and non-HR hits. We labeled the non-HR rate as H1% and the HR rate as H2%, so

$$H\% = H/(AB-K) = H1\% + H2\%$$
$$\text{where } H1\% = (H-HR)/(AB-K) \text{ and } H2\% = HR/(AB-K)$$

Our inquiry bore out our hunch: The rates indeed have distinct components. Our chosen regression of H2% is this:

$$xH2\% = FB\%*[0.0013\ PX - 0.0002\ SX - 0.057]$$
$$+ GB\%*[0.0006\ PX]$$

Not surprisingly for a rate of home runs, FB% and PX dominate. The negative term for FB*SX is logical – faster players tend to have lower rates of HRs than their PX implies, because a good portion of their doubles and triples are the product of speed, not power.

The GB*PX term is unexpected, but it was vital – the regression improved markedly with this term. Keep in mind that PX is *deduced* power based on rates of extra-base hits. But extra-base hits are rarer on ground balls, and homers are nigh impossible. The GB*PX term says that batters with higher rates of GB% have higher rates of HR than we would expect from their (GB-depressed) PX.

What about H1% – the rate of non-homer hits on hit balls? In particular, we wondered about the role of speed – is it linear? When we plotted SX vs. H1%, we found that the relationship was better described as *logarithmic*. A logarithmic curve is based on the power of the number. So, for example, the log of 100 is twice the log of 10, since 100 is 10 to the 2nd power (that is, squared). Unlike a line, a logarithmic curve rises and then settles toward a plateau.

A logarithmic relationship of speed to non-homer hits makes sense. After all, the goal is to reach first base before the throw. The important increases in speed occur among the slower batters. After a certain point, the gains in H1% diminish – being twice as fast as Scott Podsednik won't get you twice as many hits.

So, for our regression for H1%, we used $ln(SX)$ – the natural log of SX – rather than SX. Here is our result:

$$xH1\% = GB\%*[0.0004\ PX + 0.062\ ln(SX)]$$
$$+ LD\%*[0.93 - 0.086\ ln(SX)]$$
$$+ FB\%*0.12$$

In this equation, GB% and SX are pivotal. As with the current formula for xH%, there are "core" rates for non-homer hits on LD (87%) and FB (15%) but not on GB – getting a hit on a grounder depends on the batter's speed and power. However, unlike xH%, where power is about twice as important as speed, in xH1% speed is about four times as important. Success is beating the throw to first.

Here, then, is xBA for 2007 *(xH1% and xH2% defined above)*:

$$xBA = xCT\% * [xH1\% + xH2\%]$$

Forward-looking PQS
by John Burnson

One of the projects tackled at Baseball HQ in 2006 was trying to predict winners of individual games. Many of the writers engaged in this effort turned for guidance to HQ's method for appraising starting pitchers, Pure Quality Starts (PQS). In every start, PQS awards up to five points, one for each of the following criteria:

- The pitcher must have lasted at least 6 innings.
- He must have recorded at least IP-2 strikeouts.
- He must have allowed no more than one home run.
- He must have allowed no more hits than IP.
- He must have had a Command (K/BB) of at least 2.0.

Our exercises showed that we have a ways to go in predicting Wins. For sure, part of the difficulty is that a Win depends on many factors besides pitching skill. However, it is also plausible that PQS is not the best guide for this job. PQS says whether a pitcher performed ably in a *past* start – it doesn't say anything about how he'll do in the *next* start.

We decided to build a version of PQS that does that. We looked at all starts in 2006. For each series of five starts for a pitcher, we looked at his average IP, K/9, HR/9, H/9, and K/BB, and then we looked at whether the pitcher won his next start. We catalogued the results by indicator and calculated the observed future winning percentage for each data point. (We used all points that had at least 10 events, but small sample sizes still led to some sharp fluctuations.)

Innings

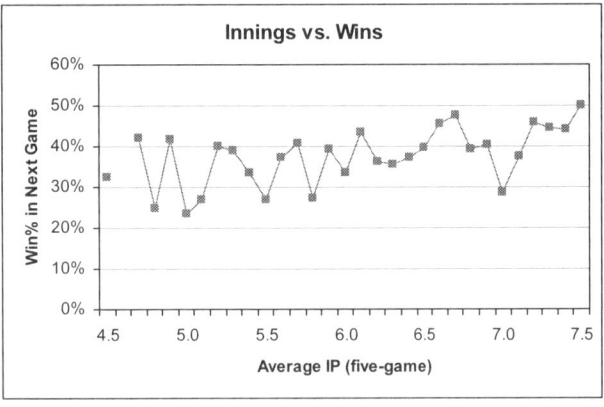

Innings pitched is not a strong gauge of future winning percentage. Standard PQS puts the threshold for quality at 6.0 IP, but this chart doesn't see substantial gains until 6.2 IP. Of the 10 data points beyond 6-1/2 IP, six have a future winning percentage above 44%, which is higher than the odds for any point below 6-1/2 IP.

The probability of a pitcher getting a Win in a game is strongly related to the number of innings that he completes. In that light, a cut-off of 6.2 IP doesn't seem to have an edge on one of 6.0 IP, since in neither case does the pitcher leave as the pitcher of record for the seventh inning. Note, though, that we're using five-game averages. A pitcher who has recently averaged 6.2 IP is just a tiny bit of managerial patience away from owning seven of the nine innings.

Strikeouts

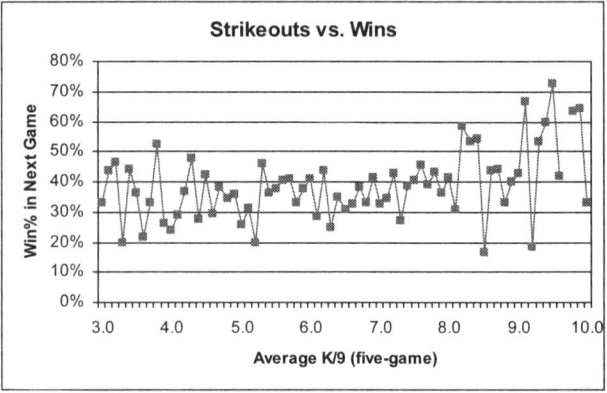

This graph does not exhibit the placidness of the previous one. There are three bands: a quivering band of 5.0 K/9 and below, where future winning percentage regularly hits only 30% or less; a steadier band from 5.0 K/9 to 8.0 K/9, where the winning percentage hovers around 35%; and a more pronounced band of 8.0 K/9 and above, where almost half of all data points top 50%. If we set the threshold for our new PQS at 8.0 K/9, that translates into a desired number of strikeouts of IP-1, versus IP-2 for standard PQS. As with innings, we suspect that the real threshold for greatness is a bit higher (namely, 9.0 K/9, at which the future winning percentage hits an amazing 70%), but an average rate over five games of 8.0 K/9 gives us a good shot at that summit.

Home runs

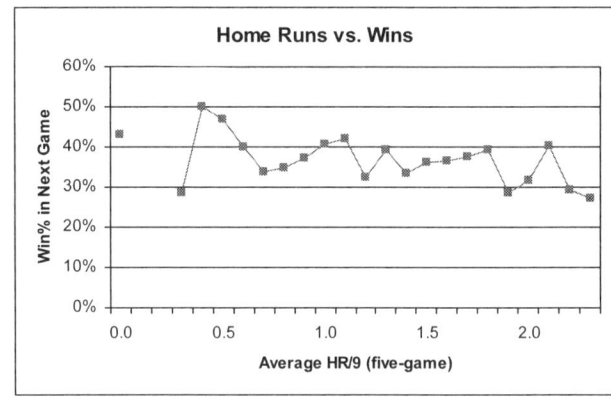

The graph is quieter than the one for strikeouts, but the trend is clearer than that for IP. The line essentially starts at a future winning percentage of 43% for 0.0 HR/9 and traipses down to 27% for 2.3 HR/9. A rate of 0.5 HR/9 or lower seems favorable; in 6 IP, that translates to one-third of a homer. We could probably stick with a ceiling of 1 HR per game, but we'll be tougher and demand 0.

We might expect that a high HR/9 would be a greater cause for alarm (and a low one, a greater reason for joy); however, for a stat like HR where two events is a big deal, outcomes can be skewed by a handful of really bad pitches or really keen batters. Recall, too, that we are studying only those pitchers who gave up 2.3 HR/9 in five games and yet got another chance; they are likely those who were deemed by their managers to have the best talent or the worst luck.

Hits

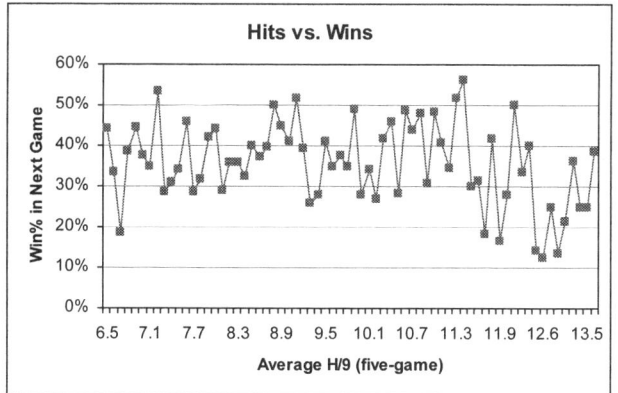

As we might expect from an indicator like hit rate, which we know has a large element of pitcher-independence, this graph paints a picture of volatility. The best future winning percentage occurs at 11.4 H/9, the next-best is down at 7.2 H/9. Still, we have to say that things start falling apart at 11.5 H/9; beyond that, only one point tops 42%, and five points fall below 20%. Curiously, a rate of 11.5 H/9 gives us a threshold for hits of IP *plus two*. That is, this new PQS is *less* strict when it comes to hits than is standard PQS! Again, we think that the reason is the luck-heavy incidence of hits on balls in play. This graph says that averaging even two more hits than IP should earn no particular scorn.

Command

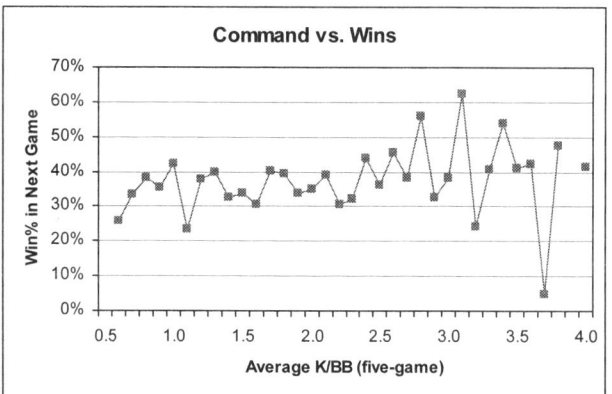

Due to having relatively few examples of excellent Command, the right side of this graph swings quite a bit. Regardless, the lesson of this graph is a little surprising. It seems that, in terms of future winning percentage, Command can't really be called "bad" until about 1.0 K/BB, and even that low rate doesn't bode terribly poorly. (As with the high-HR pitchers, the weak Commanders in this study are probably biased to those who generally see better days.)

However, there *is* such a thing as terrific Command, and it kicks in at an average rate of 2.5 K/BB, as opposed to the 2.0 K/BB favored by standard PQS. In fact, a command of 3.0 K/BB portends a winning percentage of 60% by itself. This fact places a high Command as the second-strongest determinant of future success, after a high strikeout rate. However, the disparity is not great enough for us to weight these indicators more heavily than the other three.

To recap, this research suggests that a forward-looking version of PQS should have *these* criteria:

- The pitcher must have lasted at least 6.2 innings.
- He must have recorded at least IP-1 strikeouts.
- He must have allowed zero home runs.
- He must have allowed no more hits than IP+2.
- He must have had a Command (K/BB) of at least 2.5.

Among these criteria, that of a high strikeout rate is "first among equals;" as we learn from xERA, nothing succeeds like simply keeping the ball out of play. Otherwise, forward-looking PQS generally demands more of a pitcher than does standard PQS. The reason is that the future is uncertain – to ensure a good level of play tomorrow, we need a premium level of play today. We know that a 2.0 K/BB is a good sign of pitching prowess; this research says that, to have a fair shot of hitting that 2.0 mark, we need a recent Command of 2.5. The exception to this rule is hits per game, where forward-looking PQS is more forgiving (and, perhaps, standard PQS is harsher than it needs to be).

This version of PQS does not supplant the existing one. Standard PQS points us to pitchers who *should have* done well; forward-looking PQS points us to pitchers who *ought to* do well (in the next game, anyway). Both versions highlight opportunities for buying.

There is an analog in stock-picking. The price of a stock can be set against either its actual earnings or its projected earnings; thus, the stock can be cheap (or expensive) relative to what it has done, or cheap (or expensive) relative to what it is expected to do. As in stocks, the future in baseball is shrouded in darkness; forward-looking PQS helps pierce the veil.

Relievers' secret edge
by John Burnson

Q: Which of these pitchers should have the lower ERA?

	IP	K/9	BB/9	HR/9	Role
Pitcher A	100	6.0	3.0	1.0	Starting
Pitcher B	100	6.0	3.0	1.0	Relief

Since ERA rests on a pitcher's rates of strikeouts, walks, and ground balls (and since the listed rates already account for any leap in skills from pitching in relief), the ERA's should be identical. But a reliever accrues his IP over many more games than does a starter. More to the point, the reliever often enters a game not at the top of the inning, when there are no outs, but later, when there are 1 or 2 down. The more outs gone, the smaller the window for a pitcher's runners to advance. Overall, then, the reliever should have the lower ERA. (Note, we're not discussing baserunners whom a reliever *inherits* – they aren't applied to his ERA. We are concerned only with baserunners that the reliever allows.)

For purposes of discussion, let's christen a new metric, *Edge*, defined as *(Outs Gone)/Game*. Edge is usually 0 for starters and closers but above zero for relievers. Data show it's not unusual for a reliever to have an Edge of 0.7 (i.e. he enters play with an average of $^2/_3$ of an out gone).

At bottom, our reliever creates baserunners at the same rate as does the starter, but he abandons a greater fraction of those runners – that is, the reliever sees an improvement in his *strand rate*. Strand rate, a favored gauge at HQ and a key component of Expected ERA, refers to the proportion of baserunners who do not score. All else equal, the higher the strand rate, the lower the ERA. And, in fact, we do often see better-than-expected ERA's by relievers. Some of the gain must certainly derive from relievers' often facing favorable match-ups, but a chunk must also be due to Edge.

To get a handle on the benefit, we took a LIMA-caliber reliever (6 K/9, 2 K/BB, 1 HR/9) and simulated his strand rate under two regimes, one where he always enters at the top of the inning, and one where he randomly enters with 0, 1, or 2 outs gone. We required that, whenever the reliever enters a game, he faces at least 4 men. Here are the results:

	Start w/0 Outs	Start randomly
Strand Rate	70.5%	72.1%

We can characterize the gain in strand rate by saying that, in doing away with outs, Edge effectively raises a pitcher's strikeout rate. Since each extra K/9 raises strand rate by 1.2 points, our reliever gains the equivalent of 1.3 K/9 (so he effectively has a 7.3 K/9 and 2.4 K/BB). That is a gift, especially for pitchers who already have a high dominance.

What's more, HQ's Doug Dennis has observed that Edge is greatest among *left-handed set-up men*. These pitchers are often called into a game to take on a particular batter or two, not to start an inning in relief of a dismissed starter. Thus, these relievers' odds of entering mid-inning are good. If we relax our simulation so that the reliever is a specialist who can face as few as two batters, his strand rate shoots to 72.9%. That's an effective gain in strikeout rate of 2 K/9! And Joe Reliever becomes an 8 K/9 star you have to own.

The impact of handedness
by John Burnson

When we look at deviations between ERA and xERA, we often point to the rate of hits on balls in play, or homers on fly balls. Those rates are largely pitcher-independent, so we compare the pitcher's rates vs. "normal" rates of 30% and 10%. However, the stated figures are *averages* of the entire pool of batters. A given batter's rates of hits and homers are not unpredictable but are functions of power and speed.

So maybe we can explain odd hit and homer rates for a pitcher by studying the qualities of the batters that he faces. A simple place to start is the *handedness* of the batters.

We can define pitchers by two pairs of traits: RH vs. LH, and starter vs. reliever. For relievers, we can further break out closers and non-closers. For each group, we found the percentage of AB versus LH batters. Here are the results:

	Pitcher's handedness	
Type of pitcher	**RH**	**LH**
Starter	51%	21%
Closer	50%	27%
Non-closer reliever	44%	43%

Note that the ratios for closers echo those for starters. The reason is that, like starters, closers generally don't get pulled from games on the basis of the handedness of the batter at the plate. Now, we might have imagined that *non-closer* relievers would face a more skewed bunch of batters, as opposing managers bring specialist hitters off the bench, but it seems not: relievers of either handedness face essentially the league-average ratio of lefties. HQ's Doug Dennis suggests that the ratios are similar because it is the manager of the *reliever* who ultimately determines which pitchers face which batters; therefore, relievers are removed from many unfavorable match-ups. That's especially true for LH relievers, since RH understudies tend to be more plentiful.

For our groups, we can plot H% and S% vs. LH%. We expect H% to rise and S% to fall as a pitcher faces more opposite-handed batters. When we created these graphs for starting pitchers, we found that the lines are *flat* – a starter's hit and strand rates do not appreciably worsen with more opposite-handed batters. Perhaps the need for starting batters to also be decent fielders means that managers cannot stack the line-up with masters of opposite-handed pitchers.

For relievers, the story was even stranger – we found that RH relievers had *better* H% and S% with increasing LH%, and vice versa for LH relievers. These trends are contrary to expectations. However, maybe we have the relationship backwards: Maybe it's not that relievers who faced more opposite-handed batters did better, but that better relievers faced more opposite-handed batters. In other words, opposing managers substitute more often vs. superior relievers. The correlations between K/BB and LH% back this notion:

	Correlation with LH%
RH K/BB	+0.17
LH K/BB	-0.19

In the future, then, maybe we should beware of talented relievers who haven't been tested by enough bad matchups.

A LOOK BACK AT 2006
Examining the Coors Field effect
by Brandon Kruse

The humidor that the Colorado Rockies use to keep baseballs from drying out in the thin Denver air was a hot topic in 2006. It was the subject of much speculation, hand-wringing and even some conspiracy theories from opposing teams. This was understandably so, as the Rockies did things in 2006 that once seemed utterly impossible. Their pitching staff posted a 4.66 ERA, the lowest mark in team history and only the second time in Colorado's 13-year existence that their pitching staff featured an ERA below 5.00. And they allowed the third-fewest home runs in all of baseball, just five years after setting an NL record with 239 HR allowed in the 2001 season.

But this wasn't the first year the Rockies used the humidor — they started back during the 2002 season. So what changed this year? Depending on who you ask, there are three different answers to that question: baseballs were left in the humidor longer this season, the infield grass was grown longer, and the Rockies simply had a better pitching staff.

Dan Fox of *Baseball Prospectus* and Mitchell Lichtman at *insidethebook.com* did some analysis back in June showing that the humidor had reduced the average fly ball distance at Coors by 11 feet since 2001 (down to 329 feet, just four feet above the average of all other outdoor parks), and had cut the number of those fly balls that go for home runs by 8%. Fox also found that fewer ground balls were making it through the infield, supporting the longer infield grass theory.

BP's Joe Sheehan revisited the issue in early August and concluded that park effects and balls-in-play data showed that Coors had basically become a slight pitchers' park (though he gave some credit to an improved Rockies pitching staff). And in September, Baseball HQ took a look at the first five months of Coors Field data and noted that 2006 appeared to be part of a greater trend of long-term offensive decline:

Yr	NATIONAL LEAGUE				COORS FIELD			
	R/G	BA	AB/HR	AB/D	R/G	BA	AB/HR	AB/D
00	5.00	.266	29.5	19.2	7.19	.318	23.9	16.3
01	4.70	.261	29.8	19.1	6.70	.310	21.5	15.5
02	4.45	.259	33.8	19.6	6.15	.298	24.4	17.4
03	4.61	.262	32.7	19.0	5.97	.292	24.7	16.4
04	4.64	.263	31.1	18.9	6.35	.305	26.0	15.1
05	4.45	.262	34.2	18.5	5.54	.297	33.8	16.9
06	4.76	.265	31.3	18.4	5.36	.288	33.6	17.2

One of the first things that jumps out at you is that, with the exception of 2004, R/G at Coors have been on a perfect downward trend. In seven years, Coors has steadily gone from being two-plus runs over the league average in runs scored per game to about half a run above average, and from a homer haven to a park where it's just slightly tougher than most to hit one out. Doubles are down as well. Viewed in the context of this seven-year window, suddenly 2006 starts to look like another point along an already-existing trend — perhaps we shouldn't have been quite so surprised by this season's results.

Of course, the most surprising thing about 2006 may have been the way the season ended. In 14 September games, offense exploded and Coors Field looked like the run factory of old:

COORS FIELD OFFENSE

Month	R/G	BA	AB/HR	AB/D	bb%	ct%	Eye
April	5.17	.278	36.0	19.7	10	83	0.64
May	3.55	.253	51.1	15.5	8	82	0.45
June	5.13	.288	34.3	17.7	9	81	0.51
July	4.18	.253	29.9	25.1	8	85	0.58
Aug	5.37	.300	43.8	16.8	9	82	0.55
Sept	8.39	.339	23.3	12.9	12	83	0.78

September featured everything — a high BA, lots of doubles and homers, and more walks. What to make of that? Considering the small sample size and the fact that there were no consistent trends in the other months, it could just be an outlier. At least one report suggests that the Rockies simply ran out of pre-treated balls. We should probably consider it a reminder that it's still possible to put up big numbers in the "new" Coors environment.

For further proof of this, we need look no further than a pair of young Rockies, Garrett Atkins and Matt Holliday:

HOME SPLITS

Atkins	BA	PX	AB/HR	AB/D
2005	.339	99	28.2	18.1
2006	.346	133	19.7	12.8

Holliday	BA	PX	AB/HR	AB/D
2004	.338	154	20.4	11.3
2005	.357	142	20.1	18.5
2006	.373	179	13.4	12.3

Atkins and Holliday posted the best Coors numbers of their young careers in 2006, as we might expect from two 26-year-old hitters in their pre-peak years. The humidor seemed to hardly affect them at all. Neither did the Coors park factors. Traditionally, Coors Field has given a slight advantage to LHB for HR (26% to 18%) and to RHB for BA (17% to 15%), which makes sense given that it's 375 feet to right-center and 390 feet to left-center. Did those factors hold up this year?

Type	BA	AB/HR
LHB	.289	32.9
RHB	.287	34.1

The lefty/righty BA advantage flipped this year, and the home run gap narrowed. Overall, compared to the league average, BA is still high, but home runs from both sides of the plate are now below-average.

However, the legitimacy of that lefty AB/HR mark may be in question — Colorado's two big lefties, Brad Hawpe and Todd Helton, both had odd home run figures this year. Hawpe hit just 6 HR at home compared to 16 on the road, and Helton posted the lowest HR total of his career, possibly due to lingering health issues. And as a group,

Rockies lefties had an anemic 52.8 AB/HR rate. Among visiting hitters, lefties hit home runs at a rate (25.6 AB/HR) that was significantly higher, and more in line with what we'd expect from Coors.

Let's move over to the pitching side. Have there been any shifts in the fundamental pitching skills of Colorado pitchers and their opponents that might shed some light on what's happening in Coors?

OPPOSING PITCHERS IN COORS

Year	ERA	Ctl	Dom	Cmd	hr/9	hr/f	G/L/F
2003	6.20	4.3	6.4	1.5	1.5	15%	43/24/33
2004	5.83	4.0	6.8	1.7	1.4	14%	44/21/36
2005	5.36	3.5	6.4	1.8	1.1	12%	43/25/32
2006	5.41	3.8	6.2	1.7	1.0	10%	45/23/32

ROCKIES PITCHERS IN COORS

Year	ERA	Ctl	Dom	Cmd	hr/9	hr/f	G/L/F
2003	5.10	3.0	5.8	1.9	1.4	14%	44/23/33
2004	6.27	4.6	6.0	1.3	1.4	13%	44/21/36
2005	5.19	3.6	6.2	1.7	1.0	11%	46/23/31
2006	4.72	3.4	5.9	1.8	1.1	12%	48/20/32

There is a slight trend of fewer walks for Colorado. Have pitchers become less afraid of throwing strikes now that the humidor's got their back? Home runs are down, and HR/FB rates have moved much closer to the 10% level we expect for pitchers — both trends that back up the humidor effect.

The most interesting stat is the increase in ground balls this year. It's been said before that breaking pitches break as much as 25% less in the thin air. It's also been a common complaint of pitchers that the drier baseballs were harder to grip properly. If the humidor is keeping the balls moister and heavier, it seems to make sense that they would be a little easier to grip and a little more likely to give a truer break. Certainly that would aid in throwing a sinking fastball or some other pitch that breaks downward, and throwing those pitches more effectively would result in more ground balls. The Rockies led the majors in double plays turned in 2006, probably a factor in their improved strand rate and likely an effect of the longer infield grass.

And how has all of this impacted the five pitchers who log the most innings in Coors, the members of the Rockies rotation? The chart below is a look at their last two seasons.

With the exception of Fogg, who was pretty much the same pitcher he was in 2005, Colorado's starting pitchers showed some modest skill growth this year. Cook's strikeouts went up and his homers allowed went down, Francis allowed fewer homers and line drives, Jennings improved his command and cut down on line drives, and Kim improved his command.

How much of this do we attribute to the humidor? If we saw these pitching lines minus the context of Coors Field, the general consensus would probably be "Hey, these guys have improved their skills." Their xERAs read like a fanalytic dream rotation. There's some question as to whether those below-average line drive rates are sustainable, but this is definitely an improved rotation.

So where do we go from here in terms of our expectations for Coors Field?

The data analyzed here all indicate that the humidor and the longer infield grass are both doing exactly what the Rockies hoped they would do — reduce offense. Assuming those two elements remain in place in 2007, it doesn't seem likely that offensive levels will bounce back to previous levels. There appears to be some wiggle room with home runs, given the extreme nature of the Helton/Hawpe drop and the fact that Atkins and Holliday are managing just fine. Even with the humidor effect, it shouldn't be a stretch for Coors to maintain at least a league-average home run rate. It would be stunning to see runs drop another 10-15% next year, the way they have over the past two years. Predicting a plateau or even a slight rebound feels like a better bet.

COOK

	ERA	Ctl	Dom	Cmd	hr/9	hr/f	G/L/F	xERA
05	3.68	1.7	2.6	1.5	0.9	14%	62/20/19	3.87
06	4.23	2.3	3.9	1.7	0.7	11%	60/17/22	3.57

FOGG

	ERA	Ctl	Dom	Cmd	hr/9	hr/f	G/L/F	xERA
05	5.06	2.8	4.5	1.6	1.4	12%	41/21/38	4.48
06	5.49	3.1	4.9	1.6	1.3	11%	45/18/37	4.12

FRANCIS

	ERA	Ctl	Dom	Cmd	hr/9	hr/f	G/L/F	xERA
05	5.70	3.4	6.3	1.8	1.3	11%	40/22/38	4.33
06	4.16	3.1	5.3	1.7	0.8	8%	46/17/37	3.78

JENNINGS

	ERA	Ctl	Dom	Cmd	hr/9	hr/f	G/L/F	xERA
05	5.02	4.6	5.5	1.2	0.8	10%	48/25/27	4.28
06	3.78	3.6	6.0	1.7	0.7	7%	46/17/37	3.75

KIM

	ERA	Ctl	Dom	Cmd	hr/9	hr/f	G/L/F	xERA
05	4.86	4.3	7.0	1.6	1.0	10%	42/20/39	4.26
06	5.57	3.5	7.5	2.1	1.0	11%	42/23/35	3.56

The case for Chien-Ming Wang
by Ray Murphy

In our continuing quest to better understand what makes pitchers successful, one fertile area for further study is the pool of ground-ball pitchers, and to what extent their sinkerball style can cover up deficiencies in their other BPIs. One very interesting pitcher who fits this description is Chien-Ming Wang, who continues to find success in the Yankee rotation despite BPIs that don't meet our preferred minimum thresholds.

Let's start with a look at Wang's skills:

Year	CTL	DOM	CMD	HR/9	BPV
2005*	2.3	3.9	1.7	0.8	36
2006	2.1	3.1	1.5	0.5	35

* - includes MLEs

From our "traditional" skills point of view, there's nothing remarkable here. CTL is solid but not elite, and the DOM and CMD levels are well below our LIMA filters. Yet, the results are far better than you would expect to get from this skill set:

Year	IP	ERA	WHIP	Wins	R$
2005	150	4.21	1.30	10	$10
2006	218	3.63	1.31	19	$15

How do we explain this skills-vs-stats disconnect? It's not luck, at least not according to our usual measurements of good fortune:

Year	H%	S%
2005	29	69
2006	29	72

With Wang's performance not fully explained by the above numbers, let's double back and take a look at some other pieces of his skill set:

Year	GB%	LD%	FB%	HR/FB%
2005	64	14	22	11
2006	63	17	20	8

Here, of course, are the beginnings of an explanation. An extreme groundball rate allows Wang to generate outs in bunches, and keeps the ball in the park. His ability to avoid line drives further limits extra base hits. But a groundball profile is no guarantee of success. (If only this game were that easy.) Here is a quick look at MLB's top SP by ground-ball rate in 2006, and their performances:

Pitcher	GB%	ERA	WHIP
B.Webb	66%	3.10	1.13
D.Lowe	67%	3.63	1.27
CMWang	63%	3.63	1.31
J.Westbrook	61%	4.18	1.43
Jm.Wright	58%	5.19	1.48
F.Hernandez	58%	4.52	1.34
A.Cook	58%	4.24	1.40
T.Hudson	58%	4.87	1.44

Eight pitchers with over 100 IP in 2006 and a GB% of 58% or higher, and we see a healthy variance in terms of effectiveness. Clearly, considering a blend of GB% and our "traditional" BPIs above would provide a much better correlation with pitcher effectiveness. But as we saw above, Wang's skill set above is one that we wouldn't consider rostering on its own. His skills map more toward the lousy performers on this list as opposed to Webb. So what reason do we have for optimism?

First, there is the infield defense behind Wang. Across MLB this season, ground balls were turned into outs 53% of the time. The Yankees check in at an above-average 55%. With Wang pitching, the NYY infield defense tightens even more, as Wang turns 56% of ground balls into outs.

This may seem surprising given the less-than-sterling reputation of the Yankee defense. Perhaps that reputation is not deserved, or perhaps some creative grounds-keeping at Yankee Stadium benefits Wang in his home starts:

	H/9	ERA
Home	0.86	2.76
Road	1.25	4.87

The personnel in the Yankee infield — Cano, Jeter, and Rodriguez — are entrenched, more or less. If the Yankees are legally tailoring their infield grounds to suit Wang, the success they have had in that endeavor this year would likely inspire them to continue that process. And as Wang's career unfolds, his split data should fairly quickly tell us what ballparks are good and bad for him, setting up a great micro-managing opportunity.

For another, rather speculative cause for optimism, consider the notion that Wang *can* strike out more batters, but *chooses not to*. For such an extreme ground-ball pitcher, most situations in a typical start set themselves up well for the ground ball. With nobody on, generating a ground ball is more economical than attempting to strike out a batter. Even if one or two of those ground balls get through the infield in an inning, continuing to generate grounders could yield a double play that ends the threat.

In short, a good ground ball pitcher faces relatively few situations that call for a strikeout. But unlike some of the other noteworthy ground ball pitchers, Wang has a power pitcher's velocity: he tops out in the mid-90s. To test the idea that Wang might be self-suppressing his strikeout ability, we took a look at a few on-base situations from this year where a strikeout would be advantageous:

Situation	AB/K
none on	12.5
runners on	10.1
scoring pos	11.8
on 2nd	8.5
on 3rd	5.3
2nd/3rd	10.0

Some of these individual situational samples are far too small to draw meaningful conclusions. But looking at the aggregate of these situations, the trend seems clear: in any situation where a strikeout would seem particularly beneficial to Wang, he is noticeably more effective at generating that outcome.

For a final point, consider Wang's consistently low LD%. LDs are the most damaging type of hit to a pitcher, and Wang is among the "best" at limiting them. We use quotation marks around "best" because LD-avoidance is not a skill generally within a pitcher's control. But as we continue our research, including some very preliminary work by Neil Bonner on process-based pitching metrics, we may well discover other skill measurements in which Wang grades out much higher, perhaps even at an elite level. For now, we're left to speculate on the subject.

TACTICAL IN-SEASON ROSTER MANAGEMENT
Pinpointing skills changes
by John Burnson

For more than two months last year, Erik Bedard was a disappointment. In 2005, Bedard had 7.9 K/9, 2.2 K/BB, and a 4.00 ERA, but in his first 11 starts of 2006, he averaged only 5.4 K/9, 1.4 K/BB – and a 5.67 ERA. And then, on June 11, Bedard recorded nine strikeouts. That performance raised his strikeout rate in his most recent three-game stretch to 9.0 K/9. Should fantasy owners have pounced?

It's a question that arises every season: When does a shift in apparent skills become meaningful? We decided to examine this topic for starting pitchers. Using data for 2006, we identified seasons that could be broken into three parts:

1. A period of at least five games at the start of the season (the "baseline").
2. A span of 3-5 games where the strikeout rate differed from the baseline by at least 2 K/9 (the "outburst").
3. A period of at least five games from after the outburst to the end of the season (the "shake-out").

For each span (3, 4, or 5 games), we considered only the earliest outburst for a pitcher, since we desire to pounce on legitimate gains as early as possible, and since subsequent outbursts in the same direction are often correlated.

Here are the results for an outburst of at least 2 K/9 (a pitcher's kept gain can be larger than 100% if the strikeout rate in the shake-out is above the outburst, or negative if the strikeout rate in the shake-out is below the baseline):

Shake-out from Positive Outburst

	[- AVERAGE K/9 -]			Median
Span	Base	Move	Final	Gain Kept
3	5.2	+3.0	6.8	40%
4	5.4	+3.0	7.0	45%
5	5.5	+2.8	6.9	50%

On average, a pitcher who experiences a positive outburst of at least 2 K/9 ends up keeping about half the rise, regardless of the span of the outburst. However, at smaller spans, the gains are distributed among fewer heirs. The median gain rises by five points for each extra game over which the outburst is kept up, and it reaches 50% only at five games.

Here is a depiction of the positive outbursts for all spans:

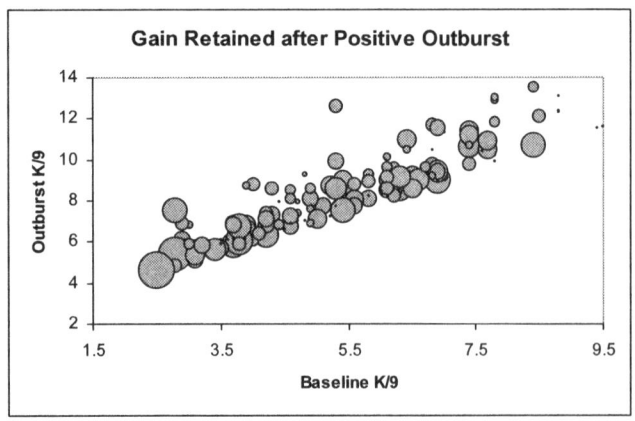

The size of the 'bubble' reflects the percentage of the outburst that is kept. Bubbles of various sizes are well distributed. However, pitchers with high baselines often retain little of their outburst. Let's sort the data by baseline K/9:

Median Gain Retained (%/Raw)

	[- Baseline Strikeout Rate -]		
Span	<5 K/9	5-7 K/9	>7 K/9
3	38%/1.0	57%/1.9	27%/1.3
4	63%/1.6	78%/2.1	21%/1.0
5	51%/1.1	59%/1.6	31%/0.9

Dominant pitchers (those with a baseline strikeout rate of at least 7 K/9) kept about 1 K/9 in the shake-out, a goodly gain. However, these pitchers retained the poorest *share* of their outburst, presumably since these pitchers can become only so much more formidable. On the other hand, so-called "soft tossers" – those with a baseline strikeout rate below 5 K/9 – keep a larger share of their outburst; however, because soft-tossers operate from a lower level, their absolute gains are on par with those for the top echelon.

The pitchers who enjoyed the most lasting effect in both absolute and relative terms were those who had a baseline strikeout rate of 5-7 K/9. Apparently, these are pitchers of skill who, in the early going, faced stronger-than-usual foes or were just mechanically off. These pitchers often boosted their dominance by two full strikeouts in the shake-out.

What about negative outbursts (losses of at least 2 K/9)?

Shake-out from Negative Outburst

	[- AVERAGE K/9 -]			Median
Span	Base	Move	Final	Drop Kept
3	7.0	-2.9	6.0	30%
4	7.0	-2.7	6.1	29%
5	7.1	-2.5	6.0	47%

Again, the duration mattered little – the pitchers in each span opened the season at about 7 K/9 and finished at about 6 K/9. At smaller spans, though, the losses were concentrated in few pitchers; most suffered lightly. Only at a span of five games did half the pitchers endure half the loss.

Median Loss Retained (%/Raw)

	[- Baseline Strikeout Rate -]		
Span	<6 K/9	6-8 K/9	>=8 K/9
3	28%/0.8	25%/0.7	69%/2.1
4	8%/0.3	29%/0.8	62%/2.1
5	20%/0.7	32%/0.8	73%/2.2

Watch out for seemingly high performers! A dominance over 8 K/9 is so difficult to maintain that negative outbursts should be viewed with concern; the bulk of the shortfall is genuine. Pitchers with more-mortal strikeout rates plod on.

And what of Erik Bedard? With a baseline strikeout rate of 5.4 K/9, Bedard fell among the pitchers who generally keep much of their positive outbursts. Indeed, Bedard never looked back after that 9-K game – he ended the season with a run of 9 K/9. His leap should have led to one of our own.

Timing, streaming and investor returns
by John Burnson

In 2006, the research company Morningstar announced that it would add a dimension to its ratings of mutual funds. In addition to tallying the return for a fund from one date to another, Morningstar will adjust the return *for the timing of purchases and sales in that period*. In other words, the performance in a given period will be weighted by the volume of deposits that actually enjoyed the performance. Morningstar refers to this new metric as "investor returns."

This approach is ideally suited to Roto. In leagues that allow weekly or daily transactions, many owners flit from hot player to hot player. But published dollar values don't capture this traffic – they assume that players are owned from April to October. For many leagues, this may be unrealistic.

We decided to calculate investor returns for 2006. We do not have data showing the percentage of owners who were "in" a player (such data could be gleaned from commercial leagues). So we devised a model. For each week, we identified the top players by one statistic – BA for hitters, ERA for pitchers – and took the top 100 hitters and top 50 pitchers. We then said that, at the end of the week, the #1 player was picked up (or already owned) by 100% of teams, the #2 player was picked up or owned by 99% of teams, and so on, down to the 100th player, who was on 1% of teams. (For pitchers, we stepped by 2%.) Last, we tracked each player's performance in the *next* week, when ownership matters.

We ran this process anew for every week of the season, tabulating each player's "investor returns" along the way. If a player was owned by 100% of teams, then we awarded him 100% of his performance. If the player was owned by half the teams, we gave him half his performance. If he was owned by no one (that is, he was not among the top players in the prior week), his performance was ignored. A player's cumulative performance over the season was his investor return. To target players who would draw interest, we set a weekly minimum of 20 AB and 6 IP.

We tackled pitchers first. As you might guess, very good pitchers were usually hurt by active trading, since their periodic bad week drove panicked owners from partaking in their strong skills. Of the top 25 ML pitchers in ERA, 15 had a higher investor ERA than actual ERA. Here are the numbers for the top 10 (bolded lines indicate pitchers who had worse investor ERA's than actual ERA's):

PITCHER	ActERA	InvERA	Diff
Johnson Jo	2.90	2.90	---
Carpenter	**2.96**	**3.64**	**+0.68**
Webb	2.99	2.48	-0.51
Santana Jo	**3.01**	**3.21**	**+0.20**
Halladay	**3.12**	**4.31**	**+1.19**
Oswalt	**3.23**	**3.56**	**+0.33**
Schmidt	3.23	2.61	-0.62
Kazmir	**3.24**	**3.31**	**+0.07**
Sabathia	**3.30**	**3.56**	**+0.26**
Zambrano	3.31	3.18	-0.13

Florida's Josh Johnson is a rare picture of consistency – among qualifying hurlers, 60% had a swing of half a run or more between their actual and investor ERA's. And traders were more hurt than helped by their bustle – on average, a pitcher's investor ERA was 0.40 *higher* than his true ERA.

The full list reveals some real migraine-inducers. Do you look at your roster and see a 3.75-ERA Noah Lowry? Not if you were an active trader – you got the 5.17-ERA model. Dust off Kelvim Escobar (3.87 ERA) and find a 5.56 ERA. Unhappy with a 3.92 ERA, Jeremy Bonderman sits at 6.18.

Owners who hopped in and out of Roy Halladay had especially good reason to curse. Halladay in 2006 gave up 1 ER or fewer on eight occasions. In the next starts, he had a 3.73 ERA (vs. a 3.12 ERA for the year) and three Wins. On eight other occasions, Halladay gave up 4 ER or more. In the following starts, he had a 2.59 ERA and *seven* Wins!

Not all good pitchers suffered from trading – those who followed bad starts with bad starts, or good starts with good starts, "rewarded" active traders. Using investor ERA, Greg Maddux went from 40th-best to 4th-best, and Scott Olsen catapulted from #47 to #9. This good fortune isn't shocking – there are always traders who get lucky. The hitch is that, on the evidence of this research, most unusually bad and good starts aren't commencements of trends but accidents.

What of hitters? Here are the ML leaders in BA:

HITTER	ActBA	InvBA	Diff
Mauer	.356	.339	-.017
Sanchez	.346	.313	-.034
Cabrera M	.340	.303	-.037
Jeter	.337	.326	-.011
Holliday	.330	.363	+.033
Tejeda	.330	.339	+.010
Guerrero	.327	.347	+.021
Dye	.326	.314	-.012
Ramirez M	.326	.317	-.008

With active trading, the BA leader was not Joe Mauer but Matt Holliday. Holliday "won" because his hot and cold spells were distinct – Holliday had two months when he had to be avoided (April and July, when he hit .262 and .253), and three months when he had to be owned (May, June, and August, when he hit .400, .388., and .345). Mauer was great for two months (May and June, when he hit .386 and .452) but a mere .300 hitter the rest. More traders got socked by Mauer's rough weeks than by Holliday's. Again, unless traders had some secret insights, this was mere luck.

That said, the fate of batters under active trading is not the fate of pitchers. About 55% of batters had poorer investor returns (vs. 60% of pitchers), and the average difference was virtually 0. Chasing performance among hitters doesn't help, but it doesn't hurt, either. The implication is that BA is "streakier" than ERA – good and bad weeks are more correlated (though still not well correlated) for hitters than pitchers. Maybe the large role of chance in pitchers' hit and homer rates leads to swings in ERA that are more extreme (and less tied to skill) than are swings in BA. Conversely, changes in batters' mechanics might be more durable.

This model was simple – we looked at only one category, and traders had no patience and (notably) no costs. Still, the results (for pitchers particularly) reinforce the emptiness of much trading. Don't be swayed by short-term results – do your homework, find skilled players, and stick with them.

Home field advantage
by John Burnson

A growing number of fantasy leagues put a premium on guessing the outcomes of single games, so let's look at how Runs Allowed and Runs Scored affect winning percentage. Although the true odds of winning are a function of the *spread* of possible outcomes, here we will consider only the *differences* between the expected outcomes for the teams.

For ease of use, we built our model for the casual gamer. When figuring the expected Runs Allowed for a team, we looked only at the starting pitcher, not the bullpen, and we used the pitcher's actual rate of RA/9 heading into the contest rather than a metric like xRA. Similarly, instead of using Runs Created or some such for hitters, we tapped each team's RS/9 – again, as of the date of the contest. We pulled data for 2006 for only those contests in which both starting pitchers had already started at least five games.

There is one other variable: *home-field advantage*. For the games under study, that advantage was about 0.6 Runs. This sum is not inconsiderable – in fact, it is often critical:

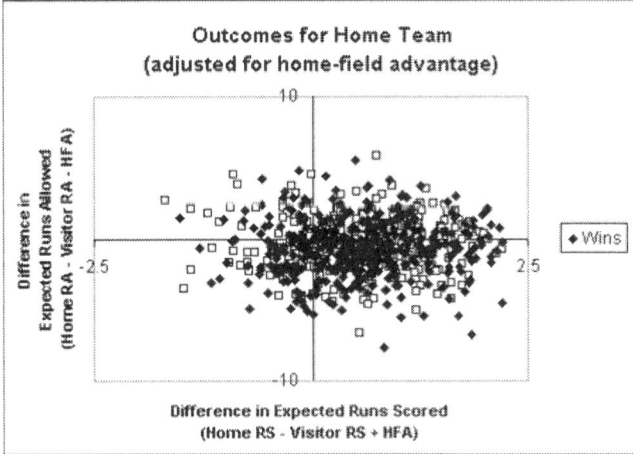

You can see how home-field advantage drags the results to the lower right, the most favorable quadrant for the home team. All in all, the mission for the home team should be to allow fewer runs. The Win rate for the home team in the lower half (where the visiting team is predicted to allow more runs) is about four percentage points higher than that in the upper half. The left-right break in Runs Scored is nowhere near as favorable. This finding reinforces a fact of baseball: *Run prevention is king*. A team that scores 10 runs can still lose, but a team that allows 0 runs can't.

Many Roto players are more interested in Wins for starting pitchers than for teams. In our study, the home starter got a Win in 38% of games (69% of the 55% of games won by the home team); the visiting starter got a Win in 33% of games (but 74% of the 45% of games won by the visitors). As the home starter fares better when the expected difference in RA is negative, the visiting starter fares better when the difference is positive. In fact, even accounting for home-field, the home and visiting starters are on roughly equal footing in the upper quadrants.

Conclusions? If you are betting on single games, go with pitching, and do not underestimate home-field advantage.

The short-term predictive value of xBA
by Brandon Kruse

On June 9, Mets shortstop Jose Reyes was hitting .247. But thanks to a combination of good skills and bad luck, he had an expected batting average of .293, which put him on the Potential BA Surgers list in our weekly Baseball HQ Top 10 Hotlists. Over the next two weeks, Reyes went 26-for-55, a .473 clip. And from June 9 to the All-Star break, Reyes hit .421 with two homers, 12 RBI, 32 runs scored and 16 steals. If you had rostered Reyes on June 9, you would have hit the fantasy baseball jackpot.

Reyes' outburst warrants a look at the short-term predictive value of xBA — specifically those hitters with large gaps between their BA and their xBA. Baseball is a streaky game, and finding a way to predict those hot and cold streaks has long been a fanalytic holy grail. Perhaps with hitters, xBA could turn a dart-throwing crapshoot into an act with a bit more precision and accuracy. If so, that could prove useful for salary cap and shallow leagues, where there's a large pool of available players to draw from and a high level of roster churn, and also for roster management in leagues with benches, where owners need to decide who to start and who to sit.

To test this out, players were gathered into several groups and their results tracked over a two-week period, from June 26 to July 9.

- **xBA Surgers**: hitters with a BA lower than their xBA
- **xBA Faders**: hitters with a BA higher than their xBA
- **xBA studs**: players who were hitting well, with an xBA/BA difference between +10/-10.
- **Control group**: a group of hitters whose last names start with B (let's call them The Killer B's).

Each group contained 24 players. The Killer B's contained four hitters who appeared in one of the other groups; in total, there were 92 players. As always, small sample size caveats apply — this is only one two-week sampling out of a 26-week season.

Here's a quick stat breakdown for the groups, looking at their combined BA and their mean xBA figures:

Group	BA	xBA	Diff
Faders	.307	.258	-49
Studs	.290	.291	1
Killer B's	.274	.266	-8
Surgers	.249	.278	29

The Studs are legitimate studs. As for the others, going by xBA, we'd expect the Surgers to perform better than people just looking at BA would anticipate. Here's what did happen:

Group	BA	AB	H
Studs	.317	1088	345
Surgers	.295	995	294
Killer B's	.292	1021	298
Faders	.260	1091	284

As expected, the Studs just kept on raking. And as we hoped, the Surgers got hot, and the Faders cooled off, nearly matching their June 26 xBA. But any excitement over the Surgers' results has to be tempered slightly by the fact that the random approach would have been just as successful as targeting hot hitters during this two-week period.

Let's examine the results from another angle. If we're trying to catch hot hands in the short-term, we'd like to own as many .300+ hitters as possible during a given period of time. Overall, 42 of the 92 hitters batted .300+ during the two-week period, or 46%. So how many .300+ hitters did each group produce during the two-week period? (In the chart below, Group% tells you what percentage of each group hit .300+, and Overall% tells you what percentage of .300+ hitters each group produced out of the 42 .300+ hitters.)

Group	.300+	Sub-.300	Group%	Overall%
Studs	14	10	58%	33%
Surgers	11	13	46%	26%
Killer B's	9	15	38%	21%
Faders	8	16	33%	19%

Again, targeting good hitters with solid skills was your best bet for getting .300 hitters. But from this point of view, the Surgers method was slightly more effective than the random Killer B's approach — though its 46% group rate matched the overall total hitter average. And once again, Faders posted the worst results. What about downside risk? How did each group fare in terms of cold hitters to avoid? Here's how many sub-.250 BA hitters each group produced (overall, 32 of the 92 hitters hit less than .250 during the two-week period, or 35%):

Group	Sub-.250	.250+	Group%	Overall%
Faders	11	13	46%	34%
Killer B's	9	15	38%	28%
Surgers	7	17	29%	22%
Studs	5	19	21%	16%

xBA Faders had the most downside risk, and the Studs had the least. And once again, the Surgers fared better than the random approach, and better than the overall average.

Finally, one more thing to look at — with the Surgers and Faders, did players' overall BA move in the direction predicted by their June 26 xBA? In this one case, the results were more definitive:

Group	BA Up	BA Down	BA Same
Surgers	18	5	1
Faders	7	17	0

Nice to see that xBA's predictive value worked well at the individual level, even in such a short period of time.

So what has this study shown us? For one, it confirms something pretty obvious — good hitters are good hitters, especially those with skills that support their output. And it does seem that xBA can provide valuable input when it comes to making weekly lineup decisions — if you've got two hitters to choose from, and one is a Surger and one is a Fader, going with the Surger looks like the better strategy. That doesn't mean xBA should be your only decision-making resource, but it's certainly one worth adding into the mix.

But if you're trying to predict the next Jose Reyes-esque hot streak, looks like you might as well break out the darts.

Late season performances of rookie SP
by Ray Murphy

This season saw a bumper crop of rookie starting pitchers who found immediate success: Justin Verlander, Francisco Liriano, and Jered Weaver top the list. However, we often caution that a rookie's second tour of the league provides insight as to future success. By that token, do rookie pitchers typically run out of gas? To find out, we went back over the past five seasons and identified 56 rookie SP who threw at least 75 IP in their rookie season. We assembled their PQS logs and sliced them a few different ways.

First we checked out the performance of the entire set of pitchers:

All rookies	#	#GS/P	DOM%	DIS%	qERA
before 7/31	56	13.3	42%	21%	4.56
after 7/31	56	9.3	37%	29%	4.82

As you might have expected, rookie pitchers on the whole tend to fade later in the season. However, a quarter-run degradation in qERA is hardly cause for panic. What if we start shrinking our study class? Let's isolate rookies who made at least 16 starts before 7/31:

16+ starts	#	#GS/P	DOM%	DIS%	qERA
before 7/31	23	17.7	43%	19%	4.44
after 7/31	23	8.6	32%	34%	5.08

It makes sense that these "busiest" rookie SPs would fare better up until July 31 than the group as a whole did: less successful pitchers lose their jobs. The hardest-working rookies crashed much harder than their rookie brethren. But "busy" rookie pitchers aren't necessarily the "best." Are the very best rookie pitchers immune from this emerging trend of late-season fades? 22 of our 56 pitchers had a pre-August average PQS score of 3.0 or more. Here's how they fared down the stretch:

avg PQS>3.0	#	#GS/P	DOM%	DIS%	qERA
before 7/31	22	11.0	57%	11%	3.97
after 7/31	22	8.2	43%	24%	4.56

These very best rookie SP suffered a fairly dramatic crash in the season's final two months. In addition, they post the lowest GS/P number. Since these are the most effective rookie pitchers, they are likely pitching less due to injury rather than ineffectiveness.

Finally, we took a look at the 8 pitchers who intersect the two groups above:

PQS>3+GS>15	#	#GS/P	DOM%	DIS%	qERA
before 7/31	8	19.1	51%	12%	4.23
after 7/31	8	9.6	34%	30%	5.08

While the sample size here is smaller, the degree of flameout by these guys is startling: their qERA rose by nearly a full run after July.

The 2006 trio bears out this phenomenon. From August 1 on, Verlander posted an ERA of 5.82 and Liriano hit the DL. Weaver had a 3.38 mark in August and September, a solid level but still nearly two full runs higher per game than his pre-August ERA. This data shows the merit in the idea of "cashing in your profits" on these young arms, particularly in single-year leagues. They may be largely responsible for putting your team in contention, but it is not a good percentage play to bet on them to bring home your league title.

Reviewing past September call-ups
by Brandon Kruse

For fanalytic owners caught up in a last-season battle for first place, September call-ups can often be viewed as potential saviors. They're usually highly regarded prospects, and in many cases are coming off of a great season in the minors. But pursuing potential, particularly untested potential, can be a risky play, and may wind up doing more harm than good.

What we'd like to do here is take a look back at recent performances by September call-ups and see if it can help guide our expectations for future call-ups, and examine whether their minor-league skills could have aided us in forecasting success or failure.

For this study, we'll look at 38 September call-ups from 2003-05. Players targeted were under 26 years of age at the time of promotion, and called up no earlier than August 22, 10 days before the roster expansion date. For the majority of these players, this was their first exposure to the majors, though there were a couple who had a little bit of experience in a previous season.

Batter	PRE-CALLUP BA	Eye	h%	ISO	POST-CALLUP BA	HR
J.Reed	.289	1.05	30	.147	.397	0
Zimmerman	.326	0.44	35	.202	.397	0
Atkins	.366	1.27	38	.212	.357	1
W.Aybar	.297	0.71	34	.122	.326	1
Adams	.288	0.73	32	.120	.306	4
Kubel	.343	0.85	35	.217	.300	2
Botts	.286	0.44	36	.230	.296	0
V.Diaz	.292	0.23	35	.199	.294	3
Hermida	.293	1.24	34	.225	.293	4
Bay	.303	0.77	34	.238	.291	3
Howard	.270	0.38	32	.334	.282	2
Laird	.260	0.61	29	.169	.273	1
Denorfia	.310	0.76	34	.195	.263	1
Swisher	.269	0.94	30	.268	.250	2
Granderson	.303	0.84	34	.212	.240	0
McPherson	.313	0.18	42	.367	.225	3
Greene	.288	0.38	32	.154	.215	2
M.Izturis	.338	1.90	36	.085	.206	1
J.Kroeger	.332	0.32	39	.255	.167	0
LaForest	.269	0.64	31	.298	.167	0

Pitcher	PRE-CALLUP ERA	Ctl	Dom	Cmd	POST-CALLUP ERA	Cmd
C.Cordero	2.05	3.4	5.9	1.7	1.64	4.0
Riley	3.59	3.6	9.9	2.8	1.80	1.6
Maholm	3.53	3.0	5.3	1.8	2.18	1.5
Cain	4.39	4.5	10.9	2.4	2.33	1.6
E.Jackson	2.19	3.2	9.5	3.0	2.45	1.7
Chacin	2.82	3.0	7.2	2.4	2.57	2.0
Duchscherer	3.25	1.0	6.8	6.5	3.31	5.0
Waechter	3.35	2.1	6.2	2.9	3.33	1.9
Floyd	5.10	2.7	5.4	2.0	3.49	1.5
Tsao	8.53	3.5	9.9	2.8	3.86	11.0
C.Young	1.48	2.7	10.2	3.8	4.71	2.7
Francis	2.85	1.5	10.8	7.0	5.15	2.5
Heilman	4.33	3.9	7.3	1.9	5.46	1.7
Kazmir	1.59	3.5	9.4	2.7	5.67	2.0
Liriano	1.78	2.4	11.1	4.7	5.70	4.7
D.Bautista	3.50	4.1	9.1	2.2	6.51	1.6
L.Martinez	1.00	3.8	9.2	2.4	9.92	0.5
Capellan	2.51	3.1	7.7	2.5	11.25	0.8

Starting with the hitters, one thing that stood out as we collected the data (though not listed in the table) was the **generally low AB totals**. Playing time was spotty and inconsistent for most hitters, and only three players got 75+ ABs (and only one topped the 100-AB mark). That's certainly less playing time than you'd like to see from a player in one month.

Other than BA, the category totals weren't very large — the high marks were 4 HR, 12 RBI and 4 SB. When deciding whether to roster a September call-up, this gives us a baseline expectation for consideration. Is the player you're replacing already capable of putting up those kind of numbers over the final month? If so, even if it's a close call, it's probably better to go with the player who has a major-league track record than the one who doesn't.

As for skills analysis and forecasting, it seems we found something useful. Among the success stories, **plate discipline was a key skill**. Seven of the 10 hitters with a .290+ BA had a batting eye of 0.70 or higher in the minors. Among the hitters who struggled, lack of plate discipline and excessively high hit rates in the minors were a leading indicators to steer clear (see Dallas McPherson and Josh Kroeger).

With the pitchers, playing time was less of an issue - most starters got four or more starts, and the relievers got 10+ games in, but **forecasting performance was a real crapshoot**, due mostly to luck in the form of hit and strand rates. And that's not a big surprise when you're dealing with a short time period like this. A pitcher can have great minor-league skills and maintain those skills in the majors, and still get torpedoed by a bad hit rate or strand rate (see Scott Kazmir and Francisco Liriano). Likewise, the pitchers with the five best ERAs all had favorable hit and strand rates. In other words, they got lucky.

There's also **risk of fatigue and excessive innings.** For many of these young pitchers, by the time they hit September, they're at or nearing personal highs in innings pitched. So there's always the possibility of a dead arm, a breakdown in mechanics that ruins command, or simply the team deciding to shut him down for the year.

All in all, September call-ups should be approached with caution. This is especially true if you're leading your league or very close to doing so. Betting on potential is not a good move for the risk-averse. If you're a little further out of contention and have less to lose, taking a gamble on a fresh horse makes a little more sense. And with any of these players, do your homework, analyze the skills. It may not give you a definitive answer, but it will always help shed some more light.

III.
GAMING

Core Fanalytic Strategies

The LIMA Plan

The LIMA Plan is a strategy for Rotisserie leagues (though the underlying concept can be used in other fantasy formats) that allows you to target high skills pitchers at very low cost, thereby freeing up dollars for offense. LIMA is an acronym for Low Investment Mound Aces, and also pays tribute to Jose Lima, a $1 pitcher in 1998 who exemplified the power of the strategy. In short:

1. *Budget a maximum of $60 (out of $260) for your pitching staff.*
2. *Allot no more than $30 of that budget for acquiring saves.* In 5x5 leagues, it is a reasonable strategy to completely forego saves at the draft table (and acquire them during the season) and re-allocate this $30 to starting pitchers ($20) and offense ($10).
3. *Draft only pitchers with:*
- Command ratio (K/BB) of 2.0 or better.
- Strikeout rate of 5.6 or better.
- Expected home run rate of 1.0 or less.
4. *Draft as few innings as your league rules will allow.* This is intended to manage risk. For some game formats, this should be a secondary consideration.
5. *Maximize your batting slots.* Target batters with:
- Contact rate of at least 80%
- Walk rate of at least 10%
- PX or SX level of at least 100

Spend no more than $29 for any player and try to keep the $1 picks to a minimum.

The overall goal is to ace the batting categories and carefully pick your pitching staff so that it will finish in the upper third in ERA/WHIP, with a little luck in the upper third in saves (and IP or strikeouts in 5x5), and somewhere around 9th-12th in wins. In a competitive league, that should be enough to win, and definitely enough to finish in the money. Worst case, you should have an excess of offense available that you can deal for pitching.

The LIMA Plan works because it better allocates resources. Fantasy leaguers who spend a lot for pitching are not only paying for expected performance, they are also paying for better defined roles – #1 and #2 rotation starters, ace closers, etc. – which are expected to translate into more innings, more wins and more saves. But roles are highly variable, changing often during the course of a season. A pitcher's role will ultimately come down to his skill and performance; if he doesn't perform, he'll lose the role.

The LIMA Plan says, let's invest in skill and let the roles fall where they may. In the long run, better skills should translate into more innings, wins and saves anyway. And as it turns out, pitching skill costs less than pitching roles do.

In *straight draft leagues*, don't start drafting starting pitchers until Round 10. In *shallow mixed leagues*, the LIMA Plan may not be necessary; just focus on the BPI benchmarks. In *simulation leagues*, also build your staff around BPIs. Depending upon your particular game, wins and saves can be ignored completely.

The RIMA Plan

LIMA is based on optimal resource allocation. These days, however, no matter how good of a team you draft, player inconsistency, injuries and unexpected *risk factors* can wreak havoc with your season. The RIMA Plan adds the element of **RI**sk **MA**nagement.

Players are not risks by virtue of their price tags alone. A $30 Johan Santana, for example, might be a very good buy since he is a healthy, stable commodity. But most LIMA drafters would not consider him because of the price.

The RIMA Plan involves setting up two pools of players. The first pool consists of those who meet the LIMA criteria. The second pool includes players with high Reliability scores. The set of players who appear in both pools are our prime draft targets. We then evaluate the two pools further, integrating different levels of skill and risk, and creating six hierarchical tiers of players to draft from:

TIER A: LIMA-caliber with high Reliability scores
TIER B: LIMA-caliber with moderate Reliability scores
TIER C: Non-LIMA with high Reliability scores
TIER D: LIMA-caliber with low Reliability scores
TIER E: Non—LIMA with moderate Reliability scores.
TIER F: Non-LIMA with low Reliability scores.

Tier C is where RIMA opens up more opportunities. While we'd typically stay away from low-skilled players, carefully-chosen "C" bodies can provide valuable support if you are careful. In this group you might find inning-eater hurlers who could help boost your strikeout totals, though might have elevated ERAs. If the rest of your staff has a solid skills foundation, you can often weather the mediocre numbers that come along with these arms. The fact that they are low risk means that you know exactly what you will be getting and so you can better plan for it.

One of the beauties of RIMA is that, for those who don't play in Rotisserie auction leagues, you can still apply the RIMA concept into your draft prep. The process of integrating skill and risk management is universal for all types of league formats.

Another beauty of RIMA… There are many of you who don't feel comfortable coming out of your draft unless you have a staff "anchor." If this is a direction you want to go, there will be many higher-priced high tier pitchers that could be worth pursuing. If a Tier A pitcher comes to you at a good value, you can feel more confident going after him, knowing that his low risk profile increases the odds that you'll get a fair return on your investment.

The overall goal for your roster is to assemble a balanced, diversified portfolio of solid performers and steady at-bat and inning-eaters that have strong odds of providing good return on your investment.

Alternative Gaming Formats

Rotisserie7

Rules:

1. Mixed league. Any number of teams.

2. 25-man roster, stocked any way you like so long as all your positions are covered. Each week, 16 of those players will be designated as "active:" 9 position players (1B, 2B, 3B, SS, CA, OF, OF, OF, DH), 5 man starting rotation and 2 relief pitchers. Nine reserves at any position.

3. 4x4 game with the following categories:

> **BATTERS:** HR, (Runs scored + RBIs - HR), SB, BatAvg
> **PITCHERS:** Wins, Saves, Strikeouts, ERA

4. Snake draft or auction is fine. For auctions, budget for the 16 active players only, followed by a snake draft for the remaining 9 players.

5. Rotisserie's category ranking system is converted into a weekly won-loss record. Depending upon where your team finishes for that week's isolated statistics determines how many games you win for that week. Each week, your team will play seven games, hence Rotisserie7.

*Place	Record	*Place	Record
1st	7-0	7th	3-4
2nd	6-1	8th	2-5
3rd	6-1	9th	2-5
4th	5-2	10th	1-6
5th	5-2	11th	1-6
6th	4-3	12th	0-7

* Based on overall Rotisserie category ranking for the week.

At the end of each week, all the roto stats revert to zero and you start over. You never dig a hole in any category that you can't climb out of, because all categories themselves are incidental to the standings.

6. There is unlimited once-weekly movement allowed between the active and reserve rosters during the season. Access to the free agent pool is limited to one player per week per team. Free agents are acquired via a straight draft in reverse order of the standings.

7. The regular season lasts for 23 weeks, which is 161 games. Weeks 24, 25 and 26 are for play-offs. The top six teams make the play-offs. In larger leagues (minimum 15 teams), the top eight teams can make the play-offs. Here it becomes a head-to-head game, but Rotisserie standings again determine the victors.

> **Week 24**: Teams 1 and 2 get byes. Team 3 meets Team 6, Team 4 meets Team 5. In larger leagues, Teams 1 and 2 would meet teams 8 and 7, respectively.
> **Week 25**: Team 1 versus Team 4 or Team 5; Team 2 versus Team 3 or Team 6
> **Week 26**: Two winners meet for the championship

The pot is divided 70% for regular season standing and 30% for play-off results.

Stratified Rotisserie

Rules:

1. Start with the same basic rules as a standard Rotisserie competition, but this is a pick-a-player contest.

2. A league may include any number of owners. You will be drafting from both American and National leagues.

3. Each team will have a 25-man roster and a 15-man reserve squad. Each active roster will have 15 batters and 10 pitchers. Standard roto positional structure applies, with two DH/utility slots on the offense side. Reserve rosters have no positional restrictions.

4. *The only players available are those who posted a dollar value of $5 or less in the previous season.*

5. Each team stocks its roster individually. There is no draft or auction. While players may end up on more than one team, the narrow spread of talent will likely ensure that no two teams look exactly alike.

6. There is unlimited once-weekly movement allowed between the active and reserve rosters during the season. There is no trading in this league.

7. On June 1 and August 1, you may select up to five new players to add to your team. For each player who is added, an active or reserve player must be dropped. New players cannot come from the original list of ineligibles (over $5).

Strategic considerations

The players with the best upside value are last year's injury rehabs and minor leaguers looking at significant playing time.

In drafting for your active roster, your key goal is to accumulate quality playing time.

Since you will be playing most of the season from the roster you draft, your reserve squad becomes very important. Naturally, you'll want to grab as many positional backups as possible to protect against injury and excessive bench-sitting of your active players. Your reserve also is a good place to stash upwardly mobile minor leaguers who could get promoted mid-season and have an impact.

Rule modification options for the truly masochistic

1. Draft from only one league, rather than both.

2. Reduce the strata threshold to $3 instead of $5.

3. Make all injury rehabs ineligible if they posted a roto value over $5 in their last healthy season.

4. Limit the number of players with less than 20 games of major league experience to 5 per roster.

5. No more than 3 players with less than 20 games of major league experience can be active at any time.

Quint-Inning

Object: To assemble a group of players that will amass the most points during a single baseball game.

Auction draft: A player auction is conducted among five "owners" before the ballgame (and must be completed prior to the start of the game). Each owner must acquire 5 players from the current 25-man rosters of the two major league teams playing in that game, at a cost not to exceed $55. There are no positional requirements for the 5 players other than one must be a pitcher. All 5 roster spots must be filled.

An owner need not spend his entire auction dollar allotment. Any unspent dollars may be added to an owner's Free Agent Acquisition Budget (FAAB).

The "salaries" paid for the five players have no further relevance once the draft is over. They are essentially acquisition costs only.

Points and standings: Team standings are calculated based on a ranking of points accumulated by players at the time they are on an owner's roster.

BATTERS accumulate points for bases gained or lost:
- Single = +1
- BB = +1
- HBP = +1
- SB = +1
- CS = -1
- Double = +2
- Triple = +3
- Home run = +4
- Error = -2

Batting stats accumulated by pitchers in the National League do count, however, the pitcher must be drafted or acquired separately as a batter. A pitcher may appear as both a batter and a pitcher in a given game, accumulate points separately, and appear on two different rosters.

PITCHERS accumulate points for IP minus ER:
- IP = +1
- Earned Run allowed = -1

The IP point is awarded to the pitcher who is on the mound when the third out of the inning is registered.

Win = +5   Save = +3

These points are awarded to the owner who has the pitcher of record on his team at the end of the game, even if the owner did not draft that pitcher. If an unrostered pitcher gets a win or save, these points are not awarded.

"The Quint:" At the beginning of the 5th inning, any owner has the option of doubling the points (positive and negative) for one player on his roster for the remainder of the game. Should that player be traded, or dropped and then re-acquired, his "Quint" status remains for the entire game.

Ninth Inning: Beginning in the 9th inning, all batting points (positive and negative) are doubled.

FAAB points: Unused FAAB units can be converted to scoring points at the end of the game. The conversion rate is 10 FAAB = 1 point.

In-game roster management: The five drafted players must remain on each owner's roster for at least the first inning. Then, players may be dropped, added or traded, and all roster size restrictions are then lifted, except:
- Rosters must contain at least one player at all times.
- Rosters must contain at least one pitcher at all times.

All player moves take effect at the beginning of each half inning. All player moves must be announced prior to the first pitch of that half inning; otherwise, the move will not take effect until the following half inning.

Dropping players: Any player can be cut from an owner's roster at any time after the first inning. Players who are cut may not be re-acquired by the original owner.

Adding players: Each owner is allotted a free agent acquisition budget (FAAB) of $50 per game for the purpose of acquiring players. Available for FAABing are...
- undrafted players on one of the 25-man rosters
- players that had been cut by other owners
- players of those owners who drop out of the game

An owner can announce that he is placing a bid on a free agent at any time after the first inning. Other owners can then bid until a winner is determined. No other player needs to be dropped. All players accumulate points from the half inning after which they were acquired. Owners are limited to one player per half inning acquired via FAAB.

Trading: A trade can be consummated at any time after the first inning, between any two or more owners. The only commodities that may be traded are rostered players and FAAB dollars. Uneven trades are allowed and roster sizes do not have to be squared up at any time. However, should a team's only pitcher be traded to another owner, a pitcher must be received in return or a free agent pitcher acquired immediately. If a pitcher is not added to a roster before the first pitch of the next half-inning, the trade is nullified.

Stakes: Quint-Inning can be played as a no-stakes, low stakes, moderate or higher stakes competition.
- It costs ($1/$5/$55) to get in the game.
- It costs (25 cents/$1/$5) per inning to stay in the game for the first four innings.
- Beginning with the 5th inning, the stakes go up to (50 cents/$2/$10) per inning to stay in the game.
- Should the game go into extra innings, the stakes rise to ($1/$5/$25) to stay in the game until its conclusion.

Each owner has to decide whether he is still in the game at the end of each full inning. Owners can drop out at the end of any inning, thus forfeiting any monies they've already contributed to the pot. When an owner drops, his players go back into the pool and can be FAABed by the other owners.

Determining the winner: The winner is the owner who finishes the game with the most points. Tie-breakers:
- Team with the most number of players contributing positive scoring points.
- Team with the most pitching points.
- Team with the most FAAB remaining.

Scorekeeping: A Quint-Inning scoresheet, along with more detailed rules and strategies, can be downloaded from http://www.baseballhq.com/free/free050819.shtml

---

The anti-Internet gambling bill that was signed into law in October has carve-out language that clearly defines the legality of fantasy sports. This language states that fantasy games are exempt as long as they follow several stipulations. The second stipulation states:

2. Winning outcomes are determined by skill for contests that use results from multiple real-life games.

Quint-Inning fails at this stipulation, which only means we won't be setting up QI games on the internet. But you can feel free to continue playing at home.

Gaming Abstracts

The changing face of fantasy

According to latest estimates, we are among over 15 million people who participate in fantasy sports. Most play fantasy football — heck, it requires one tenth the commitment — while us baseball aficionados are a distant second. Perhaps being second means we try harder. At minimum, we have been around longer, at least in the Rotisserie Era (which was just after the Mesozoic). And during our two-plus decades of playing with dollar values, we've gone through numerous evolutions.

By our mere growth alone, one would think that we are on the right path. However, this past fall, the following program description appeared in a brochure for a conference put on by *Street & Smith's* and the Fantasy Sports Association:

> "*Fantasy Sports Track: Developing Games That Expand the Player Universe*" *The success of fantasy football is well documented, but where will the growth come? In order to expand the universe, the industry must develop new games that are not as intensive when it comes to time, statistics or even sports knowledge.*

The "dumbing down" of fantasy baseball is a problem I've written about at Baseball HQ for several years now. It started with *Baseball Weekly's* transition to *Sports Weekly*, continued with the loss of several valuable STATS, Inc. books, and took a leap with many public leagues' increased focus on payout over punditry. It's one of the key reasons why I've tried to separate fanalytics — what we do here — from pure fantasy.

I personally think the game we play — the one that provides the type of intellectual challenge that makes this book necessary — is far more enriching of an experience. However, I am but one person, and there are over 14,999,999 others who might disagree,

The core issues are how we play the game and what we want to get out of this experience. At Baseball HQ, we've tried to keep tabs on these ongoing trends by means of our weekly HQ Poll, which we've been running since December 1998. As a new feature in the *Forecaster*, we'll be looking back at some of these questions and sharing the results. Currently, there are about three dozen questions and issues that we've been tracking periodically over the years. We'll look at about a dozen of these in each year's edition of this book.

Since these questions are asked at Baseball HQ, they only represent the opinions of folks who a) visit Baseball HQ, and b) respond to online polls. So these are clearly not 100% scientific representations of the industry as a whole. However, even from among our smaller group, we can glean some interesting tidbits about where our hobby may be headed...

(Note that all poll results had at least 500 responses.)

Which of the following best describes your current fantasy experience?

	2003	2004	2005	2006
100% baseball. Anything else is pure heresy.	54%	49%	48%	48%
Baseball is tops, but I'm prepping for my football draft now.	38	42	42	43
Baseball is a diversion, but football is where the real action is.	4	5	4	4
Baseball and football, but also basketball and maybe hockey.	3	3	4	4
The four major sports, more or less, plus a smattering of golf, tennis, NASCAR and bass fishing.	1	1	2	2

I ask this question each year to see the makeup of the poll respondents. Not surprisingly, the vast majority continue to cite baseball as the fantasy sport of choice. However, you can see the small but growing encroachment by fantasy football. Still, at the rate this trend is taking, Felix Hernandez will be long retired by the time it becomes a problem, at least among whatever Baseball HQ subscribers are left.

PRIVATE MIXED LEAGUERS: How many teams are in your league?

	2001	2003	2005
10 or fewer	22%	22%	24%
11-12	32	30	36
13-14	14	21	16
15-16	12	12	13
17-18	5	4	4
19-20	6	6	5
21-22	1	2	1
More than 22	4	4	1
Mean	12.9	13.0	12.4

This might seem surprising to some of you, but as recently as 10 years ago, mixed league participation was more the exception rather than the rule. Back then, most fantasy/Rotisserie participants were in fairly deep AL-only or NL-only leagues. The growth of mixed league participation over the past decade was, in part, a response to the need for a game that could better fit into the growing demands on our time. Probably the bigger impetus, though, was that mixed league play was an easier format for the hordes of casual fans finding fantasy baseball through the internet.

Still, the leap from a 12-team AL or NL-only league to a 12-team mixed league seemed steep. The level of knowledge required for each format almost created two separate games. As such, for several years, we had been assuming that most mixed leagues were at least 18 teams deep. We were wrong. By about 5 teams.

The 2005 data point shows a slight movement towards even shallower league play. Pretty soon, nobody is going to need to keep track of third string catchers any more. Not that there's anything necessarily wrong with that.

What transaction frequency does your primary, or favorite league use?

	2003	2004	2006
Daily transactions	23%	22%	27%
Daily for reserve moves, weekly for trades and free agent pickups	6	4	3
Daily for reserve moves and trades, weekly for free agent pickups	1	9	7
Weekly transactions	59	55	53
Weekly for reserve moves/trades, less than weekly for free agent pickups	5	7	5
Some other frequency	6	3	4

Along with the rise of mixed league participation has been participation in daily transaction leagues, a phenomenon driven by the internet's real-time accessibility to information. The nuevo-fantasy-types are embracing simpler, yet higher maintenance games.

There is minor movement within the categories, but the number of folks in leagues that require at least *some* daily management has grown from 30% to 37% over the past three years.

What will be the most prevalent pitching trend on draft day?

	2001	2002	2006
Higher prices for top starting pitchers	43%	23%	39%
Lower prices for top starting pitchers	4	9	7
Inflated prices for middle relievers	4	11	4
Lower prices for frontline closers	4	14	10
Lower overall budgets for pitching	26	27	27
Higher overall budgets for pitching	15	16	12

This question is an important indicator of changes in the major league talent pool and fantasy leaguers' perception of how to deal with those changes. It would have been interesting to have a few earlier data points, though this scan does somewhat show the devaluing of pitching.

In your league, what would be the best way to turn around a struggling pitching staff?

	1999	2004	2005	2006
Start trading	26	24	25	26
Stay the course but drop the worst 1-3 killers	46	53	41	42
Wait for free agents to become available			13	14
Bail out and play for next year	5	1	3	4
Forget pitching and pump up offense	8	7	4	4
Prayer	16	14	14	11

This question was intended to gauge in-season management techniques, and more specifically, the prevalence of trading in leagues. The trend is essentially flat — taking into account the addition of the third option in the 2005 poll — though it was nice to see a 5% decline in reliance on a higher deity.

Would you trade a BIG BAT even up for a BIG ARM?

	2001	2004	2005
Absolutely. There are few pitchers that can have as much impact	47%	7%	17%
Yes, but not without a decent batting throw-in	19	13	18
Probably not. [BIG BAT] production will be tough to replace.	16	37	34
No way. Never deal a batter for a pitcher even up.	16	43	31

When we first ran this poll in 2001, the question was, "Would you trade Luis Gonzalez for Curt Schilling even up?" At the time, Gonzalez was amidst his 57 HR, .325 BA season and Schilling was en route to 22 wins and a 3.03 ERA. The honest truth at the time was, this was a trade that I had just consummated in LABR in the year that I took home the title. And nearly half of the respondents gave the deal a "thumbs up."

In 2004, we asked the same question, but replaced the two players with Albert Pujols and Randy Johnson, who were posting comparable stats to the 2001 duo. And then in 2005, the players were Derrek Lee and Chris Carpenter. Perhaps the identity of the players may have affected the radical shift in results, but the last option in the poll should not have been impacted to any great degree.

Well, what is it? Does it make sense to deal a batter for a pitcher even up? Obviously, everything is dependent upon league context, but in general, is it something you would do? Perhaps the perception of pitching unpredictability has risen in the past few years. Maybe Randy Johnson's age played a factor in 2004. But heck, that's quite a swing.

How does your league handle players who are traded "out of the league?"

	2002	2004	2005	2006
LOSE THE PLAYER				
No compensation	31%	35%	29%	24%
Salary added back to FAAB	20	21	22	22
First rights on players coming back	19	14	14	15
KEEP THE PLAYER				
For this year only	25%	22%	31%	35%
For this year and beyond	4	7	4	3
Salary is deducted from FAAB	1	1	1	1

This controversy has been raging for over a decade, a battle between traditionalists versus realists. Traditionalists believe that the separation of leagues is sacrosanct; the realists eschew being penalized for a wanton act made by a major league club.

The traditionalists are still winning, though their lead has begun to narrow over the past two years. In 2002, 70% played by traditional rules; this year, that percentage has dropped to 61%.

Of course, for mixed leaguers, this is all moot. Since the respondents to this question are in the declining group of AL or NL-only leagues, it is not surprising that a traditionalist game format would be dominated by a traditionalist mindset.

PRIVATE KEEPER LEAGUERS: In what month is your trading deadline?

	2001	2004	2006
June or earlier	1%	2%	1%
July	32	26	23
August	49	55	57
September	11	11	13
No deadline. Trading all year.	5	5	4
No deadline. No trading allowed.	0	1	1

One of the negative impacts of the explosion of internet fantasy leagues has been the decline of the continuity offered by keeper leagues. For all the effort made by online game companies to attract customers, it is surprising that they would not be more aggressive in offering games that lock up these customers for more than one season at a time. But the percentage of non-private keeper leagues is tiny.

For those private leagues that do allow carryovers, there are many reasons why the trading deadline matters, but much depends upon the level of trading activity in the league. Early deadlines are often set to combat dumping activity but tend to also suppress late season interest. Late deadlines can help maintain interest but also open up opportunities for those owners not preparing for their football drafts to take advantage of those who *are* distracted. Over the past five years, there has been a clear shift toward later deadlines, which may, in fact, be a small sign of the game's attempts at its own self-preservation.

Does your league use an in-season salary cap?

	2002	2004	2006
No, we don't	68%	62%	62%
Yes, up to $325	14	18	18
Yes, up to $350	7	8	9
Yes, up to $375	3	4	4
Yes, up to $400	5	5	4
Yes, over $400	2	3	3

There has been a good deal of controversy over the years about "dump trading." While detractors cite the potential negative impact on league chemistry, purists prefer to stick to the free market system. The use of an in-season salary cap is one method that has been widely suggested to maintain the free market while still discouraging player dumping. However, adoption has been slow. This rule is still being used in fewer than 40% of leagues.

KEEPER LEAGUES: What is the maximum number of major and minor league players you are allowed to protect from one year to the next?

	2003	2004	2006
5 or fewer	20%	16%	17%
6-9	14	20	19
10-14	23	29	27
15-19	29	27	29
20 or more	14	9	12
Mean	12.5	12.1	12.8

A bunch of small movement within the tiers here. There were significant gains and losses in 2004, which then regressed a bit in 2006. This may be a grudge match between those leagues seeking more continuity (and perhaps shorter draft days) and those trying to discourage dump trades (by reducing the number of keepers allowed).

If you could make just one change to improve your league, which of the following would it be?

	2000	2004	2005
Find ways to encourage more trading	25%	25%	31%
Boot owners to improve league harmony	15	17	14
Find ways to keep interest alive into Sept.	38	37	29
Close loopholes in constitution	9	8	9
Increase the stakes	4	7	8
Find ways to reduce the time investment	6	5	9

The dominant responses have not been surprising; trading and maintaining interest over a long season are key hot buttons. What may be unexpected is the shift in the percentages for these responses. Maintaining interest may be of declining importance to this group, however, the next question shows that it is a trend that perhaps we should be paying more attention to.

Which of the following best describes your current fantasy BASEBALL experience?

	2003	2004	2006
I thoroughly enjoy everything about it.	69%	62%	58%
I enjoy it, but sometimes lose interest if my teams are not contending.	13	19	22
I'm revved up in the spring, but usually burnt out by August.	6	8	7
I love to draft, but then pretty much sit back and put my teams on auto-pilot.	1	1	2
Each year, it seems that playing this game is less fun and more work.	11	10	11

Over the past three years, there is an ever-gnawing feeling that the dog days are taking more and more of a toll. This is nothing new; had we run the poll back in 2000, the top three choices might have garnered 75%, 10% and 5%, respectively. It's a long season, but that's all the more reason we should be looking for ways to keep our interest up. There are game design issues we can consider as well as simple rule tweaks. But we have to be willing to make changes, and the long-standing Rotisserie traditionalism worries me (and not just for that one rule above).

The funny thing is that this is not a new problem. We've got an essay at RotoHQ.com called "15 Rule Changes to Keep the Fire Burning in September" that was published in 1997, and compiled from notes written well over a decade ago. Today, we could probably add at least a half dozen more ideas to the list. The ideas are there; again, we have to be willing to change.

It all boils down to — are you having a good time? The answer to that question appears to be, "Yes, but..." Some of the rule changes and different game formats I've been writing about are attempts to address this slow-growing discontent. The answer, however, is *not* dumbing down the game, as others might suggest. The answer is finding robust new challenges. Rotisserie was a masterpiece of design intelligence. The recent minor resurgence in Strat-O-Matic play may be a response to this as well.

There are great games out there yet to be played. We just have to keep an open mind.

The 75% solution

Based on poll results over the past few years, the percentage of leagues that have at least some element of daily roster management has gone from 30% in 2003 to 37% in 2006. This is both good and bad news.

For someone who cut his teeth playing this game as a 6-month chess match, my gut reaction to daily games is that they don't require much thought. See a hot player, pick him up. See a cold player, drop him. This is not a game of intellect, it is a game of reflexes.

Admittedly, weekly transaction periods are artificial. They were originally created out of necessity because we did not have the tools to support daily roster management. But they also served the purpose of providing us with a more manageable structure. One of the reasons fantasy football is so popular is because there are only 16 decision points. Weekly baseball transactions mean a manageable 26 decision points. No matter what you think about weekly versus daily, 26 is far less onerous than the 180 decision points of a daily baseball game.

But here's the kicker... If you believe that an underlying goal of fantasy is to approximate *real* baseball as best as possible, then we have to accept the fact that *real baseball is a daily game*. Daily player movement is a part of the real game. But where we get into trouble is if we allow the availability of these daily decision points to *exceed the logic and spirit of the game*. Let's look...

Injury replacements: When a player goes down in the majors, his team can replace him immediately. Fantasy teams should be able to do likewise.

Trades: When players are traded in the majors, the trade takes effect immediately. Fantasy teams should be able to do likewise.

Call-ups: When a player is called up from the minors, his team can activate him immediately. Fantasy teams should be able to do likewise.

Free agent signings: When a free agent is signed in the majors, his team can activate him immediately. Fantasy teams should be able to do likewise.

However... there is a major grey area here.

In the majors, the vast majority of new players come from a limited pool — a team's own minor league system. This pool accounts for probably 99% of the new blood that enters a league in any given year. The pool is also already under the ownership of a given team and the caliber of talent is unproven. Free agent signings are limited to unaffiliated players, which constitutes the other 1%.

In fantasy baseball, the minor league pool "owned" by any team is typically small. The pool of unaffiliated free agents is typically *huge*, its size dependent upon the player penetration of each particular league. This distinction has a major impact on how we play the game, daily or otherwise.

The larger the free agent pool, the higher the caliber of talent available for replacement purposes. In shallow mixed leagues, for example, the active roster penetration may be under 50%, leaving over half of the major league population floating out in the free agent pool. That is a ton of names to sift through. Owners end up making roster decisions involving many highly talented players, *something that would never happen in the majors.*

At its extreme, the huge depth of available talent combined with daily roster management can promote the streaming of players. Some online games allow owners to turn over their entire starting rotation daily to take advantage of favorable match-ups. This is where fantasy fails the litmus test of *the logic and spirit of the game.*

But even before we reach that extreme, we must first deal with an environment that allows, and encourages, fantasy owners to make these type of roster decisions. The Athletics did not immediately jettison Dan Johnson from their active roster this year, mostly because their other options at the time were limited. Johnson's fantasy owners might not have that level of patience, but this decision should not be a no-brainer due to the availability of Shea Hillenbrand-caliber talent in the free agent pool.

At the fantasy level, shallow player penetration has the following potential impacts:

- It diminishes the importance of the draft, which is ironic considering how much effort we put into that.
- It diminishes the need for trading, which diminishes the need for owner interaction, which diminishes the social aspect of the game.
- It makes player injuries almost desirable, because relatively high caliber replacement talent exists in great supply.
- With considerably less disparity between the top and bottom players chosen at the draft, luck plays a greater role in the final results.

The bottom line is that many daily leagues are problematic not due to the frequency of transactions but due to the skewed availability of talent during the season. Fixing the problem means taking control of the talent pool.

A few years ago, I wrote a column on player pool penetration. I suggested that the optimal league penetration was 75%. That 75% represents the percentage of the major league player pool that is drafted onto a fantasy league's rosters — active *and* reserve. Why 75%?

Twelve-team AL or 13-team NL leagues — what we might consider standard, or deep leagues — have upwards of 90% penetration (which includes 6-man reserve lists). These have thin free agent pools and less opportunity for roster management. It is difficult to compete if you have a bad draft or injury problems. These leagues represent the pinnacle of fantasy challenges, which is probably why most of the experts competitions continue to use this deep format.

Shallow leagues typically have 50% penetration, or less. The deep free agent pool often requires a high maintenance approach, and most leagues have significant roster churn.

The 75% figure is a good middle ground:

- It maintains the importance of the draft. You can't just mail it in and hope to FAAB your way to a title.
- It increases the need for trading because you won't likely be able to fix all your weaknesses from the free agent pool alone.
- Still, 75% provides for a fruitful, but not overflowing, free agent pool. There will be well-skilled players who

are worth FAABing every week (or day), but not overwhelming options that force you to choose between several highly talented commodities.
- There will be decent options for injury replacements, but few will have the skills level of the player who is on the DL. Injuries *should* hurt, at least a little.

At 75%, each team would typically have a decent starting rotation, plus a few extra starters that could be shuttled in and out to play match-ups and 2-start weeks. On the batting side, 75% prevents deep league love affairs with Alexis Gomez-level players, nor shallow league dilemmas over which of Shawn Green or Jay Gibbons to start this week.

So how do we achieve 75%?

In basic terms, 75% penetration represents the number of draftable players in your league (numerator) divided by the entire player population (denominator). That 75% can be achieved by modifying the numerator and/or denominator.

The numerator can be adjusted by changing the number of teams in your league, or roster size. The denominator can be adjusted by changing the size of the draftable player pool (i.e. single league versus mixed, or drafting from a select group of major league teams). Either of these levers — numerator or denominator — can be moved up or down to reach the 75% figure. Here are some existing formats and how they might be modified to achieve that 75% level:

15-team mixed league (NFBC format)

The National Fantasy Baseball Championship runs 15-team mixed leagues with 30-man rosters (23 active, 7 reserve). That's a 60% penetration. While many of its participants probably think that goes deep enough, the reality is that each owner has to sift through at least 300 free agents every transaction period. These leagues can dig down to 75% without affecting too much. Adding three teams gets the percentage up to 72%. Increasing roster size to 37 gets the percentage up to 75%. A hybrid — 16 teams with 35-man rosters — would be another alternative.

12-team mixed league

Perhaps the most prevalent mixed league format, these shallow leagues typically only draft to 50% penetration on the high end (and 36% on the low end). With more than half of the major league player population available as free agents, leagues with daily transactions are just primed for streaming. That might be fine if you've got unlimited free time, but it does not promote much of a social life.

Similar to the NFBC format, these leagues would have to increase to 18 teams with 30-man rosters to reach anything close to 75%, but that's quite a jump. The primary reason most play with only 12 teams is it's easier to get 12 people together for a draft than it is 15 or 18, particularly in private leagues. But to achieve even 72% with a 12-team league would require 45-man rosters.

A second reason 12-team mixed leagues are popular is simply because they do not require as deep of a knowledge of the major league population. However, that leaves a free agent pool with potentially over 400 names to evaluate each transaction period. That leaves too much to chance; too many valuable, non-drafted players will come out of that 400. It begs the question, "why bother drafting at all?"

The solution I think might work best here starts with increasing the number of teams only slightly, perhaps to 14 or 15. We'll still need to increase roster sizes, though, and that is problematic for those with limited knowledge of the player population. A 15-team league with 35-man rosters (23 active, 12 reserve) gets the percentage up to 70%. But those 12 reserve players are the killer.

One way around this is to randomly assign reserve players. This is something that automated systems could easily handle. Assigning names via a snake-draft in reverse order of projected value (using a source that is agreed upon by all owners in advance) accomplishes the goal. It's not perfect, but it creates the optimal allotment of owned players versus free agents. For those who think this method is unfair or random, remember that in the real world, new GMs inherit already existing teams. Here, you get to draft your active roster — which you would hope generates the most value — but you "inherit" your reserves.

To add even a bit more realism, you could institute a rule whereby injury replacements must come from your reserve list before the free agent pool can be accessed.

12-team AL-only or 13-team NL-only league

For these leagues, particularly those that have 6-man reserve lists, player pool penetration can exceed 90%. While this is the "standard" that was set down by the Founding Fathers, perhaps it is just a tad too onerous. In the Tout Wars-AL league this year, for example, there were never more than about 20 available batters in the free agent pool at any time. Half of them were typically catchers; only a few had more than 100 AB potential. A team struggling on offense was pretty much sunk.

There are three ways these leagues could achieve 75% player pool penetration:

1. Draft active rosters only. The 75% benchmark just covers the 23-man active rosters in these leagues. By eliminating reserve lists, the free agent pool would be stocked with some decent talent. If you have to access that pool, you really have to want the player because he's going to be on your active roster.

2. Reduce active roster size. Active rosters could be reduced to as few as 16 players (one at each defensive position, two DH/UT types and seven pitchers), leaving a 6-man reserve and a 23-man total roster.

3. Limit reserve lists to minor leaguers. Full, 23-man active rosters could be maintained, but any reserve list must be filled with players who are not on a 25-man MLB roster, or not in a major league camp at the time of the March draft. This holds intriguing tactical possibilities on Draft Day. Do you fill your reserve with players who are final MLB cuts in hopes that they are close to returning to the majors, or more talented commodities that may be a bit further from a call-up? Either way, the 750-player MLB population would only be drafted to 75% penetration.

Achieving 75% penetration might seem like an artificial goal. But I think that finding an optimal balance between owned players and free agents is important, both for realism's sake and for successfully integrating fantasy baseball into our lifestyles for the long haul.

Taming the serpentine draft

When Rotisserie's Founding Fathers wrote their first book in 1984, rosters were stocked by means of an auction draft. After all, Rotisserie was one part baseball and one part economics. As team owners, we had to consider how to build a roster within the limits of a fixed budget. There was no such thing as a snake, straight, or serpentine draft.

Over time, these alternative draft methods emerged, but auctions had taken such a strong foothold in the industry that they never gained comparable popularity.

The explosion of fantasy football coincided with the explosion of the internet in the late 1990's. In part due to the technical limitations of conducting auctions online in the earlygoing, snake drafts became the method *de rigueur*. When these hordes of football snake drafters decided to try their hand at fantasy baseball, the expectation was that snake drafting was the standard. *Um, no.*

In recent years, fantasy football has started to dip their toe in the auction pool. On one fantasy football site, there is this note: "It is interesting to see that baseball is also starting to try its hand at auction drafts." *Um, no again.*

The reality is that, over the past five years, fantasy baseball is only first starting to embrace *snake drafts*. Though I've written this before, here is why I don't particularly care for snake drafts:

- It takes control away from me. My picks are just whatever everyone else leaves behind.
- I want a shot at Albert Pujols, dammit.
- I can't successfully spread my risk if I'm forced to take high-value players in the early rounds.
- Leveraging my poker face has less impact when I'm just calling out a name.
- Draft Day should be a major event each year. Two hours and done is anti-climatic.
- Easier is not necessarily better.

Of course, everyone has their own way of enjoying the sport, so my opinion has about as much relevance as a Barry Bonds public statement.

Perhaps the bigger issue is that I am so tuned in to auction values that I have no point of reference for snake drafts. I can assume that a $40 Albert Pujols is the same thing as a snake 1st rounder, but what is the comparable round for a $15 Orlando Cabrera? So I thought I'd find out.

I created some simple grids containing our projected player values, slotted into their appropriate cell in a round-by-round snake draft. The only assumption I made was that everyone took the best player available when it was their turn. (Playing the positional scarcity card might skew the results slightly, but not likely enough to make a huge difference.) I created grids for the following leagues: 12-team AL-only, 13-team NL-only and 15-team mixed. Here were the average player values by round.

Rd	AL	NL	Mxd	Avg
1	$34	$35	$34	$35
2	$26	$29	$26	$27
3	$23	$25	$23	$24
4	$20	$22	$20	$21
5	$18	$19	$18	$18
6	$17	$17	$16	$17
7	$16	$16	$15	$15
8	$15	$15	$13	$14
9	$13	$14	$12	$13
10	$12	$12	$11	$12
11	$11	$11	$10	$11
12	$10	$9	$9	$9
13	$9	$8	$8	$8
14	$8	$7	$8	$7
15	$7	$6	$7	$7
16	$6	$4	$6	$6
17	$5	$4	$6	$5
18	$4	$3	$5	$4
19	$3	$2	$4	$3
20	$2	$1	$4	$2
21	$1	$1	$3	$2
22	$1	$1	$2	$1
23	$1	$1	$1	$1

So here are some benchmarks for us auction vets:
- All $30 players will go in the first round.
- All $20-plus players will go in the first four rounds.
- Double-digit value ends pretty much after Round 11.
- The $1 end game starts at about Round 20.

And so I should be able to get Cabrera at about Round 8.

Every year, snake drafters ask, "What is the best seed to draft from?" Most responders like mid-round so they never have to wait too long for their next player. Some responders like the swing pick, suggesting that getting two players at 15 and 16 is better than a 1 and a 30. I always assumed that the swing pick meant you'd be getting something like two $30 players instead of a $40 and $20.

A scan of the projected player values revealed the following alarming facts about the first two rounds:

In an AL-only league, the top seed would get a $44 player (at #1) and a $24 player (at #24) for a total of $68; the 12th seed would get two $29s (at #12 and #13) for $58.

In an NL-only league, the top seed would get a $48 and a $28 ($76); the 13th seed would get two $30s ($60).

In a mixed league, the top seed would get a $47 and a $24 ($71); the 15th seed would get two $28s ($56).

Since the talent level flattens out after the 2nd round, low seeds never get a chance to catch up. The total value each seed accumulates at the end of the draft is hardly equitable:

Seed	AL	NL	Mxd
1	$266	$274	$273
2	$264	$265	$269
3	$263	$265	$261
4	$262	$266	$262
5	$259	$259	$260
6	$261	$260	$260
7	$260	$261	$260
8	$261	$260	$260
9	$261	$258	$258
10	$257	$259	$260
11	$257	$257	$257
12	$258	$255	$257
13		$254	$257
14			$255
15			$256

Of course, the draft is just the starting point for managing your roster and player values are variable. Even still, it's tough to imagine a scenario where the #1 seed wouldn't have a clear advantage over the bottom seeds. Using our projections, that advantage could be as much as $20, which is huge. Can you imagine if these were the starting budgets for all teams at the beginning of an auction?

Total Control Drafting

"Irwin Zwilling... could name nineteen players he wanted before the draft and walk out owning every one of them."
— *Fantasyland*

When I read that in Sam Walker's book, it took me back to the early days of LABR, when Irwin and partner Lenny Melnick were perennial contenders. They *did* have a knack for knowing the marketplace so well that they could build their roster before even sitting down at the draft. The duo always seemed in control of the table and won many titles.

Part of the reason we play this game is the aura of "control," our ability to create a team of players we want and manage them to a championship. We make every effort to control as many elements as possible. But in reality, the players that end up on our teams are largely controlled by the other owners. *Their* bidding affects your ability to roster the players you want. In a snake draft, the other owners control your roster to an even greater extent. We are really only able to get the players we want within the limitations set by others.

The control freak in me says, "that's not good enough any more." I want who I want.

We are at the point where an optimal roster can be constructed from a fanalytic assessment of skill and risk. I want to create my team from that "perfect player pool" and not be forced to roster players that don't fit my criteria. It's now possible. It's just a matter of taking *Total Control*.

Why this makes sense

1. Our obsession with projected player values is really holding us back. Fact: The most advanced prognosticating systems are only going to be "on target" about 70% of the time. That leaves a huge variability in player value. Look at how our 2005 projected versus actual 5x5 values fared:

$$ Variance	Pct Batters	Pct Pitchers
$10+	8%	6%
$6-$9	9%	9%
$3-$5	11%	12%
$0-$2	23%	18%
-$1-$2	13%	19%
-$3-$5	16%	17%
-$6-$9	12%	9%
-$10+	8%	11%

Most of us would be pleased if the players we draft earn between +/- $5 of their drafted value. However, only about 65% of players provided that accurate of a return that year. To get that percentage up to about 85%, we had to open the range to +/- $9. This is not indicative of poor forecasting; no other system is going to be more than a few points better, or worse. It's the nature of the beast.

So, if a player on your draft list is valued at $20 and you agonize when the bidding hits $23, odds are about 2 chances in 3 that he could really earn anywhere from $15 to $25. What this means is, in some cases, you should just pay what it takes to get the players you want.

2. There are no such things as bargains. Most of us *don't* just pay what it takes because we are always on the lookout for players who go under value. But we really don't know which players will cost less than they will earn because prices are still driven by the draft table. The concept of "bargain" assumes that we even know what a player's true value is. If we target Hideki Matsui at $23 and land him for $20, we might *think* we got a bargain. In reality, Matsui might earn anywhere from $19 to $26 (which was, incidentally, his career range coming into 2006), making those $3 "saved" virtually irrelevant.

Of course, if you land him for $15, then we can talk, but it is rare that a player goes that far under projection. All players tend to get purchased within a general range of expected value. And that range is usually narrower than the variability in projected to actual value. An example:

Proj. value	Likely Bidding Range	65% Probability of Final Value Range
$25		$25
$24		|
$23		|
$22		|
$21	$21	|
$20	$20	|
$19	|	|
$18	|	|
$17	$17	|
$16		|
$15		$15

All this means two things: 1) We should be much freer with our bidding, and 2) there is no such thing as a bargain.

3. "Control" is there for the taking. Most owners are so focused on their own team that they really don't pay much attention to what you're doing. There are some exceptions, and bidding wars do happen, but in general, other owners will not provide that much resistance. You *can* take much more control than you've been doing up until now.

How it's done, Part 1

1. Create your optimal draft pool.
2. Get those players.

I'm not trying to be flip, but the purpose of all this is to fill your roster with the optimal talent group. We can't be distracted from that goal. Some detailed instructions...

Start by identifying which players will be draftable commodities. Filter for these players by looking for:

- Batters with a minimum contact rate of 80%, walk rate of 10% and PX or SX of at least 100. These are our standard LIMA criteria. Filter further by isolating those hitters with a Reliability score of at least 50.
- Starting pitchers with a minimum BPV of 50 and Reliability score of 50.
- Relief pitchers with a minimum BPV of 75 and Reliability score of 30.

As you get further into the draft, you will have to relax the targets. Relax Rel before you relax skills benchmarks.

The result of this exercise will help you plan your budget worksheet. Decide what salary range to earmark for each position. Your final plan will include a draftable pool of perhaps 60-75 players to fill your 23 roster spots.

The plan is then put into action at the draft table.

How it's done, Part 2

Bid openers: Forget about selecting bid openers with the intent of drawing out dollars. The other owners are going to spend their money eventually whether you help or not. Your focus has to be on *your roster only*.

So when it's your bid opener, *toss a player you need* at

about 50%-75% of your projected value. Bid aggressively, which means you need to be in everyone's face and keep a fast pace. *Forget about bargain-hunting;* just pay what you need to pay. Of course, don't spend $40 for a $25 player, but it's okay to exceed your projected value within reason, because that projection is going to be off by a fair percentage anyway.

Mix up the caliber of openers. Instead of tossing out an Albert Pujols at $35 in the first round, toss out a Randy Winn at $11. *Wise Guy Baseball's* Gene McCaffrey suggests tossing all lower-end players in the early-going, which does make a lot of sense. It helps you bottom-fill your roster with players most others won't chase early, and you can always build the top end of your roster with players others toss out.

Another good early tactic is to gauge the market value of scarce commodities with a $19 opener for Mariano Rivera or a $29 opener for Jose Reyes.

It is true that other owners will eventually pick up on the fact that you are only throwing out names of players you want; that's okay. You have two choices here. You can mix in a few non-targets to throw them off, though that could slow down the process of building your roster. However, odds are, even if you continue to toss your target names, two things will happen:

1. You won't be able to purchase them all anyway. The other owners won't know for sure whether you truly wanted the players that you lost.

2. Other owners may get scared out of getting into aggressive bidding wars with you for fear that you might stick them with a player or two.

Also, bid aggressively on *every player*; it will obscure which players you really want.

The Mid-Game: We've never really separated out the middle of the draft before, but Total Control Drafting may afford us the opportunity to adjust our strategy mid-stream.

If you've successfully rostered 10-12 players with high skills and Reliability scores, you will have likely built a solid foundation for your team. At that point, you could consider relaxing some of the reliability constraints and taking a few chances on players with high upside, but higher risk, like upwardly mobile rookies. I'd limit these picks to just a few, and then return to the plan, but the entire risk management approach gives you the chance to diversify a bit.

End game: You will need to relax the reliability targets for your last picks, so it might be a good idea to make sure those last buys are all pitchers (who are inherently more risky). You'll note that most high-skilled end-game LIMA pitchers have low reliability scores by nature.

At the conclusion of the draft, you may have rostered 23 players who could have been purchased at somewhat lower cost. It's tough to say. Those extra dollars likely won't mean much anyway; in fact, you might have just left them on the table. Total Control Drafting almost ensures that you'll end up spending all your money.

In the end, it's okay to pay a slight premium to make sure you get the players with the highest potential to provide a good return on your investment. It's really no different than the premium you'd pay to get that last valuable shortstop, or the few dollars extra you'd pay for the position flexibility a player like Ryan Freel provides. With this approach, you're just spending those extra dollars up front on players you know you want — players with high skill and low risk.

The best part is that you take more control of your destiny. You build your roster with what you consider are the best assemblage of players. You keep the focus on your team. And you don't just roster whatever bargains the rest of the table leaves for you, because a bargain is just a fleeting perception of value we have in March.

Dissenters

After TCD appeared on Baseball HQ, many readers wrote to disagree with the approach. For most of us, our indoctrination into fantasy baseball included strict schooling in the importance of the draft day *bargain*. It's a mindset that's tough to break. The entire Rotisserie gaming format requires that there is an economic structure that guides us during the bidding process. My contention is that this structure sits on a pretty weak foundation, not that the structure does not, or should not, exist at all.

I've pulled out a few dissenting comments to respond to. Hopefully this will provide some clarification...

"I don't want to control an auction by going in with a specific plan or groups of players which I must buy, especially if that approach includes overpaying. I want to control an auction by reacting to the auction dynamics in such a way that I come out of the auction with as much value as possible. I think flexibility is key to this."

This is the "old school" approach, which is fine if you know that your $20 "pre-draft bid values" are going to yield $20 in value. The reality is that they don't, so any expectation of bargains is faulty. What's more, you don't "control an auction" by "reacting to auction dynamics." The truth is that the auction is controlling you.

"I think TCD is mis-named. Perhaps you are in control in the sense that you purchase the players you target, but you don't seem to be in control of the price. The "new" approach is essentially, "Spend and think nothing of it, because you got what you wanted." It sounds to me like TCD drafters are getting less value than they could if they paid more attention to values."

It is true that you are not in control of the price, but the price is almost irrelevant. The goal is to get the best set of stats, not necessarily the best value. Why? Because in March, we really can't define what value is. Still, many folks can't extricate themselves from terms like "value" and "bargain."

For there to be any such animal as a "bargain," we have to start with a value that represents the point of comparison. A $15 Hideki Matsui means nothing in a vacuum; it is only when we have an expectation of $23 that $15 becomes a "bargain" and $25 becomes an "overpay." The truth is that $23 is never a real, firm number; it's just a point along a scale where it's convenient for us to stop. It might represent a "most likely" outcome, but "most likely" is still a very small percentage play.

"Then what is the difference between a $30 player and a $28 player? If there is no difference, why aren't they both

$29 players? The difference must mean something."

They might just as well both be $29 players. The *only* reason why one is $30 and the other is $28 is that we have to commit to *something* regarding what we expect them to produce. The variance is so small that we could have valued the $28 player at $31 and the $30 player at $26 and still have been within a statistically insignificant range for those variances.

"So $3 is irrelevant? The $3 you save on Matsui gets added to the $2, $3, $1, $4, you "saved" on the other guys you bought. Those dollars can be used to upgrade an $11 pitcher to a $16 pitcher or a $15 closer to a $20 closer."

This is a fallacy because those few dollars "saved" over time are not real. It is *your* perception based on *your* expectations. It does not reflect the marketplace at all (otherwise, someone else would have stayed in the bidding to eat up that "savings"). As shown above, it most likely will not reflect what actually happens next season either. You may *think* you are saving money, but the first $20 buy (who you might have gotten $3 under your expectation) who finishes at $16 (well within random statistical variance) effectively wipes out your perceived savings.

The only real fallout here is if *poor budgeting* prevents you from buying commodities you need. But I advocate setting up your budget with these buffers built in. So, a $30 slot should be created for players you'd be willing to pay $30 for, even if your projections value him at $25. Then you can manipulate your perceived "savings" all you want.

"And maybe this is Ron's core point on projected dollar values: regardless of balance sheets, PE ratios and cash flow, ultimately, what determines a stock's price is the market, and the market, for better or for worse, does not value all these variables equally for all stocks. People don't think that way and markets do not operate that way."

Correct. Here is another interesting question to ponder... Let's say, at your draft, whenever a player was opened (by you or someone else), you immediately jumped to your maximum bid. Someone opened Albert Pujols at $20; you jumped to $45. Someone opened Vicente Padilla at $1; you jumped to $14. You opened Danny Haren at exactly $22.

What do you think would happen? For one, you likely would not get every player. This is because other owners may have higher max bids than you or have greater needs than you. For those players that you *do* land, how many of them would you have "overpaid" for? You might be inclined to respond with "all, or most of them." I'd respond, "perhaps a few." However, it's also still possible that you might have gotten some "bargains." Some owners might have been frozen by your pre-emptive bid. Some might have not been willing to go to their own max bid. Others might have had that roster need already filled.

The point is, a "bargain" is defined by your particular marketplace at the time of your particular draft, not by any list of canned values, or an "expectation" of what the market value of any player might be. So the contention that TCD forces you to overpay for your players is false.

"My take is that Ron is currently trying to find a way to incorporate (a) variability of performance (rather than mean performance) and (b) risk assessment into the actual pricing strategy. Ultimately this could be a new valuation method. This is especially applicable when I see this:

	Proj$	Rel
Wood,K	$8	9
Hernandez,L	$8	90

This tells me that Wood's value is very speculative around $8, but Hernandez is more or less a lock to earn $7-9, and that gives me much better control in the draft. I can decide to bid Wood up to about $5 while knowing that Hernandez is available if I don't get Wood."

Bingo. What I suggest is to go into your draft with actually three data points for every player:

A gauge that assesses a rate of skill: I use BPV for pitchers and the LIMA benchmarks for batters (or BPV, if available). You might opt for something else.

A gauge that assesses risk management: We use reliability scores. These are not perfect, but they are a start.

A gauge that assesses general dollar value: We use the draft grids at Baseball HQ to slot players into value cells. Since those cells represent $5 ranges, we already build in some buffer for market tendencies. But you should be willing to exceed those boundaries if necessary.

Should these dollars represent market value or your expected value? Optimally both; however, we really don't know market value until we get to the table, so expected value should suffice for planning.

If you don't use the grids, then a player ranking sheet might look like this *(actual 2006 pre-draft data)*:

Rnk	PLAYER	R$	BPV	REL
1	Pujols,Albert	$46	109	93
2	Rodriguez,Alex	$46	86	64
3	Lee,Derrek	$39	93	44
4	Guerrero,Vlad	$39	88	78
5	Bay,Jason	$35	81	48
6	Helton,Todd	$34	108	70
7	Ortiz,David	$34	93	90
8	Ramirez,Manny	$34	92	91
9	Teixeira,Mark	$34	86	88
10	Crawford,Carl	$33	48	93

Decisions I might have made as a result of this list:
- Pay more for Pujols than A-Rod (higher BPV and Rel)
- Pay more for Guerrero than Lee (higher Rel)
- Pay more for Ortiz or Ramirez than Helton (higher Rel)
- Drop out of the bidding early on Lee and Bay (low Rel)

This shapes my general bidding tendencies but not my actual bidding. If any player on the bottom of this list gets bid past $35, that's not necessarily a sign for me to drop out. But these three data points do help me decide which players are better bets to stay in for.

Finally: *"If several owners are employing TCD, and others are just after "bargains" and "value," who wins?"*

Quite possibly one of those owners who was targeting bargains. This is because he would also have been targeting higher risk players, and if he had a few Frank Thomases who panned out big, then yes, he could very well win it all.

But this gets down to the next logical question: "Would you rather build a team that's positioned to contend every year or one that might strike gold every so often? Do you want to be the St. Louis Cardinals or the Florida Marlins?"

It all comes down to your own tolerance for risk. I'd prefer to be positioned for consistent contention. You might not. It's just personal preference.

Waiting

In April, we preach patience. Excruciating patience, if necessary. Those who wait are rewarded far more often than those who act too hastily. But are there times when waiting is not the best approach? And when waiting is warranted, how long are we supposed to sit in agony?

Clearly, for daily leagues that rely on roster churn for success, waiting is not a good thing. For rebuilding teams that need to take risks, waiting may not be prudent either. Still, there are good percentage plays and bad percentage plays. Riding streaks and slumps is a dangerous activity, but identifying players whose BPIs are not reflected in their outward stats can always reduce your risk.

For those in it for the long haul, particularly if your team is struggling, how long do you wait to start making moves?

The question of "how long" has come up in the past, but we've never been able to adequately address it. There is a different, more basic question though. That question is, "how can we tell if this performance is real?" When we wonder how long to wait before cutting a struggling player, for instance, what we're really wondering is whether his poor performance is a short-term aberration or a harbinger of long-term woes. If we knew the answer to that, then the "wait" decision becomes a no-brainer.

In the early-going, the problem is in the size of the data sets. If we had the luxury of waiting for 300 ABs to see if a batter is going to turn his season around, then we'd have better information with which to make a decision. But today's fantasy games don't afford *that* much patience. So how many AB or IP are enough? The simple answer is: more is always better. The not-so-simple answer: it depends. I could toss out numbers like 150 AB or 50 IP, but these have little value in a vacuum. It's best to approach this issue from a slightly higher level perspective.

Here are some general rules of thumb about minimizing the "wait" time on decisions...

1. Move quicker with batters. By the end of April, most full-time batters will have between 75-100 AB. Regular starting pitchers might have 5 starts, perhaps 30 IP; relievers will have a fraction of that. Just by virtue of the larger sample sizes, better decisions can be made with offensive numbers. (As a point of perspective, if we are willing to make a decision based on 100 AB for a hitter, we'd have to wait until *June or July* to have a comparable amount of information for a starting pitcher.)

2. Cut bait on struggling pitchers. We isolated all 2005 players who earned at least $10 more or $10 less than we had projected in March. Then we looked at the April performances of these players to see if we could have picked out the $10 outliers after just one month. Results:

Earned $10+ more than projected

	No.	Identifiable in April	Pct
BATTERS	41	16	39%
PITCHERS	32	14	44%

Earned $10+ less than projected

	No.	Identifiable in April	Pct
BATTERS	43	24	56%
PITCHERS	54	40	74%

Nearly three out of every four pitchers who earned at least $10 less than projected also struggled in April. For all the other 2005 surprises — batters or pitchers — April was *not* a strong leading indicator. Another look:

	April	2005	Pct.
Batters who finished +$25	44	20	45%
Pitchers who finished +$20	34	15	44%
Batters who finished under $0	42	25	60%
Pitchers who finished under -$5	60	47	78%

Essentially, April surgers are less than a 50/50 proposition to maintain that level all season. Those who finished April at the bottom of the roto rankings were more likely to continue struggling, especially pitchers. In fact, if we selected only those pitchers who finished April with a roto value *under -$10,* an overwhelming 21 of 23 (91%) finished the season in the red. Holes are tough to dig out of.

However, before you go cutting all your April slackers, you need to know what players were in the other 22%. They included names like Tom Glavine, Chris Capuano, Tomo Ohka and Vicente Padilla. So experience and track record still count for something. Which leads us to...

3. Hang tight with veterans. This is standard advice as players with a long-term track record will almost always revert to form at some point. Teams rarely even consider sitting a struggling veteran. There will always be those occasional lost seasons, but the percentage play is to always wait it out as long as you possibly can.

4. Use "second tour of league" for rookies and crossover players. Until opposing players get a second look, we often can't get a true sense of how a league's newcomers are really doing. Watch how hot starters fare against return opponents and sell off at the first sign of danger. Poor starters can probably be cut quickly. Good teams typically won't allow a struggling rookie to accumulate too many bad numbers. Bad teams often have no choice, so you have to make the decision first.

5. Avoid trying to time batting streaks and slumps. These will kill you every time and provide more frustration than they are worth. By time you grab the surger or punt the dog, the curve will likely have already swung the other way. *See the research abstracts in the previous section.*

6. Have confidence in your draft. Early in the season, use your draft results as a rough guide as to how long to hang onto a struggling player. This ties into the planning and confidence you had in your draft, which should count for something at this early stage of the season. Simply, higher draft picks should be given more rope.

7. The cost of making a mistake is less than you think. In many cases, we should *just do it* and not look back. In April, with so much still in flux, it doesn't make sense to try to over-analyze the situation.

For one thing, baseball reality is going to change tomorrow no matter what we decide today. Waiting may provide more information with which to make a decision, but it could open up more risks as well. The sooner we make a decision, the more time we provide ourselves to recover in case of a mistake.

And there will be mistakes, no matter how much information we have.

FAAB is in the eye of the beholder
by Doug Dennis

Suppose an outfielder called up from AAA is having a banner season after three mediocre seasons. Owners can only speculate that the "true" value (in standard Rotisserie terms) is some amount between $0 and $20 and each possible value has equal probability. As far as owners are concerned, someone has thrown a 21-sided die with each face having an integer between 0 and 20 to determine the value of the player in R$.

To add to the desire to purchase this player, the current opportunity cost has value. The R$ is worth 50% more than the player's current value to the owner's team if the owner wins the FAAB bid. That is--after the owner acquires the player, the player's R$ will increase 50% from V to 1.5V for trade purposes.

Finally, the owner's competitors' highest bid will exactly match the player's true R$. To win the player, you must bid more than R$. How much do you bid?

There is a quirk to this problem. Since any value between $0 and $20 is equally likely, on average the player is worth $10. But if you bid $10, notice that you can only win if the player's R$ is less than $10. Otherwise, you don't get the player--some competitor does.

So if you win with a bid of $10, the player is worth at most $10 and on average $5. Not only must you necessarily overbid to win, but even with the synergies that give you 1.5V for the player, on average, your winning bid of $10 would net only $7.5. This is true no matter how much you bid, and yet, if you do not bid, you are certain to get no value for your FAAB money.

On the Baseball HQ forums, *GoldenEagle* notes that FAAB money has no further utility value, so just bid $21. Yet on the other hand, "the more you bid, the more you lose (on an aggregate expected value basis)." It is a matter of whether you can do better than 1.5V for your $21.

JonE notes the "value" is less important than the incremental statistical increase that brings about some change in the standings. But here, the idea is that you can always get your 1.5V out of the purchase--but you will never really know what V is at the time of the bid. You only know that V is most likely to be more than the $0 and that you don't know what else you might be able to get for your FAAB money.

Josh Paley notes that it is the $15 expected value to the buying owner that is important. For that reason, Josh says to get the player because to hit $21--break even for that owner--the player has to be at a value of $14. There is really a 30% chance of coming out at or above the value spent--in FAAB money—the question is: is that enough?

ajc730 notes that with perfect substitutability (a word only an economist could love) between player talent and R$, the other teams would *always* win the bid, because the commodity goes to the party who derives the most utility from it. But will you get more later for your $21? We simply do not have enough information to know.

The chart below shows how five options play out.

Note that a "losing" bid is worth 0.0. It really is worth 0.0 + opportunity cost down the road — we just do not know if that has a value, and if some, what that value might be. On the other hand, it is not very comforting to know that the precious $21 might well bring only $1.5 or $3.0 or $4.5 in value, either.

There is always a "winner's penalty" that goes with the lack of perfect information — uncertainty creates some combination of foregone opportunity cost and overpayment. An owner's risk aversion is based on his own knowledge of many of the factors that have been held equal here — other competitors tendencies, opportunities to get this kind of player later or at better price, a better idea of what this player will really do, the amount of fit between this player and the owner's needs, or his ability to trade this player to fit needs.

This conundrum is an inherent part of FAAB bidding — so owners must be prepared to gamble a little during the course of the FAAB season. Even when you breathe life into the scenario with real names and real owners, these issues remain fundamental to the process.

Spent	0	1	2	3	4	5	6	7	8	9	10
$21	0.0	1.5	3.0	4.5	6.0	7.5	9.0	10.5	12.0	13.5	15.0
$16	0.0	1.5	3.0	4.5	6.0	7.5	9.0	10.5	12.0	13.5	15.0
$11	0.0	1.5	3.0	4.5	6.0	7.5	9.0	10.5	12.0	13.5	15.0
$6	0.0	1.5	3.0	4.5	6.0	7.5	0.0	0.0	0.0	0.0	0.0
$0	0.0	0.0	0.0	0.0	0.0	0.0	0.0	0.0	0.0	0.0	0.0

Spent	11	12	13	14	15	16	17	18	19	20
$21	16.5	18.0	19.5	21.0	22.5	24.0	25.5	27.0	28.5	30.0
$16	16.5	18.0	19.5	21.0	22.5	0.0	0.0	0.0	0.0	0.0
$11	0.0	0.0	0.0	0.0	0.0	0.0	0.0	0.0	0.0	0.0
$6	0.0	0.0	0.0	0.0	0.0	0.0	0.0	0.0	0.0	0.0
$0	0.0	0.0	0.0	0.0	0.0	0.0	0.0	0.0	0.0	0.0

Loss aversion and scarcity in trading
by Frank Noto

Social science research shows people are far more motivated to avoid losses than to gain new benefits. Researchers asked folks how much they would pay to reduce traffic on their street by one car an hour (a new benefit), and the average payment offered was $2.20. Then the same people were asked how much they would pay to avoid adding one more car per hour (a new loss), and their average payment was more than $9, four times as much. The threat of loss is more credible and more persuasive.

A similar aversion to taking a loss is common in the stock market. Inexperienced investors hold on to stocks that have tanked for too long, because they don't want to irrevocably take a loss. They resist cutting their losses on a crappy stock, convincing themselves that it has to rebound sometime... until it's too late.

The tendency is the same in fanalytic games and real baseball. GMs too often are loath to cut bait until it's unavoidable. Your pitcher has thrown three straight PQS 0 outings, and his Command for the season is below 1.0. If you trade him in June when his trade value is sinking and his ERA is 5.99, you may reason that your team will lose the benefit from his potential second half 3.00 ERA. Your thinking is that he's just in a slump and is "due" to improve.

There are two fallacies to this way of thinking. One is the coin-toss analogy known as the gambler's fallacy. Every time a balanced coin is tossed, the chance of getting heads is 50 percent. If perchance the coin ends up tails on the first ten tosses, does that mean the next ten tosses are statistically more likely to end up heads? No, each toss has a 50 percent chance of ending up heads. Similarly, if your pitcher has been losing the coin toss every outing, there is no reason to expect him to win his outings from here on in.

A second fallacy is the expectation that a pitcher throwing a series of DIS starts is suddenly going to turn things around. As Ron Shandler's research has shown, the odds are far greater that this starter will either continue to throw poorly or lose his job entirely.

But why do teams tend to hang on to that pitcher who won 20 games back in the last century, despite ample evidence that he's lost it? Because as human beings, we are convinced that we may miss out on the rebound that is just around the corner. We don't want to take the loss. To cut or trade him when he is below value is to admit to ourselves that we made a mistake – and his awful stats will be ours for the rest of the season, with no hope of redemption.

The cure for loss avoidance is to examine our reasons for trading or dropping a player. Fortunately, *Forecaster* readers and HQ subscribers have a variety of tools at our disposal to help us decide whether it's time to dispose of our bad investments or to expect a rebound. Every week HQ Buyers' Guides and Top 10 Hot Lists assess whether individual player performances are fact or fluke. HQ's analysis tools such as hit rate, strand rate, xERA, xBA, Eye and others help us determine whether it's just an unlucky slump or there is real skill decline.

If your season is slipping away on you, it's time to overcome that aversion to loss. Act based on the reality you see.

Another negative can result from loss aversion – premature trading. Here's how it works on the stock market: Investors see that their securities have significantly increased in value. Then they sell off prematurely, to avoid the potential for future loss, if the stock declines from its current high point. If investors neglect the stock's potential for further increase in value, then they are selling it short.

I did this once when I sold a player flying high in mid-May of his first full MLB season, batting .325+ with power. Feeling that this result was unsustainable, I determined to sell high and avoid the future loss in his value. By trading Miguel Cabrera too cheaply, I missed out not only on most of his .294-33 HR that year, but also his following All-Star caliber seasons.

Loss aversion has other implications for fanalytic game trading. For example, when trying to trade a player who provides a scarce commodity (e.g., SBs, saves, keepers for next year), GMs may find more success by focusing on what your trading partner might lose from *not* taking the deal. Remember, human nature makes us value new benefits less than potential losses, so instead of emphasizing what a team stands to gain from the trade, emphasize the potential for loss.

Rather than saying to your trading partner, "Adding a speedster to your roster could gain you 5 standings points in stolen bases," instead use language such as, "Passing on this opportunity could cost you 5 standings points in stolen bases." Call his attention to the fact that 1) stolen bases are a scarce commodity and 2) time is running out. There may never be another opportunity like it.

You can also add to the motivation by using the scarcity principle to your advantage, since opportunities appear more valuable when they are less available. Try this approach: "There is a lot of movement in the SB category in our league this year, and good base stealers are scarcer than ever. Five teams are all closely lumped together in SB and you could lose several points in the category. Someone is going to rack up all those points. Do you want to lose out on this opportunity?"

Using the principles of loss aversion and scarcity can help you overcome barriers to trading. They can also help you better understand your own motivations to trade or not to trade.

Losing interest

In our weekly Baseball HQ Poll, 22% of respondents noted that, while you like fantasy baseball, you tend to lose interest if your teams are not in contention. That percentage was up from 19% in 2004 and 13% in 2003. I find that trend troubling; our fraternity is growing impatient.

The core issue is maintaining the perception that you can still compete even when there are many teams ahead of you in the standings. When it's August and you're ranked 12th of 15, and the 11th place team is 20 points away, no level of optimism can magically will you any higher than you are. In the major national competitions, where hundreds or thousands of teams compete for a grand prize, I can't imagine maintaining interest when you're ranked 1,528, or even 152.

There is an essay at RotoHQ.com called "15 Rule Changes to Keep the Fire Burning in September." It includes some artificial rules enhancements (e.g. category pots, split season prizes, etc.) and a few "outside the game" ideas (e.g. holding a pre-winter meeting in September, etc.). I've got two more ideas…

Divisional Play

Think about dividing your league into two divisions. This accomplishes two things...

1. It provides two divisional champions. There's nothing wrong with spreading around the Yoo Hoo a little bit.

2. If you're in last place, it's a lot closer to first when you only have five other teams to jump over.

The divisional alignment would change every year. Each season's even numbered finishers would form one division the following year; odd numbers form the other division.

While the actual number of teams that finish "in the money" might not change from its current configuration, two divisions can give more teams the *perception* that they are closer to contention. It's all about perception anyway, isn't it?

This amounts to a simple cosmetic tweak that could help keep owners in the hunt longer.

Post-season play-offs

There is talk about a play-off system in the RotoHQ essay above, though that idea involves a head-to-head simulation program using regular season stats. In this new scenario, we keep the Rotisserie system and use the MLB play-offs and World Series stats instead.

The top two teams from each division move on to the post-season. These four teams would have to designate a fixed 23-man roster for all post-season games, obviously only containing players on MLB post-season teams. In order to fill the roster holes that will likely exist, these play-off-bound teams can (for the sake of the post-season only), cherry-pick players off the non-play-off teams.

This would be in the form of a mini-roster-stocking snake draft done on the Monday following the final day of the season. Draft order would be regular season finish, so the play-off team with the most regular season points — regardless of division — would get first pick. You might want to cap the number of players vultured off of other teams to five, or something like that.

It is conceivable that filling all 23 roster spots with post-season participants might present a challenge. This might require some late season tactical moves on the part of the play-off bound Roto teams. In 2006, a club comfortably in position to advance might have dealt off an overpriced Carl Crawford for a less valuable Craig Monroe to ensure he had a productive body for the playoffs. Still, it is possible that some teams might not be able to fill all 23 roster spots. They would have to go into October short-handed.

Regular Rotisserie scoring would be used for all games during October. The team with the best play-off stats at the end of the World Series is the overall champ.

What all this essentially says that, if you can manage to finish in the top four of the league, you have a shot at the title. If you prefer, you can split the pot so that 70% goes to the regular season finishers and 30% to the post-season champ.

And for four teams, at least, watching baseball in October will have meaning for your fantasy league. If you want to get creative, the non-play-off teams could place side bets on who they think will win.

At first glance, this doesn't seem to resolve the problem of a 12th place team. However, you might be in 6th place out of eight teams in your division, and depending upon how the balance of power shakes out, you could be close enough to 2nd — and a play-off spot — to keep playing for this year.

When I presented this idea as a rules proposal to the folks in the XFL, it was summarily defeated. One comment was that we were stepping too far outside the box. Another owner said that he liked that the fantasy season ended in time for him to enjoy the Major League post-season. One final objection was that a lower ranked team could conceivably win the championship, a typical complaint with MLB's own play-off structure.

Yes, it's true. The Seattle Mariners won 116 games in 2001 and never made it out of the American League Championship Series. The 2006 St. Louis Cardinals won only 83 games but managed to take the World Series. It happens all the time, in every sport. It's a part of the game. The regular season only gets you so far; you have to take that last step and survive the post-season in order to claim the top prize.

Why should Rotisserie be any different?

IV.
MAJOR LEAGUES

The Teams

The following four pages contain stat boxes for all 30 major league teams plus summary boxes for both leagues. The stats themselves will be mostly familiar to you from the player boxes, however, we have included both batter and pitcher BPIs on each line.

Each team box is divided into three sections.

At Home represents all batting and pitching statistics accumulated by that team in its home ballpark.

Away represents all batting and pitching statistics accumulated by that team in its games on the road.

Opp@ represents all batting and pitching statistics accumulated by all visiting teams when they played at the home ballpark.

Within each section are BPIs from the past three years, 2004-2006. Teams that have changed ballparks during that time may cause some inconsistent data.

To get a sense of ballpark effects, look at both the At Home and Opp@ sections in tandem. If the levels are similar, then it may indicate a particular ballpark tendency. If the levels are not similar, then it may be team dependent. You can compare this data from one team's box to another for additional insight.

As an example, Houston's batters have a contact rate at home in the low 80%'s but the opposition at the Astros' ballpark has levels consistently about 5% lower. This could indicate the success of the HOU pitching staff as opposed to any park effects.

In contrast, Milwaukee's At Home and Opp@ contact rates are both in the high 70%'s, which might be more telling of Miller Park park effects.

We've added a few new pieces of data this year. In the pitching section of each chart, we now show the number of wins (W) each team had, the Pythagorean projected wins (Py) they should have had based on their runs scored and runs allowed, and the percentage of save opportunities successfully converted.

This last data point is interesting. We never really consider that a closer's success might hinge on the friendliness of his environment. However, look at teams like Boston and the White Sox. Opposing relief pitchers visiting Fenway and U.S. Cellular converted barely 50% of their opportunities while the home-team arms were as much as 20% more successful. The reverse was true in Baltimore where visiting bullpens outpitched the Orioles' relievers.

Other things to look at include a team's SX and SBO rates, which provide insight into which teams are easier or more difficult to run on. Note that opposing teams visiting ANA ran under 10% of the time with SX rates far below league average. Compare that to the opposition coming into Coors Field, which ran just as frequently but with much greater success.

Some other interesting tidbits…

Pitchers tend to fare better in their home park than batters. You find much larger variances between Home and Away BPVs than you do for RC/G.

Opposing pitchers have a horrible time in Fenway Park, posting a 5.79 ERA there the past three years. Visiting teams have under-performed their Pythagorean projection by 6 wins in each of the past two years. Fantasy leaguers should just sit their pitchers whenever they visit Boston.

Home runs per fly ball tend to regress to 10%, but there are a few ballparks where the base rate is higher, including Arizona, both Chicago parks (the Windy City indeed!), Cincinnati, Colorado and Philadelphia. As you'd expect, consistent sub-10% rates can be found in places like Florida, San Diego and Washington.

How has Washington D.C's RFK Stadium compared to Olympic Stadium in Montreal? A look at OPS, ct%, G/L/F, PX and hr/f from 2004 to 2005-2006 reveals the answer.

How does the new Busch Stadium compare to the old? A look at 2004-2005 versus 2006 seems to indicate that it is a bit more pitcher-friendly.

BATTING / PITCHING

ANA	Yr	Avg	OB	Slg	OPS	bb%	ct%	h%	Eye	G	L	F	PX	SX	SBO	xBA	RC/G	W	Py	Sv%	ERA	WHIP	H%	S%	xERA	Ctl	Dom	Cmd	hr/f	hr/9	BPV
At Home	04	282	333	418	750	7	83	32	0.46	45	19	36	82	111	13%	260	4.68	45	41	78%	4.28	1.36	31%	72%	3.93	3.0	7.2	2.4	10%	1.1	60
	05	268	324	406	730	8	85	29	0.55	44	19	37	83	112	15%	267	4.51	49	46	80%	3.46	1.23	29%	75%	3.44	2.6	6.9	2.7	8%	0.9	76
	06	279	339	418	757	8	84	31	0.55	44	18	38	87	103	13%	260	4.86	45	43	81%	3.76	1.27	30%	73%	3.64	2.7	7.2	2.7	8%	0.9	78
Away	04	283	338	440	777	8	83	32	0.50	45	20	35	95	119	11%	277	5.06	47	49	71%	4.28	1.36	31%	71%	4.05	3.2	7.3	2.3	9%	1.0	65
	05	273	324	412	736	7	85	30	0.50	42	22	36	85	110	14%	275	4.55	46	47	72%	3.90	1.32	30%	74%	3.61	2.9	7.0	2.4	10%	1.1	64
	06	270	326	432	757	8	84	30	0.51	45	20	36	99	110	14%	279	4.82	44	42	77%	4.33	1.32	29%	70%	4.03	3.2	7.2	2.3	10%	1.1	62
Opp @ ANA	04	265	323	417	741	8	80	30	0.42	43	16	41	97	87	8%	245	4.59	36	40	58%	4.60	1.40	31%	69%	4.23	2.7	5.8	2.2	9%	1.0	50
	05	247	300	387	686	7	80	29	0.37	41	19	40	91	81	8%	250	3.90	32	35	66%	4.38	1.37	30%	70%	4.25	2.9	5.3	1.8	8%	0.9	43
	06	257	310	392	702	7	79	30	0.37	42	19	39	90	91	9%	247	4.10	36	38	71%	4.38	1.45	31%	71%	4.18	3.2	5.8	1.8	8%	0.9	45

ARI	Yr	Avg	OB	Slg	OPS	bb%	ct%	h%	Eye	G	L	F	PX	SX	SBO	xBA	RC/G	W	Py	Sv%	ERA	WHIP	H%	S%	xERA	Ctl	Dom	Cmd	hr/f	hr/9	BPV
At Home	04	266	321	423	743	7	83	30	0.48	43	19	37	102	92	5%	274	4.65	29	30	65%	4.71	1.46	30%	71%	3.95	4.1	7.4	1.8	14%	1.3	45
	05	258	330	427	758	10	81	29	0.57	45	20	35	108	96	5%	277	4.90	36	28	66%	5.27	1.51	32%	67%	4.45	3.5	6.3	1.8	13%	1.2	38
	06	283	342	461	803	8	84	31	0.57	46	20	35	114	105	7%	293	5.42	39	38	64%	4.81	1.45	31%	70%	4.06	3.5	6.9	2.0	13%	1.2	46
Away	04	240	295	363	658	7	80	28	0.39	47	19	35	85	80	7%	251	3.59	22	23	55%	5.28	1.53	31%	67%	4.60	4.3	7.1	1.6	12%	1.1	43
	05	254	328	415	743	10	80	29	0.54	45	20	34	109	83	7%	275	4.73	41	38	80%	4.45	1.40	31%	71%	3.83	3.1	6.5	2.1	13%	1.2	48
	06	251	312	388	701	8	82	28	0.48	43	19	38	92	101	8%	260	4.15	37	42	62%	4.16	1.34	31%	70%	3.88	3.1	6.9	2.2	9%	0.8	65
Opp @ ARI	04	262	340	447	787	11	79	30	0.55	47	19	34	121	115	10%	283	5.32	52	51	72%	3.94	1.33	30%	73%	3.77	2.8	5.9	2.1	9%	1.0	52
	05	284	349	470	819	9	82	32	0.56	46	22	32	122	110	7%	302	5.65	45	53	58%	3.96	1.40	29%	76%	3.47	3.7	6.6	1.8	13%	1.2	43
	06	273	340	453	793	9	80	31	0.51	47	20	33	117	110	8%	287	5.33	42	43	60%	4.55	1.46	31%	71%	4.08	3.2	5.6	1.8	10%	1.1	36

ATL	Yr	Avg	OB	Slg	OPS	bb%	ct%	h%	Eye	G	L	F	PX	SX	SBO	xBA	RC/G	W	Py	Sv%	ERA	WHIP	H%	S%	xERA	Ctl	Dom	Cmd	hr/f	hr/9	BPV
At Home	04	265	338	434	772	10	78	31	0.50	46	19	36	114	111	8%	270	5.11	49	47	70%	3.60	1.35	30%	77%	3.22	3.2	6.6	2.1	11%	1.0	56
	05	284	352	462	814	10	81	32	0.55	43	23	34	118	121	9%	294	5.62	53	49	69%	3.82	1.33	29%	73%	3.61	3.0	5.7	1.9	9%	0.8	54
	06	280	342	457	800	9	80	32	0.46	42	22	36	118	84	5%	280	5.37	40	43	59%	4.33	1.41	31%	73%	3.70	3.2	7.1	2.2	13%	1.2	54
Away	04	274	341	433	774	9	80	32	0.51	47	19	34	106	103	7%	274	5.11	47	48	71%	3.91	1.41	30%	74%	3.63	3.3	6.1	1.8	9%	0.9	49
	05	247	309	409	718	8	80	28	0.44	46	19	35	107	97	8%	270	4.32	37	41	55%	4.16	1.45	30%	74%	3.68	3.5	5.8	1.7	12%	1.0	39
	06	261	324	453	777	9	79	29	0.44	45	19	36	126	94	6%	279	5.06	39	42	54%	4.87	1.51	31%	70%	4.37	3.9	6.0	1.5	11%	1.1	35
Opp @ ATL	04	263	325	398	723	8	81	30	0.47	48	19	33	89	82	9%	259	4.40	32	34	62%	4.78	1.45	31%	70%	4.12	3.8	7.6	2.0	12%	1.2	54
	05	262	321	390	711	8	83	30	0.52	48	22	31	85	92	8%	275	4.30	28	32	50%	5.21	1.52	32%	68%	4.47	3.7	6.7	1.8	12%	1.2	42
	06	271	333	433	765	8	80	31	0.46	44	22	33	107	106	9%	280	4.93	41	38	71%	4.79	1.47	32%	71%	4.04	3.3	7.2	2.2	13%	1.3	49

BAL	Yr	Avg	OB	Slg	OPS	bb%	ct%	h%	Eye	G	L	F	PX	SX	SBO	xBA	RC/G	W	Py	Sv%	ERA	WHIP	H%	S%	xERA	Ctl	Dom	Cmd	hr/f	hr/9	BPV
At Home	04	280	339	428	767	8	85	31	0.58	42	19	39	92	91	8%	268	4.96	38	36	56%	4.94	1.52	31%	69%	4.50	4.2	6.5	1.6	10%	1.0	41
	05	263	328	427	755	9	85	28	0.64	42	19	38	96	83	7%	272	4.85	36	35	73%	4.22	1.39	29%	72%	3.87	3.7	6.6	1.8	11%	1.1	48
	06	290	344	454	798	8	86	31	0.57	43	20	36	96	109	10%	283	5.27	40	41	55%	4.73	1.47	30%	71%	4.09	3.6	6.2	1.7	13%	1.3	35
Away	04	283	345	435	780	9	82	32	0.53	44	20	36	95	93	9%	269	5.14	40	46	59%	4.46	1.47	30%	71%	4.16	4.3	7.0	1.6	9%	0.9	51
	05	274	318	441	759	6	83	30	0.38	43	21	36	104	101	10%	281	4.73	38	39	61%	4.93	1.47	31%	69%	4.19	3.6	6.7	1.9	13%	1.2	43
	06	265	323	393	717	8	83	30	0.51	46	19	35	82	97	10%	263	4.37	30	29	72%	6.02	1.63	32%	65%	5.11	4.2	6.7	1.6	13%	1.4	26
Opp @ BAL	04	269	346	413	759	11	82	30	0.64	44	19	37	88	97	7%	259	4.98	43	45	72%	4.63	1.45	31%	70%	4.36	3.2	5.1	1.7	9%	1.0	36
	05	256	328	395	724	10	81	29	0.56	46	19	35	86	91	8%	256	4.47	45	46	73%	4.03	1.39	28%	75%	3.79	3.4	5.2	1.6	11%	1.2	30
	06	277	345	442	787	9	82	31	0.57	44	20	36	99	81	9%	273	5.22	41	40	71%	4.91	1.49	31%	70%	4.29	2.9	5.2	1.8	12%	1.3	26

BOS	Yr	Avg	OB	Slg	OPS	bb%	ct%	h%	Eye	G	L	F	PX	SX	SBO	xBA	RC/G	W	Py	Sv%	ERA	WHIP	H%	S%	xERA	Ctl	Dom	Cmd	hr/f	hr/9	BPV
At Home	04	304	375	504	880	10	80	35	0.56	42	18	40	132	94	6%	279	6.48	55	51	70%	4.09	1.29	30%	70%	3.81	2.7	7.1	2.6	9%	0.9	72
	05	280	360	459	819	11	81	32	0.67	42	23	35	116	100	3%	289	5.77	54	48	70%	4.46	1.37	31%	69%	4.12	2.8	6.2	2.2	9%	1.0	54
	06	285	360	448	808	10	82	32	0.65	41	20	39	106	72	3%	271	5.61	48	42	65%	4.70	1.41	32%	68%	4.27	3.0	6.8	2.2	9%	0.9	60
Away	04	260	337	441	778	10	79	30	0.55	41	18	40	114	89	6%	263	5.20	43	45	77%	4.30	1.30	30%	69%	3.93	2.8	6.9	2.5	10%	1.0	65
	05	281	351	450	801	10	82	31	0.59	41	23	36	104	86	3%	279	5.43	41	42	63%	5.04	1.41	31%	66%	4.55	2.7	5.9	2.2	10%	1.1	47
	06	253	335	422	757	11	80	28	0.62	39	20	41	105	82	6%	262	4.93	38	39	69%	4.97	1.48	31%	70%	4.24	3.3	6.6	2.0	13%	1.4	39
Opp @ BOS	04	255	309	406	715	7	80	30	0.38	46	17	36	101	112	10%	262	4.29	26	30	52%	6.40	1.72	36%	65%	5.17	4.2	7.6	1.8	12%	1.4	33
	05	269	324	436	759	7	83	30	0.46	43	21	36	108	109	8%	284	4.86	27	33	57%	5.68	1.62	32%	67%	4.89	4.5	6.7	1.5	12%	1.2	33
	06	274	332	432	764	8	81	32	0.45	44	20	35	106	111	8%	276	4.94	33	39	45%	5.28	1.60	32%	68%	4.78	4.2	6.4	1.5	9%	1.1	36

CHC	Yr	Avg	OB	Slg	OPS	bb%	ct%	h%	Eye	G	L	F	PX	SX	SBO	xBA	RC/G	W	Py	Sv%	ERA	WHIP	H%	S%	xERA	Ctl	Dom	Cmd	hr/f	hr/9	BPV
At Home	04	274	334	484	818	8	82	29	0.50	42	20	38	130	101	6%	293	5.50	45	48	59%	3.94	1.29	30%	73%	3.46	3.2	8.1	2.6	12%	1.1	73
	05	271	321	447	768	7	84	29	0.45	44	21	35	112	92	8%	293	4.87	38	40	55%	4.04	1.32	29%	73%	3.48	3.5	7.9	2.3	14%	1.2	66
	06	279	327	440	767	7	84	31	0.44	47	20	33	102	116	12%	286	4.88	36	35	60%	4.68	1.35	29%	70%	3.94	3.8	8.5	2.2	15%	1.5	57
Away	04	262	319	433	752	8	80	30	0.41	43	21	37	114	91	7%	275	4.72	44	45	68%	3.71	1.32	30%	75%	3.36	3.5	8.5	2.4	10%	0.9	79
	05	268	320	433	754	7	83	29	0.46	45	21	34	107	79	7%	286	4.73	41	40	74%	4.36	1.37	30%	71%	3.77	3.7	7.8	2.1	13%	1.2	60
	06	256	305	405	710	7	83	28	0.41	47	19	34	92	111	13%	271	4.17	30	34	67%	4.81	1.55	31%	71%	4.38	4.8	7.1	1.5	10%	1.1	44
Opp @ CHC	04	248	312	406	718	9	76	29	0.39	44	20	36	108	97	10%	259	4.33	37	34	60%	4.97	1.43	29%	71%	4.07	3.2	6.3	2.0	16%	1.7	28
	05	247	316	405	722	9	77	29	0.44	46	21	33	109	89	10%	268	4.42	43	41	55%	4.30	1.33	29%	72%	3.80	2.6	5.7	2.2	13%	1.3	43
	06	244	321	441	762	10	75	28	0.46	43	18	39	132	121	10%	267	4.96	45	46	63%	4.36	1.37	31%	71%	3.88	2.5	5.7	2.3	11%	1.0	50

CHW	Yr	Avg	OB	Slg	OPS	bb%	ct%	h%	Eye	G	L	F	PX	SX	SBO	xBA	RC/G	W	Py	Sv%	ERA	WHIP	H%	S%	xERA	Ctl	Dom	Cmd	hr/f	hr/9	BPV
At Home	04	276	340	491	831	9	82	29	0.53	40	17	43	126	88	9%	274	5.67	46	43	71%	5.09	1.43	30%	69%	4.25	3.0	6.5	2.1	15%	1.5	37
	05	257	315	442	756	8	82	28	0.46	43	20	37	110	98	16%	279	4.73	47	43	73%	3.82	1.28	28%	74%	3.43	2.9	6.4	2.2	13%	1.2	53
	06	281	342	480	822	8	82	30	0.51	42	20	38	118	91	9%	284	5.55	49	46	70%	4.43	1.36	30%	72%	3.92	2.8	6.3	2.2	12%	1.3	45
Away	04	260	316	424	740	8	81	29	0.44	42	19	40	103	90	9%	263	4.57	37	41	77%	4.73	1.41	29%	70%	4.28	3.6	6.3	1.7	12%	1.3	38
	05	267	317	409	727	7	82	30	0.41	45	21	35	87	96	13%	267	4.37	52	48	75%	3.39	1.23	28%	75%	3.39	2.7	6.3	2.3	8%	0.9	67
	06	280	336	448	785	8	81	32	0.44	42	20	38	105	94	10%	269	5.13	41	41	76%	4.82	1.36	31%	67%	4.36	2.5	6.3	2.5	10%	1.1	55
Opp @ CHW	04	281	338	470	808	8	82	31	0.47	44	19	37	113	90	9%	277	5.37	35	38	55%	5.63	1.46	29%	67%	4.70	3.5	6.5	1.9	15%	1.9	22
	05	254	313	412	725	8	81	28	0.45	44	22	34	96	101	11%	275	4.38	34	38	50%	4.47	1.29	27%	70%	3.91	2.9	6.2	2.2	15%	1.5	43
	06	268	322	440	763	7	82	29	0.45	43	18	39	104	108	10%	269	4.82	32	35	50%	5.47	1.47	30%	68%	4.46	3.3	6.4	2.0	16%	1.7	26

CIN	Yr	Avg	OB	Slg	OPS	bb%	ct%	h%	Eye	G	L	F	PX	SX	SBO	xBA	RC/G	W	Py	Sv%	ERA	WHIP	H%	S%	xERA	Ctl	Dom	Cmd	hr/f	hr/9	BPV
At Home	04	242	315	403	718	10	76	28	0.45	45	19	37	111	91	6%	258	4.39	40	32	60%	4.75	1.38	29%	71%	4.12	3.2	6.4	2.0	14%	1.6	36
	05	268	340	472	812	10	78	30	0.49	42	22	36	138	94	6%	290	5.56	42	40	71%	5.16	1.50	32%	69%	4.29	2.9	6.2	2.1	13%	1.4	34
	06	271	350	459	809	11	78	30	0.56	43	19	38	122	94	10%	274	5.54	42	38	58%	4.78	1.38	31%	70%	4.10	2.8	6.9	2.5	13%	1.4	50
Away	04	258	331	431	763	10	75	31	0.44	45	19	35	122	111	8%	268	5.01	36	35	62%	5.71	1.63	33%	68%	4.77	3.9	6.0	1.5	13%	1.4	21
	05	254	329	422	750	10	75	31	0.45	45	22	33	119	94	7%	272	4.85	31	35	61%	5.19	1.50	31%	68%	4.57	3.2	5.8	1.8	11%	1.3	31
	06	244	314	407	721	9	78	28	0.47	44	19	37	112	100	11%	267	4.43	38	38	62%	4.28	1.44	31%	74%	3.73	3.0	6.2	2.1	11%	1.2	43
Opp @ CIN	04	264	326	465	791	8	82	28	0.50	41	19	40	130	96	6%	286	5.21	41	49	63%	4.06	1.31	29%	73%	3.62	3.6	8.0	2.2	12%	1.2	65
	05	294	347	495	842	8	83	32	0.48	42	21	37	131	103	7%	300	5.81	39	42	62%	5.28	1.47	31%	68%	4.25	3.8	7.8	2.0	16%	1.6	42
	06	273	327	460	788	7	80	31	0.41	41	20	39	123	73	5%	277	5.12	39	43	60%	4.84	1.51	30%	73%	3.95	4.2	7.5	1.8	16%	1.6	35

BATTING / PITCHING

CLE	Yr	Avg	OB	Slg	OPS	bb%	ct%	h%	Eye	G	L	F	PX	SX	SBO	xBA	RC/G	W	Py	Sv%	ERA	WHIP	H%	S%	xERA	Ctl	Dom	Cmd	hr/f	hr/9	BPV
At Home	04	270	348	424	772	11	82	31	0.67	47	18	35	102	91	8%	270	5.21	44	39	58%	4.73	1.45	31%	70%	4.15	3.6	7.0	1.9	11%	1.1	50
	05	267	333	437	770	9	81	30	0.52	45	20	34	110	79	6%	278	5.04	43	48	82%	3.32	1.16	27%	75%	3.16	2.3	6.5	2.8	11%	1.0	77
	06	280	349	458	807	10	78	33	0.49	41	21	38	118	91	4%	273	5.55	44	47	58%	4.05	1.36	31%	72%	3.72	2.7	6.1	2.2	9%	0.9	57
Away	04	281	343	462	805	9	82	31	0.53	41	19	41	110	98	10%	271	5.41	36	42	48%	4.91	1.46	31%	70%	4.28	3.5	6.7	1.9	12%	1.3	40
	05	276	329	467	797	7	80	31	0.41	44	20	36	118	94	8%	282	5.25	50	48	74%	3.91	1.29	29%	73%	3.65	2.8	6.5	2.3	10%	1.0	61
	06	281	342	456	798	8	79	33	0.43	43	20	37	114	98	6%	271	5.36	34	42	46%	4.84	1.47	32%	70%	4.22	2.7	5.9	2.2	11%	1.2	42
Opp @ CLE	04	271	339	436	775	9	80	31	0.51	45	20	35	107	101	9%	272	5.12	37	42	57%	4.84	1.50	31%	69%	4.52	4.2	6.2	1.5	9%	0.9	43
	05	240	289	378	667	6	81	27	0.35	45	21	33	89	88	10%	265	3.61	38	33	81%	4.33	1.42	30%	73%	3.78	3.5	6.8	1.9	12%	1.2	47
	06	273	325	408	733	7	83	31	0.45	46	21	34	85	105	12%	268	4.49	37	34	71%	5.21	1.52	33%	68%	4.45	3.8	7.6	2.0	12%	1.2	50

COL	Yr	Avg	OB	Slg	OPS	bb%	ct%	h%	Eye	G	L	F	PX	SX	SBO	xBA	RC/G	W	Py	Sv%	ERA	WHIP	H%	S%	xERA	Ctl	Dom	Cmd	hr/f	hr/9	BPV
At Home	04	303	373	506	879	10	81	34	0.59	44	21	36	133	88	4%	297	6.44	38	38	50%	6.27	1.75	34%	66%	5.23	4.6	6.0	1.3	13%	1.4	17
	05	300	362	460	822	9	82	34	0.55	43	25	32	104	109	6%	294	5.67	40	41	58%	5.19	1.57	33%	68%	4.41	3.6	6.2	1.7	11%	1.0	39
	06	294	362	459	821	10	82	34	0.60	45	23	32	107	117	9%	292	5.74	44	44	55%	4.72	1.47	31%	70%	4.09	3.4	5.9	1.8	12%	1.1	38
Away	04	246	310	403	713	8	76	29	0.39	47	17	36	109	83	6%	251	4.27	30	35	53%	4.77	1.50	30%	71%	4.34	4.1	5.9	1.4	11%	1.1	33
	05	232	293	359	652	8	78	28	0.39	45	20	35	88	81	6%	248	3.50	27	28	59%	5.08	1.54	31%	69%	4.51	4.1	6.3	1.5	11%	1.2	33
	06	247	312	408	720	9	78	29	0.43	42	19	38	111	96	9%	263	4.41	32	36	60%	4.60	1.43	31%	69%	4.47	3.5	5.9	1.7	7%	0.8	48
Opp @ COL	04	307	385	501	886	11	83	34	0.77	44	21	36	123	121	8%	300	6.58	43	43	66%	5.83	1.66	34%	67%	4.72	4.0	6.8	1.7	14%	1.4	28
	05	295	359	457	816	9	83	33	0.58	46	23	31	108	103	7%	297	5.63	41	40	67%	5.36	1.61	34%	68%	4.44	3.5	6.4	1.8	12%	1.1	38
	06	282	345	454	800	9	83	31	0.57	48	20	32	110	115	8%	292	5.40	37	37	71%	5.41	1.57	33%	66%	4.72	3.8	6.3	1.7	10%	1.0	41

DET	Yr	Avg	OB	Slg	OPS	bb%	ct%	h%	Eye	G	L	F	PX	SX	SBO	xBA	RC/G	W	Py	Sv%	ERA	WHIP	H%	S%	xERA	Ctl	Dom	Cmd	hr/f	hr/9	BPV
At Home	04	273	335	437	772	9	81	31	0.49	44	19	37	98	107	9%	265	5.04	38	37	65%	4.75	1.41	30%	69%	4.26	3.2	6.1	1.9	11%	1.1	43
	05	277	324	442	766	6	82	31	0.40	44	20	36	97	106	4%	274	4.84	39	39	67%	4.07	1.36	30%	73%	3.76	2.9	5.8	2.0	10%	1.0	47
	06	273	325	424	749	7	81	31	0.41	43	19	37	94	97	6%	261	4.68	46	45	72%	3.92	1.33	29%	73%	3.70	3.0	6.1	2.0	10%	1.0	52
Away	04	272	332	461	793	8	78	31	0.42	42	19	40	120	108	9%	268	5.27	34	42	47%	5.12	1.48	31%	68%	4.50	3.5	6.4	1.8	11%	1.2	39
	05	266	313	415	727	6	81	31	0.35	45	20	35	96	98	9%	265	4.37	32	36	63%	5.01	1.38	29%	67%	4.34	2.9	5.5	1.9	14%	1.4	32
	06	276	327	472	799	7	79	31	0.35	41	19	40	123	93	8%	270	5.25	49	51	76%	3.78	1.31	29%	74%	3.52	3.1	6.4	2.1	10%	1.0	56
Opp @ DET	04	273	334	437	771	8	83	30	0.52	46	19	36	99	99	9%	271	5.00	43	44	83%	4.54	1.41	31%	70%	4.09	3.2	6.6	2.0	11%	1.1	50
	05	270	327	419	746	8	83	30	0.50	45	19	35	89	80	6%	265	4.67	42	42	71%	4.09	1.35	31%	73%	3.64	2.4	6.2	2.5	11%	1.1	56
	06	259	318	404	722	8	82	29	0.50	46	19	35	89	85	6%	262	4.41	35	36	59%	4.53	1.37	31%	69%	4.12	2.7	6.6	2.4	10%	1.0	60

FLA	Yr	Avg	OB	Slg	OPS	bb%	ct%	h%	Eye	G	L	F	PX	SX	SBO	xBA	RC/G	W	Py	Sv%	ERA	WHIP	H%	S%	xERA	Ctl	Dom	Cmd	hr/f	hr/9	BPV
At Home	04	260	323	404	727	9	82	29	0.52	45	18	37	94	97	10%	261	4.50	40	39	66%	3.72	1.30	29%	75%	3.54	3.4	7.4	2.2	10%	1.0	66
	05	269	340	398	737	10	82	31	0.60	43	22	34	86	94	7%	270	4.72	45	41	78%	3.83	1.34	31%	72%	3.68	3.4	7.6	2.2	7%	0.6	77
	06	258	326	427	754	9	77	31	0.44	44	19	37	116	105	11%	264	4.87	42	39	63%	4.07	1.43	31%	74%	3.81	3.9	7.3	1.9	9%	1.0	57
Away	04	265	326	406	732	8	82	30	0.51	45	19	36	92	108	9%	268	4.54	41	42	77%	4.47	1.36	30%	69%	4.07	3.1	6.5	2.1	11%	1.1	54
	05	276	329	420	750	7	85	31	0.51	45	23	32	95	105	11%	291	4.74	38	38	61%	4.56	1.47	32%	70%	4.18	3.6	6.4	1.8	9%	0.8	51
	06	270	324	442	766	7	78	32	0.36	44	20	37	118	112	12%	271	4.91	36	41	58%	4.69	1.48	30%	71%	4.25	3.9	6.4	1.6	11%	1.1	39
Opp @ FLA	04	246	314	395	709	9	78	29	0.45	43	17	39	101	101	10%	251	4.27	38	39	69%	3.83	1.34	29%	74%	3.71	3.2	6.2	1.9	9%	0.9	54
	05	257	325	383	708	9	77	32	0.45	46	22	33	90	116	11%	259	4.33	36	40	58%	4.12	1.43	31%	72%	3.99	3.7	6.2	1.7	8%	0.7	52
	06	262	337	415	752	10	79	31	0.54	41	20	39	102	90	7%	259	4.90	39	42	74%	4.15	1.37	31%	73%	3.70	3.5	7.9	2.3	11%	1.1	66

HOU	Yr	Avg	OB	Slg	OPS	bb%	ct%	h%	Eye	G	L	F	PX	SX	SBO	xBA	RC/G	W	Py	Sv%	ERA	WHIP	H%	S%	xERA	Ctl	Dom	Cmd	hr/f	hr/9	BPV
At Home	04	277	350	453	803	10	82	31	0.64	43	20	37	111	111	7%	281	5.49	48	46	67%	3.91	1.26	30%	73%	3.42	2.9	8.5	2.9	12%	1.1	84
	05	271	334	436	771	9	82	30	0.52	43	20	37	104	116	12%	275	5.00	53	51	87%	3.08	1.13	27%	77%	2.82	2.4	7.3	3.0	12%	1.0	87
	06	254	328	430	758	10	81	28	0.57	42	19	40	114	89	5%	270	4.91	44	41	72%	4.03	1.27	29%	72%	3.58	2.7	7.2	2.6	12%	1.1	69
Away	04	257	327	420	747	9	81	29	0.55	42	20	38	108	104	8%	273	4.77	44	45	68%	4.21	1.43	31%	73%	3.72	3.7	7.5	2.0	11%	1.1	58
	05	242	299	381	681	8	80	28	0.41	44	19	37	96	98	11%	260	3.88	36	40	68%	3.98	1.33	30%	73%	3.56	3.1	7.2	2.3	11%	1.0	66
	06	256	325	390	714	9	80	29	0.52	45	19	36	89	94	10%	256	4.36	38	42	68%	4.16	1.33	29%	72%	3.78	3.2	7.0	2.2	11%	1.1	59
Opp @ HOU	04	249	308	409	717	8	75	30	0.34	45	19	36	111	111	11%	257	4.30	33	35	76%	4.86	1.51	30%	71%	4.31	3.9	6.1	1.6	12%	1.3	32
	05	233	285	369	654	7	78	27	0.33	48	20	31	91	78	8%	258	3.43	28	30	78%	4.34	1.41	30%	73%	3.87	3.3	6.3	1.9	12%	1.2	43
	06	255	310	419	729	7	79	29	0.38	46	20	35	110	96	7%	272	4.43	37	40	59%	4.43	1.36	28%	71%	4.13	3.7	6.5	1.8	12%	1.2	43

KC	Yr	Avg	OB	Slg	OPS	bb%	ct%	h%	Eye	G	L	F	PX	SX	SBO	xBA	RC/G	W	Py	Sv%	ERA	WHIP	H%	S%	xERA	Ctl	Dom	Cmd	hr/f	hr/9	BPV
At Home	04	259	319	378	697	8	82	30	0.50	46	17	37	75	84	6%	243	4.13	33	32	62%	4.89	1.46	31%	69%	4.50	3.0	5.8	1.9	9%	1.1	39
	05	269	324	395	719	8	84	31	0.49	46	20	34	82	93	6%	264	4.41	34	32	74%	5.21	1.51	32%	66%	4.74	3.4	5.8	1.7	9%	1.0	39
	06	289	348	437	785	8	81	34	0.49	47	20	32	97	104	6%	276	5.23	34	35	59%	5.68	1.62	31%	67%	4.97	4.1	5.4	1.3	12%	1.3	20
Away	04	258	313	415	728	7	80	30	0.39	45	17	38	99	84	10%	253	4.40	25	33	43%	5.45	1.58	32%	69%	4.64	3.5	5.5	1.5	13%	1.5	15
	05	256	307	397	704	7	80	30	0.36	44	20	37	90	85	6%	256	4.10	22	28	40%	5.95	1.64	33%	66%	4.98	4.0	6.0	1.5	12%	1.3	23
	06	254	308	385	693	7	81	29	0.42	48	19	33	86	92	7%	262	4.05	28	28	49%	5.66	1.59	32%	67%	4.87	3.9	6.0	1.5	12%	1.4	22
Opp @ KC	04	285	341	457	799	8	84	31	0.53	41	19	40	107	112	9%	277	5.34	47	48	78%	3.95	1.32	30%	71%	3.97	3.0	6.0	2.0	7%	0.7	60
	05	285	348	445	793	9	84	32	0.59	44	20	36	101	87	6%	278	5.34	47	49	62%	4.07	1.34	30%	70%	4.04	2.8	5.7	2.0	7%	0.6	59
	06	294	367	477	844	10	85	32	0.76	44	21	36	112	87	5%	293	6.02	47	46	72%	4.80	1.50	34%	69%	4.22	3.2	6.6	2.0	9%	0.8	55

LA	Yr	Avg	OB	Slg	OPS	bb%	ct%	h%	Eye	G	L	F	PX	SX	SBO	xBA	RC/G	W	Py	Sv%	ERA	WHIP	H%	S%	xERA	Ctl	Dom	Cmd	hr/f	hr/9	BPV
At Home	04	260	323	417	740	8	80	29	0.47	46	18	36	98	97	8%	261	4.57	49	45	86%	3.71	1.25	28%	74%	3.50	2.9	6.8	2.4	11%	1.1	62
	05	248	325	399	724	10	80	28	0.58	46	21	34	102	82	7%	272	4.52	40	41	75%	3.94	1.24	28%	72%	3.58	2.7	6.8	2.5	12%	1.1	66
	06	293	369	463	831	11	84	32	0.74	42	21	37	108	116	12%	286	5.90	49	47	71%	4.11	1.37	31%	72%	3.73	3.2	7.1	2.2	10%	0.9	63
Away	04	263	331	429	759	9	80	30	0.51	45	19	37	105	107	11%	268	4.88	44	44	84%	4.32	1.38	29%	71%	4.11	3.6	6.4	1.8	10%	1.1	47
	05	258	317	392	708	8	80	30	0.42	42	22	36	92	87	6%	261	4.23	31	34	63%	4.86	1.44	30%	69%	4.28	3.3	5.8	1.8	12%	1.2	36
	06	260	324	404	727	9	82	30	0.53	46	19	36	93	124	9%	269	4.55	39	40	61%	4.35	1.39	31%	70%	3.96	2.9	6.1	2.1	10%	0.9	53
Opp @ LA	04	249	307	394	702	8	80	28	0.42	42	19	39	93	97	9%	254	4.08	32	36	57%	4.44	1.36	29%	71%	3.88	3.2	6.8	2.1	13%	1.3	49
	05	250	305	406	710	7	80	28	0.39	47	18	34	105	100	11%	269	4.19	41	40	71%	4.07	1.36	28%	73%	3.75	3.8	6.7	1.7	11%	1.0	51
	06	265	326	408	734	8	80	31	0.45	48	17	35	99	106	12%	261	4.56	32	34	74%	5.36	1.63	32%	69%	4.78	4.3	5.8	1.4	10%	1.1	26

MIL	Yr	Avg	OB	Slg	OPS	bb%	ct%	h%	Eye	G	L	F	PX	SX	SBO	xBA	RC/G	W	Py	Sv%	ERA	WHIP	H%	S%	xERA	Ctl	Dom	Cmd	hr/f	hr/9	BPV
At Home	04	249	323	393	716	10	75	31	0.45	44	19	37	106	116	13%	255	4.46	36	37	66%	4.14	1.27	29%	70%	3.90	2.9	7.1	2.5	10%	1.0	70
	05	259	329	433	762	9	79	30	0.49	42	22	36	118	98	7%	279	4.95	46	45	66%	3.76	1.27	28%	74%	3.49	3.5	7.7	2.2	11%	1.1	67
	06	260	329	438	767	9	77	30	0.46	41	19	40	123	101	7%	267	5.02	48	39	71%	4.46	1.31	30%	68%	4.12	3.2	7.7	2.5	10%	1.0	72
Away	04	247	307	381	688	8	77	30	0.38	46	19	34	94	105	12%	253	3.95	31	31	66%	4.40	1.39	31%	71%	4.02	3.1	6.5	2.1	10%	1.1	53
	05	260	321	414	735	8	79	30	0.43	44	22	34	109	86	9%	275	4.57	35	39	72%	4.21	1.44	31%	73%	3.85	3.6	7.0	1.9	10%	1.0	53
	06	256	312	403	715	8	77	30	0.36	44	20	36	103	78	8%	259	4.26	27	32	55%	5.22	1.46	31%	66%	4.59	3.3	6.7	2.0	11%	1.2	45
Opp @ MIL	04	251	309	410	719	8	79	29	0.40	44	18	38	110	104	9%	265	4.35	45	44	69%	3.74	1.36	31%	75%	3.49	3.8	8.5	2.2	9%	0.8	78
	05	235	308	390	697	10	77	27	0.46	42	21	37	107	84	9%	261	4.13	35	36	76%	4.57	1.38	30%	70%	4.05	3.6	7.3	2.1	12%	1.2	55
	06	251	314	412	725	8	77	30	0.41	43	19	38	113	113	9%	264	4.47	33	42	52%	4.54	1.39	30%	71%	4.02	3.6	7.8	2.2	12%	1.3	58

BATTING / PITCHING

MIN	Yr	Avg	OB	Slg	OPS	bb%	ct%	h%	Eye	G	L	F	PX	SX	SBO	xBA	RC/G	W	Py	Sv%	ERA	WHIP	H%	S%	xERA	Ctl	Dom	Cmd	hr/f	hr/9	BPV
At Home	04	268	332	429	761	9	83	30	0.54	47	17	36	100	104	11%	270	4.90	49	45	76%	3.89	1.28	31%	72%	3.51	2.3	7.3	3.2	10%	1.0	82
	05	264	324	399	723	8	82	30	0.48	50	20	31	85	100	10%	266	4.43	45	42	73%	3.62	1.16	28%	72%	3.46	1.8	6.1	3.3	10%	1.0	82
	06	298	351	439	790	8	84	33	0.52	45	23	32	84	106	8%	281	5.21	54	52	95%	3.40	1.16	30%	74%	3.17	1.8	7.5	4.1	10%	1.0	106
Away	04	263	323	433	756	8	83	29	0.50	45	17	38	104	91	11%	266	4.79	43	42	67%	4.20	1.37	30%	72%	3.90	3.0	6.4	2.1	10%	1.1	53
	05	254	313	384	697	8	83	29	0.51	50	18	31	81	96	9%	263	4.12	38	42	73%	3.83	1.31	30%	75%	3.51	2.5	5.7	2.3	11%	1.1	51
	06	276	338	412	750	9	84	31	0.60	49	20	31	83	95	9%	273	4.79	42	41	71%	4.54	1.41	32%	72%	3.76	2.6	7.1	2.7	13%	1.3	57
Opp @ MIN	04	266	312	397	709	6	79	31	0.32	45	19	36	83	83	8%	246	4.09	32	36	55%	4.80	1.40	30%	68%	4.35	3.3	6.1	1.8	11%	1.1	43
	05	252	291	390	681	5	82	28	0.30	45	20	35	85	82	6%	260	3.72	36	39	56%	4.07	1.35	30%	72%	3.71	3.1	6.4	2.1	10%	0.9	59
	06	251	289	392	681	5	78	30	0.24	44	19	37	92	84	8%	250	3.71	27	29	59%	4.91	1.51	33%	68%	4.34	2.9	5.5	1.9	9%	0.9	42

NYM	Yr	Avg	OB	Slg	OPS	bb%	ct%	h%	Eye	G	L	F	PX	SX	SBO	xBA	RC/G	W	Py	Sv%	ERA	WHIP	H%	S%	xERA	Ctl	Dom	Cmd	hr/f	hr/9	BPV
At Home	04	254	317	406	723	8	80	29	0.46	44	18	39	102	104	8%	260	4.41	38	39	44%	3.76	1.39	30%	75%	3.63	3.5	6.2	1.8	8%	0.8	53
	05	261	324	411	735	9	81	29	0.50	45	20	35	98	121	14%	273	4.57	48	46	66%	3.48	1.27	29%	75%	3.45	2.9	6.3	2.2	8%	0.8	66
	06	256	325	434	759	9	81	28	0.54	44	17	38	117	128	13%	278	4.92	50	45	70%	3.77	1.27	29%	73%	3.62	3.1	7.2	2.3	10%	1.0	68
Away	04	244	308	411	719	8	78	28	0.43	42	19	39	113	104	10%	265	4.33	33	37	76%	4.46	1.43	29%	72%	4.10	3.8	5.9	1.5	11%	1.1	36
	05	256	313	421	733	8	80	29	0.41	44	21	35	109	114	13%	277	4.50	35	43	63%	4.10	1.35	29%	72%	3.87	3.3	6.4	1.9	9%	0.9	54
	06	272	335	455	790	9	81	31	0.48	42	20	38	120	121	12%	282	5.26	47	45	79%	4.58	1.38	30%	70%	4.01	3.4	7.1	2.1	12%	1.3	52
Opp @ NYM	04	260	329	384	713	9	82	30	0.57	47	18	35	84	83	9%	255	4.37	43	42	70%	3.96	1.32	29%	73%	3.70	3.2	6.9	2.2	10%	1.1	59
	05	253	312	377	689	8	81	29	0.45	44	21	35	85	104	10%	264	4.00	33	35	66%	4.27	1.37	30%	72%	3.87	3.3	6.6	2.0	11%	1.1	52
	06	245	309	388	697	9	79	29	0.44	43	19	38	98	94	12%	255	4.08	31	36	54%	4.56	1.37	29%	70%	4.18	3.5	6.5	1.9	11%	1.2	45

NYY	Yr	Avg	OB	Slg	OPS	bb%	ct%	h%	Eye	G	L	F	PX	SX	SBO	xBA	RC/G	W	Py	Sv%	ERA	WHIP	H%	S%	xERA	Ctl	Dom	Cmd	hr/f	hr/9	BPV
At Home	04	270	348	463	811	11	82	29	0.68	44	18	38	114	95	8%	275	5.56	57	47	91%	4.11	1.30	30%	71%	3.81	2.6	6.9	2.6	10%	1.1	67
	05	290	362	478	839	10	82	31	0.64	46	18	36	110	99	7%	279	5.87	53	49	68%	4.22	1.34	31%	71%	3.83	2.5	6.4	2.6	10%	1.0	63
	06	284	358	470	829	10	82	31	0.66	44	18	37	113	108	10%	280	5.79	50	49	74%	3.97	1.29	29%	72%	3.81	2.9	6.2	2.1	10%	1.0	54
Away	04	267	347	453	799	11	82	29	0.69	46	17	37	113	90	6%	276	5.46	44	42	67%	5.31	1.44	32%	65%	4.70	2.9	6.2	2.1	11%	1.2	44
	05	263	338	423	761	10	82	29	0.65	47	17	36	97	83	6%	263	4.96	42	41	69%	4.87	1.40	30%	67%	4.47	3.3	6.0	1.8	11%	1.1	42
	06	285	358	453	811	10	80	33	0.58	46	20	34	107	104	10%	278	5.61	47	46	69%	4.90	1.42	31%	67%	4.49	3.3	6.5	2.0	10%	1.1	49
Opp @ NYY	04	262	314	413	727	7	80	30	0.38	42	18	39	97	85	8%	254	4.38	24	34	45%	5.34	1.52	29%	69%	4.54	4.2	6.2	1.5	15%	1.6	20
	05	272	320	414	734	7	82	31	0.39	47	18	35	88	106	12%	260	4.46	28	32	52%	5.69	1.62	32%	69%	4.55	4.1	6.4	1.6	15%	1.7	18
	06	253	311	400	711	8	82	28	0.47	44	18	38	93	90	10%	258	4.25	31	32	67%	5.47	1.58	31%	69%	4.63	4.1	6.3	1.5	13%	1.5	24

OAK	Yr	Avg	OB	Slg	OPS	bb%	ct%	h%	Eye	G	L	F	PX	SX	SBO	xBA	RC/G	W	Py	Sv%	ERA	WHIP	H%	S%	xERA	Ctl	Dom	Cmd	hr/f	hr/9	BPV
At Home	04	272	347	439	786	10	83	30	0.66	41	20	39	103	76	4%	270	5.29	52	44	56%	4.06	1.33	29%	72%	3.84	3.2	6.3	2.0	10%	1.0	53
	05	268	331	415	746	9	87	29	0.71	42	22	36	90	57	3%	285	4.80	45	45	73%	3.82	1.25	27%	72%	3.73	3.2	6.5	2.0	10%	0.9	61
	06	259	334	409	743	10	83	28	0.67	42	18	41	91	90	4%	257	4.77	49	43	75%	3.97	1.38	30%	73%	3.90	3.1	5.9	1.9	8%	0.9	51
Away	04	268	333	426	759	9	81	31	0.50	42	18	40	104	81	5%	259	4.90	39	42	55%	4.29	1.41	30%	72%	3.89	3.5	6.3	1.8	11%	1.0	48
	05	257	323	399	722	9	84	28	0.62	44	20	36	87	80	4%	266	4.47	43	48	65%	3.57	1.26	28%	75%	3.33	3.1	6.9	2.2	11%	1.0	64
	06	261	342	414	756	11	82	29	0.67	43	21	36	95	90	6%	270	4.96	44	42	71%	4.47	1.46	31%	72%	3.99	3.5	6.6	1.9	11%	1.2	45
Opp @ OAK	04	255	319	405	724	9	82	29	0.51	46	18	36	95	83	8%	260	4.46	20	37	57%	4.79	1.52	30%	72%	4.30	4.1	6.2	1.5	11%	1.3	31
	05	239	304	372	676	9	81	27	0.49	44	22	35	85	97	9%	263	3.85	36	36	69%	4.68	1.42	29%	68%	4.57	3.3	4.7	1.4	8%	0.9	31
	06	268	328	410	738	8	83	30	0.53	43	19	38	89	96	8%	261	4.64	32	38	64%	4.33	1.43	29%	72%	4.20	3.9	5.9	1.5	9%	1.1	37

PHI	Yr	Avg	OB	Slg	OPS	bb%	ct%	h%	Eye	G	L	F	PX	SX	SBO	xBA	RC/G	W	Py	Sv%	ERA	WHIP	H%	S%	xERA	Ctl	Dom	Cmd	hr/f	hr/9	BPV
At Home	04	266	344	450	795	11	80	29	0.61	41	20	38	119	108	7%	279	5.39	42	43	53%	4.33	1.32	29%	72%	3.81	2.9	6.7	2.3	13%	1.4	50
	05	281	357	453	810	11	83	31	0.69	41	24	34	109	120	8%	293	5.62	46	43	60%	4.48	1.32	30%	70%	3.69	2.7	7.3	2.8	15%	1.3	64
	06	274	346	462	808	10	80	31	0.54	46	20	34	123	109	6%	287	5.52	41	43	61%	4.70	1.42	31%	71%	3.74	3.1	7.5	2.4	16%	1.5	51
Away	04	268	340	436	775	10	80	31	0.53	44	20	36	112	102	8%	275	5.13	44	43	71%	4.61	1.40	30%	71%	4.16	3.3	6.4	2.0	11%	1.3	43
	05	259	333	395	728	10	78	31	0.51	43	23	34	94	108	9%	266	4.58	42	46	68%	3.93	1.28	28%	73%	3.63	3.5	7.2	2.1	12%	1.1	62
	06	260	334	433	767	10	78	30	0.51	42	20	38	114	118	8%	269	5.04	44	43	68%	4.52	1.42	31%	71%	4.08	3.2	6.5	2.0	10%	1.1	48
Opp @ PHI	04	260	318	444	762	8	80	29	0.44	43	19	39	117	115	9%	275	4.83	39	38	63%	5.02	1.49	30%	70%	4.37	4.2	6.8	1.6	13%	1.4	34
	05	265	317	450	767	7	79	30	0.36	45	24	32	124	101	8%	295	4.88	35	38	77%	5.22	1.57	31%	69%	4.54	4.2	6.1	1.4	12%	1.2	29
	06	275	334	471	805	8	79	31	0.42	45	21	34	130	109	9%	292	5.40	40	38	68%	5.10	1.50	31%	70%	4.17	3.9	7.2	1.9	15%	1.4	39

PIT	Yr	Avg	OB	Slg	OPS	bb%	ct%	h%	Eye	G	L	F	PX	SX	SBO	xBA	RC/G	W	Py	Sv%	ERA	WHIP	H%	S%	xERA	Ctl	Dom	Cmd	hr/f	hr/9	BPV
At Home	04	263	312	414	726	7	82	30	0.39	48	19	33	98	97	6%	272	4.38	39	38	73%	3.85	1.36	30%	73%	3.79	3.4	6.6	2.0	7%	0.7	62
	05	265	327	407	734	8	81	31	0.47	44	22	34	97	108	5%	275	4.61	34	36	64%	4.26	1.43	30%	72%	3.91	3.6	6.3	1.8	10%	1.0	47
	06	283	339	423	762	8	80	33	0.42	43	21	35	98	99	7%	268	4.90	43	42	68%	4.09	1.44	32%	73%	3.83	3.5	6.5	1.8	8%	0.8	55
Away	04	258	313	389	702	7	80	30	0.39	49	17	34	89	94	9%	251	4.12	33	36	61%	4.79	1.48	31%	70%	4.20	3.9	7.1	1.8	12%	1.2	45
	05	254	308	394	701	7	80	29	0.39	47	19	34	93	96	9%	262	4.08	33	36	84%	4.62	1.46	29%	70%	4.34	4.1	5.7	1.4	10%	1.1	35
	06	243	299	370	669	7	77	29	0.35	46	19	36	90	80	5%	244	3.66	24	29	62%	5.06	1.58	32%	71%	4.31	4.3	6.8	1.6	13%	1.2	37
Opp @ PIT	04	262	329	391	720	9	81	31	0.51	45	20	35	91	78	7%	259	4.47	41	42	71%	3.97	1.29	30%	72%	3.57	2.5	6.4	2.5	11%	1.0	64
	05	269	337	420	758	9	82	30	0.57	44	22	34	101	86	7%	279	4.92	47	45	68%	3.94	1.37	31%	73%	3.73	3.2	6.7	2.1	8%	0.7	64
	06	275	342	408	750	9	81	32	0.54	46	20	34	92	92	10%	267	4.85	38	39	68%	4.40	1.44	33%	71%	3.94	3.0	7.1	2.4	9%	0.9	65

SD	Yr	Avg	OB	Slg	OPS	bb%	ct%	h%	Eye	G	L	F	PX	SX	SBO	xBA	RC/G	W	Py	Sv%	ERA	WHIP	H%	S%	xERA	Ctl	Dom	Cmd	hr/f	hr/9	BPV
At Home	04	256	333	387	720	10	83	29	0.68	44	19	37	86	89	4%	261	4.57	42	39	64%	3.85	1.26	30%	72%	3.68	2.4	6.7	2.8	9%	0.9	74
	05	255	327	377	704	10	82	30	0.58	41	22	37	80	101	10%	260	4.30	46	39	79%	3.52	1.24	29%	74%	3.47	3.0	7.3	2.4	8%	0.8	78
	06	245	316	388	705	9	80	28	0.51	41	18	41	94	114	10%	251	4.25	43	38	73%	3.77	1.23	28%	73%	3.59	2.8	7.1	2.5	10%	1.1	68
Away	04	288	346	438	784	8	84	32	0.56	44	20	36	98	92	6%	277	5.18	45	47	74%	4.22	1.36	30%	74%	3.60	2.9	6.8	2.4	13%	1.4	50
	05	259	334	404	738	10	83	29	0.65	43	22	35	95	103	9%	279	4.74	36	37	59%	4.79	1.45	32%	69%	4.24	3.2	6.6	2.1	10%	1.0	51
	06	279	344	443	786	9	81	32	0.51	43	21	36	111	115	10%	280	5.25	45	48	68%	4.00	1.31	29%	73%	3.81	2.9	6.4	2.2	10%	1.1	55
Opp @ SD	04	260	309	409	718	7	80	30	0.36	43	19	38	101	103	8%	264	4.28	39	42	76%	3.92	1.41	29%	73%	3.98	3.9	5.8	1.5	7%	0.7	47
	05	241	303	378	682	8	78	29	0.41	43	22	36	96	110	8%	262	3.92	35	42	73%	3.64	1.35	29%	74%	3.74	3.6	6.2	1.7	7%	0.7	57
	06	244	302	396	698	8	79	28	0.40	41	20	40	100	116	12%	258	4.04	38	43	65%	3.74	1.32	29%	74%	3.72	3.5	6.9	1.9	9%	0.9	59

SEA	Yr	Avg	OB	Slg	OPS	bb%	ct%	h%	Eye	G	L	F	PX	SX	SBO	xBA	RC/G	W	Py	Sv%	ERA	WHIP	H%	S%	xERA	Ctl	Dom	Cmd	hr/f	hr/9	BPV
At Home	04	255	319	385	703	9	80	30	0.47	46	18	36	84	86	11%	247	4.19	38	33	67%	4.30	1.35	28%	72%	4.03	3.5	6.8	1.9	11%	1.3	47
	05	260	317	390	708	8	81	30	0.44	45	20	34	85	103	11%	260	4.22	39	40	61%	4.15	1.35	29%	71%	4.09	3.1	5.8	1.9	8%	0.9	48
	06	265	315	416	731	7	82	30	0.41	45	18	37	91	108	10%	263	4.43	44	39	71%	4.26	1.38	29%	72%	4.01	3.7	6.9	1.9	10%	1.0	54
Away	04	284	336	407	743	7	83	32	0.46	49	19	32	78	95	8%	260	4.64	25	36	48%	5.26	1.50	31%	68%	4.72	3.6	6.0	1.7	11%	1.3	30
	05	252	310	393	703	8	83	28	0.51	46	21	33	88	101	10%	273	4.20	30	36	73%	4.86	1.42	29%	69%	4.38	3.1	5.4	1.7	12%	1.3	28
	06	277	325	432	757	7	83	31	0.42	44	19	37	93	111	9%	271	4.73	34	39	69%	4.96	1.47	31%	69%	4.30	3.3	6.3	1.9	12%	1.2	40
Opp @ SEA	04	251	319	426	745	9	80	28	0.51	38	19	43	112	66	6%	261	4.70	44	49	74%	3.57	1.34	30%	76%	3.39	3.2	6.9	2.1	9%	0.9	63
	05	261	322	394	717	8	83	29	0.54	41	20	40	82	82	9%	256	4.36	42	41	76%	4.09	1.33	30%	70%	3.88	2.9	6.6	2.3	8%	0.8	66
	06	255	327	410	737	10	80	29	0.53	42	19	39	101	83	8%	260	4.67	37	42	73%	4.35	1.30	30%	69%	4.05	2.5	6.2	2.5	10%	1.0	59

SF	Yr	Avg	OB	Slg	OPS	bb%	ct%	h%	Eye	G	L	F	PX	SX	SBO	xBA	RC/G	W	Py	Sv%	ERA	WHIP	H%	S%	xERA	Ctl	Dom	Cmd	hr/f	hr/9	BPV
At Home	04	284	367	463	831	12	85	31	0.88	46	19	35	113	105	4%	294	5.96	47	44	68%	4.47	1.41	31%	70%	4.04	3.1	6.6	2.1	10%	0.9	56
	05	260	316	396	711	8	85	29	0.54	47	19	33	88	92	9%	274	4.30	37	34	62%	4.26	1.37	29%	70%	4.20	3.5	6.0	1.7	8%	0.8	51
	06	264	329	415	744	9	85	29	0.63	44	19	37	98	117	6%	278	4.81	43	40	67%	4.38	1.33	29%	68%	4.35	3.4	6.4	1.9	8%	0.8	57
Away	04	257	339	415	754	11	83	28	0.75	43	17	39	100	72	4%	263	4.94	44	45	58%	4.19	1.38	28%	72%	4.04	3.6	6.0	1.6	10%	1.1	42
	05	262	315	396	711	7	82	30	0.43	41	22	37	91	87	6%	269	4.24	38	37	62%	4.45	1.47	30%	72%	4.12	3.9	6.1	1.6	10%	1.0	39
	06	254	312	428	740	8	83	28	0.49	43	18	39	108	97	6%	271	4.59	33	36	60%	4.92	1.48	30%	69%	4.59	3.9	6.1	1.6	10%	1.1	37
Opp @ SF	04	272	332	426	759	9	81	31	0.48	46	20	34	102	113	7%	276	4.89	34	37	69%	5.25	1.62	30%	69%	4.73	4.6	5.3	1.1	11%	1.1	20
	05	259	328	397	725	9	82	29	0.58	42	21	37	90	92	8%	265	4.54	44	47	74%	3.76	1.28	28%	73%	3.73	2.7	5.1	1.8	9%	0.8	48
	06	253	321	392	713	9	81	29	0.54	42	19	38	93	107	9%	262	4.38	38	41	61%	4.49	1.38	29%	68%	4.49	3.3	5.3	1.6	7%	0.8	44

STL	Yr	Avg	OB	Slg	OPS	bb%	ct%	h%	Eye	G	L	F	PX	SX	SBO	xBA	RC/G	W	Py	Sv%	ERA	WHIP	H%	S%	xERA	Ctl	Dom	Cmd	hr/f	hr/9	BPV
At Home	04	284	352	459	811	10	81	32	0.55	42	20	38	116	108	10%	279	5.57	53	50	73%	3.54	1.24	29%	74%	3.32	2.7	6.7	2.5	10%	0.9	69
	05	271	336	437	773	9	84	29	0.62	46	20	34	105	94	8%	287	5.08	50	49	67%	3.44	1.28	29%	77%	3.02	2.7	6.3	2.4	12%	1.0	61
	06	273	339	429	768	9	84	30	0.62	44	20	36	99	92	5%	279	5.03	49	45	70%	3.93	1.30	28%	73%	3.60	3.1	6.0	2.0	12%	1.1	49
Away	04	272	334	461	794	8	80	30	0.47	45	20	36	122	98	10%	284	5.25	52	50	83%	3.96	1.27	28%	73%	3.55	2.7	6.2	2.3	13%	1.2	54
	05	269	332	410	741	9	82	31	0.51	46	23	31	92	103	8%	278	4.67	50	49	80%	3.54	1.27	28%	75%	3.28	2.9	5.8	2.0	11%	0.9	55
	06	265	327	434	761	8	83	29	0.53	45	19	36	108	91	7%	280	4.87	34	38	63%	5.20	1.48	31%	68%	4.41	3.3	6.2	1.9	13%	1.3	35
Opp @ STL	04	248	305	390	695	8	80	29	0.41	49	18	33	96	85	6%	259	4.03	28	31	59%	4.93	1.52	32%	70%	4.30	3.7	6.8	1.8	11%	1.2	41
	05	258	312	398	710	7	81	29	0.42	51	19	30	92	54	4%	265	4.20	31	32	72%	4.65	1.44	30%	71%	4.15	3.5	5.5	1.6	12%	1.2	32
	06	253	315	410	725	8	82	28	0.51	47	19	34	101	85	7%	273	4.44	31	35	56%	4.78	1.46	30%	69%	4.36	3.5	5.7	1.6	10%	1.1	35

TAM	Yr	Avg	OB	Slg	OPS	bb%	ct%	h%	Eye	G	L	F	PX	SX	SBO	xBA	RC/G	W	Py	Sv%	ERA	WHIP	H%	S%	xERA	Ctl	Dom	Cmd	hr/f	hr/9	BPV
At Home	04	253	317	404	721	9	83	28	0.56	44	17	40	91	124	14%	260	4.45	40	37	79%	4.18	1.33	28%	72%	4.07	3.4	6.0	1.8	10%	1.1	44
	05	279	333	429	761	7	82	32	0.46	45	21	34	92	124	14%	274	4.87	40	36	72%	4.94	1.46	31%	68%	4.50	3.6	6.4	1.8	10%	1.1	42
	06	259	321	437	758	8	80	29	0.45	44	18	38	109	114	14%	267	4.83	41	37	66%	4.70	1.49	31%	71%	4.17	3.8	6.4	1.7	11%	1.2	37
Away	04	262	316	405	721	7	82	30	0.45	46	18	36	90	108	11%	263	4.37	29	31	76%	5.42	1.54	31%	67%	4.90	4.0	5.8	1.5	11%	1.3	25
	05	268	315	421	736	6	82	30	0.38	44	20	36	95	109	14%	270	4.47	27	29	55%	5.90	1.62	31%	65%	5.27	4.3	5.6	1.3	11%	1.3	19
	06	250	300	403	703	7	80	29	0.35	44	20	36	97	99	13%	262	4.06	20	29	53%	5.26	1.62	33%	69%	4.69	3.9	6.0	1.5	9%	1.1	32
Opp @ TAM	04	251	318	411	729	9	83	28	0.56	41	17	41	99	85	8%	260	4.54	38	41	69%	4.25	1.33	28%	70%	4.22	3.3	5.8	1.8	8%	1.0	48
	05	272	339	433	772	9	82	30	0.56	41	21	39	98	98	7%	269	5.06	41	45	68%	4.76	1.40	32%	67%	4.33	2.8	6.2	2.2	9%	0.9	55
	06	275	345	446	791	10	82	31	0.59	43	19	37	106	99	10%	274	5.33	40	44	67%	4.34	1.34	29%	72%	3.83	3.1	7.0	2.2	12%	1.3	53

TEX	Yr	Avg	OB	Slg	OPS	bb%	ct%	h%	Eye	G	L	F	PX	SX	SBO	xBA	RC/G	W	Py	Sv%	ERA	WHIP	H%	S%	xERA	Ctl	Dom	Cmd	hr/f	hr/9	BPV
At Home	04	285	347	486	833	9	82	31	0.51	38	20	42	122	109	7%	278	5.75	51	47	84%	4.58	1.42	30%	71%	4.08	3.2	6.1	1.9	11%	1.2	41
	05	278	338	509	847	8	81	29	0.49	38	20	41	136	113	6%	289	5.85	44	44	70%	4.80	1.44	31%	68%	4.34	3.0	5.7	1.9	10%	1.0	43
	06	283	343	458	801	8	81	32	0.47	42	20	38	114	84	5%	277	5.38	39	42	61%	4.68	1.42	31%	69%	4.16	3.2	5.9	1.9	11%	1.0	44
Away	04	246	305	428	733	8	79	28	0.41	40	18	42	115	83	8%	260	4.47	38	40	74%	4.50	1.48	31%	72%	4.12	3.7	6.2	1.7	10%	1.1	40
	05	258	314	430	743	8	80	29	0.40	41	21	38	109	99	6%	271	4.60	35	37	66%	5.15	1.50	32%	67%	4.57	3.5	6.0	1.7	10%	1.0	40
	06	272	331	434	765	8	82	31	0.48	44	20	37	102	92	5%	271	4.92	41	44	68%	4.54	1.45	32%	71%	4.05	3.1	6.3	2.0	10%	1.0	49
Opp @ TEX	04	272	332	436	768	8	83	30	0.53	45	20	36	100	91	7%	275	4.96	30	34	52%	5.96	1.52	32%	63%	5.13	3.4	6.6	2.0	12%	1.5	33
	05	277	334	430	764	8	84	31	0.53	46	20	34	95	100	5%	279	4.93	37	37	72%	5.66	1.48	30%	68%	4.54	3.3	6.7	2.0	16%	2.0	22
	06	273	333	420	753	8	83	30	0.53	47	21	33	91	85	7%	275	4.78	42	39	83%	5.12	1.49	33%	68%	4.42	3.2	6.9	2.1	11%	1.2	48

TOR	Yr	Avg	OB	Slg	OPS	bb%	ct%	h%	Eye	G	L	F	PX	SX	SBO	xBA	RC/G	W	Py	Sv%	ERA	WHIP	H%	S%	xERA	Ctl	Dom	Cmd	hr/f	hr/9	BPV
At Home	04	264	333	423	756	9	81	30	0.54	46	20	34	100	102	6%	274	4.90	40	37	78%	5.00	1.52	31%	69%	4.39	3.8	6.3	1.6	11%	1.1	37
	05	275	331	434	766	8	83	31	0.51	44	21	34	99	101	8%	283	4.96	43	45	59%	3.84	1.28	29%	75%	3.31	2.4	6.3	2.6	13%	1.2	57
	06	295	352	505	858	8	84	31	0.57	41	20	39	126	95	6%	295	6.01	50	49	65%	4.04	1.31	29%	73%	3.55	3.0	7.0	2.3	13%	1.1	60
Away	04	256	313	384	697	8	80	30	0.41	46	21	33	85	80	6%	258	4.08	27	33	62%	4.85	1.46	29%	69%	4.51	3.9	5.8	1.5	10%	1.2	34
	05	256	317	381	698	8	82	29	0.51	45	20	34	80	98	7%	261	4.15	37	43	66%	4.30	1.38	29%	71%	3.98	3.1	5.6	1.8	10%	1.1	42
	06	274	337	421	758	9	83	31	0.57	44	19	37	93	82	7%	266	4.89	37	37	71%	4.74	1.43	31%	70%	4.13	3.3	6.6	2.0	12%	1.2	45
Opp @ TOR	04	279	350	440	790	10	82	31	0.61	46	19	35	100	91	9%	273	5.32	41	44	68%	4.46	1.43	30%	71%	4.00	3.6	6.6	1.8	11%	1.0	49
	05	264	312	422	734	7	82	29	0.39	46	20	34	96	93	11%	272	4.41	38	36	71%	4.81	1.41	31%	67%	4.39	3.0	5.9	2.0	10%	1.0	47
	06	252	313	409	722	8	80	29	0.44	47	20	33	98	110	11%	269	4.36	31	32	81%	5.60	1.53	31%	67%	4.73	3.2	5.6	1.8	13%	1.6	20

WAS	Yr	Avg	OB	Slg	OPS	bb%	ct%	h%	Eye	G	L	F	PX	SX	SBO	xBA	RC/G	W	Py	Sv%	ERA	WHIP	H%	S%	xERA	Ctl	Dom	Cmd	hr/f	hr/9	BPV
At Home	04	251	319	425	745	9	84	27	0.64	46	18	36	112	103	11%	288	4.77	28	27	65%	4.15	1.41	30%	74%	3.71	3.6	6.5	1.8	12%	1.1	46
	05	236	304	362	665	9	80	28	0.48	44	21	35	89	83	7%	259	3.79	41	37	77%	3.56	1.28	29%	74%	3.64	3.1	6.6	2.1	8%	0.8	66
	06	262	334	409	743	10	80	30	0.55	41	19	40	100	103	10%	259	4.76	41	37	59%	4.66	1.36	29%	68%	4.51	3.1	6.1	2.0	9%	1.1	48
Away	04	251	312	391	703	8	83	28	0.51	45	19	37	90	105	11%	264	4.17	31	34	59%	4.64	1.47	30%	72%	4.05	3.8	6.6	1.7	12%	1.3	37
	05	266	323	407	731	8	80	31	0.42	47	22	31	98	68	6%	273	4.51	40	40	70%	4.19	1.46	31%	73%	3.96	3.6	5.7	1.6	9%	0.9	40
	06	261	334	425	759	10	78	31	0.49	46	20	34	116	88	14%	274	4.95	30	33	58%	5.43	1.60	31%	69%	4.80	4.3	5.9	1.4	11%	1.3	22
Opp @ WAS	04	265	335	427	762	10	81	30	0.56	45	21	34	107	83	7%	280	4.97	31	32	86%	4.10	1.32	27%	72%	3.90	3.4	5.3	1.6	11%	1.1	36
	05	247	310	371	680	8	81	29	0.47	39	22	39	85	85	8%	257	3.90	40	44	69%	3.49	1.22	28%	72%	3.68	3.2	6.7	2.1	6%	0.6	74
	06	263	323	423	746	8	82	29	0.50	39	18	43	103	113	9%	263	4.70	40	44	57%	4.37	1.40	30%	71%	4.21	3.7	6.7	1.8	9%	0.9	54

AL	Yr	Avg	OB	Slg	OPS	bb%	ct%	h%	Eye	G	L	F	PX	SX	SBO	xBA	RC/G	W	Py	Sv%	ERA	WHIP	H%	S%	xERA	Ctl	Dom	Cmd	hr/f	hr/9	BPV
At Home	04	272	338	437	775	9	82	30	0.55	44	18	38	100	100	8%	266	5.09	45	41	71%	4.49	1.39	30%	70%	4.08	3.2	6.6	2.1	11%	1.1	50
	05	271	332	433	765	8	83	30	0.53	44	20	36	100	100	8%	277	4.94	44	42	71%	4.14	1.33	30%	71%	3.85	2.9	6.2	2.2	10%	1.0	55
	06	280	342	447	789	9	82	31	0.53	43	20	37	100	100	8%	271	5.23	45	43	69%	4.30	1.37	30%	71%	3.94	3.1	6.4	2.1	10%	1.1	52
Away	04	268	329	430	758	8	81	30	0.48	44	19	38	100	100	9%	265	4.84	36	40	63%	4.79	1.45	30%	69%	4.32	3.5	6.3	1.8	11%	1.2	41
	05	264	321	416	737	8	82	30	0.46	44	20	35	100	100	8%	275	4.56	38	40	66%	4.60	1.40	30%	70%	4.16	3.2	6.1	1.9	11%	1.1	44
	06	270	331	427	758	8	82	30	0.49	44	20	36	100	100	8%	271	4.85	38	39	67%	4.84	1.46	31%	69%	4.27	3.3	6.5	2.0	11%	1.2	43

NL	Yr	Avg	OB	Slg	OPS	bb%	ct%	h%	Eye	G	L	F	PX	SX	SBO	xBA	RC/G	W	Py	Sv%	ERA	WHIP	H%	S%	xERA	Ctl	Dom	Cmd	hr/f	hr/9	BPV
At Home	04	266	335	433	768	9	81	30	0.54	44	19	37	100	100	7%	267	5.02	47	46	64%	4.17	1.35	30%	72%	3.78	3.2	6.9	2.1	11%	1.1	56
	05	266	333	424	757	9	81	30	0.54	44	22	35	100	100	8%	277	4.89	50	47	69%	4.07	1.34	30%	72%	3.71	3.1	6.7	2.2	11%	1.0	59
	06	271	338	437	775	9	81	31	0.53	43	20	37	100	100	9%	268	5.11	50	47	65%	4.33	1.36	30%	71%	3.90	3.2	7.0	2.1	11%	1.1	56
Away	04	260	324	415	739	9	80	30	0.48	45	19	36	100	100	8%	264	4.63	44	46	68%	4.48	1.42	30%	71%	4.02	3.5	6.6	1.9	11%	1.1	46
	05	257	319	405	724	8	80	30	0.46	45	21	34	100	100	8%	272	4.43	42	44	67%	4.40	1.42	30%	71%	3.98	3.5	6.4	1.8	11%	1.1	47
	06	259	321	418	739	8	80	30	0.46	44	19	37	100	100	9%	264	4.62	41	44	63%	4.67	1.45	31%	70%	4.21	3.6	6.5	1.8	11%	1.1	44

The Batters

QUALIFICATION: All batters who accumulated at least 100 at bats in the majors in 2006 have been included. Nearly all who accumulated 50-99 AB are also included. A handful of players with fewer than 50 AB are included if we believe that they will have an impact in 2007. Players who may have a role in 2007 but have spent several years battling injuries are often not included, though an injury status update will appear on page 175. All of these players will appear on BaseballHQ.com over the winter as their roles and projected impacts become clearer.

POSITIONS: Up to three positions are listed for each batter and represent those for which he appeared a minimum of 20 games in 2006. Positions are shown with their numeric designation (2=CA, 3=1B, 7=LF, 0=DH, etc.)

AGE: Each batter's current age is shown, along with a description of the associated stage in his career.

BATS: Shows which side of the plate he bats from — right (R), left (L) or switch-hitter (S).

RELIABILITY SCORE: An analysis of each player's forecast risk, on a 0-100 scale. High scores go those batters who receive regular playing time, are healthy, are in a stable age range and have displayed consistent performance over the past three years (using RC/G).

DL DAYS: Total number of days spent on the disabled list in 2006, followed by 2005.

LIMA PLAN GRADE: Rating that evaluates how well a batter would fit into a team using the LIMA Plan. Best grades go to batters who have excellent base skills, are expected to see a good amount of playing time, and are in the $10-$30 Rotisserie value range. Lowest grades will go to poor skills, few at bats and values under $5 or over $30.

BATTING AVERAGE POTENTIAL (BAvg Potl): The probability that a batter will improve his batting average in 2007 over 2006, based on an evaluation of contact rate, xBA variance and walk rate. These percentages are in 5% increments, ranging from 10% to 90%, though most will be centered closer to the mean. If a batter's BAvg Potl says 60%, for instance, it means that he has a 60% chance of improving his batting average in 2007. This is a strict, computer-generated calculation; often, the projection will not reflect the percentage play cited here.

PLAYER STAT LINES: The past five year's statistics represent the total accumulated in the majors as well as in Triple-A, Double-A ball and various foreign leagues during each year. All non-major league stats used have been converted to their equivalent major league performance level. Minor league levels below AA are not included.

Nearly all baseball publications separate a player's statistical experiences in the major leagues from the minor leagues and outside leagues. While this may be appropriate for the sake of official record-keeping, it is not an accurate snapshot of a player's complete performance for the year.

Bill James has proven that minor league statistics, at Double-A level or above, are accurate indicators of future potential. Other researchers have also devised conversion factors for foreign leagues. Since these are accurate barometers of potential performance, then we should be including them in the pool of historical data.

TEAM DESIGNATIONS: An asterisk (*) appearing with a team name means that major league equivalent Triple-A and/or Double-A numbers are included in that year's stat line. A designation of "a/a" means the stats were accumulated at both Triple-A and Double-A levels that year. "JPN" means Japan, "MEX" means Mexico, "KOR" means Korea, "TWN" means Taiwan, "CUB" means Cuba and "ind" means independent league. All stats that appear with these designations are converted to major league equivalents.

The designation "2TM" appears whenever a player was on more than one major league team, crossing leagues, in a season. "2AL" and "2NL" represent more than one team in the same league. Complete season stats are presented for players who crossed leagues during the season.

SABERMETRIC CATEGORIES: Descriptions of all the sabermetric categories appear in the glossary. The decimal point has been suppressed on several categories to conserve space. *Notes:*

- Platoon data (vL, vR) and Ball-in-play data (G/L/F) are for major league performance only.
- xBA only appears for years in which G/L/F data is available.

2007 FORECASTS: It is far too early to be making definitive projections for 2007, especially on playing time. Focus on the skill levels and trends, then consult Baseball HQ for playing time revisions as players change teams and roles become finalized. A free projections update will also be available online at BaseballForecaster.com in March.

Forecasts are computed from a player's trends over the past five years. Adjustments were made for leading indicators and variances between skill and statistical output. After reviewing the leading indicators, you might opt to make further adjustments.

Although each year's numbers include all playing time at the Double-A level or above, the 2007 forecast only represents potential playing time at the major league level, and again is highly preliminary.

CAPSULE COMMENTARIES: For each player, a brief analysis of their BPIs and the potential impact on performance in 2007 is provided. For those who played only a portion of 2006 at the major league level, and whose isolated MLB stats are significantly different from their full-season total, their MLB stats are listed here. Note that these commentaries generally look at performance related issues only. Playing time expectations may impact these analyses, so you will have to adjust accordingly, especially as we get closer to Opening Day. Upside (UP) and downside (DN) statistical potential appears for some players. These are less grounded in hard data and more speculative of skills potential.

Abercrombie,Reg			AB	R	H	HR	RBI	SB	Avg	vL	vR	OB	Slg	OPS	bb%	ct%	h%	Eye	G	L	F	PX	SX	SBO	xHR	xBA	RC/G	RAR	R$
Pos	8	02	0	0	0	0	0	0	0							0							0		0				
Age	25	03 aa	448	56	107	14	51	27	239			265	404	669	3	64	34	0.10				129	155	45%	16		3.76	-15.1	$15
Pre-Peak		04 aa	168	14	24	4	17	3	141			160	260	420	2	62	20	0.06				90	137	33%	4		-0.05	-27.3	($1)
Bats	Right	05 aa	178	23	37	7	18	5	207			245	379	625	5	77	23	0.22				106	123	34%	6		2.92	-8.6	$4
Reliability	5	06 FLA	255	39	54	5	24	6	212	220	208	264	333	597	7	69	28	0.23	54	12	34	89	117	21%	6	223	2.71	-14.0	$4
DL		1st Half	179	25	39	3	14	4	218			275	335	610	7	65	32	0.23	54	12	34	96	101	21%	5	214	2.99	-8.2	$2
BAvg Potl	40%	2nd Half	76	14	15	2	10	2	197			237	329	566	5	79	22	0.25	54	11	35	75	150	21%	2	243	2.29	-5.2	$1
LIMA Plan	F	07 Proj	200	28	40	6	21	6	200			239	339	578	5	72	25	0.18	54	11	35	92	136	28%	6	233	2.32	-14.3	$3

Another "toolsy" OF with no concept of the strike zone fails utterly in the majors. But given his MLE's, did anyone expect better? Until his awful CT% and Eye improve, the road will remain rocky.

Abreu,Bobby			AB	R	H	HR	RBI	SB	Avg	vL	vR	OB	Slg	OPS	bb%	ct%	h%	Eye	G	L	F	PX	SX	SBO	xHR	xBA	RC/G	RAR	R$
Pos	9	02 PHI	572	102	176	20	85	31	308	302	310	414	521	935	15	80	36	0.89	43	23	34	149	128	21%	24	310	7.56	36.1	$32
Age	33	03 PHI	577	99	173	20	101	22	300	272	312	411	468	879	16	78	35	0.87	50	23	27	114	91	14%	23	292	6.82	19.6	$29
Past Peak		04 PHI	574	118	173	30	105	40	301	267	318	428	544	972	18	80	33	1.09	42	21	37	154	115	20%	32	309	8.05	44.0	$37
Bats	Left	05 PHI	588	104	168	24	102	31	286	275	292	404	474	879	17	77	33	0.87	47	24	29	129	101	18%	27	297	6.84	26.7	$32
Reliability	73	06 2TM	548	98	163	15	107	30	297	293	299	427	462	889	18	75	37	0.90	45	26	29	117	105	16%	21	283	7.23	30.8	$27
DL		1st Half	251	52	72	8	52	15	287			453	474	927	23	76	35	1.25	48	25	26	128	114	16%	11	296	7.95	19.6	$13
BAvg Potl	40%	2nd Half	297	46	91	7	55	15	306			403	451	854	14	74	39	0.62	41	28	31	108	87	15%	10	272	6.54	10.8	$14
LIMA Plan	B+	07 Proj	563	102	167	20	104	28	297			418	482	900	17	77	36	0.89	45	25	30	127	104	16%	24	291	7.22	33.1	$29

Much was made of his "power outage," as judged by another HR dip. But PX shows he still hit with authority, just more LD, fewer FB. xHR says expect a return to 20+ HR, other skills suggest continued excellence.

Adams,Russ			AB	R	H	HR	RBI	SB	Avg	vL	vR	OB	Slg	OPS	bb%	ct%	h%	Eye	G	L	F	PX	SX	SBO	xHR	xBA	RC/G	RAR	R$
Pos	46	02	0	0	0	0	0	0	0							0							0		0				
Age	26	03 aa	271	34	67	3	20	7	247			309	336	645	8	89	27	0.78				53	113	10%	3		3.72	-4.4	$5
Pre-Peak		04 aaa	483	49	132	5	46	5	273			326	391	718	7	89	30	0.73				79	71	6%	9		4.53	2.6	$9
Bats	Left	05 TOR	481	68	123	8	63	11	256	195	264	326	383	708	9	88	28	0.88	46	20	33	80	116	10%	9	288	4.51	5.3	$12
Reliability	49	06 TOR *	412	49	103	3	42	4	249	135	234	310	340	650	8	85	29	0.58	36	20	44	62	80	7%	5	242	3.70	-5.2	$5
DL		1st Half	237	34	62	2	24	1	263			320	375	695	8	87	29	0.66	38	20	43	76	77	5%	4	263	4.27	1.1	$4
BAvg Potl	50%	2nd Half	175	16	40	1	18	3	230			297	292	589	9	81	28	0.52	32	20	48	43	72	10%	2	213	2.88	-6.6	$1
LIMA Plan	F	07 Proj	192	23	48	2	20	3	250			313	343	655	8	86	28	0.67	41	20	39	62	82	8%	3	256	3.79	-1.8	$3

3-28-.219 in 251 AB at TOR. When the GM says he's "going to be in Triple-A," let's just say the '07 outlook isn't rosy. J.P.'s assessment seems on the money, as skills regressed across the board. Stay away.

Alfonzo,Eliezer			AB	R	H	HR	RBI	SB	Avg	vL	vR	OB	Slg	OPS	bb%	ct%	h%	Eye	G	L	F	PX	SX	SBO	xHR	xBA	RC/G	RAR	R$
Pos	2	02 aa	244	19	57	6	32	2	234			258	373	631	3	80	27	0.17				94	58	11%	6		3.03	-6.2	$4
Age	28	03 ind	253	46	45	5	38	0	178			206	277	483	3	81	20	0.19				66	97	0%	5		1.25	-24.0	$2
Peak		04 aa	0	0	0	0	0	0	0							0							0		0				
Bats	Right	05 a/a	186	23	45	5	23	1	242			263	373	636	3	81	27	0.16				85	56	2%	5		3.03	-4.9	$4
Reliability	7	06 SF *	425	37	102	14	49	2	240	246	271	269	397	666	4	75	29	0.16	41	19	40	101	62	2%	14	245	3.44	-11.4	$7
DL		1st Half	192	18	41	5	18	1	215			260	343	603	6	76	26	0.26	37	9	53	79	74	2%	5	199	2.74	-9.5	$1
BAvg Potl	40%	2nd Half	233	18	61	9	30	1	261			277	442	719	2	74	32	0.08	42	22	37	120	46	2%	9	261	4.05	-2.0	$5
LIMA Plan	D	07 Proj	324	35	75	9	40	1	232			257	372	629	3	78	27	0.16	41	19	39	91	67	3%	9	250	2.95	-11.4	$5

12-39-.266 in 286 AB at SF.
Notable PX trend:
Jun-Jul - 167
Aug - 111
Sep - 83
Since PX is his only positive skill, this bodes ill for '07.

Alomar Jr.,Sandy			AB	R	H	HR	RBI	SB	Avg	vL	vR	OB	Slg	OPS	bb%	ct%	h%	Eye	G	L	F	PX	SX	SBO	xHR	xBA	RC/G	RAR	R$
Pos	2	02 2TM	283	29	79	7	37	0	279	247	292	301	410	711	3	88	30	0.27	48	18	33	79	41	0%	7	278	4.06	1.5	$7
Age	40	03 CHW	194	22	52	5	26	0	268	233	284	283	407	690	2	91	27	0.24	44	24	32	84	32	0%	5	306	3.83	-1.5	$4
Decline		04 CHW	146	15	35	2	14	0	240	200	252	293	308	601	7	91	25	0.85	53	16	31	39	28	0%	2	245	3.19	-5.0	$1
Bats	Right	05 TEX	128	11	35	0	14	0	273	385	245	301	328	629	4	91	30	0.42	55	14	31	44	25	0%	1	236	3.34	-2.5	$2
Reliability	0	06 2TM	108	8	30	1	17	0	278	327	232	297	380	677	3	87	31	0.21	45	21	34	72	18	0%	2	267	3.70	-2.1	$2
DL		1st Half	58	3	20	0	9	0	345			345	431	776	0	88	39	0.00	53	25	22	68	9	0%	1	290	4.65	0.4	$2
BAvg Potl	45%	2nd Half	50	5	10	1	8	0	200			245	320	565	6	86	21	0.43	36	16	49	77	32	0%	1	239	2.55	-2.9	$0
LIMA Plan	F	07 Proj	125	11	33	1	17	0	264			293	352	645	4	89	29	0.36	48	18	35	60	23	0%	2	253	3.44	-2.6	$2

The old geezer keeps hitting lefties, and keeps adding a "veteran presence," so it looks like he'll get another hundred AB or so. But unless your league is deeper than the Mariana Trench, really, don't bother.

Alou,Moises			AB	R	H	HR	RBI	SB	Avg	vL	vR	OB	Slg	OPS	bb%	ct%	h%	Eye	G	L	F	PX	SX	SBO	xHR	xBA	RC/G	RAR	R$
Pos	9	02 CHC	484	50	133	15	61	8	275	322	260	339	419	758	9	87	29	0.77	40	23	37	88	78	6%	14	290	4.93	-5.1	$15
Age	40	03 CHC	565	83	158	22	91	3	280	346	260	352	462	814	10	88	29	0.94	38	24	39	108	59	2%	20	306	5.64	0.5	$20
Decline		04 CHC	601	106	176	39	106	3	293	298	292	365	557	922	10	87	28	0.85	39	19	43	144	79	2%	32	316	6.78	24.9	$28
Bats	Right	05 SF	427	67	137	19	63	5	321	372	303	400	518	917	12	90	32	1.30	42	20	38	109	85	4%	16	309	6.90	18.8	$21
Reliability	49	06 SF	345	52	104	22	74	2	301	349	286	354	571	925	8	91	28	0.90	40	20	40	142	52	4%	17	335	6.65	17.8	$17
DL	49 31	1st Half	122	21	38	9	31	0	311			378	574	952	10	93	28	1.63	44	18	38	125	25	0%	6	321	7.01	7.4	$7
BAvg Potl	70%	2nd Half	223	31	66	13	43	2	296			340	570	910	6	90	28	0.65	38	21	40	151	60	6%	11	339	6.45	10.4	$10
LIMA Plan	C+	07 Proj	368	57	111	18	69	3	302			366	515	881	9	90	30	1.00	40	20	39	118	63	3%	15	312	6.32	12.9	$16

Still has elite skills, but declining AB totals tell you all you need to know. He's great when he's on the field, but old guys who get hurt a lot never suddenly get healthy... and they NEVER get any younger.

Amezaga,Alfredo			AB	R	H	HR	RBI	SB	Avg	vL	vR	OB	Slg	OPS	bb%	ct%	h%	Eye	G	L	F	PX	SX	SBO	xHR	xBA	RC/G	RAR	R$
Pos	84	02 aaa	518	58	113	5	39	17	218			266	305	571	6	86	25	0.46				57	110	29%	7		2.67	-35.7	$7
Age	29	03 aaa	317	44	98	2	36	11	309			342	403	745	5	90	34	0.52				61	105	23%	4		4.67	-1.7	$11
Peak		04 aaa	135	11	29	1	10	5	216			263	280	543	6	90	23	0.65				38	101	15%	1		2.51	-9.0	$1
Bats	Both	05 aaa	185	20	54	1	9	10	293			337	375	712	6	89	33	0.59				58	99	35%	2		4.37	-0.3	$6
Reliability	9	06 FLA	334	42	87	3	19	20	260	91	294	327	332	659	9	86	29	0.72	51	17	33	41	111	30%	3	248	3.85	-6.0	$9
DL		1st Half	117	13	29	2	10	6	248			313	359	671	9	84	28	0.58	45	18	36	67	97	28%	2	255	3.90	-1.9	$3
BAvg Potl	55%	2nd Half	217	29	58	1	9	14	267			335	318	653	9	88	30	0.81	53	16	31	28	112	32%	1	244	3.82	-4.1	$6
LIMA Plan	D	07 Proj	324	37	85	3	20	17	263			318	336	654	8	87	29	0.65	50	17	33	46	104	29%	3	255	3.73	-8.0	$8

CONS: No power, declining contact rate, inflated batting average, can't hit left-handers, advanced age for his status, sim league killer.
PRO: Will steal some bags, ambidextrous.

Anderson,Brian			AB	R	H	HR	RBI	SB	Avg	vL	vR	OB	Slg	OPS	bb%	ct%	h%	Eye	G	L	F	PX	SX	SBO	xHR	xBA	RC/G	RAR	R$
Pos	8	02	0	0	0	0	0	0	0							0							0		0				
Age	25	03	0	0	0	0	0	0	0							0							0		0				
Pre-Peak		04 aa	185	25	49	4	26	3	265			330	400	730	9	84	30	0.62				81	98	10%	4		4.62	-0.3	$5
Bats	Right	05 CHW *	474	61	124	17	48	4	262	83	227	314	424	738	7	78	30	0.34	36	27	36	107	71	5%	17	278	4.49	2.9	$12
Reliability	30	06 CHW	365	46	82	8	33	4	225	226	223	284	359	642	8	75	28	0.33	44	21	35	97	68	14%	10	254	3.37	-14.6	$4
DL		1st Half	155	22	27	5	18	2	174			264	303	568	11	70	21	0.41	48	15	37	89	69	8%	5	220	2.32	-11.8	$1
BAvg Potl	45%	2nd Half	210	24	55	3	15	2	262			299	400	699	5	79	32	0.25	41	25	34	103	72	18%	5	279	4.04	-3.9	$3
LIMA Plan	D	07 Proj	384	49	94	10	39	4	245			301	390	691	7	78	29	0.36	43	21	35	97	77	10%	11	263	3.97	-7.0	$7

CHW kept sticking with him, but wasn't rewarded. Irony is, it was all so predictable, given so-so MLE's. 2nd half was more representative, but the ceiling appears lower now.

Anderson,Garret			AB	R	H	HR	RBI	SB	Avg	vL	vR	OB	Slg	OPS	bb%	ct%	h%	Eye	G	L	F	PX	SX	SBO	xHR	xBA	RC/G	RAR	R$
Pos	70	02 ANA	638	93	195	29	123	6	306	284	316	337	539	876	4	87	31	0.38	37	23	39	139	77	7%	26	326	5.98	20.2	$28
Age	34	03 ANA	638	80	201	29	116	6	315	310	318	347	541	888	5	87	33	0.37	44	20	36	134	73	6%	26	319	6.11	13.4	$28
Past Peak		04 ANA	442	57	133	14	75	2	301	262	321	344	446	790	6	83	34	0.39	42	23	35	87	56	2%	13	278	5.07	1.5	$15
Bats	Left	05 ANA	575	68	163	17	96	1	283	330	259	311	435	746	4	85	31	0.27	42	21	38	97	43	1%	16	282	4.45	-4.4	$17
Reliability	78	06 ANA	543	63	152	17	85	1	280	248	294	327	433	760	7	83	31	0.40	41	22	37	94	51	1%	17	275	4.75	-6.5	$14
DL		1st Half	262	23	69	7	44	0	263			306	416	722	6	82	30	0.33	42	20	38	99	31	0%	8	267	4.29	-6.7	$5
BAvg Potl	45%	2nd Half	281	40	83	10	41	1	295			347	448	795	7	83	33	0.47	41	24	36	89	59	1%	9	279	5.18	-0.0	$9
LIMA Plan	C	07 Proj	528	65	152	17	86	2	288			328	448	776	6	84	32	0.37	41	22	37	98	57	2%	16	283	4.90	-1.7	$16

The last few seasons are what we really can expect from him now... nagging injuries dragging him down to replacement-level production. A bigger year isn't impossible, but at this point, it's not the smart money.

ROD TRUESDELL

Anderson,Marlon

Anderson,Marlon		AB	R	H	HR	RBI	SB	Avg	vL	vR	OB	Slg	OPS	bb%	ct%	h%	Eye	G	L	F	PX	SX	SBO	xHR	xBA	RC/G	RAR	R$
Pos 47	02 PHI	539	64	139	8	48	5	258	220	269	312	380	692	7	87	28	0.59	48	22	29	79	104	4%	10	294	4.16	-4.0	$11
Age 33	03 TAM	482	59	130	6	67	19	270	315	262	327	376	702	8	88	30	0.68	45	24	31	69	112	16%	8	287	4.32	2.6	$15
Past Peak	04 STL	253	31	60	8	28	6	237	160	246	272	379	651	5	85	25	0.32	48	19	33	85	82	15%	7	279	3.37	-9.5	$6
Bats Left	05 NYM	235	31	62	7	19	6	264	267	264	316	391	708	7	81	30	0.40	42	22	36	82	79	11%	7	264	4.12	-3.0	$7
Reliability 21	06 2NL	279	43	83	12	38	4	297	254	310	355	513	868	8	82	33	0.51	39	23	38	123	90	13%	11	296	6.16	12.3	$11
DL	1st Half	107	12	26	2	10	0	243			283	364	648	5	81	28	0.30	40	20	39	75	69	8%	2	251	3.39	-4.0	$1
BAvg Potl 45%	2nd Half	172	31	57	10	28	4	331			398	605	1003	10	83	35	0.66	38	24	38	152	106	15%	9	321	7.84	15.1	$10
LIMA Plan D	07 Proj	**236**	**33**	**65**	**8**	**27**	**5**	**275**			**327**	**447**	**774**	**7**	**83**	**30**	**0.46**	**42**	**22**	**36**	**102**	**97**	**13%**	**8**	**285**	**4.98**	**2.8**	**$8**

Tore it up after trade to LA. Could benefit from a platoon: 59 PX vs. LH, 138 PX vs RH. Combined with FB% trend, there's profit potential on the low end here.

Ardoin,Danny

Ardoin,Danny		AB	R	H	HR	RBI	SB	Avg	vL	vR	OB	Slg	OPS	bb%	ct%	h%	Eye	G	L	F	PX	SX	SBO	xHR	xBA	RC/G	RAR	R$
Pos 2	02 a/a	183	15	34	4	16	1	186			251	290	541	8	74	23	0.34				75	40	3%	5		1.98	-11.0	$0
Age 32	03 aaa	239	27	50	6	27	0	209			260	346	607	6	77	24	0.30				89	65	4%	6		2.84	-10.1	$2
Past Peak	04 aaa	237	34	60	8	30	1	254			333	399	732	11	77	30	0.50				93	45	3%	8		4.58	3.6	$6
Bats Right	05 COL *	352	43	86	11	36	3	244	277	220	306	395	701	8	73	30	0.34	45	18	37	111	64	5%	12	249	4.14	3.7	$7
Reliability 2	06 2TM	122	14	22	0	3	0	180	250	173	237	238	474	7	73	25	0.27	51	13	37	47	76	0%	1	197	1.14	-12.7	($1)
DL 64	1st Half	94	8	18	0	2	0	191			232	266	498	5	79	24	0.25	47	14	39	56	68	0%	1	218	1.57	-8.3	($1)
BAvg Potl 50%	2nd Half	28	6	4	0	1	0	143			250	143	393	12	54	27	0.31	67	7	27	0	84	0%	0	124	-0.57	-4.7	($0)
LIMA Plan F	07 Proj	**32**	**4**	**7**	**1**	**3**	**0**	**216**			**276**	**340**	**616**	**8**	**76**	**26**	**0.35**	**53**	**13**	**34**	**91**	**44**	**3%**	**1**	**236**	**3.03**	**-1.1**	**$0**

Even the crickets keep quiet when his name is called on draft day. He did throw out nearly 50% of baserunners in 2005, so he's got upside in formats where hitting is ignored and defensive CS% is weighted heavily.

Atkins,Garrett

Atkins,Garrett		AB	R	H	HR	RBI	SB	Avg	vL	vR	OB	Slg	OPS	bb%	ct%	h%	Eye	G	L	F	PX	SX	SBO	xHR	xBA	RC/G	RAR	R$
Pos 5	02 aa	510	51	132	11	44	4	259			316	380	697	8	90	27	0.83				73	54	8%	11		4.26	-4.0	$10
Age 27	03 aaa	439	60	134	12	50	1	305			355	458	813	7	92	31	0.94				91	43	5%	12		5.53	14.0	$14
Peak	04 COL *	473	63	157	13	72	0	332	333	385	386	510	896	8	93	34	1.31	58	15	27	105	40	0%	14	315	6.55	18.4	$19
Bats Right	05 COL	519	62	149	13	89	0	287	291	285	344	426	770	8	86	31	0.63	46	24	30	90	34	1%	14	295	5.02	3.5	$17
Reliability 24	06 COL	602	117	198	29	120	4	329	341	327	407	556	963	12	87	34	1.04	37	22	41	131	67	2%	27	314	7.44	30.9	$32
DL 23	1st Half	283	49	88	10	53	2	311			385	498	883	11	87	33	0.94	37	24	39	113	54	2%	10	307	6.51	7.8	$12
BAvg Potl 55%	2nd Half	319	68	110	19	67	2	345			426	608	1034	12	87	35	1.13	37	20	43	146	64	2%	17	322	8.26	22.7	$20
LIMA Plan B	07 Proj	**568**	**91**	**179**	**32**	**100**	**2**	**315**			**382**	**564**	**946**	**10**	**88**	**31**	**0.93**	**39**	**22**	**39**	**140**	**48**	**2%**	**28**	**329**	**7.07**	**29.5**	**$27**

Became a FB hitter overnight and voilà, the power arrived. Monster second half and strong base skills make this one a keeper.

UP: 40 HR

Aurilia,Rich

Aurilia,Rich		AB	R	H	HR	RBI	SB	Avg	vL	vR	OB	Slg	OPS	bb%	ct%	h%	Eye	G	L	F	PX	SX	SBO	xHR	xBA	RC/G	RAR	R$
Pos 536	02 SF	538	76	138	15	61	1	257	241	261	304	413	717	6	83	28	0.41	33	17	50	105	64	2%	16	259	4.28	-4.8	$13
Age 35	03 SF	505	65	140	13	58	2	277	277	277	325	410	735	7	84	31	0.44	37	25	39	85	57	3%	13	276	4.49	3.4	$13
Decline	04 2TM	399	49	98	6	44	1	246	257	240	310	353	663	8	82	29	0.52	40	18	42	72	67	1%	8	242	3.77	-14.3	$6
Bats Right	05 CIN	426	61	120	14	68	2	282	272	286	339	444	783	8	84	31	0.55	41	21	38	101	70	2%	13	283	5.13	4.2	$15
Reliability 15	06 CIN	440	61	132	23	70	3	300	347	276	350	518	868	7	88	30	0.67	38	20	42	117	59	3%	19	303	6.00	6.2	$18
DL 15 18	1st Half	184	28	50	10	31	1	272			320	505	825	7	88	26	0.57	34	19	48	131	49	3%	8	300	5.48	-0.0	$7
BAvg Potl 60%	2nd Half	256	33	82	13	39	2	320			372	527	899	8	89	32	0.75	41	21	38	108	54	3%	10	305	6.37	6.0	$11
LIMA Plan D+	07 Proj	**421**	**58**	**120**	**17**	**62**	**2**	**285**			**339**	**462**	**801**	**8**	**86**	**30**	**0.58**	**39**	**20**	**41**	**103**	**61**	**2%**	**15**	**284**	**5.29**	**1.8**	**$14**

Only his 2001 breakout was better. Comeback was fueled by a 192 PX vs. LH, but power was mediocre against LH in three of his previous four seasons. Skills will keep him productive, but he'll regress.

Ausmus,Brad

Ausmus,Brad		AB	R	H	HR	RBI	SB	Avg	vL	vR	OB	Slg	OPS	bb%	ct%	h%	Eye	G	L	F	PX	SX	SBO	xHR	xBA	RC/G	RAR	R$
Pos 2	02 HOU	447	57	115	6	50	2	257	307	245	315	353	669	8	84	29	0.54	51	19	31	64	75	4%	7	263	3.84	-3.6	$9
Age 38	03 HOU	450	43	103	4	47	5	229	237	227	300	291	592	9	85	26	0.70	49	21	31	40	70	6%	5	251	3.03	-17.3	$5
Decline	04 HOU	403	38	100	5	31	2	248	308	234	305	325	630	8	86	28	0.59	52	18	30	48	49	4%	6	251	3.40	-4.9	$5
Bats Right	05 HOU	387	35	100	3	47	5	258	293	251	345	331	675	12	88	29	1.06	54	21	25	52	47	6%	5	274	4.25	5.2	$7
Reliability 7	06 HOU	439	37	101	2	39	3	230	266	220	302	285	586	9	84	27	0.63	53	19	28	38	52	3%	4	243	2.95	-18.5	$2
DL	1st Half	225	17	56	1	17	3	249			307	316	623	8	84	29	0.54	51	17	32	46	59	6%	2	243	3.33	-6.7	$2
BAvg Potl 55%	2nd Half	214	20	45	1	22	0	210			296	252	548	11	83	25	0.72	56	20	24	30	23	0%	2	234	2.53	-12.0	$0
LIMA Plan D	07 Proj	**379**	**35**	**91**	**3**	**37**	**3**	**240**			**314**	**306**	**620**	**10**	**85**	**28**	**0.72**	**53**	**19**	**28**	**45**	**54**	**4%**	**4**	**255**	**3.41**	**-8.0**	**$4**

Used to have value as a catcher who'd give you a .270 BA in a full-time role. That was 6 years ago. But 6 years ago, I had no grey hair and the Yankees were champs. Things change.

Aybar,Erick

Aybar,Erick		AB	R	H	HR	RBI	SB	Avg	vL	vR	OB	Slg	OPS	bb%	ct%	h%	Eye	G	L	F	PX	SX	SBO	xHR	xBA	RC/G	RAR	R$
Pos 6	02	0	0	0	0	0	0	0							0							0		0				
Age 23	03	0	0	0	0	0	0	0							0							0		0				
Growth	04	0	0	0	0	0	0	0							0							0		0				
Bats Both	05 aa	535	78	142	7	42	38	265			294	376	670	4	93	28	0.55				65	144	53%	8		3.84	-6.9	$19
Reliability 0	06 ANA *	379	56	98	5	39	27	259	250	250	291	370	660	4	91	27	0.48	70	3	27	66	137	58%	6	280	3.70	-8.5	$13
DL	1st Half	196	38	49	2	22	14	250			293	357	650	6	86	28	0.44	58	0	42	64	169	49%	3		3.59	-5.0	$7
BAvg Potl 60%	2nd Half	183	18	49	3	17	13	269			288	383	670	3	96	27	0.63	78	6	17	67	91	69%	3	308	3.82	-3.4	$6
LIMA Plan F	07 Proj	**163**	**23**	**43**	**2**	**15**	**12**	**263**			**292**	**366**	**659**	**4**	**92**	**27**	**0.52**	**72**	**4**	**24**	**61**	**128**	**56%**	**3**	**284**	**3.69**	**-4.0**	**$6**

0-2-.250 in 40 AB at ANA. Didn't hit a lick in majors, but there's hope. He's green, showed good pop in minors before, makes great contact, and can run.

UP: .280 BA, 30 SB

Aybar,Willy

Aybar,Willy		AB	R	H	HR	RBI	SB	Avg	vL	vR	OB	Slg	OPS	bb%	ct%	h%	Eye	G	L	F	PX	SX	SBO	xHR	xBA	RC/G	RAR	R$
Pos 5	02	0	0	0	0	0	0	0							0							0		0				
Age 24	03	0	0	0	0	0	0	0							0							0		0				
Growth	04 aa	482	51	120	14	70	7	249			313	384	697	9	85	27	0.63				81	46	14%	14		4.16	-12.1	$11
Bats Both	05 LA *	487	44	126	4	51	4	258	250	382	320	350	669	8	91	28	0.96	53	16	31	62	50	11%	7	270	4.08	-10.2	$8
Reliability 23	06 2NL *	450	57	125	11	62	2	278	328	263	346	420	766	9	87	30	0.82	44	14	42	86	42	6%	12	260	5.10	-5.0	$12
DL 20	1st Half	252	29	69	9	47	2	274			335	444	779	8	88	28	0.79	47	13	40	98	37	7%	9	271	5.15	-2.5	$8
BAvg Potl 55%	2nd Half	198	28	56	2	15	0	283			360	389	749	11	86	32	0.86	41	16	43	71	52	5%	3	244	5.04	-2.5	$4
LIMA Plan D	07 Proj	**318**	**36**	**85**	**6**	**38**	**2**	**267**			**334**	**386**	**720**	**9**	**88**	**29**	**0.83**	**45**	**15**	**40**	**75**	**47**	**9%**	**7**	**256**	**4.59**	**-5.2**	**$7**

4-30-.280 in 243 AB at ATL and LA. It's easy to sour on failed top prospects. But this one's still young and controls the plate well. Improvement in both mediocre PX and shaky defense could spark some quick growth.

Baker,Jeff

Baker,Jeff		AB	R	H	HR	RBI	SB	Avg	vL	vR	OB	Slg	OPS	bb%	ct%	h%	Eye	G	L	F	PX	SX	SBO	xHR	xBA	RC/G	RAR	R$
Pos 9	02	0	0	0	0	0	0	0							0							0		0				
Age 25	03	0	0	0	0	0	0	0							0							0		0				
Pre-Peak	04	0	0	0	0	0	0	0							0							0		0				
Bats Right	05 aaa	228	25	60	8	26	2	263			294	439	733	4	89	27	0.38				105	66	6%	7		4.37	-4.0	$6
Reliability 0	06 COL *	539	65	158	22	101	7	292	438	341	335	497	832	6	83	32	0.38	44	28	28	120	89	6%	20	319	5.59	12.3	$21
DL	1st Half	263	25	79	7	42	2	301			350	433	783	7	83	34	0.46				78	48	4%	7		5.07	2.1	$8
BAvg Potl 50%	2nd Half	276	41	78	15	60	5	284			321	558	878	5	82	30	0.31	44	28	28	160	111	10%	13	343	6.10	10.3	$12
LIMA Plan D+	07 Proj	**332**	**39**	**93**	**13**	**53**	**4**	**280**			**318**	**483**	**801**	**5**	**85**	**30**	**0.37**	**44**	**28**	**28**	**120**	**89**	**7%**	**12**	**327**	**5.18**	**1.4**	**$11**

5-21-.368 in 57 AB at COL. Extreme hacker, as shown by his 1 BB and 14 K in those 57 AB. We need to see how he'll react once pitchers adjust. Bid, but do so without inflated expectations.

Bako,Paul

Bako,Paul		AB	R	H	HR	RBI	SB	Avg	vL	vR	OB	Slg	OPS	bb%	ct%	h%	Eye	G	L	F	PX	SX	SBO	xHR	xBA	RC/G	RAR	R$
Pos 2	02 MIL	234	24	55	4	20	0	235	167	245	295	329	624	8	80	28	0.43	49	23	28	63	46	3%	4	259	3.19	-6.6	$3
Age 34	03 CHC	188	19	43	0	17	0	229	200	233	310	330	639	10	75	30	0.47	46	22	32	82	80	2%	2	250	3.62	-3.9	$1
Past Peak	04 CHC	138	13	28	1	10	1	203	95	222	281	283	564	10	79	25	0.52	49	19	33	63	46	3%	2	239	2.57	-5.4	($0)
Bats Left	05 LA	40	1	10	0	4	0	250	250	250	362	300	662	15	70	36	0.58	67	19	15	52	0	0%	0	118	4.02	0.3	$0
Reliability 0	06 KC	153	7	32	0	10	0	209	200	210	262	229	491	7	70	30	0.24	56	19	24	20	11	0%	1	179	1.21	-15.2	($1)
DL 25 127	1st Half	80	4	20	0	6	0	250			302	275	577	7	69	36	0.24	58	22	20	26	10	0%	0	190	2.45	-4.6	$0
BAvg Potl 30%	2nd Half	73	3	12	0	4	0	164			218	178	396	6	71	23	0.24	55	17	28	14	12	0%	0	168	-0.10	-10.8	($1)
LIMA Plan F	07 Proj	**129**	**9**	**27**	**0**	**9**	**0**	**210**			**274**	**259**	**533**	**8**	**74**	**28**	**0.34**	**52**	**20**	**28**	**43**	**28**	**1%**	**1**	**214**	**1.96**	**-9.1**	**($0)**

A PX of 20 means his power skills are 80% below league average. Though his xBA rebounded strongly from 2005, he's still a solid 45th round pick in a 30-round league.

STEPHEN NICKRAND

Baldelli,Rocco

		AB	R	H	HR	RBI	SB	Avg	vL	vR	OB	Slg	OPS	bb%	ct%	h%	Eye	G	L	F	PX	SX	SBO	xHR	xBA	RC/G	RAR	R$
Pos 8	02 a/a	166	22	56	4	19	4	337			353	494	847	2	84	39	0.15				99	100	30%	4		5.56	3.4	$8
Age 25	03 TAM	637	89	185	11	78	27	290	298	285	322	418	740	4	80	35	0.23	50	20	30	84	137	23%	13	271	4.47	-5.0	$23
Pre-Peak	04 TAM	518	79	145	16	74	17	280	331	264	319	436	756	5	83	31	0.34	52	13	35	94	119	16%	15	273	4.65	-0.9	$19
Bats Right	05 TAM	0	0	0	0	0	0	0							0							0		0				
Reliability 0	06 TAM	* 411	66	128	16	61	10	311	297	303	340	527	867	4	81	36	0.22	51	16	34	134	134	13%	15	299	5.96	14.6	$18
DL 74 180	1st Half	118	18	42	3	14	0	354			405	566	971	8	84	40	0.52	47	18	35	136	80	3%	4	309	7.48	8.5	$5
BAvg Potl 35%	2nd Half	293	48	86	13	47	10	294			312	512	824	3	79	33	0.13	52	15	33	132	143	18%	11	294	5.32	5.4	$13
LIMA Plan C	07 Proj	**534**	**81**	**157**	**17**	**73**	**15**	**294**			**327**	**473**	**800**	**5**	**82**	**33**	**0.26**	**51**	**16**	**34**	**113**	**122**	**17%**	**17**	**287**	**5.17**	**8.8**	**$20**

16-57-.301-10 in 364 AB at TAM. Nice return from injury. Breakout time? PRO: PX growth, solid xBA. CON: High H% lifted BA, weak 2H Eye, high GB% caps power. That breakout? Probably a year or two away.

Barajas,Rod

		AB	R	H	HR	RBI	SB	Avg	vL	vR	OB	Slg	OPS	bb%	ct%	h%	Eye	G	L	F	PX	SX	SBO	xHR	xBA	RC/G	RAR	R$
Pos 2	02 ARI	* 170	14	42	4	24	1	247	196	252	293	382	675	6	85	27	0.42	29	18	53	93	36	3%	4	251	3.80	-1.6	$3
Age 31	03 ARI	220	19	48	3	28	0	218	244	212	265	327	592	6	80	26	0.33	32	21	47	83	25	0%	5	245	2.76	-10.3	$2
Past Peak	04 TEX	362	51	91	15	58	0	251	248	249	277	453	730	3	82	27	0.20	29	13	57	125	55	2%	14	255	4.22	-1.2	$9
Bats Right	05 TEX	410	53	104	21	60	0	254	272	251	298	466	764	6	83	26	0.37	29	20	51	131	27	0%	18	284	4.70	8.2	$12
Reliability 54	06 TEX	344	49	88	11	41	0	256	156	279	291	410	701	5	85	27	0.33	32	17	51	94	41	0%	11	255	3.97	-4.4	$7
DL	1st Half	201	25	56	6	25	0	279			310	428	737	4	86	30	0.31	35	17	48	92	30	0%	6	256	4.38	-0.2	$5
BAvg Potl 45%	2nd Half	143	24	32	5	16	0	224			265	385	650	5	85	23	0.36	26	18	55	97	58	0%	5	251	3.40	-4.4	$2
LIMA Plan D+	07 Proj	**432**	**59**	**112**	**16**	**57**	**0**	**259**			**297**	**431**	**728**	**5**	**84**	**28**	**0.33**	**30**	**18**	**53**	**106**	**40**	**0%**	**15**	**260**	**4.28**	**0.5**	**$10**

Bad April and injury-plagued September depressed power; otherwise, PX was close to '04/'05 level, so HR could return. Other skills are stable. Bidding for '06 production could yield a small profit.

Bard,Josh

		AB	R	H	HR	RBI	SB	Avg	vL	vR	OB	Slg	OPS	bb%	ct%	h%	Eye	G	L	F	PX	SX	SBO	xHR	xBA	RC/G	RAR	R$
Pos 2	02 aaa	344	33	98	6	49	0	285			320	416	736	5	88	31	0.43				88	32	0%	8		4.51	6.3	$9
Age 29	03 aaa	115	13	36	5	19	1	310			379	499	879	10	86	33	0.80				114	31	8%	5		6.35	6.9	$5
Peak	04 a/a	186	22	36	3	16	0	194			245	285	530	6	86	21	0.47				60	42	0%	3		2.17	-11.2	$0
Bats Both	05 CLE	83	6	16	1	9	0	193	148	214	272	277	549	10	87	21	0.82	43	18	39	59	16	0%	1	238	2.63	-3.6	($0)
Reliability 5	06 2TM	249	30	83	9	40	1	333	333	333	405	522	927	11	83	37	0.71	52	21	27	120	30	1%	10	301	7.05	17.4	$10
DL	1st Half	106	14	37	5	16	0	349			400	566	966	8	82	39	0.47	48	25	27	134	18	0%	5	315	7.28	7.9	$5
BAvg Potl 40%	2nd Half	143	16	46	4	24	1	322			409	490	898	13	84	36	0.91	55	17	27	110	31	2%	5	288	6.87	9.5	$5
LIMA Plan F	07 Proj	**255**	**29**	**74**	**8**	**36**	**1**	**290**			**354**	**446**	**800**	**9**	**85**	**32**	**0.65**	**52**	**20**	**27**	**99**	**33**	**2%**	**8**	**291**	**5.42**	**8.8**	**$8**

A surprise? Not really. Promise was shown in minors. H% probably aberrant, but xBA still shows a potential .300 hitter. High GB% caps power potential, but overall solid skills awaits opportunity.

Barfield,Josh

		AB	R	H	HR	RBI	SB	Avg	vL	vR	OB	Slg	OPS	bb%	ct%	h%	Eye	G	L	F	PX	SX	SBO	xHR	xBA	RC/G	RAR	R$
Pos 4	02	0	0	0	0	0	0	0							0							0		0				
Age 24	03	0	0	0	0	0	0	0							0							0		0				
Growth	04 aa	521	71	117	15	81	4	225			282	367	649	7	80	26	0.40				90	82	5%	15		3.44	-14.4	$10
Bats Right	05 aaa	512	61	142	11	60	17	277			335	386	721	8	84	31	0.55				71	88	15%	11		4.42	1.2	$16
Reliability 41	06 SD	539	72	151	13	58	21	280	331	266	318	423	741	5	85	31	0.37	39	19	42	87	110	20%	14	266	4.52	-1.3	$18
DL	1st Half	255	31	66	4	22	8	259			289	369	658	4	81	31	0.23	36	21	43	70	109	15%	5	240	3.44	-8.6	$6
BAvg Potl 40%	2nd Half	284	41	85	9	36	13	299			343	472	815	6	88	31	0.58	42	17	40	101	100	23%	9	288	5.44	6.7	$12
LIMA Plan C+	07 Proj	**523**	**68**	**142**	**13**	**62**	**17**	**272**			**320**	**405**	**726**	**7**	**84**	**30**	**0.45**	**40**	**19**	**42**	**84**	**102**	**16%**	**13**	**260**	**4.40**	**-2.6**	**$17**

Slow start hides second half growth across the board. Given mediocre performance vs. RHP, he could still see some growing pains. But if he starts to figure them out...
UP: .290, 20/20

Barmes,Clint

		AB	R	H	HR	RBI	SB	Avg	vL	vR	OB	Slg	OPS	bb%	ct%	h%	Eye	G	L	F	PX	SX	SBO	xHR	xBA	RC/G	RAR	R$
Pos 6	02 aa	438	44	111	14	42	11	253			288	404	692	5	89	26	0.43				87	78	25%	12		3.93	-4.1	$11
Age 28	03 aaa	493	47	129	7	40	9	262			286	375	662	3	91	28	0.39				74	69	16%	9		3.66	-8.8	$9
Peak	04 aaa	533	70	155	13	35	14	292			316	442	758	3	93	30	0.48				88	95	20%	13		4.71	6.3	$16
Bats Right	05 COL	350	55	101	10	46	6	289	289	283	320	434	754	4	90	30	0.44	36	23	41	87	90	11%	9	288	4.63	6.7	$13
Reliability 32	06 COL	478	57	105	7	56	5	220	267	209	254	335	589	4	85	25	0.31	34	18	48	72	92	10%	8	241	2.75	-23.8	$5
DL 88	1st Half	263	32	55	3	41	3	209			232	319	552	3	84	24	0.20	34	17	48	72	102	12%	4	238	2.25	-17.4	$3
BAvg Potl 60%	2nd Half	215	25	50	4	15	2	233			279	353	633	6	86	26	0.45	34	19	47	71	83	8%	4	245	3.35	-6.6	$2
LIMA Plan F	07 Proj	**167**	**21**	**42**	**4**	**17**	**3**	**251**			**284**	**380**	**664**	**4**	**88**	**27**	**0.38**	**34**	**20**	**46**	**77**	**90**	**13%**	**4**	**261**	**3.65**	**-2.7**	**$3**

A product of the new Coors? Low H% only partially to blame for this debacle; ct% dropped RHers killed him. PX declined for second straight year. Still owns that pre-injury '05, but approach with caution for now.

Barrett,Michael

		AB	R	H	HR	RBI	SB	Avg	vL	vR	OB	Slg	OPS	bb%	ct%	h%	Eye	G	L	F	PX	SX	SBO	xHR	xBA	RC/G	RAR	R$
Pos 2	02 MON	376	41	99	12	49	6	263	261	264	334	418	752	10	83	29	0.62	53	16	31	100	66	8%	12	280	4.84	8.0	$11
Age 30	03 MON	226	33	47	10	30	0	208	205	209	275	398	674	9	84	21	0.57	48	17	35	109	73	0%	8	286	3.81	-3.4	$4
Peak	04 CHC	456	55	131	16	65	1	287	248	299	335	489	824	7	86	31	0.52	48	20	32	118	70	5%	15	310	5.59	22.9	$14
Bats Right	05 CHC	424	48	117	16	61	0	276	320	254	338	479	817	9	86	29	0.66	43	24	33	127	44	3%	16	319	5.60	22.1	$13
Reliability 67	06 CHC	375	54	115	16	53	0	307	313	305	363	517	880	8	89	31	0.80	45	20	36	116	50	1%	14	311	6.27	19.7	$14
DL 28	1st Half	195	26	60	8	30	0	308			369	508	877	9	89	32	0.86	45	20	35	104	59	0%	7	303	6.28	10.3	$7
BAvg Potl 60%	2nd Half	180	28	55	8	23	0	306			356	528	883	7	89	31	0.74	44	19	37	128	35	2%	7	318	6.25	9.4	$7
LIMA Plan C	07 Proj	**451**	**60**	**140**	**20**	**63**	**0**	**311**			**366**	**528**	**894**	**8**	**87**	**32**	**0.68**	**45**	**20**	**34**	**126**	**46**	**2%**	**18**	**315**	**6.42**	**28.3**	**$17**

Improved eye, higher ct%, and xBA all say the .300 BA is real. Approaching the age for a catcher power spike, and second half PX growth could indicate that on the horizon. Go the extra buck. UP: 25 HR.

Bartlett,Jason

		AB	R	H	HR	RBI	SB	Avg	vL	vR	OB	Slg	OPS	bb%	ct%	h%	Eye	G	L	F	PX	SX	SBO	xHR	xBA	RC/G	RAR	R$
Pos 6	02	0	0	0	0	0	0	0							0							0		0				
Age 27	03	0	0	0	0	0	0	0							0							0		0				
Peak	04 aaa	269	46	83	2	25	6	309			376	439	815	10	88	35	0.88				76	129	10%	3		5.81	11.2	$9
Bats Right	05 MIN	* 453	68	123	7	44	6	272	290	226	339	375	714	9	85	31	0.68	47	18	35	67	92	6%	8	262	4.47	-1.2	$11
Reliability 26	06 MIN	* 568	85	172	3	51	16	303	314	307	339	407	746	5	87	35	0.42	44	22	34	72	112	15%	7	279	4.69	4.4	$16
DL	1st Half	283	46	87	1	24	7	307			341	431	772	5	85	36	0.35	50	25	25	90	114	16%	4	308	5.00	4.6	$8
BAvg Potl 40%	2nd Half	285	39	85	2	27	9	298			338	382	720	6	88	33	0.50	43	22	35	55	108	14%	3	266	4.39	-0.1	$8
LIMA Plan C+	07 Proj	**616**	**93**	**175**	**6**	**58**	**14**	**284**			**337**	**388**	**725**	**7**	**86**	**32**	**0.58**	**45**	**21**	**35**	**68**	**114**	**11%**	**9**	**272**	**4.55**	**1.4**	**$16**

2-32-.306-10 in 333 AB at MIN Nice growth, but there's less here than meets the eye. 2nd half xBA plummeted, making a .300 repeat questionable. Low walk rate limited SB opps. Don't overbid. DN: .265 BA.

Batista,Tony

		AB	R	H	HR	RBI	SB	Avg	vL	vR	OB	Slg	OPS	bb%	ct%	h%	Eye	G	L	F	PX	SX	SBO	xHR	xBA	RC/G	RAR	R$
Pos 5	02 BAL	615	90	150	31	87	5	244	234	247	301	457	758	8	83	25	0.47	30	15	55	127	66	7%	27	264	4.73	4.7	$18
Age 33	03 BAL	631	76	148	26	99	4	235	193	249	267	393	660	4	84	24	0.27	33	20	47	90	61	5%	21	258	3.38	-21.5	$15
Past Peak	04 MON	610	76	147	32	110	14	241	230	245	272	454	726	4	87	23	0.33	36	16	48	116	97	18%	25	281	4.19	-16.0	$21
Bats Right	05 JPN	559	76	137	16	88	3	245			269	389	658	3	81	28	0.17				95	76	4%	16		3.33	-21.8	$14
Reliability 55	06 MIN	178	24	42	5	21	0	236	212	246	295	388	683	8	85	25	0.56	40	22	38	97	42	3%	5	283	3.98	-5.5	$3
DL	1st Half	178	24	42	5	21	0	236			295	388	683	8	85	25	0.56	40	22	38	97	42	3%	5	283	3.98	-5.5	$3
BAvg Potl 65%	2nd Half	0	0	0	0	0	0	0							0									0				
LIMA Plan F	07 Proj	**132**	**17**	**32**	**5**	**20**	**1**	**242**			**282**	**410**	**693**	**5**	**84**	**25**	**0.36**	**36**	**19**	**45**	**102**	**57**	**7%**	**5**	**269**	**3.88**	**-3.7**	**$3**

Once was a low BA, high power hitter, but declining FB% has sapped the power, making him simply a low BA hitter. xBA says he might do better, but at age 33 opportunity to redeem himself is limited. DN: 0 AB

Bautista,Jose

		AB	R	H	HR	RBI	SB	Avg	vL	vR	OB	Slg	OPS	bb%	ct%	h%	Eye	G	L	F	PX	SX	SBO	xHR	xBA	RC/G	RAR	R$
Pos 859	02	0	0	0	0	0	0	0							0							0		0				
Age 26	03	0	0	0	0	0	0	0							0							0		0				
Pre-Peak	04 2TM	88	6	18	0	2	0	205			263	239	502	7	55	38	0.18				44	31	5%	1		1.54	-8.7	($1)
Bats Right	05 PIT	* 515	53	122	16	69	7	238			294	390	684	7	82	26	0.45				98	66	10%	16		3.80	10.5	$12
Reliability 14	06 PIT	* 501	70	122	18	60	4	243	283	216	323	420	743	11	74	20	0.46	40	13	47	117	71	7%	20	238	4.79	5.2	$11
DL	1st Half	238	33	58	11	30	3	243			332	465	797	12	77	27	0.58	37	7	56	144	69	8%	12	247	5.51	7.7	$6
BAvg Potl 45%	2nd Half	263	37	64	7	30	1	243			314	380	694	9	72	31	0.37	42	16	43	92	71	6%	8	223	4.11	-2.6	$5
LIMA Plan C	07 Proj	**509**	**64**	**122**	**14**	**64**	**5**	**240**			**309**	**386**	**695**	**9**	**77**	**28**	**0.45**	**40**	**13**	**47**	**98**	**69**	**8%**	**16**	**234**	**4.11**	**-6.8**	**$10**

16-51-.235 in 396 AB at PIT. Hit 10 HR in first 143 MLB AB, but pitchers got wise. FB% and ct% dropped in second half as he struggled against RHers. Still has some potential, but must make better contact.

HAROLD NICHOLS

Bay,Jason

Bay,Jason			AB	R	H	HR	RBI	SB	Avg	vL	vR	OB	Slg	OPS	bb%	ct%	h%	Eye	G	L	F	PX	SX	SBO	xHR	xBA	RC/G	RAR	R$
Pos	7	02 aa	188	29	48	7	27	14	255			340	441	781	11	76	30	0.53				118	146	37%	7		5.32	-1.7	$9
Age	28	03 aaa	307	52	80	15	49	19	261			353	443	796	13	80	28	0.72				106	113	24%	13		5.44	-0.2	$15
Peak		04 PIT	411	61	116	26	82	4	282	265	287	347	550	897	9	69	35	0.32	40	17	43	183	81	10%	25	274	6.97	18.1	$19
Bats	Right	05 PIT	599	110	183	32	101	21	306	342	292	401	559	960	14	76	36	0.67	38	22	40	170	133	11%	33	301	7.76	39.6	$34
Reliability	74	06 PIT	570	101	163	35	109	11	286	304	280	394	532	926	15	73	34	0.65	41	15	44	155	87	7%	35	268	7.43	35.0	$27
DL		1st Half	284	49	80	20	56	6	282			396	546	942	16	76	31	0.78	41	15	44	154	80	8%	18	277	7.51	18.3	$14
BAvg Potl	40%	2nd Half	286	52	83	15	53	5	290			392	517	910	14	70	37	0.55	40	16	44	157	81	5%	16	258	7.37	16.9	$13
LIMA Plan	B+	07 Proj	**575**	**100**	**166**	**33**	**105**	**15**	**289**			**384**	**531**	**915**	**13**	**73**	**34**	**0.58**	**39**	**18**	**42**	**158**	**104**	**10%**	**33**	**276**	**7.21**	**29.8**	**$29**

Consistent output, but buyers might hope for more than consistency from 28-year-old. Mid-70 ct% is a headwind for further gains and makes 40 HR elusive. On the plus side, he has 30-SB speed laying in wait.

Bellhorn,Mark

Bellhorn,Mark			AB	R	H	HR	RBI	SB	Avg	vL	vR	OB	Slg	OPS	bb%	ct%	h%	Eye	G	L	F	PX	SX	SBO	xHR	xBA	RC/G	RAR	R$
Pos	5	02 CHC	445	86	115	27	56	7	258	303	241	367	512	879	15	68	32	0.53	34	22	44	186	106	9%	28	273	6.99	31.5	$19
Age	32	03 2NL *	303	34	73	6	37	6	241	211	225	361	363	724	16	72	32	0.66	48	20	32	92	75	11%	8	242	4.86	5.6	$6
Past Peak		04 BOS	528	96	142	18	85	6	269	298	246	374	456	831	14	66	37	0.50	42	20	38	147	98	4%	25	250	6.51	24.3	$17
Bats	Both	05 2AL	300	43	63	8	30	3	210	230	198	327	357	683	15	63	31	0.46	41	20	39	133	62	3%	12	226	4.36	-1.3	$4
Reliability	23	06 SD	253	26	48	8	27	0	190	224	175	281	344	625	11	64	26	0.36	35	15	50	114	49	0%	10	203	3.25	-18.0	$1
DL	33	1st Half	128	14	28	5	20	0	219			296	430	725	10	61	32	0.28	33	15	51	166	67	0%	6	223	5.01	-1.9	$2
BAvg Potl	40%	2nd Half	125	12	20	3	7	0	160			266	256	522	13	68	21	0.45	36	15	49	67	21	0%	4	180	1.69	-15.7	($1)
LIMA Plan	F	07 Proj	**91**	**12**	**19**	**3**	**10**	**1**	**208**			**312**	**356**	**668**	**13**	**65**	**29**	**0.43**	**38**	**18**	**44**	**118**	**43**	**3%**	**4**	**217**	**3.95**	**-3.4**	**$1**

Dribbling toward irrelevance. Since '04, when lucky bounces nudged his BA close to 270, he has increasingly little to show for his efforts. He managed 8 HR last year only by hitting fully half his balls in the air!

Belliard,Ron

Belliard,Ron			AB	R	H	HR	RBI	SB	Avg	vL	vR	OB	Slg	OPS	bb%	ct%	h%	Eye	G	L	F	PX	SX	SBO	xHR	xBA	RC/G	RAR	R$
Pos	4	02 MIL	289	30	61	3	26	2	211	200	217	257	287	545	6	84	24	0.39	52	17	31	56	56	8%	4	249	2.26	-19.5	$2
Age	32	03 COL	447	73	124	8	50	7	277	345	254	349	409	758	10	84	32	0.69	50	23	27	90	97	7%	11	298	5.04	8.1	$13
Past Peak		04 CLE	599	78	169	12	70	3	282	319	263	347	426	773	9	84	32	0.61	44	19	37	98	54	3%	16	276	5.17	18.4	$14
Bats	Right	05 CLE	536	71	152	17	78	2	284	287	285	327	450	777	6	87	30	0.49	45	18	37	105	50	3%	17	290	4.98	12.8	$17
Reliability	96	06 2TM	544	63	148	13	67	2	272	220	295	317	403	720	6	85	30	0.44	46	19	35	81	44	4%	14	267	4.31	-0.7	$12
DL		1st Half	278	34	80	5	34	2	288			329	399	728	6	88	31	0.50	46	20	35	71	54	3%	6	273	4.44	0.6	$7
BAvg Potl	50%	2nd Half	266	29	68	8	33	0	256			305	406	711	7	82	28	0.40	46	17	36	92	41	5%	8	262	4.19	-1.3	$5
LIMA Plan	C	07 Proj	**526**	**65**	**145**	**13**	**66**	**2**	**275**			**325**	**417**	**742**	**7**	**85**	**30**	**0.48**	**46**	**19**	**36**	**90**	**53**	**4%**	**14**	**275**	**4.62**	**4.1**	**$13**

Cruising until mid-season trade. Had .757 OPS with CLE but only .666 OPS with STL. Small gains vs RH are masking big drops vs LH, dragging down overall OBP. Usual output should last for at least one more year.

Bell,David

Bell,David			AB	R	H	HR	RBI	SB	Avg	vL	vR	OB	Slg	OPS	bb%	ct%	h%	Eye	G	L	F	PX	SX	SBO	xHR	xBA	RC/G	RAR	R$
Pos	5	02 SF	552	82	144	20	73	1	261	263	260	327	429	756	9	86	27	0.68	36	20	44	104	59	2%	19	279	4.87	4.5	$16
Age	34	03 PHI	297	32	58	4	37	0	195	169	204	293	283	576	12	87	21	1.03	42	20	38	59	28	0%	5	251	3.06	-11.2	$1
Past Peak		04 PHI	533	67	155	18	77	1	291	296	289	359	458	817	10	86	31	0.76	40	23	37	100	37	1%	18	292	5.65	8.7	$17
Bats	Right	05 PHI	557	53	138	10	61	0	248	400	201	306	361	667	8	88	27	0.68	40	24	36	74	27	1%	12	282	3.89	-14.7	$8
Reliability	50	06 2NL	504	60	136	10	63	3	270	281	266	336	399	735	9	87	30	0.74	44	23	33	77	70	3%	11	285	4.72	-11.1	$11
DL		1st Half	237	25	59	4	25	0	249			326	350	676	10	86	27	0.84	41	22	37	64	21	0%	5	263	4.10	-9.7	$3
BAvg Potl	60%	2nd Half	267	35	77	6	38	3	288			345	442	787	8	87	32	0.64	47	24	29	88	92	5%	6	302	5.27	-1.7	$8
LIMA Plan	D+	07 Proj	**415**	**48**	**115**	**9**	**52**	**2**	**277**			**341**	**409**	**750**	**9**	**87**	**30**	**0.73**	**42**	**23**	**35**	**81**	**55**	**2%**	**10**	**284**	**4.88**	**-3.1**	**$10**

Unlike in 2005, he was rewarded for doing what he does well -- making contact in seven out of every eight at-bats. Speed won't make up for lack of pop -- he broke 2 SB for only second time in his career.

Beltran,Carlos

Beltran,Carlos			AB	R	H	HR	RBI	SB	Avg	vL	vR	OB	Slg	OPS	bb%	ct%	h%	Eye	G	L	F	PX	SX	SBO	xHR	xBA	RC/G	RAR	R$
Pos	8	02 KC	637	114	174	29	105	35	273	244	283	346	501	847	10	79	31	0.53	47	20	33	144	148	25%	29	303	6.05	23.6	$32
Age	30	03 KC	521	102	160	26	100	41	307	325	300	391	522	913	12	84	32	0.89	47	20	33	113	164	25%	21	303	6.88	30.6	$34
Peak		04 2TM	599	121	160	38	104	42	267	276	264	365	548	912	13	83	27	0.91	39	15	46	157	167	27%	33	304	6.92	38.9	$35
Bats	Both	05 NYM	582	83	155	16	78	17	266	308	254	331	414	745	9	84	30	0.58	44	19	37	96	102	14%	17	277	4.75	3.2	$20
Reliability	21	06 NYM	510	127	140	41	116	18	275	247	288	388	594	983	16	81	27	0.96	37	17	47	186	108	14%	36	318	7.87	50.2	$31
DL		1st Half	247	57	71	21	60	12	287			401	615	1017	16	79	29	0.89	37	15	48	194	88	19%	19	313	8.36	27.5	$17
BAvg Potl	70%	2nd Half	263	70	69	20	56	6	262			376	574	950	15	83	25	1.04	36	19	45	178	110	8%	18	323	7.45	22.9	$14
LIMA Plan	C	07 Proj	**517**	**109**	**149**	**37**	**108**	**19**	**288**			**382**	**578**	**959**	**13**	**82**	**29**	**0.84**	**40**	**18**	**43**	**168**	**119**	**15%**	**32**	**316**	**7.45**	**42.3**	**$31**

Superb season waylaid from even greater heights by measly 27% hit rate. A .300 BA is there for the taking. Drop from elite level of speed might be lasting - he has only 3 triples in his last 290 games. UP: .300, dangit!

Beltre,Adrian

Beltre,Adrian			AB	R	H	HR	RBI	SB	Avg	vL	vR	OB	Slg	OPS	bb%	ct%	h%	Eye	G	L	F	PX	SX	SBO	xHR	xBA	RC/G	RAR	R$
Pos	5	02 LA	587	70	151	21	75	7	257	302	245	301	426	727	6	84	28	0.39	42	15	43	102	92	9%	19	267	4.33	-4.5	$17
Age	29	03 LA	559	50	134	23	80	2	240	232	242	287	424	711	6	82	26	0.36	43	20	37	114	46	3%	21	283	4.11	-2.3	$12
Peak		04 LA	598	104	200	48	121	7	334	291	347	389	629	1017	8	85	33	0.61	41	18	40	159	61	5%	36	326	7.67	41.0	$38
Bats	Right	05 SEA	603	69	154	19	87	3	255	281	249	300	413	712	6	82	28	0.35	46	19	35	104	56	3%	19	277	4.16	-6.0	$15
Reliability	22	06 SEA	620	88	166	25	89	11	268	280	264	319	465	784	7	81	30	0.40	37	21	42	121	98	11%	24	282	5.07	1.1	$19
DL		1st Half	302	45	78	7	34	10	258			309	397	706	7	80	30	0.37	40	21	39	90	120	16%	8	262	4.16	-7.5	$8
BAvg Potl	50%	2nd Half	318	43	88	18	55	1	277			329	528	858	7	81	29	0.42	35	21	44	151	58	6%	16	302	5.93	8.4	$11
LIMA Plan	C+	07 Proj	**619**	**84**	**169**	**23**	**81**	**7**	**273**			**323**	**454**	**777**	**7**	**82**	**30**	**0.41**	**40**	**20**	**40**	**112**	**83**	**7%**	**22**	**280**	**4.98**	**2.8**	**$18**

Better? No, just more FB-prone, and that only for a half. Momentum aside, the massive clobberer of 2004 did not return - bb%, ct%, h% all point to same-old skills. Bid as if the halves had been reversed.

Bennett,Gary

Bennett,Gary			AB	R	H	HR	RBI	SB	Avg	vL	vR	OB	Slg	OPS	bb%	ct%	h%	Eye	G	L	F	PX	SX	SBO	xHR	xBA	RC/G	RAR	R$
Pos	2	02 COL	291	26	77	4	26	1	265	365	237	301	354	655	5	85	30	0.33	53	22	26	57	59	5%	4	271	3.48	-5.4	$5
Age	35	03 SD	307	26	73	2	42	3	238	218	248	293	306	599	7	84	28	0.50	47	24	29	52	55	4%	4	266	3.01	-11.8	$4
Decline		04 MIL	219	18	49	3	20	1	224	256	217	295	329	623	9	85	25	0.69	50	14	36	72	35	2%	4	247	3.43	-2.6	$1
Bats	Right	05 WAS	199	11	44	1	21	0	221	200	241	295	271	567	10	81	27	0.57	43	25	32	40	14	2%	2	243	2.63	-7.1	$0
Reliability	26	06 STL	157	13	35	4	22	0	223	400	172	274	331	605	7	81	25	0.37	48	20	31	65	16	0%	4	244	2.84	-7.2	$2
DL		1st Half	76	7	15	0	9	0	197			247	263	510	6	79	25	0.31	57	17	27	57	32	0%	1	233	1.76	-6.2	($0)
BAvg Potl	55%	2nd Half	81	6	20	4	13	0	247			299	395	694	7	83	25	0.43	40	24	36	72	2	0%	3	256	3.82	-1.2	$2
LIMA Plan	F	07 Proj	**134**	**10**	**30**	**3**	**16**	**0**	**224**			**284**	**319**	**602**	**8**	**82**	**26**	**0.47**	**47**	**21**	**32**	**61**	**23**	**1%**	**3**	**249**	**2.94**	**-4.8**	**$1**

When you have no power and no speed, every point of ct% is like water in a desert, and Bennett's canteen is slowly draining. BA would have been worse had he not rapped 14 hits in 35 AB against LH.

Berkman,Lance

Berkman,Lance			AB	R	H	HR	RBI	SB	Avg	vL	vR	OB	Slg	OPS	bb%	ct%	h%	Eye	G	L	F	PX	SX	SBO	xHR	xBA	RC/G	RAR	R$
Pos	39	02 HOU	578	106	169	42	128	8	292	240	307	403	578	981	16	80	30	0.91	40	18	42	178	75	6%	38	315	7.90	37.3	$34
Age	31	03 HOU	538	110	155	25	93	5	288	282	290	406	515	921	17	80	32	0.99	41	20	38	142	99	4%	26	298	7.34	27.7	$24
Past Peak		04 HOU	544	104	172	30	106	9	316	272	329	446	566	1012	19	81	34	1.26	40	21	39	151	74	7%	31	310	8.57	38.9	$30
Bats	Both	05 HOU	468	76	137	24	82	4	293	296	295	408	524	931	16	85	30	1.26	46	23	32	142	62	3%	24	327	7.37	23.0	$21
Reliability	29	06 HOU	536	95	169	45	136	3	315	266	335	421	621	1042	15	80	32	0.92	39	19	42	173	35	3%	38	313	8.58	37.4	$32
DL	37	1st Half	263	41	83	22	70	1	316			406	616	1022	13	82	31	0.85	37	19	43	164	25	2%	18	312	8.13	15.1	$16
BAvg Potl	55%	2nd Half	273	54	86	23	66	2	315			435	626	1061	18	78	33	0.98	41	19	40	181	39	3%	20	314	9.03	22.3	$17
LIMA Plan	D+	07 Proj	**556**	**100**	**171**	**35**	**121**	**5**	**308**			**421**	**565**	**986**	**16**	**81**	**33**	**1.05**	**41**	**20**	**38**	**153**	**58**	**4%**	**33**	**310**	**8.03**	**33.1**	**$30**

Can you have a five-year peak? xBA and Eye point to superlative play over a sustained period. However, the road ahead at 31 isn't what it was at 26. Pay for 2007 but not for 2008.

Berroa,Angel

Berroa,Angel			AB	R	H	HR	RBI	SB	Avg	vL	vR	OB	Slg	OPS	bb%	ct%	h%	Eye	G	L	F	PX	SX	SBO	xHR	xBA	RC/G	RAR	R$
Pos	6	02 aaa	372	38	76	7	33	8	204			243	328	571	5	80	24	0.25				81	117	19%	8		2.41	-21.6	$4
Age	29	03 KC	567	92	164	17	73	21	289	313	276	324	453	777	5	82	33	0.29	43	26	32	100	139	18%	16	292	4.89	7.4	$23
Peak		04 KC *	563	78	147	10	51	16	261	259	263	293	385	678	4	83	30	0.26	53	16	32	77	126	20%	11	268	3.72	-12.4	$14
Bats	Right	05 KC	608	68	164	11	55	7	270	278	266	291	375	666	3	82	31	0.17	49	20	31	66	88	8%	11	261	3.44	-19.8	$13
Reliability	65	06 KC	474	45	111	9	54	3	234	217	241	256	333	589	3	81	27	0.16	53	17	30	63	65	4%	9	251	2.51	-27.2	$5
DL		1st Half	261	23	63	4	27	3	241			258	333	592	2	83	28	0.13	54	18	28	62	58	8%	5	257	2.54	-14.6	$3
BAvg Potl	45%	2nd Half	213	22	48	5	27	0	225			253	333	587	4	80	26	0.19	50	17	33	65	52	0%	5	241	2.46	-12.6	$2
LIMA Plan	D	07 Proj	**444**	**49**	**110**	**9**	**47**	**5**	**247**			**273**	**358**	**631**	**3**	**82**	**29**	**0.19**	**51**	**18**	**31**	**69**	**92**	**9%**	**9**	**260**	**3.05**	**-18.7**	**$7**

Eye slipped even further from last year's dismal level. Could be why he managed to hit less than one-third of his balls into the air, which is no way to be productive unless you're Ichiro Suzuki. And Berroa ain't.

JOHN BURNSON

Betancourt,Yuniesky

Betancourt,Yuniesky			AB	R	H	HR	RBI	SB	Avg	vL	vR	OB	Slg	OPS	bb%	ct%	h%	Eye	G	L	F	PX	SX	SBO	xHR	xBA	RC/G	RAR	R$
Pos	6	02	0	0	0	0	0	0	0							0							0		0				
Age	25	03	0	0	0	0	0	0	0							0							0		0				
Pre-Peak		04	0	0	0	0	0	0	0							0							0		0				
Bats	Right	05 SEA *	621	57	157	7	58	17	253	283	248	282	367	649	4	91	27	0.47	38	17	45	66	113	25%	8	257	3.60	-18.0	$12
Reliability	6	06 SEA	558	68	161	8	47	11	289	240	303	310	403	713	3	90	31	0.31	46	18	36	67	101	14%	9	276	4.16	-3.9	$13
DL		1st Half	258	36	74	4	30	7	287			308	415	723	3	91	30	0.33	47	18	35	72	124	18%	4	283	4.30	-0.8	$8
BAvg Potl	45%	2nd Half	300	32	87	4	17	4	290			311	393	704	3	90	31	0.30	46	18	36	62	75	11%	5	269	4.04	-3.1	$6
LIMA Plan	C	07 Proj	**609**	**66**	**167**	**8**	**53**	**14**	**274**			**298**	**387**	**685**	**3**	**91**	**29**	**0.37**	**45**	**18**	**38**	**65**	**104**	**18%**	**9**	**272**	**3.92**	**-9.8**	**$13**

Flirted with .300, but xBA shows he's not there yet. High ct% and decent speed with no power or patience puts him on Neifi Perez career path. (Shudder) With few signs of growth, expect more of the same in '07.

Betemit,Wilson

Betemit,Wilson			AB	R	H	HR	RBI	SB	Avg	vL	vR	OB	Slg	OPS	bb%	ct%	h%	Eye	G	L	F	PX	SX	SBO	xHR	xBA	RC/G	RAR	R$
Pos	5	02 aaa	343	40	82	7	32	7	239			300	356	656	8	80	28	0.44				80	77	15%	8		3.60	-9.8	$7
Age	25	03 aaa	478	57	132	9	68	9	276			330	428	758	7	80	33	0.40				95	117	11%	10		4.91	7.2	$14
Pre-Peak		04 aaa	356	42	91	11	52	3	256			310	421	731	7	76	31	0.33				111	70	7%	12		4.48	-5.3	$9
Bats	Both	05 ATL	246	36	75	4	20	1	305	260	323	362	435	797	8	78	38	0.40	48	25	27	88	91	5%	5	276	5.44	4.5	$7
Reliability	39	06 2NL	373	49	98	18	53	3	263	189	281	328	469	797	9	73	32	0.35	42	21	37	139	48	4%	18	270	5.40	-1.0	$11
DL		1st Half	138	18	37	5	16	2	268			336	464	799	9	75	33	0.40	40	23	37	139	51	9%	6	281	5.51	0.1	$4
BAvg Potl	40%	2nd Half	235	31	61	13	37	1	260			323	472	795	9	71	31	0.33	44	20	36	138	37	2%	12	263	5.34	-1.0	$7
LIMA Plan	C+	07 Proj	**513**	**68**	**140**	**22**	**64**	**4**	**273**			**333**	**470**	**803**	**8**	**75**	**32**	**0.37**	**42**	**23**	**35**	**130**	**74**	**6%**	**22**	**279**	**5.44**	**4.4**	**$16**

Nice jump in PX, complete with FB% gains, though struggles vs. LH and drop in ct% raise small red flags. The seeds of a power breakout are here, but lack of a full-season skill sample means you should bid cautiously.

Biggio,Craig

Biggio,Craig			AB	R	H	HR	RBI	SB	Avg	vL	vR	OB	Slg	OPS	bb%	ct%	h%	Eye	G	L	F	PX	SX	SBO	xHR	xBA	RC/G	RAR	R$
Pos	4	02 HOU	577	96	146	15	58	16	253	183	271	313	404	716	8	81	29	0.45	48	15	37	104	130	13%	17	271	4.35	-1.0	$18
Age	41	03 HOU	628	102	166	15	62	8	264	267	264	326	412	738	8	82	30	0.49	46	23	32	102	96	7%	18	288	4.65	4.5	$17
Decline		04 HOU	633	100	178	24	63	7	281	303	276	324	469	793	6	85	30	0.43	39	23	38	116	78	6%	23	300	5.12	9.2	$21
Bats	Right	05 HOU	590	94	156	26	69	11	264	243	269	308	468	776	6	85	27	0.41	43	17	41	127	102	10%	24	296	4.89	5.6	$21
Reliability	74	06 HOU	548	79	135	21	62	3	246	297	233	298	422	719	7	85	26	0.48	39	19	41	104	56	4%	20	278	4.29	-5.0	$13
DL		1st Half	284	41	77	6	28	1	271			326	419	745	7	86	30	0.59	38	22	40	97	48	3%	8	285	4.76	1.3	$6
BAvg Potl	60%	2nd Half	264	38	58	15	34	2	220			267	424	691	6	83	21	0.38	41	16	43	111	59	6%	12	271	3.78	-6.6	$6
LIMA Plan	D	07 Proj	**360**	**55**	**92**	**15**	**40**	**1**	**256**			**304**	**438**	**742**	**6**	**84**	**27**	**0.44**	**41**	**19**	**40**	**111**	**53**	**3%**	**13**	**283**	**4.53**	**-0.5**	**$9**

Low 2H H% means BA should return - greater concerns are:
- Three-year xBA trend.
- 2H drop in Eye and LD%.
- Career-worst SX and SBO%.
- Last four half-season OPS marks: .806, .749, .745, .691.

Blake,Casey

Blake,Casey			AB	R	H	HR	RBI	SB	Avg	vL	vR	OB	Slg	OPS	bb%	ct%	h%	Eye	G	L	F	PX	SX	SBO	xHR	xBA	RC/G	RAR	R$
Pos	9	02 aaa	502	60	123	12	39	16	245			297	371	667	7	86	27	0.51				78	96	21%	12		3.75	-21.4	$12
Age	33	03 CLE	557	80	143	17	67	7	257	245	261	304	411	715	6	80	29	0.35	42	21	37	104	64	12%	18	274	4.21	-15.6	$14
Past Peak		04 CLE	587	93	159	28	88	5	271	243	284	347	486	832	10	76	31	0.49	43	17	40	137	70	8%	28	274	5.88	20.2	$20
Bats	Right	05 CLE	523	72	126	23	58	4	241	241	241	299	438	736	8	78	27	0.37	37	20	42	132	63	8%	22	277	4.49	-3.3	$13
Reliability	41	06 CLE	401	63	113	19	68	6	282	272	286	354	479	833	10	77	33	0.48	40	23	37	124	82	5%	18	279	5.84	2.1	$15
DL	47	1st Half	214	33	65	10	36	5	304			379	519	898	11	79	34	0.59	40	23	37	134	89	8%	10	295	6.70	6.1	$9
BAvg Potl	45%	2nd Half	187	30	48	9	32	1	257			325	433	758	9	74	30	0.39	41	23	36	111	52	2%	8	261	4.82	-4.6	$6
LIMA Plan	D	07 Proj	**314**	**47**	**83**	**14**	**46**	**4**	**265**			**331**	**459**	**790**	**9**	**77**	**30**	**0.44**	**40**	**21**	**39**	**125**	**75**	**7%**	**14**	**276**	**5.25**	**0.3**	**$10**

Has some pop, but xBAs reveal how decidedly average the rest of his skills are. Mediocrity only has value when it comes with full-time AB; injuries and younger competition are pushing him to the margins. It happens.

Blalock,Hank

Blalock,Hank			AB	R	H	HR	RBI	SB	Avg	vL	vR	OB	Slg	OPS	bb%	ct%	h%	Eye	G	L	F	PX	SX	SBO	xHR	xBA	RC/G	RAR	R$
Pos	50	02 TEX *	534	69	148	10	69	2	277	67	248	338	412	750	8	84	31	0.58	37	25	38	92	53	2%	13	284	4.85	5.8	$14
Age	26	03 TEX	567	89	170	29	90	2	300	209	329	350	522	872	7	83	32	0.45	33	21	45	132	63	3%	25	292	6.08	24.6	$23
Pre-Peak		04 TEX	627	108	173	33	114	2	276	282	273	356	504	858	11	76	30	0.51	34	18	48	144	68	2%	32	271	6.23	23.5	$24
Bats	Left	05 TEX	647	80	170	25	92	1	263	196	290	317	431	748	7	80	30	0.39	39	24	36	111	38	1%	24	283	4.61	2.1	$18
Reliability	75	06 TEX	591	76	157	16	89	1	266	216	284	324	401	725	8	83	30	0.52	42	21	37	81	62	1%	16	267	4.44	-9.7	$14
DL		1st Half	300	46	87	11	54	1	290			358	450	808	10	89	30	1.00	43	20	37	90	45	1%	10	288	5.55	4.5	$10
BAvg Potl	50%	2nd Half	291	30	70	5	35	0	241			287	351	638	6	77	30	0.29	41	23	37	71	62	0%	6	244	3.25	-15.3	$3
LIMA Plan	C	07 Proj	**580**	**77**	**154**	**19**	**87**	**1**	**266**			**324**	**423**	**748**	**8**	**81**	**30**	**0.45**	**39**	**22**	**39**	**99**	**56**	**1%**	**19**	**270**	**4.68**	**-2.3**	**$15**

Sore shoulder hindered him in 2H, but three-year decline in PX, xHR combined with rise in GB% says it's not just the shoulder. At 26, a rebound is likely - just don't go chasing after those 2003-04 levels.

Blanco,Henry

Blanco,Henry			AB	R	H	HR	RBI	SB	Avg	vL	vR	OB	Slg	OPS	bb%	ct%	h%	Eye	G	L	F	PX	SX	SBO	xHR	xBA	RC/G	RAR	R$
Pos	2	02 ATL	221	17	45	6	22	0	204	211	202	270	335	605	8	77	24	0.39	38	15	48	90	40	4%	6	224	2.87	-8.7	$1
Age	35	03 ATL	151	11	30	1	13	0	199	281	176	248	272	520	6	86	22	0.48	30	22	48	54	23	0%	2	240	2.10	-10.4	($0)
Decline		04 MIN	315	36	65	10	37	0	206	204	207	256	368	624	6	82	22	0.38	36	14	50	101	52	5%	10	247	3.13	-11.9	$3
Bats	Right	05 CHC	161	16	39	6	25	0	242	194	254	291	391	682	6	85	25	0.46	42	17	41	88	19	0%	5	256	3.81	0.1	$4
Reliability	29	06 CHC	241	23	64	6	37	0	266	325	236	306	419	725	5	84	29	0.37	38	24	38	93	42	0%	6	284	4.35	0.1	$5
DL		1st Half	92	10	21	3	16	0	228			276	402	678	6	88	23	0.55	30	23	47	96	54	0%	3	282	3.89	-1.2	$2
BAvg Potl	50%	2nd Half	149	13	43	3	21	0	289			325	430	754	5	82	34	0.30	43	25	32	92	39	0%	4	285	4.68	1.4	$4
LIMA Plan	F	07 Proj	**197**	**19**	**48**	**6**	**28**	**0**	**243**			**289**	**394**	**683**	**6**	**84**	**26**	**0.40**	**38**	**21**	**42**	**93**	**46**	**1%**	**6**	**269**	**3.85**	**-1.5**	**$3**

Posted a career-high BA thanks to H% and LD% rates that are probably not sustainable. It was a neat trick, but Trix are for kids, and he's 35 now.

Bloomquist,Willie

Bloomquist,Willie			AB	R	H	HR	RBI	SB	Avg	vL	vR	OB	Slg	OPS	bb%	ct%	h%	Eye	G	L	F	PX	SX	SBO	xHR	xBA	RC/G	RAR	R$
Pos	8	02 aaa	337	42	82	5	42	18	243			298	338	636	7	88	26	0.67				58	115	33%	5		3.52	-13.6	$10
Age	29	03 SEA	196	30	49	1	14	4	250	242	257	316	321	638	9	80	31	0.49	49	21	30	49	111	9%	2	248	3.47	-7.3	$3
Peak		04 SEA	188	27	46	2	18	13	245	281	212	283	330	613	5	74	32	0.21	42	20	38	67	121	34%	3	227	2.87	-10.4	$6
Bats	Right	05 SEA	249	27	64	0	22	14	257	247	262	288	333	622	4	85	30	0.29	45	24	32	59	131	26%	2	269	3.16	-8.1	$6
Reliability	34	06 SEA	251	36	62	1	15	16	247	253	243	313	299	612	9	84	29	0.60	46	17	37	32	132	25%	2	227	3.22	-10.8	$6
DL	32	1st Half	111	18	30	0	7	7	270			319	306	626	7	86	32	0.50	45	20	35	22	133	29%	0	232	3.31	-4.4	$3
BAvg Potl	50%	2nd Half	140	18	32	1	8	9	229			308	293	601	10	83	27	0.67	48	14	38	41	125	21%	1	224	3.13	-6.5	$3
LIMA Plan	F	07 Proj	**228**	**30**	**57**	**1**	**17**	**14**	**250**			**303**	**322**	**625**	**7**	**83**	**30**	**0.44**	**45**	**20**	**35**	**49**	**137**	**26%**	**2**	**247**	**3.27**	**-8.9**	**$6**

Uptick in bb% led to career-high SB; similar patience in '03 gives hope that this is a repeatable skill. Has little to offer when he swings the bat, but SX and SBO strength mean he's good for another year of end-game profit.

Blum,Geoff

Blum,Geoff			AB	R	H	HR	RBI	SB	Avg	vL	vR	OB	Slg	OPS	bb%	ct%	h%	Eye	G	L	F	PX	SX	SBO	xHR	xBA	RC/G	RAR	R$
Pos	65	02 HOU	368	45	104	10	52	2	283	185	304	367	440	807	12	81	33	0.70	43	16	41	103	81	2%	11	262	5.69	18.6	$12
Age	34	03 HOU	420	51	110	10	52	0	262	135	274	295	379	674	5	88	28	0.40	42	23	35	71	34	0%	10	279	3.72	-4.7	$9
Past Peak		04 TAM	339	38	73	8	35	2	215	288	193	267	348	615	7	83	24	0.41	46	14	40	87	51	7%	9	250	3.08	-14.5	$3
Bats	Both	05 2TM	319	32	73	6	25	3	229	213	236	291	345	636	8	87	25	0.65	40	21	39	73	69	8%	6	268	3.52	-7.2	$4
Reliability	46	06 SD	276	27	70	4	34	0	254	167	267	297	366	663	6	82	30	0.33	36	23	41	77	41	2%	6	257	3.62	-6.0	$4
DL	16	1st Half	86	8	22	1	9	0	256			289	337	626	4	77	32	0.20	39	18	43	60	24	0%	1	212	3.00	-3.4	$1
BAvg Potl	45%	2nd Half	190	19	48	3	25	0	253			300	379	679	6	84	29	0.42	35	25	40	83	48	2%	4	275	3.90	-2.6	$3
LIMA Plan	F	07 Proj	**229**	**23**	**57**	**4**	**25**	**1**	**249**			**299**	**368**	**667**	**7**	**83**	**28**	**0.42**	**39**	**21**	**40**	**79**	**54**	**4%**	**5**	**258**	**3.73**	**-3.1**	**$3**

Four straight seasons of lousy skills and sub-replacement level performance with no end in sight. Judging by his shrinking AB totals, teams are slowly realizing there's not much value in playing him. You should too.

Bonds,Barry

Bonds,Barry			AB	R	H	HR	RBI	SB	Avg	vL	vR	OB	Slg	OPS	bb%	ct%	h%	Eye	G	L	F	PX	SX	SBO	xHR	xBA	RC/G	RAR	R$
Pos	7	02 SF	403	117	149	46	110	9	370	384	363	577	799	1376	33	88	33	4.21	32	19	49	237	82	4%	42	390	13.51	71.5	$40
Age	42	03 SF	390	111	133	45	90	7	341	363	331	522	749	1271	28	85	31	2.55	30	24	46	221	80	3%	38	370	11.90	63.6	$34
Decline		04 SF	373	129	135	45	101	6	362	307	395	607	812	1419	38	89	31	5.66	35	19	46	230	82	2%	43	391	14.33	83.3	$37
Bats	Left	05 SF	42	8	12	5	10	0	286	600	243	412	667	1078	18	86	23	1.50	32	16	51	198	14	0%	4	338	8.80	4.1	$3
Reliability	0	06 SF	367	74	99	26	77	3	270	255	276	444	545	989	24	86	25	2.25	30	20	50	149	46	2%	25	311	8.39	33.0	$17
DL	171	1st Half	162	37	41	11	34	1	253			472	519	990	29	85	24	2.79	31	22	47	146	37	1%	11	311	8.72	16.5	$7
BAvg Potl	80%	2nd Half	205	37	58	15	43	2	283			419	566	985	19	87	26	1.78	30	19	51	152	42	3%	13	312	8.04	16.1	$10
LIMA Plan	B+	07 Proj	**347**	**89**	**95**	**23**	**71**	**2**	**274**			**441**	**543**	**984**	**23**	**83**	**27**	**1.72**	**30**	**19**	**51**	**157**	**64**	**1%**	**23**	**300**	**8.34**	**29.3**	**$18**

Hit .319 w/12 HR and 174 PX over final two months despite bone chips in his elbow. Even in decline, skills are strong, and chasing Aaron should provide enough motivation for one last season of double-digit value.

BRANDON KRUSE

Boone,Aaron

Boone,Aaron			AB	R	H	HR	RBI	SB	Avg	vL	vR	OB	Slg	OPS	bb%	ct%	h%	Eye	G	L	F	PX	SX	SBO	xHR	xBA	RC/G	RAR	R$
Pos	5	02 CIN	606	83	146	26	87	32	241	233	243	305	439	744	8	82	26	0.50	41	18	41	128	121	29%	25	288	4.65	1.1	$24
Age	34	03 2TM	592	92	158	24	96	23	267	216	285	320	453	772	7	82	29	0.44	38	22	40	114	126	18%	22	285	4.92	9.3	$25
Past Peak		04 2AL	0	0	0	0	0	0	0							0							0		0				
Bats	Right	05 CLE	511	61	124	16	60	9	243	229	246	291	378	669	6	82	27	0.38	43	21	35	84	82	10%	15	269	3.62	-13.4	$12
Reliability	1	06 CLE	354	50	89	7	46	5	251	280	239	304	370	675	7	82	29	0.44	36	25	40	78	79	10%	8	264	3.81	-12.6	$7
DL		1st Half	252	27	63	3	27	2	250			295	353	648	6	83	29	0.38	34	26	40	71	63	10%	4	266	3.49	-11.5	$3
BAvg Potl	55%	2nd Half	102	23	26	4	19	3	255			327	412	739	10	80	28	0.55	40	21	40	94	102	10%	4	263	4.62	-1.2	$4
LIMA Plan	F	07 Proj	**129**	**20**	**32**	**4**	**19**	**3**	**247**			**305**	**391**	**696**	**8**	**82**	**27**	**0.46**	**39**	**22**	**39**	**89**	**82**	**13%**	**4**	**268**	**4.02**	**-3.1**	**$4**

Stable core skills with steadily poorer results point to a usually irreversible age-related decline, made worse by devastating '04 ACL tear. At his peak, a 20-20-$20 guy; now a spare part if he has any role at all.

Borchard,Joe

Borchard,Joe			AB	R	H	HR	RBI	SB	Avg	vL	vR	OB	Slg	OPS	bb%	ct%	h%	Eye	G	L	F	PX	SX	SBO	xHR	xBA	RC/G	RAR	R$
Pos	9	02 aaa	474	60	120	22	57	2	253			321	464	785	9	71	31	0.34	41	23	36	155	47	5%	24	276	5.32	2.3	$13
Age	28	03 CHW	* 484	59	112	14	51	2	231	176	188	276	362	638	6	78	27	0.28	61	15	24	85	55	6%	14	258	3.17	-29.3	$8
Peak		04 CHW	* 502	64	109	25	62	4	217	177	171	282	416	698	8	77	23	0.38	43	20	37	123	65	7%	23	273	3.98	-11.2	$10
Bats	Both	05 aaa	486	52	114	25	51	5	236			292	425	717	7	76	26	0.33				121	43	9%	22		4.15	-12.2	$12
Reliability	43	06 2TM	239	33	55	10	28	0	230	148	258	311	393	704	10	71	28	0.41	48	18	34	104	52	5%	10	241	4.20	-7.4	$4
DL		1st Half	122	20	28	6	18	0	230			309	377	686	10	71	27	0.40	46	20	34	84	46	8%	5	229	3.83	-5.3	$3
BAvg Potl	45%	2nd Half	117	13	27	4	10	0	231			313	410	723	11	71	29	0.41	51	17	33	126	50	0%	5	253	4.60	-2.2	$1
LIMA Plan	F	07 Proj	**191**	**24**	**44**	**8**	**21**	**1**	**230**			**300**	**411**	**711**	**9**	**73**	**27**	**0.38**	**48**	**18**	**34**	**115**	**59**	**5%**	**8**	**257**	**4.22**	**-5.3**	**$4**

"Switch-hitter" flails helplessly against LHP (1-3-.148 in 61 AB) and isn't hugely effective against RHP (.258/.353/.449, '69% ct%). PX shows his ability to deliver HR, but PT and BA risks abound.

Botts,Jason

Botts,Jason			AB	R	H	HR	RBI	SB	Avg	vL	vR	OB	Slg	OPS	bb%	ct%	h%	Eye	G	L	F	PX	SX	SBO	xHR	xBA	RC/G	RAR	R$
Pos	0	02	0	0	0	0	0	0	0							0							0		0				
Age	26	03 aa	194	22	47	4	22	5	240			303	365	668	8	80	28	0.45				86	94	12%	5		3.77	-4.9	$4
Pre-Peak		04 aa	476	68	130	23	74	6	273			356	475	831	11	77	31	0.54				126	69	7%	22		5.89	8.0	$17
Bats	Both	05 TEX	* 533	67	136	20	73	1	255		308	318	437	755	9	78	29	0.43	50	36	14	118	59	4%	19		4.81	-19.1	$13
Reliability	25	06 TEX	* 286	45	72	13	38	5	252	100	250	334	466	800	11	72	31	0.44	38	24	38	151	90	7%	14	277	5.61	-6.9	$8
DL		1st Half	191	34	58	11	33	5	301			367	567	933	9	72	37	0.36	37	27	37	186	100	10%	11	301	7.38	5.0	$9
BAvg Potl	45%	2nd Half	95	11	15	2	5	0	154			272	263	535	14	73	19	0.59	50	0	50	81		0%	3		2.08	-13.7	($1)
LIMA Plan	F	07 Proj	**63**	**8**	**15**	**2**	**8**	**1**	**240**			**321**	**412**	**733**	**11**	**75**	**29**	**0.48**	**42**	**21**	**37**	**120**	**48**	**5%**	**3**	**266**	**4.65**	**-2.6**	**$1**

1-6-.220 in 50 AB at TEX. Prodigious but rapidly aging minor-league hitter who's scuffled in two short tries at MLB. Plate patience transfers well, but mediocre AAA 72% ct% collapsed to 60% at MLB.

Bradley,Milton

Bradley,Milton			AB	R	H	HR	RBI	SB	Avg	vL	vR	OB	Slg	OPS	bb%	ct%	h%	Eye	G	L	F	PX	SX	SBO	xHR	xBA	RC/G	RAR	R$
Pos	9	02 CLE	* 359	52	90	9	42	8	251	293	230	319	396	715	9	82	28	0.57	50	20	30	90	102	14%	10	284	4.41	-6.6	$9
Age	29	03 CLE	377	61	121	10	56	17	321	402	287	420	501	921	15	81	38	0.88	42	25	33	126	98	17%	14	303	7.33	22.5	$19
Peak		04 LA	516	72	138	19	67	15	267	295	257	356	424	780	12	76	32	0.58	47	19	34	102	66	16%	20	259	5.30	0.2	$18
Bats	Both	05 LA	283	49	82	13	38	6	290	278	294	347	484	832	8	83	31	0.53	45	23	32	117	99	9%	11	305	5.65	3.2	$13
Reliability	48	06 OAK	351	53	97	14	52	10	276	293	270	368	447	815	13	81	31	0.78	52	15	33	99	94	10%	13	275	5.75	0.9	$13
DL	69 87	1st Half	94	13	20	3	8	2	213			321	351	672	14	77	25	0.68	51	8	40	71	108	10%	2	217	3.96	-5.0	$1
BAvg Potl	50%	2nd Half	257	40	77	11	44	8	300			386	482	868	12	83	33	0.84	52	18	31	109	74	10%	11	293	6.36	5.0	$11
LIMA Plan	C	07 Proj	**398**	**61**	**109**	**15**	**54**	**11**	**274**			**357**	**443**	**800**	**11**	**81**	**31**	**0.67**	**49**	**18**	**33**	**102**	**95**	**11%**	**15**	**276**	**5.49**	**3.1**	**$14**

Injury risk defined: A 500-AB year at career rates would be 18-68-15-.276, a $20 stud. But he's only seen 500 AB once in his 6-year career, and lost 150 AB in '06 to quadriceps, knee, oblique, hip and shoulder woes.

Branyan,Russ

Branyan,Russ			AB	R	H	HR	RBI	SB	Avg	vL	vR	OB	Slg	OPS	bb%	ct%	h%	Eye	G	L	F	PX	SX	SBO	xHR	xBA	RC/G	RAR	R$
Pos	95	02 2TM	378	50	86	24	56	4	228	233	226	319	458	777	12	60	31	0.34	38	18	44	179	62	7%	25	237	5.71	6.3	$11
Age	31	03 CIN	176	22	38	9	26	0	216	250	205	320	438	758	13	61	30	0.39	31	20	49	187	20	0%	11	243	5.49	-0.6	$4
Past Peak		04 2TM	* 499	76	120	32	97	7	240	167	250	330	493	823	12	62	32	0.35	29	19	53	190	86	7%	34	242	6.37	20.5	$10
Bats	Left	05 MIL	202	23	52	12	31	1	257	50	280	378	490	868	16	60	36	0.49	29	24	47	192	24	1%	14	251	7.36	12.4	$7
Reliability	11	06 2TM	241	37	55	18	36	2	228	220	230	324	498	822	12	63	28	0.38	29	19	52	194	49	3%	18	252	6.18	7.0	$7
DL	31	1st Half	104	14	22	9	19	0	212			281	529	810	9	64	22	0.27	28	22	50	226	17	0%	8	283	5.77	1.8	$3
BAvg Potl	40%	2nd Half	137	23	33	9	17	2	241			354	474	828	15	62	32	0.46	29	17	53	170	55	5%	10	229	6.46	5.1	$4
LIMA Plan	C	07 Proj	**394**	**56**	**92**	**27**	**62**	**3**	**233**			**335**	**483**	**818**	**13**	**62**	**30**	**0.40**	**29**	**21**	**50**	**189**	**49**	**3%**	**28**	**247**	**6.28**	**13.7**	**$12**

Assume 350 PA against RHP. Likely outcome, based on 2002-06: 23-53-.237, 60 walks (14%) and 130 Ks (62% Ct%). 50 more ABs against LHP, 4-9-.200, 3 walks, 24 Ks. Add 'em up, it equals this projection.

Broussard,Ben

Broussard,Ben			AB	R	H	HR	RBI	SB	Avg	vL	vR	OB	Slg	OPS	bb%	ct%	h%	Eye	G	L	F	PX	SX	SBO	xHR	xBA	RC/G	RAR	R$
Pos	30	02 CLE	* 452	64	109	20	55	4	241	167	255	325	431	756	11	78	27	0.55	44	17	39	121	70	4%	20	269	4.90	-12.9	$12
Age	30	03 CLE	* 506	67	123	19	68	8	243	175	276	299	417	716	7	80	27	0.39	39	22	38	107	100	9%	18	274	4.23	-17.3	$13
Peak		04 CLE	418	57	115	17	82	4	275	362	258	355	488	843	11	77	32	0.55	40	18	42	136	92	5%	18	275	6.12	13.5	$14
Bats	Left	05 CLE	466	59	119	19	68	2	255	225	264	303	464	767	6	79	29	0.33	41	22	37	136	80	4%	18	294	4.86	-3.2	$13
Reliability	59	06 2AL	432	61	125	21	63	2	289	177	308	330	484	813	6	76	34	0.25	40	19	41	123	47	3%	19	265	5.34	-1.0	$15
DL		1st Half	197	33	64	9	35	0	325			370	513	882	7	76	39	0.30	46	20	34	121	34	0%	8	269	6.30	4.6	$9
BAvg Potl	35%	2nd Half	235	28	61	12	28	2	260			296	460	755	5	76	29	0.21	35	19	46	126	47	6%	11	260	4.54	-6.1	$6
LIMA Plan	D+	07 Proj	**451**	**61**	**123**	**20**	**68**	**3**	**273**			**323**	**471**	**795**	**7**	**77**	**31**	**0.33**	**40**	**20**	**40**	**127**	**70**	**4%**	**19**	**274**	**5.20**	**-1.2**	**$14**

Branyan Lite: Whiffs 20% while raking RHPs (.308/.343/.505) but fans 1/3 of ABs in struggling vs LHP (.177/.261/.355). Maybe more valuable in a full platoon, but BA success vs RHP in '06 was driven by 36% Hit Rate.

Brown,Emil

Brown,Emil			AB	R	H	HR	RBI	SB	Avg	vL	vR	OB	Slg	OPS	bb%	ct%	h%	Eye	G	L	F	PX	SX	SBO	xHR	xBA	RC/G	RAR	R$
Pos	79	02 aaa	422	48	106	10	48	9	251			298	391	689	6	82	28	0.37				91	105	11%	11		3.93	-20.9	$10
Age	32	03 aaa	369	44	96	10	47	14	260			298	406	704	5	83	29	0.32				93	112	20%	10		4.04	-15.4	$12
Past Peak		04 aaa	149	14	38	2	15	4	257			287	373	660	4	84	30	0.26				79	84	23%	3		3.54	-7.4	$3
Bats	Right	05 KC	545	75	156	17	86	10	286	315	273	344	455	799	8	80	33	0.44	42	24	34	110	108	7%	17	288	5.36	9.8	$20
Reliability	20	06 KC	527	77	151	15	81	6	287	236	308	358	457	816	10	82	33	0.62	44	18	38	113	75	6%	18	281	5.70	7.8	$17
DL		1st Half	247	32	70	6	37	3	283			349	445	795	9	84	32	0.63	42	17	41	107	66	9%	7	274	5.42	1.7	$7
BAvg Potl	50%	2nd Half	280	45	81	9	44	3	289			366	468	834	11	80	33	0.62	46	20	34	118	78	4%	10	286	5.96	6.1	$10
LIMA Plan	C	07 Proj	**481**	**64**	**130**	**13**	**69**	**5**	**270**			**331**	**431**	**762**	**8**	**82**	**31**	**0.50**	**44**	**20**	**36**	**106**	**78**	**7%**	**15**	**281**	**4.94**	**-1.1**	**$13**

At face value, 2005-06 were two very similar seasons, with one exception... An 80-point drop in BA vs LHP might be an aberration, but at 32, it's more likely a forewarning of a potential crack in the skills set.

Bruntlett,Eric

Bruntlett,Eric			AB	R	H	HR	RBI	SB	Avg	vL	vR	OB	Slg	OPS	bb%	ct%	h%	Eye	G	L	F	PX	SX	SBO	xHR	xBA	RC/G	RAR	R$
Pos	46	02 a/a	532	75	127	2	41	30	239			309	301	610	9	89	27	0.90				44	119	29%	5		3.40	-13.5	$13
Age	29	03 aaa	324	43	80	2	24	8	248			313	296	609	9	86	28	0.66				35	78	12%	3		3.21	-10.3	$6
Peak		04 aaa	332	38	73	5	28	11	219			276	313	589	7	83	25	0.45				56	115	19%	5		2.81	-15.9	$5
Bats	Right	05 HOU	109	19	24	4	14	7	220	295	125	286	413	699	8	77	25	0.40	31	28	41	122	172	39%	4	270	4.11	-1.5	$4
Reliability	15	06 HOU	* 192	21	47	1	16	5	245	350	241	341	313	653	13	81	30	0.78	41	20	38	52	57	13%	2	235	3.90	-4.1	$7
DL		1st Half	78	6	22	0	9	2	282			364	359	723	11	86	33	0.91	38	21	41	62	44	8%	1	252	4.81	0.5	$2
BAvg Potl	50%	2nd Half	114	15	25	1	7	3	219			326	281	606	14	78	27	0.72	48	19	32	45	60	16%	2	227	3.23	-5.0	$1
LIMA Plan	F	07 Proj	**125**	**16**	**29**	**2**	**12**	**5**	**231**			**312**	**339**	**650**	**10**	**81**	**27**	**0.61**	**37**	**23**	**39**	**71**	**104**	**20%**	**2**	**251**	**3.71**	**-3.3**	**$2**

0-10-.277 in 119 AB at HOU. Good speed in AAA and '04-05 in HOU. The question: Can he get on base? Underwhelming BPIs limit BA potential, maybe with enough walks to reach a .340 OBP. Make a reserve pick.

Buck,John

Buck,John			AB	R	H	HR	RBI	SB	Avg	vL	vR	OB	Slg	OPS	bb%	ct%	h%	Eye	G	L	F	PX	SX	SBO	xHR	xBA	RC/G	RAR	R$
Pos	2	02 aa	448	38	108	10	70	2	241			280	382	661	5	83	27	0.32				92	60	7%	11		3.57	-3.9	$8
Age	26	03 aaa	274	29	68	2	35	1	248			280	350	630	4	82	29	0.25				75	77	2%	4		3.20	-8.0	$4
Pre-Peak		04 2TM	* 465	61	118	22	58	1	254	222	241	300	437	737	6	77	29	0.28	45	16	39	113	38	3%	20	254	4.37	4.2	$12
Bats	Right	05 KC	401	40	97	12	47	2	242	310	214	283	389	672	5	77	29	0.24	44	17	40	103	51	5%	13	247	3.60	-5.1	$7
Reliability	49	06 KC	371	37	91	11	50	0	245	246	245	295	396	691	7	77	29	0.31	45	20	35	101	32	2%	12	258	3.91	-5.5	$6
DL		1st Half	171	22	44	7	23	0	257			314	439	752	8	79	29	0.39	41	22	37	116	33	2%	7	278	4.68	1.4	$4
BAvg Potl	45%	2nd Half	200	15	47	4	27	0	235			278	360	638	6	76	29	0.25	50	18	33	88	41	2%	5	244	3.23	-7.1	$2
LIMA Plan	D	07 Proj	**367**	**38**	**91**	**12**	**48**	**0**	**248**			**293**	**407**	**700**	**6**	**78**	**29**	**0.28**	**45**	**18**	**36**	**105**	**36**	**3%**	**12**	**258**	**3.98**	**-2.9**	**$7**

Catchers often bloom late as hitters, but not much reason for optimism for now. Consistently low BPIs, especially a sub-80% ct%, set a .250-ish BA cap. Power promise of 2004 faded with a big 2H jump in GB%.

PATRICK DAVITT

Burke,Chris

Burke,Chris			AB	R	H	HR	RBI	SB	Avg	vL	vR	OB	Slg	OPS	bb%	ct%	h%	Eye	G	L	F	PX	SX	SBO	xHR	xBA	RC/G	RAR	R$
Pos	48	02 aa	481	52	116	3	29	13	241			286	326	612	6	90	26	0.61				51	113	26%	4		3.28	-14.2	$7
Age	27	03 aa	549	69	147	3	32	26	269			322	345	667	7	91	29	0.92				46	124	23%	5		4.02	-4.2	$14
Peak		04 aaa	483	74	138	13	41	29	286			343	447	790	8	88	30	0.71				94	128	35%	13		5.30	13.5	$20
Bats	Right	05 HOU	* 408	60	104	7	34	18	254	265	239	304	384	688	7	82	29	0.40	38	19	42	87	137	24%	9	256	3.98	-7.0	$12
Reliability	30	06 HOU	366	58	101	9	40	11	276	327	257	326	418	744	7	79	33	0.35	36	23	41	95	102	13%	10	258	4.62	0.2	$12
DL	15	1st Half	150	26	46	4	21	6	307			362	493	855	8	81	36	0.45	30	30	40	125	113	15%	5	293	6.11	6.2	$7
BAvg Potl	35%	2nd Half	216	32	55	5	19	5	255			300	366	666	6	78	31	0.29	40	17	42	73	81	11%	5	229	3.55	-6.7	$5
LIMA Plan	C	07 Proj	**419**	**63**	**110**	**9**	**39**	**16**	**263**			**314**	**400**	**714**	**7**	**82**	**30**	**0.42**	**37**	**21**	**42**	**89**	**124**	**21%**	**10**	**261**	**4.30**	**-3.4**	**$13**

Battled shoulder woes all year.
PRO: first-half LD, OBA
CON: 2H LD, drop in SBO, ct%.
Will need to improve plate patience and run more often to make an impact.
DN: .250, under 10 SB

Burnitz,Jeromy

Burnitz,Jeromy			AB	R	H	HR	RBI	SB	Avg	vL	vR	OB	Slg	OPS	bb%	ct%	h%	Eye	G	L	F	PX	SX	SBO	xHR	xBA	RC/G	RAR	R$
Pos	9	02 NYM	479	65	103	19	54	10	215	174	229	300	365	665	11	72	26	0.43	38	16	46	104	71	13%	19	226	3.66	-24.6	$11
Age	38	03 2NL	464	63	111	31	77	5	239	250	235	293	487	780	7	76	25	0.31	33	21	45	156	57	10%	26	285	4.91	-9.8	$16
Decline		04 COL	541	94	153	37	110	5	283	279	285	352	558	910	10	77	31	0.46	40	17	43	167	84	8%	32	295	6.76	22.7	$26
Bats	Left	05 CHC	605	84	156	24	87	5	258	236	267	322	435	756	9	82	28	0.52	43	18	39	111	71	6%	22	278	4.80	-7.9	$19
Reliability	30	06 PIT	313	35	72	16	49	1	230	224	231	281	422	702	7	76	25	0.30	43	15	41	115	33	3%	14	249	3.93	-8.0	$7
DL		1st Half	225	25	52	12	33	1	231			270	440	710	5	76	25	0.22	41	17	42	130	37	5%	11	260	3.97	-5.5	$5
BAvg Potl	50%	2nd Half	88	10	20	4	16	0	227			306	375	681	10	78	25	0.53	49	11	39	80	18	0%	3	211	3.82	-2.5	$2
LIMA Plan	F	07 Proj	**293**	**38**	**71**	**13**	**43**	**1**	**243**			**308**	**416**	**724**	**9**	**78**	**27**	**0.43**	**43**	**16**	**41**	**105**	**53**	**3%**	**11**	**252**	**4.34**	**-6.1**	**$7**

Two years removed from COL, the slide continues. Struggled vs RHP, and GB% remains high. High 1st-half PX not sustained in 2nd half, when playing time dropped sharply. Expect drop-off to continue in 2007.

Burrell,Pat

Burrell,Pat			AB	R	H	HR	RBI	SB	Avg	vL	vR	OB	Slg	OPS	bb%	ct%	h%	Eye	G	L	F	PX	SX	SBO	xHR	xBA	RC/G	RAR	R$
Pos	7	02 PHI	586	96	165	37	116	1	282	311	274	376	544	921	13	74	32	0.58	33	23	44	181	54	1%	36	298	7.22	13.7	$27
Age	30	03 PHI	522	57	109	21	64	0	209	198	212	305	404	709	12	73	25	0.51	35	22	44	136	51	0%	23	262	4.39	-19.4	$7
Peak		04 PHI	448	66	115	24	84	2	257	271	253	367	455	822	15	71	31	0.60	35	20	45	130	43	1%	24	247	6.00	7.3	$16
Bats	Right	05 PHI	562	78	158	32	117	0	281	318	269	389	504	892	15	72	34	0.62	31	24	45	153	27	0%	33	273	7.00	26.3	$24
Reliability	78	06 PHI	462	80	119	29	95	0	258	290	244	388	502	890	18	72	30	0.75	31	21	48	158	32	0%	30	268	7.03	24.0	$18
DL		1st Half	238	37	60	19	54	0	252			375	534	909	16	71	27	0.69	33	16	51	175	15	0%	18	266	7.16	13.3	$10
BAvg Potl	50%	2nd Half	224	43	59	10	41	0	263			400	469	869	19	72	32	0.81	30	26	45	139	49	0%	12	266	6.90	10.7	$8
LIMA Plan	B	07 Proj	**524**	**83**	**138**	**30**	**103**	**0**	**263**			**382**	**489**	**871**	**16**	**72**	**31**	**0.68**	**32**	**22**	**46**	**150**	**39**	**0%**	**31**	**267**	**6.74**	**20.6**	**$20**

Continued foot problems limited playing time. h% normalization led to decrease in BA, but xBA and increased plate patience say BA should rebound. FB% rise means he should return to 30-HR range if healthy.

Bynum,Freddie

Bynum,Freddie			AB	R	H	HR	RBI	SB	Avg	vL	vR	OB	Slg	OPS	bb%	ct%	h%	Eye	G	L	F	PX	SX	SBO	xHR	xBA	RC/G	RAR	R$
Pos	7	02	0	0	0	0	0	0	0							0							0		0				
Age	27	03 aa	510	66	113	4	46	17	223			284	299	582	8	77	28	0.37				51	129	20%	5		2.66	-44.5	$8
Peak		04 a/a	523	62	124	2	37	30	237			283	304	587	6	81	29	0.33				47	130	33%	4		2.71	-39.9	$11
Bats	Left	05 aaa	378	44	90	2	31	18	238			292	320	612	7	83	28	0.44				55	133	28%	3		3.13	-22.1	$5
Reliability	4	06 CHC	136	20	35	4	12	8	257	130	283	303	456	759	6	68	35	0.20	45	25	30	127	143	40%	4	259	5.13	-0.5	$5
DL	57	1st Half	73	9	19	2	6	6	260			280	425	705	3	67	36	0.08	54	26	20	91	146	50%	1	254	4.16	-2.4	$3
BAvg Potl	30%	2nd Half	63	11	16	2	6	2	254			329	492	821	10	68	34	0.35	36	24	40	168	128	29%	2	268	6.21	1.8	$2
LIMA Plan	D	07 Proj	**177**	**24**	**45**	**3**	**15**	**9**	**255**			**307**	**398**	**705**	**7**	**74**	**33**	**0.29**	**43**	**25**	**32**	**94**	**144**	**31%**	**4**	**258**	**4.23**	**-6.1**	**$5**

High SX and SBO are enticing, but beware the inflated h%, low OBA and ct%. Those are major warning signs. The magic number is a .300 OBA, which he barely managed to reach in '06. He needs to build on that.

Byrd,Marlon

Byrd,Marlon			AB	R	H	HR	RBI	SB	Avg	vL	vR	OB	Slg	OPS	bb%	ct%	h%	Eye	G	L	F	PX	SX	SBO	xHR	xBA	RC/G	RAR	R$
Pos	8	02 aaa	538	85	147	12	52	13	273			325	429	754	7	83	31	0.46				104	133	11%	14		4.81	-0.2	$17
Age	29	03 PHI	495	86	150	7	45	11	303	315	299	360	418	778	8	81	36	0.47	50	25	25	80	124	8%	10	286	5.16	2.5	$18
Peak		04 PHI	* 498	58	112	7	46	4	225	213	232	269	325	594	6	83	26	0.35	58	14	28	65	79	9%	8	258	2.81	-28.3	$5
Bats	Right	05 2NL	* 329	38	94	8	38	8	287	326	228	338	434	772	7	82	33	0.44	38	22	40	100	92	11%	9	274	5.01	4.2	$11
Reliability	10	06 WAS	* 352	44	79	10	42	6	223	188	242	293	361	654	9	78	26	0.44	45	21	34	87	71	11%	11	256	3.54	-9.8	$6
DL	26	1st Half	183	27	43	4	17	3	235			317	355	672	11	77	29	0.51	45	20	35	79	81	12%	5	245	3.89	-3.1	$3
BAvg Potl	60%	2nd Half	169	17	36	6	25	3	211			266	368	634	7	79	23	0.36	40	30	30	96	54	11%	6		3.16	-6.7	$3
LIMA Plan	F	07 Proj	**125**	**15**	**30**	**3**	**14**	**2**	**241**			**299**	**381**	**680**	**8**	**80**	**28**	**0.42**	**46**	**20**	**34**	**89**	**88**	**11%**	**3**	**267**	**3.87**	**-2.5**	**$3**

5-18-.223 in 197 AB at WAS. Rising GB% and a lack of speed resulted in poor BA. Variations in h% and BA vs LHP over the years have defined his success. At 29, opportunities are going to get tougher to come by.

Byrnes,Eric

Byrnes,Eric			AB	R	H	HR	RBI	SB	Avg	vL	vR	OB	Slg	OPS	bb%	ct%	h%	Eye	G	L	F	PX	SX	SBO	xHR	xBA	RC/G	RAR	R$
Pos	8	02 OAK	* 213	36	48	6	23	7	225	279	216	257	376	632	4	87	23	0.32	39	17	44	86	153	21%	5	263	3.22	-10.1	$5
Age	31	03 OAK	414	64	109	12	51	10	263	286	251	331	459	790	9	83	29	0.59	38	19	44	119	137	12%	12	280	5.38	7.7	$13
Past Peak		04 OAK	569	91	161	20	73	17	283	344	260	337	467	804	7	80	32	0.41	34	18	47	117	122	12%	21	264	5.37	10.7	$21
Bats	Right	05 2TM	412	49	93	10	40	7	226	263	205	282	371	653	7	83	25	0.45	32	20	48	96	102	10%	11	256	3.58	-10.6	$7
Reliability	38	06 ARI	562	82	150	26	79	25	267	323	244	309	482	791	6	84	28	0.39	38	18	44	124	120	24%	23	287	5.06	10.0	$23
DL		1st Half	234	37	67	12	30	8	286			343	534	877	8	80	31	0.43	34	19	47	155	97	17%	12	293	6.27	12.0	$10
BAvg Potl	50%	2nd Half	328	45	83	14	49	17	253			284	445	729	4	88	25	0.34	40	17	43	104	123	30%	11	284	4.27	-1.7	$12
LIMA Plan	B	07 Proj	**538**	**77**	**140**	**20**	**68**	**18**	**260**			**307**	**450**	**757**	**6**	**83**	**28**	**0.41**	**36**	**18**	**46**	**115**	**126**	**18%**	**19**	**275**	**4.74**	**2.9**	**$19**

SB spike was more a product of opportunity than skill. Power spike seems like a 1st half aberration - PX dropped and GB rose in 2nd half despite more HRs. This is shaky ground. Expect a drop-off.

Cabrera,Melky

Cabrera,Melky			AB	R	H	HR	RBI	SB	Avg	vL	vR	OB	Slg	OPS	bb%	ct%	h%	Eye	G	L	F	PX	SX	SBO	xHR	xBA	RC/G	RAR	R$
Pos	7	02	0	0	0	0	0	0	0							0							0		0				
Age	22	03	0	0	0	0	0	0	0							0							0		0				
Growth		04	0	0	0	0	0	0	0							0							0		0				
Bats	Both	05 a/a	523	63	133	12	68	12	255			297	371	669	6	86	28	0.44				72	100	11%	11		3.71	-20.3	$14
Reliability	0	06 NYY	* 582	93	175	11	73	15	301	286	278	372	423	794	10	89	33	0.98	49	17	33	73	99	11%	13	279	5.50	5.2	$20
DL		1st Half	283	42	88	6	42	6	312			379	439	817	10	92	32	1.35	54	12	34	68	95	9%	6	276	5.77	4.6	$11
BAvg Potl	55%	2nd Half	299	51	87	5	31	9	291			365	408	773	10	85	33	0.80	47	20	33	79	84	12%	7	277	5.25	0.6	$10
LIMA Plan	D	07 Proj	**298**	**43**	**84**	**6**	**37**	**7**	**282**			**342**	**400**	**742**	**8**	**87**	**31**	**0.72**	**49**	**18**	**33**	**72**	**92**	**11%**	**6**	**275**	**4.75**	**-2.3**	**$9**

7-50-.280 in 460 AB at NYY. Solid plate patience led to a strong debut for the 22-year old. Needs to hit fewer ground balls to become a power contributor, but that could come as he fills out.

Cabrera,Miguel

Cabrera,Miguel			AB	R	H	HR	RBI	SB	Avg	vL	vR	OB	Slg	OPS	bb%	ct%	h%	Eye	G	L	F	PX	SX	SBO	xHR	xBA	RC/G	RAR	R$
Pos	5	02	0	0	0	0	0	0	0							0							0		0				
Age	24	03 FLA	* 580	82	179	20	117	8	309	364	247	368	519	886	9	78	37	0.43	48	20	32	145	95	10%	23	303	6.56	36.9	$26
Growth		04 FLA	603	101	177	33	112	5	294	262	302	365	512	878	10	75	34	0.46	45	19	35	138	70	4%	31	281	6.43	23.0	$27
Bats	Right	05 FLA	613	106	198	33	116	1	323	304	329	387	561	948	9	80	36	0.51	38	24	37	154	59	1%	31	311	7.22	39.7	$32
Reliability	70	06 FLA	576	112	195	26	114	9	339	321	344	424	568	992	13	81	38	0.80	40	24	35	144	74	7%	28	312	8.02	38.3	$32
DL		1st Half	274	57	94	12	52	7	343			438	573	1010	14	82	38	0.94	42	22	36	144	79	12%	13	312	8.33	20.6	$16
BAvg Potl	35%	2nd Half	302	55	101	14	62	2	334			412	563	975	12	80	38	0.68	38	27	35	143	62	3%	14	313	7.73	17.7	$16
LIMA Plan	D	07 Proj	**613**	**110**	**199**	**29**	**120**	**6**	**324**			**400**	**551**	**951**	**11**	**80**	**37**	**0.61**	**41**	**23**	**36**	**145**	**74**	**5%**	**30**	**306**	**7.39**	**36.9**	**$32**

Power took a slight dip, but you gotta love the improved plate patience. High h% means his BA will come down a bit, but he's a legitimate .300 hitter. Plus a few SBs - what more could you want?

Cabrera,Orlando

Cabrera,Orlando			AB	R	H	HR	RBI	SB	Avg	vL	vR	OB	Slg	OPS	bb%	ct%	h%	Eye	G	L	F	PX	SX	SBO	xHR	xBA	RC/G	RAR	R$
Pos	6	02 MON	563	64	148	7	56	25	263	264	263	321	380	701	8	91	28	0.91	45	19	36	82	100	22%	11	291	4.40	8.4	$17
Age	32	03 MON	626	95	186	17	80	24	297	311	293	351	460	811	8	90	31	0.81	40	21	39	101	116	15%	18	301	5.53	24.7	$27
Past Peak		04 2TM	621	75	163	10	62	17	262	295	249	307	382	689	6	91	27	0.74	44	18	38	72	104	14%	12	279	4.14	-2.8	$15
Bats	Right	05 ANA	540	70	139	8	57	21	257	242	266	306	365	671	7	91	27	0.76	41	19	39	67	123	17%	9	273	3.96	-9.5	$15
Reliability	83	06 ANA	607	95	171	9	72	27	282	243	297	337	404	741	8	90	30	0.88	39	17	43	79	114	18%	12	270	4.82	7.0	$20
DL	15	1st Half	298	54	91	5	44	12	305			365	436	801	9	92	32	1.22	37	17	46	81	112	14%	6	271	5.57	9.4	$12
BAvg Potl	60%	2nd Half	309	41	80	4	28	15	259			310	372	682	7	89	28	0.66	41	18	41	77	102	22%	6	269	4.08	-3.0	$8
LIMA Plan	B	07 Proj	**585**	**82**	**158**	**9**	**64**	**24**	**270**			**322**	**390**	**712**	**7**	**90**	**29**	**0.80**	**41**	**18**	**41**	**76**	**113**	**18%**	**11**	**275**	**4.45**	**-0.3**	**$17**

Value is driven by SBs; skills are flat but as long as they let him run, he'll have value. Hit rate correction and slight decline in plate patience led to 2nd-half BA fade. Pay for .270; anything else is gravy.

DAVE ADLER

Cairo,Miguel		AB	R	H	HR	RBI	SB	Avg	vL	vR	OB	Slg	OPS	bb%	ct%	h%	Eye	G	L	F	PX	SX	SBO	xHR	xBA	RC/G	RAR	R$
Pos 4	02 STL	184	28	46	2	23	1	250	273	237	299	353	653	7	80	30	0.36	47	18	36	73	103	4%	3	250	3.55	-4.7	$4
Age 32	03 STL	261	41	64	5	32	4	245	244	246	281	375	657	5	89	26	0.43	40	18	42	81	120	9%	5	271	3.62	-6.1	$6
Past Peak	04 NYY	360	48	105	6	42	11	292	336	267	325	417	742	5	86	32	0.37	44	20	36	73	128	15%	6	272	4.54	4.7	$11
Bats Right	05 NYM	327	31	82	2	19	13	251	191	273	292	324	616	5	91	27	0.61	44	22	34	53	88	20%	4	275	3.30	-12.3	$6
Reliability 35	06 NYY	222	28	53	0	30	13	239	279	221	281	320	601	6	86	28	0.42	53	16	31	55	148	27%	1	263	3.05	-7.1	$5
DL 34 17	1st Half	109	14	25	0	12	6	229			282	294	576	7	83	28	0.42	49	16	35	47	130	26%	1	237	2.70	-4.7	$2
BAvg Potl 60%	2nd Half	113	14	28	0	18	7	248			280	345	625	4	89	28	0.42	55	17	28	63	155	29%	1	287	3.37	-2.5	$3
LIMA Plan F	07 Proj	232	28	60	1	26	10	259			298	348	646	5	87	29	0.44	48	18	33	60	124	21%	3	269	3.55	-3.8	$6

Falling LD% hurt his BA. Gains in SX and SBO% suggest value, even at age 32. Poor OBA shows why he'll again have to rely on injuries to get playing time.

Callaspo,Alberto		AB	R	H	HR	RBI	SB	Avg	vL	vR	OB	Slg	OPS	bb%	ct%	h%	Eye	G	L	F	PX	SX	SBO	xHR	xBA	RC/G	RAR	R$
Pos 6	02	0	0	0	0	0	0	0							0							0		0				
Age 24	03	0	0	0	0	0	0	0							0							0		0				
Growth	04 aa	550	62	139	4	39	12	253			301	325	626	6	96	26	1.81				45	70	19%	6		3.69	-10.1	$9
Bats Right	05 a/a	557	60	147	8	59	8	264			299	357	656	5	96	26	1.27				56	57	17%	8		3.85	-6.9	$12
Reliability 22	06 ARI *	532	74	162	6	59	6	305	278	208	362	427	789	8	95	31	1.78	46	8	46	63	94	8%	7	247	5.50	16.9	$16
DL	1st Half	303	41	94	2	28	5	310			369	396	765	8	97	32	3.11				46	87	10%	3		5.31	8.0	$9
BAvg Potl 60%	2nd Half	229	33	68	4	31	1	297			353	467	821	8	92	31	1.11	46	8	46	88	91	5%	4	264	5.79	9.1	$7
LIMA Plan D	07 Proj	112	14	30	1	12	1	268			317	368	686	7	95	27	1.47	46	8	46	56	83	12%	2	239	4.28	0.3	$2

0-6-.238 in 42 AB with ARI. Outstanding Eye and ct% in minors hint at BA potential, but needs to show skills in majors. Even if he gets ABs, lack of power and speed limits value.

Cameron,Mike		AB	R	H	HR	RBI	SB	Avg	vL	vR	OB	Slg	OPS	bb%	ct%	h%	Eye	G	L	F	PX	SX	SBO	xHR	xBA	RC/G	RAR	R$
Pos 8	02 SEA	545	84	130	25	80	31	239	239	238	335	442	777	13	68	31	0.45	37	17	46	144	135	25%	27	240	5.46	11.4	$22
Age 34	03 SEA	534	74	135	18	76	17	253	286	240	339	431	770	12	74	31	0.51	32	28	40	122	113	16%	20	266	5.23	7.8	$17
Past Peak	04 NYM	493	76	114	30	76	22	231	216	235	311	479	790	10	71	26	0.40	31	16	53	167	108	25%	29	259	5.36	10.8	$20
Bats Right	05 NYM	308	47	84	12	39	13	273	311	261	335	477	813	9	72	34	0.34	42	21	38	151	126	18%	14	277	5.71	10.1	$13
Reliability 58	06 SD	552	88	148	22	83	25	268	252	273	352	482	833	11	74	32	0.50	38	17	45	137	134	22%	23	260	6.08	26.5	$23
DL 23 78	1st Half	233	41	60	9	30	12	258			337	433	771	11	70	33	0.41	47	17	36	117	125	21%	10	247	5.23	5.4	$9
BAvg Potl 40%	2nd Half	319	47	88	13	53	13	276			362	517	879	12	77	32	0.59	32	17	51	151	120	23%	14	271	6.68	20.9	$13
LIMA Plan B+	07 Proj	518	80	136	22	75	23	263			341	478	819	11	73	32	0.44	37	19	44	145	135	21%	24	263	5.85	19.8	$21

Good health and improved plate discipline delivered 20-20 season. 2H trend in FB% and PX say he's got plenty of pop left, but strikes out too much to get BA above .270.

Cano,Robinson		AB	R	H	HR	RBI	SB	Avg	vL	vR	OB	Slg	OPS	bb%	ct%	h%	Eye	G	L	F	PX	SX	SBO	xHR	xBA	RC/G	RAR	R$
Pos 4	02	0	0	0	0	0	0	0							0							0		0				
Age 24	03 aa	164	18	43	1	12	0	263			294	346	640	4	92	28	0.59				54	54	0%	2		3.55	-3.4	$2
Growth	04 a/a	508	58	135	12	66	2	267			316	413	729	7	89	28	0.67				83	71	7%	11		4.57	3.3	$11
Bats Right	05 NYY *	630	95	189	17	83	1	299	270	305	322	466	788	3	88	32	0.27	50	21	29	103	76	3%	17	310	4.95	14.3	$21
Reliability 30	06 NYY	482	62	165	15	78	5	342	287	363	366	525	891	4	89	36	0.33	52	20	28	112	66	6%	15	321	6.10	24.8	$20
DL 42	1st Half	271	34	88	4	27	3	325			351	439	790	4	90	35	0.39	56	19	25	72	70	6%	5	296	5.05	6.7	$8
BAvg Potl 35%	2nd Half	211	28	77	11	51	2	365			385	635	1020	3	88	38	0.27	47	21	32	164	46	4%	10	352	7.49	17.7	$12
LIMA Plan D+	07 Proj	557	73	176	20	85	3	316			343	512	855	4	89	33	0.37	50	20	29	116	69	4%	19	323	5.72	24.2	$21

H% the reason he competed for batting title in first full year. 2H G/L/F says 20 HR are within reach, but Eye and bb% say no way he repeats .340. In short, expect more power, less BA.

Cantu,Jorge		AB	R	H	HR	RBI	SB	Avg	vL	vR	OB	Slg	OPS	bb%	ct%	h%	Eye	G	L	F	PX	SX	SBO	xHR	xBA	RC/G	RAR	R$
Pos 4	02 aa	512	45	122	3	39	2	238			267	322	589	4	88	27	0.33				62	44	8%	6		2.83	-21.7	$4
Age 25	03 a/a	358	39	93	6	45	2	260			291	391	683	4	88	28	0.37				88	57	8%	8		3.88	-4.1	$7
Pre-Peak	04 TAM *	541	76	157	20	89	3	290	373	270	320	505	825	4	82	32	0.25	46	20	34	140	79	0%	21	310	5.45	20.7	$18
Bats Right	05 TAM	598	73	171	28	117	1	286	256	296	308	497	805	3	86	29	0.23	42	21	37	128	44	1%	24	312	5.03	15.1	$22
Reliability 45	06 TAM	413	40	103	14	62	1	249	233	256	294	404	698	6	78	29	0.29	42	20	38	97	50	2%	13	255	3.93	-2.3	$8
DL 41	1st Half	142	18	42	3	23	0	296			338	430	767	6	81	35	0.33	43	21	36	93	29	0%	4	267	4.86	2.9	$4
BAvg Potl 45%	2nd Half	271	22	61	11	39	1	225			271	391	662	6	76	26	0.27	41	19	40	99	51	4%	10	248	3.43	-5.7	$4
LIMA Plan C	07 Proj	529	59	151	21	84	1	285			320	475	794	5	82	32	0.27	42	20	38	117	49	2%	20	286	5.04	13.8	$16

Broke a bone in his foot in April and it was all downhill. Huge dropoff in PX and xBA aided by decline in ct%. If there's reason for optimism, bb% improved.

Carroll,Jamey		AB	R	H	HR	RBI	SB	Avg	vL	vR	OB	Slg	OPS	bb%	ct%	h%	Eye	G	L	F	PX	SX	SBO	xHR	xBA	RC/G	RAR	R$
Pos 4	02 MON *	501	62	127	8	45	6	253	400	295	302	363	666	7	91	27	0.76				67	84	13%	8	0	3.89	-7.8	$10
Age 33	03 MON	227	31	59	1	10	5	260	268	255	317	326	643	8	83	31	0.49	47	22	31	49	95	11%	2	254	3.53	-5.9	$4
Past Peak	04 MON	219	36	63	0	16	5	288	250	310	378	370	748	13	90	32	1.52	48	23	29	57	103	8%	2	291	5.31	4.3	$6
Bats Right	05 WAS	303	44	76	0	22	3	251	293	235	326	284	610	10	82	31	0.62	53	26	21	27	76	7%	1	261	3.23	-12.1	$4
Reliability 9	06 COL	463	84	139	5	36	10	300	359	283	376	404	780	11	86	34	0.85	49	23	29	64	95	14%	7	281	5.39	10.3	$15
DL	1st Half	213	39	70	3	13	5	329			399	441	840	11	85	37	0.81	56	23	21	65	101	15%	3	296	6.06	8.6	$8
BAvg Potl 50%	2nd Half	250	45	69	2	23	5	276			356	372	728	11	86	31	0.89	43	22	35	62	94	12%	4	268	4.81	1.5	$7
LIMA Plan D	07 Proj	219	36	61	1	17	4	279			355	361	716	11	86	32	0.82	49	24	27	54	100	11%	2	277	4.63	0.4	$5

Career year didn't amount to much. xBA says .300 season was a fluke, aided by H%. With no speed or power, BPIs say he reverts back to an aging utility infielder. Or a frog.

Casey,Sean		AB	R	H	HR	RBI	SB	Avg	vL	vR	OB	Slg	OPS	bb%	ct%	h%	Eye	G	L	F	PX	SX	SBO	xHR	xBA	RC/G	RAR	R$
Pos 3	02 CIN	433	58	115	7	44	2	266	231	275	333	372	705	9	89	28	0.94	48	23	30	72	53	2%	9	292	4.45	-14.3	$10
Age 32	03 CIN	573	71	167	14	80	4	291	320	278	349	408	758	8	90	31	0.88	45	27	27	65	80	2%	12	306	4.93	-9.3	$18
Past Peak	04 CIN	571	101	185	24	99	2	324	306	332	374	534	909	7	94	32	1.28	43	23	34	115	74	1%	21	337	6.57	9.3	$27
Bats Left	05 CIN	529	75	165	9	58	2	312	335	298	369	423	793	8	91	33	1.00	52	19	29	73	53	1%	11	290	5.40	-2.9	$18
Reliability 23	06 2TM	397	47	108	8	59	0	272	287	266	328	388	716	8	89	29	0.77	44	23	33	71	28	1%	9	284	4.45	-14.3	$9
DL 44	1st Half	131	17	38	3	15	0	290			354	443	797	9	89	31	0.93	43	20	38	97	27	0%	4	290	5.48	-0.8	$3
BAvg Potl 60%	2nd Half	266	30	70	5	44	0	263			315	361	676	7	89	28	0.69	45	24	31	58	30	1%	5	281	3.94	-13.7	$6
LIMA Plan C	07 Proj	515	69	155	12	71	0	301			357	430	786	8	90	32	0.90	46	22	32	78	30	0%	13	292	5.27	-4.2	$16

Ct% remains solid, though fading. xBA says drop in BA was a fluke. Dropoff in 2H Eye is thanks to 3 walks in his first 93 PA in AL. Return to .300 a possibility, but 2004 power is long gone.

Castilla,Vinny		AB	R	H	HR	RBI	SB	Avg	vL	vR	OB	Slg	OPS	bb%	ct%	h%	Eye	G	L	F	PX	SX	SBO	xHR	xBA	RC/G	RAR	R$
Pos 5	02 ATL	543	56	126	12	61	4	232	224	233	262	348	610	4	87	25	0.32	43	17	41	72	80	5%	11	259	2.96	-26.6	$9
Age 39	03 ATL	542	65	150	22	76	1	277	290	273	310	461	771	5	84	29	0.30	52	16	33	110	56	2%	19	286	4.75	7.6	$17
Decline	04 COL	583	93	158	35	131	0	271	267	273	330	535	865	8	81	28	0.45	41	17	42	160	53	0%	31	302	6.07	16.8	$25
Bats Right	05 WAS	494	53	125	12	66	4	253	314	234	313	403	716	8	83	28	0.52	43	18	39	103	62	5%	14	275	4.39	-5.7	$11
Reliability 6	06 2NL	275	26	63	5	27	0	229	203	239	254	320	574	3	82	26	0.18	41	21	38	57	28	0%	5	240	2.34	-26.2	$2
DL	1st Half	217	22	51	3	20	0	235			265	323	588	4	83	27	0.24	41	20	39	58	30	0%	4	241	2.61	-18.7	$2
BAvg Potl	2nd Half	58	4	12	2	7	0	207			207	310	517	0	79	23	0.00	41	24	35	52	15	0%	1	240	1.30	-7.6	$0
LIMA Plan	07 Proj	0	0	0	0	0	0	0																				

PX, bb% and Eye in a free fall, then around the bend, over the hill and out into the night.
Avg season in Colorado:
34-103-.294
Avg season everywhere else:
14-61-.249

Castillo,Jose		AB	R	H	HR	RBI	SB	Avg	vL	vR	OB	Slg	OPS	bb%	ct%	h%	Eye	G	L	F	PX	SX	SBO	xHR	xBA	RC/G	RAR	R$
Pos 4	02	0	0	0	0	0	0	0							0							0		0				
Age 26	03 aa	498	62	137	4	60	17	275			324	363	687	7	86	31	0.52				59	107	20%	6		4.06	-3.1	$14
Pre-Peak	04 PIT	383	44	98	8	39	3	256	267	253	298	368	666	6	76	32	0.25	59	16	24	75	75	5%	9	251	3.55	-11.9	$7
Bats Right	05 PIT	370	49	99	11	53	2	268	258	271	310	416	727	6	84	29	0.39	46	23	31	90	76	5%	10	288	4.34	-2.4	$11
Reliability 52	06 PIT	518	54	131	14	65	6	253	259	251	296	382	679	6	81	29	0.33	46	19	34	81	51	8%	14	259	3.72	-13.5	$11
DL 68	1st Half	264	35	73	11	42	4	277			330	458	788	7	84	29	0.51	45	17	38	106	54	10%	10	280	5.11	3.9	$9
BAvg Potl 45%	2nd Half	254	19	58	3	23	2	228			260	303	564	4	78	28	0.19	47	22	31	53	42	5%	4	237	2.20	-18.6	$2
LIMA Plan F	07 Proj	231	26	59	5	28	3	255			298	377	675	6	81	29	0.32	48	20	31	77	70	8%	6	264	3.69	-6.0	$5

Tale of two halves: One says he's a starting 2B and the other says he's a utility infielder. 2H dips in bb%, ct% and PX all worrisome. At age 26, running out of time to prove himself. We're betting against.

JEFFREY TOMICH

68

Castillo,Luis

	Year	AB	R	H	HR	RBI	SB	Avg	vL	vR	OB	Slg	OPS	bb%	ct%	h%	Eye	G	L	F	PX	SX	SBO	xHR	xBA	RC/G	RAR	R$
Pos 4	02 FLA	606	86	185	2	39	48	305	329	297	363	361	724	8	87	35	0.72	61	21	18	37	134	29%	4	289	4.60	3.2	$27
Age 31	03 FLA	595	99	187	6	39	21	314	320	312	380	397	777	10	90	34	1.05	56	25	18	48	111	18%	7	309	5.30	15.0	$22
Past Peak	04 FLA	564	91	164	2	47	21	291	308	285	374	348	722	12	88	33	1.10	65	17	19	32	131	11%	3	278	4.81	3.1	$18
Bats Both	05 FLA	439	72	132	4	30	10	301	423	259	391	374	764	13	93	32	2.03	63	22	15	41	96	10%	4	312	5.47	11.2	$14
Reliability 81	06 MIN	584	84	173	3	49	25	296	256	316	358	370	728	9	90	33	0.97	61	18	21	44	117	18%	5	289	4.74	10.2	$18
DL	1st Half	276	43	75	2	29	7	272			328	341	668	8	92	29	1.05	67	15	19	43	95	14%	3	290	4.05	-0.6	$7
BAvg Potl 60%	2nd Half	308	41	98	1	20	18	318			384	396	780	10	88	36	0.92	57	20	23	46	126	21%	2	285	5.38	10.6	$11
LIMA Plan B+	07 Proj	565	86	169	4	43	22	299			371	375	747	10	90	33	1.17	62	19	19	44	115	16%	5	296	5.04	14.8	$18

At bats and more SBOs were all he needed for SB rebound. Leg pains nagged him all year, though, so further gains are iffy. There is some hidden latent power here; he could challenge his career high of 6.

Castro,Bernie

	Year	AB	R	H	HR	RBI	SB	Avg	vL	vR	OB	Slg	OPS	bb%	ct%	h%	Eye	G	L	F	PX	SX	SBO	xHR	xBA	RC/G	RAR	R$
Pos 4	02 aa	419	53	95	0	28	47	227			302	265	567	10	84	27	0.69				29	133	54%	2		2.77	-19.6	$14
Age 27	03 aaa	424	47	114	2	20	40	269			302	330	632	5	92	29	0.56				38	131	49%	3		3.43	-10.8	$15
Peak	04 aaa	308	31	70	0	16	14	228			268	257	525	5	92	25	0.69				20	96	31%	1		2.35	-19.5	$4
Bats Both	05 BAL *	582	83	164	1	38	41	281	200	308	333	336	669	7	91	31	0.84	61	21	18	37	132	27%	3	300	4.00	-2.1	$20
Reliability 18	06 WAS *	378	48	90	2	31	26	237	182	258	283	293	576	6	86	27	0.47	63	18	18	30	144	30%	2	276	2.72	-21.5	$9
DL	1st Half	189	20	44	2	12	13	231			268	287	555	5	86	26	0.36				30	121	30%	2		2.34	-12.9	$4
BAvg Potl 60%	2nd Half	189	28	46	0	19	13	243			297	300	597	7	87	28	0.58	63	18	18	29	155	29%	0	277	3.09	-8.6	$5
LIMA Plan F	07 Proj	197	25	49	1	14	14	249			297	303	600	6	89	28	0.60	63	19	18	32	137	32%	1	284	3.11	-8.7	$5

0-10-.227 in 110 AB at WAS. Combine high GB rate plus tremendous speed, xBA says he can do better. Not good enough in the field to play every day, but given enough at bats...
UP: .275, 25 SB

Castro,Juan

	Year	AB	R	H	HR	RBI	SB	Avg	vL	vR	OB	Slg	OPS	bb%	ct%	h%	Eye	G	L	F	PX	SX	SBO	xHR	xBA	RC/G	RAR	R$
Pos 65	02 CIN *	99	7	21	2	13	0	212	222	217	271	303	574	7	80	25	0.40	55	8	38	61	14	0%	2	184	2.50	-4.3	$1
Age 34	03 CIN	320	28	81	9	33	2	253	193	276	293	388	680	5	82	28	0.31	43	17	40	85	51	7%	9	252	3.72	-3.7	$6
Past Peak	04 CIN	299	36	73	5	26	1	244	238	247	278	378	656	4	83	28	0.27	45	16	40	90	80	2%	7	260	3.50	-5.6	$4
Bats Right	05 MIN	272	27	70	5	33	0	257	247	262	281	386	667	3	86	29	0.23	50	19	31	87	47	2%	6	281	3.58	-7.8	$5
Reliability 38	06 2TM	251	18	63	3	28	1	251	268	244	282	351	633	4	86	28	0.31	49	21	29	59	65	5%	3	271	3.25	-8.4	$3
DL 22	1st Half	169	10	39	1	14	1	231			257	302	559	3	85	27	0.24	53	20	27	42	69	5%	1	259	2.35	-10.5	$0
BAvg Potl 50%	2nd Half	82	8	24	2	14	0	293			333	451	785	6	87	32	0.45	41	24	35	93	63	5%	2	295	5.09	1.6	$2
LIMA Plan F	07 Proj	167	16	44	3	20	0	263			296	384	680	4	85	29	0.31	46	20	34	77	54	4%	3	271	3.77	-2.7	$3

xBA hints at a little more, but with no power or speed, he's strictly injury-replacement material for the desperate... though position flexibility may make him desperation-worthy.

Castro,Ramon

	Year	AB	R	H	HR	RBI	SB	Avg	vL	vR	OB	Slg	OPS	bb%	ct%	h%	Eye	G	L	F	PX	SX	SBO	xHR	xBA	RC/G	RAR	R$
Pos 2	02 FLA	101	11	24	6	18	0	238	160	263	330	455	786	12	76	25	0.58	34	21	45	140	0	0%	5	263	5.25	3.4	$3
Age 31	03 FLA	53	6	15	5	8	0	283	409	194	333	604	937	7	79	27	0.36	24	24	53	185	0	0%	4	346	6.71	3.6	$2
Past Peak	04 FLA *	312	31	56	4	28	4	179	143	134	254	279	532	9	81	21	0.52	32	11	58	61	100	13%	5	192	2.18	-16.7	($0)
Bats Right	05 NYM *	339	43	76	13	59	2	223	290	236	293	412	705	9	76	26	0.41	36	19	45	133	61	3%	14	265	4.19	4.2	$8
Reliability 0	06 NYM	126	13	30	4	12	0	238	269	230	319	389	708	11	68	32	0.38	36	22	42	112	17	0%	5	232	4.40	0.2	$2
DL 62 18	1st Half	86	10	22	3	8	0	256			340	419	759	11	70	33	0.42	42	19	39	118	18	0%	4	236	5.12	2.0	$2
BAvg Potl 35%	2nd Half	40	3	8	1	4	0	200			273	325	598	9	65	28	0.29	23	27	50	99	12	0%	1	225	2.79	-1.9	$0
LIMA Plan F	07 Proj	189	21	41	6	23	1	217			297	371	668	10	76	26	0.47	37	18	44	101	61	5%	6	242	3.76	-2.0	$3

A lost season: first a strained oblique, then knee surgery. If healthy, he'll give you a handful of homers, but at the expense of BA.

Catalanotto,Frank

	Year	AB	R	H	HR	RBI	SB	Avg	vL	vR	OB	Slg	OPS	bb%	ct%	h%	Eye	G	L	F	PX	SX	SBO	xHR	xBA	RC/G	RAR	R$
Pos 70	02 TEX	228	43	59	3	25	9	259	231	274	335	430	764	10	88	28	0.93	43	26	32	100	153	24%	4	312	5.29	3.1	$7
Age 33	03 TOR	489	83	146	13	59	2	299	176	318	345	472	818	7	87	32	0.56	42	24	34	105	93	3%	13	309	5.54	2.8	$16
Past Peak	04 TOR	249	27	73	1	26	1	293	227	307	338	390	728	6	87	33	0.52	44	27	29	70	58	1%	3	295	4.56	-2.7	$5
Bats Left	05 TOR	419	56	126	8	59	0	301	290	302	357	451	809	8	87	33	0.70	45	21	35	96	64	2%	10	295	5.56	9.7	$13
Reliability 41	06 TOR	437	56	131	7	56	1	300	237	306	374	439	814	11	92	32	1.41	48	19	34	88	46	3%	10	296	5.86	8.2	$11
DL	1st Half	179	24	59	5	37	0	330			431	508	940	15	92	34	2.13	53	19	28	106	41	1%	6	318	7.53	11.2	$7
BAvg Potl 70%	2nd Half	258	32	72	2	19	1	279			331	391	722	7	91	30	0.91	44	19	38	76	59	4%	4	282	4.65	-3.9	$4
LIMA Plan C	07 Proj	400	53	119	6	50	1	297			361	436	796	9	89	32	0.93	46	21	33	89	58	2%	9	298	5.52	5.6	$10

Steady contact hitter faded in September after playing regularly in 2nd half. Legitimate .300 hitter vs. righties. Traditional platoon role suits him best.

Cedeno,Ronny

	Year	AB	R	H	HR	RBI	SB	Avg	vL	vR	OB	Slg	OPS	bb%	ct%	h%	Eye	G	L	F	PX	SX	SBO	xHR	xBA	RC/G	RAR	R$
Pos 6	02	0	0	0	0	0	0	0							0							0		0				
Age 24	03	0	0	0	0	0	0	0							0							0		0				
Growth	04 aa	384	34	96	5	42	9	250			291	349	640	5	82	29	0.32				64	83	22%	6		3.32	-11.4	$7
Bats Right	05 CHC *	325	48	105	8	35	10	323	256	341	365	454	819	6	89	34	0.63	61	14	25	79	91	14%	8	297	5.48	13.3	$15
Reliability 4	06 CHC	534	51	131	6	41	8	245	230	251	269	339	608	3	80	30	0.16	47	16	37	58	96	14%	7	232	2.76	-25.8	$7
DL	1st Half	271	26	75	2	21	5	277			300	373	673	3	83	33	0.20	50	18	32	56	103	15%	3	253	3.63	-5.7	$5
BAvg Potl 40%	2nd Half	263	25	56	4	20	3	213			236	304	540	3	76	27	0.13	43	15	42	59	83	12%	4	209	1.81	-21.0	$1
LIMA Plan D	07 Proj	368	41	94	6	34	8	256			290	364	653	5	83	29	0.28	48	16	36	67	96	16%	7	250	3.42	-8.4	$8

151 games of mediocrity. Horrendous eye, average speed, lack of power and a 2nd half that was truly scary. That 2nd half is your benchmark. Sim game nightmare. Be afraid.
DN: 250 AB, .225

Chavez,Endy

	Year	AB	R	H	HR	RBI	SB	Avg	vL	vR	OB	Slg	OPS	bb%	ct%	h%	Eye	G	L	F	PX	SX	SBO	xHR	xBA	RC/G	RAR	R$
Pos 978	02 MON *	530	79	169	5	45	21	319	316	292	359	447	806	6	91	34	0.69	50	27	23	83	128	26%	8	330	5.45	2.2	$22
Age 29	03 MON	483	66	121	5	47	18	251	304	238	296	354	650	6	88	28	0.53	55	22	23	66	133	21%	7	302	3.64	-28.6	$12
Peak	04 MON *	567	72	157	5	39	36	277	241	290	319	369	688	6	92	29	0.78	57	15	28	52	143	29%	6	285	4.15	-18.8	$19
Bats Left	05 2NL *	203	27	42	1	14	6	207	381	179	257	285	542	6	91	23	0.71	57	21	23	46	137	19%	1	294	2.57	-17.2	$2
Reliability 9	06 NYM	353	48	108	4	42	12	306	333	298	350	431	781	6	88	34	0.55	55	20	25	76	120	15%	6	301	5.15	3.7	$13
DL	1st Half	153	22	42	1	14	6	275			319	399	718	6	84	32	0.42	57	23	20	84	125	16%	2	310	4.42	-1.5	$4
BAvg Potl 45%	2nd Half	200	26	66	3	28	6	330			374	455	829	7	90	36	0.70	54	18	28	70	102	14%	3	293	5.69	4.9	$8
LIMA Plan D+	07 Proj	389	52	114	4	38	15	293			337	398	735	6	89	32	0.62	56	20	25	64	124	18%	5	297	4.64	-4.4	$13

xBA has long shown .300 potential, and he finally delivered. SX, ct%, and LD rate all concur. Thrived in part-time role. If circumstances provide more playing time...
UP: .300 again, 25 SB

Chavez,Eric

	Year	AB	R	H	HR	RBI	SB	Avg	vL	vR	OB	Slg	OPS	bb%	ct%	h%	Eye	G	L	F	PX	SX	SBO	xHR	xBA	RC/G	RAR	R$
Pos 5	02 OAK	585	87	161	34	109	8	275	209	301	348	513	861	10	80	29	0.55	35	17	48	142	84	7%	30	280	6.11	27.5	$25
Age 29	03 OAK	588	94	166	29	101	8	282	220	312	351	514	864	10	85	29	0.70	40	25	35	136	98	7%	26	321	6.16	27.4	$24
Peak	04 OAK	475	87	131	29	77	6	276	306	257	396	501	898	17	79	29	0.96	41	18	42	131	57	5%	27	278	6.91	27.3	$20
Bats Left	05 OAK	625	92	168	27	101	6	269	260	271	331	466	796	8	79	30	0.45	39	18	43	130	77	4%	26	277	5.29	14.2	$22
Reliability 72	06 OAK	485	74	117	22	72	3	241	197	257	353	435	788	15	79	26	0.84	39	18	44	118	68	2%	22	266	5.50	7.1	$12
DL	1st Half	243	37	61	14	46	1	251			366	469	835	15	79	26	0.88	38	19	42	126	52	1%	13	276	6.05	7.4	$8
BAvg Potl 60%	2nd Half	242	37	56	8	26	2	231			340	401	741	14	79	26	0.80	39	16	45	110	71	3%	9	255	4.95	-0.5	$4
LIMA Plan B	07 Proj	527	82	140	25	80	5	266			361	469	829	13	80	29	0.73	39	18	43	126	75	3%	24	274	5.93	16.9	$17

Steady BPIs, but nagging injuries depressed his numbers. Three straight years of so-so BA vs. RHP no longer offset plummeting BA vs LHP. If healthy, should rebound, but he may have already peaked.

Choo,Shin-Soo

	Year	AB	R	H	HR	RBI	SB	Avg	vL	vR	OB	Slg	OPS	bb%	ct%	h%	Eye	G	L	F	PX	SX	SBO	xHR	xBA	RC/G	RAR	R$
Pos 9	02	0	0	0	0	0	0	0							0							0		0				
Age 24	03	0	0	0	0	0	0	0							0							0		0				
Growth	04 aa	517	80	149	13	76	36	288			356	416	771	9	83	33	0.60				72	141	27%	12		5.09	1.3	$25
Bats Left	05 aaa	444	61	106	9	45	16	239		91	332	356	688	12	80	28	0.70	57	7	36	78	102	20%	10		4.22	-10.4	$11
Reliability 5	06 2AL *	532	84	153	14	63	27	288	278	281	358	444	801	10	78	35	0.50	56	24	20	102	126	22%	16	300	5.53	-2.0	$21
DL	1st Half	305	47	86	7	31	15	282			350	410	760	9	81	33	0.55				80	116	21%	8		4.96	-6.1	$11
BAvg Potl 45%	2nd Half	227	37	67	7	32	12	295			368	489	857	10	74	37	0.45	56	24	20	134	132-	23%	8	305	6.38	4.6	$10
LIMA Plan C+	07 Proj	438	66	119	11	53	21	272			350	415	764	11	79	32	0.57	56	23	21	92	120	22%	12	293	5.10	-1.6	$16

3-22-.295 in 146 AB at CLE. 35% hit rate masked problems adjusting to MLB pitching (1 K every 3.1 AB), but the seeds are there. Excellent speed, limited power until GB rate drops below 50%. Still, invest.

TOM TODARO

Church,Ryan			AB	R	H	HR	RBI	SB	Avg	vL	vR	OB	Slg	OPS	bb%	ct%	h%	Eye	G	L	F	PX	SX	SBO	xHR	xBA	RC/G	RAR	R$
Pos	8	02 aa	291	34	80	12	45	1	275			301	474	776	4	81	30	0.20				123	79	2%	11		4.76	-0.5	$9
Age	28	03 aa	371	41	87	11	45	4	236			288	382	670	7	83	26	0.44				89	74	8%	11		3.71	-12.9	$7
Peak		04 aaa	347	54	107	14	58	0	307			374	537	911	10	86	33	0.78				135	73	1%	13		6.78	19.9	$14
Bats	Left	05 WAS	268	41	77	9	42	3	287	367	277	346	466	812	8	74	36	0.34	46	24	30	125	102	7%	10	280	5.64	8.2	$10
Reliability	10	06 WAS	* 390	47	91	17	60	10	232	265	279	316	425	741	11	72	28	0.44	39	18	43	130	79	12%	18	251	4.76	3.7	$11
DL	35	1st Half	208	23	36	8	27	7	174			275	325	600	12	76	19	0.57	41	15	43	88	92	16%	8	230	2.86	-10.7	$3
BAvg Potl	45%	2nd Half	182	24	54	9	33	3	299			364	539	903	9	68	40	0.32	37	20	43	183	50	9%	10	272	7.24	14.1	$8
LIMA Plan	C	07 Proj	386	52	103	15	61	6	267			335	468	803	9	75	32	0.41	43	22	36	134	95	8%	16	280	5.52	10.8	$13

10-35-.276 in 196 AB at WAS. Power is legitimate, and spike in SBO% was an unexpected bonus. Declining ct% introduces some BA risk, but if he gets a full-time job...
UP: 25 HR.

Cintron,Alex			AB	R	H	HR	RBI	SB	Avg	vL	vR	OB	Slg	OPS	bb%	ct%	h%	Eye	G	L	F	PX	SX	SBO	xHR	xBA	RC/G	RAR	R$
Pos	64	02 ARI	* 426	51	119	3	24	7	279	182	226	312	371	683	4	91	30	0.54	61	11	27	63	85	12%	5	278	3.99	1.2	$9
Age	28	03 ARI	* 555	86	181	15	67	3	326	365	296	366	501	867	6	93	33	0.92	45	27	29	98	96	4%	14	338	6.07	29.0	$22
Peak		04 ARI	564	56	148	4	49	3	262	295	250	301	363	664	5	90	29	0.53	45	18	37	63	82	4%	7	267	3.81	-5.2	$8
Bats	Both	05 ARI	330	36	90	8	48	1	273	301	267	298	415	713	4	90	28	0.36	43	22	34	86	61	4%	8	299	4.17	2.0	$9
Reliability	68	06 CHW	288	35	82	5	41	10	285	274	288	309	392	701	3	88	31	0.29	46	23	31	60	115	18%	5	280	3.97	-3.6	$9
DL		1st Half	127	13	35	2	14	7	276			303	378	681	4	91	29	0.42	50	21	29	52	127	21%	2	283	3.85	-2.0	$4
BAvg Potl	45%	2nd Half	161	22	47	3	27	3	292			313	404	717	3	86	33	0.22	43	25	33	67	89	15%	3	279	4.09	-1.5	$5
LIMA Plan	D	07 Proj	303	36	85	5	40	9	281			308	399	708	4	89	30	0.36	45	22	33	69	111	15%	5	286	4.12	-3.0	$9

Re-emergence of long-dormant running game puts him back on our radar screen. Getting a handful of HR and double-digit SB out of your $1 MI purchase is never a bad thing, and should be repeatable.

Cirillo,Jeff			AB	R	H	HR	RBI	SB	Avg	vL	vR	OB	Slg	OPS	bb%	ct%	h%	Eye	G	L	F	PX	SX	SBO	xHR	xBA	RC/G	RAR	R$
Pos	5	02 SEA	485	51	121	6	54	8	249	304	226	295	328	622	6	86	28	0.46	41	17	42	52	67	10%	7	237	3.22	-18.1	$9
Age	37	03 SEA	258	24	53	2	23	1	205	227	194	273	271	544	9	88	23	0.75	40	23	37	46	41	3%	3	257	2.55	-15.8	$0
Decline		04 SD	75	12	16	1	7	0	213	207	217	263	293	556	6	81	25	0.36	49	14	37	55	60	0%	1	224	2.30	-6.4	$1
Bats	Right	05 MIL	185	29	52	4	23	4	281	400	231	361	427	788	11	88	30	1.05	50	16	34	99	71	11%	5	293	5.50	3.8	$6
Reliability	0	06 MIL	263	33	84	3	23	1	319	413	282	370	414	784	7	87	36	0.64	46	20	34	64	38	2%	4	267	5.20	-2.0	$8
DL	69	1st Half	99	16	32	2	11	1	323			396	434	831	11	87	36	0.92	45	25	31	68	48	5%	2	285	5.92	1.1	$4
BAvg Potl	40%	2nd Half	164	17	52	1	12	0	317			353	402	755	5	88	36	0.45	46	18	36	61	22	0%	2	251	4.75	-3.2	$4
LIMA Plan	F	07 Proj	211	27	60	3	21	2	285			345	387	732	8	88	31	0.73	45	20	35	69	52	5%	4	269	4.67	-2.8	$5

His late-career ability to mash LH pitching keeps him in the majors. Hopefully his manager is smart enough to limit his AB vs. RHP. He's a serviceable end-gamer, especially for daily matchup gamers.

Clark,Brady			AB	R	H	HR	RBI	SB	Avg	vL	vR	OB	Slg	OPS	bb%	ct%	h%	Eye	G	L	F	PX	SX	SBO	xHR	xBA	RC/G	RAR	R$
Pos	8	02 2NL	* 187	21	42	1	22	1	225	143	220	260	294	554	5	90	25	0.47	46	25	28	52	59	13%	2	289	2.55	-13.6	$2
Age	34	03 MIL	* 349	37	93	6	43	14	266	263	279	312	393	704	6	87	29	0.50	44	18	38	85	102	19%	8	275	4.22	-7.7	$11
Past Peak		04 MIL	354	41	99	7	46	15	280	250	291	373	395	769	13	86	31	1.08	42	19	39	72	79	18%	8	262	5.35	7.2	$12
Bats	Right	05 MIL	599	94	183	13	53	10	306	302	305	356	426	782	7	91	32	0.85	37	26	37	74	70	12%	13	294	5.18	10.3	$21
Reliability	63	06 MIL	415	51	109	4	29	3	263	273	258	332	335	667	9	86	30	0.72	40	23	37	45	58	5%	5	252	3.93	-6.1	$6
DL	15	1st Half	230	28	64	2	17	2	278			364	339	703	12	87	31	1.07	33	24	44	39	39	6%	3	244	4.55	0.7	$4
BAvg Potl	55%	2nd Half	185	23	45	2	12	1	243			289	330	619	6	83	28	0.39	49	23	28	51	85	4%	2	265	3.13	-7.2	$2
LIMA Plan	F	07 Proj	256	33	70	4	23	4	273			335	368	703	9	87	30	0.71	41	23	36	59	75	10%	4	267	4.32	-1.7	$6

Across-the-board BPI erosion signals that his brief tenure as a full-timer is coming to a close. Regardless of role, declining SX and SBO% say that his only fantasy asset has moved to the liability side of the ledger.

Clark,Tony			AB	R	H	HR	RBI	SB	Avg	vL	vR	OB	Slg	OPS	bb%	ct%	h%	Eye	G	L	F	PX	SX	SBO	xHR	xBA	RC/G	RAR	R$
Pos	3	02 BOS	275	25	57	3	29	0	207	159	228	264	291	554	7	79	25	0.37	50	15	35	59	43	0%	4	224	2.30	-30.4	$1
Age	34	03 NYM	254	29	59	10	40	0	232	279	215	299	472	771	9	71	26	0.33	49	19	33	164	15	0%	15	272	4.99	-4.0	$7
Past Peak		04 NYY	253	37	56	16	49	0	221	196	236	294	458	752	9	64	28	0.28	52	12	30	170	31	0%	16	240	5.04	0.4	$7
Bats	Both	05 ARI	349	47	106	30	87	0	304	313	299	370	636	1007	10	75	33	0.42	43	22	34	215	35	0%	25	331	8.04	23.2	$20
Reliability	3	06 ARI	132	13	26	6	16	0	197	125	213	269	364	633	9	70	23	0.33	38	22	40	109	16	0%	6	235	3.11	-12.0	$1
DL	39	1st Half	100	12	19	5	14	0	190			277	380	657	11	72	21	0.43	38	22	40	122	23	0%	5	254	3.51	-7.9	$1
BAvg Potl	50%	2nd Half	32	1	7	1	2	0	219			242	312	555	3	63	32	0.08	40	20	40	60	1	0%	1	167	1.87	-4.1	$0
LIMA Plan	F	07 Proj	231	29	58	14	41	0	251			322	475	797	9	71	30	0.36	45	19	36	149	19	0%	13	261	5.40	-3.0	$7

Battled shoulder issues all year, eventually undergoing surgery. Power should return, but he will once again have to earn his ABs. Set your expectations against 2003-04 levels.

Clayton,Royce			AB	R	H	HR	RBI	SB	Avg	vL	vR	OB	Slg	OPS	bb%	ct%	h%	Eye	G	L	F	PX	SX	SBO	xHR	xBA	RC/G	RAR	R$
Pos	6	02 CHW	342	51	86	7	35	5	251	238	257	293	365	658	6	80	29	0.30	52	21	27	73	106	7%	7	272	3.48	-11.1	$8
Age	37	03 MIL	483	49	110	11	39	5	228	240	225	299	333	632	9	81	26	0.53	54	16	29	67	66	5%	11	251	3.34	-11.4	$6
Decline		04 COL	574	95	160	8	54	10	279	288	276	334	397	732	8	78	34	0.38	57	17	26	84	110	9%	12	267	4.58	7.3	$16
Bats	Right	05 ARI	522	59	141	2	44	13	270	296	259	320	351	670	7	80	33	0.36	58	20	22	62	109	11%	6	270	3.79	-2.6	$12
Reliability	69	06 2NL	454	49	117	2	40	14	258	303	239	304	341	645	6	81	31	0.35	53	20	27	64	86	18%	6	263	3.46	-12.0	$8
DL		1st Half	260	29	69	0	21	4	265			313	346	659	6	83	32	0.40	51	21	27	64	73	10%	3	269	3.71	-5.0	$4
BAvg Potl	45%	2nd Half	194	20	48	2	19	10	247			291	335	626	6	79	30	0.30	55	17	28	65	84	28%	3	253	3.14	-7.1	$4
LIMA Plan	D	07 Proj	383	45	97	3	34	11	253			303	346	649	7	80	31	0.36	55	19	26	68	104	15%	6	265	3.50	-7.8	$8

Good news: skills are quite stable into his late 30s.
Bad news: Those skills were never that exciting to begin with. His speed is still relatively intact, which is only thing keeping his R$ positive.

Clevlen,Brent			AB	R	H	HR	RBI	SB	Avg	vL	vR	OB	Slg	OPS	bb%	ct%	h%	Eye	G	L	F	PX	SX	SBO	xHR	xBA	RC/G	RAR	R$
Pos	8	02	0	0	0	0	0	0	0							0							0		0				
Age	23	03	0	0	0	0	0	0	0							0							0		0				
Growth		04	0	0	0	0	0	0	0							0							0		0				
Bats	Right	05	0	0	0	0	0	0	0							0							0		0				
Reliability	0	06 aa	434	53	97	13	49	6	224	333	200	298	359	657	10	67	30	0.32	58	17	25	97	85	7%	15	236	3.64	-12.2	$7
DL		1st Half	270	27	52	4	23	5	193			264	281	545	9	70	26	0.32				70	70	10%	6		2.03	-21.6	$1
BAvg Potl	35%	2nd Half	164	26	45	9	26	1	274			353	488	841	11	63	38	0.33	58	17	25	147	89	4%	9	250	6.59	9.6	$6
LIMA Plan	F	07 Proj	126	17	30	5	16	1	238			315	402	717	10	66	32	0.32	58	17	25	116	83	6%	5	242	4.55	-0.1	$3

3-6-.282 in 39 AB at DET. Toolsy prospect with a high ceiling. Needs more time to develop skills, especially ct% and Eye. Power-speed combo make him worth stashing as a longer-term project.

Closser,J.D.			AB	R	H	HR	RBI	SB	Avg	vL	vR	OB	Slg	OPS	bb%	ct%	h%	Eye	G	L	F	PX	SX	SBO	xHR	xBA	RC/G	RAR	R$
Pos	2	02 aa	315	31	85	12	45	6	270			337	470	807	9	85	28	0.70				127	60	13%	12		5.52	15.1	$10
Age	27	03 aa	410	48	111	13	42	2	270			330	445	775	8	85	29	0.62				107	70	4%	13		5.10	10.8	$10
Peak		04 aaa	298	36	80	6	37	0	268			329	393	722	8	90	28	0.90				74	39	4%	7		4.59	4.5	$6
Bats	Both	05 COL	237	31	52	7	27	1	219	270	210	312	376	688	12	80	25	0.67	44	19	37	102	78	2%	7	267	4.17	2.8	$4
Reliability	29	06 COL	* 322	33	80	9	33	6	249	83	212	321	394	716	10	84	27	0.67	36	23	41	86	71	10%	9	272	4.46	1.1	$6
DL		1st Half	192	18	51	4	18	4	265			326	407	734	8	86	29	0.64	26	26	49	90	68	12%	5	271	4.68	1.9	$4
BAvg Potl	60%	2nd Half	130	16	29	5	16	2	225			313	375	689	11	82	24	0.71	52	19	29	80	71	8%	4	272	4.11	-0.9	$2
LIMA Plan	F	07 Proj	126	15	31	4	14	1	247			323	398	721	10	84	27	0.70	43	20	37	90	71	6%	4	273	4.54	1.6	$3

2-11-.192 in 97 AB at COL. One-time prospect has never gotten a clear shot in the bigs, now moves to MIL. If he gets a chance to display that MLE PX:
UP: 300 AB, 15 HR.

Conine,Jeff			AB	R	H	HR	RBI	SB	Avg	vL	vR	OB	Slg	OPS	bb%	ct%	h%	Eye	G	L	F	PX	SX	SBO	xHR	xBA	RC/G	RAR	R$
Pos	379	02 BAL	451	44	123	15	63	8	273	292	266	311	448	759	5	85	29	0.38	42	15	44	104	100	8%	14	272	4.70	-14.9	$14
Age	40	03 2TM	577	88	163	20	95	5	282	288	281	340	459	799	8	88	29	0.71	38	23	39	105	93	3%	19	300	5.36	-1.5	$21
Decline		04 FLA	521	55	146	14	83	5	280	275	282	341	432	773	8	85	31	0.62	35	21	43	96	53	7%	15	274	5.08	-12.9	$16
Bats	Right	05 FLA	335	42	102	3	33	2	304	288	311	375	403	778	10	83	36	0.66	40	27	33	72	70	2%	5	275	5.32	-2.6	$9
Reliability	50	06 2TM	489	54	131	10	66	3	268	260	271	323	399	722	8	87	29	0.62	46	19	35	78	70	4%	11	274	4.48	-17.3	$11
DL		1st Half	205	25	52	6	20	2	254			329	424	753	10	85	27	0.77	41	16	43	97	88	5%	6	269	4.97	-4.5	$4
BAvg Potl	60%	2nd Half	284	29	79	4	46	1	278			319	380	699	6	88	31	0.49	50	21	29	64	52	3%	5	277	4.12	-12.8	$7
LIMA Plan	F	07 Proj	225	26	63	4	30	2	280			339	406	745	8	85	31	0.61	43	21	36	80	60	4%	5	274	4.77	-5.1	$6

Turned back the clock a bit with 1st half power outburst, but there's very little left in this skill set. xBA says he might have another year of empty BA to offer, but that's it.

RAY MURPHY

Cora,Alex

Cora,Alex		AB	R	H	HR	RBI	SB	Avg	vL	vR	OB	Slg	OPS	bb%	ct%	h%	Eye	G	L	F	PX	SX	SBO	xHR	xBA	RC/G	RAR	R$
Pos 6	02 LA	258	37	75	5	28	7	291	318	288	356	434	790	9	85	33	0.68	50	18	31	90	121	12%	6	289	5.38	10.8	$9
Age 31	03 LA	477	39	119	4	34	4	249	308	240	274	338	611	3	88	28	0.27	46	21	33	59	75	6%	6	270	3.01	-15.5	$5
Past Peak	04 LA	405	47	107	10	47	3	264	239	267	341	380	721	10	90	27	1.15	46	17	37	59	70	5%	8	261	4.67	6.4	$9
Bats Left	05 2AL	250	25	58	3	24	7	232	281	227	264	332	596	4	88	25	0.37	52	17	30	57	121	17%	3	272	2.91	-12.5	$4
Reliability 39	06 BOS	235	31	56	1	18	6	238	333	219	295	298	593	7	88	27	0.66	51	16	32	37	108	12%	2	248	3.06	-9.6	$3
DL	1st Half	83	15	25	0	9	2	301			370	361	731	10	93	32	1.50	53	18	30	36	103	13%	0	270	4.94	1.2	$3
BAvg Potl 60%	2nd Half	152	16	31	1	9	4	204			253	263	516	6	85	23	0.43	51	16	34	37	101	11%	1	236	1.98	-11.5	$0
LIMA Plan F	07 Proj	**209**	**25**	**51**	**2**	**19**	**5**	**244**			**297**	**327**	**624**	**7**	**88**	**27**	**0.64**	**51**	**17**	**32**	**49**	**104**	**12%**	**2**	**260**	**3.39**	**-6.8**	**$3**

Marvel at the lack of power... then realize PX would've been even lower if Alex Rios hadn't slapped Cora's only HR over Fenway's short RF fence with his bare hand. You can't make this stuff up.

Costa,Shane

Costa,Shane		AB	R	H	HR	RBI	SB	Avg	vL	vR	OB	Slg	OPS	bb%	ct%	h%	Eye	G	L	F	PX	SX	SBO	xHR	xBA	RC/G	RAR	R$
Pos 98	02	0	0	0	0	0	0	0							0							0		0				
Age 25	03	0	0	0	0	0	0	0							0							0		0				
Pre-Peak	04	0	0	0	0	0	0	0							0							0		0				
Bats Left	05 KC	* 370	41	88	7	41	4	238		268	282	357	639	6	92	24	0.79	63	19	18	71	84	6%	7	321	3.60	-12.2	$6
Reliability 0	06 KC	* 444	51	128	10	47	5	288	244	281	314	443	758	4	89	31	0.33	43	24	33	94	92	5%	11	306	4.67	-12.2	$11
DL 20	1st Half	174	17	46	5	17	1	262			286	432	718	3	88	27	0.29	49	23	29	98	76	3%	5	313	4.19	-7.4	$3
BAvg Potl 50%	2nd Half	270	34	83	5	30	4	306			332	451	783	4	89	33	0.35	35	26	39	91	94	6%	6	298	4.98	-5.0	$8
LIMA Plan F	07 Proj	**134**	**15**	**38**	**3**	**14**	**1**	**284**			**316**	**422**	**738**	**5**	**90**	**30**	**0.47**	**47**	**23**	**30**	**82**	**77**	**5%**	**3**	**306**	**4.53**	**-2.6**	**$3**

3-23-.274 in 237 AB at KC. Improved LD and FB%, solid ct% suggest BA upside, especially in a platoon. As a corner OF, though, we need to see more PX growth before getting too excited.

Coste,Chris

Coste,Chris		AB	R	H	HR	RBI	SB	Avg	vL	vR	OB	Slg	OPS	bb%	ct%	h%	Eye	G	L	F	PX	SX	SBO	xHR	xBA	RC/G	RAR	R$
Pos 2	02 aaa	478	49	134	7	56	0	280			320	387	707	6	88	31	0.51				71	35	0%	9		4.23	4.9	$11
Age 34	03 aaa	96	4	15	1	6	0	159			182	234	417	3	81	19	0.15				56	10	0%	1		0.50	-11.7	($1)
Past Peak	04 aaa	262	25	63	2	20	2	240			280	337	617	5	87	27	0.42				68	64	8%	4		3.20	-6.9	$2
Bats Right	05 aaa	499	50	116	15	59	2	233			273	368	641	5	86	24	0.39				81	40	6%	14		3.31	-9.0	$8
Reliability 20	06 PHI	* 345	36	88	9	45	1	256	288	345	293	394	688	5	82	29	0.30	40	29	31	89	35	2%	10	294	3.82	-5.2	$7
DL	1st Half	174	15	32	2	15	1	186			222	269	491	4	82	22	0.26	42	38	19	59	49	6%	3	313	1.50	-15.9	($1)
BAvg Potl 50%	2nd Half	171	21	56	7	30	0	328			365	522	887	6	82	37	0.33	40	27	33	119	19	0%	7	308	6.19	8.3	$7
LIMA Plan F	07 Proj	**242**	**25**	**67**	**6**	**30**	**1**	**277**			**315**	**409**	**723**	**5**	**84**	**31**	**0.35**	**40**	**28**	**32**	**84**	**34**	**3%**	**6**	**296**	**4.28**	**1.2**	**$6**

7-32-.328 in 198 AB at PHI. Talk about a late-bloomer. This 33-year-old rookie simply hit line drive after line drive. But can he do it again? 2002 and prior seasons suggest it wasn't entirely a fluke.

Cota,Humberto

Cota,Humberto		AB	R	H	HR	RBI	SB	Avg	vL	vR	OB	Slg	OPS	bb%	ct%	h%	Eye	G	L	F	PX	SX	SBO	xHR	xBA	RC/G	RAR	R$
Pos 2	02 aaa	404	42	99	7	45	4	245			289	366	655	6	80	29	0.30				89	59	14%	9		3.50	-4.5	$7
Age 28	03 aaa	200	20	38	6	23	2	190			253	325	578	8	76	22	0.35				92	56	5%	6		2.48	-10.9	$1
Peak	04 PIT	66	10	15	5	8	0	227	188	240	261	500	761	4	70	24	0.15	43	15	41	164	90	0%	4	266	4.66	1.7	$2
Bats Right	05 PIT	297	29	72	7	43	0	242	294	222	283	387	671	5	73	31	0.21	40	22	38	112	40	0%	9	253	3.66	-1.2	$5
Reliability 4	06 PIT	100	5	19	0	5	0	190	125	211	250	200	450	7	74	26	0.31	55	16	29	9	13	0%	0	168	0.77	-11.4	($1)
DL 17	1st Half	66	3	15	0	4	0	227			282	242	524	7	82	28	0.42	57	19	24	13	9	0%	0	197	1.98	-4.7	($0)
BAvg Potl 40%	2nd Half	34	2	4	0	1	0	118			189	118	307	8	59	20	0.21	48	10	43	0	25	0%	0	107	-1.94	-7.4	($1)
LIMA Plan F	07 Proj	**121**	**10**	**29**	**3**	**13**	**1**	**239**			**291**	**359**	**650**	**7**	**78**	**28**	**0.33**	**48**	**17**	**35**	**79**	**31**	**3%**	**3**	**234**	**3.38**	**-2.7**	**$2**

Possibly the biggest power outage since the '77 NYC blackout. Stunningly bad. But one must assume that he didn't suddenly forget how to hit FB while riding the bench, and so he'll rebound somewhere.

Counsell,Craig

Counsell,Craig		AB	R	H	HR	RBI	SB	Avg	vL	vR	OB	Slg	OPS	bb%	ct%	h%	Eye	G	L	F	PX	SX	SBO	xHR	xBA	RC/G	RAR	R$
Pos 6	02 ARI	436	63	123	2	51	7	282	269	289	349	351	700	9	88	32	0.87	52	19	29	51	80	8%	5	271	4.42	6.5	$12
Age 36	03 ARI	303	40	71	3	21	11	234	219	239	326	304	629	12	89	25	1.28	51	22	27	38	116	15%	3	275	3.78	-3.1	$6
Decline	04 MIL	476	60	116	2	24	17	244	184	254	327	317	644	11	82	30	0.67	47	23	30	50	120	14%	4	255	3.72	-5.9	$8
Bats Left	05 ARI	578	85	148	9	42	26	256	269	253	345	375	720	12	88	28	1.13	49	20	31	77	123	18%	12	292	4.79	14.2	$17
Reliability 16	06 ARI	372	56	95	4	30	15	255	256	255	313	347	659	8	87	28	0.66	48	20	31	53	118	22%	5	269	3.81	-6.1	$9
DL 38	1st Half	268	37	74	2	24	9	276			310	358	668	5	86	31	0.35	50	22	28	49	115	21%	3	272	3.69	-5.2	$7
BAvg Potl 60%	2nd Half	104	19	21	2	6	6	202			320	317	637	15	90	21	1.80	46	15	39	62	124	25%	2	262	4.06	-1.0	$2
LIMA Plan D+	07 Proj	**249**	**38**	**62**	**3**	**18**	**11**	**249**			**332**	**347**	**679**	**11**	**87**	**27**	**0.99**	**48**	**19**	**32**	**60**	**117**	**19%**	**4**	**271**	**4.24**	**0.4**	**$6**

Spent much of 2nd half watching as ARI went young. BB% recovered and SX still solid, so his two redeeming skills remain. But at 36, there's nowhere to go but down. Days as a regular may be over.

Crawford,Carl

Crawford,Carl		AB	R	H	HR	RBI	SB	Avg	vL	vR	OB	Slg	OPS	bb%	ct%	h%	Eye	G	L	F	PX	SX	SBO	xHR	xBA	RC/G	RAR	R$
Pos 7	02 TAM	* 612	79	176	9	80	34	288	200	276	319	430	748	4	84	33	0.29	53	20	27	83	152	33%	10	294	4.62	-3.7	$24
Age 25	03 TAM	630	80	177	5	54	55	281	263	288	309	362	671	4	84	33	0.25	54	23	23	49	159	38%	6	276	3.64	-30.8	$25
Pre-Peak	04 TAM	626	104	185	11	55	59	296	295	296	333	450	783	5	87	33	0.43	48	20	33	82	180	45%	10	289	5.10	2.8	$31
Bats Left	05 TAM	644	101	194	15	81	46	301	244	326	329	469	798	4	87	33	0.32	45	20	35	97	172	34%	14	295	5.15	7.7	$32
Reliability 99	06 TAM	600	89	183	18	77	58	305	288	311	345	482	827	6	86	33	0.44	52	18	30	92	168	40%	15	298	5.55	6.2	$33
DL	1st Half	289	49	88	10	37	26	304			350	478	827	6	88	32	0.59	55	15	30	90	160	39%	8	300	5.56	3.1	$16
BAvg Potl 50%	2nd Half	311	40	95	8	40	32	305			341	486	827	5	84	35	0.33	50	21	29	95	165	42%	6	295	5.56	3.3	$17
LIMA Plan D+	07 Proj	**617**	**92**	**185**	**20**	**84**	**49**	**300**			**335**	**488**	**823**	**5**	**86**	**32**	**0.38**	**49**	**20**	**31**	**100**	**166**	**37%**	**16**	**302**	**5.45**	**7.5**	**$32**

Baby step up in bb% helped spur SB rebound. We keep waiting for that breakout year, but he's still just 25. This is the plateau before the spike; history says that could come in '07 but more likely in 2008.

Crede,Joe

Crede,Joe		AB	R	H	HR	RBI	SB	Avg	vL	vR	OB	Slg	OPS	bb%	ct%	h%	Eye	G	L	F	PX	SX	SBO	xHR	xBA	RC/G	RAR	R$
Pos 5	02 CHW	* 559	78	164	36	92	0	293	259	295	333	538	871	6	85	29	0.40	33	22	45	137	21	2%	28	307	5.87	21.8	$24
Age 29	03 CHW	536	68	140	19	75	1	261	300	246	303	433	736	6	86	27	0.43	35	21	44	103	56	2%	17	283	4.45	-1.0	$14
Peak	04 CHW	490	67	117	21	69	1	239	256	230	288	418	707	6	83	25	0.42	34	16	49	105	44	3%	19	259	4.07	-12.3	$11
Bats Right	05 CHW	432	54	109	22	62	1	252	277	246	293	454	747	5	85	25	0.38	36	18	45	119	38	2%	18	283	4.47	-0.4	$12
Reliability 74	06 CHW	544	76	154	30	94	0	283	273	288	318	506	824	5	89	27	0.48	31	18	51	121	28	2%	23	292	5.34	5.1	$19
DL 15	1st Half	262	44	79	14	54	0	302			337	519	856	5	90	29	0.56	29	21	50	117	41	2%	11	299	5.72	5.1	$11
BAvg Potl 55%	2nd Half	282	32	75	16	40	0	266			301	493	794	5	88	25	0.42	34	15	51	124	22	2%	12	282	4.98	-0.2	$8
LIMA Plan C	07 Proj	**549**	**73**	**149**	**31**	**96**	**0**	**271**			**310**	**498**	**808**	**5**	**87**	**26**	**0.43**	**33**	**18**	**49**	**127**	**26**	**2%**	**25**	**290**	**5.17**	**5.5**	**$19**

Actually, no big skills jump. Instead, a few small gains and better hit rate luck fueled this apparent breakout. Assuming his back is sound, this looks like a level he can sustain for a while.

Crisp,Coco

Crisp,Coco		AB	R	H	HR	RBI	SB	Avg	vL	vR	OB	Slg	OPS	bb%	ct%	h%	Eye	G	L	F	PX	SX	SBO	xHR	xBA	RC/G	RAR	R$
Pos 8	02 CLE	* 461	79	135	9	52	33	293	270	256	347	406	752	8	85	33	0.56	40	22	38	72	122	33%	10	266	4.79	0.2	$22
Age 27	03 CLE	* 639	94	187	4	49	33	293	321	245	341	396	737	7	89	33	0.64	44	26	29	65	136	27%	7	295	4.71	-0.5	$22
Peak	04 CLE	491	78	146	15	71	20	297	311	290	345	446	791	7	86	32	0.52	50	19	31	86	103	23%	14	289	5.16	6.3	$21
Bats Both	05 CLE	594	86	178	16	69	15	300	252	325	348	465	813	7	86	33	0.54	46	20	34	106	105	13%	17	300	5.47	19.7	$22
Reliability 57	06 BOS	413	58	109	8	36	22	264	277	259	315	385	700	7	84	30	0.46	48	16	36	77	125	24%	9	263	4.14	-6.3	$12
DL 47 15	1st Half	144	26	42	3	13	5	292			338	410	747	6	85	33	0.45	53	13	34	71	115	19%	3	261	4.65	-0.0	$5
BAvg Potl 50%	2nd Half	269	32	67	5	23	17	249			303	372	675	7	83	28	0.47	46	17	37	81	120	27%	6	263	3.86	-6.4	$7
LIMA Plan C+	07 Proj	**554**	**82**	**165**	**17**	**68**	**30**	**298**			**347**	**459**	**806**	**7**	**85**	**33**	**0.50**	**48**	**18**	**34**	**97**	**118**	**24%**	**17**	**287**	**5.34**	**11.8**	**$24**

Broke his finger in the first week, and PX dip shows he never really recovered. All his other skills remained solid, though, so with health, he should resume his prior growth, and rebound nicely.

Crosby,Bobby

Crosby,Bobby		AB	R	H	HR	RBI	SB	Avg	vL	vR	OB	Slg	OPS	bb%	ct%	h%	Eye	G	L	F	PX	SX	SBO	xHR	xBA	RC/G	RAR	R$
Pos 6	02 aa	228	27	57	6	27	8	250			299	390	690	7	85	27	0.46				92	85	19%	6		3.98	-1.8	$7
Age 27	03 aaa	465	69	125	18	72	19	269			340	462	802	10	80	30	0.55				122	123	19%	18		5.47	16.2	$19
Peak	04 OAK	545	70	130	22	64	7	239	194	254	312	426	737	10	74	28	0.41	45	17	38	127	73	8%	24	263	4.65	3.1	$12
Bats Right	05 OAK	333	66	92	9	38	0	276	314	260	345	456	802	10	84	31	0.65	54	18	28	118	86	0%	10	308	5.53	9.1	$10
Reliability 21	06 OAK	358	42	82	9	40	8	229	185	242	299	338	637	9	79	27	0.47	47	18	35	69	75	9%	9	241	3.64	-11.6	$6
DL 58 73	1st Half	254	31	63	8	32	7	248			310	382	692	8	80	28	0.45	48	17	35	83	78	10%	8	253	3.98	-3.2	$6
BAvg Potl 50%	2nd Half	104	11	19	1	8	1	183			274	231	504	11	76	23	0.52	45	21	35	33	51	7%	1	212	1.68	-9.2	($0)
LIMA Plan C	07 Proj	**506**	**70**	**134**	**13**	**55**	**7**	**265**			**336**	**396**	**731**	**10**	**79**	**31**	**0.51**	**48**	**18**	**33**	**86**	**83**	**6%**	**14**	**259**	**4.59**	**1.9**	**$12**

Two hand injuries & debilitating lower back woes derailed this season. Folks are starting to forget about him, which means he could be a huge bargain. But back troubles can linger, so be sure he's sound.

ROD TRUEDSELL

Cruz,Jose		AB	R	H	HR	RBI	SB	Avg	vL	vR	OB	Slg	OPS	bb%	ct%	h%	Eye	G	L	F	PX	SX	SBO	xHR	xBA	RC/G	RAR	R$
Pos 79	02 TOR	466	64	114	18	70	7	245	225	253	319	438	757	10	77	28	0.48	40	18	42	123	109	7%	18	267	4.92	1.2	$13
Age 33	03 SF	539	90	135	20	68	5	250	304	233	370	414	783	16	78	29	0.84	41	21	38	107	59	7%	22	264	5.53	-0.9	$16
Past Peak	04 TAM	545	76	132	21	78	11	242	264	233	335	433	768	12	79	27	0.65	37	16	47	114	113	11%	20	254	5.17	3.8	$15
Bats Both	05 2TM	370	46	93	18	50	0	251	325	232	365	473	838	15	73	30	0.65	43	20	37	157	36	2%	20	279	6.27	13.6	$10
Reliability 18	06 LA	223	34	52	5	17	5	233	313	199	357	381	738	16	76	29	0.80	36	14	50	105	85	8%	7	231	5.06	-1.3	$4
DL 29	1st Half	179	31	41	4	14	5	229			367	369	736	18	77	28	0.93	39	14	47	101	71	10%	6	233	5.09	-0.9	$4
BAvg Potl 50%	2nd Half	44	3	11	1	3	0	250			312	432	744	8	73	32	0.33	22	16	63	124	55	0%	1	223	4.88	-0.5	$0
LIMA Plan D	07 Proj	**238**	**36**	**58**	**8**	**29**	**4**	**243**			**355**	**417**	**772**	**15**	**76**	**28**	**0.74**	**35**	**17**	**48**	**115**	**75**	**8%**	**10**	**247**	**5.36**	**-0.1**	**$6**

Even worse-than-usual line vs RHers sealed his fate in LA. If a team would realize what he is -- a platoon player who can damage lefties from the top of the order -- he could be useful again.

Cruz,Nelson		AB	R	H	HR	RBI	SB	Avg	vL	vR	OB	Slg	OPS	bb%	ct%	h%	Eye	G	L	F	PX	SX	SBO	xHR	xBA	RC/G	RAR	R$
Pos 9	02	0	0	0	0	0	0	0							0							0		0				
Age 25	03 aaa	3	1	1	0	0	0	300			300	300	600	0	63	48	0.00					0	0%	0		2.54	-0.2	$0
Pre-Peak	04 a/a	275	43	74	12	36	6	268			319	451	770	7	77	31	0.32				116	91	14%	11		4.88	-0.9	$9
Bats Right	05 a/a	455	57	111	20	60	14	244			313	438	752	9	76	28	0.42				134	73	21%	20		4.77	-2.8	$15
Reliability 25	06 2TM	* 501	75	133	25	87	16	265	217	226	327	465	792	8	75	31	0.36	46	12	42	126	91	18%	23	255	5.23	0.3	$20
DL	1st Half	271	41	68	13	41	13	249			325	445	770	10	70	31	0.38				137	91	23%	13		5.16	-0.4	$10
BAvg Potl 35%	2nd Half	230	34	65	12	47	3	285			328	489	818	6	81	31	0.33	46	12	42	116	72	11%	10	263	5.33	0.7	$10
LIMA Plan D	07 Proj	**257**	**37**	**67**	**12**	**40**	**7**	**260**			**320**	**452**	**772**	**8**	**76**	**30**	**0.37**	**46**	**12**	**42**	**123**	**73**	**17%**	**11**	**255**	**4.94**	**-1.4**	**$9**

6-22-.223 in 130 AB at TEX. Low ct% limits BA upside, but his power skills are intriguing. Should enter 2007 as at least a platoon player, and there's an opportunity for full-time AB. UP: 500 AB, 25 HR, 15 SB

Cuddyer,Michael		AB	R	H	HR	RBI	SB	Avg	vL	vR	OB	Slg	OPS	bb%	ct%	h%	Eye	G	L	F	PX	SX	SBO	xHR	xBA	RC/G	RAR	R$
Pos 9	02 MIN	442	63	119	18	52	11	269			321	468	790	7	80	30	0.38	50	17	33	120	114	19%	16	288	5.16	1.8	$15
Age 28	03 MIN	* 288	36	80	6	39	5	278	245	262	354	424	778	11	78	34	0.53	49	22	29	101	88	11%	8	277	5.31	1.3	$8
Peak	04 MIN	339	49	89	12	45	5	263	293	245	335	440	775	10	78	30	0.50	39	19	42	116	75	11%	13	265	5.14	4.4	$10
Bats Right	05 MIN	422	55	111	12	42	3	263	280	260	328	422	750	9	78	31	0.44	53	18	29	109	72	6%	13	277	4.81	1.4	$10
Reliability 59	06 MIN	557	102	158	24	109	6	284	297	276	355	504	860	10	77	33	0.48	44	21	35	145	110	4%	25	292	6.28	9.7	$22
DL 15	1st Half	224	41	61	11	44	3	272			366	513	879	13	76	31	0.61	44	20	36	158	97	5%	12	297	6.68	6.5	$9
BAvg Potl 45%	2nd Half	333	61	97	13	65	3	291			348	498	847	8	77	34	0.38	44	21	35	136	103	3%	14	289	5.99	3.1	$13
LIMA Plan B	07 Proj	**570**	**91**	**156**	**21**	**88**	**7**	**274**			**343**	**469**	**812**	**10**	**77**	**32**	**0.47**	**46**	**20**	**34**	**129**	**96**	**7%**	**22**	**284**	**5.63**	**6.8**	**$19**

Finally! Those with patience were rewarded, as breakout came at typical age 27. Power skills tailed off some in the 2nd half, so this is about as good as it gets. But a near-repeat seems reasonable.

Damon,Johnny		AB	R	H	HR	RBI	SB	Avg	vL	vR	OB	Slg	OPS	bb%	ct%	h%	Eye	G	L	F	PX	SX	SBO	xHR	xBA	RC/G	RAR	R$
Pos 8	02 BOS	623	118	178	14	63	31	286	306	279	353	443	796	9	89	30	0.93	44	22	34	89	162	20%	14	299	5.51	12.9	$26
Age 33	03 BOS	609	103	166	12	67	30	273	275	272	346	404	750	10	88	29	0.92	46	23	31	79	137	20%	13	296	4.99	4.4	$22
Past Peak	04 BOS	627	126	192	20	94	20	306	278	319	381	477	858	11	89	32	1.07	49	17	34	95	125	14%	19	299	6.24	26.6	$29
Bats Left	05 BOS	624	117	197	10	75	18	316	327	310	369	439	808	8	89	34	0.77	45	23	32	77	136	10%	12	295	5.53	21.0	$26
Reliability 84	06 NYY	593	115	169	24	80	25	285	297	280	358	482	840	10	86	30	0.79	41	19	40	113	124	20%	22	293	5.93	21.7	$26
DL	1st Half	302	58	89	11	42	16	295			372	477	849	11	85	32	0.84	42	17	41	110	116	21%	11	284	6.10	12.2	$14
BAvg Potl 60%	2nd Half	291	57	80	13	38	9	275			343	488	831	9	86	28	0.73	41	21	38	117	129	19%	11	302	5.76	9.4	$12
LIMA Plan B+	07 Proj	**588**	**113**	**173**	**20**	**76**	**20**	**294**			**362**	**471**	**832**	**10**	**87**	**31**	**0.83**	**44**	**20**	**36**	**101**	**127**	**15%**	**18**	**297**	**5.84**	**20.9**	**$25**

The evolution continues. Knows how to use his home park, with more pulled FB netting career-best PX. Ran twice as often, but only gained 1/3 more SB. He's following a typical career path for an aging star.

DaVanon,Jeff		AB	R	H	HR	RBI	SB	Avg	vL	vR	OB	Slg	OPS	bb%	ct%	h%	Eye	G	L	F	PX	SX	SBO	xHR	xBA	RC/G	RAR	R$
Pos 8	02 aaa	130	18	32	5	17	5	246			319	462	781	10	81	27	0.56				144	105	31%	5		5.24	1.7	$4
Age 33	03 ANA	* 390	64	108	14	53	20	277	312	274	356	446	802	11	83	30	0.72	41	25	35	103	114	22%	14	291	5.52	8.9	$17
Past Peak	04 ANA	285	41	79	7	34	18	277	136	289	378	418	795	14	81	32	0.85	40	12	48	82	132	20%	7	220	5.66	7.8	$11
Bats Both	05 ANA	225	42	52	2	15	11	231	393	206	345	311	656	15	80	28	0.89	44	19	37	59	111	22%	3	241	4.00	-2.0	$5
Reliability 7	06 ARI	221	38	64	5	35	10	290	205	308	377	448	825	12	81	34	0.74	51	20	29	95	129	19%	6	285	5.99	9.8	$9
DL 50	1st Half	153	26	43	3	24	7	281			371	418	790	13	82	33	0.81	55	20	25	83	119	17%	4	288	5.56	4.9	$6
BAvg Potl 50%	2nd Half	68	12	21	2	11	3	309			390	515	904	12	78	37	0.60	42	21	38	124	120	23%	2	279	7.02	5.0	$3
LIMA Plan D+	07 Proj	**218**	**37**	**60**	**5**	**28**	**11**	**275**			**368**	**420**	**789**	**13**	**80**	**32**	**0.75**	**45**	**19**	**36**	**91**	**129**	**21%**	**6**	**265**	**5.55**	**6.4**	**$9**

Nice rebound season cut short by ankle injury. Should be good for more of the same in '07. But should he platoon? Yes, against LHP... no wait, against RHers... Uh, no, against lefties! Nope, against righties....

DeJesus,David		AB	R	H	HR	RBI	SB	Avg	vL	vR	OB	Slg	OPS	bb%	ct%	h%	Eye	G	L	F	PX	SX	SBO	xHR	xBA	RC/G	RAR	R$
Pos 78	02 aa	79	6	19	2	13	3	241			302	430	733	8	89	25	0.78				109	111	24%	2		4.74	-2.1	$2
Age 27	03 a/a	286	52	84	6	27	7	294			369	437	806	11	90	31	1.13				89	100	16%	7		5.70	2.0	$10
Peak	04 KC	* 560	89	163	12	52	14	291	224	309	349	429	778	8	87	32	0.67	50	17	33	81	102	19%	13	281	5.16	3.6	$18
Bats Left	05 KC	461	69	135	9	56	5	293	270	303	352	445	797	8	84	34	0.55	45	22	32	100	99	8%	11	292	5.41	9.0	$14
Reliability 72	06 KC	491	83	145	8	56	6	295	307	291	352	446	798	8	86	33	0.61	49	22	29	95	113	7%	11	303	5.45	3.7	$14
DL 38	1st Half	126	19	36	3	12	1	286			366	452	819	11	84	32	0.80	41	21	38	101	92	10%	3	283	5.85	2.4	$3
BAvg Potl 55%	2nd Half	365	64	109	5	44	5	299			347	444	791	7	86	34	0.54	51	23	26	93	126	5%	7	310	5.30	1.2	$11
LIMA Plan B	07 Proj	**575**	**93**	**173**	**11**	**63**	**10**	**301**			**362**	**450**	**812**	**9**	**86**	**34**	**0.66**	**47**	**22**	**31**	**94**	**105**	**11%**	**13**	**296**	**5.62**	**9.7**	**$19**

Maintained improvement vs LHP, the key to his steady xBA growth. Should break that .300 barrier in '07. Otherwise, well, he really doesn't do much else. If he returned to near 20% SBO, then we'd have something.

Delgado,Carlos		AB	R	H	HR	RBI	SB	Avg	vL	vR	OB	Slg	OPS	bb%	ct%	h%	Eye	G	L	F	PX	SX	SBO	xHR	xBA	RC/G	RAR	R$
Pos 3	02 TOR	505	103	140	33	108	1	277	238	297	399	549	947	17	75	31	0.81	36	17	47	175	61	1%	33	288	7.71	26.4	$24
Age 34	03 TOR	570	117	172	42	145	0	302	284	310	414	593	1007	16	76	33	0.80	36	26	39	187	40	0%	40	320	8.39	47.0	$32
Past Peak	04 TOR	458	74	123	32	99	0	269	271	267	364	535	899	13	75	29	0.60	36	21	43	167	24	1%	30	290	6.82	24.1	$19
Bats Left	05 FLA	521	81	157	33	115	0	301	229	327	386	582	968	12	77	34	0.60	40	23	37	186	47	0%	32	320	7.71	30.1	$27
Reliability 61	06 NYM	524	89	139	38	114	0	265	226	282	356	548	904	12	77	28	0.62	42	18	40	168	40	0%	33	297	6.78	11.8	$22
DL 19	1st Half	286	47	75	22	55	0	262			332	538	871	9	77	27	0.45	43	17	40	162	27	0%	18	287	6.16	1.3	$12
BAvg Potl 60%	2nd Half	238	42	64	16	59	0	269			383	559	942	16	78	28	0.83	41	19	40	175	53	0%	15	308	7.50	10.2	$11
LIMA Plan C+	07 Proj	**516**	**87**	**150**	**36**	**116**	**0**	**291**			**384**	**571**	**955**	**13**	**77**	**32**	**0.65**	**40**	**20**	**40**	**175**	**41**	**0%**	**33**	**304**	**7.55**	**24.4**	**$25**

Consistent skills; BA drop was not seen in xBA, so expect that to rebound. Despite his home ballpark, there is another .300 season still in his bat.

Dellucci,David		AB	R	H	HR	RBI	SB	Avg	vL	vR	OB	Slg	OPS	bb%	ct%	h%	Eye	G	L	F	PX	SX	SBO	xHR	xBA	RC/G	RAR	R$
Pos 79	02 ARI	* 244	35	58	7	30	2	238	111	262	319	389	708	11	76	28	0.50	62	9	29	105	85	9%	8	258	4.34	-15.2	$6
Age 33	03 2TM	216	26	49	3	23	12	227	132	247	301	352	653	10	73	30	0.40	47	21	32	92	150	22%	4	250	3.67	-11.8	$5
Past Peak	04 TEX	335	59	80	17	61	9	239	107	254	332	436	768	12	73	28	0.53	40	17	43	124	98	14%	16	252	5.11	1.7	$12
Bats Left	05 TEX	435	97	109	29	65	5	251	242	254	362	513	875	15	72	28	0.63	41	16	43	170	113	6%	27	279	6.68	25.3	$18
Reliability 46	06 PHI	264	41	77	13	39	1	292	200	299	360	530	890	10	77	34	0.45	37	19	44	142	84	5%	12	276	6.62	10.2	$10
DL	1st Half	86	11	26	4	14	0	302			355	570	925	8	71	39	0.28	39	19	42	181	79	10%	4	284	7.32	5.0	$3
BAvg Potl 40%	2nd Half	178	30	51	9	25	1	287			362	511	873	11	79	32	0.57	36	19	45	126	92	4%	8	272	6.36	5.6	$7
LIMA Plan C+	07 Proj	**399**	**68**	**109**	**20**	**60**	**5**	**273**			**355**	**506**	**860**	**11**	**74**	**32**	**0.50**	**40**	**18**	**42**	**146**	**105**	**8%**	**19**	**273**	**6.35**	**11.3**	**$16**

Despite fewer AB, proved his '05 breakout was no fluke. Now, his stated goal is to find a team which will give him a more prominent role. Of course, that's every player's dream, and there are just so many roles. Still...

Denorfia,Chris		AB	R	H	HR	RBI	SB	Avg	vL	vR	OB	Slg	OPS	bb%	ct%	h%	Eye	G	L	F	PX	SX	SBO	xHR	xBA	RC/G	RAR	R$
Pos 9	02	0	0	0	0	0	0	0							0							0		0				
Age 26	03	0	0	0	0	0	0	0							0							0		0				
Pre-Peak	04 aa	221	26	48	6	23	4	219			298	348	646	10	82	24	0.63				79	77	10%	6		3.60	-9.6	$3
Bats Right	05 CIN	* 549	76	145	17	69	11	264	273	259	324	422	746	8	84	29	0.55	66	10	24	98	98	12%	16	291	4.71	-8.7	$17
Reliability 9	06 CIN	* 418	57	133	8	49	15	318	317	262	380	437	817	9	85	36	0.69	59	17	24	75	88	12%	9	286	5.66	10.0	$17
DL	1st Half	240	33	81	4	29	13	336			395	441	836	9	88	37	0.84	43	14	43	66	83	16%	5		5.88	7.0	$12
BAvg Potl 40%	2nd Half	178	24	52	4	20	2	293			360	431	791	10	81	34	0.56	60	17	23	89	67	5%	5	281	5.37	3.0	$5
LIMA Plan D	07 Proj	**255**	**34**	**71**	**6**	**30**	**6**	**279**			**343**	**415**	**759**	**9**	**84**	**31**	**0.61**	**60**	**16**	**24**	**86**	**85**	**11%**	**7**	**288**	**4.93**	**-0.7**	**$8**

1-7-.274 in 106 AB at CIN. Extreme groundball hitter with otherwise solid all-around skills. GB profile limits his viability as a corner OF, but he gets on, and can steal a few bags. Decent end-gamer that won't hurt you.

ROD TRUESDELL

DeRosa,Mark			AB	R	H	HR	RBI	SB	Avg	vL	vR	OB	Slg	OPS	bb%	ct%	h%	Eye	G	L	F	PX	SX	SBO	xHR	xBA	RC/G	RAR	R$
Pos	954	02 ATL	* 267	32	75	5	28	4	281	293	299	322	397	719	6	90	30	0.62	52	18	30	70	88	10%	5	288	4.38	-7.0	$8
Age	32	03 ATL	266	40	70	6	22	1	263	277	257	305	383	688	6	82	30	0.33	45	20	35	82	62	2%	7	264	3.86	-13.4	$6
Past Peak		04 ATL	309	33	74	3	31	1	239	233	242	292	320	613	7	83	28	0.43	48	20	32	58	41	5%	5	250	3.10	-20.5	$3
Bats	Right	05 TEX	148	26	36	8	20	1	243	322	188	317	439	756	10	76	27	0.46	47	19	35	123	60	3%	7	273	4.76	0.3	$5
Reliability	16	06 TEX	520	78	154	13	74	4	296	342	278	351	456	807	8	80	35	0.43	49	23	29	109	70	6%	16	292	5.48	-2.7	$16
DL	15	1st Half	201	31	69	3	25	2	343			394	502	897	8	82	41	0.46	48	31	21	121	55	5%	6	328	6.65	5.2	$8
BAvg Potl	45%	2nd Half	319	47	85	10	49	2	266			324	426	750	8	80	31	0.42	49	17	34	101	77	6%	10	269	4.72	-8.7	$9
LIMA Plan	D+	07 Proj	**451**	**67**	**123**	**15**	**58**	**3**	**273**			**330**	**439**	**769**	**8**	**80**	**31**	**0.44**	**48**	**19**	**33**	**107**	**65**	**5%**	**16**	**279**	**4.95**	**-3.5**	**$13**

Compare 2nd half line to past few full seasons. They're a dead-on skills match. The smart money says that's his true level. This includes FB%, so he keeps the HR. But the BA is headed down in '07.

Diaz,Matt			AB	R	H	HR	RBI	SB	Avg	vL	vR	OB	Slg	OPS	bb%	ct%	h%	Eye	G	L	F	PX	SX	SBO	xHR	xBA	RC/G	RAR	R$
Pos	7	02 aa	449	58	109	9	41	26	243			287	365	652	6	85	27	0.42				81	119	36%	10		3.54	-28.4	$14
Age	29	03 a/a	480	58	155	10	75	13	323			363	477	840	6	86	36	0.45				102	90	15%	12		5.74	3.7	$20
Peak		04 aaa	503	68	147	16	78	13	293			323	484	807	4	83	33	0.25				123	109	16%	17		5.25	0.8	$19
Bats	Right	05 KC	* 374	44	103	10	51	8	276	370	143	303	436	739	4	83	31	0.23	51	20	29	101	106	15%	10	295	4.40	-3.5	$11
Reliability	24	06 ATL	297	37	97	7	32	5	327	295	358	351	475	825	4	84	37	0.22	50	24	27	87	92	12%	7	294	5.39	1.1	$11
DL	37	1st Half	124	12	42	2	13	3	339			364	484	848	4	81	40	0.22	50	22	28	85	97	14%	2	280	5.76	1.7	$5
BAvg Potl	30%	2nd Half	173	25	55	5	19	2	318			341	468	809	3	85	35	0.23	50	25	26	88	73	11%	5	303	5.13	-0.6	$6
LIMA Plan	F	07 Proj	**235**	**29**	**70**	**6**	**29**	**5**	**297**			**325**	**458**	**783**	**4**	**84**	**34**	**0.25**	**50**	**23**	**27**	**98**	**103**	**15%**	**6**	**301**	**4.93**	**-3.0**	**$8**

PRO:
- Maintained solid LD%
- Boosted xBA in 2nd half

CON:
- High GB% limits HR potential
- Low bb%, so value tied to BA

Nice 4th OF -- that's his ceiling.

Doumit,Ryan			AB	R	H	HR	RBI	SB	Avg	vL	vR	OB	Slg	OPS	bb%	ct%	h%	Eye	G	L	F	PX	SX	SBO	xHR	xBA	RC/G	RAR	R$
Pos	3	02	0	0	0	0	0	0	0							0							0		0				
Age	26	03	0	0	0	0	0	0	0							0							0		0				
Pre-Peak		04 aa	221	24	51	8	26	0	233			286	421	707	7	83	25	0.43				123	31	2%	8		4.19	-8.6	$3
Bats	Both	05 PIT	* 396	56	110	15	62	3	278	296	243	317	455	772	5	81	31	0.31	51	16	33	114	64	9%	14	281	4.82	-8.9	$14
Reliability	1	06 PIT	* 171	18	38	6	24	0	222	208	208	292	397	689	9	73	27	0.37	46	17	38	118	44	0%	7	248	4.01	-10.4	$2
DL	100	1st Half	78	8	19	2	14	0	243			279	422	701	5	76	30	0.21	40	19	40	122	63	0%	2	263	4.06	-4.5	$1
BAvg Potl	45%	2nd Half	93	10	19	4	10	0	204			302	376	678	12	71	24	0.48	49	15	36	115	16	0%	4	227	3.91	-6.1	$1
LIMA Plan	F	07 Proj	**129**	**15**	**31**	**5**	**18**	**0**	**240**			**298**	**411**	**709**	**8**	**77**	**28**	**0.36**	**48**	**16**	**36**	**115**	**39**	**3%**	**5**	**260**	**4.16**	**-6.5**	**$3**

6-17-.208 in 149 AB at PIT. He had marginal offensive value as a catcher. Now at 1B, that value is truly offensive. Some pop in his bat, but not enough to shoulder the risk.

Drew,J.D.			AB	R	H	HR	RBI	SB	Avg	vL	vR	OB	Slg	OPS	bb%	ct%	h%	Eye	G	L	F	PX	SX	SBO	xHR	xBA	RC/G	RAR	R$
Pos	9	02 STL	424	61	107	18	56	8	252	262	250	341	429	770	12	75	29	0.55	42	18	39	120	83	8%	18	262	5.14	-2.0	$14
Age	31	03 STL	287	60	83	15	42	2	289	218	306	368	512	881	11	83	30	0.75	44	23	33	128	101	5%	13	312	6.42	6.6	$13
Past Peak		04 ATL	518	118	158	31	93	12	305	287	313	434	569	1003	19	78	34	1.02	43	19	38	158	126	7%	30	300	8.52	46.0	$30
Bats	Left	05 LA	252	48	72	15	36	1	286	235	304	406	520	926	17	80	30	1.02	46	15	39	142	57	2%	14	290	7.30	14.6	$11
Reliability	50	06 LA	494	84	140	20	100	2	283	244	296	393	498	891	15	79	33	0.84	45	19	36	133	76	3%	22	287	6.94	30.4	$19
DL	89	1st Half	241	38	68	9	46	2	282			378	473	851	13	80	32	0.77	46	17	37	110	87	5%	9	273	6.29	10.4	$9
BAvg Potl	55%	2nd Half	253	46	72	11	54	0	285			407	522	928	17	77	33	0.90	44	20	35	156	58	1%	13	300	7.57	20.0	$10
LIMA Plan	B+	07 Proj	**412**	**76**	**118**	**20**	**74**	**3**	**286**			**400**	**514**	**914**	**16**	**79**	**32**	**0.89**	**45**	**18**	**37**	**140**	**86**	**4%**	**20**	**292**	**7.21**	**25.2**	**$18**

Dynamite finish shows what he can do when healthy. Alas, that has happened for exactly one full season in his career. Do you feel lucky? Then go ahead, make my draft day, and take him. Too risky for me.

Drew,Stephen			AB	R	H	HR	RBI	SB	Avg	vL	vR	OB	Slg	OPS	bb%	ct%	h%	Eye	G	L	F	PX	SX	SBO	xHR	xBA	RC/G	RAR	R$
Pos	6	02	0	0	0	0	0	0	0							0							0		0				
Age	24	03	0	0	0	0	0	0	0							0							0		0				
Growth		04	0	0	0	0	0	0	0							0							0		0				
Bats	Left	05 aa	101	10	20	3	10	2	198			277	327	604	10	74	24	0.42				90	54	21%	3		2.85	-4.6	$1
Reliability	0	06 ARI	* 551	69	154	16	62	4	279	350	308	328	452	780	7	84	31	0.45	36	24	40	98	89	6%	15	281	5.07	11.2	$15
DL		1st Half	311	37	81	8	32	2	260			311	386	697	7	88	27	0.64				70	50	7%	7		4.14	-2.0	$6
BAvg Potl	50%	2nd Half	240	32	73	8	30	2	304			350	537	888	7	78	36	0.33	36	24	40	139	97	3%	8	290	6.51	14.1	$8
LIMA Plan	C	07 Proj	**479**	**56**	**130**	**15**	**52**	**6**	**272**			**330**	**443**	**773**	**8**	**79**	**32**	**0.42**	**36**	**24**	**40**	**106**	**88**	**10%**	**15**	**271**	**5.03**	**11.7**	**$13**

5-23-.316 in 209 AB at ARI. Solid debut for uber-prospect, with nice 2nd half gains. On the darker side, ct% can go, and won't play unless he's 150% healthy (Sound familiar?) Only limited by long-term health.

Duffy,Chris			AB	R	H	HR	RBI	SB	Avg	vL	vR	OB	Slg	OPS	bb%	ct%	h%	Eye	G	L	F	PX	SX	SBO	xHR	xBA	RC/G	RAR	R$
Pos	8	02	0	0	0	0	0	0	0							0							0		0				
Age	27	03 aa	494	74	125	1	37	30	253			308	320	628	7	86	29	0.56				47	138	31%	4		3.42	-21.5	$14
Peak		04 aa	453	65	122	6	31	23	268			306	369	675	5	86	30	0.40				62	131	27%	7		3.80	-11.7	$13
Bats	Both	05 PIT	* 434	64	126	6	33	15	291	355	337	320	396	716	4	85	33	0.30	62	18	20	49	129	24%	6	292	4.18	-4.7	$15
Reliability	29	06 PIT	* 420	63	116	4	35	39	276	229	264	322	377	699	6	80	34	0.34	58	19	23	67	154	37%	6	274	4.11	-4.0	$17
DL	36	1st Half	98	13	19	0	4	3	194			218	276	493	3	73	26	0.12	61	12	27	67	140	20%	1	236	1.30	-9.7	$0
BAvg Potl	40%	2nd Half	322	50	97	4	31	36	301			353	408	761	7	82	36	0.45	57	22	21	67	151	40%	5	287	4.91	4.2	$17
LIMA Plan	C+	07 Proj	**530**	**78**	**147**	**5**	**39**	**38**	**277**			**316**	**375**	**691**	**5**	**82**	**33**	**0.32**	**59**	**17**	**23**	**64**	**154**	**33%**	**7**	**277**	**3.95**	**-9.1**	**$20**

2-18-.255-26 in 314 AB at PIT. Big 2nd half fuels hope for big SB totals in '07. That said, simply doubling the 2nd half isn't a smart projection. But if those OB gains are real...
UP: 50 SB

Duncan,Chris			AB	R	H	HR	RBI	SB	Avg	vL	vR	OB	Slg	OPS	bb%	ct%	h%	Eye	G	L	F	PX	SX	SBO	xHR	xBA	RC/G	RAR	R$
Pos	79	02	0	0	0	0	0	0	0							0							0		0				
Age	25	03 aa	25	1	5	1	3	0	200			200	360	560	0	76	22	0.00				104	0	0%	1		1.84	-2.8	$0
Pre-Peak		04 aa	387	47	98	13	52	7	253			342	406	748	12	79	29	0.65				99	54	10%	14		4.90	-3.3	$10
Bats	Left	05 aaa	430	45	100	16	58	1	233			314	395	709	11	80	25	0.61				104	33	4%	16		4.32	-9.3	$8
Reliability	12	06 STL	* 461	81	128	28	71	1	277	170	318	351	519	870	10	75	31	0.45	44	21	35	148	63	2%	25	286	6.34	14.4	$18
DL		1st Half	209	26	54	9	36	1	256			324	446	770	9	72	32	0.35	44	11	44	127	54	6%	9	235	5.10	-0.9	$6
BAvg Potl	45%	2nd Half	252	55	74	19	35	0	294			373	579	952	11	77	31	0.56	44	23	34	163	68	0%	16	311	7.32	14.5	$12
LIMA Plan	C	07 Proj	**406**	**59**	**110**	**24**	**58**	**2**	**271**			**349**	**507**	**855**	**11**	**78**	**30**	**0.53**	**44**	**21**	**35**	**143**	**56**	**4%**	**21**	**294**	**6.10**	**8.6**	**$15**

22-43-.293 in 280 AB at STL.
Why he's likely to regress:
- Debut far exceeded MLEs, & 2 1/2 years' data is better

Why he just might not:
- Did it at MLB level
- Fully supported by skills

Dunn,Adam			AB	R	H	HR	RBI	SB	Avg	vL	vR	OB	Slg	OPS	bb%	ct%	h%	Eye	G	L	F	PX	SX	SBO	xHR	xBA	RC/G	RAR	R$
Pos	7	02 CIN	535	84	133	26	71	19	249	254	246	394	454	848	19	68	32	0.75	40	20	40	154	92	14%	31	259	6.71	5.2	$21
Age	27	03 CIN	381	70	82	27	57	8	215	202	221	343	465	807	16	67	24	0.59	31	18	51	171	94	9%	27	249	5.86	3.2	$14
Peak		04 CIN	568	105	151	46	102	6	266	256	271	383	569	952	16	66	32	0.55	33	19	48	215	62	4%	46	278	8.14	44.3	$27
Bats	Left	05 CIN	543	107	134	40	101	4	247	199	273	377	540	917	17	69	28	0.68	36	17	47	209	77	4%	41	288	7.50	34.8	$24
Reliability	76	06 CIN	561	99	131	40	92	7	234	270	215	361	490	851	17	65	28	0.58	28	24	49	176	66	4%	41	256	6.63	23.3	$20
DL		1st Half	267	55	60	24	46	1	225			373	539	912	19	67	23	0.72	32	20	48	208	42	1%	23	280	7.43	17.7	$10
BAvg Potl	45%	2nd Half	294	44	71	16	46	6	241			350	446	795	14	64	32	0.46	24	27	49	147	65	7%	18	236	5.87	5.4	$9
LIMA Plan	B+	07 Proj	**554**	**100**	**134**	**38**	**94**	**6**	**242**			**368**	**503**	**871**	**17**	**66**	**29**	**0.59**	**31**	**21**	**48**	**184**	**74**	**4%**	**40**	**263**	**6.91**	**25.4**	**$21**

No matter how impressive all his skills are, a sub-70% ct% means that there is downside potential everywhere. BA is the first to go. 2nd half power slide cannot be ignored. Pay your $20, however:
DN: 30 HR, .225

Durham,Ray			AB	R	H	HR	RBI	SB	Avg	vL	vR	OB	Slg	OPS	bb%	ct%	h%	Eye	G	L	F	PX	SX	SBO	xHR	xBA	RC/G	RAR	R$
Pos	4	02 2AL	564	114	163	15	70	26	289	255	301	370	450	821	11	84	32	0.78	44	20	36	100	144	18%	16	282	5.85	29.0	$26
Age	35	03 SF	410	61	117	8	33	7	285	370	258	363	441	805	11	80	34	0.61	41	24	35	108	100	11%	11	283	5.68	15.0	$17
Decline		04 SF	471	95	133	17	65	10	282	333	263	360	484	844	11	87	29	0.95	44	16	40	112	136	10%	16	294	6.08	19.7	$19
Bats	Both	05 SF	497	67	144	12	62	6	290	290	292	352	429	781	9	88	31	0.81	47	21	32	90	61	6%	13	298	5.24	9.5	$16
Reliability	18	06 SF	498	79	146	26	93	7	293	341	277	359	538	897	9	88	29	0.84	46	17	37	130	102	7%	22	316	6.51	26.6	$22
DL	15	1st Half	206	28	50	8	35	2	243			328	442	769	11	87	25	0.96	51	16	33	108	89	4%	7	300	5.21	3.7	$5
BAvg Potl	65%	2nd Half	292	51	96	18	58	5	329			382	606	988	8	88	32	0.74	43	17	40	146	100	9%	14	326	7.41	21.8	$17
LIMA Plan	B	07 Proj	**507**	**82**	**147**	**18**	**79**	**8**	**290**			**358**	**481**	**839**	**10**	**87**	**30**	**0.82**	**45**	**18**	**36**	**110**	**103**	**8%**	**17**	**301**	**5.92**	**19.2**	**$20**

For perspective: he was two shy of a career-high in HR -- in the 2nd half alone! A Brady Anderson-esque explosion, for three months at least. At 35, a repeat is unlikely; if he does, the whispers will begin.

ROD TRUESDELL

Dye,Jermaine			AB	R	H	HR	RBI	SB	Avg	vL	vR	OB	Slg	OPS	bb%	ct%	h%	Eye	G	L	F	PX	SX	SBO	xHR	xBA	RC/G	RAR	R$
Pos	9	02 OAK	504	76	125	24	87	2	248	212	262	320	452	772	10	78	27	0.49	39	18	43	129	66	2%	23	273	5.02	-0.0	$16
Age	33	03 OAK	* 270	34	49	6	26	1	181	260	146	271	278	548	11	81	20	0.63	41	12	47	61	52	1%	6	208	2.37	-24.1	$1
Past Peak		04 OAK	532	87	141	23	80	4	265	280	259	327	464	791	8	76	31	0.38	39	18	43	127	91	4%	22	263	5.27	8.8	$17
Bats	Right	05 CHW	529	74	145	31	86	11	274	252	278	324	512	836	7	81	29	0.39	38	21	41	145	86	12%	26	301	5.60	13.8	$22
Reliability	51	06 CHW	539	103	170	44	120	7	315	337	305	383	622	1004	10	78	33	0.50	39	20	40	179	84	6%	35	314	7.86	32.1	$31
DL		1st Half	235	45	72	20	54	3	306			392	617	1009	12	80	31	0.69	38	20	42	177	72	7%	16	316	7.98	15.0	$14
BAvg Potl	40%	2nd Half	304	58	98	24	66	4	322			376	625	1001	8	77	35	0.37	40	21	39	180	90	6%	19	313	7.76	17.1	$18
LIMA Plan	C+	07 Proj	**574**	**97**	**170**	**38**	**108**	**8**	**296**			**358**	**555**	**913**	**9**	**79**	**32**	**0.45**	**39**	**20**	**41**	**155**	**86**	**7%**	**32**	**297**	**6.69**	**23.5**	**$27**

His power output has grossly exceeded his xHR for two years now, and you'd have to think that he's already reached the crest. Still a solid buy, but stop well short of $30.

Easley,Damion			AB	R	H	HR	RBI	SB	Avg	vL	vR	OB	Slg	OPS	bb%	ct%	h%	Eye	G	L	F	PX	SX	SBO	xHR	xBA	RC/G	RAR	R$
Pos	65	02 DET	* 330	33	71	8	30	1	215	313	198	285	339	624	9	87	23	0.74	41	17	42	74	42	8%	8	254	3.41	-12.1	$3
Age	37	03 TAM	107	8	20	1	7	0	187	184	188	202	262	464	2	83	22	0.11	45	20	35	46	62	0%	1	242	1.07	-11.5	($1)
Decline		04 FLA	223	26	53	9	43	4	238	149	294	312	457	769	10	84	25	0.67	41	18	41	138	77	11%	9	302	5.10	6.5	$6
Bats	Right	05 FLA	267	37	64	9	30	4	240	333	218	307	419	727	9	82	26	0.55	40	23	37	119	87	8%	9	295	4.52	4.5	$7
Reliability	28	06 ARI	189	24	44	9	28	1	233	245	217	310	418	728	10	84	23	0.70	45	15	40	99	57	4%	7	266	4.50	0.8	$4
DL		1st Half	110	15	25	6	21	0	227			336	455	790	14	88	21	1.38	42	14	43	117	55	3%	5	288	5.55	4.0	$3
BAvg Potl	70%	2nd Half	79	9	19	3	7	1	241			268	367	635	4	78	27	0.18	50	16	34	69	51	6%	2	236	2.93	-3.4	$1
LIMA Plan	F	07 Proj	**129**	**16**	**31**	**5**	**17**	**1**	**241**			**303**	**419**	**721**	**8**	**83**	**26**	**0.52**	**44**	**18**	**38**	**104**	**76**	**6%**	**4**	**276**	**4.37**	**0.7**	**$3**

Outward stats make it look like he's been holding steady. But xBA, PX reveal the true trend, and 2nd half brings it in laser-sharp focus. The descent will continue in '07, and the end of the line looms.

Eckstein,David			AB	R	H	HR	RBI	SB	Avg	vL	vR	OB	Slg	OPS	bb%	ct%	h%	Eye	G	L	F	PX	SX	SBO	xHR	xBA	RC/G	RAR	R$
Pos	6	02 ANA	608	107	178	8	63	21	293	302	289	342	388	730	7	93	31	1.02	42	25	33	53	126	18%	8	289	4.66	1.4	$22
Age	32	03 ANA	452	59	114	3	31	16	252	256	251	307	325	633	7	90	27	0.80	50	20	30	50	102	17%	5	276	3.58	-11.3	$9
Past Peak		04 ANA	566	92	156	2	35	16	276	279	274	326	332	658	7	91	30	0.86	50	21	30	38	104	12%	5	273	3.87	-9.7	$13
Bats	Right	05 STL	630	90	185	8	61	11	294	262	306	353	395	748	8	93	31	1.32	46	23	31	59	100	9%	9	296	5.00	18.4	$19
Reliability	27	06 STL	500	68	146	2	23	7	292	280	298	333	344	677	6	92	32	0.76	49	22	29	34	67	8%	4	271	4.00	-5.0	$10
DL	23	1st Half	304	45	97	1	18	5	319			363	375	738	6	93	34	1.00	49	22	29	36	74	8%	2	278	4.74	3.2	$9
BAvg Potl	55%	2nd Half	196	23	49	1	5	2	250			286	296	582	5	90	27	0.50	49	22	29	30	56	10%	2	261	2.82	-9.0	$2
LIMA Plan	C	07 Proj	**523**	**73**	**142**	**4**	**32**	**10**	**272**			**320**	**338**	**658**	**7**	**92**	**29**	**0.85**	**48**	**22**	**30**	**42**	**91**	**11%**	**5**	**278**	**3.84**	**-5.3**	**$11**

Given that '05 saw a career best in almost every stat, some drop-off was inevitable. Still, he was fine before nagging injuries cut sharply into skills. Even if healthy, xBA says bid on '03 with fewer SB, not '05.

Edmonds,Jim			AB	R	H	HR	RBI	SB	Avg	vL	vR	OB	Slg	OPS	bb%	ct%	h%	Eye	G	L	F	PX	SX	SBO	xHR	xBA	RC/G	RAR	R$
Pos	8	02 STL	476	96	148	28	83	4	311	262	329	416	561	977	15	72	38	0.64	37	25	38	178	76	4%	29	295	8.24	43.7	$26
Age	36	03 STL	447	89	123	39	89	1	275	225	292	382	617	999	15	72	30	0.61	34	20	47	231	58	3%	36	316	8.38	43.6	$23
Decline		04 STL	498	102	150	42	111	8	301	330	293	419	643	1062	17	70	35	0.67	34	21	45	231	89	7%	41	309	9.54	67.3	$31
Bats	Left	05 STL	467	88	123	29	89	5	263	296	251	384	533	917	16	70	31	0.65	35	19	47	198	65	7%	32	287	7.49	40.1	$21
Reliability	19	06 STL	350	52	90	19	70	4	257	156	295	355	471	826	13	71	31	0.52	35	20	44	142	55	4%	19	257	6.00	15.9	$13
DL		1st Half	200	28	51	7	38	3	255			358	405	763	14	78	30	0.71	37	19	44	94	54	4%	7	244	5.15	4.2	$6
BAvg Potl	45%	2nd Half	150	24	39	12	32	1	260			351	560	911	12	63	33	0.38	32	23	45	220	38	3%	12	275	7.64	13.9	$7
LIMA Plan	C+	07 Proj	**389**	**68**	**103**	**23**	**78**	**4**	**265**			**372**	**511**	**883**	**15**	**70**	**32**	**0.56**	**34**	**21**	**45**	**172**	**73**	**5%**	**24**	**270**	**6.95**	**27.0**	**$17**

Nagging injuries, then post-concussion syndrome combined to drag him down. There are still skills flashes, and a small rebound can't be ruled out. But the halcyon days are over, and he won't stop getting nicked up.

Ellis,Mark			AB	R	H	HR	RBI	SB	Avg	vL	vR	OB	Slg	OPS	bb%	ct%	h%	Eye	G	L	F	PX	SX	SBO	xHR	xBA	RC/G	RAR	R$
Pos	4	02 OAK	* 429	68	115	6	39	7	268	296	268	342	389	731	10	85	30	0.75	35	17	48	77	115	7%	8	243	4.76	8.9	$11
Age	29	03 OAK	553	78	137	9	52	6	248	217	259	308	371	679	8	83	28	0.51	40	22	38	81	104	6%	11	266	3.96	-2.9	$10
Peak		04 OAK	0	0	0	0	0	0	0							0							0		0				
Bats	Right	05 OAK	434	76	137	13	52	1	316	313	318	379	477	856	9	88	34	0.86	47	18	35	93	78	3%	12	292	6.10	23.1	$17
Reliability	3	06 OAK	441	64	110	11	52	4	249	278	242	312	385	697	8	83	28	0.53	39	19	42	87	82	4%	12	260	4.15	0.3	$9
DL	29	1st Half	164	21	37	3	11	3	226			282	323	606	7	83	26	0.46	40	21	39	63	74	8%	3	250	2.99	-5.6	$2
BAvg Potl	55%	2nd Half	277	43	73	8	41	1	264			329	422	751	9	83	29	0.50	39	18	43	101	68	1%	9	266	4.83	5.7	$7
LIMA Plan	C	07 Proj	**484**	**74**	**129**	**13**	**54**	**4**	**266**			**330**	**416**	**746**	**9**	**84**	**29**	**0.61**	**41**	**19**	**40**	**91**	**86**	**4%**	**14**	**271**	**4.76**	**9.0**	**$12**

Good things:
- Another 2nd half rebound
- 2nd half xHR shows upside

Bad things:
- Entire 1st half
- 2nd half not as good as '05
- He keeps getting hurt

Encarnacion,Edwin			AB	R	H	HR	RBI	SB	Avg	vL	vR	OB	Slg	OPS	bb%	ct%	h%	Eye	G	L	F	PX	SX	SBO	xHR	xBA	RC/G	RAR	R$
Pos	5	02	0	0	0	0	0	0	0							0							0		0				
Age	24	03 aa	254	34	68	5	30	6	269			317	393	709	7	87	29	0.55				78	92	14%	6		4.27	-0.8	$7
Growth		04 aa	469	65	123	13	67	15	262			328	418	746	9	85	28	0.66				100	90	15%	15		4.80	-2.5	$15
Bats	Right	05 CIN	* 501	63	134	23	77	9	268	246	234	331	479	810	9	80	30	0.47	41	24	35	142	70	9%	23	306	5.47	10.0	$18
Reliability	36	06 CIN	406	60	112	15	72	6	276	248	287	342	473	815	9	81	31	0.53	41	21	37	127	72	9%	16	292	5.62	1.5	$14
DL	29	1st Half	185	27	50	6	36	0	270			345	481	826	10	79	31	0.55	39	24	37	143	53	2%	7	303	5.88	2.1	$6
BAvg Potl	50%	2nd Half	221	33	62	9	36	6	281			340	466	806	8	82	31	0.50	44	19	38	113	71	14%	9	281	5.39	-0.6	$9
LIMA Plan	B	07 Proj	**511**	**71**	**144**	**20**	**82**	**10**	**282**			**344**	**474**	**818**	**9**	**82**	**31**	**0.53**	**42**	**21**	**37**	**123**	**82**	**10%**	**20**	**294**	**5.60**	**6.7**	**$19**

Nice follow-up in first full ML season. Late HR drought cut into PX, but that's all part of the unsteady growth of a 23-year-old; he's got good skills. Ironic tidbit: the "throw-in" in the Ruben Mateo/Rob Bell trade.

Encarnacion,Juan			AB	R	H	HR	RBI	SB	Avg	vL	vR	OB	Slg	OPS	bb%	ct%	h%	Eye	G	L	F	PX	SX	SBO	xHR	xBA	RC/G	RAR	R$
Pos	98	02 2NL	584	77	158	24	85	21	271	233	282	324	449	772	7	81	30	0.41	43	21	36	109	116	20%	21	281	4.91	-6.7	$24
Age	31	03 FLA	601	80	162	19	94	19	270	267	270	312	446	758	6	86	29	0.45	42	21	37	106	121	20%	18	298	4.75	-15.0	$22
Past Peak		04 2NL	484	63	114	16	62	5	236	217	241	291	405	696	7	82	26	0.44	43	16	41	106	78	9%	16	267	4.05	-18.2	$10
Bats	Right	05 FLA	506	59	145	16	76	6	287	309	282	340	447	787	7	79	33	0.39	39	24	38	106	71	8%	16	275	5.16	-1.4	$18
Reliability	66	06 STL	557	74	155	19	79	6	278	316	261	315	443	759	5	85	30	0.35	45	20	35	93	85	8%	17	283	4.66	-1.8	$17
DL		1st Half	284	38	80	10	43	3	282			304	465	769	3	85	30	0.21	43	20	37	101	95	10%	9	286	4.67	-0.8	$9
BAvg Potl	45%	2nd Half	273	36	75	9	36	3	275			327	421	748	7	84	30	0.49	48	20	32	83	66	7%	8	278	4.64	-1.1	$8
LIMA Plan	C	07 Proj	**501**	**64**	**137**	**17**	**71**	**7**	**274**			**320**	**436**	**756**	**6**	**83**	**30**	**0.40**	**43**	**20**	**36**	**97**	**81**	**9%**	**16**	**278**	**4.69**	**-5.0**	**$16**

Outwardly, one of the more stable skills sets. Behind the curtain, small signs of decline. GB rise, PX drop, widening platoon splits are problematic. But $15 will buy you $15 and sim gamers still stay away.

Ensberg,Morgan			AB	R	H	HR	RBI	SB	Avg	vL	vR	OB	Slg	OPS	bb%	ct%	h%	Eye	G	L	F	PX	SX	SBO	xHR	xBA	RC/G	RAR	R$
Pos	5	02 HOU	* 424	56	109	10	50	10	257	320	224	349	394	743	12	82	29	0.77	40	20	40	87	106	11%	11	259	4.94	4.3	$12
Age	31	03 HOU	385	69	112	25	60	7	291	316	282	370	530	899	11	84	29	0.80	38	21	41	133	84	8%	20	304	6.54	24.7	$19
Past Peak		04 HOU	411	51	113	10	66	6	275	282	273	333	411	745	8	89	29	0.78	45	20	35	78	85	9%	10	285	4.79	-3.2	$13
Bats	Right	05 HOU	526	86	149	36	101	6	283	293	278	383	557	940	14	77	30	0.71	37	17	45	173	71	8%	33	297	7.36	38.8	$26
Reliability	33	06 HOU	387	67	91	23	58	1	235	245	232	393	463	856	21	75	25	1.05	38	15	48	138	34	3%	24	255	6.61	13.2	$11
DL	22	1st Half	249	43	60	18	41	1	241			378	514	892	18	74	25	0.85	37	17	47	167	50	4%	17	277	6.96	11.0	$9
BAvg Potl	65%	2nd Half	138	24	31	5	17	0	225			418	370	788	25	78	25	1.48	40	11	49	89	25	3%	6	211	5.98	2.1	$3
LIMA Plan	B	07 Proj	**519**	**84**	**142**	**31**	**91**	**4**	**274**			**397**	**508**	**905**	**17**	**79**	**29**	**0.97**	**39**	**16**	**45**	**139**	**51**	**5%**	**29**	**276**	**7.05**	**28.7**	**$21**

Look at that 2nd half, and try to convince us he wasn't playing hurt. 1st half PX was as good as '05, and xBA shows BA skills were fine before his shoulder injury. If healthy, a strong rebound candidate.

Erstad,Darin			AB	R	H	HR	RBI	SB	Avg	vL	vR	OB	Slg	OPS	bb%	ct%	h%	Eye	G	L	F	PX	SX	SBO	xHR	xBA	RC/G	RAR	R$
Pos	8	02 ANA	625	99	177	10	73	23	283	280	285	313	389	702	4	89	30	0.40	48	21	32	63	135	16%	10	284	4.07	-12.5	$22
Age	32	03 ANA	258	35	65	4	17	9	252	302	227	301	333	634	7	84	29	0.45	50	23	27	49	109	14%	4	271	3.31	-10.9	$6
Past Peak		04 ANA	495	79	146	7	69	16	295	253	316	344	400	744	7	85	34	0.50	57	16	27	70	114	12%	9	278	4.68	-0.4	$18
Bats	Left	05 ANA	609	86	166	7	66	10	273	232	291	325	371	696	7	82	32	0.43	48	22	30	71	100	8%	10	270	4.10	-3.1	$15
Reliability	29	06 ANA	95	8	21	0	5	1	221	192	232	267	326	594	6	81	27	0.33	51	12	37	82	82	11%	1	245	2.91	-5.2	($0)
DL	112	1st Half	91	8	20	0	5	1	220			260	319	579	5	81	27	0.29	52	11	37	76	91	12%	1	241	2.69	-5.6	($0)
BAvg Potl	50%	2nd Half	4	0	1	0	0	0	250			400	500	900	20	75	33	1.00	33	33	33	234	-10	0%	0		7.83	0.4	($0)
LIMA Plan	D	07 Proj	**329**	**43**	**86**	**3**	**31**	**5**	**262**			**307**	**361**	**668**	**6**	**84**	**30**	**0.40**	**52**	**17**	**31**	**69**	**92**	**8%**	**5**	**264**	**3.75**	**-8.0**	**$6**

Finally succumbed to an injury, rather than playing through it as usual. Now that his contract is up, finding someone to pay for his meager production will be tougher. But someone will overpay. Don't be like them.

ROD TRUESDELL

Escobar,Alex

		Year	AB	R	H	HR	RBI	SB	Avg	vL	vR	OB	Slg	OPS	bb%	ct%	h%	Eye	G	L	F	PX	SX	SBO	xHR	xBA	RC/G	RAR	R$
Pos	8	02 CLE	0	0	0	0	0	0	0							0							0		0				
Age	28	03 CLE	* 538	72	131	28	84	8	243	350	220	282	446	728	5	71	29	0.18	44	24	32	138	83	10%	26	273	4.29	-7.2	$17
Peak		04 CLE	* 215	28	46	4	20	1	214	200	216	299	344	643	11	72	28	0.43	47	16	37	95	85	6%	6	233	3.54	-7.9	$2
Bats	Right	05 WAS	0	0	0	0	0	0	0							0							0		0				
Reliability	0	06 WAS	* 209	29	58	7	37	4	278	400	333	348	454	802	10	78	33	0.49	44	16	40	108	85	9%	7	260	5.48	6.2	$7
DL	83	1st Half	107	14	23	2	14	2	217			310	336	646	12	78	26	0.61				81	59	14%	3		3.61	-2.8	$2
BAvg Potl	40%	2nd Half	102	16	35	5	23	1	343			391	576	967	7	79	40	0.37	44	16	40	136	93	4%	4	283	7.40	7.8	$6
LIMA Plan	F	07 Proj	191	26	50	6	29	2	262			329	434	763	9	75	32	0.40	45	17	38	113	92	7%	7	257	5.00	2.5	$6

4-18-.356 in 87 AB at WAS
Opened up his swing, and high h% produced this result. 1st half line is still part of his package. Sept shoulder surgery increases risk.
DN: sub- .250 BA

Estrada,Johnny

		Year	AB	R	H	HR	RBI	SB	Avg	vL	vR	OB	Slg	OPS	bb%	ct%	h%	Eye	G	L	F	PX	SX	SBO	xHR	xBA	RC/G	RAR	R$
Pos	2	02 aaa	451	40	110	9	56	1	244			282	364	646	5	89	26	0.47				78	37	1%	10		3.50	-4.9	$7
Age	30	03 ATL	* 390	38	117	10	62	0	300	167	333	345	446	791	6	92	31	0.84	42	21	36	90	17	0%	10	296	5.25	10.3	$12
Peak		04 ATL	462	56	145	9	76	0	314	272	329	367	450	817	8	86	35	0.59	43	22	36	92	24	0%	12	283	5.60	22.2	$16
Bats	Both	05 ATL	357	31	93	4	39	0	261	214	277	300	367	667	5	89	28	0.53	36	26	38	76	22	0%	6	294	3.82	0.3	$5
Reliability	37	06 ARI	414	43	125	11	71	0	302	296	304	323	444	768	3	90	31	0.33	39	20	41	83	21	0%	11	279	4.70	4.1	$13
DL	16	1st Half	212	25	65	6	41	0	307			329	458	786	3	92	31	0.39	36	22	42	87	25	0%	6	292	4.93	3.4	$8
BAvg Potl	45%	2nd Half	202	18	60	5	30	0	297			317	431	748	3	89	31	0.27	43	18	39	79	16	0%	5	264	4.46	0.7	$6
LIMA Plan	D+	07 Proj	401	40	116	10	60	0	289			322	435	757	5	89	30	0.45	39	22	39	89	22	0%	11	289	4.69	6.5	$11

Rising FB trend validates double-digit HR, so he could reach that mark again. But 2nd half xBA decline calls BA into question, and he's being less and less selective. Another .300 season may be a stretch.

Ethier,Andre

		Year	AB	R	H	HR	RBI	SB	Avg	vL	vR	OB	Slg	OPS	bb%	ct%	h%	Eye	G	L	F	PX	SX	SBO	xHR	xBA	RC/G	RAR	R$
Pos	7	02	0	0	0	0	0	0	0							0							0		0				
Age	25	03	0	0	0	0	0	0	0							0							0		0				
Pre-Peak		04	0	0	0	0	0	0	0							0							0		0				
Bats	Left	05 a/a	516	81	145	14	64	1	281			332	424	756	7	85	31	0.52				91	58	4%	14		4.78	-3.6	$16
Reliability	0	06 LA	* 482	62	148	12	64	7	307	351	298	366	469	835	9	81	36	0.50	41	22	37	95	98	9%	12	273	5.87	8.2	$17
DL		1st Half	217	31	68	5	29	3	313			374	461	835	9	81	37	0.51	44	21	35	89	87	10%	5	269	5.87	3.7	$8
BAvg Potl	35%	2nd Half	265	31	80	7	35	4	302			360	475	835	8	82	35	0.49	40	23	38	100	97	8%	7	276	5.86	4.5	$9
LIMA Plan	C+	07 Proj	520	73	149	13	67	5	286			343	443	786	8	83	32	0.51	41	22	37	94	94	7%	14	278	5.21	-2.5	$16

11-56-.308 in 396 AB at LA
Solid debut and a bright future. But xBA and high h% suggest he won't repeat .300 BA, and PX is still below average. May still have some growing pains, so don't overbid for '07.

Everett,Adam

		Year	AB	R	H	HR	RBI	SB	Avg	vL	vR	OB	Slg	OPS	bb%	ct%	h%	Eye	G	L	F	PX	SX	SBO	xHR	xBA	RC/G	RAR	R$
Pos	6	02 HOU	* 433	56	108	2	26	14	249	261	169	303	339	642	7	83	30	0.45	30	26	43	61	146	15%	4	243	3.52	-4.8	$9
Age	30	03 HOU	* 487	71	122	9	59	11	251	324	240	299	372	671	7	84	28	0.43	38	24	38	78	124	11%	10	266	3.77	-4.9	$12
Peak		04 HOU	384	66	105	8	31	13	273	235	282	304	385	690	4	85	30	0.30	41	15	45	66	134	15%	8	239	3.84	-3.2	$12
Bats	Right	05 HOU	549	58	136	11	54	21	248	227	255	282	364	646	5	81	29	0.25	39	19	42	79	107	23%	12	249	3.30	-10.9	$14
Reliability	73	06 HOU	514	52	123	6	59	9	239	250	237	286	352	639	6	86	27	0.48	37	20	43	76	95	13%	8	255	3.48	-13.7	$8
DL		1st Half	244	25	59	2	28	2	242			286	336	622	6	88	27	0.50	39	18	42	60	73	7%	3	249	3.31	-7.7	$3
BAvg Potl	60%	2nd Half	270	27	64	4	31	7	237			287	367	654	7	85	27	0.46	35	22	43	78	104	18%	5	259	3.65	-5.8	$4
LIMA Plan	C	07 Proj	515	60	127	8	53	12	247			289	363	652	6	84	28	0.38	38	19	43	73	110	15%	9	252	3.53	-10.2	$10

SX continues to decline, so double-digit SB may soon be a thing of the past. Growth in eye and ct%, along with a low h%, mean BA may rebound some. But slowing .250 hitters are not in great demand these days.

Everett,Carl

		Year	AB	R	H	HR	RBI	SB	Avg	vL	vR	OB	Slg	OPS	bb%	ct%	h%	Eye	G	L	F	PX	SX	SBO	xHR	xBA	RC/G	RAR	R$
Pos	0	02 TEX	374	47	100	16	62	2	267	220	283	327	439	765	8	79	30	0.43	42	17	41	105	39	5%	15	255	4.84	-7.5	$12
Age	36	03 2AL	526	93	151	28	92	8	287	254	299	352	510	862	9	84	30	0.63	34	23	43	128	92	8%	24	299	6.06	21.4	$23
Decline		04 2TM	281	29	73	7	35	1	260	233	272	300	402	702	5	84	29	0.36	47	18	35	90	56	2%	7	271	4.05	-10.2	$6
Bats	Both	05 CHW	490	58	123	23	87	4	251	265	244	310	435	745	8	80	27	0.42	43	17	40	111	56	7%	20	265	4.56	-21.3	$15
Reliability	32	06 SEA	308	37	70	11	33	1	227	186	239	294	360	654	9	81	25	0.51	37	16	46	76	37	5%	10	232	3.51	-27.6	$4
DL		1st Half	244	32	59	9	28	1	242			315	381	696	10	82	26	0.59	36	18	45	80	40	4%	8	243	4.09	-17.2	$5
BAvg Potl	60%	2nd Half	64	5	11	2	5	0	172			209	281	490	4	80	18	0.23	41	8	51	62	38	9%	2	188	1.25	-11.0	($0)
LIMA Plan	F	07 Proj	163	18	38	5	21	0	233			286	357	643	7	81	26	0.39	41	15	44	74	35	4%	5	228	3.30	-13.5	$2

Power fade accelerated. LD rate has dropped for three straight years. So he's now a powerless low BA injury risk who's capable of putting up ugly numbers without the benefit of bad luck. And he's looking for a job.

Fahey,Brandon

		Year	AB	R	H	HR	RBI	SB	Avg	vL	vR	OB	Slg	OPS	bb%	ct%	h%	Eye	G	L	F	PX	SX	SBO	xHR	xBA	RC/G	RAR	R$
Pos	7	02	0	0	0	0	0	0	0							0							0		0				
Age	26	03	0	0	0	0	0	0	0							0							0		0				
Pre-Peak		04 aa	208	17	44	1	13	3	210			265	261	526	7	88	23	0.63				32	73	8%	1		2.28	-18.9	$0
Bats	Left	05 aa	500	58	133	3	43	15	266			320	333	653	7	86	31	0.57				46	99	15%	5		3.68	-19.8	$11
Reliability	17	06 BAL	* 319	44	77	2	26	7	241	190	244	312	307	618	9	83	28	0.62	56	21	23	41	102	14%	3	264	3.32	-18.1	$4
DL		1st Half	189	28	50	2	19	6	264			324	332	656	8	88	29	0.77	50	21	29	36	107	18%	2	264	3.80	-7.8	$4
BAvg Potl	60%	2nd Half	130	16	27	0	7	1	208			295	269	564	11	76	27	0.52	61	21	17	50	80	6%	1	255	2.58	-10.6	($0)
LIMA Plan	F	07 Proj	160	19	38	1	12	3	237			303	302	605	9	84	28	0.58	58	21	21	44	88	12%	1	271	3.14	-9.2	$2

2-23-.235 in 251 AB at BAL
If speed is your only skill, a .300 OBA won't cut it.
WARNING to sim gamers: Cover your eyes. Do not look at RAR. I repeat - DO NOT LOOK.

Fasano,Sal

		Year	AB	R	H	HR	RBI	SB	Avg	vL	vR	OB	Slg	OPS	bb%	ct%	h%	Eye	G	L	F	PX	SX	SBO	xHR	xBA	RC/G	RAR	R$
Pos	2	02 aaa	173	13	32	5	14	1	185			212	324	536	3	77	21	0.15				96	44	4%	5		1.79	-11.5	$0
Age	35	03	0	0	0	0	0	0	0							0							0		0				
Decline		04 aaa	236	16	43	8	26	0	183			207	343	550	3	82	19	0.17				97	30	0%	7		2.04	-15.3	$0
Bats	Right	05 BAL	* 205	30	50	15	29	0	243	317	224	281	485	766	5	73	26	0.19	38	19	43	153	31	0%	12	270	4.63	3.7	$7
Reliability	0	06 2TM	189	12	41	5	15	0	217	241	207	245	360	605	4	68	29	0.11	45	13	41	113	18	3%	6	209	2.70	-9.8	$1
DL	17	1st Half	131	9	32	4	10	0	244			272	397	669	4	66	34	0.11	43	14	43	121	18	4%	5	209	3.68	-2.7	$1
BAvg Potl	35%	2nd Half	58	3	9	1	5	0	155			183	276	459	3	72	20	0.13	50	12	38	95	15	0%	1	206	0.75	-7.0	($1)
LIMA Plan	F	07 Proj	135	11	27	5	14	0	200			231	364	594	4	73	24	0.15	45	15	41	113	27	1%	5	234	2.47	-7.2	$1

PRO: Occasional power.
CON: Everything else.
After extensive and painstaking research, it's been determined that there are no existing fantasy game formats that would benefit from use of this player.

Feliz,Pedro

		Year	AB	R	H	HR	RBI	SB	Avg	vL	vR	OB	Slg	OPS	bb%	ct%	h%	Eye	G	L	F	PX	SX	SBO	xHR	xBA	RC/G	RAR	R$
Pos	5	02 SF	146	14	37	2	13	0	253	184	289	283	336	619	4	82	30	0.22	42	21	37	53	54	0%	2	240	2.93	-7.1	$2
Age	32	03 SF	235	31	58	16	48	2	247	231	251	278	515	792	4	77	25	0.19	46	18	36	159	95	10%	12	302	4.93	4.7	$9
Past Peak		04 SF	503	72	139	22	84	5	276	291	269	308	485	793	4	83	30	0.27	47	15	37	125	89	7%	20	292	5.01	-0.8	$18
Bats	Right	05 SF	569	69	142	20	81	0	250	271	245	297	422	718	6	82	27	0.37	44	17	39	108	55	2%	19	272	4.24	-9.0	$14
Reliability	91	06 SF	603	75	147	22	98	1	244	212	253	283	428	711	5	81	27	0.29	40	16	43	110	69	2%	21	266	4.10	-25.0	$14
DL		1st Half	300	40	80	10	49	0	267			299	447	746	4	81	30	0.25	42	18	40	109	62	0%	10	272	4.49	-8.6	$8
BAvg Potl	50%	2nd Half	303	35	67	12	49	1	221			267	409	676	6	82	23	0.34	39	15	46	112	66	4%	11	260	3.70	-16.6	$5
LIMA Plan	C	07 Proj	526	65	131	20	82	2	249			289	434	722	5	82	27	0.30	43	17	41	112	71	3%	18	272	4.23	-14.2	$13

Outwardly, decent counting stats, and he's been very steady. But RAR is a better indicator of his true value, and you have to think THAT trend is going to eventually affect his opportunities. Don't overbid.

Fick,Robert

		Year	AB	R	H	HR	RBI	SB	Avg	vL	vR	OB	Slg	OPS	bb%	ct%	h%	Eye	G	L	F	PX	SX	SBO	xHR	xBA	RC/G	RAR	R$
Pos	2	02 DET	556	66	150	17	63	0	270	281	265	326	433	759	8	84	30	0.51	39	20	41	103	41	1%	18	276	4.85	19.6	$13
Age	33	03 ATL	409	52	110	11	80	1	269	135	289	337	418	755	9	89	28	0.89	35	24	41	92	53	1%	12	294	4.98	8.1	$12
Past Peak		04 2TM	226	14	45	6	26	0	199	111	207	270	319	589	9	84	21	0.61	35	18	47	64	37	0%	5	232	2.87	-8.5	$1
Bats	Left	05 SD	* 262	29	70	5	38	1	267	297	259	352	379	731	12	87	29	0.97	42	19	39	69	57	3%	5	258	4.82	7.8	$6
Reliability	0	06 WAS	* 177	20	43	3	10	3	242	273	262	300	316	617	8	81	28	0.45	34	18	48	46	53	9%	3	213	3.09	-6.7	$2
DL	75	1st Half	95	12	21	2	5	3	219			278	305	583	8	79	26	0.39	29	20	51	54	70	14%	2	210	2.61	-5.1	$1
BAvg Potl	45%	2nd Half	82	8	22	1	5	0	268			326	329	655	8	84	31	0.54	37	18	46	37	29	4%	1	212	3.63	-1.7	$1
LIMA Plan	F	07 Proj	96	10	23	2	9	1	241			308	329	637	9	84	27	0.61	37	19	44	54	40	5%	2	231	3.46	-1.9	$1

2-9-.266 in 128 AB at WAS
PX, which once upon a time was his one real strong suit, is now in a major free-fall. Eye, ct% and xBA all point to more problems. Stay far away.

HAROLD NICHOLS

Fielder,Prince

			AB	R	H	HR	RBI	SB	Avg	vL	vR	OB	Slg	OPS	bb%	ct%	h%	Eye	G	L	F	PX	SX	SBO	xHR	xBA	RC/G	RAR	R$
Pos	3	02	0	0	0	0	0	0	0							0							0		0				
Age	22	03	0	0	0	0	0	0	0							0							0		0				
Growth		04 aa	497	72	139	25	81	12	279			364	496	860	12	83	29	0.76				129	73	13%	23		6.22	10.7	$20
Bats	Left	05 MIL	* 437	58	123	25	80	7	281	500	281	351	510	860	10	81	30	0.58	37	35	28	142	49	11%	22	339	6.06	5.8	$19
Reliability	42	06 MIL	569	82	154	28	81	7	271	247	280	339	483	822	9	78	30	0.47	42	18	39	132	70	6%	27	279	5.66	-5.6	$19
DL		1st Half	285	38	82	16	42	5	288			345	533	878	8	77	32	0.38	39	18	43	153	71	9%	15	286	6.31	2.5	$11
BAvg Potl	45%	2nd Half	284	44	72	12	39	2	254			333	433	766	11	79	28	0.57	46	19	35	111	51	4%	12	271	5.02	-8.2	$8
LIMA Plan	C	07 Proj	599	85	164	31	95	9	274			346	491	837	10	80	30	0.55	43	20	38	133	63	9%	29	290	5.84	-0.2	$23

Superb debut, bright future. Sophomore slump possible? CASE FOR: xBA, PX and FB% dropped in second half. CASE AGAINST: ct% and eye improved, Sept. PX rebound VERDICT: Invest.

Fields,Josh

			AB	R	H	HR	RBI	SB	Avg	vL	vR	OB	Slg	OPS	bb%	ct%	h%	Eye	G	L	F	PX	SX	SBO	xHR	xBA	RC/G	RAR	R$
Pos	5	02	0	0	0	0	0	0	0							0							0		0				
Age	24	03	0	0	0	0	0	0	0							0							0		0				
Growth		04	0	0	0	0	0	0	0							0							0		0				
Bats	Right	05 aa	474	55	98	14	57	5	207			267	338	605	8	73	25	0.31				95	60	12%	15		2.79	-27.8	$7
Reliability	0	06 aaa	482	82	140	21	66	26	290	167	143	362	500	862	10	72	36	0.41	58	8	33	143	126	22%	23		6.42	15.9	$23
DL		1st Half	265	44	88	13	39	12	332			406	581	987	11	72	42	0.45				174	109	19%	14		8.24	21.3	$15
BAvg Potl	25%	2nd Half	217	38	52	8	27	14	240			307	401	708	9	73	29	0.36	58	8	33	106	139	27%	8		4.21	-6.8	$8
LIMA Plan	F	07 Proj	32	5	8	1	4	1	251			317	423	741	9	73	31	0.36	58	8	33	123	74	20%	1	250	4.69	-0.3	$1

1-2-.150 in 20 AB at CHW Why he's not yet ready — 1st half BA fueled by gigantic hit rate. 2nd half shows effect of a more typical h%. Low ct% creates BA risk. Probably a couple of years away.

Figgins,Chone

			AB	R	H	HR	RBI	SB	Avg	vL	vR	OB	Slg	OPS	bb%	ct%	h%	Eye	G	L	F	PX	SX	SBO	xHR	xBA	RC/G	RAR	R$
Pos	85	02 aaa	511	77	136	6	47	30	266			319	380	699	7	88	29	0.65				67	158	29%	7		4.27	-8.3	$18
Age	29	03 ANA	* 525	78	149	3	51	26	284	284	303	338	392	730	8	87	32	0.65	43	29	28	63	145	26%	4	296	4.68	-0.9	$17
Peak		04 ANA	577	83	171	5	60	34	296	314	289	351	419	771	8	84	35	0.52	37	25	39	69	150	27%	6	259	5.12	6.8	$22
Bats	Both	05 ANA	642	113	186	8	57	62	290	244	313	354	397	751	9	84	33	0.63	41	22	37	66	162	38%	9	260	4.92	11.8	$32
Reliability	99	06 ANA	604	93	161	9	62	52	267	233	280	338	376	714	10	83	31	0.65	44	21	36	65	151	37%	10	258	4.48	-3.3	$24
DL		1st Half	300	52	76	4	25	27	253			323	347	670	9	82	30	0.56	44	22	34	57	153	37%	5	252	3.89	-7.0	$11
BAvg Potl	50%	2nd Half	304	41	85	5	37	25	280			352	405	757	10	85	31	0.76	44	19	37	73	141	36%	5	265	5.05	3.5	$13
LIMA Plan	B	07 Proj	618	96	169	8	62	50	273			339	386	726	9	84	31	0.63	42	22	36	67	157	35%	9	261	4.62	0.7	$25

xBA has projected this BA dip since '04. Signs conflict for '07: 2nd half uptick says he might rebound, but xBA, declining LD% and ct% show there's still room for slippage. Net 10 SB hang in the balance.

Finley,Steve

			AB	R	H	HR	RBI	SB	Avg	vL	vR	OB	Slg	OPS	bb%	ct%	h%	Eye	G	L	F	PX	SX	SBO	xHR	xBA	RC/G	RAR	R$
Pos	8	02 ARI	505	82	145	25	89	16	287	297	282	368	499	867	11	86	29	0.89	45	15	40	123	112	13%	21	296	6.28	20.1	$26
Age	41	03 ARI	516	82	148	22	70	15	287	245	306	358	500	858	10	82	32	0.61	43	21	36	124	132	15%	20	296	6.15	17.3	$22
Decline		04 2NL	628	92	170	36	94	9	271	245	282	335	490	826	9	87	26	0.74	40	20	40	118	64	10%	29	301	5.58	17.0	$24
Bats	Left	05 ANA	406	41	90	12	54	8	222	271	201	269	374	643	6	83	24	0.37	40	18	43	96	93	15%	12	262	3.35	-11.7	$7
Reliability	1	06 SF	426	66	105	6	40	7	246	255	244	320	394	714	10	87	27	0.84	46	15	38	81	131	6%	7	270	4.63	2.3	$8
DL	23	1st Half	226	37	57	5	31	4	252			321	420	742	9	87	27	0.79	49	11	40	83	126	7%	4	264	4.87	2.9	$6
BAvg Potl	65%	2nd Half	200	29	48	1	9	3	240			318	365	683	10	87	27	0.88	43	20	37	78	118	6%	3	277	4.35	-0.6	$2
LIMA Plan	D	07 Proj	251	35	62	7	28	5	247			314	411	725	9	86	27	0.67	43	17	40	94	119	9%	7	276	4.58	0.2	$6

The descent continues. Still has a fine Eye, and xBA says he might do better. But advancing age and rapidly declining PX and LD rate make a rebound less likely. Bet against.

Floyd,Cliff

			AB	R	H	HR	RBI	SB	Avg	vL	vR	OB	Slg	OPS	bb%	ct%	h%	Eye	G	L	F	PX	SX	SBO	xHR	xBA	RC/G	RAR	R$
Pos	7	02 2TM	520	86	150	28	79	15	288	247	306	379	533	912	13	80	32	0.72	42	22	36	161	79	13%	28	316	6.97	20.0	$25
Age	34	03 NYM	365	57	106	18	68	3	290	262	305	377	518	895	12	82	31	0.77	38	18	44	141	77	3%	17	294	6.71	11.4	$16
Past Peak		04 NYM	396	55	103	18	63	11	260	239	269	339	462	801	11	74	31	0.46	43	18	40	138	74	14%	19	269	5.53	1.0	$15
Bats	Left	05 NYM	550	85	150	34	98	12	273	224	290	347	505	853	10	82	28	0.64	41	18	42	135	94	9%	28	293	5.97	9.9	$26
Reliability	16	06 NYM	332	45	81	11	44	6	244	179	266	305	407	711	8	83	27	0.50	42	18	40	99	85	8%	11	268	4.27	-9.7	$8
DL	48	1st Half	181	25	43	6	19	4	238			310	403	713	10	87	25	0.79	38	18	44	94	90	9%	6	271	4.45	-4.3	$4
BAvg Potl	55%	2nd Half	151	20	38	5	25	2	252			298	411	709	6	77	29	0.29	46	19	36	105	61	6%	5	262	4.10	-5.1	$4
LIMA Plan	D+	07 Proj	400	57	104	13	62	6	260			328	417	745	9	80	30	0.51	42	18	40	101	82	7%	13	264	4.73	-7.5	$12

Why a rebound is no given: Declining PX & eye, increasing fragility and struggles vs LHP. In fact, the last 4 years of his LH/RH splits are a perfect exhibition of the evolution of a platoon player.

Ford,Lew

			AB	R	H	HR	RBI	SB	Avg	vL	vR	OB	Slg	OPS	bb%	ct%	h%	Eye	G	L	F	PX	SX	SBO	xHR	xBA	RC/G	RAR	R$
Pos	79	02 a/a	566	85	147	14	52	20	260			312	403	715	7	89	27	0.70				87	122	19%	14		4.41	-20.0	$18
Age	30	03 MIN	* 284	45	82	5	42	6	289	329	361	329	447	776	6	87	32	0.47	44	22	34	103	110	16%	7	304	5.05	-2.3	$10
Peak		04 MIN	569	89	170	15	72	20	299	293	301	373	446	819	11	87	32	0.89	52	17	31	87	120	12%	15	290	5.77	13.0	$22
Bats	Right	05 MIN	522	70	138	7	53	13	264	224	278	323	377	700	8	84	30	0.53	54	16	30	78	105	13%	10	273	4.23	-7.4	$13
Reliability	32	06 MIN	234	40	53	4	18	9	226	206	242	276	312	588	6	82	26	0.37	52	16	32	51	131	17%	4	245	2.68	-15.7	$4
DL	28	1st Half	176	30	38	2	11	8	216			277	295	573	8	81	26	0.45	52	14	34	52	136	20%	2	237	2.61	-14.0	$2
BAvg Potl	50%	2nd Half	58	10	15	2	7	1	259			271	362	633	2	83	28	0.10	52	23	25	51	87	7%	1	268	2.84	-3.9	$2
LIMA Plan	F	07 Proj	230	36	58	4	24	5	253			300	349	649	6	84	29	0.42	52	18	29	59	102	10%	4	263	3.46	-10.6	$5

Skills have been screaming "4th OF" for years, even as MIN kept putting him out there every day. Declining PX, Eye, ct%, and increasing struggles vs both RHP and LHP have removed "full-time" from the vocabulary.

Francoeur,Jeff

			AB	R	H	HR	RBI	SB	Avg	vL	vR	OB	Slg	OPS	bb%	ct%	h%	Eye	G	L	F	PX	SX	SBO	xHR	xBA	RC/G	RAR	R$
Pos	9	02	0	0	0	0	0	0	0							0							0		0				
Age	23	03	0	0	0	0	0	0	0							0							0		0				
Growth		04 aa	76	7	13	2	8	1	171			171	263	434	0	79	19	0.00				53	10	10%	2		0.34	-11.5	$0
Bats	Right	05 ATL	* 592	76	161	25	99	14	272	403	268	306	483	789	5	79	31	0.23	40	19	41	144	96	17%	25	290	5.02	-3.9	$23
Reliability	1	06 ATL	651	83	169	29	103	1	260	292	248	285	449	733	3	80	29	0.17	45	18	37	107	60	5%	24	270	4.20	-11.0	$18
DL		1st Half	327	37	83	15	57	1	254			269	437	707	2	80	28	0.11	48	21	31	101	63	10%	12	279	3.77	-9.7	$9
BAvg Potl	45%	2nd Half	324	46	86	14	46	0	265			300	460	760	5	79	30	0.24	42	15	42	114	65	1%	12	261	4.62	-1.4	$9
LIMA Plan	C	07 Proj	638	83	169	25	92	2	265			295	449	743	4	79	30	0.20	43	18	38	115	64	5%	23	272	4.39	-11.9	$18

High AB total masks base skill declines, so he'll likely be overvalued. However, small 2nd half growth gives reason for hope. Ah, the unpredictablity of youth.
UP: 30 HR, .290 BA.
DN: 20 HR, 250 BA

Franco,Julio

			AB	R	H	HR	RBI	SB	Avg	vL	vR	OB	Slg	OPS	bb%	ct%	h%	Eye	G	L	F	PX	SX	SBO	xHR	xBA	RC/G	RAR	R$
Pos	3	02 ATL	338	51	96	6	30	5	284	382	256	358	382	740	10	78	35	0.52	44	29	27	69	82	5%	7	269	4.75	-8.1	$10
Age	48	03 ATL	197	28	58	5	31	0	294	351	243	374	447	821	11	78	36	0.58	55	25	20	102	68	2%	6	295	5.86	1.9	$7
Decline		04 ATL	320	37	99	6	57	4	309	306	312	379	441	820	10	79	38	0.53	54	24	22	88	80	6%	8	285	5.81	-1.3	$12
Bats	Right	05 ATL	233	30	64	9	42	4	275	267	278	350	451	801	10	76	33	0.47	57	21	22	120	83	6%	9	289	5.51	-0.6	$9
Reliability	8	06 NYM	165	14	45	2	26	6	273	227	303	326	370	696	7	70	38	0.27	55	27	18	80	63	15%	4	258	4.14	-8.8	$5
DL		1st Half	62	6	19	1	12	4	306			368	435	803	9	79	38	0.46	53	18	29	95	66	21%	2	271	5.53	-0.8	$3
BAvg Potl	30%	2nd Half	103	8	26	1	14	2	252			300	330	630	6	65	38	0.19	57	33	10	69	46	11%	2	251	3.27	-8.4	$2
LIMA Plan	F	07 Proj	96	10	24	2	16	2	251			317	365	683	9	74	32	0.37	55	24	21	85	60	11%	3	266	3.94	-5.4	$2

Professional hitter began to show his age in the 2nd half. Diminished skills will mean diminished PT, so the end is clearly near. His retirement will leave Roger Clemens as the oldest active ballplayer.

Frandsen,Kevin

			AB	R	H	HR	RBI	SB	Avg	vL	vR	OB	Slg	OPS	bb%	ct%	h%	Eye	G	L	F	PX	SX	SBO	xHR	xBA	RC/G	RAR	R$
Pos	4	02	0	0	0	0	0	0	0							0							0		0				
Age	24	03	0	0	0	0	0	0	0							0							0		0				
Growth		04	0	0	0	0	0	0	0							0							0		0				
Bats	Right	05 a/a	218	31	61	3	26	6	280			296	394	690	2	93	29	0.33				77	89	23%	4		3.95	-2.5	$7
Reliability	0	06 SF	* 386	47	99	4	30	5	256	200	217	279	368	647	3	90	28	0.32	48	13	39	71	80	14%	6	264	3.49	-12.7	$6
DL	15	1st Half	198	23	51	1	13	3	258			283	354	636	3	89	28	0.33	50	17	33	65	78	19%	3	272	3.39	-7.2	$3
BAvg Potl	55%	2nd Half	188	24	48	3	17	2	255			275	383	658	3	91	27	0.31	44	7	48	77	86	8%	4	245	3.59	-5.6	$3
LIMA Plan	F	07 Proj	136	18	36	2	13	3	264			284	375	658	3	92	28	0.33	47	12	40	73	78	17%	2	265	3.61	-3.9	$3

2-6-.204 in 93 AB at SF. Makes good contact, but poor plate patience and below average power and speed limit his upside. Still has time to grow, but probably a couple of years away.

HAROLD NICHOLS

Freel,Ryan

Freel,Ryan			AB	R	H	HR	RBI	SB	Avg	vL	vR	OB	Slg	OPS	bb%	ct%	h%	Eye	G	L	F	PX	SX	SBO	xHR	xBA	RC/G	RAR	R$
Pos	89	02 aaa	448	54	107	7	41	31	239			288	359	647	6	90	25	0.67				75	137	41%	8		3.68	-15.7	$14
Age	31	03 CIN *	352	52	92	7	22	28	261	326	266	310	378	688	7	89	28	0.64	44	30	27	70	138	42%	7	310	4.07	-9.6	$14
Past Peak		04 CIN	505	74	140	3	28	37	277	235	290	362	368	730	12	83	33	0.76	50	20	29	58	150	27%	5	263	4.84	2.8	$18
Bats	Right	05 CIN	369	69	100	4	21	36	271	302	263	360	371	731	12	84	31	0.86	53	24	24	68	149	37%	6	291	4.86	3.3	$17
Reliability	80	06 CIN	454	67	123	8	27	37	271	303	261	352	399	751	11	78	33	0.58	44	21	35	89	114	34%	11	261	4.99	7.4	$17
DL	51	1st Half	221	34	65	4	13	17	294			371	430	801	11	81	35	0.63	43	22	35	93	109	30%	6	272	5.61	7.4	$9
BAvg Potl	40%	2nd Half	233	33	58	4	14	20	249			335	369	704	11	76	31	0.55	45	20	35	85	112	39%	6	250	4.38	-0.4	$8
LIMA Plan	B	07 Proj	454	70	122	11	27	33	269			350	415	765	11	81	31	0.67	47	22	31	94	129	32%	13	283	5.12	7.7	$18

Shift in GB to FB is taking away his BA upside, and hence, a bit of his speed game. The give-back is a bit more power. Potential net gain for real-world productivity. Potential net loss for long-term Rotisserie value.

Freeman,Choo

Freeman,Choo			AB	R	H	HR	RBI	SB	Avg	vL	vR	OB	Slg	OPS	bb%	ct%	h%	Eye	G	L	F	PX	SX	SBO	xHR	xBA	RC/G	RAR	R$
Pos	8	02 aa	430	58	120	11	46	11	279			349	419	767	10	84	31	0.68				83	97	20%	11		5.08	3.3	$14
Age	27	03 aaa	327	33	79	7	27	1	242			279	352	631	5	85	27	0.35				63	65	13%	6		3.19	-16.8	$4
Peak		04 COL *	450	54	114	9	45	6	253	205	176	301	398	699	6	84	29	0.42	57	17	26	85	109	10%	9	287	4.13	-7.0	$9
Bats	Right	05 aaa	354	29	86	8	37	3	243			280	358	638	5	87	26	0.38				64	74	8%	7		3.31	-11.8	$5
Reliability	29	06 COL	173	24	41	2	18	5	237	276	206	294	341	635	7	76	30	0.33	54	22	24	66	123	25%	2	257	3.32	-6.1	$3
DL		1st Half	84	10	22	1	9	2	262			303	357	661	6	75	34	0.24	52	21	27	63	101	14%	1	245	3.53	-2.2	$2
BAvg Potl	45%	2nd Half	89	14	19	1	9	3	213			286	326	612	9	76	27	0.43	56	23	21	68	133	36%	1	268	3.12	-3.9	$1
LIMA Plan	F	07 Proj	65	8	16	1	7	1	245			296	357	653	7	81	29	0.38	54	21	24	66	111	19%	1	272	3.52	-2.1	$1

Struggled to make contact, as COL didn't follow up on promise for more PT. Second half SX shows his potential, but as long as he can't hit right-handed pitching - again - his role will be limited.

Furcal,Rafael

Furcal,Rafael			AB	R	H	HR	RBI	SB	Avg	vL	vR	OB	Slg	OPS	bb%	ct%	h%	Eye	G	L	F	PX	SX	SBO	xHR	xBA	RC/G	RAR	R$
Pos	6	02 ATL	636	95	175	8	47	27	275	288	272	321	387	708	6	82	32	0.38	48	25	27	75	137	25%	10	282	4.21	5.9	$21
Age	29	03 ATL	664	130	194	15	61	25	292	247	306	351	443	794	8	89	31	0.79	48	23	29	88	163	14%	15	309	5.38	23.6	$27
Peak		04 ATL	563	103	157	14	59	29	279	276	280	346	414	760	9	87	30	0.82	50	16	34	76	139	20%	13	278	5.01	14.3	$23
Bats	Both	05 ATL	616	100	175	12	58	46	284	288	280	350	429	778	9	87	31	0.79	47	24	30	86	163	31%	12	302	5.27	23.1	$29
Reliability	99	06 LA	654	113	196	15	63	37	300	324	293	370	445	815	10	85	33	0.74	50	21	29	83	133	23%	15	290	5.70	24.8	$28
DL		1st Half	315	58	82	4	26	17	260			338	343	681	11	84	30	0.73	51	22	27	50	119	23%	5	267	4.12	-2.3	$10
BAvg Potl	50%	2nd Half	339	55	114	11	37	20	336			400	540	940	10	86	37	0.77	49	20	31	114	134	24%	11	313	7.14	25.2	$18
LIMA Plan	B+	07 Proj	639	119	188	17	62	38	294			361	455	815	9	86	32	0.75	49	21	30	92	152	25%	17	299	5.66	26.5	$30

Why he could be primed for a career year:
- Growing OPS trend
- Growing bb%
- 2nd half PX

UP: 20 HR, 40 SB, .310 BA

Garciaparra,Nomar

Garciaparra,Nomar			AB	R	H	HR	RBI	SB	Avg	vL	vR	OB	Slg	OPS	bb%	ct%	h%	Eye	G	L	F	PX	SX	SBO	xHR	xBA	RC/G	RAR	R$
Pos	3	02 BOS	635	101	197	24	120	5	310	305	311	352	528	880	6	90	32	0.65	33	21	46	128	92	5%	23	311	6.17	5.4	$28
Age	33	03 BOS	658	120	198	28	105	19	301	357	281	340	524	864	6	91	30	0.64	33	20	47	119	151	15%	22	300	5.95	10.4	$31
Past Peak		04 2TM	326	55	103	10	44	4	316	240	329	365	494	859	7	91	33	0.83	34	24	42	101	97	5%	10	303	6.02	4.8	$13
Bats	Right	05 CHC	230	28	65	9	30	0	283	281	285	318	452	770	5	90	28	0.50	40	25	35	99	26	0%	8	311	4.80	-5.1	$7
Reliability	8	06 LA	469	82	142	20	93	3	303	341	294	360	505	865	8	94	29	1.40	38	20	42	107	76	2%	17	312	6.15	1.9	$21
DL	33 106	1st Half	229	46	83	10	47	3	362			423	590	1012	9	94	35	1.85	39	25	36	123	79	4%	9	347	7.84	10.5	$14
BAvg Potl	70%	2nd Half	240	36	59	10	46	0	246			298	425	723	7	93	23	1.06	38	15	47	91	51	0%	8	276	4.52	-10.5	$7
LIMA Plan	C+	07 Proj	419	66	129	17	71	3	308			355	498	854	7	92	31	0.90	38	21	41	105	74	3%	14	308	5.91	0.7	$18

There has never been a question about his superb skills. The REAL issue here, still, is health. Highest AB since 2003, but still sidelined a lot. Face it, to roster Nomar is to roster injury risk.

Garko,Ryan

Garko,Ryan			AB	R	H	HR	RBI	SB	Avg	vL	vR	OB	Slg	OPS	bb%	ct%	h%	Eye	G	L	F	PX	SX	SBO	xHR	xBA	RC/G	RAR	R$
Pos	3	02	0	0	0	0	0	0	0							0							0		0				
Age	26	03	0	0	0	0	0	0	0							0							0		0				
Pre-Peak		04 a/a	192	25	57	4	34	1	297			341	438	779	6	86	33	0.48				93	48	2%	5		5.06	-2.2	$6
Bats	Right	05 aaa	452	58	119	13	59	1	263			315	409	724	7	84	29	0.46				93	52	4%	13		4.38	-12.8	$11
Reliability	27	06 CLE *	549	69	137	20	100	4	250	333	281	321	413	734	9	81	28	0.56	42	17	41	102	43	6%	20	259	4.58	-13.7	$14
DL		1st Half	275	32	62	9	47	3	227			307	374	681	10	82	25	0.63				92	46	10%	9		3.99	-12.1	$5
BAvg Potl	50%	2nd Half	274	37	75	11	54	1	273			336	451	787	9	81	30	0.50	42	17	41	111	40	3%	11	265	5.17	-1.9	$9
LIMA Plan	C	07 Proj	515	66	136	16	85	2	264			323	419	743	8	83	29	0.51	42	17	41	98	52	5%	16	262	4.65	-9.7	$14

7-45-.292 in 185 AB at CLE Might be overvalued due to hype from small MLB sample. There has been BPI erosion upon each promotion, and RAR tells us where he stands among his peers. Bid with caution.

Gathright,Joey

Gathright,Joey			AB	R	H	HR	RBI	SB	Avg	vL	vR	OB	Slg	OPS	bb%	ct%	h%	Eye	G	L	F	PX	SX	SBO	xHR	xBA	RC/G	RAR	R$
Pos	8	02	0	0	0	0	0	0	0							0							0		0				
Age	25	03 aa	85	11	31	0	5	11	365			400	376	776	6	84	44	0.36				10	100	40%	0		4.90	0.1	$6
Pre-Peak		04 a/a	362	51	112	0	14	39	309			357	356	714	7	81	38	0.39				36	128	48%	2		4.30	-4.0	$17
Bats	Left	05 TAM *	429	62	114	1	26	42	266	353	269	315	336	651	7	83	32	0.42	72	15	13	47	160	46%	3	289	3.59	-9.0	$16
Reliability	33	06 2AL	383	59	91	1	41	22	238	232	239	313	292	605	10	80	29	0.56	67	16	17	38	129	26%	3	261	3.13	-18.1	$9
DL		1st Half	168	30	36	0	13	12	214			309	256	565	12	82	26	0.74	63	17	20	36	115	31%	1	255	2.78	-10.0	$4
BAvg Potl	55%	2nd Half	215	29	55	1	28	10	256			316	321	637	8	80	32	0.43	70	16	14	40	128	23%	1	264	3.41	-8.1	$5
LIMA Plan	C	07 Proj	404	60	105	1	33	32	260			321	319	640	8	81	32	0.48	69	16	16	40	140	36%	2	269	3.49	-13.3	$13

Bad luck 1H hit rate depressed BA but note xBA and rising bb%. Extreme GB hitter of the Ichiro mold, but makes 10% less contact, which is why he doesn't hit .350. Still, could surprise. UP: .280 BA, 45 SB.

German,Esteban

German,Esteban			AB	R	H	HR	RBI	SB	Avg	vL	vR	OB	Slg	OPS	bb%	ct%	h%	Eye	G	L	F	PX	SX	SBO	xHR	xBA	RC/G	RAR	R$
Pos	4057	02 aaa	458	54	105	1	32	19	229			315	275	590	11	89	25	1.16				32	93	26%	3		3.31	-13.3	$8
Age	29	03 aaa	467	68	124	2	41	26	266			329	338	667	9	88	30	0.81				46	133	25%	4		4.01	-3.6	$14
Peak		04 OAK *	291	34	80	2	28	14	275	167	271	317	344	661	6	88	31	0.50	67	13	20	40	124	20%	2	274	3.71	-3.1	$8
Bats	Right	05 aaa	489	68	128	4	46	29	262			323	348	671	8	89	29	0.81				56	132	26%	6		4.03	-4.5	$16
Reliability	17	06 KC	279	44	91	3	34	7	326	347	311	411	459	869	13	82	39	0.82	58	18	24	86	118	10%	5	290	6.62	18.7	$10
DL		1st Half	110	20	37	1	10	2	336			425	409	834	13	87	38	1.21	61	17	22	49	60	6%	2	269	6.19	6.0	$4
BAvg Potl	40%	2nd Half	169	24	54	2	24	5	320			401	491	892	12	79	39	0.66	56	19	25	113	116	12%	3	297	6.96	13.1	$6
LIMA Plan	D	07 Proj	251	36	74	2	27	10	294			366	396	762	10	86	34	0.78	59	18	23	65	117	16%	3	286	5.15	7.4	$8

What does a guy have to do to get a full-time gig? Hit rate says BA will drop, but these are solid skills. Drop in SBO says he didn't get green light often. If that changes, SB could spike.

Giambi,Jason

Giambi,Jason			AB	R	H	HR	RBI	SB	Avg	vL	vR	OB	Slg	OPS	bb%	ct%	h%	Eye	G	L	F	PX	SX	SBO	xHR	xBA	RC/G	RAR	R$
Pos	03	02 NYY	560	120	176	41	122	2	314	299	320	426	598	1024	16	80	33	0.97	31	24	45	169	54	2%	37	313	8.48	44.7	$33
Age	36	03 NYY	535	97	134	41	107	2	250	192	272	396	527	923	19	74	26	0.92	27	20	53	176	38	2%	39	283	7.42	44.2	$23
Decline		04 NYY	264	33	55	12	40	0	208	263	185	328	379	707	15	77	23	0.76	41	9	50	104	22	1%	12	212	4.39	-7.5	$4
Bats	Left	05 NYY	417	74	113	32	87	0	271	261	276	421	535	956	21	74	29	0.99	33	19	48	167	18	0%	30	278	7.92	22.6	$19
Reliability	12	06 NYY	446	92	113	37	113	2	253	213	270	401	558	959	20	76	25	1.04	30	16	53	185	48	1%	34	293	7.84	18.4	$21
DL		1st Half	229	49	62	23	62	1	271			414	624	1038	20	75	26	0.98	30	16	54	213	39	1%	20	308	8.86	15.9	$13
BAvg Potl	65%	2nd Half	217	43	51	14	51	1	235			387	488	876	20	77	24	1.10	31	17	53	157	45	1%	14	276	6.80	2.4	$8
LIMA Plan	B	07 Proj	449	83	113	33	100	1	252			395	517	912	19	76	26	0.98	33	16	51	163	37	1%	31	277	7.22	15.8	$19

Comparisons with 2003:
- Near-Mendoza Line vs LHP
- Over 50% FB rate
- Undershot xBA by 30+ points
- PX over 175

Also the PED use in '03, but you certainly can't link that here...

Gibbons,Jay

Gibbons,Jay			AB	R	H	HR	RBI	SB	Avg	vL	vR	OB	Slg	OPS	bb%	ct%	h%	Eye	G	L	F	PX	SX	SBO	xHR	xBA	RC/G	RAR	R$
Pos	09	02 BAL	490	71	121	28	69	1	247	235	250	310	482	792	8	87	23	0.68	41	14	45	132	47	4%	23	292	5.19	-4.9	$15
Age	30	03 BAL	625	80	173	23	100	0	277	273	279	329	456	785	7	86	29	0.55	40	24	36	109	36	1%	22	301	5.12	8.9	$19
Peak		04 BAL	346	36	85	10	47	1	246	257	241	304	379	683	8	82	28	0.45	46	13	40	80	44	2%	10	237	3.87	-14.6	$6
Bats	Left	05 BAL	488	72	135	26	79	0	277	250	286	316	516	832	5	89	27	0.50	37	17	47	138	52	0%	21	307	5.51	-7.0	$18
Reliability	35	06 BAL	343	34	95	13	46	0	277	258	281	339	458	796	9	86	29	0.67	38	16	46	109	13	0%	13	265	5.32	-10.8	$8
DL	61	1st Half	190	22	52	10	29	0	274			310	495	805	5	87	27	0.42	38	14	47	125	19	0%	8	279	5.14	-7.0	$6
BAvg Potl	55%	2nd Half	153	12	43	3	17	0	281			371	412	783	13	84	32	0.92	38	18	44	89	8	0%	4	249	5.49	-4.1	$3
LIMA Plan	D+	07 Proj	483	54	136	19	67	0	282			340	466	806	8	86	30	0.62	39	16	45	111	33	1%	18	275	5.40	-8.4	$14

Only twice on the DL in his 6-year career, but my $18 Tout Wars bid was still deemed "foolish" for a player so injury-prone. Bah! Window for big year still open, IF he stays healthy. UP: 30 HR, .300 BA Bah!

HAROLD NICHOLS

Giles,Brian

Giles,Brian		AB	R	H	HR	RBI	SB	Avg	vL	vR	OB	Slg	OPS	bb%	ct%	h%	Eye	G	L	F	PX	SX	SBO	xHR	xBA	RC/G	RAR	R$
Pos 9	02 PIT	497	95	148	38	103	15	298	231	325	448	622	1070	21	85	29	1.82	30	18	52	190	98	10%	35	333	9.25	55.0	$32
Age 36	03 2NL	492	93	147	20	88	4	299	286	305	422	514	936	18	88	31	1.81	34	23	43	125	89	4%	20	309	7.58	26.9	$22
Decline	04 SD	609	97	173	23	94	10	284	237	309	375	475	850	13	87	30	1.11	37	20	44	106	106	7%	22	285	6.24	16.3	$24
Bats Left	05 SD	545	92	164	15	83	13	301	289	306	426	483	909	18	88	32	1.86	37	24	39	110	111	8%	17	306	7.35	31.8	$24
Reliability 45	06 SD	604	87	159	14	83	9	263	217	282	371	397	769	15	90	27	1.73	40	18	43	79	63	6%	16	270	5.53	13.4	$16
DL	1st Half	286	41	80	6	44	5	280			387	388	775	15	90	30	1.67	40	19	41	63	55	6%	7	260	5.59	6.7	$9
BAvg Potl 70%	2nd Half	318	46	79	8	39	4	248			358	406	763	15	91	25	1.80	40	16	44	93	63	6%	9	279	5.48	6.7	$7
LIMA Plan A	07 Proj	**573**	**90**	**164**	**16**	**85**	**7**	**286**			**398**	**450**	**848**	**16**	**89**	**30**	**1.66**	**38**	**20**	**42**	**96**	**81**	**5%**	**18**	**285**	**6.47**	**23.2**	**$20**

Can he rebound?
CON: Drop in LD% and SX, declining PX trend.
PRO: Superb eye and ct%, PX spike in Aug/Sept, low 2H H%.
VERDICT: Power is likely gone; .300 potential still there.

Giles,Marcus

Giles,Marcus		AB	R	H	HR	RBI	SB	Avg	vL	vR	OB	Slg	OPS	bb%	ct%	h%	Eye	G	L	F	PX	SX	SBO	xHR	xBA	RC/G	RAR	R$
Pos 4	02 ATL	* 328	49	83	11	37	4	253	158	246	327	409	735	10	84	27	0.67	41	20	38	98	80	5%	11	278	4.66	2.4	$9
Age 28	03 ATL	551	101	174	21	69	14	316	283	325	382	526	908	10	85	34	0.74	41	21	38	135	106	11%	22	315	6.74	34.9	$27
Peak	04 ATL	379	61	118	8	48	17	311	402	282	371	443	814	9	82	37	0.51	42	22	35	86	116	17%	9	270	5.60	10.3	$17
Bats Right	05 ATL	577	104	168	15	63	16	291	304	289	362	461	823	10	81	34	0.59	41	19	40	117	124	11%	18	281	5.81	20.2	$23
Reliability 69	06 ATL	550	87	144	11	60	10	262	229	273	337	387	724	10	81	31	0.59	42	22	36	82	87	9%	14	264	4.58	-0.3	$14
DL	1st Half	294	43	70	5	25	7	238			321	354	675	11	81	28	0.63	44	20	36	75	96	13%	6	254	4.02	-5.2	$5
BAvg Potl 50%	2nd Half	256	44	74	6	35	3	289			355	426	780	9	81	34	0.54	40	24	36	91	65	5%	7	275	5.21	4.4	$9
LIMA Plan B	07 Proj	**506**	**94**	**147**	**13**	**59**	**12**	**291**			**360**	**441**	**801**	**10**	**81**	**34**	**0.58**	**42**	**21**	**37**	**99**	**107**	**10%**	**15**	**275**	**5.49**	**13.0**	**$19**

Why he'll rebound:
- Hitting skills still solid
- 1st half h% below his norm
- 2nd half PX rebound
- Actual HR below xHR
- Low 2nd half SBO%

He could easily repeat '05.

Glaus,Troy

Glaus,Troy		AB	R	H	HR	RBI	SB	Avg	vL	vR	OB	Slg	OPS	bb%	ct%	h%	Eye	G	L	F	PX	SX	SBO	xHR	xBA	RC/G	RAR	R$
Pos 5	02 ANA	569	99	142	30	111	10	250	298	230	350	453	804	13	75	28	0.61	39	20	41	129	87	7%	29	265	5.61	19.3	$22
Age 30	03 ANA	319	53	79	16	50	7	248	303	226	342	464	806	13	77	27	0.63	35	22	43	137	100	10%	15	278	5.63	10.6	$11
Peak	04 ANA	207	47	52	18	42	2	251	242	255	349	575	924	13	75	25	0.60	39	16	45	196	88	9%	15	305	7.07	13.4	$10
Bats Right	05 ARI	538	78	139	37	97	4	258	244	263	359	522	881	14	73	29	0.58	37	17	46	177	54	4%	35	282	6.66	29.5	$22
Reliability 59	06 TOR	540	105	136	38	104	3	252	292	238	355	513	868	14	75	27	0.64	34	17	49	162	55	3%	35	275	6.40	22.1	$21
DL	1st Half	274	54	68	21	53	2	248			348	533	881	13	74	26	0.60	35	17	48	178	61	3%	19	287	6.56	12.5	$11
BAvg Potl 60%	2nd Half	266	51	68	17	51	1	256			361	492	854	14	76	28	0.69	33	16	51	145	46	4%	16	263	6.25	9.7	$10
LIMA Plan B	07 Proj	**514**	**95**	**130**	**36**	**97**	**4**	**253**			**354**	**517**	**871**	**14**	**75**	**27**	**0.62**	**36**	**17**	**47**	**166**	**65**	**5%**	**33**	**280**	**6.46**	**24.9**	**$21**

Second half power decline was the result of knee problems, which led to a 115 PX in September. With an increasing FB rate, he could return to the 40 HR level if his knee is healthy.

Gload,Ross

Gload,Ross		AB	R	H	HR	RBI	SB	Avg	vL	vR	OB	Slg	OPS	bb%	ct%	h%	Eye	G	L	F	PX	SX	SBO	xHR	xBA	RC/G	RAR	R$
Pos 3	02 aaa	442	43	123	13	44	6	278			297	439	736	3	92	28	0.33				91	80	12%	11		4.38	-17.1	$12
Age 31	03 aaa	508	60	143	17	58	5	281			316	467	783	5	89	29	0.47				109	82	7%	16		5.01	-6.3	$15
Past Peak	04 CHW	234	28	75	7	44	0	321	425	299	374	479	853	8	84	36	0.54	39	25	35	100	22	4%	7	294	5.96	6.2	$9
Bats Left	05 aaa	236	34	73	13	34	0	308			353	555	909	6	86	32	0.50				149	44	2%	11		6.45	7.1	$10
Reliability 19	06 CHW	156	22	51	3	18	6	327	308	333	352	462	813	4	90	35	0.40	51	21	27	76	121	14%	3	306	5.29	-0.5	$6
DL	1st Half	53	5	14	0	6	1	264			278	340	617	2	87	30	0.14	49	23	28	46	104	8%	0	274	3.01	-3.7	$1
BAvg Potl 45%	2nd Half	103	17	37	3	12	5	359			389	524	913	5	92	37	0.63	53	20	27	91	116	16%	3	323	6.41	2.6	$6
LIMA Plan F	07 Proj	**100**	**13**	**31**	**3**	**13**	**2**	**311**			**345**	**480**	**825**	**5**	**88**	**33**	**0.44**	**49**	**22**	**29**	**99**	**91**	**9%**	**3**	**313**	**5.46**	**0.5**	**$4**

Has never been able to transfer minor league power skills to the majors, and as long as he's hitting so few fly balls, it won't happen. Nice BA, but gets so few AB it's pretty irrelevant.

Gomes,Jonny

Gomes,Jonny		AB	R	H	HR	RBI	SB	Avg	vL	vR	OB	Slg	OPS	bb%	ct%	h%	Eye	G	L	F	PX	SX	SBO	xHR	xBA	RC/G	RAR	R$
Pos 0	02	0	0	0	0	0	0	0							0							0		0				
Age 26	03 a/a	461	64	110	15	52	21	239			313	419	732	10	69	31	0.35				136	140	21%	18		4.74	1.7	$14
Pre-Peak	04 aaa	390	63	89	20	67	7	228			306	451	758	10	69	27	0.37				150	80	16%	21		5.00	-3.6	$12
Bats Right	05 TAM	* 510	86	141	30	87	14	276	287	280	354	524	877	11	71	33	0.42	29	23	48	166	118	14%	28	268	6.62	8.8	$24
Reliability 16	06 TAM	385	53	83	20	59	1	216	297	187	323	431	754	14	70	25	0.53	29	17	54	149	44	6%	21	243	5.04	-16.7	$8
DL 34	1st Half	257	40	64	17	48	1	249			357	510	866	14	68	30	0.53	26	21	52	179	50	8%	17	265	6.69	2.1	$9
BAvg Potl 50%	2nd Half	128	13	19	3	11	0	148			253	273	527	12	73	18	0.51	34	8	57	93	27	0%	4	187	1.92	-19.3	($1)
LIMA Plan C+	07 Proj	**441**	**63**	**113**	**25**	**63**	**7**	**256**			**343**	**491**	**835**	**12**	**71**	**31**	**0.45**	**31**	**16**	**54**	**160**	**75**	**9%**	**25**	**252**	**6.08**	**0.8**	**$15**

Shoulder woes killed his entire 2nd half. Rising Eye and FB rate presents a real buying opportunity. If the shoulder's healthy, there's big time power here.
UP: 2005 stat line

Gomez,Alexis

Gomez,Alexis		AB	R	H	HR	RBI	SB	Avg	vL	vR	OB	Slg	OPS	bb%	ct%	h%	Eye	G	L	F	PX	SX	SBO	xHR	xBA	RC/G	RAR	R$
Pos 79	02 aa	461	64	131	13	67	32	284			339	443	781	8	84	31	0.53				93	134	45%	12		5.12	-6.8	$22
Age 28	03 aaa	456	39	115	7	46	3	252			284	373	656	4	85	28	0.29				75	74	9%	8		3.51	-26.5	$7
Peak	04 aaa	383	35	87	6	26	6	228			256	344	601	4	81	27	0.20				71	106	17%	6		2.75	-28.9	$3
Bats Left	05 aaa	421	43	115	6	46	18	273			309	404	713	5	81	33	0.27				87	137	25%	7		4.21	-10.1	$13
Reliability 8	06 DET	* 329	49	86	10	38	11	260	188	287	306	449	756	6	79	30	0.32	37	28	35	118	141	20%	10	289	4.76	-4.1	$10
DL	1st Half	167	22	37	3	18	7	224			266	339	605	5	79	27	0.27	34	30	36	68	142	26%	3	254	2.83	-12.2	$3
BAvg Potl 45%	2nd Half	162	26	48	7	20	4	298			347	564	911	7	80	33	0.38	43	25	32	168	125	13%	7	328	6.73	7.0	$6
LIMA Plan F	07 Proj	**175**	**22**	**48**	**4**	**19**	**6**	**275**			**315**	**441**	**757**	**6**	**81**	**32**	**0.30**	**38**	**28**	**34**	**104**	**122**	**20%**	**5**	**287**	**4.74**	**-1.4**	**$5**

1-6-.272-4 in 103 AB at DET
Pigeon-holed as a minor league journeyman, but 2nd half shows what a peaking 28-year-old can do. The question is opportunity. Will he experience that peak in AAA or MLB?

Gomez,Chris

Gomez,Chris		AB	R	H	HR	RBI	SB	Avg	vL	vR	OB	Slg	OPS	bb%	ct%	h%	Eye	G	L	F	PX	SX	SBO	xHR	xBA	RC/G	RAR	R$
Pos 3	02 TAM	461	51	122	10	46	1	265	172	286	297	410	707	4	87	28	0.36	40	20	40	91	58	4%	11	280	4.13	-23.2	$9
Age 35	03 MIN	175	14	44	1	15	2	251	251	252	280	354	635	4	93	27	0.54	48	22	30	61	90	8%	2	296	3.51	-9.7	$2
Decline	04 TOR	341	41	96	3	37	3	282	300	274	336	346	682	8	88	31	0.68	45	25	30	40	63	5%	4	270	4.05	-9.1	$7
Bats Right	05 BAL	219	27	61	1	18	2	279	317	243	358	342	700	11	92	30	1.59	52	20	28	46	49	4%	2	278	4.64	-2.8	$4
Reliability 19	06 BAL	132	14	45	2	17	1	341	333	345	374	439	813	5	92	36	0.64	51	21	28	61	36	7%	2	286	5.38	-0.1	$5
DL 60	1st Half	45	6	10	1	4	0	222			286	311	597	8	87	24	0.67	54	15	31	50	38	0%	1	243	3.00	-3.3	$0
BAvg Potl 40%	2nd Half	87	8	35	1	13	1	402			422	506	928	3	94	42	0.60	49	23	27	66	33	10%	1	308	6.50	2.3	$4
LIMA Plan F	07 Proj	**160**	**17**	**45**	**2**	**18**	**1**	**282**			**326**	**373**	**699**	**6**	**91**	**30**	**0.75**	**48**	**23**	**30**	**57**	**57**	**5%**	**2**	**288**	**4.26**	**-4.7**	**$3**

No speed or power. Total of 7 HR and 8 SB the past four seasons. BA driven by a gigantic second half h%. At his age, don't expect a repeat.
DN: .250 BA

Gonzalez,Adrian

Gonzalez,Adrian		AB	R	H	HR	RBI	SB	Avg	vL	vR	OB	Slg	OPS	bb%	ct%	h%	Eye	G	L	F	PX	SX	SBO	xHR	xBA	RC/G	RAR	R$
Pos 3	02 aa	508	60	125	14	83	5	246			310	398	708	8	82	27	0.52				102	65	7%	15		4.27	-22.1	$13
Age 24	03 a/a	449	42	119	5	45	2	265			318	356	675	7	87	30	0.58				59	61	2%	6		3.93	-19.6	$7
Growth	04 TEX	* 499	55	144	13	77	1	289		286	334	435	769	6	88	31	0.58	34	20	46	87	48	2%	13	271	4.93	-0.8	$14
Bats Left	05 TEX	* 478	60	133	20	63	0	278	71	243	325	458	783	6	86	29	0.49	39	20	41	105	40	0%	17	285	5.00	-1.3	$14
Reliability 47	06 SD	570	83	173	24	82	0	304	312	301	362	500	862	8	80	34	0.46	44	23	33	122	35	1%	24	292	6.10	1.5	$21
DL	1st Half	257	37	71	10	27	0	276			319	451	770	6	82	31	0.34	47	21	32	107	32	0%	9	282	4.81	-8.7	$7
BAvg Potl 40%	2nd Half	313	46	102	14	55	0	326			395	540	935	10	79	38	0.55	41	25	35	135	37	1%	14	300	7.18	9.8	$14
LIMA Plan D+	07 Proj	**550**	**87**	**165**	**26**	**90**	**0**	**300**			**354**	**507**	**861**	**8**	**83**	**32**	**0.49**	**43**	**23**	**35**	**123**	**49**	**1%**	**23**	**303**	**5.98**	**2.0**	**$22**

Superb breakout season. High h% drove second half BA, but xBA still marks him as a potential .300 hitter. Rising PX and FB% in 2nd half indicate there's more to come.
UP: 30 HR, 100 RBI

Gonzalez,Alex

Gonzalez,Alex		AB	R	H	HR	RBI	SB	Avg	vL	vR	OB	Slg	OPS	bb%	ct%	h%	Eye	G	L	F	PX	SX	SBO	xHR	xBA	RC/G	RAR	R$
Pos 6	02 FLA	151	15	34	2	18	3	225	200	231	282	325	607	7	79	27	0.38	29	24	47	72	92	11%	3	233	2.96	-4.3	$2
Age 30	03 FLA	528	52	135	18	77	0	256	274	251	299	443	743	6	80	29	0.31	35	20	45	121	54	4%	18	271	4.55	6.8	$12
Peak	04 FLA	561	67	130	23	79	3	232	278	220	267	419	686	5	78	26	0.21	33	16	51	118	79	4%	22	247	3.71	-7.1	$12
Bats Right	05 FLA	435	45	115	5	45	5	264	216	277	313	368	681	7	81	32	0.38	37	18	45	80	57	7%	8	241	3.90	-0.8	$9
Reliability 85	06 BOS	388	48	99	9	50	1	255	278	244	295	397	692	5	83	29	0.33	37	20	43	91	68	1%	10	261	3.93	-5.4	$7
DL 15	1st Half	209	28	56	5	24	1	268			314	388	701	6	85	29	0.45	39	21	40	74	51	2%	5	261	4.09	-1.9	$4
BAvg Potl 45%	2nd Half	179	20	43	4	26	0	240			273	408	681	4	80	28	0.22	34	19	47	113	67	0%	5	261	3.77	-3.4	$3
LIMA Plan D	07 Proj	**458**	**52**	**115**	**13**	**58**	**1**	**251**			**293**	**411**	**704**	**6**	**81**	**28**	**0.31**	**35**	**19**	**46**	**105**	**51**	**2%**	**14**	**260**	**4.05**	**-5.6**	**$9**

Recovery from elbow surgery affected 1st half PX, but 2nd half rebound shows that he still owns those skills from 2003-04. A return to double-digit power seems likely.

HAROLD NICHOLS

Gonzalez,Luis

			AB	R	H	HR	RBI	SB	Avg	vL	vR	OB	Slg	OPS	bb%	ct%	h%	Eye	G	L	F	PX	SX	SBO	xHR	xBA	RC/G	RAR	R$
Pos	7	02 ARI	524	90	151	28	103	9	288	272	297	399	496	896	16	85	29	1.28	41	18	42	118	90	6%	24	290	6.84	6.7	$26
Age	39	03 ARI	579	92	176	26	104	5	304	223	354	401	532	933	14	88	31	1.40	40	21	40	135	77	4%	25	321	7.28	27.0	$26
Decline		04 ARI	379	69	98	17	48	2	259	244	266	371	493	865	15	85	27	1.17	36	16	48	137	91	3%	17	291	6.55	12.4	$12
Bats	Left	05 ARI	579	90	157	24	79	4	271	269	272	358	459	817	12	84	29	0.87	38	20	42	118	59	3%	23	290	5.74	6.7	$20
Reliability	41	06 ARI	586	93	159	15	73	0	271	259	277	348	444	792	11	90	28	1.19	40	19	41	105	44	1%	18	298	5.55	5.1	$15
DL	18	1st Half	272	47	70	6	34	0	257			353	404	757	13	91	27	1.60	42	19	38	88	54	1%	7	289	5.32	0.6	$6
BAvg Potl	70%	2nd Half	314	46	89	9	39	0	283			344	478	822	8	89	29	0.88	38	20	43	120	41	0%	10	305	5.74	4.3	$9
LIMA Plan	C+	07 Proj	**384**	**62**	**105**	**9**	**51**	**1**	**274**			**360**	**436**	**796**	**12**	**88**	**29**	**1.08**	**39**	**19**	**42**	**102**	**71**	**2%**	**11**	**285**	**5.63**	**2.8**	**$11**

Now a fringe MLB full-timer. PX trend tells the story. In fact, taking out a monster July, he'd be left with a 98 PX. Probably has a better shot at a .280 BA than 15 HR.

Gonzalez,Luis A.

			AB	R	H	HR	RBI	SB	Avg	vL	vR	OB	Slg	OPS	bb%	ct%	h%	Eye	G	L	F	PX	SX	SBO	xHR	xBA	RC/G	RAR	R$
Pos	7	02 a/a	282	38	69	6	23	4	245			276	358	634	4	87	26	0.32				67	111	6%	5		3.23	-19.9	$6
Age	27	03 aa	431	63	124	7	54	1	288			348	399	747	8	91	30	1.00				67	70	1%	8		4.92	-6.6	$12
Peak		04 COL	322	42	94	12	40	1	292	268	302	323	469	792	4	79	34	0.22	44	23	33	110	63	8%	11	282	5.02	-3.8	$11
Bats	Right	05 COL	404	51	118	9	44	3	292	380	237	325	421	746	5	84	33	0.32	52	21	27	87	51	7%	10	289	4.52	-9.3	$12
Reliability	15	06 COL *	231	14	53	3	18	2	230	259	277	252	335	586	3	85	26	0.20	46	17	37	65	62	7%	4	253	2.64	-18.3	$1
DL		1st Half	186	12	42	3	11	2	226			245	346	591	2	85	25	0.17	45	13	41	73	71	9%	3	244	2.67	-14.7	$1
BAvg Potl	55%	2nd Half	45	2	11	0	7	0	244			277	289	565	4	87	28	0.33	48	25	28	35	9	0%	0	257	2.52	-3.6	$0
LIMA Plan	F	07 Proj	**134**	**15**	**36**	**3**	**13**	**1**	**269**			**302**	**406**	**707**	**4**	**85**	**30**	**0.30**	**48**	**22**	**30**	**84**	**74**	**6%**	**3**	**286**	**4.07**	**-5.0**	**$3**

2-14-.242 in 149 AB at COL. BA remains erratic due to unstable H%. Has shown pop just once in five years. Poor skill foundation and lack of wheels are other reasons to stay away.

Gordon,Alex

			AB	R	H	HR	RBI	SB	Avg	vL	vR	OB	Slg	OPS	bb%	ct%	h%	Eye	G	L	F	PX	SX	SBO	xHR	xBA	RC/G	RAR	R$
Pos	5	02	0	0	0	0	0	0	0							0							0		0				
Age	23	03	0	0	0	0	0	0	0							0							0		0				
Growth		04	0	0	0	0	0	0	0							0							0		0				
Bats	Left	05	0	0	0	0	0	0	0							0							0		0				
Reliability	1	06 aa	486	87	139	20	79	17	286			361	490	851	10	83	31	0.67				127	104	15%	20		6.09	11.6	$21
DL		1st Half	253	39	64	7	27	13	253			332	407	739	11	86	27	0.83				94	116	20%	8		4.83	-3.1	$8
BAvg Potl	40%	2nd Half	233	48	75	13	52	4	322			392	579	972	10	79	36	0.55				165	69	10%	13		7.61	14.9	$13
LIMA Plan	C+	07 Proj	**336**	**62**	**99**	**15**	**59**	**10**	**295**			**369**	**515**	**884**	**10**	**82**	**32**	**0.64**	**35**	**18**	**47**	**140**	**98**	**14%**	**15**	**286**	**6.49**	**14.3**	**$16**

A great full-season at Double-A has him knocking on MLB's door. Good control of strike zone. Enticing power/speed combo. Hits both LHers and RHers well. For the optimistic: UP: 30-100-.290-15

Graffanino,Tony

			AB	R	H	HR	RBI	SB	Avg	vL	vR	OB	Slg	OPS	bb%	ct%	h%	Eye	G	L	F	PX	SX	SBO	xHR	xBA	RC/G	RAR	R$
Pos	45	02 CHW	229	35	60	6	31	2	262	261	263	327	428	755	9	83	29	0.58	45	18	37	98	108	5%	6	277	4.91	5.8	$6
Age	34	03 CHW	250	51	65	7	23	8	260	303	176	325	428	753	9	85	28	0.65	41	26	32	102	148	13%	7	303	4.89	5.4	$8
Past Peak		04 KC	278	37	73	3	26	10	263	265	262	328	335	662	9	86	30	0.71	46	19	35	47	88	14%	4	251	3.86	-1.8	$7
Bats	Right	05 2AL	379	68	117	7	38	7	309	297	317	361	425	786	8	87	34	0.61	50	22	28	72	109	7%	7	290	5.20	11.1	$14
Reliability	34	06 2TM	456	68	125	7	59	5	274	275	274	339	406	745	9	85	31	0.66	41	19	40	86	83	7%	10	268	4.86	6.6	$11
DL		1st Half	168	21	42	4	23	2	250			308	387	695	8	85	28	0.54	45	21	35	88	56	10%	5	278	4.12	-1.2	$4
BAvg Potl	55%	2nd Half	288	47	83	3	36	3	288			357	417	774	10	85	33	0.74	39	18	43	86	94	6%	5	262	5.29	7.5	$8
LIMA Plan	D+	07 Proj	**348**	**54**	**97**	**8**	**40**	**6**	**279**			**341**	**416**	**757**	**9**	**86**	**31**	**0.65**	**41**	**20**	**39**	**85**	**95**	**9%**	**9**	**274**	**4.92**	**5.7**	**$11**

No sign of skill erosion as he enters his mid-30s. In fact, xHR and PX suggest double-digit HR remain possible if given regular AB. But we can never assume he'll get those regular AB.

Granderson,Curtis

			AB	R	H	HR	RBI	SB	Avg	vL	vR	OB	Slg	OPS	bb%	ct%	h%	Eye	G	L	F	PX	SX	SBO	xHR	xBA	RC/G	RAR	R$
Pos	8	02	0	0	0	0	0	0	0							0							0		0				
Age	26	03	0	0	0	0	0	0	0							0							0		0				
Pre-Peak		04 aa	462	75	122	16	79	12	265			354	433	787	12	82	29	0.78				93	118	14%	14		5.42	10.1	$17
Bats	Left	05 DET *	607	87	167	20	77	20	275	364	257	332	488	820	8	75	34	0.34	48	17	35	137	137	19%	20	279	5.77	26.2	$22
Reliability	59	06 DET	596	90	155	19	68	8	260	218	274	334	438	772	10	71	34	0.38	39	22	39	122	116	8%	21	251	5.28	10.8	$15
DL		1st Half	298	52	86	11	42	5	289			380	487	867	13	71	37	0.51	38	25	37	137	107	9%	13	266	6.72	17.5	$11
BAvg Potl	35%	2nd Half	298	38	69	8	26	3	232			284	389	674	7	70	30	0.25	40	20	40	107	114	6%	9	236	3.79	-7.9	$4
LIMA Plan	B	07 Proj	**508**	**75**	**130**	**16**	**63**	**7**	**256**			**324**	**442**	**767**	**9**	**74**	**32**	**0.39**	**41**	**21**	**39**	**120**	**115**	**10%**	**17**	**261**	**5.11**	**7.9**	**$13**

Reasons for concern, even after a torrid September...
- Big overall 2nd half fade
- Problems with LHers
- xBA and ct% trends

Future remains bright, but he'll be overvalued in '07.

Greene,Khalil

			AB	R	H	HR	RBI	SB	Avg	vL	vR	OB	Slg	OPS	bb%	ct%	h%	Eye	G	L	F	PX	SX	SBO	xHR	xBA	RC/G	RAR	R$
Pos	6	02	0	0	0	0	0	0	0							0							0		0				
Age	27	03 a/a	548	54	137	10	58	6	250			289	365	654	5	83	29	0.32				79	55	11%	12		3.47	-13.2	$9
Peak		04 SD	484	67	132	15	65	4	273	291	266	345	446	791	10	81	31	0.56	36	18	45	110	86	4%	16	263	5.37	17.2	$14
Bats	Right	05 SD	436	51	109	15	70	5	250	200	267	291	431	722	5	79	29	0.27	33	22	44	124	92	6%	16	273	4.25	3.7	$12
Reliability	55	06 SD	412	56	101	15	55	5	245	271	237	310	427	738	9	79	28	0.45	35	19	46	115	83	6%	15	261	4.60	3.0	$10
DL	15 68	1st Half	268	33	61	10	40	5	228			308	410	718	10	79	25	0.56	37	16	46	115	77	9%	10	259	4.44	0.7	$6
BAvg Potl	50%	2nd Half	144	23	40	5	15	0	278			316	458	774	5	78	33	0.25	29	25	46	115	64	0%	5	267	4.90	2.2	$4
LIMA Plan	C+	07 Proj	**507**	**67**	**135**	**17**	**67**	**5**	**266**			**318**	**440**	**758**	**7**	**79**	**31**	**0.36**	**33**	**21**	**46**	**113**	**83**	**5%**	**17**	**264**	**4.79**	**8.7**	**$14**

On the surface, growth continues to stall. We'll blame a torn ligament in his finger for making him useless in Aug/Sept. If healthy, his first 20 HR season is coming.
UP: 20-80-.275

Greene,Todd

			AB	R	H	HR	RBI	SB	Avg	vL	vR	OB	Slg	OPS	bb%	ct%	h%	Eye	G	L	F	PX	SX	SBO	xHR	xBA	RC/G	RAR	R$
Pos	2	02 TEX *	389	48	103	22	68	2	265	271	266	283	491	774	3	84	27	0.16	36	10	54	132	52	3%	18	265	4.59	10.9	$14
Age	35	03 TEX	205	25	47	10	20	0	229	211	240	237	434	671	1	77	25	0.04	31	23	46	129	58	0%	9	273	3.30	-4.9	$4
Decline		04 COL	195	23	55	10	35	0	282	366	234	327	508	835	6	81	31	0.34	35	15	51	141	19	0%	9	269	5.60	9.8	$7
Bats	Right	05 COL	126	10	32	7	23	0	254	294	227	293	452	746	5	83	26	0.33	36	21	43	113	0	0%	5	263	4.38	2.2	$4
Reliability	0	06 SF	159	16	46	2	17	0	289	250	301	331	428	759	6	72	39	0.22	36	18	46	106	59	0%	4	228	5.00	2.9	$3
DL	71	1st Half	79	7	26	0	6	0	329			361	468	830	5	72	46	0.18	37	23	40	121	56	0%	1	255	6.02	3.5	$2
BAvg Potl	15%	2nd Half	80	9	20	2	11	0	250			302	387	690	7	71	33	0.26	35	12	53	91	63	0%	2	200	3.98	-0.8	$1
LIMA Plan	F	07 Proj	**151**	**15**	**37**	**4**	**22**	**0**	**245**			**286**	**401**	**687**	**5**	**77**	**29**	**0.25**	**35**	**18**	**47**	**105**	**52**	**0%**	**5**	**244**	**3.83**	**-1.3**	**$3**

Hacked his way to a .289 BA, but crazy 39% H% simply is not repeatable. On top of the BA downside, his dwindling PX has eroded his HR upside. Very limited value at this point in his career.

Green,Nick

			AB	R	H	HR	RBI	SB	Avg	vL	vR	OB	Slg	OPS	bb%	ct%	h%	Eye	G	L	F	PX	SX	SBO	xHR	xBA	RC/G	RAR	R$
Pos	46	02 aa	355	39	72	11	40	2	203			261	338	599	7	78	23	0.35				88	55	11%	11		2.74	-16.8	$4
Age	28	03 aaa	399	38	94	10	48	7	236			279	378	657	6	81	27	0.32				96	71	15%	11		3.51	-9.3	$7
Peak		04 ATL *	341	47	98	3	36	1	287	354	236	321	393	714	5	79	36	0.24	42	21	37	73	82	7%	5	248	4.21	-3.9	$8
Bats	Right	05 TAM	318	53	76	5	29	3	239	290	217	311	346	656	9	73	31	0.38	38	21	41	81	100	5%	7	229	3.65	-4.6	$6
Reliability	19	06 2AL *	204	17	39	3	9	2	190	150	203	250	275	526	8	67	27	0.25	37	21	41	71	44	14%	4	204	1.69	-16.1	($1)
DL		1st Half	129	9	21	1	5	1	160			229	211	440	8	71	22	0.31	52	11	37	41	41	14%	2	176	0.55	-15.6	($2)
BAvg Potl	40%	2nd Half	75	8	18	2	4	1	240			287	387	674	6	61	36	0.17	28	28	44	130	53	13%	3	225	4.07	-0.1	$1
LIMA Plan	F	07 Proj	**65**	**8**	**15**	**1**	**5**	**1**	**231**			**287**	**330**	**616**	**7**	**71**	**31**	**0.27**	**36**	**23**	**41**	**77**	**55**	**9%**	**2**	**222**	**2.97**	**-2.3**	**$1**

2-4-.184 in 114 AB at NYY and TAM. Speaking of hacking, this one is taking it to a new level. Problem is he hasn't shown any semblance of power in three years. MLB teams will stop giving him the call soon.

Green,Shawn

			AB	R	H	HR	RBI	SB	Avg	vL	vR	OB	Slg	OPS	bb%	ct%	h%	Eye	G	L	F	PX	SX	SBO	xHR	xBA	RC/G	RAR	R$
Pos	9	02 LA	582	110	166	42	114	8	285	270	291	384	558	942	14	81	29	0.83	52	18	29	167	74	7%	36	329	7.26	32.4	$32
Age	34	03 LA	611	84	171	19	85	6	280	252	295	352	460	812	10	82	32	0.61	48	20	32	122	78	5%	22	299	5.65	0.7	$20
Past Peak		04 LA	590	92	157	28	86	5	266	232	281	345	459	804	11	81	29	0.62	54	15	30	115	65	4%	26	284	5.47	3.0	$20
Bats	Left	05 ARI	581	87	166	22	73	8	286	226	309	355	477	831	10	84	31	0.65	51	18	31	120	92	7%	21	304	5.81	9.2	$22
Reliability	83	06 2NL	530	73	147	15	66	4	277	267	282	334	432	766	8	85	30	0.55	54	18	28	93	68	6%	15	288	4.95	2.7	$15
DL		1st Half	271	40	81	8	33	4	299			345	458	802	7	85	33	0.48	56	20	24	89	97	7%	7	302	5.29	3.9	$9
BAvg Potl	50%	2nd Half	259	33	66	7	33	0	255			323	405	728	9	84	28	0.62	52	16	33	96	29	4%	8	266	4.58	-1.4	$5
LIMA Plan	C	07 Proj	**522**	**76**	**144**	**16**	**69**	**1**	**276**			**343**	**433**	**776**	**9**	**83**	**31**	**0.61**	**53**	**17**	**30**	**98**	**48**	**3%**	**16**	**280**	**5.14**	**1.6**	**$15**

PX and FB declines paint a grim picture. Let's face it - this is now basically a middle infielder's profile. He's a $10M investment in MLB, and is becoming a $10 investment in fantasy leagues.

STEPHEN NICKRAND

Griffey Jr.,Ken		AB	R	H	HR	RBI	SB	Avg	vL	vR	OB	Slg	OPS	bb%	ct%	h%	Eye	G	L	F	PX	SX	SBO	xHR	xBA	RC/G	RAR	R$
Pos 8	02 CIN	197	17	52	8	23	1	264	217	285	356	426	782	12	80	29	0.72	37	22	41	103	19	5%	8	269	5.30	2.5	$5
Age 37	03 CIN	166	34	41	13	26	1	247	250	245	352	566	919	14	73	26	0.61	37	25	39	212	85	2%	12	322	7.18	10.8	$7
Decline	04 CIN	300	49	76	20	60	1	253	198	286	349	513	862	13	78	26	0.66	37	16	47	160	42	1%	18	284	6.27	14.2	$12
Bats Left	05 CIN	491	85	148	35	92	0	301	278	314	371	576	947	10	81	31	0.58	34	22	44	168	29	1%	29	315	7.09	34.2	$26
Reliability 15	06 CIN	428	62	108	27	72	0	252	204	278	315	486	801	8	82	25	0.50	42	15	43	130	25	0%	22	273	5.21	9.7	$14
DL 28 26	1st Half	201	26	53	15	44	0	264			318	527	845	7	83	25	0.46	38	17	45	142	15	0%	11	285	5.63	6.9	$8
BAvg Potl 60%	2nd Half	227	36	55	12	28	0	242			312	449	761	9	81	25	0.53	46	13	41	120	34	0%	11	263	4.82	2.6	$6
LIMA Plan C	07 Proj	**441**	**69**	**117**	**25**	**76**	**0**	**265**			**338**	**491**	**829**	**10**	**80**	**28**	**0.56**	**39**	**17**	**43**	**134**	**37**	**1%**	**22**	**280**	**5.69**	**14.5**	**$16**

4 reasons not to expect another comeback...
- PX and FB% trends
- 111 PX vs. LHers
- Eroding bb% and Eye
- '05 H% looks like the outlier
- DL or no DL? -- DL!

Gross,Gabe		AB	R	H	HR	RBI	SB	Avg	vL	vR	OB	Slg	OPS	bb%	ct%	h%	Eye	G	L	F	PX	SX	SBO	xHR	xBA	RC/G	RAR	R$
Pos 87	02 aa	403	44	85	7	42	6	211			284	320	604	9	87	23	0.76				67	95	8%	8		3.22	-20.1	$5
Age 27	03 a/a	492	63	139	10	63	3	283			373	437	810	13	81	33	0.77				109	62	4%	14		5.84	13.6	$13
Peak	04 aaa	377	44	106	8	46	3	281			358	430	788	11	82	33	0.66				102	47	8%	11		5.43	8.1	$10
Bats Left	05 TOR	* 482	62	130	6	44	12	270	91	272	341	391	732	10	82	32	0.59	30	21	49	88	104	11%	10	245	4.74	6.3	$12
Reliability 19	06 MIL	208	42	57	9	38	1	274	95	294	381	476	857	15	71	35	0.60	34	23	42	143	52	1%	11	264	6.61	12.9	$8
DL	1st Half	99	22	26	7	19	0	263			348	505	853	12	72	30	0.46	37	18	45	148	46	0%	6	260	6.17	5.0	$4
BAvg Potl 40%	2nd Half	109	20	31	2	19	1	284			409	450	859	17	71	39	0.72	33	28	40	139	49	3%	4	269	6.98	7.8	$4
LIMA Plan D	07 Proj	**244**	**39**	**67**	**10**	**45**	**3**	**274**			**366**	**476**	**842**	**13**	**77**	**32**	**0.62**	**34**	**23**	**43**	**136**	**72**	**5%**	**11**	**279**	**6.19**	**11.5**	**$9**

Why he may be closer to a mini-breakout than we think...
- bb% spike
- PX spike
- Mashes RHers

If he solves LHP even a little... UP: 20-75-.280

Grudzielanek,Mark		AB	R	H	HR	RBI	SB	Avg	vL	vR	OB	Slg	OPS	bb%	ct%	h%	Eye	G	L	F	PX	SX	SBO	xHR	xBA	RC/G	RAR	R$
Pos 4	02 LA	536	56	145	9	50	4	271	257	274	299	364	663	4	83	31	0.25	45	23	32	64	59	4%	10	265	3.48	-14.4	$12
Age 36	03 CHC	481	73	151	3	38	6	314	360	302	354	416	770	6	87	36	0.47	48	27	26	77	87	6%	7	305	4.98	7.5	$15
Decline	04 CHC	257	32	79	6	23	1	307	220	349	346	432	777	6	88	33	0.47	41	24	34	73	56	3%	6	286	4.95	2.4	$8
Bats Right	05 STL	528	64	155	8	59	8	294	296	288	327	407	734	5	85	33	0.32	48	24	28	77	85	10%	10	289	4.42	-2.1	$16
Reliability 58	06 KC	548	85	163	7	52	3	297	277	305	332	409	740	5	87	33	0.41	52	23	25	71	88	3%	9	299	4.55	6.5	$14
DL	1st Half	273	39	78	3	22	1	286			323	385	708	5	88	32	0.44	50	23	27	62	78	3%	4	289	4.20	0.6	$5
BAvg Potl 50%	2nd Half	275	46	85	4	30	2	309			340	433	773	5	87	34	0.37	54	23	23	79	92	4%	5	308	4.90	5.8	$8
LIMA Plan C	07 Proj	**533**	**75**	**159**	**6**	**53**	**4**	**299**			**333**	**400**	**733**	**5**	**86**	**34**	**0.38**	**49**	**24**	**27**	**67**	**83**	**5%**	**8**	**289**	**4.45**	**4.9**	**$14**

Remains a decent end-game infield pickup in deep leagues. Just buy him for his .300 BA, not his power. FB% trend suggests his minimal power will become even less noticeable.

Guerrero,Vladimir		AB	R	H	HR	RBI	SB	Avg	vL	vR	OB	Slg	OPS	bb%	ct%	h%	Eye	G	L	F	PX	SX	SBO	xHR	xBA	RC/G	RAR	R$
Pos 90	02 MON	614	106	206	39	111	40	336	290	347	415	593	1008	12	89	33	1.20	43	19	38	146	102	28%	32	334	7.89	43.5	$45
Age 31	03 MON	394	71	130	25	79	9	330	393	313	422	586	1009	14	87	33	1.19	45	21	34	141	90	10%	21	329	8.04	25.6	$25
Past Peak	04 ANA	612	124	206	39	126	15	337	342	335	389	598	987	8	88	33	0.70	42	20	38	142	107	10%	31	328	7.35	42.5	$37
Bats Right	05 ANA	520	95	165	32	108	13	317	313	319	389	565	954	10	91	30	1.27	44	17	39	135	100	9%	25	329	7.17	34.5	$31
Reliability 93	06 ANA	607	92	200	33	116	15	329	401	307	381	552	932	8	89	33	0.74	44	19	37	121	76	11%	27	313	6.73	17.4	$32
DL 20	1st Half	300	37	87	16	56	5	290			326	490	816	5	87	29	0.40	46	16	37	108	62	7%	12	290	5.22	-3.7	$12
BAvg Potl 50%	2nd Half	307	55	113	17	60	10	368			431	612	1043	10	91	37	1.21	42	21	37	133	79	14%	14	333	8.16	19.5	$20
LIMA Plan D+	07 Proj	**595**	**102**	**191**	**32**	**118**	**11**	**321**			**383**	**547**	**929**	**9**	**89**	**32**	**0.93**	**44**	**19**	**38**	**124**	**86**	**9%**	**26**	**317**	**6.82**	**25.7**	**$31**

Monster 2nd half came with elite skills, but was also fueled by 37% hit rate. 171 PX vs. LHers, 117 PX against RHers. SX dip may foretell a SB decline. OPS trend shows he's not getting any younger.

Guiel,Aaron		AB	R	H	HR	RBI	SB	Avg	vL	vR	OB	Slg	OPS	bb%	ct%	h%	Eye	G	L	F	PX	SX	SBO	xHR	xBA	RC/G	RAR	R$
Pos 9	02 KC	* 455	62	120	11	75	7	264	169	254	323	389	712	8	80	31	0.44	45	22	32	82	75	10%	12	267	4.27	-10.0	$14
Age 34	03 KC	* 544	90	143	21	74	5	263	275	278	325	454	779	8	82	29	0.51	40	22	37	122	79	0%	21	291	5.10	-0.8	$17
Past Peak	04 KC	* 271	39	52	12	33	3	192	171	149	287	358	645	12	71	22	0.46	49	15	36	109	60	9%	12	237	3.39	-11.4	$1
Bats Left	05 KC	* 605	84	138	22	74	6	228	200	315	288	398	686	8	82	25	0.47	38	13	48	107	80	7%	21	253	3.93	-14.3	$13
Reliability 18	06 2AL	* 359	59	80	18	50	2	222	174	257	313	428	740	12	76	24	0.54	41	17	41	131	68	3%	17	265	4.70	-10.5	$8
DL	1st Half	223	34	44	10	32	0	199			310	406	715	14	76	21	0.67	42	16	42	135	48	0%	11	265	4.51	-8.1	$3
BAvg Potl 65%	2nd Half	136	25	35	8	18	2	260			318	463	781	8	75	30	0.33	41	18	41	125	73	9%	7	261	5.01	-2.6	$5
LIMA Plan F	07 Proj	**145**	**23**	**35**	**6**	**22**	**1**	**242**			**315**	**425**	**740**	**10**	**77**	**27**	**0.46**	**42**	**17**	**40**	**117**	**59**	**6%**	**6**	**261**	**4.61**	**-2.6**	**$4**

7-18-.242 in 132 AB at NYY and KC. Low hit rate is his own personal level, though xBA says there could be more upside. However, MLB clubs don't give extended chances to 34-year-olds with extreme platoon splits.

Guillen,Carlos		AB	R	H	HR	RBI	SB	Avg	vL	vR	OB	Slg	OPS	bb%	ct%	h%	Eye	G	L	F	PX	SX	SBO	xHR	xBA	RC/G	RAR	R$
Pos 6	02 SEA	475	73	124	9	56	4	261	221	275	326	394	720	9	81	31	0.51	42	18	40	84	102	7%	10	254	4.48	-1.4	$12
Age 31	03 SEA	388	63	107	7	52	4	276	265	280	361	394	756	12	84	32	0.81	43	24	33	76	83	6%	8	275	5.10	7.5	$11
Past Peak	04 DET	522	97	166	20	97	12	318	269	348	380	542	922	9	83	35	0.60	41	22	37	132	134	11%	19	306	6.91	34.7	$25
Bats Both	05 DET	334	48	107	5	23	2	320	368	306	366	434	800	7	87	36	0.53	44	23	33	70	82	5%	6	280	5.33	6.9	$10
Reliability 31	06 DET	543	100	174	19	85	20	320	291	332	399	519	918	12	84	35	0.82	42	20	38	122	114	16%	20	297	7.01	38.6	$26
DL 61	1st Half	268	42	80	9	44	10	299			380	489	868	12	82	34	0.73	41	21	38	124	90	18%	10	294	6.42	15.2	$12
BAvg Potl 45%	2nd Half	275	58	94	10	41	10	342			418	549	967	12	86	37	0.92	42	19	39	121	126	14%	10	301	7.57	22.9	$15
LIMA Plan B	07 Proj	**536**	**93**	**170**	**16**	**73**	**13**	**317**			**384**	**490**	**874**	**10**	**85**	**35**	**0.71**	**42**	**21**	**37**	**105**	**112**	**11%**	**16**	**290**	**6.38**	**28.0**	**$23**

Terrific year with strong skill support. Got better as season went along. Made most of green light, and loves Comerica. Good bet for strong follow-up, if he can stop pattern of alternating 500 AB seasons.

Guillen,Jose		AB	R	H	HR	RBI	SB	Avg	vL	vR	OB	Slg	OPS	bb%	ct%	h%	Eye	G	L	F	PX	SX	SBO	xHR	xBA	RC/G	RAR	R$
Pos 9	02 CIN	* 286	30	71	10	40	4	248	252	226	286	399	684	5	83	27	0.31	56	15	29	96	52	16%	9	273	3.73	-13.6	$8
Age 30	03 2TM	485	77	151	31	86	1	311	315	310	344	569	913	5	80	33	0.25	45	23	32	156	53	4%	25	320	6.40	13.5	$24
Peak	04 ANA	565	88	166	27	104	5	294	299	292	337	497	835	6	84	31	0.40	47	18	34	116	80	6%	23	295	5.56	13.5	$23
Bats Right	05 WAS	551	81	156	24	76	1	283	215	303	321	479	800	5	81	31	0.30	44	22	34	124	61	2%	22	297	5.14	-1.8	$20
Reliability 20	06 WAS	241	28	52	9	40	1	216	200	221	262	398	660	6	80	23	0.31	41	14	45	113	61	2%	9	257	3.50	-9.4	$4
DL 88	1st Half	188	24	39	7	27	0	207			247	388	636	5	81	22	0.28	43	14	43	110	58	0%	7	259	3.17	-9.4	$2
BAvg Potl 60%	2nd Half	53	4	13	2	13	1	245			310	434	744	9	77	28	0.42	34	15	51	126	32	8%	2	249	4.69	-0.1	$2
LIMA Plan F	07 Proj	**300**	**36**	**77**	**13**	**54**	**2**	**257**			**304**	**449**	**753**	**6**	**80**	**28**	**0.35**	**42**	**17**	**41**	**120**	**67**	**5%**	**12**	**275**	**4.63**	**-3.5**	**$9**

Tommy John surgery in July puts his '07 up in the air. A free agent, getting out of WAS would do wonders once he's healthy. 21 of 24 HR in '05 came on road.

Gutierrez,Franklin		AB	R	H	HR	RBI	SB	Avg	vL	vR	OB	Slg	OPS	bb%	ct%	h%	Eye	G	L	F	PX	SX	SBO	xHR	xBA	RC/G	RAR	R$
Pos 9	02	0	0	0	0	0	0	0							0							0		0				
Age 24	03 aa	67	12	20	4	12	3	298			367	564	931	10	72	36	0.39				173	127	33%	4		7.32	3.8	$4
Growth	04 a/a	289	36	77	4	33	5	265			313	400	712	6	75	34	0.28				105	83	14%	7		4.30	-5.9	$7
Bats Right	05 a/a	450	65	104	8	40	13	231			278	358	635	6	83	26	0.38				88	114	21%	10		3.33	-22.7	$9
Reliability 3	06 CLE	* 485	81	129	9	44	12	266	262	277	336	396	732	10	77	33	0.46	43	23	34	97	83	15%	13	268	4.66	-14.3	$12
DL	1st Half	267	44	66	3	21	10	247			323	341	664	10	76	32	0.46	47	25	28	74	94	18%	5	258	3.81	-14.9	$6
BAvg Potl 45%	2nd Half	218	37	63	6	23	2	289			351	463	815	9	79	34	0.47	41	23	36	124	58	10%	8	288	5.65	-0.1	$6
LIMA Plan F	07 Proj	**129**	**20**	**33**	**2**	**12**	**3**	**255**			**313**	**390**	**703**	**8**	**79**	**31**	**0.41**	**42**	**23**	**35**	**99**	**78**	**16%**	**3**	**274**	**4.20**	**-3.9**	**$3**

1-8-.272 in 136 AB at CLE. Long-time prospect still just 24. Stagnant growth gives gloomy short-term outlook. PX trend coupled with high GB% limits power upside. Don't invest now, but keep him on your radar.

Guzman,Cristian		AB	R	H	HR	RBI	SB	Avg	vL	vR	OB	Slg	OPS	bb%	ct%	h%	Eye	G	L	F	PX	SX	SBO	xHR	xBA	RC/G	RAR	R$
Pos 6	02 MIN	623	80	170	9	59	12	273	257	281	292	385	677	3	87	30	0.22	55	18	27	69	106	18%	10	287	3.69	-16.3	$15
Age 29	03 MIN	534	78	142	3	53	18	266	268	276	305	363	668	5	85	31	0.38	50	21	29	54	146	19%	3	270	3.77	-10.4	$14
Peak	04 MIN	576	84	158	8	46	10	274	326	250	310	384	694	5	89	30	0.47	57	16	27	67	104	10%	10	286	4.06	-6.6	$13
Bats Both	05 WAS	456	39	100	4	31	7	219	161	242	260	314	573	5	83	26	0.33	56	20	24	62	106	11%	5	276	2.58	-19.4	$3
Reliability 6	06 WAS	0	0	0	0	0	0	0																				
DL 183	1st Half	0	0	0	0	0	0	0																				
BAvg Potl	2nd Half	0	0	0	0	0	0	0																				
LIMA Plan D	07 Proj	**333**	**42**	**90**	**3**	**28**	**5**	**270**			**305**	**371**	**676**	**5**	**86**	**31**	**0.35**	**54**	**19**	**27**	**61**	**106**	**11%**	**4**	**277**	**3.80**	**-3.8**	**$7**

Shoulder surgery wiped out his season. Even when healthy, he's carried negative RAR since 2001. Speed is his sole asset, but with just one SX over 106 in five years, even that isn't worth much speculation.

STEPHEN NICKRAND

Guzman,Freddy			AB	R	H	HR	RBI	SB	Avg	vL	vR	OB	Slg	OPS	bb%	ct%	h%	Eye	G	L	F	PX	SX	SBO	xHR	xBA	RC/G	RAR	R$
Pos	8	02	0	0	0	0	0	0	0							0							0		0				
Age	26	03 a/a	187	27	45	1	10	36	241			321	289	609	11	83	28	0.71				31	157	72%	1		3.26	-9.4	$11
Pre-Peak		04 a/a	402	59	105	2	22	56	261			327	338	665	9	84	31	0.62				49	168	55%	3		3.90	-9.4	$19
Bats	Right	05 SD	0	0	0	0	0	0	0							0							0		0				
Reliability	0	06 aaa	383	48	98	3	22	33	256	500		326	339	664	9	89	28	0.91	80	0	20	49	130	40%	4		4.03	-6.1	$12
DL	180	1st Half	239	27	62	2	15	18	261			330	356	687	9	91	28	1.11				59	112	41%	3		4.35	-1.5	$7
BAvg Potl	50%	2nd Half	144	21	36	1	7	15	248			318	310	627	9	85	28	0.70	80	0	20	32	153	39%	1		3.47	-4.7	$5
LIMA Plan	F	07 Proj	63	9	16	0	3	8	252			322	334	656	9	86	29	0.72				48	151	51%	1		3.86	-1.4	$3

0-0-.286 in 7 AB at TEX. Still young enough to earn more chances, yet zero power and poor arm strength expose him as a regular. Needs to land in a perfect situation to bring those SB to the majors.

Guzman,Joel			AB	R	H	HR	RBI	SB	Avg	vL	vR	OB	Slg	OPS	bb%	ct%	h%	Eye	G	L	F	PX	SX	SBO	xHR	xBA	RC/G	RAR	R$
Pos	5	02	0	0	0	0	0	0	0							0							0		0				
Age	22	03	0	0	0	0	0	0	0							0							0		0				
Growth		04 aa	182	25	51	9	35	1	278			327	508	835	7	80	31	0.35				138	86	8%	8		5.68	3.6	$7
Bats	Right	05 aa	439	54	112	14	63	6	256			309	414	723	7	77	30	0.34				110	72	10%	15		4.34	-3.9	$12
Reliability	4	06 aaa	424	46	111	12	59	8	261	143	250	309	404	713	6	83	29	0.41	41	18	41	85	77	13%	12	257	4.20	-13.1	$11
DL		1st Half	254	26	67	7	37	3	263			312	397	709	7	85	29	0.47	41	18	41	80	59	13%	7	256	4.21	-7.9	$6
BAvg Potl	50%	2nd Half	170	20	44	6	22	4	259			304	414	718	6	81	29	0.34				93	93	14%	5		4.21	-5.2	$5
LIMA Plan	F	07 Proj	65	8	17	2	10	1	260			310	405	715	7	80	30	0.36	41	18	41	92	54	11%	2	251	4.18	-1.5	$2

0-3-.211 in 19 AB at TAM. He's scaled minor league levels without addressing the holes in his swing. His power should surface first, but he'll need to make adjustments once MLB pitchers expose them.

Gwynn Jr.,Tony			AB	R	H	HR	RBI	SB	Avg	vL	vR	OB	Slg	OPS	bb%	ct%	h%	Eye	G	L	F	PX	SX	SBO	xHR	xBA	RC/G	RAR	R$
Pos	8	02	0	0	0	0	0	0	0							0							0		0				
Age	24	03	0	0	0	0	0	0	0							0							0		0				
Growth		04 aa	534	73	126	2	36	33	236			303	300	602	9	83	28	0.55				44	130	32%	4		3.09	-26.4	$12
Bats	Left	05 aa	505	65	117	1	32	24	232			313	286	599	10	88	26	0.94				38	108	27%	3		3.32	-17.4	$9
Reliability	30	06 MIL	* 524	71	145	4	42	30	277	167	268	329	361	690	7	82	33	0.44	50	23	27	54	120	28%	6	268	4.05	-6.0	$16
DL		1st Half	300	44	87	2	26	16	289			336	381	718	7	83	34	0.43				60	119	28%	4		4.38	-0.5	$10
BAvg Potl	45%	2nd Half	224	27	58	2	16	14	260			320	333	653	8	81	31	0.46	50	23	27	46	111	27%	3	257	3.60	-5.6	$6
LIMA Plan	D	07 Proj	224	29	56	1	16	12	250			316	320	636	9	84	29	0.60	50	23	27	45	123	28%	2	267	3.52	-7.0	$6

0-4-.260 in 77 AB at MIL. A speedy slap hitter who makes the most out of getting the green light. A 2% bb% and 77% ct% over 57 AB in September suggest his learning curve might be a long one.

Hafner,Travis			AB	R	H	HR	RBI	SB	Avg	vL	vR	OB	Slg	OPS	bb%	ct%	h%	Eye	G	L	F	PX	SX	SBO	xHR	xBA	RC/G	RAR	R$
Pos	0	02 TEX	* 463	66	137	18	64	2	296	333	232	386	473	859	13	84	32	0.93	38	17	45	105	52	2%	17	268	6.31	10.1	$17
Age	29	03 CLE	* 391	49	99	16	49	4	253	190	280	327	450	777	10	73	31	0.41	43	22	35	136	82	6%	17	273	5.24	7.2	$10
Peak		04 CLE	482	96	150	28	109	3	311	244	344	396	583	979	12	77	36	0.61	38	19	44	175	82	3%	28	301	7.90	34.1	$25
Bats	Left	05 CLE	486	94	148	33	108	0	305	269	319	402	595	996	14	75	35	0.64	43	20	37	201	30	0%	33	316	8.26	29.6	$26
Reliability	72	06 CLE	454	100	140	42	117	0	308	321	300	433	659	1092	18	76	30	0.90	39	21	40	216	37	0%	38	330	9.57	38.7	$28
DL	18	1st Half	258	60	80	21	62	0	310			451	620	1071	20	79	32	1.20	37	22	41	183	44	0%	19	319	9.33	20.2	$15
BAvg Potl	55%	2nd Half	196	40	60	21	55	0	306			409	709	1118	15	71	33	0.61	40	21	39	265	23	0%	18	342	9.99	19.0	$13
LIMA Plan	D+	07 Proj	514	103	161	45	121	0	313			416	656	1072	15	75	34	0.71	40	20	39	219	40	1%	40	330	9.20	44.0	$30

Few guys can boast his surging trends over the last four years. Growth against LHers has made him a complete hitter. A broken hand on Sept. 1 prevented this: UP: 50-130-.325

Hairston Jr.,Jerry			AB	R	H	HR	RBI	SB	Avg	vL	vR	OB	Slg	OPS	bb%	ct%	h%	Eye	G	L	F	PX	SX	SBO	xHR	xBA	RC/G	RAR	R$
Pos	74	02 BAL	426	55	114	5	32	21	268	263	269	322	376	697	7	87	30	0.62	36	26	38	70	124	23%	7	276	4.24	-7.4	$13
Age	30	03 BAL	218	25	59	2	21	14	271	255	276	340	372	712	10	89	30	0.92	37	24	39	65	112	29%	3	273	4.58	-4.8	$7
Peak		04 BAL	287	43	87	2	24	13	303	316	296	367	397	764	9	90	33	1.00	37	23	40	64	100	22%	4	271	5.18	2.0	$10
Bats	Right	05 CHC	380	51	99	4	30	8	261	255	263	316	368	685	8	88	29	0.67	43	22	34	75	92	17%	6	285	4.13	-13.7	$8
Reliability	12	06 2TM	170	25	35	0	10	5	206	153	245	262	253	515	7	80	26	0.38	42	17	41	36	119	17%	1	212	1.87	-18.0	$1
DL	15	1st Half	112	15	24	0	6	5	214			254	277	531	5	82	26	0.30	36	22	42	45	138	21%	1	228	2.06	-10.9	$1
BAvg Potl	50%	2nd Half	58	10	11	0	4	0	190			277	207	484	11	76	25	0.50	56	7	37	16	74	12%	0	169	1.43	-7.3	($0)
LIMA Plan	F	07 Proj	142	21	37	1	10	6	260			322	338	660	8	83	31	0.55	43	19	38	55	113	22%	2	243	3.80	-5.9	$3

A lost season puts his career at a crossroads.
PRO: SX hasn't disappeared
CON: Nearly everything else has, including, most likely, his window of opportunity. His new upside? A .280 BA and 15 SB.

Hairston,Scott			AB	R	H	HR	RBI	SB	Avg	vL	vR	OB	Slg	OPS	bb%	ct%	h%	Eye	G	L	F	PX	SX	SBO	xHR	xBA	RC/G	RAR	R$
Pos	7	02	0	0	0	0	0	0	0							0							0		0				
Age	26	03 a/a	337	40	85	8	36	5	252			300	415	715	6	83	28	0.40				101	114	9%	8		4.31	-11.5	$7
Pre-Peak		04 ARI	* 454	59	116	17	43	3	256	307	223	300	458	758	6	78	30	0.28	38	19	44	123	99	10%	16	265	4.76	-9.2	$11
Bats	Right	05 ARI	* 229	31	59	12	28	2	259	182		305	471	776	6	85	26	0.43	29	7	64	119	87	4%	9		4.85	-3.2	$7
Reliability	6	06 aaa	396	64	116	20	63	2	292	375	429	358	510	868	9	83	31	0.62	50	30	20	126	62	2%	18		6.15	10.3	$16
DL	43 62	1st Half	254	39	79	15	42	2	310			372	546	918	9	85	32	0.66	50	50	0	132	63	3%	12		6.70	10.2	$11
BAvg Potl	40%	2nd Half	142	25	37	6	21	0	260			333	445	778	10	81	29	0.56	50	17	33	115	42	0%	6		5.14	-0.3	$4
LIMA Plan	D	07 Proj	207	31	56	9	28	1	270			327	476	804	8	82	29	0.48	38	18	44	121	82	4%	8	279	5.33	0.8	$7

0-2-.400 in 15 AB at ARI. Sleeper here if opportunity and health align. Good power, improving base skills, and at an age when some players break out. If he nabs more AB than projected here... UP: 25-75-.275

Hall,Bill			AB	R	H	HR	RBI	SB	Avg	vL	vR	OB	Slg	OPS	bb%	ct%	h%	Eye	G	L	F	PX	SX	SBO	xHR	xBA	RC/G	RAR	R$
Pos	6	02 aaa	465	34	105	4	29	16	226			262	299	561	5	81	27	0.26				54	82	27%	6		2.30	-28.3	$5
Age	27	03 MIL	* 496	75	131	10	49	10	264	185	278	307	403	711	6	80	31	0.31	48	22	30	98	99	21%	12	281	4.19	1.2	$13
Peak		04 MIL	394	44	95	10	55	13	241	190	256	278	383	661	5	70	32	0.17	43	20	37	104	116	23%	12	237	3.53	-7.2	$10
Bats	Right	05 MIL	501	69	146	17	62	18	291	328	277	343	495	838	7	79	34	0.38	43	23	34	138	124	20%	18	301	5.83	26.5	$21
Reliability	37	06 MIL	537	101	145	35	85	8	270	300	261	347	553	900	11	70	32	0.39	33	19	48	192	92	13%	35	279	7.01	41.7	$23
DL		1st Half	250	46	68	16	39	3	272			326	576	902	7	71	32	0.27	32	18	50	202	116	10%	15	287	6.90	18.3	$10
BAvg Potl	35%	2nd Half	287	55	77	19	46	5	268			364	533	897	13	69	32	0.48	34	20	46	182	58	15%	19	273	7.07	23.1	$13
LIMA Plan	B	07 Proj	513	90	134	28	81	10	261			324	508	832	8	73	31	0.34	38	21	42	165	110	17%	27	283	5.86	25.4	$21

Age 26 explosion. Doubled HR total supported by PX and FB%. SB should return if green light comes back. Expect regression while skills stabilize, but most of the power should stay.

Hall,Toby			AB	R	H	HR	RBI	SB	Avg	vL	vR	OB	Slg	OPS	bb%	ct%	h%	Eye	G	L	F	PX	SX	SBO	xHR	xBA	RC/G	RAR	R$
Pos	2	02 TAM	* 422	48	114	8	58	0	270	200	272	303	386	689	5	91	28	0.56	43	15	42	70	43	1%	8	258	4.02	4.9	$9
Age	31	03 TAM	463	50	117	12	47	0	253	253	252	288	380	668	5	91	26	0.58	33	23	44	75	29	1%	11	281	3.77	-4.4	$8
Past Peak		04 TAM	404	35	103	8	60	0	255	294	242	297	366	663	6	90	27	0.59	40	15	44	67	20	2%	8	243	3.75	-6.9	$7
Bats	Right	05 TAM	432	28	124	5	48	0	287	302	281	313	368	681	4	91	31	0.41	41	21	39	54	12	0%	6	256	3.84	-2.2	$8
Reliability	68	06 2TM	278	17	72	8	31	0	259	292	248	285	406	691	3	92	26	0.45	37	16	47	84	0	4%	7	220	3.96	-3.4	$4
DL		1st Half	221	15	51	8	23	0	231			258	398	656	3	92	22	0.47	35	16	50	92	14	5%	7	266	3.57	-5.4	$2
BAvg Potl	55%	2nd Half	57	2	21	0	8	0	368			390	439	828	3	91	40	0.40	43	17	40	53	1	0%	1	215	5.47	1.5	$2
LIMA Plan	F	07 Proj	202	13	54	6	25	0	268			296	418	714	4	91	27	0.46	40	18	42	87	11	1%	6	269	4.20	0.1	$4

Power returned from the ashes during 1st half, but rode the bench after trade to LA. PX and FB% spikes give hope he can reach double-digit HR again. BA recovery will be tougher to come by.

Hardy,J.J.			AB	R	H	HR	RBI	SB	Avg	vL	vR	OB	Slg	OPS	bb%	ct%	h%	Eye	G	L	F	PX	SX	SBO	xHR	xBA	RC/G	RAR	R$
Pos	6	02 aa	145	13	33	1	12	1	228			268	290	558	5	90	25	0.53				43	48	9%	2		2.59	-7.4	$1
Age	24	03 aa	416	61	109	11	57	5	262			343	401	744	11	88	28	1.04				87	60	7%	12		4.94	8.2	$12
Growth		04 aaa	101	15	27	4	18	0	270			320	489	808	7	93	26	1.10				125	34	0%	4		5.48	3.4	$3
Bats	Right	05 MIL	372	46	92	9	50	0	247	245	240	327	384	711	11	87	26	0.92	44	20	35	88	38	0%	10	282	4.54	6.3	$8
Reliability	0	06 MIL	128	13	31	5	14	1	242	294	223	297	398	696	7	82	26	0.43	47	19	34	90	36	6%	4	265	3.96	-1.5	$2
DL	138	1st Half	128	13	31	5	14	1	242			297	398	696	7	82	26	0.43	47	18	35	90	36	6%	4	262	3.96	-1.5	$2
BAvg Potl	55%	2nd Half	0	0	0	0	0	0	0							0							0		0				
LIMA Plan	D	07 Proj	386	47	97	12	51	2	251			312	406	718	8	88	26	0.71	46	19	35	93	44	4%	12	285	4.44	2.9	$9

Ankle surgery ended season. Pre-injury skill decline is worrisome, but he's usually a slow starter. Keep 157 PX vs. LHers in your pocket on draft day. He'd emerge quickly with improvement against RHers.

STEPHEN NICKRAND

Harper,Brandon		AB	R	H	HR	RBI	SB	Avg	vL	vR	OB	Slg	OPS	bb%	ct%	h%	Eye	G	L	F	PX	SX	SBO	xHR	xBA	RC/G	RAR	R$
Pos 2	02	0	0	0	0	0	0	0							0							0		0				
Age 31	03 aa	195	13	36	2	14	2	183			253	255	508	9	81	22	0.49				55	44	4%	3		1.86	-14.6	($1)
Past Peak	04 a/a	224	27	44	9	27	2	197			249	349	598	6	82	20	0.37				90	60	8%	8		2.73	-9.5	$3
Bats Right	05 aaa	248	26	51	5	25	4	205			272	308	580	8	86	22	0.67				65	84	6%	5		2.87	-8.0	$2
Reliability 9	06 WAS	* 161	20	40	4	15	3	248	258	400	315	388	702	9	84	28	0.60	39	11	50	91	59	9%	5	235	4.27	-0.3	$3
DL	1st Half	71	6	14	1	4	1	190			256	279	535	8	77	24	0.38				66	49	12%	1		2.02	-5.3	($0)
BAvg Potl 45%	2nd Half	90	14	26	3	11	2	293			360	473	833	9	89	30	0.98	39	11	50	108	60	7%	3	267	5.89	3.9	$3
LIMA Plan F	07 Proj	**137**	**16**	**31**	**3**	**14**	**2**	**226**			**291**	**355**	**646**	**8**	**84**	**25**	**0.57**	**39**	**11**	**50**	**83**	**60**	**8%**	**4**	**230**	**3.57**	**-2.3**	**$2**

2-6-.293 in 41 AB at WAS. His MLB debut came at age 30. As it stands, he's never maintained good skills over long stretches. His history suggests any power flashes will be offset by a lagging BA.

Hart,Corey		AB	R	H	HR	RBI	SB	Avg	vL	vR	OB	Slg	OPS	bb%	ct%	h%	Eye	G	L	F	PX	SX	SBO	xHR	xBA	RC/G	RAR	R$
Pos 97	02 a/a	376	46	91	3	47	8	242			328	322	650	11	86	27	0.94				54	83	15%	5		3.90	-14.5	$7
Age 25	03 aa	334	34	88	4	40	10	263			342	326	669	11	84	31	0.73				41	66	12%	5		3.95	-14.0	$8
Pre-Peak	04 aaa	441	59	119	14	59	15	269			322	450	772	7	84	30	0.48				109	117	22%	14		5.01	0.2	$15
Bats Both	05 MIL	* 486	73	126	15	59	25	259	211	184	318	440	759	8	84	28	0.54	54	22	24	112	146	29%	15	319	4.89	-5.2	$19
Reliability 28	06 MIL	* 337	47	94	13	50	14	279	304	272	332	474	806	7	75	34	0.32	42	17	41	128	105	29%	13	263	5.47	6.9	$14
DL	1st Half	140	22	45	4	25	14	321			383	507	890	9	78	39	0.45	66	13	22	126	121	43%	5	302	6.66	7.3	$9
BAvg Potl 35%	2nd Half	197	25	49	9	25	0	249			295	450	745	6	73	30	0.25	36	18	45	129	68	14%	8	252	4.59	-1.1	$4
LIMA Plan C	07 Proj	**410**	**57**	**110**	**15**	**56**	**7**	**268**			**326**	**460**	**786**	**8**	**80**	**30**	**0.42**	**43**	**18**	**39**	**120**	**88**	**16%**	**15**	**276**	**5.17**	**1.6**	**$13**

9-33-.283 in 237 AB at MIL. Two reasons for optimism:
1. Jun/Jul/Aug PX: 63, 118, 160.
2. Even LH/RH splits.
Expect BA dip until ct% improves, but seeds for PX growth apparent.

Hatteberg,Scott		AB	R	H	HR	RBI	SB	Avg	vL	vR	OB	Slg	OPS	bb%	ct%	h%	Eye	G	L	F	PX	SX	SBO	xHR	xBA	RC/G	RAR	R$
Pos 3	02 OAK	492	58	138	15	61	0	280	233	291	368	433	801	12	89	29	1.21	46	18	37	85	44	0%	14	277	5.66	-2.8	$13
Age 37	03 OAK	541	63	137	12	61	0	253	255	253	334	383	717	11	90	26	1.25	45	20	35	81	24	1%	14	284	4.71	-10.7	$9
Decline	04 OAK	550	87	156	15	82	0	284	285	283	367	420	787	12	91	29	1.50	42	18	40	78	33	0%	15	273	5.52	8.2	$16
Bats Left	05 OAK	464	52	119	7	59	0	256	214	271	330	343	673	10	88	28	0.94	47	20	33	56	26	1%	8	258	4.09	-13.6	$8
Reliability 27	06 CIN	456	62	132	13	51	2	289	231	302	389	436	825	14	91	30	1.80	46	21	33	84	34	2%	14	295	6.11	1.4	$13
DL	1st Half	210	31	61	6	22	0	290			399	452	852	15	93	29	2.71	46	20	34	93	25	3%	7	303	6.57	3.4	$6
BAvg Potl 70%	2nd Half	246	31	71	7	29	2	289			379	423	802	13	89	30	1.33	45	22	33	76	42	2%	7	288	5.72	-1.9	$7
LIMA Plan C+	07 Proj	**430**	**56**	**115**	**11**	**53**	**1**	**267**			**357**	**395**	**752**	**12**	**90**	**28**	**1.41**	**45**	**20**	**35**	**76**	**36**	**2%**	**11**	**282**	**5.17**	**-8.4**	**$10**

Nice rebound season, but there are still signs of wear. 2nd half is skewed by an other-worldly July. A .226 BA and 43 PX over final two months point to a looming decline.
DN: 8-45-.250

Hawpe,Brad		AB	R	H	HR	RBI	SB	Avg	vL	vR	OB	Slg	OPS	bb%	ct%	h%	Eye	G	L	F	PX	SX	SBO	xHR	xBA	RC/G	RAR	R$
Pos 9	02	0	0	0	0	0	0	0							0							0		0				
Age 27	03 aa	346	39	90	16	51	1	260			308	471	779	6	81	28	0.37				136	31	5%	15		4.96	-4.3	$10
Peak	04 COL	* 450	54	126	28	66	3	280	154	261	332	524	856	7	79	30	0.38	53	21	26	142	59	6%	23	310	5.88	7.5	$17
Bats Left	05 COL	305	38	80	9	47	2	262	250	264	353	403	757	12	77	31	0.61	52	17	32	90	76	4%	9	255	5.04	-1.9	$9
Reliability 30	06 COL	499	67	146	22	84	5	293	232	302	384	515	899	13	75	35	0.60	42	22	36	142	77	6%	23	285	6.98	31.0	$19
DL 54	1st Half	255	33	78	14	45	2	306			392	553	945	12	73	37	0.53	38	24	39	153	76	6%	13	283	7.59	19.9	$11
BAvg Potl 40%	2nd Half	244	34	68	8	39	3	279			376	475	851	13	77	33	0.69	47	20	34	131	75	7%	10	287	6.40	11.3	$8
LIMA Plan B	07 Proj	**510**	**65**	**142**	**25**	**91**	**4**	**278**			**360**	**505**	**865**	**11**	**77**	**32**	**0.56**	**46**	**20**	**34**	**141**	**74**	**6%**	**24**	**292**	**6.35**	**19.1**	**$19**

Gotta love the PX and FB% growth, especially in 1st half. In fact, he managed a 130 PX in every month except July. Once he fixes his .232 BA / 110 PX vs. LHers and halts his ct% slide...
UP: 30-100-.300

Helms,Wes		AB	R	H	HR	RBI	SB	Avg	vL	vR	OB	Slg	OPS	bb%	ct%	h%	Eye	G	L	F	PX	SX	SBO	xHR	xBA	RC/G	RAR	R$
Pos 35	02 ATL	210	20	51	6	22	1	243	167	269	281	405	685	5	73	31	0.19	37	17	46	129	41	5%	7	247	3.82	-11.2	$4
Age 30	03 MIL	476	56	124	23	67	0	261	314	249	322	450	771	8	72	31	0.33	38	22	39	128	21	1%	22	259	5.00	-7.1	$14
Peak	04 MIL	278	25	74	4	29	0	266	306	248	325	367	691	8	78	33	0.39	43	18	39	71	37	1%	5	231	4.04	-15.3	$4
Bats Right	05 MIL	168	18	50	4	24	0	298	305	294	352	458	810	8	82	34	0.47	44	18	38	111	46	2%	5	276	5.51	-0.4	$5
Reliability 14	06 FLA	240	30	79	10	47	0	329	336	323	383	575	958	8	77	39	0.38	38	26	36	155	66	6%	10	306	7.48	9.6	$11
DL	1st Half	97	8	25	5	15	0	258			308	474	782	7	72	31	0.26	49	15	35	135	49	9%	5	259	5.10	-2.6	$2
BAvg Potl 25%	2nd Half	143	22	54	5	32	0	378			433	643	1076	9	80	45	0.50	31	33	36	166	76	5%	6	332	8.97	10.6	$8
LIMA Plan D+	07 Proj	**323**	**37**	**98**	**15**	**52**	**0**	**303**			**358**	**535**	**892**	**8**	**78**	**35**	**0.39**	**40**	**22**	**38**	**147**	**57**	**4%**	**14**	**297**	**6.53**	**6.1**	**$12**

Nearly half of all his balls-in-play fell for hits in the 2nd half. The problem: those 143 magical ABs are going to color everyone's expectations. But power growth does bear watching.
UP: 2003, plus 40 pts of BA.

Helton,Todd		AB	R	H	HR	RBI	SB	Avg	vL	vR	OB	Slg	OPS	bb%	ct%	h%	Eye	G	L	F	PX	SX	SBO	xHR	xBA	RC/G	RAR	R$
Pos 3	02 COL	553	107	182	30	109	5	329	327	331	431	577	1008	15	84	35	1.09	38	26	37	154	88	3%	29	327	8.24	38.6	$33
Age 33	03 COL	583	135	209	33	117	0	358	387	344	461	630	1091	16	88	37	1.54	33	28	39	158	56	2%	31	349	9.22	55.0	$37
Past Peak	04 COL	547	115	190	32	96	3	347	320	360	470	620	1090	19	87	36	1.76	35	21	44	158	68	1%	32	329	9.42	48.5	$33
Bats Left	05 COL	509	92	163	20	79	3	320	245	351	437	534	972	17	84	35	1.33	33	24	42	140	69	1%	23	312	8.01	32.7	$24
Reliability 48	06 COL	546	94	165	15	81	3	302	326	295	402	476	878	14	88	32	1.42	35	24	41	102	76	3%	17	297	6.74	11.2	$20
DL 15 15	1st Half	228	47	70	8	38	0	307			432	500	932	18	87	32	1.72	36	20	44	114	47	2%	9	294	7.57	9.9	$10
BAvg Potl 65%	2nd Half	318	47	95	7	43	3	299			379	459	838	11	89	32	1.17	35	26	39	93	89	3%	8	299	6.12	1.1	$10
LIMA Plan A	07 Proj	**531**	**97**	**164**	**20**	**84**	**3**	**309**			**417**	**516**	**934**	**16**	**87**	**33**	**1.41**	**35**	**24**	**41**	**124**	**77**	**2%**	**21**	**309**	**7.44**	**23.0**	**$23**

Another disappointing year. Blame lingering effects of early-season intestinal ailment. Besides PX, otherwise solid BPIs remain unchanged. He should rebound - but then, we thought that last year.

Hermida,Jeremy		AB	R	H	HR	RBI	SB	Avg	vL	vR	OB	Slg	OPS	bb%	ct%	h%	Eye	G	L	F	PX	SX	SBO	xHR	xBA	RC/G	RAR	R$
Pos 9	02	0	0	0	0	0	0	0							0							0		0				
Age 23	03	0	0	0	0	0	0	0							0							0		0				
Growth	04	0	0	0	0	0	0	0							0							0		0				
Bats Left	05 FLA	* 427	77	115	19	67	22	269	200	306	415	480	895	20	78	31	1.12	31	24	45	142	114	14%	22	281	7.20	24.0	$21
Reliability 0	06 FLA	307	37	77	5	28	4	251	219	261	324	368	692	10	77	31	0.47	45	20	35	84	72	6%	7	251	4.15	-5.6	$5
DL 39	1st Half	129	20	38	2	11	2	295			364	450	813	10	76	38	0.45	50	19	31	116	85	5%	4	275	5.82	3.8	$4
BAvg Potl 45%	2nd Half	178	17	39	3	17	2	219			294	309	603	10	78	26	0.49	41	21	38	61	45	6%	4	234	2.97	-9.9	$1
LIMA Plan C+	07 Proj	**453**	**65**	**122**	**12**	**53**	**13**	**269**			**370**	**425**	**795**	**14**	**77**	**32**	**0.71**	**44**	**20**	**35**	**106**	**101**	**10%**	**15**	**268**	**5.66**	**8.1**	**$15**

Hampered by hip and ankle injuries, but flashed upside. Healthy June saw a .345 BA and 130 PX over 87 AB. Still has 20-20 upside if he can stay sound and loft the ball a bit more.

Hernandez,Anderson		AB	R	H	HR	RBI	SB	Avg	vL	vR	OB	Slg	OPS	bb%	ct%	h%	Eye	G	L	F	PX	SX	SBO	xHR	xBA	RC/G	RAR	R$
Pos 4	02	0	0	0	0	0	0	0							0							0		0				
Age 24	03	0	0	0	0	0	0	0							0							0		0				
Growth	04 aa	394	56	97	4	25	15	246			284	332	617	5	81	30	0.28				57	128	23%	5		3.00	-16.0	$8
Bats Both	05 a/a	526	65	151	7	44	28	287			323	373	696	5	84	33	0.33				55	107	32%	8		3.95	-6.1	$19
Reliability 7	06 NYM	* 480	47	110	1	25	15	229	211	128	261	277	539	4	84	27	0.27	49	15	36	30	107	18%	2	222	2.09	-36.9	$4
DL 35	1st Half	226	19	51	0	11	11	226			268	265	533	5	85	26	0.39	52	18	30	25	104	26%	1	239	2.18	-17.0	$2
BAvg Potl 45%	2nd Half	254	28	59	1	14	4	232			256	287	543	3	82	28	0.17	45	10	45	36	98	9%	2	195	2.03	-19.8	$2
LIMA Plan F	07 Proj	**100**	**11**	**22**	**1**	**7**	**2**	**220**			**255**	**292**	**548**	**5**	**83**	**26**	**0.28**	**49**	**15**	**37**	**45**	**105**	**18%**	**1**	**229**	**2.21**	**-7.4**	**$1**

1-3-.152 in 66 AB at NYM. Great glove, no bat, and no signs of that changing. SB history was driven by SBO% more than SX; don't expect it to translate into success on MLB basepaths.

Hernandez,Jose		AB	R	H	HR	RBI	SB	Avg	vL	vR	OB	Slg	OPS	bb%	ct%	h%	Eye	G	L	F	PX	SX	SBO	xHR	xBA	RC/G	RAR	R$
Pos 9	02 MIL	525	72	151	24	73	3	288	253	296	352	478	830	9	64	41	0.28	49	22	29	150	60	5%	26	254	6.30	14.9	$20
Age 37	03 2NL	519	58	117	13	57	2	225	235	221	288	347	635	8	66	32	0.26	47	20	33	92	74	2%	15	222	3.31	-36.3	$7
Decline	04 LA	211	32	61	13	29	3	289	310	259	367	540	907	11	71	35	0.43	45	15	40	167	74	7%	13	274	7.05	10.4	$9
Bats Right	05 CLE	234	28	54	6	31	1	231	269	169	274	338	612	6	74	29	0.23	50	18	32	74	48	7%	6	233	2.78	-13.8	$4
Reliability 0	06 2NL	152	12	40	3	19	0	263	290	244	317	362	679	7	74	34	0.30	45	21	34	63	36	0%	3	226	3.79	-4.3	$2
DL	1st Half	65	5	12	2	6	0	185			243	277	520	7	83	19	0.45	57	11	32	45	15	0%	2	196	1.84	-6.1	($0)
BAvg Potl 30%	2nd Half	87	7	28	1	13	0	322			372	425	798	7	67	47	0.24	35	30	35	80	50	0%	2	230	5.78	2.3	$3
LIMA Plan F	07 Proj	**134**	**14**	**32**	**2**	**17**	**0**	**239**			**296**	**333**	**629**	**8**	**72**	**32**	**0.30**	**46**	**20**	**34**	**67**	**71**	**3%**	**2**	**225**	**3.19**	**-7.4**	**$2**

Days are numbered. Posted a 43 PX in 90 AB against RHers. Who needs a whiffer who can't hit RHers? The chubby 3rd grader with his own backdraft issues would be picked before him in a sandlot game now.

STEPHEN NICKRAND

Hernandez,Ramon

		Season	AB	R	H	HR	RBI	SB	Avg	vL	vR	OB	Slg	OPS	bb%	ct%	h%	Eye	G	L	F	PX	SX	SBO	xHR	xBA	RC/G	RAR	R$
Pos	2	02 OAK	403	51	94	7	42	0	233	257	224	307	335	642	10	84	26	0.67	49	18	34	67	33	0%	8	251	3.60	-0.2	$5
Age	30	03 OAK	483	70	132	21	78	0	273	208	302	320	458	777	6	84	29	0.42	41	22	37	110	43	0%	18	289	4.90	11.2	$16
Peak		04 SD	384	45	106	18	63	1	276	310	264	337	477	813	8	88	27	0.78	47	19	34	113	33	1%	16	303	5.48	18.2	$13
Bats	Right	05 SD	369	36	107	12	58	1	290	238	304	323	450	773	5	89	30	0.45	46	21	33	93	53	1%	10	302	4.84	10.8	$12
Reliability	50	06 BAL	501	66	138	23	91	1	275	291	270	333	479	812	8	84	29	0.54	44	19	38	119	53	1%	20	293	5.42	14.4	$16
DL	54	1st Half	275	32	79	15	59	1	287			342	524	866	8	87	29	0.64	42	21	37	133	45	1%	13	318	6.02	12.4	$10
BAvg Potl	55%	2nd Half	226	34	59	8	32	0	261			321	425	746	8	81	29	0.47	46	16	38	100	51	0%	8	260	4.66	1.6	$6
LIMA Plan	D+	07 Proj	**450**	**56**	**129**	**18**	**73**	**1**	**287**			**338**	**470**	**808**	**7**	**86**	**30**	**0.54**	**45**	**19**	**36**	**107**	**50**	**1%**	**16**	**291**	**5.36**	**14.0**	**$14**

Leveraged his solid skills over an extra 130 AB. Spent a combined three months on DL over 2004-05, so this is likely his maximal output. Don't underrate the burden of his position (note the 2nd-half slide).

Hillenbrand,Shea

		Season	AB	R	H	HR	RBI	SB	Avg	vL	vR	OB	Slg	OPS	bb%	ct%	h%	Eye	G	L	F	PX	SX	SBO	xHR	xBA	RC/G	RAR	R$
Pos	305	02 BOS	634	94	186	18	83	4	293	269	299	320	459	779	4	85	32	0.26	47	21	32	103	87	4%	18	299	4.86	-17.6	$21
Age	31	03 2TM	515	60	144	20	97	1	280	298	271	312	468	780	4	86	29	0.34	44	25	31	115	49	1%	18	318	4.87	-8.4	$17
Past Peak		04 ARI	562	68	174	15	80	2	310	323	304	338	464	802	4	91	32	0.49	47	20	33	89	69	1%	14	304	5.19	-11.6	$19
Bats	Right	05 TOR	594	91	173	18	82	5	291	325	279	321	449	770	4	87	31	0.33	43	20	37	99	89	4%	17	292	4.77	-5.3	$20
Reliability	97	06 2TM	530	73	147	21	68	1	277	338	256	305	451	756	4	85	29	0.26	46	20	34	100	53	3%	18	287	4.51	-18.1	$15
DL		1st Half	251	35	78	11	35	0	311			347	498	845	5	86	33	0.40	47	19	35	104	45	3%	9	290	5.62	-0.6	$9
BAvg Potl	45%	2nd Half	279	38	69	10	33	1	247			266	409	674	2	84	26	0.16	45	21	34	97	60	2%	9	284	3.49	-18.3	$6
LIMA Plan	C	07 Proj	**538**	**74**	**155**	**19**	**73**	**2**	**288**			**316**	**457**	**772**	**4**	**86**	**31**	**0.29**	**45**	**20**	**34**	**100**	**69**	**3%**	**17**	**294**	**4.75**	**-12.4**	**$17**

Bombed after trade to SF in July, hitting .248 (with only 7 BB) after batting .301 for TOR. However, xBA doesn't see a difference in the two halves, and a .300-level BA is a truer measure of his recent skills.

Hill,Aaron

		Season	AB	R	H	HR	RBI	SB	Avg	vL	vR	OB	Slg	OPS	bb%	ct%	h%	Eye	G	L	F	PX	SX	SBO	xHR	xBA	RC/G	RAR	R$
Pos	46	02	0	0	0	0	0	0	0							0							0		0				
Age	25	03	0	0	0	0	0	0	0							0							0		0				
Pre-Peak		04 aa	480	75	134	11	77	3	279			360	417	777	11	88	30	1.03				84	70	3%	12		5.36	13.9	$15
Bats	Right	05 TOR	* 517	67	143	7	55	4	277	298	269	325	398	723	7	89	30	0.67	43	22	36	81	83	4%	10	291	4.54	6.0	$12
Reliability	53	06 TOR	546	70	159	6	50	5	291	298	288	342	386	728	7	88	32	0.64	46	19	35	61	80	4%	8	267	4.57	6.9	$12
DL		1st Half	249	32	70	2	23	1	281			325	382	706	6	90	31	0.64	49	18	34	64	73	3%	3	273	4.33	1.5	$5
BAvg Potl	50%	2nd Half	297	38	89	4	27	4	300			356	391	747	8	86	34	0.63	44	21	35	58	75	5%	5	260	4.78	5.4	$8
LIMA Plan	C+	07 Proj	**549**	**73**	**151**	**8**	**59**	**5**	**275**			**331**	**386**	**716**	**8**	**88**	**30**	**0.71**	**45**	**20**	**35**	**71**	**83**	**4%**	**10**	**277**	**4.48**	**5.7**	**$12**

It is unusual for a guy with a 61 PX to put up a 32% hit rate, and xBA confirms the disconnect. Could get a bump in power from maturation but the net effect is likely to be a wash.

Hinske,Eric

		Season	AB	R	H	HR	RBI	SB	Avg	vL	vR	OB	Slg	OPS	bb%	ct%	h%	Eye	G	L	F	PX	SX	SBO	xHR	xBA	RC/G	RAR	R$
Pos	90	02 TOR	566	99	158	24	84	13	279	202	301	365	481	846	12	76	33	0.56	40	21	39	136	106	8%	26	278	6.20	18.9	$23
Age	29	03 TOR	449	74	109	12	63	12	243	256	237	331	437	767	12	77	29	0.57	36	26	39	144	119	13%	17	290	5.26	1.5	$13
Peak		04 TOR	570	66	140	15	69	12	246	268	236	311	375	686	9	81	28	0.50	43	18	39	79	86	13%	15	250	3.98	-12.3	$12
Bats	Left	05 TOR	477	79	125	15	68	8	262	172	281	327	430	757	9	75	32	0.38	41	20	39	122	99	10%	17	263	4.91	3.0	$15
Reliability	26	06 2AL	277	43	75	13	34	2	271	167	293	353	487	840	11	71	34	0.44	40	16	43	148	77	5%	14	259	6.18	4.2	$8
DL		1st Half	91	17	23	4	10	0	253			340	429	768	12	78	28	0.60	41	15	44	109	51	4%	4	250	5.07	-1.6	$2
BAvg Potl	35%	2nd Half	186	26	52	9	24	2	280			359	516	875	11	68	36	0.39	40	17	43	170	86	6%	10	263	6.86	6.3	$6
LIMA Plan	D	07 Proj	**251**	**39**	**66**	**10**	**32**	**3**	**263**			**339**	**446**	**785**	**10**	**75**	**32**	**0.45**	**41**	**18**	**41**	**125**	**76**	**8%**	**10**	**259**	**5.33**	**0.8**	**$7**

Steep and coinciding drops in PT, ct%, and SBO make him tantalizing. If not for BA vs LHP, there might be a sleeper here. Bright spot: Had .896 OPS vs RH, against whom he was on pace for 30 HR in 600 AB.

Hollandsworth,Todd

		Season	AB	R	H	HR	RBI	SB	Avg	vL	vR	OB	Slg	OPS	bb%	ct%	h%	Eye	G	L	F	PX	SX	SBO	xHR	xBA	RC/G	RAR	R$
Pos	97	02 2TM	430	55	122	16	67	8	284	228	292	345	463	807	9	77	34	0.41	52	17	31	123	67	14%	17	279	5.48	4.0	$16
Age	34	03 FLA	228	32	58	3	20	2	254	250	255	320	421	741	9	76	32	0.40	41	21	38	131	103	10%	6	277	4.87	-5.0	$4
Past Peak		04 CHC	148	28	47	8	22	1	318	353	313	388	547	935	10	82	34	0.65	50	21	28	127	93	4%	7	313	7.03	7.0	$7
Bats	Left	05 2NL	303	26	74	6	36	4	244	275	234	298	373	670	7	78	29	0.35	46	19	35	91	71	13%	7	258	3.73	-13.9	$5
Reliability	2	06 2TM	224	27	55	7	35	0	246	174	254	278	429	706	4	77	29	0.19	46	18	36	126	60	5%	8	273	4.04	-7.9	$5
DL		1st Half	96	10	19	3	16	0	198			222	396	618	3	75	23	0.13	47	15	38	138	88	10%	3	272	2.89	-7.1	$1
BAvg Potl	45%	2nd Half	128	17	36	4	19	0	281			319	453	772	5	78	33	0.25	45	20	35	118	40	3%	5	275	4.87	-1.3	$4
LIMA Plan	F	07 Proj	**197**	**24**	**54**	**6**	**28**	**0**	**274**			**320**	**444**	**764**	**6**	**78**	**32**	**0.31**	**47**	**19**	**34**	**114**	**54**	**5%**	**7**	**272**	**4.84**	**-1.6**	**$5**

Despite being healthy again, BA didn't recover. But note that PX, SX, and ct% were same as in 2002, when he hit .281 (which is also what he batted in the 2nd half). His power will get him another chance.

Holliday,Matt

		Season	AB	R	H	HR	RBI	SB	Avg	vL	vR	OB	Slg	OPS	bb%	ct%	h%	Eye	G	L	F	PX	SX	SBO	xHR	xBA	RC/G	RAR	R$
Pos	7	02 aa	463	57	122	9	46	12	263			334	369	703	10	85	29	0.72				66	96	10%	9		4.33	-17.1	$12
Age	27	03 aa	522	49	126	12	55	12	241			286	375	662	6	89	25	0.59				79	89	19%	12		3.75	-27.2	$10
Peak		04 COL	400	65	116	14	57	3	290	237	307	341	488	829	7	79	34	0.36	50	17	32	131	86	6%	15	290	5.71	3.1	$15
Bats	Right	05 COL	479	68	147	19	87	14	307	324	302	355	505	861	7	84	34	0.46	48	21	31	118	125	13%	17	306	5.98	8.4	$24
Reliability	67	06 COL	602	119	196	34	114	10	326	327	325	374	586	961	7	82	35	0.43	45	21	34	153	104	9%	30	320	7.19	31.2	$33
DL	40	1st Half	298	56	105	15	54	4	352			383	614	997	5	84	38	0.31	47	20	33	156	95	8%	14	330	7.46	16.9	$17
BAvg Potl	40%	2nd Half	304	63	91	19	60	6	299			366	559	925	10	80	32	0.52	42	22	36	151	99	11%	16	310	6.88	13.8	$16
LIMA Plan	D+	07 Proj	**583**	**109**	**183**	**37**	**101**	**11**	**314**			**365**	**586**	**951**	**7**	**82**	**33**	**0.45**	**46**	**20**	**33**	**159**	**111**	**11%**	**31**	**327**	**7.03**	**26.2**	**$32**

Lofty heights, but there are reasons to expect more growth:
- Contact rate was only 82%.
- .373 at Coors w/the humidor
- GB% continues to slip.

At minimum, we like odds of a repeat.

Hollins,Damon

		Season	AB	R	H	HR	RBI	SB	Avg	vL	vR	OB	Slg	OPS	bb%	ct%	h%	Eye	G	L	F	PX	SX	SBO	xHR	xBA	RC/G	RAR	R$
Pos	98	02 aaa	498	54	120	8	48	8	241			281	357	639	5	86	27	0.39				78	87	9%	11		3.36	-26.8	$9
Age	32	03 aaa	307	34	74	10	39	6	240			283	421	704	6	80	27	0.29				119	104	14%	10		4.05	-12.2	$7
Past Peak		04 aaa	356	40	89	16	53	4	250			288	458	746	5	85	26	0.35				120	72	9%	14		4.49	-5.4	$10
Bats	Left	05 TAM	* 423	51	103	14	57	10	243	248	250	298	396	694	7	82	27	0.43	44	18	38	97	85	13%	13	268	3.98	-9.1	$11
Reliability	35	06 TAM	333	37	76	15	33	3	228	240	221	270	423	693	5	81	24	0.30	41	19	40	121	50	10%	14	280	3.84	-18.6	$6
DL		1st Half	199	22	46	9	17	2	231			278	427	705	6	82	24	0.36	39	20	42	120	47	13%	8	282	4.03	-10.0	$3
BAvg Potl	60%	2nd Half	134	15	30	6	16	1	224			257	418	675	4	79	24	0.21	46	18	36	123	50	5%	6	277	3.54	-8.6	$2
LIMA Plan	F	07 Proj	**231**	**26**	**58**	**9**	**28**	**3**	**251**			**293**	**428**	**721**	**6**	**82**	**27**	**0.32**	**43**	**18**	**38**	**110**	**56**	**9%**	**9**	**275**	**4.19**	**-7.0**	**$5**

Despite 25-HR power and a 121 PX, he had only a 24% hit rate. His skills are borderline tolerable across the board. He will never earn $20, but between his HR and his SB, you are probably assured of $5.

Howard,Ryan

		Season	AB	R	H	HR	RBI	SB	Avg	vL	vR	OB	Slg	OPS	bb%	ct%	h%	Eye	G	L	F	PX	SX	SBO	xHR	xBA	RC/G	RAR	R$
Pos	3	02	0	0	0	0	0	0	0							0							0		0				
Age	27	03	0	0	0	0	0	0	0							0							0		0				
Peak		04 a/a	485	75	119	35	105	1	246			315	516	831	9	68	28	0.32				182	47	3%	32		5.93	6.7	$19
Bats	Left	05 PHI	* 522	82	160	36	106	0	307	148	320	381	584	965	11	71	37	0.41	44	27	29	193	43	1%	34	311	7.84	31.9	$27
Reliability	19	06 PHI	581	104	182	58	149	0	313	279	331	421	659	1080	16	69	36	0.60	42	22	36	220	24	0%	51	305	9.69	57.7	$36
DL		1st Half	280	42	80	27	68	0	286			353	618	971	9	71	31	0.36	45	20	35	201	27	0%	22	301	7.63	12.8	$15
BAvg Potl	30%	2nd Half	301	62	102	31	81	0	339			476	698	1174	21	66	42	0.78	39	24	37	239	15	0%	30	308	11.59	43.6	$22
LIMA Plan	D+	07 Proj	**555**	**94**	**168**	**52**	**129**	**0**	**303**			**395**	**641**	**1036**	**13**	**69**	**35**	**0.50**	**42**	**24**	**34**	**223**	**29**	**1%**	**46**	**313**	**8.93**	**46.9**	**$33**

Awesome power, but beware sub-70% contact rate. Growth relies on ever-higher PX. Furthermore, teams will simply stop pitching to him. In 2006, he lost 5% of PA to intentional walks, and 20% to all walks.

Huber,Justin

		Season	AB	R	H	HR	RBI	SB	Avg	vL	vR	OB	Slg	OPS	bb%	ct%	h%	Eye	G	L	F	PX	SX	SBO	xHR	xBA	RC/G	RAR	R$
Pos	0	02	0	0	0	0	0	0	0							0							0		0				
Age	24	03 aa	193	13	44	5	29	0	228			284	363	646	7	77	27	0.33				96	15	5%	6		3.37	-7.4	$2
Growth		04 a/a	252	40	63	10	31	2	250			355	444	799	14	79	28	0.79				124	65	5%	11		5.66	2.7	$7
Bats	Right	05 KC	* 526	73	144	15	81	8	274	167	263	345	426	771	10	81	31	0.58	47	19	34	100	84	8%	16	276	5.10	-13.9	$17
Reliability	22	06 aaa	362	43	93	12	40	3	257	125	500	326	431	757	9	77	31	0.44	17	33	50	115	66	5%	13		4.91	-16.2	$8
DL		1st Half	223	23	51	8	22	3	229			295	399	694	9	76	27	0.40	17	33	50	106	78	10%	8		4.03	-16.4	$3
BAvg Potl	35%	2nd Half	139	20	42	4	18	0	302			374	482	856	10	77	37	0.50				130	27	0%	5		6.31	-0.5	$4
LIMA Plan	F	07 Proj	**126**	**16**	**33**	**4**	**16**	**1**	**262**			**336**	**420**	**756**	**10**	**78**	**31**	**0.52**	**43**	**21**	**36**	**107**	**45**	**5%**	**4**	**268**	**4.92**	**-4.1**	**$3**

0-1-.200 in 10 AB in KC. Had a decent second half... unfortunately, it was in Triple-A. Lack of Sept call-up suggests he is not in KC's plans. Could be a winning reserve pick with a change of scenery.

JOHN BURNSON

Hudson,Orlando

Hudson,Orlando			AB	R	H	HR	RBI	SB	Avg	vL	vR	OB	Slg	OPS	bb%	ct%	h%	Eye	G	L	F	PX	SX	SBO	xHR	xBA	RC/G	RAR	R$
Pos	4	02 TOR	* 609	70	168	12	53	6	276	184	308	319	419	738	6	89	30	0.56	43	22	35	86	87	9%	13	294	4.62	10.3	$14
Age	29	03 TOR	474	54	127	9	57	5	268	160	297	324	395	718	8	82	31	0.45	47	26	28	79	92	7%	10	284	4.38	3.3	$11
Peak		04 TOR	489	73	132	12	58	7	270	262	272	339	438	777	9	80	32	0.52	48	20	32	107	112	8%	14	282	5.22	16.1	$13
Bats	Both	05 TOR	461	62	125	10	63	7	271	227	288	316	412	728	6	86	30	0.46	52	20	28	88	108	7%	10	297	4.45	4.2	$13
Reliability	66	06 ARI	579	87	166	15	67	9	287	338	270	355	454	809	10	87	31	0.78	49	19	32	95	100	9%	15	295	5.62	16.8	$18
DL		1st Half	268	35	70	5	29	5	261			329	399	728	9	84	30	0.63	53	19	28	82	98	12%	6	283	4.64	0.3	$6
BAvg Potl	55%	2nd Half	311	52	96	10	38	4	309			377	502	878	10	89	32	0.97	47	19	35	106	98	6%	10	306	6.43	15.6	$12
LIMA Plan	B	07 Proj	**550**	**79**	**159**	**13**	**66**	**8**	**289**			**349**	**450**	**798**	**8**	**85**	**32**	**0.63**	**49**	**20**	**31**	**95**	**108**	**8%**	**14**	**295**	**5.42**	**13.1**	**$18**

With $5 more in earnings, this *feels* like a breakout, but mostly it was Hudson collecting a few more HR and SB on a few more hits on a few more balls in play. Climbing Eye may herald true breakout.

Huff,Aubrey

Huff,Aubrey			AB	R	H	HR	RBI	SB	Avg	vL	vR	OB	Slg	OPS	bb%	ct%	h%	Eye	G	L	F	PX	SX	SBO	xHR	xBA	RC/G	RAR	R$
Pos	59	02 TAM	* 580	83	180	26	76	4	310	307	315	362	503	865	7	89	32	0.71	47	18	36	110	55	3%	22	302	6.01	24.3	$23
Age	30	03 TAM	636	91	198	34	107	2	311	318	308	364	555	919	8	87	31	0.66	47	21	32	141	49	3%	29	333	6.64	36.9	$28
Peak		04 TAM	600	92	178	29	104	5	297	304	293	357	493	850	9	88	30	0.76	46	18	36	106	77	3%	24	297	5.88	16.1	$24
Bats	Left	05 TAM	575	70	150	22	92	8	261	254	262	319	428	747	8	85	28	0.56	48	15	37	100	69	10%	20	275	4.66	2.7	$18
Reliability	29	06 2TM	454	57	121	21	66	0	267	233	278	339	469	808	10	86	27	0.78	45	19	36	114	35	0%	19	294	5.51	3.4	$13
DL	24	1st Half	191	19	48	5	22	0	251			329	377	706	10	88	26	1.00	49	17	34	69	37	0%	5	264	4.46	-4.4	$3
BAvg Potl	60%	2nd Half	263	38	73	16	44	0	278			347	536	883	10	84	28	0.67	41	20	38	148	37	0%	14	315	6.33	8.1	$10
LIMA Plan	C	07 Proj	**537**	**80**	**157**	**25**	**93**	**1**	**292**			**356**	**493**	**849**	**9**	**86**	**30**	**0.70**	**46**	**18**	**36**	**114**	**49**	**2%**	**22**	**294**	**5.91**	**13.9**	**$21**

A 140-level PX, a high-80 ct%, a healthy Eye – we must be talking about 2003, right? No, 2006. A career-low H% squelched a return to level of 2002-04. The skills are alive! They're alive! Bid as such.

Hunter,Torii

Hunter,Torii			AB	R	H	HR	RBI	SB	Avg	vL	vR	OB	Slg	OPS	bb%	ct%	h%	Eye	G	L	F	PX	SX	SBO	xHR	xBA	RC/G	RAR	R$
Pos	8	02 MIN	561	89	162	29	94	23	289	296	286	331	524	855	6	79	32	0.30	51	16	34	147	123	24%	26	303	5.86	17.4	$28
Age	31	03 MIN	581	83	145	26	102	6	250	250	249	309	451	760	8	82	27	0.47	48	18	34	122	82	10%	23	293	4.80	1.1	$18
Past Peak		04 MIN	520	79	141	23	81	21	271	255	278	323	475	798	7	81	30	0.40	48	15	37	129	96	23%	22	287	5.23	7.9	$21
Bats	Right	05 MIN	372	63	100	14	56	23	269	283	263	330	452	782	8	83	29	0.52	49	14	36	118	119	32%	14	288	5.13	9.2	$17
Reliability	77	06 MIN	557	86	155	31	98	12	278	319	262	332	490	822	7	81	30	0.42	45	18	37	121	88	12%	26	283	5.46	12.7	$23
DL	15 64	1st Half	283	45	75	12	46	6	265			346	431	777	11	81	29	0.66	43	17	40	98	66	11%	11	261	5.15	4.0	$10
BAvg Potl	50%	2nd Half	274	41	80	19	52	6	292			317	551	868	4	80	30	0.18	47	19	35	145	97	14%	14	304	5.74	8.3	$13
LIMA Plan	C+	07 Proj	**585**	**92**	**161**	**29**	**98**	**17**	**275**			**327**	**484**	**811**	**7**	**81**	**30**	**0.40**	**47**	**17**	**36**	**125**	**100**	**17%**	**26**	**288**	**5.33**	**12.7**	**$24**

Launched a few more liners, and had a few more balls leave the park, but in general, this was same old Hunter. Swung harder in the second half, but also stopped taking walks, so his gains are vulnerable.

Iannetta,Chris

Iannetta,Chris			AB	R	H	HR	RBI	SB	Avg	vL	vR	OB	Slg	OPS	bb%	ct%	h%	Eye	G	L	F	PX	SX	SBO	xHR	xBA	RC/G	RAR	R$
Pos	2	02	0	0	0	0	0	0	0							0							0		0				
Age	24	03	0	0	0	0	0	0	0							0							0		0				
Growth		04	0	0	0	0	0	0	0							0							0		0				
Bats	Right	05 aa	60	6	12	1	9	0	200			284	283	567	10	72	26	0.41				64	25	0%	1		2.39	-2.9	$0
Reliability	0	06 COL	* 384	59	118	14	47	1	307	231	266	386	495	880	11	85	33	0.88	52	23	25	108	59	2%	14	316	6.51	22.7	$14
DL		1st Half	156	28	48	9	19	1	305			375	560	934	10	88	30	0.94				135	81	2%	7		6.97	11.2	$7
BAvg Potl	55%	2nd Half	228	31	70	5	28	0	309			393	450	843	12	84	35	0.84	52	23	25	89	39	1%	6	292	6.17	11.4	$7
LIMA Plan	C	07 Proj	**372**	**57**	**109**	**11**	**46**	**1**	**293**			**373**	**464**	**837**	**11**	**85**	**32**	**0.87**	**52**	**23**	**25**	**102**	**66**	**2%**	**12**	**312**	**6.01**	**19.7**	**$12**

2-10-.260 in 77 AB at COL. Leapt onto the scene with fully developed plate patience and contact rate, which set a nice floor under his BA. On the other hand, a very high G/F sets a ceiling above his power.

Ibanez,Raul

Ibanez,Raul			AB	R	H	HR	RBI	SB	Avg	vL	vR	OB	Slg	OPS	bb%	ct%	h%	Eye	G	L	F	PX	SX	SBO	xHR	xBA	RC/G	RAR	R$
Pos	7	02 KC	497	70	146	24	103	5	294	274	300	346	537	884	7	85	31	0.53	42	19	39	143	92	7%	21	314	6.28	20.1	$22
Age	34	03 KC	608	95	179	18	90	8	294	245	319	347	454	801	7	87	32	0.60	42	23	35	95	95	7%	17	294	5.35	0.2	$22
Past Peak		04 SEA	481	67	146	16	62	1	304	295	307	352	472	824	7	85	33	0.50	44	21	35	102	47	2%	16	280	5.56	8.1	$16
Bats	Left	05 SEA	614	92	172	20	89	9	280	274	283	355	436	791	10	84	31	0.72	46	21	34	98	82	7%	20	287	5.37	11.3	$21
Reliability	73	06 SEA	626	103	181	33	123	2	289	243	308	356	516	872	9	82	31	0.57	42	19	39	132	65	3%	29	294	6.22	18.4	$25
DL		1st Half	306	50	88	16	62	2	288			361	529	890	10	84	30	0.70	44	19	37	137	86	6%	14	308	6.51	11.5	$12
BAvg Potl	50%	2nd Half	320	53	93	17	61	0	291			351	503	855	9	80	32	0.46	40	20	40	126	50	1%	15	280	5.95	6.9	$13
LIMA Plan	C	07 Proj	**605**	**94**	**168**	**23**	**98**	**1**	**278**			**343**	**458**	**800**	**9**	**83**	**30**	**0.58**	**43**	**20**	**37**	**109**	**57**	**3%**	**22**	**284**	**5.38**	**6.1**	**$19**

Five seasons and almost no sign of erosion. Still, he's 34, so we ought not get complacent. In particular, a declining ct% says that his bat is slowing. 2007 could be his first sub-.280 BA since 2000.

Iguchi,Tadahito

Iguchi,Tadahito			AB	R	H	HR	RBI	SB	Avg	vL	vR	OB	Slg	OPS	bb%	ct%	h%	Eye	G	L	F	PX	SX	SBO	xHR	xBA	RC/G	RAR	R$
Pos	4	02 JPN	428	62	103	11	52	19	242			278	357	636	5	81	27	0.27				72	125	27%	10		3.14	-14.1	$13
Age	33	03 JPN	515	109	163	16	106	38	317			393	488	882	11	85	35	0.85				109	129	26%	18		6.53	31.9	$34
Past Peak		04 JPN	510	94	158	14	87	16	311			358	474	832	7	83	35	0.44				102	117	15%	15		5.68	18.7	$24
Bats	Right	05 CHW	511	74	142	15	71	15	278	274	279	339	438	777	8	78	33	0.41	48	22	30	106	118	14%	16	280	5.13	14.6	$18
Reliability	92	06 CHW	555	97	156	18	67	11	281	252	298	350	422	772	10	80	32	0.54	51	16	34	88	80	9%	18	259	5.05	14.7	$18
DL		1st Half	277	55	82	8	37	5	296			346	430	775	7	78	35	0.35	49	19	33	87	84	10%	8	259	4.97	6.6	$10
BAvg Potl	45%	2nd Half	278	42	74	10	30	6	266			354	414	768	12	82	29	0.76	52	13	35	88	67	9%	10	257	5.13	8.2	$8
LIMA Plan	C+	07 Proj	**542**	**90**	**148**	**15**	**74**	**10**	**273**			**338**	**410**	**749**	**9**	**81**	**32**	**0.51**	**50**	**17**	**32**	**88**	**94**	**10%**	**16**	**266**	**4.77**	**10.2**	**$17**

Outwardly similar season, but both PX and SX sank, in a continuation of 3-year trends. After having six triples in '05, he had none in '06, which isn't what we'd expect from a healthy guy who has speed. Caution.

Infante,Omar

Infante,Omar			AB	R	H	HR	RBI	SB	Avg	vL	vR	OB	Slg	OPS	bb%	ct%	h%	Eye	G	L	F	PX	SX	SBO	xHR	xBA	RC/G	RAR	R$
Pos	4	02 aaa	436	51	127	3	53	20	291			338	394	733	7	92	31	0.84				57	130	29%	4		4.71	6.2	$15
Age	25	03 DET	* 445	54	100	2	27	29	225	155	253	290	279	569	8	86	26	0.65	46	18	36	39	117	30%	4	240	2.76	-19.0	$9
Pre-Peak		04 DET	503	69	133	16	55	13	264	277	257	319	449	768	7	78	31	0.36	35	18	46	114	130	17%	16	254	4.97	13.2	$14
Bats	Right	05 DET	406	36	90	9	43	8	222	178	236	251	367	618	4	82	25	0.22	33	16	51	101	101	12%	10	247	2.98	-14.3	$6
Reliability	17	06 DET	224	35	62	4	25	3	277	286	273	319	415	735	6	80	33	0.31	38	19	43	86	122	9%	4	247	4.50	2.5	$6
DL		1st Half	99	13	26	2	12	1	263			298	404	702	5	77	32	0.22	37	12	51	88	110	9%	2	217	4.03	-0.3	$2
BAvg Potl	30%	2nd Half	125	22	36	2	13	2	288			336	424	760	7	82	34	0.41	39	24	37	85	121	9%	2	270	4.87	2.7	$4
LIMA Plan	F	07 Proj	**198**	**26**	**51**	**4**	**21**	**4**	**258**			**300**	**403**	**703**	**6**	**81**	**30**	**0.32**	**37**	**18**	**45**	**92**	**121**	**13%**	**4**	**250**	**4.11**	**0.0**	**$4**

Don't read much into his BA in only 277 AB. His xBA remains dour, and his career BA is a fitting .251. If he can't pick up a few more bases, he might become truly useless.

Inge,Brandon

Inge,Brandon			AB	R	H	HR	RBI	SB	Avg	vL	vR	OB	Slg	OPS	bb%	ct%	h%	Eye	G	L	F	PX	SX	SBO	xHR	xBA	RC/G	RAR	R$
Pos	5	02 DET	* 386	36	82	9	36	2	212	229	195	276	368	644	8	70	28	0.30	41	18	41	106	86	10%	10	233	3.46	-12.3	$3
Age	29	03 DET	* 472	46	102	12	44	7	216	245	182	270	354	624	7	79	25	0.35	42	20	38	91	84	12%	13	256	3.11	-20.6	$6
Peak		04 DET	408	43	117	13	64	5	287	327	258	339	453	792	7	82	32	0.44	44	17	39	93	91	8%	11	265	5.21	13.4	$13
Bats	Both	05 DET	616	75	161	16	72	7	261	288	257	330	419	749	9	77	32	0.45	40	18	42	105	98	8%	17	253	4.84	6.2	$15
Reliability	96	06 DET	542	83	137	27	83	7	253	243	256	308	463	771	7	76	28	0.34	40	14	46	133	85	9%	25	261	4.90	-1.8	$17
DL		1st Half	262	43	62	16	46	3	237			296	489	784	8	75	26	0.33	38	11	51	158	96	13%	14	264	5.09	0.7	$8
BAvg Potl	45%	2nd Half	280	40	75	11	37	4	268			319	439	758	7	78	31	0.34	41	18	41	110	70	6%	11	259	4.73	-2.3	$8
LIMA Plan	C+	07 Proj	**581**	**76**	**150**	**22**	**79**	**7**	**258**			**316**	**438**	**754**	**8**	**77**	**30**	**0.38**	**41**	**16**	**43**	**114**	**90**	**8%**	**21**	**257**	**4.76**	**-0.9**	**$16**

Highly reliable at being OK. In the first half, he rode a late-20's power spike, abetted by a nine-point jump in FB%. 2007 should be likewise hunky-dory - maybe a little more hunky, a little less dory.

Inglett,Joe

Inglett,Joe			AB	R	H	HR	RBI	SB	Avg	vL	vR	OB	Slg	OPS	bb%	ct%	h%	Eye	G	L	F	PX	SX	SBO	xHR	xBA	RC/G	RAR	R$
Pos	4	02	0	0	0	0	0	0	0							0							0		0				
Age	28	03 aa	276	33	67	4	21	1	241			315	339	654	10	87	27	0.81				65	52	3%	5		3.85	-3.5	$3
Peak		04 aa	266	37	66	1	15	3	249			307	343	651	8	89	28	0.79				61	97	11%	3		3.85	-4.0	$3
Bats	Left	05 aaa	322	41	86	1	29	10	268			295	360	655	4	89	30	0.36				60	127	21%	3		3.62	-6.9	$8
Reliability	21	06 CLE	* 422	59	122	5	39	13	288	217	292	341	390	731	7	83	34	0.47	47	24	29	67	112	14%	6	276	4.56	5.2	$12
DL		1st Half	226	33	62	3	18	9	275			335	376	711	8	86	31	0.62				66	108	21%	4		4.41	1.9	$6
BAvg Potl	45%	2nd Half	196	26	60	2	21	4	304			348	406	753	6	81	37	0.35	46	24	30	68	107	7%	3	268	4.76	3.4	$6
LIMA Plan	F	07 Proj	**219**	**29**	**60**	**2**	**19**	**5**	**274**			**322**	**371**	**693**	**7**	**86**	**31**	**0.49**	**47**	**24**	**29**	**64**	**104**	**13%**	**3**	**282**	**4.12**	**0.0**	**$5**

2-21-.284 in 201 AB at CLE. Opened with a .354 July, and then hit .270 from there, in line with xBA. MLE's suggest that his ct% could acclimate, which would make up for his lack of power. Note the speed.

JOHN BURNSON

Iwamura,Akinori

Iwamura,Akinori			AB	R	H	HR	RBI	SB	Avg	vL	vR	OB	Slg	OPS	bb%	ct%	h%	Eye	G	L	F	PX	SX	SBO	xHR	xBA	RC/G	RAR	R$
Pos	5	02 JPN	510	65	152	14	69	5	298			357	459	816	8	79	36	0.43				112	74	6%	16		5.62	15.6	$18
Age	28	03 JPN	232	42	57	7	34	5	245			299	391	690	7	78	29	0.34				87	136	10%	6		3.90	-3.3	$7
Peak		04 JPN	533	97	149	27	100	7	280			349	464	813	10	69	36	0.34				123	74	7%	26		5.72	11.1	$23
Bats	Left	05 JPN	548	81	163	18	99	5	298			357	475	832	8	75	37	0.37				122	99	5%	19		5.90	19.2	$22
Reliability	15	06 JPN	546	82	158	19	75	7	290			357	456	813	9	78	34	0.47				104	94	4%	19		5.59	5.1	$19
DL		1st Half																											
BAvg Potl	30%	2nd Half																											
LIMA Plan	C+	07 Proj	511	82	145	17	82	7	284			347	440	787	9	75	35	0.39				103	97	6%	18		5.26	4.1	$18

From a BPI perspective, he'd be a solid contributor, a free-swinger with declining power, but still some good years ahead of him. His real value, though... Had these been MLB stats, he'd have a Reliability score of 99.

Izturis,Cesar

Izturis,Cesar			AB	R	H	HR	RBI	SB	Avg	vL	vR	OB	Slg	OPS	bb%	ct%	h%	Eye	G	L	F	PX	SX	SBO	xHR	xBA	RC/G	RAR	R$
Pos	56	02 LA	439	43	102	1	31	7	232	306	195	256	303	559	3	91	25	0.36	53	21	27	52	88	16%	4	288	2.58	-27.1	$4
Age	27	03 LA	558	47	140	1	40	10	251	263	246	283	315	598	4	87	29	0.36	49	25	25	43	99	11%	3	282	2.94	-21.8	$7
Peak		04 LA	670	90	193	4	62	25	288	269	295	331	381	712	6	90	32	0.61	49	19	31	56	129	18%	7	281	4.38	-13.0	$21
Bats	Both	05 LA	444	48	114	2	31	8	257	303	242	296	322	618	5	89	29	0.49	52	22	26	46	81	14%	4	279	3.24	-20.4	$7
Reliability	39	06 2NL	252	21	61	1	20	1	240	206	253	296	308	603	7	94	25	1.23	52	16	31	43	44	8%	2	261	3.41	-15.9	$1
DL	103 54	1st Half	88	11	22	0	3	0	245			327	278	606	11	93	26	1.78	58	21	21	24	30	0%	0	269	3.64	-4.8	$0
BAvg Potl	75%	2nd Half	164	10	39	1	17	1	238			277	323	601	5	94	25	0.90	51	16	33	53	48	14%	2	267	3.27	-11.2	$1
LIMA Plan	D	07 Proj	351	35	88	1	27	5	251			298	320	618	6	91	27	0.78	51	20	29	45	75	11%	3	275	3.42	-18.1	$4

Lost first 2-1/2 months to recovery from TJ surgery and much of last 6 weeks to strained hamstring. In between, he showed practically none of the speed on which his value rests. In truth, he's shown it only once.

Izturis,Maicer

Izturis,Maicer			AB	R	H	HR	RBI	SB	Avg	vL	vR	OB	Slg	OPS	bb%	ct%	h%	Eye	G	L	F	PX	SX	SBO	xHR	xBA	RC/G	RAR	R$
Pos	5	02 aa	253	30	66	0	29	7	261			302	348	650	6	90	29	0.60				54	128	17%	1		3.74	-5.9	$6
Age	26	03 a/a	519	67	132	3	45	26	254			311	347	658	8	91	28	0.91				58	128	28%	5		3.95	-6.8	$13
Pre-Peak		04 aaa	376	50	116	2	28	11	309			378	383	761	10	94	32	1.91				48	71	19%	4		5.30	3.4	$12
Bats	Both	05 ANA *	222	25	59	1	16	12	265	191	268	331	369	700	9	89	29	0.91	45	20	35	66	128	28%	2	277	4.48	-0.2	$6
Reliability	12	06 ANA	352	64	103	5	44	14	293	247	307	362	412	773	10	90	31	1.09	49	19	32	73	119	18%	6	291	5.31	3.0	$13
DL	46 52	1st Half	49	14	13	0	8	4	265			379	327	706	16	94	28	3.00	60	15	26	46	121	26%	0	288	5.11	0.1	$2
BAvg Potl	65%	2nd Half	303	50	90	5	36	10	297			358	426	784	9	89	32	0.91	47	20	33	77	114	16%	6	291	5.34	2.8	$11
LIMA Plan	C+	07 Proj	384	52	109	6	36	15	284			346	407	753	9	91	30	1.03	50	19	32	73	108	21%	7	292	5.01	2.2	$12

Fulfilled the promise of his high ct% and SX. Now his ceiling is set by a lack of power, but as he is approaching his late 20's, we can't count even that out (the second half may show a hint).

Jackson,Conor

Jackson,Conor			AB	R	H	HR	RBI	SB	Avg	vL	vR	OB	Slg	OPS	bb%	ct%	h%	Eye	G	L	F	PX	SX	SBO	xHR	xBA	RC/G	RAR	R$
Pos	3	02	0	0	0	0	0	0	0							0							0		0				
Age	24	03	0	0	0	0	0	0	0							0							0		0				
Growth		04 aa	226	24	62	5	27	2	274			331	416	747	8	88	29	0.73				83	66	10%	5		4.81	-4.3	$5
Bats	Right	05 ARI *	418	54	123	8	59	2	294	258	157	387	455	841	13	92	31	1.91	44	12	44	105	52	4%	11	283	6.35	8.7	$13
Reliability	9	06 ARI	485	75	141	15	79	1	291	296	288	362	441	803	10	85	32	0.74	38	21	41	89	52	1%	15	271	5.50	-6.8	$16
DL		1st Half	218	33	60	6	39	0	275			373	417	790	13	89	29	1.36	43	17	40	84	27	0%	6	267	5.64	-2.2	$7
BAvg Potl	45%	2nd Half	267	42	81	9	40	1	303			352	461	813	7	82	34	0.42	34	24	42	94	62	1%	9	269	5.40	-4.4	$10
LIMA Plan	B	07 Proj	501	69	140	13	74	2	279			355	432	788	11	88	30	0.97	39	20	42	94	57	3%	14	281	5.43	-5.9	$15

A more-than-respectable year for a 24-year-old, but a lower bb% and ct% in the second half suggest that he got greedy. A .300 BA is over his head barring a power spike, which is probably more than one season off.

Jackson,Damian

Jackson,Damian			AB	R	H	HR	RBI	SB	Avg	vL	vR	OB	Slg	OPS	bb%	ct%	h%	Eye	G	L	F	PX	SX	SBO	xHR	xBA	RC/G	RAR	R$
Pos	8	02 DET	245	31	63	1	25	12	257	217	270	316	359	675	8	85	30	0.58	43	18	39	77	113	24%	4	263	4.03	-5.4	$7
Age	33	03 BOS	161	34	42	1	13	16	261	241	284	296	323	619	5	83	31	0.29	28	34	38	47	147	57%	2	252	3.03	-8.5	$7
Past Peak		04 aaa	262	45	65	9	28	11	247			324	433	757	10	83	27	0.67				112	132	20%	9		4.97	2.3	$9
Bats	Right	05 SD *	326	54	84	7	30	16	256	289	242	337	363	700	11	84	29	0.76	40	22	39	68	115	18%	7	257	4.34	-2.2	$11
Reliability	13	06 WAS	116	16	23	4	10	1	198	233	178	273	371	644	9	66	26	0.31	34	19	47	125	91	17%	5	224	3.47	-3.6	$1
DL	17	1st Half	95	13	21	4	9	1	221			275	432	706	7	71	27	0.25	34	19	47	144	100	24%	4	251	4.19	-0.7	$2
BAvg Potl	45%	2nd Half	21	3	2	0	1	0	95			269	95	364	19	48	20	0.45	30	20	50	0	42	0%	0		-1.45	-4.4	($1)
LIMA Plan	F	07 Proj	161	26	39	2	15	4	242			305	353	658	8	80	29	0.44	36	23	42	77	105	18%	3	247	3.68	-4.3	$3

Decided to play "power-hitter" by swatting fly balls and striking out a lot. It didn't work out, but he should find a job somewhere (he played six positions in 2006). If he can, it could be off-to-the-races again.

Jacobs,Mike

Jacobs,Mike			AB	R	H	HR	RBI	SB	Avg	vL	vR	OB	Slg	OPS	bb%	ct%	h%	Eye	G	L	F	PX	SX	SBO	xHR	xBA	RC/G	RAR	R$
Pos	3	02	0	0	0	0	0	0	0							0							0		0				
Age	26	03 aa	407	46	118	14	67	0	290			326	477	803	5	82	33	0.30				124	32	4%	15		5.22	-2.6	$13
Pre-Peak		04 aaa	96	7	16	1	5	0	167			231	219	450	8	67	24	0.25				41	23	0%	1		0.54	-15.5	($1)
Bats	Right	05 NYM *	533	67	148	30	91	1	277	400	305	322	522	843	6	81	29	0.34	41	23	37	156	41	3%	26	316	5.68	1.2	$21
Reliability	8	06 FLA	469	54	123	20	77	3	262	182	281	327	473	800	9	78	30	0.43	40	20	40	138	55	3%	21	282	5.41	-8.1	$14
DL		1st Half	228	27	62	10	41	2	272			357	482	839	12	78	31	0.59	37	22	41	138	39	3%	11	284	6.05	0.3	$8
BAvg Potl	50%	2nd Half	241	27	61	10	36	1	253			297	465	762	6	78	29	0.28	42	18	39	138	52	2%	10	281	4.77	-8.7	$6
LIMA Plan	D+	07 Proj	456	54	128	21	75	2	281			331	500	831	7	79	31	0.37	40	20	40	142	46	3%	21	292	5.65	-2.5	$16

Did his job - hit for power in first half, hit for power in second half. If he can maintain his PX and regain a few points of ct% - both fair propositions - we could be looking at a .300 BA.

Jenkins,Geoff

Jenkins,Geoff			AB	R	H	HR	RBI	SB	Avg	vL	vR	OB	Slg	OPS	bb%	ct%	h%	Eye	G	L	F	PX	SX	SBO	xHR	xBA	RC/G	RAR	R$
Pos	9	02 MIL	243	35	59	10	29	1	243	200	258	306	444	750	8	75	28	0.37	50	16	34	144	66	6%	11	281	4.76	-3.9	$6
Age	32	03 MIL	487	81	144	28	95	0	296	270	308	371	538	909	11	75	34	0.48	42	25	33	159	50	0%	27	303	6.89	17.2	$22
Past Peak		04 MIL	621	89	164	27	93	3	264	215	281	315	472	787	7	75	31	0.30	44	19	37	134	93	3%	26	275	5.16	-2.3	$20
Bats	Left	05 MIL	538	87	157	25	86	0	292	261	307	359	513	872	9	74	35	0.41	40	27	34	159	43	0%	27	301	6.44	17.7	$22
Reliability	29	06 MIL	484	62	131	17	70	4	271	133	306	346	434	780	10	73	34	0.43	44	22	34	110	59	3%	19	259	5.28	7.1	$14
DL		1st Half	284	28	73	7	45	3	257			322	391	712	9	69	35	0.31	46	22	33	102	47	4%	9	241	4.41	-3.0	$6
BAvg Potl	35%	2nd Half	200	34	58	10	25	1	290			380	495	875	13	79	32	0.69	42	22	36	120	60	3%	9	284	6.48	9.6	$8
LIMA Plan	C	07 Proj	437	65	121	19	64	2	277			348	475	823	10	75	33	0.44	43	23	35	131	68	2%	19	279	5.78	9.3	$15

So his BA swung by 20 points again, ho-hum. A low ct% increases the unpredictability of his average. But still packs a punch. If you can pay $10 for a guy who recently earned $20 (several times), that's a deal.

Jeter,Derek

Jeter,Derek			AB	R	H	HR	RBI	SB	Avg	vL	vR	OB	Slg	OPS	bb%	ct%	h%	Eye	G	L	F	PX	SX	SBO	xHR	xBA	RC/G	RAR	R$
Pos	6	02 NYY	644	124	191	18	75	32	297	315	292	368	421	789	10	82	34	0.64	54	21	24	77	115	16%	18	286	5.31	13.1	$30
Age	32	03 NYY	482	87	156	10	52	11	324	370	312	379	450	829	8	82	38	0.49	54	25	21	83	102	10%	11	298	5.74	17.1	$20
Past Peak		04 NYY	643	111	188	23	78	23	292	314	285	340	471	811	7	85	32	0.46	49	19	32	109	111	16%	23	300	5.38	16.5	$26
Bats	Right	05 NYY	654	122	202	19	70	14	309	317	305	382	450	831	11	82	35	0.66	60	19	21	86	108	8%	18	295	5.87	23.4	$27
Reliability	85	06 NYY	623	118	214	14	97	34	343	390	328	409	483	892	10	84	39	0.68	59	22	18	90	125	17%	16	313	6.61	35.7	$34
DL		1st Half	284	51	94	5	46	15	331			415	458	873	13	83	39	0.85	59	24	18	83	119	15%	7	308	6.59	16.4	$15
BAvg Potl	35%	2nd Half	339	67	120	9	51	19	354			403	504	908	8	84	40	0.52	60	21	19	96	116	19%	10	316	6.61	19.1	$20
LIMA Plan	C+	07 Proj	634	118	196	17	85	26	309			374	453	827	9	83	35	0.62	58	21	21	91	124	15%	18	305	5.77	22.7	$29

A sub-100 PX, a mid-80 ct%, a .343 BA. Which of these doesn't belong? Sure, he's fleet of foot, but a 39 h% is the province of the titans. As long as you keep thinking "300 BA," you'll be fine.

Johjima,Kenji

Johjima,Kenji			AB	R	H	HR	RBI	SB	Avg	vL	vR	OB	Slg	OPS	bb%	ct%	h%	Eye	G	L	F	PX	SX	SBO	xHR	xBA	RC/G	RAR	R$
Pos	2	02 JPN	463	59	114	15	72	7	246			283	382	665	5	92	24	0.62				75	68	14%	12		3.71	-2.1	$13
Age	30	03 JPN	628	98	170	21	116	8	270			317	439	756	6	92	27	0.90				96	94	8%	18		4.86	12.1	$22
Peak		04 JPN	498	89	134	22	89	5	269			323	456	779	7	91	26	0.93				99	83	8%	18		5.09	14.8	$19
Bats	Right	05 JPN	411	68	118	14	56	3	288			331	477	808	6	93	28	0.88				102	100	7%	12		5.41	17.5	$15
Reliability	80	06 SEA	506	61	147	18	76	3	291	263	298	317	451	768	4	91	29	0.43	45	19	36	88	56	3%	15	293	4.73	4.6	$15
DL		1st Half	246	33	73	10	41	0	297			332	480	812	5	91	29	0.59	44	15	40	102	32	2%	8	286	5.29	6.0	$8
BAvg Potl	60%	2nd Half	260	28	74	8	35	3	285			303	423	726	3	91	29	0.29	45	22	32	74	72	5%	6	297	4.20	-1.5	$7
LIMA Plan	C+	07 Proj	508	72	144	16	77	4	283			319	441	760	5	92	28	0.62	45	20	35	86	80	6%	14	298	4.77	7.5	$16

This was his "rookie year" so you have to look at his 2nd half with slight concern. High ct% will keep his BA near .300 territory, but power is at some risk, at least in the short term.

JOHN BURNSON

Johnson,Ben			AB	R	H	HR	RBI	SB	Avg	vL	vR	OB	Slg	OPS	bb%	ct%	h%	Eye	G	L	F	PX	SX	SBO	xHR	xBA	RC/G	RAR	R$
Pos	7	02 aa	456	52	98	8	50	10	215			302	325	627	11	74	27	0.48				80	90	16%	10		3.31	-33.2	$7
Age	25	03 aa	127	7	21	1	6	0	165			221	220	441	7	74	22	0.27				44	26	4%	2		0.63	-20.3	($2)
Pre-Peak		04 aa	475	70	104	18	74	4	219			288	406	695	9	74	26	0.37				123	95	10%	19		4.06	-16.7	$10
Bats	Right	05 SD	* 489	72	125	19	79	5	256	185	250	330	442	771	10	81	28	0.57	36	26	38	123	72	6%	19	296	5.08	-3.7	$16
Reliability	5	06 SD	* 318	46	74	9	29	8	231	275	232	301	378	680	9	75	28	0.40	46	17	37	94	116	11%	10	245	3.89	-13.1	$6
DL	27	1st Half	184	27	41	6	21	4	222			301	389	690	10	74	27	0.43	43	20	37	109	108	9%	6	254	4.08	-6.6	$4
BAvg Potl	40%	2nd Half	134	19	33	3	8	4	245			302	364	665	8	76	30	0.34	50	13	37	76	101	14%	3	230	3.64	-6.5	$3
LIMA Plan	D	07 Proj	250	35	60	7	28	5	240			309	394	702	9	76	29	0.42	45	18	37	100	102	10%	8	254	4.19	-8.9	$6

4-12-.250 in 120 AB at SD. Second year with contact rate of 70% in the majors is not going to cut it. History shows signs of a better ct% and PX, but those are not well-grounded hopes.

Johnson,Dan			AB	R	H	HR	RBI	SB	Avg	vL	vR	OB	Slg	OPS	bb%	ct%	h%	Eye	G	L	F	PX	SX	SBO	xHR	xBA	RC/G	RAR	R$
Pos	3	02	0	0	0	0	0	0	0							0							0		0				
Age	27	03 a/a	542	71	134	21	89	6	247			313	419	732	9	87	25	0.75				97	76	8%	18		4.59	-13.9	$15
Peak		04 aaa	536	72	140	23	84	0	260			342	449	791	11	86	27	0.89				106	45	1%	20		5.39	-1.3	$15
Bats	Left	05 OAK	* 557	81	153	21	89	0	275	276	275	361	453	814	12	87	29	1.04	38	24	38	110	25	1%	21	306	5.74	10.4	$18
Reliability	37	06 OAK	* 458	56	113	14	70	0	246	217	238	338	398	736	12	85	26	0.95	49	15	36	91	38	1%	14	265	4.86	-7.7	$9
DL		1st Half	209	25	53	6	24	0	254			347	392	740	13	87	27	1.07	48	18	34	83	21	0%	6	267	4.94	-2.9	$4
BAvg Potl	65%	2nd Half	249	31	60	8	46	0	239			330	402	732	12	84	26	0.86	52	6	41	97	52	1%	8	244	4.79	-4.7	$5
LIMA Plan	D	07 Proj	358	47	93	12	57	0	260			345	425	771	12	86	27	0.94	45	19	37	99	39	1%	12	282	5.22	-0.8	$9

9-37-.234 in 286 AB at OAK. Indicators seemed generally steady but he shed 100 points of OPS in the majors. No one could survive a 6% line-drive rate, as he had in the second half. We'll call this an off-year.

Johnson,Kelly			AB	R	H	HR	RBI	SB	Avg	vL	vR	OB	Slg	OPS	bb%	ct%	h%	Eye	G	L	F	PX	SX	SBO	xHR	xBA	RC/G	RAR	R$
Pos	7	02	0	0	0	0	0	0	0							0							0		0				
Age	25	03 aa	334	43	88	6	42	9	263			328	404	732	9	78	32	0.44				98	115	13%	8		4.64	-8.0	$9
Pre-Peak		04 aa	479	62	125	14	45	8	261			323	424	747	8	82	29	0.50				105	74	15%	15		4.75	-6.3	$12
Bats	Left	05 ATL	* 445	77	114	16	59	8	256	257	236	357	438	795	14	79	29	0.74	44	26	30	117	115	7%	17	294	5.61	3.5	$15
Reliability	0	06 aaa	* 39	3	12	1	7	1	308			400	487	887	13	85	34	1.00				121	32	8%	1		6.81	1.7	$2
DL	183	1st Half	39	3	12	1	7	1	308			400	487	887	13	85	34	1.00				121	32	8%	1		6.81	1.7	$2
BAvg Potl	40%	2nd Half	0	0	0	0	0	0	0							0									0				
LIMA Plan	D	07 Proj	314	45	82	10	38	4	261			338	432	769	10	79	30	0.56	44	26	30	110	87	8%	10	291	5.13	-0.6	$8

Lost season to TJ surgery. We won't read much into a .333 BA in 39 AB in the minors, but he is showing the consistent power that could lead to .300 BA in the majors. If healthy, meaty HR upside.

Johnson,Nick			AB	R	H	HR	RBI	SB	Avg	vL	vR	OB	Slg	OPS	bb%	ct%	h%	Eye	G	L	F	PX	SX	SBO	xHR	xBA	RC/G	RAR	R$
Pos	3	02 NYY	389	57	93	15	58	1	239	175	257	324	393	718	11	74	29	0.49	43	21	35	102	39	4%	15	251	4.41	-17.0	$10
Age	28	03 NYY	324	60	92	14	47	5	284	282	285	411	472	883	18	82	31	1.23	45	27	28	117	60	5%	15	314	6.89	13.9	$13
Peak		04 MON	251	35	63	7	33	6	251	323	228	354	398	752	14	77	30	0.69	47	20	33	103	65	11%	9	264	5.08	-6.5	$7
Bats	Left	05 WAS	453	66	131	15	74	3	289	328	277	396	479	875	15	81	33	0.92	44	21	35	129	59	7%	18	296	6.73	14.6	$17
Reliability	30	06 WAS	500	100	145	23	77	10	290	303	285	418	520	938	18	80	32	1.11	42	22	36	148	69	7%	26	309	7.65	23.1	$22
DL	6 29	1st Half	250	51	77	12	33	6	308			425	548	973	17	84	33	1.31	42	26	32	147	67	9%	13	335	7.96	13.5	$12
BAvg Potl	60%	2nd Half	250	49	68	11	44	4	272			411	492	903	19	76	32	0.98	42	18	40	150	60	5%	14	283	7.33	9.5	$10
LIMA Plan	B	07 Proj	510	88	147	20	79	8	288			405	489	893	16	79	33	0.94	43	21	35	133	70	7%	23	294	7.02	16.9	$21

Finally lasted 500 AB, and his indicators held up just fine. Lost some of his judgment in the second half, but his power permits a few slip-ups. There's no reason not to expect a solid encore.

Johnson,Reed			AB	R	H	HR	RBI	SB	Avg	vL	vR	OB	Slg	OPS	bb%	ct%	h%	Eye	G	L	F	PX	SX	SBO	xHR	xBA	RC/G	RAR	R$
Pos	79	02 aaa	159	21	33	2	8	1	208			254	321	575	6	89	22	0.56				70	106	19%	2		2.83	-14.3	$1
Age	30	03 TOR	* 513	91	151	12	66	8	294	328	279	325	425	750	4	85	33	0.29	42	29	29	81	108	9%	12	298	4.53	-11.5	$18
Peak		04 TOR	537	68	145	10	61	6	270	301	255	306	380	686	5	82	31	0.29	55	19	26	71	83	7%	11	270	3.81	-17.6	$12
Bats	Right	05 TOR	398	55	107	8	58	5	269	279	262	307	412	719	5	79	32	0.27	51	22	27	95	110	12%	9	284	4.27	-5.3	$11
Reliability	26	06 TOR	461	86	147	12	49	8	319	323	316	364	479	844	7	82	37	0.41	47	20	33	105	101	8%	14	288	5.83	8.0	$18
DL		1st Half	167	45	62	4	18	6	371			432	533	965	10	86	42	0.75	44	23	33	98	137	11%	4	299	7.46	9.5	$10
BAvg Potl	35%	2nd Half	294	41	85	8	31	2	289			324	449	773	5	81	34	0.26	49	18	33	110	57	4%	9	278	4.86	-2.7	$8
LIMA Plan	C	07 Proj	428	71	122	10	49	6	285			328	428	755	6	82	33	0.35	49	21	30	93	104	9%	11	284	4.72	-3.6	$13

Broke into positive RAR for first time, but he did not deserve the BA. Inflated hit rate and flat xBA cry fluke! Age 30 is pretty late to start setting a new foundation. Expect a pullback.

Jones,Adam			AB	R	H	HR	RBI	SB	Avg	vL	vR	OB	Slg	OPS	bb%	ct%	h%	Eye	G	L	F	PX	SX	SBO	xHR	xBA	RC/G	RAR	R$
Pos	8	02	0	0	0	0	0	0	0							0							0		0				
Age	21	03	0	0	0	0	0	0	0							0							0		0				
Growth		04	0	0	0	0	0	0	0							0							0		0				
Bats	Right	05 aa	228	32	65	6	19	8	286			349	428	777	9	81	33	0.51				89	107	18%	6		5.11	4.5	$8
Reliability	0	06 SEA	* 454	71	124	16	66	15	273	235	211	317	441	758	6	81	31	0.34	44	27	29	102	111	19%	15	297	4.69	0.3	$16
DL		1st Half	298	45	80	10	44	9	269			313	428	741	6	83	30	0.36				93	114	15%	9		4.48	-1.5	$10
BAvg Potl	50%	2nd Half	156	26	44	7	22	6	279			326	465	790	6	78	32	0.32	44	27	29	120	88	28%	6	298	5.11	2.0	$6
LIMA Plan	F	07 Proj	148	22	41	5	18	5	277			330	440	769	7	81	32	0.40	44	27	29	100	106	21%	5	293	4.91	1.4	$5

1-8-.216 in 74 AB at SEA. A 70% contact rate with little power doomed his debut. He did attempt a steal in 4 of 13 trips to first base (31% SBO). That's a rate that justifies a reserve pick.

Jones,Andruw			AB	R	H	HR	RBI	SB	Avg	vL	vR	OB	Slg	OPS	bb%	ct%	h%	Eye	G	L	F	PX	SX	SBO	xHR	xBA	RC/G	RAR	R$
Pos	8	02 ATL	560	91	148	35	94	8	264	228	270	359	513	872	13	76	29	0.61	43	17	40	166	66	7%	33	293	6.46	25.9	$25
Age	30	03 ATL	595	101	165	36	116	4	277	260	282	336	513	849	8	79	30	0.42	40	20	40	143	76	5%	31	291	5.84	14.7	$27
Peak		04 ATL	570	85	149	29	91	6	261	265	260	343	488	831	11	74	30	0.48	48	16	36	147	78	8%	29	278	5.94	21.6	$20
Bats	Right	05 ATL	586	95	154	51	128	5	263	254	265	335	575	910	10	81	24	0.57	42	16	42	180	73	6%	39	320	6.56	34.1	$30
Reliability	98	06 ATL	565	107	148	41	129	4	262	260	263	355	531	886	13	78	27	0.65	39	19	42	158	59	3%	36	294	6.54	34.4	$26
DL		1st Half	294	47	83	18	65	3	282			347	517	864	9	78	31	0.45	40	20	40	140	54	5%	16	285	6.09	13.7	$13
BAvg Potl	60%	2nd Half	271	60	65	23	64	1	240			364	546	910	16	77	23	0.85	39	18	43	179	51	1%	20	303	6.98	20.5	$13
LIMA Plan	B	07 Proj	586	104	160	44	124	5	273			359	551	910	12	78	28	0.61	41	18	41	165	66	4%	37	299	6.79	37.6	$29

HR retreated as xHR said. More surprising is a second straight year of underperforming BA. It is incredible for Jones to not break .280. Even if his hit rate is merely 30%, his BA becomes .290. It's gonna happen.

Jones,Chipper			AB	R	H	HR	RBI	SB	Avg	vL	vR	OB	Slg	OPS	bb%	ct%	h%	Eye	G	L	F	PX	SX	SBO	xHR	xBA	RC/G	RAR	R$
Pos	5	02 ATL	548	90	179	26	100	8	327	320	328	437	536	973	16	84	35	1.20	42	22	36	132	71	4%	26	309	7.90	48.1	$30
Age	35	03 ATL	555	103	169	27	106	2	305	306	304	405	517	922	14	85	32	1.13	38	22	40	126	61	2%	25	304	7.14	43.9	$27
Decline		04 ATL	472	69	117	30	96	2	248	268	238	362	485	847	15	80	25	0.88	46	15	39	137	51	1%	27	283	6.16	15.3	$17
Bats	Both	05 ATL	358	66	106	21	72	5	296	254	303	414	556	970	17	84	30	1.29	42	23	35	162	62	5%	20	336	7.84	30.3	$19
Reliability	41	06 ATL	411	87	133	26	86	6	324	293	332	411	596	1007	13	82	34	0.84	41	19	40	156	93	5%	23	314	8.07	28.2	$24
DL	45 42	1st Half	243	44	70	8	38	5	288			382	453	835	13	78	34	0.70	46	22	32	105	84	7%	9	277	6.10	4.2	$10
BAvg Potl	50%	2nd Half	168	43	63	18	48	1	375			453	804	1257	12	88	35	1.20	35	15	50	221	83	2%	13	373	10.65	21.3	$15
LIMA Plan	B	07 Proj	390	77	115	21	84	4	295			396	539	935	14	84	31	1.02	41	19	40	144	87	4%	20	309	7.29	23.2	$20

At age 35, and with his risk profile, we are more apt to see a 105 PX again (as in first half) than a 221 PX (as in second half). This could be the season of the sub-20 HR.

Jones,Jacque			AB	R	H	HR	RBI	SB	Avg	vL	vR	OB	Slg	OPS	bb%	ct%	h%	Eye	G	L	F	PX	SX	SBO	xHR	xBA	RC/G	RAR	R$
Pos	9	02 MIN	577	96	173	27	85	6	300	213	333	342	511	853	6	78	35	0.29	54	16	29	137	78	9%	26	293	5.88	13.9	$24
Age	32	03 MIN	517	76	157	16	69	12	304	304	317	331	462	793	4	80	36	0.20	59	20	21	106	101	10%	16	300	5.01	-1.9	$20
Past Peak		04 MIN	555	69	141	24	80	13	254	245	258	304	427	731	7	79	28	0.34	57	13	30	104	77	17%	21	268	4.34	-6.0	$17
Bats	Left	05 MIN	523	74	130	23	73	13	249	201	268	315	438	753	9	77	28	0.43	59	15	26	120	110	13%	21	287	4.76	1.0	$17
Reliability	85	06 CHC	533	73	152	27	81	9	285	234	303	329	499	828	6	78	32	0.30	56	19	26	131	80	8%	24	300	5.53	11.4	$21
DL		1st Half	252	30	75	13	37	2	298			327	512	839	4	79	33	0.21	54	21	25	130	41	5%	11	300	5.52	5.2	$10
BAvg Potl	45%	2nd Half	281	43	77	14	44	7	274			331	488	819	8	77	31	0.38	58	16	26	132	93	10%	13	295	5.53	6.1	$11
LIMA Plan	C+	07 Proj	535	75	151	23	79	8	282			332	471	803	7	78	32	0.34	57	17	26	119	82	8%	22	287	5.28	3.8	$20

It's hard to imagine any power upside with a GB% in the high 50's. That, and his widening platoon splits are worrisome. I've been right about previous BA swings, but no, I did not make him cry.

JOHN BURNSON

Jordan,Brian			AB	R	H	HR	RBI	SB	Avg	vL	vR	OB	Slg	OPS	bb%	ct%	h%	Eye	G	L	F	PX	SX	SBO	xHR	xBA	RC/G	RAR	R$
Pos	3	02 LA	471	65	134	18	80	2	285	303	279	333	469	802	7	82	32	0.40	43	20	37	119	73	3%	17	288	5.27	-4.4	$18
Age	40	03 LA	224	28	67	6	28	1	299	397	265	364	420	784	9	87	32	0.77	52	18	31	73	38	3%	6	267	5.23	-1.7	$7
Decline		04 TEX	212	27	47	5	23	2	222	259	197	276	363	640	7	83	24	0.46	43	18	38	90	83	9%	6	268	3.42	-10.3	$3
Bats	Right	05 ATL	231	25	57	3	24	2	247	260	239	290	338	627	6	80	30	0.30	52	12	36	60	89	3%	3	229	3.14	-16.8	$4
Reliability	0	06 ATL	91	11	21	3	10	0	231	180	293	286	352	637	7	75	28	0.30	40	14	46	73	29	0%	3	205	3.14	-7.8	$1
DL	75 57	1st Half	84	10	18	3	10	0	214			267	345	612	7	76	25	0.30	42	11	47	78	30	0%	3	202	2.80	-8.3	$1
BAvg Potl	35%	2nd Half	7	1	3	0	0	0	429			500	429	928	12	57	75	0.33				0	20	0%	0		8.97	0.5	$0
LIMA Plan	F	07 Proj	**33**	**4**	**8**	**1**	**4**	**0**	**242**			**295**	**354**	**648**	**7**	**81**	**28**	**0.39**	**43**	**12**	**45**	**68**	**45**	**3%**	**1**	**216**	**3.38**	**-2.4**	**$1**

The Steve Carlton Path to Retirement is littered with PX and xBA levels like the ones he's posted the last two years. When your last remaining skill - hitting LHPs - disappears, it's time to tip your cap and wave good-bye.

Kapler,Gabe			AB	R	H	HR	RBI	SB	Avg	vL	vR	OB	Slg	OPS	bb%	ct%	h%	Eye	G	L	F	PX	SX	SBO	xHR	xBA	RC/G	RAR	R$
Pos	97	02 2TM	* 332	42	95	3	38	12	286	250	293	323	392	714	5	83	34	0.33	41	25	34	71	126	18%	5	272	4.25	-8.6	$11
Age	31	03 2TM	* 263	43	67	4	29	9	255	326	233	324	376	701	9	80	30	0.52	48	20	32	85	124	15%	6	270	4.28	-8.6	$7
Past Peak		04 BOS	290	51	79	6	33	5	272	317	238	308	390	698	5	83	31	0.31	49	16	34	74	103	12%	6	260	3.95	-6.3	$8
Bats	Right	05 BOS	97	15	24	1	9	1	247	314	210	270	351	621	3	85	28	0.20	54	16	30	78	81	5%	2	273	3.03	-4.8	$2
Reliability	16	06 BOS	* 155	23	38	2	14	1	244	265	242	313	359	672	9	86	27	0.73	47	14	38	76	77	5%	3	258	4.04	-7.5	$2
DL	15	1st Half	36	4	10	1	7	0	272			303	517	820	4	80	32	0.22	50	10	40	165	71	0%	1		5.57	-0.1	$1
BAvg Potl	60%	2nd Half	119	19	28	1	7	1	235			316	311	627	11	88	26	1.00	47	15	38	52	63	6%	2	242	3.64	-7.3	$1
LIMA Plan	F	07 Proj	**129**	**21**	**33**	**2**	**12**	**1**	**256**			**316**	**366**	**682**	**8**	**84**	**29**	**0.54**	**49**	**16**	**35**	**72**	**89**	**7%**	**2**	**258**	**4.03**	**-4.5**	**$2**

2-12-.254 in 130 AB at BOS. Power and speed are gone, low LD rates indicate he hasn't hit the ball squarely for years. Remaining skills (good ct%, BA vs. LHP) are worth more to his real team than to yours.

Kearns,Austin			AB	R	H	HR	RBI	SB	Avg	vL	vR	OB	Slg	OPS	bb%	ct%	h%	Eye	G	L	F	PX	SX	SBO	xHR	xBA	RC/G	RAR	R$
Pos	9	02 CIN	* 417	76	130	17	68	7	312	330	310	401	516	916	13	79	36	0.70	46	20	34	137	96	7%	18	298	7.12	20.7	$21
Age	26	03 CIN	292	39	77	15	58	5	264	266	263	354	455	810	12	77	30	0.60	51	20	29	120	56	8%	14	280	5.61	0.0	$12
Pre-Peak		04 CIN	* 300	43	72	11	44	4	240	213	235	335	423	759	13	70	31	0.48	49	12	39	128	95	7%	13	244	5.17	-1.0	$8
Bats	Right	05 CIN	* 498	81	127	24	84	0	254	233	240	331	483	813	10	73	30	0.43	49	23	29	166	46	0%	26	300	5.72	6.8	$17
Reliability	37	06 2NL	537	86	142	24	86	9	264	336	236	356	467	823	12	75	31	0.56	42	19	39	132	78	8%	25	270	5.91	17.8	$19
DL		1st Half	279	46	76	13	44	5	272			343	477	820	10	73	33	0.41	42	21	37	137	73	7%	14	273	5.75	7.8	$11
BAvg Potl	45%	2nd Half	258	40	66	11	42	4	256			368	457	826	15	76	30	0.75	42	17	41	127	78	10%	12	266	6.07	10.0	$8
LIMA Plan	B	07 Proj	**522**	**82**	**141**	**20**	**85**	**6**	**270**			**359**	**456**	**816**	**12**	**74**	**33**	**0.54**	**45**	**19**	**36**	**128**	**77**	**6%**	**22**	**268**	**5.84**	**12.2**	**$18**

As expected, move to WAS hurt: GAB - .279 BA, 144 PX RFK - .254 BA, 93 PX Overall, this is still a good skill set, but there's more plateau than progress. He may hang here for a few years.

Kemp,Matt			AB	R	H	HR	RBI	SB	Avg	vL	vR	OB	Slg	OPS	bb%	ct%	h%	Eye	G	L	F	PX	SX	SBO	xHR	xBA	RC/G	RAR	R$
Pos	8	02	0	0	0	0	0	0	0							0							0		0				
Age	22	03	0	0	0	0	0	0	0							0							0		0				
Growth		04	0	0	0	0	0	0	0							0							0		0				
Bats	Right	05	0	0	0	0	0	0	0							0							0		0				
Reliability	2	06 LA	* 535	93	157	16	84	28	293	229	264	343	464	806	7	79	34	0.36	40	24	36	107	134	24%	17	278	5.40	14.5	$25
DL		1st Half	287	57	88	14	51	15	307			366	537	903	9	76	36	0.40	39	25	36	146	127	22%	14	293	6.73	18.0	$17
BAvg Potl	35%	2nd Half	248	36	69	2	33	13	278			314	379	693	5	83	33	0.31	40	24	36	65	132	27%	3	261	3.99	-3.3	$9
LIMA Plan	C	07 Proj	**393**	**65**	**109**	**10**	**59**	**21**	**277**			**324**	**429**	**753**	**6**	**80**	**32**	**0.35**	**40**	**24**	**36**	**98**	**148**	**26%**	**10**	**274**	**4.73**	**2.0**	**$17**

7-23-.253 in 154 AB at LA. Put up 212 PX in June, then pitchers stopped throwing him fastballs. More of a gap hitter in minors, and LD% backs up that notion. Target the speed; whatever else you get is gravy.

Kendall,Jason			AB	R	H	HR	RBI	SB	Avg	vL	vR	OB	Slg	OPS	bb%	ct%	h%	Eye	G	L	F	PX	SX	SBO	xHR	xBA	RC/G	RAR	R$
Pos	2	02 PIT	545	59	154	3	44	15	283	275	284	342	356	698	8	95	29	1.69	51	19	30	48	93	13%	5	288	4.51	6.3	$14
Age	32	03 PIT	587	84	191	6	58	8	325	310	331	377	416	793	8	93	34	1.23	47	25	28	56	77	7%	8	304	5.42	17.8	$21
Past Peak		04 PIT	574	86	183	3	51	11	319	291	325	383	390	774	9	93	34	1.46	51	20	29	49	67	9%	7	282	5.35	24.1	$19
Bats	Right	05 OAK	601	70	163	0	53	8	271	293	264	327	321	648	8	94	29	1.28	53	21	26	38	72	6%	4	283	3.92	-1.8	$11
Reliability	74	06 OAK	552	76	163	1	50	11	295	331	285	357	342	699	9	90	33	0.98	50	24	26	35	72	8%	4	279	4.41	0.1	$13
DL		1st Half	225	22	61	1	22	2	271			336	320	656	9	90	30	1.00	50	20	29	34	38	8%	2	258	3.93	-2.5	$3
BAvg Potl	60%	2nd Half	327	54	102	0	28	9	312			372	358	729	9	90	35	0.97	50	26	24	36	89	8%	2	291	4.75	3.0	$10
LIMA Plan	C+	07 Proj	**512**	**68**	**144**	**1**	**46**	**9**	**281**			**342**	**334**	**676**	**9**	**92**	**30**	**1.14**	**51**	**22**	**27**	**38**	**71**	**8%**	**4**	**281**	**4.19**	**-0.7**	**$11**

Saved his season with big 2nd half, but H% and LD% will be tough to repeat. xBA, downward Eye trend give reason to feel nervous about future BA output. If H% drops like it did in '05... DN: .260 BA.

Kendrick,Howie			AB	R	H	HR	RBI	SB	Avg	vL	vR	OB	Slg	OPS	bb%	ct%	h%	Eye	G	L	F	PX	SX	SBO	xHR	xBA	RC/G	RAR	R$
Pos	34	02	0	0	0	0	0	0	0							0							0		0				
Age	24	03	0	0	0	0	0	0	0							0							0		0				
Growth		04	0	0	0	0	0	0	0							0							0		0				
Bats	Right	05 aa	190	27	57	5	33	9	300			318	484	802	3	92	31	0.31				117	118	37%	5		5.14	-1.1	$9
Reliability	0	06 ANA	* 557	70	171	14	79	15	307	264	295	329	476	804	3	85	34	0.22	52	15	33	107	109	15%	15	296	5.14	-4.3	$20
DL		1st Half	281	44	91	10	46	9	323			343	527	870	3	87	35	0.23	76	5	19	121	115	19%	9	328	5.83	3.1	$13
BAvg Potl	40%	2nd Half	276	26	80	4	33	6	290			314	424	738	3	84	33	0.21	50	16	34	92	93	10%	6	276	4.41	-7.7	$7
LIMA Plan	C+	07 Proj	**510**	**66**	**149**	**8**	**78**	**18**	**292**			**313**	**440**	**753**	**3**	**88**	**32**	**0.24**	**52**	**15**	**33**	**98**	**113**	**23%**	**11**	**296**	**4.60**	**-10.1**	**$18**

4-30-.285 in 267 AB at ANA. Nice debut, but be cautious:
- Notable slip in ct%
- 2H drops in PX, SX and xBA
- .264 BA, 82% CT in Aug-Sept

These are bumps along the growth curve. Exercise patience.

Kennedy,Adam			AB	R	H	HR	RBI	SB	Avg	vL	vR	OB	Slg	OPS	bb%	ct%	h%	Eye	G	L	F	PX	SX	SBO	xHR	xBA	RC/G	RAR	R$
Pos	4	02 ANA	474	65	148	7	52	17	312	275	319	339	449	788	4	83	36	0.24	33	27	40	90	131	17%	9	273	5.03	12.9	$18
Age	31	03 ANA	449	71	121	13	49	22	269	235	281	336	399	735	9	84	30	0.62	31	27	42	78	105	23%	12	266	4.60	6.1	$17
Past Peak		04 ANA	468	70	130	10	48	15	278	250	286	336	406	742	8	80	33	0.45	40	21	39	79	125	15%	11	251	4.67	7.9	$14
Bats	Left	05 ANA	416	49	125	2	37	19	300	296	302	346	370	716	7	85	35	0.45	41	24	35	55	90	18%	5	261	4.34	2.5	$14
Reliability	77	06 ANA	451	50	123	4	55	16	273	193	291	331	384	714	8	84	32	0.54	41	27	32	72	113	21%	6	280	4.44	4.3	$11
DL	37	1st Half	242	28	62	2	29	7	256			313	355	668	8	82	30	0.47	40	25	35	69	96	19%	4	265	3.84	-2.1	$5
BAvg Potl	50%	2nd Half	209	22	61	2	26	9	292			351	416	767	8	86	33	0.66	42	29	30	76	120	23%	3	298	5.13	6.0	$6
LIMA Plan	C	07 Proj	**449**	**54**	**120**	**5**	**49**	**18**	**267**			**322**	**372**	**694**	**8**	**84**	**31**	**0.50**	**40**	**26**	**34**	**69**	**115**	**20%**	**7**	**271**	**4.14**	**0.4**	**$12**

PRO: Three-year xBA trend, resurgent LD%, SX rebound, great reliability score.
CON: FB% slide has killed xHR, can't hit .300 without high H%, big drop in BA vs. LH.
'07 value depends on new home.

Kent,Jeff			AB	R	H	HR	RBI	SB	Avg	vL	vR	OB	Slg	OPS	bb%	ct%	h%	Eye	G	L	F	PX	SX	SBO	xHR	xBA	RC/G	RAR	R$
Pos	4	02 SF	623	102	195	37	108	5	313	366	297	366	565	931	8	84	33	0.51	36	19	45	155	80	4%	31	310	6.78	39.8	$33
Age	39	03 HOU	505	77	150	22	93	6	297	361	282	347	509	856	7	83	32	0.46	36	21	43	135	80	6%	21	298	5.94	21.4	$22
Decline		04 HOU	540	96	156	27	107	7	289	284	290	348	531	880	8	82	31	0.51	36	20	44	141	121	7%	24	296	6.29	25.6	$25
Bats	Right	05 LA	553	100	160	29	105	6	289	306	285	371	512	883	12	85	30	0.85	31	21	48	136	69	5%	26	297	6.46	29.5	$27
Reliability	74	06 LA	407	61	119	14	68	1	292	347	275	377	477	853	12	83	32	0.80	34	23	43	111	57	2%	15	282	6.24	18.6	$14
DL	36	1st Half	207	35	56	9	40	1	271			366	473	839	13	84	28	0.94	36	24	40	118	64	2%	9	298	6.08	8.8	$8
BAvg Potl	50%	2nd Half	200	26	63	5	28	0	315			388	480	868	11	82	36	0.67	32	21	47	104	52	3%	6	265	6.41	9.9	$7
LIMA Plan	C+	07 Proj	**451**	**72**	**133**	**19**	**79**	**0**	**295**			**370**	**501**	**871**	**11**	**83**	**32**	**0.71**	**34**	**21**	**45**	**124**	**59**	**2%**	**18**	**288**	**6.34**	**22.2**	**$18**

Wrist and oblique injuries sapped his power, especially in 2H. Since the rest of his BPIs held strong, there's reason to believe he'll bounce back. How much depends on him staying healthy, a big if at age 39.

Keppinger,Jeff			AB	R	H	HR	RBI	SB	Avg	vL	vR	OB	Slg	OPS	bb%	ct%	h%	Eye	G	L	F	PX	SX	SBO	xHR	xBA	RC/G	RAR	R$
Pos	5	02	0	0	0	0	0	0	0							0							0		0				
Age	27	03	0	0	0	0	0	0	0							0							0		0				
Peak		04 a/a	389	47	113	1	31	10	292			340	357	696	7	95	30	1.61				42	83	15%	3		4.42	-6.2	$10
Bats	Right	05 aaa	255	34	78	3	25	4	307			340	412	752	5	96	31	1.16				63	94	7%	4		4.84	1.4	$8
Reliability	30	06 KC	* 510	67	152	6	50	0	298	222	303	354	378	732	8	93	31	1.25	58	19	23	48	31	2%	7	279	4.77	-3.4	$11
DL		1st Half	268	28	79	2	20	0	293			350	351	701	8	93	31	1.33				37	23	4%	3		4.45	-4.3	$4
BAvg Potl	65%	2nd Half	242	39	73	4	29	0	303			359	408	767	8	92	32	1.17	58	19	23	61	53	0%	4	297	5.14	0.8	$7
LIMA Plan	D	07 Proj	**131**	**18**	**37**	**1**	**13**	**1**	**282**			**331**	**376**	**707**	**7**	**94**	**29**	**1.24**	**58**	**19**	**23**	**55**	**80**	**6%**	**2**	**303**	**4.47**	**-1.3**	**$3**

2-8-.267 in 60 AB at KC.
PRO: Promsing ct% and eye
CON: - Low PX and SX
- Only qualifies at 3b
- 27-year-olds have officially passed from prospect to suspect.

BRANDON KRUSE

Kielty,Bobby			AB	R	H	HR	RBI	SB	Avg	vL	vR	OB	Slg	OPS	bb%	ct%	h%	Eye	G	L	F	PX	SX	SBO	xHR	xBA	RC/G	RAR	R$
Pos	79	02 MIN	296	49	87	12	46	4	294	264	303	401	486	888	15	77	35	0.79	38	20	41	121	94	5%	12	268	6.89	16.9	$12
Age	30	03 2AL	427	71	104	13	57	8	244	300	216	351	400	752	14	78	28	0.77	38	24	39	107	84	8%	15	270	5.09	-3.1	$12
Peak		04 OAK	238	29	51	7	31	1	214	259	172	315	370	685	13	80	24	0.74	42	16	42	100	57	2%	8	255	4.18	-5.5	$3
Bats	Both	05 OAK	377	55	99	10	57	3	263	322	227	349	395	744	12	82	30	0.75	45	20	36	89	53	4%	11	267	4.88	1.8	$10
Reliability	53	06 OAK	270	35	73	8	36	2	270	325	229	325	441	766	8	82	31	0.45	49	17	34	111	69	3%	9	284	4.94	-1.9	$7
DL		1st Half	112	11	32	2	14	0	286			355	429	783	10	84	33	0.67	51	22	27	93	47	0%	3	294	5.34	0.5	$2
BAvg Potl	50%	2nd Half	158	24	41	6	22	2	259			304	449	753	6	80	29	0.32	48	13	39	124	70	6%	6	276	4.64	-2.5	$4
LIMA Plan	D	07 Proj	**265**	**36**	**73**	**9**	**37**	**2**	**275**			**348**	**447**	**795**	**10**	**81**	**31**	**0.60**	**44**	**18**	**38**	**110**	**66**	**3%**	**9**	**275**	**5.41**	**3.0**	**$8**

Wild swings in BA; xBA shows he's actually pretty stable. Took more aggressive approach in 2H and posted career-high PX. Has a 20-HR season in his bat, but given his poor BA vs. RHP, he probably won't get the chance.

Kinsler,Ian			AB	R	H	HR	RBI	SB	Avg	vL	vR	OB	Slg	OPS	bb%	ct%	h%	Eye	G	L	F	PX	SX	SBO	xHR	xBA	RC/G	RAR	R$
Pos	4	02	0	0	0	0	0	0	0							0							0		0				
Age	24	03	0	0	0	0	0	0	0							0							0		0				
Growth		04 aa	271	42	78	8	37	6	288			352	454	806	9	85	31	0.68				106	71	13%	9		5.51	9.0	$10
Bats	Right	05 aaa	526	71	127	18	64	13	241			291	395	687	7	88	24	0.61				91	89	16%	16		3.98	-5.7	$14
Reliability	12	06 TEX	423	65	121	14	55	11	286	271	292	348	454	802	9	85	31	0.63	35	21	44	103	89	13%	14	276	5.40	15.4	$15
DL	43	1st Half	113	17	32	5	22	2	283			357	496	853	10	83	30	0.68	35	13	52	125	85	13%	5	265	6.09	6.4	$4
BAvg Potl	50%	2nd Half	310	48	89	9	33	9	287			344	439	783	8	85	31	0.60	35	23	41	95	85	13%	9	281	5.16	9.1	$10
LIMA Plan	C+	07 Proj	**565**	**83**	**157**	**19**	**76**	**14**	**278**			**337**	**443**	**780**	**8**	**86**	**30**	**0.63**	**35**	**19**	**46**	**100**	**82**	**13%**	**19**	**273**	**5.12**	**16.3**	**$19**

2nd half PX and FB% should guide expectations for his power output. Otherwise, his skills are remarkably stable for a young player. Low AB total could leave him undervalued. Healthy, he's a potential Top 10 2B.

Klesko,Ryan			AB	R	H	HR	RBI	SB	Avg	vL	vR	OB	Slg	OPS	bb%	ct%	h%	Eye	G	L	F	PX	SX	SBO	xHR	xBA	RC/G	RAR	R$
Pos	3	02 SD	540	90	162	29	95	6	300	287	305	386	537	923	12	84	31	0.88	40	21	39	148	73	5%	27	317	7.01	21.1	$27
Age	35	03 SD	397	47	100	21	67	2	252	194	272	357	456	813	14	79	27	0.78	40	17	44	126	24	6%	20	264	5.73	2.5	$12
Decline		04 SD	402	58	117	9	66	3	291	325	278	400	448	848	15	83	33	1.09	44	22	35	104	66	3%	12	289	6.45	5.7	$14
Bats	Left	05 SD	443	61	110	18	58	3	248	200	263	357	418	775	14	82	27	0.94	42	17	41	104	50	5%	17	265	5.34	-3.5	$12
Reliability	0	06 SD	4	0	3	0	2	0	750	******	667	833	******	1833	33	100	75		25	50	25	172	0	0%	0		19.36	0.5	$1
DL	172	1st Half	0	0	0	0	0	0	0																				
BAvg Potl		2nd Half	4	0	3	0	2	0	750			833	******	1833	33	100	75		25	50	25	172		0%	0		19.36	0.5	$1
LIMA Plan	D	07 Proj	**210**	**29**	**56**	**9**	**33**	**1**	**267**			**371**	**454**	**824**	**14**	**82**	**29**	**0.90**	**41**	**18**	**40**	**115**	**37**	**5%**	**9**	**274**	**5.94**	**0.6**	**$7**

Bum shoulder led to a lost year, and hangs a cloud over his future. PX was already in 4-year decline, though likely departure from Petco (-22% LH HR) will help. Reliability score speaks volumes about '07 uncertainty.

Konerko,Paul			AB	R	H	HR	RBI	SB	Avg	vL	vR	OB	Slg	OPS	bb%	ct%	h%	Eye	G	L	F	PX	SX	SBO	xHR	xBA	RC/G	RAR	R$
Pos	3	02 CHW	570	81	173	27	104	0	304	279	310	353	498	852	7	87	31	0.61	44	18	38	110	26	0%	23	289	5.81	-0.8	$24
Age	31	03 CHW	444	49	104	18	65	0	234	327	187	302	399	700	9	89	23	0.86	40	22	38	92	20	0%	15	291	4.25	-15.0	$9
Past Peak		04 CHW	563	84	156	41	117	1	277	288	273	356	535	891	11	81	28	0.64	42	17	41	144	33	1%	33	290	6.42	22.8	$24
Bats	Right	05 CHW	575	98	163	40	100	0	283	261	289	372	534	906	12	81	29	0.74	33	25	42	148	26	0%	33	309	6.71	26.1	$26
Reliability	99	06 CHW	566	97	177	35	113	1	313	318	310	379	551	930	10	82	33	0.58	33	25	42	139	41	1%	30	303	6.88	22.2	$27
DL		1st Half	280	49	88	19	60	0	314			383	571	954	10	83	32	0.66	31	24	45	145	28	0%	16	310	7.14	13.0	$14
BAvg Potl	45%	2nd Half	286	48	89	16	53	1	311			375	531	906	9	80	34	0.51	35	26	39	132	44	1%	14	298	6.61	9.2	$13
LIMA Plan	C	07 Proj	**574**	**94**	**175**	**36**	**109**	**1**	**305**			**376**	**541**	**917**	**10**	**82**	**32**	**0.63**	**36**	**23**	**41**	**137**	**36**	**0%**	**30**	**301**	**6.75**	**22.8**	**$26**

Constantly outperforms his xHR due to dearth of doubles. With three years of stable skills and consistent production, he's been as close to a sure thing as you can get. Death, taxes and... Konerko?

Koskie,Corey			AB	R	H	HR	RBI	SB	Avg	vL	vR	OB	Slg	OPS	bb%	ct%	h%	Eye	G	L	F	PX	SX	SBO	xHR	xBA	RC/G	RAR	R$
Pos	5	02 MIN	490	71	131	15	69	10	267	253	274	361	447	808	13	74	33	0.57	41	20	39	129	85	14%	19	265	5.84	20.0	$16
Age	33	03 MIN	469	76	137	14	69	11	292	292	331	392	452	844	14	76	36	0.68	38	26	36	112	89	9%	17	272	6.33	24.1	$18
Past Peak		04 MIN	422	68	106	25	71	9	251	233	260	329	495	824	10	76	28	0.48	36	15	49	153	98	12%	23	270	5.74	10.3	$16
Bats	Left	05 TOR	354	49	88	11	36	4	249	211	265	332	398	730	11	75	30	0.49	46	19	35	109	61	5%	13	256	4.63	1.4	$8
Reliability	7	06 MIL	257	29	67	12	33	1	261	263	260	336	490	826	10	77	29	0.50	47	17	35	152	27	5%	13	287	5.81	2.4	$7
DL	87 68	1st Half	233	25	61	10	30	0	262			336	485	821	10	77	30	0.48	47	17	35	152	18	4%	11	281	5.77	1.9	$6
BAvg Potl	50%	2nd Half	24	4	6	2	3	1	250			333	542	875	11	83	22	0.75	50	15	35	155	59	17%	2	316	6.18	0.5	$1
LIMA Plan	D	07 Proj	**342**	**48**	**89**	**14**	**47**	**1**	**260**			**343**	**461**	**804**	**11**	**76**	**31**	**0.52**	**42**	**19**	**39**	**136**	**53**	**5%**	**15**	**273**	**5.60**	**4.6**	**$10**

Concussion ended a strong comeback season.
PRO: Return to 2004 PX level, best xBA in five years.
CON: Did not return to '04 FB% level, AB history says don't expect a full season of health.

Kotchman,Casey			AB	R	H	HR	RBI	SB	Avg	vL	vR	OB	Slg	OPS	bb%	ct%	h%	Eye	G	L	F	PX	SX	SBO	xHR	xBA	RC/G	RAR	R$
Pos	3	02	0	0	0	0	0	0	0							0							0		0				
Age	24	03	0	0	0	0	0	0	0							0							0		0				
Growth		04 a/a	313	42	108	6	46	0	346			383	507	889	6	92	36	0.79				103	28	0%	8		6.31	6.8	$13
Bats	Left	05 ANA	* 489	63	128	14	66	1	263	250	277	327	408	735	9	91	27	1.02	55	21	24	86	43	4%	14	312	4.74	-5.0	$12
Reliability	0	06 ANA	79	6	12	1	6	0	152	214	138	221	215	436	8	84	17	0.54	67	11	23	40	37	6%	1	222	1.04	-11.7	($1)
DL	145	1st Half	79	6	12	1	6	0	152			221	215	436	8	84	17	0.54	67	11	23	40	37	6%	1	222	1.04	-11.7	($1)
BAvg Potl	65%	2nd Half	0	0	0	0	0	0	0																				
LIMA Plan	F	07 Proj	**250**	**33**	**69**	**8**	**35**	**1**	**276**			**329**	**435**	**764**	**7**	**89**	**28**	**0.71**	**54**	**21**	**25**	**96**	**44**	**4%**	**8**	**312**	**4.93**	**-2.6**	**$7**

Bad case of mono forces us to toss '06 out the window. Going back to 2005, he had a 131 PX and .347 xBA in 2H. Upside is still there, playing time may not be. Keep him on your radar.

Kotsay,Mark			AB	R	H	HR	RBI	SB	Avg	vL	vR	OB	Slg	OPS	bb%	ct%	h%	Eye	G	L	F	PX	SX	SBO	xHR	xBA	RC/G	RAR	R$
Pos	8	02 SD	578	82	169	17	61	11	292	324	277	358	452	809	9	85	32	0.66	40	24	36	97	101	11%	16	290	5.55	11.2	$21
Age	31	03 SD	482	64	128	7	38	6	266	236	278	342	384	726	10	83	31	0.68	46	26	29	80	90	6%	10	286	4.68	-4.2	$10
Past Peak		04 OAK	606	78	190	15	63	8	314	336	239	371	459	829	8	88	34	0.79	38	21	41	86	71	7%	16	282	5.76	17.3	$20
Bats	Left	05 OAK	582	75	163	15	82	5	280	324	261	326	421	747	6	91	29	0.78	40	25	35	86	58	7%	15	307	4.75	7.9	$17
Reliability	83	06 OAK	502	57	138	7	59	6	275	265	278	333	386	720	8	89	30	0.80	46	19	35	70	77	6%	9	275	4.56	-1.4	$10
DL		1st Half	276	33	72	6	28	3	261			320	384	704	8	89	28	0.77	44	17	40	70	76	8%	6	263	4.33	-2.7	$5
BAvg Potl	60%	2nd Half	226	24	66	1	31	3	292			350	389	739	8	89	32	0.83	48	22	30	69	71	4%	3	289	4.85	1.2	$5
LIMA Plan	C+	07 Proj	**516**	**62**	**144**	**9**	**63**	**6**	**279**			**336**	**405**	**741**	**8**	**89**	**30**	**0.78**	**43**	**22**	**35**	**78**	**78**	**7%**	**11**	**287**	**4.77**	**2.8**	**$13**

Chronic back woes and drop in BA vs. LH cut into his value, and it has now been five years since he had even league-average power or speed. He can maintain this level, but those $20 seasons are over.

Kouzmanoff,Kevin			AB	R	H	HR	RBI	SB	Avg	vL	vR	OB	Slg	OPS	bb%	ct%	h%	Eye	G	L	F	PX	SX	SBO	xHR	xBA	RC/G	RAR	R$
Pos	0	02	0	0	0	0	0	0	0							0							0		0				
Age	25	03	0	0	0	0	0	0	0							0							0		0				
Pre-Peak		04 aa	24	3	4	1	5	0	167			231	333	564	8	75	18	0.33				107	41	0%	1		2.21	-2.4	$0
Bats	Right	05	0	0	0	0	0	0	0							0							0		0				
Reliability	9	06 CLE	* 402	65	129	20	78	4	321	167	227	376	546	922	8	85	34	0.61	59	9	32	132	61	7%	18	301	6.71	3.1	$19
DL		1st Half	180	30	63	6	32	2	350			406	535	941	9	88	37	0.81				108	68	7%	6		7.02	2.8	$9
BAvg Potl	50%	2nd Half	222	35	66	14	46	2	297			350	556	906	8	83	30	0.49	59	9	32	153	52	6%	12	307	6.47	0.2	$10
LIMA Plan	F	07 Proj	**129**	**21**	**36**	**5**	**25**	**1**	**279**			**337**	**456**	**793**	**8**	**85**	**30**	**0.59**	**47**	**18**	**35**	**110**	**59**	**7%**	**5**	**293**	**5.26**	**-2.8**	**$5**

3-11-.214 in 56 AB at CLE. Hit over .300 with plus power at every level of minors, but beat too many balls into the dirt in Sept call-up. Now with SD. Worth tucking away.

Kubel,Jason			AB	R	H	HR	RBI	SB	Avg	vL	vR	OB	Slg	OPS	bb%	ct%	h%	Eye	G	L	F	PX	SX	SBO	xHR	xBA	RC/G	RAR	R$
Pos	70	02	0	0	0	0	0	0	0							0							0		0				
Age	24	03	0	0	0	0	0	0	0							0							0		0				
Growth		04 a/a	488	85	162	18	89	14	332			393	547	940	9	89	35	0.91				127	107	14%	18		7.07	24.4	$26
Bats	Left	05 MIN	0	0	0	0	0	0	0							0							0		0				
Reliability	0	06 MIN	* 340	41	86	12	48	4	253	243	240	302	415	717	7	80	29	0.35	49	21	31	99	83	5%	11	277	4.21	-9.7	$8
DL	180	1st Half	230	32	66	10	41	4	287			336	483	819	7	80	32	0.36	48	22	31	117	97	7%	9	292	5.47	1.9	$9
BAvg Potl	45%	2nd Half	110	9	20	2	7	0	182			231	273	503	6	80	21	0.32	49	20	31	60	25	0%	2	238	1.59	-12.7	($1)
LIMA Plan	C	07 Proj	**403**	**54**	**108**	**13**	**56**	**6**	**268**			**323**	**433**	**756**	**7**	**83**	**29**	**0.49**	**49**	**20**	**31**	**103**	**89**	**8%**	**13**	**293**	**4.79**	**-2.7**	**$12**

8-26-.241 in 220 AB at MIN. Hasn't been the same since blowing out his left knee two years ago. Ongoing pain ruined his 2nd half, and overall drops in ct%, Eye and PX create doubts about his future.

BRANDON KRUSE

Laird,Gerald		Year	AB	R	H	HR	RBI	SB	Avg	vL	vR	OB	Slg	OPS	bb%	ct%	h%	Eye	G	L	F	PX	SX	SBO	xHR	xBA	RC/G	RAR	R$
Pos	2	02 aa	442	62	116	10	60	7	262			324	389	713	8	81	30	0.49				82	92	11%	11		4.32	5.9	$13
Age	27	03 TEX	* 382	53	96	10	41	8	251	294	259	319	411	730	9	84	28	0.60	36	30	33	98	116	11%	10	298	4.62	6.0	$9
Peak		04 TEX	147	20	33	1	16	0	224	317	189	283	286	569	8	76	29	0.34	44	19	36	48	51	3%	2	218	2.43	-8.6	$1
Bats	Right	05 TEX	* 321	43	86	14	42	8	269			315	457	772	6	85	28	0.44	39	15	45	108	104	14%	11	270	4.86	7.8	$11
Reliability	10	06 TEX	243	46	72	7	22	3	296	400	241	329	473	803	5	78	36	0.22	34	19	46	124	99	7%	8	263	5.27	5.8	$8
DL		1st Half	90	23	30	4	12	3	333			362	567	928	4	82	37	0.25	30	19	51	152	112	19%	4	291	6.64	5.3	$5
BAvg Potl	25%	2nd Half	153	23	42	3	10	0	275			311	418	729	5	75	35	0.21	38	19	43	105	68	0%	4	246	4.41	0.0	$3
LIMA Plan	C	07 Proj	404	66	108	15	43	6	267			311	448	759	6	80	30	0.31	37	19	44	116	101	9%	15	268	4.72	5.6	$12

3 reasons he'll be overvalued:
- Gap between BA and xBA
- Low BA vs. RHP
- Huge 1H hid 2H drop-off

1 reason to target him anyway:
- Peak age catcher w/power and some speed who's likely in TEX.

Lamb,Mike		Year	AB	R	H	HR	RBI	SB	Avg	vL	vR	OB	Slg	OPS	bb%	ct%	h%	Eye	G	L	F	PX	SX	SBO	xHR	xBA	RC/G	RAR	R$
Pos	35	02 TEX	* 342	56	99	9	36	0	289	211	293	354	409	763	9	85	32	0.67	42	22	36	72	38	0%	9	269	4.96	-8.6	$10
Age	31	03 aaa	274	36	71	8	37	1	259			341	431	772	11	85	28	0.83				105	76	3%	8		5.24	-1.6	$7
Past Peak		04 HOU	278	38	80	14	58	1	288	349	277	359	511	870	10	77	33	0.49	44	22	34	135	70	3%	13	290	6.33	2.9	$12
Bats	Left	05 HOU	322	41	76	12	53	1	236	182	243	285	419	704	6	80	26	0.34	42	22	36	111	94	3%	11	280	4.06	-14.9	$8
Reliability	11	06 HOU	381	70	117	12	45	2	307	211	324	365	475	840	8	86	33	0.64	40	20	39	97	75	5%	12	282	5.86	-1.5	$14
DL		1st Half	162	32	53	6	20	0	327			381	506	887	8	85	36	0.58	36	21	43	107	46	4%	6	283	6.33	1.4	$7
BAvg Potl	50%	2nd Half	219	38	64	6	25	2	292			354	452	806	9	86	32	0.68	44	20	36	90	96	6%	6	282	5.51	-3.0	$7
LIMA Plan	D+	07 Proj	353	56	100	12	51	1	283			343	463	806	8	83	31	0.53	42	21	37	106	85	4%	12	283	5.43	-4.2	$12

PX trending downward despite rising FB% doesn't speak very highly of his power. .307 BA might garner some interest, but xBA pegs him as .280-ish hitter. You can fool some of the people some of the time, but not xBA.

Lane,Jason		Year	AB	R	H	HR	RBI	SB	Avg	vL	vR	OB	Slg	OPS	bb%	ct%	h%	Eye	G	L	F	PX	SX	SBO	xHR	xBA	RC/G	RAR	R$
Pos	9	02 HOU	* 495	68	131	19	82	12	265	349	192	316	471	786	7	81	29	0.39	26	21	53	139	106	15%	19	277	5.14	-2.4	$19
Age	30	03 aaa	248	32	70	7	34	2	282			350	431	782	9	90	29	1.04				91	48	4%	7		5.31	-0.5	$8
Peak		04 HOU	136	21	37	4	19	1	272	280	267	349	463	812	11	76	33	0.48	34	19	47	129	99	3%	5	259	5.78	1.9	$4
Bats	Right	05 HOU	517	65	138	26	78	6	267	237	277	310	499	809	6	80	29	0.30	30	19	51	148	88	8%	23	281	5.29	0.6	$19
Reliability	49	06 HOU	288	44	58	15	45	1	201	198	203	318	392	710	15	74	22	0.65	28	14	58	137	38	4%	15	225	4.36	-3.7	$6
DL		1st Half	208	35	43	11	29	1	207			335	404	739	16	77	21	0.83	30	14	57	117	44	3%	11	234	4.83	0.4	$4
BAvg Potl	60%	2nd Half	80	9	15	4	16	0	187			270	362	632	10	66	22	0.33	23	16	61	117	31	6%	4	202	3.14	-4.2	$1
LIMA Plan	D	07 Proj	220	30	56	12	36	1	255			330	479	809	10	75	29	0.45	29	17	55	142	62	5%	11	255	5.53	3.2	$7

Getting demoted at 29 is not a good career move. Neither is a .225 xBA or 66% ct in 2nd half. Sky-high FB% still gives hope for HR output, but opportunity is the big question now.

Langerhans,Ryan		Year	AB	R	H	HR	RBI	SB	Avg	vL	vR	OB	Slg	OPS	bb%	ct%	h%	Eye	G	L	F	PX	SX	SBO	xHR	xBA	RC/G	RAR	R$
Pos	78	02 aa	391	48	88	7	52	8	225			321	338	658	12	83	26	0.81				77	75	12%	9		3.92	-20.5	$7
Age	27	03 a/a	468	52	117	9	46	11	250			325	389	714	10	78	30	0.50				100	85	18%	12		4.46	-14.2	$10
Peak		04 aaa	456	91	126	18	63	4	276			363	471	834	12	79	32	0.65				125	79	10%	19		6.01	10.9	$17
Bats	Left	05 ATL	326	48	87	8	42	0	267	298	261	342	426	768	10	77	33	0.49	40	26	33	114	66	2%	10	282	5.16	-1.7	$9
Reliability	43	06 ATL	315	46	76	7	28	1	241	308	232	345	378	723	14	71	32	0.55	41	21	38	96	72	3%	9	237	4.76	-4.6	$5
DL		1st Half	188	22	45	4	16	0	239			325	372	698	11	72	31	0.45	42	18	40	87	75	4%	5	225	4.30	-5.4	$2
BAvg Potl	40%	2nd Half	127	24	31	3	12	1	244			373	386	758	17	70	33	0.68	41	26	34	110	54	2%	5	253	5.41	0.6	$3
LIMA Plan	F	07 Proj	153	24	39	4	17	1	255			350	403	753	13	74	32	0.58	41	24	35	104	75	5%	5	260	5.08	-1.3	$4

Signs that the "4th Outfielder" label is about to stick for good:
- PX and ct% in decline
- 45-point plunge in xBA
- Growing platoon differential
- You've passed the magic age "26" and no cover story in SI.

LaRoche,Adam		Year	AB	R	H	HR	RBI	SB	Avg	vL	vR	OB	Slg	OPS	bb%	ct%	h%	Eye	G	L	F	PX	SX	SBO	xHR	xBA	RC/G	RAR	R$
Pos	3	02 aa	173	14	45	3	16	1	260			319	358	678	8	82	30	0.48				68	31	4%	4		3.88	-9.4	$3
Age	27	03 a/a	483	70	134	19	67	2	277			353	466	818	10	79	32	0.55				125	49	4%	20		5.70	3.5	$16
Peak		04 ATL	324	45	90	13	45	0	278	250	280	333	488	821	8	76	33	0.35	46	19	35	145	45	0%	14	284	5.67	-2.6	$10
Bats	Left	05 ATL	451	53	117	20	78	0	259	191	269	318	455	773	8	81	28	0.45	44	21	34	127	21	2%	19	289	4.95	-8.5	$14
Reliability	37	06 ATL	492	89	140	32	90	0	285	241	297	356	561	917	10	74	33	0.43	38	21	41	180	41	2%	31	298	7.02	14.1	$21
DL		1st Half	232	34	56	12	40	0	241			326	474	800	11	74	28	0.48	39	21	40	153	31	2%	13	282	5.53	-3.3	$6
BAvg Potl	45%	2nd Half	260	55	84	20	50	0	323			385	638	1023	9	74	37	0.38	37	21	42	201	59	1%	18	311	8.35	16.3	$15
LIMA Plan	C	07 Proj	573	88	165	35	96	0	288			352	544	896	9	77	32	0.42	39	21	40	165	38	2%	32	298	6.59	11.9	$24

Breakout season came in part thanks to growth vs. LH:
2005 - .191 BA, 71 PX
2006 - .241 BA, 166 PX
PX and xBA surges in 2H give hope there's more to come.
UP: 40 HR, .300 BA

LaRue,Jason		Year	AB	R	H	HR	RBI	SB	Avg	vL	vR	OB	Slg	OPS	bb%	ct%	h%	Eye	G	L	F	PX	SX	SBO	xHR	xBA	RC/G	RAR	R$
Pos	2	02 CIN	353	42	88	12	52	1	249	207	264	303	405	708	7	67	34	0.23	44	21	36	123	55	4%	14	240	4.30	1.9	$9
Age	33	03 CIN	379	52	87	16	50	3	230	210	237	291	422	713	8	71	28	0.30	41	18	41	140	74	8%	17	256	4.30	0.1	$9
Past Peak		04 CIN	390	46	98	14	55	0	251	274	244	298	431	729	6	72	31	0.24	43	19	38	126	49	2%	15	256	4.44	7.2	$9
Bats	Right	05 CIN	361	38	94	14	60	0	260	257	262	336	452	787	10	72	33	0.41	42	23	36	145	16	0%	16	271	5.42	17.1	$10
Reliability	18	06 CIN	191	22	37	8	21	1	194	235	179	294	346	639	12	73	22	0.53	44	20	36	94	37	2%	8	239	3.34	-6.0	$2
DL	23	1st Half	101	8	18	4	11	0	178			252	317	569	9	76	19	0.42	40	23	37	81	11	0%	4	244	2.32	-6.6	$0
BAvg Potl	60%	2nd Half	90	14	19	4	10	1	211			336	378	714	16	70	25	0.63	48	16	35	109	47	3%	4	234	4.53	0.5	$2
LIMA Plan	F	07 Proj	214	26	55	9	28	1	257			325	424	749	9	72	32	0.36	43	20	37	115	36	2%	9	249	4.78	4.2	$5

Spring knee injury and David Ross put the kibosh on hopes for a late career power spike. Still owns those skills, but age and opportunity are conspiring against him now. And the bb% increase? 9 intentional walks.

LeCroy,Matt		Year	AB	R	H	HR	RBI	SB	Avg	vL	vR	OB	Slg	OPS	bb%	ct%	h%	Eye	G	L	F	PX	SX	SBO	xHR	xBA	RC/G	RAR	R$
Pos	2	02 MIN	* 355	45	99	15	63	1	279	289	231	326	468	794	7	82	31	0.38	39	16	45	113	56	3%	13	265	5.13	15.3	$12
Age	31	03 MIN	345	39	99	17	64	0	287	287	280	335	490	825	7	76	33	0.30	40	24	37	133	18	1%	16	283	5.56	14.2	$12
Past Peak		04 MIN	264	25	71	9	39	0	269	322	241	311	424	735	6	77	32	0.27	51	18	31	102	16	0%	9	250	4.39	0.4	$6
Bats	Right	05 MIN	304	33	79	17	50	0	260	303	228	348	444	792	12	72	31	0.48	42	17	40	116	0	0%	15	195	5.37	11.9	$9
Reliability	23	06 WAS	67	5	16	2	9	0	239	229	250	346	373	719	14	75	29	0.65	53	12	35	90	0	0%	2	125	4.61	0.5	$1
DL		1st Half	62	5	14	2	8	0	226			324	371	695	13	76	27	0.60	52	13	35	95	8	0%	2	209	4.22	-0.2	$1
BAvg Potl	35%	2nd Half	5	0	2	0	1	0	400			571	400	971	29	60	67	1.00	67	0	33	0		0%	0		10.07	0.7	$0
LIMA Plan	F	07 Proj	32	3	8	1	5	0	250			319	404	723	9	76	29	0.42	47	17	36	96	19	0%	1	237	4.36	0.2	$1

Can't catch. Can't play first base. Can't run. Can't hit line drives. Can't hit for power anymore. Can't hit lefties anymore either. And according to xBA, can't hit at all, period. This might be the fanalytic equivalent of a flatline.

Lee,Carlos		Year	AB	R	H	HR	RBI	SB	Avg	vL	vR	OB	Slg	OPS	bb%	ct%	h%	Eye	G	L	F	PX	SX	SBO	xHR	xBA	RC/G	RAR	R$
Pos	7	02 CHW	492	82	130	26	80	1	264	295	255	362	484	845	13	85	26	1.03	32	21	47	124	49	3%	23	292	6.11	18.4	$18
Age	30	03 CHW	623	100	181	31	113	18	291	218	317	330	499	830	6	85	30	0.41	39	21	40	122	98	15%	26	300	5.45	2.1	$29
Peak		04 CHW	591	103	180	31	99	11	305	308	303	363	525	887	8	85	31	0.63	33	20	47	126	76	10%	27	290	6.30	22.2	$27
Bats	Right	05 MIL	618	85	164	32	114	13	265	261	267	327	487	814	8	86	26	0.66	34	20	46	134	76	11%	28	300	5.47	2.4	$26
Reliability	76	06 2TM	624	102	187	37	116	19	300	313	296	359	540	899	9	90	29	0.89	40	20	40	128	95	12%	29	318	6.42	20.8	$31
DL		1st Half	297	51	82	25	63	10	276			345	576	920	9	89	24	0.94	37	18	45	152	81	16%	18	327	6.60	11.8	$16
BAvg Potl	65%	2nd Half	327	51	105	12	53	9	321			373	508	881	8	90	33	0.84	42	21	36	106	94	9%	11	311	6.26	9.1	$15
LIMA Plan	B	07 Proj	609	96	184	33	109	15	302			361	529	891	8	88	30	0.75	37	20	43	128	86	11%	27	307	6.34	19.2	$30

PRO: Rising trends in ct%, eye, PX and xBA might indicate yet another level to come.
CON: 2nd straight year that HR and FB% dropped in 2H.
His new home park could decide over/under on .300 BA, 35 HR.

Lee,Derrek		Year	AB	R	H	HR	RBI	SB	Avg	vL	vR	OB	Slg	OPS	bb%	ct%	h%	Eye	G	L	F	PX	SX	SBO	xHR	xBA	RC/G	RAR	R$
Pos	3	02 FLA	581	95	157	27	86	19	270	264	272	376	494	870	14	72	33	0.60	35	23	42	159	121	15%	29	274	6.75	19.6	$26
Age	31	03 FLA	539	91	146	31	92	21	271	333	256	373	508	882	14	76	31	0.67	42	22	36	154	100	17%	30	296	6.68	18.4	$27
Past Peak		04 CHC	605	90	168	32	98	12	278	306	271	351	504	855	10	79	31	0.53	41	19	40	141	75	10%	30	288	6.09	2.4	$25
Bats	Right	05 CHC	594	120	199	46	107	15	335	333	339	418	662	1080	13	82	35	0.78	39	22	39	202	104	10%	40	347	8.91	51.7	$41
Reliability	11	06 CHC	175	30	50	8	30	8	286	292	283	375	474	849	13	77	33	0.61	41	20	38	118	75	21%	8	268	6.19	1.0	$8
DL	100	1st Half	61	12	18	4	12	5	295			411	557	968	16	79	32	0.92	50	12	38	158	79	32%	4	297	7.84	3.3	$4
BAvg Potl	45%	2nd Half	114	18	32	4	18	3	281			354	430	784	10	75	34	0.46	36	25	39	96	63	14%	4	256	5.27	-2.4	$4
LIMA Plan	D+	07 Proj	552	97	163	36	95	21	295			383	558	941	12	78	32	0.64	41	20	39	162	90	17%	33	304	7.28	22.4	$31

Rushed June return from wrist injury - looked much better in Aug/Sept, when he hit .339 w/4 HR in 56 AB. Should be fully recovered by spring, so put more stock in '05 skills than '06.
UP: 40+ HR, again.

BRANDON KRUSE

Lee,Travis

	Yr	AB	R	H	HR	RBI	SB	Avg	vL	vR	OB	Slg	OPS	bb%	ct%	h%	Eye	G	L	F	PX	SX	SBO	xHR	xBA	RC/G	RAR	R$
Pos 3	02 PHI	536	55	142	13	70	5	265	282	259	332	394	726	9	81	31	0.52	43	23	33	87	63	5%	14	272	4.51	-16.9	$14
Age 31	03 TAM	542	75	149	19	70	6	275	285	269	351	459	811	11	82	31	0.66	42	20	38	118	80	5%	20	288	5.64	4.0	$17
Past Peak	04 NYY	19	1	2	0	2	0	105		154	150	158	308	5	84	13	0.33	50	6	44	44	32	0%	0	184	-0.47	-3.6	($1)
Bats Left	05 TAM	404	54	110	12	49	7	272	245	277	330	426	756	8	84	30	0.53	44	21	34	98	85	10%	12	286	4.82	-3.1	$12
Reliability 1	06 TAM	343	35	77	11	31	5	224	226	224	309	364	674	11	79	25	0.58	46	20	34	84	71	7%	11	256	3.87	-16.2	$4
DL 18	1st Half	193	16	39	4	13	1	202			270	301	571	9	78	24	0.42	50	19	30	66	35	4%	4	238	2.47	-18.0	($0)
BAvg Potl 60%	2nd Half	150	19	38	7	18	4	253			356	447	803	14	80	27	0.80	40	20	39	107	95	10%	6	270	5.63	0.9	$4
LIMA Plan F	07 Proj	188	22	47	6	21	3	250			328	403	731	10	81	28	0.60	44	21	36	93	73	8%	6	269	4.60	-3.9	$4

Since 2002, his 1H/2H splits:
1H - .236 BA, 53.6 AB/HR
2H - .284 BA, 24.6 AB/HR
Posted higher 2H PX and xBA every year except '04, when hurt. Just wait for him to hit the waiver wire in June.

Lewis,Fred

	Yr	AB	R	H	HR	RBI	SB	Avg	vL	vR	OB	Slg	OPS	bb%	ct%	h%	Eye	G	L	F	PX	SX	SBO	xHR	xBA	RC/G	RAR	R$
Pos 8	02	0	0	0	0	0	0	0							0							0		0				
Age 26	03	0	0	0	0	0	0	0							0							0		0				
Pre-Peak	04	0	0	0	0	0	0	0							0							0		0				
Bats Left	05 aa	508	62	121	5	38	24	238			311	340	651	10	78	29	0.49				73	128	27%	7		3.68	-11.7	$11
Reliability 2	06 aaa	439	64	106	9	43	14	241			320	379	698	10	82	28	0.64				80	130	20%	9		4.31	-3.3	$10
DL	1st Half	257	41	58	6	28	8	227			324	374	697	12	80	26	0.70				89	122	20%	7		4.36	-1.5	$5
BAvg Potl 45%	2nd Half	182	24	48	3	15	6	261			313	386	700	7	86	29	0.53				67	128	18%	3		4.20	-1.9	$4
LIMA Plan D	07 Proj	254	34	62	4	22	10	244			315	365	680	9	81	29	0.55	51	10	39	75	127	22%	4	240	4.04	-4.1	$6

0-2-.455 in 11 AB at SF. Speed skills are being held back by low OB%. Even with 30% hit rate, BA would only top out near .260, though 2H ct% growth was encouraging. For now, end-game SB flyer material.

Lieberthal,Mike

	Yr	AB	R	H	HR	RBI	SB	Avg	vL	vR	OB	Slg	OPS	bb%	ct%	h%	Eye	G	L	F	PX	SX	SBO	xHR	xBA	RC/G	RAR	R$
Pos 2	02 PHI	476	46	133	15	52	0	279	346	260	333	443	776	7	88	29	0.66	36	22	41	102	33	1%	14	294	5.06	12.8	$12
Age 35	03 PHI	508	68	159	13	81	0	313	319	311	361	453	814	7	88	33	0.64	37	27	37	86	34	0%	13	300	5.47	16.1	$19
Decline	04 PHI	476	58	129	17	61	1	271	284	267	324	447	771	7	86	29	0.54	33	21	46	106	46	2%	16	282	4.95	15.6	$13
Bats Right	05 PHI	392	48	103	12	47	0	263	276	259	323	418	742	8	91	26	1.00	38	21	40	94	27	0%	12	296	4.79	11.4	$10
Reliability 49	06 PHI	209	22	57	9	36	0	273	286	269	300	469	768	4	91	27	0.42	38	17	45	108	18	0%	8	285	4.73	2.3	$6
DL 62	1st Half	84	4	21	0	9	0	250			259	345	604	1	89	28	0.11	43	26	31	73	12	0%	1	296	2.93	-3.5	$0
BAvg Potl 60%	2nd Half	125	18	36	9	27	0	288			326	552	878	5	92	25	0.70	35	11	54	130	22	0%	6	285	5.91	5.5	$6
LIMA Plan D	07 Proj	316	36	86	12	47	0	272			313	451	764	6	90	27	0.59	37	19	43	104	27	0%	11	290	4.83	6.5	$9

Skills have held up well despite all the injuries. Went swinging for the fences in 2H to salvage his season and sure enough, it worked. Target the overall skill stability and hope for some bonus power upside.

Linden,Todd

	Yr	AB	R	H	HR	RBI	SB	Avg	vL	vR	OB	Slg	OPS	bb%	ct%	h%	Eye	G	L	F	PX	SX	SBO	xHR	xBA	RC/G	RAR	R$
Pos 7	02 a/a	492	72	134	11	54	10	272			363	407	769	12	76	34	0.60				95	94	10%	14		5.28	-4.7	$15
Age 26	03 aaa	471	61	114	7	45	11	242			290	346	636	6	82	28	0.38				69	106	14%	8		3.33	-30.3	$9
Pre-Peak	04 aaa	489	70	107	14	56	6	219			286	362	648	9	77	26	0.41				94	82	12%	15		3.46	-26.5	$8
Bats Both	05 SF	* 511	77	128	23	69	7	251	300	199	321	454	775	9	76	29	0.43	46	23	31	137	97	8%	23	293	5.10	-3.7	$17
Reliability 9	06 SF	* 264	38	66	6	22	5	249	208	302	326	397	723	10	80	29	0.56	42	28	30	92	116	7%	7	283	4.59	-5.1	$5
DL	1st Half	147	17	31	2	14	4	211			291	323	614	10	80	25	0.55				71	110	11%	3		3.23	-9.2	$1
BAvg Potl 55%	2nd Half	117	21	35	4	9	1	296			370	490	860	11	79	34	0.57	42	28	30	117	101	3%	4	300	6.30	3.4	$4
LIMA Plan D	07 Proj	253	38	66	8	26	4	261			333	430	763	10	78	31	0.50	43	25	32	108	104	7%	8	282	5.02	-2.6	$7

2-5-.273 in 77 AB at SF.
Reasons to keep an eye on him:
- 115 PX, 120 SX in majors
- LD tendency should translate to higher BA
- Slight growth in bb%, ct%, eye
- Right age for a spike

Lind,Adam

	Yr	AB	R	H	HR	RBI	SB	Avg	vL	vR	OB	Slg	OPS	bb%	ct%	h%	Eye	G	L	F	PX	SX	SBO	xHR	xBA	RC/G	RAR	R$
Pos 0	02	0	0	0	0	0	0	0							0							0		0				
Age 23	03	0	0	0	0	0	0	0							0							0		0				
Growth	04	0	0	0	0	0	0	0							0							0		0				
Bats Left	05	0	0	0	0	0	0	0							0							0		0				
Reliability 7	06 TOR	* 517	66	171	26	91	3	331	444	353	389	559	948	9	79	38	0.44	35	19	46	148	39	3%	26	284	7.21	10.6	$23
DL	1st Half	282	32	84	13	49	2	299			342	502	844	6	75	36	0.26				138	38	4%	13		5.86	-4.4	$10
BAvg Potl 25%	2nd Half	235	34	87	13	43	1	369			441	627	1068	12	83	40	0.77	35	19	46	159	30	1%	13	308	8.73	13.4	$13
LIMA Plan D+	07 Proj	381	50	110	15	68	2	289			355	487	842	9	80	33	0.51	35	19	46	133	45	3%	16	277	5.95	-0.7	$13

2-8-.367 in 60 AB at TOR. Impressive debut, with strong 2H growth in multiple skills. H% got a little high; xBA says he'll likely dip back below .300. Expect an adjustment period, but all in all, looks good for 2007.

LoDuca,Paul

	Yr	AB	R	H	HR	RBI	SB	Avg	vL	vR	OB	Slg	OPS	bb%	ct%	h%	Eye	G	L	F	PX	SX	SBO	xHR	xBA	RC/G	RAR	R$
Pos 2	02 LA	580	74	163	10	64	3	281	307	273	321	402	723	6	95	28	1.10	45	21	33	76	64	3%	11	307	4.55	7.2	$15
Age 35	03 LA	568	64	155	7	52	0	273	281	270	325	377	702	7	90	29	0.81	45	27	29	68	43	1%	9	305	4.35	0.9	$10
Decline	04 2NL	535	68	153	13	80	4	286	314	276	331	421	752	6	91	30	0.73	44	20	36	78	64	6%	13	288	4.78	14.8	$16
Bats Right	05 FLA	445	45	126	6	57	4	283	314	277	334	380	714	7	93	29	1.10	45	24	30	61	57	5%	7	300	4.52	9.2	$11
Reliability 80	06 NYM	512	80	163	5	49	3	318	336	311	349	428	777	4	93	34	0.63	45	21	34	71	70	2%	8	295	5.02	9.4	$16
DL	1st Half	244	34	69	3	22	3	283			316	398	714	5	94	29	0.80	49	18	34	73	69	5%	4	293	4.41	0.5	$6
BAvg Potl 50%	2nd Half	268	46	94	2	27	0	351			379	455	834	4	91	38	0.52	42	25	33	69	55	0%	4	297	5.61	8.6	$10
LIMA Plan D+	07 Proj	463	63	138	7	52	3	298			337	413	750	6	92	31	0.77	45	23	33	72	67	3%	9	299	4.79	8.7	$13

Ended four-year run of 2H fades thanks to huge H%. Superb ct% and LD% skills should keep him hovering around .300. Posted career-high in doubles, creating some xHR upside, though Shea (-22% RH HR) doesn't help.

Lofton,Kenny

	Yr	AB	R	H	HR	RBI	SB	Avg	vL	vR	OB	Slg	OPS	bb%	ct%	h%	Eye	G	L	F	PX	SX	SBO	xHR	xBA	RC/G	RAR	R$
Pos 8	02 2TM	532	98	139	11	51	29	261	248	265	349	414	763	12	86	29	0.99	42	21	37	92	155	25%	12	285	5.26	6.9	$20
Age 39	03 2NL	547	97	162	12	46	30	296	244	313	351	450	800	8	91	31	0.90	44	21	36	89	155	25%	12	300	5.47	7.5	$24
Decline	04 NYY	276	51	76	3	18	7	275	308	272	349	395	743	10	90	30	1.15	51	16	33	62	140	11%	3	276	5.03	2.6	$7
Bats Left	05 PHI	367	67	123	2	36	22	335	348	333	388	420	808	8	89	37	0.78	49	26	25	53	149	19%	3	298	5.57	9.7	$19
Reliability 35	06 LA	469	79	141	3	41	32	301	214	319	362	403	765	9	91	33	1.07	45	22	33	52	155	24%	3	277	5.20	9.9	$19
DL 15 17	1st Half	217	34	63	0	16	14	290			347	378	725	8	89	32	0.83	46	21	33	43	151	21%	0	265	4.71	1.6	$8
BAvg Potl 60%	2nd Half	252	45	78	3	25	18	310			374	425	799	9	92	33	1.37	44	22	34	60	145	26%	3	288	5.62	8.2	$12
LIMA Plan C+	07 Proj	255	45	74	2	22	15	290			354	395	748	9	90	32	1.00	47	22	32	58	155	22%	3	284	5.00	3.2	$10

Continues to laugh in the face of advancing age while running on legs that surely must be bionic. Power is the only skill that's waning, and that's not why you buy him anyway. With enough AB, can steal 25+ again.

Logan,Nook

	Yr	AB	R	H	HR	RBI	SB	Avg	vL	vR	OB	Slg	OPS	bb%	ct%	h%	Eye	G	L	F	PX	SX	SBO	xHR	xBA	RC/G	RAR	R$
Pos 8	02	0	0	0	0	0	0	0							0							0		0				
Age 27	03 aa	514	62	116	3	33	32	226			288	302	590	8	82	27	0.50				46	150	34%	4		2.90	-31.6	$11
Peak	04 DET	* 560	71	140	2	34	41	250	395	222	291	330	621	5	81	30	0.30	51	17	32	48	166	39%	3	244	3.13	-26.9	$15
Bats Both	05 DET	322	47	83	1	17	23	258	284	246	303	335	639	6	84	30	0.40	54	17	29	51	157	34%	2	260	3.43	-8.2	$10
Reliability 40	06 WAS	* 232	32	54	1	13	12	233	350	286	302	298	601	9	74	31	0.38	47	18	35	45	129	26%	2	213	2.91	-11.0	$4
DL	1st Half	65	8	11	0	4	3	164			253	224	477	11	75	22	0.47				41	128	31%	0		1.37	-6.8	($0)
BAvg Potl 35%	2nd Half	167	24	43	1	10	9	259			322	327	649	8	73	35	0.34	47	18	35	46	123	25%	2	213	3.52	-4.6	$4
LIMA Plan D	07 Proj	212	29	50	1	12	13	236			295	308	604	8	78	30	0.39	51	17	31	48	144	31%	2	236	2.98	-10.3	$5

1-8-.300 in 90 AB at WAS. Someone's going to see the speed and .300 BA in Sept and wildly overbid. And you're going to let them, safe in the knowledge that he barely has the skills of a .250 hitter.

Loney,James

	Yr	AB	R	H	HR	RBI	SB	Avg	vL	vR	OB	Slg	OPS	bb%	ct%	h%	Eye	G	L	F	PX	SX	SBO	xHR	xBA	RC/G	RAR	R$
Pos 3	02	0	0	0	0	0	0	0							0							0		0				
Age 22	03	0	0	0	0	0	0	0							0							0		0				
Growth	04 aa	395	37	88	4	34	5	223			295	303	598	9	83	26	0.60				54	59	11%	6		3.04	-29.8	$3
Bats Left	05 aa	500	59	121	9	51	0	242			306	350	656	8	86	27	0.65				71	37	4%	10		3.74	-24.2	$7
Reliability 0	06 LA	* 468	73	156	10	74	8	333	350	268	379	503	882	7	92	35	0.96	49	12	39	96	96	11%	11	292	6.32	4.0	$21
DL	1st Half	270	32	86	3	33	5	317			357	429	786	6	94	33	0.97	50	13	37	66	80	12%	4	272	5.24	-5.6	$9
BAvg Potl 50%	2nd Half	198	40	70	7	40	3	356			408	604	1012	8	91	37	0.95	48	11	41	139	114	9%	7	323	7.84	9.4	$12
LIMA Plan C+	07 Proj	433	61	126	12	58	7	291			347	460	808	8	88	31	0.74	42	20	38	100	92	10%	12	292	5.50	-4.3	$15

4-18-.284 in 102 AB at LA. Major growth season, with nice jumps in ct%, Eye and SX, plus a hint of emerging power in the 2nd half. But lack of experience means there will be some growing pains. Be patient.

BRANDON KRUSE

Lopez,Felipe			AB	R	H	HR	RBI	SB	Avg	vL	vR	OB	Slg	OPS	bb%	ct%	h%	Eye	G	L	F	PX	SX	SBO	xHR	xBA	RC/G	RAR	R$
Pos	6	02 TOR	* 455	64	117	10	48	16	257	303	204	327	400	727	9	74	33	0.40	47	21	31	102	123	16%	13	262	4.60	0.2	$13
Age	26	03 CIN	* 340	46	80	4	28	10	235	196	219	312	335	647	10	74	31	0.43	49	24	27	78	103	22%	6	255	3.58	-5.6	$6
Pre-Peak		04 CIN	* 557	75	135	15	66	3	242	292	226	299	384	683	7	75	30	0.33	44	18	38	96	72	6%	17	245	3.87	-4.4	$11
Bats	Both	05 CIN	580	97	169	23	85	15	291	244	312	355	486	841	9	81	33	0.51	54	20	27	124	115	13%	22	308	5.89	31.6	$26
Reliability	35	06 2NL	617	98	169	11	52	44	274	246	285	358	381	739	12	80	33	0.64	50	19	30	69	118	27%	13	258	4.83	8.5	$24
DL		1st Half	311	49	83	8	28	22	267			350	395	746	11	80	31	0.63	51	17	32	81	110	28%	9	260	4.87	4.7	$12
BAvg Potl	45%	2nd Half	306	49	86	3	24	22	281			366	366	732	12	79	35	0.65	50	22	29	57	120	26%	5	255	4.79	3.9	$12
LIMA Plan	C+	07 Proj	**597**	**93**	**162**	**9**	**53**	**28**	**271**			**345**	**381**	**726**	**10**	**79**	**33**	**0.53**	**51**	**20**	**29**	**75**	**122**	**20%**	**12**	**261**	**4.62**	**7.5**	**$20**

PRO: bb%, Eye, SX trends
CON: - Yearly & 2H PX trend
- Monthy PX's: 112, 79, 66, 45
- SB spike driven by opportunity (SBO), not skill (SX)
- Power ended after leaving CIN
Lots and lots of downside here.

Lopez,Javy			AB	R	H	HR	RBI	SB	Avg	vL	vR	OB	Slg	OPS	bb%	ct%	h%	Eye	G	L	F	PX	SX	SBO	xHR	xBA	RC/G	RAR	R$
Pos	2	02 ATL	347	31	81	11	52	0	233	255	230	287	372	659	7	82	26	0.41	52	17	31	90	20	1%	11	256	3.53	-6.1	$6
Age	36	03 ATL	457	89	150	43	109	0	328	336	326	373	687	1061	7	80	33	0.37	40	23	37	211	60	1%	32	353	8.25	47.8	$31
Decline		04 BAL	579	83	183	23	86	0	316	313	317	367	503	870	8	83	35	0.48	46	18	36	110	47	0%	21	283	6.11	27.6	$22
Bats	Right	05 BAL	395	47	110	15	49	0	278	287	276	312	458	770	5	83	30	0.28	46	22	32	115	38	1%	14	295	4.74	8.1	$11
Reliability	10	06 2AL	342	36	86	8	35	0	251	270	245	293	386	679	6	78	30	0.26	44	21	35	92	36	0%	9	256	3.73	-6.8	$5
DL	15 61	1st Half	217	24	60	6	26	0	276			317	429	746	6	79	33	0.28	42	22	36	101	44	0%	6	267	4.57	1.0	$5
BAvg Potl	40%	2nd Half	125	12	26	2	9	0	208			250	312	562	5	76	26	0.23	48	19	33	78	30	0%	3	237	2.23	-8.5	($0)
LIMA Plan	F	07 Proj	**231**	**27**	**61**	**5**	**27**	**0**	**264**			**306**	**399**	**705**	**6**	**80**	**31**	**0.30**	**46**	**20**	**34**	**90**	**47**	**0%**	**6**	**263**	**4.07**	**-1.2**	**$4**

Across-the-board declines since his '03 comeback. Stats say it's time for him to start his second career, but is he ready to give up a major league paycheck? Some people just don't know how to say good-bye.

Lopez,Jose			AB	R	H	HR	RBI	SB	Avg	vL	vR	OB	Slg	OPS	bb%	ct%	h%	Eye	G	L	F	PX	SX	SBO	xHR	xBA	RC/G	RAR	R$
Pos	4	02	0	0	0	0	0	0	0							0							0		0				
Age	23	03 aa	538	84	140	12	70	19	260			298	396	694	5	91	27	0.60				84	108	24%	13		4.10	-2.7	$18
Growth		04 SEA	* 482	66	130	17	60	5	270	214	238	304	440	744	5	89	27	0.44	42	21	38	99	66	8%	16	297	4.52	6.2	$13
Bats	Right	05 SEA	* 372	44	103	6	54	6	277	273	235	303	430	733	4	88	30	0.30	41	19	40	110	67	17%	9	295	4.43	3.2	$10
Reliability	53	06 SEA	603	78	170	10	79	5	282	331	265	312	405	716	4	87	31	0.33	49	18	33	72	100	5%	10	274	4.21	1.5	$15
DL		1st Half	311	47	88	9	56	2	283			312	479	791	4	86	31	0.30	44	17	38	112	116	3%	8	295	5.07	8.3	$10
BAvg Potl	45%	2nd Half	292	31	82	1	23	3	281			311	325	637	4	87	32	0.35	53	19	28	30	69	6%	2	251	3.31	-6.7	$5
LIMA Plan	C	07 Proj	**613**	**79**	**170**	**11**	**78**	**8**	**277**			**308**	**408**	**716**	**4**	**88**	**30**	**0.36**	**47**	**19**	**34**	**82**	**89**	**10%**	**13**	**284**	**4.23**	**2.0**	**$16**

Low FB% zaps power. OK wheels + no green light = few SB. Hit the wall in 2nd half, but did rebound a bit in September. For now, we'll put most of blame on stamina.

Loretta,Mark			AB	R	H	HR	RBI	SB	Avg	vL	vR	OB	Slg	OPS	bb%	ct%	h%	Eye	G	L	F	PX	SX	SBO	xHR	xBA	RC/G	RAR	R$
Pos	4	02 2NL	283	33	86	4	27	1	304	309	302	375	410	784	10	87	34	0.86	39	24	37	75	36	2%	6	280	5.39	7.6	$8
Age	35	03 SD	589	74	186	13	72	5	316	307	318	373	445	818	8	89	34	0.87	36	31	33	76	69	5%	13	311	5.64	19.8	$21
Decline		04 SD	620	108	208	16	76	5	335	352	329	392	495	887	9	93	34	1.29	40	22	38	94	72	4%	17	307	6.47	30.3	$27
Bats	Right	05 SD	404	54	113	3	38	8	280	309	269	352	347	698	10	92	30	1.32	40	28	32	44	80	9%	4	287	4.52	-0.5	$11
Reliability	18	06 BOS	635	75	181	5	59	4	285	274	290	336	361	697	7	90	31	0.78	35	27	38	51	56	3%	8	278	4.27	2.6	$12
DL	60	1st Half	309	37	98	2	32	2	317			353	395	748	5	91	34	0.61	38	27	35	54	49	3%	4	288	4.71	4.9	$8
BAvg Potl	60%	2nd Half	326	38	83	3	27	2	255			321	328	649	9	89	28	0.91	33	27	40	49	52	2%	4	270	3.82	-2.8	$4
LIMA Plan	C	07 Proj	**545**	**71**	**155**	**3**	**54**	**3**	**284**			**345**	**360**	**704**	**8**	**91**	**31**	**0.98**	**37**	**26**	**36**	**52**	**58**	**3%**	**6**	**280**	**4.47**	**5.4**	**$11**

Tanked in September for second straight year, but skill foundation's still good. Mention his 2nd half fade on draft day, get him cheap, then sell him mid-season while he's still got a .300 BA.

Lowell,Mike			AB	R	H	HR	RBI	SB	Avg	vL	vR	OB	Slg	OPS	bb%	ct%	h%	Eye	G	L	F	PX	SX	SBO	xHR	xBA	RC/G	RAR	R$
Pos	5	02 FLA	597	88	165	24	92	4	276	255	283	347	471	818	10	85	29	0.71	30	22	49	126	53	4%	24	291	5.65	18.1	$22
Age	33	03 FLA	492	76	136	32	105	3	276	295	271	350	530	881	10	84	27	0.72	33	22	45	147	61	3%	26	310	6.29	28.6	$23
Past Peak		04 FLA	598	87	175	27	85	5	293	344	279	361	505	866	10	87	30	0.83	32	19	49	124	64	4%	25	292	6.19	18.8	$23
Bats	Right	05 FLA	500	56	118	8	58	4	236	308	222	300	360	660	8	88	25	0.79	32	21	47	84	75	3%	11	268	3.91	-13.0	$8
Reliability	28	06 BOS	573	79	163	20	80	2	284	241	302	339	475	813	8	89	29	0.77	38	22	41	114	48	3%	20	308	5.53	8.4	$17
DL		1st Half	274	39	84	9	40	1	307			360	507	868	8	92	31	1.00	37	25	38	120	59	1%	9	329	6.19	8.8	$9
BAvg Potl	60%	2nd Half	299	40	79	11	40	1	264			319	445	764	7	87	27	0.63	38	19	43	108	41	4%	11	287	4.90	-0.9	$7
LIMA Plan	C+	07 Proj	**545**	**73**	**158**	**18**	**75**	**3**	**290**			**349**	**470**	**819**	**8**	**88**	**30**	**0.77**	**35**	**21**	**44**	**110**	**54**	**3%**	**18**	**293**	**5.62**	**12.3**	**$17**

Reversed LH/RH split from year before. End result was what we've come to expect. 120+ PX in four of six months, but with FB% trend and xBA, a .300 BA may be more likely than 20 HR.

Lugo,Julio			AB	R	H	HR	RBI	SB	Avg	vL	vR	OB	Slg	OPS	bb%	ct%	h%	Eye	G	L	F	PX	SX	SBO	xHR	xBA	RC/G	RAR	R$
Pos	64	02 HOU	322	45	84	8	35	9	261	270	258	320	388	708	8	77	32	0.38	47	21	32	90	101	14%	9	261	4.21	2.9	$10
Age	31	03 2TM	498	64	135	15	55	12	271	240	284	330	410	740	8	80	31	0.44	47	23	30	84	101	11%	14	274	4.58	4.5	$15
Past Peak		04 TAM	581	83	160	7	75	21	275	300	267	337	396	733	9	82	33	0.51	49	18	33	84	121	16%	11	269	4.67	3.4	$18
Bats	Right	05 TAM	616	89	182	6	57	39	295	306	291	359	403	762	9	88	33	0.85	49	20	31	71	131	26%	9	288	5.11	9.6	$24
Reliability	84	06 2TM	435	69	121	12	37	24	278	263	284	338	421	758	8	83	31	0.51	47	20	34	87	114	27%	12	274	4.86	6.0	$16
DL	31	1st Half	201	36	60	8	18	11	299			359	488	847	9	85	32	0.61	50	19	31	115	96	26%	8	305	5.91	8.6	$9
BAvg Potl	45%	2nd Half	234	33	61	4	19	13	261			319	363	682	8	81	31	0.44	44	20	36	63	125	27%	4	247	3.92	-3.2	$7
LIMA Plan	C+	07 Proj	**504**	**80**	**141**	**15**	**58**	**26**	**280**			**340**	**435**	**776**	**8**	**83**	**31**	**0.55**	**48**	**20**	**33**	**95**	**120**	**24%**	**15**	**285**	**5.08**	**11.0**	**$20**

Hit the wall after trade to LA:

	BA	PX
TAM	.308	114
LA	.219	34

Recent PX and FB% trends put 15 HR within reach. Should rebound; profit potential here.

Luna,Hector			AB	R	H	HR	RBI	SB	Avg	vL	vR	OB	Slg	OPS	bb%	ct%	h%	Eye	G	L	F	PX	SX	SBO	xHR	xBA	RC/G	RAR	R$
Pos	46	02	0	0	0	0	0	0	0							0							0		0				
Age	27	03 aa	462	78	126	2	34	16	273			333	329	662	8	87	31	0.68				41	112	14%	4		3.86	-5.5	$13
Peak		04 STL	173	25	43	3	22	6	249	240	255	301	364	665	7	79	30	0.35	42	24	35	74	125	20%	3	254	3.66	-4.9	$5
Bats	Right	05 STL	* 360	45	83	3	35	19	231	304	256	281	333	614	6	85	26	0.45	49	21	30	73	134	33%	5	279	3.19	-15.3	$8
Reliability	31	06 2TM	350	41	100	6	38	5	286	315	261	337	409	745	7	83	33	0.45	44	23	33	80	75	9%	8	274	4.70	3.4	$9
DL		1st Half	170	23	54	3	14	3	318			363	441	804	7	86	36	0.50	43	24	32	77	77	12%	4	286	5.35	4.6	$6
BAvg Potl	45%	2nd Half	180	18	46	3	24	2	256			313	378	691	8	80	30	0.42	44	21	34	83	68	7%	4	262	4.05	-1.7	$3
LIMA Plan	F	07 Proj	**209**	**27**	**55**	**3**	**22**	**5**	**263**			**316**	**371**	**687**	**7**	**83**	**31**	**0.45**	**44**	**22**	**33**	**74**	**92**	**14%**	**4**	**269**	**4.00**	**-2.1**	**$5**

BA will drop, but he could hit 10 HR in 400 AB if PX and FB% continue ascent. And if he gets 400 AB.

Mabry,John			AB	R	H	HR	RBI	SB	Avg	vL	vR	OB	Slg	OPS	bb%	ct%	h%	Eye	G	L	F	PX	SX	SBO	xHR	xBA	RC/G	RAR	R$
Pos	3	02 2TM	214	28	59	11	43	1	276	192	287	323	500	823	7	80	30	0.36	43	14	43	140	62	4%	10	282	5.48	-1.6	$9
Age	36	03 SEA	104	12	22	3	16	0	212		224	311	356	667	13	80	24	0.71	48	18	34	97	23	0%	3	257	3.93	-4.7	$1
Decline		04 STL	* 376	51	107	21	64	0	285	333	285	352	497	849	9	76	32	0.44	42	18	40	131	22	1%	19	266	5.97	0.2	$14
Bats	Left	05 STL	246	26	59	8	32	0	240	226	243	297	407	703	8	74	29	0.32	45	22	33	120	38	0%	9	268	4.13	-10.8	$5
Reliability	7	06 CHC	210	16	43	5	25	0	205	316	194	283	324	607	10	73	26	0.40	41	14	45	80	31	0%	6	205	2.93	-20.1	$1
DL		1st Half	87	6	19	1	5	0	218			292	299	591	9	77	27	0.45	49	16	34	59	13	0%	2	209	2.80	-8.5	($0)
BAvg Potl	50%	2nd Half	123	10	24	4	20	0	195			277	341	619	10	70	24	0.38	35	12	53	96	40	0%	4	199	3.06	-11.4	$1
LIMA Plan	F	07 Proj	**127**	**12**	**29**	**4**	**17**	**0**	**228**			**299**	**373**	**673**	**9**	**74**	**28**	**0.40**	**43**	**17**	**41**	**99**	**22**	**0%**	**4**	**231**	**3.76**	**-8.0**	**$2**

Was paid a million bucks for 19 productive AB against LHers. There's gotta be some good clubhouse CI/OF types in Triple-A with pop, and they'd come at a third of his price. Stay away.

Mackowiak,Rob			AB	R	H	HR	RBI	SB	Avg	vL	vR	OB	Slg	OPS	bb%	ct%	h%	Eye	G	L	F	PX	SX	SBO	xHR	xBA	RC/G	RAR	R$
Pos	879	02 PIT	385	57	94	16	48	9	244	302	237	319	426	744	10	69	31	0.35	44	16	40	140	82	12%	18	250	4.84	-0.3	$12
Age	30	03 PIT	* 391	37	92	8	38	12	235	257	273	288	358	646	7	75	29	0.30	48	25	27	81	121	16%	9	263	3.38	-18.9	$7
Peak		04 PIT	491	65	121	17	75	13	246	164	258	316	420	736	9	77	29	0.44	46	20	33	108	121	13%	17	270	4.62	-0.5	$15
Bats	Left	05 PIT	463	57	126	9	58	8	272	275	272	334	389	723	8	78	33	0.43	51	20	30	80	92	9%	10	261	4.45	-1.5	$13
Reliability	71	06 CHW	255	31	74	5	23	5	290	222	308	360	404	764	10	77	36	0.47	54	17	29	78	73	8%	6	249	5.06	2.9	$7
DL		1st Half	143	17	40	2	12	0	280			356	378	734	11	80	34	0.59	49	17	34	71	29	2%	3	238	4.73	0.3	$2
BAvg Potl	30%	2nd Half	112	14	34	3	11	5	304			366	437	803	9	73	39	0.37	62	16	22	88	100	16%	3	257	5.56	2.8	$4
LIMA Plan	D	07 Proj	**304**	**38**	**79**	**6**	**34**	**7**	**260**			**328**	**381**	**709**	**9**	**76**	**32**	**0.42**	**52**	**18**	**29**	**83**	**96**	**11%**	**7**	**254**	**4.31**	**-2.5**	**$7**

Hail the .290 BA, but...
- Elevated 36% hit rate
- Poor 2nd half ct%
- .249 xBA
FB%, PX, and SX trends give little hope for a power/speed rebound either.

STEPHEN NICKRAND

Markakis,Nick			AB	R	H	HR	RBI	SB	Avg	vL	vR	OB	Slg	OPS	bb%	ct%	h%	Eye	G	L	F	PX	SX	SBO	xHR	xBA	RC/G	RAR	R$
Pos	97	02	0	0	0	0	0	0	0							0							0		0				
Age	23	03	0	0	0	0	0	0	0							0							0		0				
Growth		04	0	0	0	0	0	0	0							0							0		0				
Bats	Left	05 aa	120	19	39	3	28	0	325			413	533	946	13	78	40	0.69				158	65	3%	5		7.68	8.7	$6
Reliability	0	06 BAL	491	72	143	16	62	2	291	286	293	348	448	796	8	85	32	0.60	51	20	29	92	67	1%	15	292	5.29	-5.0	$15
DL		1st Half	196	25	49	2	19	0	250			316	337	653	9	82	30	0.53	50	22	28	55	63	0%	3	258	3.67	-11.5	$2
BAvg Potl	50%	2nd Half	295	47	94	14	43	2	319			370	522	892	8	88	33	0.67	52	18	30	115	53	2%	12	312	6.30	5.1	$12
LIMA Plan	C+	07 Proj	**535**	**81**	**159**	**18**	**90**	**1**	**297**			**368**	**484**	**852**	**10**	**82**	**33**	**0.64**	**51**	**20**	**29**	**120**	**59**	**2%**	**19**	**301**	**6.12**	**13.4**	**$19**

Initially struggled with jump from Double-A, but impressed in 2H despite hitting the wall in Sept. .300 is a good possibility, and there are hints that 20 HR may be within reach soon as well.

Marrero,Eli			AB	R	H	HR	RBI	SB	Avg	vL	vR	OB	Slg	OPS	bb%	ct%	h%	Eye	G	L	F	PX	SX	SBO	xHR	xBA	RC/G	RAR	R$
Pos	7	02 STL	397	63	104	18	66	14	262	227	273	330	451	780	9	82	28	0.56	36	20	44	118	108	15%	16	277	5.09	-14.9	$17
Age	33	03 STL	107	10	24	2	20	0	224	259	222	272	355	627	6	83	25	0.39	35	13	52	77	88	4%	2	226	3.24	-7.7	$2
Past Peak		04 ATL	250	37	80	10	40	4	320	415	250	377	520	897	8	80	37	0.46	45	16	39	128	77	7%	10	281	6.57	7.6	$12
Bats	Right	05 2AL	138	19	25	7	19	1	181	247	61	242	413	655	7	72	19	0.29	39	7	54	156	110	5%	7	248	3.43	-5.7	$2
Reliability	0	06 2NL	93	11	19	6	15	5	204	138	234	315	441	756	14	67	23	0.48	38	13	49	161	65	21%	6	240	5.06	-0.6	$3
DL	66	1st Half	72	9	16	5	13	5	222			333	486	819	14	71	24	0.57	39	16	45	172	69	26%	5	271	5.88	1.4	$3
BAvg Potl	55%	2nd Half	21	2	3	1	2	0	143			250	286	536	12	52	20	0.30	33	0	67	110	15	0%	1		1.84	-2.4	($0)
LIMA Plan	D	07 Proj	**108**	**14**	**26**	**5**	**18**	**3**	**241**			**315**	**460**	**774**	**10**	**76**	**27**	**0.46**	**40**	**14**	**46**	**138**	**99**	**14%**	**5**	**265**	**5.10**	**-0.9**	**$4**

Flirted with the Mendoza line in '05 and '06 due to depressed h%. Growth in bb% offset by decline in ct%. If there's any glimmer of hope at age 33, it's his PX. Any unexpected ABs could mean some surprise HRs.

Marte,Andy			AB	R	H	HR	RBI	SB	Avg	vL	vR	OB	Slg	OPS	bb%	ct%	h%	Eye	G	L	F	PX	SX	SBO	xHR	xBA	RC/G	RAR	R$
Pos	5	02	0	0	0	0	0	0	0							0							0		0				
Age	23	03	0	0	0	0	0	0	0							0							0		0				
Growth		04 aa	387	48	101	21	64	1	260			352	499	851	12	78	29	0.63				152	38	2%	21		6.19	13.6	$12
Bats	Right	05 ATL *	446	53	117	20	76	0	262	174	118	362	468	830	14	82	28	0.88	35	13	52	130	32	3%	20	263	5.99	15.9	$14
Reliability	19	06 CLE *	521	69	128	19	69	1	246	227	225	310	433	742	8	78	28	0.42	34	17	48	125	54	1%	20	261	4.66	-5.3	$11
DL		1st Half	275	41	69	11	35	1	252			322	420	742	9	79	29	0.48				108	50	1%	11		4.65	-2.9	$6
BAvg Potl	50%	2nd Half	246	28	59	8	35	0	240			295	447	742	7	78	28	0.36	34	17	48	145	41	0%	10	275	4.67	-2.5	$4
LIMA Plan	C	07 Proj	**433**	**54**	**110**	**18**	**66**	**1**	**254**			**333**	**456**	**790**	**11**	**80**	**28**	**0.58**	**34**	**17**	**49**	**133**	**37**	**2%**	**19**	**268**	**5.36**	**6.9**	**$11**

5-23-.226 in 164 ABs at CLE. Former ATL prospect finally got a chance in 2006 with mixed results. PX is there to hit 20 HRs if he can earn enough ABs, but there's BA downside.

Martinez,Ramon			AB	R	H	HR	RBI	SB	Avg	vL	vR	OB	Slg	OPS	bb%	ct%	h%	Eye	G	L	F	PX	SX	SBO	xHR	xBA	RC/G	RAR	R$
Pos	45	02 SF	181	26	49	4	25	2	271	254	279	323	414	737	7	86	30	0.54	32	23	45	91	104	4%	4	271	4.63	1.1	$6
Age	34	03 CHC	293	30	83	3	34	0	283	346	259	338	375	713	8	83	33	0.48	43	23	33	66	42	1%	5	264	4.34	-0.5	$6
Past Peak		04 CHC	260	22	64	3	30	1	246	243	247	315	346	661	9	85	28	0.65	39	19	42	68	49	1%	4	248	3.85	-5.8	$3
Bats	Right	05 2TM	112	11	31	1	14	0	277	255	292	314	330	644	5	90	30	0.55	47	23	30	34	25	0%	1	261	3.50	-2.7	$2
Reliability	18	06 LA	176	20	49	2	24	0	278	289	275	335	364	699	8	89	31	0.75	44	19	37	51	44	0%	2	253	4.28	-1.6	$4
DL	19	1st Half	100	14	34	1	17	0	340			389	440	829	7	90	37	0.80	46	21	33	59	57	0%	1	276	5.75	3.0	$4
BAvg Potl	50%	2nd Half	76	6	15	1	7	0	197			265	263	528	8	87	22	0.70	41	17	42	39	19	0%	1	217	2.28	-5.5	($0)
LIMA Plan	F	07 Proj	**134**	**14**	**34**	**2**	**16**	**0**	**254**			**309**	**326**	**635**	**7**	**88**	**28**	**0.65**	**43**	**20**	**37**	**46**	**31**	**0%**	**2**	**248**	**3.48**	**-4.3**	**$2**

An 89% contact rate and little else. The only rising trend that we can count on with 100% certainty is his age.

Martinez,Victor			AB	R	H	HR	RBI	SB	Avg	vL	vR	OB	Slg	OPS	bb%	ct%	h%	Eye	G	L	F	PX	SX	SBO	xHR	xBA	RC/G	RAR	R$
Pos	23	02 aa	443	73	139	20	74	3	314			383	535	918	10	87	33	0.86				138	50	5%	19		6.84	35.8	$21
Age	28	03 CLE *	445	53	133	8	58	4	299	271	300	350	407	757	7	88	33	0.66	47	25	28	70	43	7%	9	293	4.86	9.6	$13
Peak		04 CLE	520	77	147	23	108	0	283	282	283	357	492	849	10	87	29	0.87	40	16	44	123	38	1%	22	290	6.05	25.2	$19
Bats	Both	05 CLE	547	73	167	20	80	0	305	274	320	377	475	852	10	86	33	0.81	48	21	32	106	22	1%	20	293	6.08	30.8	$20
Reliability	99	06 CLE	572	82	181	16	93	0	316	290	332	392	465	857	11	86	35	0.91	44	22	34	92	25	0%	17	286	6.23	27.9	$20
DL		1st Half	273	39	80	10	50	0	293			359	462	820	9	89	30	0.90	43	19	38	97	27	0%	9	286	5.66	9.5	$9
BAvg Potl	45%	2nd Half	299	43	101	6	43	0	338			421	468	889	13	84	39	0.91	45	24	31	88	24	0%	8	286	6.76	18.2	$11
LIMA Plan	C	07 Proj	**563**	**80**	**174**	**17**	**91**	**0**	**309**			**383**	**466**	**849**	**11**	**86**	**33**	**0.86**	**44**	**21**	**35**	**98**	**29**	**1%**	**18**	**288**	**6.10**	**28.3**	**$20**

PRO: Consistent BPIs and Rel score makes him as safe a bet as there is among catchers. CON: Declining PX and FB% makes '04 power output look like anomaly.

Martin,Russell			AB	R	H	HR	RBI	SB	Avg	vL	vR	OB	Slg	OPS	bb%	ct%	h%	Eye	G	L	F	PX	SX	SBO	xHR	xBA	RC/G	RAR	R$
Pos	2	02	0	0	0	0	0	0	0							0							0		0				
Age	24	03	0	0	0	0	0	0	0							0							0		0				
Growth		04	0	0	0	0	0	0	0							0							0		0				
Bats	Right	05 aa	405	67	108	7	48	12	267			361	358	719	13	86	30	1.05				57	87	14%	8		4.74	10.0	$13
Reliability	0	06 LA *	489	76	136	10	72	10	278	366	265	351	425	776	10	87	31	0.83	50	20	30	90	92	12%	12	297	5.30	13.5	$16
DL		1st Half	234	34	66	4	40	3	282			356	419	775	10	87	31	0.87	52	17	31	85	77	8%	5	285	5.31	6.5	$7
BAvg Potl	60%	2nd Half	255	42	70	6	32	7	275			346	431	778	10	86	30	0.80	50	22	29	96	99	15%	7	304	5.28	7.0	$8
LIMA Plan	C+	07 Proj	**448**	**72**	**127**	**9**	**60**	**11**	**283**			**364**	**411**	**775**	**11**	**86**	**31**	**0.92**	**50**	**20**	**30**	**79**	**94**	**13%**	**10**	**288**	**5.32**	**15.7**	**$16**

Seized starting catcher job and never let go. Maintained Eye and BPIs from minors, and .297 xBA indicates there's BA upside. Only mediocre power, but he's still developing.

Matheny,Mike			AB	R	H	HR	RBI	SB	Avg	vL	vR	OB	Slg	OPS	bb%	ct%	h%	Eye	G	L	F	PX	SX	SBO	xHR	xBA	RC/G	RAR	R$
Pos	2	02 STL	315	31	77	3	35	1	244	265	239	314	317	632	9	84	28	0.65	50	16	34	51	44	4%	4	237	3.48	-5.9	$4
Age	36	03 STL	441	43	111	8	47	1	252	340	226	320	356	676	9	82	29	0.54	40	23	37	68	48	2%	9	256	3.92	-4.9	$7
Decline		04 STL	385	28	95	5	50	0	247	247	247	289	348	637	6	78	30	0.28	50	17	34	74	27	2%	7	234	3.25	-6.4	$5
Bats	Right	05 SF	443	42	107	13	59	0	242	269	233	288	406	694	6	79	28	0.32	41	25	34	118	22	2%	15	289	3.97	2.4	$8
Reliability	15	06 SF	160	10	37	3	18	0	231	364	181	272	338	610	5	81	27	0.30	39	20	41	70	10	0%	3	236	2.90	-7.0	$1
DL	122	1st Half	160	10	37	3	18	0	231			272	338	610	5	81	27	0.30	39	20	41	70	10	0%	3	236	2.90	-7.0	$1
BAvg Potl	50%	2nd Half	0	0	0	0	0	0	0																				
LIMA Plan	F	07 Proj	**164**	**13**	**40**	**3**	**20**	**0**	**244**			**293**	**354**	**647**	**7**	**81**	**29**	**0.36**	**43**	**20**	**37**	**76**	**24**	**2%**	**4**	**248**	**3.41**	**-3.4**	**$2**

After a career season in '05, he took a foul ball to the head on the last day of May and never played another inning. Expect little if returns from post-concussion syndrome.

Mathis,Jeff			AB	R	H	HR	RBI	SB	Avg	vL	vR	OB	Slg	OPS	bb%	ct%	h%	Eye	G	L	F	PX	SX	SBO	xHR	xBA	RC/G	RAR	R$
Pos	2	02	0	0	0	0	0	0	0							0							0		0				
Age	24	03 aa	95	17	26	2	13	1	276			348	453	801	10	86	30	0.79				125	68	13%	3		5.61	3.9	$3
Growth		04 aa	432	46	87	10	45	2	201			268	331	599	8	81	23	0.47				83	70	3%	11		2.91	-15.7	$3
Bats	Right	05 aaa	427	59	105	16	56	3	246			296	420	717	7	86	25	0.52				105	76	8%	14		4.29	4.9	$11
Reliability	3	06 ANA *	439	57	106	6	41	2	241	133	150	285	364	650	6	83	28	0.37	29	12	59	85	75	3%	9	221	3.52	-11.6	$5
DL		1st Half	239	30	56	3	21	1	235			280	346	625	6	84	27	0.39				79	62	3%	4		3.26	-8.3	$2
BAvg Potl	40%	2nd Half	200	27	50	3	20	1	250			292	387	679	6	83	29	0.34	29	12	59	93	87	3%	5	225	3.85	-3.3	$3
LIMA Plan	F	07 Proj	**122**	**16**	**29**	**3**	**13**	**1**	**238**			**287**	**391**	**677**	**6**	**84**	**26**	**0.43**	**29**	**12**	**59**	**98**	**80**	**5%**	**3**	**233**	**3.86**	**-1.4**	**$2**

2-6-.145 in 55 AB with ANA. Even at Triple-A, production took a step back in almost every category, including HRs. Only bright spot is that he's young enough to rebound.

Matos,Luis			AB	R	H	HR	RBI	SB	Avg	vL	vR	OB	Slg	OPS	bb%	ct%	h%	Eye	G	L	F	PX	SX	SBO	xHR	xBA	RC/G	RAR	R$
Pos	7	02 aa	249	28	56	8	35	13	225			301	382	682	10	81	25	0.57				101	102	30%	8		3.99	-12.6	$8
Age	28	03 BAL *	614	96	181	14	68	21	295	269	314	338	440	778	6	80	35	0.33	38	27	35	97	119	18%	16	279	5.01	-5.6	$23
Peak		04 BAL	330	36	74	6	28	12	224	133	267	266	333	600	5	82	26	0.32	46	17	37	74	91	23%	7	252	2.81	-21.7	$5
Bats	Right	05 BAL	389	53	109	4	32	17	280	297	270	327	373	700	6	85	32	0.47	43	19	38	64	109	24%	6	255	4.15	-6.5	$12
Reliability	15	06 2TM	136	16	28	2	5	7	206	219	194	260	331	591	7	83	23	0.43	44	17	39	83	129	27%	3	258	2.88	-9.9	$2
DL	18 39	1st Half	112	14	23	2	5	7	205			270	339	610	8	82	23	0.50	39	17	44	87	136	30%	3	249	3.14	-7.3	$2
BAvg Potl	65%	2nd Half	24	2	5	0	0	0	208			208	292	500	0	88	24	0.00	67	14	19	66	40	0%	0	272	1.65	-2.7	($0)
LIMA Plan	D	07 Proj	**325**	**41**	**83**	**4**	**27**	**10**	**255**			**308**	**363**	**671**	**7**	**82**	**30**	**0.43**	**42**	**19**	**39**	**74**	**105**	**17%**	**6**	**252**	**3.81**	**-13.3**	**$7**

H% partially to blame for his plunging BA, and otherwise static BPIs. Let go by BAL and later cut by WAS, but SX and decent hitting skills say double-digits SBs are still possible if he can find work.

JEFFREY TOMICH

Matsui,Hideki

		Year	AB	R	H	HR	RBI	SB	Avg	vL	vR	OB	Slg	OPS	bb%	ct%	h%	Eye	G	L	F	PX	SX	SBO	xHR	xBA	RC/G	RAR	R$
Pos	7	02 JPN	500	106	156	30	102	3	312			419	552	971	16	79	34	0.88				148	70	3%	28		7.84	30.2	$28
Age	32	03 NYY	623	82	179	16	106	2	287	287	287	353	435	788	9	86	31	0.73	55	21	24	95	45	2%	18	302	5.32	-0.2	$19
Past Peak		04 NYY	584	109	174	31	108	3	298	265	314	390	522	912	13	82	32	0.85	41	19	39	131	75	2%	29	295	6.93	31.9	$26
Bats	Left	05 NYY	629	108	192	23	116	2	305	354	278	368	496	865	9	88	32	0.81	47	16	36	117	64	2%	22	303	6.18	25.1	$26
Reliability	45	06 NYY	172	32	52	8	29	1	302	226	336	397	494	891	14	87	31	1.17	39	17	44	108	49	2%	7	281	6.70	7.2	$7
DL	124	1st Half	119	21	31	5	19	0	261			353	454	807	13	87	26	1.13	40	15	44	113	37	0%	5	281	5.69	1.8	$3
BAvg Potl	55%	2nd Half	53	11	21	3	10	1	396			492	585	1077	16	85	43	1.25	36	21	43	98	47	4%	2	277	9.01	4.8	$4
LIMA Plan	B	07 Proj	**593**	**110**	**181**	**25**	**107**	**5**	**305**			**394**	**486**	**880**	**13**	**85**	**32**	**1.01**	**42**	**19**	**39**	**106**	**69**	**2%**	**23**	**285**	**6.54**	**24.5**	**$26**

Season derailed by unexpected injury to a previous Reliability stud, but Eye improved and other BPIs remained solid over small sample, so expect return to form. If FB trend continues, could take another run at 30 HR.

Matsui,Kazuo

		Year	AB	R	H	HR	RBI	SB	Avg	vL	vR	OB	Slg	OPS	bb%	ct%	h%	Eye	G	L	F	PX	SX	SBO	xHR	xBA	RC/G	RAR	R$
Pos	4	02 JPN	582	116	180	22	85	30	309			356	531	887	7	82	35	0.40				141	168	24%	22		6.38	34.5	$33
Age	31	03 JPN	587	101	167	20	82	12	284			334	468	802	7	80	33	0.38				117	126	10%	20		5.33	17.7	$23
Past Peak		04 NYM	460	65	125	7	44	14	272	306	262	330	396	726	8	79	33	0.41	48	23	29	89	107	14%	10	276	4.51	-1.3	$13
Bats	Both	05 NYM	267	31	68	3	24	6	255	279	246	292	352	644	5	84	29	0.33	51	22	27	60	123	11%	3	276	3.39	-9.2	$5
Reliability	22	06 2NL	* 370	56	98	6	40	13	266	119	299	309	375	684	6	82	31	0.35	48	20	31	69	121	15%	7	264	3.87	-7.8	$11
DL	24 51	1st Half	164	14	37	1	8	2	224			260	296	555	5	86	25	0.35	50	17	33	51	53	6%	2	250	2.42	-10.9	$0
BAvg Potl	40%	2nd Half	206	43	62	5	33	11	299			347	438	786	7	78	36	0.34	47	24	29	85	152	21%	5	271	5.17	3.3	$10
LIMA Plan	D+	07 Proj	**394**	**58**	**107**	**9**	**43**	**15**	**272**			**316**	**405**	**722**	**6**	**82**	**31**	**0.36**	**50**	**22**	**29**	**83**	**132**	**16%**	**9**	**281**	**4.32**	**-2.8**	**$13**

Quietly showed signs of life in COL after flameout in NY. SX trend says double digit SB is repeatable. Uptick in FB% and 2nd half PX give some hope of more power, too.

Matthews Jr.,Gary

		Year	AB	R	H	HR	RBI	SB	Avg	vL	vR	OB	Slg	OPS	bb%	ct%	h%	Eye	G	L	F	PX	SX	SBO	xHR	xBA	RC/G	RAR	R$
Pos	8	02 2TM	345	54	95	7	38	15	275	239	292	356	426	782	11	80	33	0.62	55	17	28	106	124	19%	9	288	5.39	5.7	$13
Age	32	03 2TM	468	71	116	6	42	12	248	287	233	311	359	670	8	80	30	0.45	50	20	30	82	102	17%	9	268	3.85	-14.3	$10
Past Peak		04 TEX	* 428	60	117	18	60	8	273	244	289	348	474	822	10	79	31	0.55	45	24	31	123	100	8%	17	296	5.74	12.6	$14
Bats	Both	05 TEX	475	72	121	17	55	9	255	241	260	322	436	758	9	81	28	0.52	51	17	32	114	116	9%	16	290	4.88	8.4	$14
Reliability	21	06 TEX	620	102	194	19	79	10	313	314	313	372	495	867	9	84	35	0.59	51	19	30	112	97	9%	20	303	6.21	26.3	$23
DL	19	1st Half	280	42	91	8	41	4	325			376	529	905	8	84	37	0.50	48	19	33	129	101	8%	9	309	6.65	14.9	$11
BAvg Potl	40%	2nd Half	340	60	103	11	38	6	303			368	468	836	9	84	33	0.66	53	19	28	99	88	10%	11	296	5.85	11.3	$12
LIMA Plan	B	07 Proj	**559**	**88**	**160**	**16**	**69**	**9**	**286**			**351**	**453**	**804**	**9**	**82**	**32**	**0.56**	**51**	**19**	**30**	**105**	**100**	**9%**	**17**	**290**	**5.49**	**14.4**	**$18**

Career year or breakout? Improved ct%, but jump in BA fueled by H%. Career-high in RBI a product of increased ABs. In other words, don't bet on a repeat.

Mauer,Joe

		Year	AB	R	H	HR	RBI	SB	Avg	vL	vR	OB	Slg	OPS	bb%	ct%	h%	Eye	G	L	F	PX	SX	SBO	xHR	xBA	RC/G	RAR	R$
Pos	2	02	0	0	0	0	0	0	0							0							0		0				
Age	24	03 aa	276	43	92	3	37	0	333			383	438	821	7	92	35	1.05				68	51	0%	4		5.70	10.9	$10
Growth		04 MIN	107	18	33	6	17	1	308	182	365	373	570	943	9	87	31	0.79	46	18	36	146	81	3%	5	328	7.04	7.9	$5
Bats	Left	05 MIN	489	61	144	9	55	13	294	232	323	373	411	784	11	87	32	0.95	52	24	24	75	93	8%	11	303	5.42	19.0	$16
Reliability	8	06 MIN	521	86	181	13	84	8	347	331	356	433	507	940	13	90	37	1.46	49	25	26	94	86	5%	15	325	7.38	40.0	$24
DL		1st Half	260	43	102	5	37	7	392			463	538	1001	12	90	43	1.26	48	27	25	93	84	7%	7	329	7.98	22.2	$14
BAvg Potl	55%	2nd Half	261	43	79	8	47	1	303			405	475	880	15	90	31	1.67	50	23	27	96	72	3%	8	319	6.78	17.1	$10
LIMA Plan	B	07 Proj	**526**	**81**	**169**	**15**	**88**	**6**	**321**			**400**	**488**	**888**	**12**	**89**	**34**	**1.18**	**50**	**23**	**27**	**98**	**84**	**4%**	**16**	**320**	**6.66**	**34.0**	**$22**

Continued growth in bb%, ct% and eye, along with xBA, say he's a legit .320 hitter. Increased FB could help some of his 36 doubles turn into HR. At 23, power is still developing. UP: 20 HR

McCann,Brian

		Year	AB	R	H	HR	RBI	SB	Avg	vL	vR	OB	Slg	OPS	bb%	ct%	h%	Eye	G	L	F	PX	SX	SBO	xHR	xBA	RC/G	RAR	R$
Pos	2	02	0	0	0	0	0	0	0							0							0		0				
Age	23	03	0	0	0	0	0	0	0							0							0		0				
Growth		04	0	0	0	0	0	0	0							0							0		0				
Bats	Left	05 ATL	* 346	43	90	10	46	3	260	344	259	337	408	744	10	86	28	0.82	42	23	35	92	55	7%	10	290	4.86	10.9	$9
Reliability	0	06 ATL	442	61	147	24	93	2	333	266	351	389	572	962	8	88	34	0.76	35	22	43	135	38	2%	21	317	7.16	32.6	$23
DL	16	1st Half	170	22	60	5	23	2	353			421	512	933	11	88	38	1.00	32	26	41	95	42	3%	5	300	7.07	11.8	$8
BAvg Potl	50%	2nd Half	272	39	87	19	70	0	320			369	610	979	7	88	31	0.62	37	19	44	160	1	0%	15	310	7.22	20.9	$15
LIMA Plan	C	07 Proj	**445**	**59**	**135**	**25**	**89**	**1**	**303**			**368**	**546**	**914**	**9**	**87**	**30**	**0.79**	**37**	**22**	**41**	**137**	**35**	**2%**	**21**	**319**	**6.66**	**31.2**	**$20**

Displayed same Eye and ct% from Double-A in 2005. Higher FB% supports jump in PX, and xBA showed that .300 average was for real. Asking for another .330+ is asking a lot, though.

McDonald,John

		Year	AB	R	H	HR	RBI	SB	Avg	vL	vR	OB	Slg	OPS	bb%	ct%	h%	Eye	G	L	F	PX	SX	SBO	xHR	xBA	RC/G	RAR	R$
Pos	6	02 CLE	264	35	66	1	12	3	250	232	256	277	326	603	4	81	31	0.20	43	27	31	52	117	5%	2	259	2.80	-13.8	$3
Age	32	03 CLE	214	21	46	1	14	3	215	215	215	253	280	534	5	86	25	0.35	40	22	38	46	79	13%	2	247	2.16	-15.2	$1
Past Peak		04 CLE	93	17	19	2	7	0	204	200	220	237	344	581	4	88	21	0.36	43	13	44	81	111	0%	2	259	2.74	-5.0	$1
Bats	Right	05 2AL	166	18	46	0	16	6	277	298	253	322	325	647	6	86	32	0.46	55	21	24	36	98	14%	1	264	3.55	-4.8	$4
Reliability	18	06 TOR	260	35	58	3	23	7	223	230	220	268	308	576	6	84	25	0.39	48	18	34	49	128	15%	3	249	2.63	-14.3	$3
DL	15	1st Half	64	11	15	0	2	4	234			269	250	519	4	88	27	0.38	58	16	25	13	120	29%	0	244	1.99	-4.7	$1
BAvg Potl	55%	2nd Half	196	24	43	3	21	3	219			268	327	594	6	83	25	0.39	45	19	37	61	112	9%	3	250	2.85	-9.4	$2
LIMA Plan	F	07 Proj	**166**	**21**	**40**	**1**	**13**	**5**	**241**			**282**	**300**	**582**	**5**	**85**	**28**	**0.37**	**49**	**20**	**31**	**39**	**106**	**15%**	**1**	**250**	**2.70**	**-8.8**	**$2**

Backed in to playing time in 2H. BA and ct% say marginal value as a SB threat if he can get on base. But that's the problem... Poor eye, declining ct% indicate he doesn't do that often enough.

McLouth,Nate

		Year	AB	R	H	HR	RBI	SB	Avg	vL	vR	OB	Slg	OPS	bb%	ct%	h%	Eye	G	L	F	PX	SX	SBO	xHR	xBA	RC/G	RAR	R$
Pos	89	02	0	0	0	0	0	0	0							0							0		0				
Age	25	03	0	0	0	0	0	0	0							0							0		0				
Pre-Peak		04 aa	515	76	153	6	59	25	297			345	414	759	7	91	32	0.81				76	116	23%	9		4.98	4.3	$20
Bats	Left	05 PIT	* 506	68	133	9	42	28	263	100	292	307	374	680	6	88	29	0.52	52	16	31	70	121	29%	10	279	3.92	-9.7	$17
Reliability	24	06 PIT	270	50	63	7	16	10	233	260	227	281	385	666	6	78	27	0.31	39	25	35	99	141	20%	8	269	3.63	-6.6	$6
DL	47	1st Half	182	32	40	3	9	8	220			276	330	605	7	79	26	0.37	42	23	35	78	115	23%	4	259	2.93	-8.5	$3
BAvg Potl	50%	2nd Half	88	18	23	4	7	2	261			293	500	793	4	76	30	0.19	33	30	37	144	146	13%	4	290	5.14	1.8	$3
LIMA Plan	D	07 Proj	**198**	**33**	**51**	**5**	**16**	**9**	**258**			**301**	**408**	**709**	**6**	**83**	**29**	**0.36**	**39**	**26**	**36**	**93**	**142**	**25%**	**5**	**282**	**4.17**	**-2.2**	**$6**

BPIs predictably slipped with jump to majors; dip in h% didn't help. Bum ankle cost him last 6 weeks. Showed surprising pop, but main attribute -- speed -- mitigated by poor OB skills.

McPherson,Dallas

		Year	AB	R	H	HR	RBI	SB	Avg	vL	vR	OB	Slg	OPS	bb%	ct%	h%	Eye	G	L	F	PX	SX	SBO	xHR	xBA	RC/G	RAR	R$
Pos	5	02	0	0	0	0	0	0	0							0							0		0				
Age	26	03 aa	102	18	29	4	23	3	285			380	504	884	13	79	33	0.72				148	106	9%	4		6.76	6.8	$5
Pre-Peak		04 a/a	521	81	139	27	95	9	266			321	514	834	7	74	31	0.30				159	113	16%	26		5.85	13.4	$20
Bats	Left	05 ANA	* 259	35	63	12	40	4	243	196	258	294	462	757	7	69	30	0.24	38	19	43	159	101	19%	12	262	4.91	3.2	$8
Reliability	0	06 ANA	* 323	42	74	20	47	3	228	231	265	266	471	736	5	66	28	0.15	40	21	39	168	95	7%	18	261	4.59	-4.2	$8
DL	69 85	1st Half	211	28	49	12	29	2	233			271	476	747	5	64	30	0.14	40	22	38	180	98	7%	12	262	4.89	-0.7	$5
BAvg Potl	40%	2nd Half	112	14	25	8	18	1	219			257	461	717	5	70	24	0.17	33	0	67	147	87	8%	6		4.08	-3.2	$3
LIMA Plan	D	07 Proj	**196**	**27**	**51**	**11**	**32**	**3**	**260**			**309**	**492**	**801**	**7**	**70**	**32**	**0.23**	**38**	**20**	**42**	**155**	**97**	**11%**	**10**	**263**	**5.43**	**3.5**	**$7**

7-13-.261 in 115 AB with ANA. PX history indicates good power when he makes contact, but that doesn't happen often enough. History of injuries, downward trend in BPIs underscore the risk.

Melhuse,Adam

		Year	AB	R	H	HR	RBI	SB	Avg	vL	vR	OB	Slg	OPS	bb%	ct%	h%	Eye	G	L	F	PX	SX	SBO	xHR	xBA	RC/G	RAR	R$
Pos	2	02 aaa	341	33	87	10	34	3	255			306	416	722	7	86	27	0.53				103	50	10%	10		4.41	5.5	$7
Age	35	03 OAK	* 224	32	56	7	27	0	250	333	283	333	406	740	11	79	29	0.58	33	19	48	107	35	2%	8	251	4.76	4.4	$5
Decline		04 OAK	214	23	55	11	31	0	257	120	275	309	463	771	7	78	28	0.34	47	20	33	126	20	2%	10	277	4.84	3.2	$5
Bats	Both	05 OAK	97	11	24	2	12	0	247	77	274	284	381	666	5	71	33	0.18	48	19	33	112	32	0%	3	244	3.60	-1.2	$2
Reliability	12	06 OAK	128	10	28	4	18	0	219	222	218	270	375	645	7	73	27	0.26	45	27	27	112	22	4%	5	276	3.31	-4.4	$1
DL		1st Half	83	8	19	3	12	0	229			289	398	686	8	77	26	0.37	45	27	28	113	29	6%	3	288	3.89	-1.3	$1
BAvg Potl	50%	2nd Half	45	2	9	1	6	0	200			234	333	567	4	67	28	0.13	45	29	26	111	3	0%	1	251	2.23	-3.1	($0)
LIMA Plan	F	07 Proj	**128**	**15**	**32**	**5**	**17**	**0**	**250**			**315**	**422**	**737**	**9**	**79**	**28**	**0.45**	**43**	**23**	**34**	**113**	**32**	**4%**	**5**	**282**	**4.57**	**1.2**	**$3**

Has a history of performing better with more consistent playing time, not unlike almost every other player on the planet. But role, circumstance and age will prevent that from happening, unfortunately.

JEFFREY TOMICH

Mench,Kevin

			AB	R	H	HR	RBI	SB	Avg	vL	vR	OB	Slg	OPS	bb%	ct%	h%	Eye	G	L	F	PX	SX	SBO	xHR	xBA	RC/G	RAR	R$
Pos	97	02 TEX	* 464	65	113	20	71	1	244	269	256	309	440	749	9	77	28	0.41	38	14	48	127	64	2%	20	253	4.71	-4.2	$12
Age	29	03 TEX	* 241	29	67	6	28	3	278	346	301	351	436	786	10	87	30	0.84	37	25	38	105	52	6%	7	302	5.39	1.7	$6
Peak		04 TEX	438	69	122	26	71	0	279	319	259	329	539	868	7	86	28	0.52	36	17	46	146	58	0%	21	306	6.00	16.0	$16
Bats	Right	05 TEX	557	71	147	25	73	4	264	296	257	325	469	793	8	88	26	0.74	38	17	45	120	67	5%	22	294	5.27	9.2	$17
Reliability	63	06 2TM	446	45	120	13	68	1	269	303	257	311	419	730	6	87	29	0.46	42	18	39	88	49	1%	12	273	4.41	-10.2	$10
DL		1st Half	248	30	70	11	42	1	282			326	472	798	6	85	29	0.44	43	15	42	106	53	2%	9	273	5.13	-0.6	$8
BAvg Potl	55%	2nd Half	198	15	50	2	26	0	253			292	354	645	5	88	28	0.48	41	22	36	66	33	0%	3	273	3.55	-9.7	$2
LIMA Plan	D	07 Proj	**326**	**38**	**88**	**12**	**47**	**1**	**270**			**320**	**450**	**770**	**7**	**87**	**28**	**0.55**	**40**	**19**	**42**	**106**	**58**	**2%**	**11**	**285**	**4.93**	**-1.8**	**$9**

3rd year of power decline, with a complete 2H collapse in both PX and FB% after a promising start. He still owns those skils but they are in a box somewhere in the basement and you know they'll be in the last place he looks.

Michaels,Jason

			AB	R	H	HR	RBI	SB	Avg	vL	vR	OB	Slg	OPS	bb%	ct%	h%	Eye	G	L	F	PX	SX	SBO	xHR	xBA	RC/G	RAR	R$
Pos	7	02 PHI	* 137	19	36	2	17	2	263	242	302	344	438	782	11	73	35	0.46	36	22	42	137	112	17%	4	265	5.59	-3.3	$4
Age	30	03 PHI	109	20	36	5	17	0	330	382	278	411	569	980	12	80	38	0.68	41	24	34	164	32	0%	6	321	7.86	6.5	$5
Peak		04 PHI	299	44	82	10	40	2	274	286	270	364	415	778	12	73	34	0.53	40	20	40	95	45	4%	11	237	5.33	-0.9	$9
Bats	Right	05 PHI	289	54	88	4	31	3	304	323	289	396	415	812	13	84	35	0.98	41	25	35	75	87	5%	6	276	5.89	4.4	$10
Reliability	20	06 CLE	494	77	132	9	55	9	267	291	252	326	391	717	8	80	32	0.43	40	23	38	87	88	11%	12	261	4.37	-11.6	$12
DL	18	1st Half	242	34	67	5	25	4	277			337	393	730	8	80	33	0.45	41	26	33	79	63	10%	6	270	4.52	-4.6	$6
BAvg Potl	45%	2nd Half	252	43	65	4	30	5	258			315	389	704	8	79	31	0.40	39	20	42	95	102	11%	6	254	4.23	-7.0	$6
LIMA Plan	D+	07 Proj	**381**	**63**	**104**	**8**	**45**	**5**	**273**			**348**	**408**	**755**	**10**	**79**	**33**	**0.56**	**40**	**23**	**37**	**93**	**88**	**8%**	**10**	**265**	**4.99**	**-0.4**	**$10**

BPIs eroded pretty much across the board in his first full-time exposure. This is expected, however, his pre-'06 levels did not have much buffer built in. With these current BPIs, he is not worthy of full time play.

Mientkiewicz,Doug

			AB	R	H	HR	RBI	SB	Avg	vL	vR	OB	Slg	OPS	bb%	ct%	h%	Eye	G	L	F	PX	SX	SBO	xHR	xBA	RC/G	RAR	R$
Pos	3	02 MIN	467	60	122	10	64	1	261	257	263	362	392	754	14	85	29	1.07	37	19	43	85	42	2%	12	262	5.20	-8.9	$11
Age	32	03 MIN	487	67	146	11	65	4	300	300	310	392	450	842	13	89	32	1.35	38	26	36	97	62	3%	14	308	6.27	11.9	$16
Past Peak		04 2AL	391	47	93	6	35	2	238	220	246	321	350	672	11	86	26	0.86	43	18	39	74	53	5%	8	258	4.10	-10.5	$4
Bats	Left	05 NYM	275	36	66	11	29	0	240	214	245	319	407	726	10	86	24	0.82	49	16	35	100	30	1%	10	273	4.59	-8.4	$6
Reliability	30	06 KC	314	37	89	4	43	3	283	274	286	355	411	766	10	84	33	0.70	41	22	37	88	74	3%	7	276	5.18	-2.1	$7
DL	67 41	1st Half	244	26	65	2	30	3	266			339	377	717	10	83	31	0.66	44	22	34	81	70	4%	4	273	4.59	-5.8	$4
BAvg Potl	50%	2nd Half	70	11	24	2	13	0	343			410	529	939	10	87	37	0.89	32	21	47	109	67	0%	2	286	7.17	3.2	$3
LIMA Plan	F	07 Proj	**125**	**17**	**35**	**3**	**17**	**0**	**280**			**357**	**434**	**791**	**11**	**86**	**31**	**0.84**	**41**	**20**	**40**	**95**	**63**	**2%**	**3**	**279**	**5.47**	**0.6**	**$3**

Never much power, and BA skills have been in steady decline since 2003. Add in season-ending back surgery, and it's hard to justify rostering him, except in formats that reward slick glovework.

Miles,Aaron

			AB	R	H	HR	RBI	SB	Avg	vL	vR	OB	Slg	OPS	bb%	ct%	h%	Eye	G	L	F	PX	SX	SBO	xHR	xBA	RC/G	RAR	R$
Pos	46	02 aa	531	55	145	8	56	21	273			318	384	702	6	91	29	0.76				72	82	26%	10		4.29	1.0	$16
Age	30	03 aaa	546	68	150	11	43	7	275			320	401	721	6	92	28	0.78				75	76	12%	11		4.48	3.3	$13
Peak		04 COL	* 576	80	168	6	52	13	292	267	301	327	365	691	5	90	32	0.54	55	17	28	43	97	13%	6	269	4.03	-9.5	$17
Bats	Both	05 COL	* 356	41	97	2	29	5	272	234	292	287	344	631	2	89	30	0.20	54	23	23	45	105	8%	3	288	3.18	-14.1	$7
Reliability	34	06 STL	426	48	112	2	30	2	263	291	256	323	347	671	8	90	29	0.90	55	20	25	51	78	2%	4	286	4.09	-6.3	$5
DL	33	1st Half	203	24	55	0	14	2	271			339	345	684	9	90	30	1.05	54	20	26	49	78	5%	1	281	4.34	-1.5	$3
BAvg Potl	70%	2nd Half	223	24	57	2	16	0	256			308	350	658	7	90	28	0.77	57	20	23	53	60	0%	2	287	3.86	-4.8	$2
LIMA Plan	F	07 Proj	**231**	**27**	**63**	**2**	**18**	**3**	**273**			**316**	**356**	**671**	**6**	**90**	**30**	**0.62**	**55**	**20**	**25**	**51**	**83**	**7%**	**2**	**287**	**3.91**	**-4.4**	**$4**

Improved his bb% modestly to boost his OBP over .300. But 55% grounders by a player who doesn't run especially well, coupled with a 50-ish PX and 30-ish age, make him not very roster-worthy-ish.

Millar,Kevin

			AB	R	H	HR	RBI	SB	Avg	vL	vR	OB	Slg	OPS	bb%	ct%	h%	Eye	G	L	F	PX	SX	SBO	xHR	xBA	RC/G	RAR	R$
Pos	30	02 FLA	* 450	59	135	17	58	0	300	317	302	357	504	862	8	82	33	0.50	32	22	46	142	24	2%	18	300	6.11	6.4	$16
Age	35	03 BOS	544	83	150	25	96	3	276	289	271	348	472	820	10	80	30	0.56	34	23	42	123	60	3%	24	283	5.64	4.0	$20
Decline		04 BOS	513	75	152	18	74	1	296	299	297	307	472	838	10	82	33	0.62	36	17	47	112	38	1%	19	264	5.92	13.2	$17
Bats	Right	05 BOS	449	57	122	9	50	0	272	246	283	350	399	749	11	84	31	0.73	34	20	46	87	37	1%	11	255	4.94	-1.9	$10
Reliability	59	06 BAL	430	64	117	15	64	1	272	244	283	360	437	797	12	83	30	0.80	35	22	42	103	38	1%	16	276	5.53	1.4	$12
DL		1st Half	194	31	47	6	31	1	242			332	376	708	12	83	26	0.79	33	21	46	81	51	3%	6	253	4.42	-5.8	$4
BAvg Potl	55%	2nd Half	236	33	70	9	33	0	297			383	487	870	12	83	33	0.80	38	23	39	122	22	0%	10	293	6.44	6.7	$7
LIMA Plan	D	07 Proj	**369**	**52**	**101**	**11**	**51**	**1**	**274**			**355**	**427**	**781**	**11**	**83**	**31**	**0.72**	**35**	**21**	**44**	**100**	**36**	**1%**	**12**	**268**	**5.31**	**0.2**	**$10**

Deliberate effort to reverse months of high-GB% paid off with a nice September surge in HR, BA. But the dropc in bb%, CT% and eye made the late success look more like luck than a turnaround.

Milledge,Lastings

			AB	R	H	HR	RBI	SB	Avg	vL	vR	OB	Slg	OPS	bb%	ct%	h%	Eye	G	L	F	PX	SX	SBO	xHR	xBA	RC/G	RAR	R$
Pos	79	02	0	0	0	0	0	0	0							0						0			0				
Age	22	03	0	0	0	0	0	0	0							0						0			0				
Growth		04	0	0	0	0	0	0	0							0						0			0				
Bats	Right	05 aa	193	27	61	3	20	9	316			354	446	800	6	81	38	0.32				99	86	29%	5		5.28	1.3	$9
Reliability	0	06 NYM	* 473	70	130	11	61	15	275	241	241	355	429	783	11	79	33	0.60	44	22	34	99	102	20%	13	274	5.39	1.9	$15
DL		1st Half	265	41	75	7	33	10	283			373	472	845	13	78	34	0.65	41	25	34	122	111	21%	9	287	6.29	8.1	$10
BAvg Potl	45%	2nd Half	208	29	55	3	28	6	265			330	373	703	9	81	31	0.52	46	20	34	70	85	18%	4	257	4.26	-6.1	$6
LIMA Plan	D+	07 Proj	**384**	**55**	**107**	**9**	**46**	**15**	**279**			**340**	**429**	**769**	**8**	**80**	**33**	**0.48**	**44**	**22**	**34**	**101**	**101**	**25%**	**11**	**278**	**5.04**	**-3.7**	**$14**

4-22-.241 in 166 AB at NYM. Solid prospect who looked overmatched in MLB (7% bb%, vs 12% at Triple-A). Immediate speed value, with potential for power to come with maturity - physical and otherwise.

Miller,Damian

			AB	R	H	HR	RBI	SB	Avg	vL	vR	OB	Slg	OPS	bb%	ct%	h%	Eye	G	L	F	PX	SX	SBO	xHR	xBA	RC/G	RAR	R$
Pos	2	02 ARI	306	41	77	11	42	0	252	275	238	334	435	769	11	71	32	0.43	52	21	28	145	28	0%	14	271	5.25	10.2	$8
Age	37	03 CHC	352	34	82	9	36	1	233	248	226	309	369	679	10	74	29	0.43	48	23	29	99	50	1%	11	261	3.93	-3.8	$5
Decline		04 OAK	397	39	108	9	58	0	272	290	264	337	403	740	9	78	33	0.45	43	24	33	92	19	1%	11	265	4.69	4.1	$8
Bats	Right	05 MIL	385	50	105	9	43	0	273	231	286	336	413	749	9	76	34	0.39	50	25	24	105	42	1%	11	279	4.83	11.5	$10
Reliability	53	06 MIL	331	34	83	6	38	0	251	280	241	319	390	708	9	74	32	0.38	44	21	35	108	21	0%	10	253	4.37	0.3	$5
DL		1st Half	189	21	50	5	24	0	265			338	439	777	10	79	31	0.53	42	21	36	124	20	0%	7	279	5.26	5.0	$4
BAvg Potl	40%	2nd Half	142	13	33	1	14	0	232			292	324	616	8	68	34	0.26	47	21	33	84	23	0%	3	220	3.12	-5.2	$1
LIMA Plan	D	07 Proj	**305**	**33**	**78**	**6**	**36**	**0**	**256**			**322**	**387**	**709**	**9**	**74**	**33**	**0.38**	**47**	**23**	**31**	**102**	**27**	**0%**	**9**	**257**	**4.34**	**2.1**	**$5**

Advancing years provide no reason to expect anything more. Mostly consistent performance and skills suggest little reason to expect anything less. BA decline looks real, so adjust expectations there.

Mirabelli,Doug

			AB	R	H	HR	RBI	SB	Avg	vL	vR	OB	Slg	OPS	bb%	ct%	h%	Eye	G	L	F	PX	SX	SBO	xHR	xBA	RC/G	RAR	R$
Pos	2	02 BOS	151	17	34	7	25	0	225	364	168	304	411	714	10	78	24	0.52	42	13	45	116	19	0%	7	240	4.29	3.1	$3
Age	36	03 BOS	163	23	42	6	18	0	258	250	261	305	448	752	6	78	30	0.31	44	22	34	133	36	0%	7	289	4.68	2.8	$4
Decline		04 BOS	160	27	45	9	32	0	281	311	270	358	525	883	11	71	34	0.41	39	18	43	170	32	0%	9	274	6.72	10.8	$6
Bats	Right	05 BOS	136	16	31	6	18	2	228	245	212	300	412	712	9	65	30	0.29	36	18	45	146	53	6%	7	233	4.46	1.8	$3
Reliability	0	06 2TM	183	13	35	6	25	0	191	200	188	253	328	580	8	68	25	0.25	39	13	48	98	10	0%	7	189	2.40	-11.5	$1
DL	24	1st Half	74	4	12	1	6	0	162			235	257	491	9	72	21	0.33	36	11	53	75	11	0%	2	176	1.33	-7.4	($1)
BAvg Potl	45%	2nd Half	109	9	23	5	19	0	211			265	376	641	7	65	27	0.21	41	14	45	115	10	0%	5	197	3.23	-3.8	$2
LIMA Plan	F	07 Proj	**128**	**13**	**28**	**5**	**19**	**0**	**219**			**285**	**386**	**671**	**9**	**69**	**28**	**0.30**	**39**	**16**	**46**	**121**	**32**	**2%**	**6**	**223**	**3.73**	**-1.8**	**$2**

It'd be nice if he could repeat 2004, but skills freefall at age 36 make that unlikely. Still a serviceable second catcher, if you need 4-5 HR badly enough to endure 150+ empty outs with 50+ Ks. Desperation $1 pick.

Molina,Ben

			AB	R	H	HR	RBI	SB	Avg	vL	vR	OB	Slg	OPS	bb%	ct%	h%	Eye	G	L	F	PX	SX	SBO	xHR	xBA	RC/G	RAR	R$
Pos	2	02 ANA	428	34	105	5	47	0	245	248	244	271	322	593	3	92	26	0.44	45	19	37	48	22	0%	6	254	2.93	-8.7	$5
Age	32	03 ANA	409	37	115	14	71	1	281	289	278	303	443	746	3	92	28	0.42	37	24	39	92	28	2%	12	307	4.49	4.6	$12
Past Peak		04 ANA	337	36	93	10	54	0	276	252	286	313	404	716	5	90	28	0.51	48	16	36	71	25	1%	9	257	4.23	-1.0	$8
Bats	Right	05 ANA	410	45	121	15	69	0	295	393	253	339	446	785	6	90	30	0.66	41	21	38	86	18	2%	12	283	5.05	11.7	$14
Reliability	48	06 TOR	433	44	123	19	57	1	284	358	246	314	467	781	4	89	28	0.40	39	23	38	99	37	2%	15	303	4.84	5.3	$12
DL	25	1st Half	193	22	59	6	18	0	306			350	440	790	6	91	31	0.76	41	26	33	74	25	2%	5	303	5.15	3.9	$5
BAvg Potl	55%	2nd Half	240	22	64	13	39	1	267			285	487	772	2	88	26	0.20	37	21	42	120	43	2%	10	304	4.59	1.3	$7
LIMA Plan	D+	07 Proj	**424**	**43**	**123**	**16**	**68**	**1**	**290**			**323**	**455**	**778**	**5**	**90**	**29**	**0.47**	**41**	**21**	**38**	**91**	**34**	**2%**	**13**	**292**	**4.86**	**7.3**	**$13**

Posted .478/.500/.826 with 2 HR vs Johan Santana, continuing recent mastery of LHPs:
2002-04: .263/.300/.421, 11 HR
2005-06: .374/.409/.630, 17 HR
Home field could be an issue - hit 12 of 19 HR in SkyDome.

PATRICK DAVITT

94

Molina,Jose

Molina,Jose		AB	R	H	HR	RBI	SB	Avg	vL	vR	OB	Slg	OPS	bb%	ct%	h%	Eye	G	L	F	PX	SX	SBO	xHR	xBA	RC/G	RAR	R$
Pos 2	02 ANA *	360	27	94	3	36	0	261	100	340	289	331	619	4	83	31	0.23	38	24	38	48	28	7%	4	244	2.97	-6.9	$5
Age 31	03 ANA	114	12	21	0	6	0	184	240	141	191	219	411	1	77	24	0.04	43	33	24	33	59	0%	1	260	0.15	-14.4	($1)
Past Peak	04 ANA	203	26	53	3	25	4	261	339	229	296	374	670	5	74	34	0.19	48	15	37	80	113	10%	4	231	3.62	-4.2	$5
Bats Right	05 ANA	184	14	42	6	25	2	228	306	186	279	348	627	7	78	26	0.32	50	20	30	74	39	4%	5	248	3.01	-5.6	$3
Reliability 33	06 ANA	225	18	54	4	22	1	240	218	254	269	369	638	4	78	29	0.18	42	18	39	96	38	2%	6	250	3.18	-8.3	$2
DL	1st Half	115	10	25	1	9	1	217			256	304	561	5	77	28	0.22	45	22	33	70	50	4%	2	245	2.24	-7.7	$0
BAvg Potl 45%	2nd Half	110	8	29	3	13	0	264			283	436	720	3	80	31	0.14	39	15	46	122	12	0%	4	251	4.11	-0.9	$2
LIMA Plan F	07 Proj	244	21	59	5	27	1	242			275	361	636	4	78	29	0.21	45	19	37	85	36	2%	6	245	3.13	-8.1	$3

Hot July-Aug (2-10-.333, 9 2B) but lack of consistent contact or patience, and utter lack of punch continue to mark his offensive performance. Don't bid on hopes of a late-career catcher's surge. Not here.

Molina,Yadier

Molina,Yadier		AB	R	H	HR	RBI	SB	Avg	vL	vR	OB	Slg	OPS	bb%	ct%	h%	Eye	G	L	F	PX	SX	SBO	xHR	xBA	RC/G	RAR	R$
Pos 2	02 0	0	0	0	0	0	0	0							0							0		0				
Age 24	03 aa	364	30	94	2	47	0	258			306	313	619	6	88	29	0.58				37	33	1%	3		3.29	-9.6	$5
Growth	04 STL *	264	28	72	3	27	0	273	250	272	340	352	692	9	89	30	0.90	46	20	34	52	26	1%	4	255	4.30	3.7	$5
Bats Right	05 STL	385	36	97	8	49	2	252	299	231	294	358	653	6	92	26	0.77	51	18	31	62	48	5%	7	280	3.70	-1.1	$7
Reliability 34	06 STL	417	29	90	6	49	1	216	213	217	262	321	583	6	90	23	0.63	42	18	39	67	26	4%	8	262	2.94	-18.0	$2
DL 41	1st Half	212	12	45	2	27	0	212			251	297	548	5	92	22	0.69	43	21	36	54	19	5%	3	267	2.61	-11.4	$0
BAvg Potl 80%	2nd Half	205	17	45	4	22	1	220			273	346	619	7	88	23	0.60	42	16	42	80	36	2%	5	258	3.31	-6.5	$1
LIMA Plan D	07 Proj	440	37	110	9	52	1	250			299	361	660	6	90	26	0.69	46	18	36	68	28	3%	9	266	3.78	-4.3	$7

The youngest Molina puts the bat on the ball consistently, and xBA points out how .216 was a fluke. Growth in FB% and PX could augur HR potential as well. UP: 10-60-.275

Monroe,Craig

Monroe,Craig		AB	R	H	HR	RBI	SB	Avg	vL	vR	OB	Slg	OPS	bb%	ct%	h%	Eye	G	L	F	PX	SX	SBO	xHR	xBA	RC/G	RAR	R$
Pos 70	02 aaa	383	58	108	8	46	6	282			341	444	784	8	86	31	0.63				104	106	11%	10		5.28	-3.6	$12
Age 30	03 DET *	472	64	119	25	76	5	252	293	209	298	466	764	6	79	27	0.32	47	16	37	130	77	7%	21	283	4.70	-8.7	$15
Peak	04 DET	447	65	131	18	72	3	293	256	314	336	488	824	6	82	32	0.37	46	16	38	117	76	6%	17	283	5.49	6.8	$16
Bats Right	05 DET	567	69	157	20	89	8	277	303	270	325	446	771	7	83	30	0.42	49	19	32	106	83	8%	19	292	4.88	2.7	$19
Reliability 88	06 DET	541	89	138	28	92	2	255	271	249	303	482	785	6	77	28	0.29	38	18	44	146	73	4%	26	277	5.04	-2.1	$17
DL	1st Half	240	39	57	11	36	1	238			274	429	703	5	74	28	0.19	40	18	41	127	66	7%	11	259	3.92	-9.2	$6
BAvg Potl 45%	2nd Half	301	50	81	17	56	1	269			325	525	850	8	79	29	0.39	36	18	46	159	77	2%	16	292	5.91	6.3	$11
LIMA Plan C	07 Proj	570	85	158	30	98	1	277			324	509	834	7	80	30	0.35	39	18	43	142	60	3%	27	287	5.61	9.6	$20

Opened his swing and started lofting the ball, boosting power but causing a BA sag. 2nd half PX/xBA indicates he can hold the power gain with a potential BA rebound. Speculate... UP: 35 HR, .290

Montero,Miguel

Montero,Miguel		AB	R	H	HR	RBI	SB	Avg	vL	vR	OB	Slg	OPS	bb%	ct%	h%	Eye	G	L	F	PX	SX	SBO	xHR	xBA	RC/G	RAR	R$
Pos 2	02	0	0	0	0	0	0	0							0							0		0				
Age 23	03	0	0	0	0	0	0	0							0							0		0				
Growth	04	0	0	0	0	0	0	0							0							0		0				
Bats Left	05 aa	108	10	24	2	10	1	225			264	323	588	5	81	26	0.28				53	97	4%	1		2.60	-4.3	$1
Reliability 0	06 a/a	439	38	118	15	66	1	269	333	231	338	426	764	9	87	28	0.81	38	15	46	91	13	5%	14		5.02	8.2	$10
DL	1st Half	247	19	64	9	35	0	259			346	428	775	12	87	27	1.07				99	7	4%	9		5.30	6.7	$5
BAvg Potl 50%	2nd Half	192	19	54	6	31	1	281			327	423	750	6	86	30	0.50	38	15	46	82	30	6%	6		4.63	1.4	$5
LIMA Plan F	07 Proj	162	14	41	4	21	1	253			307	385	692	7	84	28	0.50	38	15	46	76	52	5%	4	240	4.01	-0.8	$3

0-3-.250 in 16 AB at ARI. Fine year in the minors. Good offensive potential with plate discipline and a quick, lively bat with pull power. Will need to improve throwing, but in all, a top prospect. UP: 350+ AB

Morales,Kendry

Morales,Kendry		AB	R	H	HR	RBI	SB	Avg	vL	vR	OB	Slg	OPS	bb%	ct%	h%	Eye	G	L	F	PX	SX	SBO	xHR	xBA	RC/G	RAR	R$
Pos 3	02	0	0	0	0	0	0	0							0							0		0				
Age 23	03	0	0	0	0	0	0	0							0							0		0				
Growth	04	0	0	0	0	0	0	0							0							0		0				
Bats Both	05 aa	281	36	75	13	42	2	267			299	445	744	4	88	26	0.38				100	55	3%	10		4.41	-7.6	$9
Reliability 0	06 ANA *	453	53	119	14	63	1	263	229	235	306	413	718	6	87	28	0.47	52	15	34	86	46	6%	13	271	4.28	-15.2	$10
DL	1st Half	286	32	73	8	36	0	257			304	389	693	6	88	27	0.56	52	11	37	76	42	4%	7	249	4.05	-11.6	$5
BAvg Potl 55%	2nd Half	167	21	46	6	27	1	273			308	454	762	5	86	29	0.35	51	21	28	105	67	9%	6	308	4.69	-3.6	$5
LIMA Plan D	07 Proj	332	41	88	13	49	2	265			302	431	734	5	87	27	0.41	51	17	32	94	54	5%	11	288	4.37	-9.0	$9

5-22-.234 in 197 AB at ANA. Cuban defector didn't live up to hype. Hit far too many GB in majors. Better outcomes with lesser skills in AAA, indicating at 23 he might need more seasoning.

Mora,Melvin

Mora,Melvin		AB	R	H	HR	RBI	SB	Avg	vL	vR	OB	Slg	OPS	bb%	ct%	h%	Eye	G	L	F	PX	SX	SBO	xHR	xBA	RC/G	RAR	R$
Pos 5	02 BAL	557	86	130	19	64	16	233	240	231	319	404	723	11	81	26	0.65	34	21	45	106	108	18%	19	263	4.56	1.7	$15
Age 35	03 BAL	344	68	109	15	48	6	317	324	315	402	503	905	12	79	36	0.69	40	26	34	116	79	7%	15	291	6.87	22.1	$16
Decline	04 BAL	550	111	187	27	104	11	340	303	352	411	562	973	11	83	37	0.69	40	21	39	135	75	9%	26	303	7.54	38.0	$31
Bats Right	05 BAL	593	86	168	27	88	7	283	234	304	339	474	813	8	81	31	0.45	37	18	45	119	66	7%	24	272	5.41	15.3	$22
Reliability 35	06 BAL	624	96	171	16	83	11	274	253	282	332	391	723	8	84	30	0.55	39	20	41	71	87	7%	16	254	4.41	-10.7	$18
DL	1st Half	317	49	92	9	38	4	290			336	426	762	6	84	32	0.44	40	20	40	84	73	4%	9	264	4.78	-2.0	$10
BAvg Potl 45%	2nd Half	307	47	79	7	45	7	257			327	355	682	9	84	29	0.65	38	20	41	58	82	8%	7	243	4.01	-9.0	$8
LIMA Plan C	07 Proj	574	92	155	15	84	8	270			335	400	735	9	83	30	0.56	38	20	41	82	81	7%	16	257	4.60	-3.6	$17

Curiosity Dept: Tejada brings his B12 syringe to BAL in 2004 and Mora has a career year. Similar skills and slight FB% growth since, yet power and BA are plunging. Don't expect a big resurgence. Or even a little one.

Morneau,Justin

Morneau,Justin		AB	R	H	HR	RBI	SB	Avg	vL	vR	OB	Slg	OPS	bb%	ct%	h%	Eye	G	L	F	PX	SX	SBO	xHR	xBA	RC/G	RAR	R$
Pos 3	02 aa	494	60	137	13	66	6	277			325	431	756	7	85	31	0.47				98	92	5%	14		4.78	-13.3	$15
Age 25	03 a/a	344	47	90	18	48	0	262			321	471	792	8	82	27	0.48				122	48	2%	15		5.14	-3.1	$11
Pre-Peak	04 MIN *	568	83	157	36	112	1	276	240	283	341	537	878	9	83	28	0.58	38	16	46	152	34	1%	31	297	6.22	19.9	$22
Bats Left	05 MIN	490	62	117	22	79	0	239	205	254	301	437	738	8	81	25	0.47	42	18	41	121	56	2%	20	277	4.54	-8.0	$12
Reliability 20	06 MIN	592	97	190	34	130	3	321	315	325	377	559	936	8	84	34	0.57	36	24	41	137	49	4%	29	312	6.85	22.8	$29
DL 15	1st Half	267	39	77	19	64	1	288			343	558	901	8	79	30	0.39	31	23	46	161	35	3%	16	302	6.42	7.5	$12
BAvg Potl 45%	2nd Half	325	58	113	15	66	2	348			404	560	964	9	89	36	0.84	39	24	37	120	58	4%	13	321	7.23	15.2	$17
LIMA Plan C	07 Proj	610	91	187	37	127	2	307			364	555	919	8	83	32	0.54	38	21	41	144	51	3%	31	309	6.66	22.7	$28

Extrapolating slow April-May sets a power baseline of mid-30s HR, 120+ RBI. Upside is shown by June-July: mid-50s HR, 150+ RBI. Set expectations in between. For now.

Mueller,Bill

Mueller,Bill		AB	R	H	HR	RBI	SB	Avg	vL	vR	OB	Slg	OPS	bb%	ct%	h%	Eye	G	L	F	PX	SX	SBO	xHR	xBA	RC/G	RAR	R$
Pos 5	02 2NL	382	52	101	8	42	0	264	221	272	356	401	756	12	89	28	1.26	41	27	32	83	61	1%	9	306	5.23	7.1	$9
Age 36	03 BOS	524	85	171	19	85	1	326	295	342	395	540	935	10	85	36	0.77	39	26	35	134	62	3%	20	324	7.10	36.3	$22
Decline	04 BOS	399	75	113	12	57	2	283	255	298	364	446	811	11	86	31	0.91	43	21	36	100	68	3%	13	291	5.71	9.0	$13
Bats Both	05 BOS	519	69	153	10	62	0	295	275	299	367	430	796	10	86	33	0.80	42	25	32	90	47	0%	12	297	5.52	14.6	$14
Reliability 24	06 LA	107	12	27	3	15	1	252	280	244	355	402	757	14	92	25	1.89	49	15	35	86	35	6%	3	280	5.35	-0.4	$2
DL 142	1st Half	107	12	27	3	15	1	252			355	402	757	14	92	25	1.89	49	15	35	86	35	6%	3	280	5.35	-0.4	$2
BAvg Potl 80%	2nd Half	0	0	0	0	0	0	0																				
LIMA Plan	07 Proj	0	0	0	0	0	0	0																				

Dr. HQ reports "no known treatment at the moment" for Mueller's knee arthritis, concluding "Mueller's career is over." Miracles happen, especially in medicine, but it's hard to see him as a contributor.

Munson,Eric

Munson,Eric		AB	R	H	HR	RBI	SB	Avg	vL	vR	OB	Slg	OPS	bb%	ct%	h%	Eye	G	L	F	PX	SX	SBO	xHR	xBA	RC/G	RAR	R$
Pos 2	02 DET *	536	72	123	20	81	1	229	200	182	328	410	739	13	79	25	0.72	52	13	35	112	62	3%	20	264	4.83	19.8	$12
Age 29	03 DET	313	28	75	18	50	3	240	208	250	316	441	757	10	81	24	0.57	43	16	41	115	35	4%	15	265	4.76	6.2	$8
Peak	04 DET	321	36	68	19	49	1	212	227	208	277	445	723	8	72	23	0.32	37	16	47	149	58	3%	17	255	4.32	-0.1	$6
Bats Left	05 aaa	378	44	84	16	47	1	221			268	391	659	6	83	23	0.38				103	42	2%	14		3.48	-4.9	$7
Reliability 27	06 HOU	141	10	28	5	19	0	199	318	176	257	348	604	7	77	22	0.34	39	17	44	93	0	0%	5	198	2.78	-6.9	$1
DL	1st Half	83	7	19	4	12	0	229			281	410	691	7	83	23	0.43	36	17	47	100	8	0%	3	250	3.85	-1.2	$1
BAvg Potl 50%	2nd Half	58	3	9	1	7	0	155			222	259	481	8	69	21	0.28	45	18	38	82	9	0%	1	201	1.08	-6.3	($1)
LIMA Plan F	07 Proj	32	3	6	1	4	0	188			250	335	585	8	77	20	0.36	40	17	43	91	27	2%	1	233	2.52	-1.6	$0

HOU resurrected his career as a second- or third-string catcher with occasional pop. BA will be reliably Mendoza-ish with a solidly established 77% contact rate and 23% hit rate. And a 2% chance of getting drafted.

PATRICK DAVITT

Murton,Matt			AB	R	H	HR	RBI	SB	Avg	vL	vR	OB	Slg	OPS	bb%	ct%	h%	Eye	G	L	F	PX	SX	SBO	xHR	xBA	RC/G	RAR	R$
Pos	7	02	0	0	0	0	0	0	0							0							0		0				
Age	25	03	0	0	0	0	0	0	0							0							0		0				
Pre-Peak		04	0	0	0	0	0	0	0							0							0		0				
Bats	Right	05 CHC *	487	60	150	15	54	17	308	380	246	364	459	823	8	86	33	0.65	62	14	24	87	104	15%	13	297	5.61	3.7	$20
Reliability	4	06 CHC	455	70	135	13	62	5	297	301	295	360	444	804	9	86	32	0.73	58	18	24	84	79	5%	13	296	5.47	2.8	$16
DL		1st Half	226	33	60	4	21	3	265			331	363	693	9	84	30	0.61	61	20	19	58	76	6%	4	281	4.15	-7.2	$5
BAvg Potl	55%	2nd Half	229	37	75	9	41	2	328			389	524	913	9	89	34	0.88	54	16	29	108	72	4%	8	310	6.71	8.9	$11
LIMA Plan	C+	07 Proj	539	77	164	17	70	6	304			365	462	827	9	87	33	0.71	58	17	25	90	79	6%	16	298	5.69	4.7	$20

Consistent performance across almost all splits except home/road (.918 OPS/.708). 2nd half gains are very promising for a rookie: Here, BA/xBA growth supports a .300 BA, and G/F shift hints at future HR potential.

Nady,Xavier			AB	R	H	HR	RBI	SB	Avg	vL	vR	OB	Slg	OPS	bb%	ct%	h%	Eye	G	L	F	PX	SX	SBO	xHR	xBA	RC/G	RAR	R$
Pos	93	02 aaa	315	40	79	8	37	0	251			289	368	657	5	83	28	0.31				72	55	1%	7		3.45	-15.9	$6
Age	28	03 SD *	507	66	130	14	58	6	256	311	249	302	389	690	6	81	29	0.34	47	22	32	85	83	6%	14	272	3.88	-25.7	$13
Peak		04 SD *	368	50	102	19	66	2	277	344	178	320	492	812	6	87	27	0.49	58	17	25	119	62	2%	15	320	5.27	-0.2	$14
Bats	Right	05 SD	326	40	85	13	43	2	261	323	220	307	439	746	6	79	29	0.33	44	20	36	112	75	4%	12	277	4.54	-6.7	$9
Reliability	47	06 2NL	468	57	131	17	63	3	280	336	263	323	453	776	6	82	31	0.35	46	17	37	106	52	5%	16	272	4.91	1.9	$14
DL	19	1st Half	191	26	51	11	27	2	267			310	497	808	6	81	28	0.32	45	19	36	131	69	7%	9	292	5.20	2.4	$7
BAvg Potl	40%	2nd Half	277	31	80	6	36	1	289			332	422	755	6	83	33	0.38	47	16	37	89	34	4%	7	254	4.72	-0.4	$7
LIMA Plan	C	07 Proj	521	65	142	18	72	3	273			317	438	754	6	82	30	0.36	46	18	36	101	65	4%	17	275	4.65	-5.8	$15

Nady enters '07 with improving AB/XBH rate 2003-06: 13.7-11.0-10.9-10.2. A few doubles start clearing fences, and 20-25 HR is a possibility. But power collapsed after mid-year trade, so it's by no means a sure thing.

Napoli,Mike			AB	R	H	HR	RBI	SB	Avg	vL	vR	OB	Slg	OPS	bb%	ct%	h%	Eye	G	L	F	PX	SX	SBO	xHR	xBA	RC/G	RAR	R$
Pos	2	02	0	0	0	0	0	0	0							0							0		0				
Age	25	03	0	0	0	0	0	0	0							0							0		0				
Pre-Peak		04	0	0	0	0	0	0	0							0							0		0				
Bats	Right	05 aa	439	71	87	22	74	9	199			299	398	697	13	75	21	0.57				131	89	13%	22		4.14	3.3	$12
Reliability	0	06 ANA *	346	57	78	18	51	3	225	185	241	337	434	770	14	65	29	0.48	34	14	52	155	50	7%	21	227	5.47	11.3	$9
DL		1st Half	191	31	51	10	32	3	267			369	487	856	14	62	38	0.43	38	18	44	174	59	8%	12	242	7.01	14.5	$7
BAvg Potl	40%	2nd Half	155	23	27	8	19	0	174			297	368	664	15	68	20	0.54	31	11	58	134	37	5%	9	212	3.74	-3.4	$1
LIMA Plan	D	07 Proj	272	44	59	14	41	3	217			324	419	743	14	69	26	0.51	33	13	54	142	57	8%	15	230	4.89	5.4	$7

16-42-.228 in 268 AB at ANA. If he gets 400 AB, he's a cinch for 20 HR, but 2nd half tailspin means Mendoza territory... and 2006's MLB line becomes his upside. Scary, and risky. How much do you need his HRs?

Navarro,Dioner			AB	R	H	HR	RBI	SB	Avg	vL	vR	OB	Slg	OPS	bb%	ct%	h%	Eye	G	L	F	PX	SX	SBO	xHR	xBA	RC/G	RAR	R$
Pos	2	02	0	0	0	0	0	0	0							0									0				
Age	23	03 aa	208	25	70	4	34	2	338			387	476	863	7	90	36	0.83				88	41	10%	5		6.09	10.6	$9
Growth		04 a/a	391	46	101	3	42	2	259			332	349	681	10	88	29	0.89				59	73	2%	5		4.22	1.8	$6
Bats	Both	05 LA *	417	43	103	7	35	1	247	435	248	322	346	668	10	91	26	1.31	45	22	33	61	29	4%	8	281	4.14	4.4	$6
Reliability	12	06 2TM *	308	30	74	6	29	3	241	286	245	315	336	651	10	82	28	0.59	35	24	41	60	47	4%	7	245	3.62	-6.9	$4
DL	43	1st Half	117	7	27	2	9	2	233			321	320	641	11	81	27	0.66	32	24	44	56	36	6%	2	237	3.57	-2.8	$1
BAvg Potl	50%	2nd Half	191	23	47	4	20	1	246			311	346	657	9	83	28	0.55	36	23	41	62	44	4%	4	251	3.65	-4.1	$3
LIMA Plan	D	07 Proj	411	43	103	7	41	3	251			323	347	670	10	86	28	0.76	37	23	40	61	44	5%	8	261	3.96	-2.6	$6

6-28-.254 in 268 AB in LA, TAM One core skill (ct%) fell off, taking BA down. Low FB% limits power potential, but he's still in growth mode. There are worse catchers.

Nevin,Phil			AB	R	H	HR	RBI	SB	Avg	vL	vR	OB	Slg	OPS	bb%	ct%	h%	Eye	G	L	F	PX	SX	SBO	xHR	xBA	RC/G	RAR	R$
Pos	3	02 SD	407	53	116	12	57	4	285	337	268	346	413	759	9	79	34	0.44	47	19	34	86	63	3%	12	255	4.83	-8.8	$14
Age	36	03 SD	226	30	63	13	46	2	279	349	252	340	487	827	9	81	30	0.48	45	24	31	122	48	3%	11	299	5.55	0.2	$10
Decline		04 SD	547	78	158	26	105	0	289	324	273	365	492	857	11	78	33	0.55	45	18	37	128	34	0%	25	275	6.18	3.5	$22
Bats	Right	05 2TM	380	46	90	12	55	3	237	205	253	287	379	666	7	74	29	0.28	42	20	38	98	72	3%	12	246	3.56	-20.3	$8
Reliability	14	06 2TM	397	54	95	22	68	0	239	226	246	321	438	760	11	73	27	0.45	43	23	35	123	23	0%	20	264	4.88	-9.8	$11
DL	27	1st Half	250	35	57	15	42	0	228			303	448	751	10	78	23	0.49	46	19	36	129	26	0%	13	277	4.68	-7.8	$6
BAvg Potl	50%	2nd Half	147	19	38	7	26	0	259			351	422	773	12	65	35	0.41	37	30	34	110	1	0%	7	252	5.40	-1.3	$4
LIMA Plan	F	07 Proj	203	27	50	9	34	0	246			320	418	738	10	73	29	0.41	42	22	36	110	29	0%	9	256	4.59	-5.9	$5

Still banging out extra base hits, especially against RHP (1 every 11 AB). But started whiffing a lot more, particularly in 2nd half. Another player with late round power potential, but at a cost you might not want to incur.

Newhan,David			AB	R	H	HR	RBI	SB	Avg	vL	vR	OB	Slg	OPS	bb%	ct%	h%	Eye	G	L	F	PX	SX	SBO	xHR	xBA	RC/G	RAR	R$
Pos	8	02	0	0	0	0	0	0	0							0							0		0				
Age	33	03 aaa	244	29	73	3	19	4	299			329	410	739	4	89	33	0.39				71	85	14%	4		4.52	-2.3	$7
Past Peak		04 BAL *	635	105	188	15	80	18	296	297	316	343	454	796	7	81	35	0.38	49	18	33	95	150	11%	16	277	5.28	9.9	$23
Bats	Left	05 BAL	218	31	44	5	21	9	202	250	194	275	312	587	9	79	23	0.49	53	17	29	75	100	21%	5	259	2.74	-10.6	$4
Reliability	3	06 BAL	131	14	33	4	18	4	252	182	266	290	374	664	5	83	28	0.32	50	17	34	71	67	19%	4	255	3.49	-4.6	$3
DL	133	1st Half	34	8	9	2	7	3	265			306	441	747	6	88	25	0.50	54	14	32	82	131	33%	1	287	4.41	-0.2	$2
BAvg Potl	45%	2nd Half	97	6	24	2	11	1	247			284	351	635	5	81	29	0.28	48	17	35	67	32	13%	2	240	3.16	-4.4	$1
LIMA Plan	F	07 Proj	98	12	26	2	11	2	265			312	399	711	6	82	31	0.37	50	18	33	85	96	14%	2	269	4.21	-1.1	$2

High G/F splits and H% make 2004's eruption the outlier. (Yet another Oriole outlier during their B12 year.) At age 33, and coming off a serious leg injury, he's not likely poised for a rebound.

Niekro,Lance			AB	R	H	HR	RBI	SB	Avg	vL	vR	OB	Slg	OPS	bb%	ct%	h%	Eye	G	L	F	PX	SX	SBO	xHR	xBA	RC/G	RAR	R$
Pos	3	02 aa	297	27	81	3	28	0	273			287	370	657	2	91	29	0.21				65	40	3%	4		3.51	-19.0	$5
Age	28	03 aaa	381	35	101	3	33	2	265			293	336	629	4	92	28	0.48				44	55	6%	4		3.35	-23.4	$6
Peak		04 aaa	241	32	60	8	35	1	251			280	448	728	4	90	25	0.41				112	92	5%	7		4.39	-7.7	$6
Bats	Right	05 SF	278	32	70	12	46	0	252	324	204	295	460	755	6	81	27	0.32	40	16	44	130	64	4%	11	278	4.65	-7.8	$8
Reliability	25	06 SF *	343	47	88	15	56	0	256	246	246	289	438	727	4	85	26	0.32	45	17	38	99	53	0%	12	276	4.22	-17.8	$9
DL	31	1st Half	154	23	41	5	28	0	265			310	413	723	6	86	28	0.45	44	19	38	77	70	0%	4	265	4.31	-7.5	$4
BAvg Potl	55%	2nd Half	189	24	47	10	28	0	249			272	458	729	3	85	25	0.21	49	12	40	117	30	0%	8	271	4.13	-10.4	$5
LIMA Plan	F	07 Proj	201	25	53	8	31	0	264			296	453	749	4	86	28	0.32	43	16	41	108	69	2%	7	281	4.52	-7.7	$6

5-31-.246 in 199 AB at SF. More GBs and fewer FBs further reduce already limited power. Other skills, notably diminishing ct%, point to a BA ceiling as well. Not a pretty picture for a 1Bman.

Nixon,Trot			AB	R	H	HR	RBI	SB	Avg	vL	vR	OB	Slg	OPS	bb%	ct%	h%	Eye	G	L	F	PX	SX	SBO	xHR	xBA	RC/G	RAR	R$
Pos	9	02 BOS	532	81	136	24	94	4	256	233	262	337	470	807	11	80	28	0.60	38	18	44	136	78	4%	24	281	5.57	8.5	$18
Age	33	03 BOS	441	81	135	28	87	4	306	219	330	395	578	973	13	78	34	0.68	29	24	48	164	99	4%	25	296	7.75	31.5	$23
Past Peak		04 BOS	149	24	47	6	23	0	315	133	336	378	510	888	9	84	34	0.63	37	17	46	115	56	0%	6	272	6.44	6.9	$6
Bats	Left	05 BOS	408	64	112	13	67	2	275	229	289	358	446	804	11	86	29	0.90	39	20	40	111	61	2%	14	290	5.63	10.9	$13
Reliability	17	06 BOS	381	59	102	8	52	0	268	204	288	367	394	761	14	85	30	1.07	39	17	44	82	31	2%	10	253	5.28	-4.2	$9
DL	34 27	1st Half	233	45	77	6	42	0	330			426	494	920	14	91	35	1.77	37	20	43	102	34	0%	7	294	7.24	9.7	$10
BAvg Potl	60%	2nd Half	148	14	25	2	10	0	169			272	236	509	12	77	21	0.62	43	12	45	46	31	5%	2	185	1.82	-18.8	($1)
LIMA Plan	D	07 Proj	396	58	103	11	55	1	260			349	409	758	12	83	29	0.81	39	17	44	95	47	2%	12	259	5.09	-1.5	$9

Improving plate skills partially offset the declining H% and PX that often point to declining bat speed. The key number here is "187." That's the number of days he's spent on the DL the past three years.

Nix,Laynce			AB	R	H	HR	RBI	SB	Avg	vL	vR	OB	Slg	OPS	bb%	ct%	h%	Eye	G	L	F	PX	SX	SBO	xHR	xBA	RC/G	RAR	R$
Pos	8	02	0	0	0	0	0	0	0							0							0		0				
Age	26	03 TEX *	519	70	138	22	85	11	266	150	268	317	455	772	7	79	30	0.35	40	27	34	124	79	11%	21	295	4.90	2.4	$18
Pre-Peak		04 TEX	374	59	92	14	46	1	246	176	266	291	433	725	6	70	32	0.21	46	18	36	130	100	3%	15	253	4.44	-3.0	$8
Bats	Left	05 TEX *	265	34	66	8	36	2	249	333	232	289	419	708	5	82	28	0.31	49	17	34	105	104	5%	8	281	4.10	-1.4	$6
Reliability	20	06 2TM *	421	53	110	17	72	4	261	125	169	296	440	736	5	72	33	0.17	43	15	43	120	82	5%	17	241	4.43	-1.5	$12
DL	78	1st Half	235	28	58	9	44	2	249			276	430	706	4	71	31	0.13	38	13	50	127	76	7%	9	230	4.02	-3.7	$6
BAvg Potl	30%	2nd Half	186	26	52	8	29	2	277			321	453	774	6	73	34	0.24	46	17	38	112	77	4%	7	248	4.94	2.0	$6
LIMA Plan	F	07 Proj	199	27	51	8	30	2	256			297	440	737	5	75	31	0.23	47	18	35	120	95	5%	7	265	4.45	-0.7	$6

1-10-.164 in 67 AB at TEX, MIL. Injuries and erratic skills have taken the shine off this one-time prospect. The fact that he hasn't yet broken a 5.00 RC/G as he enters his peak years speaks volumes.

PATRICK DAVITT

Norton,Greg

			AB	R	H	HR	RBI	SB	Avg	vL	vR	OB	Slg	OPS	bb%	ct%	h%	Eye	G	L	F	PX	SX	SBO	xHR	xBA	RC/G	RAR	R$
Pos	93	02 COL	180	20	38	7	37	2	211	167	232	311	383	694	13	69	26	0.47	40	25	35	126	69	10%	8	258	4.21	-6.2	$4
Age	34	03 COL	179	19	47	6	31	2	263	273	261	323	447	770	8	74	33	0.34	43	24	33	140	47	7%	7	284	5.09	-2.7	$5
Past Peak		04 DET *	270	30	46	5	15	1	170	182	167	253	256	509	10	75	21	0.45	40	15	45	54	64	3%	5	201	1.65	-26.9	($1)
Bats	Both	05 aaa	323	41	77	14	41	0	240			309	426	735	9	82	25	0.55				115	38	2%	13		4.55	-4.2	$8
Reliability	1	06 TAM	294	47	87	17	45	1	296	283	299	371	520	891	11	77	34	0.51	38	19	42	140	32	7%	16	275	6.59	7.7	$12
DL		1st Half	81	12	24	4	9	0	296			345	494	839	7	74	36	0.29	37	24	39	129	38	5%	4	271	5.79	0.3	$3
BAvg Potl	40%	2nd Half	213	35	63	13	36	1	296			380	531	911	12	77	33	0.60	39	18	43	144	35	7%	12	278	6.88	7.3	$9
LIMA Plan	F	07 Proj	253	35	65	12	33	1	257			330	442	771	10	77	29	0.47	40	21	40	118	36	5%	11	267	5.01	-1.5	$7

Amazing what spending 2005 in AAA did for this 33-year old:
- Career HR high (31-HR pace)
- Most at bats since 1999
- Hamstring injury only kept him out for 5 days
- 2007 contract with '08 option

Nunez,Abraham O.

			AB	R	H	HR	RBI	SB	Avg	vL	vR	OB	Slg	OPS	bb%	ct%	h%	Eye	G	L	F	PX	SX	SBO	xHR	xBA	RC/G	RAR	R$
Pos	5	02 PIT	253	28	59	2	15	3	233	176	242	307	320	627	10	83	28	0.61	57	19	24	66	70	10%	4	269	3.45	-8.9	$3
Age	31	03 PIT	311	37	77	4	35	9	248	163	261	306	357	663	8	83	29	0.49	55	23	22	62	135	14%	4	285	3.76	-4.6	$7
Past Peak		04 PIT	182	17	43	2	13	1	236	158	245	276	319	595	5	80	28	0.28	63	12	25	60	43	10%	3	233	2.71	-13.1	$1
Bats	Both	05 STL	421	64	120	5	44	0	285	310	277	343	361	704	8	85	33	0.59	54	25	21	49	56	1%	6	280	4.26	-6.2	$11
Reliability	28	06 PHI	322	42	68	2	32	1	211	171	225	300	273	574	11	82	25	0.71	62	15	23	40	68	1%	3	241	2.84	-26.4	$2
DL		1st Half	90	5	14	1	3	0	156			191	222	414	4	86	17	0.31	68	4	28	43	19	0%	1	181	0.71	-14.2	($2)
BAvg Potl	65%	2nd Half	232	37	54	1	29	1	233			338	293	631	14	81	28	0.82	60	19	21	40	81	1%	2	252	3.66	-12.8	$3
LIMA Plan	F	07 Proj	274	34	63	3	25	1	230			297	301	598	9	83	27	0.55	60	16	23	48	65	3%	3	253	3.00	-17.8	$3

Obviously, it was some other Abraham Nunez that spent 2005 in St. Louis. THAT guy made above average contact, got on base and teed off on LHPs. THIS Nunez clearly does not like the state of Pennsylvania.

Olivo,Miguel

			AB	R	H	HR	RBI	SB	Avg	vL	vR	OB	Slg	OPS	bb%	ct%	h%	Eye	G	L	F	PX	SX	SBO	xHR	xBA	RC/G	RAR	R$
Pos	2	02 aa	359	44	98	6	43	25	273			341	423	764	9	82	32	0.58				97	145	38%	7		5.11	13.4	$15
Age	28	03 CHW	317	37	75	6	27	6	237	302	212	280	360	639	6	75	30	0.24	41	26	33	92	87	15%	8	261	3.25	-8.2	$5
Peak		04 2AL	301	46	70	13	40	7	233	322	196	280	439	719	6	72	28	0.24	47	14	39	134	132	22%	13	260	4.29	-0.4	$8
Bats	Right	05 2TM *	300	36	68	11	43	7	225	284	188	247	381	628	3	72	28	0.11	47	18	35	109	103	17%	11	249	2.87	-9.5	$7
Reliability	26	06 FLA	430	52	113	16	58	2	263	273	258	278	440	717	2	76	31	0.09	42	19	39	112	70	6%	15	260	3.99	-4.4	$11
DL		1st Half	179	21	52	8	29	2	291			310	492	801	3	74	35	0.11	38	20	42	135	47	11%	8	266	5.12	4.0	$7
BAvg Potl	40%	2nd Half	251	31	61	8	29	0	243			255	402	657	2	77	28	0.07	45	19	36	96	82	2%	7	256	3.22	-8.4	$4
LIMA Plan	D	07 Proj	410	51	99	12	54	2	241			267	390	658	3	75	30	0.14	44	18	37	100	77	7%	12	248	3.34	-9.5	$8

Throw away the book. BPIs do not support this output. But the key indicator in his first full season is the 2nd half plunge. Any player who can't come within 20 points of a .300 OB -- ever -- is just not of interest.

Ordonez,Magglio

			AB	R	H	HR	RBI	SB	Avg	vL	vR	OB	Slg	OPS	bb%	ct%	h%	Eye	G	L	F	PX	SX	SBO	xHR	xBA	RC/G	RAR	R$
Pos	9	02 CHW	590	116	189	38	135	7	320	288	329	376	597	973	8	87	32	0.69	42	21	37	158	74	8%	31	339	7.25	35.6	$35
Age	33	03 CHW	606	95	192	29	99	9	317	317	317	376	546	922	9	88	32	0.78	42	22	36	134	83	8%	26	327	6.76	26.4	$28
Past Peak		04 CHW	202	32	59	9	37	0	292	339	273	344	485	829	7	89	29	0.73	49	15	36	100	69	4%	7	290	5.61	5.1	$8
Bats	Right	05 DET	305	38	92	8	46	0	302	308	300	364	436	800	9	89	32	0.86	44	23	34	84	23	0%	8	291	5.45	6.2	$10
Reliability	29	06 DET	593	82	177	24	104	1	298	294	300	348	477	825	7	85	32	0.52	45	18	38	104	35	3%	21	279	5.53	-2.2	$21
DL	77	1st Half	288	43	90	15	57	1	313			365	521	886	8	85	33	0.56	43	17	40	118	36	4%	13	287	6.23	4.4	$13
BAvg Potl	50%	2nd Half	305	39	87	9	47	0	285			331	436	767	6	86	31	0.48	47	18	35	91	45	2%	9	275	4.87	-6.8	$8
LIMA Plan	C	07 Proj	582	82	169	20	99	0	290			345	456	801	8	87	31	0.63	45	19	36	97	42	2%	19	286	5.33	1.8	$19

Outhit his skills by about 20 BA points and 3 HR. That over-performance and postseason-related exuberance could drive '07 bidding past acceptable risk, especially given injury history, age, and second-half slowdown.

Orr,Pete

			AB	R	H	HR	RBI	SB	Avg	vL	vR	OB	Slg	OPS	bb%	ct%	h%	Eye	G	L	F	PX	SX	SBO	xHR	xBA	RC/G	RAR	R$
Pos	4	02 aa	305	29	67	2	29	18	220			259	275	534	5	87	25	0.41				37	113	32%	3		2.20	-19.3	$6
Age	27	03 aa	257	19	52	2	28	12	203			266	270	536	8	82	24	0.48				47	95	28%	3		2.21	-17.0	$3
Peak		04 aaa	460	60	136	1	31	21	295			321	368	689	4	89	33	0.35				42	139	25%	2		3.96	-5.1	$14
Bats	Left	05 ATL	150	32	45	1	8	7	300	409	286	327	387	714	4	85	35	0.26	57	18	25	62	147	20%	2	279	4.15	-1.7	$6
Reliability	22	06 ATL	154	22	39	1	8	2	253	182	265	277	344	621	3	81	31	0.17	53	23	25	49	119	17%	1	260	2.98	-7.6	$2
DL		1st Half	71	9	15	1	4	2	211			233	310	543	3	76	26	0.12	57	15	28	48	136	29%	1	231	1.87	-6.2	$1
BAvg Potl	45%	2nd Half	83	13	24	0	4	0	289			314	373	687	3	84	34	0.23	49	28	22	49	107	9%	0	287	3.88	-1.7	$1
LIMA Plan	F	07 Proj	115	18	31	1	7	3	270			297	356	653	4	84	32	0.24	54	21	25	52	137	20%	1	273	3.44	-3.8	$3

Scrappy scrubeenie smallball specialist -- beats the ball into the ground for leg hits and then swipes bases. It worked in the minors, but less so at MLB. BPI-wise, not a great end-gamer unless you're desperate.

Ortiz,David

			AB	R	H	HR	RBI	SB	Avg	vL	vR	OB	Slg	OPS	bb%	ct%	h%	Eye	G	L	F	PX	SX	SBO	xHR	xBA	RC/G	RAR	R$
Pos	0	02 MIN	412	52	112	20	75	1	272	203	299	341	500	841	9	79	30	0.49	35	16	49	148	40	3%	20	278	5.92	4.6	$14
Age	31	03 BOS	448	79	129	31	101	0	288	216	313	370	592	961	11	81	29	0.70	34	27	39	187	49	0%	28	344	7.42	35.1	$22
Past Peak		04 BOS	582	94	175	41	139	0	301	250	326	381	603	984	11	77	33	0.56	35	20	46	189	43	0%	38	311	7.83	40.3	$29
Bats	Left	05 BOS	601	119	180	47	148	1	300	302	297	401	604	1005	15	79	31	0.82	31	23	46	189	51	1%	41	323	8.13	34.8	$34
Reliability	97	06 BOS	558	115	160	54	137	1	287	278	292	412	636	1048	18	79	27	1.02	36	17	47	200	51	1%	45	322	8.76	36.3	$31
DL		1st Half	284	52	75	22	69	0	264			374	542	917	15	80	26	0.86	36	18	46	160	27	0%	19	294	6.98	4.5	$13
BAvg Potl	65%	2nd Half	274	63	85	32	68	1	310			449	734	1183	20	78	29	1.17	37	15	47	242	66	1%	26	351	10.60	30.9	$19
LIMA Plan	D+	07 Proj	575	112	179	50	138	1	311			417	642	1060	15	79	32	0.86	35	19	46	197	50	1%	43	323	8.87	44.2	$34

Give Ortiz a 10% bb% rather than 18%, and HR/RBI at the same AB rate, and he's 60-151-.287. DH-only constrains flexibility in standard formats, but this is the closest thing to sure offensive production.

Overbay,Lyle

			AB	R	H	HR	RBI	SB	Avg	vL	vR	OB	Slg	OPS	bb%	ct%	h%	Eye	G	L	F	PX	SX	SBO	xHR	xBA	RC/G	RAR	R$
Pos	3	02 aaa	525	62	161	15	82	0	307			345	463	808	6	88	33	0.48				100	24	0%	15		5.31	-6.0	$18
Age	30	03 ARI *	373	41	100	7	40	1	268	291	268	364	405	768	13	78	33	0.69	43	28	29	105	34	1%	11	291	5.33	-2.0	$8
Peak		04 MIL	583	84	175	16	88	2	300	298	301	386	479	864	12	78	36	0.63	45	23	31	128	48	2%	22	292	6.51	8.9	$20
Bats	Left	05 MIL	537	80	148	19	72	1	276	270	278	367	449	816	13	82	31	0.80	51	21	27	114	51	1%	20	298	5.81	3.2	$17
Reliability	87	06 TOR	581	82	181	22	92	5	312	284	322	371	508	879	9	83	34	0.57	46	22	32	124	56	5%	23	308	6.32	14.2	$22
DL		1st Half	273	39	81	11	42	2	297			375	487	862	11	83	33	0.72	45	22	33	116	57	5%	11	298	6.25	6.3	$10
BAvg Potl	45%	2nd Half	308	43	100	11	50	3	325			368	526	894	6	84	36	0.43	46	23	31	131	54	5%	12	318	6.37	7.8	$13
LIMA Plan	C	07 Proj	567	80	170	23	89	3	300			370	504	875	10	82	33	0.63	47	22	30	131	51	3%	24	310	6.36	16.7	$21

Corrected 2005 G/F imbalance and saw doubles power grow to HRs. SkyDome effect (17 home HR out of 22 total) also helped new Jays Molina (12/19) and Glaus (25/38). Raked RHP and held his own with LHP.

Ozuna,Pablo

			AB	R	H	HR	RBI	SB	Avg	vL	vR	OB	Slg	OPS	bb%	ct%	h%	Eye	G	L	F	PX	SX	SBO	xHR	xBA	RC/G	RAR	R$
Pos	7	02 aaa	261	25	67	5	22	11	257			289	372	661	4	89	27	0.40				72	99	25%	5		3.62	-15.5	$7
Age	32	03 a/a	278	21	58	1	13	10	209			230	298	528	3	91	23	0.30				53	131	36%	2		2.25	-28.6	$1
Past Peak		04 aaa	472	58	114	5	57	23	242			269	324	593	3	91	26	0.39				51	120	35%	6		2.91	-33.1	$12
Bats	Right	05 CHW	203	27	56	0	11	14	276	306	248	300	330	630	3	87	32	0.27	73	15	12	37	137	39%	1	293	3.22	-9.1	$6
Reliability	7	06 CHW	189	25	62	2	17	6	328	322	348	352	444	796	4	92	35	0.44	49	19	32	71	101	23%	3	293	5.15	-0.1	$7
DL		1st Half	87	18	37	1	13	5	425			451	540	991	4	91	46	0.50	45	26	30	69	116	29%	1	304	7.27	4.5	$6
BAvg Potl	40%	2nd Half	102	7	25	1	4	1	245			267	363	629	3	92	26	0.38	53	13	34	73	72	11%	1	279	3.37	-5.5	$0
LIMA Plan	F	07 Proj	169	21	49	1	13	7	290			314	390	705	3	90	32	0.36	57	17	26	62	119	29%	2	293	4.13	-4.3	$5

In 503 career AB: 2-33-.292, with 25 SB. Doesn't walk but makes contact. Versatility and speed make him a decent end-game pick or filler with upside should he get extra ABs.

Pagan,Angel

			AB	R	H	HR	RBI	SB	Avg	vL	vR	OB	Slg	OPS	bb%	ct%	h%	Eye	G	L	F	PX	SX	SBO	xHR	xBA	RC/G	RAR	R$
Pos	79	02	0	0	0	0	0	0	0							0							0		0				
Age	25	03	0	0	0	0	0	0	0							0							0		0				
Pre-Peak		04 a/a	494	72	129	3	55	28	261			315	360	676	7	82	31	0.43				66	153	27%	6		3.92	-18.6	$15
Bats	Both	05 aaa	509	57	124	6	32	23	244			297	338	635	7	81	29	0.41				61	121	29%	7		3.35	-26.4	$11
Reliability	10	06 CHC	170	28	42	5	18	4	247	196	272	308	394	702	8	84	27	0.54	51	15	34	81	112	14%	5	266	4.18	-5.4	$4
DL	75	1st Half	19	2	5	0	1	0	263			263	316	579	0	79	33	0.00	60	7	33	46	67	25%	0	204	2.24	-1.8	$0
BAvg Potl	55%	2nd Half	151	26	37	5	17	4	245			313	404	717	9	84	26	0.63	50	16	34	85	120	13%	4	273	4.41	-3.8	$4
LIMA Plan	F	07 Proj	134	20	34	2	13	6	254			312	379	692	8	82	29	0.48	50	16	34	76	132	22%	3	261	4.10	-5.1	$4

Excellent speed, but few on-base skills to let him take advantage. A marginal deep-league fifth OF or injury sub if you need the possibility of perhaps 10 SBs and can cope with the BA damage.

PATRICK DAVITT

Palmeiro,Orlando		AB	R	H	HR	RBI	SB	Avg	vL	vR	OB	Slg	OPS	bb%	ct%	h%	Eye	G	L	F	PX	SX	SBO	xHR	xBA	RC/G	RAR	R$
Pos 7	02 ANA	263	35	79	0	31	7	300	412	284	372	354	726	10	92	33	1.36	44	21	35	38	89	9%	2	262	4.87	0.3	$8
Age 38	03 STL	317	37	86	3	33	3	271	182	290	338	347	685	9	90	29	1.03	44	26	30	49	60	6%	4	285	4.27	-12.1	$7
Decline	04 HOU	133	19	32	3	12	2	241	167	248	331	346	677	12	86	26	0.95	40	19	42	63	60	7%	3	248	4.15	-5.2	$3
Bats Left	05 HOU	204	22	58	3	20	3	284	143	302	333	431	765	7	89	31	0.65	43	23	34	98	88	8%	4	307	5.03	-1.8	$5
Reliability 0	06 HOU	119	12	30	0	17	0	252		259	288	319	607	5	86	29	0.35	41	28	30	47	61	3%	1	276	3.04	-7.8	$1
DL	1st Half	61	10	14	0	6	0	230			277	279	556	6	85	27	0.44	46	24	30	27	99	0%	0	251	2.49	-5.1	$1
BAvg Potl 55%	2nd Half	58	2	16	0	11	0	276			300	362	662	3	86	32	0.25	37	33	31	69	18	8%	1	310	3.61	-2.8	$1
LIMA Plan F	07 Proj	**112**	**12**	**30**	**1**	**14**	**1**	**268**			**317**	**371**	**688**	**7**	**87**	**30**	**0.55**	**41**	**25**	**33**	**69**	**71**	**6%**	**2**	**284**	**4.11**	**-4.1**	**$2**

Strictly a PH/platoon option these days - only 37 ABs vs LHP in last three years. BB% is in steep decline. No power, no speed, no reason to utter his name on draft day.

Patterson,Corey		AB	R	H	HR	RBI	SB	Avg	vL	vR	OB	Slg	OPS	bb%	ct%	h%	Eye	G	L	F	PX	SX	SBO	xHR	xBA	RC/G	RAR	R$
Pos 8	02 CHC	592	71	150	14	54	18	253	188	275	277	392	668	3	76	31	0.13	48	20	32	98	134	18%	15	265	3.48	-24.3	$16
Age 27	03 CHC	329	49	98	13	55	16	298	289	301	328	511	839	4	77	36	0.19	40	26	34	134	154	28%	12	290	5.71	6.8	$17
Peak	04 CHC	631	91	168	24	72	32	266	289	258	315	452	767	7	73	33	0.27	40	19	41	123	139	27%	24	255	4.93	5.2	$25
Bats Left	05 CHC	* 542	60	121	17	44	20	223	169	231	264	362	626	5	74	27	0.22	46	18	36	92	115	23%	16	244	2.95	-26.9	$12
Reliability 24	06 BAL	463	75	128	16	53	45	276	207	301	308	443	751	4	80	32	0.22	39	21	40	99	166	50%	14	262	4.51	-2.1	$23
DL	1st Half	238	40	67	8	32	29	282			321	429	750	6	82	32	0.33	39	23	39	86	148	52%	7	264	4.54	-0.8	$14
BAvg Potl 35%	2nd Half	225	35	61	8	21	16	271			293	458	751	3	77	32	0.14	39	20	41	113	169	46%	7	260	4.49	-1.1	$9
LIMA Plan C+	07 Proj	**510**	**73**	**133**	**18**	**54**	**40**	**261**			**296**	**432**	**727**	**5**	**77**	**31**	**0.21**	**41**	**20**	**39**	**107**	**156**	**43%**	**17**	**260**	**4.25**	**-5.0**	**$21**

PRO: Improving ct%; half the time he reached 1B, he ran and was successful 83% of the time. CON: Still no walks, so low OB; struggles vs LHP. More plate patience would be nice, but speed drives his value.

Paulino,Ronny		AB	R	H	HR	RBI	SB	Avg	vL	vR	OB	Slg	OPS	bb%	ct%	h%	Eye	G	L	F	PX	SX	SBO	xHR	xBA	RC/G	RAR	R$
Pos 2	02	0	0	0	0	0	0	0							0							0		0				
Age 26	03 aa	159	17	34	5	17	0	214			265	358	623	6	81	23	0.37				88	62	6%	5		3.08	-5.5	$2
Pre-Peak	04 aa	369	43	93	12	48	2	252			298	410	709	6	87	26	0.50				93	56	5%	11		4.20	1.4	$8
Bats Right	05 a/a	436	54	115	14	46	5	265			312	412	724	6	87	28	0.51				89	79	4%	13		4.36	5.8	$11
Reliability 31	06 PIT	* 471	39	144	6	59	1	306	339	300	356	390	747	7	82	36	0.42	47	23	31	58	25	1%	8	252	4.68	4.4	$12
DL	1st Half	219	19	65	2	21	1	296			355	383	738	8	80	36	0.46	49	20	31	65	30	1%	4	245	4.68	2.1	$5
BAvg Potl 30%	2nd Half	252	20	79	4	38	0	313			357	397	754	6	83	37	0.39	45	25	30	53	11	0%	4	255	4.68	2.3	$7
LIMA Plan D	07 Proj	**410**	**41**	**107**	**9**	**49**	**2**	**261**			**311**	**379**	**690**	**7**	**84**	**29**	**0.44**	**47**	**23**	**30**	**74**	**51**	**2%**	**10**	**275**	**3.97**	**-1.7**	**$8**

6-55-.310 in 442 AB at PIT. High h% and low xBA say he's not a .300 hitter. MLEs show more PX potential, but needs to hit fewer GBs to produce power in the majors.

Paul,Josh		AB	R	H	HR	RBI	SB	Avg	vL	vR	OB	Slg	OPS	bb%	ct%	h%	Eye	G	L	F	PX	SX	SBO	xHR	xBA	RC/G	RAR	R$
Pos 2	02 CHW	* 335	26	80	0	25	11	239	250	233	290	296	585	7	81	30	0.38	37	21	43	47	84	17%	3	224	2.75	-8.8	$4
Age 31	03 aaa	210	14	40	3	16	1	190			227	257	484	5	80	22	0.24				39	56	9%	3		1.29	-19.7	($1)
Past Peak	04 ANA	70	11	17	2	10	2	243	316	216	312	371	683	9	76	29	0.41	46	15	38	86	78	16%	2	235	3.90	-0.9	$2
Bats Right	05 ANA	* 70	9	15	2	9	0	214			286	357	643	9	76	25	0.41	44	15	41	104	47	6%	2	240	3.40	-1.4	$1
Reliability 9	06 TAM	146	15	38	1	8	1	260	333	234	325	342	667	9	73	35	0.36	48	22	30	71	41	7%	2	237	3.81	-2.6	$1
DL 24	1st Half	77	7	19	1	3	0	247			284	351	635	5	74	32	0.20	48	21	31	83	36	6%	2	242	3.17	-2.9	$0
BAvg Potl 30%	2nd Half	69	8	19	0	5	1	275			367	333	700	13	72	38	0.53	48	24	28	56	46	8%	1	232	4.48	0.1	$1
LIMA Plan F	07 Proj	**148**	**13**	**35**	**1**	**10**	**2**	**236**			**293**	**300**	**593**	**7**	**77**	**30**	**0.34**	**47**	**22**	**30**	**50**	**45**	**9%**	**2**	**235**	**2.74**	**-6.8**	**$1**

No power or speed, and BA was driven by a high h%. Can't hit RHPs, strikes out a lot, and when he makes contact, it's usually a ground ball. RuPaul could put up better numbers than this.

Payton,Jay		AB	R	H	HR	RBI	SB	Avg	vL	vR	OB	Slg	OPS	bb%	ct%	h%	Eye	G	L	F	PX	SX	SBO	xHR	xBA	RC/G	RAR	R$
Pos 789	02 2NL	445	69	135	16	59	7	303	252	326	346	488	834	6	88	32	0.54	50	17	33	104	114	9%	13	305	5.62	-9.4	$19
Age 34	03 COL	600	93	181	28	89	6	302	288	307	340	512	860	7	87	31	0.56	45	23	32	119	88	6%	23	320	5.90	5.2	$26
Past Peak	04 SD	458	57	119	8	55	2	260	283	248	323	367	690	9	88	28	0.77	43	16	41	61	78	2%	8	250	4.20	-16.5	$9
Bats Right	05 2AL	408	62	109	18	63	0	267	283	258	308	444	751	6	88	27	0.51	42	19	38	98	50	1%	14	291	4.59	-1.5	$13
Reliability 88	06 OAK	557	78	165	10	59	8	296	296	296	323	418	741	4	91	31	0.42	45	22	34	73	94	8%	11	292	4.52	-10.3	$15
DL	1st Half	238	36	66	3	22	2	277			295	395	690	2	90	30	0.25	39	24	37	73	99	6%	4	286	3.89	-8.7	$5
BAvg Potl 55%	2nd Half	319	42	99	7	37	6	310			343	436	779	5	91	32	0.57	49	20	31	73	76	10%	7	295	4.98	-1.8	$11
LIMA Plan D+	07 Proj	**464**	**66**	**132**	**12**	**58**	**4**	**284**			**322**	**428**	**750**	**5**	**89**	**30**	**0.52**	**44**	**20**	**36**	**82**	**84**	**6%**	**11**	**288**	**4.65**	**-4.8**	**$13**

Ct% remains solid, but bb% continues to drop. A falling FB%, esp. in 2nd half, limits his power. Makes a great fourth OF, but he's less valuable when he plays every day.

Pedroia,Dustin		AB	R	H	HR	RBI	SB	Avg	vL	vR	OB	Slg	OPS	bb%	ct%	h%	Eye	G	L	F	PX	SX	SBO	xHR	xBA	RC/G	RAR	R$
Pos 4	02	0	0	0	0	0	0	0							0							0		0				
Age 23	03	0	0	0	0	0	0	0							0							0		0				
Growth	04	0	0	0	0	0	0	0							0							0		0				
Bats Right	05 a/a	453	63	125	10	52	7	276			343	415	758	9	92	28	1.35				85	84	8%	11		5.12	10.1	$13
Reliability 0	06 BOS	* 512	56	145	7	53	1	283	162	212	349	404	754	9	94	29	1.68	48	23	30	75	39	4%	10	308	5.16	15.1	$10
DL	1st Half	245	28	68	2	18	0	278			347	392	739	10	93	29	1.44				73	52	4%	4		5.02	6.4	$3
BAvg Potl 75%	2nd Half	267	28	77	5	35	1	288			352	416	767	9	95	29	2.00	48	23	30	77	31	4%	6	311	5.28	8.7	$6
LIMA Plan B+	07 Proj	**477**	**58**	**136**	**8**	**53**	**4**	**285**			**351**	**415**	**766**	**9**	**93**	**29**	**1.55**	**48**	**23**	**30**	**79**	**59**	**5%**	**10**	**312**	**5.25**	**15.4**	**$11**

2-7-.191 in 89 AB at BOS. Many reasons for optimism: Solid plate patience. High LD%. High ct%. Low BA in BOS was due to 19% h%. xBA shows potential. Slow start in '06 could make him a draft day bargain.

Pena,Brayan		AB	R	H	HR	RBI	SB	Avg	vL	vR	OB	Slg	OPS	bb%	ct%	h%	Eye	G	L	F	PX	SX	SBO	xHR	xBA	RC/G	RAR	R$
Pos 2	02	0	0	0	0	0	0	0							0							0		0				
Age 25	03	0	0	0	0	0	0	0							0							0		0				
Pre-Peak	04 aa	277	27	81	2	27	3	292			324	368	692	4	91	32	0.52				43	77	9%	2		4.06	-0.1	$6
Bats Both	05 aaa	282	24	85	0	22	3	301			358	379	738	8	94	32	1.47				58	55	4%	3		4.95	8.1	$6
Reliability 12	06 ATL	* 366	39	105	2	36	6	287	200	308	327	361	688	6	91	31	0.69	58	22	19	48	63	11%	4	299	4.11	-2.4	$8
DL	1st Half	203	22	52	1	14	5	256			311	320	631	7	91	28	0.84	54	23	23	44	68	11%	2	290	3.58	-4.5	$3
BAvg Potl 60%	2nd Half	163	17	53	1	22	1	325			349	411	760	4	92	35	0.46	70	20	10	54	55	13%	2		4.76	1.9	$5
LIMA Plan F	07 Proj	**132**	**13**	**37**	**1**	**13**	**2**	**280**			**324**	**360**	**684**	**6**	**92**	**30**	**0.83**	**61**	**22**	**18**	**52**	**73**	**9%**	**1**	**309**	**4.15**	**0.2**	**$3**

1-5-.268 in 41 AB at ATL. Nice ct%; he'll hit for average. But 2nd half BA was due to high h%. High GB%, no power means not much happens when he puts it in play. End-game CA who will just fill a roster spot.

Pena,Carlos		AB	R	H	HR	RBI	SB	Avg	vL	vR	OB	Slg	OPS	bb%	ct%	h%	Eye	G	L	F	PX	SX	SBO	xHR	xBA	RC/G	RAR	R$
Pos 3	02 2AL	* 572	65	131	26	76	4	229	265	230	301	427	728	9	74	26	0.40	37	20	43	126	78	4%	25	258	4.47	-24.1	$13
Age 28	03 DET	452	51	112	18	50	4	248	208	267	327	440	767	10	73	30	0.43	37	21	42	128	84	8%	18	256	5.13	-3.4	$10
Peak	04 DET	481	89	116	27	82	7	241	245	240	338	472	810	13	70	29	0.48	40	16	44	153	112	6%	27	256	5.80	11.7	$17
Bats Left	05 DET	* 517	73	131	28	82	3	254	146	255	342	462	804	12	70	31	0.45	38	18	45	146	47	5%	28	253	5.66	8.7	$17
Reliability 63	06 BOS	* 451	66	112	21	68	4	249	273	273	339	433	772	12	76	28	0.57	48	17	35	115	58	3%	21	264	5.13	-3.8	$12
DL	1st Half	221	31	49	8	28	2	223			333	379	711	14	76	26	0.67				101	50	3%	9		4.46	-6.5	$4
BAvg Potl 50%	2nd Half	230	36	63	13	40	2	274			346	485	831	10	76	31	0.47	48	17	35	129	51	3%	12	274	5.75	2.2	$8
LIMA Plan D	07 Proj	**212**	**31**	**53**	**11**	**33**	**2**	**250**			**337**	**454**	**791**	**12**	**73**	**29**	**0.50**	**40**	**18**	**43**	**131**	**69**	**4%**	**10**	**257**	**5.41**	**0.7**	**$6**

1-3-.273 in 33 AB at BOS. Power was MIA in the 1st half, but returned to form in the 2nd half. Low ct% limits BA upside, but could produce decent power numbers if he finds regular ABs.

Pena,Wily Mo		AB	R	H	HR	RBI	SB	Avg	vL	vR	OB	Slg	OPS	bb%	ct%	h%	Eye	G	L	F	PX	SX	SBO	xHR	xBA	RC/G	RAR	R$
Pos 98	02 aa	388	40	96	9	40	6	247			300	384	684	7	76	30	0.32				100	81	7%	11		3.87	-14.7	$8
Age 25	03 CIN	* 216	34	56	9	28	3	259	204	225	310	435	746	7	71	32	0.26	46	21	32	121	93	9%	9	262	4.65	-6.1	$7
Pre-Peak	04 CIN	336	45	87	26	66	5	259	302	244	304	527	831	6	68	30	0.20	50	16	33	174	72	10%	22	274	5.79	4.9	$15
Bats Right	05 CIN	311	42	79	19	51	2	254	291	234	299	492	791	6	63	34	0.17	48	20	32	189	50	5%	19	265	5.63	3.5	$11
Reliability 33	06 BOS	276	36	83	11	42	0	301	260	326	348	489	837	7	67	41	0.22	40	21	39	137	57	1%	12	247	6.16	3.8	$9
DL 51 35	1st Half	112	12	36	4	18	0	321			377	482	859	8	67	45	0.27	42	23	35	122	14	0%	5	239	6.56	2.7	$4
BAvg Potl 15%	2nd Half	164	24	47	7	24	0	287			328	494	821	6	68	38	0.19	38	20	42	147	83	3%	7	250	5.88	1.0	$5
LIMA Plan C	07 Proj	**458**	**61**	**118**	**23**	**72**	**2**	**258**			**306**	**467**	**773**	**6**	**67**	**34**	**0.21**	**44**	**20**	**36**	**151**	**67**	**4%**	**23**	**256**	**5.17**	**-0.7**	**$14**

A .300 hitter? Hardly. H%, xBA, and poor plate patience point to a signficantly lower BA next year. Rising FB% makes the PX drop unexpected; wrist surgery a likely cause. More power likely on the way. UP: 30 HR.

DAVE ADLER

Peralta,Jhonny

		Year	AB	R	H	HR	RBI	SB	Avg	vL	vR	OB	Slg	OPS	bb%	ct%	h%	Eye	G	L	F	PX	SX	SBO	xHR	xBA	RC/G	RAR	R$
Pos	6	02 aa	470	58	132	15	58	4	281			340	449	789	8	82	32	0.50				108	78	5%	15		5.23	13.2	$14
Age	24	03 aaa	237	25	64	1	21	1	269			311	348	659	6	84	32	0.37				59	58	7%	3		3.63	-4.4	$4
Growth		04 aaa	556	88	166	12	69	6	298			349	440	789	7	82	35	0.44				97	77	7%	15		5.22	14.3	$18
Bats	Right	05 CLE	504	82	147	24	78	0	292	305	288	365	520	885	10	75	35	0.45	46	19	35	158	59	1%	25	291	6.65	29.4	$19
Reliability	19	06 CLE	569	84	146	13	68	0	257	267	252	323	385	708	9	73	33	0.37	48	19	34	91	57	1%	16	241	4.30	-1.9	$11
DL		1st Half	294	53	73	7	34	0	248			326	381	707	10	72	32	0.42	44	21	35	96	62	0%	9	245	4.36	-0.5	$6
BAvg Potl	35%	2nd Half	275	31	73	6	34	0	265			320	389	709	7	74	34	0.31	51	17	33	84	53	1%	7	236	4.22	-1.5	$5
LIMA Plan	C	07 Proj	**576**	**84**	**153**	**16**	**74**	**0**	**266**			**329**	**420**	**749**	**9**	**76**	**32**	**0.39**	**47**	**19**	**34**	**106**	**56**	**2%**	**19**	**260**	**4.79**	**5.4**	**$14**

Not just a sophomore slump: low ct%, eye indicate 2006 BA was about right. PX decline is tougher to explain - G/L/F was consistent with 2005. Growth still possible, but 2005 may have been an early peak.

Perez,Antonio

		Year	AB	R	H	HR	RBI	SB	Avg	vL	vR	OB	Slg	OPS	bb%	ct%	h%	Eye	G	L	F	PX	SX	SBO	xHR	xBA	RC/G	RAR	R$
Pos	50	02 aa	240	30	59	2	24	15	246			279	313	591	4	74	33	0.17				51	121	41%	3		2.53	-14.9	$7
Age	27	03 a/a	215	39	57	7	27	5	265			342	470	811	10	76	32	0.48				143	131	13%	8		5.76	8.6	$7
Peak		04 aaa	476	64	114	16	61	15	239			301	393	694	8	87	25	0.68				85	96	26%	14		4.13	-12.7	$13
Bats	Right	* 05 LA	315	33	87	4	27	12	276	312	298	325	374	699	7	76	35	0.31	44	23	33	73	103	19%	6	248	4.09	-6.3	$9
Reliability	3	06 OAK	98	10	10	1	8	0	102	129	90	185	204	389	9	55	17	0.23	36	11	53	101	103	8%	2	160	-0.47	-19.1	($2)
DL	38	1st Half	49	3	4	1	5	0	82			167	184	350	9	51	13	0.21	40	4	56	105	21	0%	2	130	-1.36	-11.2	($1)
BAvg Potl	50%	2nd Half	49	7	6	0	3	0	122			204	224	428	9	59	21	0.25	32	18	50	97	141	14%	1	178	0.36	-8.0	($1)
LIMA Plan	F	07 Proj	**129**	**18**	**31**	**3**	**14**	**5**	**240**			**301**	**380**	**680**	**8**	**78**	**29**	**0.39**	**39**	**17**	**44**	**93**	**108**	**23%**	**3**	**242**	**3.89**	**-3.7**	**$3**

When you strike out in almost half of your AB and hit very few LDs, a .100 BA isn't surprising. Biggest problem is that, at 27, he's pretty late to the party and nobody is gonna wait around for him to figure things out.

Perez,Eduardo

		Year	AB	R	H	HR	RBI	SB	Avg	vL	vR	OB	Slg	OPS	bb%	ct%	h%	Eye	G	L	F	PX	SX	SBO	xHR	xBA	RC/G	RAR	R$
Pos	3	02 STL	154	22	31	10	26	0	201	271	143	281	455	735	10	77	19	0.47	40	16	44	167	31	0%	9	287	4.49	-5.3	$4
Age	37	03 STL	253	47	72	10	41	5	285	353	238	358	466	825	10	79	33	0.55	40	24	37	121	81	9%	10	286	5.76	1.8	$11
Decline		04 TAM	38	2	8	0	7	0	211			286	316	602	10	76	28	0.44				72	62	0%	0		3.10	-2.2	$0
Bats	Right	05 TAM	161	23	41	11	28	0	255	259	231	358	497	855	14	81	25	0.87	46	17	37	141	22	4%	9	289	6.16	5.1	$6
Reliability	0	06 2AL	186	22	47	9	33	0	253	275	152	319	452	770	9	82	26	0.55	49	19	33	118	24	2%	8	284	4.94	-2.6	$5
DL		1st Half	99	16	30	8	22	0	303			337	636	973	5	89	28	0.45	48	17	36	184	27	0%	6	354	6.95	4.1	$5
BAvg Potl	60%	2nd Half	87	6	17	1	11	0	195			300	241	541	13	75	25	0.59	50	21	29	30	20	4%	1	208	2.19	-9.0	($0)
LIMA Plan	F	07 Proj	**156**	**20**	**38**	**8**	**26**	**0**	**244**			**326**	**436**	**762**	**11**	**80**	**26**	**0.61**	**46**	**19**	**35**	**116**	**34**	**4%**	**7**	**276**	**4.92**	**-1.7**	**$4**

Doesn't see much time against RHP anymore, which is a good thing, considering his splits. High GB% suppresses power, and age limits his upside. He's fine for $1 roster filler, but not much more.

Perez,Neifi

		Year	AB	R	H	HR	RBI	SB	Avg	vL	vR	OB	Slg	OPS	bb%	ct%	h%	Eye	G	L	F	PX	SX	SBO	xHR	xBA	RC/G	RAR	R$
Pos	46	02 KC	554	65	131	3	37	8	236	227	240	263	303	566	3	90	26	0.38	39	24	37	41	99	14%	4	263	2.62	-24.0	$6
Age	33	03 SF	328	27	84	1	31	3	256	253	257	287	348	634	4	93	27	0.61	43	26	31	59	88	7%	3	299	3.54	-8.3	$4
Past Peak		04 CHC	381	40	97	4	39	1	255	252	256	299	336	635	6	89	28	0.59	46	20	34	52	51	2%	5	263	3.46	-12.8	$5
Bats	Both	05 CHC	572	59	157	9	54	8	274	267	272	297	383	679	3	92	29	0.38	44	23	33	69	72	9%	10	296	3.83	-12.0	$13
Reliability	60	06 2TM	301	31	73	2	29	1	243	265	232	262	316	578	3	92	26	0.32	40	19	41	47	60	3%	3	253	2.73	-14.6	$3
DL		1st Half	145	16	35	1	16	0	241			262	324	586	3	91	26	0.31	37	22	42	51	59	0%	2	260	2.82	-6.7	$1
BAvg Potl	60%	2nd Half	156	15	38	1	13	1	244			262	308	570	2	92	26	0.33	43	17	41	42	52	6%	2	244	2.66	-7.9	$1
LIMA Plan	D	07 Proj	**300**	**31**	**76**	**3**	**28**	**2**	**253**			**278**	**338**	**616**	**3**	**91**	**27**	**0.40**	**42**	**21**	**37**	**54**	**64**	**5%**	**4**	**268**	**3.17**	**-10.3**	**$4**

Setting the standard in offensive futility for over a decade. Doesn't get on base, doesn't run, and doesn't hit for power. His most amazing attribute is the fact that teams still trade FOR him.

Perez,Tomas

		Year	AB	R	H	HR	RBI	SB	Avg	vL	vR	OB	Slg	OPS	bb%	ct%	h%	Eye	G	L	F	PX	SX	SBO	xHR	xBA	RC/G	RAR	R$
Pos	564	02 PHI	221	24	56	5	21	1	253	250	250	318	389	707	9	81	29	0.51	38	26	36	94	57	2%	6	281	4.29	-1.9	$4
Age	33	03 PHI	298	39	79	5	33	0	265	266	265	318	379	697	7	82	31	0.43	45	23	32	79	54	1%	6	271	4.10	-1.4	$6
Past Peak		04 PHI	176	22	38	6	21	0	216	213	217	254	415	669	5	75	25	0.20	33	19	48	136	80	0%	7	260	3.60	-7.9	$2
Bats	Right	05 PHI	159	17	37	0	22	1	233	283	212	282	277	559	6	83	28	0.41	39	23	38	39	54	2%	1	238	2.46	-11.1	$2
Reliability	21	06 TAM	241	31	51	2	16	1	212	178	226	228	286	514	2	82	25	0.11	40	14	46	55	75	2%	3	215	1.62	-25.2	$0
DL		1st Half	124	15	21	2	8	1	169			202	250	452	4	81	19	0.21	42	12	46	53	81	5%	2	207	0.88	-16.7	($1)
BAvg Potl	50%	2nd Half	117	16	30	0	8	0	256			256	325	581	0	83	31	0.00	38	16	46	58	57	0%	1	223	2.37	-9.0	$1
LIMA Plan	F	07 Proj	**168**	**21**	**38**	**1**	**16**	**1**	**226**			**257**	**293**	**549**	**4**	**81**	**27**	**0.22**	**39**	**18**	**43**	**54**	**60**	**2%**	**2**	**225**	**2.15**	**-13.6**	**$1**

...OK, maybe Neifi IS the better option. Managed to walk five times all year. OB is barely above the Mendoza line. Antonio, Neifi, and Tomas - a veritable Perez-troika of offensive ineptitude.

Phillips,Andy

		Year	AB	R	H	HR	RBI	SB	Avg	vL	vR	OB	Slg	OPS	bb%	ct%	h%	Eye	G	L	F	PX	SX	SBO	xHR	xBA	RC/G	RAR	R$
Pos	3	02 a/a	477	73	118	24	70	3	247			300	470	770	7	81	26	0.39				140	72	8%	22		4.86	-12.5	$15
Age	30	03 aaa	67	6	13	2	4	0	188			233	333	566	5	78	21	0.27				100	24	0%	2		2.29	-6.7	($0)
Peak		04 a/a	476	67	121	23	75	3	254			311	450	760	8	87	25	0.64				102	90	4%	18		4.81	-9.3	$14
Bats	Right	* 05 NYY	340	54	81	18	46	2	239			297	446	743	8	80	25	0.41				127	73	2%	15		4.51	-5.9	$10
Reliability	27	06 NYY	246	30	59	7	29	3	240	195	262	284	394	678	6	77	28	0.27	44	20	35	97	102	9%	7	261	3.72	-12.6	$4
DL	15	1st Half	128	14	37	5	16	2	289			321	492	813	4	76	35	0.19	40	21	38	121	99	10%	4	269	5.39	-0.1	$4
BAvg Potl	45%	2nd Half	118	16	22	2	13	1	186			244	288	532	7	79	22	0.36	48	19	32	72	73	9%	3	250	1.99	-13.1	$0
LIMA Plan	F	07 Proj	**228**	**32**	**59**	**9**	**30**	**2**	**259**			**309**	**434**	**743**	**7**	**80**	**29**	**0.36**	**45**	**20**	**35**	**106**	**86**	**6%**	**8**	**277**	**4.55**	**-5.0**	**$6**

1H/2H BA swing was due to h%; xBA shows there wasn't much difference. Power drop was due to higher GB%. Needs to improve plate patience and improve against LHP to see more playing time.

Phillips,Brandon

		Year	AB	R	H	HR	RBI	SB	Avg	vL	vR	OB	Slg	OPS	bb%	ct%	h%	Eye	G	L	F	PX	SX	SBO	xHR	xBA	RC/G	RAR	R$
Pos	4	02 a/a	503	67	153	18	64	14	304			343	479	822	6	86	32	0.44				108	90	14%	17		5.44	16.9	$21
Age	25	* 03 CLE	524	50	104	9	46	10	198	179	218	236	302	538	5	82	23	0.27	45	19	36	70	83	19%	10	253	2.03	-35.4	$4
Pre-Peak		* 04 CLE	543	65	141	6	39	11	260	167	188	306	361	667	6	91	28	0.71	35	24	41	65	80	20%	9	274	3.91	-2.9	$10
Bats	Right	05 aaa	459	60	102	10	35	5	222			270	340	610	6	85	24	0.42				76	78	11%	10		3.02	-18.8	$6
Reliability	14	06 CIN	536	65	148	17	75	25	276	299	268	320	427	748	6	84	30	0.40	46	19	35	90	102	20%	16	277	4.58	-0.2	$20
DL		1st Half	239	36	74	7	44	14	310			355	456	812	7	87	34	0.53	44	23	34	84	112	20%	7	289	5.39	5.1	$12
BAvg Potl	45%	2nd Half	297	29	74	10	31	11	249			292	404	696	6	81	28	0.32	48	16	36	96	74	20%	10	265	3.92	-6.0	$8
LIMA Plan	C	07 Proj	**559**	**68**	**143**	**14**	**61**	**20**	**256**			**301**	**390**	**691**	**6**	**85**	**28**	**0.42**	**46**	**19**	**35**	**84**	**96**	**20%**	**15**	**275**	**3.96**	**-10.2**	**$16**

Perennial prospect finally broke out. 2nd half drop in h%, LD% led to a BA fade, but power rose as he opened his swing. That 2nd half is your benchmark for '07 so expect a slight regression.

Piazza,Mike

		Year	AB	R	H	HR	RBI	SB	Avg	vL	vR	OB	Slg	OPS	bb%	ct%	h%	Eye	G	L	F	PX	SX	SBO	xHR	xBA	RC/G	RAR	R$
Pos	2	02 NYM	478	69	134	33	98	0	280	286	278	357	544	901	11	83	28	0.70	41	20	39	155	33	2%	27	314	6.55	33.2	$22
Age	38	03 NYM	234	37	67	11	34	0	286	265	292	379	483	862	13	83	31	0.88	44	18	39	120	27	0%	10	280	6.32	13.3	$9
Decline		04 NYM	455	47	121	20	54	0	266	303	257	361	444	805	13	83	28	0.87	41	20	39	104	11	0%	19	268	5.62	23.7	$12
Bats	Right	05 NYM	398	41	100	19	62	0	251	269	248	321	452	773	9	83	26	0.61	45	19	36	124	13	0%	17	285	5.03	14.5	$11
Reliability	43	06 SD	399	39	113	22	68	0	283	359	257	339	501	841	8	83	29	0.52	40	21	39	121	16	0%	18	292	5.70	15.3	$14
DL	23	1st Half	201	18	53	11	31	0	264			324	478	802	8	83	27	0.53	40	20	40	121	5	0%	9	275	5.26	5.3	$6
BAvg Potl	50%	2nd Half	198	21	60	11	37	0	303			355	525	880	7	84	32	0.50	40	23	37	121	28	0%	9	302	6.15	9.8	$8
LIMA Plan	D	07 Proj	**304**	**32**	**84**	**15**	**49**	**0**	**276**			**344**	**478**	**822**	**9**	**83**	**29**	**0.62**	**42**	**21**	**38**	**117**	**29**	**0%**	**13**	**288**	**5.60**	**12.9**	**$10**

Defied age and park effects with best power season in four years, but xHR shows he did better than expected. Heed the warning signs - years behind the plate are taking their toll.

Pierre,Juan

		Year	AB	R	H	HR	RBI	SB	Avg	vL	vR	OB	Slg	OPS	bb%	ct%	h%	Eye	G	L	F	PX	SX	SBO	xHR	xBA	RC/G	RAR	R$
Pos	8	02 COL	592	90	170	1	35	47	287	294	285	323	343	666	5	91	31	0.60	56	26	18	37	152	34%	3	310	3.82	-17.8	$24
Age	29	03 FLA	668	100	204	1	41	65	305	311	303	358	373	731	8	95	32	1.57	52	31	17	42	150	38%	4	334	4.84	-2.7	$32
Peak		04 FLA	678	100	221	3	49	45	326	305	334	368	407	775	6	95	34	1.29	56	21	23	43	138	30%	4	305	5.19	10.1	$30
Bats	Left	05 FLA	656	96	181	2	47	57	276	284	267	319	354	672	6	93	29	0.91	55	25	20	43	170	39%	3	315	4.05	-9.9	$27
Reliability	88	06 CHC	699	87	204	3	40	58	292	293	291	323	388	711	4	95	31	0.84	55	21	24	52	147	41%	5	311	4.40	-0.8	$26
DL		1st Half	322	36	81	1	12	24	252			285	323	608	4	92	27	0.58	59	18	23	41	137	39%	2	289	3.21	-11.9	$8
BAvg Potl	65%	2nd Half	377	51	123	2	28	34	326			355	443	798	4	97	33	1.42	52	24	24	61	149	43%	3	329	5.38	9.8	$18
LIMA Plan	B	07 Proj	**678**	**93**	**205**	**3**	**44**	**60**	**302**			**339**	**389**	**728**	**5**	**94**	**32**	**0.96**	**55**	**23**	**22**	**48**	**154**	**40%**	**4**	**314**	**4.62**	**1.4**	**$30**

Simple formula for success: keep the ball on the ground, don't strike out, use your blinding speed, wreak havoc on the bases. More BB would be nice, but high BA is fully supported by these BPIs.

DAVE ADLER

Pierzynski,A.J.

			AB	R	H	HR	RBI	SB	Avg	vL	vR	OB	Slg	OPS	bb%	ct%	h%	Eye	G	L	F	PX	SX	SBO	xHR	xBA	RC/G	RAR	R$
Pos	2	02 MIN	440	54	132	6	49	1	300	270	308	320	439	759	3	86	34	0.21	47	24	29	89	84	3%	8	302	4.65	12.5	$12
Age	30	03 MIN	487	63	152	11	74	3	312	312	324	344	464	808	5	89	33	0.44	47	23	30	95	74	3%	12	312	5.30	15.9	$17
Peak		04 SF	471	45	128	11	77	0	272	227	283	300	410	710	4	94	27	0.70	47	19	35	78	39	1%	10	293	4.27	6.2	$11
Bats	Left	05 CHW	460	61	118	18	56	0	257	230	262	292	420	711	5	85	27	0.34	46	22	32	98	35	2%	15	291	4.05	0.5	$11
Reliability	80	06 CHW	509	65	150	16	64	1	295	270	304	324	436	760	4	86	32	0.31	44	23	33	84	43	1%	14	285	4.60	2.7	$14
DL		1st Half	246	28	78	4	23	0	317			349	435	784	5	87	35	0.39	42	26	32	78	25	0%	5	295	5.00	3.9	$6
BAvg Potl	45%	2nd Half	263	37	72	12	41	1	274			300	437	738	4	84	29	0.24	46	20	34	89	51	2%	9	276	4.22	-1.5	$8
LIMA Plan	D+	07 Proj	**489**	**61**	**137**	**16**	**65**	**1**	**280**			**310**	**429**	**740**	**4**	**87**	**30**	**0.34**	**45**	**22**	**33**	**88**	**49**	**1%**	**14**	**290**	**4.40**	**2.1**	**$13**

BA rebound was driven by high 1st half h% and improved BA vs. LHP. All but one of his HRs came against RHPs. No reason to expect deviation from these consistent BPIs.

Podsednik,Scott

			AB	R	H	HR	RBI	SB	Avg	vL	vR	OB	Slg	OPS	bb%	ct%	h%	Eye	G	L	F	PX	SX	SBO	xHR	xBA	RC/G	RAR	R$
Pos	7	02 aaa	458	56	111	8	57	30	242			305	360	665	8	85	27	0.59				75	131	38%	9		3.83	-25.3	$15
Age	31	03 MIL	558	100	174	9	58	43	312	270	329	375	441	815	9	84	36	0.62	43	27	30	82	160	29%	11	289	5.68	1.4	$30
Past Peak		04 MIL	645	86	157	12	39	70	243	224	249	306	363	669	8	84	27	0.55	48	17	35	71	162	49%	13	261	3.85	-31.3	$26
Bats	Left	05 CHW	507	80	147	0	25	59	290	330	284	350	349	699	8	85	34	0.63	56	20	23	49	129	50%	4	277	4.31	-6.2	$24
Reliability	94	06 CHW	524	86	137	3	45	40	261	216	278	330	353	684	9	82	32	0.56	49	23	28	63	146	38%	6	269	4.12	-16.9	$18
DL	16	1st Half	260	54	68	2	31	24	262			351	388	740	12	82	31	0.77	47	23	30	81	172	42%	4	279	5.02	-1.3	$11
BAvg Potl	50%	2nd Half	264	32	69	1	14	16	261			309	318	627	6	81	32	0.37	51	23	27	45	93	34%	3	257	3.21	-15.8	$6
LIMA Plan	C	07 Proj	**489**	**75**	**131**	**3**	**35**	**39**	**268**			**331**	**357**	**687**	**9**	**83**	**32**	**0.55**	**50**	**22**	**28**	**61**	**134**	**39%**	**6**	**271**	**4.13**	**-13.1**	**$17**

Reversed SX slide, but lower SBO contributed to a drop in SBs. Struggled vs. LHPs and slipped into platoon role. Add in 3-year trend of increasing CS%, and elite SB output is at risk.

Polanco,Placido

			AB	R	H	HR	RBI	SB	Avg	vL	vR	OB	Slg	OPS	bb%	ct%	h%	Eye	G	L	F	PX	SX	SBO	xHR	xBA	RC/G	RAR	R$
Pos	4	02 2NL	548	75	158	9	49	5	288	338	270	321	403	724	5	93	30	0.63	50	22	27	73	84	6%	10	311	4.43	0.3	$15
Age	31	03 PHI	492	87	142	14	63	14	289	292	288	345	447	792	8	92	29	1.11	50	21	29	92	125	12%	13	323	5.36	13.2	$20
Past Peak		04 PHI	503	74	150	17	55	7	298	327	287	334	441	775	5	92	30	0.69	48	23	29	77	69	8%	14	310	4.91	4.3	$18
Bats	Right	05 2TM	501	84	166	9	56	4	331	348	324	373	447	820	6	95	34	1.32	48	27	25	69	78	4%	9	330	5.60	16.6	$20
Reliability	21	06 DET	461	58	136	4	52	1	295	272	305	320	364	685	4	94	31	0.63	51	21	28	42	53	2%	5	284	3.98	-1.8	$10
DL	38 15	1st Half	283	33	82	3	29	1	290			314	367	681	3	93	31	0.48	49	22	29	49	44	4%	4	284	3.88	-1.9	$6
BAvg Potl	55%	2nd Half	178	25	54	1	23	0	303			330	360	689	4	97	31	1.17	54	20	26	32	60	0%	1	283	4.13	0.0	$4
LIMA Plan	C	07 Proj	**505**	**73**	**154**	**6**	**58**	**3**	**305**			**338**	**391**	**729**	**5**	**94**	**31**	**0.88**	**50**	**23**	**27**	**51**	**75**	**4%**	**7**	**300**	**4.54**	**5.9**	**$14**

Skills were mixed even before late shoulder injury:
PRO: High ct% supports BA
CON: drop in bb%, LD%; continued slide in PX, SX
Other than BA, this is an empty skill set. Don't overbid.

Posada,Jorge

			AB	R	H	HR	RBI	SB	Avg	vL	vR	OB	Slg	OPS	bb%	ct%	h%	Eye	G	L	F	PX	SX	SBO	xHR	xBA	RC/G	RAR	R$
Pos	2	02 NYY	511	79	137	20	99	1	268	326	247	368	468	836	14	72	34	0.57	42	21	37	146	51	1%	24	272	6.27	38.9	$18
Age	35	03 NYY	481	83	135	30	101	1	281	295	276	397	518	915	16	77	31	0.85	43	21	36	148	25	3%	29	290	7.16	42.2	$21
Decline		04 NYY	449	72	122	21	81	1	272	275	270	391	481	872	16	80	30	0.96	52	17	31	133	29	3%	22	284	6.68	30.4	$15
Bats	Both	05 NYY	474	67	124	19	71	1	262	281	246	352	430	782	12	80	29	0.70	43	17	39	108	39	1%	19	264	5.30	17.6	$14
Reliability	21	06 NYY	465	65	129	23	93	3	277	263	284	365	492	857	12	79	31	0.66	38	20	42	132	63	2%	22	282	6.24	24.1	$17
DL		1st Half	215	30	62	10	42	0	288			388	474	862	14	80	32	0.81	37	19	44	112	19	0%	10	262	6.39	11.9	$8
BAvg Potl	50%	2nd Half	250	35	67	13	51	3	268			344	508	852	10	78	30	0.54	38	21	41	150	86	5%	12	295	6.11	12.2	$9
LIMA Plan	C	07 Proj	**414**	**60**	**112**	**19**	**77**	**2**	**271**			**365**	**474**	**839**	**13**	**79**	**30**	**0.70**	**42**	**19**	**39**	**128**	**52**	**2%**	**19**	**280**	**6.06**	**21.5**	**$14**

A brief power resurgence late in his career. As usual, most of the damage was done from the left side (LHB: 20 HRs/.540 Slg). With stable BPIs, the decline should be gradual.

Prado,Martin

			AB	R	H	HR	RBI	SB	Avg	vL	vR	OB	Slg	OPS	bb%	ct%	h%	Eye	G	L	F	PX	SX	SBO	xHR	xBA	RC/G	RAR	R$
Pos	4	02	0	0	0	0	0	0	0							0							0		0				
Age	23	03	0	0	0	0	0	0	0							0							0		0				
Growth		04	0	0	0	0	0	0	0							0							0		0				
Bats	Right	05 aa	143	15	37	1	10	3	259			329	336	665	9	90	28	1.00				50	76	14%	2		4.06	-1.2	$2
Reliability	0	06 ATL	* 459	48	124	4	45	4	270	310	154	315	349	664	6	85	31	0.44	49	14	37	49	65	6%	5	233	3.70	-12.0	$8
DL		1st Half	238	22	64	1	18	4	269			320	345	665	7	84	32	0.46	40	20	40	48	85	9%	2		3.78	-5.7	$4
BAvg Potl	45%	2nd Half	221	26	60	3	27	0	271			309	353	662	5	87	30	0.41	50	13	37	51	34	3%	3	229	3.62	-6.3	$4
LIMA Plan	F	07 Proj	**139**	**15**	**37**	**1**	**12**	**2**	**266**			**320**	**350**	**670**	**7**	**87**	**30**	**0.62**	**49**	**14**	**37**	**53**	**76**	**9%**	**2**	**243**	**3.91**	**-2.7**	**$2**

1-9-.262 in 42 AB at ATL. Solid ct% potential is a plus, but complete lack of power or speed kills his value. Projects to utility role for the short term.

Pratt,Todd

			AB	R	H	HR	RBI	SB	Avg	vL	vR	OB	Slg	OPS	bb%	ct%	h%	Eye	G	L	F	PX	SX	SBO	xHR	xBA	RC/G	RAR	R$
Pos	2	02 PHI	106	14	33	3	16	2	311	417	280	438	500	938	18	74	40	0.86	38	19	42	155	46	5%	5	275	7.99	11.1	$5
Age	40	03 PHI	125	16	34	4	20	0	272	267	274	381	464	845	15	70	36	0.58	41	24	34	149	51	0%	5	272	6.61	8.3	$4
Decline		04 PHI	128	16	33	3	16	0	258	318	245	349	367	717	12	70	34	0.47	43	23	34	80	25	0%	4	229	4.56	2.8	$3
Bats	Right	05 PHI	175	17	44	7	23	0	251	300	231	325	394	719	10	71	31	0.38	43	18	38	95	13	0%	7	222	4.36	2.9	$4
Reliability	0	06 ATL	135	14	28	4	19	1	207	176	239	272	341	613	8	68	27	0.28	41	18	41	97	43	3%	5	217	2.92	-6.0	$1
DL		1st Half	87	10	17	2	13	1	195			255	287	543	7	67	27	0.24	44	10	46	65	56	5%	2	173	1.85	-6.8	$1
BAvg Potl	35%	2nd Half	48	4	11	2	6	0	229			302	437	739	9	71	28	0.36	35	32	32	152	8	0%	2	302	4.75	0.6	$1
LIMA Plan	F	07 Proj	**62**	**7**	**15**	**2**	**9**	**0**	**242**			**328**	**375**	**704**	**11**	**70**	**32**	**0.42**	**43**	**18**	**39**	**99**	**36**	**2%**	**2**	**224**	**4.34**	**0.4**	**$1**

BPIs - including h% - are in a four-year slide. Usual strength vs. LHP has abandoned him. He's just about done - look elsewhere for your backup catcher.

Pujols,Albert

			AB	R	H	HR	RBI	SB	Avg	vL	vR	OB	Slg	OPS	bb%	ct%	h%	Eye	G	L	F	PX	SX	SBO	xHR	xBA	RC/G	RAR	R$
Pos	3	02 STL	590	118	185	34	127	2	314	309	315	388	561	949	11	88	31	1.04	45	20	35	145	64	3%	29	335	7.17	25.2	$34
Age	27	03 STL	591	137	212	43	124	5	359	387	350	434	667	1101	12	89	35	1.22	42	22	36	175	77	3%	35	363	8.91	50.7	$42
Peak		04 STL	592	133	196	46	123	5	331	379	319	414	657	1071	12	91	30	1.62	41	17	41	174	74	6%	36	358	8.58	41.4	$38
Bats	Right	05 STL	591	129	195	41	117	16	330	300	340	424	609	1034	14	89	32	1.49	42	20	38	156	106	9%	34	343	8.30	42.2	$41
Reliability	95	06 STL	535	119	177	49	137	7	331	336	329	429	671	1100	15	91	29	1.84	37	18	45	170	67	5%	37	348	8.98	42.0	$38
DL	18	1st Half	212	55	65	26	67	2	307			435	712	1147	18	89	24	2.09	38	13	49	195	53	3%	18	352	9.61	20.8	$17
BAvg Potl	75%	2nd Half	323	64	112	23	70	5	347			425	644	1069	12	92	33	1.63	37	21	42	154	68	7%	18	346	8.53	21.2	$21
LIMA Plan	C	07 Proj	**595**	**132**	**202**	**50**	**137**	**9**	**339**			**431**	**668**	**1098**	**14**	**90**	**31**	**1.62**	**40**	**19**	**42**	**171**	**86**	**6%**	**39**	**353**	**8.94**	**48.0**	**$42**

The scary thing is that nagging injuries and a depressed h% kept his numbers DOWN. Improved Eye, increased FB%, and xBA point to a monster '07. UP: .350, 55 HR, 150 RBI. Triple crown!

Punto,Nick

			AB	R	H	HR	RBI	SB	Avg	vL	vR	OB	Slg	OPS	bb%	ct%	h%	Eye	G	L	F	PX	SX	SBO	xHR	xBA	RC/G	RAR	R$
Pos	56	02 aaa	449	62	111	1	24	35	247			346	298	645	13	82	30	0.86				35	136	27%	2		3.84	-9.3	$13
Age	29	03 PHI	* 203	31	53	1	12	8	261	278	179	306	330	636	6	83	31	0.38	56	24	20	50	125	18%	2	283	3.34	-5.4	$5
Peak		04 MIN	91	17	23	2	12	6	253	250	254	340	319	658	12	79	30	0.63	32	29	39	34	105	18%	2	229	3.70	-3.2	$4
Bats	Both	05 MIN	394	45	94	4	26	13	239	210	246	302	335	637	8	78	30	0.42	51	21	28	69	113	20%	6	260	3.41	-13.1	$7
Reliability	23	06 MIN	459	73	133	1	45	17	290	331	267	356	373	728	9	85	34	0.69	46	24	30	53	133	15%	3	270	4.72	-3.7	$13
DL	30	1st Half	139	23	39	0	10	6	281			375	353	728	13	86	33	1.11	46	22	32	47	125	13%	1	261	4.98	-0.1	$4
BAvg Potl	50%	2nd Half	320	50	94	1	35	11	294			347	381	728	8	85	34	0.53	47	24	29	56	130	15%	3	274	4.60	-3.7	$10
LIMA Plan	D	07 Proj	**381**	**55**	**102**	**2**	**30**	**16**	**268**			**335**	**347**	**682**	**9**	**83**	**32**	**0.59**	**48**	**23**	**29**	**54**	**123**	**18%**	**4**	**265**	**4.10**	**-8.0**	**$9**

The boosts in ct% and Eye are promising. But jump in h% inflated his BA, so don't expect a repeat performance. Good end-game infielder with speed; just don't bid to 2006 value.

Quentin,Carlos

			AB	R	H	HR	RBI	SB	Avg	vL	vR	OB	Slg	OPS	bb%	ct%	h%	Eye	G	L	F	PX	SX	SBO	xHR	xBA	RC/G	RAR	R$
Pos	9	02	0	0	0	0	0	0	0							0							0		0				
Age	24	03	0	0	0	0	0	0	0							0							0		0				
Growth		04 aa	210	29	68	5	28	0	324			366	486	852	6	92	34	0.82				101	34	14%	6		5.92	5.5	$8
Bats	Right	05 aaa	452	68	121	16	62	6	268			345	445	789	10	89	27	1.08				104	91	5%	15		5.43	5.9	$15
Reliability	21	06 ARI	* 484	74	127	16	72	5	262	171	280	331	469	800	9	86	28	0.72	46	16	38	125	99	4%	17	302	5.51	10.3	$14
DL		1st Half	268	39	69	6	28	3	257			323	425	749	9	88	27	0.84				103	89	5%	7		4.94	1.4	$6
BAvg Potl	65%	2nd Half	216	35	58	10	44	2	269			342	523	865	10	82	29	0.63	46	16	38	153	95	4%	10	312	6.27	9.3	$8
LIMA Plan	B	07 Proj	**476**	**72**	**131**	**20**	**71**	**5**	**275**			**343**	**498**	**841**	**9**	**87**	**28**	**0.82**	**46**	**16**	**38**	**130**	**84**	**6%**	**19**	**311**	**5.93**	**12.2**	**$17**

9-32-.253 in 166 AB in ARI. Struggled with ct% and vs. LHP after call-up, but xBA and 2nd half PX hint at big upside. Power may arrive before BA, but both are on the way.

DAVE ADLER

Quinlan,Robb

			AB	R	H	HR	RBI	SB	Avg	vL	vR	OB	Slg	OPS	bb%	ct%	h%	Eye	G	L	F	PX	SX	SBO	xHR	xBA	RC/G	RAR	R$
Pos	3	02 aaa	528	72	154	17	85	6	292			331	468	799	6	87	31	0.44				103	109	6%	15		5.20	-7.9	$20
Age	30	03 ANA *	487	56	133	7	56	9	273	286	288	309	374	682	5	87	30	0.40	49	24	27	61	92	12%	8	289	3.86	-21.4	$12
Peak		04 ANA *	268	33	81	6	34	4	302	390	317	360	459	819	8	86	33	0.65	47	22	31	101	71	8%	7	302	5.65	4.9	$8
Bats	Right	05 ANA	134	17	31	5	14	0	231	289	137	270	403	672	5	81	25	0.27	51	18	30	114	45	4%	5	283	3.58	-6.1	$2
Reliability	3	06 ANA	234	28	75	9	32	2	321	326	313	340	491	832	3	88	34	0.25	53	17	30	95	60	5%	7	294	5.32	-0.6	$9
DL	53	1st Half	103	11	28	3	9	0	272			272	417	689	0	86	29	0.00	58	19	23	89	41	5%	3	293	3.56	-5.5	$2
BAvg Potl	40%	2nd Half	131	17	47	6	23	2	359			391	550	941	5	89	37	0.50	49	15	36	99	72	5%	5	293	6.65	4.1	$7
LIMA Plan	F	07 Proj	**234**	**29**	**69**	**8**	**30**	**2**	**295**			**327**	**463**	**789**	**5**	**86**	**32**	**0.33**	**51**	**18**	**31**	**100**	**64**	**6%**	**7**	**293**	**4.98**	**-2.0**	**$7**

H% fueled a 2nd half surge, but his hacking ways (didn't take a walk until July) will keep him from repeating. High GB% restricts power. Despite gains vs. RHP, best in a platoon role - bid accordingly.

Quintanilla,Omar

			AB	R	H	HR	RBI	SB	Avg	vL	vR	OB	Slg	OPS	bb%	ct%	h%	Eye	G	L	F	PX	SX	SBO	xHR	xBA	RC/G	RAR	R$
Pos	6	02	0	0	0	0	0	0	0							0							0		0				
Age	25	03	0	0	0	0	0	0	0							0							0		0				
Pre-Peak		04	0	0	0	0	0	0	0							0							0		0				
Bats	Left	05 COL *	474	59	123	4	30	3	259	67	239	299	338	637	5	90	28	0.57	42	26	32	48	80	6%	5	283	3.49	-6.5	$7
Reliability	2	06 COL *	342	39	85	3	25	4	249	250	167	298	360	657	7	86	28	0.51	52	20	28	73	84	8%	5	285	3.74	-6.3	$4
DL	19	1st Half	212	29	58	2	10	1	274			319	363	682	6	85	31	0.44	56	6	38	59	63	5%	3	222	3.92	-2.7	$3
BAvg Potl	60%	2nd Half	130	10	27	1	15	3	208			264	354	618	7	88	23	0.67	44	44	11	94	100	14%	2		3.47	-3.6	$1
LIMA Plan	F	07 Proj	**80**	**9**	**22**	**1**	**6**	**1**	**275**			**320**	**388**	**708**	**6**	**88**	**31**	**0.56**	**47**	**20**	**33**	**72**	**88**	**7%**	**1**	**280**	**4.33**	**0.3**	**$2**

0-3-.176 in 34 AB at COL. High ct% should eventually lead to a decent BA, but with no power or speed, he offers little else. No reason to have him on your draft radar.

Rabe,Josh

			AB	R	H	HR	RBI	SB	Avg	vL	vR	OB	Slg	OPS	bb%	ct%	h%	Eye	G	L	F	PX	SX	SBO	xHR	xBA	RC/G	RAR	R$
Pos	0	02 aa	183	16	39	1	15	3	213			246	284	530	4	85	25	0.30				55	69	11%	2		2.07	-19.6	$1
Age	28	03 a/a	497	66	129	13	71	17	260			307	384	691	6	84	29	0.43				77	111	17%	12		3.96	-9.7	$16
Peak		04 aaa	429	45	101	6	37	21	235			291	337	628	7	84	27	0.49				71	95	26%	8		3.33	-25.8	$9
Bats	Right	05 aaa	277	42	60	9	41	4	217			280	368	648	8	82	24	0.48				100	79	10%	9		3.48	-21.8	$6
Reliability	23	06 MIN *	404	56	113	9	52	7	279	375	200	336	398	734	8	87	30	0.66	42	21	37	72	75	10%	9	273	4.61	-21.1	$11
DL		1st Half	270	35	75	3	33	6	279			344	379	723	9	88	31	0.84				67	80	11%	4		4.66	-13.8	$7
BAvg Potl	55%	2nd Half	134	21	37	6	18	1	280			317	437	754	5	85	29	0.37	42	21	37	84	58	6%	5	275	4.51	-7.4	$4
LIMA Plan	F	07 Proj	**130**	**18**	**33**	**3**	**16**	**3**	**254**			**306**	**380**	**687**	**7**	**85**	**28**	**0.49**	**42**	**21**	**37**	**78**	**69**	**12%**	**3**	**269**	**3.94**	**-8.0**	**$3**

3-7-.286 in 49 AB at MIN. Posted the rookie dream week (3 homers), which drove his 116 PX in the bigs. Don't count on a repeat. BPIs don't indicate any power potential. In fact, RAR makes him a sim nightmare.

Ramirez,Aramis

			AB	R	H	HR	RBI	SB	Avg	vL	vR	OB	Slg	OPS	bb%	ct%	h%	Eye	G	L	F	PX	SX	SBO	xHR	xBA	RC/G	RAR	R$
Pos	5	02 PIT	522	51	122	18	71	2	234	260	226	274	387	661	5	82	25	0.31	37	16	46	100	46	2%	17	253	3.47	-17.6	$10
Age	28	03 2NL	607	75	165	27	106	2	272	285	268	319	465	784	6	84	29	0.42	36	18	46	116	55	3%	24	276	4.99	12.8	$21
Peak		04 CHC	547	99	174	36	103	0	318	267	328	374	578	952	8	89	31	0.79	34	23	43	139	37	1%	28	325	6.96	28.0	$29
Bats	Right	05 CHC	463	72	140	31	92	0	302	355	284	351	568	919	7	87	29	0.58	39	20	41	153	28	1%	24	327	6.52	22.1	$23
Reliability	86	06 CHC	594	93	173	38	119	2	291	261	301	346	561	907	8	89	27	0.79	35	18	47	141	66	2%	29	316	6.46	16.1	$27
DL	37	1st Half	277	35	69	14	42	1	249			302	466	768	7	91	23	0.81	38	16	46	114	52	3%	11	293	4.93	-4.6	$7
BAvg Potl	60%	2nd Half	317	58	104	24	77	1	328			384	644	1028	8	88	31	0.78	32	20	47	165	70	1%	18	334	7.84	19.6	$19
LIMA Plan	C+	07 Proj	**592**	**93**	**176**	**40**	**116**	**1**	**297**			**350**	**567**	**917**	**8**	**88**	**28**	**0.67**	**36**	**20**	**45**	**147**	**53**	**2%**	**31**	**320**	**6.53**	**22.7**	**$28**

1st half season struggles were due to a low h%, but made up for it with a strong run after the Break. That finish plus FB% gains say that he could take another step forward...
UP: 45 HR, 130 RBI, .325 BA

Ramirez,Hanley

			AB	R	H	HR	RBI	SB	Avg	vL	vR	OB	Slg	OPS	bb%	ct%	h%	Eye	G	L	F	PX	SX	SBO	xHR	xBA	RC/G	RAR	R$
Pos	6	02	0	0	0	0	0	0	0							0							0		0				
Age	23	03	0	0	0	0	0	0	0							0							0		0				
Growth		04 aa	129	23	39	4	13	11	301			344	472	816	6	84	33	0.42				101	140	39%	4		5.41	4.1	$7
Bats	Both	05 aa	461	57	119	5	45	22	258			308	360	668	7	89	28	0.65				64	122	29%	6		3.90	-5.0	$13
Reliability	10	06 FLA	633	119	185	17	59	51	292	307	288	350	480	830	8	80	34	0.44	44	21	35	118	164	40%	19	286	5.83	26.6	$31
DL		1st Half	284	56	76	3	20	22	268			329	394	723	8	77	34	0.40	50	21	29	86	172	34%	5	266	4.56	1.7	$11
BAvg Potl	40%	2nd Half	349	63	109	14	39	29	312			367	550	917	8	82	35	0.48	39	21	40	143	149	44%	14	303	6.81	24.1	$20
LIMA Plan	B	07 Proj	**584**	**96**	**165**	**13**	**56**	**40**	**283**			**335**	**440**	**775**	**7**	**84**	**32**	**0.49**	**43**	**21**	**36**	**97**	**154**	**36%**	**15**	**283**	**5.07**	**15.0**	**$26**

Hot start, cool middle, strong finish -- driven by h% variations. Owns the speed skills, so SBs weren't a surprise. Okay, maybe a litte. And the power? Hmm. Skills spike was too high, too soon. No possible way to repeat.

Ramirez,Manny

			AB	R	H	HR	RBI	SB	Avg	vL	vR	OB	Slg	OPS	bb%	ct%	h%	Eye	G	L	F	PX	SX	SBO	xHR	xBA	RC/G	RAR	R$
Pos	7	02 BOS *	466	86	155	34	109	0	333	438	331	429	620	1050	14	80	36	0.84	45	25	30	174	23	0%	31	332	8.71	47.3	$28
Age	34	03 BOS	569	117	185	37	104	3	325	385	305	423	587	1010	15	83	34	1.03	36	24	40	154	58	2%	33	322	8.16	42.6	$31
Past Peak		04 BOS	568	108	175	43	130	2	308	306	309	395	613	1008	13	78	33	0.66	41	15	43	188	38	4%	39	309	8.13	49.6	$31
Bats	Right	05 BOS	554	112	162	45	144	1	292	236	313	382	594	976	13	79	30	0.67	37	24	39	185	56	1%	38	326	7.63	44.8	$32
Reliability	27	06 BOS	449	79	144	35	102	0	321	326	319	444	619	1064	18	77	35	0.98	36	22	42	181	26	1%	32	313	9.19	48.1	$24
DL		1st Half	245	47	74	20	53	0	302			439	604	1043	20	73	34	0.92	35	23	42	187	40	0%	19	303	9.14	26.6	$13
BAvg Potl	45%	2nd Half	204	32	70	15	49	0	343			451	637	1088	16	82	36	1.08	37	22	42	174	15	1%	14	323	9.25	21.5	$12
LIMA Plan	B	07 Proj	**533**	**99**	**168**	**40**	**127**	**0**	**315**			**420**	**608**	**1028**	**15**	**79**	**34**	**0.85**	**38**	**22**	**41**	**178**	**34**	**1%**	**36**	**317**	**8.51**	**50.2**	**$30**

Knee problems cost him most of September, depressing his final numbers. Got back to crushing LHPs, PX is steady. If healthy, count on a return to the $30+ level. That's just Manny being Manny.

Randa,Joe

			AB	R	H	HR	RBI	SB	Avg	vL	vR	OB	Slg	OPS	bb%	ct%	h%	Eye	G	L	F	PX	SX	SBO	xHR	xBA	RC/G	RAR	R$
Pos	5	02 KC	549	63	155	11	80	2	282	321	270	338	426	764	8	87	31	0.67	43	24	34	89	73	2%	13	297	5.01	8.4	$15
Age	37	03 KC	502	80	146	16	72	1	291	311	282	344	452	797	8	88	31	0.67	35	25	40	98	60	1%	15	298	5.30	11.0	$17
Decline		04 KC	485	65	139	8	56	0	287	299	282	341	408	749	8	84	33	0.52	40	19	41	80	48	1%	10	256	4.78	-1.7	$11
Bats	Right	05 2NL	555	71	153	17	68	0	276	306	264	332	452	784	8	85	30	0.58	37	25	39	115	44	1%	18	304	5.19	6.5	$15
Reliability	42	06 PIT	206	23	55	4	28	0	267	275	263	320	388	708	7	87	29	0.62	37	20	43	77	24	0%	5	261	4.31	-7.0	$4
DL	37	1st Half	103	9	25	2	10	0	243			284	350	634	6	87	26	0.46	38	17	45	65	19	0%	2	241	3.34	-6.6	$1
BAvg Potl	55%	2nd Half	103	14	30	2	18	0	291			354	427	781	9	87	32	0.77	36	22	42	88	28	0%	3	280	5.27	-0.6	$3
LIMA Plan	F	07 Proj	**291**	**36**	**79**	**7**	**39**	**0**	**271**			**327**	**414**	**741**	**8**	**86**	**30**	**0.61**	**38**	**21**	**41**	**91**	**48**	**0%**	**8**	**279**	**4.71**	**-3.6**	**$7**

Foot injury contributed to a drop in playing time. Consistent BPIs, but PX drop shows 2005 power output was a fluke. Days as a starter are probably over.

Redmond,Mike

			AB	R	H	HR	RBI	SB	Avg	vL	vR	OB	Slg	OPS	bb%	ct%	h%	Eye	G	L	F	PX	SX	SBO	xHR	xBA	RC/G	RAR	R$
Pos	2	02 FLA	256	19	78	2	28	0	305	286	312	357	387	744	8	87	35	0.62	52	25	23	62	15	2%	4	283	4.76	4.6	$6
Age	36	03 FLA	125	12	30	0	11	0	240	314	211	280	312	592	5	87	28	0.44	49	23	28	53	58	0%	1	275	2.96	-5.0	$1
Decline		04 FLA	246	19	63	2	25	1	256	179	279	296	341	638	5	89	28	0.50	47	21	32	60	36	2%	4	272	3.47	-2.5	$3
Bats	Right	05 MIN	148	17	46	1	26	0	311	345	289	338	392	730	4	91	34	0.43	53	24	23	59	30	0%	2	295	4.41	1.6	$5
Reliability	19	06 MIN	179	20	61	0	23	0	341	443	275	355	413	769	2	90	38	0.22	46	27	27	57	29	0%	2	297	4.73	1.5	$5
DL		1st Half	85	9	32	0	12	0	376			376	447	824	0	88	43	0.00	43	29	28	56	25	0%	1	297	5.13	1.5	$3
BAvg Potl	30%	2nd Half	94	11	29	0	11	0	309			337	383	720	4	91	34	0.50	48	25	26	57	32	0%	1	298	4.39	-0.1	$2
LIMA Plan	F	07 Proj	**159**	**17**	**46**	**1**	**21**	**0**	**289**			**315**	**368**	**684**	**4**	**90**	**32**	**0.37**	**49**	**25**	**27**	**59**	**35**	**0%**	**2**	**293**	**3.91**	**-1.5**	**$3**

Big swings in h% have been driving the wild variations in his BA. He posts solid LD%, but high GB% limit his power. End-game catcher who offers BA but nothing else. Not that there's anything wrong with that.

Reed,Jeremy

			AB	R	H	HR	RBI	SB	Avg	vL	vR	OB	Slg	OPS	bb%	ct%	h%	Eye	G	L	F	PX	SX	SBO	xHR	xBA	RC/G	RAR	R$
Pos	8	02	0	0	0	0	0	0	0							0							0		0				
Age	25	03 aa	242	48	96	8	41	17	397			461	579	1040	11	93	41	1.61				103	110	31%	8		8.25	21.3	$19
Pre-Peak		04 aaa	509	74	132	11	64	22	259			333	385	718	10	90	27	1.10				69	121	21%	11		4.65	-0.5	$16
Bats	Left	05 SEA	488	61	124	3	45	12	254	200	269	321	352	673	9	85	29	0.65	49	19	33	73	90	17%	7	270	4.04	-3.5	$9
Reliability	27	06 SEA	212	27	46	6	17	2	217		243	256	377	633	5	85	23	0.35	51	13	37	83	115	13%	5	266	3.26	-9.3	$2
DL	90	1st Half	196	27	45	6	17	2	230			271	393	663	5	86	24	0.39	52	13	35	86	116	13%	5	274	3.63	-6.2	$3
BAvg Potl	65%	2nd Half	16	0	1	0	0	0	62			62	187	250	0	81	8	0.00	31	8	62	54						-3.6	($1)
LIMA Plan	D	07 Proj	**298**	**44**	**80**	**7**	**34**	**10**	**268**			**330**	**411**	**741**	**8**	**88**	**29**	**0.77**	**51**	**15**	**34**	**81**	**115**	**21%**	**7**	**281**	**4.78**	**1.8**	**$9**

Tough to show growth when wrist/thumb injuries derail your season. Low h% depressed his BA; xBA shows he's capable of much more. High GB% will limit power, but he could contribute SBs in 2007.

DAVE ADLER

Renteria,Edgar		AB	R	H	HR	RBI	SB	Avg	vL	vR	OB	Slg	OPS	bb%	ct%	h%	Eye	G	L	F	PX	SX	SBO	xHR	xBA	RC/G	RAR	R$
Pos 6	02 STL	544	77	166	11	83	22	305	288	310	363	439	802	8	90	33	0.86	47	23	30	87	107	17%	13	308	5.48	23.9	$25
Age 31	03 STL	587	96	194	13	100	34	330	391	316	397	480	878	10	91	35	1.20	44	23	32	96	109	21%	16	316	6.46	36.9	$34
Past Peak	04 STL	586	84	168	10	72	17	287	366	264	331	401	732	6	87	32	0.50	47	22	31	75	83	18%	12	287	4.51	6.4	$20
Bats Right	05 BOS	623	100	172	8	70	9	276	326	253	335	385	720	8	84	32	0.55	47	24	29	76	99	7%	11	284	4.48	-1.4	$17
Reliability 97	06 ATL	598	100	175	14	70	17	293	333	281	359	436	796	9	85	33	0.70	47	22	31	90	97	13%	16	294	5.43	18.0	$22
DL	1st Half	280	44	84	8	30	8	300			376	439	815	11	83	34	0.72	48	22	30	86	72	11%	8	284	5.69	10.3	$11
BAvg Potl 55%	2nd Half	318	56	91	6	40	9	286			344	434	778	8	87	31	0.67	46	23	31	94	105	15%	8	301	5.20	7.6	$11
LIMA Plan C	07 Proj	**600**	**97**	**174**	**13**	**73**	**16**	**290**			**350**	**424**	**775**	**8**	**86**	**32**	**0.65**	**47**	**23**	**30**	**86**	**102**	**13%**	**15**	**294**	**5.13**	**16.0**	**$22**

Nice comeback year across the board, completely supported by BPIs. Getting away from Boston provided more SBOs, as predicted. Skills a notch below '03 level, but he's a reliable pick.

Repko,Jason		AB	R	H	HR	RBI	SB	Avg	vL	vR	OB	Slg	OPS	bb%	ct%	h%	Eye	G	L	F	PX	SX	SBO	xHR	xBA	RC/G	RAR	R$
Pos 8	02	0	0	0	0	0	0	0							0							0		0				
Age 26	03 aa	416	59	91	9	22	20	219			289	327	616	9	79	26	0.47				67	127	27%	9		3.10	-23.1	$8
Pre-Peak	04 a/a	491	64	126	11	47	18	257			291	397	688	5	84	29	0.30				89	112	28%	12		3.86	-12.1	$13
Bats Right	05 LA	* 307	47	71	10	34	6	231	235	216	269	397	667	5	73	29	0.19	43	17	40	116	139	10%	10	249	3.54	-9.5	$8
Reliability 9	06 LA	130	21	33	3	16	10	254	239	262	331	377	708	10	82	29	0.63	44	21	35	73	120	36%	3	259	4.37	-0.3	$5
DL 75	1st Half	69	13	21	3	12	8	304			377	522	898	10	80	35	0.57	49	24	27	128	148	43%	3	309	6.71	4.4	$5
BAvg Potl 55%	2nd Half	61	8	12	0	4	2	197			279	213	493	10	84	24	0.70	38	18	44	14	75	28%	0	198	1.85	-5.3	$0
LIMA Plan F	07 Proj	**161**	**24**	**40**	**4**	**16**	**8**	**248**			**309**	**371**	**680**	**8**	**80**	**29**	**0.43**	**43**	**19**	**38**	**79**	**120**	**27%**	**4**	**250**	**3.88**	**-3.3**	**$5**

Did all his damage in April prior to DL stint, aided by 35% H%. Ct% and on-base skills not optimal for a speedster. Power/speed useful in small doses, but anything more will come with a .250 BA.

Reyes,Jose		AB	R	H	HR	RBI	SB	Avg	vL	vR	OB	Slg	OPS	bb%	ct%	h%	Eye	G	L	F	PX	SX	SBO	xHR	xBA	RC/G	RAR	R$
Pos 6	02 aa	275	44	79	2	23	25	287			324	411	735	5	89	32	0.48				76	174	57%	3		4.61	3.0	$13
Age 23	03 NYM	* 434	77	129	5	46	41	297	225	340	340	406	745	6	87	33	0.50	47	25	29	65	176	39%	6	289	4.69	7.1	$23
Growth	04 NYM	220	33	56	2	14	19	255	326	237	271	373	644	2	86	29	0.16	43	19	38	80	176	51%	3	271	3.32	-5.3	$8
Bats Both	05 NYM	696	99	190	7	58	60	273	288	269	300	386	687	4	89	30	0.35	47	20	33	63	182	44%	7	278	3.93	-0.5	$29
Reliability 21	06 NYM	647	122	194	19	81	64	300	330	288	353	487	840	8	87	32	0.65	45	21	34	98	168	45%	16	300	5.85	27.4	$37
DL	1st Half	334	67	98	8	36	34	293			350	482	832	8	88	31	0.73	46	22	32	101	174	47%	8	309	5.84	14.2	$19
BAvg Potl 55%	2nd Half	313	55	96	11	45	30	307			356	492	848	7	87	33	0.59	44	20	36	94	158	43%	9	290	5.86	13.3	$19
LIMA Plan D+	07 Proj	**619**	**104**	**182**	**12**	**65**	**57**	**294**			**333**	**447**	**780**	**6**	**88**	**32**	**0.47**	**45**	**20**	**34**	**84**	**179**	**44%**	**12**	**288**	**5.05**	**15.3**	**$32**

Could this all be the result of better plate patience? Higher BA; power spike a bonus (tho' PX says it's not as big as it appears). The best news -- injury-free for two years! But bid aggressively, not recklessly.

Rios,Alexis		AB	R	H	HR	RBI	SB	Avg	vL	vR	OB	Slg	OPS	bb%	ct%	h%	Eye	G	L	F	PX	SX	SBO	xHR	xBA	RC/G	RAR	R$
Pos 9	02	0	0	0	0	0	0	0							0							0		0				
Age 26	03 aa	514	71	168	9	68	9	327			367	469	836	6	86	37	0.47				89	113	8%	10		5.72	4.7	$20
Pre-Peak	04 TOR	* 611	67	168	4	47	17	275	287	286	318	376	695	6	82	33	0.36	57	20	23	68	125	13%	8	280	4.07	-11.0	$13
Bats Right	05 TOR	481	71	126	10	59	14	262	249	271	303	397	700	6	79	31	0.28	49	19	31	90	129	20%	11	269	4.02	-9.8	$14
Reliability 20	06 TOR	450	68	136	17	82	15	302	295	305	353	516	868	7	80	35	0.39	37	22	41	134	123	18%	17	288	6.18	6.5	$20
DL 27	1st Half	270	46	89	15	53	9	330			384	585	970	8	83	36	0.51	34	21	45	152	99	18%	13	305	7.33	12.2	$15
BAvg Potl 35%	2nd Half	180	22	47	2	29	6	261			304	411	715	6	77	33	0.26	42	23	36	104	136	18%	3	265	4.35	-6.9	$5
LIMA Plan C+	07 Proj	**525**	**72**	**154**	**20**	**90**	**16**	**293**			**337**	**500**	**837**	**6**	**80**	**33**	**0.34**	**44**	**21**	**35**	**127**	**126**	**17%**	**19**	**294**	**5.72**	**7.4**	**$22**

Breakout season derailed in mid-year by bacterial infection in leg. BA in first half was boosted by 35% hit rate, but power/ speed combo is exceptional. Expect big things.
UP: 30-100-20-.300

Rivera,Juan		AB	R	H	HR	RBI	SB	Avg	vL	vR	OB	Slg	OPS	bb%	ct%	h%	Eye	G	L	F	PX	SX	SBO	xHR	xBA	RC/G	RAR	R$
Pos 798	02 NYY	* 348	42	90	8	44	5	284	200	274	318	428	746	5	88	31	0.40	45	15	40	90	76	8%	9	274	4.58	-2.5	$10
Age 28	03 NYY	* 481	62	136	13	50	1	283	340	236	327	432	760	6	88	30	0.54	47	23	30	95	36	3%	14	304	4.82	-7.0	$13
Peak	04 MON	394	49	121	12	49	6	307	276	328	362	464	827	8	89	32	0.76	49	20	31	93	70	7%	12	301	5.67	2.5	$14
Bats Right	05 ANA	350	46	95	15	59	1	271	252	286	316	454	771	6	87	27	0.52	46	17	37	106	43	12%	13	288	4.85	1.4	$11
Reliability 22	06 ANA	448	65	139	23	85	0	310	351	293	358	525	882	7	87	32	0.56	51	16	33	121	23	3%	19	293	6.13	11.7	$18
DL 16	1st Half	151	18	39	6	27	0	258			309	437	746	7	89	26	0.69	52	15	33	101	32	6%	5	286	4.67	-2.3	$4
BAvg Potl 50%	2nd Half	297	47	100	17	58	0	337			382	569	951	7	86	35	0.51	51	17	33	132	27	2%	14	302	6.92	13.6	$15
LIMA Plan C	07 Proj	**518**	**70**	**153**	**22**	**92**	**0**	**295**			**343**	**486**	**828**	**7**	**87**	**30**	**0.57**	**49**	**17**	**34**	**110**	**34**	**5%**	**19**	**293**	**5.55**	**7.7**	**$19**

Big jump in power - but all of it came in July (11 HRs); otherwise, PX was 100. High GB rate doesn't support HR level, but early-season injury may have been a factor.
DN: 15 HR

Rivera,Mike		AB	R	H	HR	RBI	SB	Avg	vL	vR	OB	Slg	OPS	bb%	ct%	h%	Eye	G	L	F	PX	SX	SBO	xHR	xBA	RC/G	RAR	R$
Pos 2	02 aaa	265	38	56	15	48	0	211			299	426	725	11	78	21	0.58				130	49	2%	13		4.43	4.7	$7
Age 30	03 aaa	295	30	74	11	44	0	251			286	403	688	5	79	28	0.23				94	25	3%	10		3.69	-4.4	$7
Peak	04 aaa	210	12	35	4	18	1	168			207	270	477	5	79	19	0.23				63	65	6%	4		1.19	-19.8	($2)
Bats Right	05 aaa	213	23	47	11	29	2	222			245	432	676	3	86	21	0.21				121	69	9%	9		3.53	-2.4	$5
Reliability 7	06 MIL	* 355	40	91	14	61	3	257	226	279	298	429	727	6	83	28	0.33	38	14	48	103	43	7%	13	249	4.26	-0.8	$10
DL	1st Half	195	21	49	7	33	3	249			289	411	699	5	80	28	0.28				99	49	13%	7		3.90	-2.6	$5
BAvg Potl 45%	2nd Half	160	20	43	7	28	0	266			309	451	760	6	85	27	0.43	38	14	48	106	24	0%	6	257	4.69	1.6	$5
LIMA Plan F	07 Proj	**171**	**18**	**40**	**7**	**26**	**1**	**234**			**272**	**402**	**675**	**5**	**83**	**25**	**0.31**	**38**	**14**	**48**	**100**	**42**	**5%**	**6**	**248**	**3.60**	**-2.6**	**$4**

6-24-.268 in 142 AB at MIL. Spent bulk of last five years at Triple-A. Showed some gains in ct% and PX last two years, but at age 30, he's strictly backup material.

Rivera,Rene		AB	R	H	HR	RBI	SB	Avg	vL	vR	OB	Slg	OPS	bb%	ct%	h%	Eye	G	L	F	PX	SX	SBO	xHR	xBA	RC/G	RAR	R$
Pos 2	02	0	0	0	0	0	0	0							0							0		0				
Age 23	03	0	0	0	0	0	0	0							0							0		0				
Growth	04 aaa	15	3	6	1	1	0	367			367	660	1027	0	82	39	0.00				173	0	0%	1		7.36	1.2	$1
Bats Right	05 a/a	257	19	60	2	21	1	233			257	323	580	3	84	27	0.19				66	54	4%	4		2.54	-10.6	$2
Reliability 0	06 SEA	99	8	15	2	4	1	152	87	171	176	253	429	3	71	19	0.10	44	11	44	75	65	8%	2	197	0.21	-13.8	($1)
DL	1st Half	40	5	7	1	1	0	175			214	325	539	5	65	24	0.14	42	0	58	128	53	0%	1	185	1.86	-3.3	($0)
BAvg Potl 55%	2nd Half	59	3	8	1	3	1	136			150	203	353	2	75	16	0.07	45	18	36	44	55	14%	1	208	-0.74	-10.3	($1)
LIMA Plan F	07 Proj	**68**	**4**	**14**	**1**	**4**	**1**	**206**			**224**	**275**	**499**	**2**	**78**	**25**	**0.10**	**45**	**18**	**36**	**48**	**42**	**7%**	**1**	**219**	**1.28**	**-6.3**	**($0)**

He sports a .256 career BA in 1400 minor-league AB, with a 0.35 Eye and 82 PX. Yes, he's only 23, but big trees only grow from healthy young acorns. Yes, we give you stats, projections and horticulture lessons.

Roberts,Brian		AB	R	H	HR	RBI	SB	Avg	vL	vR	OB	Slg	OPS	bb%	ct%	h%	Eye	G	L	F	PX	SX	SBO	xHR	xBA	RC/G	RAR	R$
Pos 4	02 BAL	* 441	61	106	4	37	28	240	146	264	316	322	638	10	86	27	0.79	34	24	42	49	144	26%	5	243	3.67	-4.9	$12
Age 29	03 BAL	* 638	99	174	5	55	41	273	264	272	346	364	709	10	89	30	1.03	40	32	28	59	130	27%	8	302	4.60	8.6	$22
Peak	04 BAL	641	107	175	4	53	29	273	215	299	346	376	721	10	85	32	0.75	39	21	39	75	112	22%	10	265	4.68	11.3	$19
Bats Both	05 BAL	561	92	176	18	73	27	314	273	332	387	515	902	11	85	34	0.81	35	27	37	128	125	21%	19	314	6.78	41.0	$28
Reliability 31	06 BAL	563	85	161	10	55	36	286	235	308	350	410	760	9	88	31	0.83	44	21	35	77	126	25%	12	283	5.04	14.8	$21
DL 24 12	1st Half	229	36	72	1	30	19	314			389	415	804	11	88	36	1.00	41	26	33	69	129	27%	3	287	5.75	10.2	$11
BAvg Potl 55%	2nd Half	334	49	89	9	25	17	266			321	407	729	7	89	28	0.71	45	18	37	82	110	24%	9	280	4.55	4.2	$10
LIMA Plan B	07 Proj	**592**	**92**	**170**	**15**	**60**	**34**	**287**			**356**	**443**	**799**	**10**	**87**	**31**	**0.81**	**41**	**23**	**36**	**96**	**126**	**24%**	**16**	**294**	**5.49**	**23.3**	**$24**

Keeps teasing us with power spurts: 13 HR in 1st half of '05, 9 HR in 2nd half of '06. Elbow problem affected his swing early in season. If everything falls into place... UP: 18 HR

Roberts,Dave		AB	R	H	HR	RBI	SB	Avg	vL	vR	OB	Slg	OPS	bb%	ct%	h%	Eye	G	L	F	PX	SX	SBO	xHR	xBA	RC/G	RAR	R$
Pos 7	02 LA	422	63	117	3	34	45	277	400	270	351	365	716	10	88	31	0.94	49	28	23	53	168	39%	4	299	4.66	-21.3	$21
Age 34	03 LA	388	56	97	2	16	40	250	265	246	325	307	632	10	90	27	1.10	50	28	22	30	155	43%	2	294	3.72	-22.3	$14
Past Peak	04 2TM	319	64	81	4	35	38	254	179	270	333	379	713	11	85	29	0.79	50	16	35	72	198	44%	5	266	4.60	-5.6	$16
Bats Left	05 SD	411	65	113	8	38	23	275	258	278	358	428	786	11	86	31	0.90	50	22	28	89	146	27%	8	302	5.50	1.9	$16
Reliability 51	06 SD	499	80	146	2	44	49	293	292	293	358	393	751	9	88	33	0.84	56	19	25	54	164	34%	3	287	5.04	-3.0	$23
DL 17 20	1st Half	220	36	65	2	18	19	295			357	432	789	9	88	33	0.78	55	19	26	70	154	34%	2	295	5.44	1.2	$10
BAvg Potl 55%	2nd Half	279	44	81	0	26	30	290			359	362	721	10	88	33	0.88	56	20	24	42	159	33%	1	280	4.72	-4.2	$13
LIMA Plan B+	07 Proj	**440**	**72**	**123**	**4**	**40**	**40**	**280**			**352**	**391**	**744**	**10**	**87**	**31**	**0.86**	**53**	**20**	**27**	**63**	**170**	**34%**	**5**	**288**	**4.97**	**-5.2**	**$20**

Reached career highs in AB and SB, thanks to relatively good health and more SBOs. BA reached high end of expectations. Odds are against a repeat.

TOM TODARO

Rodriguez,Alex

		Year	AB	R	H	HR	RBI	SB	Avg	vL	vR	OB	Slg	OPS	bb%	ct%	h%	Eye	G	L	F	PX	SX	SBO	xHR	xBA	RC/G	RAR	R$
Pos	5	02 TEX	624	125	187	57	142	9	300	239	320	385	623	1009	12	80	29	0.71	40	16	44	182	82	7%	44	318	7.91	59.6	$39
Age	31	03 TEX	607	124	181	47	118	17	298	305	295	386	600	986	13	79	31	0.69	39	22	39	176	124	11%	39	320	7.77	54.9	$36
Past Peak		04 NYY	601	112	172	36	106	28	286	311	279	370	512	883	12	78	31	0.61	46	16	39	132	117	17%	32	280	6.48	26.6	$32
Bats	Right	05 NYY	605	124	194	48	130	21	321	300	330	409	610	1019	13	77	35	0.65	45	16	40	179	94	13%	41	308	8.29	61.9	$41
Reliability	42	06 NYY	572	113	166	35	121	15	290	294	289	387	523	909	14	76	33	0.65	42	18	40	143	93	10%	33	279	6.99	31.9	$29
DL		1st Half	280	56	78	16	55	8	279			384	496	881	15	76	32	0.71	46	16	38	133	92	11%	15	272	6.67	13.4	$13
BAvg Potl	45%	2nd Half	292	57	88	19	66	7	301			389	548	937	13	76	34	0.59	39	20	41	153	77	8%	17	285	7.29	18.4	$16
LIMA Plan	D+	07 Proj	609	121	179	40	127	16	294			386	538	923	13	77	33	0.64	43	17	40	149	93	10%	36	286	7.09	38.8	$33

No longer the slam-dunk #1 pick of old. The changes in five years are a slowly-eroding ct% and inconsistent PX. Still, when his off year is better than 99% of all hitters, it's hard to quibble.

Rodriguez,Ivan

		Year	AB	R	H	HR	RBI	SB	Avg	vL	vR	OB	Slg	OPS	bb%	ct%	h%	Eye	G	L	F	PX	SX	SBO	xHR	xBA	RC/G	RAR	R$
Pos	2	02 TEX	408	67	128	19	60	5	314	306	317	353	542	895	6	83	34	0.35	39	24	36	142	85	9%	18	314	6.31	30.0	$19
Age	35	03 FLA	511	90	152	16	85	10	297	376	274	366	474	839	10	82	34	0.60	47	27	26	116	100	11%	17	313	5.95	23.8	$22
Decline		04 DET	527	72	176	19	86	7	334	343	330	382	510	892	7	83	38	0.45	45	22	33	108	71	7%	18	291	6.38	28.5	$23
Bats	Right	05 DET	504	71	139	14	50	7	276	294	271	291	444	736	2	82	31	0.12	48	22	30	111	112	10%	14	298	4.26	3.4	$14
Reliability	44	06 DET	547	74	164	13	69	8	300	340	284	332	437	769	5	84	34	0.30	50	21	28	83	96	8%	13	289	4.77	5.5	$17
DL		1st Half	276	38	83	7	38	3	301			325	446	771	3	85	33	0.24	51	22	27	84	99	6%	7	296	4.73	2.4	$9
BAvg Potl	40%	2nd Half	271	36	81	6	31	5	299			338	428	766	6	83	34	0.36	50	20	30	82	82	9%	7	280	4.81	3.0	$8
LIMA Plan	C	07 Proj	510	71	150	12	65	7	294			328	441	768	5	83	33	0.30	48	22	30	93	94	8%	13	289	4.80	7.9	$16

Power is fading, pushed along by a rising GB%. LD rate still solid, but not what it once was. Has another .290 season in him, but at age 35, the next level of decline is in sight.
DN: 10 HR, .275

Rodriguez,John

		Year	AB	R	H	HR	RBI	SB	Avg	vL	vR	OB	Slg	OPS	bb%	ct%	h%	Eye	G	L	F	PX	SX	SBO	xHR	xBA	RC/G	RAR	R$
Pos	7	02 aa	354	43	67	13	53	11	189			253	356	609	8	75	21	0.34				111	115	21%	13		2.85	-31.3	$7
Age	29	03 aaa	232	30	54	9	28	5	235			295	393	687	8	81	25	0.46				94	92	9%	8		3.90	-10.9	$6
Peak		04 aaa	378	65	97	14	57	9	257			326	459	785	9	80	29	0.51				123	140	13%	13		5.28	1.0	$13
Bats	Left	05 STL *	439	48	111	19	72	6	252	296	295	311	440	752	8	78	28	0.39	45	29	25	121	80	6%	18	306	4.69	-8.4	$14
Reliability	25	06 STL	183	31	55	2	19	0	301	308	300	373	432	804	10	75	39	0.47	52	18	30	92	80	0%	3	257	5.75	2.5	$5
DL		1st Half	126	21	38	0	10	0	302			358	397	754	8	77	39	0.38	55	18	27	71	84	0%	1	253	4.98	-0.9	$3
BAvg Potl	25%	2nd Half	57	10	17	2	9	0	298			403	509	912	15	72	38	0.63	44	19	37	143	76	0%	2	268	7.47	3.5	$2
LIMA Plan	F	07 Proj	126	19	33	4	18	0	262			337	441	779	10	76	32	0.48	48	20	32	116	88	1%	4	275	5.28	-0.3	$3

Needed a sky-high hit rate just to touch .300, so you know where his BA is headed. Enough power to be acceptable in spots, but low ct% makes for inconsistent results.

Rodriguez,Luis

		Year	AB	R	H	HR	RBI	SB	Avg	vL	vR	OB	Slg	OPS	bb%	ct%	h%	Eye	G	L	F	PX	SX	SBO	xHR	xBA	RC/G	RAR	R$
Pos	5	02 aa	455	40	86	5	26	2	189			255	262	516	8	89	20	0.83				44	60	4%	6		2.28	-32.7	($1)
Age	26	03 aaa	199	18	40	2	8	2	201			264	271	535	8	78	25	0.40				48	76	4%	3		2.05	-14.5	($0)
Pre-Peak		04 aaa	486	56	116	4	40	3	239			300	326	626	8	90	26	0.89				59	56	4%	7		3.57	-20.7	$5
Bats	Both	05 MIN *	305	34	79	3	34	2	260	233	276	328	358	686	9	88	29	0.84	43	21	36	66	62	6%	4	271	4.25	-2.3	$5
Reliability	21	06 MIN	115	11	27	2	6	0	235	250	231	318	322	640	11	86	26	0.88	46	19	34	53	19	0%	2	244	3.68	-4.6	$1
DL		1st Half	57	7	13	2	4	0	228			333	368	702	14	86	23	1.13	46	19	35	79	21	0%	2	262	4.49	-0.9	$1
BAvg Potl	65%	2nd Half	58	4	14	0	2	0	241			302	276	577	8	86	28	0.63	47	20	33	28	17	0%	0	226	2.85	-3.7	($0)
LIMA Plan	F	07 Proj	154	15	37	2	11	0	240			312	320	632	9	87	27	0.80	46	20	35	54	35	2%	2	253	3.57	-5.7	$1

With power like this, you'd better be either very fast, or skilled at hitting them where they ain't. Or a wizard with a glove.

Rolen,Scott

		Year	AB	R	H	HR	RBI	SB	Avg	vL	vR	OB	Slg	OPS	bb%	ct%	h%	Eye	G	L	F	PX	SX	SBO	xHR	xBA	RC/G	RAR	R$
Pos	5	02 2NL	580	89	154	31	110	8	266	288	260	347	503	850	11	82	28	0.71	37	20	44	142	107	8%	27	297	6.06	24.8	$25
Age	32	03 STL	559	98	160	28	104	13	286	283	287	378	528	905	13	81	31	0.79	33	25	42	157	94	10%	29	313	6.89	41.5	$27
Past Peak		04 STL	500	109	157	34	124	4	314	371	302	400	598	998	13	82	33	0.78	30	21	49	164	92	4%	29	305	7.93	38.9	$31
Bats	Right	05 STL	196	28	46	5	28	1	235	237	234	321	383	704	11	86	25	0.89	35	23	42	95	70	6%	6	280	4.47	-1.9	$4
Reliability	10	06 STL	521	94	154	22	95	7	296	259	310	364	518	882	10	87	31	0.81	33	20	48	133	77	8%	22	301	6.42	13.6	$23
DL	109	1st Half	241	49	83	10	50	4	344			408	568	977	10	86	37	0.76	34	22	44	138	63	11%	10	310	7.53	13.0	$14
BAvg Potl	60%	2nd Half	280	45	71	12	45	3	254			326	475	801	10	88	25	0.86	31	18	50	129	80	5%	12	293	5.49	-0.0	$9
LIMA Plan	B	07 Proj	531	92	153	23	96	6	288			365	502	866	11	85	30	0.82	33	21	46	129	79	6%	22	296	6.29	17.2	$23

Shoulder surgeries cost him some oomph, but PX still well above average, supported by high FB. Better ct% two years' running a plus. Enough risk to require a cautious bid, but if he's healthy... UP: 30-100-.300

Rollins,Jimmy

		Year	AB	R	H	HR	RBI	SB	Avg	vL	vR	OB	Slg	OPS	bb%	ct%	h%	Eye	G	L	F	PX	SX	SBO	xHR	xBA	RC/G	RAR	R$
Pos	6	02 PHI	637	82	156	11	60	31	245	243	246	304	380	684	8	84	28	0.52	43	21	36	87	148	28%	12	275	4.04	2.8	$18
Age	28	03 PHI	628	85	165	8	62	20	263	262	263	321	387	708	8	82	31	0.48	39	27	34	87	119	20%	12	280	4.33	4.1	$17
Peak		04 PHI	657	119	190	14	73	30	289	303	285	346	455	801	8	89	31	0.78	43	21	36	96	157	22%	15	299	5.49	25.3	$27
Bats	Both	05 PHI	677	115	196	12	54	41	290	278	292	336	431	767	6	90	31	0.66	44	24	32	85	166	26%	13	303	5.01	20.0	$29
Reliability	99	06 PHI	689	127	191	25	83	36	277	277	277	332	478	810	8	88	28	0.71	44	19	37	111	149	24%	23	306	5.49	22.2	$30
DL		1st Half	324	57	85	9	29	18	262			317	426	743	7	90	27	0.76	44	19	37	94	129	28%	9	296	4.76	3.8	$12
BAvg Potl	60%	2nd Half	365	70	106	16	54	18	290			346	523	869	8	87	30	0.67	44	19	37	125	160	20%	14	315	6.15	18.2	$18
LIMA Plan	D+	07 Proj	676	119	200	19	73	35	296			348	471	819	7	88	31	0.68	44	21	35	101	155	22%	18	301	5.61	26.8	$31

We predicted power growth, still, a 30-point PX jump from 1H to 2H is extreme. Expect an adjustment. Streaky hitter, he's been much better in 2H in each of last three seasons. And a .300 BA is there for the taking.

Ross,Cody

		Year	AB	R	H	HR	RBI	SB	Avg	vL	vR	OB	Slg	OPS	bb%	ct%	h%	Eye	G	L	F	PX	SX	SBO	xHR	xBA	RC/G	RAR	R$
Pos	798	02 aa	400	60	97	13	59	13	243			308	415	723	9	84	26	0.58				108	126	16%	13		4.48	-13.5	$13
Age	26	03 aaa	470	75	132	17	61	15	281			328	494	822	6	84	30	0.44				128	139	20%	16		5.55	1.2	$19
Pre-Peak		04 aaa	238	30	52	10	34	1	218			256	408	664	5	87	21	0.39				107	71	3%	8		3.58	-11.8	$4
Bats	Right	05 aaa	388	49	78	14	40	3	201			258	353	611	7	83	21	0.45				92	71	8%	12		2.99	-25.0	$5
Reliability	8	06 2NL *	319	45	78	16	52	1	244	245	216	317	447	764	10	76	27	0.45	36	21	43	122	59	5%	15	264	4.91	-3.2	$9
DL	21	1st Half	136	22	41	7	26	1	300			386	520	906	12	79	34	0.65	46	19	35	124	82	7%	6	283	6.86	6.1	$6
BAvg Potl	50%	2nd Half	183	23	37	9	26	0	202			263	393	656	8	74	22	0.32	31	22	47	120	36	3%	8	255	3.39	-10.7	$3
LIMA Plan	F	07 Proj	258	35	64	11	37	2	248			308	434	742	8	80	27	0.44	36	21	43	112	66	6%	10	270	4.56	-6.3	$7

13-46-.227 in 269 AB at LA, CIN and FLA. High 1st half hit rate couldn't hide his problems with ct% for long. Some upside in xBA, but if he hits .240, you really can't complain.

Ross,David

		Year	AB	R	H	HR	RBI	SB	Avg	vL	vR	OB	Slg	OPS	bb%	ct%	h%	Eye	G	L	F	PX	SX	SBO	xHR	xBA	RC/G	RAR	R$
Pos	2	02 aaa	303	36	72	12	50	1	238			300	409	709	8	78	27	0.40				111	55	3%	11		4.17	2.8	$7
Age	30	03 LA *	210	28	48	14	30	0	229	258	258	302	476	778	9	69	26	0.34	33	18	49	172	28	4%	13	262	5.17	5.6	$6
Peak		04 LA	165	13	28	5	15	0	170	125	198	239	291	530	8	62	23	0.24	33	15	52	87	42	0%	5	176	1.68	-11.5	($1)
Bats	Right	05 2NL	125	11	30	3	15	0	240	200	253	275	392	667	5	78	29	0.21	38	15	47	108	52	0%	3	243	3.56	-0.9	$2
Reliability	5	06 CIN	247	37	63	21	52	0	255	316	228	352	579	931	13	70	28	0.49	32	17	51	211	34	0%	19	287	7.44	22.4	$10
DL	18	1st Half	103	17	33	10	26	0	320			402	680	1081	12	74	35	0.52	35	19	45	213	46	0%	8	314	9.18	13.3	$7
BAvg Potl	50%	2nd Half	144	20	30	11	26	0	208			317	507	824	14	67	22	0.48	30	15	55	210	16	0%	11	267	6.08	7.8	$4
LIMA Plan	D	07 Proj	320	39	79	19	52	0	247			321	487	808	10	71	29	0.37	34	16	50	160	46	0%	18	257	5.62	14.3	$9

Terrific power, whiffs a lot, draws walks. Didn't CIN already have someone like this? Name of Dunn? You decide if the upside of 25 HR at catcher is worth the downside of a .235 average.

Rowand,Aaron

		Year	AB	R	H	HR	RBI	SB	Avg	vL	vR	OB	Slg	OPS	bb%	ct%	h%	Eye	G	L	F	PX	SX	SBO	xHR	xBA	RC/G	RAR	R$
Pos	8	02 CHW	302	41	78	7	29	0	258	265	255	287	394	681	4	82	29	0.22	50	20	30	86	71	2%	7	276	3.69	-9.6	$6
Age	29	03 CHW *	277	35	71	9	35	0	256	338	250	299	412	711	6	89	26	0.55	43	25	32	93	31	0%	8	308	4.23	-4.2	$6
Peak		04 CHW	487	94	151	24	69	17	310	302	315	350	544	894	6	81	34	0.33	46	19	35	145	120	19%	22	309	6.32	21.5	$25
Bats	Right	05 CHW	578	77	156	13	69	16	270	303	259	308	407	715	5	80	32	0.28	52	21	28	92	119	15%	14	281	4.18	-1.7	$17
Reliability	25	06 PHI	405	59	106	12	47	10	262	222	275	293	425	718	4	81	30	0.24	44	22	34	101	110	16%	12	282	4.15	-3.5	$12
DL	56	1st Half	231	31	63	8	25	4	273			300	446	746	4	82	30	0.21	44	24	32	102	92	16%	7	291	4.42	-0.1	$7
BAvg Potl	50%	2nd Half	174	28	43	4	22	6	247			284	397	681	5	80	29	0.26	45	19	37	98	122	17%	5	269	3.77	-3.5	$5
LIMA Plan	C+	07 Proj	514	77	143	15	63	13	278			313	441	754	5	81	32	0.27	47	21	33	104	114	14%	16	285	4.62	1.0	$18

Tough season. First he crashed face-first into a wall, then he fractured his ankle. Decent across-the-board skills provide value, but not as one of your primary outfielders.

TOM TODARO

Ruiz,Carlos

Ruiz,Carlos		AB	R	H	HR	RBI	SB	Avg	vL	vR	OB	Slg	OPS	bb%	ct%	h%	Eye	G	L	F	PX	SX	SBO	xHR	xBA	RC/G	RAR	R$
Pos 2	02	0	0	0	0	0	0	0							0							0		0				
Age 28	03 aa	169	17	38	2	12	1	225			266	292	558	5	92	24	0.69				42	50	5%	2		2.67	-7.9	$1
Peak	04 aa	349	33	77	12	37	6	222			256	361	617	4	89	22	0.44				74	72	16%	9		3.10	-10.5	$5
Bats Right	05 aaa	339	37	89	4	30	3	263			307	401	707	6	89	29	0.56				85	99	11%	5		4.34	4.4	$6
Reliability 15	06 PHI	* 437	58	126	20	76	4	289	263	260	354	488	842	9	85	30	0.68	47	19	34	113	53	5%	18	297	5.85	18.5	$17
DL	1st Half	194	29	57	8	27	3	294			362	480	842	10	85	31	0.74				111	54	8%	7		5.93	8.6	$7
BAvg Potl 55%	2nd Half	243	29	69	13	49	1	285			347	495	842	9	85	29	0.63	47	19	34	114	42	3%	10	296	5.78	9.9	$9
LIMA Plan D	07 Proj	**315**	**37**	**85**	**10**	**42**	**3**	**270**			**323**	**430**	**753**	**7**	**87**	**28**	**0.62**	**47**	**19**	**34**	**92**	**67**	**8%**	**9**	**290**	**4.77**	**6.1**	**$9**

3-10-.261 in 69 AB at PHI. Good contact hitter with line-drive bat and growing power. Increase in patience a plus. Sleeper who could get his opportunity in '07.
UP: 12-75-.285

Saenz,Olmedo

Saenz,Olmedo		AB	R	H	HR	RBI	SB	Avg	vL	vR	OB	Slg	OPS	bb%	ct%	h%	Eye	G	L	F	PX	SX	SBO	xHR	xBA	RC/G	RAR	R$
Pos 3	02 OAK	156	15	43	6	18	1	276	317	247	331	468	799	8	80	31	0.42	45	6	49	122	57	5%	6	246	5.31	-2.4	$4
Age 36	03	0	0	0	0	0	0	0							0							0		0				
Decline	04 LA	111	17	31	8	22	0	279	338	196	350	505	854	10	70	33	0.36	33	19	48	135	23	0%	7	242	6.11	0.5	$5
Bats Right	05 LA	319	39	84	15	63	0	263	261	266	321	480	800	8	80	29	0.43	39	24	37	144	25	1%	15	306	5.30	-2.8	$11
Reliability 2	06 LA	179	30	53	11	48	0	296	397	248	347	564	911	7	74	35	0.30	37	19	44	179	31	0%	11	290	6.82	4.0	$9
DL	1st Half	119	19	36	6	33	0	303			325	555	880	3	76	36	0.14	34	20	45	172	36	0%	6	294	6.17	0.6	$6
BAvg Potl 30%	2nd Half	60	11	17	5	15	0	283			386	583	969	14	70	32	0.56	42	16	42	193	23	0%	5	279	8.00	3.4	$3
LIMA Plan F	07 Proj	**123**	**18**	**35**	**8**	**27**	**0**	**285**			**350**	**534**	**884**	**9**	**75**	**33**	**0.40**	**39**	**19**	**43**	**163**	**31**	**1%**	**7**	**282**	**6.47**	**2.1**	**$6**

Terrific power, and crushes lefties, but his playing time depends on the health of his teammates. Makes a great insurance policy if you've got a reserve roster.

Salazar,Jeff

Salazar,Jeff		AB	R	H	HR	RBI	SB	Avg	vL	vR	OB	Slg	OPS	bb%	ct%	h%	Eye	G	L	F	PX	SX	SBO	xHR	xBA	RC/G	RAR	R$
Pos 8	02	0	0	0	0	0	0	0							0							0		0				
Age 26	03	0	0	0	0	0	0	0							0							0		0				
Pre-Peak	04 aa	224	33	48	1	15	9	212			300	299	599	11	88	24	1.09				57	122	19%	2		3.43	-8.8	$3
Bats Left	05 a/a	497	59	117	8	40	11	236			308	353	661	9	85	26	0.71				77	89	18%	10		3.89	-8.2	$8
Reliability 22	06 COL	* 381	59	96	8	37	11	252		294	331	390	721	10	84	28	0.73	32	21	47	79	120	15%	8	247	4.62	2.0	$9
DL	1st Half	96	13	27	2	13	2	278			346	402	748	9	85	31	0.70				71	85	10%	2		4.86	1.2	$3
BAvg Potl 55%	2nd Half	285	46	69	6	24	9	244			326	386	712	11	83	27	0.73	32	21	47	82	123	17%	6	248	4.53	0.8	$7
LIMA Plan D	07 Proj	**166**	**23**	**40**	**3**	**15**	**4**	**241**			**318**	**363**	**680**	**10**	**85**	**27**	**0.76**	**32**	**21**	**47**	**74**	**109**	**16%**	**3**	**248**	**4.15**	**-2.0**	**$3**

1-8-.283 in 53 AB at COL. Speedster who makes contact but needs to hit far fewer fly balls to be successful. Hit just .264 in two years at Triple-A. Projects as a reserve OF.

Salmon,Tim

Salmon,Tim		AB	R	H	HR	RBI	SB	Avg	vL	vR	OB	Slg	OPS	bb%	ct%	h%	Eye	G	L	F	PX	SX	SBO	xHR	xBA	RC/G	RAR	R$
Pos 0	02 ANA	483	84	138	22	88	6	286	299	280	377	503	880	13	79	32	0.70	35	20	45	142	74	6%	23	283	6.62	14.9	$21
Age 38	03 ANA	528	78	145	19	72	3	275	274	275	367	464	831	13	82	30	0.83	34	23	43	119	74	2%	20	287	6.01	21.0	$16
Decline	04 ANA	186	15	47	2	23	1	253	147	234	305	323	628	7	78	31	0.34	32	24	44	51	35	2%	3	227	3.16	-11.7	$2
Bats Right	05 ANA	0	0	0	0	0	0	0							0							0		0				
Reliability 0	06 ANA	211	30	56	9	27	0	265	298	234	354	450	804	12	79	30	0.66	34	20	46	108	57	3%	8	259	5.58	-5.2	$5
DL 180	1st Half	139	19	39	6	18	0	281			375	482	857	13	82	31	0.84	31	21	48	114	65	2%	5	271	6.31	-0.5	$4
BAvg Potl	2nd Half	72	11	17	3	9	0	236			312	389	701	10	74	28	0.42	40	19	42	96	46	5%	3	235	4.10	-5.1	$1
LIMA Plan	07 Proj	**0**	**0**	**0**	**0**	**0**	**0**	**0**																				

Retired after 14 seasons and 299 homers. You younger folks or those of us with failing memories might not know that he put up a 33-129-.296 season ten years ago. He and Jim Edmonds were the Angel studs.

Sanchez,Freddy

Sanchez,Freddy		AB	R	H	HR	RBI	SB	Avg	vL	vR	OB	Slg	OPS	bb%	ct%	h%	Eye	G	L	F	PX	SX	SBO	xHR	xBA	RC/G	RAR	R$
Pos 564	02 a/a	494	67	141	5	52	19	285			336	387	723	7	89	31	0.68				69	108	18%	8		4.54	0.2	$17
Age 29	03 aaa	216	40	68	4	21	7	315			388	449	838	11	87	35	0.90				92	93	10%	6		6.04	9.6	$9
Peak	04 PIT	* 144	10	32	1	11	3	222		176	263	306	569	5	90	24	0.53	63	13	25	53	78	13%	2	269	2.75	-10.3	$1
Bats Right	05 PIT	453	54	132	5	35	2	291	326	278	331	400	731	6	92	31	0.75	46	23	31	68	73	3%	7	300	4.60	-2.2	$11
Reliability 20	06 PIT	582	85	200	6	85	3	344	442	316	377	473	849	5	91	37	0.60	37	28	36	85	60	3%	11	311	5.85	5.4	$23
DL	1st Half	257	42	91	4	39	1	354			385	506	891	5	92	37	0.65	34	30	36	93	72	3%	6	325	6.28	5.2	$11
BAvg Potl 40%	2nd Half	325	43	109	2	46	2	335			370	446	816	5	90	37	0.56	40	25	35	79	48	3%	5	299	5.50	0.1	$12
LIMA Plan C	07 Proj	**566**	**73**	**174**	**10**	**74**	**3**	**307**			**346**	**444**	**790**	**6**	**91**	**33**	**0.64**	**41**	**26**	**34**	**85**	**69**	**4%**	**12**	**309**	**5.21**	**1.1**	**$18**

Is .344 for real? 37% hit rate says no. But is .300 for real? Ct% and LD% say he's legit. And, based on rising PX and FB, xHR says that double-digit homers are in reach.
UP: 12-15 HRs

Sanders,Reggie

Sanders,Reggie		AB	R	H	HR	RBI	SB	Avg	vL	vR	OB	Slg	OPS	bb%	ct%	h%	Eye	G	L	F	PX	SX	SBO	xHR	xBA	RC/G	RAR	R$
Pos 9	02 SF	505	75	126	23	85	18	250	289	237	313	455	769	9	76	29	0.39	41	14	45	134	136	20%	21	263	4.97	-5.0	$21
Age 39	03 PIT	453	74	129	31	87	15	285	301	278	340	567	907	8	76	31	0.35	37	23	40	180	120	19%	27	306	6.67	13.7	$25
Decline	04 STL	446	64	116	22	67	21	260	230	270	311	482	793	7	74	31	0.28	37	22	40	147	126	27%	21	274	5.25	-0.5	$19
Bats Right	05 STL	295	49	80	21	54	14	271	245	281	334	546	880	9	75	30	0.37	36	14	50	176	126	21%	18	281	6.35	9.4	$17
Reliability 4	06 KC	325	45	80	11	49	7	246	268	237	306	425	731	8	74	30	0.33	43	19	39	127	85	19%	13	261	4.54	-11.1	$8
DL 52 56	1st Half	215	36	53	9	38	6	247			302	442	744	7	71	31	0.27	42	21	37	138	108	21%	10	262	4.70	-6.3	$7
BAvg Potl 40%	2nd Half	110	9	27	2	11	1	245			314	391	705	9	79	29	0.48	44	15	41	109	36	15%	3	253	4.33	-4.5	$1
LIMA Plan D	07 Proj	**321**	**44**	**82**	**12**	**49**	**5**	**255**			**317**	**443**	**759**	**8**	**75**	**30**	**0.36**	**40**	**17**	**43**	**128**	**75**	**13%**	**13**	**261**	**4.88**	**-3.3**	**$9**

BPIs have held up well for his age, but Reliability Score sums up where his career is now. Looks like speed is finally starting to go. A return to $15 value is not impossible, but don't pay for it.

Schneider,Brian

Schneider,Brian		AB	R	H	HR	RBI	SB	Avg	vL	vR	OB	Slg	OPS	bb%	ct%	h%	Eye	G	L	F	PX	SX	SBO	xHR	xBA	RC/G	RAR	R$
Pos 2	02 MON	207	21	57	5	29	1	275	280	275	342	459	801	9	80	32	0.51	46	19	35	133	65	6%	7	295	5.54	8.5	$6
Age 30	03 MON	335	34	77	9	46	0	230	179	243	306	394	700	10	78	27	0.50	51	18	32	118	39	3%	11	272	4.26	-0.4	$5
Peak	04 MON	436	40	112	12	49	0	257	244	260	322	399	721	9	86	28	0.67	49	20	32	83	42	1%	12	277	4.49	8.7	$8
Bats Left	05 WAS	369	38	99	10	44	1	268	265	269	322	409	731	7	87	29	0.60	47	21	33	88	46	1%	10	287	4.53	7.8	$9
Reliability 68	06 WAS	410	30	105	4	55	2	256	271	251	319	329	648	8	84	30	0.57	47	23	30	50	28	3%	6	255	3.62	-8.7	$6
DL 15	1st Half	195	11	44	2	27	0	226			298	297	595	9	84	26	0.65	49	17	34	48	12	2%	3	222	3.04	-7.8	$1
BAvg Potl 50%	2nd Half	215	19	61	2	28	2	284			339	358	697	8	83	33	0.50	45	28	27	52	38	4%	3	277	4.15	-1.2	$5
LIMA Plan D	07 Proj	**385**	**34**	**101**	**7**	**49**	**1**	**262**			**323**	**374**	**698**	**8**	**84**	**30**	**0.57**	**47**	**22**	**31**	**72**	**41**	**3%**	**8**	**272**	**4.19**	**0.9**	**$7**

Consistent line-drive hitter whose BA can swing wildly from month to month. The real concern is the five-year fade in PX, which makes him a whole lot less interesting than he used to be. Draft him as your #2 CA.

Scott,Luke

Scott,Luke		AB	R	H	HR	RBI	SB	Avg	vL	vR	OB	Slg	OPS	bb%	ct%	h%	Eye	G	L	F	PX	SX	SBO	xHR	xBA	RC/G	RAR	R$
Pos 7	02	0	0	0	0	0	0	0							0							0		0				
Age 28	03 aa	183	17	43	6	31	0	235			271	410	681	5	79	27	0.24				117	48	3%	6		3.71	-9.7	$3
Peak	04 aa	208	31	49	14	44	0	236			312	500	812	10	81	23	0.59				155	33	4%	12		5.45	1.6	$7
Bats Left	05 HOU	* 478	56	110	23	67	3	230	286	178	287	446	733	7	79	24	0.39	43	11	46	134	82	6%	20	267	4.44	-13.1	$12
Reliability 15	06 HOU	* 532	79	153	26	85	7	287	240	366	369	517	887	11	81	31	0.68	36	24	40	133	95	5%	24	297	6.58	19.9	$21
DL	1st Half	284	46	73	15	44	5	255			338	458	796	11	82	27	0.68				113	82	6%	13		5.36	0.9	$10
BAvg Potl 55%	2nd Half	248	34	80	11	42	2	324			405	585	990	12	80	37	0.68	36	24	40	156	82	5%	11	311	8.02	18.4	$11
LIMA Plan C	07 Proj	**380**	**51**	**106**	**19**	**63**	**3**	**279**			**348**	**508**	**856**	**10**	**80**	**30**	**0.54**	**37**	**23**	**40**	**138**	**79**	**5%**	**17**	**296**	**6.09**	**7.8**	**$14**

10-37-.336 in 214 AB at HOU. Finally, some growth to go with all that power. Renewed patience resulted in a bunch of LDs and xBA spike. If he grabs a starting job...
UP: 25 HR, 85 RBI

Scutaro,Marco

Scutaro,Marco		AB	R	H	HR	RBI	SB	Avg	vL	vR	OB	Slg	OPS	bb%	ct%	h%	Eye	G	L	F	PX	SX	SBO	xHR	xBA	RC/G	RAR	R$
Pos 64	02 aaa	390	44	108	7	30	6	277			320	405	726	6	82	32	0.36				82	95	16%	8		4.39	1.7	$9
Age 31	03 NYM	* 319	46	83	10	34	12	260	95	259	344	426	771	11	85	28	0.85	46	10	44	103	101	20%	10	262	5.22	10.6	$11
Past Peak	04 OAK	455	50	124	7	43	0	273	276	271	297	393	691	3	87	30	0.28	43	20	36	80	41	0%	9	276	3.89	-7.4	$8
Bats Right	05 OAK	381	48	94	9	37	5	247	171	262	312	391	703	9	87	26	0.75	43	21	36	90	89	7%	9	288	4.34	-2.4	$8
Reliability 61	06 OAK	365	52	97	5	41	5	266	218	279	354	397	751	12	82	31	0.76	44	21	36	84	111	5%	7	268	5.11	7.3	$8
DL	1st Half	152	15	35	0	14	1	230			304	309	613	10	81	28	0.55	42	21	37	57	85	2%	1	242	3.28	-5.2	$1
BAvg Potl 55%	2nd Half	213	37	62	5	27	4	291			389	460	849	14	83	33	0.92	45	21	35	103	118	7%	6	285	6.38	11.7	$7
LIMA Plan D	07 Proj	**344**	**46**	**90**	**6**	**36**	**4**	**262**			**332**	**396**	**728**	**10**	**84**	**30**	**0.67**	**43**	**21**	**36**	**85**	**98**	**6%**	**7**	**275**	**4.67**	**2.1**	**$7**

His one hope of having some fantasy value is speed -- but he's gotten the green light exactly 13 times in three years with OAK. Otherwise, he's your garden-variety utility infielder. See? More horticulture!

TOM TODARO

Sexson,Richie

			AB	R	H	HR	RBI	SB	Avg	vL	vR	OB	Slg	OPS	bb%	ct%	h%	Eye	G	L	F	PX	SX	SBO	xHR	xBA	RC/G	RAR	R$
Pos	3	02 MIL	570	86	159	29	102	0	279	238	288	358	504	861	11	76	32	0.51	45	21	34	154	43	0%	29	296	6.29	11.1	$23
Age	32	03 MIL	606	97	165	45	124	2	272	279	271	374	548	921	14	75	29	0.65	47	19	34	173	48	3%	40	302	7.13	28.1	$28
Past Peak		04 ARI	90	20	21	9	23	0	233	222	236	337	578	914	13	77	20	0.67	48	14	38	201	44	0%	7	318	6.81	2.3	$5
Bats	Right	05 SEA	558	99	147	39	121	1	263	333	244	365	541	906	14	70	31	0.53	40	19	41	197	48	1%	39	292	7.16	33.5	$25
Reliability	31	06 SEA	591	75	156	34	107	1	264	204	282	336	504	840	10	74	30	0.42	42	18	40	160	28	1%	33	278	5.97	9.4	$19
DL		1st Half	295	32	66	14	55	1	224			293	420	714	9	71	27	0.34	43	18	39	135	32	3%	14	254	4.28	-10.3	$6
BAvg Potl	45%	2nd Half	296	43	90	20	52	0	304			378	588	965	11	77	34	0.51	41	17	41	183	18	0%	19	300	7.56	17.3	$13
LIMA Plan	C+	07 Proj	588	87	159	37	113	1	270			355	529	884	12	74	31	0.50	42	18	40	171	41	1%	36	286	6.63	22.6	$22

A lesson in the value of fantasy patience. Slumped badly in April/May; hit .367 over final two months. 2nd half power shows that another 40-HR year is not out of reach.

Shealy,Ryan

			AB	R	H	HR	RBI	SB	Avg	vL	vR	OB	Slg	OPS	bb%	ct%	h%	Eye	G	L	F	PX	SX	SBO	xHR	xBA	RC/G	RAR	R$
Pos	3	02	0	0	0	0	0	0	0							0							0		0				
Age	27	03	0	0	0	0	0	0	0							0							0		0				
Peak		04 aa	469	68	134	27	77	1	286			350	532	881	9	77	32	0.42				154	60	1%	25		6.40	12.2	$18
Bats	Right	05 COL	* 498	65	143	21	69	4	286	125	373	336	484	820	7	86	30	0.52	45	25	30	121	70	3%	19	321	5.47	-1.8	$18
Reliability	24	06 2TM	* 424	58	112	19	76	1	264	185	311	312	472	784	6	81	28	0.37	37	18	45	125	61	2%	18	276	5.01	-8.6	$13
DL	44	1st Half	166	20	44	10	31	0	263			311	521	831	6	89	25	0.60				142	39	0%	8		5.57	-0.7	$5
BAvg Potl	50%	2nd Half	258	38	68	10	45	1	265			312	441	754	6	77	31	0.30	37	18	45	113	65	3%	10	251	4.67	-7.7	$8
LIMA Plan	C	07 Proj	572	78	157	23	93	1	274			325	463	788	7	82	30	0.42	38	19	43	117	58	2%	22	277	5.11	-7.4	$18

7-36-.280 in 193 AB at KC. Finally got his opportunity with trade to KC. Poor batting eye and high Ks will keep his BA modest, but 20-25 homers looks like a no-brainer, with an upside of 30.

Sheffield,Gary

			AB	R	H	HR	RBI	SB	Avg	vL	vR	OB	Slg	OPS	bb%	ct%	h%	Eye	G	L	F	PX	SX	SBO	xHR	xBA	RC/G	RAR	R$
Pos	9	02 ATL	492	82	151	25	84	12	307	293	310	395	512	908	13	89	30	1.36	42	17	41	118	79	8%	21	304	6.83	20.6	$26
Age	38	03 ATL	576	126	190	39	132	18	330	341	327	417	604	1021	13	90	31	1.56	47	18	35	149	109	11%	31	348	8.08	37.8	$40
Decline		04 NYY	573	117	166	36	121	5	290	314	282	388	534	922	14	86	29	1.11	42	17	41	134	60	6%	31	302	7.01	37.4	$28
Bats	Right	05 NYY	584	104	170	34	123	10	291	359	266	375	512	887	12	87	29	1.03	42	17	41	125	75	6%	28	302	6.47	28.9	$29
Reliability	23	06 NYY	151	22	45	6	25	5	298	344	286	354	450	804	8	89	30	0.81	49	15	37	81	73	13%	5	274	5.34	-1.3	$6
DL	127	1st Half	123	19	38	4	19	5	309			370	439	809	9	87	33	0.75	48	16	36	72	76	14%	3	264	5.47	-0.7	$6
BAvg Potl	55%	2nd Half	28	3	7	2	6	0	250			276	500	776	3	100	19		50	11	39	113	11	0%	1	290	4.90	-0.6	$1
LIMA Plan	B	07 Proj	512	88	147	24	89	3	287			371	473	844	12	87	29	1.05	45	17	38	104	47	4%	21	286	6.02	11.7	$20

BPIs have held up remarkably well for his age, but you have to be concerned about lingering effects of wrist surgery. For a 28-year-old, we'd expect a quick rebound. For a 38-year-old, this projection could be optimistic.

Shelton,Chris

			AB	R	H	HR	RBI	SB	Avg	vL	vR	OB	Slg	OPS	bb%	ct%	h%	Eye	G	L	F	PX	SX	SBO	xHR	xBA	RC/G	RAR	R$
Pos	3	02	0	0	0	0	0	0	0							0							0		0				
Age	26	03 aa	122	15	32	0	13	0	262			301	358	659	5	83	32	0.33				76	72	3%	1		3.67	-6.3	$2
Pre-Peak		04 DET	* 108	10	28	1	9	0	259			365	315	680	14	73	35	0.62				42	16	0%	2		4.16	-2.6	$1
Bats	Right	05 DET	* 569	92	170	25	94	0	300	277	303	362	510	872	9	80	34	0.48	38	24	38	138	50	1%	25	299	6.27	18.6	$23
Reliability	17	06 DET	* 482	68	129	19	60	2	268	276	273	337	454	791	9	71	34	0.36	33	20	48	124	83	3%	20	238	5.47	0.7	$13
DL		1st Half	269	37	73	14	35	0	271			329	494	823	8	70	34	0.28	29	23	48	148	68	1%	13	255	5.82	3.1	$8
BAvg Potl	25%	2nd Half	213	31	56	5	25	2	264			348	402	750	11	71	35	0.45	41	13	46	94	99	4%	6	214	5.04	-2.4	$5
LIMA Plan	C	07 Proj	414	57	105	17	52	1	254			328	449	777	10	75	30	0.43	36	20	44	127	74	3%	17	260	5.18	-1.4	$10

16-47-.273 in 373 AB at DET. Hit 9 HR in his first 13 games, then 7 HR in the next 119 gms. A one month minor league stint didn't help. Has 25 HR pop, but with .250 BA and a ton of K's. At 26, it's really now or never.

Shoppach,Kelly

			AB	R	H	HR	RBI	SB	Avg	vL	vR	OB	Slg	OPS	bb%	ct%	h%	Eye	G	L	F	PX	SX	SBO	xHR	xBA	RC/G	RAR	R$
Pos	2	02	0	0	0	0	0	0	0							0							0		0				
Age	27	03 aa	340	38	88	10	50	0	260			318	442	760	8	78	31	0.39				131	44	0%	12		4.93	7.3	$8
Peak		04 aaa	399	50	85	17	52	0	213			280	404	683	8	73	25	0.34				132	30	0%	18		3.86	-2.6	$6
Bats	Right	05 aaa	370	46	84	19	57	0	227			294	423	716	9	76	25	0.39				127	24	0%	17		4.22	3.5	$9
Reliability	20	06 CLE	* 188	18	46	6	25	0	247	314	213	298	409	708	7	63	36	0.20	43	15	42	137	23	2%	8	216	4.51	0.6	$3
DL		1st Half	102	12	24	3	11	0	239			300	401	701	8	67	33	0.26	60	7	33	133	36	4%	4	221	4.30	-0.3	$1
BAvg Potl	15%	2nd Half	86	6	22	3	14	0	256			297	419	715	5	58	40	0.14	38	18	44	144	1	0%	4	193	4.89	1.2	$2
LIMA Plan	F	07 Proj	130	14	30	5	19	0	231			288	407	695	7	69	30	0.26	41	16	42	133	26	1%	6	235	4.06	-0.7	$2

3-16-.245 in 110 AB at CLE. Even a .220 Triple-A average can buy you a ticket to The Show if you're a catcher with power. But with low ct%, it will probably be a round-trip ticket. Hello Buffalo! (Or wherever...)

Sizemore,Grady

			AB	R	H	HR	RBI	SB	Avg	vL	vR	OB	Slg	OPS	bb%	ct%	h%	Eye	G	L	F	PX	SX	SBO	xHR	xBA	RC/G	RAR	R$
Pos	8	02	0	0	0	0	0	0	0							0							0		0				
Age	24	03 aa	496	88	143	12	71	9	288			344	442	785	8	86	31	0.62				91	117	14%	12		5.22	5.2	$18
Growth		04 CLE	* 556	74	142	10	65	15	255	178	280	315	381	696	8	84	29	0.53	47	16	37	77	111	19%	11	261	4.17	-9.1	$13
Bats	Left	05 CLE	640	111	185	22	81	22	289	245	308	342	484	827	8	79	34	0.39	44	24	31	125	145	19%	22	298	5.70	25.8	$27
Reliability	39	06 CLE	655	134	190	28	76	22	290	214	329	366	533	898	11	77	34	0.51	33	20	47	158	152	16%	30	281	6.86	40.6	$28
DL		1st Half	319	65	98	15	39	13	307			370	552	922	9	81	34	0.52	35	18	47	145	153	17%	14	285	6.92	19.7	$16
BAvg Potl	40%	2nd Half	336	69	92	13	37	9	274			361	515	876	12	73	34	0.50	32	22	47	172	135	15%	16	278	6.81	20.9	$12
LIMA Plan	B+	07 Proj	635	116	180	32	97	16	283			350	536	886	9	79	32	0.49	37	21	41	156	131	16%	30	299	6.50	34.8	$28

Hit just six more HR, but PX jumped 33 points. Why? 55 doubles. Add in a higher FB%, and some of those doubles could go over the fence. 30 HRs is probably a no-brainer, so... UP: 35-40 HR

Sledge,Termel

			AB	R	H	HR	RBI	SB	Avg	vL	vR	OB	Slg	OPS	bb%	ct%	h%	Eye	G	L	F	PX	SX	SBO	xHR	xBA	RC/G	RAR	R$
Pos	7	02 a/a	476	68	123	8	43	10	258			330	376	706	10	84	29	0.69				74	101	14%	9		4.40	-17.2	$12
Age	30	03 aaa	497	70	139	16	68	10	280			338	445	783	8	86	30	0.61				97	101	12%	15		5.16	-4.3	$17
Peak		04 MON	402	46	108	15	63	3	269	241	277	335	460	795	9	84	29	0.61	42	18	40	109	81	6%	14	280	5.35	-1.1	$12
Bats	Left	05 WAS	37	7	9	1	8	2	243		250	364	378	742	16	78	29	0.88	35	23	42	69	134	21%	1	235	5.04	-0.3	$2
Reliability	11	06 SD	* 437	56	103	17	59	4	237	400	215	316	405	721	10	81	26	0.60	53	17	30	96	74	6%	15	274	4.46	-10.4	$9
DL	151	1st Half	229	26	44	5	25	3	192			277	292	569	10	83	21	0.68	62	5	33	62	56	6%	5	220	2.71	-18.5	$1
BAvg Potl	65%	2nd Half	208	30	59	12	34	1	285			359	529	888	10	78	31	0.54	47	25	28	136	80	6%	10	307	6.52	7.5	$8
LIMA Plan	F	07 Proj	63	8	16	2	9	1	254			326	445	771	10	82	28	0.60	44	18	38	110	94	8%	2	281	5.09	-0.5	$2

2-7-.229 in 70 AB at SD. SD had zero patience for his slow start, demoting him in mid-April. Has the skills to be a useful backup OF, but there is not much upside at age 30.

Smith,Jason

			AB	R	H	HR	RBI	SB	Avg	vL	vR	OB	Slg	OPS	bb%	ct%	h%	Eye	G	L	F	PX	SX	SBO	xHR	xBA	RC/G	RAR	R$
Pos	4	02 TAM	* 271	34	65	4	30	7	240		217	267	358	625	4	77	30	0.16	46	17	37	78	142	15%	5	242	2.99	-8.5	$6
Age	29	03 aaa	515	65	135	13	61	12	262			276	425	701	2	77	32	0.08				100	135	22%	12		3.86	-6.3	$14
Peak		04 DET	* 277	35	66	7	43	5	238	242	238	272	408	680	4	78	28	0.22	42	19	39	104	129	15%	7	263	3.75	-2.8	$5
Bats	Left	05 aaa	180	19	34	5	20	7	191			231	336	567	5	74	23	0.20				101	128	32%	5		2.23	-12.3	$2
Reliability	6	06 COL	* 240	26	61	8	28	5	256	400	255	305	418	723	7	75	31	0.28	43	19	38	98	103	10%	7	247	4.34	-1.8	$6
DL		1st Half	129	15	33	4	15	3	254			328	388	715	10	74	31	0.43	43	20	37	82	80	8%	4	237	4.37	-0.9	$3
BAvg Potl	35%	2nd Half	111	11	29	4	14	2	259			277	452	730	2	75	31	0.10	41	18	41	116	101	14%	3	254	4.26	-1.1	$3
LIMA Plan	F	07 Proj	67	7	16	2	8	2	239			276	399	675	5	75	29	0.21	42	19	39	103	112	16%	2	252	3.66	-1.9	$1

5-13-.263 in 99 AB at COL. Baseball's Pure Obstacles:
- Has power, but can't make contact.
- Has speed, but can't reach base.
- Has hope but is too old.

Snelling,Chris

			AB	R	H	HR	RBI	SB	Avg	vL	vR	OB	Slg	OPS	bb%	ct%	h%	Eye	G	L	F	PX	SX	SBO	xHR	xBA	RC/G	RAR	R$
Pos	9	02 aa	89	11	29	1	13	5	326			412	483	895	13	89	36	1.30				108	104	19%	2		6.95	4.3	$4
Age	25	03 a/a	253	35	78	5	35	2	307			343	432	774	5	85	35	0.36				80	63	15%	6		4.88	-3.6	$9
Pre-Peak		04	0	0	0	0	0	0	0							0							0		0				
Bats	Left	05 aaa	246	42	81	7	38	2	329			406	484	890	12	85	37	0.84				99	62	7%	8		6.66	11.2	$11
Reliability	0	06 SEA	* 337	44	70	7	41	5	208	91	271	292	335	627	11	73	26	0.44	38	21	41	92	92	10%	9	234	3.28	-25.2	$4
DL	60 49	1st Half	118	21	29	2	21	2	246			341	381	722	13	78	30	0.65				103	74	6%	3		4.72	-3.3	$3
BAvg Potl	50%	2nd Half	219	23	41	5	20	3	187			264	311	575	10	70	24	0.35	38	21	41	86	91	12%	6	222	2.47	-22.6	$1
LIMA Plan	F	07 Proj	189	28	50	4	26	2	265			339	403	742	10	79	31	0.54	38	21	41	94	76	9%	5	255	4.79	-2.4	$5

3-8-.250 in 96 AB at SEA. Good prospect forever slowed by injuries, most recently to his shoulder. Line-drive hitter with moderate power, but needs to prove that he's healthy.

TOM TODARO

Snyder,Chris

Snyder,Chris		AB	R	H	HR	RBI	SB	Avg	vL	vR	OB	Slg	OPS	bb%	ct%	h%	Eye	G	L	F	PX	SX	SBO	xHR	xBA	RC/G	RAR	R$
Pos 2	02	0	0	0	0	0	0	0							0						0			0				
Age 26	03 aa	188	15	34	3	19	0	181			238	298	535	7	89	19	0.67				79	24	0%	4		2.43	-10.6	($1)
Pre-Peak	04 ARI	* 442	57	114	16	55	2	258	250	234	331	446	776	10	85	27	0.72	38	21	42	118	45	3%	17	292	5.18	17.7	$11
Bats Right	05 ARI	326	24	66	6	28	0	202	260	185	290	301	590	11	73	26	0.46	51	19	29	75	16	1%	8	224	2.76	-10.5	$0
Reliability 8	06 ARI	184	19	51	6	32	0	277	246	294	354	424	778	11	79	32	0.56	45	22	33	93	14	0%	6	260	5.20	4.5	$5
DL	1st Half	76	7	21	3	19	0	276			375	447	822	14	82	31	0.86	50	17	33	103	7	0%	3	250	5.90	3.4	$3
BAvg Potl 40%	2nd Half	108	12	30	3	13	0	278			339	407	746	8	77	34	0.40	42	26	33	85	20	0%	3	262	4.70	1.1	$3
LIMA Plan F	07 Proj	220	21	57	6	30	0	259			334	397	732	10	79	30	0.55	47	21	32	92	21	1%	7	261	4.62	3.2	$5

With Estrada, gave ARI a solid CA tandem. Kept bb% gains, and brought earlier BA and PX up this time. xBA suggests BA will dip a bit, but you can do worse for your $1 end-game catcher.

Soriano,Alfonso

Soriano,Alfonso		AB	R	H	HR	RBI	SB	Avg	vL	vR	OB	Slg	OPS	bb%	ct%	h%	Eye	G	L	F	PX	SX	SBO	xHR	xBA	RC/G	RAR	R$
Pos 7	02 NYY	696	128	209	39	102	41	300	316	297	323	547	870	3	77	34	0.15	35	21	45	160	139	39%	35	290	5.92	21.3	$40
Age 31	03 NYY	682	114	198	38	91	35	290	312	285	328	525	853	5	81	31	0.29	34	22	45	140	134	27%	32	289	5.73	7.7	$35
Past Peak	04 TEX	613	77	170	28	91	18	277	266	284	314	480	794	5	80	31	0.27	33	19	48	121	108	17%	25	264	5.05	1.9	$23
Bats Right	05 TEX	637	102	171	36	104	30	268	257	272	304	512	816	5	80	28	0.26	34	19	47	155	133	26%	31	293	5.29	10.4	$31
Reliability 75	06 WAS	647	119	179	46	95	41	277	293	271	345	560	904	9	75	30	0.42	29	20	51	175	113	37%	41	283	6.70	27.6	$36
DL	1st Half	321	56	87	24	51	18	271			333	542	875	9	77	28	0.41	34	17	49	159	91	32%	20	281	6.17	8.7	$17
BAvg Potl 45%	2nd Half	326	63	92	22	44	23	282			355	577	932	10	74	32	0.43	24	22	54	191	125	42%	21	284	7.25	19.1	$19
LIMA Plan D+	07 Proj	640	108	179	40	96	35	280			331	538	870	7	77	31	0.34	31	20	49	161	126	31%	35	284	6.12	13.7	$34

Not just good, but when RFK is considered, a terrific season. More selective; ct% took a hit, but he hit his pitch. A lot. And far. Position switch let him focus on offense. Seems LF wasn't so bad after all!

Spiezio,Scott

Spiezio,Scott		AB	R	H	HR	RBI	SB	Avg	vL	vR	OB	Slg	OPS	bb%	ct%	h%	Eye	G	L	F	PX	SX	SBO	xHR	xBA	RC/G	RAR	R$
Pos 57	02 ANA	491	80	140	12	82	6	285	368	248	371	436	807	12	89	30	1.29	32	21	47	92	73	8%	14	278	5.78	18.5	$17
Age 34	03 ANA	521	69	138	16	83	6	265	223	282	325	453	777	8	87	28	0.70	38	23	39	112	102	7%	16	303	5.17	10.0	$15
Past Peak	04 SEA	367	38	79	10	41	4	215	203	218	285	346	631	9	84	23	0.60	33	18	49	74	82	6%	9	236	3.38	-17.3	$4
Bats Both	05 SEA	* 105	12	20	2	9	0	190			227	276	503	5	73	24	0.18				62	45	0%	2		1.31	-10.6	$0
Reliability 4	06 STL	276	44	75	13	52	1	272	318	251	358	496	854	12	76	31	0.56	34	20	46	137	85	1%	13	269	6.28	6.2	$10
DL	1st Half	122	17	34	3	22	0	279			362	434	797	12	76	34	0.55	38	22	40	106	55	0%	4	258	5.61	0.4	$4
BAvg Potl 45%	2nd Half	154	27	41	10	30	1	266			354	545	900	12	76	29	0.57	32	18	50	162	94	2%	9	279	6.81	5.9	$6
LIMA Plan D	07 Proj	222	31	58	8	33	1	261			331	432	763	9	78	30	0.47	34	20	46	106	77	2%	8	251	4.95	-1.2	$6

Revived his flagging career subbing for various injured Redbirds, and showed his best skills since... well, since ever. Maybe it was the Cardinal-red goatee. Anyway, he's back to relevance, albeit as a part-timer.

Spilborghs,Ryan

Spilborghs,Ryan		AB	R	H	HR	RBI	SB	Avg	vL	vR	OB	Slg	OPS	bb%	ct%	h%	Eye	G	L	F	PX	SX	SBO	xHR	xBA	RC/G	RAR	R$
Pos 8	02	0	0	0	0	0	0	0							0							0		0				
Age 27	03	0	0	0	0	0	0	0							0							0		0				
Peak	04	0	0	0	0	0	0	0							0							0		0				
Bats Right	05 a/a	478	63	134	7	51	11	281			337	429	766	8	85	32	0.55				103	108	15%	11		5.06	8.8	$14
Reliability 4	06 COL	* 436	62	129	8	46	11	295	323	267	348	422	770	7	85	33	0.53	51	21	29	78	103	11%	9	285	5.01	7.0	$14
DL	1st Half	208	28	62	4	20	3	297			346	432	778	7	86	33	0.52	44	23	33	82	84	8%	4	285	5.09	3.8	$6
BAvg Potl 45%	2nd Half	228	34	67	4	25	8	294			349	413	762	8	84	33	0.54	56	19	25	73	104	14%	5	284	4.94	3.2	$8
LIMA Plan F	07 Proj	162	22	47	3	17	4	290			344	433	777	8	85	33	0.54	51	20	28	91	107	13%	3	295	5.15	2.7	$5

4-21-.287 in 167 AB at COL. Gets the most out of limited tools. GB ways limit PX, but has BA upside. Wild guess: has a .300+ breakout season sometime in the next few years, then fades slowly away.

Stairs,Matt

Stairs,Matt		AB	R	H	HR	RBI	SB	Avg	vL	vR	OB	Slg	OPS	bb%	ct%	h%	Eye	G	L	F	PX	SX	SBO	xHR	xBA	RC/G	RAR	R$
Pos 0	02 MIL	270	41	66	16	41	2	244	154	249	333	478	811	12	81	25	0.72	43	13	44	145	54	3%	14	287	5.56	0.3	$9
Age 39	03 PIT	305	49	89	20	57	0	292	188	304	383	561	944	13	79	31	0.70	35	20	45	168	41	1%	18	304	7.32	23.0	$14
Decline	04 KC	439	48	117	18	66	1	267	223	278	340	451	791	10	79	30	0.53	50	13	37	112	55	1%	17	260	5.32	0.2	$11
Bats Left	05 KC	396	55	109	13	66	1	275	259	278	371	444	815	13	83	31	0.87	40	19	42	111	42	2%	14	275	5.84	-2.1	$12
Reliability 34	06 2AL	348	42	86	13	51	0	247	217	252	325	420	744	10	75	29	0.47	43	17	39	117	22	0%	14	250	4.76	-17.1	$7
DL	1st Half	148	18	38	7	29	0	257			337	459	797	11	76	30	0.50	38	16	46	133	18	0%	7	253	5.44	-4.3	$4
BAvg Potl 50%	2nd Half	200	24	48	6	22	0	240			315	390	705	10	75	29	0.44	47	19	34	105	25	0%	7	249	4.26	-12.9	$3
LIMA Plan F	07 Proj	187	24	45	7	29	0	241			325	417	742	11	78	27	0.57	43	17	40	116	32	1%	8	260	4.75	-7.1	$4

Decline is best seen in BA vs RHP, his specialty. Had to open up his swing just to maintain PX. Even his last vestige of fanalytic value, as a platoon player in sim formats, is just about gone.

Stewart,Shannon

Stewart,Shannon		AB	R	H	HR	RBI	SB	Avg	vL	vR	OB	Slg	OPS	bb%	ct%	h%	Eye	G	L	F	PX	SX	SBO	xHR	xBA	RC/G	RAR	R$
Pos 7	02 TOR	577	103	175	10	45	14	303	302	304	363	442	805	9	90	33	0.90	48	20	32	84	128	9%	12	300	5.57	11.7	$20
Age 33	03 2AL	573	90	176	13	73	4	307	331	300	365	459	824	8	88	33	0.79	44	23	33	97	66	6%	15	307	5.72	6.2	$20
Past Peak	04 MIN	378	46	115	11	47	6	304	257	325	381	447	828	11	88	32	1.07	42	22	37	80	72	7%	10	268	5.90	10.0	$13
Bats Right	05 MIN	551	69	151	10	56	7	274	244	283	316	388	705	6	87	30	0.47	46	20	35	73	83	8%	11	274	4.16	-8.8	$13
Reliability 24	06 MIN	174	21	51	2	21	3	293	288	295	346	368	714	7	89	32	0.74	48	14	39	43	78	7%	2	236	4.41	-3.7	$5
DL 118	1st Half	141	19	42	2	17	3	298			353	376	729	8	90	32	0.86	50	14	35	41	91	6%	2	246	4.61	-2.2	$5
BAvg Potl 45%	2nd Half	33	2	9	0	4	0	273			314	333	648	6	85	32	0.40	36	11	54	50	31	11%	0	193	3.53	-1.6	$0
LIMA Plan D	07 Proj	376	52	104	8	43	2	277			337	393	731	8	89	30	0.81	46	19	35	69	69	4%	8	274	4.65	-4.0	$9

Plantar facia woes continue to decimate skills, but it's not all the feet. BPIs were already sliding before this injury-driven debacle. Should rebound, but unlike a J.D. Drew, the reward is meager with all that risk.

Sullivan,Cory

Sullivan,Cory		AB	R	H	HR	RBI	SB	Avg	vL	vR	OB	Slg	OPS	bb%	ct%	h%	Eye	G	L	F	PX	SX	SBO	xHR	xBA	RC/G	RAR	R$
Pos 8	02	0	0	0	0	0	0	0							0							0		0				
Age 27	03 aa	557	61	155	5	46	13	278			314	384	698	5	88	31	0.46				68	102	19%	7		4.14	-11.8	$13
Peak	04 COL	0	0	0	0	0	0	0							0							0		0				
Bats Left	05 COL	378	64	111	4	30	12	294	250	301	342	386	729	7	78	37	0.34	44	32	24	65	136	13%	5	276	4.47	-0.9	$13
Reliability 2	06 COL	386	47	103	2	30	10	267	280	266	323	402	725	8	74	36	0.32	36	32	33	95	119	16%	5	265	4.64	2.2	$8
DL	1st Half	237	33	64	1	11	5	270			311	414	724	6	75	36	0.24	35	31	35	100	128	11%	3	266	4.54	0.7	$4
BAvg Potl 30%	2nd Half	149	14	39	1	19	5	262			341	383	724	11	72	36	0.44	38	33	29	88	102	23%	2	263	4.76	1.5	$3
LIMA Plan D	07 Proj	324	43	90	3	28	9	278			332	394	726	8	77	35	0.36	40	32	28	80	128	17%	4	275	4.55	-0.0	$8

Didn't follow up well, as ct% regressed further. Speed skills and bb% each imply SB upside, but not with this BA. With his fine LD%, all it would take is a few more balls in play for... UP: .295 BA, 15 SB

Suzuki,Ichiro

Suzuki,Ichiro		AB	R	H	HR	RBI	SB	Avg	vL	vR	OB	Slg	OPS	bb%	ct%	h%	Eye	G	L	F	PX	SX	SBO	xHR	xBA	RC/G	RAR	R$
Pos 98	02 SEA	647	111	208	8	51	31	321	356	308	386	425	811	10	90	35	1.10	56	22	22	59	129	20%	9	306	5.70	12.2	$28
Age 33	03 SEA	679	111	212	13	62	34	312	359	291	347	436	783	5	90	33	0.52	49	24	27	70	143	21%	12	307	5.03	-2.2	$29
Past Peak	04 SEA	704	101	262	8	60	36	372	404	359	413	455	868	7	91	40	0.78	64	18	18	47	109	17%	9	301	6.07	24.3	$35
Bats Left	05 SEA	679	111	206	15	68	33	303	352	284	349	436	785	7	90	32	0.73	54	21	24	71	150	20%	12	311	5.17	8.9	$29
Reliability 95	06 SEA	695	110	224	9	49	45	322	352	312	367	416	783	7	90	35	0.69	51	22	28	50	150	20%	9	285	5.15	-9.6	$30
DL	1st Half	338	61	121	4	27	25	358			404	447	851	7	90	39	0.76	56	21	23	46	151	21%	4	295	5.93	2.3	$19
BAvg Potl 45%	2nd Half	357	49	103	5	22	20	289			332	387	718	6	90	31	0.62	46	22	33	54	138	19%	5	277	4.40	-12.6	$12
LIMA Plan C+	07 Proj	654	102	200	9	53	37	306			352	407	759	7	90	33	0.71	53	21	26	55	145	20%	9	295	4.89	-5.9	$26

He is the special case that has caused the repeated revisiting the xBA calculation. Now that we think we've got it right, his xBA once again dips below .300. Perhaps this time it's for real. Or he's just messing with us again.

Sweeney,Mark

Sweeney,Mark		AB	R	H	HR	RBI	SB	Avg	vL	vR	OB	Slg	OPS	bb%	ct%	h%	Eye	G	L	F	PX	SX	SBO	xHR	xBA	RC/G	RAR	R$
Pos 37	02 SD	65	3	11	1	4	0	169	89	189	217	262	479	6	71	22	0.21	33	22	46	77	0	0%	1	211	1.02	-9.7	($1)
Age 37	03 COL	* 262	29	67	7	37	1	256		275	337	408	745	11	81	29	0.63	26	27	47	104	45	9%	8	274	4.87	-5.1	$6
Decline	04 COL	177	25	47	9	40	1	266	556	250	378	508	886	15	71	32	0.63	39	15	45	166	77	2%	10	267	7.04	5.6	$7
Bats Left	05 SD	221	31	65	8	40	4	294	200	302	402	466	868	15	74	37	0.69	37	25	38	121	79	5%	9	266	6.74	7.0	$10
Reliability 10	06 SF	259	32	65	5	37	0	251	135	270	324	382	706	10	81	29	0.56	42	22	36	85	54	1%	6	265	4.35	-12.6	$5
DL	1st Half	158	17	42	3	23	0	266			314	430	744	7	82	31	0.38	46	20	34	108	62	0%	4	284	4.70	-5.9	$3
BAvg Potl 55%	2nd Half	101	15	23	2	14	0	228			339	307	646	14	79	27	0.81	37	25	38	47	38	3%	2	238	3.72	-7.1	$1
LIMA Plan F	07 Proj	231	31	60	4	38	0	260			355	369	723	13	77	32	0.65	39	23	39	77	50	2%	5	245	4.71	-7.7	$5

Weird that while his other skills swing wildly, xBA is so steady. Maybe because two of his seasons equals one regular's -- it's sample size. Keeps hitting RHers, so he'll keep getting his 250-ish AB.

ROD TRUESDELL

Sweeney,Mike

			AB	R	H	HR	RBI	SB	Avg	vL	vR	OB	Slg	OPS	bb%	ct%	h%	Eye	G	L	F	PX	SX	SBO	xHR	xBA	RC/G	RAR	R$
Pos	0	02 KC	483	83	163	25	89	9	337	357	334	413	563	976	11	90	34	1.29	42	24	34	125	69	10%	22	333	7.52	25.6	$27
Age	33	03 KC	392	62	115	16	83	3	293	277	300	393	467	859	14	86	31	1.14	42	21	37	100	56	3%	15	290	6.38	19.2	$16
Past Peak		04 KC	411	56	118	22	79	3	287	221	312	340	504	844	7	89	28	0.75	37	15	47	117	47	5%	18	288	5.74	5.1	$16
Bats	Right	05 KC	470	63	141	21	83	3	300	279	308	346	517	863	7	87	31	0.54	36	17	47	136	54	3%	19	300	5.96	-0.8	$19
Reliability	33	06 KC	217	23	56	8	33	2	258	266	255	343	438	781	11	78	30	0.58	35	21	44	121	40	3%	9	268	5.29	-7.2	$5
DL	98 15	1st Half	68	8	12	2	6	0	176			291	309	600	14	75	20	0.65	33	12	56	90	26	0%	2	201	2.98	-7.6	($0)
BAvg Potl	50%	2nd Half	149	15	44	6	27	2	295			367	497	864	10	79	34	0.55	36	25	39	134	39	5%	6	295	6.28	-0.6	$5
LIMA Plan	C	07 Proj	**410**	**51**	**117**	**17**	**68**	**3**	**285**			**356**	**479**	**835**	**10**	**83**	**31**	**0.63**	**36**	**19**	**45**	**121**	**47**	**3%**	**17**	**279**	**5.84**	**-2.1**	**$14**

Let's invent something called the "Risk Threat Index" (RTI). Any time a player's analysis has the phrase, "if he's healthy," raise the RTI one threat level. If he's healthy, Sweeney should post solid numbers again.

Swisher,Nick

			AB	R	H	HR	RBI	SB	Avg	vL	vR	OB	Slg	OPS	bb%	ct%	h%	Eye	G	L	F	PX	SX	SBO	xHR	xBA	RC/G	RAR	R$
Pos	37	02	0	0	0	0	0	0	0							0							0		0				
Age	26	03 aa	287	29	57	4	35	0	199			274	321	595	9	78	24	0.48				93	48	2%	7		2.94	-22.7	$1
Pre-Peak		04 aaa	443	83	105	23	70	2	237			350	456	806	15	81	25	0.90				132	59	5%	22		5.71	3.2	$14
Bats	Both	05 OAK *	485	69	117	21	75	0	241	197	248	321	447	768	11	76	28	0.49	38	19	43	144	39	2%	22	276	5.09	-0.0	$12
Reliability	39	06 OAK	556	106	141	35	95	1	254	291	241	364	493	857	15	73	29	0.64	33	19	48	152	55	2%	34	264	6.42	16.3	$20
DL	23	1st Half	274	58	76	19	49	1	277			389	547	936	15	76	30	0.76	33	19	48	163	78	2%	17	282	7.42	15.6	$12
BAvg Potl	50%	2nd Half	282	48	65	16	46	0	230			340	440	780	14	70	27	0.55	33	20	47	140	34	1%	16	247	5.39	-0.2	$7
LIMA Plan	B	07 Proj	**547**	**91**	**141**	**33**	**87**	**1**	**258**			**356**	**496**	**852**	**13**	**75**	**29**	**0.61**	**35**	**19**	**46**	**153**	**43**	**2%**	**32**	**276**	**6.24**	**15.1**	**$19**

The only fly in this ointment of skills is the dwindling ct%, which is holding back his BA. Otherwise, PX is solid, bb% is outstanding, and Triple-A MLE's show there's still room for growth. Bid accordingly.

Taguchi,So

			AB	R	H	HR	RBI	SB	Avg	vL	vR	OB	Slg	OPS	bb%	ct%	h%	Eye	G	L	F	PX	SX	SBO	xHR	xBA	RC/G	RAR	R$
Pos	78	02 a/a	426	42	84	4	36	7	197			228	270	498	4	86	22	0.28	73	0	27	52	81	14%	6		1.67	-53.4	$2
Age	37	03 STL *	312	35	70	5	33	12	224	259	259	280	317	597	7	84	25	0.49	53	21	26	57	110	22%	5	275	2.93	-25.7	$6
Decline		04 STL *	234	30	66	4	31	11	282	266	318	320	406	726	5	85	32	0.37	48	20	32	78	119	23%	5	279	4.37	-7.2	$9
Bats	Right	05 STL	396	45	114	8	53	11	288	277	294	322	412	734	5	84	33	0.32	46	24	30	81	102	13%	9	288	4.39	-10.5	$14
Reliability	40	06 STL	316	46	84	2	31	11	266	280	252	333	351	685	9	85	31	0.67	48	21	30	60	95	15%	4	269	4.16	-10.0	$8
DL		1st Half	198	34	56	2	26	8	283			340	364	703	8	86	32	0.61	49	22	29	55	90	18%	3	271	4.28	-5.5	$7
BAvg Potl	55%	2nd Half	118	12	28	0	5	3	237			323	331	654	11	83	29	0.75	47	20	33	70	84	9%	1	265	3.95	-4.6	$1
LIMA Plan	F	07 Proj	**259**	**32**	**70**	**3**	**26**	**8**	**270**			**325**	**369**	**694**	**8**	**84**	**31**	**0.52**	**47**	**22**	**31**	**68**	**97**	**14%**	**4**	**273**	**4.14**	**-9.2**	**$7**

STL keeps finding AB for him, and he keeps responding with this level of okay-ness. Nice bb% spike, but modest power dwindled (at least, until the playoffs). At 37, it's not like he's going to break out or anything.

Tatis,Fernando

			AB	R	H	HR	RBI	SB	Avg	vL	vR	OB	Slg	OPS	bb%	ct%	h%	Eye	G	L	F	PX	SX	SBO	xHR	xBA	RC/G	RAR	R$
Pos	5	02 MON	381	43	87	15	55	2	228	230	228	293	399	692	8	76	26	0.39				115	53	5%	15		3.96	-7.3	$8
Age	32	03 MON	175	15	34	2	15	2	194	240	176	269	263	532	9	77	24	0.45				51	51	7%	3		2.03	-12.4	$0
Past Peak		04	0	0	0	0	0	0	0							0							0		0				
Bats	Both	05	0	0	0	0	0	0	0							0							0		0				
Reliability	10	06 BAL *	382	47	100	8	41	7	260	286	214	329	387	716	9	80	31	0.51	44	15	41	83	88	8%	10	241	4.41	-6.6	$8
DL		1st Half	268	32	72	6	24	7	269			327	390	717	8	80	32	0.44				77	88	11%	7		4.33	-5.3	$6
BAvg Potl	40%	2nd Half	114	15	28	2	17	0	241			334	380	714	12	79	29	0.67	44	15	41	96	66	3%	3	247	4.60	-1.4	$2
LIMA Plan	F	07 Proj	**158**	**17**	**36**	**3**	**18**	**2**	**228**			**303**	**351**	**654**	**10**	**78**	**27**	**0.50**	**44**	**15**	**41**	**83**	**74**	**6%**	**4**	**235**	**3.66**	**-5.6**	**$2**

2-8-.250 in 56 AB at BAL. A comeback of monocarpic proportions. That he's trying to come back at all is a proud testament to the human spirit. Or he has some bills to pay, not sure. Still, good for him.

Taveras,Willy

			AB	R	H	HR	RBI	SB	Avg	vL	vR	OB	Slg	OPS	bb%	ct%	h%	Eye	G	L	F	PX	SX	SBO	xHR	xBA	RC/G	RAR	R$
Pos	8	02	0	0	0	0	0	0	0							0							0		0				
Age	25	03	0	0	0	0	0	0	0							0							0		0				
Pre-Peak		04 aa	409	62	126	2	22	45	308			355	357	712	7	85	36	0.50				33	128	41%	3		4.29	-4.5	$21
Bats	Right	05 HOU	592	82	172	3	29	34	291	233	311	319	341	661	4	83	35	0.24	55	19	26	33	134	25%	4	249	3.46	-18.6	$20
Reliability	61	06 HOU	529	83	147	1	30	33	278	254	285	321	338	660	6	83	33	0.39	56	18	27	40	137	27%	3	254	3.64	-12.2	$16
DL		1st Half	262	41	70	0	18	12	267			314	324	639	6	84	32	0.42	55	18	27	38	130	22%	1	253	3.44	-7.8	$7
BAvg Potl	35%	2nd Half	267	42	77	1	12	21	288			329	352	681	6	83	34	0.36	56	17	27	43	136	31%	2	253	3.85	-4.5	$10
LIMA Plan	C	07 Proj	**520**	**78**	**150**	**2**	**27**	**36**	**288**			**327**	**346**	**673**	**5**	**83**	**34**	**0.35**	**55**	**18**	**27**	**38**	**139**	**29%**	**4**	**253**	**3.73**	**-12.2**	**$19**

You don't look at his BA and think, "30 game hit streak," but that's what he had, saving his SB numbers. With speedsters, it's all about the OB; if he can build on those 2nd half gains: UP: 45 SB

Teahen,Mark

			AB	R	H	HR	RBI	SB	Avg	vL	vR	OB	Slg	OPS	bb%	ct%	h%	Eye	G	L	F	PX	SX	SBO	xHR	xBA	RC/G	RAR	R$
Pos	5	02	0	0	0	0	0	0	0							0							0		0				
Age	25	03	0	0	0	0	0	0	0							0							0		0				
Pre-Peak		04 a/a	512	55	140	12	58	0	273			333	422	756	8	81	32	0.48				100	43	1%	14		4.89	-1.5	$11
Bats	Left	05 KC *	474	63	116	7	58	7	245	200	263	310	371	682	9	76	31	0.39	53	23	24	96	105	8%	11	279	3.99	-7.1	$9
Reliability	7	06 KC *	472	83	141	20	82	10	298	274	296	374	527	900	11	80	34	0.60	49	16	35	136	136	7%	19	296	6.78	23.0	$20
DL	20	1st Half	232	33	64	6	32	2	275			347	451	798	10	80	32	0.56	54	11	35	103	105	3%	6	266	5.52	3.4	$6
BAvg Potl	40%	2nd Half	240	50	77	14	50	8	321			399	600	999	11	80	36	0.63	46	18	36	167	141	11%	13	319	8.00	19.1	$14
LIMA Plan	B	07 Proj	**506**	**78**	**149**	**23**	**86**	**9**	**294**			**363**	**521**	**884**	**10**	**79**	**34**	**0.50**	**45**	**19**	**36**	**141**	**114**	**7%**	**22**	**298**	**6.51**	**23.8**	**$21**

18-69-.290 in 393 AB at KC.

Yr-Half	FB	PX	HR
'05-1H	23	82	2
'05-2H	25	107	5
'06-1H	35	103	6
'06-2H	36	167	14

This is growth to pay for.

Teixeira,Mark

			AB	R	H	HR	RBI	SB	Avg	vL	vR	OB	Slg	OPS	bb%	ct%	h%	Eye	G	L	F	PX	SX	SBO	xHR	xBA	RC/G	RAR	R$
Pos	3	02 aa	171	28	52	9	25	3	304			387	556	942	12	82	33	0.74				149	109	9%	8		7.27	7.3	$8
Age	26	03 TEX	529	66	137	26	84	1	259	295	242	316	480	796	8	77	29	0.37	36	28	36	140	66	2%	24	299	5.26	-1.9	$16
Pre-Peak		04 TEX	549	102	154	38	112	4	281	313	267	360	557	917	11	79	29	0.58	40	21	40	166	78	3%	33	309	6.87	29.1	$25
Bats	Both	05 TEX	644	112	194	43	144	4	301	292	301	372	575	946	10	81	32	0.58	40	21	38	168	81	2%	37	321	7.14	36.1	$34
Reliability	95	06 TEX	628	99	177	33	110	2	282	302	275	371	514	885	12	80	31	0.70	39	20	41	146	51	1%	32	294	6.61	21.0	$23
DL		1st Half	313	43	86	8	44	0	275			357	441	798	11	80	32	0.65	40	22	38	115	42	0%	10	280	5.58	1.4	$7
BAvg Potl	50%	2nd Half	315	56	91	25	66	2	289			385	587	972	13	79	29	0.74	39	18	43	177	47	2%	21	309	7.63	19.4	$15
LIMA Plan	D+	07 Proj	**620**	**113**	**183**	**45**	**145**	**2**	**295**			**376**	**585**	**961**	**11**	**80**	**31**	**0.64**	**39**	**21**	**40**	**175**	**65**	**2%**	**39**	**318**	**7.41**	**36.3**	**$32**

Hit 27 doubles in 1H with those 8 HR; that flipped to 18/25 in 2nd half, as FB% highlights the adjustments. Eye growth shows it's all sustainable. At 26-with-experience, the upside: UP: 50-150-.300

Tejada,Miguel

			AB	R	H	HR	RBI	SB	Avg	vL	vR	OB	Slg	OPS	bb%	ct%	h%	Eye	G	L	F	PX	SX	SBO	xHR	xBA	RC/G	RAR	R$
Pos	6	02 OAK	662	108	204	34	131	7	308	285	314	346	508	853	5	87	31	0.45	47	15	38	110	72	5%	27	291	5.68	19.8	$32
Age	30	03 OAK	636	98	177	27	106	10	278	269	281	334	472	806	8	90	28	0.82	45	20	36	112	85	6%	24	314	5.40	17.5	$24
Peak		04 BAL	653	107	203	34	150	4	311	327	306	358	534	893	7	89	31	0.66	47	19	34	122	71	3%	28	319	6.26	31.8	$31
Bats	Right	05 BAL	654	89	199	26	98	5	304	293	309	344	515	860	6	87	32	0.48	48	19	33	129	85	4%	24	322	5.90	23.9	$25
Reliability	98	06 BAL	648	99	214	24	100	6	330	335	329	375	498	873	7	88	35	0.58	51	22	27	98	61	4%	22	312	6.06	28.1	$27
DL		1st Half	318	57	102	16	57	4	321			370	522	892	7	90	32	0.81	53	21	26	108	71	4%	13	329	6.27	15.7	$15
BAvg Potl	45%	2nd Half	330	42	112	8	43	2	339			379	476	855	6	85	38	0.44	49	23	28	87	41	4%	9	293	5.86	12.5	$12
LIMA Plan	D+	07 Proj	**623**	**93**	**198**	**22**	**103**	**5**	**318**			**361**	**489**	**850**	**6**	**88**	**34**	**0.55**	**49**	**20**	**31**	**102**	**67**	**4%**	**20**	**306**	**5.80**	**22.3**	**$25**

Maybe it was just the 6-point FB% dip, and maybe there was more to it than that. In any case, PX dipped to lowest value this millennium. Other skills solid as ever. This looks like his new level for awhile.

Thames,Marcus

			AB	R	H	HR	RBI	SB	Avg	vL	vR	OB	Slg	OPS	bb%	ct%	h%	Eye	G	L	F	PX	SX	SBO	xHR	xBA	RC/G	RAR	R$
Pos	70	02 aaa	399	43	72	12	38	4	180			247	331	577	8	84	18	0.56	29	0	71	93	80	12%	12		2.73	-37.4	$2
Age	30	03 TEX *	333	42	78	5	34	4	234	250	95	296	342	638	8	78	29	0.39	42	18	40	80	75	11%	7	239	3.37	-20.0	$5
Peak		04 DET *	399	72	107	29	83	4	268	284	226	339	564	903	10	80	27	0.54	33	19	48	176	75	7%	25	310	6.58	18.9	$18
Bats	Right	05 DET *	364	54	95	24	63	4	262	212	186	341	522	863	11	75	29	0.47	27	14	59	165	89	5%	21	262	6.25	16.2	$14
Reliability	48	06 DET	348	61	89	26	60	1	256	238	266	327	549	876	10	74	27	0.40	26	15	59	185	72	3%	23	274	6.38	12.3	$13
DL		1st Half	178	37	53	15	30	1	298			359	629	988	9	76	31	0.40	25	17	58	208	57	5%	13	305	7.68	12.4	$9
BAvg Potl	45%	2nd Half	170	24	36	11	30	0	212			295	465	759	11	71	23	0.40	27	13	60	160	66	0%	10	241	4.92	-1.3	$4
LIMA Plan	C	07 Proj	**347**	**55**	**91**	**23**	**59**	**1**	**262**			**335**	**526**	**860**	**10**	**75**	**29**	**0.44**	**27**	**15**	**58**	**166**	**67**	**3%**	**20**	**267**	**6.16**	**11.6**	**$13**

Forecaster readers have been aware of his power potential for years; happily for him, DET finally became aware of it also. Ct% will hold BA down, but that bat's a powder keg. UP (with 500 AB): 35 HR

ROD TRUESDELL

Theriot,Ryan

		AB	R	H	HR	RBI	SB	Avg	vL	vR	OB	Slg	OPS	bb%	ct%	h%	Eye	G	L	F	PX	SX	SBO	xHR	xBA	RC/G	RAR	R$
Pos 4	02	0	0	0	0	0	0	0							0							0		0				
Age 27	03 aa	178	18	38	1	8	8	213			317	245	562	13	88	24	1.25				21	67	25%	1		3.01	-7.3	$2
Peak	04	0	0	0	0	0	0	0							0							0		0				
Bats Right	05 aa	445	41	113	1	43	19	253			309	324	632	7	91	28	0.93				50	99	24%	4		3.67	-9.1	$9
Reliability 4	06 CHC	* 414	71	122	3	35	26	294	346	317	358	399	756	9	88	33	0.81	50	27	24	62	148	23%	5	302	5.06	5.4	$16
DL	1st Half	234	30	66	0	17	13	282			344	332	676	9	88	32	0.77	67	0	33	33	114	17%	1		4.10	-3.3	$7
BAvg Potl 60%	2nd Half	180	41	56	3	18	13	309			375	486	861	10	88	34	0.85	49	27	24	101	161	32%	4	331	6.31	8.6	$9
LIMA Plan C+	07 Proj	386	55	109	3	33	21	282			348	377	725	9	89	31	0.92	49	27	24	58	129	24%	4	305	4.74	1.9	$13

3-16-.328 in 134 AB at CHC. A monster Sept. 36% hit rate deserves much of the credit, but he'll never hit for much power. Speed is real; if he keeps getting the green light...
UP: .300 BA, 30 SB

Thomas,Frank

		AB	R	H	HR	RBI	SB	Avg	vL	vR	OB	Slg	OPS	bb%	ct%	h%	Eye	G	L	F	PX	SX	SBO	xHR	xBA	RC/G	RAR	R$
Pos 0	02 CHW	523	77	132	28	92	3	252	214	264	360	472	832	14	78	27	0.77	23	18	58	137	60	2%	27	258	6.02	7.6	$18
Age 38	03 CHW	546	87	146	42	105	0	267	315	249	381	562	943	15	79	27	0.87	24	20	55	181	18	0%	38	307	7.39	43.5	$23
Decline	04 CHW	240	53	65	18	49	0	271	200	289	424	563	987	21	76	28	1.12	28	18	53	181	31	2%	18	293	8.34	21.1	$11
Bats Right	05 CHW	* 147	21	29	13	29	0	199	281	192	290	489	779	11	74	17	0.48	25	21	55	179	19	0%	10	287	4.99	-4.8	$4
Reliability 0	06 OAK	466	77	126	39	114	0	270	245	278	378	545	923	15	83	25	1.00	24	19	57	145	19	0%	30	288	6.96	7.0	$22
DL 15 138	1st Half	184	28	44	16	39	0	239			349	522	871	14	84	20	1.07	28	15	57	145	16	0%	12	283	6.26	-0.9	$7
BAvg Potl 65%	2nd Half	282	49	82	23	75	0	291			398	560	958	15	82	29	0.96	21	22	57	144	20	0%	18	291	7.43	7.8	$15
LIMA Plan C	07 Proj	455	76	124	35	100	0	273			381	539	920	15	79	27	0.83	25	19	56	153	23	0%	30	282	7.02	12.9	$20

Almost lost his starting job in May, then a trip back to CHW lit his fire. Was vintage Frank after that. Bulk likely will keep foot and ankle problems a concern, so be aware of the risk.

Thome,Jim

		AB	R	H	HR	RBI	SB	Avg	vL	vR	OB	Slg	OPS	bb%	ct%	h%	Eye	G	L	F	PX	SX	SBO	xHR	xBA	RC/G	RAR	R$
Pos 0	02 CLE	480	101	146	52	118	1	304	245	333	445	677	1122	20	71	33	0.88	35	19	45	233	46	2%	46	315	10.28	62.7	$32
Age 36	03 PHI	578	111	154	47	131	0	266	254	272	385	573	957	16	69	31	0.61	38	22	39	210	50	2%	45	298	8.03	57.1	$29
Decline	04 PHI	508	97	139	42	105	0	274	239	294	397	581	978	17	72	30	0.72	38	18	45	198	33	1%	40	292	8.17	41.7	$25
Bats Left	05 PHI	193	26	40	7	30	0	207	164	233	357	352	709	19	69	26	0.76	45	18	37	105	21	0%	8	227	4.62	-8.4	$3
Reliability 3	06 CHW	490	108	141	42	109	0	288	236	321	415	598	1013	18	70	33	0.73	37	20	43	204	30	0%	40	293	8.80	32.4	$26
DL 110	1st Half	251	60	71	24	63	0	283			410	606	1015	18	69	32	0.69	34	19	47	207	35	0%	22	288	8.80	16.8	$14
BAvg Potl 45%	2nd Half	239	48	70	18	46	0	293			421	590	1011	18	71	34	0.77	40	21	40	200	26	0%	18	299	8.80	15.7	$11
LIMA Plan C+	07 Proj	496	94	137	40	100	0	276			407	569	976	18	70	31	0.74	39	19	41	194	25	0%	39	287	8.26	31.6	$23

LHers still give him fits, but that's nitpicking. Stayed mostly healthy, and this comeback season was the result. There aren't many guys who can give you 40 HR almost every year. Ride him until he breaks down.

Thorman,Scott

		AB	R	H	HR	RBI	SB	Avg	vL	vR	OB	Slg	OPS	bb%	ct%	h%	Eye	G	L	F	PX	SX	SBO	xHR	xBA	RC/G	RAR	R$
Pos 7	02	0	0	0	0	0	0	0							0							0		0				
Age 25	03	0	0	0	0	0	0	0							0							0		0				
Pre-Peak	04 aa	345	28	81	10	45	4	235			305	371	676	9	82	26	0.56				81	59	8%	10		3.89	-13.6	$6
Bats Left	05 a/a	550	63	149	19	81	2	271			312	440	752	6	81	30	0.32				107	65	3%	18		4.61	-6.7	$16
Reliability 23	06 ATL	* 437	49	118	19	60	5	270	189	253	324	469	793	7	85	28	0.52	40	17	43	114	62	7%	17	280	5.19	-0.8	$13
DL	1st Half	281	33	82	14	43	3	292			362	505	868	10	84	31	0.69	36	9	55	118	61	6%	12	252	6.19	7.4	$10
BAvg Potl 55%	2nd Half	156	16	36	5	17	2	231			250	404	654	2	86	24	0.18	41	19	40	107	60	9%	5	286	3.36	-8.9	$2
LIMA Plan F	07 Proj	99	11	27	4	13	1	273			317	441	758	6	83	30	0.39	41	18	41	105	41	5%	3	271	4.70	-1.9	$3

5-14-.234 in 128 AB at ATL. A cat-and-mouse game with SP:
- Jun: 29 PX, .192 xBA
- Jul: 218 PX, .329 xBA
- Aug: 77 PX, .293 xBA
- Sept: 152 PX, .219 xBA

Consistency, hitting LHers key.

Torrealba,Yorvit

		AB	R	H	HR	RBI	SB	Avg	vL	vR	OB	Slg	OPS	bb%	ct%	h%	Eye	G	L	F	PX	SX	SBO	xHR	xBA	RC/G	RAR	R$
Pos 2	02 SF	136	17	38	2	14	0	279	385	255	347	397	744	9	85	32	0.70	53	21	26	86	29	0%	3	285	4.85	2.8	$3
Age 28	03 SF	200	22	52	4	29	1	200	212	260	308	390	698	7	81	31	0.36	55	22	23	85	77	2%	4	286	4.07	-1.3	$4
Peak	04 SF	172	19	39	6	23	2	227	286	170	296	407	703	9	82	24	0.55	59	10	31	102	98	5%	5	276	4.20	2.2	$3
Bats Right	05 2TM	201	32	47	3	15	1	234	314	209	290	338	629	7	75	30	0.32	60	14	26	84	69	2%	4	247	3.19	-4.3	$3
Reliability 10	06 COL	* 259	23	61	7	44	4	234	246	247	273	407	680	5	79	27	0.25	63	13	25	112	85	15%	8	282	3.76	-4.6	$5
DL 91	1st Half	88	2	15	1	13	1	166			217	266	484	6	79	20	0.31	63	12	24	75	25	15%	2	230	1.40	-8.6	($1)
BAvg Potl 50%	2nd Half	171	21	46	6	31	3	269			302	480	781	4	78	31	0.22	62	13	25	131	108	15%	6	300	4.99	3.2	$6
LIMA Plan F	07 Proj	196	21	49	5	26	2	250			299	402	701	7	79	30	0.33	60	14	26	101	89	7%	5	275	4.11	-0.0	$4

7-43-.247 in 223 AB at COL. 125+ PX over regular duty in July and August, but all those GB means a HR ceiling. Huge BA downside too, but worth a $1 investment with the hope of 10 HR upside.

Tracy,Chad

		AB	R	H	HR	RBI	SB	Avg	vL	vR	OB	Slg	OPS	bb%	ct%	h%	Eye	G	L	F	PX	SX	SBO	xHR	xBA	RC/G	RAR	R$
Pos 5	02 aa	514	63	163	6	58	2	317			354	438	791	5	93	33	0.76				77	66	4%	9		5.25	10.1	$16
Age 26	03 aaa	522	71	156	8	62	0	299			339	412	751	6	93	31	0.82				69	54	1%	9		4.82	6.2	$14
Pre-Peak	04 ARI	* 521	51	150	10	62	4	288	215	305	351	418	770	9	87	31	0.77	36	20	44	81	60	4%	12	266	5.14	1.1	$13
Bats Left	05 ARI	503	73	155	27	72	3	308	236	324	353	553	906	7	84	32	0.45	33	24	42	147	77	3%	23	317	6.43	22.6	$23
Reliability 24	06 ARI	597	91	168	20	80	5	281	231	304	341	451	792	8	78	33	0.42	36	21	43	112	63	4%	22	265	5.27	-3.7	$19
DL	1st Half	304	45	84	12	42	4	276			333	464	797	8	74	34	0.33	36	23	41	128	63	6%	13	266	5.37	-1.1	$10
BAvg Potl 40%	2nd Half	293	46	84	8	38	1	287			349	437	786	9	83	32	0.55	36	20	45	97	48	1%	9	263	5.23	-2.1	$9
LIMA Plan C	07 Proj	563	79	156	19	74	3	277			333	453	786	8	83	31	0.50	35	22	43	110	67	3%	19	280	5.16	0.3	$17

Why he may underwhelm in age 26/27 peak years...
- Plummeting ct%
- xBA dip
- 73 PX vs. LHers

Don't expect him to take another step up just yet.

Treanor,Matt

		AB	R	H	HR	RBI	SB	Avg	vL	vR	OB	Slg	OPS	bb%	ct%	h%	Eye	G	L	F	PX	SX	SBO	xHR	xBA	RC/G	RAR	R$
Pos 2	02 a/a	251	23	51	6	32	3	203			283	323	606	10	84	22	0.68				74	66	6%	6		3.15	-5.6	$3
Age 31	03 aaa	315	32	70	8	29	7	222			288	352	640	8	88	23	0.78				78	73	16%	8		3.61	-5.7	$5
Past Peak	04 FLA	* 253	27	52	5	25	1	206	182	250	282	300	583	10	81	23	0.57	56	24	20	60	44	2%	5	276	2.77	-8.2	$1
Bats Right	05 FLA	134	10	27	0	13	0	201	120	215	287	261	548	11	79	25	0.57	49	19	32	55	20	0%	1	229	2.44	-5.6	($0)
Reliability 18	06 FLA	157	12	36	2	14	0	229	268	216	313	318	631	11	78	28	0.56	44	18	38	59	42	2%	3	224	3.42	-4.4	$1
DL 15	1st Half	84	6	18	1	7	0	214			298	298	595	11	75	27	0.48	41	25	34	63	22	4%	2	238	2.89	-3.8	($0)
BAvg Potl 45%	2nd Half	73	6	18	1	7	0	247			329	342	672	11	82	29	0.69	48	10	42	55	52	0%	1	210	4.01	-0.7	$1
LIMA Plan F	07 Proj	125	10	28	1	12	0	224			305	316	621	10	80	27	0.59	47	17	36	61	53	2%	2	234	3.33	-3.0	$1

If throwing out runners was a leading indicator, he'd be a breakout target: 21%, 27%, 47% CS% last three years. Yet another CA who'd be valuable in leagues where they don't count offense.

Tulowitzki,Troy

		AB	R	H	HR	RBI	SB	Avg	vL	vR	OB	Slg	OPS	bb%	ct%	h%	Eye	G	L	F	PX	SX	SBO	xHR	xBA	RC/G	RAR	R$
Pos 6	02	0	0	0	0	0	0	0							0							0		0				
Age 22	03	0	0	0	0	0	0	0							0							0		0				
Growth	04	0	0	0	0	0	0	0							0							0		0				
Bats Right	05	0	0	0	0	0	0	0							0							0		0				
Reliability 2	06 COL	* 519	73	139	12	53	8	268	150	263	326	410	737	8	85	29	0.59	49	21	30	89	78	10%	14	292	4.65	4.4	$13
DL	1st Half	252	33	68	8	27	3	270			319	440	759	7	87	28	0.56				100	64	15%	8		4.83	3.5	$7
BAvg Potl 60%	2nd Half	267	40	71	4	26	5	266			333	382	715	9	84	31	0.61	49	21	30	77	90	7%	6	278	4.48	0.9	$6
LIMA Plan C	07 Proj	450	64	123	10	46	7	273			333	412	744	8	85	30	0.59	49	21	30	89	85	9%	11	292	4.76	7.4	$12

1-6-.240 in 96 AB at COL. Showed decent base skills but not much else in MLB debut. Seventh overall pick from 2005, and just turned 22, so he's got plenty of time. For 2007:
UP: 15-60-.280-10

Tyner,Jason

		AB	R	H	HR	RBI	SB	Avg	vL	vR	OB	Slg	OPS	bb%	ct%	h%	Eye	G	L	F	PX	SX	SBO	xHR	xBA	RC/G	RAR	R$
Pos 7	02 TAM	* 519	67	131	0	32	24	252	189	221	301	299	600	6	92	28	0.84				28	131	22%	2		3.24	-24.8	$11
Age 30	03 TAM	* 365	41	107	0	26	11	293	167	295	344	370	713	7	90	33	0.78				50	102	18%	2		4.51	-8.6	$9
Peak	04 aaa	382	58	105	1	29	21	276			328	328	656	7	90	31	0.76				36	118	23%	3		3.82	-15.2	$12
Bats Left	05 MIN	* 580	72	146	1	34	16	252	333	318	303	296	599	7	90	28	0.73	57	20	22	30	101	13%	3	277	3.17	-26.8	$9
Reliability 30	06 MIN	* 534	76	161	0	38	11	301	269	325	342	356	697	6	88	34	0.52	52	27	21	35	112	9%	2	291	4.16	-15.1	$13
DL	1st Half	279	38	80	0	19	7	287			339	342	681	7	86	33	0.55				37	113	9%	1		4.03	-9.0	$6
BAvg Potl 45%	2nd Half	255	38	81	0	19	4	317			345	370	715	4	91	35	0.47	52	27	21	32	100	9%	1	297	4.28	-6.2	$7
LIMA Plan F	07 Proj	131	18	37	0	9	4	282			327	331	657	6	89	32	0.62	52	26	21	31	103	13%	1	291	3.76	-4.7	$3

0-18-.312 in 218 AB at MIN. His OBP was inflated by a 34 h%. He'd have an outside shot at 30 SB over 500 AB, but few teams will give a weak-armed slap hitter that much work.

STEPHEN NICKRAND

Uggla,Dan		AB	R	H	HR	RBI	SB	Avg	vL	vR	OB	Slg	OPS	bb%	ct%	h%	Eye	G	L	F	PX	SX	SBO	xHR	xBA	RC/G	RAR	R$
Pos 4	02	0	0	0	0	0	0	0							0							0		0				
Age 27	03	0	0	0	0	0	0	0							0							0		0				
Peak	04 aa	294	20	65	3	21	7	220			249	301	549	4	86	25	0.28				51	77	25%	4		2.27	-19.3	$2
Bats Right	05 aa	495	62	124	16	61	11	251			305	420	725	7	82	28	0.44				110	90	17%	16		4.40	0.8	$14
Reliability 21	06 FLA	611	105	172	27	90	6	282	307	273	334	480	813	7	80	31	0.39	41	17	42	113	95	8%	24	266	5.42	14.4	$23
DL	1st Half	266	49	83	13	43	4	312			360	530	890	7	83	34	0.44	38	17	44	118	110	8%	11	277	6.29	12.3	$13
BAvg Potl 35%	2nd Half	345	56	89	14	47	2	258			314	441	754	8	77	30	0.36	43	16	40	110	81	7%	13	257	4.72	1.2	$10
LIMA Plan C	07 Proj	**522**	**73**	**136**	**18**	**66**	**3**	**261**			**310**	**428**	**739**	**7**	**81**	**29**	**0.39**	**41**	**17**	**42**	**101**	**73**	**9%**	**17**	**261**	**4.51**	**-1.0**	**$14**

Surprisingly strong rookie season, but H%, ct%, xBA all dipped in 2nd half, while GB% rose. Look for a sophomore slump, perhaps a very pronounced one.
DN: .250, 12 HR.

Upton,B.J.		AB	R	H	HR	RBI	SB	Avg	vL	vR	OB	Slg	OPS	bb%	ct%	h%	Eye	G	L	F	PX	SX	SBO	xHR	xBA	RC/G	RAR	R$
Pos 5	02	0	0	0	0	0	0	0							0									0				
Age 22	03 aa	105	14	31	1	17	2	295			393	410	803	14	79	37	0.77				93	50	16%	2		5.87	4.6	$4
Growth	04 TAM *	527	104	159	16	63	24	302	410	163	385	469	853	12	75	38	0.55	56	13	31	113	125	18%	19	268	6.36	21.3	$24
Bats Right	05 aaa	536	75	147	13	56	35	275			349	425	773	10	84	31	0.72				96	118	34%	15		5.21	9.0	$22
Reliability 20	06 TAM *	573	90	148	8	50	56	258	298	227	345	357	702	12	79	31	0.63	54	19	27	65	135	41%	10	259	4.38	-11.1	$23
DL	1st Half	284	42	74	4	28	30	259			358	370	728	13	80	31	0.76				75	126	48%	6		4.83	-1.6	$12
BAvg Potl 50%	2nd Half	289	48	75	4	22	26	258			332	344	675	10	79	32	0.52	54	19	27	54	141	35%	5	251	3.92	-9.4	$11
LIMA Plan C+	07 Proj	**496**	**78**	**130**	**9**	**51**	**36**	**262**			**346**	**381**	**727**	**11**	**80**	**31**	**0.63**	**55**	**17**	**28**	**80**	**122**	**33%**	**12**	**268**	**4.69**	**-2.0**	**$19**

1-10-.246 in 175 AB at TAM. Still very young, but 2006 power outage is a concern, as is his iron glove. Will provide SB immediately, but a few years away from five-category stud status.

Uribe,Juan		AB	R	H	HR	RBI	SB	Avg	vL	vR	OB	Slg	OPS	bb%	ct%	h%	Eye	G	L	F	PX	SX	SBO	xHR	xBA	RC/G	RAR	R$
Pos 6	02 COL	566	69	136	6	49	9	240	241	240	283	341	624	6	79	30	0.28	46	20	34	71	128	8%	8	250	3.12	-13.2	$9
Age 27	03 COL	316	45	80	10	33	7	253	301	236	291	427	719	5	81	28	0.28	37	26	37	111	122	14%	10	286	4.21	0.9	$9
Peak	04 CHW	502	82	142	23	74	9	283	264	293	326	506	832	6	81	31	0.33	38	18	45	133	107	18%	21	281	5.59	16.5	$19
Bats Right	05 CHW	481	58	121	16	71	4	252	311	234	301	412	713	7	84	27	0.44	38	19	42	98	68	9%	15	271	4.21	-5.0	$12
Reliability 63	06 CHW	463	53	109	21	71	1	235	224	244	256	441	697	3	82	24	0.16	38	17	45	123	58	3%	18	277	3.76	-9.1	$10
DL	1st Half	229	28	53	8	32	0	231			251	402	653	3	83	25	0.16	39	17	44	99	75	3%	7	264	3.27	-7.9	$4
BAvg Potl 60%	2nd Half	234	25	56	13	39	1	239			261	479	740	3	81	24	0.16	37	17	46	147	40	3%	11	289	4.25	-1.1	$6
LIMA Plan C	07 Proj	**535**	**67**	**143**	**22**	**78**	**4**	**267**			**300**	**459**	**759**	**4**	**82**	**29**	**0.26**	**38**	**18**	**43**	**117**	**72**	**8%**	**20**	**276**	**4.61**	**2.2**	**$15**

Bad luck on H% masked a nice PX rebound. Don't get hung up on the 3-year decline in BA, xBA has been steady over that time. Speed has gone dormant, but otherwise...
UP: see 2004.

Utley,Chase		AB	R	H	HR	RBI	SB	Avg	vL	vR	OB	Slg	OPS	bb%	ct%	h%	Eye	G	L	F	PX	SX	SBO	xHR	xBA	RC/G	RAR	R$
Pos 4	02 aaa	464	64	119	15	61	7	256			320	446	766	8	84	28	0.57				128	83	10%	17		5.01	10.7	$13
Age 28	03 PHI *	565	85	162	18	90	11	287	333	230	344	457	800	8	83	32	0.52	40	23	37	108	101	10%	18	291	5.35	15.1	$22
Peak	04 PHI *	390	55	102	18	78	7	262	200	279	314	462	776	7	83	27	0.45	44	22	34	114	97	11%	15	297	4.94	3.7	$15
Bats Left	05 PHI	543	93	158	28	105	16	291	220	313	371	540	911	11	80	32	0.63	35	23	42	159	125	12%	27	305	6.89	35.4	$29
Reliability 26	06 PHI	658	131	203	32	102	15	309	301	312	369	527	896	9	80	35	0.48	37	20	43	131	111	10%	30	280	6.53	34.8	$32
DL	1st Half	306	63	89	15	45	7	291			352	503	856	9	82	31	0.53	39	19	42	124	99	12%	14	285	5.98	11.9	$14
BAvg Potl 35%	2nd Half	352	68	114	17	57	8	324			383	548	932	9	78	38	0.44	35	20	45	137	110	8%	16	277	7.04	22.9	$19
LIMA Plan B	07 Proj	**605**	**107**	**178**	**27**	**103**	**14**	**294**			**358**	**506**	**864**	**9**	**81**	**33**	**0.52**	**37**	**21**	**42**	**130**	**119**	**10%**	**25**	**286**	**6.17**	**27.0**	**$28**

Solved LHPs, but ridiculously high AB total and 2nd half h% spike masked some BPI erosion. Still an elite producer at a scarce position, but another 30-100-.300 might be just out of reach.

Valentin,Javier		AB	R	H	HR	RBI	SB	Avg	vL	vR	OB	Slg	OPS	bb%	ct%	h%	Eye	G	L	F	PX	SX	SBO	xHR	xBA	RC/G	RAR	R$
Pos 2	02 aaa	455	48	108	14	55	0	237			283	398	681	6	83	26	0.38				104	38	1%	14		3.82	-0.7	$8
Age 31	03 TAM	135	13	30	3	15	0	222	231	221	250	356	606	4	77	27	0.16	38	19	43	91	54	0%	3	242	2.71	-5.7	$1
Past Peak	04 CIN	202	18	47	6	20	0	233	109	269	292	381	673	8	82	26	0.47	35	22	43	91	37	0%	6	265	3.80	-0.1	$2
Bats Both	05 CIN	221	36	62	14	50	0	281	184	298	367	520	887	12	83	28	0.81	34	23	43	141	26	0%	12	308	6.47	16.7	$11
Reliability 6	06 CIN	186	24	50	8	27	0	269	111	286	317	441	757	7	84	28	0.45	33	23	43	92	44	0%	7	274	4.67	1.7	$5
DL	1st Half	101	11	21	1	10	0	208			279	297	576	9	84	24	0.63	37	21	43	55	59	0%	1	240	2.84	-4.7	$0
BAvg Potl 50%	2nd Half	85	13	29	7	17	0	341			364	612	975	3	85	34	0.23	29	26	44	136	19	0%	5	319	6.80	5.4	$5
LIMA Plan F	07 Proj	**231**	**30**	**63**	**11**	**38**	**0**	**273**			**327**	**469**	**796**	**7**	**83**	**28**	**0.49**	**33**	**23**	**43**	**110**	**41**	**0%**	**9**	**285**	**5.16**	**6.9**	**$8**

Struggled early, then got more aggressive in 2nd half, and found his power stroke. Should continue as an attractive power source for your 2nd CA slot.
UP: 400 AB, 20 HR.

Valentin,Jose		AB	R	H	HR	RBI	SB	Avg	vL	vR	OB	Slg	OPS	bb%	ct%	h%	Eye	G	L	F	PX	SX	SBO	xHR	xBA	RC/G	RAR	R$
Pos 4	02 CHW	474	70	118	25	75	3	249	152	259	311	479	790	8	79	27	0.43	35	21	44	139	84	6%	22	284	5.18	16.1	$15
Age 37	03 CHW	503	79	119	28	74	8	237	131	265	311	463	774	10	77	25	0.47	32	22	46	142	89	9%	25	278	5.02	13.4	$16
Decline	04 CHW	450	73	97	30	70	8	216	191	226	284	473	757	9	69	24	0.31	29	14	56	170	109	16%	28	247	4.86	11.0	$13
Bats Both	05 LA	147	17	25	2	14	3	170	316	148	315	265	580	17	74	21	0.82	40	14	47	64	100	8%	2	200	2.91	-7.9	$0
Reliability 0	06 NYM	384	56	104	18	62	6	271	219	288	335	490	825	9	82	29	0.52	31	16	53	129	87	8%	17	265	5.65	11.6	$14
DL 88	1st Half	149	19	44	8	26	2	295			340	544	883	6	85	31	0.43	33	19	48	142	70	9%	7	298	6.16	6.5	$6
BAvg Potl 50%	2nd Half	235	37	60	10	36	4	255			332	455	787	10	80	28	0.56	30	13	56	120	95	8%	10	244	5.29	4.8	$8
LIMA Plan C	07 Proj	**374**	**53**	**93**	**16**	**54**	**6**	**249**			**331**	**442**	**773**	**11**	**78**	**28**	**0.54**	**33**	**16**	**51**	**121**	**96**	**9%**	**16**	**249**	**5.14**	**6.4**	**$11**

Nice rebound from 2005 knee injury. Infielders with fly ball tendency and good power get your attention. Despite 2006's improved ct%, be wary of the long track record of poor BA.
UP: 20 HR. DN: .220 BA.

Varitek,Jason		AB	R	H	HR	RBI	SB	Avg	vL	vR	OB	Slg	OPS	bb%	ct%	h%	Eye	G	L	F	PX	SX	SBO	xHR	xBA	RC/G	RAR	R$
Pos 2	02 BOS	467	58	124	10	61	4	266	263	266	325	392	717	8	80	31	0.43	43	22	35	87	64	6%	12	263	4.35	10.0	$11
Age 35	03 BOS	451	63	123	25	85	3	273	309	257	347	512	859	10	76	31	0.48	42	23	35	158	54	4%	24	301	6.19	27.1	$17
Decline	04 BOS	467	68	139	19	76	10	298	350	273	380	488	868	12	73	37	0.49	42	21	37	132	78	9%	21	267	6.56	29.0	$19
Bats Both	05 BOS	470	70	132	22	70	2	281	320	267	365	489	854	12	75	33	0.53	45	23	32	144	57	1%	23	291	6.27	29.8	$17
Reliability 17	06 BOS	365	46	87	12	55	1	238	229	244	324	400	724	11	76	28	0.53	45	17	38	106	55	3%	13	252	4.55	1.6	$7
DL 33	1st Half	219	31	56	7	37	1	256			345	406	752	12	84	28	0.88	47	17	36	88	55	4%	7	268	5.00	3.8	$5
BAvg Potl 50%	2nd Half	146	15	31	5	18	0	212			290	390	681	10	64	30	0.30	41	17	41	142	50	0%	6	229	4.14	-1.2	$1
LIMA Plan C	07 Proj	**436**	**57**	**117**	**17**	**65**	**3**	**268**			**349**	**452**	**801**	**11**	**74**	**33**	**0.47**	**44**	**20**	**37**	**127**	**64**	**3%**	**18**	**264**	**5.59**	**16.9**	**$12**

Hampered by injuries early and late in the year, punished by a low h%. May rebound if health cooperates, but good health and 35-year old catchers don't often mix. Acquire only at a discount.

Victorino,Shane		AB	R	H	HR	RBI	SB	Avg	vL	vR	OB	Slg	OPS	bb%	ct%	h%	Eye	G	L	F	PX	SX	SBO	xHR	xBA	RC/G	RAR	R$
Pos 879	02 aa	481	58	116	4	32	43	241			306	299	605	9	90	26	0.94				37	119	42%	5		3.32	-22.5	$16
Age 26	03 a/a	307	37	80	3	21	14	261			306	345	651	6	87	29	0.49				49	123	27%	3		3.60	-11.7	$8
Pre-Peak	04 a/a	493	77	121	15	50	13	245			280	389	670	5	83	27	0.29				82	119	22%	13		3.58	-16.5	$13
Bats Right	05 aaa	494	73	138	16	55	13	279			332	468	800	7	88	29	0.68				102	126	19%	13		5.37	13.6	$18
Reliability 22	06 PHI	415	70	119	6	46	4	287	273	293	326	414	740	5	87	32	0.44	45	21	34	72	117	6%	6	277	4.60	1.9	$12
DL	1st Half	130	22	40	4	14	1	308			338	485	823	4	85	34	0.32	37	20	43	99	98	3%	4	275	5.40	3.4	$5
BAvg Potl 50%	2nd Half	285	48	79	2	32	3	277			320	382	703	6	88	31	0.51	48	22	30	59	118	8%	3	279	4.25	-1.6	$7
LIMA Plan D+	07 Proj	**329**	**52**	**91**	**7**	**35**	**7**	**277**			**319**	**421**	**741**	**6**	**87**	**30**	**0.48**	**44**	**21**	**35**	**80**	**127**	**15%**	**7**	**281**	**4.60**	**0.5**	**$10**

Got to play regularly in 2nd half, unfortunately his power/speed combo from the minors did not show up. He still owns those skills, but for now a fairly empty BA is his primary offering.

Vidro,Jose		AB	R	H	HR	RBI	SB	Avg	vL	vR	OB	Slg	OPS	bb%	ct%	h%	Eye	G	L	F	PX	SX	SBO	xHR	xBA	RC/G	RAR	R$
Pos 4	02 MON	604	103	190	19	96	2	315	297	321	377	490	867	9	88	33	0.86	51	18	31	110	75	2%	19	312	6.22	29.4	$26
Age 32	03 MON	509	77	158	15	65	3	310	315	309	393	470	862	12	90	32	1.38	52	20	28	98	48	3%	16	313	6.38	27.4	$19
Past Peak	04 MON	416	51	121	14	60	3	291	267	306	366	450	815	11	89	30	1.11	51	19	30	92	45	3%	13	298	5.71	12.8	$14
Bats Both	05 WAS	309	38	85	7	32	0	275	258	280	341	424	765	9	90	29	1.03	44	25	31	92	47	0%	8	315	5.15	5.2	$7
Reliability 45	06 WAS	463	52	134	7	47	1	289	323	276	347	395	742	8	90	31	0.85	46	22	32	65	45	1%	9	282	4.81	2.8	$10
DL 24 61	1st Half	285	36	89	5	29	1	312			364	411	774	7	88	34	0.70	45	23	33	57	53	1%	5	274	5.06	3.6	$8
BAvg Potl 55%	2nd Half	178	16	45	2	18	0	253			321	371	692	9	92	27	1.20	49	20	31	78	18	0%	3	287	4.44	-0.8	$2
LIMA Plan D+	07 Proj	**413**	**49**	**116**	**9**	**46**	**1**	**281**			**347**	**413**	**760**	**9**	**90**	**30**	**1.02**	**47**	**22**	**31**	**81**	**47**	**1%**	**10**	**298**	**5.08**	**5.9**	**$10**

Four years of declining bb% and Eye, and five years of declining PX and BA v. RHP. Long history of leg problems make him a very old 32. Don't expect those trends to reverse.

RAY MURPHY

Vizcaino,Jose

Vizcaino,Jose		AB	R	H	HR	RBI	SB	Avg	vL	vR	OB	Slg	OPS	bb%	ct%	h%	Eye	G	L	F	PX	SX	SBO	xHR	xBA	RC/G	RAR	R$
Pos 6	02 HOU	406	53	123	5	37	3	303	337	292	342	397	738	6	90	33	0.60	42	21	37	60	66	7%	6	271	4.60	7.9	$12
Age 39	03 HOU	189	14	47	3	26	0	249	222	255	279	365	644	4	88	27	0.36	50	21	29	66	65	2%	3	285	3.44	-3.8	$3
Decline	04 HOU	358	34	98	3	33	1	274	250	279	312	374	686	5	89	30	0.51	52	21	27	64	62	2%	5	288	4.04	-0.9	$6
Bats Both	05 HOU	187	15	46	1	23	2	246	295	222	302	337	639	7	79	31	0.38	47	20	33	68	84	4%	2	248	3.42	-3.0	$3
Reliability 20	06 2NL	142	19	33	2	8	0	232	214	240	314	317	631	11	90	25	1.21	57	14	28	51	39	5%	2	254	3.74	-2.7	$1
DL	1st Half	93	14	23	1	4	0	247			352	312	664	14	89	27	1.50	58	16	27	39	39	3%	1	249	4.27	-0.2	$1
BAvg Potl 80%	2nd Half	49	5	10	1	4	0	204			235	327	562	4	92	20	0.50	57	11	32	73	53	13%	1	271	2.64	-2.7	$0
LIMA Plan F	07 Proj	64	7	17	1	6	0	266			326	343	668	8	87	30	0.69	53	17	30	52	39	3%	1	251	3.92	-0.5	$1

Somehow managed an 11% walk rate to accompany his robust 51 PX. Question to MLB pitchers: what exactly are you afraid of?

As for Vizcaino, he's done.

Vizquel,Omar

Vizquel,Omar		AB	R	H	HR	RBI	SB	Avg	vL	vR	OB	Slg	OPS	bb%	ct%	h%	Eye	G	L	F	PX	SX	SBO	xHR	xBA	RC/G	RAR	R$
Pos 6	02 CLE	582	85	160	14	72	18	275	281	273	339	418	756	9	89	29	0.88	36	21	43	83	108	17%	14	276	4.98	6.8	$20
Age 40	03 CLE	250	43	61	2	19	8	244	224	251	323	336	659	10	92	26	1.45	41	26	33	58	120	15%	3	291	4.16	-2.0	$5
Decline	04 CLE	567	82	165	7	59	19	291	258	308	356	388	744	9	89	32	0.92	43	21	36	60	108	14%	9	271	4.89	6.9	$18
Bats Both	05 SF	568	66	154	3	45	24	271	253	279	337	350	687	9	90	30	0.97	44	24	32	53	106	19%	6	281	4.30	5.7	$15
Reliability 65	06 SF	579	88	171	4	58	24	295	340	281	357	389	746	9	91	32	1.10	40	22	38	51	132	16%	5	268	4.99	10.2	$19
DL	1st Half	264	47	80	3	23	8	303			387	402	788	12	90	33	1.38	38	23	39	53	113	12%	3	265	5.62	9.3	$9
BAvg Potl 60%	2nd Half	315	41	91	1	35	16	289			331	378	709	6	92	31	0.80	41	22	37	49	136	21%	2	270	4.43	0.6	$10
LIMA Plan B+	07 Proj	543	77	150	2	52	20	276			340	359	699	9	91	30	1.01	41	23	36	50	126	16%	5	270	4.45	4.1	$15

No sign of slowdown here, BPIs are rock-solid across the board. Maybe 40 really is the new 20. At least in San Francisco...

Walker,Todd

Walker,Todd		AB	R	H	HR	RBI	SB	Avg	vL	vR	OB	Slg	OPS	bb%	ct%	h%	Eye	G	L	F	PX	SX	SBO	xHR	xBA	RC/G	RAR	R$
Pos 435	02 CIN	612	79	183	11	64	8	299	278	306	352	431	783	8	87	33	0.62	43	22	34	90	79	7%	14	292	5.21	13.5	$20
Age 33	03 BOS	587	92	166	13	85	1	283	234	301	337	428	765	8	91	29	0.89	37	23	40	87	69	1%	14	294	5.05	15.0	$17
Past Peak	04 CHC	372	60	102	15	50	0	274	268	275	349	468	817	10	86	29	0.83	39	23	38	108	69	3%	13	299	5.68	11.5	$12
Bats Left	05 CHC	* 434	52	127	12	42	1	293	352	292	342	454	796	7	90	30	0.74	39	22	39	97	57	2%	12	299	5.30	8.9	$12
Reliability 56	06 2NL	442	56	123	9	53	2	278	204	302	358	398	756	11	91	29	1.45	39	20	41	68	54	2%	9	271	5.19	7.4	$11
DL 44	1st Half	243	31	72	3	33	0	296			376	391	767	11	91	32	1.41	38	23	40	57	40	1%	4	271	5.34	5.0	$6
BAvg Potl 70%	2nd Half	199	25	51	6	20	2	256			336	407	743	11	92	25	1.50	41	16	43	81	62	3%	6	273	5.01	2.4	$4
LIMA Plan D+	07 Proj	362	48	101	10	41	2	279			348	425	772	10	90	29	1.06	39	20	40	84	63	3%	9	284	5.22	6.6	$10

Still controls the strike zone, but three-year declining PX trend signals skills erosion. A stint in a hitter's park might slow the decline, but the handwriting is on the wall.

Ward,Daryle

Ward,Daryle		AB	R	H	HR	RBI	SB	Avg	vL	vR	OB	Slg	OPS	bb%	ct%	h%	Eye	G	L	F	PX	SX	SBO	xHR	xBA	RC/G	RAR	R$
Pos 9	02 HOU	453	41	125	12	72	1	276	204	286	325	424	749	7	82	31	0.40	37	21	42	104	23	3%	14	270	4.67	-8.1	$13
Age 31	03 LA	* 253	18	50	3	28	0	198	400	173	231	265	496	4	82	23	0.24	48	17	36	46	24	0%	3	220	1.49	-32.7	($0)
Past Peak	04 PIT	* 387	50	95	21	71	0	245	296	238	293	478	771	6	83	25	0.41	38	16	47	134	47	0%	18	284	4.82	-5.4	$12
Bats Left	05 PIT	407	46	106	12	63	0	260	200	281	322	405	727	8	85	28	0.62	40	21	39	91	34	2%	12	275	4.52	-8.7	$10
Reliability 17	06 2NL	130	17	40	7	26	0	308	59	345	379	546	925	10	79	34	0.56	36	21	43	149	21	3%	7	293	7.00	8.0	$6
DL	1st Half	59	10	19	5	14	0	322			437	661	1098	17	88	30	1.71	33	20	47	182	23	5%	4	348	9.20	7.1	$4
BAvg Potl 40%	2nd Half	71	7	21	2	12	0	296			324	451	775	4	72	39	0.15	39	22	39	115	18	0%	2	247	4.99	0.4	$2
LIMA Plan F	07 Proj	110	13	31	5	20	0	282			341	474	815	8	81	31	0.47	38	20	42	120	27	2%	5	278	5.48	1.4	$4

Skill history is all over the map due to small samples, but power is for real. Opportunities are tough to find on the wrong side of 30, but still has 15-20 HR pop in the right role.

Weeks,Rickie

Weeks,Rickie		AB	R	H	HR	RBI	SB	Avg	vL	vR	OB	Slg	OPS	bb%	ct%	h%	Eye	G	L	F	PX	SX	SBO	xHR	xBA	RC/G	RAR	R$
Pos 4	02	0	0	0	0	0	0	0							0							0		0				
Age 24	03	0	0	0	0	0	0	0							0							0		0				
Growth	04 aa	479	66	121	8	41	11	253			327	397	724	10	78	31	0.50				101	105	18%	12		4.62	4.0	$10
Bats Right	05 MIL	* 563	88	143	22	78	23	254	229	244	327	446	773	10	76	30	0.45	49	20	31	124	151	18%	21	284	5.12	9.3	$22
Reliability 25	06 MIL	359	73	100	8	34	19	279	271	280	334	404	738	8	74	36	0.33	46	20	33	83	141	23%	9	246	4.62	0.2	$14
DL 64	1st Half	273	57	77	7	26	15	282			342	410	753	8	75	36	0.36	44	21	36	82	134	23%	7	242	4.82	1.7	$12
BAvg Potl 25%	2nd Half	86	16	23	1	8	4	267			308	384	691	5	73	35	0.22	55	20	25	85	142	24%	2	258	3.99	-1.5	$3
LIMA Plan B	07 Proj	500	86	132	12	54	21	264			325	414	739	8	75	33	0.36	50	20	30	101	149	21%	14	267	4.68	1.5	$18

Lots of talent, but holes in these skills too. bb%, ct%, Eye, PX all trending the wrong way. Add in season-ending wrist surgery, and it may be 2008 before immense potential becomes reality.

Wells,Vernon

Wells,Vernon		AB	R	H	HR	RBI	SB	Avg	vL	vR	OB	Slg	OPS	bb%	ct%	h%	Eye	G	L	F	PX	SX	SBO	xHR	xBA	RC/G	RAR	R$
Pos 8	02 TOR	608	87	167	23	100	9	275	260	280	306	457	763	4	86	29	0.32	41	22	37	106	104	10%	20	297	4.66	-2.0	$22
Age 28	03 TOR	678	118	215	33	117	4	317	347	307	357	550	907	6	88	32	0.53	39	21	40	134	90	3%	28	319	6.39	30.1	$31
Peak	04 TOR	536	82	146	23	67	9	272	287	267	336	472	808	9	85	29	0.61	45	17	38	118	93	8%	21	293	5.44	11.2	$18
Bats Right	05 TOR	620	78	167	28	97	8	269	347	243	321	463	784	7	86	27	0.55	41	19	40	113	82	7%	24	293	5.04	13.6	$21
Reliability 73	06 TOR	611	91	185	32	106	17	303	333	292	359	542	901	8	85	31	0.60	42	18	40	136	105	13%	28	308	6.48	30.7	$28
DL	1st Half	291	44	91	20	62	9	313			381	605	986	10	85	31	0.74	41	16	42	161	102	15%	16	323	7.53	22.8	$16
BAvg Potl 55%	2nd Half	320	47	94	12	44	8	294			339	484	824	6	85	31	0.47	42	20	38	113	101	11%	11	296	5.51	7.6	$12
LIMA Plan C+	07 Proj	615	89	177	29	98	13	288			341	502	843	7	86	30	0.56	42	19	39	124	102	10%	25	301	5.77	20.5	$24

After two off years, reclaimed '03's elite skill levels, complete with an SBO spike. But 2nd half looked a lot like 2004-05, so don't get caught overpaying for that big 1st half.

White,Rondell

White,Rondell		AB	R	H	HR	RBI	SB	Avg	vL	vR	OB	Slg	OPS	bb%	ct%	h%	Eye	G	L	F	PX	SX	SBO	xHR	xBA	RC/G	RAR	R$
Pos 7	02 NYY	455	59	109	14	62	1	240	286	226	279	378	657	5	81	27	0.29	50	18	32	87	48	3%	14	263	3.41	-19.4	$9
Age 35	03 2TM	488	62	141	22	87	1	289	299	285	331	488	819	6	84	31	0.39	45	20	35	115	55	4%	19	294	5.38	-1.1	$18
Decline	04 DET	448	76	121	19	67	1	270	293	258	329	453	782	8	83	29	0.51	49	13	38	106	65	3%	17	269	5.06	1.6	$14
Bats Right	05 DET	374	49	117	12	53	1	313	325	309	343	489	832	4	87	33	0.35	55	17	29	108	68	1%	11	306	5.49	7.8	$14
Reliability 21	06 MIN	337	32	83	7	38	1	246	271	235	270	365	635	3	84	28	0.20	44	21	34	75	50	3%	7	268	3.13	-20.5	$4
DL 31 47	1st Half	181	15	33	0	15	1	182			204	215	420	3	83	22	0.17	45	21	34	28	59	3%	1	232	0.62	-26.5	($2)
BAvg Potl 50%	2nd Half	156	17	50	7	23	0	321			346	538	884	4	85	34	0.25	43	22	35	129	42	3%	6	311	6.01	3.5	$6
LIMA Plan F	07 Proj	267	32	74	8	36	1	277			310	436	745	5	85	30	0.30	48	19	33	97	54	2%	8	283	4.48	-4.1	$7

A hot September (.952 OPS) showed that he can still put up numbers when his body cooperates. But his AB trend shows that those periods are increasingly rare. Rosterable as a short-term fill-in, nothing more.

Wigginton,Ty

Wigginton,Ty		AB	R	H	HR	RBI	SB	Avg	vL	vR	OB	Slg	OPS	bb%	ct%	h%	Eye	G	L	F	PX	SX	SBO	xHR	xBA	RC/G	RAR	R$
Pos 345	02 NYM	* 499	62	139	11	61	6	279	314	296	339	417	756	8	87	30	0.71	45	12	42	91	74	7%	12	263	4.93	-9.5	$15
Age 29	03 NYM	573	73	146	11	71	12	255	297	239	310	396	706	7	78	31	0.37	45	20	34	99	124	10%	14	269	4.23	-21.5	$14
Peak	04 2NL	494	63	129	17	66	7	261	222	272	323	433	756	8	83	28	0.55	45	19	36	105	85	6%	17	286	4.83	-16.0	$14
Bats Right	05 PIT	* 435	58	109	17	62	6	251	247	268	322	428	750	9	83	27	0.63	42	22	36	111	66	11%	16	293	4.80	-10.5	$13
Reliability 59	06 TAM	444	55	122	24	79	4	275	316	260	324	498	821	7	78	30	0.33	40	19	41	138	55	7%	21	283	5.46	0.6	$15
DL 33	1st Half	280	30	72	13	46	3	257			300	446	746	6	79	28	0.29	42	17	41	117	45	8%	12	264	4.47	-7.8	$8
BAvg Potl 40%	2nd Half	164	25	50	11	33	1	305			363	585	948	8	77	34	0.39	37	24	40	174	65	5%	10	310	7.20	8.0	$8
LIMA Plan C	07 Proj	427	56	121	20	69	3	283			341	492	833	8	80	31	0.45	41	21	39	129	61	6%	18	290	5.71	5.1	$15

A little more aggression and a few more fly balls paid off. BA gains came mostly in 117 AB v. LHPs, could be a sample size fluke. Five-year rising PX trend says power is legit.

Wilkerson,Brad

Wilkerson,Brad		AB	R	H	HR	RBI	SB	Avg	vL	vR	OB	Slg	OPS	bb%	ct%	h%	Eye	G	L	F	PX	SX	SBO	xHR	xBA	RC/G	RAR	R$
Pos 7	02 MON	507	92	135	20	59	7	266	230	274	367	469	837	14	68	35	0.50	40	19	40	150	116	9%	23	256	6.44	0.8	$18
Age 29	03 MON	504	78	135	19	77	13	268	281	263	378	464	842	15	69	35	0.57	40	24	36	147	97	14%	24	267	6.53	14.0	$19
Peak	04 MON	573	112	146	32	67	13	255	278	245	371	497	869	16	73	29	0.70	31	21	47	162	94	11%	34	275	6.66	20.8	$22
Bats Left	05 WAS	565	76	140	11	57	8	248	296	228	345	405	750	13	74	32	0.57	31	24	45	120	96	11%	16	254	5.14	-3.4	$12
Reliability 60	06 TEX	320	56	71	15	44	3	222	190	230	303	422	724	10	64	30	0.32	35	15	50	149	100	7%	17	224	4.73	-4.4	$7
DL 47	1st Half	239	50	58	13	32	3	243			320	469	788	10	63	33	0.31	37	13	50	166	117	8%	14	232	5.73	4.0	$8
BAvg Potl 35%	2nd Half	81	6	13	2	12	0	160			253	284	537	11	65	22	0.36	31	20	49	99	14	0%	3	206	1.90	-8.8	($0)
LIMA Plan C+	07 Proj	491	71	125	22	63	6	255			347	463	809	12	69	33	0.45	33	20	47	150	77	7%	25	250	5.90	12.8	$14

Shoulder issues from March on ruined his season. His ability to sustain PX despite the injury and good post-surgical reports both point to a rebound in 2007. UP: 2004, always. He still owns those skills, after all.

RAY MURPHY

Williams,Bernie

		Yr	AB	R	H	HR	RBI	SB	Avg	vL	vR	OB	Slg	OPS	bb%	ct%	h%	Eye	G	L	F	PX	SX	SBO	xHR	xBA	RC/G	RAR	R$
Pos	980	02 NYY	612	102	204	19	102	8	333	354	326	413	493	906	12	84	37	0.86	50	23	27	99	77	5%	20	304	6.87	29.9	$29
Age	38	03 NYY	445	77	117	15	64	5	263	280	256	364	411	776	14	86	28	1.16	51	17	32	86	82	3%	14	284	5.40	3.2	$14
Decline		04 NYY	561	105	147	22	70	1	262	265	261	359	435	794	13	83	28	0.89	44	18	38	103	46	3%	22	273	5.53	13.6	$16
Bats	Both	05 NYY	485	53	121	12	64	1	249	231	263	323	367	690	10	85	27	0.71	44	18	38	73	40	2%	12	255	4.16	-7.8	$9
Reliability	12	06 NYY	420	65	118	12	61	2	281	323	261	333	436	769	7	87	30	0.62	50	18	32	96	60	2%	13	294	4.98	-8.0	$12
DL		1st Half	232	33	64	6	34	0	276			320	414	734	6	89	29	0.58	52	16	32	84	36	0%	6	276	4.52	-7.5	$6
BAvg Potl	60%	2nd Half	188	32	54	6	27	2	287			350	463	812	9	86	31	0.67	48	21	31	111	66	4%	6	307	5.56	-0.5	$6
LIMA Plan	F	07 Proj	**235**	**36**	**64**	**7**	**33**	**1**	**272**			**342**	**422**	**764**	**10**	**86**	**29**	**0.73**	**48**	**19**	**34**	**93**	**51**	**3%**	**7**	**282**	**5.02**	**-1.3**	**$7**

BPIs are in free-fall, and if he returns in 2007 he won't come anywhere near 400 AB. If he does hang 'em up, he does so as MLB's all-time postseason HR leader.

Willingham,Josh

		Yr	AB	R	H	HR	RBI	SB	Avg	vL	vR	OB	Slg	OPS	bb%	ct%	h%	Eye	G	L	F	PX	SX	SBO	xHR	xBA	RC/G	RAR	R$
Pos	7	02	0	0	0	0	0	0	0							0							0		0				
Age	28	03 aa	67	12	17	4	11	0	255			364	482	846	15	72	30	0.60				142	80	0%	4		6.31	1.7	$2
Peak		04 aa	338	60	75	15	57	5	221			356	413	769	17	75	25	0.85				126	60	7%	17		5.36	1.8	$9
Bats	Right	05 aaa	219	39	57	12	37	4	261			360	492	852	13	81	27	0.82				140	99	7%	11		6.22	7.6	$9
Reliability	38	06 FLA	502	62	139	26	74	2	277	299	269	347	496	843	10	78	31	0.50	43	16	41	132	51	1%	24	273	5.92	9.6	$17
DL	16	1st Half	222	22	59	9	38	1	266			332	455	787	9	77	31	0.42	41	14	44	125	28	2%	9	250	5.24	-0.0	$6
BAvg Potl	45%	2nd Half	280	40	80	17	36	1	286			359	529	888	10	80	31	0.56	44	17	39	138	58	1%	15	288	6.45	9.4	$10
LIMA Plan	C+	07 Proj	**553**	**84**	**151**	**29**	**87**	**6**	**273**			**362**	**493**	**855**	**12**	**79**	**30**	**0.66**	**43**	**16**	**41**	**134**	**78**	**4%**	**27**	**280**	**6.20**	**13.1**	**$21**

It's always promising when a rookie shows BPI growth in the 2nd half. Others may dismiss him because CA eligibility is gone, but skill growth should keep him on your radar.
UP: .285, 35 HR.

Wilson,Craig

		Yr	AB	R	H	HR	RBI	SB	Avg	vL	vR	OB	Slg	OPS	bb%	ct%	h%	Eye	G	L	F	PX	SX	SBO	xHR	xBA	RC/G	RAR	R$
Pos	39	02 PIT	368	48	97	16	57	2	264	313	242	323	443	765	8	68	34	0.28	38	23	39	133	58	5%	17	251	5.06	-5.8	$12
Age	30	03 PIT	309	49	81	18	49	3	262	308	238	337	505	842	10	71	31	0.39	44	18	38	163	96	5%	17	277	6.11	5.3	$12
Peak		04 PIT	561	97	148	29	82	2	264	259	265	324	499	823	8	70	33	0.30	46	19	36	162	92	3%	29	276	5.86	-1.4	$20
Bats	Right	05 PIT	197	23	52	5	22	3	264	275	259	361	421	783	13	65	38	0.43	45	22	33	136	80	5%	8	245	5.83	1.3	$5
Reliability	46	06 2TM	359	53	90	17	49	1	251	278	235	305	446	751	7	66	33	0.23	38	17	45	137	74	1%	17	231	4.91	-8.4	$9
DL	104	1st Half	216	35	60	12	36	1	278			347	509	857	10	67	36	0.32	33	17	50	159	82	2%	12	242	6.54	5.0	$8
BAvg Potl	30%	2nd Half	143	18	30	5	13	0	210			236	350	586	3	65	28	0.10	46	16	38	103	44	0%	5	211	2.37	-14.8	$1
LIMA Plan	D	07 Proj	**312**	**44**	**78**	**13**	**39**	**2**	**250**			**313**	**436**	**749**	**8**	**67**	**33**	**0.27**	**43**	**19**	**39**	**137**	**79**	**3%**	**14**	**242**	**4.96**	**-5.6**	**$8**

To survive with Adam Dunn-like ct%, you need Adam Dunn-like power. Wilson's got nice power, but it's not Dunn-like. For mere mortals, sub-70% contact rates aren't going to cut it.

Wilson,Jack

		Yr	AB	R	H	HR	RBI	SB	Avg	vL	vR	OB	Slg	OPS	bb%	ct%	h%	Eye	G	L	F	PX	SX	SBO	xHR	xBA	RC/G	RAR	R$
Pos	6	02 PIT	527	77	133	4	47	5	252	360	223	301	332	633	7	86	29	0.50	44	19	38	54	105	5%	6	250	3.42	-7.5	$10
Age	29	03 PIT	558	58	143	9	62	5	256	261	255	301	357	658	6	87	28	0.49	42	25	33	61	77	7%	9	277	3.65	-7.7	$11
Peak		04 PIT	652	82	201	11	59	8	308	261	318	335	459	793	4	89	33	0.37	45	20	36	87	113	7%	12	292	5.12	17.7	$20
Bats	Right	05 PIT	587	60	151	8	52	7	257	255	256	294	363	657	5	90	27	0.53	48	18	34	62	100	7%	8	275	3.69	-4.6	$11
Reliability	77	06 PIT	543	70	148	8	35	4	273	301	262	314	370	684	6	88	30	0.51	47	23	30	61	60	5%	9	281	3.96	-6.5	$10
DL		1st Half	274	36	73	7	23	2	266			304	391	695	5	89	28	0.48	47	20	32	72	54	4%	7	281	4.01	-2.8	$6
BAvg Potl	55%	2nd Half	269	34	75	1	12	2	279			324	349	673	6	87	32	0.53	46	26	28	49	65	5%	3	281	3.90	-3.5	$4
LIMA Plan	C	07 Proj	**535**	**65**	**146**	**7**	**41**	**5**	**273**			**312**	**376**	**688**	**5**	**88**	**30**	**0.49**	**46**	**21**	**32**	**63**	**86**	**6%**	**8**	**279**	**4.01**	**-2.7**	**$11**

2004 continues to look like an outlier here. 2006 SX decline was likely due to an early-season hamstring injury. But even with two healthy wheels, this skill set is empty and unremarkable.

Wilson,Preston

		Yr	AB	R	H	HR	RBI	SB	Avg	vL	vR	OB	Slg	OPS	bb%	ct%	h%	Eye	G	L	F	PX	SX	SBO	xHR	xBA	RC/G	RAR	R$
Pos	79	02 FLA	510	80	124	23	65	20	243	242	244	320	429	750	10	73	29	0.41	49	16	35	129	107	23%	23	264	4.82	-24.4	$19
Age	32	03 COL	600	94	169	36	141	14	282	274	285	341	537	878	8	77	31	0.39	41	22	37	168	88	15%	33	307	6.30	12.3	$31
Past Peak		04 COL	202	24	50	6	29	2	248	290	226	306	391	697	8	76	30	0.35	44	22	35	99	53	6%	7	258	4.04	-8.4	$5
Bats	Right	05 2NL	520	73	135	25	90	6	260	262	259	319	467	786	8	72	32	0.30	52	21	27	147	73	10%	25	284	5.25	-1.4	$19
Reliability	15	06 2NL	501	58	132	17	72	12	263	292	255	304	423	727	5	76	32	0.24	55	18	27	103	89	12%	17	271	4.29	-13.9	$15
DL		1st Half	287	30	81	8	41	5	282			316	415	730	5	74	36	0.19	56	20	25	84	79	9%	8	256	4.32	-7.6	$9
BAvg Potl	40%	2nd Half	214	28	51	9	31	7	238			288	435	723	7	78	27	0.32	54	16	29	127	85	17%	9	289	4.28	-6.2	$6
LIMA Plan	D+	07 Proj	**391**	**50**	**102**	**14**	**61**	**8**	**261**			**312**	**427**	**739**	**7**	**75**	**32**	**0.30**	**51**	**19**	**29**	**113**	**84**	**11%**	**14**	**271**	**4.54**	**-9.5**	**$12**

Gave back 2005's PX gains, although he did start to find that power stroke again in 2nd half. As GB% continues to rise, it's less and less likely that he has another big HR year in him.

Wilson,Vance

		Yr	AB	R	H	HR	RBI	SB	Avg	vL	vR	OB	Slg	OPS	bb%	ct%	h%	Eye	G	L	F	PX	SX	SBO	xHR	xBA	RC/G	RAR	R$
Pos	2	02 NYM	163	19	40	5	26	0	245	125	275	268	380	648	3	80	28	0.16	41	19	40	89	43	3%	5	254	3.16	-4.6	$4
Age	34	03 NYM	268	28	65	8	39	1	243	243	242	283	373	656	5	79	28	0.27	43	23	34	82	55	5%	7	262	3.37	-7.4	$5
Past Peak		04 NYM	157	18	43	4	21	1	274	200	299	321	427	748	7	85	30	0.46	41	16	43	95	65	3%	4	263	4.69	3.9	$4
Bats	Right	05 DET	152	18	30	3	19	0	197	231	193	252	283	534	7	83	22	0.42	48	10	42	54	40	0%	3	207	2.08	-9.3	$1
Reliability	0	06 DET	152	18	43	5	18	0	283	326	266	292	441	733	1	78	33	0.06	43	21	36	105	41	13%	5	268	4.11	-1.3	$4
DL		1st Half	74	9	22	3	11	0	297			297	500	797	0	77	35	0.00	40	25	35	139	44	8%	3	296	4.88	1.0	$2
BAvg Potl	35%	2nd Half	78	9	21	2	7	0	269			287	385	672	2	79	32	0.13	46	17	37	74	48	17%	2	241	3.42	-2.3	$1
LIMA Plan	F	07 Proj	**152**	**18**	**39**	**4**	**19**	**0**	**257**			**285**	**385**	**670**	**4**	**81**	**29**	**0.21**	**44**	**17**	**39**	**83**	**42**	**7%**	**4**	**247**	**3.50**	**-3.4**	**$3**

Backup CA who hasn't heard about the vagaries of small sample sizes. Every year it's the same thing with him: 150ish AB, 18 Runs, 43ish Hits, handful of HRs, 20ish RBI. And a Reliability score of 0.

Winn,Randy

		Yr	AB	R	H	HR	RBI	SB	Avg	vL	vR	OB	Slg	OPS	bb%	ct%	h%	Eye	G	L	F	PX	SX	SBO	xHR	xBA	RC/G	RAR	R$
Pos	987	02 TAM	607	87	181	14	75	27	298	347	283	356	461	818	8	82	35	0.50	47	21	32	103	135	20%	16	290	5.66	10.8	$25
Age	32	03 SEA	600	103	177	11	75	23	295	314	288	340	425	765	6	82	35	0.38	51	20	29	88	132	17%	14	283	4.88	-4.5	$24
Past Peak		04 SEA	626	84	179	14	81	21	286	257	299	342	427	768	8	84	32	0.54	53	18	29	85	116	16%	15	285	5.00	5.4	$21
Bats	Both	05 2TM	617	85	189	20	63	19	306	269	317	356	499	856	7	85	33	0.53	50	21	29	123	107	18%	20	320	5.99	17.4	$25
Reliability	30	06 SF	573	82	150	11	56	10	262	219	278	319	396	715	8	89	28	0.76	50	17	33	79	92	12%	12	284	4.48	-4.7	$13
DL		1st Half	298	49	82	8	35	3	275			345	440	785	10	91	28	1.14	51	17	32	89	86	12%	8	299	5.41	5.6	$9
BAvg Potl	60%	2nd Half	275	33	68	3	21	7	247			289	349	638	5	87	27	0.46	48	17	35	67	96	13%	4	266	3.44	-10.8	$5
LIMA Plan	C+	07 Proj	**584**	**81**	**164**	**13**	**61**	**12**	**281**			**333**	**428**	**761**	**7**	**86**	**31**	**0.58**	**50**	**18**	**32**	**90**	**100**	**13%**	**14**	**291**	**4.92**	**-1.9**	**$18**

Power continues to be limited by high GB%. Speed is in a long-term decline as well. H% was artificially low, BA should rebound toward .280s. But don't expect much else.

Woodward,Chris

		Yr	AB	R	H	HR	RBI	SB	Avg	vL	vR	OB	Slg	OPS	bb%	ct%	h%	Eye	G	L	F	PX	SX	SBO	xHR	xBA	RC/G	RAR	R$
Pos	4	02 TOR	312	48	86	13	45	3	276	149	315	331	468	799	8	77	32	0.36	35	22	43	117	107	4%	12	263	5.32	11.4	$11
Age	30	03 TOR	349	49	91	7	45	1	261	307	242	316	395	711	7	79	31	0.39	31	23	45	94	68	3%	9	256	4.27	1.4	$8
Peak		04 TOR	213	21	50	1	24	1	235	254	227	282	347	629	6	78	30	0.30	39	21	40	78	97	7%	3	246	3.29	-5.1	$2
Bats	Right	05 NYM	173	16	49	3	18	0	283	260	316	333	393	726	7	73	37	0.28	35	32	33	88	18	0%	4	271	4.46	-0.5	$4
Reliability	16	06 NYM	222	25	48	3	25	1	216	226	209	290	311	601	9	75	27	0.42	44	18	38	67	62	4%	4	225	2.91	-11.6	$2
DL		1st Half	80	10	19	1	12	1	238			315	338	652	10	70	33	0.38	49	21	30	83	52	9%	2	233	3.65	-2.3	$1
BAvg Potl	50%	2nd Half	142	15	29	2	13	0	204			276	296	571	9	78	25	0.45	42	17	42	59	52	0%	2	218	2.56	-9.0	$0
LIMA Plan	F	07 Proj	**170**	**19**	**41**	**3**	**19**	**1**	**241**			**303**	**350**	**653**	**8**	**75**	**31**	**0.36**	**40**	**23**	**37**	**79**	**62**	**3%**	**4**	**243**	**3.56**	**-5.1**	**$2**

Doesn't make consistent contact. Power and speed skills are both well below league average. Add in a winter featuring shoulder surgery and rehab, and there is no good reason to roster him.

Wright,David

		Yr	AB	R	H	HR	RBI	SB	Avg	vL	vR	OB	Slg	OPS	bb%	ct%	h%	Eye	G	L	F	PX	SX	SBO	xHR	xBA	RC/G	RAR	R$
Pos	5	02 0	0	0	0	0	0	0	0							0							0		0				
Age	24	03 0	0	0	0	0	0	0	0							0							0		0				
Growth		04 NYM *	600	97	188	31	91	26	313	309	288	378	557	934	9	85	33	0.69	35	20	46	146	90	23%	29	308	6.97	31.7	$33
Bats	Right	05 NYM	575	99	176	27	102	17	306	336	300	383	523	907	11	80	34	0.64	39	25	35	143	86	13%	27	310	6.82	32.4	$31
Reliability	86	06 NYM	582	96	181	26	116	20	311	285	321	381	531	912	10	81	35	0.58	36	19	44	133	110	14%	25	283	6.85	21.6	$30
DL		1st Half	299	50	98	18	64	11	328			396	592	988	10	80	36	0.58	34	20	46	154	108	14%	16	295	7.73	17.9	$18
BAvg Potl	40%	2nd Half	283	46	83	8	52	9	293			365	466	832	10	81	34	0.59	39	19	42	111	101	14%	9	271	5.91	3.4	$12
LIMA Plan	B	07 Proj	**596**	**99**	**178**	**27**	**109**	**20**	**299**			**372**	**517**	**888**	**10**	**81**	**33**	**0.62**	**38**	**22**	**41**	**136**	**106**	**16%**	**26**	**296**	**6.55**	**23.4**	**$30**

PRO: Growth in FB% and SX, improving trend vs. RHP
CON: PX drop in 2nd half, xBA didn't support .300+ BA
Might need another year of consolidation before he really explodes. But it's coming.

RAY MURPHY

Youkilis,Kevin			AB	R	H	HR	RBI	SB	Avg	vL	vR	OB	Slg	OPS	bb%	ct%	h%	Eye	G	L	F	PX	SX	SBO	xHR	xBA	RC/G	RAR	R$
Pos	3	02 aa	160	26	49	4	19	4	306			393	444	837	13	91	32	1.64				85	62	16%	4		6.17	2.0	$7
Age	28	03 a/a	421	70	111	6	44	6	264			389	371	759	17	87	29	1.54				72	80	4%	9		5.52	0.9	$10
Peak		04 BOS	* 365	58	92	9	50	2	252	250	265	342	389	731	12	82	29	0.75	37	21	42	91	56	3%	11	260	4.76	-2.5	$8
Bats	Right	05 BOS	* 231	33	66	7	29	1	284	300	265	390	474	865	15	82	32	0.96	32	28	40	133	49	5%	9	310	6.61	10.1	$7
Reliability	27	06 BOS	569	100	159	13	72	5	279	270	283	379	429	808	14	79	33	0.76	31	24	45	104	79	4%	18	262	5.85	6.9	$16
DL		1st Half	277	54	88	9	38	4	318			420	498	918	15	78	38	0.82	31	26	42	122	83	4%	11	279	7.32	14.1	$12
BAvg Potl	45%	2nd Half	292	46	71	4	34	1	243			338	363	701	13	79	29	0.70	30	23	47	88	64	3%	7	247	4.47	-8.4	$4
LIMA Plan	B	07 Proj	**513**	**88**	**140**	**12**	**65**	**4**	**273**			**373**	**424**	**797**	**14**	**81**	**32**	**0.85**	**31**	**24**	**44**	**104**	**66**	**5%**	**16**	**272**	**5.70**	**6.0**	**$14**

2H decline was not supported by BPIs, suggesting injury or fatigue may have contributed. Big swing in h% was a factor as well. xHR and increasing FB% point to power increase.
UP: 20 HR

Young,Chris			AB	R	H	HR	RBI	SB	Avg	vL	vR	OB	Slg	OPS	bb%	ct%	h%	Eye	G	L	F	PX	SX	SBO	xHR	xBA	RC/G	RAR	R$
Pos	8	02	0	0	0	0	0	0	0							0							0		0				
Age	23	03	0	0	0	0	0	0	0							0							0		0				
Growth		04	0	0	0	0	0	0	0							0							0		0				
Bats	Right	05 aa	462	72	115	24	61	25	249			330	489	819	11	78	27	0.54				161	126	29%	24		5.72	18.1	$20
Reliability	0	06 ARI	* 472	67	114	18	66	14	241	360	178	307	440	747	9	86	25	0.66	42	20	37	116	99	20%	18	301	4.78	4.9	$14
DL		1st Half	232	27	54	10	32	5	233			294	426	720	8	86	23	0.63				109	71	17%	9		4.41	-0.2	$5
BAvg Potl	75%	2nd Half	240	40	60	9	34	10	249			320	453	773	9	85	26	0.69	42	20	37	123	117	23%	9	303	5.15	5.1	$8
LIMA Plan	B	07 Proj	**520**	**81**	**137**	**23**	**71**	**21**	**263**			**334**	**479**	**813**	**10**	**82**	**28**	**0.60**	**42**	**20**	**37**	**133**	**113**	**22%**	**22**	**302**	**5.58**	**15.8**	**$21**

2-10-.243 in 70 AB at ARI. Improved ct% is encouraging, xBA says he is capable of higher BA. PX dip may have been related to pre-season hand injury. Invest, future is very bright.

Young,Delmon			AB	R	H	HR	RBI	SB	Avg	vL	vR	OB	Slg	OPS	bb%	ct%	h%	Eye	G	L	F	PX	SX	SBO	xHR	xBA	RC/G	RAR	R$
Pos	9	02	0	0	0	0	0	0	0							0							0		0				
Age	21	03	0	0	0	0	0	0	0							0							0		0				
Growth		04	0	0	0	0	0	0	0							0							0		0				
Bats	Right	05 a/a	558	75	163	21	81	28	292			321	463	784	4	88	30	0.35				96	120	32%	17		4.90	-1.3	$26
Reliability	0	06 TAM	* 468	68	152	11	71	25	325	379	299	348	485	834	3	83	38	0.20	47	26	27	102	136	26%	12	305	5.51	-2.0	$22
DL		1st Half	115	18	41	0	15	15	354			389	421	810	5	87	41	0.43				47	145	43%	1		5.39	-0.8	$8
BAvg Potl	30%	2nd Half	353	50	112	11	55	10	316			334	507	841	3	82	36	0.15	47	26	27	121	117	17%	11	313	5.56	-1.0	$15
LIMA Plan	C	07 Proj	**538**	**76**	**155**	**17**	**79**	**24**	**288**			**316**	**458**	**774**	**4**	**85**	**31**	**0.28**	**47**	**26**	**27**	**100**	**130**	**28%**	**15**	**312**	**4.80**	**-6.5**	**$22**

3-10-.317 in 126 AB at TAM. Put on a show in 2nd half after return from bat-throwing suspension. Power and speed skills are obvious, needs to bump ct% and bb% to become a star.

Young,Dmitri			AB	R	H	HR	RBI	SB	Avg	vL	vR	OB	Slg	OPS	bb%	ct%	h%	Eye	G	L	F	PX	SX	SBO	xHR	xBA	RC/G	RAR	R$
Pos	0	02 DET	201	25	57	7	27	2	284	296	279	324	458	782	6	81	32	0.31	52	19	29	115	55	4%	7	289	4.97	-3.1	$6
Age	33	03 DET	562	78	167	29	85	2	297	293	299	363	537	900	9	77	34	0.45	44	27	29	152	79	2%	27	312	6.71	32.5	$22
Past Peak		04 DET	389	72	106	18	60	0	272	248	286	329	481	810	8	82	29	0.46	46	20	34	124	69	1%	16	296	5.40	1.1	$13
Bats	Both	05 DET	469	61	127	21	72	1	271	277	269	313	471	784	6	79	30	0.29	47	20	33	129	67	1%	19	291	4.99	-13.8	$15
Reliability	27	06 DET	172	19	43	7	23	1	250	136	267	295	407	702	6	77	29	0.28	52	14	34	91	59	5%	6	247	3.93	-12.8	$4
DL	80	1st Half	59	5	10	0	4	1	169			222	220	443	6	69	24	0.22	46	7	46	51	63	9%	1	166	0.58	-11.2	($1)
BAvg Potl	40%	2nd Half	113	14	33	7	19	0	292			333	504	838	6	81	31	0.33	55	17	28	109	54	3%	5	285	5.48	-3.0	$4
LIMA Plan	F	07 Proj	**262**	**33**	**71**	**11**	**37**	**1**	**271**			**318**	**444**	**761**	**6**	**78**	**31**	**0.31**	**49**	**17**	**33**	**107**	**58**	**3%**	**10**	**266**	**4.72**	**-9.8**	**$7**

A lost year due to injuries and off-field issues, but 2nd half shows he can still hit. Don't pay for more than part-time ABs, but in the right situation he could turn a nice profit.

Young,Eric			AB	R	H	HR	RBI	SB	Avg	vL	vR	OB	Slg	OPS	bb%	ct%	h%	Eye	G	L	F	PX	SX	SBO	xHR	xBA	RC/G	RAR	R$
Pos	7	02 MIL	496	57	139	3	28	31	280	282	278	333	369	702	7	92	30	1.03	47	21	33	60	119	29%	6	289	4.43	-28.2	$16
Age	39	03 2NL	475	80	119	15	34	28	251	240	252	331	302	722	11	91	25	1.30	42	23	35	79	117	29%	10	207	4.71	-12.7	$17
Decline		04 TEX	344	55	99	1	27	14	288	329	250	367	381	748	11	92	31	1.54	41	20	39	64	105	20%	4	275	5.22	2.0	$10
Bats	Right	05 SD	142	22	39	2	12	7	275	318	219	356	380	737	11	92	29	1.50	39	29	33	70	83	28%	3	308	5.02	-1.4	$5
Reliability	0	06 2TM	138	20	28	3	15	8	203	268	134	276	326	602	9	88	21	0.82	44	20	36	70	131	31%	3	273	3.23	-8.7	$3
DL	85	1st Half	90	12	21	2	8	6	233			296	344	640	8	91	24	1.00	48	24	29	64	95	35%	2	299	3.69	-4.2	$3
BAvg Potl	75%	2nd Half	48	8	7	1	7	2	146			241	292	532	11	81	16	0.67	37	12	51	85	159	22%	1	226	2.30	-4.7	$0
LIMA Plan	D	07 Proj	**122**	**18**	**30**	**1**	**10**	**7**	**246**			**320**	**325**	**645**	**10**	**91**	**26**	**1.27**	**43**	**23**	**33**	**54**	**94**	**29%**	**2**	**283**	**3.94**	**-4.7**	**$3**

Seemed to find his legs again, but SX spike is likely a sample size fluke. He can still swipe the occasional bag, but inability to hit RHPs limits him to a bench role.

Young,Michael			AB	R	H	HR	RBI	SB	Avg	vL	vR	OB	Slg	OPS	bb%	ct%	h%	Eye	G	L	F	PX	SX	SBO	xHR	xBA	RC/G	RAR	R$
Pos	6	02 TEX	573	77	150	9	62	6	262	290	251	311	382	693	7	80	31	0.37	50	20	30	77	102	9%	10	265	4.03	-9.2	$13
Age	30	03 TEX	666	106	204	14	72	13	306	308	306	342	446	788	5	85	35	0.35	44	27	29	85	131	8%	14	298	5.06	11.6	$24
Peak		04 TEX	693	115	216	22	100	12	312	330	307	355	481	835	6	87	33	0.52	38	25	38	93	120	8%	19	292	5.65	22.3	$28
Bats	Right	05 TEX	668	114	221	24	91	5	331	340	327	384	513	898	8	86	36	0.64	45	26	29	111	87	3%	22	320	6.47	33.6	$30
Reliability	76	06 TEX	691	93	217	14	103	7	314	295	320	359	459	817	6	86	35	0.50	48	25	27	94	76	5%	17	310	5.52	20.7	$23
DL		1st Half	334	45	109	5	50	4	326			375	452	827	7	88	36	0.63	49	25	26	86	57	6%	7	309	5.70	11.5	$12
BAvg Potl	45%	2nd Half	357	48	108	9	53	3	303			343	465	808	6	85	34	0.40	47	25	28	102	82	4%	10	309	5.35	9.2	$11
LIMA Plan	C	07 Proj	**653**	**98**	**205**	**17**	**92**	**7**	**314**			**360**	**472**	**832**	**7**	**86**	**35**	**0.51**	**46**	**25**	**29**	**97**	**92**	**5%**	**18**	**307**	**5.67**	**21.3**	**$24**

xHR says his HR total was a shade low, but 2005's PX is an outlier. Consistent .310+ BA over massive AB totals drives his value, and that should continue. Any power or speed is just gravy.

Zaun,Gregg			AB	R	H	HR	RBI	SB	Avg	vL	vR	OB	Slg	OPS	bb%	ct%	h%	Eye	G	L	F	PX	SX	SBO	xHR	xBA	RC/G	RAR	R$
Pos	2	02 HOU	185	18	41	3	24	1	222	316	197	269	319	588	6	81	26	0.33	42	19	38	66	69	2%	3	242	2.67	-8.2	$2
Age	35	03 2NL	166	15	38	4	21	1	229	308	205	308	349	658	10	87	24	0.90	43	21	35	75	34	4%	4	276	3.88	-2.1	$2
Decline		04 TOR	338	46	91	6	36	0	269	272	268	358	393	752	12	82	31	0.77	45	24	32	87	29	2%	9	277	5.07	7.2	$7
Bats	Both	05 TOR	434	61	109	11	61	2	251	278	241	359	373	732	14	84	28	1.04	46	19	35	77	49	3%	12	263	4.91	11.5	$10
Reliability	46	06 TOR	290	39	79	12	40	0	272	373	251	363	462	825	12	86	28	0.98	38	20	42	113	23	2%	12	287	5.88	12.2	$8
DL	15 16	1st Half	119	15	39	6	21	0	328			398	555	953	11	90	33	1.17	39	25	36	128	20	3%	5	332	7.22	8.9	$5
BAvg Potl	65%	2nd Half	171	24	40	6	19	0	234			338	398	736	14	82	25	0.90	36	17	47	102	32	2%	6	256	4.86	2.3	$3
LIMA Plan	D	07 Proj	**306**	**40**	**82**	**11**	**41**	**1**	**268**			**359**	**431**	**791**	**12**	**84**	**29**	**0.91**	**41**	**20**	**39**	**101**	**29**	**3%**	**11**	**279**	**5.48**	**11.0**	**$8**

Even in mid-30s, he's an ideal 2nd CA on your roster: double-digit HRs and a serviceable BA. As 2005 shows, more AB may just wear him out. Set your expectations for 300 AB.

Zimmerman,Ryan			AB	R	H	HR	RBI	SB	Avg	vL	vR	OB	Slg	OPS	bb%	ct%	h%	Eye	G	L	F	PX	SX	SBO	xHR	xBA	RC/G	RAR	R$
Pos	5	02	0	0	0	0	0	0	0							0							0		0				
Age	22	03	0	0	0	0	0	0	0							0							0		0				
Growth		04	0	0	0	0	0	0	0							0							0		0				
Bats	Right	05 WAS	* 291	39	90	7	32	1	309	400	395	343	481	824	5	86	34	0.38	43	38	19	120	41	10%	9	365	5.50	5.9	$10
Reliability	0	06 WAS	614	84	176	20	110	11	287	280	289	351	471	822	9	80	33	0.51	42	22	36	119	78	11%	22	288	5.71	3.8	$23
DL		1st Half	291	37	78	10	48	5	268			328	454	782	8	77	32	0.39	42	22	36	125	70	13%	11	280	5.18	-2.6	$9
BAvg Potl	50%	2nd Half	323	47	98	10	62	6	303			372	486	858	10	84	34	0.66	42	21	36	114	77	10%	11	295	6.18	6.2	$14
LIMA Plan	C	07 Proj	**602**	**82**	**179**	**17**	**92**	**7**	**297**			**350**	**478**	**827**	**7**	**83**	**33**	**0.47**	**42**	**24**	**34**	**119**	**68**	**11%**	**20**	**303**	**5.68**	**9.2**	**$22**

Here's another rookie who showed nice 2nd half BPI growth. Power may take more time to develop, but .300 BA should come soon, perhaps even in 2007.
UP: .310 BA, 25 HR.

Zobrist,Ben			AB	R	H	HR	RBI	SB	Avg	vL	vR	OB	Slg	OPS	bb%	ct%	h%	Eye	G	L	F	PX	SX	SBO	xHR	xBA	RC/G	RAR	R$
Pos	6	02	0	0	0	0	0	0	0							0							0		0				
Age	25	03	0	0	0	0	0	0	0							0							0		0				
Pre-Peak		04	0	0	0	0	0	0	0							0							0		0				
Bats	Both	05	0	0	0	0	0	0	0							0							0		0				
Reliability	14	06 TAM	* 567	68	150	5	48	12	265	212	229	340	372	712	10	86	30	0.82	47	22	30	67	103	13%	8	281	4.58	2.9	$10
DL		1st Half	275	41	76	2	20	5	275			359	383	742	12	86	31	0.93				76	81	10%	4		5.04	5.0	$5
BAvg Potl	60%	2nd Half	292	27	75	3	29	8	256			321	362	683	9	86	29	0.71	47	22	30	59	110	16%	3	276	4.15	-2.3	$5
LIMA Plan	D	07 Proj	**252**	**29**	**66**	**2**	**22**	**6**	**262**			**335**	**372**	**707**	**10**	**86**	**30**	**0.80**	**47**	**22**	**30**	**68**	**102**	**14%**	**3**	**282**	**4.52**	**0.4**	**$5**

No longer young by prospect standards. Lack of any above-average skills limits his upside. Could hang around in a utility role, but any fanalytic impact will be minimal.

RAY MURPHY

The Pitchers

QUALIFICATION: All pitchers who accumulated at least 40 IP in the majors in 2006 are included. Some select players with fewer than 40 IP are included if we believe they will have an impact in 2007. Players who may have a role in 2007 but have spent several years battling injuries are often not included, though an injury status update will appear on page 175. All of these players will appear on BaseballHQ.com over the winter as their 2007 roles and projected impacts become clearer.

THROWS: How he throws — right (RH) or left (LH).

ROLE: Pitchers are classified as Starters (projected 18+ batters faced per game) or Relievers (under 18 BF/G).

AGE: Each pitcher's current age is shown, along with a description of the associated stage in his career.

TYPE evaluates the extent to which a pitcher allows the ball to be put into play. FINESSE represents those pitchers who allow the ball to be put into play a great deal. POWER represents those with high strikeout and/or walk totals who keep the ball out of play.

RELIABILITY SCORE: An analysis of each player's forecast risk, on a 0-100 scale. High scores go those pitchers who throw many innings, are healthy (and have not been overused at a young age), are in a stable age range and have displayed consistent performance over the past two years (using xERA).

DL DAYS: Total number of days spent on the disabled list in 2006, followed by 2005.

LIMA PLAN GRADE: Rating that evaluates how well that pitcher would be a good fit for a team employing the LIMA Plan. Best grades will go to pitchers who have excellent base skills and had a 2006 Roto value under $20. Lowest grades will go to poor skills and values over $20.

ERA POTENTIAL (ERA Potl): The probability that a pitcher will improve his ERA in 2007 over 2006, based on an evaluation of strand rate, hit rate, xERA variance and base performance value. These percentages are in 5% increments, ranging from 10% to 90%, though most will be centered closer to the mean. If a pitcher's ERA Potl says 60%, for instance, it means that he has a 60% chance of improving his ERA in 2007.

PLAYER STAT LINES: The past five year's statistics represent the total accumulated in the majors as well as in Triple-A, Double-A ball and various foreign leagues during each year. All non-major league stats used have been converted to their equivalent major league performance level. Minor league levels below AA are not included.

Nearly all baseball publications separate a player's statistical experiences in the major leagues from the minor leagues and outside leagues. While this may be an appropriate approach for the sake of official record-keeping, it is not an accurate measure of a player's complete performance for the year.

Bill James has proven that minor league statistics, at Double-A level or above, are accurate indicators of future potential. Other researchers have also devised conversion factors for foreign leagues that place them on a comparable playing field as MLB stats. Since these conversions are accurate barometers of potential performance, then we should be including them in the pool of historical data.

TEAM DESIGNATIONS: An asterisk (*) appearing with a team name means that major league equivalent Triple-A and/or Double-A numbers are included in that year's stat line. A designation of "a/a" means the stats were accumulated at both Triple-A and Double-A levels that year. "JPN" means Japan, "MEX" means Mexico, "KOR" means Korea, "TWN" means Taiwan, "CUB" means Cuba and "ind" means independent league. All stats that appear with these designations are converted to major league equivalents.

The designation "2TM" appears whenever a player was on more than one major league team, crossing leagues, in a season. "2AL" and "2NL" represent more than one team in the same league. Complete season stats are presented for players who crossed leagues during the season.

SABERMETRIC CATEGORIES: Descriptions of all the sabermetric categories appear in the glossary. The decimal point has been suppressed on several categories to conserve space. *Notes:*
- Platoon data (vL, vR) and Ball-in-play data (G/L/F) are for major league performance only.
- The xERA2 formula is used for years in which G/L/F data is available. The old formula is used otherwise.

2007 FORECASTS: It is far too early to be making definitive projections for 2007, especially on playing time. Focus on the skill levels and trends, then consult Baseball HQ for playing time revisions as players change teams and roles become finalized. A free projections update will also be available online at BaseballForecaster.com in March.

Forecasts are computed from a player's trends over the past five years. Adjustments were made for leading indicators and variances between skill and statistical output. After reviewing the leading indicators, you might opt to make further adjustments.

Although each year's numbers include all playing time at the Double-A level or above, the 2007 forecast only represents potential playing time at the major league level, and again is highly preliminary.

CAPSULE COMMENTARIES: For each player, a brief analysis of their BPIs and the potential impact on performance in 2007 is provided. For those who played only a portion of 2006 at the major league level, and whose isolated MLB stats are significantly different from their full-season total, their MLB stats are listed here. Note that these commentaries generally look at performance related issues only. Playing time expectations may impact these analyses, so you will have to adjust accordingly, especially as we get closer to Opening Day. Upside (UP) and downside (DN) statistical potential appears for some players. These are less grounded in hard data and more speculative of skills potential.

Aardsma,David

Aardsma,David		W	L	Sv	IP	K	ERA	WHIP	OBA	vL	vR	BF/G	H%	S%	xERA	G	L	F	Ctl	Dom	Cmd	hr/f	hr/9	RAR	BPV	R$
RH Reliever	02	0	0	0	0	0	0.00	0.00											0.0	0.0						
Age 25	03	0	0	0	0	0	0.00	0.00											0.0	0.0						
Growth	04 aaa	6	4	11	55	47	2.96	1.28	227			5.3	29%	75%	2.77				4.0	7.7	1.9		0.2	9.4	91	$11
Type Power	05 aa	10	3	2	96	62	4.34	1.52	287			10.2	33%	71%	4.49				3.5	5.8	1.7		0.5	-0.4	53	$7
Reliability 0	06 CHC *	5	3	8	89	81	4.24	1.38	239	190	225	5.2	29%	72%	4.06	37	19	44	4.4	8.2	1.8	9%	1.0	2.7	65	$10
DL	1st Half	3	1	5	40	37	4.24	1.32	225			5.0	27%	71%	3.85	41	17	41	4.5	8.3	1.9	11%	1.1	1.2	65	$6
ERA Potl 50%	2nd Half	2	2	3	49	44	4.24	1.43	251			5.3	30%	72%	4.22	34	20	45	4.4	8.1	1.8	8%	0.9	1.5	64	$4
LIMA Plan B+	07 Proj	5	2	0	59	47	4.15	1.42	257			6.3	31%	71%	4.30	37	19	44	4.0	7.2	1.8	5%	0.6	0.5	67	$5

3-0, 4.08 in 53.0 IP at CHC. Ctl is shaky, and FB tendency could foretell HR problems. But spike in DOM puts this one-time prospect back on our radar screen. Worth tucking away.

Accardo,Jeremy

Accardo,Jeremy		W	L	Sv	IP	K	ERA	WHIP	OBA	vL	vR	BF/G	H%	S%	xERA	G	L	F	Ctl	Dom	Cmd	hr/f	hr/9	RAR	BPV	R$
RH Reliever	02	0	0	0	0	0	0.00	0.00											0.0	0.0						
Age 25	03	0	0	0	0	0	0.00	0.00											0.0	0.0						
Growth	04 a/a	3	0	7	42	38	1.71	1.07	228			5.1	30%	82%	2.11				2.1	8.1	3.8		0.0	13.6	138	$9
Type	05 SF *	4	5	7	73	59	3.45	1.19	234	182	265	4.9	29%	71%	3.67	39	23	38	3.0	7.3	2.5	5%	0.5	7.1	89	$10
Reliability 7	06 2TM	2	4	3	69	54	5.35	1.39	281	241	307	4.6	33%	62%	3.62	42	25	32	2.6	7.0	2.7	10%	0.9	-7.0	70	$4
DL	1st Half	0	1	2	31	32	4.35	1.16	236			4.7	33%	58%	3.03	42	24	34	2.6	9.3	3.6	0%	0.0	0.6	138	$3
ERA Potl 65%	2nd Half	2	3	1	38	22	6.16	1.58	314			4.5	33%	64%	4.13	42	27	31	2.6	5.2	2.0	17%	1.7	-7.7	16	$0
LIMA Plan A	07 Proj	3	3	0	59	47	3.85	1.28	260			4.7	31%	70%	3.54	42	25	33	2.6	7.2	2.8	7%	0.6	6.4	86	$5

Battered by unlucky H% and S%, but 1st half BPIs were closer-worthy. 2H loss of DOM gives us pause, but his longer-term track record makes him a solid LIMA option/speculative saves source.

Adkins,Jon

Adkins,Jon		W	L	Sv	IP	K	ERA	WHIP	OBA	vL	vR	BF/G	H%	S%	xERA	G	L	F	Ctl	Dom	Cmd	hr/f	hr/9	RAR	BPV	R$
RH Reliever	02 aaa	11	8	0	143	90	5.22	1.64	324			23.3	37%	68%	5.52				2.6	5.7	2.2		0.7	-16.8	50	$3
Age 29	03 aaa	7	8	1	122	52	5.31	1.48	297			20.7	31%	66%	5.19				2.7	3.9	1.5		1.1	-13.9	15	$3
Peak	04 CHW	2	3	0	62	44	4.65	1.53	300	327	288	5.5	32%	77%	3.84	46	21	33	2.9	6.4	2.2	19%	1.9	-1.6	23	$2
Type	05 aaa	4	9	0	124	71	7.01	1.82	339			26.7	35%	65%	7.44				3.4	5.1	1.5		1.9	-41.5	-8	($8)
Reliability 1	06 SD *	3	1	7	66	39	3.27	1.30	255	287	259	4.2	29%	75%	4.35	41	18	41	3.0	5.3	1.8	3%	0.4	9.9	61	$8
DL	1st Half	1	1	7	33	23	2.99	1.42	272			4.5	33%	77%	4.15	41	23	36	3.3	6.3	1.9	0%	0.0	6.1	78	$5
ERA Potl 45%	2nd Half	2	0	0	33	16	3.55	1.18	238			3.9	25%	72%	4.48	40	15	45	2.7	4.4	1.6	6%	0.8	3.8	43	$3
LIMA Plan C+	07 Proj	2	2	0	44	26	4.55	1.49	290			6.4	32%	72%	4.40	43	19	39	3.1	5.4	1.7	9%	1.0	-0.2	35	$1

2-1, 3.98 in 54 IP at SD. Don't mistake 2006 for a breakout. BPIs remain unremarkable, DOM not LIMA-worthy. Improvement came from plunging HR/9, but HR/F says that was more luck than skill.

Affeldt,Jeremy

Affeldt,Jeremy		W	L	Sv	IP	K	ERA	WHIP	OBA	vL	vR	BF/G	H%	S%	xERA	G	L	F	Ctl	Dom	Cmd	hr/f	hr/9	RAR	BPV	R$
LH Reliever	02 KC	3	4	0	77	67	4.68	1.58	281	283	271	10.2	34%	72%	4.04	42	22	36	4.3	7.8	1.8	10%	0.9	-2.1	56	$3
Age 27	03 KC	7	6	4	126	98	3.93	1.30	262	223	272	14.8	31%	72%	3.71	43	20	37	2.7	7.0	2.6	8%	0.9	9.3	73	$13
Pre-Peak	04 KC	3	4	13	76	49	4.97	1.62	298	271	312	9.1	34%	69%	4.35	46	21	33	3.8	5.8	1.5	7%	0.7	-5.0	41	$6
Type Power	05 KC	0	2	0	49	39	5.30	1.73	288	263	283	4.7	35%	68%	4.06	53	22	25	5.3	7.1	1.3	8%	0.5	-5.7	52	($1)
Reliability 8	06 2TM	8	8	1	97	48	6.21	1.62	271	212	289	8.2	28%	63%	4.89	50	17	33	5.1	4.4	0.9	12%	1.2	-20.2	10	$1
DL 67	1st Half	3	5	0	55	22	7.02	1.83	292			15.4	30%	62%	5.64	49	17	34	6.0	3.6	0.6	12%	1.3	-17.0	-8	($3)
ERA Potl 55%	2nd Half	5	3	1	42	26	5.14	1.33	243			4.8	26%	63%	3.98	51	17	32	3.9	5.6	1.4	12%	1.1	-3.2	38	$4
LIMA Plan C+	07 Proj	4	6	0	81	52	5.14	1.58	275			6.6	31%	68%	4.34	49	19	31	4.6	5.8	1.3	10%	0.9	0.8	35	$2

xERA says he's not the disaster that his ERA implies, but Cmd is in a four-year spiral. High GB% offers a glimmer of optimism, but there's little other reason to hold out hope.

Albers,Matt

Albers,Matt		W	L	Sv	IP	K	ERA	WHIP	OBA	vL	vR	BF/G	H%	S%	xERA	G	L	F	Ctl	Dom	Cmd	hr/f	hr/9	RAR	BPV	R$
RH Starter	02	0	0	0	0	0	0.00	0.00																		
Age 24	03	0	0	0	0	0	0.00	0.00																		
Growth	04	0	0	0	0	0	0.00	0.00																		
Type Power	05	0	0	0	0	0	0.00	0.00																		
Reliability 2	06 HOU *	12	5	0	156	113	3.23	1.38	258	333	267	24.9	31%	77%	3.89	43	26	30	3.6	6.5	1.8	5%	0.5	24.2	66	$15
DL	1st Half	9	2	0	91	60	2.55	1.36	257			26.0	30%	81%					3.5	5.9	1.7		0.3	21.8	66	$11
ERA Potl 45%	2nd Half	3	3	0	65	53	4.19	1.42	260			23.5	31%	71%	3.76	43	26	30	3.9	7.3	1.9	8%	0.7	2.4	66	$4
LIMA Plan B	07 Proj	6	5	0	110	82	4.11	1.40	259			24.9	31%	70%	3.86	43	26	30	3.7	6.7	1.8	6%	0.5	6.8	67	$7

0-2, 6.00 in 15 IP at HOU. Decent DOM and GB tendency are what make him a prospect. Doesn't have much room for error, so even mild Ctl problems are worrisome. Upside of a mid-rotation SP.

Aquino,Greg

Aquino,Greg		W	L	Sv	IP	K	ERA	WHIP	OBA	vL	vR	BF/G	H%	S%	xERA	G	L	F	Ctl	Dom	Cmd	hr/f	hr/9	RAR	BPV	R$
RH Reliever	02	0	0	0	0	0	0.00	0.00											0.0	0.0						
Age 29	03 aa	7	3	0	106	76	4.07	1.62	309			24.1	37%	74%	5.02				3.2	6.4	2.0		0.4	4.3	61	$5
Pre-Peak	04 ARI *	1	6	17	64	41	5.20	1.61	261	167	224	5.3	29%	68%	4.51	53	16	31	5.5	5.8	1.1	9%	0.8	-7.4	34	$5
Type Power	05 ARI	0	1	1	31	34	7.81	1.90	324	309	329	4.3	39%	62%	3.78	44	23	33	4.9	9.8	2.0	22%	2.0	-13.7	30	($3)
Reliability 0	06 ARI	2	0	0	48	51	4.49	1.62	285	280	286	5.2	35%	77%	3.41	48	22	30	4.5	9.5	2.1	19%	1.5	-0.0	55	$2
DL 19 64	1st Half	2	0	0	27	27	4.65	1.59	282			4.9	34%	74%	3.44	49	22	29	4.3	9.0	2.1	17%	1.3	-0.5	56	$1
ERA Potl 45%	2nd Half	0	0	0	21	24	4.29	1.67	288			5.7	36%	81%	3.39	46	23	32	4.7	10.3	2.2	21%	1.7	0.5	53	$0
LIMA Plan C+	07 Proj	2	2	0	79	78	5.01	1.70	295			5.4	36%	74%	3.72	47	22	31	4.7	8.9	1.9	18%	1.5	6.3	45	$0

A bit of a paradox here:
PRO: overpowering DOM
CON: LD%, HR/9, high H% all say that he gets hit very hard. No evidence of either trend changing, which means he'll remain flammable.

Armas Jr.,Tony

Armas Jr.,Tony		W	L	Sv	IP	K	ERA	WHIP	OBA	vL	vR	BF/G	H%	S%	xERA	G	L	F	Ctl	Dom	Cmd	hr/f	hr/9	RAR	BPV	R$
RH Starter	02 MON	12	12	0	164	131	4.45	1.38	244	309	190	24.3	28%	71%	3.87	46	20	34	4.3	7.2	1.7	13%	1.2	-6.9	48	$11
Age 29	03 MON	2	1	0	31	23	2.61	1.06	222	250	209	24.7	25%	83%	3.89	33	17	50	2.3	6.7	2.9	9%	1.2	6.4	76	$4
Pre-Peak	04 MON	2	4	0	72	54	4.88	1.54	245	231	258	20.1	26%	73%	4.81	35	23	42	5.6	6.8	1.2	14%	1.6	-5.4	23	$1
Type	05 WAS *	8	9	0	125	76	4.93	1.53	267	276	241	23.2	28%	71%	4.90	36	21	43	4.6	5.5	1.2	11%	1.4	-10.6	18	$4
Reliability 21	06 WAS	9	12	0	154	97	5.03	1.50	278	274	284	22.7	30%	68%	4.54	39	22	40	3.7	5.7	1.5	10%	1.1	-10.2	32	$6
DL 27 57	1st Half	6	4	0	79	57	4.44	1.41	262			22.8	31%	69%	4.42	34	22	44	3.6	6.5	1.8	6%	0.7	0.4	59	$6
ERA Potl 50%	2nd Half	3	8	0	75	40	5.64	1.60	294			22.6	30%	68%	4.68	42	22	36	3.8	4.8	1.3	14%	1.6	-10.7	4	($0)
LIMA Plan C	07 Proj	9	12	0	164	106	4.90	1.50	268			22.6	29%	71%	4.60	38	22	40	4.2	5.8	1.4	11%	1.3	-4.8	26	$6

Finally hit a stretch of relatively good health, but cumulative injury history appears to have taken its toll. No longer carries the "would be valuable if healthy" tag. Former prospect luster has worn away.

Arroyo,Bronson

Arroyo,Bronson		W	L	Sv	IP	K	ERA	WHIP	OBA	vL	vR	BF/G	H%	S%	xERA	G	L	F	Ctl	Dom	Cmd	hr/f	hr/9	RAR	BPV	R$
RH Starter	02 PIT *	10	7	0	170	120	3.71	1.27	267			23.0	31%	71%	3.57				2.2	6.4	2.9		0.6	8.4	84	$14
Age 30	03 aaa	12	6	0	149	127	4.46	1.36	297			26.6	36%	67%	4.34				1.5	7.7	5.1		0.6	-1.3	130	$13
Peak	04 BOS	10	9	0	178	142	4.04	1.22	254	269	227	23.1	30%	69%	3.58	41	20	39	2.4	7.2	3.0	8%	0.9	8.6	85	$16
Type	05 BOS	14	10	0	205	100	4.52	1.30	269	286	234	24.7	29%	67%	4.52	38	18	44	2.4	4.4	1.9	7%	1.0	-3.7	37	$14
Reliability 67	06 CIN	14	11	0	240	184	3.30	1.19	247	282	206	28.2	28%	78%	3.68	38	21	41	2.4	6.9	2.9	11%	1.2	35.3	73	$26
DL	1st Half	9	4	0	111	84	2.59	1.12	245			28.1	28%	82%	3.60	39	18	42	1.9	6.8	3.7	8%	0.9	26.0	97	$16
ERA Potl 45%	2nd Half	5	7	0	129	100	3.91	1.25	248			28.3	27%	74%	3.76	37	24	39	2.9	7.0	2.4	13%	1.4	9.2	57	$11
LIMA Plan D+	07 Proj	15	10	0	239	188	3.81	1.24	257			26.1	30%	72%	3.71	39	20	41	2.4	7.1	3.0	9%	1.0	19.3	78	$22

Recovered 2005's lost DOM, and performance bounced back to 2004 levels. Workload concerns, home ballpark and 2nd half fade all conspire against further growth, but sub-4.00 ERA should be sustainable.

Astacio,Ezequiel

Astacio,Ezequiel		W	L	Sv	IP	K	ERA	WHIP	OBA	vL	vR	BF/G	H%	S%	xERA	G	L	F	Ctl	Dom	Cmd	hr/f	hr/9	RAR	BPV	R$
RH Starter	02	0	0	0	0	0	0.00	0.00											0.0	0.0						
Age 27	03	0	0	0	0	0	0.00	0.00											0.0	0.0						
Pre-Peak	04 aa	13	10	0	176	147	4.90	1.38	272			27.0	33%	64%	4.14				3.0	7.5	2.5		0.7	-12.1	78	$12
Type	05 HOU *	7	10	1	146	113	4.62	1.33	277	313	290	17.7	30%	72%	3.90	36	18	46	2.2	7.0	3.1	14%	1.8	-6.7	54	$9
Reliability 2	06 aaa	8	4	0	92	62	5.84	1.67	298			20.1	32%	68%	6.04				4.2	6.1	1.4		1.6	-15.0	14	$2
DL	1st Half	3	2	0	38	20	5.59	1.78	315			20.0	34%	69%					4.4	4.8	1.1		1.0	-5.0	15	($0)
ERA Potl 50%	2nd Half	5	2	0	54	42	6.01	1.58	285			20.3	30%	68%					4.1	7.0	1.7		2.1	-9.9	13	$2
LIMA Plan C+	07 Proj	5	4	0	73	53	5.21	1.50	286			20.0	32%	69%	4.42	36	18	46	3.4	6.6	2.0	11%	1.5	-0.0	34	$3

2-0, 11.12 in 6 IP at HOU. Banished to Triple-A in May and never returned, not a good indicator of his value within the organization. MLEs certainly didn't warrant that recall. Stay away.

RAY MURPHY

Astacio,Pedro

	Yr	Tm	W	L	Sv	IP	K	ERA	WHIP	OBA	vL	vR	BF/G	H%	S%	xERA	G	L	F	Ctl	Dom	Cmd	hr/f	hr/9	RAR	BPV	R$
RH Starter	02	NYM	12	11	0	191	152	4.81	1.34	263	237	283	26.2	29%	69%	3.80	41	18	40	3.0	7.2	2.4	14%	1.5	-16.5	51	$12
Age 37	03	NYM	3	2	0	36	20	7.46	1.80	315	324	300	24.4	32%	61%	5.25	29	33	39	4.5	5.0	1.1	16%	2.0	-14.2	-15	($2)
Decline	04	BOS *	0	1	0	21	16	6.00	1.67	313			12.0	36%	66%	6.11				3.4	6.9	2.0		1.3	-4.1	37	($1)
Type Finesse	05	2TM	6	10	0	126	78	4.71	1.35	272	244	306	22.4	29%	68%	4.05	42	22	37	2.6	5.6	2.1	11%	1.2	-6.3	42	$6
Reliability 0	06	WAS	5	5	0	90	42	5.99	1.55	300	270	330	23.7	31%	63%	5.04	37	18	46	3.1	4.2	1.4	10%	1.4	-16.7	7	$0
DL 91 31	1st Half		1	1	0	18	5	7.22	1.42	304			19.5	30%	48%					1.7	2.3	1.4		1.1	-6.1	3	($0)
ERA Potl 50%	2nd Half		4	4	0	72	38	5.69	1.59	299			25.0	31%	67%	5.02	37	18	46	3.5	4.7	1.4	10%	1.5	-10.7	8	$0
LIMA Plan C	07	Proj	6	8	0	116	61	5.12	1.50	292			23.3	31%	69%	4.70	36	22	41	3.0	4.7	1.6	11%	1.4	-4.8	16	$3

Injured most of 1st half, when he returned he could not sustain 2005's skills rebound. Could surprise us one more time, but age and injury history say the percentage play is to bet against.

Ayala,Luis

	Yr	Tm	W	L	Sv	IP	K	ERA	WHIP	OBA	vL	vR	BF/G	H%	S%	xERA	G	L	F	Ctl	Dom	Cmd	hr/f	hr/9	RAR	BPV	R$
RH Reliever	02	MEX *	0	0	1	11	11	6.55	1.55	295			5.5	35%	60%	5.70				3.3	9.0	2.8		1.6	-3.1	59	$0
Age 29	03	MON	10	3	5	71	46	2.92	1.10	245	337	188	4.4	27%	79%	2.98	58	17	25	1.6	5.8	3.5	14%	1.0	11.9	85	$13
Pre-Peak	04	MON	6	12	2	90	63	2.70	1.19	266	246	282	4.6	31%	79%	3.06	54	19	26	1.5	6.3	4.2	8%	0.6	17.4	110	$11
Type Finesse	05	WAS	8	7	1	71	40	2.66	1.25	273	350	230	4.4	30%	83%	3.82	43	23	34	1.8	5.1	2.9	9%	0.9	13.9	64	$10
Reliability 0	06	WAS	0	0	0	0	0	0.00	0.00																		
DL 183	1st Half		0	0	0	0	0	0.00	0.00																		
ERA Potl	2nd Half		0	0	0	0	0	0.00	0.00																		
LIMA Plan C+	07	Proj	5	4	3	43	27	3.77	1.26	266			4.5	30%	72%	3.47	51	20	29	2.1	5.7	2.7	10%	0.8	4.7	67	$6

Torn labrum in March made him the most notable casualty of the WBC. Aiming to be ready for spring training. Typical 18-month recovery would put him at full strength much later in the season.

Backe,Brandon

	Yr	Tm	W	L	Sv	IP	K	ERA	WHIP	OBA	vL	vR	BF/G	H%	S%	xERA	G	L	F	Ctl	Dom	Cmd	hr/f	hr/9	RAR	BPV	R$
RH Starter	02	aa	4	6	2	105	42	6.26	1.65	299			16.5	31%	63%	5.65				4.0	3.6	0.9		1.2	-25.7	-0	($3)
Age 29	03	TAM	3	2	0	77	59	5.73	1.53	267	302	220	7.8	31%	62%	4.37	26	42	32	4.6	6.9	1.5	9%	0.8	-11.4	50	$2
Pre-Peak	04	HOU *	11	8	0	131	114	3.84	1.48	276	347	253	11.1	32%	78%	3.90	40	21	39	3.6	7.8	2.2	12%	1.2	6.8	55	$10
Type	05	HOU	10	8	0	149	97	4.77	1.46	264	260	266	25.1	29%	70%	4.43	42	20	38	4.0	5.9	1.4	10%	1.1	-9.6	33	$7
Reliability 0	06	HOU	3	2	0	43	19	3.77	1.42	262	317	205	23.3	28%	75%	5.09	36	20	44	3.8	4.0	1.1	6%	0.8	3.8	24	$3
DL 141 40	1st Half		1	0	0	8	3	2.25	0.75	151			14.7	9%	100%	3.68	52	9	39	2.3	3.4	1.5	22%	2.3	2.2	9	$2
ERA Potl	2nd Half		2	2	0	35	16	4.11	1.57	283			26.2	31%	74%	5.41	33	22	45	4.1	4.1	1.0	4%	0.5	1.6	29	$1
LIMA Plan	07	Proj	0	0	0	0	0	0.00	0.00																		

Had Tommy John surgery in September, will likely miss all of 2007.

Baek,Cha Seung

	Yr	Tm	W	L	Sv	IP	K	ERA	WHIP	OBA	vL	vR	BF/G	H%	S%	xERA	G	L	F	Ctl	Dom	Cmd	hr/f	hr/9	RAR	BPV	R$
RH Starter	02		0	0	0	0	0	0.00	0.00																		
Age 26	03	aa	3	3	0	56	40	3.31	1.36	268			26.6	32%	75%	3.67				3.0	6.4	2.1		0.3	7.5	75	$5
Growth	04	aaa	3	4	0	72	52	4.74	1.62	314			23.4	36%	72%	5.54				3.0	6.5	2.2		0.9	-3.5	51	$2
Type	05	aaa	8	8	0	112	65	7.05	1.73	334			21.7	36%	61%	6.74				2.8	5.2	1.8		1.5	-38.0	12	($3)
Reliability 0	06	SEA *	16	5	0	181	113	3.62	1.28	260	211	206	25.4	28%	77%	4.03	43	17	40	2.6	5.6	2.2	11%	1.2	21.0	46	$20
DL 15	1st Half		7	4	0	86	46	3.88	1.45	292			25.1	31%	78%					2.6	4.8	1.8		1.3	7.2	25	$7
ERA Potl 40%	2nd Half		9	1	0	95	68	3.38	1.13	229			25.6	25%	75%	3.69	43	17	40	2.6	6.4	2.5	11%	1.2	13.8	65	$14
LIMA Plan D+	07	Proj	10	12	0	174	112	4.55	1.44	286			24.5	32%	71%	4.20	43	17	40	2.7	5.8	2.1	10%	1.1	6.2	43	$10

4-1, 3.67 in 34.3 IP at SEA. Regained prospect status after getting DFA'd last winter, then went PQS-DOM in 4 of 6 Sept. starts. Marginal DOM limits upside, but an intriguing speculative pick.

Baez,Danys

	Yr	Tm	W	L	Sv	IP	K	ERA	WHIP	OBA	vL	vR	BF/G	H%	S%	xERA	G	L	F	Ctl	Dom	Cmd	hr/f	hr/9	RAR	BPV	R$
RH Reliever	02	CLE	10	11	6	165	130	4.42	1.47	256	278	233	18.6	30%	71%	4.30	40	20	40	4.5	7.1	1.6	7%	0.8	0.8	57	$12
Age 29	03	CLE	2	9	25	75	66	3.84	1.17	235	285	165	4.2	28%	71%	3.32	44	19	37	2.8	7.9	2.9	12%	1.1	6.3	83	$16
Peak	04	TAM	4	4	30	68	52	3.57	1.31	238	252	223	4.6	28%	75%	4.12	42	16	43	3.8	6.9	1.8	7%	0.8	7.2	62	$17
Type	05	TAM	5	4	41	72	51	2.87	1.33	245	268	215	4.6	28%	82%	3.90	47	20	33	3.7	6.4	1.7	10%	0.9	13.3	54	$21
Reliability 49	06	2NL	5	6	9	59	39	4.56	1.30	264	295	244	4.4	31%	64%	4.17	40	17	43	2.6	5.9	2.3	4%	0.5	-0.5	72	$8
DL 38	1st Half		4	4	9	39	25	4.36	1.35	289			4.7	33%	67%	4.08	39	20	41	1.8	5.7	3.1	4%	0.5	0.6	83	$7
ERA Potl 60%	2nd Half		1	2	0	20	14	4.95	1.20	210			3.9	25%	57%	4.36	41	12	47	4.0	6.3	1.6	4%	0.4	-1.1	70	$1
LIMA Plan C+	07	Proj	4	5	8	64	45	3.97	1.29	245			4.5	28%	70%	4.09	42	17	41	3.4	6.4	1.9	6%	0.7	2.1	62	$8

BPIs stayed largely intact as he lost grip on LA closer role, then got sent to ATL. Skills were never classically closer-worthy, so even if he lands in the role again, don't assume success.

Bailey,Homer

	Yr	Tm	W	L	Sv	IP	K	ERA	WHIP	OBA	vL	vR	BF/G	H%	S%	xERA	G	L	F	Ctl	Dom	Cmd	hr/f	hr/9	RAR	BPV	R$
RH Starter	02		0	0	0	0	0	0.00	0.00																		
Age 21	03		0	0	0	0	0	0.00	0.00																		
Green	04		0	0	0	0	0	0.00	0.00																		
Type Power	05		0	0	0	0	0	0.00	0.00																		
Reliability 0	06	aa	7	1	0	68	68	2.02	1.25	230			21.8	31%	83%	2.62				3.7	9.0	2.5		0.1	21.0	111	$12
DL	1st Half		2	0	0	12	10	0.75	0.83	171			22.5	23%	90%					2.3	7.5	3.3		0.0	5.6	136	$3
ERA Potl 50%	2nd Half		5	1	0	56	58	2.29	1.34	241			21.7	33%	82%					4.0	9.4	2.4		0.2	15.4	108	$8
LIMA Plan B+	07	Proj	5	2	0	58	66	3.26	1.47	258			21.2	36%	76%	3.58				4.3	10.2	2.4		0.2	6.0	110	$7

Was lights-out in Double-A, CIN resisted moving him to Triple-A or the majors late in the year. Not that there has to be one every year, but: if you're looking for 2007's Verlander, this is an excellent candidate.

Baker,Scott

	Yr	Tm	W	L	Sv	IP	K	ERA	WHIP	OBA	vL	vR	BF/G	H%	S%	xERA	G	L	F	Ctl	Dom	Cmd	hr/f	hr/9	RAR	BPV	R$
RH Starter	02		0	0	0	0	0	0.00	0.00											0.0	0.0						
Age 25	03		0	0	0	0	0	0.00	0.00											0.0	0.0						
Growth	04	a/a	6	6	0	124	96	4.42	1.26	266			27.3	32%	63%	3.43				2.1	7.0	3.3		0.4	-1.2	102	$9
Type	05	MIN *	8	11	0	187	125	3.60	1.23	263	221	257	24.3	29%	74%	3.86	40	19	41	2.0	6.0	3.0	9%	1.0	17.8	72	$17
Reliability 14	06	MIN *	10	12	0	167	119	5.19	1.54	310	349	299	26.6	35%	68%	4.42	34	19	47	2.4	6.4	2.6	8%	1.2	-13.0	51	$7
DL	1st Half		4	6	0	84	66	4.94	1.51	300			26.6	35%	70%	4.45	28	21	51	2.7	7.0	2.6	8%	1.2	-4.0	57	$4
ERA Potl 60%	2nd Half		6	6	0	83	54	5.43	1.57	320			26.7	35%	67%	4.30	42	17	42	2.2	5.8	2.7	9%	1.2	-9.0	46	$3
LIMA Plan C	07	Proj	11	11	0	195	136	4.29	1.39	289			26.3	33%	72%	4.17	36	19	45	2.2	6.3	2.8	8%	1.0	7.7	64	$14

5-8, 6.37 in 83 IP at MIN. Skills were far better than his ERA would suggest, elevated H% did him in. Needs to figure out LH hitters and keep the ball down more, but if he does... UP: 15 Wins, 3.80 ERA.

Bannister,Brian

	Yr	Tm	W	L	Sv	IP	K	ERA	WHIP	OBA	vL	vR	BF/G	H%	S%	xERA	G	L	F	Ctl	Dom	Cmd	hr/f	hr/9	RAR	BPV	R$
RH Starter	02		0	0	0	0	0	0.00	0.00																		
Age 26	03		0	0	0	0	0	0.00	0.00																		
Growth	04	aa	3	3	0	44	23	4.84	1.57	293			24.7	33%	68%	4.68				3.6	4.8	1.3		0.4	-2.7	40	$1
Type	05	a/a	13	5	0	154	115	3.19	1.29	266			25.0	31%	77%	3.77				2.4	6.7	2.8		0.7	21.2	81	$17
Reliability 0	06	NYM *	5	4	0	68	40	4.78	1.52	285	286	185	21.6	31%	71%	4.77	40	15	45	3.6	5.3	1.5	9%	1.2	-2.5	25	$3
DL 130	1st Half		2	1	0	28	14	2.88	1.42	225			20.3	24%	82%	5.28	43	12	44	5.4	4.5	0.8	5%	0.6	5.6	35	$3
ERA Potl 50%	2nd Half		3	3	0	40	26	6.12	1.59	321			22.5	35%	64%	4.55	31	23	46	2.3	5.8	2.6	11%	1.6	-8.0	32	$0
LIMA Plan C	07	Proj	8	6	0	108	69	4.33	1.45	281			23.6	31%	72%	4.51	40	15	45	3.2	5.8	1.8	7%	0.9	-2.0	44	$6

2-1, 4.26 in 38 IP at NYM. Soft-tosser was hampered by injuries in 2006. Needs to recapture prior skills to have value, don't bid more than a buck on that possibility.

Batista,Miguel

	Yr	Tm	W	L	Sv	IP	K	ERA	WHIP	OBA	vL	vR	BF/G	H%	S%	xERA	G	L	F	Ctl	Dom	Cmd	hr/f	hr/9	RAR	BPV	R$
RH Starter	02	ARI	8	9	0	184	112	4.30	1.32	249	269	223	21.6	28%	67%	3.90	54	15	32	3.4	5.5	1.6	7%	0.6	-4.5	54	$10
Age 36	03	ARI	10	9	0	193	142	3.54	1.33	266	297	241	22.8	31%	74%	3.40	53	19	27	2.8	6.6	2.4	8%	0.6	17.5	73	$15
Decline	04	TOR	10	13	5	198	104	4.81	1.52	269	264	285	23.2	29%	70%	4.38	52	18	29	4.4	4.7	1.1	11%	1.0	-9.3	22	$7
Type	05	TOR	5	8	31	74	54	4.12	1.44	277	256	282	4.6	31%	74%	3.84	48	19	33	3.3	6.5	2.0	12%	1.1	2.3	48	$15
Reliability 78	06	ARI	11	8	0	206	110	4.59	1.53	284	321	257	27.0	31%	71%	4.21	52	20	28	3.7	4.8	1.3	9%	0.8	-2.5	31	$7
DL	1st Half		7	5	0	96	58	5.24	1.73	317			27.9	35%	71%	4.23	50	23	27	3.7	5.4	1.5	13%	1.1	-8.9	21	$1
ERA Potl 45%	2nd Half		4	3	0	110	52	4.01	1.36	253			26.1	28%	70%	4.18	54	17	29	3.6	4.3	1.2	6%	0.5	6.4	40	$6
LIMA Plan C	07	Proj	10	10	0	174	103	4.40	1.47	275			26.3	30%	72%	4.08	51	19	30	3.6	5.3	1.5	10%	0.9	6.2	37	$8

Returned to the rotation and gradually regained former GB%. Cmd has always been questionable as an SP, but a high GB% can make an otherwise ugly skill set serviceable.

RAY MURPHY

Bauer,Rick

	Yr	Tm	W	L	Sv	IP	K	ERA	WHIP	OBA	vL	vR	BF/G	H%	S%	xERA	G	L	F	Ctl	Dom	Cmd	hr/f	hr/9	RAR	BPV	R$
RH Reliever	02	BAL	6	8	1	87	46	4.24	1.46	266	288	253	6.7	27%	76%	4.29	50	19	31	3.9	4.8	**1.2**	16%	1.4	2.3	12	$5
Age 30	03	BAL *	3	1	0	97	60	4.08	1.36	258	247	261	9.9	29%	70%	4.19	46	18	36	3.4	5.6	**1.6**	5%	0.6	5.3	54	$6
Peak	04	BAL *	5	6	0	119	70	5.06	1.54	297	293	193	15.2	33%	67%	3.95	56	16	28	3.2	5.3	**1.7**	8%	0.7	-9.2	42	$2
Type Finesse	05	aaa	3	8	0	73	34	5.43	1.93	336			12.2	34%	77%	7.59				4.5	4.2	**0.9**		1.9	-10.1	-23	($3)
Reliability 3	06	TEX	3	1	2	71	35	3.55	1.38	267	231	299	5.3	29%	74%	4.11	53	17	30	3.2	4.4	**1.4**	6%	0.5	8.8	42	$6
DL	1st Half		2	1	1	39	23	3.44	1.61	294			6.3	34%	76%	4.37	49	21	30	3.9	5.3	**1.4**	0%	0.0	5.4	56	$3
ERA Potl 40%	2nd Half		1	0	1	32	12	3.68	1.10	231			4.3	23%	71%	3.78	57	13	30	2.3	3.4	**1.5**	13%	1.1	3.4	27	$3
LIMA Plan D+	07	Proj	**2**	**3**	**1**	**59**	**29**	**4.31**	**1.50**	**286**			**4.7**	**30%**	**74%**	**4.24**	**53**	**16**	**30**	**3.4**	**4.5**	**1.3**	**11%**	**1.1**	**1.8**	**20**	**$2**

Manages to survive with low DOM by generating GBs in bunches. With no shot at saves and very few K's, the risks of rostering him far outweigh the rewards.

Bautista,Denny

	Yr	Tm	W	L	Sv	IP	K	ERA	WHIP	OBA	vL	vR	BF/G	H%	S%	xERA	G	L	F	Ctl	Dom	Cmd	hr/f	hr/9	RAR	BPV	R$
RH Starter	02		0	0	0	0	0	0.00	0.00											0.0	0.0						
Age 26	03	aa	4	5	0	53	58	4.36	1.58	245			21.7	32%	73%	4.32				6.0	9.8	**1.6**		0.8	0.2	75	$4
Growth	04	aa	7	8	0	144	119	5.39	1.63	292			25.2	35%	67%	5.07				4.2	7.4	**1.8**		0.7	-18.6	56	$2
Type Power	05	KC	2	2	0	35	23	5.88	1.51	266	288	220	22.3	31%	59%	3.64	64	13	23	4.3	5.9	**1.4**	8%	0.5	-6.6	50	$1
Reliability 0	06	2TM *	3	12	0	121	79	7.90	2.02	336	272	294	21.4	38%	59%	4.95	49	19	32	5.3	5.9	**1.1**	8%	0.8	-50.6	22	($11)
DL 25 140	1st Half		0	4	0	47	31	7.17	1.74	303			19.9	34%	59%	4.49	50	17	32	4.6	5.9	**1.3**	12%	1.2	-15.4	22	($3)
ERA Potl 65%	2nd Half		3	8	0	74	49	8.36	2.19	355			22.3	41%	59%	5.30	42	29	29	5.7	5.9	**1.0**	6%	0.6	-35.2	22	($9)
LIMA Plan D	07	Proj	**3**	**7**	**0**	**83**	**58**	**5.53**	**1.81**	**304**			**21.8**	**35%**	**69%**	**4.25**	**58**	**16**	**27**	**5.2**	**6.3**	**1.2**	**9%**	**0.8**	**1.8**	**35**	**($2)**

0-3, 5.62 ERA in 41.7 IP at KC and COL. Once displayed a tantalizing combo of high DOM/ high GB%, but both of those former strengths are trending down. Too young to write off, but a very dangerous play.

Beckett,Josh

	Yr	Tm	W	L	Sv	IP	K	ERA	WHIP	OBA	vL	vR	BF/G	H%	S%	xERA	G	L	F	Ctl	Dom	Cmd	hr/f	hr/9	RAR	BPV	R$
RH Starter	02	FLA	6	7	0	107	113	4.12	1.28	236	246	218	19.5	30%	71%	3.52	34	23	43	3.7	9.5	**2.6**	11%	1.1	-0.2	86	$9
Age 26	03	FLA	9	8	0	142	152	3.04	1.32	248	220	267	25.1	33%	78%	3.15	44	24	32	3.5	9.6	**2.7**	7%	0.6	21.7	103	$16
Growth	04	FLA	9	9	0	156	152	3.80	1.22	237	281	192	24.9	30%	71%	3.25	46	17	37	3.1	8.8	**2.8**	10%	0.9	8.8	92	$16
Type Power	05	FLA	15	8	0	178	166	3.38	1.18	233	217	252	25.2	29%	73%	3.28	43	22	36	2.9	8.4	**2.9**	8%	0.7	18.9	98	$22
Reliability 62	06	BOS	16	11	0	204	158	5.02	1.30	249	251	238	26.1	27%	66%	3.73	45	17	38	3.3	7.0	**2.1**	16%	1.6	-11.8	44	$18
DL 30	1st Half		10	3	0	97	82	4.64	1.18	233			24.8	25%	68%	3.52	44	14	43	2.9	7.6	**2.6**	17%	1.9	-1.0	54	$12
ERA Potl 60%	2nd Half		6	8	0	107	76	5.37	1.41	263			27.3	29%	64%	3.91	46	20	33	3.6	6.4	**1.8**	14%	1.3	-10.8	37	$6
LIMA Plan C	07	Proj	**15**	**11**	**0**	**203**	**176**	**4.30**	**1.27**	**244**			**25.0**	**29%**	**69%**	**3.52**	**44**	**19**	**37**	**3.2**	**7.8**	**2.4**	**12%**	**1.2**	**24.1**	**69**	**$21**

Spike in HR/9 destroyed him. HR/F says some of that was unlucky, but DOM is in four-year decline. Finally threw 200 IP, but if he traded dominance for endurance, the end result is far less appealing.

Bedard,Erik

	Yr	Tm	W	L	Sv	IP	K	ERA	WHIP	OBA	vL	vR	BF/G	H%	S%	xERA	G	L	F	Ctl	Dom	Cmd	hr/f	hr/9	RAR	BPV	R$
LH Starter	02	aa	6	3	0	68	54	2.38	1.18	204			21.4	26%	78%	2.03				4.1	7.1	**1.7**		0.0	15.8	94	$10
Age 28	03		0	0	0	0	0	0.00	0.00											0.0	0.0						
Pre-Peak	04	BAL	6	10	0	137	121	4.60	1.60	278	277	269	23.0	34%	72%	4.36	38	19	42	4.7	7.9	**1.7**	7%	0.9	-2.8	57	$5
Type Power	05	BAL	6	8	0	141	125	4.02	1.39	259	252	263	25.3	32%	72%	3.77	40	23	37	3.6	8.0	**2.2**	7%	0.6	6.2	78	$11
Reliability 54	06	BAL	15	11	0	196	171	3.76	1.35	262	200	272	25.4	32%	73%	3.35	49	21	30	3.2	7.8	**2.5**	9%	0.7	19.2	80	$21
DL 53	1st Half		8	6	0	95	75	4.73	1.46	277			24.5	32%	69%	3.61	49	22	29	3.4	7.1	**2.1**	12%	0.9	-2.0	57	$7
ERA Potl 55%	2nd Half		7	5	0	101	96	2.85	1.25	246			26.3	32%	78%	3.12	49	20	31	2.9	8.6	**2.9**	7%	0.5	21.3	102	$14
LIMA Plan C	07	Proj	**15**	**10**	**0**	**203**	**180**	**3.50**	**1.33**	**257**			**24.6**	**32%**	**75%**	**3.48**	**45**	**21**	**34**	**3.1**	**8.0**	**2.5**	**7%**	**0.6**	**25.1**	**86**	**$23**

Long-anticipated breakout came in June, as he reeled of 16 PQS-DOM outings over 18 starts. GB% and CMD both rising, carrying him into the AL's elite. If he can sustain 2nd half: UP: 20 Wins, 3.00 ERA.

Beimel,Joe

	Yr	Tm	W	L	Sv	IP	K	ERA	WHIP	OBA	vL	vR	BF/G	H%	S%	xERA	G	L	F	Ctl	Dom	Cmd	hr/f	hr/9	RAR	BPV	R$
LH Reliever	02	PIT	2	5	0	85	53	4.66	1.56	269	262	269	7.2	30%	72%	4.30	47	27	27	4.0	5.6	**1.2**	12%	1.0	-5.8	31	$1
Age 30	03	PIT	1	3	0	62	42	5.07	1.64	283	311	288	4.1	32%	71%	4.52	35	36	29	4.8	6.1	**1.3**	12%	1.0	-0.1	31	($1)
Peak	04	aaa	2	4	2	62	37	8.71	2.02	361			6.3	39%	58%	8.28				3.8	5.4	**1.4**		1.8	-33.4	-10	($7)
Type Finesse	05	aaa	1	2	0	52	29	4.08	1.61	301			4.9	34%	74%	4.82				3.5	5.0	**1.4**		0.4	1.5	43	$1
Reliability 1	06	LA *	5	1	2	83	37	2.73	1.26	252	234	277	4.8	27%	81%	3.97	57	11	32	2.8	4.0	**1.5**	8%	0.8	18.0	37	$9
DL	1st Half		5	1	1	41	16	2.88	1.17	245			5.0	26%	76%	3.88	57	12	31	2.3	3.6	**1.6**	5%	0.4	8.2	47	$6
ERA Potl 25%	2nd Half		0	0	1	42	21	2.58	1.34	258			4.7	27%	86%	4.05	56	11	33	3.2	4.5	**1.4**	11%	1.1	9.8	28	$3
LIMA Plan C+	07	Proj	**2**	**2**	**0**	**69**	**36**	**4.20**	**1.50**	**285**			**5.1**	**31%**	**74%**	**4.26**	**48**	**22**	**30**	**3.4**	**4.7**	**1.4**	**10%**	**0.9**	**0.9**	**28**	**$2**

2-1, 2.96 ERA in 70 IP at LA. Infield defense worked wonders behind him, turning GBs into outs at a remarkable rate. xERA shows what these skills should have yielded. Don't expect another sub-4.00 ERA.

Belisle,Matt

	Yr	Tm	W	L	Sv	IP	K	ERA	WHIP	OBA	vL	vR	BF/G	H%	S%	xERA	G	L	F	Ctl	Dom	Cmd	hr/f	hr/9	RAR	BPV	R$
RH Reliever	02	aa	5	9	0	159	103	5.03	1.37	287			26.3	32%	65%	4.65				2.1	5.8	**2.8**		1.1	-15.0	59	$5
Age 26	03	a/a	8	12	0	171	102	5.21	1.62	319			27.7	36%	67%	5.33				2.7	5.4	**2.0**		0.6	-17.2	48	$2
Growth	04	aaa	9	11	0	162	89	5.88	1.60	316			26.2	34%	64%	5.66				2.7	4.9	**1.8**		1.0	-30.8	30	($0)
Type	05	CIN	4	8	1	85	59	4.44	1.49	296	331	273	6.3	33%	73%	3.54	52	21	26	2.7	6.2	**2.3**	15%	1.2	-2.0	46	$4
Reliability 0	06	CIN	2	0	0	40	26	3.60	1.55	276	240	295	6.0	30%	81%	4.36	48	17	35	4.3	5.9	**1.4**	11%	1.1	4.4	30	$2
DL 65	1st Half		2	0	0	19	14	3.75	1.46	260			5.6	30%	77%	4.22	47	15	38	4.2	6.6	**1.6**	9%	0.9	1.7	47	$2
ERA Potl 30%	2nd Half		0	0	0	21	12	3.46	1.63	290			6.3	31%	84%	4.49	49	19	32	4.3	5.2	**1.2**	13%	1.3	2.6	14	$0
LIMA Plan C+	07	Proj	**4**	**3**	**0**	**87**	**55**	**4.24**	**1.55**	**292**			**7.6**	**32%**	**76%**	**4.11**	**50**	**19**	**32**	**3.5**	**5.7**	**1.6**	**12%**	**1.1**	**2.7**	**31**	**$3**

Hit the DL twice with back problems, which likely led to the BPI dip. Got a late-season audition as SP. If he can recover 2004's skills, he could have some value in that role. Worth a flier.

Benitez,Armando

	Yr	Tm	W	L	Sv	IP	K	ERA	WHIP	OBA	vL	vR	BF/G	H%	S%	xERA	G	L	F	Ctl	Dom	Cmd	hr/f	hr/9	RAR	BPV	R$
RH Reliever	02	NYM	1	0	33	67	79	2.28	1.06	196	160	220	4.3	26%	86%	3.13	29	23	48	3.4	10.6	**3.2**	11%	1.1	15.1	114	$20
Age 34	03	2TM	4	4	21	73	75	2.96	1.37	223	214	221	4.5	29%	81%	3.94	35	22	43	5.1	9.2	**1.8**	7%	0.7	12.9	82	$15
Past Peak	04	FLA	2	2	47	69	62	1.30	0.82	156	168	140	4.0	18%	92%	3.48	30	17	53	2.7	8.1	**3.0**	7%	0.8	25.3	111	$27
Type Power	05	SF	2	3	19	30	23	4.50	1.37	228	212	246	4.3	25%	72%	4.64	32	18	50	4.8	6.9	**1.4**	12%	1.5	-0.9	36	$8
Reliability 8	06	SF	4	2	17	38	31	3.54	1.57	266	270	265	4.2	30%	83%	4.71	32	21	47	5.0	7.3	**1.5**	11%	1.4	4.4	34	$9
DL 36 110	1st Half		4	1	6	18	14	2.49	1.71	271			4.7	31%	90%	5.25	30	23	46	6.0	7.0	**1.2**	8%	1.0	4.5	37	$5
ERA Potl 30%	2nd Half		0	1	11	20	17	4.50	1.45	262			3.8	29%	76%	4.25	34	19	47	4.0	7.6	**1.9**	14%	1.8	-0.0	34	$4
LIMA Plan C	07	Proj	**3**	**2**	**10**	**43**	**36**	**3.98**	**1.47**	**257**			**4.3**	**30%**	**77%**	**4.47**	**32**	**20**	**48**	**4.4**	**7.5**	**1.7**	**10%**	**1.3**	**-0.6**	**47**	**$6**

Chronic knee problems have knocked him from the ranks of elite closers, and the possibility of more surgery looms. Even if he does get back to closing, there's little reason to think he can succeed.

Benoit,Joaquin

	Yr	Tm	W	L	Sv	IP	K	ERA	WHIP	OBA	vL	vR	BF/G	H%	S%	xERA	G	L	F	Ctl	Dom	Cmd	hr/f	hr/9	RAR	BPV	R$
RH Reliever	02	TEX *	12	9	1	182	148	4.65	1.46	252	275	268	24.2	30%	68%	4.41	38	18	44	4.6	7.3	**1.6**	6%	0.7	-4.2	61	$12
Age 29	03	TEX *	10	6	0	138	113	5.48	1.42	256	222	272	19.3	28%	66%	4.21	35	20	44	4.0	7.4	**1.8**	15%	1.8	-16.2	33	$8
Peak	04	TEX	3	5	0	103	95	5.68	1.40	280	249	311	15.9	32%	63%	3.81	34	19	47	2.7	8.3	**3.1**	13%	1.7	-15.8	63	$4
Type Power	05	TEX	4	4	0	87	78	3.72	1.23	220	227	196	11.3	26%	72%	3.99	33	19	48	3.9	8.1	**2.1**	8%	0.9	6.9	75	$9
Reliability 23	06	TEX	1	1	0	79	85	4.89	1.34	233	191	245	6.0	31%	62%	3.67	37	19	44	4.3	9.7	**2.2**	5%	0.6	-3.2	96	$5
DL 53	1st Half		0	1	0	37	41	5.08	1.45	228			5.6	31%	63%	3.89	39	19	42	5.6	9.9	**1.8**	5%	0.5	-2.4	92	$2
ERA Potl 75%	2nd Half		1	0	0	42	44	4.71	1.24	238			6.5	31%	61%	3.49	36	18	46	3.2	9.4	**2.9**	6%	0.6	-0.8	106	$4
LIMA Plan B+	07	Proj	**2**	**2**	**0**	**73**	**71**	**4.10**	**1.32**	**241**			**8.5**	**30%**	**71%**	**3.82**	**35**	**19**	**46**	**3.8**	**8.8**	**2.3**	**8%**	**0.9**	**6.0**	**82**	**$6**

Finally stranded some runners in 2005, but couldn't sustain that. Skills have outshined performance for years. Tempting to give up, but you can't ignore the BPV trend. Great end-game target.

Benson,Kris

	Yr	Tm	W	L	Sv	IP	K	ERA	WHIP	OBA	vL	vR	BF/G	H%	S%	xERA	G	L	F	Ctl	Dom	Cmd	hr/f	hr/9	RAR	BPV	R$
RH Starter	02	PIT *	10	8	0	154	102	4.32	1.48	280	313	281	22.6	31%	74%	4.39	42	17	41	3.4	6.0	**1.7**	10%	1.2	-4.1	36	$7
Age 32	03	PIT	5	9	0	105	68	4.97	1.55	300	339	260	26.1	33%	70%	4.69	34	20	47	3.1	5.8	**1.9**	8%	1.2	-9.0	34	$2
Peak	04	2NL	12	12	0	200	134	4.32	1.31	264	276	251	27.3	30%	67%	3.99	42	20	38	2.7	6.0	**2.2**	6%	0.7	-1.4	64	$13
Type Finesse	05	NYM	10	8	0	174	95	4.14	1.26	258	268	240	26.0	27%	71%	4.06	44	19	37	2.5	4.9	**1.9**	12%	1.2	2.4	36	$12
Reliability 73	06	BAL	11	12	0	183	88	4.82	1.40	278	303	270	26.4	28%	71%	4.51	41	19	39	2.9	4.3	**1.5**	13%	1.6	-5.9	8	$10
DL 17 31	1st Half		9	5	0	104	49	4.23	1.31	254			26.0	26%	71%	4.52	42	18	39	3.2	4.2	**1.3**	10%	1.1	4.2	24	$9
ERA Potl 40%	2nd Half		2	7	0	79	39	5.60	1.52	308			26.9	30%	71%	4.48	40	21	40	2.4	4.5	**1.9**	18%	2.3	-10.1	-9	$1
LIMA Plan D+	07	Proj	**10**	**11**	**0**	**178**	**97**	**4.65**	**1.38**	**277**			**26.4**	**29%**	**71%**	**4.31**	**42**	**19**	**39**	**2.7**	**4.9**	**1.8**	**12%**	**1.4**	**3.9**	**24**	**$10**

DOM and CMD continue to erode. 23/37 DOM/DIS says that he's not good that often, and when he's bad he's really bad. Even Leo Mazzone can't turn this skill set into lemonade.

RAY MURPHY

Bergmann,Jason

			W	L	Sv	IP	K	ERA	WHIP	OBA	vL	vR	BF/G	H%	S%	xERA	G	L	F	Ctl	Dom	Cmd	hr/f	hr/9	RAR	BPV	R$
RH	Reliever	02	0	0	0	0	0	0.00	0.00																		
Age	25	03	0	0	0	0	0	0.00	0.00																		
Growth		04	0	0	0	0	0	0.00	0.00																		
Type	Power	05 a/a	5	2	7	74	66	2.31	1.12	212			7.3	26%	84%	2.80				3.3	8.0	**2.4**		0.9	18.2	87	$13
Reliability	0	06 WAS *	8	4	4	124	105	5.38	1.54	289	255	353	10.1	34%	67%	4.25	32	24	45	3.5	7.6	**2.2**	10%	1.2	-13.6	52	$6
DL		1st Half	4	1	4	46	36	4.11	1.61	290			6.3	34%	76%	4.38	38	25	38	4.1	7.0	**1.7**	7%	0.8	2.1	51	$4
ERA Potl	60%	2nd Half	4	3	0	78	70	6.13	1.49	289			15.7	34%	61%	4.11	29	24	47	3.1	8.0	**2.6**	12%	1.5	-15.8	54	$2
LIMA Plan	C+	07 Proj	**4**	**3**	**0**	**73**	**63**	**4.10**	**1.38**	**260**			**8.7**	**31%**	**74%**	**4.03**	**32**	**24**	**44**	**3.5**	**7.8**	**2.3**	**10%**	**1.1**	**3.0**	**64**	**$5**

0-2, 6.68 ERA in 65 IP at WAS. Massive blowup coming off a promising 2005, but skill levels were basically the same. Auditioned as a starter late in the season, so role is unclear. Worth a minimum bid.

Betancourt,Rafael

			W	L	Sv	IP	K	ERA	WHIP	OBA	vL	vR	BF/G	H%	S%	xERA	G	L	F	Ctl	Dom	Cmd	hr/f	hr/9	RAR	BPV	R$
RH	Reliever	02	0	0	0	0	0	0.00	0.00											0.0	0.0						
Age	32	03 CLE *	2	2	18	90	95	2.40	1.27	244	270	133	5.5	32%	83%	3.94	21	19	59	3.2	9.5	**3.0**	4%	0.6	23.6	108	$18
Peak		04 CLE	5	6	4	66	76	3.94	1.34	276	272	264	4.2	37%	73%	3.18	38	19	44	2.4	10.3	**4.2**	9%	1.0	4.0	122	$9
Type	Power	05 CLE	4	3	1	67	73	2.81	1.10	231	264	204	5.0	31%	77%	3.11	33	22	44	2.3	9.8	**4.3**	6%	0.7	12.9	138	$11
Reliability	20	06 CLE	3	4	3	56	48	3.84	1.12	247	221	254	4.5	29%	70%	3.74	23	25	51	1.8	7.7	**4.4**	8%	1.1	5.0	110	$8
DL	25 / 17	1st Half	0	3	0	23	19	3.90	1.08	235			4.0	27%	68%	3.68	25	27	48	1.9	7.4	**3.8**	9%	1.2	1.9	97	$2
ERA Potl	60%	2nd Half	3	1	3	33	29	3.81	1.15	255			5.0	30%	71%	3.78	22	24	54	1.6	7.9	**4.8**	8%	1.1	3.1	120	$6
LIMA Plan	A	07 Proj	**3**	**4**	**5**	**58**	**57**	**3.41**	**1.17**	**248**			**4.7**	**31%**	**74%**	**3.51**	**28**	**23**	**49**	**2.2**	**8.8**	**4.1**	**8%**	**0.9**	**7.0**	**116**	**$9**

Was lights-out outside of one stretch in June. Despite chaos in CLE pen, never got save opps. One reason: a perception he can't pitch on consecutive days. He's a safe pick, with upside.

Billingsley,Chad

			W	L	Sv	IP	K	ERA	WHIP	OBA	vL	vR	BF/G	H%	S%	xERA	G	L	F	Ctl	Dom	Cmd	hr/f	hr/9	RAR	BPV	R$
RH	Starter	02	0	0	0	0	0	0.00	0.00																		
Age	22	03	0	0	0	0	0	0.00	0.00																		
Growth		04 aa	4	1	0	42	42	3.26	1.31	224			22.3	30%	74%	2.85				4.5	9.0	**2.0**		0.2	5.6	100	$5
Type	Power	05 aa	13	6	0	146	136	3.64	1.16	229			21.3	29%	70%	2.99				2.9	8.4	**2.9**		0.7	12.0	98	$19
Reliability	0	06 LA *	13	7	0	160	128	3.79	1.47	247	328	213	22.7	29%	76%	4.12	48	16	36	4.9	7.2	**1.5**	8%	0.8	13.7	57	$13
DL		1st Half	6	4	0	86	75	4.13	1.34	234			23.0	28%	71%	3.46	55	15	30	4.3	7.9	**1.8**	10%	0.8	3.8	69	$8
ERA Potl	50%	2nd Half	7	3	0	74	53	3.41	1.61	262			22.3	30%	81%	4.67	47	16	37	5.5	6.4	**1.2**	7%	0.7	9.9	44	$6
LIMA Plan	C+	07 Proj	**12**	**6**	**0**	**142**	**122**	**4.26**	**1.39**	**246**			**22.6**	**30%**	**70%**	**3.80**	**48**	**16**	**36**	**4.2**	**7.8**	**1.8**	**7%**	**0.7**	**9.8**	**70**	**$12**

7-4, 3.80 ERA in 90 IP at LA. Battled CMD problems that got worse in the majors (1.0 CMD w/LA). Hype and MLB ERA will drive up interest, percentage play is to expect more growing pains.

Blanton,Joe

			W	L	Sv	IP	K	ERA	WHIP	OBA	vL	vR	BF/G	H%	S%	xERA	G	L	F	Ctl	Dom	Cmd	hr/f	hr/9	RAR	BPV	R$
RH	Starter	02	0	0	0	0	0	0.00	0.00											0.0	0.0						
Age	26	03 aa	3	1	1	35	26	1.53	0.85	188			19.0	23%	83%	1.31				1.8	6.6	**3.7**		0.3	12.4	128	$8
Growth		04 aaa	11	8	0	176	121	4.40	1.39	299			27.1	35%	69%	4.54				1.7	6.2	**3.7**		0.7	-1.1	89	$11
Type	Finesse	05 OAK	12	12	0	201	116	3.54	1.22	239	228	246	25.2	26%	75%	4.05	46	17	38	3.0	5.2	**1.7**	10%	1.0	20.7	44	$19
Reliability	58	06 OAK	16	12	0	194	107	4.82	1.54	306	314	304	27.1	34%	69%	4.43	43	20	37	2.7	5.0	**1.8**	7%	0.8	-6.3	39	$10
DL		1st Half	7	7	0	98	53	4.86	1.49	290			27.0	32%	67%	4.53	43	19	39	3.0	4.9	**1.6**	6%	0.7	-3.7	38	$5
ERA Potl	55%	2nd Half	9	5	0	96	54	4.78	1.59	321			27.1	35%	71%	4.34	43	21	36	2.3	5.1	**2.2**	7%	0.8	-2.6	41	$5
LIMA Plan	C	07 Proj	**15**	**11**	**0**	**203**	**121**	**4.12**	**1.37**	**280**			**25.6**	**31%**	**71%**	**4.10**	**44**	**19**	**37**	**2.5**	**5.4**	**2.2**	**7%**	**0.8**	**9.6**	**53**	**$16**

2005's favorable H% corrected, resulting in a major decline. But skills and xERA were similar across the two seasons. If he finally has a luck-neutral year, expect an outcome right between 2005 and 2006.

Bonderman,Jeremy

			W	L	Sv	IP	K	ERA	WHIP	OBA	vL	vR	BF/G	H%	S%	xERA	G	L	F	Ctl	Dom	Cmd	hr/f	hr/9	RAR	BPV	R$
RH	Starter	02	0	0	0	0	0	0.00	0.00											0.0	0.0						
Age	24	03 DET	6	19	0	162	108	5.56	1.55	297	306	277	21.9	33%	66%	4.15	45	20	35	3.2	6.0	**1.9**	12%	1.3	-20.6	32	$3
Growth		04 DET	11	13	0	184	168	4.89	1.31	245	255	223	23.6	29%	65%	3.39	48	18	34	3.6	8.2	**2.3**	14%	1.2	-10.4	68	$14
Type	Power	05 DET	14	13	0	189	145	4.57	1.35	272	287	249	27.9	31%	68%	3.58	48	19	33	2.7	6.9	**2.5**	11%	1.0	-4.7	65	$15
Reliability	68	06 DET	14	8	0	214	202	4.08	1.30	262	284	235	26.6	33%	70%	3.16	48	20	32	2.7	8.5	**3.2**	9%	0.8	12.6	97	$23
DL		1st Half	7	4	0	106	102	3.65	1.16	239			27.0	31%	68%	2.87	51	20	29	2.5	8.7	**3.5**	7%	0.5	11.9	118	$14
ERA Potl	65%	2nd Half	7	4	0	108	100	4.50	1.44	283			26.1	35%	71%	3.44	46	19	35	2.9	8.3	**2.9**	11%	1.0	0.8	78	$9
LIMA Plan	C	07 Proj	**16**	**9**	**0**	**203**	**186**	**3.64**	**1.23**	**248**			**24.8**	**30%**	**74%**	**3.16**	**48**	**19**	**33**	**2.7**	**8.2**	**3.1**	**12%**	**1.0**	**33.2**	**91**	**$25**

Breakout is edging closer as predicted, would have been even bigger without spike in 2nd half H%. Sell that plus playoff run as burnout risk, and scoop him up while you still can.
UP: Many Cy Young awards.

Bonser,Boof

			W	L	Sv	IP	K	ERA	WHIP	OBA	vL	vR	BF/G	H%	S%	xERA	G	L	F	Ctl	Dom	Cmd	hr/f	hr/9	RAR	BPV	R$
RH	Starter	02 aa	1	2	0	24	21	5.98	1.78	313			22.7	38%	66%	5.76				4.5	7.8	**1.8**		0.7	-5.1	54	($1)
Age	25	03 a/a	8	12	0	158	117	3.91	1.31	240			23.9	28%	70%	3.41				3.7	6.6	**1.8**		0.6	9.5	66	$13
Growth		04 a/a	13	10	0	161	136	5.31	1.56	297			25.8	35%	69%	5.57				3.4	7.6	**2.3**		1.3	-19.2	49	$7
Type	Power	05 aaa	11	9	0	160	147	4.89	1.47	280			25.1	33%	70%	4.99				3.3	8.3	**2.5**		1.3	-11.6	62	$9
Reliability	2	06 MIN *	13	10	0	186	154	4.21	1.37	266	251	280	25.0	31%	72%	3.91	42	15	43	3.1	7.4	**2.4**	9%	1.1	8.1	63	$17
DL		1st Half	5	3	0	81	63	3.67	1.35	255			24.8	28%	78%	3.94	47	12	42	3.5	6.9	**2.0**	12%	1.3	8.9	48	$8
ERA Potl	50%	2nd Half	8	7	0	105	91	4.62	1.39	274			25.1	33%	68%	3.86	39	17	44	2.9	7.8	**2.7**	8%	0.9	-0.8	76	$9
LIMA Plan	C+	07 Proj	**8**	**7**	**0**	**116**	**98**	**4.27**	**1.41**	**272**			**25.1**	**32%**	**73%**	**3.94**	**41**	**15**	**43**	**3.3**	**7.6**	**2.3**	**10%**	**1.2**	**7.8**	**60**	**$10**

7-6, 4.22 ERA in 100 IP at MIN. Finished strong with five PQS-DOM outings in Sept. Not as hyped as some other young arms, but this is a solid and stable skill set worth targeting.

Borkowski,Dave

			W	L	Sv	IP	K	ERA	WHIP	OBA	vL	vR	BF/G	H%	S%	xERA	G	L	F	Ctl	Dom	Cmd	hr/f	hr/9	RAR	BPV	R$
RH	Reliever	02 aa	0	2	0	8	6	7.88	1.75	347			18.7	42%	50%	5.55				2.3	6.8	**3.0**		0.0	-3.6	89	($1)
Age	30	03 aa	6	8	0	128	53	4.71	1.62	333			19.4	35%	72%	5.90				2.0	3.7	**1.9**		0.9	-5.0	23	$1
Peak		04 BAL *	9	13	0	141	93	5.80	1.60	316	270	307	19.3	36%	63%	4.14	44	22	34	2.7	5.9	**2.2**	8%	0.8	-23.9	49	$2
Type	Finesse	05 aaa	10	10	0	182	85	5.74	1.69	343			29.0	36%	67%	6.43				2.0	4.2	**2.1**		1.1	-32.2	23	($2)
Reliability	6	06 HOU	3	2	0	71	52	4.69	1.31	259	262	255	7.5	29%	66%	3.74	47	17	36	2.9	6.6	**2.3**	10%	1.0	-1.8	60	$4
DL		1st Half	1	0	0	34	32	4.49	1.29	261			7.2	33%	66%	3.19	45	22	32	2.6	8.4	**3.2**	9%	0.8	0.0	97	$2
ERA Potl	50%	2nd Half	2	2	0	37	20	4.88	1.33	257			7.8	27%	66%	4.28	48	13	39	3.2	4.9	**1.5**	11%	1.2	-1.8	29	$2
LIMA Plan	C+	07 Proj	**2**	**2**	**0**	**44**	**26**	**4.97**	**1.47**	**298**			**7.6**	**33%**	**68%**	**4.12**	**46**	**18**	**36**	**2.5**	**5.4**	**2.2**	**9%**	**1.0**	**1.3**	**42**	**$1**

For one short 34-IP stretch in the 1st half, he almost looked rosterable. Chronically low S% means he loses composure with men on base. That's curable, but consistent BPIs have to be there, and they're not.

Borowski,Joe

			W	L	Sv	IP	K	ERA	WHIP	OBA	vL	vR	BF/G	H%	S%	xERA	G	L	F	Ctl	Dom	Cmd	hr/f	hr/9	RAR	BPV	R$
RH	Reliever	02 CHC	4	4	2	95	97	2.75	1.19	239	209	260	5.3	30%	82%	3.21	39	22	39	2.7	9.2	**3.3**	10%	0.9	15.9	104	$12
Age	36	03 CHC	2	2	33	68	66	2.65	1.06	217	212	204	4.0	28%	78%	3.22	38	20	42	2.5	8.7	**3.5**	7%	0.7	13.7	117	$20
Decline		04 CHC	2	4	9	21	17	8.10	1.99	312	344	281	4.7	36%	59%	5.51	33	21	46	6.4	7.3	**1.1**	9%	1.3	-10.0	21	$1
Type	Power	05 2TM	1	5	0	46	27	4.49	1.08	226	192	244	4.3	23%	64%	3.67	47	17	36	2.3	5.3	**2.3**	16%	1.6	-1.1	42	$3
Reliability	0	06 FLA	3	3	36	69	64	3.77	1.39	244	167	291	4.1	30%	75%	4.21	33	18	50	4.3	8.3	**1.9**	7%	0.9	6.1	70	$18
DL	51	1st Half	0	1	14	29	25	3.39	1.40	233			4.1	28%	79%	4.51	32	20	49	4.9	7.7	**1.6**	7%	0.9	4.0	60	$7
ERA Potl	50%	2nd Half	3	2	22	40	39	4.05	1.37	252			4.2	32%	73%	4.01	33	17	50	3.8	8.8	**2.3**	7%	0.9	2.2	78	$11
LIMA Plan	C	07 Proj	**3**	**4**	**30**	**73**	**62**	**3.72**	**1.24**	**236**			**4.2**	**28%**	**73%**	**3.86**	**37**	**18**	**45**	**3.4**	**7.7**	**2.3**	**9%**	**1.0**	**4.5**	**72**	**$16**

Found a formula for success: spiked both his DOM and CTL, but survived by getting buckets of fly balls in FLA's expansive OF. Not the most closer-worthy BPIs, so the line between success and failure is very thin.

Bradford,Chad

			W	L	Sv	IP	K	ERA	WHIP	OBA	vL	vR	BF/G	H%	S%	xERA	G	L	F	Ctl	Dom	Cmd	hr/f	hr/9	RAR	BPV	R$
RH	Reliever	02 OAK	4	2	2	75	56	3.12	1.16	257	267	247	4.1	31%	72%	2.64	65	15	21	1.7	6.7	**4.0**	4%	0.2	12.4	121	$10
Age	32	03 OAK	7	4	2	77	62	3.04	1.26	236	326	190	4.5	28%	79%	2.75	64	19	17	3.5	7.2	**2.1**	18%	0.8	14.1	70	$11
Peak		04 OAK	5	7	1	59	34	4.42	1.27	235	298	211	3.6	26%	66%	3.54	61	16	23	3.7	5.2	**1.4**	12%	0.8	0.1	46	$5
Type		05 BOS	2	1	0	23	10	3.90	1.43	308	409	282	3.2	34%	72%	2.90	65	23	12	1.6	3.9	**2.5**	10%	0.4	1.4	58	$2
Reliability	1	06 NYM	4	2	2	62	45	2.90	1.16	252	250	256	3.6	31%	73%	2.75	63	21	16	1.9	6.5	**3.5**	3%	0.1	12.1	112	$9
DL	107	1st Half	3	2	2	28	24	2.55	0.96	217			3.2	27%	73%	2.34	64	15	21	1.6	7.7	**4.8**	6%	0.3	6.7	149	$6
ERA Potl	55%	2nd Half	1	0	0	34	21	3.20	1.33	280			4.0	33%	73%	3.11	63	17	20	2.1	5.6	**2.6**	0%	0.0	5.4	88	$3
LIMA Plan	B	07 Proj	**4**	**3**	**0**	**58**	**40**	**3.41**	**1.24**	**252**			**3.8**	**30%**	**72%**	**2.88**	**63**	**18**	**18**	**2.6**	**6.2**	**2.4**	**9%**	**0.5**	**10.6**	**77**	**$6**

Recovered the DOM he lost following back surgery in 2005, and everything else fell into place. Miniscule HR/9 indicates some good fortune, but he's back to being a classic LIMA reliever.

RAY MURPHY

Braun,Ryan

Profile	Year	W	L	Sv	IP	K	ERA	WHIP	OBA	vL	vR	BF/G	H%	S%	xERA	G	L	F	Ctl	Dom	Cmd	hr/f	hr/9	RAR	BPV	R$
RH Reliever	02	0	0	0	0	0	0.00	0.00																		
Age 26	03	0	0	0	0	0	0.00	0.00																		
Growth	04	0	0	0	0	0	0.00	0.00																		
Type Power	05	0	0	0	0	0	0.00	0.00																		
Reliability 6	06 KC *	1	9	13	75	76	3.22	1.35	253	357	296	6.2	33%	77%	3.48	39	25	36	3.6	9.1	2.5	5%	0.5	12.4	98	$11
DL	1st Half	1	5	10	38	48	2.13	1.13	213			6.4	31%	83%					3.3	11.3	3.4		0.5	11.4	138	$10
ERA Potl 55%	2nd Half	0	4	3	37	28	4.34	1.58	290			6.0	35%	72%	4.31	39	25	36	3.9	6.8	1.8	5%	0.5	1.0	60	$2
LIMA Plan B+	07 Proj	4	5	0	65	62	4.19	1.43	266			6.2	34%	70%	3.66	39	25	36	3.6	8.7	2.4	4%	0.4	6.6	91	$6

0-1, 6.75 ERA in 11 IP at KC. Strong rebound from 2005 shoulder problems. Old for a prospect, but if shoulder is sound he could quickly earn a prominent role in unsettled KC pen.

Bray,Bill

Profile	Year	W	L	Sv	IP	K	ERA	WHIP	OBA	vL	vR	BF/G	H%	S%	xERA	G	L	F	Ctl	Dom	Cmd	hr/f	hr/9	RAR	BPV	R$
LH Reliever	02	0	0	0	0	0	0.00	0.00																		
Age 23	03	0	0	0	0	0	0.00	0.00																		
Growth	04	0	0	0	0	0	0.00	0.00																		
Type Power	05	0	0	0	0	0	0.00	0.00																		
Reliability 0	06 2NL *	7	3	7	81	77	4.42	1.39	273	333	252	5.1	33%	71%	3.29	44	25	31	3.0	8.5	2.9	13%	1.1	0.7	78	$10
DL	1st Half	5	2	5	45	50	4.97	1.37	269			5.9	34%	67%	3.21	39	22	39	3.0	9.9	3.3	14%	1.4	-2.7	89	$6
ERA Potl 55%	2nd Half	2	1	2	36	27	3.74	1.41	277			4.3	32%	75%	3.62	46	26	28	3.0	6.7	2.3	9%	0.7	3.3	65	$3
LIMA Plan B	07 Proj	6	2	8	73	65	3.97	1.39	274			4.8	33%	74%	3.36	45	25	30	3.0	8.1	2.7	12%	1.0	9.0	76	$9

3-2, 4.09 ERA in 51 IP at WAS and CIN. Mixes a healthy DOM and solid CMD with GB tendency. Possible closer of the future if he can overcome the LH closer bias. Quality LIMA option in the meantime.

Brazoban,Yhency

Profile	Year	W	L	Sv	IP	K	ERA	WHIP	OBA	vL	vR	BF/G	H%	S%	xERA	G	L	F	Ctl	Dom	Cmd	hr/f	hr/9	RAR	BPV	R$
RH Reliever	02	0	0	0	0	0	0.00	0.00											0.0	0.0						
Age 26	03 aa	2	2	3	27	16	9.26	1.88	325			6.5	34%	51%	7.41				4.6	5.3	1.1		2.0	-16.3	-14	($2)
Growth	04 a/a	6	5	14	63	65	2.65	1.23	238			5.6	31%	81%	3.31				3.1	9.3	3.0		0.7	13.2	104	$14
Type Power	05 LA	4	10	21	72	61	5.36	1.41	256	267	250	4.2	29%	65%	3.97	39	22	39	4.0	7.6	1.9	13%	1.4	-9.9	48	$10
Reliability 0	06 LA	0	0	0	5	4	5.40	1.80	332	333	364	4.7	41%	67%	5.35	18	24	59	3.6	7.2	2.0	0%	0.0	-0.6	74	($0)
DL 170	1st Half	0	0	0	5	4	5.40	1.80	332			4.7	41%	67%	5.35	18	24	59	3.6	7.2	2.0	0%	0.0	-0.6	74	($0)
ERA Potl 65%	2nd Half	0	0	0	0	0	0.00	0.00																		
LIMA Plan C	07 Proj	2	3	0	29	27	4.34	1.34	248			4.8	30%	71%	3.68	39	22	39	3.7	8.4	2.3	12%	1.2	2.5	66	$2

Had Tommy John surgery in May. Worthy of your Draft Day consideration only if you're eyeing 2008.

Britton,Chris

Profile	Year	W	L	Sv	IP	K	ERA	WHIP	OBA	vL	vR	BF/G	H%	S%	xERA	G	L	F	Ctl	Dom	Cmd	hr/f	hr/9	RAR	BPV	R$
RH Reliever	02	0	0	0	0	0	0.00	0.00																		
Age 24	03	0	0	0	0	0	0.00	0.00																		
Growth	04	0	0	0	0	0	0.00	0.00																		
Type Power	05	0	0	0	0	0	0.00	0.00																		
Reliability 0	06 BAL *	1	2	3	69	62	3.38	1.23	238	301	186	4.4	30%	73%	3.95	31	19	50	3.1	8.1	2.6	4%	0.5	10.0	94	$8
DL	1st Half	1	1	2	37	37	2.18	1.19	235			4.6	31%	83%	3.70	32	18	51	2.9	8.8	3.0	4%	0.5	10.9	110	$6
ERA Potl 55%	2nd Half	0	1	1	32	25	4.79	1.27	242			4.2	29%	61%	4.26	30	20	50	3.4	7.2	2.1	4%	0.6	-0.9	78	$2
LIMA Plan B+	07 Proj	1	2	3	56	49	3.84	1.24	240			4.3	30%	69%	4.04	31	19	50	3.2	7.8	2.5	4%	0.5	3.1	91	$6

0-2, 3.35 ERA in 54 IP at BAL. Another young power arm with the skills of a future closer. High FB% could cause some trouble down the road, but there's a lot to like here. Now with NYY.

Brown,Andrew

Profile	Year	W	L	Sv	IP	K	ERA	WHIP	OBA	vL	vR	BF/G	H%	S%	xERA	G	L	F	Ctl	Dom	Cmd	hr/f	hr/9	RAR	BPV	R$
RH Reliever	02	0	0	0	0	0	0.00	0.00																		
Age 26	03 aa	0	0	0	1	1	0.00	0.00	0			2.9	0%		-2.83				0.0	9.0				0.5	109	$0
Growth	04 a/a	5	10	0	122	110	4.86	1.42	255			20.4	31%	67%	4.23				4.1	8.1	2.0		1.0	-7.8	66	$6
Type Power	05 aaa	4	2	4	69	71	3.51	1.05	220			5.6	28%	69%	2.65				2.3	9.2	3.9		0.8	6.8	126	$11
Reliability 0	06 CLE *	5	4	5	72	54	3.40	1.58	250	286	95	6.8	29%	80%	4.94	39	18	43	5.8	6.7	1.2	5%	0.6	10.3	51	$7
DL	1st Half	4	3	2	45	35	3.02	1.68	245			7.7	29%	83%					6.8	6.9	1.0		0.6	8.6	50	$5
ERA Potl 45%	2nd Half	1	1	3	27	19	4.04	1.42	257			5.6	30%	72%	4.47	39	18	43	4.0	6.3	1.6	6%	0.7	1.7	54	$3
LIMA Plan B+	07 Proj	2	2	0	44	37	4.14	1.33	241			6.6	29%	70%	4.01	39	18	43	3.9	7.7	1.9	7%	0.8	2.6	69	$4

0-0, 3.60 ERA in 10 IP at CLE. CMD turned from a strength to a liability in 2006. Electric arm, but durability concerns limit his upside. Potential LIMA option if he reclaims previous CMD levels.

Broxton,Jonathan

Profile	Year	W	L	Sv	IP	K	ERA	WHIP	OBA	vL	vR	BF/G	H%	S%	xERA	G	L	F	Ctl	Dom	Cmd	hr/f	hr/9	RAR	BPV	R$
RH Reliever	02	0	0	0	0	0	0.00	0.00																		
Age 22	03	0	0	0	0	0	0.00	0.00																		
Growth	04	0	0	0	0	0	0.00	0.00																		
Type Power	05 aa	5	3	5	96	90	3.27	1.16	234			11.9	30%	71%	2.73				2.7	8.4	3.1		0.4	12.2	113	$13
Reliability 0	06 LA *	5	1	8	87	113	2.27	1.18	213	244	196	4.5	31%	84%	2.85	39	20	40	3.7	11.6	3.1	9%	0.7	23.8	126	$16
DL	1st Half	2	0	5	42	56	2.13	1.10	205			4.5	29%	88%	2.72	42	13	45	3.4	11.9	3.5	12%	1.1	12.3	127	$9
ERA Potl 50%	2nd Half	3	1	3	45	57	2.40	1.24	221			4.6	33%	81%	2.98	37	26	37	4.0	11.4	2.9	5%	0.4	11.6	127	$8
LIMA Plan B	07 Proj	4	2	15	78	90	2.65	1.18	223			4.7	31%	79%	3.07	39	21	40	3.3	10.4	3.1	7%	0.6	12.5	121	$16

3 Sv, 2.59 ERA in 76 IP at LA. Power reliever gave up a few too many LDs, but double-digit DOM will cover up a lot of sins. Clearly a future closer, only question is how soon?
UP: 40 Saves

Bruney,Brian

Profile	Year	W	L	Sv	IP	K	ERA	WHIP	OBA	vL	vR	BF/G	H%	S%	xERA	G	L	F	Ctl	Dom	Cmd	hr/f	hr/9	RAR	BPV	R$
RH Reliever	02 aa	0	2	0	12	13	3.75	1.25	245			5.0	32%	71%	3.42				3.0	9.8	3.3		0.8	0.8	110	$1
Age 25	03 a/a	3	3	26	63	56	3.00	1.33	239			4.5	31%	76%	3.02				4.0	8.0	2.0		0.1	10.9	93	$15
Growth	04 ARI *	5	5	5	69	75	2.87	1.20	163	214	172	4.7	23%	76%	3.81	33	26	41	5.9	9.8	1.7	5%	0.4	11.9	104	$11
Type Power	05 ARI	1	3	12	46	51	7.43	1.98	302	280	314	4.8	39%	62%	4.46	41	22	37	6.8	10.0	1.5	12%	1.2	-18.1	50	$0
Reliability 0	06 NYY *	2	3	3	37	48	4.84	1.69	245	115	229	5.0	34%	74%	4.13	35	18	47	7.0	11.6	1.7	12%	1.2	-1.3	74	$3
DL	1st Half	0	1	0	2	4	49.09	6.82	639			5.4	80%	23%					16.4	16.4	1.0		8.2	-12.1	******	($3)
ERA Potl 60%	2nd Half	2	2	3	35	44	2.06	1.37	189			5.0	27%	89%	3.78	35	18	47	6.4	11.3	1.8	8%	0.8	10.8	99	$6
LIMA Plan B+	07 Proj	3	4	0	58	64	4.19	1.41	212			4.7	29%	71%	3.91	37	22	41	5.9	9.9	1.7	7%	0.6	4.1	89	$5

1-1, 0.87 ERA in 21 IP at NYY. Had a great late-season run in NY, but it was driven by H%/S% rather than skills. Until he learns some CTL, the results will continue to be rocky.

Buchholz,Taylor

Profile	Year	W	L	Sv	IP	K	ERA	WHIP	OBA	vL	vR	BF/G	H%	S%	xERA	G	L	F	Ctl	Dom	Cmd	hr/f	hr/9	RAR	BPV	R$
RH Starter	02 aa	0	2	0	23	16	9.00	1.70	337			26.5	36%	47%	7.08				2.3	6.3	2.7		2.0	-13.4	22	($2)
Age 25	03 aa	9	11	0	144	100	3.93	1.26	267			24.1	30%	71%	3.92				2.1	6.2	2.9		0.9	8.2	75	$13
Growth	04 aaa	6	7	0	98	62	6.15	1.51	303			21.7	32%	62%	5.75				2.6	5.7	2.2		1.6	-21.9	28	$1
Type	05 aaa	6	0	0	74	36	5.46	1.46	286			17.1	31%	67%	5.47				2.9	4.4	1.5		1.7	-10.6	4	$2
Reliability 0	06 HOU *	7	13	0	157	108	5.85	1.34	265	249	248	23.1	29%	58%	3.95	44	18	38	2.9	6.2	2.1	12%	1.3	-26.3	44	$5
DL	1st Half	4	6	0	83	55	5.84	1.23	259			23.0	27%	55%	3.69	45	18	37	2.2	5.9	2.8	14%	1.5	-13.9	51	$4
ERA Potl 60%	2nd Half	3	7	0	74	53	5.85	1.48	273			23.2	31%	61%	4.35	40	19	41	3.8	6.5	1.7	9%	1.1	-12.4	42	$1
LIMA Plan C	07 Proj	7	7	0	116	73	4.81	1.36	270			20.7	29%	69%	4.10	43	18	39	2.9	5.7	2.0	12%	1.4	3.8	35	$6

6-10, 5.89 ERA in 113 IP at HOU. Attracted some attention with five straight PQS-DOM outings in June. xERA shows upside. Needs to cut down on HR/9, which would help S%.
UP: 12 Wins, 4.00.

Buehrle,Mark

Profile	Year	W	L	Sv	IP	K	ERA	WHIP	OBA	vL	vR	BF/G	H%	S%	xERA	G	L	F	Ctl	Dom	Cmd	hr/f	hr/9	RAR	BPV	R$
LH Starter	02 CHW	19	12	0	239	134	3.58	1.24	259	228	271	29.3	28%	74%	3.82	48	18	34	2.3	5.0	2.2	10%	0.9	26.0	51	$24
Age 28	03 CHW	14	14	0	230	119	4.15	1.35	278	263	285	28.1	30%	71%	4.21	46	17	37	2.4	4.7	2.0	8%	0.9	10.7	42	$16
Pre-Peak	04 CHW	16	10	0	245	165	3.89	1.26	271	271	267	29.2	30%	73%	3.46	49	19	32	1.9	6.1	3.2	13%	1.2	16.3	69	$22
Type Finesse	05 CHW	16	8	0	236	149	3.12	1.19	265	271	260	29.4	30%	76%	3.51	46	21	33	1.5	5.7	3.7	8%	0.8	36.3	91	$27
Reliability 75	06 CHW	12	13	0	204	98	4.99	1.45	300	238	322	27.8	31%	70%	4.29	44	19	37	2.1	4.3	2.0	13%	1.6	-10.8	16	$9
DL	1st Half	9	4	0	111	47	3.24	1.26	263			29.0	27%	78%	4.28	46	17	37	2.3	3.8	1.7	9%	1.0	18.1	31	$12
ERA Potl 50%	2nd Half	3	9	0	93	51	7.08	1.67	340			26.6	35%	63%	4.29	43	20	37	1.9	4.9	2.6	19%	2.3	-28.9	0	($3)
LIMA Plan C	07 Proj	13	12	0	218	122	4.51	1.37	290			28.3	31%	70%	3.96	45	19	35	1.9	5.0	2.6	11%	1.2	14.0	47	$14

Did burnout finally get him? Lost CMD in 1st half, then had HR/9 problems later. Expect some recovery, since CMD rebounded some in 2nd half and HR/F should revert. But unlikely he'll get back below 4.00 ERA.

RAY MURPHY

Burgos,Ambiorix

	Yr	Tm	W	L	Sv	IP	K	ERA	WHIP	OBA	vL	vR	BF/G	H%	S%	xERA	G	L	F	Ctl	Dom	Cmd	hr/f	hr/9	RAR	BPV	R$
RH Reliever	02		0	0	0	0	0	0.00	0.00											0.0	0.0						
Age 23	03		0	0	0	0	0	0.00	0.00											0.0	0.0						
Growth	04		0	0	0	0	0	0.00	0.00											0.0	0.0						
Type Power	05	KC *	4	6	3	76	83	4.26	1.43	243	300	216	4.7	32%	72%	3.38	50	15	35	4.7	9.8	**2.1**	11%	0.9	1.1	80	$7
Reliability 0	06	KC	4	5	18	73	72	5.54	1.64	287	345	249	4.9	33%	72%	3.90	43	18	39	4.6	8.9	**1.9**	19%	2.0	-8.9	33	$8
DL 24	1st Half		1	3	13	35	39	6.65	1.65	277			4.7	32%	65%	4.03	35	18	47	5.1	10.0	**2.0**	20%	2.3	-9.1	31	$4
ERA Potl 50%	2nd Half		3	2	5	38	33	4.51	1.64	296			5.1	34%	78%	3.79	50	17	33	4.0	7.8	**1.9**	18%	1.7	0.2	34	$4
LIMA Plan C+	07	Proj	**3**	**4**	**15**	**58**	**59**	**4.50**	**1.57**	**272**			**4.8**	**33%**	**77%**	**3.72**	**46**	**17**	**37**	**4.7**	**9.2**	**2.0**	**16%**	**1.6**	**5.5**	**50**	**$8**

H% and HR/F were both higher than he deserved, leading to major gap between ERA and xERA. Blew 40% of save opps after being rushed into the closer role, but he should get more opps down the road.

Burnett,A.J.

	Yr	Tm	W	L	Sv	IP	K	ERA	WHIP	OBA	vL	vR	BF/G	H%	S%	xERA	G	L	F	Ctl	Dom	Cmd	hr/f	hr/9	RAR	BPV	R$
RH Starter	02	FLA	12	9	0	204	203	3.31	1.19	210	242	177	27.1	27%	73%	3.44	39	24	37	4.0	9.0	**2.3**	6%	0.5	20.1	98	$23
Age 30	03	FLA	0	2	0	23	21	4.70	1.57	217	234	194	25.8	27%	71%	4.38	47	20	33	7.0	8.2	**1.2**	10%	0.8	-1.2	62	$0
Peak	04	FLA	7	6	0	120	113	3.68	1.17	232	247	211	24.5	29%	69%	3.06	50	17	33	2.9	8.5	**3.0**	8%	0.7	8.7	102	$13
Type Power	05	FLA	12	12	0	209	198	3.44	1.26	238	226	249	27.3	31%	73%	2.79	58	19	22	3.4	8.5	**2.5**	9%	0.5	20.6	96	$21
Reliability 38	06	TOR	10	8	0	135	118	3.99	1.31	266	261	267	27.2	32%	72%	3.15	50	20	29	2.6	7.9	**3.0**	12%	0.9	9.4	85	$15
DL 83	1st Half		1	1	0	25	24	3.24	1.04	246			24.8	29%	77%	2.22	59	18	23	1.1	8.6	**8.0**	25%	1.4	4.1	182	$4
ERA Potl 60%	2nd Half		9	7	0	110	94	4.17	1.37	270			27.8	33%	71%	3.38	49	21	31	2.9	7.7	**2.6**	10%	0.8	5.3	77	$11
LIMA Plan B	07	Proj	**12**	**10**	**0**	**189**	**174**	**3.63**	**1.23**	**246**			**26.9**	**30%**	**72%**	**2.93**	**53**	**19**	**28**	**2.8**	**8.3**	**3.0**	**12%**	**0.8**	**36.1**	**94**	**$22**

Missed most of 1st half with elbow trouble, but BPIs were intact when he returned. Health issues make him a risky play, but xERA history shows the upside. If health cooperates... UP: 18 Wins, 3.20 ERA.

Bush,David

	Yr	Tm	W	L	Sv	IP	K	ERA	WHIP	OBA	vL	vR	BF/G	H%	S%	xERA	G	L	F	Ctl	Dom	Cmd	hr/f	hr/9	RAR	BPV	R$
RH Starter	02		0	0	0	0	0	0.00	0.00											0.0	0.0						
Age 27	03	aa	7	3	0	81	62	3.44	1.31	274			24.5	33%	74%	3.72				2.2	6.9	**3.1**		0.4	9.5	93	$9
Growth	04	TOR *	11	10	0	196	141	4.45	1.36	286	289	206	26.3	33%	69%	3.94	42	16	42	2.1	6.5	**3.1**	7%	0.9	-0.3	73	$13
Type Finesse	05	TOR *	7	13	0	191	110	4.77	1.33	287	269	269	23.9	31%	67%	3.85	46	19	35	1.8	5.2	**2.9**	12%	1.3	-9.4	51	$9
Reliability 53	06	MIL	12	11	0	210	166	4.41	1.14	253	258	246	25.1	29%	64%	3.18	47	19	34	1.6	7.1	**4.4**	12%	1.1	1.9	105	$20
DL	1st Half		5	6	0	111	93	4.46	1.17	249			26.7	29%	65%	3.30	45	17	37	2.1	7.5	**3.6**	12%	1.1	0.4	91	$10
ERA Potl 65%	2nd Half		7	5	0	99	73	4.37	1.10	258			23.4	29%	63%	3.03	48	21	31	1.1	6.6	**6.1**	13%	1.1	1.5	138	$11
LIMA Plan C+	07	Proj	**13**	**9**	**0**	**203**	**145**	**3.72**	**1.23**	**269**			**25.5**	**30%**	**73%**	**3.45**	**46**	**19**	**35**	**1.7**	**6.4**	**3.7**	**11%**	**1.1**	**22.8**	**86**	**$19**

Pushed skill set from "intriguing" to "elite", at least in terms of CMD. xERA shows what he'd have done with a better S%. There's more growth to come if DOM increase sustains. UP: 16 Wins, 3.25 ERA.

Byrd,Paul

	Yr	Tm	W	L	Sv	IP	K	ERA	WHIP	OBA	vL	vR	BF/G	H%	S%	xERA	G	L	F	Ctl	Dom	Cmd	hr/f	hr/9	RAR	BPV	R$
RH Starter	02	KC	17	11	0	228	129	3.91	1.15	258	269	241	28.1	27%	72%	4.10				1.5	5.1	**3.4**		1.4	15.5	63	$24
Age 36	03	aa	0	0	0	4	3	13.17	3.17	509			25.0	56%	58%	15.01				2.2	6.6	**3.0**		2.2	-4.4	-10	($2)
Decline	04	ATL *	9	8	0	126	85	4.43	1.30	281	329	219	24.2	31%	71%	4.04	36	18	46	1.8	6.1	**3.4**	11%	1.4	-2.5	64	$9
Type Finesse	05	ANA	12	11	0	204	102	3.75	1.20	273	306	234	27.1	29%	72%	4.12	38	20	42	1.2	4.5	**3.6**	8%	1.0	15.7	75	$18
Reliability 58	06	CLE	10	9	0	179	88	4.88	1.51	315	369	256	25.6	33%	71%	4.40	39	24	37	1.9	4.4	**2.3**	11%	1.3	-7.1	28	$7
DL	1st Half		6	5	0	92	52	4.39	1.25	263			25.6	28%	67%	4.25	37	20	44	2.1	5.1	**2.4**	8%	1.1	1.9	50	$8
ERA Potl 50%	2nd Half		4	4	0	87	36	5.39	1.79	362			25.5	37%	74%	4.55	40	29	31	1.7	3.7	**2.3**	14%	1.6	-8.9	6	($1)
LIMA Plan C	07	Proj	**11**	**10**	**0**	**189**	**98**	**4.49**	**1.40**	**300**			**26.2**	**32%**	**72%**	**4.23**	**38**	**23**	**39**	**1.7**	**4.7**	**2.8**	**11%**	**1.3**	**5.9**	**43**	**$11**

Such is the life of the soft-tosser: a couple more walks, a couple more HR, and your ERA jumps by a full run. Troubles with LH hitters are getting worse; if he doesn't solve those: DN: 5.00 ERA.

Cabrera,Daniel

	Yr	Tm	W	L	Sv	IP	K	ERA	WHIP	OBA	vL	vR	BF/G	H%	S%	xERA	G	L	F	Ctl	Dom	Cmd	hr/f	hr/9	RAR	BPV	R$
RH Starter	02		0	0	0	0	0	0.00	0.00											0.0	0.0						
Age 25	03		0	0	0	0	0	0.00	0.00											0.0	0.0						
Growth	04	BAL *	12	9	1	174	104	4.75	1.50	243	249	270	23.3	27%	69%	4.96	43	17	40	5.3	5.4	**1.0**	7%	0.8	-6.9	37	$8
Type Power	05	BAL	10	13	0	161	157	4.53	1.43	241	285	174	24.2	30%	69%	3.45	53	18	30	4.9	8.8	**1.8**	11%	0.8	-3.1	74	$12
Reliability 3	06	BAL	9	10	0	148	157	4.74	1.58	238	231	251	25.6	31%	70%	4.12	41	18	41	6.3	9.5	**1.5**	8%	0.7	-3.4	76	$10
DL 21 20	1st Half		4	5	0	68	75	5.15	1.74	235			24.5	32%	70%	4.67	40	20	40	7.9	9.9	**1.3**	7%	0.7	-5.0	74	$3
ERA Potl 65%	2nd Half		5	5	0	80	82	4.40	1.44	240			26.8	31%	70%	3.69	42	24	35	5.0	9.2	**1.9**	8%	0.7	1.6	81	$7
LIMA Plan B	07	Proj	**12**	**13**	**0**	**189**	**186**	**4.39**	**1.47**	**240**			**25.9**	**31%**	**71%**	**3.80**	**45**	**20**	**35**	**5.2**	**8.9**	**1.7**	**8%**	**0.7**	**16.0**	**75**	**$15**

Progressed from "unbelievably wild" to merely "wild" in 2nd half. Keeps flirting with the important 2.0 CMD level, but can't get over the hump. Has a high ceiling, but will test your patience along the way.

Cabrera,Fernando

	Yr	Tm	W	L	Sv	IP	K	ERA	WHIP	OBA	vL	vR	BF/G	H%	S%	xERA	G	L	F	Ctl	Dom	Cmd	hr/f	hr/9	RAR	BPV	R$
RH Reliever	02	aa	1	2	1	27	26	6.67	1.56	283			17.3	37%	54%	4.32				4.0	8.7	**2.2**		0.3	-8.0	86	$0
Age 25	03	aa	9	4	5	109	98	3.96	1.45	272			13.2	33%	74%	4.40				3.6	8.1	**2.3**		0.8	5.8	72	$11
Growth	04	aaa	4	3	5	75	83	3.77	1.30	213			7.2	28%	73%	3.32				4.8	10.0	**2.1**		0.9	5.3	88	$9
Type Power	05	CLE *	8	2	3	81	88	1.33	1.03	213	196	224	7.1	29%	90%	2.89	35	29	36	2.4	9.7	**4.0**	5%	0.4	30.5	142	$18
Reliability 1	06	CLE	3	3	0	60	71	5.23	1.41	238	235	248	5.1	29%	68%	3.54	33	23	43	4.8	10.6	**2.2**	18%	1.8	-5.0	64	$5
DL 15	1st Half		1	1	0	26	27	5.86	1.61	238			4.9	29%	66%	4.38	31	30	39	6.6	9.3	**1.4**	15%	1.4	-4.2	52	$1
ERA Potl 60%	2nd Half		2	2	0	34	44	4.75	1.26	238			5.3	30%	71%	2.99	35	18	47	3.4	11.6	**3.4**	21%	2.1	-0.8	85	$4
LIMA Plan A	07	Proj	**4**	**2**	**5**	**58**	**65**	**3.88**	**1.29**	**231**			**5.6**	**29%**	**75%**	**3.42**	**34**	**24**	**42**	**4.0**	**10.1**	**2.5**	**13%**	**1.2**	**7.6**	**85**	**$9**

Got rocked (6 ER) on Opening Night and went into tailspin. CMD came back in 2nd half, but spike in HR/F drove up his ERA. Still a "future closer", just may take longer to get there.

Cain,Matt

	Yr	Tm	W	L	Sv	IP	K	ERA	WHIP	OBA	vL	vR	BF/G	H%	S%	xERA	G	L	F	Ctl	Dom	Cmd	hr/f	hr/9	RAR	BPV	R$
RH Starter	02		0	0	0	0	0	0.00	0.00											0.0	0.0						
Age 22	03		0	0	0	0	0	0.00	0.00											0.0	0.0						
Growth	04	aa	6	4	0	86	64	3.99	1.38	250			24.7	29%	72%	3.85				4.0	6.7	**1.7**		0.7	3.8	60	$7
Type Power	05	SF *	12	6	0	191	201	3.35	1.06	192	160	143	23.1	24%	72%	3.53	29	18	53	3.5	9.5	**2.7**	8%	0.9	21.2	104	$25
Reliability 33	06	SF	13	12	0	190	179	4.16	1.28	226	217	227	25.0	28%	69%	3.95	36	16	48	4.1	8.5	**2.1**	7%	0.9	7.6	78	$18
DL	1st Half		6	6	0	81	67	5.22	1.37	237			23.2	27%	63%	4.22	42	13	46	4.4	7.4	**1.7**	9%	1.1	-7.3	54	$5
ERA Potl 60%	2nd Half		7	6	0	109	112	3.38	1.22	218			26.6	29%	74%	3.75	31	19	49	3.9	9.2	**2.4**	6%	0.7	14.9	97	$13
LIMA Plan C+	07	Proj	**13**	**9**	**0**	**189**	**180**	**3.82**	**1.21**	**218**			**25.1**	**27%**	**70%**	**3.83**	**35**	**17**	**49**	**3.9**	**8.6**	**2.2**	**7%**	**0.8**	**12.3**	**85**	**$20**

Top prospect scuffled early, then the light bulb went on in the 2nd half. Skills are ace-caliber, workload has been well-managed to date. If he can carry over his 2nd half skills... UP: 18 Wins, 3.20 ERA.

Calero,Kiko

	Yr	Tm	W	L	Sv	IP	K	ERA	WHIP	OBA	vL	vR	BF/G	H%	S%	xERA	G	L	F	Ctl	Dom	Cmd	hr/f	hr/9	RAR	BPV	R$
RH Reliever	02	a/a	8	7	0	141	90	4.85	1.48	292			24.8	32%	69%	5.01				2.9	5.7	**2.0**		1.1	-10.1	41	$5
Age 32	03	STL	1	1	1	38	51	2.84	1.29	213	222	205	6.2	30%	84%	3.29	24	29	48	4.7	12.1	**2.6**	12%	1.2	6.7	103	$5
Peak	04	STL *	3	1	3	70	73	2.82	1.06	205	175	177	5.3	25%	80%	3.02	44	16	40	3.0	9.4	**3.2**	13%	1.2	12.4	102	$10
Type Power	05	OAK	4	1	1	55	52	3.26	1.14	224	319	162	3.9	27%	75%	3.57	34	19	47	2.9	8.5	**2.9**	9%	1.0	7.6	92	$8
Reliability 15	06	OAK	3	2	2	58	67	3.41	1.28	234	278	208	3.5	32%	74%	3.36	35	21	44	3.7	10.4	**2.8**	6%	0.6	8.2	111	$8
DL 27	1st Half		2	1	1	31	36	3.48	1.26	222			3.6	31%	73%	3.59	29	21	51	4.1	10.5	**2.6**	5%	0.6	4.1	110	$5
ERA Potl 60%	2nd Half		1	1	1	27	31	3.33	1.30	247			3.3	34%	76%	3.09	42	21	38	3.3	10.3	**3.1**	8%	0.7	4.1	113	$4
LIMA Plan A	07	Proj	**3**	**2**	**3**	**65**	**70**	**3.31**	**1.21**	**230**			**4.0**	**30%**	**75%**	**3.36**	**36**	**20**	**44**	**3.3**	**9.7**	**2.9**	**8%**	**0.8**	**9.1**	**103**	**$9**

Note the trend in BF/G: he just shreds RH batters, and he is increasingly being used as a RH specialist. Won't likely close despite having the skills, but he remains an ideal LIMA guy.

Camp,Shawn

	Yr	Tm	W	L	Sv	IP	K	ERA	WHIP	OBA	vL	vR	BF/G	H%	S%	xERA	G	L	F	Ctl	Dom	Cmd	hr/f	hr/9	RAR	BPV	R$
RH Reliever	02	aaa	4	1	2	58	49	4.19	1.26	265			6.2	32%	68%	3.75				2.2	7.6	**3.5**		0.8	0.6	98	$6
Age 31	03	a/a	0	3	0	72	53	7.36	1.89	343			6.8	40%	59%	6.55				3.7	6.6	**1.8**		0.7	-26.4	41	($6)
Peak	04	KC *	3	3	3	88	68	4.59	1.45	297	287	283	6.8	34%	72%	3.23	58	15	27	2.3	6.9	**3.0**	15%	1.2	-1.7	63	$5
Type	05	KC *	4	10	1	116	62	5.26	1.62	319	407	274	10.6	35%	68%	4.04	57	14	29	2.7	4.8	**1.8**	10%	0.9	-12.8	30	$0
Reliability 22	06	TAM	7	4	4	75	53	4.68	1.49	305	370	284	4.4	35%	71%	3.29	57	18	24	2.3	6.4	**2.8**	15%	1.1	-1.1	58	$7
DL	1st Half		2	0	3	36	19	3.25	1.44	288			4.4	32%	78%	3.43	60	21	19	2.8	4.8	**1.7**	9%	0.5	5.8	47	$4
ERA Potl 50%	2nd Half		5	4	1	39	34	6.00	1.54	321			4.5	37%	64%	3.14	55	16	30	1.8	7.8	**4.3**	18%	1.6	-6.9	79	$3
LIMA Plan C	07	Proj	**4**	**5**	**3**	**73**	**50**	**4.97**	**1.53**	**308**			**5.8**	**35%**	**70%**	**3.46**	**57**	**17**	**26**	**2.5**	**6.2**	**2.5**	**14%**	**1.1**	**9.2**	**50**	**$4**

Has raw elements of a quality RP: strong CMD, acceptable DOM, healthy GB. Consistently high H% suggests he is an exception to McCracken's law. Splits show LHers are doing most of that damage. Stay clear.

RAY MURPHY

Capellan,Jose

	Yr	W	L	Sv	IP	K	ERA	WHIP	OBA	vL	vR	BF/G	H%	S%	xERA	G	L	F	Ctl	Dom	Cmd	hr/f	hr/9	RAR	BPV	R$
RH Reliever	02	0	0	0	0	0	0.00	0.00											0.0	0.0						
Age 26	03	0	0	0	0	0	0.00	0.00											0.0	0.0						
Growth	04 a/a	9	3	0	93	78	3.09	1.43	276			25.3	35%	77%	3.75				3.2	7.5	**2.4**		0.1	14.3	92	$10
Type Power	05 MIL *	6	4	6	105	80	3.93	1.47	270	235	317	8.7	33%	73%	4.22	40	22	38	3.8	6.8	**1.8**	4%	0.4	4.1	66	$8
Reliability 11	06 MIL	4	2	0	71	58	4.42	1.35	245	248	242	5.0	27%	72%	4.17	32	24	44	3.9	7.3	**1.9**	12%	1.4	0.6	48	$5
DL 15	1st Half	2	0	0	41	32	4.61	1.24	237			5.3	26%	67%	3.96	33	24	43	3.3	7.0	**2.1**	12%	1.3	-0.6	55	$3
ERA Potl 50%	2nd Half	2	2	0	30	26	4.17	1.49	254			4.6	29%	78%	4.46	30	24	46	4.8	7.7	**1.6**	12%	1.5	1.2	40	$2
LIMA Plan C+	07 Proj	**4**	**2**	**1**	**58**	**47**	**4.03**	**1.41**	**258**			**6.8**	**30%**	**74%**	**4.28**	**32**	**24**	**44**	**3.9**	**7.3**	**1.9**	**8%**	**0.9**	**0.6**	**59**	**$5**

Still hasn't quite replicated 2004 MLEs in majors. Ctl creeping upward, rising FB% is yielding HRs. Still some nuggets of hope, but expectations of future closer role may be unfounded.

Capps,Matt

	Yr	W	L	Sv	IP	K	ERA	WHIP	OBA	vL	vR	BF/G	H%	S%	xERA	G	L	F	Ctl	Dom	Cmd	hr/f	hr/9	RAR	BPV	R$
RH Reliever	02	0	0	0	0	0	0.00	0.00																		
Age 23	03	0	0	0	0	0	0.00	0.00																		
Growth	04	0	0	0	0	0	0.00	0.00																		
Type Finesse	05 aa	0	2	7	24	23	3.75	1.29	293			4.8	37%	72%	4.21				1.1	8.6	**7.7**		0.8	1.6	187	$4
Reliability 0	06 PIT	9	1	1	80	56	3.82	1.16	264	250	275	3.8	29%	73%	3.55	41	20	40	1.3	6.3	**4.7**	12%	1.3	6.6	98	$11
DL	1st Half	2	1	0	40	31	3.82	1.17	271			4.1	31%	71%	3.13	45	23	33	1.1	7.0	**6.2**	12%	1.1	3.3	139	$4
ERA Potl 55%	2nd Half	7	0	1	40	25	3.82	1.15	256			3.6	27%	74%	3.95	37	17	47	1.6	5.6	**3.6**	12%	1.6	3.3	65	$7
LIMA Plan B	07 Proj	**5**	**3**	**13**	**58**	**40**	**3.88**	**1.21**	**272**			**3.9**	**30%**	**74%**	**3.67**	**40**	**19**	**41**	**1.4**	**6.2**	**4.4**	**12%**	**1.4**	**5.0**	**89**	**$10**

Another young reliever who didn't quite replicate his MLEs in his big-league debut, but there is still much to like. 2nd half DOM plunge is a concern, if he reverses that he might earn some save opps.

Capuano,Chris

	Yr	W	L	Sv	IP	K	ERA	WHIP	OBA	vL	vR	BF/G	H%	S%	xERA	G	L	F	Ctl	Dom	Cmd	hr/f	hr/9	RAR	BPV	R$
LH Starter	02 aaa	4	1	0	36	24	3.00	1.19	245			24.7	29%	74%	2.84				2.5	6.0	**2.4**		0.3	5.6	85	$5
Age 28	03 aaa	9	5	0	142	94	4.05	1.36	275			26.4	32%	70%	4.05				2.6	5.9	**2.3**		0.6	6.0	65	$11
Pre-Peak	04 MIL	6	8	0	88	80	5.01	1.45	268	207	282	22.7	30%	72%	3.91	38	19	43	3.8	8.2	**2.2**	16%	1.8	-8.1	41	$5
Type	05 MIL	18	12	0	219	176	3.99	1.38	256	201	270	26.9	29%	76%	4.06	38	21	41	3.7	7.2	**1.9**	12%	1.3	7.0	50	$18
Reliability 68	06 MIL	11	12	0	221	174	4.03	1.25	269	273	264	27.1	31%	72%	3.58	40	20	40	1.9	7.1	**3.7**	11%	1.2	12.5	86	$19
DL	1st Half	9	4	0	116	105	3.10	1.16	252			27.9	31%	76%	3.26	41	20	39	1.9	8.1	**4.2**	8%	0.8	19.8	118	$16
ERA Potl 50%	2nd Half	2	8	0	105	69	5.05	1.34	286			26.3	31%	67%	3.94	39	20	41	1.9	5.9	**3.1**	13%	1.6	-7.3	50	$4
LIMA Plan D+	07 Proj	**12**	**12**	**0**	**203**	**159**	**4.26**	**1.33**	**267**			**26.1**	**30%**	**72%**	**3.83**	**39**	**20**	**41**	**2.7**	**7.0**	**2.6**	**11%**	**1.3**	**13.3**	**60**	**$15**

Went out and posted the skills that would have supported 2005's breakout. 2nd half DOM plunge may be sign of burnout; formerly brittle arm has thrown a ton of IP in last two years. Bid cautiously.

Carmona,Fausto

	Yr	W	L	Sv	IP	K	ERA	WHIP	OBA	vL	vR	BF/G	H%	S%	xERA	G	L	F	Ctl	Dom	Cmd	hr/f	hr/9	RAR	BPV	R$
RH Reliever	02	0	0	0	0	0	0.00	0.00																		
Age 23	03 aa	0	0	0	6	3	5.45	1.52	350			26.6	38%	67%	6.33				0.0	5.0			1.4	-0.8	-26	($0)
Growth	04 a/a	5	9	0	93	62	5.01	1.52	312			25.8	37%	64%	4.68				2.1	6.0	**2.8**		0.3	-7.7	80	$3
Type	05 a/a	13	9	0	173	97	3.86	1.25	272			26.7	30%	70%	3.84				1.7	5.0	**2.9**		0.7	9.5	69	$15
Reliability 0	06 CLE *	2	13	0	102	85	5.75	1.55	294	299	298	10.4	35%	63%	3.36	60	13	27	3.4	7.5	**2.2**	12%	1.0	-15.0	58	$2
DL	1st Half	1	5	0	56	49	5.17	1.35	274			12.6	33%	61%	3.01	61	9	29	2.5	7.8	**3.1**	10%	0.8	-4.2	89	$3
ERA Potl 65%	2nd Half	1	8	0	46	36	6.45	1.80	316			8.7	36%	65%	3.83	58	16	25	4.5	7.0	**1.6**	15%	1.2	-10.7	31	($1)
LIMA Plan B	07 Proj	**4**	**6**	**0**	**73**	**51**	**4.72**	**1.46**	**291**			**9.6**	**33%**	**69%**	**3.41**	**59**	**14**	**27**	**2.7**	**6.3**	**2.3**	**11%**	**0.9**	**9.6**	**57**	**$4**

1-10, 5.42 ERA in 75 IP at CLE. Brutal outward numbers in CLE. But rising DOM and strong GB% will yield better results, as suggested by xERA. Future role is unclear, but worth stashing away.

Carpenter,Chris

	Yr	W	L	Sv	IP	K	ERA	WHIP	OBA	vL	vR	BF/G	H%	S%	xERA	G	L	F	Ctl	Dom	Cmd	hr/f	hr/9	RAR	BPV	R$
RH Starter	02 TOR *	4	7	0	97	56	6.40	1.76	327	329	276	23.9	35%	67%	6.91				3.5	5.2	**1.5**		1.7	-23.2	2	($3)
Age 32	03 a/a	0	1	0	11	4	12.05	2.77	452			15.9	48%	53%	11.12				4.0	3.2	**0.8**		0.8	-10.6	-23	($4)
Peak	04 STL	15	5	0	182	152	3.46	1.14	248	268	226	26.4	29%	75%	2.92	52	18	29	1.9	7.5	**4.0**	15%	1.2	18.0	99	$22
Type	05 STL	21	5	0	241	213	2.84	1.06	231	264	199	29.1	28%	76%	2.67	55	19	26	1.9	7.9	**4.2**	10%	0.7	41.9	124	$35
Reliability 97	06 STL	15	8	0	221	184	3.09	1.07	237	266	210	27.6	28%	75%	2.82	53	18	28	1.7	7.5	**4.3**	12%	0.9	38.1	117	$30
DL 17	1st Half	6	4	0	98	88	2.85	1.21	252			27.0	31%	81%	2.89	51	23	26	2.4	8.1	**3.4**	14%	0.8	19.8	97	$12
ERA Potl 60%	2nd Half	9	4	0	123	96	3.29	0.96	225			28.1	26%	68%	2.76	55	15	30	1.2	7.0	**5.6**	10%	0.8	18.2	147	$18
LIMA Plan C+	07 Proj	**18**	**7**	**0**	**218**	**178**	**3.23**	**1.14**	**247**			**27.6**	**29%**	**76%**	**2.91**	**54**	**18**	**28**	**1.9**	**7.4**	**3.8**	**13%**	**1.0**	**38.9**	**101**	**$28**

After years of inconsistency and injury, he's been remarkably consistent over three years in STL. Has everything you seek in an ace: elite CMD, high GB%, RH hitters can't touch him. Bid full value.

Carrasco,Hector

	Yr	W	L	Sv	IP	K	ERA	WHIP	OBA	vL	vR	BF/G	H%	S%	xERA	G	L	F	Ctl	Dom	Cmd	hr/f	hr/9	RAR	BPV	R$
RH Reliever	02 TEX	0	0	0	0	0	0.00	0.00											0.0	0.0						
Age 37	03 BAL *	6	8	5	82	66	3.94	1.47	256	288	256	4.9	30%	75%	4.32				4.5	7.2	**1.6**		0.9	6.0	55	$9
Decline	04 JPN	8	8	5	76	74	6.91	1.65	270			6.6	32%	60%	5.60				5.4	8.7	**1.6**		1.6	-24.1	40	$3
Type Power	05 WAS	5	4	2	88	75	2.04	1.10	192	206	178	5.5	23%	85%	3.59	42	21	37	3.9	7.7	**2.0**	7%	0.6	23.9	86	$13
Reliability 2	06 ANA	7	3	1	100	72	3.42	1.20	248	249	240	7.4	28%	75%	3.39	50	19	31	2.4	6.5	**2.7**	11%	0.9	14.1	73	$13
DL	1st Half	2	2	1	50	37	4.13	1.26	250			8.0	29%	68%	3.60	47	20	33	2.9	6.6	**2.3**	8%	0.7	2.6	72	$5
ERA Potl 50%	2nd Half	5	1	0	50	35	2.70	1.14	246			6.8	27%	82%	3.17	53	18	29	2.0	6.3	**3.2**	14%	1.1	11.5	78	$8
LIMA Plan C+	07 Proj	**7**	**4**	**0**	**87**	**69**	**3.62**	**1.26**	**239**			**6.4**	**28%**	**74%**	**3.55**	**48**	**19**	**33**	**3.4**	**7.1**	**2.1**	**11%**	**0.9**	**10.0**	**66**	**$10**

No surprise that 2005's ERA wasn't sustained, that was a H%-induced fluke. Swingman role means more IP and more vulture win opps, and keeps him off the radar. Nice profit opportunity.

Casilla,Santiago

	Yr	W	L	Sv	IP	K	ERA	WHIP	OBA	vL	vR	BF/G	H%	S%	xERA	G	L	F	Ctl	Dom	Cmd	hr/f	hr/9	RAR	BPV	R$
RH Reliever	02	0	0	0	0	0	0.00	0.00																		
Age 26	03	0	0	0	0	0	0.00	0.00																		
Growth	04	0	0	0	0	0	0.00	0.00																		
Type Power	05	0	0	0	0	0	0.00	0.00																		
Reliability 0	06 OAK *	2	0	4	35	29	4.10	1.14	227	400		5.3	28%	63%	3.02	40	40	20	2.8	7.4	**2.6**	10%	0.5	2.0	94	$5
DL	1st Half	2	0	4	35	29	4.11	1.14	227			5.3	28%	63%	3.02	40	40	20	2.8	7.5	**2.6**	10%	0.5	1.9	94	$5
ERA Potl 75%	2nd Half	0	0	0	0	0	0.00	0.00																		
LIMA Plan A	07 Proj	**3**	**0**	**0**	**45**	**41**	**4.45**	**1.26**	**246**			**4.9**	**31%**	**64%**	**3.29**				**3.0**	**8.3**	**2.7**		**0.6**	**6.6**	**95**	**$5**

0-0, 11.57 ERA in 2 IP at OAK. Formerly known as Jairo Garcia. By any name, he's another power arm and excellent LIMA option out of the OAK pen.

Cassidy,Scott

	Yr	W	L	Sv	IP	K	ERA	WHIP	OBA	vL	vR	BF/G	H%	S%	xERA	G	L	F	Ctl	Dom	Cmd	hr/f	hr/9	RAR	BPV	R$
RH Reliever	02	0	0	0	0	0	0.00	0.00																		
Age 31	03 aaa	3	4	4	80	60	4.59	1.82	297			6.7	36%	74%	5.40				5.7	6.8	**1.2**		0.5	-1.9	47	$1
Peak	04 aaa	5	3	1	80	56	4.44	1.60	282			13.0	31%	76%	5.36				4.4	6.3	**1.4**		1.2	-1.0	29	$3
Type Power	05 aaa	6	4	11	79	66	4.63	1.42	265			8.0	32%	68%	4.14				3.6	7.6	**2.1**		0.8	-3.2	69	$9
Reliability 5	06 SD	6	4	0	42	49	2.56	1.37	247	237	255	4.3	31%	92%	3.28	36	26	38	4.1	10.5	**2.6**	19%	1.7	10.0	71	$7
DL	1st Half	4	3	0	36	39	2.25	1.31	251			4.5	30%	95%	3.19	36	27	37	3.3	9.8	**3.0**	19%	1.8	9.9	74	$6
ERA Potl 25%	2nd Half	2	1	0	6	10	4.35	1.77	222			3.6	35%	80%	3.83	31	23	46	8.7	14.5	**1.7**	17%	1.5	0.1	89	$1
LIMA Plan C	07 Proj	**3**	**2**	**0**	**44**	**37**	**3.93**	**1.52**	**273**			**7.1**	**32%**	**78%**	**4.09**	**36**	**27**	**37**	**4.1**	**7.7**	**1.9**	**12%**	**1.2**	**1.5**	**48**	**$3**

One time-tested way to post a low ERA is to strand 92% of your runners. To be fair, he showed some nice growth in DOM, too. That may be sustainable, but the S% certainly is not.

Chacin,Gustavo

	Yr	W	L	Sv	IP	K	ERA	WHIP	OBA	vL	vR	BF/G	H%	S%	xERA	G	L	F	Ctl	Dom	Cmd	hr/f	hr/9	RAR	BPV	R$
LH Starter	02 aa	6	5	1	119	59	5.29	1.69	301			15.7	32%	69%	5.51				4.2	4.5	**1.1**		0.9	-14.9	16	($0)
Age 26	03 a/a	3	4	2	69	48	5.34	1.71	314			7.0	37%	66%	5.04				3.8	6.3	**1.7**		0.1	-8.1	61	$1
Growth	04 a/a	18	3	0	153	107	3.88	1.38	267			24.4	30%	76%	4.53				3.2	6.3	**1.9**		1.2	8.7	45	$15
Type	05 TOR	13	9	0	203	121	3.72	1.39	271	225	288	25.8	30%	76%	4.28	41	22	37	3.1	5.4	**1.7**	8%	0.9	16.2	43	$15
Reliability 16	06 TOR	9	4	0	87	47	5.06	1.47	268	268	266	22.5	26%	72%	4.86	35	21	44	3.9	4.9	**1.2**	15%	2.0	-5.4	-2	$6
DL 94	1st Half	6	2	0	51	28	5.64	1.51	273			22.6	26%	70%	4.90	33	24	43	4.1	4.9	**1.2**	18%	2.3	-6.8	-13	$3
ERA Potl 40%	2nd Half	3	2	0	36	19	4.25	1.42	262			22.3	27%	76%	4.81	38	17	44	3.7	4.7	**1.3**	11%	1.5	1.4	13	$3
LIMA Plan D+	07 Proj	**14**	**7**	**0**	**160**	**93**	**4.46**	**1.45**	**272**			**20.5**	**29%**	**74%**	**4.63**	**38**	**21**	**42**	**3.6**	**5.2**	**1.5**	**11%**	**1.4**	**-2.8**	**22**	**$11**

Already-marginal BPIs deteriorated quite a bit in his sophomore year. Elbow problems were likely a factor. Even if healthy, skill set is uninspiring. Let someone else gamble on a return to '05 form.

RAY MURPHY

Chacon,Shawn

Chacon,Shawn		Yr	Tm	W	L	Sv	IP	K	ERA	WHIP	OBA	vL	vR	BF/G	H%	S%	xERA	G	L	F	Ctl	Dom	Cmd	hr/f	hr/9	RAR	BPV	R$
RH	Starter	02	COL *	7	11	0	139	80	5.76	1.56	274	319	220	24.9	28%	68%	4.74	45	15	40	4.5	5.2	1.2	16%	1.9	-28.4	-1	($0)
Age	29	03	COL	11	8	0	137	93	4.60	1.33	243	254	230	25.3	28%	66%	4.36	40	17	43	3.8	6.1	1.6	7%	0.8	-5.4	53	$10
Pre-Peak		04	COL	1	9	35	63	52	7.13	1.95	285	236	326	4.7	32%	66%	5.73	33	19	48	7.4	7.4	1.0	13%	1.7	-22.3	12	$6
Type	Power	05	2TM	8	10	0	151	79	3.45	1.33	240	232	252	23.8	26%	76%	4.64	40	21	39	3.9	4.7	1.2	7%	0.8	15.9	35	$11
Reliability	10	06	2TM	7	6	0	109	62	6.36	1.72	287	305	274	19.4	29%	67%	5.59	33	18	50	5.2	5.1	1.0	13%	1.9	-24.7	-8	($1)
DL	25 33	1st Half		4	2	0	52	29	5.70	1.69	290			20.0	31%	67%	5.46	36	17	47	4.8	5.0	1.0	7%	1.0	-7.6	18	$0
ERA Potl	40%	2nd Half		3	4	0	57	33	6.96	1.74	285			18.9	27%	67%	5.72	29	18	52	5.5	5.2	0.9	17%	2.7	-17.1	-32	($2)
LIMA Plan	F	07	Proj	6	8	0	106	64	5.72	1.63	273			18.5	28%	69%	5.27	35	18	46	5.1	5.5	1.1	12%	1.6	-11.0	7	$1

Outside of his lucky 2005, his skills have been brutally MIA for five years, with no sign of change. I just spent 15 minutes trying to find a reason why any team - real or fantasy - would want him, and I couldn't.

Chen,Bruce

Chen,Bruce		Yr	Tm	W	L	Sv	IP	K	ERA	WHIP	OBA	vL	vR	BF/G	H%	S%	xERA	G	L	F	Ctl	Dom	Cmd	hr/f	hr/9	RAR	BPV	R$
LH	Reliever	02	2NL	2	5	0	77	80	5.61	1.66	281	252	287	6.4	36%	66%	4.95				5.0	9.4	1.9		0.8	-14.3	69	($0)
Age	29	03	aaa	5	5	1	85	60	5.61	1.33	288			22.6	32%	60%	4.87				1.7	6.4	3.8		1.4	-12.8	73	$4
Peak		04	BAL *	6	5	0	152	130	4.20	1.39	271	200	227	19.9	31%	76%	3.83	41	17	43	3.1	7.7	2.5	13%	1.5	4.4	53	$10
Type	Power	05	BAL	13	10	0	197	133	3.84	1.27	252	324	224	24.3	27%	76%	3.98	39	21	40	2.9	6.1	2.1	14%	1.5	13.0	40	$18
Reliability	53	06	BAL	0	7	0	98	70	6.97	1.75	331	328	337	11.5	35%	67%	4.70	33	21	47	3.2	6.4	2.0	17%	2.6	-29.2	-8	($5)
DL		1st Half		0	6	0	60	37	6.75	1.72	329			16.4	33%	68%	4.98	30	20	50	3.0	5.6	1.9	17%	2.7	-16.2	-20	($3)
ERA Potl	50%	2nd Half		0	1	0	38	33	7.30	1.81	334			7.8	37%	64%	4.27	37	22	41	3.5	7.8	2.2	19%	2.4	-12.9	10	($2)
LIMA Plan	F	07	Proj	2	4	0	73	56	5.34	1.53	294			12.4	32%	72%	4.22	36	21	43	3.2	7.0	2.2	16%	2.0	2.4	24	$2

He's always had issues with allowing HR, but 2.6 HR/9 is just absurd. HR/F says some of that was bad luck, but not all of it. xERA filters out the bad luck and says it wasn't THAT bad. I'd speculate with a reserve pick.

Chulk,Vinnie

Chulk,Vinnie		Yr	Tm	W	L	Sv	IP	K	ERA	WHIP	OBA	vL	vR	BF/G	H%	S%	xERA	G	L	F	Ctl	Dom	Cmd	hr/f	hr/9	RAR	BPV	R$
RH	Reliever	02	a/a	13	6	1	156	95	3.52	1.36	261			24.7	29%	76%	3.88				3.3	5.5	1.7		0.7	14.5	50	$14
Age	28	03	aaa	8	10	0	119	79	5.52	1.57	294			23.3	32%	67%	5.48				3.6	6.0	1.7		1.3	-16.5	29	$3
Pre-Peak		04	TOR *	4	5	4	84	65	4.29	1.56	278	308	228	5.8	31%	76%	4.34	40	20	39	4.3	7.0	1.6	12%	1.3	1.5	37	$5
Type	Power	05	TOR	0	1	0	72	39	3.88	1.31	251	283	231	4.9	26%	74%	4.36	42	19	39	3.3	4.9	1.5	10%	1.1	4.4	32	$3
Reliability	12	06	2TM *	4	5	1	78	78	4.45	1.37	244	206	282	5.0	30%	71%	3.56	43	18	39	4.1	9.0	2.2	14%	1.3	0.7	67	$7
DL		1st Half		4	2	1	44	43	5.00	1.44	274			6.0	32%	72%	3.45	40	25	34	3.4	8.7	2.6	21%	1.9	-2.6	49	$4
ERA Potl	50%	2nd Half		0	3	0	34	36	3.72	1.28	202			4.1	27%	71%	3.67	46	11	43	5.1	9.4	1.9	6%	0.5	3.4	94	$3
LIMA Plan	C+	07	Proj	2	3	7	58	51	4.19	1.38	248			5.3	29%	73%	3.85	43	18	39	4.0	7.9	2.0	11%	1.1	4.1	61	$6

1-3, 5.24 ERA in 46 IP at TOR and SF. Dramatic spike in DOM puts him back on our radar screen. Also reversed his L/R splits, indicating some new approach. Could be a speculative saves source.

Claussen,Brandon

Claussen,Brandon		Yr	Tm	W	L	Sv	IP	K	ERA	WHIP	OBA	vL	vR	BF/G	H%	S%	xERA	G	L	F	Ctl	Dom	Cmd	hr/f	hr/9	RAR	BPV	R$
LH	Starter	02	aaa	2	8	0	93	65	3.68	1.47	262			27.2	31%	74%	3.89				4.3	6.3	1.5		0.4	6.8	60	$4
Age	28	03	aaa	2	2	0	84	47	4.71	1.26	257			25.1	28%	64%	3.88				2.6	5.0	2.0		1.0	-3.3	46	$4
Pre-Peak		04	CIN *	10	14	0	166	137	5.64	1.62	287	375	278	23.6	34%	66%	4.47	37	20	43	4.3	7.4	1.7	9%	1.1	-28.1	45	$2
Type		05	CIN	10	11	0	166	121	4.22	1.41	275	233	275	24.8	31%	74%	4.23	37	19	44	3.1	6.6	2.1	10%	1.3	0.4	45	$10
Reliability	22	06	CIN	3	8	0	77	57	6.19	1.57	300	164	331	24.7	33%	64%	4.40	36	20	44	3.3	6.7	2.0	13%	1.6	-16.2	29	($0)
DL	106	1st Half		3	8	0	77	57	6.19	1.57	300			24.7	33%	64%	4.40	36	20	44	3.3	6.7	2.0	13%	1.6	-16.2	29	($0)
ERA Potl	55%	2nd Half		0	0	0	0	0	0.00	0.00																		
LIMA Plan	D	07	Proj	5	9	0	116	84	4.97	1.49	281			24.4	32%	69%	4.41	36	20	44	3.5	6.5	1.9	10%	1.2	-0.6	40	$4

Was sustaining 2005's growth before shoulder surgery shut him down. Supposed to be ready for spring, but this skill set isn't so attractive that you would want to own it at less than 100%.

Clemens,Roger

Clemens,Roger		Yr	Tm	W	L	Sv	IP	K	ERA	WHIP	OBA	vL	vR	BF/G	H%	S%	xERA	G	L	F	Ctl	Dom	Cmd	hr/f	hr/9	RAR	BPV	R$
RH	Starter	02	NYY	13	7	0	187	197	4.24	1.29	253	220	283	26.3	33%	69%	3.13	41	25	34	3.0	9.5	3.1	10%	0.9	5.2	101	$20
Age	44	03	NYY	17	9	0	211	190	3.92	1.22	251	215	288	26.5	30%	71%	3.31	42	22	36	2.5	8.1	3.3	11%	1.0	15.6	92	$25
Decline		04	HOU	18	4	0	214	218	2.98	1.16	219	218	217	26.5	29%	76%	3.02	49	18	33	3.3	9.2	2.8	8%	0.6	33.7	105	$29
Type	Power	05	HOU	13	8	0	211	185	1.88	1.01	202	195	202	25.9	25%	84%	2.95	50	20	30	2.6	7.9	3.0	7%	0.5	61.7	110	$33
Reliability	61	06	HOU	7	6	0	113	102	2.31	1.04	218	254	185	23.6	27%	80%	3.02	49	16	35	2.3	8.1	3.5	7%	0.6	30.4	117	$18
DL		1st Half		0	2	0	11	7	2.43	1.17	223			22.7	27%	77%	3.51	53	22	25	3.2	5.7	1.8	0%	0.0	2.8	81	$1
ERA Potl	50%	2nd Half		7	4	0	102	95	2.29	1.03	218			23.7	27%	81%	2.97	49	15	36	2.2	8.4	3.8	7%	0.6	27.6	123	$17
LIMA Plan	B	07	Proj	6	4	0	101	96	2.94	1.13	228			25.6	29%	76%	2.97	49	19	32	2.7	8.6	3.2	9%	0.7	17.4	107	$13

No other human in the history of the game has been able to consistently post this caliber of BPIs at this age. We can just watch in awe, or demand to look behind the curtain so future generations can benefit. Okay?

Clement,Matt

Clement,Matt		Yr	Tm	W	L	Sv	IP	K	ERA	WHIP	OBA	vL	vR	BF/G	H%	S%	xERA	G	L	F	Ctl	Dom	Cmd	hr/f	hr/9	RAR	BPV	R$
RH	Starter	02	CHC	12	11	0	205	215	3.60	1.20	219	219	212	26.4	28%	72%	3.01	47	23	30	3.7	9.4	2.5	11%	0.8	12.8	97	$22
Age	32	03	CHC	14	12	0	201	171	4.12	1.23	230	246	209	26.1	27%	69%	3.20	53	19	28	3.5	7.7	2.2	14%	1.0	3.9	71	$19
Peak		04	CHC	9	13	0	181	190	3.68	1.28	233	234	224	25.4	29%	76%	3.08	50	17	33	3.8	9.4	2.5	15%	1.1	13.0	83	$17
Type	Finesse	05	BOS	13	6	0	191	146	4.57	1.36	263	275	244	25.6	31%	67%	3.74	45	21	34	3.2	6.9	2.1	9%	0.8	-4.7	63	$14
Reliability	28	06	BOS	5	5	0	65	43	6.64	1.77	295	307	272	25.4	33%	63%	4.77	49	16	35	5.3	5.9	1.1	10%	1.1	-16.7	22	($1)
DL	107	1st Half		5	5	0	65	43	6.64	1.77	295			25.4	33%	63%	4.77	49	16	35	5.3	5.9	1.1	10%	1.1	-16.7	22	($1)
ERA Potl		2nd Half		0	0	0	0	0	0.00	0.00																		
LIMA Plan		07	Proj	0	0	0	0	0	0.00	0.00								49	18	33								

Finally diagnosed with a torn labrum and rotator cuff in late September, which probably explains the complete collapse of his skill set going back to the 2nd half of 2005. Expected to miss all of 2007.

Coffey,Todd

Coffey,Todd		Yr	Tm	W	L	Sv	IP	K	ERA	WHIP	OBA	vL	vR	BF/G	H%	S%	xERA	G	L	F	Ctl	Dom	Cmd	hr/f	hr/9	RAR	BPV	R$
RH	Reliever	02		0	0	0	0	0	0.00	0.00											0.0	0.0						
Age	26	03		0	0	0	0	0	0.00	0.00											0.0	0.0						
Growth		04	a/a	5	2	24	59	52	3.77	1.10	261			4.3	32%	67%	3.36				0.9	8.0	8.5		0.8	4.1	205	$15
Type		05	CIN	4	1	1	58	26	4.50	1.64	339	337	348	4.6	36%	73%	4.04	51	23	26	1.7	4.0	2.4	9%	0.8	-1.8	38	$1
Reliability	24	06	CIN	6	7	8	78	60	3.58	1.44	279	347	242	4.2	33%	77%	3.48	52	21	27	3.1	6.9	2.2	10%	0.8	8.8	63	$10
DL		1st Half		3	2	6	41	28	2.63	1.31	252			4.8	29%	82%	3.31	57	21	22	3.3	6.1	1.9	11%	0.7	9.4	61	$7
ERA Potl	45%	2nd Half		3	5	2	37	32	4.63	1.57	307			3.7	37%	72%	3.63	47	20	33	2.9	7.8	2.7	10%	1.0	-0.7	67	$3
LIMA Plan	B	07	Proj	4	4	3	58	40	3.88	1.40	288			4.2	33%	74%	3.49	51	22	27	2.3	6.2	2.7	10%	0.8	6.3	67	$5

Recovered some of his lost DOM, and rode it all the way into a stint as CIN closer, where he acquitted himself decently. Good LIMA option and speculative save source if he can sustain 2nd half CMD.

Colon,Bartolo

Colon,Bartolo		Yr	Tm	W	L	Sv	IP	K	ERA	WHIP	OBA	vL	vR	BF/G	H%	S%	xERA	G	L	F	Ctl	Dom	Cmd	hr/f	hr/9	RAR	BPV	R$
RH	Starter	02	2TM	20	8	0	233	149	2.94	1.24	250	242	261	29.4	28%	79%	3.83	47	18	36	2.7	5.8	2.1	8%	0.8	38.4	61	$27
Age	33	03	CHW	15	13	0	242	173	3.87	1.20	246	250	246	29.3	27%	72%	3.90	39	18	44	2.5	6.4	2.6	9%	1.1	19.6	65	$25
Past Peak		04	ANA	18	12	0	208	158	5.02	1.37	268	273	256	26.3	29%	69%	4.09	39	17	45	3.1	6.8	2.2	13%	1.6	-15.0	40	$15
Type	Finesse	05	ANA	21	8	0	222	157	3.48	1.16	255	250	258	27.5	29%	74%	3.56	44	17	39	1.7	6.4	3.7	10%	1.1	24.3	87	$28
Reliability	33	06	ANA	1	5	0	56	31	5.13	1.46	310	354	261	24.6	32%	70%	4.11	41	22	37	1.8	5.0	2.8	15%	1.8	-4.0	29	$1
DL	125	1st Half		0	3	0	26	18	5.84	1.83	357			24.9	38%	76%	4.34	37	25	37	2.4	6.2	2.6	19%	2.4	-4.1	3	($1)
ERA Potl	45%	2nd Half		1	2	0	30	13	4.51	1.14	262			24.3	27%	63%	3.89	44	20	36	1.2	3.9	3.3	11%	1.2	0.2	58	$2
LIMA Plan	C+	07	Proj	7	9	0	138	86	4.50	1.33	281			25.5	30%	71%	3.94	42	20	39	2.0	5.6	2.8	13%	1.4	9.3	48	$9

Poster child for burnout risk and bad conditioning finally broke down. Elected to rehab a torn rotator cuff rather than have surgery, which elevates the risk for 2007. Bid cautiously, if at all.

Colon,Roman

Colon,Roman		Yr	Tm	W	L	Sv	IP	K	ERA	WHIP	OBA	vL	vR	BF/G	H%	S%	xERA	G	L	F	Ctl	Dom	Cmd	hr/f	hr/9	RAR	BPV	R$
RH	Reliever	02		0	0	0	0	0	0.00	0.00											0.0	0.0						
Age	27	03	aa	11	3	2	107	47	4.78	1.57	305			12.3	32%	71%	5.39				3.0	3.9	1.3		1.0	-5.1	16	$6
Pre-Peak		04	a/a	5	2	0	77	57	4.55	1.46	292			6.2	34%	69%	4.56				2.7	6.7	2.5		0.6	-2.0	70	$4
Type		05	2TM	2	6	0	69	47	5.60	1.49	296	304	282	8.7	31%	70%	3.62	50	21	29	2.7	6.1	2.2	26%	2.2	-11.0	13	$1
Reliability	5	06	DET	2	0	1	38	25	4.95	1.57	299	271	323	8.6	33%	72%	4.52	40	17	43	3.3	5.9	1.8	11%	1.4	-1.8	26	$2
DL	41	1st Half		0	0	0	19	14	5.68	1.58	300			9.5	31%	72%	4.52	30	23	47	3.3	6.6	2.0	17%	2.4	-2.6	6	($0)
ERA Potl	40%	2nd Half		2	0	1	19	11	4.22	1.56	298			7.8	34%	72%	4.47	51	11	38	3.3	5.2	1.6	4%	0.5	0.8	45	$2
LIMA Plan	C+	07	Proj	3	1	0	44	28	4.76	1.54	298			8.4	32%	73%	4.24	45	18	37	3.1	5.8	1.9	13%	1.4	1.3	26	$2

Looked like a sleeper entering 2006; could not win a job in suddenly pitching-rich DET. BPIs showed some erosion, but sample is small. Still holds some marginal intrigue, but opps may be tough to come by.

RAY MURPHY

Contreras,Jose		W	L	Sv	IP	K	ERA	WHIP	OBA	vL	vR	BF/G	H%	S%	xERA	G	L	F	Ctl	Dom	Cmd	hr/f	hr/9	RAR	BPV	R$
RH Starter	02 CUB	13	4	0	143	149	1.76	0.29	0			22.9	0%		-2.15				2.6	9.4	3.6			44.2	188	$39
Age 35	03 NYY *	9	2	0	87	88	2.90	1.14	209	203	202	16.0	28%	76%	3.03	47	21	32	3.5	9.1	2.6	7%	0.5	17.5	107	$15
Past Peak	04 2AL	13	9	0	170	150	5.50	1.47	257	251	254	24.1	29%	67%	3.97	44	16	40	4.4	7.9	1.8	16%	1.6	-22.5	39	$9
Type	05 CHW	15	7	0	204	154	3.61	1.23	235	231	233	26.5	27%	74%	3.71	44	20	36	3.3	6.8	2.1	11%	1.0	19.1	61	$22
Reliability 88	06 CHW	13	9	0	196	134	4.27	1.27	260	267	248	27.4	29%	68%	3.86	45	16	39	2.5	6.2	2.4	8%	0.9	6.9	64	$18
DL 16	1st Half	8	0	0	91	64	3.16	1.10	226			28.2	25%	75%	3.60	47	13	39	2.5	6.3	2.6	9%	0.9	15.7	75	$14
ERA Potl 55%	2nd Half	5	9	0	105	70	5.23	1.42	287			26.8	32%	64%	4.08	43	19	39	2.6	6.0	2.3	8%	0.9	-8.7	54	$5
LIMA Plan D+	07 Proj	13	8	0	189	144	4.15	1.25	243			25.3	28%	69%	3.73	44	18	38	3.1	6.9	2.3	10%	1.0	17.7	65	$19

CTL is improving and DOM declining. That approach will cause problems as DOM drops toward key 5.6 level. Signs of decline are creeping in, don't get caught holding him when the cliff comes.

Cook,Aaron		W	L	Sv	IP	K	ERA	WHIP	OBA	vL	vR	BF/G	H%	S%	xERA	G	L	F	Ctl	Dom	Cmd	hr/f	hr/9	RAR	BPV	R$
RH Starter	02 a/a	13	7	0	194	93	3.29	1.28	269	295	295	24.7	29%	77%	3.99				2.2	4.3	1.9		0.9	23.4	41	$17
Age 28	03 COL *	5	7	0	140	53	5.66	1.66	303	342	298	14.3	32%	65%	4.49	59	16	25	3.9	3.4	0.9	8%	0.7	-23.8	12	($3)
Pre-Peak	04 COL *	9	5	0	142	61	3.92	1.37	271	267	324	26.5	29%	71%	3.92	58	16	26	2.9	3.9	1.3	6%	0.5	5.9	37	$8
Type Finesse	05 COL	7	2	0	83	24	3.68	1.41	301	313	281	27.7	31%	76%	3.60	62	20	19	1.7	2.6	1.5	14%	0.9	5.8	16	$5
Reliability 24	06 COL	9	15	0	212	92	4.24	1.40	288	314	258	28.6	31%	70%	3.75	58	18	24	2.3	3.9	1.7	10%	0.7	6.4	34	$10
DL 127	1st Half	6	7	0	108	48	3.50	1.33	281			28.7	30%	75%	3.47	60	19	21	2.1	4.0	1.9	10%	0.7	13.2	43	$8
ERA Potl 45%	2nd Half	3	8	0	104	44	5.01	1.47	295			28.6	31%	66%	4.04	56	18	27	2.6	3.8	1.5	9%	0.8	-6.8	26	$1
LIMA Plan C	07 Proj	11	10	0	203	80	4.39	1.41	289			26.6	30%	70%	3.78	59	18	23	2.3	3.5	1.5	10%	0.8	14.6	28	$9

Another low-DOM guy whose fate rests in the hands of his infield defense. That worked reasonably well in COL this year (longer grass?), but don't expect another step forward without a strikeout pitch.

Corcoran,Tim		W	L	Sv	IP	K	ERA	WHIP	OBA	vL	vR	BF/G	H%	S%	xERA	G	L	F	Ctl	Dom	Cmd	hr/f	hr/9	RAR	BPV	R$
RH Reliever	02 aa	0	5	1	49	39	4.41	2.10	343			7.0	40%	81%	7.21				5.7	7.2	1.3		0.9	-0.8	28	($2)
Age 29	03 aa	4	1	3	44	26	6.14	1.62	283			7.7	33%	59%	4.44				4.5	5.3	1.2		0.2	-9.5	48	$2
Pre-Peak	04 a/a	3	4	0	67	41	5.07	1.77	292			8.1	32%	72%	5.62				5.5	5.4	1.0		0.9	-6.0	23	($1)
Type Power	05 aaa	5	1	0	56	40	2.88	1.32	250			8.2	30%	78%	3.31				3.4	6.4	1.9		0.3	9.9	73	$7
Reliability 5	06 TAM *	10	10	1	127	84	3.87	1.48	265	281	262	14.0	30%	76%	4.45	40	23	37	4.2	5.9	1.4	8%	0.9	10.8	42	$11
DL	1st Half	6	1	1	45	29	2.53	1.33	267			8.4	31%	82%	4.04	38	27	35	2.7	5.8	2.1	4%	0.4	11.3	68	$7
ERA Potl 40%	2nd Half	4	9	0	82	55	4.61	1.56	264			21.6	29%	73%	4.67	40	23	37	4.9	6.0	1.2	10%	1.1	-0.5	31	$4
LIMA Plan C+	07 Proj	5	4	0	73	48	4.22	1.52	271			11.9	31%	73%	4.51	40	23	37	4.2	6.0	1.4	7%	0.7	-0.2	44	$4

5-9, 4.38 ERA in 90 IP at TAM. Built on 2005's CMD gains early, then couldn't sustain when he got moved to the rotation in June. Might be better suited to bullpen, but there's little value here.

Cordero,Chad		W	L	Sv	IP	K	ERA	WHIP	OBA	vL	vR	BF/G	H%	S%	xERA	G	L	F	Ctl	Dom	Cmd	hr/f	hr/9	RAR	BPV	R$
RH Reliever	02	0	0	0	0	0	0.00	0.00											0.0	0.0						
Age 24	03 MON	1	0	1	11	12	1.64	0.64	114			3.3	14%	83%	0.47				2.5	9.8	4.0		0.8	3.6	151	$3
Growth	04 MON	7	3	14	82	83	2.96	1.35	227	243	205	5.1	29%	82%	4.12	29	20	51	4.7	9.1	1.9	7%	0.9	13.2	78	$14
Type Power	05 WAS	2	4	47	74	61	1.82	0.97	208	186	205	3.9	24%	90%	3.52	35	16	49	2.1	7.4	3.6	9%	1.1	22.2	100	$26
Reliability 56	06 WAS	7	4	29	73	69	3.20	1.11	223	219	212	4.3	25%	81%	3.56	35	13	52	2.7	8.5	3.1	13%	1.6	11.6	79	$21
DL	1st Half	2	3	13	35	31	3.34	1.14	209			4.4	21%	84%	3.66	39	15	46	3.6	8.0	2.2	18%	2.1	4.9	46	$9
ERA Potl 40%	2nd Half	5	1	16	38	38	3.07	1.08	235			4.2	29%	78%	3.47	32	11	57	1.9	9.0	4.8	9%	1.2	6.7	126	$12
LIMA Plan C	07 Proj	5	4	43	73	66	2.73	1.09	218			4.3	25%	83%	3.63	34	15	51	2.7	8.2	3.0	10%	1.2	6.6	86	$25

Had some mild CTL and HR problems in 1st half, but posted career best BPIs down the stretch. Strong finishes are often obscured by slow starts, so he could be undervalued. That's good news for you. Buy!

Cordero,Francisco		W	L	Sv	IP	K	ERA	WHIP	OBA	vL	vR	BF/G	H%	S%	xERA	G	L	F	Ctl	Dom	Cmd	hr/f	hr/9	RAR	BPV	R$
RH Reliever	02 TEX *	2	2	12	57	58	2.84	1.23	237	189	216	4.7	31%	79%	3.37	40	19	41	3.2	9.2	2.9	6%	0.6	11.4	104	$11
Age 31	03 TEX	5	8	15	82	90	2.96	1.32	232	236	223	4.8	32%	78%	3.07	47	24	29	4.2	9.9	2.4	7%	0.4	15.8	104	$16
Peak	04 TEX	3	4	49	71	79	2.15	1.29	230	235	216	4.5	33%	82%	3.36	42	18	40	4.0	10.0	2.5	1%	0.1	20.1	117	$26
Type Power	05 TEX	3	1	37	69	79	3.39	1.32	239	250	214	4.2	33%	76%	3.21	43	19	38	3.9	10.3	2.6	7%	0.7	8.3	105	$19
Reliability 75	06 2TM	10	5	22	75	84	3.72	1.34	246	286	219	4.2	33%	74%	3.32	40	21	39	3.8	10.1	2.6	9%	0.8	7.5	96	$18
DL	1st Half	6	4	5	37	39	5.08	1.26	250			4.0	32%	60%	3.01	44	23	33	2.9	9.4	3.3	12%	1.0	-2.6	101	$7
ERA Potl 60%	2nd Half	4	1	17	38	45	2.37	1.42	241			4.3	33%	86%	3.64	35	19	46	4.7	10.7	2.3	7%	0.7	10.0	97	$12
LIMA Plan B	07 Proj	6	3	45	73	82	3.23	1.34	241			4.3	33%	77%	3.32	41	20	39	4.0	10.2	2.6	7%	0.6	9.8	103	$24

BPIs were still strong when he lost closer role in TEX, so made sense that he had success in MIL. There is minor decline, but much less than most think. He is one of the lowest risk closer options out there right now.

Cormier,Lance		W	L	Sv	IP	K	ERA	WHIP	OBA	vL	vR	BF/G	H%	S%	xERA	G	L	F	Ctl	Dom	Cmd	hr/f	hr/9	RAR	BPV	R$
RH Reliever	02	0	0	0	0	0	0.00	0.00											0.0	0.0						
Age 26	03 a/a	3	4	0	69	33	5.48	1.75	328			23.0	36%	68%	5.78				3.4	4.3	1.3		0.5	-9.2	26	($1)
Growth	04 ARI *	6	10	0	158	109	4.38	1.59	302	387	297	20.4	34%	74%	4.00	48	21	31	3.3	6.2	1.9	10%	0.9	-2.3	44	$4
Type	05 ARI	7	3	0	79	63	5.12	1.63	278	300	273	5.4	33%	69%	4.00	50	23	27	4.9	7.2	1.5	10%	0.8	-8.5	49	$3
Reliability 20	06 ATL *	8	8	0	127	66	5.23	1.77	323	271	351	15.7	35%	71%	4.55	50	21	29	3.8	4.7	1.2	10%	0.9	-11.7	16	($0)
DL	1st Half	3	3	0	40	16	6.56	2.04	325			9.0	34%	68%	5.42	56	18	26	6.1	3.6	0.6	10%	0.9	-10.3	-4	($3)
ERA Potl 45%	2nd Half	5	5	0	87	50	4.62	1.65	322			25.0	36%	74%	4.25	45	24	31	2.8	5.2	1.8	9%	0.9	-1.4	32	$2
LIMA Plan C+	07 Proj	3	2	0	44	26	5.17	1.72	310			10.6	35%	70%	4.37	50	22	28	4.1	5.4	1.3	9%	0.8	-0.1	28	$0

A Tale of Two Cormier's: You'd think this was a "Prince and the Pauper" story (this one's the pauper) but the truth is both are void of skill. The dearth of 2.0 CMD ratios is the tip-off that you're wasting your time here.

Cormier,Rheal		W	L	Sv	IP	K	ERA	WHIP	OBA	vL	vR	BF/G	H%	S%	xERA	G	L	F	Ctl	Dom	Cmd	hr/f	hr/9	RAR	BPV	R$
LH Reliever	02 PHI	5	6	0	60	49	5.25	1.55	265	291	253	5.0	31%	67%	3.55	56	22	22	4.8	7.4	1.5	15%	0.9	-8.5	51	$2
Age 40	03 PHI	8	0	1	84	67	1.82	0.95	188	119	207	5.0	23%	83%	2.93	56	16	29	2.7	7.2	2.7	6%	0.4	25.5	104	$16
Decline	04 PHI	4	5	0	81	46	3.56	1.19	235	250	230	4.0	26%	72%	3.69	53	16	30	2.9	5.1	1.8	9%	0.8	7.1	53	$7
Type Finesse	05 PHI	4	2	0	47	34	5.92	1.53	297	256	324	3.7	32%	65%	3.52	50	25	25	3.1	6.5	2.1	24%	1.7	-9.7	28	$1
Reliability 1	06 2NL	2	3	0	48	19	2.44	1.35	262	289	247	3.2	27%	87%	4.49	45	22	33	3.2	3.6	1.1	9%	0.9	12.1	19	$4
DL 15	1st Half	2	1	0	26	11	1.37	1.03	196			3.0	22%	85%	3.92	53	19	29	3.1	3.8	1.2	0%	0.0	10.1	64	$4
ERA Potl 20%	2nd Half	0	2	0	22	8	3.72	1.74	328			3.4	32%	88%	5.17	38	25	37	3.3	3.3	1.0	16%	2.1	2.1	-32	($0)
LIMA Plan C+	07 Proj	2	3	0	44	24	4.34	1.40	273			3.5	29%	73%	4.04	47	22	30	3.1	5.0	1.6	14%	1.2	1.7	27	$2

A 2.44 ERA makes him the Prince of the Cormiers. But the wide differences in ERA are due entirely to H%/S% variations. Pass on the bidding here too.

Corpas,Manuel		W	L	Sv	IP	K	ERA	WHIP	OBA	vL	vR	BF/G	H%	S%	xERA	G	L	F	Ctl	Dom	Cmd	hr/f	hr/9	RAR	BPV	R$
RH Reliever	02	0	0	0	0	0	0.00	0.00																		
Age 24	03	0	0	0	0	0	0.00	0.00																		
Growth	04	0	0	0	0	0	0.00	0.00																		
Type	05	0	0	0	0	0	0.00	0.00																		
Reliability 0	06 COL *	3	3	19	77	63	2.22	1.06	238	281	290	4.0	29%	81%	3.12	45	20	34	1.6	7.3	4.5	5%	0.5	21.6	132	$17
DL	1st Half	2	1	19	37	31	1.46	0.84	205			4.0	26%	83%					1.0	7.5	7.8		0.2	13.9	215	$14
ERA Potl 50%	2nd Half	1	2	0	40	32	2.92	1.27	266			4.0	32%	79%	3.44	45	20	34	2.2	7.2	3.2	7%	0.7	7.8	92	$4
LIMA Plan A	07 Proj	2	2	5	44	35	3.10	1.08	241			4.0	30%	71%	3.17	45	20	34	1.7	7.2	4.4	5%	0.4	6.4	130	$7

Emerged in 2nd half as COL's primary setup man. Appears well-suited for the role, with raw skills to develop into closer candidate. One of those guys that could conceivably earn $20 on your $1 investment.

Correia,Kevin		W	L	Sv	IP	K	ERA	WHIP	OBA	vL	vR	BF/G	H%	S%	xERA	G	L	F	Ctl	Dom	Cmd	hr/f	hr/9	RAR	BPV	R$
RH Reliever	02	0	0	0	0	0	0.00	0.00											0.0	0.0						
Age 26	03 a/a	6	7	0	105	81	3.68	1.26	256			23.1	31%	70%	3.33				2.6	6.9	2.7		0.4	9.2	89	$10
Growth	04 aaa	3	7	0	105	59	4.54	1.46	292			15.9	32%	69%	4.70				2.7	5.1	1.9		0.8	-2.5	44	$3
Type	05 SF *	5	7	7	104	74	5.21	1.57	277	311	242	10.0	30%	71%	4.56	37	24	39	4.4	6.4	1.4	13%	1.5	-12.4	24	$4
Reliability 16	06 SF	2	0	0	69	57	3.51	1.24	247	275	218	6.0	30%	73%	3.88	34	22	44	2.9	7.4	2.6	6%	0.7	8.3	85	$6
DL	1st Half	0	0	0	34	24	3.16	1.35	243			7.3	27%	81%	4.13	42	21	37	3.9	6.3	1.6	10%	1.1	5.6	46	$2
ERA Potl 50%	2nd Half	2	0	0	35	33	3.86	1.14	251			5.1	33%	64%	3.66	25	23	52	1.8	8.5	4.7	2%	0.3	2.7	147	$4
LIMA Plan C+	07 Proj	4	4	1	108	82	4.17	1.35	264			11.0	31%	71%	4.17	33	23	44	3.1	6.8	2.2	7%	0.8	2.6	65	$7

Figured something out in 2nd half, in a big way. Spike in FB% while reducing HR/9 means some of this might be a mirage. But the CMD spike makes him a breakout candidate. Watch what role he gets.

RAY MURPHY

Cotts,Neal

Cotts,Neal	Yr	W	L	Sv	IP	K	ERA	WHIP	OBA	vL	vR	BF/G	H%	S%	xERA	G	L	F	Ctl	Dom	Cmd	hr/f	hr/9	RAR	BPV	R$
LH Reliever	02	0	0	0	0	0	0.00	0.00											0.0	0.0						
Age 27	03 aa	9	7	0	108	117	3.16	1.37	220			22.1	31%	76%	2.96				5.2	9.7	**1.9**		0.2	16.4	102	$13
Growth	04 CHW	4	4	0	65	58	5.67	1.40	249	269	231	5.0	28%	64%	3.68	44	20	35	4.1	8.0	**1.9**	20%	1.8	-9.9	40	$3
Type Power	05 CHW	4	0	0	60	58	1.95	1.11	183	206	155	3.5	25%	82%	3.41	46	18	36	4.3	8.7	**2.0**	2%	0.1	18.0	108	$10
Reliability 17	06 CHW	1	2	1	54	43	5.17	1.63	296	263	314	3.5	32%	75%	4.15	42	21	37	4.0	7.2	**1.8**	19%	2.0	-4.1	16	$1
DL	1st Half	0	2	1	29	20	3.09	1.13	234			3.7	24%	82%	3.68	43	18	40	2.5	6.2	**2.5**	15%	1.5	5.3	52	$3
ERA Potl 40%	2nd Half	1	0	0	25	23	7.59	2.21	357			3.4	40%	71%	4.70	42	24	35	5.8	8.3	**1.4**	24%	2.5	-9.3	-12	($2)
LIMA Plan B	07 Proj	**3**	**2**	**0**	**58**	**52**	**4.19**	**1.45**	**258**			**3.9**	**30%**	**76%**	**3.79**	**43**	**20**	**36**	**4.2**	**8.1**	**1.9**	**15%**	**1.4**	**5.0**	**50**	**$4**

Why RPs are so unpredictable: If you combine his 2005-06 values for H%, S%, and HR/F, they all end up where we'd expect them. But the one-year fluctuations lead to ERA swings. xERA shows the truth.

Crain,Jesse

Crain,Jesse	Yr	W	L	Sv	IP	K	ERA	WHIP	OBA	vL	vR	BF/G	H%	S%	xERA	G	L	F	Ctl	Dom	Cmd	hr/f	hr/9	RAR	BPV	R$
RH Reliever	02	0	0	0	0	0	0.00	0.00											0.0	0.0						
Age 25	03 a/a	4	2	19	65	75	2.08	1.00	194			5.7	29%	77%	1.47				2.9	10.4	**3.6**		0.0	18.6	154	$18
Growth	04 aaa	3	2	19	50	57	3.05	1.20	233			5.0	31%	78%	3.30				3.0	10.2	**3.4**		0.9	8.0	113	$13
Type	05 MIN	12	5	1	79	25	2.73	1.14	215	194	225	4.3	22%	79%	4.62	46	16	37	3.3	2.8	**0.9**	6%	0.7	16.1	27	$13
Reliability 6	06 MIN	4	5	1	76	60	3.54	1.27	269	259	263	4.7	32%	74%	2.98	55	21	24	2.1	7.1	**3.3**	11%	0.7	9.5	92	$9
DL	1st Half	1	4	0	34	30	5.26	1.55	328			4.8	39%	67%	2.77	57	22	21	1.6	7.9	**5.0**	17%	1.1	-3.0	110	$1
ERA Potl 55%	2nd Half	3	1	1	42	30	2.14	1.05	213			4.6	25%	81%	3.16	53	19	27	2.6	6.4	**2.5**	6%	0.4	12.5	91	$8
LIMA Plan B+	07 Proj	**6**	**4**	**3**	**73**	**55**	**3.10**	**1.19**	**241**			**4.7**	**29%**	**75%**	**3.25**	**52**	**19**	**29**	**2.6**	**6.8**	**2.6**	**8%**	**0.6**	**11.1**	**84**	**$11**

Nice growth year was covered up by the 10% rise in H%. Increasing GB% is a positive. But this wild DOM swing -- 10.2 to 2.8 to 7.1 -- what's the deal with that? Seriously, what really happened in 2005?

Cruceta,Francisco

Cruceta,Francisco	Yr	W	L	Sv	IP	K	ERA	WHIP	OBA	vL	vR	BF/G	H%	S%	xERA	G	L	F	Ctl	Dom	Cmd	hr/f	hr/9	RAR	BPV	R$
RH Starter	02	0	0	0	0	0	0.00	0.00																		
Age 25	03 aa	13	9	0	163	115	4.14	1.47	269			26.5	32%	71%	4.12				3.9	6.3	**1.6**		0.5	5.1	58	$12
Growth	04 a/a	10	13	0	171	91	4.73	1.47	274			25.9	30%	69%	4.55				3.7	4.8	**1.3**		0.8	-8.2	31	$6
Type Power	05 aaa	7	5	0	111	93	5.18	1.55	307			15.5	36%	69%	5.61				2.7	7.5	**2.8**		1.3	-12.1	59	$4
Reliability 0	06 SEA	* 13	9	0	166	166	5.35	1.59	277	200	471	23.4	33%	70%	4.50	31	12	58	4.6	9.0	**2.0**	11%	1.6	-16.3	47	$10
DL	1st Half	6	4	0	81	86	4.37	1.58	268			24.3	35%	74%					4.9	9.6	**1.9**		0.9	1.9	72	$6
ERA Potl 50%	2nd Half	7	5	0	85	80	6.29	1.60	285			22.6	32%	67%	4.54	31	12	58	4.3	8.5	**2.0**	14%	2.2	-18.2	23	$3
LIMA Plan C+	07 Proj	**6**	**7**	**0**	**104**	**89**	**5.19**	**1.55**	**283**			**21.1**	**33%**	**70%**	**5.27**				**3.9**	**7.7**	**2.0**		**1.4**	**-10.1**	**45**	**$5**

0-0, 10.80 ERA in 7 IP at SEA. Rising DOM and CMD trends are enticing, will need to cut down on HR to succeed in majors. Moving from SEA to TEX isn't going to help that problem.

Cruz,Juan

Cruz,Juan	Yr	W	L	Sv	IP	K	ERA	WHIP	OBA	vL	vR	BF/G	H%	S%	xERA	G	L	F	Ctl	Dom	Cmd	hr/f	hr/9	RAR	BPV	R$
RH Reliever	02 CHC	3	11	1	97	81	3.99	1.47	235	250	234	9.5	27%	76%	4.31	41	21	37	5.5	7.5	**1.4**	11%	1.0	1.4	51	$5
Age 28	03 CHC	* 6	7	0	111	106	4.38	1.32	255	292	265	13.8	32%	67%	3.34	42	25	33	3.2	8.6	**2.7**	8%	0.6	-1.4	93	$9
Pre-Peak	04 ATL	6	2	0	72	70	2.75	1.24	225	239	214	6.0	28%	82%	3.35	45	20	35	3.8	8.8	**2.3**	10%	0.6	13.4	85	$10
Type Power	05 OAK	* 5	4	0	107	111	4.03	1.32	235	283	296	11.1	31%	70%	3.34	45	19	35	4.0	9.3	**2.3**	9%	0.8	4.5	90	$10
Reliability 28	06 ARI	5	6	0	94	88	4.20	1.35	231	263	199	13.0	29%	69%	3.80	40	23	37	4.5	8.4	**1.9**	7%	0.7	3.3	78	$8
DL 26	1st Half	3	3	0	46	41	4.09	1.26	207			13.8	26%	67%	3.86	43	18	39	4.7	8.0	**1.7**	6%	0.6	2.3	80	$5
ERA Potl 60%	2nd Half	2	3	0	48	47	4.31	1.44	254			12.3	32%	71%	3.74	37	28	35	4.3	8.8	**2.0**	8%	0.7	1.0	78	$3
LIMA Plan B+	07 Proj	**3**	**3**	**3**	**58**	**56**	**3.88**	**1.33**	**234**			**10.7**	**29%**	**72%**	**3.61**	**41**	**23**	**36**	**4.2**	**8.7**	**2.1**	**9%**	**0.8**	**5.4**	**81**	**$6**

One disastrous start in June (2 outs, 9 ER) ruined what would have been a very nice year. Looked good in rotation (47% PQS-DOM), but ended up in bullpen. Risk is in his health, not his skills.

Davies,Kyle

Davies,Kyle	Yr	W	L	Sv	IP	K	ERA	WHIP	OBA	vL	vR	BF/G	H%	S%	xERA	G	L	F	Ctl	Dom	Cmd	hr/f	hr/9	RAR	BPV	R$
RH Starter	02	0	0	0	0	0	0.00	0.00											0.0	0.0						
Age 23	03	0	0	0	0	0	0.00	0.00											0.0	0.0						
Growth	04 a/a	4	2	0	67	70	3.33	1.09	208			22.4	25%	76%	3.11				3.2	9.5	**3.0**		1.3	8.4	94	$9
Type Power	05 ATL	* 12	8	0	160	119	4.57	1.57	274	264	295	21.2	32%	72%	4.67	34	25	41	4.6	6.7	**1.5**	7%	0.8	-6.3	46	$7
Reliability 0	06 ATL	3	7	0	63	51	8.42	1.95	336	333	331	21.9	37%	59%	4.72	37	24	39	4.7	7.3	**1.5**	17%	2.0	-30.6	4	($5)
DL 108	1st Half	2	3	0	42	36	6.18	1.56	292			23.7	31%	67%	4.26	33	20	47	3.6	7.7	**2.1**	18%	2.3	-8.8	17	$0
ERA Potl 65%	2nd Half	1	4	0	21	15	12.92	2.73	410			19.7	46%	50%	5.70	44	31	25	6.9	6.5	**0.9**	14%	1.3	-21.7	-7	($6)
LIMA Plan D	07 Proj	**9**	**11**	**0**	**131**	**105**	**4.97**	**1.66**	**290**			**20.6**	**34%**	**71%**	**4.33**	**39**	**27**	**35**	**4.6**	**7.2**	**1.6**	**10%**	**1.0**	**0.5**	**45**	**$4**

Torn groin cost him the middle of the season, and got rocked before and (especially) after the DL stint. BPIs were steady, so he probably deserves a mulligan. Set your expectations against 2005.

Davis,Doug

Davis,Doug	Yr	W	L	Sv	IP	K	ERA	WHIP	OBA	vL	vR	BF/G	H%	S%	xERA	G	L	F	Ctl	Dom	Cmd	hr/f	hr/9	RAR	BPV	R$
LH Starter	02 TEX	* 7	8	0	120	68	5.48	1.51	304	243	312	28.0	33%	65%	4.56	41	15	44	2.5	5.1	**2.1**	8%	1.1	-15.0	37	$3
Age 31	03 MIL	* 12	10	0	177	93	4.47	1.57	297	293	283	25.6	32%	75%	4.75	42	18	40	3.4	4.7	**1.4**	9%	1.2	-4.3	18	$6
Peak	04 MIL	12	12	0	215	168	3.26	1.28	243	259	244	26.6	29%	75%	3.65	47	19	34	3.3	7.0	**2.1**	6%	0.6	26.5	75	$20
Type Power	05 MIL	11	11	0	222	208	3.85	1.30	238	259	228	26.8	29%	74%	3.50	44	20	36	3.8	8.4	**2.2**	12%	1.1	10.9	73	$19
Reliability 90	06 MIL	11	11	0	203	159	4.92	1.52	265	307	253	26.5	31%	68%	4.19	44	20	36	4.5	7.0	**1.6**	9%	0.8	-10.8	52	$8
DL	1st Half	4	5	0	97	73	4.82	1.56	266			25.5	31%	70%	4.35	45	19	36	4.8	6.8	**1.4**	9%	0.9	-4.0	44	$3
ERA Potl 55%	2nd Half	7	6	0	106	86	5.00	1.48	263			27.5	31%	66%	4.06	43	22	35	4.2	7.3	**1.7**	8%	0.8	-6.8	59	$5
LIMA Plan C+	07 Proj	**12**	**12**	**0**	**218**	**174**	**4.22**	**1.41**	**254**			**26.9**	**30%**	**72%**	**3.95**	**44**	**20**	**36**	**4.1**	**7.2**	**1.8**	**9%**	**0.9**	**11.0**	**59**	**$14**

Case study in the importance of a 2.0+ CMD. Prospered just above that line in '04-05, slipped below it in 2006. 2005 DOM is an outlier, and CTL is in 3-year decline, so don't expect full recovery.

Davis,Jason

Davis,Jason	Yr	W	L	Sv	IP	K	ERA	WHIP	OBA	vL	vR	BF/G	H%	S%	xERA	G	L	F	Ctl	Dom	Cmd	hr/f	hr/9	RAR	BPV	R$
RH Reliever	02 aa	6	2	0	59	39	4.58	1.56	311			26.4	36%	70%	4.90				2.6	5.9	**2.3**		0.5	-2.2	63	$3
Age 27	03 CLE	8	11	0	165	85	4.69	1.33	270	259	289	26.0	28%	69%	4.05	49	17	35	2.6	4.6	**1.8**	13%	1.4	-3.4	26	$9
Growth	04 CLE	* 5	9	0	168	105	4.77	1.62	301	305	317	21.8	34%	72%	4.16	52	18	30	3.7	5.6	**1.5**	10%	0.9	-6.9	33	$2
Type	05 CLE	* 12	7	0	135	98	4.76	1.50	290	193	333	22.1	34%	69%	3.68	49	23	28	3.1	6.5	**2.1**	10%	0.8	-6.4	57	$9
Reliability 14	06 CLE	3	2	1	55	37	3.76	1.47	301	316	294	6.2	36%	73%	3.80	49	20	32	2.3	6.0	**2.6**	2%	0.2	5.4	82	$4
DL	1st Half	2	1	0	30	21	5.08	1.50	309			6.3	37%	64%	3.87	45	21	34	2.1	6.3	**3.0**	3%	0.3	-2.0	85	$2
ERA Potl 60%	2nd Half	1	1	1	25	16	2.16	1.44	291			6.1	35%	83%	3.71	53	19	28	2.5	5.8	**2.3**	0%	0.0	7.4	79	$3
LIMA Plan B+	07 Proj	**3**	**3**	**10**	**58**	**39**	**3.72**	**1.41**	**281**			**6.4**	**33%**	**73%**	**3.76**	**50**	**20**	**31**	**2.8**	**6.1**	**2.2**	**5%**	**0.5**	**5.2**	**67**	**$8**

Third straight year of CMD growth triggered this breakout. Favorable HR/F won't sustain, but neither should elevated H%. If he can take one more step forward on rising BPV trend... UP: 3.00 ERA, save opps.

De La Rosa,Jorge

De La Rosa,Jorge	Yr	W	L	Sv	IP	K	ERA	WHIP	OBA	vL	vR	BF/G	H%	S%	xERA	G	L	F	Ctl	Dom	Cmd	hr/f	hr/9	RAR	BPV	R$
LH Reliever	02 aa	1	2	0	18	14	5.50	1.61	272			20.4	33%	64%	4.49				5.0	7.0	**1.4**		0.5	-2.7	57	$0
Age 26	03 aa	7	5	1	124	101	3.77	1.48	276			20.2	34%	74%	4.16				3.6	7.3	**2.0**		0.4	9.5	73	$9
Growth	04 MIL	* 5	9	0	109	78	5.45	1.54	279			19.5	32%	65%	4.78				4.0	6.4	**1.6**		0.9	-16.0	44	$1
Type Power	05 MIL	2	2	0	42	42	4.49	2.04	288	321	273	5.5	38%	76%	4.76	49	23	28	8.1	9.0	**1.1**	3%	0.2	-1.3	68	($1)
Reliability 0	06 2TM	* 8	7	0	109	85	5.72	1.66	286	250	269	14.7	33%	67%	4.50	41	20	39	4.7	7.0	**1.5**	11%	1.2	-16.1	34	$3
DL 45	1st Half	2	2	0	34	32	7.65	1.62	256			8.1	31%	51%	4.35	42	19	39	5.8	8.4	**1.5**	10%	1.1	-13.2	53	($1)
ERA Potl 55%	2nd Half	6	5	0	75	53	4.83	1.67	299			22.9	33%	75%	4.57	40	21	38	4.2	6.4	**1.5**	12%	1.3	-2.9	25	$3
LIMA Plan B	07 Proj	**5**	**5**	**0**	**77**	**64**	**4.94**	**1.59**	**271**			**9.9**	**32%**	**70%**	**4.20**	**44**	**21**	**34**	**4.9**	**7.5**	**1.5**	**9%**	**0.8**	**2.1**	**53**	**$3**

5-6, 6.49 ERA in 79 IP at MIL and KC. Traded off some DOM for improved CTL, with poor results. PQS DOM/DIS split of 8/46 suggests that he isn't suited for the rotation... or your roster.

Delcarmen,Manny

Delcarmen,Manny	Yr	W	L	Sv	IP	K	ERA	WHIP	OBA	vL	vR	BF/G	H%	S%	xERA	G	L	F	Ctl	Dom	Cmd	hr/f	hr/9	RAR	BPV	R$
RH Reliever	02	0	0	0	0	0	0.00	0.00																		
Age 25	03	0	0	0	0	0	0.00	0.00																		
Growth	04	0	0	0	0	0	0.00	0.00																		
Type Power	05 a/a	7	5	5	59	62	3.20	1.44	248			5.7	33%	78%	3.68				4.6	9.5	**2.1**		0.5	8.0	92	$9
Reliability 0	06 BOS	* 2	1	0	70	62	4.62	1.44	283	319	302	5.1	36%	66%	3.46	45	26	30	3.0	8.0	**2.7**	3%	0.3	-0.6	95	$4
DL	1st Half	1	1	0	34	30	3.97	1.29	244			5.5	31%	67%	3.25	47	27	25	3.4	7.9	**2.3**	4%	0.3	2.5	94	$3
ERA Potl 75%	2nd Half	1	0	0	36	32	5.24	1.58	316			4.8	40%	64%	3.58	43	25	32	2.5	8.0	**3.2**	3%	0.2	-3.0	99	$1
LIMA Plan A+	07 Proj	**2**	**1**	**3**	**29**	**28**	**3.72**	**1.38**	**262**			**5.2**	**34%**	**72%**	**3.33**	**44**	**26**	**30**	**3.4**	**8.7**	**2.5**	**4%**	**0.3**	**4.1**	**99**	**$4**

A rookie with 2nd-half CMD over 3.0 is eye-catching. Elite skills were masked by unfavorable H%/S%. Likely not ready to close yet, but great LIMA option with potential for larger role in the future.

RAY MURPHY

Dempster,Ryan

Dempster,Ryan	Yr	Tm	W	L	Sv	IP	K	ERA	WHIP	OBA	vL	vR	BF/G	H%	S%	xERA	G	L	F	Ctl	Dom	Cmd	hr/f	hr/9	RAR	BPV	R$
RH Reliever	02	2NL	10	13	0	209	153	5.38	1.54	279	332	248	28.2	33%	64%	4.38	41	21	39	4.0	6.6	**1.6**	6%	0.7	-32.9	53	$3
Age 30	03	CIN	3	7	0	115	84	6.57	1.77	292	300	288	24.5	33%	63%	4.80	44	20	36	5.5	6.6	**1.2**	10%	1.1	-32.6	28	($5)
Peak	04	CHC *	2	2	2	41	34	4.37	1.55	251	222	200	6.4	31%	71%	3.98	52	21	28	5.5	7.4	**1.4**	6%	0.4	-0.5	65	$2
Type: Power	05	CHC	5	3	33	92	89	3.13	1.43	242	278	216	6.4	32%	78%	3.13	58	21	21	4.8	8.7	**1.8**	7%	0.4	12.7	85	$19
Reliability: 44	06	CHC	1	9	24	75	67	4.80	1.51	267	310	226	4.5	33%	68%	3.64	52	18	30	4.3	8.0	**1.9**	7%	0.6	-2.9	71	$10
DL	1st Half		1	4	12	34	33	4.47	1.37	243			4.3	31%	67%	3.61	45	19	36	4.2	8.7	**2.1**	6%	0.5	0.1	86	$6
ERA Potl 60%	2nd Half		0	5	12	41	34	5.07	1.62	286			4.6	35%	68%	3.64	57	17	26	4.4	7.5	**1.7**	9%	0.7	-2.9	59	$4
LIMA Plan C+	07	Proj	**2**	**6**	**15**	**73**	**64**	**4.47**	**1.52**	**260**			**5.6**	**33%**	**70%**	**3.67**	**53**	**19**	**28**	**4.7**	**7.9**	**1.7**	**7%**	**0.5**	**6.2**	**71**	**$8**

For closers with sub-standard skills, everything has to go just right. A BPI slip here, a H% spike there, and you get this 2nd half collapse. Still in the mix for saves, but 2005's ERA isn't coming back.

Dessens,Elmer

Dessens,Elmer	Yr	Tm	W	L	Sv	IP	K	ERA	WHIP	OBA	vL	vR	BF/G	H%	S%	xERA	G	L	F	Ctl	Dom	Cmd	hr/f	hr/9	RAR	BPV	R$
RH Reliever	02	CIN	7	8	0	178	93	3.03	1.25	256	244	268	24.7	27%	82%	3.94	49	16	34	2.5	4.7	**1.9**	12%	1.2	23.6	35	$14
Age 35	03	ARI	8	8	0	175	113	5.09	1.54	300	364	242	22.9	33%	69%	3.99	49	19	32	2.9	5.8	**2.0**	12%	1.1	-17.5	37	$4
Past Peak	04	2NL	2	6	2	105	73	4.46	1.47	293	316	264	9.2	33%	73%	3.71	49	20	31	2.7	6.3	**2.4**	14%	1.3	-2.5	45	$3
Type	05	LA	1	2	0	65	37	3.59	1.26	255	236	254	9.7	28%	74%	3.77	50	19	31	2.6	5.1	**1.9**	9%	0.8	5.3	51	$4
Reliability: 22	06	2TM	5	8	2	77	52	4.56	1.40	284	267	292	5.4	32%	69%	3.77	45	23	31	2.6	6.1	**2.4**	10%	0.9	-0.4	56	$6
DL 15 56	1st Half		4	6	1	42	30	4.07	1.29	280			5.4	33%	69%	3.37	46	24	29	1.7	6.4	**3.8**	8%	0.6	2.3	97	$5
ERA Potl 50%	2nd Half		1	2	1	35	22	5.14	1.54	288			5.4	31%	69%	4.28	44	22	34	3.6	5.7	**1.6**	13%	1.3	-2.7	26	$1
LIMA Plan C	07	Proj	**2**	**4**	**0**	**58**	**37**	**4.34**	**1.40**	**278**			**7.2**	**31%**	**72%**	**3.85**	**47**	**21**	**32**	**2.8**	**5.7**	**2.1**	**12%**	**1.1**	**4.1**	**44**	**$3**

Four straight years of BPV upticks. If that trend holds, he'll be closer-worthy in 2016. Until then, a marginal reserve round LIMA pick.

Devine,Joey

Devine,Joey	Yr	Tm	W	L	Sv	IP	K	ERA	WHIP	OBA	vL	vR	BF/G	H%	S%	xERA	G	L	F	Ctl	Dom	Cmd	hr/f	hr/9	RAR	BPV	R$
RH Reliever	02		0	0	0	0	0	0.00	0.00																		
Age 23	03		0	0	0	0	0	0.00	0.00																		
Growth	04		0	0	0	0	0	0.00	0.00																		
Type: Power	05	ATL *	1	2	5	26	28	5.88	1.96	297			5.3	36%	74%	6.91				6.9	9.7	**1.4**		1.7	-5.3	31	$1
Reliability: 0	06	ATL *	2	0	0	17	28	5.26	1.64	212	333	286	4.6	35%	69%	3.71	13	38	50	7.9	14.7	**1.9**	12%	1.1	-1.6	109	$1
DL	1st Half		0	0	0	1	2	72.00	12.00	680			5.0	86%	36%	110.39	17	50	33	54.0	18.0	**0.3**	44%	9.0	-8.3	******	($3)
ERA Potl 75%	2nd Half		2	0	0	16	26	1.12	0.99	134			4.5	24%	93%	2.79	10	30	60	5.0	14.5	**2.9**	6%	0.6	6.7	159	$4
LIMA Plan B+	07	Proj	**3**	**3**	**7**	**44**	**52**	**3.72**	**1.22**	**175**			**4.3**	**23%**	**73%**	**2.80**				**5.6**	**10.8**	**1.9**		**1.0**	**8.4**	**94**	**$8**

0-0, 9.95 ERA in 6 IP at ATL. Missed 1st half with back troubles, then came back and re-established himself as future closer material. Definitely worth targeting, even if Saves don't come until 2008.

Dohmann,Scott

Dohmann,Scott	Yr	Tm	W	L	Sv	IP	K	ERA	WHIP	OBA	vL	vR	BF/G	H%	S%	xERA	G	L	F	Ctl	Dom	Cmd	hr/f	hr/9	RAR	BPV	R$
RH Reliever	02		0	0	0	0	0	0.00	0.00											0.0	0.0						
Age 29	03	aa	9	4	4	93	80	6.66	1.76	333			8.7	38%	66%	7.16				3.2	7.7	**2.4**		1.9	-26.1	28	$2
Pre-Peak	04	COL *	1	4	2	68	74	3.31	1.34	256	211	255	4.9	33%	80%	3.59	35	16	50	3.3	9.8	**3.0**	10%	1.2	8.0	89	$6
Type: Power	05	aaa	2	1	1	39	43	4.86	1.57	296			5.1	37%	73%	5.61				3.4	9.9	**2.9**		1.5	-2.7	72	$2
Reliability: 5	06	2TM	2	4	1	48	44	7.11	1.91	303	357	293	4.8	35%	65%	4.73	40	22	38	6.2	8.2	**1.3**	16%	1.7	-15.4	21	($2)
DL 19	1st Half		1	0	1	20	21	5.35	1.63	269			4.4	35%	68%	4.29	35	19	46	5.3	9.4	**1.8**	8%	0.9	-2.1	67	$1
ERA Potl 60%	2nd Half		1	4	0	28	23	8.39	2.11	326			5.2	36%	63%	5.06	43	24	33	6.8	7.4	**1.1**	22%	2.3	-13.3	-10	($3)
LIMA Plan D	07	Proj	**2**	**3**	**0**	**44**	**43**	**5.79**	**1.66**	**285**			**5.1**	**34%**	**69%**	**4.08**	**39**	**21**	**41**	**4.8**	**8.9**	**1.9**	**15%**	**1.7**	**1.8**	**41**	**$1**

Attractive DOM, but history of elevated H% and HR/9 tells us that he gets hit very hard. Until his CTL evaporated, we would have bet on a H% reversion making him rosterable. Now, we just steer clear.

Donnelly,Brendan

Donnelly,Brendan	Yr	Tm	W	L	Sv	IP	K	ERA	WHIP	OBA	vL	vR	BF/G	H%	S%	xERA	G	L	F	Ctl	Dom	Cmd	hr/f	hr/9	RAR	BPV	R$
RH Reliever	02	ANA *	5	1	7	82	88	2.96	1.13	214	242	148	4.7	28%	77%	3.15	36	26	38	3.3	9.7	**2.9**	9%	0.8	15.1	109	$14
Age 35	03	ANA	2	2	3	74	79	1.58	1.07	209	199	202	4.7	29%	86%	3.41	28	22	50	2.9	9.6	**3.3**	2%	0.2	26.9	133	$14
Decline	04	ANA	5	2	0	42	56	3.00	1.17	223	211	237	4.3	32%	80%	2.92	34	16	50	3.2	12.0	**3.7**	10%	1.1	7.4	129	$8
Type: Power	05	ANA	9	3	0	65	53	3.73	1.21	246	213	274	4.1	28%	74%	3.84	34	20	46	2.6	7.3	**2.8**	10%	1.2	5.1	71	$10
Reliability: 5	06	ANA	6	0	0	64	53	3.94	1.34	243	290	204	4.4	28%	74%	3.83	44	19	37	3.9	7.5	**1.9**	12%	1.1	4.9	57	$7
DL	1st Half		1	0	0	32	25	2.80	1.21	243			4.3	27%	85%	3.81	42	13	45	2.8	7.0	**2.5**	12%	1.4	6.9	59	$4
ERA Potl 55%	2nd Half		5	0	0	32	28	5.08	1.47	244			4.5	30%	66%	3.83	46	26	29	5.1	7.9	**1.6**	11%	0.8	-2.0	61	$4
LIMA Plan B	07	Proj	**5**	**3**	**0**	**65**	**61**	**4.14**	**1.32**	**246**			**4.4**	**30%**	**72%**	**3.67**	**39**	**20**	**41**	**3.6**	**8.4**	**2.3**	**11%**	**1.1**	**6.5**	**72**	**$7**

ERA and WHIP have climbed four years running, BPV is in a corresponding plunge. 2nd half CMD level suggests that the decline may be picking up steam. Next stop: ERA over 4.00

Dotel,Octavio

Dotel,Octavio	Yr	Tm	W	L	Sv	IP	K	ERA	WHIP	OBA	vL	vR	BF/G	H%	S%	xERA	G	L	F	Ctl	Dom	Cmd	hr/f	hr/9	RAR	BPV	R$
RH Reliever	02	HOU	6	4	6	97	118	1.86	0.88	175	190	159	4.4	25%	83%	2.84	25	25	50	2.5	10.9	**4.4**	7%	0.6	26.9	158	$20
Age 33	03	HOU	6	4	4	87	97	2.48	0.97	178	152	186	4.4	23%	80%	3.00	35	22	43	3.2	10.0	**3.1**	10%	0.9	19.3	117	$16
Peak	04	2TM	6	6	36	85	122	3.70	1.19	221	245	188	4.5	32%	75%	2.90	28	19	54	3.5	12.9	**3.7**	13%	1.4	6.7	125	$24
Type: Power	05	OAK	1	2	7	15	16	3.58	1.39	190	269	107	4.3	23%	79%	4.44	24	26	50	6.6	9.5	**1.5**	11%	1.2	1.5	69	$4
Reliability: 0	06	NYY	0	0	0	10	7	10.80	2.90	390	333	414	4.2	43%	63%	7.83	37	20	44	9.9	6.3	**0.6**	12%	1.8	-7.7	-26	($3)
DL 145 137	1st Half		0	0	0	3	5	9.17	2.04	419			5.1	57%	60%					0.0	13.8			3.1	-1.8	-38	($0)
ERA Potl 70%	2nd Half		0	0	0	7	2	11.53	3.29	375			3.9	38%	64%	11.92	37	20	44	14.3	2.9	**0.2**	7%	1.2	-5.9	-35	($3)
LIMA Plan C	07	Proj	**3**	**4**	**0**	**64**	**66**	**3.80**	**1.41**	**243**			**4.9**	**30%**	**77%**	**3.88**	**35**	**20**	**45**	**4.5**	**9.3**	**2.1**	**10%**	**1.1**	**4.8**	**72**	**$6**

Rocky return not unexpected in recovery from TJ surgery. Should be much closer to full strength in 2007. Vintage skills and save opps may be too much to ask, but at minimum a decent LIMA option.

Downs,Scott

Downs,Scott	Yr	Tm	W	L	Sv	IP	K	ERA	WHIP	OBA	vL	vR	BF/G	H%	S%	xERA	G	L	F	Ctl	Dom	Cmd	hr/f	hr/9	RAR	BPV	R$
LH Reliever	02	aaa	2	1	0	23	13	8.22	1.78	369			6.4	37%	59%	8.63				1.2	5.1	**4.3**		2.7	-11.2	20	($1)
Age 31	03	aaa	8	9	0	121	43	4.90	1.44	285			25.2	29%	68%	4.82				2.9	3.2	**1.1**		1.0	-7.6	9	$4
Peak	04	MON *	13	12	0	198	90	4.68	1.52	311	286	315	25.9	32%	73%	4.05	53	18	29	2.3	4.1	**1.8**	13%	1.3	-10.2	17	$6
Type	05	TOR *	6	6	0	133	104	4.82	1.38	281	234	262	17.3	32%	68%	3.12	54	22	24	2.5	7.1	**2.8**	18%	1.2	-7.4	63	$7
Reliability: 29	06	TOR	6	2	1	77	61	4.09	1.34	252	232	258	5.6	29%	72%	3.31	56	18	26	3.5	7.1	**2.0**	15%	1.1	4.4	59	$8
DL	1st Half		1	0	0	36	27	4.99	1.39	239			5.6	27%	65%	3.58	60	13	27	4.5	6.7	**1.5**	14%	1.0	-1.9	49	$2
ERA Potl 45%	2nd Half		5	2	1	41	34	3.30	1.30	262			5.6	31%	79%	3.08	52	22	26	2.6	7.5	**2.8**	16%	1.1	6.3	74	$6
LIMA Plan C	07	Proj	**4**	**3**	**0**	**62**	**43**	**4.21**	**1.39**	**274**			**6.7**	**31%**	**73%**	**3.43**	**55**	**20**	**26**	**2.9**	**6.2**	**2.2**	**16%**	**1.2**	**8.1**	**48**	**$5**

xERA likes his combo of healthy CMD and GB%, but failure in SP role and limitation to situational relief work limits his value to vulture wins. End-gamer.

Duchscherer,Justin

Duchscherer,Justin	Yr	Tm	W	L	Sv	IP	K	ERA	WHIP	OBA	vL	vR	BF/G	H%	S%	xERA	G	L	F	Ctl	Dom	Cmd	hr/f	hr/9	RAR	BPV	R$
RH Reliever	02	aaa	2	4	0	63	44	5.43	1.43	297			19.6	34%	62%	4.73				2.1	6.3	**2.9**		0.9	-9.0	69	$1
Age 29	03	aaa	14	2	0	155	99	3.60	1.18	274			26.5	31%	71%	3.65				1.0	5.7	**5.5**		0.7	15.2	129	$18
Pre-Peak	04	OAK	7	6	0	96	59	3.28	1.22	239	247	235	7.5	25%	79%	4.08	43	17	40	3.0	5.5	**1.8**	11%	1.2	13.7	43	$10
Type	05	OAK	7	4	5	85	85	2.22	1.01	218	225	208	5.2	28%	82%	2.85	44	19	37	2.0	9.0	**4.5**	9%	0.7	22.6	137	$17
Reliability: 23	06	OAK	2	1	9	55	51	2.93	1.11	250	248	241	4.2	31%	75%	3.10	37	26	38	1.5	8.3	**5.7**	7%	0.7	11.1	154	$11
DL 47	1st Half		2	1	2	18	18	2.98	1.44	301			4.6	39%	80%	3.73	23	32	45	2.0	9.0	**4.5**	4%	0.5	3.5	128	$3
ERA Potl 55%	2nd Half		0	0	7	37	33	2.91	0.94	223			4.0	27%	72%	2.79	44	22	34	1.2	8.0	**6.6**	9%	0.7	7.5	175	$7
LIMA Plan B+	07	Proj	**4**	**3**	**3**	**73**	**63**	**3.10**	**1.13**	**247**			**5.2**	**30%**	**75%**	**3.29**	**39**	**23**	**38**	**1.9**	**7.8**	**4.2**	**8%**	**0.7**	**10.7**	**118**	**$11**

Shook off early-season injury to post elite skills. Worthy closer-in-waiting behind sometimes-fragile Street. Good health and more IP should yield a 2005-like combo of W and Sv.

Duckworth,Brandon

Duckworth,Brandon	Yr	Tm	W	L	Sv	IP	K	ERA	WHIP	OBA	vL	vR	BF/G	H%	S%	xERA	G	L	F	Ctl	Dom	Cmd	hr/f	hr/9	RAR	BPV	R$
RH Starter	02	PHI	8	9	0	163	167	5.41	1.45	266	248	273	23.7	33%	66%	3.69	35	23	42	3.8	9.2	**2.4**	14%	1.4	-26.2	65	$6
Age 31	03	PHI *	6	8	0	113	80	4.85	1.55	285	246	297	18.1	31%	72%	5.33				3.9	6.4	**1.6**		1.4	-8.0	30	$3
Peak	04	aaa	5	5	0	70	49	6.91	1.81	331			23.7	37%	64%	6.92				3.7	6.3	**1.7**		1.5	-22.2	17	($2)
Type	05	aaa	8	6	0	115	67	5.50	1.77	337			27.0	36%	72%	6.82				3.0	5.3	**1.8**		1.5	-17.0	12	($1)
Reliability: 2	06	KC *	9	8	0	119	70	4.69	1.72	314	232	390	25.1	35%	73%	4.54	47	21	32	3.8	5.3	**1.4**	6%	0.6	-1.9	34	$4
DL 62	1st Half		9	4	0	90	54	4.00	1.64	310			27.4	35%	76%	4.35	44	25	31	3.4	5.4	**1.6**	7%	0.7	6.2	40	$6
ERA Potl 50%	2nd Half		0	4	0	29	16	6.80	1.96	328			20.3	37%	64%	5.20	49	19	33	5.3	4.9	**0.9**	6%	0.6	-8.1	20	($2)
LIMA Plan C+	07	Proj	**2**	**3**	**0**	**37**	**23**	**5.11**	**1.70**	**311**			**24.4**	**35%**	**71%**	**4.63**	**43**	**21**	**36**	**3.9**	**5.6**	**1.4**	**9%**	**1.0**	**-0.7**	**27**	**$0**

1-5, 6.11 ERA in 46 IP at KC. Decent early-season run in the minors earned him a look in KC, where he displayed the same old skills that have made him unrosterable for years.

RAY MURPHY

Duke,Zach

Duke,Zach		Yr	Tm	W	L	Sv	IP	K	ERA	WHIP	OBA	vL	vR	BF/G	H%	S%	xERA	G	L	F	Ctl	Dom	Cmd	hr/f	hr/9	RAR	BPV	R$
LH	Starter	02		0	0	0	0	0	0.00	0.00											0.0	0.0						
Age	24	03		0	0	0	0	0	0.00	0.00											0.0	0.0						
Growth		04	aa	5	1	0	51	30	1.94	1.08	242			22.7	28%	83%	2.66				1.6	5.3	3.3		0.4	15.2	98	$8
Type	Finesse	05	PIT	*20	5	0	192	117	2.49	1.21	260	150	273	26.5	30%	81%	3.43	48	26	26	2.0	5.5	2.7	7%	0.5	41.6	78	$26
Reliability	31	06	PIT	10	15	0	215	117	4.48	1.50	296	264	310	28.0	33%	71%	4.03	51	20	29	2.8	4.9	1.7	8%	0.7	0.3	40	$8
DL	20	1st Half		5	7	0	100	59	4.86	1.52	286			27.8	32%	69%	4.24	49	18	33	3.5	5.3	1.5	9%	0.9	-4.6	34	$3
ERA Potl	50%	2nd Half		5	8	0	115	58	4.14	1.49	304			28.2	34%	72%	3.85	53	22	25	2.3	4.5	2.0	7%	0.5	4.9	47	$5
LIMA Plan	C+	07	Proj	15	10	0	203	116	4.03	1.33	277			27.0	31%	70%	3.69	51	21	28	2.3	5.1	2.2	7%	0.6	16.8	60	$15

Could not sustain solid CMD from rookie season. DOM went from borderline acceptable to red flag level, 2nd half dip heightens the concern. GB% is promising, but won't succeed without more DOM.

Eaton,Adam

Eaton,Adam		Yr	Tm	W	L	Sv	IP	K	ERA	WHIP	OBA	vL	vR	BF/G	H%	S%	xERA	G	L	F	Ctl	Dom	Cmd	hr/f	hr/9	RAR	BPV	R$
RH	Starter	02	SD	2	2	0	45	30	5.00	1.29	230	333	162	23.7	24%	66%	4.40	36	20	44	4.0	6.0	1.5	13%	1.6	-5.0	28	$2
Age	29	03	SD	9	12	0	183	146	4.08	1.32	251	276	222	25.0	29%	71%	3.73	45	19	36	3.3	7.2	2.1	10%	1.0	4.4	63	$13
Pre-Peak		04	SD	10	14	0	199	153	4.61	1.29	267	260	272	25.4	30%	68%	3.80	40	18	42	2.4	6.9	2.9	11%	1.3	-8.6	67	$13
Type		05	SD	11	5	0	128	100	4.28	1.44	279	309	255	23.3	33%	72%	3.86	41	24	35	3.1	7.0	2.3	10%	1.0	-0.6	60	$9
Reliability	12	06	TEX	7	4	0	65	43	5.12	1.57	299	320	279	22.4	32%	71%	4.40	37	24	38	3.3	6.0	1.8	13%	1.5	-4.5	23	$4
DL	117 66	1st Half		0	0	0	0	0	0.00	0.00																		
ERA Potl	50%	2nd Half		7	4	0	65	43	5.12	1.57	299			22.4	32%	71%	4.40	37	24	38	3.3	6.0	1.8	13%	1.5	-4.5	23	$4
LIMA Plan	B	07	Proj	13	10	0	174	132	4.41	1.38	268			23.3	30%	71%	3.95	39	22	39	3.1	6.8	2.2	11%	1.2	11.4	53	$14

Besides a slight drop in DOM, BPIs were basically intact upon return from finger injury. HR troubles should continue and will lead to continued volatility, as shown by 2006's 31/31 DOM%/DIS% split.

Elarton,Scott

Elarton,Scott		Yr	Tm	W	L	Sv	IP	K	ERA	WHIP	OBA	vL	vR	BF/G	H%	S%	xERA	G	L	F	Ctl	Dom	Cmd	hr/f	hr/9	RAR	BPV	R$
RH	Starter	02	COL	0	0	0	0	0	0.00	0.00											0.0	0.0						
Age	31	03	COL	*10	12	0	169	96	7.24	1.88	351	318	344	26.2	37%	65%	5.03	40	17	43	3.2	5.1	1.6	13%	2.0	-61.8	-10	($10)
Peak		04	2TM	*4	12	0	178	111	5.66	1.43	271	226	306	24.2	28%	65%	4.70	34	18	49	3.4	5.6	1.6	12%	1.7	-28.9	17	$2
Type	Finesse	05	CLE	11	9	0	181	103	4.62	1.31	270	275	261	24.7	28%	70%	4.40	33	22	45	2.4	5.1	2.1	12%	1.6	-5.5	29	$12
Reliability	38	06	KC	4	9	0	114	49	5.36	1.48	266	253	278	25.1	25%	71%	5.51	29	18	52	4.1	3.9	0.9	13%	2.0	-11.3	-17	$2
DL	75	1st Half		3	9	0	98	45	5.14	1.46	264			25.3	25%	72%	5.50	27	18	55	4.0	4.1	1.0	12%	2.0	-7.0	-12	$2
ERA Potl	30%	2nd Half		1	0	0	16	4	6.71	1.61	284			24.3	25%	64%	5.58	42	20	38	4.5	2.2	0.5	18%	2.2	-4.3	-45	($0)
LIMA Plan	C	07	Proj	3	7	0	105	48	5.23	1.50	281			24.5	28%	70%	5.10	35	20	45	3.6	4.1	1.1	12%	1.7	-8.0	-4	$1

Will miss the beginning of 2007 after tearing his labrum this past summer. We share this info just in case the -17 BPV wasn't enough of a reason to avoid him.

Embree,Alan

Embree,Alan		Yr	Tm	W	L	Sv	IP	K	ERA	WHIP	OBA	vL	vR	BF/G	H%	S%	xERA	G	L	F	Ctl	Dom	Cmd	hr/f	hr/9	RAR	BPV	R$
LH	Reliever	02	2TM	4	6	2	62	81	2.03	1.08	212	156	244	3.6	30%	87%	2.38	43	26	31	2.9	11.8	4.1	14%	0.9	17.1	142	$12
Age	37	03	BOS	4	1	1	55	45	4.25	1.18	240	263	221	3.5	29%	65%	3.46	44	20	37	2.6	7.4	2.8	9%	0.8	1.8	86	$7
Decline		04	BOS	2	2	0	53	37	4.07	1.15	250	240	247	3.0	28%	69%	3.62	38	24	38	1.9	6.3	3.4	11%	1.2	2.4	78	$5
Type	Power	05	2AL	2	5	1	52	38	7.62	1.46	297	320	278	3.4	32%	48%	3.85	40	23	36	2.4	6.6	2.7	16%	1.7	-20.8	40	($1)
Reliability	11	06	SD	4	3	0	52	53	3.28	1.25	254	240	258	3.0	33%	75%	3.15	43	20	37	2.6	9.2	3.5	8%	0.7	7.7	113	$7
DL	15	1st Half		2	1	0	27	31	3.99	1.25	268			3.1	36%	71%	2.81	49	12	39	2.0	10.3	5.2	10%	1.0	1.7	142	$3
ERA Potl	55%	2nd Half		2	2	0	25	22	2.52	1.24	238			2.8	30%	80%	3.55	37	29	34	3.2	7.9	2.4	4%	0.4	6.1	95	$4
LIMA Plan	B+	07	Proj	3	3	0	44	39	3.72	1.31	268			3.1	32%	75%	3.42	41	23	36	2.5	8.1	3.3	11%	1.0	5.1	87	$4

Rediscovered his DOM and the ability to strand runners, driving ERA rebound. 2nd half skills were less impressive, but should continue to be reasonably effective. Expect ERA to creep toward 4.00.

Escobar,Kelvim

Escobar,Kelvim		Yr	Tm	W	L	Sv	IP	K	ERA	WHIP	OBA	vL	vR	BF/G	H%	S%	xERA	G	L	F	Ctl	Dom	Cmd	hr/f	hr/9	RAR	BPV	R$
RH	Starter	02	TOR	5	7	38	78	85	4.27	1.53	254	245	246	4.6	33%	75%	3.78	39	22	39	5.1	9.8	1.9	12%	1.2	1.8	69	$19
Age	31	03	TOR	13	9	4	180	159	4.30	1.48	271	233	308	19.3	33%	72%	3.65	47	22	31	3.9	8.0	2.0	9%	0.8	5.0	69	$16
Peak		04	ANA	11	12	0	208	191	3.94	1.29	247	252	236	26.5	30%	72%	3.57	43	17	40	3.3	8.3	2.5	9%	0.9	12.7	81	$19
Type	Power	05	ANA	3	2	1	59	63	3.04	1.11	212	278	138	14.9	28%	74%	3.01	47	15	38	3.2	9.6	3.0	7%	0.6	9.7	115	$9
Reliability	39	06	ANA	11	14	0	189	147	3.62	1.28	265	258	270	26.5	31%	74%	3.57	45	19	36	2.4	7.0	2.9	8%	0.8	21.9	81	$20
DL	15 127	1st Half		5	9	0	93	70	4.15	1.39	280			26.8	32%	73%	3.74	47	17	36	2.7	6.8	2.5	9%	1.0	4.7	63	$7
ERA Potl	60%	2nd Half		6	5	0	96	77	3.10	1.17	250			26.1	30%	75%	3.42	42	21	37	2.1	7.2	3.5	7%	0.7	17.3	102	$13
LIMA Plan	C+	07	Proj	14	11	0	189	168	3.53	1.23	248			18.2	30%	73%	3.37	45	18	37	2.7	8.0	3.0	8%	0.8	25.9	94	$23

Seems like he has been on the verge of stardom for years, 2nd half skill growth gets our hopes up once again. If health and skills ever align for a full year... UP: 18 Wins, 3.00 ERA.

Eyre,Scott

Eyre,Scott		Yr	Tm	W	L	Sv	IP	K	ERA	WHIP	OBA	vL	vR	BF/G	H%	S%	xERA	G	L	F	Ctl	Dom	Cmd	hr/f	hr/9	RAR	BPV	R$
LH	Reliever	02	2TM	2	4	0	74	58	4.50	1.57	277	233	317	4.7	34%	71%	4.21	45	20	35	4.4	7.1	1.6	5%	0.5	-2.1	61	$2
Age	34	03	SF	2	1	1	57	35	3.32	1.51	272	219	305	3.4	31%	79%	4.57	44	18	38	4.1	5.5	1.3	6%	0.6	6.8	43	$3
Past Peak		04	SF	2	2	1	52	49	4.14	1.34	226	200	240	2.7	26%	74%	3.96	41	13	46	4.7	8.4	1.8	12%	1.4	0.8	57	$4
Type	Power	05	SF	2	2	0	68	65	2.64	1.09	200	182	213	3.2	26%	76%	3.49	38	18	43	3.4	8.6	2.5	4%	0.4	13.5	107	$9
Reliability	15	06	CHC	1	3	0	61	73	3.39	1.49	261	273	261	3.6	33%	85%	3.30	42	20	38	4.4	10.8	2.4	18%	1.6	8.3	70	$4
DL	16	1st Half		0	1	0	37	39	2.18	1.29	217			4.1	28%	89%	3.29	47	20	33	4.6	9.5	2.1	13%	1.0	10.5	82	$4
ERA Potl	35%	2nd Half		1	2	0	24	34	5.25	1.79	321			3.1	43%	81%	3.28	34	21	45	4.1	12.7	3.1	24%	2.6	-2.3	53	$0
LIMA Plan	B+	07	Proj	2	3	3	58	63	3.72	1.38	245			3.2	30%	79%	3.51	40	19	42	4.2	9.8	2.3	14%	1.4	6.1	72	$5

2nd half explosion was caused by ridiculous H% and HR/F, so don't treat it as a decline. Still a safe situational lefty whose DOM offers surprising value for your $1 investment.

Eyre,Willie

Eyre,Willie		Yr	Tm	W	L	Sv	IP	K	ERA	WHIP	OBA	vL	vR	BF/G	H%	S%	xERA	G	L	F	Ctl	Dom	Cmd	hr/f	hr/9	RAR	BPV	R$
RH	Reliever	02	aa	6	4	2	50	35	4.32	1.42	254			7.8	31%	67%	3.46				4.1	6.3	1.5		0.2	-0.3	69	$5
Age	28	03	a/a	6	7	0	120	71	5.36	1.77	311			16.1	35%	69%	5.71				4.5	5.3	1.2		0.7	-14.4	29	($1)
Pre-Peak		04	aaa	6	7	4	136	79	4.50	1.54	286			16.8	31%	72%	4.94				3.7	5.2	1.4		0.9	-2.7	32	$5
Type		05	aaa	1	3	7	82	62	3.57	1.54	292			6.5	35%	76%	4.47				3.3	6.8	2.0		0.3	7.4	69	$5
Reliability	16	06	MIN	1	0	0	59	26	5.33	1.64	310	379	257	6.4	32%	70%	4.83	46	18	36	3.4	4.0	1.2	10%	1.2	-5.6	5	($1)
DL		1st Half		0	0	0	26	14	5.84	1.79	321			5.9	35%	68%	4.73	48	20	32	4.1	4.8	1.2	10%	1.0	-4.1	13	($1)
ERA Potl	50%	2nd Half		1	0	0	33	12	4.92	1.52	301			7.0	30%	71%	4.90	43	16	40	2.7	3.3	1.2	10%	1.4	-1.5	-1	$1
LIMA Plan	D	07	Proj	1	1	0	29	16	4.97	1.59	300			7.3	33%	70%	4.57	45	18	37	3.4	5.0	1.5	8%	0.9	-0.3	27	$0

DOM didn't translate to majors in debut. 2nd half was even rockier than first, so expect continued struggles even if he can retain a job.

Farnsworth,Kyle

Farnsworth,Kyle		Yr	Tm	W	L	Sv	IP	K	ERA	WHIP	OBA	vL	vR	BF/G	H%	S%	xERA	G	L	F	Ctl	Dom	Cmd	hr/f	hr/9	RAR	BPV	R$
RH	Reliever	02	CHC	4	7	1	49	48	7.35	1.63	288	392	216	4.7	34%	57%	4.07	34	24	42	4.4	8.8	2.0	16%	1.8	-19.6	37	($0)
Age	31	03	CHC	3	2	0	76	92	3.32	1.17	198	189	199	4.0	28%	73%	2.83	44	25	31	4.3	10.9	2.6	11%	0.7	9.0	113	$9
Peak		04	CHC	4	5	0	66	78	4.76	1.51	264	267	255	4.1	34%	72%	3.50	40	19	41	4.5	10.6	2.4	14%	1.4	-4.1	75	$4
Type	Power	05	2TM	1	1	16	70	87	2.19	1.01	182	198	165	3.8	26%	82%	2.65	43	21	36	3.5	11.2	3.2	9%	0.6	18.3	134	$16
Reliability	30	06	NYY	3	6	6	66	75	4.36	1.36	250	215	264	3.9	33%	71%	3.46	34	22	44	3.8	10.2	2.7	11%	1.1	1.6	90	$8
DL		1st Half		2	4	1	35	40	4.89	1.69	278			4.2	38%	70%	4.17	31	25	45	5.4	10.3	1.9	5%	0.5	-1.4	86	$2
ERA Potl	60%	2nd Half		1	2	5	31	35	3.77	1.00	215			3.6	26%	72%	2.73	39	19	43	2.0	10.2	5.0	18%	1.7	3.0	126	$6
LIMA Plan	A	07	Proj	2	4	10	58	68	3.72	1.26	231			3.9	31%	74%	3.17	38	21	41	3.7	10.6	2.8	12%	1.1	9.4	99	$10

Skills were rock-solid outside of 1st half CTL issues. That 2nd half remains the benchmark for his future performance. Good speculative saves option.

Feldman,Scott

Feldman,Scott		Yr	Tm	W	L	Sv	IP	K	ERA	WHIP	OBA	vL	vR	BF/G	H%	S%	xERA	G	L	F	Ctl	Dom	Cmd	hr/f	hr/9	RAR	BPV	R$
RH	Reliever	02		0	0	0	0	0	0.00	0.00																		
Age	24	03		0	0	0	0	0	0.00	0.00																		
Growth		04		0	0	0	0	0	0.00	0.00																		
Type		05	aa	1	2	14	61	35	3.10	1.21	229			5.5	26%	76%	3.02				3.4	5.2	1.5		0.6	9.1	54	$9
Reliability	0	06	TEX	*2	4	4	68	52	3.57	1.26	259	280	259	4.8	30%	76%	2.81	59	22	19	2.5	6.8	2.7	20%	1.1	8.3	70	$8
DL		1st Half		0	2	1	35	33	4.60	1.16	250			4.5	29%	66%	2.69	51	22	26	2.0	8.4	4.1	23%	1.5	-0.2	96	$3
ERA Potl	45%	2nd Half		2	2	3	33	19	2.46	1.37	268			5.2	30%	84%	2.66	68	22	10	3.0	5.1	1.7	18%	0.5	8.5	52	$5
LIMA Plan	B	07	Proj	1	2	0	36	24	3.72	1.27	250			5.1	28%	72%	2.99	61	22	17	3.0	6.0	2.0	15%	0.7	6.7	60	$3

0-2, 3.92 ERA in 41 IP at TEX. Skills eroded in 2nd half, a definite warning sign for a rookie. But superior GB% will cover a lot of ills. Projects as a LIMA-worthy setup option.

RAY MURPHY

Feliciano,Pedro

Feliciano,Pedro		W	L	Sv	IP	K	ERA	WHIP	OBA	vL	vR	BF/G	H%	S%	xERA	G	L	F	Ctl	Dom	Cmd	hr/f	hr/9	RAR	BPV	R$
LH Reliever	02 a/a	3	2	6	74	42	4.01	1.58	324			6.3	36%	76%	5.43				2.1	5.1	2.5		0.7	2.3	51	$4
Age 30	03 NYM *	3	2	1	70	57	3.97	1.47	277	304	259	8.1	32%	76%	4.68				3.5	7.3	2.1		1.0	2.7	57	$4
Peak	04 NYM *	5	4	2	53	34	6.79	1.62	280			4.5	31%	58%	5.26				4.8	5.8	1.2		1.2	-16.5	24	$0
Type Power	05 JPN	3	2	0	37	38	4.83	1.31	236			4.2	26%	71%	4.64				3.9	9.2	2.4		2.0	-2.4	52	$3
Reliability 7	06 NYM	7	2	0	60	54	2.10	1.26	248	231	266	3.9	31%	86%	3.17	49	21	29	3.0	8.1	2.7	8%	0.6	17.7	93	$10
DL	1st Half	1	2	0	29	27	1.86	1.03	227			3.7	30%	83%	2.80	49	20	31	1.9	8.4	4.5	4%	0.3	9.4	145	$5
ERA Potl 30%	2nd Half	6	0	0	31	27	2.32	1.48	267			4.1	32%	88%	3.54	50	22	28	4.1	7.8	1.9	12%	0.9	8.3	63	$5
LIMA Plan C+	07 Proj	6	2	0	58	50	3.72	1.38	258			4.3	31%	77%	3.40	50	21	29	3.6	7.8	2.2	14%	1.1	6.9	63	$6

Productive 2005 in Japan, he developed a taste for sushi and a strikeout pitch. Upon return to US, 2nd half dip in CMD tempers our optimism, but should have a few years as a dependable LH setup option.

Flores,Randy

Flores,Randy		W	L	Sv	IP	K	ERA	WHIP	OBA	vL	vR	BF/G	H%	S%	xERA	G	L	F	Ctl	Dom	Cmd	hr/f	hr/9	RAR	BPV	R$
LH Reliever	02 2TM *	3	5	2	85	50	5.93	1.72	311			7.9	34%	66%	5.87				4.0	5.3	1.3		1.1	-17.4	21	($2)
Age 31	03 aaa	10	8	0	142	94	7.28	1.92	335			24.6	36%	64%	7.41				4.5	5.9	1.3		1.7	-50.7	0	($7)
Peak	04 STL *	6	7	2	136	86	4.10	1.43	276			13.2	31%	72%	4.23				3.2	5.7	1.8		0.7	2.7	51	$7
Type Power	05 STL	3	1	1	41	43	3.50	1.21	242	173	304	3.4	30%	76%	3.03	43	22	35	2.8	9.4	3.3	13%	1.1	3.8	100	$5
Reliability 6	06 STL	1	1	0	41	40	5.68	1.72	297	258	329	2.9	37%	68%	4.19	39	22	39	4.8	8.7	1.8	10%	1.1	-6.1	54	($0)
DL 15	1st Half	0	1	0	22	21	4.86	1.49	269			3.1	36%	64%	4.00	40	18	42	4.1	8.5	2.1	0%	0.0	-1.0	96	$0
ERA Potl 60%	2nd Half	1	0	0	19	19	6.63	2.00	327			2.8	38%	73%	4.42	38	25	37	5.7	9.0	1.6	23%	2.4	-5.0	6	($1)
LIMA Plan D+	07 Proj	2	1	0	44	39	4.55	1.49	268			3.7	32%	73%	3.92	40	23	37	4.1	8.1	2.0	12%	1.2	2.4	53	$2

Anomalies like 37% hit rates are more likely to happen in small sample sizes, and that's what happened in Flores' 41 IP. CTL problems may keep him from regaining 2005's success, but he will improve.

Floyd,Gavin

Floyd,Gavin		W	L	Sv	IP	K	ERA	WHIP	OBA	vL	vR	BF/G	H%	S%	xERA	G	L	F	Ctl	Dom	Cmd	hr/f	hr/9	RAR	BPV	R$
RH Starter	02	0	0	0	0	0	0.00	0.00											0.0	0.0						
Age 24	03	0	0	0	0	0	0.00	0.00											0.0	0.0						
Growth	04 a/a	7	9	0	149	104	3.16	1.26	243			25.0	29%	75%	3.24				3.2	6.3	1.9		0.5	21.8	71	$14
Type	05 PHI *	7	11	0	163	103	7.33	1.67	297	283	283	24.1	33%	55%	4.78	42	19	39	4.2	5.7	1.3	8%	1.0	-62.0	29	($7)
Reliability 2	06 PHI *	11	7	0	169	105	6.81	1.74	317	306	323	28.1	34%	62%	4.72	39	24	37	3.9	5.6	1.4	13%	1.5	-48.5	11	($4)
DL	1st Half	6	4	0	86	59	7.52	1.80	327			25.4	35%	61%	4.58	39	24	37	3.9	6.2	1.6	17%	2.0	-32.2	1	($4)
ERA Potl 55%	2nd Half	5	3	0	83	46	6.08	1.68	306			31.8	33%	64%					3.9	5.0	1.3		1.0	-16.3	21	($1)
LIMA Plan D	07 Proj	2	2	0	44	27	5.79	1.63	298			28.3	33%	65%	4.66	40	23	37	3.9	5.6	1.4	9%	1.0	-1.6	28	($0)

Still young, but not exactly full of promise. Has yet to post a 2.0 CMD above Single-A, and trends are only getting worse. Sent to AFL to learn some CMD, until that happens he's unrosterable.

Fogg,Josh

Fogg,Josh		W	L	Sv	IP	K	ERA	WHIP	OBA	vL	vR	BF/G	H%	S%	xERA	G	L	F	Ctl	Dom	Cmd	hr/f	hr/9	RAR	BPV	R$
RH Starter	02 PIT	12	12	0	194	113	4.36	1.38	267	292	243	25.3	28%	73%	4.19	47	16	37	3.2	5.2	1.6	12%	1.3	-6.1	29	$10
Age 30	03 PIT	10	9	0	142	71	5.26	1.45	293	320	273	23.0	30%	67%	4.30	46	17	37	2.5	4.5	1.8	12%	1.4	-17.2	19	$5
Peak	04 PIT	11	10	0	178	82	4.65	1.45	278	282	285	24.3	30%	69%	4.49	48	18	34	3.3	4.1	1.2	8%	0.9	-8.5	25	$7
Type Finesse	05 PIT	6	11	0	169	85	5.06	1.47	291	340	249	21.8	30%	69%	4.52	41	21	38	2.8	4.5	1.6	12%	1.4	-16.9	14	$2
Reliability 82	06 COL	11	9	0	172	93	5.49	1.55	298	309	291	24.8	32%	67%	4.53	43	20	37	3.1	4.9	1.6	11%	1.3	-21.4	19	$4
DL	1st Half	5	5	0	83	42	5.09	1.56	293			24.8	31%	69%	4.80	40	22	38	3.6	4.5	1.3	8%	1.0	-6.2	21	$2
ERA Potl 45%	2nd Half	6	4	0	89	51	5.87	1.53	303			24.7	32%	64%	4.27	45	19	36	2.7	5.2	1.9	13%	1.5	-15.2	19	$2
LIMA Plan C	07 Proj	9	9	0	162	84	5.07	1.50	292			23.8	31%	69%	4.47	43	20	37	3.0	4.7	1.6	11%	1.3	-2.1	19	$4

Soft-tosser continues to struggle to nudge his CMD to acceptable levels. Gave it a good run in 2nd half. xERA history is consistent, and says he's a league-average innings-eater at best.

Fossum,Casey

Fossum,Casey		W	L	Sv	IP	K	ERA	WHIP	OBA	vL	vR	BF/G	H%	S%	xERA	G	L	F	Ctl	Dom	Cmd	hr/f	hr/9	RAR	BPV	R$
LH Starter	02 BOS *	5	7	1	131	125	3.78	1.44	292	277	265	11.9	36%	76%	3.46	42	21	38	2.5	8.6	3.5	9%	0.9	11.0	94	$10
Age 29	03 BOS *	7	6	2	96	80	5.53	1.50	274	230	286	15.7	32%	64%	4.38	33	21	46	3.9	7.5	1.9	0%	1.0	-11.0	51	$6
Pre-Peak	04 ARI *	6	16	0	161	134	5.98	1.60	293	257	316	22.8	33%	67%	4.08	41	21	38	3.9	7.5	1.9	16%	1.7	-34.1	30	($0)
Type Power	05 TAM	8	12	0	162	128	4.94	1.42	271	234	278	19.5	31%	67%	3.97	39	22	39	3.3	7.1	2.1	11%	1.2	-11.3	53	$8
Reliability 48	06 TAM	6	6	0	130	88	5.33	1.53	271	271	263	23.1	30%	67%	4.26	46	21	33	4.4	6.1	1.4	13%	1.2	-12.4	29	$4
DL 15	1st Half	3	3	0	78	29	5.06	1.52	276			24.8	27%	70%	4.80	47	21	32	4.0	3.3	0.8	14%	1.4	-4.9	-4	$1
ERA Potl 50%	2nd Half	3	3	0	52	59	5.73	1.54	263			21.0	35%	64%	3.49	43	22	35	4.9	10.3	2.1	12%	1.0	-7.5	77	$3
LIMA Plan B	07 Proj	7	9	0	139	115	4.94	1.42	260			20.0	30%	68%	3.87	43	21	36	3.9	7.5	1.9	13%	1.2	10.5	51	$8

Spiked his DOM in 2nd half, xERA shows what a little better luck might have yielded. Surgery to repair frayed labrum in September, so make him show the DOM again in 2007 before you commit.

Foulke,Keith

Foulke,Keith		W	L	Sv	IP	K	ERA	WHIP	OBA	vL	vR	BF/G	H%	S%	xERA	G	L	F	Ctl	Dom	Cmd	hr/f	hr/9	RAR	BPV	R$
RH Reliever	02 CHW	2	4	11	77	58	2.92	1.01	230	266	185	4.7	27%	75%	3.37	41	19	41	1.5	6.8	4.5	8%	0.8	14.6	119	$14
Age 34	03 OAK	9	1	43	88	88	2.09	0.90	190	158	210	4.6	23%	85%	3.20	26	21	53	2.1	9.2	4.4	9%	1.0	25.8	133	$34
Past Peak	04 BOS	5	3	32	83	79	2.17	0.94	212	185	232	4.4	26%	83%	3.20	34	16	49	1.6	8.6	5.3	7%	0.9	23.2	149	$25
Type	05 BOS	5	5	15	45	34	5.97	1.57	294	255	333	4.7	32%	65%	4.86	26	19	55	3.6	6.8	1.9	10%	1.6	-8.9	29	$7
Reliability 0	06 BOS	3	1	0	49	36	4.39	1.20	273	301	236	4.6	30%	70%	4.10	24	20	56	1.3	6.6	5.1	10%	1.6	1.0	99	$5
DL 67 57	1st Half	2	1	0	32	23	5.63	1.22	279			4.6	30%	58%	4.38	18	17	64	1.1	6.5	5.8	9%	1.7	-4.2	108	$2
ERA Potl 55%	2nd Half	1	0	0	17	13	2.09	1.16	260			4.7	28%	94%	3.57	35	24	42	1.6	6.8	4.3	14%	1.6	5.2	88	$3
LIMA Plan B	07 Proj	3	2	15	44	34	3.72	1.22	260			4.6	29%	76%	3.99	29	20	51	2.1	7.0	3.4	10%	1.4	2.7	73	$10

Recovered elite CMD level from his days as a closer. Ongoing durability concerns and increasing FB% make it less likely he'll return to closing effectively, but we can't rule it out. Worth a speculative bid.

Francisco,Frank

Francisco,Frank		W	L	Sv	IP	K	ERA	WHIP	OBA	vL	vR	BF/G	H%	S%	xERA	G	L	F	Ctl	Dom	Cmd	hr/f	hr/9	RAR	BPV	R$
RH Reliever	02 aa	2	2	0	16	15	6.19	1.69	196			8.2	27%	59%	3.22				9.0	8.4	0.9		0.0	-3.8	86	$1
Age 27	03 aa	2	3	0	35	18	11.79	2.11	357			25.2	37%	42%	8.37				4.9	4.6	0.9		1.8	-32.0	-23	($7)
Pre-Peak	04 TEX *	6	5	6	68	84	3.30	1.23	186	247	165	4.7	27%	75%	3.68	28	19	54	5.3	11.1	2.1	6%	0.7	9.5	109	$12
Type Power	05 TEX	0	0	0	0	0	0.00	0.00											0.0	0.0						
Reliability 0	06 TEX *	0	1	0	22	25	3.26	1.22	243		444	4.4	31%	79%	2.84	50	13	38	2.9	10.2	3.6	14%	1.2	3.5	106	$2
DL 88 180	1st Half	0	0	0	7	8	0.00	0.84	192			3.9	29%	100%					1.5	10.4	6.9		0.0	4.0	224	$2
ERA Potl 55%	2nd Half	0	1	0	15	17	4.83	1.41	265			4.6	32%	72%	3.09	50	13	38	3.5	10.1	2.9	20%	1.8	-0.5	69	$1
LIMA Plan A	07 Proj	4	5	3	58	65	3.88	1.24	231			6.9	30%	72%	3.28	40	15	44	3.6	10.1	2.8	11%	1.1	8.6	96	$8

0-1, 4.91 ERA in 7 IP at TEX. Displayed his former skill set in a brief late-season return from Tommy John surgery. Will be two full years post-surgery in May, so return to LIMA-worthiness is likely.

Francis,Jeff

Francis,Jeff		W	L	Sv	IP	K	ERA	WHIP	OBA	vL	vR	BF/G	H%	S%	xERA	G	L	F	Ctl	Dom	Cmd	hr/f	hr/9	RAR	BPV	R$
LH Starter	02	0	0	0	0	0	0.00	0.00											0.0	0.0						
Age 26	03	0	0	0	0	0	0.00	0.00											0.0	0.0						
Growth	04 a/a	16	3	0	154	164	2.80	1.00	225			25.2	29%	77%	2.80				1.6	9.6	5.9		1.0	29.3	161	$27
Type	05 COL	14	12	0	183	128	5.70	1.63	306	285	317	25.2	34%	67%	4.37	40	22	38	3.4	6.3	1.8	11%	1.3	-32.8	32	$3
Reliability 41	06 COL	13	11	0	199	117	4.16	1.29	250	241	252	26.2	28%	69%	4.12	45	19	36	3.1	5.3	1.7	8%	0.8	8.0	48	$16
DL	1st Half	5	7	0	97	64	4.26	1.30	235			25.6	26%	69%	4.38	39	18	43	3.9	5.9	1.5	8%	0.9	2.7	48	$7
ERA Potl 50%	2nd Half	8	4	0	102	53	4.06	1.28	264			26.7	29%	69%	3.87	50	20	31	2.4	4.7	2.0	8%	0.7	5.3	50	$9
LIMA Plan D+	07 Proj	14	10	0	189	130	4.34	1.36	268			26.0	30%	70%	3.95	43	20	37	3.0	6.2	2.1	10%	1.0	9.5	53	$14

Promise of rising GB% is negated by dropping DOM. Both trends picked up speed in 2nd half. Until he shows he can do both concurrently, don't expect to see the ERA slip below 4.00.

Franklin,Ryan

Franklin,Ryan		W	L	Sv	IP	K	ERA	WHIP	OBA	vL	vR	BF/G	H%	S%	xERA	G	L	F	Ctl	Dom	Cmd	hr/f	hr/9	RAR	BPV	R$
RH Reliever	02 SEA	7	5	0	118	65	4.04	1.18	260	265	247	11.8	28%	69%	4.22	38	14	48	1.7	5.0	3.0	8%	1.1	6.1	63	$11
Age 34	03 SEA	11	13	0	212	99	3.57	1.23	250	267	233	27.5	25%	78%	4.73	35	15	51	2.6	4.2	1.6	10%	1.4	25.1	21	$19
Past Peak	04 SEA	4	16	0	200	104	4.90	1.42	284	275	297	27.2	29%	70%	4.69	35	20	45	2.7	4.7	1.7	11%	1.5	-11.6	18	$4
Type	05 SEA	8	15	0	190	93	5.11	1.44	283	266	295	25.9	29%	67%	4.63	42	16	42	2.9	4.4	1.5	10%	1.3	-17.3	16	$5
Reliability 66	06 2NL	6	7	0	77	43	4.55	1.54	283	265	294	5.2	30%	75%	4.46	47	18	35	3.9	5.0	1.3	14%	1.5	-0.6	10	$4
DL	1st Half	1	4	0	41	20	4.15	1.43	279			5.0	27%	80%	4.26	50	14	35	3.1	4.4	1.4	18%	2.0	1.7	-4	$1
ERA Potl 35%	2nd Half	5	3	0	36	23	5.01	1.67	288			5.5	32%	71%	4.70	43	22	34	4.8	5.8	1.2	10%	1.1	-2.3	27	$2
LIMA Plan C	07 Proj	2	2	0	29	16	4.66	1.48	281			8.5	30%	72%	4.56	42	18	39	3.4	5.0	1.5	10%	1.2	-0.7	22	$1

BPV fell 6 whole points after 2005 suspension for steroid use. What's worse: getting caught cheating, or being unable to gain anything positive from cheating in the first place?

RAY MURPHY

Frasor,Jason

	Yr	Tm	W	L	Sv	IP	K	ERA	WHIP	OBA	vL	vR	BF/G	H%	S%	xERA	G	L	F	Ctl	Dom	Cmd	hr/f	hr/9	RAR	BPV	R$
RH Reliever	02		0	0	0	0	0	0.00	0.00											0.0	0.0						
Age 29	03	aa	1	0	17	36	38	4.23	1.69	301			4.8	40%	75%	5.10				4.2	9.4	2.2		0.5	0.7	83	$7
Peak	04	TOR	4	6	17	68	54	4.10	1.47	250	232	274	4.7	30%	72%	4.13	47	19	35	4.8	7.1	1.5	6%	0.5	2.8	63	$10
Type Power	05	TOR	3	5	1	74	62	3.27	1.28	243	236	257	4.7	29%	78%	3.43	50	18	32	3.4	7.5	2.2	12%	1.0	10.0	69	$8
Reliability 26	06	TOR *	6	3	1	70	81	4.50	1.49	265	211	262	4.5	34%	73%	3.26	43	23	34	4.2	10.4	2.5	16%	1.3	0.5	78	$7
DL	1st Half		3	2	0	36	40	4.97	1.49	255			4.6	33%	69%	3.66	36	25	39	4.7	9.9	2.1	13%	1.2	-1.9	71	$3
ERA Potl 60%	2nd Half		3	1	1	34	41	3.99	1.48	274			4.4	36%	78%	2.73	53	20	27	3.7	10.9	2.9	20%	1.3	2.4	87	$4
LIMA Plan B	07	Proj	4	3	3	58	59	4.03	1.45	262			4.6	33%	75%	3.40	47	20	33	4.0	9.2	2.3	13%	1.1	7.8	73	$6

3-2, 4.32 ERA in 50 IP at TOR. Skills all trending in good directions, and reached elite levels in 2nd half. Worthy LIMA option and speculative saves source.

Fuentes,Brian

	Yr	Tm	W	L	Sv	IP	K	ERA	WHIP	OBA	vL	vR	BF/G	H%	S%	xERA	G	L	F	Ctl	Dom	Cmd	hr/f	hr/9	RAR	BPV	R$
LH Reliever	02	COL *	5	3	1	75	89	4.56	1.61	267			4.7	37%	71%	3.91	30	28	42	5.3	10.7	2.0	5%	0.5	-4.2	94	$4
Age 31	03	COL	3	3	4	75	82	2.76	1.31	232	238	227	4.2	31%	82%	3.56	32	25	43	4.1	9.8	2.4	8%	0.8	14.0	93	$10
Peak	04	COL	2	4	0	44	48	5.70	1.47	270	213	300	4.1	35%	62%	3.69	34	23	44	3.9	9.8	2.5	9%	1.0	-7.8	82	$1
Type Power	05	COL	2	5	31	74	91	2.91	1.26	220	167	236	4.0	31%	79%	3.03	38	26	36	4.1	11.1	2.7	9%	0.7	12.2	112	$18
Reliability 38	06	COL	3	4	30	65	73	3.46	1.17	214	186	217	4.0	28%	75%	3.39	35	16	50	3.6	10.1	2.8	10%	1.1	8.3	99	$18
DL	1st Half		1	1	15	31	43	2.31	1.03	178			3.8	26%	83%	2.80	30	21	49	3.8	12.4	3.3	10%	0.9	8.4	137	$10
ERA Potl 55%	2nd Half		2	3	15	34	30	4.51	1.30	245			4.2	28%	69%	3.97	38	12	50	3.5	8.0	2.3	10%	1.3	-0.1	62	$8
LIMA Plan B	07	Proj	3	5	33	73	82	3.72	1.27	230			4.1	30%	74%	3.41	35	20	45	3.8	10.2	2.6	10%	1.0	8.6	96	$18

One bad July outing (0.1 IP, 6 ER) ruined an otherwise strong year. Spike in FB% and 2nd half BPV dip trigger some alarms. If 2007 1st half is like 2006 2nd half, closer role could be at risk. Don't overbid.

Fultz,Aaron

	Yr	Tm	W	L	Sv	IP	K	ERA	WHIP	OBA	vL	vR	BF/G	H%	S%	xERA	G	L	F	Ctl	Dom	Cmd	hr/f	hr/9	RAR	BPV	R$
LH Reliever	02	SF *	3	5	3	63	48	4.57	1.59	280	302	284	4.7	33%	72%	4.48	39	22	39	4.4	6.9	1.5	6%	0.7	-3.6	51	$2
Age 33	03	TEX	1	3	0	67	53	5.24	1.52	284	218	345	4.7	33%	68%	3.83	46	21	32	3.6	7.1	2.0	13%	1.2	-5.9	46	$1
Past Peak	04	MIN	3	3	1	50	37	5.04	1.46	262	212	314	4.0	30%	66%	4.30	42	18	40	4.1	6.7	1.6	8%	0.9	-3.7	49	$3
Type Power	05	PHI	4	0	0	72	54	2.25	0.97	188	220	170	4.5	22%	81%	3.53	40	22	39	2.9	6.7	2.3	8%	0.7	17.8	85	$11
Reliability 25	06	PHI	3	1	0	71	62	4.56	1.52	285	277	293	4.8	35%	71%	3.98	38	23	39	3.5	7.8	2.2	8%	0.9	-0.6	65	$3
DL	1st Half		1	0	0	41	41	4.38	1.41	284			5.6	35%	72%	3.41	39	22	38	2.6	9.0	3.4	11%	1.1	0.5	91	$2
ERA Potl 55%	2nd Half		2	1	0	30	21	4.80	1.67	287			4.0	33%	71%	4.87	37	23	40	4.8	6.3	1.3	5%	0.6	-1.2	45	$1
LIMA Plan B	07	Proj	3	2	0	65	51	4.14	1.39	258			4.5	30%	72%	4.07	39	22	39	3.7	7.0	1.9	8%	0.8	2.3	60	$4

Biggest difference between brilliant 2005 and rocky 2006 was h%. 2nd half loss of CMD likely due to shoulder troubles. xERA history is stable and tells us what to expect in 2007.

Gagne,Eric

	Yr	Tm	W	L	Sv	IP	K	ERA	WHIP	OBA	vL	vR	BF/G	H%	S%	xERA	G	L	F	Ctl	Dom	Cmd	hr/f	hr/9	RAR	BPV	R$
RH Reliever	02	LA	4	1	52	82	114	1.98	0.87	192	213	163	4.0	29%	82%	2.21	31	29	40	1.8	12.5	7.1	9%	0.7	21.6	222	$32
Age 31	03	LA	2	3	55	82	137	1.21	0.70	138	130	135	3.8	27%	84%	1.49	38	33	29	2.2	15.0	6.9	5%	0.2	31.1	255	$37
Peak	04	LA	7	3	45	82	114	2.19	0.91	186	233	129	4.5	29%	79%	2.24	42	18	40	2.4	12.5	5.2	7%	0.5	21.0	185	$30
Type Power	05	LA	1	0	8	13	22	2.75	0.99	213	217	185	3.7	35%	82%	1.64	52	11	37	2.1	15.1	7.3	22%	1.4	2.4	216	$5
Reliability 0	06	LA	0	0	1	2	3	0.00	0.50	0			3.4	0%		2.40	33	0	67	4.5	13.5	3.0	0%		1.1	199	$1
DL 175 150	1st Half		0	0	1	2	3	0.00	0.50	0			3.4	0%		2.40	33	0	67	4.5	13.5	3.0	0%		1.1	199	$1
ERA Potl	2nd Half		0	0	0	0	0	0.00	0.00																		
LIMA Plan A+	07	Proj	2	1	20	44	64	2.28	0.94	180			4.2	30%	77%	2.09	44	21	35	2.9	13.2	4.6	7%	0.4	12.2	182	$15

Elbow and back injuries sidelined him almost all season. Back should be 100% by spring, questions about elbow remain. Elite skills, but Rel Score and DL time tell the story...
UP: 40 Svs. DN: Long DL stint.

Garcia,Freddy

	Yr	Tm	W	L	Sv	IP	K	ERA	WHIP	OBA	vL	vR	BF/G	H%	S%	xERA	G	L	F	Ctl	Dom	Cmd	hr/f	hr/9	RAR	BPV	R$
RH Starter	02	SEA	16	10	0	223	181	4.40	1.30	265	255	265	27.7	31%	70%	3.62	42	19	39	2.5	7.3	2.9	12%	1.2	1.7	70	$20
Age 30	03	SEA	12	14	0	201	144	4.52	1.33	257	281	223	25.9	28%	70%	4.02	41	18	41	3.2	6.4	2.0	12%	1.4	0.1	43	$15
Peak	04	2AL	13	11	0	210	184	3.81	1.22	245	236	248	28.0	29%	71%	3.47	43	17	40	2.7	7.9	2.9	9%	0.9	16.0	85	$21
Type	05	CHW	14	8	0	228	146	3.87	1.25	259	268	249	28.8	29%	72%	3.57	49	21	31	2.4	5.8	2.4	12%	1.0	14.2	58	$20
Reliability 99	06	CHW	17	9	0	216	135	4.54	1.28	272	262	271	27.5	29%	68%	3.95	41	18	41	2.0	5.6	2.8	11%	1.3	0.5	53	$20
DL	1st Half		10	4	0	102	60	4.67	1.35	280			27.3	29%	71%	4.13	42	17	41	2.3	5.3	2.3	14%	1.7	-1.4	29	$9
ERA Potl 55%	2nd Half		7	5	0	114	75	4.42	1.21	265			27.7	29%	66%	3.80	40	19	41	1.7	5.9	3.4	9%	1.0	1.9	78	$11
LIMA Plan D+	07	Proj	14	9	0	203	139	4.26	1.26	264			28.3	29%	70%	3.76	43	19	38	2.3	6.2	2.7	11%	1.2	18.1	62	$19

ERA doesn't show it, but skills bounced back nicely in 2nd half. xERA and PQS DOM/DIS of 52/9 also hint at better outcomes. Needs to hold DOM near 6.0, if he does...
UP: 3.50 ERA.

Garland,Jon

	Yr	Tm	W	L	Sv	IP	K	ERA	WHIP	OBA	vL	vR	BF/G	H%	S%	xERA	G	L	F	Ctl	Dom	Cmd	hr/f	hr/9	RAR	BPV	R$
RH Starter	02	CHW	12	12	0	192	112	4.59	1.41	258	287	220	25.2	28%	70%	4.52	44	16	40	3.9	5.3	1.3	9%	1.1	-3.2	31	$11
Age 27	03	CHW	12	13	0	191	108	4.52	1.37	259	278	234	25.6	27%	71%	4.23	48	16	36	3.5	5.1	1.5	13%	1.3	0.0	25	$12
Pre-Peak	04	CHW	12	11	0	217	113	4.89	1.38	267	269	277	27.4	27%	68%	4.35	46	17	38	3.2	4.7	1.5	12%	1.4	-12.4	19	$10
Type Finesse	05	CHW	18	10	0	221	115	3.50	1.17	254	267	242	28.3	27%	74%	3.70	47	21	32	1.9	4.7	2.4	11%	1.1	23.7	52	$24
Reliability 67	06	CHW	18	7	0	211	112	4.52	1.36	293	290	297	27.4	31%	69%	4.12	42	20	38	1.7	4.8	2.7	9%	1.1	1.0	49	$17
DL	1st Half		6	3	0	95	50	5.77	1.45	298			27.7	30%	65%	4.34	43	17	40	2.3	4.7	2.1	14%	1.8	-14.3	14	$3
ERA Potl 50%	2nd Half		12	4	0	116	62	3.49	1.29	289			27.2	32%	73%	3.94	42	23	36	1.3	4.8	3.6	5%	0.5	15.3	86	$14
LIMA Plan D	07	Proj	16	9	0	203	108	4.26	1.32	276			27.7	29%	71%	4.06	44	20	36	2.2	4.8	2.2	10%	1.1	10.6	42	$17

As expected, could not sustain 2005 success, although he did return to those skill levels in 2nd half. This kind of volatility is not unusual in low-DOM/high-CMD pitchers, and should continue unless DOM rises.

Garza,Matt

	Yr	Tm	W	L	Sv	IP	K	ERA	WHIP	OBA	vL	vR	BF/G	H%	S%	xERA	G	L	F	Ctl	Dom	Cmd	hr/f	hr/9	RAR	BPV	R$
RH Starter	02		0	0	0	0	0	0.00	0.00																		
Age 23	03		0	0	0	0	0	0.00	0.00																		
Growth	04		0	0	0	0	0	0.00	0.00																		
Type Power	05		0	0	0	0	0	0.00	0.00																		
Reliability 0	06	MIN *	12	9	0	141	123	4.15	1.30	255	245	356	23.8	31%	68%	3.75	35	25	40	3.0	7.8	2.6	6%	0.6	7.2	87	$16
DL	1st Half		4	2	0	41	44	4.82	1.34	257			21.9	34%	63%					3.3	9.6	2.9		0.7	-1.3	103	$5
ERA Potl 65%	2nd Half		8	7	0	100	79	3.87	1.28	254			24.7	30%	70%	3.88	35	25	40	2.9	7.1	2.5	6%	0.6	8.5	80	$11
LIMA Plan B	07	Proj	10	7	0	139	125	4.22	1.31	255			23.4	32%	68%	3.70	35	25	40	3.1	8.1	2.7	6%	0.6	13.4	89	$14

3-6, 5.76 ERA in 50 IP at MIN. Despite getting hit hard in majors, had a decent Sept. skill-wise (86 BPV, 3.75 xERA). If you can scoop him up at a discount, do so... excellent longer-term investment.

Gaudin,Chad

	Yr	Tm	W	L	Sv	IP	K	ERA	WHIP	OBA	vL	vR	BF/G	H%	S%	xERA	G	L	F	Ctl	Dom	Cmd	hr/f	hr/9	RAR	BPV	R$
RH Reliever	02		0	0	0	0	0	0.00	0.00																		
Age 24	03	TAM *	4	0	0	59	44	2.59	1.12	220	269	218	13.2	26%	79%	3.99	28	28	44	2.9	6.7	2.3	5%	0.6	14.1	82	$9
Growth	04	TAM *	2	5	2	90	80	5.00	1.54	299	403	301	9.3	36%	70%	3.95	36	23	41	3.1	8.0	2.6	10%	1.1	-6.3	64	$3
Type	05	TOR *	10	11	0	163	117	4.64	1.36	285	481	462	24.9	32%	68%	3.61	40	29	31	2.2	6.5	3.0	12%	1.0	-5.4	68	$11
Reliability 0	06	OAK *	7	2	2	88	58	2.45	1.31	210	253	201	6.3	25%	81%	4.73	39	16	45	5.0	5.9	1.2	3%	0.3	22.9	64	$12
DL	1st Half		3	2	1	52	41	2.75	1.30	213			9.2	26%	79%	4.28	38	23	40	4.8	7.1	1.5	3%	0.3	11.6	75	$7
ERA Potl 30%	2nd Half		4	0	1	36	17	2.01	1.31	205			4.3	23%	85%	5.36	41	10	49	5.3	4.3	0.8	2%	0.3	11.2	49	$6
LIMA Plan B	07	Proj	4	2	0	51	35	4.26	1.42	259			8.2	30%	71%	4.53	38	17	45	3.9	6.2	1.6	6%	0.7	-0.3	53	$4

4-2, 3.09 ERA in 62 IP at OAK. Despite outward success in OAK after previous debacles, BPIs show that he's still not ready. But you can't ignore the earlier CMD ratios. Either a deep REM sleeper or AAAA lifer.

Geary,Geoff

	Yr	Tm	W	L	Sv	IP	K	ERA	WHIP	OBA	vL	vR	BF/G	H%	S%	xERA	G	L	F	Ctl	Dom	Cmd	hr/f	hr/9	RAR	BPV	R$
RH Reliever	02	aaa	4	2	1	101	73	3.74	1.61	310			12.1	36%	79%	5.43				3.1	6.5	2.1		0.9	6.6	49	$4
Age 30	03	aaa	9	4	5	87	67	2.79	1.19	266			7.8	32%	76%	3.19				1.5	6.9	4.5		0.3	17.3	128	$14
Peak	04	PHI *	2	2	8	67	48	4.55	1.61	286	322	261	5.6	32%	75%	4.68	39	17	44	4.3	6.4	1.5	9%	1.2	-2.4	32	$3
Type	05	PHI	2	1	0	58	42	3.72	1.29	248	192	294	6.1	29%	73%	3.75	44	23	32	3.3	6.5	2.0	9%	0.8	3.7	63	$4
Reliability 25	06	PHI	7	1	1	91	60	2.96	1.35	286	348	249	4.8	33%	79%	3.59	50	19	31	2.0	5.9	3.0	6%	0.6	17.1	79	$10
DL 15	1st Half		4	0	0	42	27	3.64	1.69	333			5.0	38%	79%	3.90	49	24	27	2.6	5.8	2.3	7%	0.6	4.4	51	$3
ERA Potl 40%	2nd Half		3	1	1	49	33	2.38	1.06	241			4.7	28%	80%	3.32	51	14	35	1.5	6.0	4.1	6%	0.5	12.7	113	$8
LIMA Plan C+	07	Proj	3	1	0	58	40	3.41	1.36	275			5.5	32%	77%	3.76	47	20	33	2.6	6.2	2.4	8%	0.8	4.3	63	$5

Emerging as a dependable setup option. 2nd half growth is promising, and compares nicely with 2003 MLEs. Trouble vs. LH hitters should limit him to setup work, but he's a nice LIMA/ vulture win option.

RAY MURPHY

Glavine,Tom

	Yr	W	L	Sv	IP	K	ERA	WHIP	OBA	vL	vR	BF/G	H%	S%	xERA	G	L	F	Ctl	Dom	Cmd	hr/f	hr/9	RAR	BPV	R$
LH Starter	02 ATL	18	11	0	224	127	2.97	1.29	250	244	254	26.2	27%	80%	4.33	41	19	40	3.1	5.1	**1.6**	7%	0.8	31.3	45	$22
Age 41	03 NYM	9	14	0	183	82	4.52	1.48	284	285	289	25.2	30%	72%	4.59	48	16	36	3.2	4.0	**1.2**	9%	1.0	-5.6	17	$6
Decline	04 NYM	11	14	0	212	109	3.61	1.29	254	242	255	27.1	27%	74%	3.94	51	19	30	3.0	4.6	**1.6**	10%	0.8	17.1	39	$15
Type Finesse	05 NYM	13	13	0	211	105	3.54	1.36	276	323	267	27.4	30%	74%	4.08	47	23	30	2.6	4.5	**1.7**	6%	0.5	18.4	47	$15
Reliability 80	06 NYM	15	7	0	198	131	3.82	1.33	266	200	287	26.3	30%	74%	3.82	44	23	32	2.8	6.0	**2.1**	11%	1.0	16.3	52	$18
DL	1st Half	11	2	0	102	75	3.35	1.23	250			26.5	28%	79%	3.43	46	24	30	2.6	6.6	**2.5**	15%	1.2	14.4	60	$13
ERA Potl 45%	2nd Half	4	5	0	96	56	4.32	1.44	282			26.1	31%	71%	4.24	43	23	34	3.0	5.3	**1.8**	7%	0.8	2.0	44	$4
LIMA Plan D	07 Proj	**12**	**10**	**0**	**189**	**108**	**4.01**	**1.35**	**268**			**26.8**	**30%**	**72%**	**4.02**	**46**	**22**	**32**	**2.9**	**5.2**	**1.8**	**9%**	**0.8**	**8.0**	**46**	**$13**

Gains in Ctl, CMD disappeared with summer. H% and S% corrections also fueled 2H fade; blood clot in shoulder didn't help. Better at Shea (2.88 ERA), so adjust expectations if he changes teams.

Gobble,Jimmy

	Yr	W	L	Sv	IP	K	ERA	WHIP	OBA	vL	vR	BF/G	H%	S%	xERA	G	L	F	Ctl	Dom	Cmd	hr/f	hr/9	RAR	BPV	R$
LH Reliever	02 aa	5	7	0	69	43	4.57	1.52	307			23.6	35%	69%	4.80				2.5	5.6	**2.3**		0.5	-2.5	59	$3
Age 25	03 KC	* 16	13	0	184	114	4.45	1.45	289	263	273	25.9	32%	72%	4.79	30	17	53	2.7	5.6	**2.1**	7%	1.1	1.7	40	$13
Growth	04 KC	* 11	9	0	167	61	5.39	1.43	284	317	255	25.0	28%	66%	4.98	38	18	44	2.7	3.3	**1.2**	11%	1.6	-19.7	-6	$5
Type Power	05 KC	* 3	8	0	111	77	6.39	1.74	316	304	294	13.0	35%	65%	4.76	40	18	42	4.0	6.2	**1.6**	10%	1.3	-27.7	23	($4)
Reliability 11	06 KC	4	6	2	84	80	5.14	1.48	286	255	294	6.2	35%	68%	3.70	38	22	40	3.1	8.6	**2.8**	12%	1.3	-6.1	69	$5
DL	1st Half	2	1	1	40	34	3.82	1.20	236			5.7	27%	74%	3.68	39	18	44	2.9	7.6	**2.6**	12%	1.3	3.7	68	$5
ERA Potl 60%	2nd Half	2	5	1	44	46	6.36	1.73	326			6.6	41%	64%	3.71	38	25	38	3.3	9.4	**2.9**	12%	1.2	-9.7	70	$0
LIMA Plan C+	07 Proj	**4**	**6**	**0**	**83**	**68**	**4.77**	**1.43**	**275**			**8.8**	**32%**	**70%**	**3.99**	**38**	**20**	**41**	**3.3**	**7.4**	**2.3**	**11%**	**1.3**	**5.1**	**53**	**$5**

ERA says he lost something in the 2nd half, but xERA shows he was really much the same pitcher. 2nd half DOM and CMD give reason for optimism. Now must cut down on the walks.

Gonzalez,Edgar

	Yr	W	L	Sv	IP	K	ERA	WHIP	OBA	vL	vR	BF/G	H%	S%	xERA	G	L	F	Ctl	Dom	Cmd	hr/f	hr/9	RAR	BPV	R$
RH Starter	02	0	0	0	0	0	0.00	0.00																		
Age 24	03 a/a	10	9	0	165	96	3.86	1.22	265			26.3	31%	67%	3.26				1.8	5.2	**2.8**		0.3	10.8	84	$15
Growth	04 aaa	5	5	0	94	67	4.79	1.26	268			26.2	30%	65%	4.36				2.0	6.4	**3.2**		1.3	-5.2	68	$6
Type Finesse	05 aaa	1	5	0	160	100	4.50	1.36	289			25.3	32%	69%	4.61				1.9	5.6	**3.0**		1.0	-3.9	63	$5
Reliability 3	06 ARI	* 6	12	0	180	122	4.49	1.33	286	259	288	21.9	32%	68%	4.13	38	15	47	1.7	6.1	**3.5**	7%	0.9	-0.1	79	$10
DL	1st Half	2	6	0	101	79	4.46	1.38	294			25.6	34%	71%	4.32	26	19	56	1.8	7.0	**3.9**	7%	1.1	0.4	85	$5
ERA Potl 60%	2nd Half	4	6	0	79	43	4.54	1.26	276			18.4	31%	64%	4.15	44	13	44	1.7	5.0	**2.9**	5%	0.7	-0.5	71	$5
LIMA Plan B	07 Proj	**4**	**6**	**0**	**102**	**65**	**4.26**	**1.30**	**281**			**22.5**	**32%**	**69%**	**4.12**	**40**	**14**	**46**	**1.8**	**5.8**	**3.3**	**7%**	**0.9**	**3.1**	**75**	**$6**

3-4, 4.22 ERA in 43 IP at ARI. Sample size was limited and low LD% helped, but 24-year-olds with 3.0 Cmd can't be ignored. Good LIMA pick.

Gonzalez,Enrique

	Yr	W	L	Sv	IP	K	ERA	WHIP	OBA	vL	vR	BF/G	H%	S%	xERA	G	L	F	Ctl	Dom	Cmd	hr/f	hr/9	RAR	BPV	R$
RH Starter	02	0	0	0	0	0	0.00	0.00																		
Age 24	03	0	0	0	0	0	0.00	0.00																		
Growth	04	0	0	0	0	0	0.00	0.00																		
Type	05 aa	1	8	0	161	128	4.38	1.51	295			26.4	35%	71%	4.64				3.0	7.2	**2.4**		0.6	-1.4	72	$4
Reliability 0	06 ARI	* 7	10	0	166	97	4.55	1.38	280	288	265	22.3	31%	68%	4.13	44	19	37	2.5	5.3	**2.1**	8%	0.9	-1.3	48	$8
DL	1st Half	6	4	0	91	54	3.26	1.25	262			23.8	29%	76%	4.05	41	20	39	2.3	5.3	**2.3**	6%	0.7	13.8	63	$9
ERA Potl 55%	2nd Half	1	6	0	75	43	6.11	1.53	301			20.9	33%	60%	4.32	45	19	36	2.9	5.2	**1.8**	10%	1.1	-15.0	31	($1)
LIMA Plan B	07 Proj	**4**	**4**	**0**	**98**	**63**	**4.71**	**1.46**	**289**			**23.7**	**33%**	**68%**	**4.11**	**44**	**19**	**36**	**2.8**	**5.8**	**2.1**	**7%**	**0.7**	**3.0**	**54**	**$3**

3-7, 5.67 ERA in 106 IP at ARI. Wore down as season progressed, low S% didn't help. Hardly overpowering, but can succeed by limiting BB and HR as he did at Triple-A.

Gonzalez,Geremi

	Yr	W	L	Sv	IP	K	ERA	WHIP	OBA	vL	vR	BF/G	H%	S%	xERA	G	L	F	Ctl	Dom	Cmd	hr/f	hr/9	RAR	BPV	R$
RH Reliever	02 aaa	6	5	14	92	77	3.91	1.49	276			8.8	33%	75%	4.49				3.7	7.5	**2.0**		0.8	4.1	64	$11
Age 32	03 TAM	* 7	11	0	188	123	3.88	1.26	233	235	220	24.5	26%	72%	4.57	33	16	51	3.6	5.9	**1.6**	7%	1.0	15.0	49	$15
Peak	04 TAM	* 4	7	1	106	57	6.10	1.65	311	427	286	16.7	33%	65%	4.82	37	25	39	3.4	4.8	**1.4**	12%	1.4	-21.8	9	($2)
Type	05 BOS	* 7	3	0	125	76	4.58	1.38	287	340	246	13.8	31%	70%	4.17	39	21	40	2.2	5.5	**2.5**	9%	1.1	-3.2	48	$7
Reliability 21	06 2NL	4	2	0	56	44	5.79	1.68	310	442	236	10.7	35%	65%	4.57	31	25	45	3.7	7.1	**1.9**	12%	1.4	-9.0	27	$1
DL	1st Half	0	0	0	26	19	6.18	1.68	302			17.2	33%	67%	4.79	32	23	45	4.1	6.5	**1.6**	13%	1.7	-5.5	15	($1)
ERA Potl 50%	2nd Half	4	2	0	30	25	5.44	1.68	317			8.1	37%	71%	4.39	29	26	44	3.3	7.6	**2.3**	12%	1.5	-3.5	39	$2
LIMA Plan C+	07 Proj	**2**	**3**	**0**	**44**	**31**	**5.38**	**1.59**	**302**			**12.3**	**33%**	**69%**	**4.52**	**33**	**24**	**43**	**3.3**	**6.4**	**1.9**	**11%**	**1.4**	**-0.8**	**30**	**$0**

Nice gains in CMD and xERA indicates he's better than surface stats. Rising FB% tells us to expect continued volatility. Unlikely to escape mop-up / journeyman role.

Gonzalez,Mike

	Yr	W	L	Sv	IP	K	ERA	WHIP	OBA	vL	vR	BF/G	H%	S%	xERA	G	L	F	Ctl	Dom	Cmd	hr/f	hr/9	RAR	BPV	R$
LH Reliever	02 aa	8	4	0	85	67	4.87	1.64	280			24.2	34%	69%	4.58				4.9	7.1	**1.5**		0.4	-6.3	60	$4
Age 28	03 a/a	0	0	3	17	16	4.21	1.35	261			6.1	33%	68%	3.70				3.2	8.4	**2.7**		0.5	0.4	94	$2
Pre-Peak	04 PIT	* 5	2	3	63	83	1.14	0.95	205	213	194	4.0	32%	90%	2.09	50	19	31	2.0	11.8	**5.9**	5%	0.3	24.3	201	$14
Type Power	05 PIT	1	3	3	50	58	2.70	1.32	199	156	223	4.2	28%	80%	3.15	53	18	30	5.6	10.4	**1.9**	6%	0.4	9.5	106	$6
Reliability 15	06 PIT	3	4	24	54	64	2.17	1.35	216	163	227	4.3	32%	83%	3.45	37	27	36	5.2	10.7	**2.1**	2%	0.2	15.5	114	$16
DL 34 54	1st Half	1	3	12	30	31	2.98	1.56	260			4.4	35%	80%	3.96	38	26	36	5.1	9.2	**1.8**	3%	0.3	5.6	88	$6
ERA Potl 50%	2nd Half	2	1	12	24	33	1.13	1.09	152			4.2	26%	88%	2.84	35	30	35	5.3	12.5	**2.4**	0%	0.0	9.8	149	$9
LIMA Plan B	07 Proj	**4**	**4**	**28**	**73**	**86**	**2.48**	**1.28**	**209**			**4.6**	**31%**	**80%**	**3.17**	**43**	**24**	**33**	**4.8**	**10.7**	**2.2**	**3%**	**0.2**	**10.7**	**116**	**$19**

Handed closer role and notched 24 saves, but missed Sept. with elbow tendonitis. Superb DOM and HR/9 levels over multiple years. Ctl keeps him from elite levels, but likely good enough to hold closer role.

Gordon,Tom

	Yr	W	L	Sv	IP	K	ERA	WHIP	OBA	vL	vR	BF/G	H%	S%	xERA	G	L	F	Ctl	Dom	Cmd	hr/f	hr/9	RAR	BPV	R$
RH Reliever	02 HOU	1	3	1	43	48	3.98	1.44	262	269	255	5.2	36%	72%	3.61	33	25	42	4.0	10.0	**2.5**	4%	0.4	0.7	103	$3
Age 39	03 CHW	7	6	12	74	91	3.16	1.19	215	231	196	4.6	31%	74%	2.87	40	26	34	3.8	11.1	**2.9**	7%	0.5	12.4	126	$16
Decline	04 NYY	9	4	4	89	96	2.22	0.89	182	185	174	4.2	25%	77%	2.65	47	16	38	2.3	9.7	**4.2**	6%	0.5	24.3	149	$20
Type Power	05 NYY	5	4	2	80	69	2.58	1.10	207	187	217	4.1	24%	81%	3.23	53	12	35	3.3	7.7	**2.4**	10%	0.9	17.7	83	$13
Reliability 33	06 PHI	3	4	34	59	68	3.35	1.27	241	185	277	4.2	31%	80%	2.82	45	23	31	3.4	10.4	**3.1**	19%	1.4	8.3	93	$19
DL 15	1st Half	2	3	20	32	41	1.96	1.02	195			3.8	28%	87%	2.20	48	28	24	3.1	11.5	**3.7**	17%	0.8	10.1	138	$13
ERA Potl 45%	2nd Half	1	1	14	27	27	5.02	1.56	290			4.6	34%	75%	3.60	43	19	38	3.7	9.0	**2.5**	20%	2.0	-1.8	43	$6
LIMA Plan C+	07 Proj	**4**	**4**	**35**	**73**	**76**	**3.48**	**1.23**	**236**			**4.3**	**30%**	**76%**	**3.05**	**46**	**19**	**35**	**3.2**	**9.4**	**2.9**	**13%**	**1.1**	**11.7**	**92**	**$20**

Vintage performance until FB% and HR/9 went off the charts in 2nd half and ERA followed. HR/F was exaggerated and xERA confirms he was a victim of bad luck. Should continue to be effective when healthy.

Gorzelanny,Tom

	Yr	W	L	Sv	IP	K	ERA	WHIP	OBA	vL	vR	BF/G	H%	S%	xERA	G	L	F	Ctl	Dom	Cmd	hr/f	hr/9	RAR	BPV	R$
LH Starter	02	0	0	0	0	0	0.00	0.00																		
Age 24	03	0	0	0	0	0	0.00	0.00																		
Growth	04	0	0	0	0	0	0.00	0.00																		
Type Power	05 aa	8	5	0	129	102	3.88	1.36	264			24.0	32%	71%	3.68				3.1	7.1	**2.3**		0.4	6.8	80	$11
Reliability 0	06 PIT	* 8	10	0	160	120	3.53	1.20	227	239	223	24.5	27%	70%	3.61	49	18	33	3.4	6.7	**2.0**	5%	0.4	18.8	78	$16
DL 19	1st Half	6	5	0	99	80	3.36	1.13	229			25.1	28%	70%					2.6	7.3	**2.8**		0.5	13.8	97	$12
ERA Potl 50%	2nd Half	2	5	0	61	40	3.82	1.32	225			23.6	26%	71%	4.17	49	18	33	4.6	5.9	**1.3**	5%	0.4	5.0	59	$4
LIMA Plan C+	07 Proj	**6**	**7**	**0**	**116**	**87**	**3.72**	**1.29**	**241**			**24.4**	**28%**	**73%**	**3.70**	**49**	**18**	**33**	**3.6**	**6.8**	**1.9**	**9%**	**0.8**	**9.4**	**64**	**$10**

2-5, 3.79 ERA in 62 IP at PIT. GB% and OBA are recipe for success, but needs to reverse 2nd half Ctl problems to realize his top prospect potential. Nice LIMA choice with upside.

Grabow,John

	Yr	W	L	Sv	IP	K	ERA	WHIP	OBA	vL	vR	BF/G	H%	S%	xERA	G	L	F	Ctl	Dom	Cmd	hr/f	hr/9	RAR	BPV	R$
LH Reliever	02 aa	8	13	0	146	81	6.84	1.77	341			24.4	38%	59%	6.08				2.8	5.0	**1.8**		0.6	-46.3	36	($6)
Age 28	03 a/a	6	3	1	107	82	5.12	1.61	326			11.9	38%	69%	5.66				2.3	6.9	**3.0**		0.8	-9.6	70	$3
Pre-Peak	04 PIT	2	5	1	61	64	5.15	1.78	319	327	319	4.2	40%	73%	3.50	48	23	29	4.1	9.4	**2.3**	15%	1.2	-6.7	60	$0
Type Power	05 PIT	2	3	0	52	42	4.85	1.37	239	219	250	3.5	28%	66%	3.80	47	20	33	4.3	7.3	**1.7**	12%	1.0	-3.9	55	$2
Reliability 23	06 PIT	4	2	0	69	66	4.16	1.42	258	275	251	4.2	32%	73%	3.46	49	18	34	3.9	8.6	**2.2**	11%	0.9	2.8	74	$5
DL	1st Half	1	1	0	29	24	4.93	1.68	298			4.3	33%	77%	4.20	44	19	37	4.3	7.4	**1.7**	17%	1.8	-1.6	20	$0
ERA Potl 50%	2nd Half	3	1	0	40	42	3.60	1.22	226			4.0	31%	69%	2.93	54	16	30	3.6	9.4	**2.6**	3%	0.2	4.4	115	$5
LIMA Plan C+	07 Proj	**4**	**3**	**0**	**73**	**66**	**4.68**	**1.49**	**272**			**4.4**	**33%**	**70%**	**3.62**	**48**	**19**	**32**	**3.9**	**8.1**	**2.1**	**11%**	**1.0**	**6.7**	**63**	**$4**

Made strides in 2nd half by cutting bb%, boosting DOM and keeping the ball on the ground. Also aided by reversal in HR/F. 2nd half BPV shows potential, but it will take more consistency to convince us.

JEFFREY TOMICH

Gregg,Kevin

Gregg,Kevin			W	L	Sv	IP	K	ERA	WHIP	OBA	vL	vR	BF/G	H%	S%	xERA	G	L	F	Ctl	Dom	Cmd	hr/f	hr/9	RAR	BPV	R$
RH Reliever	02	a/a	5	8	0	96	75	6.84	1.71	316			16.5	37%	59%	5.71				3.7	7.0	**1.9**		0.8	-30.5	49	($2)
Age 28	03	a/a	11	7	0	158	109	4.78	1.37	287			22.6	33%	66%	4.41				2.2	6.2	**2.9**		0.8	-7.6	71	$10
Pre-Peak	04	ANA	5	2	1	87	84	4.23	1.31	259	260	250	6.7	33%	68%	3.40	44	18	38	2.9	8.7	**3.0**	6%	0.6	2.2	100	$8
Type: Power	05	ANA *	4	3	0	98	81	4.65	1.50	282	267	279	10.9	33%	70%	3.76	48	19	33	3.5	7.4	**2.1**	10%	0.9	-3.3	59	$4
Reliability 29	06	ANA	3	4	0	78	71	4.15	1.40	285	298	268	10.5	34%	74%	3.79	36	18	46	2.4	8.2	**3.4**	9%	1.2	3.9	83	$6
DL	1st Half		2	2	0	43	38	4.80	1.55	315			12.1	37%	73%	3.83	37	21	42	2.3	7.9	**3.5**	12%	1.5	-1.3	68	$2
ERA Potl 60%	2nd Half		1	2	0	35	33	3.34	1.20	245			9.0	31%	74%	3.74	34	14	52	2.6	8.5	**3.3**	6%	0.8	5.2	103	$4
LIMA Plan B+	07	Proj	**4**	**4**	**0**	**87**	**77**	**3.83**	**1.36**	**271**			**9.8**	**33%**	**74%**	**3.75**	**39**	**17**	**43**	**2.8**	**8.0**	**2.9**	**8%**	**0.9**	**7.9**	**81**	**$8**

As a reliever, he had a 3.45 ERA and 8.6 DOM in 63 IP. Strand rate shows improvement pitching with runners on. If you can bench him for those occasional emergency starts, he can be an asset.

Greinke,Zack

Greinke,Zack			W	L	Sv	IP	K	ERA	WHIP	OBA	vL	vR	BF/G	H%	S%	xERA	G	L	F	Ctl	Dom	Cmd	hr/f	hr/9	RAR	BPV	R$
RH Starter	02		0	0	0	0	0	0.00	0.00											0.0	0.0						
Age 23	03	aa	4	3	0	53	31	4.08	1.30	300			24.9	33%	71%	4.65				0.8	5.3	**6.2**		1.0	2.1	126	$5
Growth	04	KC *	9	12	0	173	118	3.85	1.19	262	251	262	23.7	28%	74%	3.86	35	20	45	1.7	6.1	**3.6**	12%	1.5	12.4	71	$16
Type	05	KC	5	17	0	183	114	5.80	1.56	311	340	279	24.9	34%	64%	4.31	39	23	37	2.6	5.6	**2.2**	10%	1.1	-32.3	38	($0)
Reliability 16	06	KC *	9	3	0	111	87	4.69	1.23	260	400	200	22.0	30%	63%	3.41	35	35	30	2.2	7.0	**3.2**	11%	0.9	-1.8	86	$12
DL	1st Half		2	1	0	26	17	8.31	1.62	290			19.7	32%	47%					4.2	5.9	**1.4**		1.4	-12.0	20	($1)
ERA Potl 65%	2nd Half		7	2	0	85	70	3.59	1.11	250			22.9	30%	69%	3.13	35	35	30	1.6	7.4	**4.7**	9%	0.7	10.2	125	$12
LIMA Plan C	07	Proj	**8**	**9**	**0**	**145**	**101**	**4.53**	**1.36**	**281**			**23.0**	**32%**	**69%**	**3.97**	**38**	**22**	**40**	**2.3**	**6.3**	**2.7**	**10%**	**1.1**	**9.2**	**60**	**$10**

1-0, 4.26 ERA in 6.3 IP at KC. Forgotten man after walking out of camp and spending year at AA, but he was solid in 2nd half. Potential sleeper (xERA shows the upside), but a lot will depend on attitude.

Grilli,Jason

Grilli,Jason			W	L	Sv	IP	K	ERA	WHIP	OBA	vL	vR	BF/G	H%	S%	xERA	G	L	F	Ctl	Dom	Cmd	hr/f	hr/9	RAR	BPV	R$
RH Reliever	02		0	0	0	0	0	0.00	0.00											0.0	0.0						
Age 30	03	aaa	6	2	0	66	33	3.53	1.50	270			24.4	30%	76%	4.13				4.1	4.5	**1.1**		0.4	7.0	39	$5
Peak	04	CHW *	11	12	0	197	108	6.66	1.69	312	292	296	27.6	32%	64%	4.96	40	17	43	3.7	4.9	**1.3**	14%	1.9	-54.3	-8	($4)
Type: Finesse	05	aaa	1	9	0	160	86	5.38	1.63	308			27.0	33%	69%	5.76				3.3	4.9	**1.5**		1.2	-21.2	17	($3)
Reliability 9	06	DET	2	3	0	62	31	4.21	1.39	259	292	249	5.2	28%	71%	4.55	47	15	38	3.6	4.5	**1.2**	8%	0.9	2.7	30	$3
DL	1st Half		0	0	0	25	8	3.93	1.47	252			5.0	26%	74%	5.56	46	9	45	4.6	2.9	**0.6**	5%	0.7	2.0	13	$1
ERA Potl 40%	2nd Half		2	3	0	37	23	4.40	1.33	263			5.4	29%	69%	3.89	48	19	33	2.9	5.6	**1.9**	10%	1.0	0.7	47	$3
LIMA Plan C	07	Proj	**3**	**4**	**0**	**73**	**38**	**4.59**	**1.50**	**281**			**8.9**	**30%**	**72%**	**4.62**	**46**	**15**	**39**	**3.6**	**4.7**	**1.3**	**9%**	**1.1**	**-1.2**	**21**	**$2**

Better CMD and DOM in 2nd half, but needs to do that for a full season to be a decent LIMA reliever. History says to bet against.

Guardado,Eddie

Guardado,Eddie			W	L	Sv	IP	K	ERA	WHIP	OBA	vL	vR	BF/G	H%	S%	xERA	G	L	F	Ctl	Dom	Cmd	hr/f	hr/9	RAR	BPV	R$
LH Reliever	02	MIN	1	3	45	67	70	2.96	1.06	219	263	200	3.9	27%	79%	3.30	30	20	50	2.4	9.4	**3.9**	10%	1.2	12.4	113	$24
Age 35	03	MIN	3	5	41	65	60	2.91	0.98	214	175	219	3.8	26%	75%	3.46	29	19	52	1.9	8.3	**4.3**	8%	1.0	13.0	123	$24
Decline	04	SEA	2	2	18	45	45	2.79	1.00	196	109	228	4.3	22%	84%	3.47	28	17	55	2.8	9.0	**3.2**	13%	1.6	9.1	89	$13
Type: Power	05	SEA	2	3	36	56	48	2.73	1.19	247	231	242	4.0	29%	83%	3.68	35	19	46	2.4	7.7	**3.2**	9%	1.1	11.4	85	$18
Reliability 20	06	2TM	1	3	13	37	39	3.89	1.54	297	239	324	3.8	34%	87%	3.89	33	14	54	3.2	9.5	**3.0**	17%	2.4	2.9	43	$7
DL 42	1st Half		0	3	5	21	21	5.52	1.65	295			3.7	30%	81%	4.28	35	9	55	4.2	8.9	**2.1**	23%	3.4	-2.6	-8	$2
ERA Potl 35%	2nd Half		1	0	8	16	18	1.71	1.39	299			4.0	39%	95%	3.40	29	20	51	1.7	10.3	**6.0**	9%	1.1	5.5	149	$5
LIMA Plan C+	07	Proj	**1**	**1**	**0**	**19**	**18**	**4.74**	**1.42**	**272**			**4.1**	**32%**	**71%**	**4.03**	**32**	**17**	**51**	**3.3**	**8.5**	**2.6**	**11%**	**1.4**	**0.9**	**63**	**$1**

Rejuvenated after trade to CIN before elbow soreness led to TJ surgery. Could be back in 2nd half 2007, but odds of a 35-year-old returning to form quickly are remote.

Guerrier,Matt

Guerrier,Matt			W	L	Sv	IP	K	ERA	WHIP	OBA	vL	vR	BF/G	H%	S%	xERA	G	L	F	Ctl	Dom	Cmd	hr/f	hr/9	RAR	BPV	R$
RH Reliever	02	aaa	7	12	0	157	111	5.56	1.40	284			25.1	32%	62%	4.75				2.5	6.4	**2.5**		1.1	-25.0	55	$5
Age 28	03	aaa	4	6	0	105	66	5.97	1.40	304			22.7	33%	60%	5.38				1.6	5.7	**3.6**		1.5	-20.4	61	$2
Pre-Peak	04	aaa	5	10	0	144	83	3.93	1.28	280			25.2	31%	72%	4.27				1.7	5.2	**3.1**		1.0	7.3	67	$9
Type: Finesse	05	MIN	0	3	0	71	46	3.41	1.33	261	279	247	7.0	30%	76%	3.91	47	19	34	3.0	5.8	**1.9**	8%	0.8	8.4	55	$4
Reliability 24	06	MIN	1	0	1	69	37	3.38	1.43	286	333	256	7.7	30%	81%	4.28	45	18	37	2.7	4.8	**1.8**	10%	1.2	10.0	29	$4
DL	1st Half		0	0	0	32	19	3.36	1.65	301			7.0	34%	80%	4.49	48	20	32	3.9	5.3	**1.4**	6%	0.6	4.7	38	$1
ERA Potl 30%	2nd Half		1	0	1	37	18	3.40	1.24	272			8.6	27%	82%	4.09	43	17	40	1.7	4.4	**2.6**	14%	1.7	5.3	30	$4
LIMA Plan C+	07	Proj	**1**	**2**	**0**	**58**	**34**	**3.88**	**1.36**	**278**			**9.2**	**30%**	**75%**	**4.03**	**45**	**19**	**36**	**2.5**	**5.3**	**2.1**	**10%**	**1.1**	**3.2**	**43**	**$3**

Finesse ground ball pitcher who relies on good CTL, but that's been inconsistent. Helped by high S% last two years, so ERA will climb, possibly north of 4.00.

Guzman,Angel

Guzman,Angel			W	L	Sv	IP	K	ERA	WHIP	OBA	vL	vR	BF/G	H%	S%	xERA	G	L	F	Ctl	Dom	Cmd	hr/f	hr/9	RAR	BPV	R$
RH Starter	02		0	0	0	0	0	0.00	0.00																		
Age 25	03	aa	3	3	0	89	77	3.63	1.41	280			25.8	34%	77%	4.51				2.8	7.8	**2.8**		0.9	8.4	76	$6
Growth	04	aa	0	3	0	18	13	6.00	1.44	302			19.6	33%	61%	5.51				2.0	6.5	**3.3**		1.5	-3.7	57	($0)
Type: Power	05		0	0	0	0	0	0.00	0.00																		
Reliability 2	06	CHC *	4	10	0	131	128	6.31	1.66	295	305	309	20.0	36%	62%	4.14	32	28	40	4.3	8.8	**2.0**	10%	1.1	-29.5	58	($1)
DL	1st Half		2	6	0	66	70	5.84	1.58	278			23.0	36%	63%	4.14	28	25	47	4.5	9.5	**2.1**	8%	1.0	-11.0	72	$1
ERA Potl 65%	2nd Half		2	4	0	65	58	6.79	1.74	312			17.8	37%	62%	4.20	35	30	36	4.2	8.0	**1.9**	12%	1.2	-18.5	44	($2)
LIMA Plan B	07	Proj	**3**	**6**	**0**	**102**	**94**	**5.14**	**1.53**	**283**			**21.5**	**34%**	**68%**	**3.96**	**33**	**28**	**39**	**3.7**	**8.3**	**2.2**	**10%**	**1.1**	**5.0**	**63**	**$2**

0-6, 7.39 ERA in 56 IP at CHC. Had no trouble striking out major leaguers, but home plate was much more elusive in his return year. No stamina, thanks to history of arm problems. Needs more polish.

Halladay,Roy

Halladay,Roy			W	L	Sv	IP	K	ERA	WHIP	OBA	vL	vR	BF/G	H%	S%	xERA	G	L	F	Ctl	Dom	Cmd	hr/f	hr/9	RAR	BPV	R$
RH Starter	02	TOR	19	7	0	239	168	2.94	1.19	249	259	228	28.9	30%	75%	3.00	60	17	23	2.3	6.3	**2.7**	6%	0.4	44.9	89	$30
Age 30	03	TOR	22	7	0	266	204	3.25	1.07	252	262	224	29.5	29%	73%	2.59	58	19	23	1.1	6.9	**6.4**	14%	0.9	41.9	153	$37
Peak	04	TOR	8	8	0	133	95	4.20	1.35	272	285	258	27.0	31%	70%	3.28	60	13	27	2.6	6.4	**2.4**	11%	0.9	3.9	64	$10
Type: Finesse	05	TOR	12	4	0	141	108	2.42	0.96	229	217	235	28.9	27%	78%	2.44	61	18	21	1.1	6.9	**6.0**	13%	0.7	34.0	156	$24
Reliability 41	06	TOR	16	5	0	220	132	3.19	1.10	251	259	244	27.6	28%	74%	2.94	57	21	22	1.4	5.4	**3.9**	12%	0.8	37.1	95	$29
DL 84	1st Half		9	2	0	108	57	3.08	1.05	249			28.6	27%	73%	2.97	57	21	22	1.1	4.7	**4.4**	12%	0.7	19.7	103	$16
ERA Potl 60%	2nd Half		7	3	0	112	75	3.30	1.14	253			26.8	29%	74%	2.91	58	20	22	1.7	6.0	**3.6**	13%	0.8	17.4	91	$14
LIMA Plan C+	07	Proj	**16**	**7**	**0**	**218**	**148**	**3.14**	**1.11**	**249**			**28.3**	**28%**	**74%**	**2.84**	**59**	**18**	**23**	**1.6**	**6.1**	**3.9**	**12%**	**0.7**	**44.1**	**101**	**$28**

DOM rate off a bit, but otherwise business as usual. Don't let low Rel score scare you - last two injuries were from getting hit with line drives, not arm trouble. Unless you think being a target is chronic, pay the going rate.

Halsey,Brad

Halsey,Brad			W	L	Sv	IP	K	ERA	WHIP	OBA	vL	vR	BF/G	H%	S%	xERA	G	L	F	Ctl	Dom	Cmd	hr/f	hr/9	RAR	BPV	R$
LH Reliever	02		0	0	0	0	0	0.00	0.00											0.0	0.0						
Age 26	03	aa	7	5	0	91	67	5.83	1.76	349			28.4	41%	65%	6.10				2.2	6.6	**3.0**		0.5	-16.1	74	$0
Growth	04	NYY *	12	7	0	176	116	3.73	1.35	273	143	349	23.5	31%	73%	4.06	43	17	39	2.6	5.9	**2.3**	6%	0.7	15.2	64	$15
Type	05	ARI	8	12	0	160	82	4.61	1.44	297	267	309	24.9	32%	70%	4.30	41	22	37	2.2	4.6	**2.1**	10%	1.1	-7.2	34	$6
Reliability 34	06	OAK	5	4	0	94	53	4.69	1.64	289	317	277	8.2	31%	73%	4.87	44	18	38	4.4	5.1	**1.2**	9%	1.1	-1.5	20	$3
DL	1st Half		3	2	0	60	33	3.74	1.53	277			12.2	29%	80%	4.69	43	20	38	4.0	4.9	**1.2**	11%	1.2	6.1	19	$4
ERA Potl 45%	2nd Half		2	2	0	34	20	6.37	1.83	310			5.4	35%	64%	5.18	45	16	39	5.0	5.3	**1.1**	7%	0.8	-7.6	23	($1)
LIMA Plan C+	07	Proj	**3**	**3**	**0**	**58**	**34**	**4.81**	**1.53**	**291**			**10.3**	**32%**	**70%**	**4.50**	**43**	**19**	**38**	**3.4**	**5.3**	**1.5**	**8%**	**0.9**	**-0.1**	**33**	**$2**

Took a step backward as control abandoned him and DOM has been sub-par for two years now. Trends heading in the wrong direction include xERA, BPV, CMD and BA vs LH. There's a lot not to like here.

Hamels,Cole

Hamels,Cole			W	L	Sv	IP	K	ERA	WHIP	OBA	vL	vR	BF/G	H%	S%	xERA	G	L	F	Ctl	Dom	Cmd	hr/f	hr/9	RAR	BPV	R$
LH Starter	02		0	0	0	0	0	0.00	0.00																		
Age 23	03		0	0	0	0	0	0.00	0.00																		
Growth	04		0	0	0	0	0	0.00	0.00																		
Type: Power	05	aa	2	0	0	19	18	2.84	1.32	183			26.8	22%	83%	3.04				6.2	8.5	**1.4**		0.9	3.4	70	$3
Reliability 0	06	PHI *	11	8	0	155	177	3.59	1.15	228	207	244	24.3	30%	73%	3.04	39	18	43	2.8	10.2	**3.6**	11%	1.1	17.1	113	$21
DL 15	1st Half		3	4	0	60	67	3.72	1.17	225			24.6	30%	70%	3.38	34	16	50	3.1	9.9	**3.2**	7%	0.7	5.7	114	$7
ERA Potl 60%	2nd Half		8	4	0	95	110	3.51	1.14	230			24.1	30%	76%	2.86	41	18	41	2.7	10.4	**3.9**	15%	1.3	11.5	114	$14
LIMA Plan C+	07	Proj	**13**	**10**	**0**	**189**	**214**	**3.58**	**1.15**	**228**			**24.0**	**30%**	**73%**	**3.05**	**39**	**18**	**44**	**2.9**	**10.2**	**3.6**	**11%**	**1.1**	**30.5**	**113**	**$24**

9-8, 4.08 ERA in 132 IP at PHI. As good as advertised. Struggled with control at first, but had 4.0 CMD in last 11 starts. Breakout could come any time.
UP: Sub-3.00 ERA

TOM TODARO

Hammel,Jason

Hammel,Jason		W	L	Sv	IP	K	ERA	WHIP	OBA	vL	vR	BF/G	H%	S%	xERA	G	L	F	Ctl	Dom	Cmd	hr/f	hr/9	RAR	BPV	R$
RH Starter	02	0	0	0	0	0	0.00	0.00																		
Age 24	03	0	0	0	0	0	0.00	0.00																		
Growth	04	0	0	0	0	0	0.00	0.00																		
Type	05 a/a	11	4	0	136	106	3.38	1.32	260			26.2	31%	76%	3.81				2.9	7.0	2.4		0.7	15.6	74	$14
Reliability 0	06 TAM *	5	15	0	171	132	6.10	1.62	311	372	299	23.5	36%	62%	4.10	44	19	38	3.1	6.9	2.2	9%	1.0	-32.5	51	$1
DL	1st Half	3	7	0	85	61	5.81	1.56	308			23.9	36%	62%	4.57	41	7	52	2.7	6.4	2.3	5%	0.8	-13.2	56	$1
ERA Potl 65%	2nd Half	2	8	0	86	71	6.38	1.67	314			23.2	37%	62%	3.98	44	22	34	3.5	7.4	2.2	11%	1.2	-19.4	47	($1)
LIMA Plan C+	07 Proj	8	12	0	174	136	4.76	1.44	281			24.5	33%	68%	3.87	44	19	37	3.1	7.0	2.3	9%	0.9	13.2	61	$10

0-6, 7.77 ERA in 44 IP at TAM. Pretty good command in debut, but bad hit/strand rates cost him. Better control and a few breaks could put him in the profit column.

Hampton,Mike

Hampton,Mike		W	L	Sv	IP	K	ERA	WHIP	OBA	vL	vR	BF/G	H%	S%	xERA	G	L	F	Ctl	Dom	Cmd	hr/f	hr/9	RAR	BPV	R$
LH Reliever	02 COL	7	15	0	178	74	6.17	1.79	312	376	293	28.0	32%	67%	5.07	52	15	32	4.6	3.7	0.8	11%	1.2	-45.3	-4	($8)
Age 34	03 ATL	14	8	0	190	110	3.84	1.39	258	164	278	26.4	29%	73%	4.05	53	16	31	3.7	5.2	1.4	7%	0.7	10.3	44	$14
Past Peak	04 ATL	13	9	0	172	87	4.29	1.53	290	253	300	26.4	31%	73%	4.14	52	21	27	3.4	4.5	1.3	9%	0.8	-0.6	29	$8
Type Finesse	05 ATL	5	3	0	69	27	3.52	1.33	275	338	263	24.5	29%	75%	4.12	51	20	29	2.3	3.5	1.5	7%	0.7	6.2	33	$5
Reliability 0	06 ATL	0	0	0	0	0	0.00	0.00																		
DL 183 107	1st Half	0	0	0	0	0	0.00	0.00																		
ERA Potl	2nd Half	0	0	0	0	0	0.00	0.00																		
LIMA Plan	07 Proj	8	6	0	116	56	4.19	1.46	278			25.4	30%	72%	4.22	52	18	30	3.3	4.3	1.3	9%	0.8	2.0	30	$6

Missed all of 2006 recovering from TJ surgery, but threw well in late-season rehab. Should be ready to go by spring training, but extreme GB pitchers with poor BPIs are very risky. See: Chien Ming Wang

Hancock,Josh

Hancock,Josh		W	L	Sv	IP	K	ERA	WHIP	OBA	vL	vR	BF/G	H%	S%	xERA	G	L	F	Ctl	Dom	Cmd	hr/f	hr/9	RAR	BPV	R$
RH Reliever	02 a/a	7	6	1	129	81	4.33	1.44	279			24.5	31%	71%	4.42				3.1	5.7	1.8		0.8	-0.9	48	$7
Age 29	03 aaa	10	9	0	165	106	4.85	1.35	270			25.2	30%	65%	4.18				2.8	5.8	2.1		0.9	-9.3	53	$10
Pre-Peak	04 2NL *	13	9	0	170	91	4.75	1.42	284	233	299	21.8	30%	70%	4.31	45	17	38	2.7	4.8	1.8	12%	1.4	-10.3	23	$8
Type Finesse	05 CIN *	2	2	0	58	35	5.74	1.66	323			12.1	36%	66%	5.84				2.8	5.4	1.9		0.9	-10.7	36	($1)
Reliability 6	06 STL	3	3	1	77	50	4.09	1.21	244	239	241	5.1	27%	69%	3.98	40	19	40	2.7	5.8	2.2	9%	1.1	3.8	55	$6
DL	1st Half	3	2	0	38	28	3.79	1.08	213			5.2	23%	69%	3.52	45	18	37	2.8	6.6	2.3	13%	1.2	3.3	66	$5
ERA Potl 50%	2nd Half	0	1	1	39	22	4.38	1.33	272			5.0	30%	69%	4.44	36	21	44	2.5	5.1	2.0	7%	0.9	0.5	45	$2
LIMA Plan C	07 Proj	3	3	0	68	42	4.63	1.38	276			7.9	30%	69%	4.26	40	19	41	2.8	5.6	2.0	9%	1.1	0.8	43	$3

BPIs have been straddling the line of acceptability for five years. Any growth he's shown has just been a rebound from a previous decline. In short, there has been no REAL growth and that's not good for a 29-year-old.

Hansen,Craig

Hansen,Craig		W	L	Sv	IP	K	ERA	WHIP	OBA	vL	vR	BF/G	H%	S%	xERA	G	L	F	Ctl	Dom	Cmd	hr/f	hr/9	RAR	BPV	R$
RH Reliever	02	0	0	0	0	0	0.00	0.00											0.0	0.0						
Age 23	03	0	0	0	0	0	0.00	0.00											0.0	0.0						
Growth	04	0	0	0	0	0	0.00	0.00											0.0	0.0						
Type	05 BOS *	0	0	1	13	11	2.08	1.46	304	600	333	4.7	37%	89%	3.66	50	8	42	2.1	7.6	3.7	6%	0.7	3.7	96	$1
Reliability 0	06 BOS *	4	4	0	85	63	4.76	1.51	271	344	276	6.6	32%	67%	4.20	44	22	35	4.1	6.7	1.6	5%	0.5	-2.2	59	$4
DL	1st Half	3	2	0	43	31	3.33	1.50	247			9.6	30%	77%	4.75	42	16	42	5.2	6.4	1.2	2%	0.2	6.6	64	$4
ERA Potl 60%	2nd Half	1	2	0	42	32	6.26	1.51	294			5.0	34%	58%	3.85	44	23	33	3.0	6.9	2.3	9%	0.9	-8.8	60	$0
LIMA Plan B+	07 Proj	2	3	0	58	45	4.34	1.36	265			5.9	32%	68%	3.73	44	23	33	3.1	7.0	2.3	7%	0.6	5.4	73	$4

2-2, 6.63 ERA in 38 IP at BOS. Much better BPIs in 2nd half, but terrible S% took toll on ERA. If he can get his bb% under 3.0, there's a serviceable LIMA pitcher here.

Harang,Aaron

Harang,Aaron		W	L	Sv	IP	K	ERA	WHIP	OBA	vL	vR	BF/G	H%	S%	xERA	G	L	F	Ctl	Dom	Cmd	hr/f	hr/9	RAR	BPV	R$
RH Starter	02 OAK *	10	7	0	133	113	4.06	1.48	268	237	287	21.7	33%	72%	4.49	32	18	50	4.1	7.6	1.9	4%	0.5	6.5	71	$10
Age 29	03 2TM *	13	9	0	148	96	4.62	1.37	285	272	322	21.9	32%	69%	4.03	42	18	40	2.3	5.8	2.6	9%	1.1	-4.2	55	$11
Pre-Peak	04 CIN	10	9	0	161	125	4.86	1.43	280	262	292	25.0	31%	70%	3.88	42	19	38	3.0	7.0	2.4	13%	1.5	-11.9	47	$8
Type	05 CIN	11	13	0	211	163	3.84	1.27	267	253	279	27.6	31%	72%	3.67	39	22	39	2.2	6.9	3.2	9%	0.9	10.7	82	$17
Reliability 90	06 CIN	16	11	0	234	216	3.77	1.27	268	267	270	27.3	33%	74%	3.38	39	22	40	2.2	8.3	3.9	10%	1.1	20.8	100	$24
DL	1st Half	9	5	0	112	109	3.45	1.26	263			27.5	33%	75%	3.24	40	23	38	2.2	8.8	3.9	9%	0.9	14.3	110	$14
ERA Potl 55%	2nd Half	7	6	0	122	107	4.06	1.29	273			27.0	32%	73%	3.51	38	21	41	2.1	7.9	3.8	11%	1.3	6.5	90	$11
LIMA Plan C	07 Proj	16	10	0	223	188	3.83	1.27	263			25.9	31%	73%	3.57	39	21	40	2.4	7.6	3.2	10%	1.1	21.8	82	$22

Three years in the majors - three years of growth. BPIs all trending up; heck, he doubled his BPV. Only concern is the rising flyball rate in CIN. If he can keep that in check...
UP: 20 wins, 3.25 ERA

Harden,Rich

Harden,Rich		W	L	Sv	IP	K	ERA	WHIP	OBA	vL	vR	BF/G	H%	S%	xERA	G	L	F	Ctl	Dom	Cmd	hr/f	hr/9	RAR	BPV	R$
RH Starter	02 aa	8	3	0	85	91	3.28	1.41	229			23.0	32%	75%	3.10				5.2	9.6	1.9		0.2	10.4	100	$10
Age 25	03 OAK *	16	8	0	175	164	3.55	1.25	228	271	241	22.1	29%	72%	3.25	49	21	30	3.7	8.4	2.3	8%	0.6	21.1	91	$23
Growth	04 OAK	11	7	0	189	167	4.00	1.33	243	254	227	26.0	30%	71%	3.70	45	18	37	3.9	7.9	2.1	8%	0.8	10.2	75	$16
Type Power	05 OAK	10	5	0	128	121	2.53	1.06	205	179	221	23.2	26%	78%	3.05	43	26	31	3.0	8.5	2.8	7%	0.5	29.1	109	$21
Reliability 0	06 OAK	4	0	0	46	49	4.29	1.23	192	176	211	21.3	24%	67%	3.34	43	24	32	5.1	9.5	1.9	14%	1.0	1.6	84	$6
DL 141 38	1st Half	3	0	0	35	34	3.86	1.20	196			24.0	25%	69%	3.40	44	25	31	4.6	8.7	1.9	11%	0.8	3.0	85	$5
ERA Potl 60%	2nd Half	1	0	0	11	15	5.62	1.34	181			15.9	23%	62%	3.16	42	23	35	6.4	12.1	1.9	24%	1.6	-1.5	82	$1
LIMA Plan B+	07 Proj	11	8	0	178	169	3.79	1.29	230			24.2	29%	71%	3.48	44	23	33	4.0	8.5	2.1	7%	0.6	22.1	86	$19

DOM rate just fine in return from DL, but prior years' control gains vanished. Gets a fresh start in 2007, but strained elbow raises the risk level considerably.

Haren,Danny

Haren,Danny		W	L	Sv	IP	K	ERA	WHIP	OBA	vL	vR	BF/G	H%	S%	xERA	G	L	F	Ctl	Dom	Cmd	hr/f	hr/9	RAR	BPV	R$
RH Starter	02	0	0	0	0	0	0.00	0.00											0.0	0.0						
Age 26	03 STL *	11	8	0	172	120	4.24	1.30	278	278	304	24.2	32%	70%	3.91	40	18	42	1.9	6.3	3.2	8%	1.0	0.8	75	$13
Growth	04 STL *	14	7	0	174	164	4.34	1.35	277	190	330	21.2	34%	71%	3.38	45	16	39	2.4	8.5	3.5	10%	1.1	-1.8	91	$15
Type	05 OAK	14	12	0	217	163	3.73	1.22	257	252	258	26.4	29%	73%	3.33	48	20	32	2.2	6.8	3.1	12%	1.1	17.1	76	$22
Reliability 82	06 OAK	14	13	0	223	176	4.12	1.21	263	246	268	27.1	30%	70%	3.33	45	19	36	1.8	7.1	3.9	13%	1.3	12.1	90	$24
DL	1st Half	6	6	0	108	81	3.58	1.15	251			27.5	28%	73%	3.43	44	19	37	1.8	6.7	3.7	11%	1.1	13.1	90	$13
ERA Potl 55%	2nd Half	8	7	0	115	95	4.63	1.26	274			26.7	31%	68%	3.23	47	19	34	1.8	7.4	4.1	15%	1.4	-1.0	89	$11
LIMA Plan C	07 Proj	17	8	0	203	162	3.77	1.22	262			25.5	30%	73%	3.33	46	19	35	2.0	7.2	3.6	11%	1.1	28.9	89	$24

ERA doesn't show it, but 2006 was his best year. DOM/DIS pct. was 53/6. Great command, though a touch of gopheritis. Time is right to expect a breakout.
UP: 20 wins, 3.00 ERA

Harville,Chad

Harville,Chad		W	L	Sv	IP	K	ERA	WHIP	OBA	vL	vR	BF/G	H%	S%	xERA	G	L	F	Ctl	Dom	Cmd	hr/f	hr/9	RAR	BPV	R$
RH Reliever	02 aaa	1	2	5	30	21	5.70	1.53	287			5.6	32%	64%	5.16				3.6	6.3	1.8		1.2	-5.3	36	$2
Age 30	03 aaa	3	5	18	57	47	2.37	1.19	226			4.9	27%	84%	3.12				3.3	7.4	2.2		0.8	14.2	78	$14
Peak	04 2TM	3	2	0	55	46	4.73	1.50	265	259	256	4.1	30%	72%	3.54	56	17	27	4.4	7.5	1.7	18%	1.3	-2.6	44	$2
Type Power	05 2TM	0	3	0	45	36	4.79	1.55	253	244	267	4.5	28%	74%	4.20	47	20	33	5.4	7.2	1.3	18%	1.6	-2.7	28	$0
Reliability 16	06 TAM *	0	2	2	56	37	5.41	1.69	288	284	272	6.0	33%	68%	4.28	53	19	27	5.0	6.0	1.2	10%	0.8	-5.9	34	($0)
DL	1st Half	0	1	2	36	27	4.90	1.66	267			6.4	32%	69%	3.85	62	16	22	5.7	6.8	1.2	8%	0.5	-1.5	52	$1
ERA Potl 50%	2nd Half	0	1	0	20	10	6.33	1.76	325			5.5	34%	66%	4.63	47	22	31	3.6	4.5	1.3	13%	1.4	-4.4	3	($1)
LIMA Plan C+	07 Proj	1	2	0	44	31	5.17	1.61	281			5.1	31%	70%	4.12	50	20	30	4.6	6.4	1.4	14%	1.2	1.9	30	$0

0-2, 5.93 ERA in 41 IP at TAM. Home plate is that pentagonal thing in front of the catcher. (The catcher is the crouching one with the mask. No, not the one in black.) It's been 3 years. He needs reminding.

Hawkins,LaTroy

Hawkins,LaTroy		W	L	Sv	IP	K	ERA	WHIP	OBA	vL	vR	BF/G	H%	S%	xERA	G	L	F	Ctl	Dom	Cmd	hr/f	hr/9	RAR	BPV	R$
RH Reliever	02 MIN	6	0	0	80	63	2.14	0.98	218			4.8	26%	81%	3.12	46	19	35	1.7	7.1	4.2	6%	0.6	22.9	125	$14
Age 34	03 MIN	9	3	2	77	75	1.87	1.09	241	205	263	4.2	31%	85%	3.12	37	22	40	1.8	8.8	5.0	5%	0.5	25.2	150	$16
Past Peak	04 CHC	5	4	25	82	69	2.63	1.05	237	230	236	4.2	28%	82%	3.25	38	21	41	1.5	7.6	4.9	10%	1.1	16.5	124	$19
Type Finesse	05 2NL	2	8	6	56	43	3.85	1.46	268	228	297	3.7	31%	77%	4.10	44	17	39	3.9	6.9	1.8	10%	1.1	2.7	47	$5
Reliability 26	06 BAL	3	2	0	60	27	4.49	1.46	301	323	285	4.4	33%	69%	4.41	44	21	35	2.2	4.0	1.8	5%	0.6	0.5	39	$3
DL 24	1st Half	1	1	0	33	14	4.08	1.39	284			4.1	31%	70%	4.54	43	19	37	2.4	3.8	1.6	5%	0.5	2.0	37	$2
ERA Potl 50%	2nd Half	2	1	0	27	13	5.00	1.56	321			4.8	35%	68%	4.24	45	23	31	2.0	4.3	2.2	6%	0.7	-1.5	42	$1
LIMA Plan C+	07 Proj	3	4	0	58	32	4.34	1.38	281			4.2	31%	69%	4.18	43	20	36	2.5	5.0	2.0	7%	0.8	2.2	47	$4

Four year drop in DOM has turned him into a finesse reliever. Still has good control but his ceiling is much lower now. He should no longer be on anyone's depth chart for saves.

TOM TODARO

Heilman,Aaron

	Yr	W	L	Sv	IP	K	ERA	WHIP	OBA	vL	vR	BF/G	H%	S%	xERA	G	L	F	Ctl	Dom	Cmd	hr/f	hr/9	RAR	BPV	R$
RH Reliever	02 a/a	6	7	0	146	112	4.19	1.27	255			22.6	30%	67%	3.49				2.7	6.9	**2.5**		0.6	1.4	80	$11
Age 28	03 NYM *	8	11	0	159	110	5.15	1.68	301	299	301	24.4	34%	71%	4.35	46	21	33	4.2	6.2	**1.5**	10%	1.0	-17.1	33	$1
Pre-Peak	04 NYM *	8	13	0	179	125	5.52	1.64	295	232	286	26.3	33%	68%	4.05	51	20	29	4.1	6.3	**1.5**	13%	1.1	-27.9	33	$0
Type Power	05 NYM	5	3	5	108	106	3.17	1.15	222	208	236	8.3	29%	73%	3.02	46	24	31	3.1	8.8	**2.9**	7%	0.5	14.4	109	$14
Reliability 31	06 NYM	4	5	0	87	73	3.62	1.16	229	231	231	4.8	28%	69%	3.48	45	17	38	2.9	7.6	**2.6**	5%	0.5	9.3	94	$9
DL	1st Half	0	2	0	41	36	4.39	1.37	262			5.2	32%	68%	3.48	46	21	32	3.3	7.9	**2.4**	8%	0.7	0.5	81	$2
ERA Potl 60%	2nd Half	4	3	0	46	37	2.93	0.98	198			4.5	24%	70%	3.48	43	13	43	2.5	7.2	**2.8**	4%	0.4	8.8	107	$8
LIMA Plan B+	07 Proj	**5**	**3**	**3**	**73**	**61**	**3.48**	**1.24**	**241**			**7.0**	**29%**	**73%**	**3.52**	**45**	**19**	**36**	**3.1**	**7.6**	**2.4**	**7%**	**0.6**	**7.5**	**85**	**$9**

Wants to start, but his success has been in the pen. If he stays there, he's a top LIMA reliever. If not, the outlook is murkier. But he's improved since his first shot at starting so he's good to tuck away in any case.

Hendrickson,Mark

	Yr	W	L	Sv	IP	K	ERA	WHIP	OBA	vL	vR	BF/G	H%	S%	xERA	G	L	F	Ctl	Dom	Cmd	hr/f	hr/9	RAR	BPV	R$
LH Starter	02 TOR *	10	5	0	128	76	3.87	1.32	271	194	204	15.5	30%	74%	4.06	46	15	39	2.5	5.3	**2.2**	9%	1.0	9.3	49	$11
Age 32	03 TOR	9	9	0	158	76	5.53	1.56	317	269	333	23.6	33%	67%	4.45	45	18	37	2.3	4.3	**1.9**	11%	1.4	-19.5	16	$3
Peak	04 TAM	10	15	0	183	87	4.82	1.40	290	291	295	24.7	31%	67%	4.26	46	19	36	2.3	4.3	**1.9**	9%	1.0	-8.7	31	$7
Type Finesse	05 TAM	11	8	0	178	89	5.91	1.55	311	258	328	25.7	33%	63%	4.25	46	22	32	2.5	4.5	**1.8**	12%	1.2	-33.8	21	$2
Reliability 78	06 2TM	6	15	0	164	99	4.22	1.43	272	287	264	23.0	30%	72%	4.23	48	16	36	3.4	5.4	**1.6**	9%	0.9	6.1	39	$8
DL 18 16	1st Half	4	8	0	89	51	3.83	1.29	244			28.9	26%	73%	4.28	48	11	41	3.4	5.1	**1.5**	9%	1.0	7.5	38	$7
ERA Potl 45%	2nd Half	2	7	0	75	48	4.68	1.60	303			18.8	34%	72%	4.16	47	22	31	3.4	5.8	**1.7**	9%	0.8	-1.5	40	$1
LIMA Plan C	07 Proj	**6**	**10**	**0**	**133**	**74**	**4.87**	**1.48**	**291**			**22.5**	**32%**	**69%**	**4.23**	**47**	**19**	**34**	**2.9**	**5.0**	**1.7**	**10%**	**1.0**	**3.1**	**33**	**$4**

What we might call a "precision pitcher" -- throws soft and with good location. But there is no dominance here, so patient batters will ultimate time a good pitch to hit, as reflected by his elevated oppBAs. Avoid.

Hennessey,Brad

	Yr	W	L	Sv	IP	K	ERA	WHIP	OBA	vL	vR	BF/G	H%	S%	xERA	G	L	F	Ctl	Dom	Cmd	hr/f	hr/9	RAR	BPV	R$
RH Reliever	02	0	0	0	0	0	0.00	0.00											0.0	0.0						
Age 27	03	0	0	0	0	0	0.00	0.00											0.0	0.0						
Growth	04 a/a	9	6	0	136	58	3.61	1.44	279			25.8	30%	75%	4.27				3.1	3.8	**1.2**		0.5	12.3	32	$8
Type Finesse	05 SF *	9	10	0	185	103	4.78	1.48	281	320	244	25.5	30%	69%	4.24	48	20	32	3.5	5.0	**1.4**	10%	1.0	-12.2	30	$5
Reliability 28	06 SF	5	6	1	99	42	4.27	1.35	248	230	265	12.5	25%	71%	4.73	44	19	37	3.8	3.8	**1.0**	10%	1.1	2.7	17	$6
DL	1st Half	3	1	1	48	17	2.61	1.22	223			14.3	23%	82%	4.87	41	19	39	3.7	3.2	**0.9**	6%	0.7	11.1	25	$6
ERA Potl 40%	2nd Half	2	5	0	51	25	5.83	1.47	270			11.2	28%	63%	4.58	46	19	35	3.9	4.4	**1.1**	13%	1.4	-8.5	9	$0
LIMA Plan D+	07 Proj	**5**	**6**	**0**	**102**	**48**	**4.79**	**1.49**	**278**			**16.6**	**29%**	**69%**	**4.64**	**46**	**19**	**35**	**3.6**	**4.3**	**1.2**	**9%**	**1.0**	**-3.4**	**20**	**$3**

Mixed success as a starter, they moved him into the pen with much better results (3.32 ERA), then rewarded him by moving him back to the rotation (8.22 ERA). Soft-tosser, down trends. DN: ERA north of 5.00

Hensley,Clay

	Yr	W	L	Sv	IP	K	ERA	WHIP	OBA	vL	vR	BF/G	H%	S%	xERA	G	L	F	Ctl	Dom	Cmd	hr/f	hr/9	RAR	BPV	R$
RH Starter	02	0	0	0	0	0	0.00	0.00											0.0	0.0						
Age 27	03	0	0	0	0	0	0.00	0.00											0.0	0.0						
Pre-Peak	04 aa	11	10	0	159	95	5.66	1.65	319			26.9	36%	66%	5.71				3.0	5.4	**1.8**		0.9	-25.8	36	$1
Type	05 SD *	3	3	0	137	91	2.62	1.00	205	275	103	13.8	24%	74%	3.02	59	16	25	2.5	6.0	**2.4**	6%	0.4	27.6	88	$16
Reliability 20	06 SD	11	12	0	187	122	3.71	1.34	248	263	239	21.5	28%	74%	3.78	54	17	30	3.7	5.9	**1.6**	9%	0.7	18.0	53	$15
DL	1st Half	5	6	0	91	44	4.15	1.30	237			19.2	25%	69%	4.24	53	14	33	3.8	4.3	**1.2**	8%	0.8	3.8	34	$6
ERA Potl 50%	2nd Half	6	6	0	96	78	3.28	1.38	258			24.2	31%	78%	3.35	55	19	26	3.6	7.3	**2.1**	9%	0.7	14.2	71	$9
LIMA Plan D+	07 Proj	**9**	**9**	**0**	**190**	**126**	**3.94**	**1.34**	**257**			**25.2**	**30%**	**71%**	**3.63**	**55**	**17**	**28**	**3.3**	**6.0**	**1.8**	**8%**	**0.6**	**17.2**	**59**	**$13**

By outward standards, a solid season and good 2nd half growth. But good ground ball tendencies may not be enough to offset erratic control and depressed hit rate. Don't overbid.

Herges,Matt

	Yr	W	L	Sv	IP	K	ERA	WHIP	OBA	vL	vR	BF/G	H%	S%	xERA	G	L	F	Ctl	Dom	Cmd	hr/f	hr/9	RAR	BPV	R$
RH Reliever	02 MON	2	5	6	64	50	4.08	1.66	307	315	300	4.7	35%	80%	4.03	47	19	34	3.7	7.0	**1.9**	14%	1.4	0.2	34	$3
Age 37	03 2NL	3	2	3	79	68	2.62	1.23	234	209	249	4.9	30%	79%	3.62	43	20	38	3.3	7.7	**2.3**	4%	0.3	16.2	94	$10
Decline	04 SF	4	5	23	65	39	5.25	1.71	329	366	318	4.3	36%	71%	4.55	44	18	39	2.9	5.4	**1.9**	9%	1.1	-8.0	27	$7
Type	05 2NL *	2	3	0	58	35	3.88	1.71	320	256	333	5.0	34%	83%	4.70	39	22	39	3.4	5.4	**1.6**	12%	1.6	2.6	10	$1
Reliability 23	06 FLA	2	3	0	71	36	4.31	1.72	319	300	340	5.0	35%	75%	4.64	47	22	31	3.5	4.6	**1.3**	6%	0.6	1.6	26	$0
DL	1st Half	0	2	0	33	17	4.64	1.61	306			4.7	33%	72%	4.37	50	19	31	3.3	4.6	**1.4**	8%	0.8	-0.6	27	($0)
ERA Potl 35%	2nd Half	2	1	0	38	19	4.03	1.82	331			5.3	37%	78%	4.88	44	24	31	3.8	4.5	**1.2**	5%	0.5	2.2	27	$0
LIMA Plan C	07 Proj	**2**	**2**	**0**	**44**	**24**	**4.55**	**1.70**	**317**			**4.9**	**35%**	**75%**	**4.62**	**45**	**21**	**34**	**3.5**	**5.0**	**1.4**	**9%**	**1.0**	**-1.4**	**20**	**$0**

The Frankie Frisch Fact: "Have one good year (2003) and you can fool them for five more." Even with bad CMD and chronic high hit rates/oppBAs, he still breathes life... at least until 2008, I guess.

Hermanson,Dustin

	Yr	W	L	Sv	IP	K	ERA	WHIP	OBA	vL	vR	BF/G	H%	S%	xERA	G	L	F	Ctl	Dom	Cmd	hr/f	hr/9	RAR	BPV	R$
RH Reliever	02 BOS *	1	2	0	35	21	6.17	1.74	318	325	373	9.6	36%	64%	5.03	37	21	42	3.9	5.4	**1.4**	6%	0.8	-7.4	30	($1)
Age 34	03 SF *	3	4	1	94	52	4.50	1.39	282	282	264	11.3	31%	69%	4.24	45	17	38	2.6	5.0	**1.9**	8%	1.0	-2.6	40	$4
Past Peak	04 SF	6	9	17	131	102	4.53	1.36	263	285	242	11.9	30%	69%	3.93	43	17	41	3.2	7.0	**2.2**	9%	1.0	-4.4	60	$12
Type	05 CHW	2	4	34	57	33	2.05	1.10	222	240	206	4.0	25%	85%	4.10	38	21	41	2.7	5.2	**1.9**	6%	0.6	16.4	64	$18
Reliability 3	06 CHW	0	0	0	6	5	4.35	1.13	255	167	308	4.2	24%	80%	3.10	50	10	40	1.5	7.3	**5.0**	27%	2.9	0.2	65	$1
DL 157	1st Half	0	0	0	0	0	0.00	0.00																		
ERA Potl 25%	2nd Half	0	0	0	6	5	4.36	1.13	256			4.2	24%	80%	3.10	50	10	40	1.5	7.3	**5.0**	27%	2.9	0.2	65	$1
LIMA Plan B	07 Proj	**1**	**1**	**0**	**24**	**15**	**4.50**	**1.42**	**278**			**4.7**	**31%**	**69%**	**4.28**	**44**	**15**	**40**	**3.0**	**5.6**	**1.9**	**6%**	**0.8**	**0.6**	**50**	**$1**

Serious back problem cost him almost entire season. At best, he'll deal with chronic soreness; at worst, he'll need career-ending surgery. And if he's not closing, then why gamble?

Hernandez,Felix

	Yr	W	L	Sv	IP	K	ERA	WHIP	OBA	vL	vR	BF/G	H%	S%	xERA	G	L	F	Ctl	Dom	Cmd	hr/f	hr/9	RAR	BPV	R$
RH Starter	02	0	0	0	0	0	0.00	0.00											0.0	0.0						
Age 21	03	0	0	0	0	0	0.00	0.00											0.0	0.0						
Green	04 aa	5	1	0	57	62	3.56	1.16	226			23.3	31%	68%	2.67				3.0	9.8	**3.2**		0.4	5.5	124	$8
Type Power	05 SEA *	13	8	0	172	187	2.35	1.04	194	164	224	22.0	27%	78%	2.14	67	14	19	3.3	9.8	**3.0**	10%	0.4	42.8	126	$30
Reliability 21	06 SEA	12	14	0	191	176	4.52	1.34	266	281	241	26.2	32%	69%	2.85	58	18	25	2.8	8.3	**2.9**	17%	1.1	0.8	81	$18
DL	1st Half	8	7	0	97	92	4.92	1.40	281			26.2	34%	68%	2.85	56	20	24	2.7	8.5	**3.2**	20%	1.3	-4.3	78	$9
ERA Potl 65%	2nd Half	4	7	0	94	84	4.12	1.27	249			26.2	30%	69%	2.85	60	16	25	3.0	8.0	**2.7**	14%	0.9	5.1	84	$9
LIMA Plan B	07 Proj	**15**	**11**	**0**	**204**	**204**	**3.58**	**1.20**	**235**			**26.2**	**30%**	**72%**	**2.59**	**60**	**17**	**23**	**3.1**	**9.0**	**3.0**	**13%**	**0.7**	**47.6**	**103**	**$26**

The King exhibited stellar skills but a disappointing ERA, thanks to unlucky h%, s% and hr/f. As all regress, his xERA becomes the target. He'll turn 21 soon after Opening Day. It only gets better from here.

Hernandez,Livan

	Yr	W	L	Sv	IP	K	ERA	WHIP	OBA	vL	vR	BF/G	H%	S%	xERA	G	L	F	Ctl	Dom	Cmd	hr/f	hr/9	RAR	BPV	R$
RH Starter	02 SF	12	16	0	216	134	4.38	1.41	277	295	273	28.3	31%	70%	4.09	46	19	35	3.0	5.6	**1.9**	8%	0.8	-7.2	49	$11
Age 32	03 MON	15	10	0	233	178	3.21	1.21	255	278	233	29.2	29%	78%	3.40	47	19	34	2.2	6.9	**3.1**	11%	1.0	30.8	80	$25
Peak	04 MON	11	15	0	255	186	3.60	1.24	246	258	238	30.3	28%	74%	3.67	46	19	35	2.9	6.6	**2.2**	10%	0.9	20.8	65	$21
Type	05 WAS	15	10	0	246	147	3.99	1.43	279	290	278	30.6	31%	74%	4.23	40	26	34	3.1	5.4	**1.8**	9%	0.9	7.9	41	$14
Reliability 90	06 2NL	13	13	0	216	128	4.83	1.50	288	302	275	28.1	31%	71%	4.67	37	20	44	3.3	5.3	**1.6**	9%	1.2	-9.2	28	$9
DL	1st Half	6	8	0	105	61	5.57	1.62	300			28.0	32%	68%	4.91	36	21	43	3.7	5.2	**1.4**	10%	1.4	-14.0	15	$1
ERA Potl 45%	2nd Half	7	5	0	111	67	4.14	1.39	275			28.1	30%	73%	4.45	37	19	44	2.8	5.4	**1.9**	8%	1.1	4.8	41	$7
LIMA Plan C	07 Proj	**10**	**11**	**0**	**193**	**116**	**4.52**	**1.46**	**279**			**29.1**	**31%**	**71%**	**4.44**	**40**	**21**	**39**	**3.3**	**5.4**	**1.7**	**9%**	**1.0**	**-1.9**	**36**	**$8**

The mileage is piling up and taking a toll. DOM down again; OBA getting progressively worse. And until his arm really does fall off, you're stuck with 200 IP of a bad ERA and WHIP.

Hernandez,Orlando

	Yr	W	L	Sv	IP	K	ERA	WHIP	OBA	vL	vR	BF/G	H%	S%	xERA	G	L	F	Ctl	Dom	Cmd	hr/f	hr/9	RAR	BPV	R$
RH Starter	02 NYY	9	5	1	151	117	3.58	1.17	246	224	248	24.7	28%	73%	3.57				2.2	7.0	**3.2**		1.0	16.4	84	$17
Age 41	03 NYY	0	0	0	0	0	0.00	0.00											0.0	0.0						
Decline	04 NYY	8	2	0	84	84	3.31	1.29	235	255	194	23.7	29%	78%	3.70	35	21	44	3.8	9.0	**2.3**	9%	1.0	11.6	82	$11
Type Power	05 CHW	9	9	1	128	91	5.13	1.46	275	295	257	23.4	31%	67%	4.23	39	22	39	3.5	6.4	**1.8**	11%	1.3	-12.0	39	$7
Reliability 10	06 2NL	11	11	0	162	164	4.66	1.33	253	300	199	23.8	31%	68%	3.69	34	19	47	3.4	9.1	**2.7**	10%	1.2	-3.5	79	$14
DL 52	1st Half	4	7	0	77	79	5.84	1.49	279			22.7	34%	64%	3.91	32	20	48	3.6	9.2	**2.5**	12%	1.5	-12.8	63	$3
ERA Potl 55%	2nd Half	7	4	0	85	85	3.60	1.19	229			24.9	29%	73%	3.50	35	19	45	3.2	9.0	**2.8**	9%	1.0	9.3	94	$11
LIMA Plan C+	07 Proj	**10**	**9**	**0**	**145**	**132**	**4.41**	**1.33**	**254**			**23.7**	**30%**	**70%**	**3.81**	**36**	**20**	**44**	**3.4**	**8.2**	**2.4**	**10%**	**1.2**	**10.0**	**69**	**$12**

Trade to NYM helped to reduce h% and hr/f and revive his stats. But was anyone surprised when he missed the playoffs? Risky but rosterable. And old. Perhaps very old. But since 41 is the new 31 these days....

TOM TODARO

Hernandez,Roberto

		W	L	Sv	IP	K	ERA	WHIP	OBA	vL	vR	BF/G	H%	S%	xERA	G	L	F	Ctl	Dom	Cmd	hr/f	hr/9	RAR	BPV	R$
RH Reliever	02 KC	1	3	26	53	40	4.25	1.45	293	282	317	4.3	34%	73%	3.50	50	22	29	2.5	6.8	2.7	12%	1.0	1.4	63	$11
Age 42	03 ATL	5	3	0	60	45	4.35	1.73	265	248	276	4.2	29%	80%	4.28	55	20	25	6.5	6.8	1.0	22%	1.5	-0.5	19	$2
Decline	04 PHI	3	5	0	56	44	4.80	1.69	294	278	311	4.1	33%	76%	4.04	55	13	32	4.6	7.0	1.5	16%	1.4	-3.8	27	$1
Type Power	05 NYM	8	6	4	69	61	2.60	1.23	226	244	213	4.3	28%	81%	3.69	39	22	39	3.6	7.9	2.2	7%	0.7	14.0	84	$12
Reliability 8	06 2NL	0	3	2	63	48	3.13	1.47	255	290	219	4.1	30%	81%	4.13	47	19	34	4.6	6.8	1.5	8%	0.7	10.6	55	$4
DL	1st Half	0	1	2	34	24	2.11	1.37	243			4.2	29%	87%	4.01	53	13	35	4.2	6.3	1.5	6%	0.5	10.0	60	$3
ERA Potl 35%	2nd Half	0	2	0	29	24	4.34	1.59	268			4.0	32%	74%	4.27	40	26	34	5.0	7.4	1.5	10%	0.9	0.5	50	$0
LIMA Plan B	07 Proj	2	4	0	58	46	4.19	1.47	258			4.1	30%	73%	4.01	46	20	34	4.3	7.1	1.6	10%	0.9	2.6	53	$3

All those walks, but a string of high strand rates. Why? Last four years:
- Nobody on: .273 OBA
- Runners on: .235 OBA

A few more untimely hits will send his ERA north.

Hernandez,Runelvys

		W	L	Sv	IP	K	ERA	WHIP	OBA	vL	vR	BF/G	H%	S%	xERA	G	L	F	Ctl	Dom	Cmd	hr/f	hr/9	RAR	BPV	R$
RH Starter	02 KC *	12	7	0	181	117	3.93	1.33	276	302	236	26.5	32%	71%	4.02				2.3	5.8	2.5		0.6	11.9	70	$15
Age 29	03 KC	7	5	0	91	48	4.64	1.36	253	267	231	24.4	27%	67%	4.66	35	26	39	3.7	4.7	1.3	8%	0.9	-1.3	33	$6
Pre-Peak	04 KC	0	0	0	0	0	0.00	0.00											0.0	0.0						
Type	05 KC	8	14	0	159	88	5.54	1.52	277	261	290	24.4	30%	64%	4.92	38	18	43	4.0	5.0	1.3	8%	1.0	-22.9	25	$3
Reliability 0	06 KC *	11	16	0	173	85	6.39	1.75	317	325	329	24.5	33%	65%	5.11	39	23	38	3.9	4.4	1.1	12%	1.5	-39.2	-2	($2)
DL 115 15	1st Half	5	8	0	77	37	7.27	1.76	325			22.7	33%	61%	5.07	39	23	38	3.7	4.3	1.2	13%	1.7	-25.9	-9	($3)
ERA Potl 45%	2nd Half	6	8	0	96	48	5.68	1.73	310			26.3	33%	69%	5.15	38	23	38	4.2	4.5	1.1	11%	1.3	-13.3	3	($0)
LIMA Plan C	07 Proj	6	13	0	135	71	5.62	1.59	294			24.3	31%	66%	4.91	38	22	40	3.7	4.8	1.3	10%	1.2	-7.0	15	$1

6-10, 6.48 ERA in 109 IP at KC. Two years removed from TJ surgery, his command is gone, his dominance is gone and his composure with runners on base is gone. But he still has his hair.

Hill,Rich

		W	L	Sv	IP	K	ERA	WHIP	OBA	vL	vR	BF/G	H%	S%	xERA	G	L	F	Ctl	Dom	Cmd	hr/f	hr/9	RAR	BPV	R$
LH Starter	02	0	0	0	0	0	0.00	0.00																		
Age 27	03	0	0	0	0	0	0.00	0.00																		
Growth	04	0	0	0	0	0	0.00	0.00																		
Type Power	05 a/a	10	4	0	122	152	4.34	1.23	246			24.2	31%	73%	4.36				2.8	11.2	4.0		1.8	-0.6	104	$15
Reliability 1	06 CHC *	13	8	0	199	205	3.34	1.12	222	262	220	25.1	28%	74%	3.51	30	18	52	2.8	9.3	3.3	8%	0.9	28.2	108	$26
DL	1st Half	5	5	0	89	92	4.09	1.23	240			24.7	32%	67%	3.51	42	9	49	3.1	9.3	3.0	5%	0.6	4.3	108	$9
ERA Potl 55%	2nd Half	8	3	0	110	113	2.72	1.03	207			25.5	25%	81%	3.41	26	21	52	2.6	9.3	3.5	10%	1.2	23.9	108	$18
LIMA Plan B	07 Proj	11	9	0	174	184	3.98	1.22	244			24.8	30%	72%	3.53	30	19	52	2.8	9.5	3.4	10%	1.3	17.9	96	$18

6-7, 4.17 ERA in 99 IP at CHC. Wildness earned him demotion in May; showed great command after recall. It's just two months, though; S% helped and FB rate is a concern, so curb your enthusiasm. For now.

Hirsh,Jason

		W	L	Sv	IP	K	ERA	WHIP	OBA	vL	vR	BF/G	H%	S%	xERA	G	L	F	Ctl	Dom	Cmd	hr/f	hr/9	RAR	BPV	R$
RH Starter	02	0	0	0	0	0	0.00	0.00																		
Age 25	03	0	0	0	0	0	0.00	0.00																		
Growth	04	0	0	0	0	0	0.00	0.00																		
Type	05 aa	1	8	0	172	133	4.15	1.28	263			24.9	31%	69%	3.82				2.4	6.9	2.9		0.8	3.3	80	$9
Reliability 0	06 HOU *	16	6	0	181	129	3.33	1.25	231	211	303	23.6	27%	76%	4.51	30	18	52	3.6	6.4	1.8	6%	0.8	26.0	61	$21
DL	1st Half	8	2	0	98	71	3.03	1.27	233			25.7	28%	76%					3.8	6.5	1.7		0.4	17.7	73	$12
ERA Potl 40%	2nd Half	8	4	0	83	58	3.68	1.21	230			21.5	25%	75%	4.42	30	18	52	3.4	6.3	1.9	9%	1.3	8.3	47	$10
LIMA Plan C	07 Proj	8	6	0	145	106	4.16	1.32	258			24.6	29%	71%	4.45	30	18	52	3.1	6.6	2.1	7%	1.0	-1.6	58	$10

3-4, 6.04 ERA in 44 IP at HOU. ERA was 4.29 apart from 2.2 IP 10 ER disaster on 8/22. We don't routinely give mulligans but that start was particularly brutal and there are signs he could be moderately successful.

Hoffman,Trevor

		W	L	Sv	IP	K	ERA	WHIP	OBA	vL	vR	BF/G	H%	S%	xERA	G	L	F	Ctl	Dom	Cmd	hr/f	hr/9	RAR	BPV	R$
RH Reliever	02 SD	2	5	38	59	69	2.75	1.19	238	186	275	4.0	34%	76%	3.07	32	26	41	2.7	10.5	3.8	3%	0.3	9.9	142	$19
Age 39	03 SD	0	0	0	9	11	2.00	1.11	216	182	273	4.0	29%	89%	2.64	41	25	34	3.0	11.0	3.7	14%	1.0	2.5	125	$1
Decline	04 SD	3	3	40	54	53	2.32	0.92	216	255	161	3.8	27%	80%	3.07	31	22	47	1.3	8.8	6.6	7%	0.8	13.0	179	$21
Type	05 SD	1	6	43	57	54	2.99	1.12	244	291	179	3.9	31%	74%	3.28	37	21	42	1.9	8.5	4.5	4%	0.5	8.9	138	$20
Reliability 64	06 SD	0	2	46	63	50	2.14	0.97	213	194	214	3.8	25%	84%	3.50	32	22	45	1.9	7.1	3.8	8%	0.9	18.2	110	$24
DL	1st Half	0	1	19	29	24	1.24	1.00	227			3.9	28%	89%	3.60	30	20	50	1.6	7.4	4.8	2%	0.3	11.6	146	$11
ERA Potl 40%	2nd Half	0	1	27	34	26	2.91	0.94	200			3.6	21%	78%	3.42	34	25	41	2.1	6.9	3.3	13%	1.3	6.6	85	$13
LIMA Plan C+	07 Proj	1	3	40	58	46	3.13	1.13	243			3.9	28%	76%	3.65	33	22	44	2.0	7.2	3.5	8%	0.9	5.1	96	$19

Stellar control has compensated for eroding DOM, but there are warning signs in xERA. Good for another 35+ saves, but at this stage the prudent play is to tack on a half-run to his ERA each year from now on.

Howell,J.P.

		W	L	Sv	IP	K	ERA	WHIP	OBA	vL	vR	BF/G	H%	S%	xERA	G	L	F	Ctl	Dom	Cmd	hr/f	hr/9	RAR	BPV	R$
LH Starter	02	0	0	0	0	0	0.00	0.00											0.0	0.0						
Age 24	03	0	0	0	0	0	0.00	0.00											0.0	0.0						
Growth	04	0	0	0	0	0	0.00	0.00											0.0	0.0						
Type Power	05 KC *	8	6	0	127	99	5.16	1.48	263	229	271	22.4	31%	65%	3.51	58	19	24	4.3	7.0	1.6	12%	0.8	-12.3	55	$6
Reliability 0	06 TAM *	9	8	0	133	103	4.60	1.53	298	400	281	22.8	36%	70%	3.71	45	26	29	3.0	7.0	2.3	7%	0.6	-0.7	68	$8
DL	1st Half	4	3	0	47	34	5.17	1.47	286			20.6	33%	65%					3.1	6.5	2.1		0.8	-3.6	59	$3
ERA Potl 60%	2nd Half	5	5	0	86	69	4.29	1.56	304			24.1	37%	72%	3.68	45	26	29	2.9	7.2	2.5	6%	0.5	2.9	74	$5
LIMA Plan C	07 Proj	10	12	0	174	134	4.34	1.45	273			22.4	32%	70%	3.58	51	23	27	3.5	6.9	2.0	9%	0.7	19.5	63	$12

1-3, 5.10 ERA in 42 IP at TAM. GB pitcher improved his CMD, but elevated H% hurt his bottom line. With better luck and a lower LD rate, he'll reach double-digit value. xERA really likes him. Sleeper.

Howry,Bob

		W	L	Sv	IP	K	ERA	WHIP	OBA	vL	vR	BF/G	H%	S%	xERA	G	L	F	Ctl	Dom	Cmd	hr/f	hr/9	RAR	BPV	R$
RH Reliever	02 2AL	3	5	0	68	45	4.24	1.29	259	239	280	4.3	31%	65%	3.37				2.8	6.0	2.1		0.3	1.9	76	$5
Age 33	03 aaa	2	0	0	17	7	1.59	1.12	273			5.3	29%	89%	3.34				0.5	3.7	7.0		0.5	5.9	154	$3
Past Peak	04 CLE *	5	3	0	68	58	4.09	1.20	247	291	169	5.1	29%	70%	3.58	33	28	40	2.5	7.7	3.1	11%	1.2	2.9	80	$7
Type	05 CLE	7	4	3	73	48	2.47	0.89	192	186	198	3.5	22%	74%	3.56	40	19	41	2.0	5.9	3.0	5%	0.5	17.2	100	$14
Reliability 35	06 CHC	4	5	5	76	71	3.19	1.14	246	247	244	3.7	30%	76%	3.35	38	18	44	2.0	8.4	4.2	8%	0.9	12.2	116	$11
DL	1st Half	3	2	1	36	34	3.49	1.22	256			3.8	31%	77%	3.50	37	17	47	2.2	8.5	3.8	10%	1.2	4.4	97	$5
ERA Potl 55%	2nd Half	1	3	4	40	37	2.92	1.07	236			3.6	30%	75%	3.21	39	19	42	1.8	8.3	4.6	6%	0.7	7.8	134	$6
LIMA Plan B+	07 Proj	5	4	13	73	60	3.23	1.09	233			3.8	28%	73%	3.49	38	20	43	2.1	7.4	3.5	7%	0.7	7.8	105	$14

These are the BPIs of a closer. Yes, he's 33, and yes, he's not currently on the frontline for saves, but these are the guys you have to speculate on. At minimum, you've got a great LIMA reliever, and maybe more.

Hudson,Luke

		W	L	Sv	IP	K	ERA	WHIP	OBA	vL	vR	BF/G	H%	S%	xERA	G	L	F	Ctl	Dom	Cmd	hr/f	hr/9	RAR	BPV	R$
RH Reliever	02 aaa	5	9	3	117	107	5.00	1.40	253			16.9	32%	63%	3.65				4.0	8.2	2.1		0.5	-10.5	83	$7
Age 30	03	0	0	0	0	0	0.00	0.00											0.0	0.0						
Peak	04 CIN *	13	10	0	153	116	3.82	1.34	254	160	250	23.3	29%	75%	4.41	34	15	51	3.5	6.8	2.0	8%	1.1	8.4	55	$14
Type	05 CIN	6	9	0	84	53	6.41	1.58	259	255	278	19.9	27%	61%	5.00	38	21	41	5.3	5.7	1.1	13%	1.5	-22.5	15	($0)
Reliability 11	06 KC *	9	6	1	137	80	4.82	1.41	276	258	293	15.2	31%	64%	3.91	49	23	28	3.0	5.3	1.8	6%	0.5	-4.4	55	$9
DL 68	1st Half	2	3	1	46	22	5.14	1.48	291			9.2	33%	61%	4.22	51	19	30	2.9	4.4	1.5	0%	0.0	-3.3	55	$2
ERA Potl 60%	2nd Half	7	3	0	91	58	4.65	1.38	268			23.0	30%	66%	3.76	49	23	28	3.1	5.7	1.9	9%	0.7	-1.1	54	$7
LIMA Plan C	07 Proj	9	11	0	153	95	4.53	1.38	267			20.6	30%	68%	4.10	44	22	34	3.2	5.6	1.8	9%	0.9	7.4	46	$10

7-6, 5.12 ERA in 102 IP at KC. ERA was 4.25 apart from 0.1 IP 10 ER disaster on 8/13. BPIs are marginal and DOM trend is troubling, but he's pitched in lots of bad luck as well. There's upside here, just not much.

Hudson,Tim

		W	L	Sv	IP	K	ERA	WHIP	OBA	vL	vR	BF/G	H%	S%	xERA	G	L	F	Ctl	Dom	Cmd	hr/f	hr/9	RAR	BPV	R$
RH Starter	02 OAK	15	9	0	238	152	2.99	1.26	261	283	239	29.2	30%	79%	3.42	55	16	28	2.3	5.7	2.5	9%	0.7	43.2	67	$25
Age 31	03 OAK	16	7	0	240	162	2.70	1.08	225	229	214	28.2	26%	77%	3.08	58	16	26	2.3	6.1	2.7	8%	0.6	54.0	85	$33
Peak	04 OAK	12	6	0	188	103	3.54	1.26	268	298	229	29.2	30%	71%	3.32	60	17	23	2.1	4.9	2.3	6%	0.4	20.7	69	$16
Type	05 ATL	14	9	0	192	115	3.52	1.35	264	285	240	28.3	29%	77%	3.36	59	21	21	3.0	5.4	1.8	16%	0.9	17.3	44	$16
Reliability 88	06 ATL	13	12	0	218	141	4.87	1.44	276	281	265	27.2	31%	68%	3.53	58	18	24	3.3	5.8	1.8	15%	1.0	-10.3	41	$10
DL 30	1st Half	6	7	0	111	74	4.29	1.34	254			27.9	29%	69%	3.41	59	18	23	3.4	6.0	1.8	11%	0.7	2.7	55	$8
ERA Potl 50%	2nd Half	7	5	0	107	67	5.47	1.54	298			26.5	32%	67%	3.66	57	18	25	3.1	5.6	1.8	18%	1.3	-13.0	27	$3
LIMA Plan D+	07 Proj	10	13	0	208	128	4.21	1.41	271			27.2	30%	71%	3.53	58	18	24	3.2	5.6	1.7	12%	0.8	21.3	46	$11

Declining control, marginal DOM are intrinsic weaknesses. S% drop and ridiculous hr/f rates (despite extreme GB rate) may be out of his control. xERA is optimistic; I don't see GB being the universal panacea. Caution.

TOM TODARO

Igawa,Kei

			W	L	Sv	IP	K	ERA	WHIP	OBA	vL	vR	BF/G	H%	S%	xERA	G	L	F	Ctl	Dom	Cmd	hr/f	hr/9	RAR	BPV	R$
LH Starter	02	JPN	14	9	1	210	217	3.09	1.15	228			27.5	29%	78%	3.23				2.8	9.3	3.3		1.1	30.7	103	$28
Age 27	03	JPN	20	5	0	206	189	3.47	1.31	254			30.0	31%	78%	4.03				3.1	8.2	2.6		1.1	23.4	76	$25
Pre-Peak	04	JPN	14	11	0	200	240	4.64	1.35	266			29.5	32%	75%	5.32				3.0	10.8	3.6		2.2	-7.3	77	$18
Type Power	05	JPN	13	9	0	172	153	4.81	1.67	306			29.3	35%	78%	6.55				3.9	8.0	2.1		2.0	-10.7	25	$7
Reliability 16	06	JPN	14	9	0	209	204	3.69	1.22	247			29.8	30%	75%	3.78				2.6	8.8	3.4		1.2	21.4	93	$25
DL	1st Half																										
ERA Potl 50%	2nd Half																										
LIMA Plan D	07	Proj	13	8	0	174	166	4.24	1.34	263			29.7	31%	75%	4.71				3.1	8.6	2.8		1.6	-6.3	65	$16

2006 was a rebound season after two off-years, though his BPIs have been fairly stable. His key weakness has been the longball; it will be interesting to see how that converts over to his new MLB home.

Isringhausen,Jason

			W	L	Sv	IP	K	ERA	WHIP	OBA	vL	vR	BF/G	H%	S%	xERA	G	L	F	Ctl	Dom	Cmd	hr/f	hr/9	RAR	BPV	R$
RH Reliever	02	STL	3	2	32	65	68	2.49	0.98	201	247	164	4.2	29%	72%	2.74	46	21	32	2.5	9.4	3.8	0%	0.0	12.9	151	$20
Age 34	03	STL	0	1	22	42	41	2.36	1.17	207	254	159	4.3	27%	81%	3.19	48	19	32	3.9	8.8	2.3	6%	0.4	10.0	101	$12
Past Peak	04	STL	4	2	47	75	71	2.88	1.04	206	205	195	4.0	26%	74%	3.10	44	19	37	2.8	8.5	3.1	7%	0.6	12.8	112	$25
Type Power	05	STL	1	2	39	59	51	2.14	1.19	205	170	229	3.8	25%	85%	3.34	51	20	29	4.1	7.8	1.9	9%	0.6	15.4	82	$19
Reliability 50	06	STL	4	8	33	58	52	3.56	1.46	223	270	187	4.3	25%	83%	4.20	44	18	38	5.9	8.1	1.4	16%	1.5	6.6	41	$16
DL 22 16	1st Half		2	3	24	32	34	3.91	1.65	223			4.5	26%	83%	4.29	45	20	35	7.5	9.5	1.3	21%	1.7	2.3	44	$10
ERA Potl 25%	2nd Half		2	5	9	26	18	3.13	1.24	223			4.1	24%	82%	4.10	43	16	42	3.8	6.3	1.6	13%	1.4	4.3	41	$6
LIMA Plan D+	07	Proj	1	3	10	28	23	4.18	1.50	248			4.4	29%	74%	4.18	46	19	36	5.1	7.4	1.4	10%	1.0	0.6	51	$5

CMD collapsed, as did most of his other BPIs. His season ended with more surgery on his degenerative hip. This projection may be a gift; his career could well be over.

Jackson,Edwin

			W	L	Sv	IP	K	ERA	WHIP	OBA	vL	vR	BF/G	H%	S%	xERA	G	L	F	Ctl	Dom	Cmd	hr/f	hr/9	RAR	BPV	R$
RH Reliever	02		0	0	0	0	0	0.00	0.00											0.0	0.0						
Age 23	03	aa	7	7	0	148	147	4.40	1.25	242			22.9	31%	64%	3.26				3.2	8.9	2.8		0.6	-0.1	102	$13
Growth	04	aaa	6	4	0	90	66	4.63	1.36	237			20.3	29%	64%	3.22				4.4	6.6	1.5		0.3	-3.2	71	$6
Type Power	05	LA *	11	13	0	145	78	5.57	1.53	277	333	236	21.5	29%	65%	5.08	36	19	46	4.0	4.8	1.2	9%	1.2	-23.8	18	$3
Reliability 0	06	TAM *	3	7	5	109	83	6.60	1.86	314	233	333	11.6	37%	64%	4.42	52	17	31	5.1	6.8	1.3	9%	0.8	-27.5	37	($2)
DL	1st Half		2	7	0	75	56	7.68	1.87	319			19.9	37%	58%	5.33	40	7	53	4.9	6.7	1.4	7%	1.1	-28.9	28	($5)
ERA Potl 65%	2nd Half		1	0	5	34	27	4.22	1.85	304			6.0	37%	76%	4.11	56	20	24	5.5	7.1	1.3	4%	0.3	1.4	56	$2
LIMA Plan B	07	Proj	1	3	3	44	32	4.97	1.49	264			6.0	31%	66%	3.94	51	19	30	4.3	6.6	1.5	8%	0.6	2.9	55	$2

0-0, 5.45 ERA in 36 IP at TAM. After his impressive Sept. '03 callup, it's been all downhill. Ctl has been declining, DOM fluctuates, and low strand rate may be a chronic condition. Not enough signs of life to bid on.

James,Chuck

			W	L	Sv	IP	K	ERA	WHIP	OBA	vL	vR	BF/G	H%	S%	xERA	G	L	F	Ctl	Dom	Cmd	hr/f	hr/9	RAR	BPV	R$
LH Starter	02		0	0	0	0	0	0.00	0.00																		
Age 25	03		0	0	0	0	0	0.00	0.00																		
Growth	04		0	0	0	0	0	0.00	0.00																		
Type	05	a/a	10	4	0	119	117	3.10	1.04	222			21.5	28%	72%	2.55				2.1	8.8	4.2		0.7	17.8	131	$19
Reliability 0	06	ATL *	12	4	0	152	113	3.78	1.25	243	297	215	19.9	26%	76%	4.36	28	19	53	3.1	6.7	2.1	10%	1.4	13.2	49	$16
DL 32	1st Half		2	0	0	52	36	2.93	1.11	226			14.0	25%	79%	4.36	23	21	56	2.6	6.2	2.4	7%	1.0	10.1	66	$6
ERA Potl 45%	2nd Half		10	4	0	100	77	4.23	1.33	252			25.0	27%	75%	4.40	28	19	53	3.4	6.9	2.0	11%	1.6	3.1	40	$10
LIMA Plan C	07	Proj	9	7	0	160	125	4.06	1.25	253			23.8	29%	72%	4.21	27	19	53	2.7	7.1	2.6	9%	1.2	3.0	64	$14

11-4, 3.78 ERA in 119 IP at ATL. Results were better than his BPIs, but all in all, a respectable debut. High FB rate could mean some HRs, so don't pay for a sub-4.00 ERA.

Janssen,Casey

			W	L	Sv	IP	K	ERA	WHIP	OBA	vL	vR	BF/G	H%	S%	xERA	G	L	F	Ctl	Dom	Cmd	hr/f	hr/9	RAR	BPV	R$
RH Starter	02		0	0	0	0	0	0.00	0.00																		
Age 25	03		0	0	0	0	0	0.00	0.00																		
Growth	04		0	0	0	0	0	0.00	0.00																		
Type Finesse	05	aa	3	3	0	43	39	4.63	1.62	350			21.7	43%	73%	6.09				0.9	8.2	9.3		0.9	-1.7	202	$2
Reliability 0	06	TOR *	7	15	0	136	72	5.64	1.40	295	292	261	21.0	32%	60%	3.84	53	16	31	2.0	4.7	2.4	11%	1.1	-18.2	43	$5
DL	1st Half		6	8	0	88	51	4.92	1.25	279			23.0	30%	62%	3.40	55	15	30	1.4	5.2	3.6	12%	1.0	-3.9	76	$7
ERA Potl 55%	2nd Half		1	7	0	48	21	6.95	1.67	321			18.4	34%	58%	4.74	47	17	35	3.0	3.9	1.3	9%	1.1	-14.2	8	($2)
LIMA Plan C+	07	Proj	2	4	0	44	24	4.97	1.52	306			21.4	33%	69%	4.07	51	16	33	2.5	5.0	2.0	10%	1.0	2.2	35	$1

6-10, 5.07 ERA in 94 IP at TOR. Finesse GB pitchers can pitch well and have bad results, as 1st half shows. His 2nd half command? That's just a recipe for disaster. Not a safe place for your money.

Jenks,Bobby

			W	L	Sv	IP	K	ERA	WHIP	OBA	vL	vR	BF/G	H%	S%	xERA	G	L	F	Ctl	Dom	Cmd	hr/f	hr/9	RAR	BPV	R$
RH Reliever	02	aa	3	6	0	58	50	5.74	1.74	258			27.0	33%	65%	4.44				6.8	7.8	1.1		0.3	-10.5	64	($0)
Age 26	03	aa	7	2	0	83	88	2.71	1.40	217			22.4	30%	80%	2.97				5.5	9.5	1.7		0.2	17.2	99	$11
Growth	04	aaa	0	1	0	12	12	9.75	2.25	360			20.7	44%	56%	8.47				6.0	9.0	1.5		1.5	-8.0	24	($2)
Type Power	05	CHW *	2	3	25	80	89	3.12	1.37	247	105	298	5.1	34%	78%	3.13	45	26	30	4.1	10.0	2.5	6%	0.5	12.3	104	$16
Reliability 0	06	CHW	3	4	41	69	80	4.03	1.40	253	227	268	4.5	35%	72%	2.61	59	19	22	4.0	10.4	2.6	13%	0.7	4.5	102	$20
DL	1st Half		2	1	24	36	42	2.49	1.08	216			3.9	30%	78%	2.29	54	22	23	2.7	10.5	3.8	10%	0.5	9.2	140	$14
ERA Potl 65%	2nd Half		1	3	17	33	38	5.71	1.75	289			5.2	39%	67%	2.98	63	16	21	5.4	10.3	1.9	16%	0.8	-4.7	75	$6
LIMA Plan B	07	Proj	3	4	38	73	82	3.97	1.42	252			5.0	35%	72%	2.78	57	20	23	4.2	10.2	2.4	9%	0.5	15.2	101	$19

Stuff is unquestioned - and so is his lack of control. High GB rate makes him vulnerable to swings in H%. Each half of 2006 represented his upside and downside. Take your pick.

Jennings,Jason

			W	L	Sv	IP	K	ERA	WHIP	OBA	vL	vR	BF/G	H%	S%	xERA	G	L	F	Ctl	Dom	Cmd	hr/f	hr/9	RAR	BPV	R$
RH Starter	02	COL	16	8	0	185	127	4.52	1.46	278	299	267	25.4	31%	73%	3.88	50	18	32	3.4	6.2	1.8	14%	1.3	-9.5	37	$11
Age 28	03	COL	12	13	0	181	119	5.12	1.66	293	323	271	25.9	33%	70%	4.40	48	20	32	4.4	5.9	1.4	10%	1.0	-18.8	30	$3
Pre-Peak	04	COL	11	11	0	201	133	5.51	1.70	298	340	261	28.1	33%	70%	4.37	48	22	30	4.5	6.0	1.3	13%	1.2	-30.9	22	($0)
Type	05	COL	6	9	0	122	75	5.02	1.57	274	269	279	27.4	31%	69%	4.29	48	25	27	4.6	5.5	1.2	10%	0.8	-11.6	34	$2
Reliability 70	06	COL	9	13	0	212	142	3.78	1.37	256	254	261	28.4	29%	74%	4.17	44	19	37	3.6	6.0	1.7	7%	0.7	18.5	53	$14
DL 70	1st Half		6	6	0	107	77	3.95	1.40	265			28.9	31%	74%	4.10	44	17	39	3.4	6.5	1.9	8%	0.8	7.2	55	$8
ERA Potl 45%	2nd Half		3	7	0	105	65	3.61	1.35	247			27.9	28%	74%	4.24	44	21	35	3.8	5.6	1.5	6%	0.6	11.4	52	$7
LIMA Plan D+	07	Proj	10	13	0	204	132	4.64	1.49	272			28.0	31%	70%	4.22	46	21	33	3.9	5.8	1.5	9%	0.8	3.6	42	$8

This wasn't just the Humidor Effect. Improved both his control and command, and more FBs died in the OF. But to ignore his sub-2.0 CMD and the unknown of Coors '07 is a risky play. Bet on closer to 2005 than 2006.

Johnson,Jason

			W	L	Sv	IP	K	ERA	WHIP	OBA	vL	vR	BF/G	H%	S%	xERA	G	L	F	Ctl	Dom	Cmd	hr/f	hr/9	RAR	BPV	R$
RH Starter	02	BAL	6	14	0	136	102	4.43	1.40	274	261	290	25.5	31%	72%	3.89	43	18	38	3.0	6.8	2.3	12%	1.3	0.4	51	$8
Age 33	03	BAL	10	10	0	189	118	4.19	1.57	288	283	283	26.5	32%	76%	4.49	44	19	37	3.8	5.6	1.5	9%	1.0	7.8	31	$9
Past Peak	04	DET	8	15	0	196	125	5.14	1.44	286	281	286	25.9	32%	65%	3.86	49	19	32	2.8	5.7	2.1	11%	1.0	-17.1	46	$6
Type Finesse	05	DET	8	13	0	210	93	4.54	1.34	282	310	258	27.1	30%	68%	3.98	52	17	31	2.1	4.0	1.9	10%	1.0	-4.4	33	$9
Reliability 63	06	2TM *	5	13	0	139	67	5.96	1.63	318	380	297	22.6	34%	64%	3.86	59	18	23	2.8	4.3	1.6	14%	1.0	-24.6	19	($2)
DL	1st Half		3	8	0	77	32	5.96	1.69	332			25.3	35%	66%	4.01	60	17	24	2.6	3.7	1.5	14%	1.2	-13.7	6	($2)
ERA Potl 55%	2nd Half		2	5	0	62	35	5.95	1.55	300			19.8	33%	61%	3.68	58	20	22	3.0	5.1	1.7	12%	0.9	-10.9	34	($0)
LIMA Plan C+	07	Proj	3	7	0	87	46	5.28	1.49	298			24.0	32%	66%	3.92	54	18	28	2.7	4.8	1.8	12%	1.0	5.4	30	$1

3-12, 6.10 ERA in 115 IP at CLE. Has grown into a soft-tossing extreme GB pitcher but it hasn't changed the results. Ran into more bad luck than usual in '06 (h%, s%, hr/f) but still a desperation pick at best.

Johnson,Josh

			W	L	Sv	IP	K	ERA	WHIP	OBA	vL	vR	BF/G	H%	S%	xERA	G	L	F	Ctl	Dom	Cmd	hr/f	hr/9	RAR	BPV	R$
RH Starter	02		0	0	0	0	0	0.00	0.00																		
Age 23	03		0	0	0	0	0	0.00	0.00																		
Growth	04		0	0	0	0	0	0.00	0.00																		
Type Power	05	FLA *	12	4	0	151	112	4.71	1.56	288			22.5	35%	68%	4.38				3.8	6.7	1.8		0.2	-8.6	68	$7
Reliability 0	06	FLA	12	7	0	157	133	3.10	1.30	235	246	227	21.4	28%	79%	3.69	46	19	36	3.9	7.6	2.0	9%	0.8	27.0	71	$18
DL	1st Half		7	4	0	73	64	2.34	1.28	228			18.1	29%	82%	3.65	50	13	37	4.1	7.9	1.9	4%	0.4	19.4	86	$11
ERA Potl 45%	2nd Half		5	3	0	84	69	3.76	1.31	241			25.3	28%	76%	3.72	42	24	34	3.8	7.4	2.0	13%	1.2	7.5	57	$8
LIMA Plan C	07	Proj	11	8	0	174	141	3.83	1.40	257			22.1	31%	74%	3.87	45	19	36	3.8	7.3	1.9	8%	0.7	10.7	66	$13

ERA was built on three months of high S%. Ctl was up and down all year. Impressive 63/8 DOM/DIS split shows maturity. A keeper, but will be overpriced if bidders expect another 3.10 ERA.

TOM TODARO

133

Johnson,Randy

	Yr	Tm	W	L	Sv	IP	K	ERA	WHIP	OBA	vL	vR	BF/G	H%	S%	xERA	G	L	F	Ctl	Dom	Cmd	hr/f	hr/9	RAR	BPV	R$
LH Starter	02	ARI	24	5	0	260	334	2.32	1.03	212	221	206	29.3	30%	83%	2.32	43	25	32	2.5	11.6	4.7	14%	0.9	57.3	154	$46
Age 43	03	ARI	6	8	0	114	125	4.26	1.33	280	303	276	26.9	36%	72%	2.88	40	27	32	2.1	9.9	4.6	15%	1.3	0.2	118	$9
Decline	04	ARI	16	14	0	245	290	2.61	0.90	204	163	204	26.8	28%	74%	2.39	45	18	37	1.6	10.6	6.6	8%	0.7	50.1	197	$41
Type Power	05	NYY	17	8	0	225	211	3.80	1.13	246	185	257	26.8	29%	72%	3.05	45	17	38	1.9	8.4	4.5	13%	1.3	16.0	112	$29
Reliability 60	06	NYY	17	11	0	205	172	5.00	1.24	251	194	259	25.8	29%	62%	3.63	42	16	43	2.6	7.6	2.9	11%	1.2	-11.3	73	$20
DL	1st Half		9	6	0	100	85	4.86	1.28	252			24.7	29%	65%	3.64	45	14	42	3.0	7.6	2.6	12%	1.3	-3.7	64	$10
ERA Potl 65%	2nd Half		8	5	0	105	87	5.15	1.20	251			27.0	29%	58%	3.61	39	18	43	2.3	7.5	3.2	10%	1.1	-7.6	84	$10
LIMA Plan D+	07	Proj	12	9	0	164	140	4.29	1.28	255			24.5	30%	70%	3.59	43	17	40	2.8	7.7	2.7	11%	1.2	18.1	73	$16

Age and back problems are catching up with him. PRO: still dominates LHers; low S%; 58/18 DOM/DIS. CON: DOM falling, Ctl, FB rising He's still capable of posting solid numbers, but don't bid too high.

Johnson,Tyler

	Yr	Tm	W	L	Sv	IP	K	ERA	WHIP	OBA	vL	vR	BF/G	H%	S%	xERA	G	L	F	Ctl	Dom	Cmd	hr/f	hr/9	RAR	BPV	R$
LH Reliever	02		0	0	0	0	0	0.00	0.00																		
Age 25	03	aa	1	0	0	27	36	2.32	1.29	199			5.7	31%	82%	2.56				5.3	12.0	2.3		0.3	6.9	124	$4
Growth	04	aa	2	2	4	56	66	5.62	1.64	257			4.8	35%	65%	4.50				6.0	10.6	1.8		0.7	-8.9	85	$2
Type Power	05	aaa	2	1	7	59	68	4.58	1.36	248			4.4	34%	67%	3.75				3.8	10.4	2.7		0.8	-2.0	102	$6
Reliability 2	06	STL	2	4	0	36	37	4.99	1.55	245	221	276	2.9	30%	71%	4.15	39	19	42	5.7	9.2	1.6	12%	1.2	-2.2	58	$2
DL	1st Half		0	1	0	13	14	5.45	1.36	228			2.7	28%	63%	3.83	37	16	47	4.8	9.5	2.0	12%	1.4	-1.6	68	$0
ERA Potl 55%	2nd Half		2	3	0	23	23	4.72	1.66	254			3.0	31%	74%	4.32	40	22	38	6.3	9.0	1.4	12%	1.2	-0.6	53	$1
LIMA Plan B+	07	Proj	2	3	0	44	45	4.34	1.45	232			3.8	30%	71%	3.99	39	19	42	5.4	9.3	1.7	8%	0.8	2.0	76	$3

A sore arm slowed him at the start of the year. DOM is nice, but has to cut down on the walks. There is upside, but being right-brain dominant will limit his fantasy value.

Jones,Todd

	Yr	Tm	W	L	Sv	IP	K	ERA	WHIP	OBA	vL	vR	BF/G	H%	S%	xERA	G	L	F	Ctl	Dom	Cmd	hr/f	hr/9	RAR	BPV	R$
RH Reliever	02	COL	1	4	1	82	73	4.72	1.37	266	233	301	4.4	32%	68%	3.43	44	23	33	3.1	8.0	2.6	13%	1.1	-6.2	72	$3
Age 39	03	2TM	3	5	0	68	59	7.15	1.82	327	323	323	5.5	38%	61%	4.03	45	24	31	4.1	7.8	1.9	14%	1.3	-23.1	37	($3)
Decline	04	2NL	11	5	2	82	59	4.17	1.43	266	221	290	4.6	31%	72%	4.17	41	21	38	3.6	6.5	1.8	7%	0.8	1.0	55	$9
Type Finesse	05	FLA	1	5	40	73	62	2.10	1.03	229	211	229	4.2	29%	79%	2.76	53	21	27	1.7	7.6	4.4	4%	0.2	19.4	141	$22
Reliability 5	06	DET	2	6	37	64	28	3.94	1.27	279	264	284	4.3	30%	69%	3.78	53	18	29	1.5	3.9	2.5	6%	0.6	4.9	59	$16
DL 19	1st Half		1	5	20	31	10	6.39	1.45	314			4.5	32%	55%	4.06	53	21	27	1.5	2.9	2.0	10%	0.9	-7.0	26	$6
ERA Potl 50%	2nd Half		1	1	17	33	18	1.64	1.09	244			4.1	28%	86%	3.52	53	14	32	1.6	4.9	3.0	3%	0.3	11.9	91	$10
LIMA Plan D	07	Proj	3	5	33	65	32	4.14	1.29	276			4.4	30%	69%	3.82	50	19	31	1.9	4.4	2.3	9%	0.8	5.3	50	$15

An atypical closer profile, though one seemingly adopted by many pitchers lately... pinpoint control, a non-reliance on Ks and lots of ground balls. His half-season swing shows how volatile a path that is. It's way too risky for me.

Julio,Jorge

	Yr	Tm	W	L	Sv	IP	K	ERA	WHIP	OBA	vL	vR	BF/G	H%	S%	xERA	G	L	F	Ctl	Dom	Cmd	hr/f	hr/9	RAR	BPV	R$
RH Reliever	02	BAL	5	6	25	68	55	1.99	1.21	223	213	214	4.2	27%	87%	3.93	39	17	44	3.6	7.3	2.0	6%	0.7	20.7	77	$19
Age 28	03	BAL	0	7	36	61	52	4.43	1.54	259	273	239	4.3	29%	76%	4.17	43	20	37	5.0	7.7	1.5	15%	1.5	0.7	37	$14
Pre-Peak	04	BAL	2	5	22	69	70	4.57	1.42	233	234	221	4.6	28%	72%	3.93	41	14	45	5.1	9.1	1.8	13%	1.4	-1.1	58	$12
Type Power	05	BAL	3	5	0	71	58	5.94	1.40	275	281	257	4.6	30%	62%	3.86	40	18	41	3.0	7.3	2.4	16%	1.8	-13.8	42	$2
Reliability 39	06	2NL	2	4	16	66	88	4.23	1.32	218	185	234	4.5	30%	73%	2.99	40	21	39	4.8	12.0	2.5	17%	1.4	2.1	95	$11
DL	1st Half		1	2	6	36	49	3.49	1.14	203			4.6	28%	75%	2.50	47	16	36	3.7	12.2	3.3	17%	1.2	4.4	119	$7
ERA Potl 55%	2nd Half		1	2	10	30	39	5.12	1.54	236			4.4	32%	71%	3.63	32	26	42	6.0	11.7	2.0	17%	1.5	-2.3	74	$5
LIMA Plan C+	07	Proj	2	4	10	58	64	4.66	1.40	241			4.6	30%	71%	3.54	40	19	41	4.5	9.9	2.2	14%	1.4	5.9	71	$7

Huge spike in DOM looked good for half the season while he kept his walks under control, but once he lost home plate in the 2nd half, the bottom fell out. Lots of weaknesses here; just thowing hard is not enough.

Karstens,Jeff

	Yr	Tm	W	L	Sv	IP	K	ERA	WHIP	OBA	vL	vR	BF/G	H%	S%	xERA	G	L	F	Ctl	Dom	Cmd	hr/f	hr/9	RAR	BPV	R$
RH Starter	02		0	0	0	0	0	0.00	0.00																		
Age 24	03		0	0	0	0	0	0.00	0.00																		
Growth	04		0	0	0	0	0	0.00	0.00																		
Type Finesse	05	aa	12	11	0	169	123	4.95	1.54	313			26.9	36%	69%	5.36				2.3	6.6	2.9		1.0	-13.5	63	$7
Reliability 0	06	NYY *	13	6	0	189	108	4.33	1.40	277	253	233	24.8	30%	72%	4.78	33	16	51	2.8	5.1	1.8	7%	1.1	5.2	37	$14
DL	1st Half		4	5	0	97	65	5.26	1.45	276			26.5	31%	65%					3.3	6.0	1.8		1.1	-8.4	42	$4
ERA Potl 45%	2nd Half		9	1	0	92	43	3.36	1.34	279			23.2	29%	79%	4.86	33	16	51	2.3	4.2	1.8	7%	1.1	13.7	31	$10
LIMA Plan C+	07	Proj	4	2	0	58	36	4.50	1.45	294			25.3	32%	71%	4.66	33	16	51	2.5	5.6	2.3	7%	1.1	-1.3	44	$4

2-1, 3.80 ERA in 43 IP at NYY. Posted strong numbers across three levels. DOM suffered in the majors, where ERA was helped by a low H%. Unlikely to make much of an impact in 2007

Kazmir,Scott

	Yr	Tm	W	L	Sv	IP	K	ERA	WHIP	OBA	vL	vR	BF/G	H%	S%	xERA	G	L	F	Ctl	Dom	Cmd	hr/f	hr/9	RAR	BPV	R$
LH Starter	02		0	0	0	0	0	0.00	0.00											0.0	0.0						
Age 23	03		0	0	0	0	0	0.00	0.00											0.0	0.0						
Growth	04	aa	3	3	0	51	48	1.85	1.01	184			25.0	25%	80%	1.42				3.4	8.5	2.5		0.0	15.7	123	$9
Type Power	05	TAM	10	9	0	186	174	3.77	1.46	247	174	268	25.5	31%	75%	3.98	42	20	38	4.8	8.4	1.7	6%	0.6	13.7	75	$15
Reliability 1	06	TAM	10	8	0	144	163	3.25	1.28	245	227	242	25.2	32%	78%	3.11	42	19	39	3.2	10.2	3.1	10%	0.9	23.3	105	$20
DL 52	1st Half		9	5	0	100	108	3.60	1.37	260			25.3	33%	78%	3.18	45	19	35	3.4	9.7	2.8	12%	1.1	11.9	89	$13
ERA Potl 55%	2nd Half		1	3	0	44	55	2.45	1.07	210			25.1	30%	80%	2.96	33	18	49	2.9	11.2	3.9	6%	0.6	11.5	145	$7
LIMA Plan B	07	Proj	11	8	0	178	194	3.08	1.23	230			25.5	30%	77%	3.26	40	19	41	3.5	9.8	2.8	8%	0.8	26.8	104	$24

An inflamed shoulder cut short another great growth season When healthy, he was lights-out. CMD spike was very encouraging as he both increased Ks and cut down BBs. UP: 15 wins, sub-3.00 ERA.

Kennedy,Joe

	Yr	Tm	W	L	Sv	IP	K	ERA	WHIP	OBA	vL	vR	BF/G	H%	S%	xERA	G	L	F	Ctl	Dom	Cmd	hr/f	hr/9	RAR	BPV	R$
LH Reliever	02	TAM	8	11	0	196	109	4.55	1.32	270	273	268	27.7	29%	68%	4.48	39	15	46	2.5	5.0	2.0	8%	1.1	-2.1	41	$11
Age 27	03	TAM	3	12	1	133	77	6.16	1.61	308	230	324	18.8	33%	63%	4.50	44	19	37	3.2	5.2	1.6	11%	1.3	-26.8	20	($2)
Pre-Peak	04	COL	9	7	0	162	117	3.66	1.42	263	183	289	26.0	30%	77%	3.96	48	17	34	3.7	6.5	1.7	10%	0.9	11.9	50	$11
Type	05	2TM	8	13	0	152	97	6.03	1.68	309	265	320	20.0	34%	65%	4.38	45	22	32	3.8	5.7	1.5	12%	1.2	-32.4	24	($2)
Reliability 9	06	OAK	4	1	1	35	29	2.31	1.34	256	326	220	3.8	32%	83%	3.54	49	20	31	3.3	7.5	2.2	3%	0.3	9.7	88	$6
DL 86	1st Half		2	0	1	12	9	2.23	1.74	291			3.1	36%	86%	4.57	54	10	37	5.2	6.7	1.3	0%	0.0	3.5	64	$2
ERA Potl 35%	2nd Half		2	1	0	23	20	2.36	1.14	236			4.4	30%	80%	3.04	45	27	28	2.4	7.9	3.3	6%	0.4	6.2	113	$4
LIMA Plan C+	07	Proj	3	3	0	44	31	3.93	1.40	273			4.9	31%	74%	3.81	47	20	33	3.1	6.4	2.1	9%	0.8	3.6	58	$4

Moved to pen, but lost half the year to arm woes. ERA aided by high S%, but GB, FB trends look good, as does his DOM. Worthy LIMA option if he stays in the pen.

Kim,Byung-Hyun

	Yr	Tm	W	L	Sv	IP	K	ERA	WHIP	OBA	vL	vR	BF/G	H%	S%	xERA	G	L	F	Ctl	Dom	Cmd	hr/f	hr/9	RAR	BPV	R$
RH Starter	02	ARI	8	3	36	84	92	2.04	1.07	213	220	198	4.7	29%	84%	2.64	50	20	30	2.8	9.9	3.5	8%	0.5	21.5	130	$26
Age 28	03	2TM	9	10	16	122	102	3.32	1.12	232	221	227	8.8	28%	74%	3.21	47	19	34	2.4	7.5	3.1	10%	0.9	16.2	92	$21
Pre-Peak	04	BOS *	4	7	0	77	40	6.29	1.50	310	308	185	11.8	34%	57%	4.37	45	16	39	2.1	4.7	2.2	7%	0.8	-17.7	43	$0
Type Power	05	COL	5	12	0	148	115	4.86	1.53	272	308	244	16.5	31%	70%	4.29	42	20	39	4.3	7.0	1.6	10%	1.0	-11.3	46	$3
Reliability 44	06	COL	8	12	0	155	129	5.57	1.55	291	325	265	25.7	34%	65%	3.93	42	23	35	3.5	7.5	2.1	10%	1.0	-20.8	55	$4
DL 31	1st Half		5	4	0	64	56	4.35	1.54	287			26.0	35%	72%	3.83	42	25	34	3.6	7.9	2.2	8%	0.7	1.1	69	$4
ERA Potl 60%	2nd Half		3	8	0	91	73	6.44	1.55	293			25.4	34%	59%	4.01	41	22	37	3.5	7.2	2.1	12%	1.3	-21.9	45	($1)
LIMA Plan B	07	Proj	7	10	0	131	102	4.55	1.46	276			23.8	32%	70%	3.95	42	21	36	3.4	7.0	2.0	10%	1.0	6.6	56	$7

An all-or-nothing season. His DOM/DIS of 44/37 meant that he either pitched a gem or was rocked in over 80% of his starts. There was little middle ground. Three years removed from last good season = even more risk.

King,Ray

	Yr	Tm	W	L	Sv	IP	K	ERA	WHIP	OBA	vL	vR	BF/G	H%	S%	xERA	G	L	F	Ctl	Dom	Cmd	hr/f	hr/9	RAR	BPV	R$
LH Reliever	02	MIL	3	2	0	66	51	3.00	1.32	250	219	280	3.6	30%	79%	3.46	51	22	27	3.4	7.0	2.0	9%	0.7	9.0	69	$6
Age 33	03	ATL	3	4	0	59	43	3.51	1.24	217	200	223	3.1	26%	71%	3.59	55	17	29	4.1	6.6	1.6	6%	0.5	5.6	71	$5
Peak	04	STL	5	2	0	62	40	2.61	1.08	197	150	248	2.9	24%	74%	3.64	51	19	31	3.5	5.8	1.7	2%	0.1	12.6	81	$9
Type	05	STL	4	4	0	40	23	3.38	1.55	290	244	352	2.3	32%	81%	4.16	50	22	29	3.6	5.2	1.4	10%	0.9	4.3	31	$3
Reliability 20	06	COL	1	4	1	44	23	4.48	1.72	310	303	347	3.1	33%	77%	4.34	53	22	25	4.1	4.7	1.2	15%	1.2	0.0	9	$0
DL	1st Half		1	3	0	21	7	4.25	1.60	269			3.2	28%	73%	4.40	61	22	17	5.1	3.0	0.6	8%	0.4	0.6	19	$0
ERA Potl 30%	2nd Half		0	1	1	23	16	4.70	1.83	344			3.0	37%	81%	4.18	46	22	32	3.1	6.3	2.0	19%	2.0	-0.6	7	($0)
LIMA Plan C	07	Proj	2	3	0	44	23	4.34	1.54	285			2.8	31%	74%	4.21	51	21	28	3.7	4.8	1.3	12%	1.0	0.8	22	$1

ERA took a hit in COL; no surprise. Great GB%, and hr/9 should drop as hr/f normalizes. Plummeting DOM a concern. When a situational lefty struggles against lefties, it's time to look elsewhere.

DAVE ADLER

Kline,Steve

Info	Yr	Tm	W	L	Sv	IP	K	ERA	WHIP	OBA	vL	vR	BF/G	H%	S%	xERA	G	L	F	Ctl	Dom	Cmd	hr/f	hr/9	RAR	BPV	R$
LH Reliever	02	STL	2	1	6	60	42	3.30	1.27	242	230	266	3.7	29%	74%	3.74	46	24	31	3.3	6.3	1.9	5%	0.5	6.0	71	$7
Age 34	03	STL	5	5	3	63	31	3.86	1.37	240	243	233	3.5	26%	73%	4.50	52	14	35	4.3	4.4	1.0	7%	0.7	3.3	34	$6
Past Peak	04	STL	2	2	3	50	35	1.80	1.08	208	143	269	3.0	24%	86%	3.24	58	14	28	3.1	6.3	2.1	7%	0.5	15.2	78	$8
Type	05	BAL	2	4	0	61	36	4.28	1.46	255	317	209	4.0	26%	77%	4.04	56	16	28	4.4	5.3	1.2	20%	1.6	0.7	12	$2
Reliability 12	06	SF	4	3	1	51	33	3.69	1.54	269	261	287	3.2	31%	76%	4.47	47	19	34	4.6	5.8	1.3	5%	0.5	5.0	47	$4
DL	1st Half		1	1	0	25	12	2.50	1.31	228			3.2	25%	81%	4.41	53	14	32	4.3	4.3	1.0	4%	0.4	6.2	45	$2
ERA Potl 40%	2nd Half		3	2	1	26	21	4.85	1.77	304			3.1	36%	73%	4.51	42	23	36	4.8	7.3	1.5	7%	0.7	-1.1	49	$1
LIMA Plan C+	07	Proj	4	3	0	58	38	4.03	1.47	262			3.3	30%	74%	4.14	50	18	32	4.2	5.9	1.4	9%	0.8	1.6	44	$4

Return to the NL seemed to work wonders, but xERA indicates otherwise. Here's hr/f at work - hr/9 dropped by a factor of three despite a rise in FB%. Situational lefty who doesn't make an impact.

Kolb,Danny

Info	Yr	Tm	W	L	Sv	IP	K	ERA	WHIP	OBA	vL	vR	BF/G	H%	S%	xERA	G	L	F	Ctl	Dom	Cmd	hr/f	hr/9	RAR	BPV	R$
RH Reliever	02	TEX	3	7	1	40	22	4.28	1.65	262	291	172	4.7	30%	72%	4.51	53	26	21	5.9	5.0	0.8	4%	0.2	0.9	43	$2
Age 32	03	MIL	1	2	21	41	39	1.98	1.29	227	209	230	4.7	29%	86%	2.94	58	21	21	4.2	8.6	2.1	8%	0.4	11.6	91	$11
Peak	04	MIL	0	4	39	57	21	2.99	1.14	237	256	218	3.6	25%	74%	3.36	64	17	19	2.4	3.3	1.4	8%	0.5	9.0	43	$16
Type	05	ATL	3	8	11	57	39	5.98	1.87	326	336	323	4.2	37%	68%	4.14	53	24	23	4.6	6.1	1.3	11%	0.8	-12.2	31	$1
Reliability 36	06	MIL *	6	4	9	126	86	4.97	1.51	269	323	260	6.0	31%	67%	4.10	51	17	32	4.2	6.1	1.5	9%	0.8	-7.4	45	$7
DL	1st Half		6	3	0	66	46	4.13	1.43	255			6.1	29%	73%	4.34	45	15	40	4.2	6.3	1.5	8%	0.9	2.9	47	$5
ERA Potl 50%	2nd Half		0	1	9	60	40	5.88	1.59	284			5.9	33%	62%	3.64	60	20	20	4.2	5.9	1.4	11%	0.7	-10.4	43	$2
LIMA Plan C+	07	Proj	2	4	0	58	37	4.81	1.53	278			4.9	32%	68%	3.82	56	21	24	4.0	5.7	1.4	9%	0.6	3.9	45	$1

1 save, 4.84 ERA in 48 IP at MIL. Nice to see the OBA drop, and LD% came down too. Good enough for saves again? No. BPIs were similar to 2005, and they just don't say "closer." Fact is, they never really did.

Koronka,John

Info	Yr	Tm	W	L	Sv	IP	K	ERA	WHIP	OBA	vL	vR	BF/G	H%	S%	xERA	G	L	F	Ctl	Dom	Cmd	hr/f	hr/9	RAR	BPV	R$
LH Starter	02	aa	2	8	0	95	58	5.77	1.78	311			27.9	34%	68%	5.99				4.5	5.5	1.2		1.0	-17.6	20	($4)
Age 26	03	aa	7	13	0	162	101	4.75	1.63	306			28.4	35%	70%	5.09				3.4	5.6	1.6		0.5	-7.1	46	$3
Growth	04	aaa	12	9	0	153	104	4.47	1.54	286			23.6	32%	73%	5.10				3.7	6.1	1.7		1.1	-2.4	37	$8
Type	05	aaa	9	11	0	136	84	4.68	1.44	279			25.8	31%	69%	4.53				3.1	5.6	1.8		0.9	-6.3	44	$7
Reliability 24	06	TEX	7	7	0	125	61	5.69	1.54	291	274	300	24.2	31%	65%	4.74	42	19	39	3.4	4.4	1.3	10%	1.2	-17.4	14	$2
DL	1st Half		6	4	0	86	44	5.02	1.48	284			25.2	31%	66%	4.49	45	19	36	3.2	4.6	1.4	8%	0.8	-4.9	31	$4
ERA Potl 50%	2nd Half		1	3	0	39	17	7.15	1.67	308			22.4	30%	61%	5.29	37	19	44	3.7	3.9	1.1	14%	2.1	-12.5	-23	($2)
LIMA Plan C	07	Proj	6	7	0	104	57	5.19	1.56	294			24.5	31%	69%	4.76	40	19	41	3.5	4.9	1.4	9%	1.2	-3.5	19	$3

Gangbusters out of the gate, with three wins and two PQS-DOMs in April. But posted only two more DOMs the rest of the year. Average stuff, needs pinpoint control to succeed - he's not there yet.

Kuo,Hong-Chih

Info	Yr	Tm	W	L	Sv	IP	K	ERA	WHIP	OBA	vL	vR	BF/G	H%	S%	xERA	G	L	F	Ctl	Dom	Cmd	hr/f	hr/9	RAR	BPV	R$
LH Reliever	02		0	0	0	0	0	0.00	0.00																		
Age 25	03		0	0	0	0	0	0.00	0.00																		
Growth	04		0	0	0	0	0	0.00	0.00																		
Type Power	05	aa	1	2	3	33	49	3.82	1.48	250			5.6	40%	74%	3.86				4.9	13.4	2.7		0.5	2.0	126	$4
Reliability 0	06	LA *	5	8	1	112	123	3.70	1.45	255	241	246	9.6	34%	75%	3.38	44	21	34	4.3	9.9	2.3	8%	0.6	10.8	92	$9
DL	1st Half		1	4	1	34	41	5.01	1.73	232			5.1	32%	71%	4.12	46	20	33	7.9	10.8	1.4	11%	0.8	-2.2	78	$1
ERA Potl 55%	2nd Half		4	4	0	78	83	3.13	1.33	265			16.6	35%	78%	3.12	43	22	35	2.8	9.5	3.4	7%	0.6	13.1	114	$8
LIMA Plan B+	07	Proj	7	7	0	124	135	4.21	1.49	251			23.8	33%	73%	3.54	45	21	34	4.9	9.8	2.0	9%	0.7	12.6	84	$8

1-5, 4.22 ERA in 60 IP at LA. The ultimate high-risk, high-reward gamble. Two TJ surgeries cost him 2002-04, but he throws heat and posts an elite DOM. Three PQS-DOM starts in Sept whet the appetite.

Lackey,John

Info	Yr	Tm	W	L	Sv	IP	K	ERA	WHIP	OBA	vL	vR	BF/G	H%	S%	xERA	G	L	F	Ctl	Dom	Cmd	hr/f	hr/9	RAR	BPV	R$
RH Starter	02	ANA *	17	6	0	209	139	3.27	1.29	263	208	317	25.9	30%	76%	3.84	45	19	36	2.5	6.0	2.4	6%	0.6	30.6	68	$23
Age 28	03	ANA	10	16	0	204	151	4.63	1.42	279	286	269	26.8	31%	71%	3.97	41	21	39	2.9	6.7	2.3	12%	1.4	-2.7	46	$12
Pre-Peak	04	ANA	14	13	0	198	144	4.68	1.39	278	303	248	25.9	32%	68%	3.94	44	16	40	2.7	6.5	2.4	9%	1.0	-6.0	59	$13
Type Power	05	ANA	14	5	0	209	199	3.44	1.33	261	274	241	26.9	33%	75%	3.31	45	23	33	3.1	8.6	2.8	7%	0.6	23.9	96	$22
Reliability 82	06	ANA	13	11	0	217	190	3.56	1.27	249	263	231	27.6	31%	72%	3.57	43	18	39	3.0	7.9	2.6	6%	0.6	26.6	90	$25
DL	1st Half		5	5	0	106	77	3.31	1.11	213			26.7	24%	73%	3.83	42	16	42	3.1	6.5	2.1	8%	0.5	16.3	70	$13
ERA Potl 55%	2nd Half		8	6	0	111	113	3.80	1.43	280			28.3	37%	72%	3.33	44	20	36	2.8	9.1	3.2	3%	0.3	10.3	112	$12
LIMA Plan C	07	Proj	14	10	0	214	185	3.54	1.32	261			27.4	32%	74%	3.57	44	19	37	2.9	7.8	2.7	7%	0.7	24.1	86	$23

A rough August kept him from posting career numbers. Things to like: dominates RHers, 2nd-half DOM, 61/18 DOM/DIS. This may be the year he puts it all together...
UP: 18 wins, 3.25 ERA.

Lawrence,Brian

Info	Yr	Tm	W	L	Sv	IP	K	ERA	WHIP	OBA	vL	vR	BF/G	H%	S%	xERA	G	L	F	Ctl	Dom	Cmd	hr/f	hr/9	RAR	BPV	R$
RH Reliever	02	SD	12	12	0	210	149	3.69	1.34	280	324	236	25.6	33%	74%	3.16	58	18	24	2.2	6.4	2.9	10%	0.7	10.9	77	$15
Age 31	03	SD	10	15	0	210	116	4.20	1.25	258	275	244	26.6	27%	70%	3.78	51	16	33	2.4	5.0	2.0	12%	1.2	2.0	41	$14
Peak	04	SD	15	14	0	203	121	4.12	1.38	283	301	272	25.7	31%	74%	3.69	53	18	29	2.4	5.4	2.2	13%	1.2	3.5	42	$14
Type Finesse	05	SD	7	15	0	195	109	4.84	1.37	277	300	249	25.4	30%	65%	4.02	47	21	33	2.6	5.0	1.9	8%	0.8	-14.3	45	$6
Reliability 3	06	WAS	0	0	0	0	0	0.00	0.00																		
DL 183	1st Half		0	0	0	0	0	0.00	0.00																		
ERA Potl	2nd Half		0	0	0	0	0	0.00	0.00																		
LIMA Plan	07	Proj	6	9	0	123	72	4.26	1.33	272			26.0	30%	70%	3.75	51	18	31	2.5	5.3	2.1	11%	1.0	9.2	48	$7

Missed the entire year with a torn labrum. Pre-injury BPIs were consistent and not terribly exciting. When he finds a home, check the park factors, since past numbers were posted at PETCO.

League,Brandon

Info	Yr	Tm	W	L	Sv	IP	K	ERA	WHIP	OBA	vL	vR	BF/G	H%	S%	xERA	G	L	F	Ctl	Dom	Cmd	hr/f	hr/9	RAR	BPV	R$
RH Reliever	02		0	0	0	0	0	0.00	0.00											0.0	0.0						
Age 24	03		0	0	0	0	0	0.00	0.00											0.0	0.0						
Growth	04	aa	6	4	2	104	79	4.93	1.55	283			11.3	34%	66%	4.40				3.9	6.8	1.8		0.3	-7.6	66	$4
Type	05	TOR *	5	4	0	98	50	6.57	1.67	314	333	269	11.6	33%	62%	3.83	60	19	21	3.4	4.5	1.3	21%	1.4	-26.7	5	($3)
Reliability 0	06	TOR *	4	4	9	96	66	2.80	1.33	275	276	178	6.4	33%	78%	2.50	73	13	14	2.3	6.2	2.6	7%	0.3	20.9	84	$13
DL	1st Half		2	2	6	48	35	2.99	1.60	313			8.1	38%	79%					2.8	6.5	2.3		0.0	9.3	81	$5
ERA Potl 50%	2nd Half		2	2	3	48	31	2.61	1.06	232			5.2	27%	77%	2.31	73	13	14	1.9	5.8	3.1	15%	0.6	11.6	92	$8
LIMA Plan B	07	Proj	4	3	0	83	56	3.58	1.30	264			7.8	31%	73%	2.68	70	14	16	2.6	6.1	2.3	12%	0.5	18.5	71	$7

1-2, 2.53 ERA in 43 IP at TOR. Sinkerball pitcher, does a great job keeping the ball on the ground. BPIs are trending in the right direction, and he owns righties. Count on an increased bullpen role.

Ledezma,Wil

Info	Yr	Tm	W	L	Sv	IP	K	ERA	WHIP	OBA	vL	vR	BF/G	H%	S%	xERA	G	L	F	Ctl	Dom	Cmd	hr/f	hr/9	RAR	BPV	R$
LH Reliever	02		0	0	0	0	0	0.00	0.00											0.0	0.0						
Age 26	03	DET	3	7	0	84	49	5.79	1.60	295	309	292	11.2	32%	66%	5.11	33	18	49	3.8	5.3	1.4	9%	1.3	-13.1	18	$0
Growth	04	DET *	14	6	0	164	107	3.40	1.25	261	227	285	21.4	30%	74%	3.88	46	14	39	2.3	5.9	2.5	5%	0.6	21.0	73	$18
Type	05	DET *	6	7	0	99	66	6.90	1.70	298	352	286	22.9	33%	60%	4.79	43	18	40	4.5	6.0	1.3	10%	1.2	-30.9	24	($2)
Reliability 6	06	DET *	7	6	0	131	95	3.45	1.36	263	241	261	15.6	30%	77%	4.31	34	21	46	3.2	6.5	2.1	7%	0.8	18.0	60	$13
DL	1st Half		5	3	0	74	58	3.19	1.29	256			20.8	30%	78%					2.9	7.1	2.4		0.9	12.5	71	$9
ERA Potl 45%	2nd Half		2	3	0	57	37	3.78	1.44	271			11.8	31%	75%	4.64	34	21	46	3.5	5.8	1.7	6%	0.8	5.5	47	$4
LIMA Plan C+	07	Proj	4	4	0	81	55	4.56	1.46	276			16.1	31%	70%	4.51	37	19	44	3.4	6.1	1.8	7%	0.9	-0.2	47	$4

3-3, 3.58 ERA in 60 IP at DET. Serviceable in late call-up; BPIs show slow improvement. ERA aided by high S%; the drop in GB% is also a concern. Year-to-year consistency is the challenge now. Wait on him.

Lee,Cliff

Info	Yr	Tm	W	L	Sv	IP	K	ERA	WHIP	OBA	vL	vR	BF/G	H%	S%	xERA	G	L	F	Ctl	Dom	Cmd	hr/f	hr/9	RAR	BPV	R$
LH Starter	02	a/a	12	5	0	145	138	4.53	1.30	237			23.5	28%	70%	4.13				3.8	8.6	2.3		1.5	-4.7	62	$14
Age 28	03	CLE *	10	4	0	127	104	3.97	1.47	263	278	197	25.4	31%	76%	4.32	37	19	44	4.2	7.4	1.8	8%	1.0	8.7	54	$11
Pre-Peak	04	CLE	14	8	0	179	161	5.43	1.50	271	231	277	24.0	31%	67%	4.18	34	21	45	4.1	8.1	2.0	13%	1.5	-22.0	46	$9
Type	05	CLE	18	5	0	202	143	3.79	1.22	254	293	237	26.1	29%	72%	3.96	35	21	44	2.3	6.4	2.8	8%	1.0	14.6	71	$23
Reliability 83	06	CLE	14	11	0	200	129	4.41	1.41	284	261	282	26.3	31%	73%	4.50	33	19	48	2.6	5.8	2.2	9%	1.3	3.8	41	$15
DL	1st Half		7	5	0	97	68	4.63	1.40	283			26.2	31%	71%	4.39	30	21	48	2.6	6.3	2.4	10%	1.4	-0.9	46	$7
ERA Potl 50%	2nd Half		7	6	0	103	61	4.19	1.42	285			26.3	31%	74%	4.61	35	17	48	2.6	5.3	2.0	8%	1.2	4.6	36	$8
LIMA Plan D+	07	Proj	15	10	0	204	146	4.29	1.37	272			25.7	30%	73%	4.28	34	19	47	2.9	6.5	2.2	9%	1.2	5.1	49	$17

Couldn't repeat 2005 success. BPIs regressed across the board. The main culprit was his fly ball rate. The difference between a half dozen HRs is also the difference between an ERA over 4.00 or under 4.00.

DAVE ADLER

Lester,Jon

	Yr	Tm	W	L	Sv	IP	K	ERA	WHIP	OBA	vL	vR	BF/G	H%	S%	xERA	G	L	F	Ctl	Dom	Cmd	hr/f	hr/9	RAR	BPV	R$
LH Starter	02		0	0	0	0	0	0.00	0.00																		
Age 23	03		0	0	0	0	0	0.00	0.00																		
Growth	04		0	0	0	0	0	0.00	0.00																		
Type Power	05	aa	1	6	0	148	139	3.40	1.30	244			24.1	31%	75%	3.49				3.5	8.4	2.4		0.7	16.5	87	$11
Reliability 0	06	BOS *	10	6	0	127	100	4.39	1.64	283	397	271	22.3	33%	75%	4.48	41	22	38	4.8	7.1	1.5	8%	0.9	2.7	45	$8
DL 38	1st Half		6	4	0	67	64	3.48	1.58	262			20.2	33%	81%	4.09	44	18	38	5.2	8.5	1.6	9%	0.9	8.9	61	$7
ERA Potl 50%	2nd Half		4	2	0	60	36	5.40	1.72	304			25.3	34%	69%	4.91	40	23	37	4.3	5.4	1.2	8%	0.9	-6.2	26	$1
LIMA Plan C+	07	Proj	5	4	0	95	78	4.64	1.52	270			23.4	32%	70%	4.16	40	22	37	4.3	7.4	1.7	8%	0.9	3.8	56	$5

7-2, 4.76 ERA in 81 IP at BOS. DOM regressed after callup, and control declined as well. LHers plastered him with a 1.120 OPS. For 2007, the bigger battle is against lymphoma.

Lidge,Brad

	Yr	Tm	W	L	Sv	IP	K	ERA	WHIP	OBA	vL	vR	BF/G	H%	S%	xERA	G	L	F	Ctl	Dom	Cmd	hr/f	hr/9	RAR	BPV	R$
RH Reliever	02	a/a	7	6	0	130	117	4.64	1.48	257			16.3	31%	70%	4.30				4.5	8.1	1.8		0.9	-5.9	63	$7
Age 30	03	HOU	6	3	1	85	97	3.60	1.20	200	230	179	4.5	27%	71%	3.37	35	24	41	4.4	10.3	2.3	7%	0.6	7.1	106	$11
Peak	04	HOU	6	5	29	94	157	1.91	0.92	177	191	155	4.5	31%	85%	2.03	32	21	47	2.9	15.0	5.2	10%	0.8	27.3	197	$28
Type Power	05	HOU	4	4	42	70	103	2.31	1.15	227	244	202	4.1	36%	83%	2.13	47	23	30	2.9	13.2	4.5	11%	0.6	16.8	164	$25
Reliability 69	06	HOU	1	5	32	75	104	5.28	1.40	246	286	201	4.2	35%	64%	2.72	44	23	33	4.3	12.5	2.9	17%	1.2	-7.3	105	$15
DL	1st Half		0	2	19	37	54	5.34	1.46	240			4.3	36%	64%	2.92	42	19	39	5.1	13.1	2.6	12%	1.0	-3.9	111	$8
ERA Potl 75%	2nd Half		1	3	13	38	50	5.22	1.35	252			4.0	35%	64%	2.52	45	27	28	3.6	11.9	3.3	23%	1.4	-3.4	103	$7
LIMA Plan B+	07	Proj	3	4	30	73	102	3.60	1.26	230			4.4	34%	75%	2.52	43	23	34	3.7	12.7	3.4	14%	1.0	16.5	127	$18

xERA shows that there was nothing wrong with his skill. Ctl was off, but a perfect storm of H%, S%, and hr/f killed his ERA. Still, a closer with a low S% has nobody to blame but himself. He will be undervalued; take a shot.

Lidle,Cory

	Yr	Tm	W	L	Sv	IP	K	ERA	WHIP	OBA	vL	vR	BF/G	H%	S%	xERA	G	L	F	Ctl	Dom	Cmd	hr/f	hr/9	RAR	BPV	R$
RH Starter	02	OAK	8	10	0	196	114	3.86	1.20	259	248	269	25.2	29%	69%	3.74	49	16	36	1.9	5.2	2.7	8%	0.8	14.6	68	$16
Age 35	03	TOR	12	15	0	192	112	5.77	1.44	285	265	305	27.0	31%	61%	3.91	52	18	31	2.8	5.3	1.9	12%	1.1	-29.4	35	$7
Past Peak	04	2NL	12	12	0	211	126	4.90	1.35	273	278	269	26.5	30%	66%	3.77	49	20	30	2.6	5.4	2.1	13%	1.2	-16.7	41	$10
Type	05	PHI	13	11	0	184	121	4.54	1.36	288	289	289	25.4	33%	68%	3.39	50	25	25	2.0	5.9	3.0	12%	0.9	-6.8	70	$12
Reliability 74	06	2TM	12	10	0	170	130	4.86	1.40	274	290	256	23.7	30%	70%	3.61	50	17	33	3.1	6.9	2.2	17%	1.6	-7.2	41	$12
DL 15	1st Half		4	6	0	91	73	5.13	1.45	282			24.9	33%	66%	3.56	49	21	31	3.1	7.2	2.4	13%	1.1	-6.9	59	$4
ERA Potl	2nd Half		8	4	0	79	57	4.56	1.35	264			22.5	27%	76%	3.66	51	14	35	3.1	6.5	2.1	22%	2.2	-0.4	21	$7
LIMA Plan	07	Proj	0	0	0	0	0	0.00	0.00																		

He was a personal favorite and perennial target of mine. Always decent BPIs, though not overly dominant, yet couldn't get his ERA consistently under 4.00 despite xERAs that promised better. Rest in peace, Cory.

Lieber,Jon

	Yr	Tm	W	L	Sv	IP	K	ERA	WHIP	OBA	vL	vR	BF/G	H%	S%	xERA	G	L	F	Ctl	Dom	Cmd	hr/f	hr/9	RAR	BPV	R$
RH Starter	02	CHC	6	8	0	141	87	3.70	1.17	278	308	246	27.5	31%	71%	3.83				0.8	5.6	7.3		1.0	7.0	156	$11
Age 37	03	NYY	0	0	0	0	0	0.00	0.00											0.0	0.0						
Decline	04	NYY	14	8	0	176	102	4.34	1.33	303	346	250	27.7	33%	70%	3.54	52	15	33	0.9	5.2	5.7	10%	1.0	2.0	114	$13
Type Finesse	05	PHI	17	13	0	218	149	4.21	1.21	266	305	223	25.7	29%	70%	3.41	46	22	33	1.7	6.1	3.6	15%	1.4	1.0	74	$20
Reliability 69	06	PHI	9	11	0	168	100	4.93	1.31	293	304	278	26.3	31%	66%	3.73	43	22	35	1.3	5.4	4.2	13%	1.4	-9.1	73	$9
DL 38	1st Half		3	5	0	65	42	5.81	1.29	290			24.9	31%	58%	3.58	44	21	35	1.2	5.8	4.7	14%	1.5	-10.6	84	$2
ERA Potl 60%	2nd Half		6	6	0	103	58	4.37	1.32	294			27.3	31%	72%	3.82	43	22	36	1.3	5.1	3.9	13%	1.4	1.5	66	$7
LIMA Plan B+	07	Proj	12	11	0	189	116	4.34	1.27	286			26.3	31%	70%	3.59	45	20	34	1.3	5.5	4.3	13%	1.3	17.9	81	$14

Another "precision" arm with good BPIs but one that batters are able to wait on. Rising FB rate is troublesome, especially since his hr/f has been running high in PHI. xERA is optimistic; I am less so.

Lilly,Ted

	Yr	Tm	W	L	Sv	IP	K	ERA	WHIP	OBA	vL	vR	BF/G	H%	S%	xERA	G	L	F	Ctl	Dom	Cmd	hr/f	hr/9	RAR	BPV	R$
LH Starter	02	2AL	5	7	0	100	77	3.69	1.11	221	154	231	18.3	27%	69%	4.04	33	16	51	2.8	6.9	2.5	9%	0.5	9.5	91	$11
Age 31	03	OAK	12	10	0	178	147	4.35	1.33	263	235	261	23.6	30%	71%	3.96	35	20	45	2.9	7.4	2.5	10%	1.2	3.9	64	$16
Peak	04	TOR	12	10	0	197	168	4.06	1.32	235	196	238	26.1	27%	73%	4.11	36	18	46	4.1	7.7	1.9	10%	1.2	9.0	58	$17
Type Power	05	TOR	10	11	0	126	96	5.57	1.53	275	336	248	22.4	30%	68%	4.38	37	22	41	4.1	6.9	1.7	14%	1.6	-18.6	27	$5
Reliability 65	06	TOR	15	13	0	181	160	4.32	1.43	259	202	265	24.7	30%	75%	4.04	38	19	43	4.0	7.9	2.0	12%	1.4	5.3	51	$17
DL 59	1st Half		8	7	0	90	84	3.89	1.50	257			24.9	30%	79%	4.03	38	22	40	4.7	8.4	1.8	14%	1.4	7.4	50	$9
ERA Potl 50%	2nd Half		7	6	0	91	76	4.75	1.37	262			24.4	30%	69%	4.04	37	17	46	3.4	7.5	2.2	11%	1.4	-2.1	53	$8
LIMA Plan D+	07	Proj	14	13	0	189	162	4.54	1.41	258			24.0	30%	72%	4.07	37	20	44	3.9	7.7	2.0	12%	1.3	9.7	52	$15

Returned to form after injury-plagued 2005. Still suffers from gopheritis and ceiling is limited by high Ctl. There are skills in his past and unfulfilled potential. If he ends up on the right team: UP: sub-4.00 ERA

Linebrink,Scott

	Yr	Tm	W	L	Sv	IP	K	ERA	WHIP	OBA	vL	vR	BF/G	H%	S%	xERA	G	L	F	Ctl	Dom	Cmd	hr/f	hr/9	RAR	BPV	R$
RH Reliever	02	HOU *	1	1	0	41	38	7.24	2.05	322			5.5	40%	63%	5.50	31	17	51	6.4	8.3	1.3	4%	0.7	-15.9	48	($4)
Age 30	03	2NL	3	2	0	92	68	3.33	1.40	264	275	265	7.6	30%	79%	4.36	35	20	45	3.5	6.7	1.9	7%	0.9	10.8	55	$6
Peak	04	SD	7	3	0	84	83	2.14	1.04	205	178	236	4.6	26%	85%	3.34	33	21	46	2.8	8.9	3.2	8%	0.9	22.0	109	$14
Type Power	05	SD	8	1	1	73	70	1.84	1.07	210	195	223	4.0	27%	85%	3.29	39	21	41	2.8	8.6	3.0	5%	0.5	21.7	114	$14
Reliability 40	06	SD	7	4	2	75	68	3.59	1.22	248	204	294	4.3	30%	75%	3.49	39	19	42	2.6	8.1	3.1	10%	1.1	8.3	87	$10
DL	1st Half		5	2	0	35	35	2.56	0.94	201			4.1	22%	88%	3.01	36	18	46	2.0	8.9	4.4	17%	1.8	8.4	107	$8
ERA Potl 55%	2nd Half		2	2	2	40	33	4.50	1.47	285			4.4	35%	68%	3.94	42	20	38	3.1	7.4	2.4	4%	0.4	-0.1	79	$3
LIMA Plan B	07	Proj	6	3	5	73	67	3.21	1.22	240			4.4	29%	77%	3.56	38	20	42	3.0	8.3	2.8	8%	0.9	7.2	89	$11

Despite ERA rise, his BPIs were essentially the same as 2005. hr/f normalized; he struggled against RHers (.809 OPS; .578 vs LH). Otherwise, business as usual. With saves opps, his value doubles.

Liriano,Francisco

	Yr	Tm	W	L	Sv	IP	K	ERA	WHIP	OBA	vL	vR	BF/G	H%	S%	xERA	G	L	F	Ctl	Dom	Cmd	hr/f	hr/9	RAR	BPV	R$
LH Reliever	02		0	0	0	0	0	0.00	0.00											0.0	0.0						
Age 23	03		0	0	0	0	0	0.00	0.00											0.0	0.0						
Growth	04	aa	3	2	0	39	46	3.94	1.72	313			26.0	42%	79%	5.76				3.9	10.6	2.7		0.9	2.0	86	$2
Type Finesse	05	MIN *	13	9	0	190	220	3.41	1.12	226	222	221	23.3	31%	71%	2.56	50	19	31	2.7	10.4	3.9	9%	0.6	22.6	135	$27
Reliability 0	06	MIN	12	3	1	121	144	2.16	1.00	207	202	206	16.9	29%	82%	2.11	55	21	23	2.4	10.7	4.5	13%	0.7	35.8	152	$26
DL 35	1st Half		8	1	1	73	82	2.22	1.03	214			14.4	29%	81%	2.20	56	21	23	2.3	10.1	4.3	12%	0.6	21.1	145	$16
ERA Potl	2nd Half		4	2	0	48	62	2.07	0.96	196			23.2	28%	83%	1.98	54	21	25	2.4	11.6	4.8	15%	0.8	14.7	163	$11
LIMA Plan	07	Proj	0	0	0	0	0	0.00	0.00																		

There was lots of crying in the coffee last summer when this rotation anchor went down. TJ surgery pushes his timetable back to 2008. He's the complete package but don't count on Cy Young awards until at least '09.

Littleton,Wes

	Yr	Tm	W	L	Sv	IP	K	ERA	WHIP	OBA	vL	vR	BF/G	H%	S%	xERA	G	L	F	Ctl	Dom	Cmd	hr/f	hr/9	RAR	BPV	R$
RH Reliever	02		0	0	0	0	0	0.00	0.00																		
Age 24	03		0	0	0	0	0	0.00	0.00																		
Growth	04		0	0	0	0	0	0.00	0.00																		
Type	05	aa	2	3	3	81	59	5.37	1.70	331			7.8	37%	71%	6.46				2.7	6.6	2.4		1.4	-10.7	37	($0)
Reliability 0	06	TEX *	9	2	6	80	51	1.71	1.04	202	256	157	5.0	22%	91%	2.64	71	12	17	3.0	5.7	1.9	21%	0.9	28.1	62	$18
DL	1st Half		7	1	5	43	33	1.73	1.05	214			5.9	23%	95%					2.6	6.9	2.7		1.3	15.0	71	$11
ERA Potl 25%	2nd Half		2	1	1	37	18	1.70	1.03	187			4.3	20%	86%	3.00	71	12	17	3.4	4.4	1.3	11%	0.5	13.1	56	$6
LIMA Plan C+	07	Proj	4	2	0	58	38	3.88	1.40	275			6.0	30%	76%	2.85	71	12	17	2.9	5.9	2.0	22%	1.1	11.7	45	$5

2-1, 1.73 ERA in 36 IP at TEX. H% and S% point to ERA correction. But side-armer is lethal on righties, forcing a ton of GBs. He doesn't scare lefties; expect him to be a late-inning specialist.

Loaiza,Esteban

	Yr	Tm	W	L	Sv	IP	K	ERA	WHIP	OBA	vL	vR	BF/G	H%	S%	xERA	G	L	F	Ctl	Dom	Cmd	hr/f	hr/9	RAR	BPV	R$
RH Starter	02	TOR *	11	10	0	169	99	5.43	1.49	308	308	311	26.6	34%	64%	4.11	47	16	37	2.1	5.3	2.5	8%	1.0	-20.3	50	$6
Age 35	03	CHW	21	9	0	226	207	2.91	1.12	235	259	191	26.8	29%	76%	3.02	46	21	33	2.2	8.2	3.7	8%	0.7	45.1	115	$35
Past Peak	04	2AL	10	7	0	183	117	5.70	1.57	296	298	293	26.5	32%	67%	4.49	41	18	40	3.5	5.8	1.6	13%	1.6	-28.7	18	$3
Type	05	WAS	12	10	0	217	173	3.77	1.30	271	285	255	26.9	32%	72%	3.50	44	22	35	2.3	7.2	3.1	8%	0.7	12.6	88	$18
Reliability 51	06	OAK	11	9	0	154	97	4.90	1.42	292	319	265	25.7	32%	67%	4.08	42	20	38	2.3	5.7	2.4	9%	1.0	-6.6	52	$10
DL 45	1st Half		3	4	0	44	18	6.34	1.64	307			25.1	32%	62%	5.05	42	20	38	3.5	3.7	1.1	10%	1.2	-9.7	1	($0)
ERA Potl 55%	2nd Half		8	5	0	110	79	4.33	1.33	285			26.0	33%	69%	3.73	42	20	38	1.9	6.5	3.4	8%	0.9	3.1	82	$10
LIMA Plan C+	07	Proj	12	10	0	189	126	4.54	1.42	287			26.4	32%	70%	4.02	43	20	37	2.6	6.0	2.3	9%	1.0	10.8	53	$12

Consistent winner whose inconsistent ERAs ebb and flow with K/9 swings. Age and in-season variances (38/31 DOM/DIS!) suggest not to bet your team on much ERA improvement in 2007.

DAVE ADLER

Loewen,Adam

	Yr	W	L	Sv	IP	K	ERA	WHIP	OBA	vL	vR	BF/G	H%	S%	xERA	G	L	F	Ctl	Dom	Cmd	hr/f	hr/9	RAR	BPV	R$
LH Starter	02	0	0	0	0	0	0.00	0.00																		
Age 23	03	0	0	0	0	0	0.00	0.00																		
Growth	04	0	0	0	0	0	0.00	0.00																		
Type Power	05	0	0	0	0	0	0.00	0.00																		
Reliability 2	06 BAL *	12	8	0	183	166	4.52	1.49	258	277	254	23.7	32%	69%	3.69	48	21	31	4.5	8.2	1.8	7%	0.6	0.8	72	$14
DL	1st Half	5	4	0	86	81	4.80	1.67	279			23.3	35%	72%	3.76	55	15	30	5.2	8.4	1.6	10%	0.8	-2.5	59	$4
ERA Potl 60%	2nd Half	7	4	0	97	85	4.28	1.32	240			24.2	30%	66%	3.55	46	23	31	3.9	7.9	2.0	5%	0.4	3.4	86	$10
LIMA Plan C+	07 Proj	11	7	0	160	144	4.18	1.40	250			23.7	31%	70%	3.55	48	21	31	4.1	8.1	2.0	8%	0.6	18.4	77	$14

6-6, 5.37 ERA in 112 IP at BAL. Poor MLB results hid fine skills: Two thirds of outs were GB or K, HRs infrequent. Expect growing pains, but a buying opportunity. UP: 3.50 ERA

Loe,Kameron

	Yr	W	L	Sv	IP	K	ERA	WHIP	OBA	vL	vR	BF/G	H%	S%	xERA	G	L	F	Ctl	Dom	Cmd	hr/f	hr/9	RAR	BPV	R$
RH Starter	02	0	0	0	0	0	0.00	0.00											0.0	0.0						
Age 25	03	0	0	0	0	0	0.00	0.00											0.0	0.0						
Growth	04 a/a	12	9	0	157	115	4.24	1.54	311			26.9	36%	74%	5.27				2.4	6.6	2.8		0.9	1.9	65	$9
Type Finesse	05 TEX *	11	7	1	120	65	3.97	1.37	268	284	223	9.7	29%	74%	3.48	61	16	22	3.0	4.9	1.6	15%	1.0	5.9	36	$11
Reliability 0	06 TEX	3	6	0	78	34	5.88	1.63	323	313	321	23.7	34%	65%	4.36	51	19	30	2.5	3.9	1.5	11%	1.2	-12.7	12	($1)
DL 44	1st Half	3	6	0	78	34	5.88	1.63	323			23.7	34%	65%	4.36	51	19	30	2.5	3.9	1.5	11%	1.2	-12.7	12	($1)
ERA Potl 55%	2nd Half	0	0	0	0	0	0.00	0.00																		
LIMA Plan D	07 Proj	8	8	0	123	66	4.78	1.53	306			24.8	33%	70%	3.90	54	18	28	2.6	4.8	1.9	11%	1.0	8.9	34	$5

Shut down in July with elbow pain, ending a forgettable year. A few good signs, like high GB% and unlucky H% and S%. Still too few K's and too many HR to generate much optimism.

Lohse,Kyle

	Yr	W	L	Sv	IP	K	ERA	WHIP	OBA	vL	vR	BF/G	H%	S%	xERA	G	L	F	Ctl	Dom	Cmd	hr/f	hr/9	RAR	BPV	R$
RH Reliever	02 MIN	13	8	0	180	124	4.25	1.39	263	308	213	24.3	29%	74%	4.43	36	18	46	3.5	6.2	1.8	10%	1.3	4.6	38	$14
Age 28	03 MIN	14	11	0	201	130	4.61	1.27	271	283	249	25.5	30%	67%	4.01	39	18	43	2.0	5.8	2.9	10%	1.3	-2.2	59	$16
Pre-Peak	04 MIN	9	13	0	194	111	5.34	1.63	305	290	324	25.2	33%	70%	4.57	45	18	37	3.5	5.1	1.5	11%	1.3	-21.6	17	$1
Type	05 MIN	9	13	0	178	86	4.19	1.43	296	291	305	25.0	31%	74%	4.22	44	22	34	2.2	4.3	2.0	10%	1.1	3.9	30	$9
Reliability 54	06 2TM *	7	11	0	150	106	5.30	1.48	287	288	304	17.4	33%	65%	4.09	43	20	37	3.1	6.4	2.1	9%	1.0	-14.4	50	$5
DL	1st Half	4	6	0	70	41	6.47	1.68	306			19.0	34%	61%	4.97	37	21	41	3.9	5.3	1.4	7%	0.9	-16.9	27	($1)
ERA Potl 55%	2nd Half	3	5	0	80	65	4.27	1.30	269			16.1	32%	69%	3.42	47	19	34	2.4	7.3	3.1	11%	1.0	2.4	80	$6
LIMA Plan C	07 Proj	8	11	0	166	110	4.45	1.43	283			23.3	32%	72%	4.06	43	20	37	2.9	6.0	2.1	10%	1.1	7.3	45	$9

5-10, 5.83 ERA in 126 IP at MIN and CIN. Borderline skills and bad luck in MIN improved considerably in 2nd half for CIN. A return to double-digit '02/'03 value is not impossible.

Looper,Braden

	Yr	W	L	Sv	IP	K	ERA	WHIP	OBA	vL	vR	BF/G	H%	S%	xERA	G	L	F	Ctl	Dom	Cmd	hr/f	hr/9	RAR	BPV	R$
RH Reliever	02 FLA	2	5	13	86	55	3.14	1.17	231	278	191	4.5	26%	76%	3.88	44	19	37	2.9	5.8	2.0	8%	0.8	10.3	59	$11
Age 32	03 FLA	6	4	28	80	56	3.71	1.39	267	280	250	4.7	32%	73%	3.68	53	18	29	3.3	6.3	1.9	5%	0.5	5.6	67	$16
Peak	04 NYM	2	5	29	83	60	2.71	1.23	268	311	227	4.9	32%	79%	2.83	62	15	23	1.7	6.5	3.8	8%	0.5	15.9	103	$17
Type Finesse	05 NYM	4	7	28	59	27	3.96	1.47	281	336	210	4.3	29%	76%	4.21	51	21	27	3.4	4.1	1.2	12%	1.1	2.1	17	$12
Reliability 36	06 STL	9	3	0	73	41	3.57	1.31	269	287	272	4.5	31%	72%	3.84	49	20	30	2.5	5.0	2.1	4%	0.4	8.3	63	$9
DL	1st Half	3	0	0	33	17	3.27	1.12	250			4.0	28%	71%	3.78	45	20	35	1.6	4.6	2.8	5%	0.5	4.9	76	$4
ERA Potl 50%	2nd Half	6	3	0	40	24	3.82	1.47	285			4.9	33%	72%	3.88	53	21	27	3.1	5.4	1.7	3%	0.2	3.3	60	$4
LIMA Plan C+	07 Proj	6	5	5	73	41	3.48	1.35	271			4.6	30%	75%	3.80	52	20	28	2.7	5.1	1.9	7%	0.6	5.0	52	$8

2nd half GB% hints at return to better days, but most other factors suggest caution: Vulture wins and hr/f were lucky, DOM remains substandard, plus injury, role and age risks. End-game pick.

Lopez,Javier

	Yr	W	L	Sv	IP	K	ERA	WHIP	OBA	vL	vR	BF/G	H%	S%	xERA	G	L	F	Ctl	Dom	Cmd	hr/f	hr/9	RAR	BPV	R$
LH Reliever	02 aa	2	2	6	46	35	3.52	1.28	245			3.2	29%	73%	3.36				3.3	6.8	2.1		0.6	4.3	73	$6
Age 29	03 COL	4	1	1	58	40	3.72	1.21	262	250	266	3.2	30%	71%	3.07	59	15	26	1.9	6.2	3.3	10%	0.8	4.0	87	$6
Peak	04 COL	1	2	0	40	20	7.61	1.77	284	221	350	2.9	32%	53%	4.75	55	23	22	5.8	4.5	0.8	3%	0.2	-16.6	34	($3)
Type	05 2NL *	1	2	4	40	29	6.30	1.80	294			3.2	34%	64%	5.50				5.6	6.5	1.2		0.7	-10.1	39	($1)
Reliability 4	06 BOS *	3	1	17	65	41	2.96	1.56	294	250	208	4.4	34%	82%	3.05	65	22	13	3.5	5.6	1.6	15%	0.6	12.9	46	$10
DL	1st Half	2	1	12	37	23	1.04	1.32	268			4.8	31%	93%					2.6	5.6	2.2		0.3	16.1	72	$9
ERA Potl 30%	2nd Half	1	0	5	28	18	5.47	1.88	325			4.1	36%	72%	3.46	65	22	13	4.7	5.7	1.2	24%	1.0	-3.2	19	$1
LIMA Plan B	07 Proj	1	1	0	29	19	4.34	1.48	275			3.5	32%	71%	3.53	59	20	21	3.7	5.9	1.6	10%	0.6	3.4	50	$1

1-0, 2.70 ERA in 16 IP at BOS. Smallish samples, but variant skills and difficulty with RH hitters (OPS .935 in 2003-06 at MLB) add up to a situational lefty. Tough to see much playing time or value.

Lopez,Rodrigo

	Yr	W	L	Sv	IP	K	ERA	WHIP	OBA	vL	vR	BF/G	H%	S%	xERA	G	L	F	Ctl	Dom	Cmd	hr/f	hr/9	RAR	BPV	R$
RH Starter	02 BAL	15	9	0	196	136	3.58	1.19	237	228	241	24.4	26%	74%	3.94	41	17	42	2.8	6.2	2.2	9%	1.1	21.2	59	$22
Age 31	03 BAL	7	10	0	147	103	5.82	1.57	312	308	319	25.4	34%	66%	4.03	42	22	35	2.6	6.3	2.4	14%	1.5	-23.4	37	$2
Peak	04 BAL	14	9	0	170	121	3.60	1.28	255	258	245	19.3	28%	76%	3.75	46	18	36	2.9	6.4	2.2	11%	1.1	17.6	56	$17
Type	05 BAL	15	12	0	209	118	4.91	1.41	282	288	262	25.9	30%	68%	4.17	44	21	36	2.7	5.1	1.9	11%	1.2	-13.8	32	$11
Reliability 86	06 BAL	9	18	0	189	136	5.90	1.55	305	308	296	23.5	34%	65%	3.98	43	22	35	2.8	6.5	2.3	14%	1.5	-31.4	36	$4
DL	1st Half	5	8	0	96	59	6.46	1.54	302			26.8	32%	61%	4.31	39	23	37	2.9	5.5	1.9	16%	1.8	-22.6	14	$1
ERA Potl 55%	2nd Half	4	10	0	93	77	5.33	1.56	309			20.8	36%	68%	3.64	46	21	33	2.7	7.5	2.8	13%	1.3	-8.8	58	$3
LIMA Plan C+	07 Proj	8	11	0	137	94	4.66	1.42	284			22.9	31%	70%	3.93	44	21	36	2.8	6.2	2.2	12%	1.2	9.4	45	$8

How important is luck? Nearly identical BPIs in '06 as in '04, but far worse results thanks to H%, S%, hr/f. No guarantees, but could be a sleeper given enough IPs and normal luck. UP: See 2004

Lowe,Derek

	Yr	W	L	Sv	IP	K	ERA	WHIP	OBA	vL	vR	BF/G	H%	S%	xERA	G	L	F	Ctl	Dom	Cmd	hr/f	hr/9	RAR	BPV	R$
RH Starter	02 BOS	21	8	0	219	127	2.59	0.98	212	209	213	26.7	24%	75%	2.76	66	14	20	2.0	5.2	2.6	9%	0.5	50.5	85	$35
Age 33	03 BOS	17	7	0	203	110	4.48	1.42	274	276	266	26.7	30%	69%	3.37	65	16	19	3.2	4.9	1.5	13%	0.8	1.2	39	$14
Past Peak	04 BOS	14	12	0	189	110	5.23	1.60	299	305	293	25.9	33%	67%	3.61	62	17	20	3.5	5.2	1.5	12%	0.8	-18.7	35	$5
Type Finesse	05 LA	12	15	0	222	146	3.61	1.25	263	296	219	26.5	29%	76%	2.93	64	15	21	2.2	5.9	2.7	19%	1.1	17.5	60	$18
Reliability 88	06 LA	16	8	0	218	123	3.63	1.27	264	270	255	26.1	30%	72%	2.93	67	16	17	2.3	5.1	2.2	11%	0.6	23.0	62	$20
DL	1st Half	6	4	0	111	57	3.49	1.23	246			27.1	27%	72%	3.12	67	15	18	2.8	4.6	1.7	11%	0.6	13.7	52	$10
ERA Potl 50%	2nd Half	10	4	0	107	66	3.79	1.31	283			25.1	32%	71%	2.74	68	16	17	1.8	5.6	3.1	12%	0.6	9.3	80	$11
LIMA Plan D	07 Proj	16	11	0	218	130	3.89	1.31	269			26.3	30%	71%	3.03	65	16	19	2.4	5.4	2.2	11%	0.6	35.8	61	$18

Reasons not to be concerned about DOM drop:
1. It recovered in 2nd half
2. It's at career norms
3. Extreme GB% has enabled fine results for years at roughly this DOM anyway.

Lowe,Mark

	Yr	W	L	Sv	IP	K	ERA	WHIP	OBA	vL	vR	BF/G	H%	S%	xERA	G	L	F	Ctl	Dom	Cmd	hr/f	hr/9	RAR	BPV	R$
RH Reliever	02	0	0	0	0	0	0.00	0.00																		
Age 23	03	0	0	0	0	0	0.00	0.00																		
Growth	04	0	0	0	0	0	0.00	0.00																		
Type Power	05	0	0	0	0	0	0.00	0.00																		
Reliability 0	06 SEA *	1	1	3	32	28	1.98	1.13	225	167	205	5.4	29%	83%	3.21	49	19	33	2.8	7.8	2.8	3%	0.3	10.2	106	$6
DL 42	1st Half	0	1	3	14	8	1.99	1.10	268			6.3	31%	80%					0.7	5.0	7.5		0.0	4.4	189	$3
ERA Potl 45%	2nd Half	1	0	0	18	20	1.98	1.15	189			4.9	26%	85%	3.04	49	19	33	4.5	9.9	2.2	7%	0.5	5.8	108	$3
LIMA Plan A	07 Proj	2	1	0	44	43	3.93	1.33	232			4.7	30%	71%	3.40	49	19	33	4.3	8.9	2.0	8%	0.6	5.8	86	$4

1-0, 1.93 ERA in 18 IP at SEA. Elbow surgery ended effective MLB audition. Live fastball/ sinker combo got lots of Ks and GBs. Ctl was a problem in small MLB sample, but not in minors. Worth watching.

Lowry,Noah

	Yr	W	L	Sv	IP	K	ERA	WHIP	OBA	vL	vR	BF/G	H%	S%	xERA	G	L	F	Ctl	Dom	Cmd	hr/f	hr/9	RAR	BPV	R$
LH Starter	02	0	0	0	0	0	0.00	0.00											0.0	0.0						
Age 26	03 a/a	10	6	0	137	93	4.66	1.47	282			22.3	33%	66%	4.14				3.2	6.1	1.9		0.3	-4.5	65	$8
Growth	04 SF *	13	5	0	181	134	3.98	1.35	273	338	238	23.4	32%	72%	3.93	42	17	41	2.6	6.7	2.5	7%	0.8	6.4	68	$14
Type	05 SF	13	13	0	204	172	3.79	1.32	251	213	259	26.2	30%	74%	3.78	41	20	39	3.3	7.6	2.3	9%	0.9	11.5	70	$18
Reliability 45	06 SF	7	10	0	159	84	4.75	1.40	270	312	262	25.4	28%	69%	4.74	36	18	45	3.2	4.8	1.5	9%	1.2	-5.2	25	$7
DL 31	1st Half	3	5	0	63	27	3.86	1.37	271			24.5	27%	77%	5.05	35	14	51	2.9	3.9	1.4	8%	1.3	4.9	14	$4
ERA Potl 50%	2nd Half	4	5	0	96	57	5.34	1.42	270			26.0	29%	64%	4.54	37	21	42	3.4	5.3	1.6	9%	1.1	-10.1	33	$3
LIMA Plan C	07 Proj	10	10	0	174	114	4.40	1.38	267			24.9	30%	71%	4.35	38	19	43	3.2	5.9	1.9	9%	1.1	0.3	44	$10

Positive sign: Take away three straight elbow-hampered PQS-0 starts in Sept, he finishes at 3.87 ERA. Negative sign: Even without those DISasters, BPIs (4.5 DOM/1.5 CMD) and G/F well short of the comfort zone.

PATRICK DAVITT

Lugo,Ruddy		W	L	Sv	IP	K	ERA	WHIP	OBA	vL	vR	BF/G	H%	S%	xERA	G	L	F	Ctl	Dom	Cmd	hr/f	hr/9	RAR	BPV	R$
RH Reliever	02 aa	3	1	1	33	20	5.17	1.63	300			13.7	34%	69%	5.26				3.8	5.4	**1.4**		0.8	-3.7	33	$1
Age 26	03 aa	4	15	1	118	92	7.62	1.80	321			13.6	37%	57%	6.30				4.2	7.0	**1.7**		1.1	-47.0	35	($6)
Growth	04 aa	0	1	0	15	5	6.00	1.87	299			9.0	27%	75%	7.39				6.0	3.0	**0.5**		2.4	-3.1	-48	($1)
Type Power	05 aa	1	1	2	40	37	1.50	1.41	216			6.7	28%	90%	3.01				5.7	8.3	**1.4**		0.2	13.9	84	$5
Reliability 0	06 TAM	2	4	0	85	48	3.81	1.32	238	213	264	5.6	27%	70%	4.52	44	16	40	3.9	5.1	**1.3**	4%	0.4	7.8	52	$6
DL 23	1st Half	1	2	0	42	24	3.85	1.33	233			5.8	26%	70%	4.82	39	16	45	4.3	5.1	**1.2**	3%	0.4	3.7	52	$3
ERA Potl 50%	2nd Half	1	2	0	43	24	3.78	1.31	244			5.5	28%	70%	4.22	49	16	35	3.6	5.0	**1.4**	4%	0.4	4.1	54	$3
LIMA Plan C	07 Proj	**1**	**2**	**0**	**44**	**30**	**4.34**	**1.49**	**264**			**7.1**	**30%**	**72%**	**4.43**	**45**	**16**	**39**	**4.3**	**6.2**	**1.4**	**8%**	**0.8**	**0.3**	**45**	**$2**

2-4, 3.81 ERA in 85 IP at TAM. There's less here than met the eye in '06. Sub-optimal skills yield an xERA that suggests low ERA was an illusion. Slightly low H% also implies higher WHIP.

Lyon,Brandon		W	L	Sv	IP	K	ERA	WHIP	OBA	vL	vR	BF/G	H%	S%	xERA	G	L	F	Ctl	Dom	Cmd	hr/f	hr/9	RAR	BPV	R$
RH Reliever	02 TOR *	5	13	0	137	60	6.24	1.65	329	321	289	21.6	34%	63%	4.91	44	13	43	2.4	3.9	**1.6**	8%	1.2	-30.1	12	($3)
Age 27	03 BOS	4	6	9	59	50	4.12	1.56	305	317	276	5.4	37%	76%	4.10	35	23	43	2.9	7.6	**2.6**	7%	0.9	3.0	68	$7
Pre-Peak	04 ARI	0	0	0	0	0	0.00	0.00											0.0	0.0						
Type	05 ARI	0	2	14	29	17	6.49	1.86	349	317	364	4.3	37%	69%	4.60	42	23	35	3.1	5.3	**1.7**	16%	1.9	-8.1	-3	$2
Reliability 0	06 ARI	2	4	0	69	46	3.91	1.30	259	244	270	4.3	29%	72%	3.84	43	24	33	2.9	6.0	**2.1**	10%	0.9	4.9	56	$5
DL 92	1st Half	1	2	0	36	28	5.24	1.19	256			4.2	29%	58%	3.41	41	24	35	2.0	7.0	**3.5**	13%	1.2	-3.3	82	$2
ERA Potl 50%	2nd Half	1	2	0	33	18	2.45	1.42	262			4.3	29%	84%	4.34	45	24	31	3.8	4.9	**1.3**	6%	0.5	8.3	43	$3
LIMA Plan B	07 Proj	**3**	**5**	**0**	**58**	**40**	**4.19**	**1.47**	**288**			**5.4**	**33%**	**73%**	**4.02**	**42**	**23**	**35**	**2.9**	**6.2**	**2.1**	**9%**	**0.9**	**2.5**	**51**	**$3**

Decent skills supported a solid season two years after serious elbow surgery. Never quite closer-worthy BPIs, but did that job when called upon. Don't let 2nd half ERA deceive you; xERA tells the truth.

MacDougal,Mike		W	L	Sv	IP	K	ERA	WHIP	OBA	vL	vR	BF/G	H%	S%	xERA	G	L	F	Ctl	Dom	Cmd	hr/f	hr/9	RAR	BPV	R$
RH Reliever	02 a/a	4	7	0	79	44	6.61	2.18	271			18.3	30%	69%	6.09				10.1	5.0	**0.5**		0.7	-22.8	21	($7)
Age 30	03 KC	3	5	27	64	57	4.08	1.50	262	230	314	4.2	33%	73%	3.38	55	21	24	4.5	8.0	**1.8**	9%	0.6	3.5	71	$14
Peak	04 KC *	2	3	4	43	30	5.61	2.08	303	304	321	4.9	35%	72%	5.23	51	24	24	7.7	6.2	**0.8**	8%	0.6	-6.3	30	($1)
Type	05 KC	5	6	21	70	72	3.34	1.33	259	240	270	4.4	33%	77%	2.85	57	15	28	3.1	9.2	**3.0**	11%	0.8	8.9	99	$15
Reliability 0	06 2AL	1	1	1	29	21	1.55	0.93	204	281	171	3.9	25%	85%	2.31	64	21	15	1.9	6.5	**3.5**	8%	0.3	10.8	117	$6
DL 110	1st Half	0	0	0	0	0	0.00	0.00																		
ERA Potl 35%	2nd Half	1	1	1	29	21	1.55	0.93	204			3.9	25%	85%	2.31	64	21	15	1.9	6.5	**3.5**	8%	0.3	10.7	117	$6
LIMA Plan B	07 Proj	**3**	**4**	**3**	**58**	**45**	**3.88**	**1.29**	**255**			**4.5**	**30%**	**70%**	**3.00**	**59**	**20**	**21**	**2.9**	**7.0**	**2.4**	**11%**	**0.6**	**10.6**	**77**	**$6**

Shoulder woes required former wild fireballer to reinvent himself as a control/GB artist, with great success. Low flyball rate that yields elite hr/9 helps. Excellent LIMA pick with a clear shot at closing should the chance arise.

Maddux,Greg		W	L	Sv	IP	K	ERA	WHIP	OBA	vL	vR	BF/G	H%	S%	xERA	G	L	F	Ctl	Dom	Cmd	hr/f	hr/9	RAR	BPV	R$
RH Starter	02 ATL	16	6	0	199	118	2.62	1.20	257	232	276	24.1	29%	80%	3.33	57	17	27	2.0	5.3	**2.6**	8%	0.6	36.4	72	$23
Age 41	03 ATL	16	11	0	218	123	3.96	1.18	268	271	264	24.8	29%	69%	3.38	54	17	30	1.4	5.1	**3.7**	11%	1.0	8.5	80	$20
Decline	04 CHC	16	11	0	212	151	4.03	1.18	267	271	268	26.4	29%	72%	3.10	51	20	29	1.4	6.4	**4.6**	18%	1.5	6.1	92	$21
Type Finesse	05 CHC	13	15	0	225	136	4.24	1.22	274	283	270	26.6	30%	69%	3.26	52	22	27	1.4	5.4	**3.8**	15%	1.2	0.2	77	$17
Reliability 80	06 2NL	15	14	0	210	117	4.20	1.22	270	254	284	25.6	30%	67%	3.46	51	21	28	1.6	5.0	**3.2**	10%	0.9	7.4	72	$18
DL	1st Half	7	8	0	98	56	4.95	1.29	281			25.8	31%	63%	3.54	48	24	28	1.7	5.1	**2.9**	12%	1.0	-5.6	61	$6
ERA Potl 55%	2nd Half	8	6	0	112	61	3.54	1.15	260			25.3	29%	71%	3.39	53	19	28	1.4	4.9	**3.4**	9%	0.7	13.1	82	$12
LIMA Plan D+	07 Proj	**12**	**11**	**0**	**174**	**98**	**4.03**	**1.26**	**275**			**26.0**	**30%**	**71%**	**3.48**	**52**	**21**	**28**	**1.7**	**5.1**	**3.0**	**12%**	**1.0**	**18.9**	**63**	**$14**

The decline is slow, but it is there nonetheless. Terrible luck (34% H%, 61% S%, 17% hr/f) and DOM sag (to 4.4) fed poor May-June ERA/WHIP. Age is a concern, but still a solid bet.

Madson,Ryan		W	L	Sv	IP	K	ERA	WHIP	OBA	vL	vR	BF/G	H%	S%	xERA	G	L	F	Ctl	Dom	Cmd	hr/f	hr/9	RAR	BPV	R$
RH Reliever	02 aa	16	4	0	171	121	3.84	1.33	262			28.0	31%	72%	3.77				3.0	6.4	**2.1**		0.6	9.0	66	$16
Age 26	03 aaa	12	8	0	157	122	4.36	1.45	291			26.4	35%	70%	4.46				2.6	7.0	**2.7**		0.6	0.7	77	$11
Growth	04 PHI	9	3	1	77	55	2.34	1.13	238	252	227	6.0	28%	83%	3.16	54	18	28	2.2	6.4	**2.9**	9%	0.7	18.3	86	$13
Type	05 PHI	6	5	0	87	79	4.14	1.25	255	292	233	4.7	31%	70%	2.99	48	25	27	2.6	8.2	**3.2**	16%	1.1	1.2	85	$8
Reliability 27	06 PHI	11	9	2	134	99	5.70	1.69	318	306	336	12.4	36%	68%	4.20	43	22	35	3.4	6.6	**2.0**	12%	1.3	-20.1	33	$3
DL	1st Half	7	5	0	71	46	6.45	1.80	326			19.8	35%	68%	4.71	43	18	39	3.9	5.8	**1.5**	15%	1.9	-17.2	-1	($1)
ERA Potl 60%	2nd Half	4	4	2	63	53	4.86	1.56	308			8.5	37%	69%	3.64	42	27	31	2.7	7.6	**2.8**	8%	0.7	-2.9	76	$3
LIMA Plan B	07 Proj	**6**	**4**	**5**	**73**	**57**	**4.34**	**1.38**	**274**			**7.8**	**32%**	**71%**	**3.56**	**46**	**23**	**31**	**2.9**	**7.1**	**2.5**	**11%**	**1.0**	**7.2**	**65**	**$7**

Tale of two pitchers 2003-06:
As SP: 6.56 ERA in 181 IP
As RP: 3.51 ERA in 251 IP
Moral: Best of times as RP, worst of times as SP.
Draft accordingly.

Mahay,Ron		W	L	Sv	IP	K	ERA	WHIP	OBA	vL	vR	BF/G	H%	S%	xERA	G	L	F	Ctl	Dom	Cmd	hr/f	hr/9	RAR	BPV	R$
LH Reliever	02 CHC *	2	1	2	60	56	3.75	1.17	217			4.9	25%	74%	3.73	34	17	49	3.5	8.4	**2.4**	12%	1.4	2.6	73	$6
Age 35	03 TEX *	7	5	3	87	80	4.55	1.25	241	208	190	6.0	29%	66%	4.03	28	18	54	3.2	8.3	**2.6**	8%	1.0	-0.3	80	$10
Decline	04 TEX	3	0	0	67	54	2.55	1.33	241	227	241	4.7	29%	83%	4.02	44	14	42	3.9	7.3	**1.9**	6%	0.7	15.5	69	$7
Type Power	05 TEX *	1	5	1	59	52	7.02	1.73	308	302	322	7.2	36%	62%	3.78	48	23	29	4.3	7.9	**1.9**	20%	1.7	-19.3	30	($2)
Reliability 14	06 TEX	1	3	0	57	56	3.95	1.44	251	240	258	4.0	31%	76%	3.75	41	21	38	4.4	8.8	**2.0**	12%	1.1	4.3	67	$4
DL 16	1st Half	0	1	0	23	23	1.95	1.30	235			3.9	31%	86%	3.48	43	20	37	3.9	9.0	**2.3**	4%	0.4	7.4	98	$3
ERA Potl 50%	2nd Half	1	2	0	34	33	5.31	1.53	262			4.1	31%	70%	3.95	39	22	39	4.8	8.8	**1.8**	16%	1.6	-3.1	46	$1
LIMA Plan B+	07 Proj	**1**	**3**	**0**	**54**	**50**	**4.50**	**1.44**	**258**			**4.8**	**31%**	**71%**	**3.80**	**42**	**20**	**37**	**4.2**	**8.3**	**2.0**	**10%**	**1.0**	**4.6**	**65**	**$3**

Great 1st half skills, but walks, HR shot up, feeding bad results. HRs were partly unlucky, but walks reflect steady increases since '03. Depending on role, maybe a late LIMA pick, more likely injury-replacement fodder.

Maholm,Paul		W	L	Sv	IP	K	ERA	WHIP	OBA	vL	vR	BF/G	H%	S%	xERA	G	L	F	Ctl	Dom	Cmd	hr/f	hr/9	RAR	BPV	R$
LH Starter	02	0	0	0	0	0	0.00	0.00											0.0	0.0						
Age 24	03	0	0	0	0	0	0.00	0.00											0.0	0.0						
Growth	04	0	0	0	0	0	0.00	0.00											0.0	0.0						
Type	05 PIT *	10	4	0	158	107	3.30	1.31	258	87	232	23.9	30%	75%	3.40	55	20	25	3.0	6.1	**2.1**	7%	0.5	18.5	68	$14
Reliability 2	06 PIT	8	10	0	176	117	4.76	1.61	289	233	313	26.6	33%	72%	3.99	53	20	27	4.1	6.0	**1.4**	12%	1.0	-5.8	34	$4
DL	1st Half	2	7	0	92	61	4.98	1.75	305			26.9	34%	73%	4.19	51	24	25	4.6	6.0	**1.3**	13%	1.0	-5.6	28	($1)
ERA Potl 45%	2nd Half	6	3	0	84	56	4.51	1.45	271			26.2	30%	71%	3.78	55	17	28	3.6	6.0	**1.6**	12%	1.0	-0.2	42	$5
LIMA Plan C+	07 Proj	**10**	**7**	**0**	**174**	**117**	**4.14**	**1.47**	**275**			**25.5**	**31%**	**73%**	**3.75**	**54**	**20**	**27**	**3.6**	**6.1**	**1.7**	**10%**	**0.8**	**13.1**	**48**	**$9**

Rising talent whose nifty combo of GBs and Ks predicts ERA upside, as seen in 2nd half xERA. Spotty control limits overall ceiling, but 2nd half improvement is promising.

Maine,John		W	L	Sv	IP	K	ERA	WHIP	OBA	vL	vR	BF/G	H%	S%	xERA	G	L	F	Ctl	Dom	Cmd	hr/f	hr/9	RAR	BPV	R$
RH Starter	02	0	0	0	0	0	0.00	0.00											0.0	0.0						
Age 26	03	0	0	0	0	0	0.00	0.00											0.0	0.0						
Growth	04 a/a	9	8	0	147	124	4.40	1.47	277			24.0	33%	72%	4.65				3.5	7.6	**2.1**		0.9	-1.1	62	$9
Type Power	05 BAL *	8	14	0	168	121	5.78	1.50	283	227	275	22.5	32%	63%	3.99	46	21	34	3.5	6.5	**1.9**	13%	1.2	-29.2	39	$4
Reliability 5	06 NYM *	9	10	0	146	112	4.14	1.31	250	231	191	23.8	29%	71%	4.18	38	15	47	3.3	6.9	**2.1**	8%	1.0	6.2	58	$12
DL 40	1st Half	3	6	0	61	47	5.18	1.60	302			25.2	36%	66%	4.41	33	27	40	3.4	6.8	**2.0**	4%	0.4	-5.3	65	$1
ERA Potl 50%	2nd Half	6	4	0	85	65	3.39	1.11	208			22.8	22%	78%	3.91	38	15	47	3.3	6.9	**2.1**	12%	1.5	11.5	54	$11
LIMA Plan C	07 Proj	**10**	**12**	**0**	**174**	**132**	**4.50**	**1.40**	**265**			**23.5**	**30%**	**70%**	**4.23**	**39**	**16**	**45**	**3.4**	**6.8**	**2.0**	**9%**	**1.1**	**2.9**	**52**	**$10**

6-5, 3.60 ERA in 90 IP at NYM. Five good games after recall (4.0 PQS avg) didn't last. S% normalized, Ctl doubled, hr/9 jumped, ERA soared. FB% means HRs, which limits ERA potential; otherwise decent BPIs.

Majewski,Gary		W	L	Sv	IP	K	ERA	WHIP	OBA	vL	vR	BF/G	H%	S%	xERA	G	L	F	Ctl	Dom	Cmd	hr/f	hr/9	RAR	BPV	R$
RH Reliever	02 aa	5	3	3	74	69	3.64	1.48	261			5.7	33%	75%	3.98				4.4	8.4	**1.9**		0.5	5.8	79	$7
Age 27	03 aaa	6	4	4	72	65	5.24	1.43	264			7.5	33%	62%	3.92				3.7	8.1	**2.2**		0.5	-7.5	81	$6
Growth	04 aaa	4	5	15	57	50	4.09	1.36	251			5.0	32%	68%	3.44				3.8	7.9	**2.1**		0.3	1.8	86	$10
Type	05 WAS *	4	4	1	86	50	2.93	1.36	248	236	259	4.7	29%	77%	4.32	46	20	34	3.9	5.2	**1.4**	2%	0.2	14.0	59	$7
Reliability 8	06 2NL	4	4	0	70	43	4.62	1.54	286	290	279	4.8	32%	70%	4.06	53	19	29	3.7	5.5	**1.5**	8%	0.6	-1.2	43	$3
DL 25	1st Half	3	2	0	47	31	3.63	1.38	236			5.1	27%	75%	4.13	51	17	32	4.6	5.9	**1.3**	9%	0.8	5.0	48	$4
ERA Potl 50%	2nd Half	1	2	0	23	12	6.65	1.87	369			4.4	41%	62%	3.94	56	21	23	2.0	4.7	**2.4**	5%	0.4	-6.1	48	($1)
LIMA Plan C+	07 Proj	**3**	**4**	**0**	**58**	**38**	**4.50**	**1.47**	**278**			**4.8**	**32%**	**70%**	**3.85**	**52**	**20**	**28**	**3.4**	**5.9**	**1.7**	**9%**	**0.8**	**3.7**	**48**	**$3**

2nd half ERA took a hit due to high H%; shoulder injury didn't help. High GB% is nice, but CMD just doesn't cut it the past two years. Was more impressive in the minors, marginal at best in the majors.

PATRICK DAVITT

Marcum,Shaun

	Season	W	L	Sv	IP	K	ERA	WHIP	OBA	vL	vR	BF/G	H%	S%	xERA	G	L	F	Ctl	Dom	Cmd	hr/f	hr/9	RAR	BPV	R$
RH Reliever	02	0	0	0	0	0	0.00	0.00																		
Age 25	03	0	0	0	0	0	0.00	0.00																		
Growth	04	0	0	0	0	0	0.00	0.00																		
Type Power	05 a/a	13	5	0	157	115	5.50	1.38	298			25.0	33%	64%	5.35				1.7	6.6	**4.0**		1.6	-23.2	70	$9
Reliability 0	06 TOR *	7	4	0	130	117	4.90	1.48	283	303	256	14.7	33%	71%	4.03	36	18	46	3.3	8.1	**2.4**	12%	1.5	-5.6	52	$8
DL	1st Half	4	0	0	55	56	5.36	1.48	297			11.6	36%	67%	3.77	27	27	47	2.6	9.1	**3.5**	12%	1.5	-5.5	80	$4
ERA Potl 50%	2nd Half	3	4	0	75	61	4.57	1.48	272			18.3	31%	74%	4.30	36	17	46	3.8	7.3	**1.9**	12%	1.6	-0.1	38	$4
LIMA Plan C	07 Proj	**9**	**5**	**0**	**145**	**120**	**4.72**	**1.41**	**276**			**17.4**	**31%**	**71%**	**4.04**	**36**	**17**	**46**	**3.0**	**7.4**	**2.5**	**12%**	**1.5**	**8.0**	**52**	**$10**

3-4, 5.06 ERA in 78 IP at TOR. Rotation fixture in the 2nd half. PRO: Strong DOM, xERA potential, hr/f should regress CON: High FB, 21/50 DOM/DIS. There is some upside but much still needs to improve.

Marmol,Carlos

	Season	W	L	Sv	IP	K	ERA	WHIP	OBA	vL	vR	BF/G	H%	S%	xERA	G	L	F	Ctl	Dom	Cmd	hr/f	hr/9	RAR	BPV	R$
RH Starter	02	0	0	0	0	0	0.00	0.00																		
Age 24	03	0	0	0	0	0	0.00	0.00																		
Growth	04	0	0	0	0	0	0.00	0.00																		
Type Power	05 aa	3	4	0	81	62	4.77	1.55	266			25.9	30%	73%	5.16				4.8	6.9	**1.4**		1.4	-4.7	30	$2
Reliability 0	06 CHC *	8	9	0	138	117	5.21	1.59	252	229	263	19.5	30%	68%	5.07	29	18	53	5.8	7.6	**1.3**	7%	1.0	-12.2	49	$4
DL 15	1st Half	4	4	0	86	84	4.11	1.41	248			21.9	32%	71%	4.30	28	18	54	4.3	8.8	**2.0**	4%	0.5	4.0	85	$6
ERA Potl 50%	2nd Half	4	5	0	52	33	7.01	1.89	257			16.7	27%	65%	6.59	29	18	53	8.2	5.7	**0.7**	11%	1.7	-16.2	1	($2)
LIMA Plan C+	07 Proj	**4**	**4**	**0**	**69**	**53**	**5.39**	**1.69**	**269**			**21.1**	**30%**	**71%**	**5.38**	**29**	**18**	**53**	**5.9**	**7.0**	**1.2**	**9%**	**1.3**	**-8.6**	**28**	**$0**

5-7, 6.08 ERA in 77 IP at CHC. He throws hard. He throws wild. He gives up many long flies. xERA is bad. His value is naught. Don't come out of your draft saying Marmol's been bought. (Poetry: 1, Shandler: 0)

Maroth,Mike

	Season	W	L	Sv	IP	K	ERA	WHIP	OBA	vL	vR	BF/G	H%	S%	xERA	G	L	F	Ctl	Dom	Cmd	hr/f	hr/9	RAR	BPV	R$
LH Starter	02 DET *	14	11	0	201	104	4.12	1.27	259	252	284	26.3	29%	67%	3.94	51	16	33	2.6	4.7	**1.8**	6%	0.6	8.4	52	$16
Age 29	03 DET	9	21	0	193	87	5.74	1.46	298	257	311	25.6	30%	64%	4.35	47	17	36	2.3	4.1	**1.7**	14%	1.6	-28.8	9	$4
Peak	04 DET	11	13	0	217	108	4.31	1.40	285	288	294	28.4	30%	72%	4.27	46	18	36	2.4	4.5	**1.8**	9%	1.0	3.2	32	$11
Type Finesse	05 DET	14	14	0	209	115	4.74	1.37	285	275	293	26.4	30%	69%	3.97	48	17	35	2.2	5.0	**2.3**	12%	1.3	-9.4	36	$12
Reliability 37	06 DET	5	2	0	53	24	4.23	1.50	299	250	309	18.1	30%	80%	4.64	42	18	40	2.7	4.1	**1.5**	15%	1.9	2.2	-5	$4
DL 103	1st Half	5	2	0	48	22	3.56	1.48	293			23.5	30%	83%	4.59	42	20	38	2.8	4.1	**1.5**	12%	1.5	5.9	7	$4
ERA Potl 30%	2nd Half	0	0	0	5	2	10.38	1.73	353			6.0	28%	50%	5.11	41	5	55	1.7	3.5	**2.0**	27%	5.2	-3.7	******	($1)
LIMA Plan C	07 Proj	**7**	**6**	**0**	**94**	**46**	**4.62**	**1.41**	**287**			**9.9**	**30%**	**71%**	**4.29**	**46**	**18**	**36**	**2.5**	**4.4**	**1.8**	**11%**	**1.3**	**2.2**	**24**	**$6**

Was putting up career-best numbers when elbow surgery derailed his season. But high S% meant it was a mirage anyway. In all, BPI optimism after '05 reverted to his old form, which isn't so good.

Marquis,Jason

	Season	W	L	Sv	IP	K	ERA	WHIP	OBA	vL	vR	BF/G	H%	S%	xERA	G	L	F	Ctl	Dom	Cmd	hr/f	hr/9	RAR	BPV	R$
RH Starter	02 ATL	8	10	0	119	89	4.99	1.54	284	292	276	23.1	32%	71%	4.23	41	20	39	3.8	6.7	**1.8**	13%	1.4	-13.0	33	$4
Age 28	03 ATL *	8	4	1	134	82	4.97	1.57	295	250	287	16.7	33%	68%	4.23	52	15	33	3.6	5.5	**1.5**	6%	0.6	-11.4	43	$3
Pre-Peak	04 STL	15	7	0	201	138	3.71	1.42	275	278	271	27.3	31%	78%	3.50	56	19	26	3.1	6.2	**2.0**	16%	1.2	13.6	44	$15
Type Finesse	05 STL	13	14	0	207	100	4.13	1.33	261	238	280	26.6	27%	73%	4.03	52	17	31	3.0	4.3	**1.4**	14%	1.3	2.9	22	$13
Reliability 75	06 STL	14	16	0	194	96	6.03	1.52	288	288	291	26.1	29%	64%	4.74	43	17	40	3.5	4.5	**1.3**	13%	1.6	-36.9	2	$3
DL	1st Half	9	6	0	102	45	5.82	1.41	267			27.6	26%	62%	4.83	42	15	43	3.4	4.0	**1.2**	13%	1.7	-16.8	-1	$4
ERA Potl 45%	2nd Half	5	10	0	92	51	6.25	1.65	309			24.8	32%	65%	4.63	44	19	37	3.5	5.0	**1.4**	13%	1.6	-20.1	6	($1)
LIMA Plan C	07 Proj	**13**	**14**	**0**	**189**	**103**	**4.87**	**1.48**	**282**			**25.1**	**30%**	**71%**	**4.33**	**47**	**18**	**35**	**3.3**	**4.9**	**1.5**	**13%**	**1.3**	**0.8**	**19**	**$8**

It's not often that you see a 6.03 ERA in nearly 200 IP. But it was not all bad. His ERA got as low as 2.79 on April 17! It hit 5.53 on June 21 and pretty much stayed in the 5's the rest of the way. A workhorse with bad BPIs.

Marshall,Sean

	Season	W	L	Sv	IP	K	ERA	WHIP	OBA	vL	vR	BF/G	H%	S%	xERA	G	L	F	Ctl	Dom	Cmd	hr/f	hr/9	RAR	BPV	R$
LH Starter	02	0	0	0	0	0	0.00	0.00																		
Age 24	03	0	0	0	0	0	0.00	0.00																		
Growth	04 aa	2	2	0	29	19	10.13	2.25	382			25.0	43%	53%	8.44				4.6	5.9	**1.3**		1.0	-20.7	12	($5)
Type Power	05 aa	0	1	0	25	20	4.55	1.14	239			25.4	28%	60%	3.09				2.3	7.2	**3.2**		0.8	-0.7	94	$2
Reliability 0	06 CHC *	6	11	0	146	95	5.48	1.55	271	256	273	23.4	29%	67%	4.46	47	17	36	4.6	5.8	**1.3**	12%	1.3	-17.9	24	$2
DL 40	1st Half	4	6	0	80	53	5.16	1.43	252			23.3	28%	65%	4.17	50	17	33	4.4	5.9	**1.4**	11%	1.0	-6.7	39	$3
ERA Potl 45%	2nd Half	2	5	0	66	42	5.86	1.70	293			23.4	31%	69%	4.87	42	19	40	4.8	5.7	**1.2**	14%	1.6	-11.2	7	($1)
LIMA Plan C+	07 Proj	**6**	**12**	**0**	**160**	**105**	**5.02**	**1.56**	**277**			**23.1**	**30%**	**70%**	**4.46**	**46**	**18**	**37**	**4.3**	**5.9**	**1.4**	**12%**	**1.2**	**-1.9**	**27**	**$3**

6-9, 5.59 ERA in 126 IP at CHC. Made the jump from AA, looked good until mid-May. But he was living on low H%; ERA ballooned when corrected. Expect continued growing pains until he regains CMD.

Marte,Damaso

	Season	W	L	Sv	IP	K	ERA	WHIP	OBA	vL	vR	BF/G	H%	S%	xERA	G	L	F	Ctl	Dom	Cmd	hr/f	hr/9	RAR	BPV	R$
LH Reliever	02 CHW	1	1	10	60	72	2.85	1.03	206	149	252	3.5	29%	75%	2.57	40	28	33	2.7	10.8	**4.0**	11%	0.8	11.9	140	$12
Age 32	03 CHW	4	2	11	79	87	1.59	1.06	183	168	199	4.4	26%	86%	3.25	36	22	42	3.9	9.9	**2.6**	4%	0.3	28.5	121	$18
Peak	04 CHW	6	5	6	73	68	3.44	1.23	213	143	263	4.1	25%	78%	3.86	36	17	46	4.2	8.4	**2.0**	11%	1.2	8.9	68	$11
Type Power	05 CHW	3	4	4	45	54	3.79	1.73	261	267	244	3.2	35%	81%	4.03	40	21	39	6.6	10.8	**1.6**	11%	1.0	3.2	72	$4
Reliability 28	06 PIT	1	7	0	58	63	3.72	1.41	237	225	258	3.4	31%	75%	3.76	34	25	41	4.8	9.8	**2.0**	8%	0.8	5.5	86	$4
DL 17	1st Half	0	5	0	28	37	3.51	1.49	267			3.3	38%	79%	3.22	33	27	40	4.1	11.8	**2.8**	10%	1.0	3.4	103	$2
ERA Potl 50%	2nd Half	1	2	0	30	26	3.91	1.34	207			3.4	26%	71%	4.31	35	24	41	5.4	7.8	**1.4**	6%	0.6	2.1	73	$2
LIMA Plan B+	07 Proj	**2**	**5**	**0**	**58**	**62**	**3.88**	**1.43**	**234**			**3.5**	**30%**	**75%**	**3.83**	**36**	**23**	**41**	**5.1**	**9.6**	**1.9**	**10%**	**0.9**	**3.8**	**77**	**$4**

Situational lefty who's marginally LIMA-caliber. He throws hard but his control has been off for four years now. He will ride a thin edge around a 4.00 ERA. The last few years he's been lucky. DN: 4.25 ERA

Martinez,Carlos

	Season	W	L	Sv	IP	K	ERA	WHIP	OBA	vL	vR	BF/G	H%	S%	xERA	G	L	F	Ctl	Dom	Cmd	hr/f	hr/9	RAR	BPV	R$
RH Reliever	02	0	0	0	0	0	0.00	0.00																		
Age 24	03	0	0	0	0	0	0.00	0.00																		
Growth	04	0	0	0	0	0	0.00	0.00																		
Type	05 a/a	0	0	1	3	1	9.00	2.00	371			4.9	35%	60%	9.50				3.0	3.0	**1.0**		3.0	-1.7	-70	($0)
Reliability 0	06 FLA	0	1	0	10	11	1.78	1.49	240	250	250	3.7	34%	87%	4.28	22	30	48	5.3	9.8	**1.8**	0%	0.0	3.4	104	$1
DL 146	1st Half	0	1	0	10	11	1.78	1.49	240			3.7	34%	87%	4.28	22	30	48	5.3	9.8	**1.8**	0%	0.0	3.4	104	$1
ERA Potl	2nd Half	0	0	0	0	0	0.00	0.00																		
LIMA Plan	07 Proj	**0**	**0**	**0**	**0**	**0**	**0.00**	**0.00**																		

With only 3 IP above A-ball, he surprisingly won a bullpen spot. Elbow problems sent him to the DL; after TJ surgery, could return late-2007. Keep him on your radar, but 2007 impact will be minimal.

Martinez,Pedro

	Season	W	L	Sv	IP	K	ERA	WHIP	OBA	vL	vR	BF/G	H%	S%	xERA	G	L	F	Ctl	Dom	Cmd	hr/f	hr/9	RAR	BPV	R$
RH Starter	02 BOS	20	4	0	199	239	2.26	0.92	204	203	191	25.5	29%	78%	2.42	39	25	35	1.8	10.8	**6.0**	8%	0.6	53.9	187	$41
Age 35	03 BOS	14	4	0	186	206	2.23	1.04	219	238	179	25.4	31%	79%	2.77	40	24	36	2.3	10.0	**4.4**	4%	0.3	52.7	153	$34
Decline	04 BOS	16	9	0	217	227	3.90	1.17	240	236	240	26.9	30%	70%	3.19	38	19	43	2.5	9.4	**3.7**	10%	1.1	14.3	109	$26
Type Power	05 NYM	15	8	0	217	208	2.82	0.95	206	215	192	27.1	26%	74%	3.12	38	17	45	1.9	8.6	**4.4**	8%	0.8	38.2	135	$33
Reliability 70	06 NYM	9	8	0	132	137	4.49	1.11	225	231	211	23.2	27%	63%	3.20	36	19	44	2.7	9.3	**3.5**	12%	1.3	-0.1	101	$15
DL 52	1st Half	7	4	0	101	111	3.47	1.01	206			24.8	26%	72%	3.03	34	19	47	2.5	9.9	**4.0**	12%	1.2	12.7	119	$15
ERA Potl 70%	2nd Half	2	4	0	31	26	7.84	1.45	280			19.4	32%	45%	3.80	42	20	38	3.2	7.5	**2.4**	14%	1.5	-12.8	50	($0)
LIMA Plan B	07 Proj	**5**	**5**	**0**	**74**	**73**	**3.89**	**1.15**	**235**			**23.2**	**29%**	**70%**	**3.25**	**39**	**19**	**42**	**2.6**	**8.9**	**3.5**	**11%**	**1.1**	**10.2**	**101**	**$9**

Started strong, but you could tell that something wasn't right as the season progressed. Had a 2.50 ERA on May 31 and 7.11 the rest of the way. Future cloudy at best; should return from rotator cuff surgery mid-'07.

Martin,Tom

	Season	W	L	Sv	IP	K	ERA	WHIP	OBA	vL	vR	BF/G	H%	S%	xERA	G	L	F	Ctl	Dom	Cmd	hr/f	hr/9	RAR	BPV	R$
LH Reliever	02 TAM *	0	0	2	4	5	9.00	2.50	415			3.6	56%	60%	8.80				4.5	11.3	**2.5**		0.0	-2.2	92	($0)
Age 36	03 LA	1	2	0	51	51	3.53	1.18	200	189	211	2.6	24%	74%	3.14	49	20	31	4.2	9.0	**2.1**	15%	1.1	4.7	82	$5
Decline	04 2NL	0	2	1	45	30	3.99	1.51	278	310	247	2.6	30%	79%	4.53	39	19	42	3.8	6.0	**1.6**	11%	1.4	1.5	27	$1
Type Power	05 ATL *	0	0	5	29	12	5.28	1.97	334			5.9	33%	78%	7.70				5.0	3.7	**0.8**		1.9	-3.7	-30	($1)
Reliability 0	06 COL	2	0	0	60	46	5.09	1.45	268	268	261	3.9	32%	64%	3.71	49	22	28	3.7	6.9	**1.8**	8%	0.6	-4.5	63	$2
DL	1st Half	1	0	0	28	22	4.82	1.39	248			3.9	31%	63%	3.85	45	25	30	4.2	7.1	**1.7**	4%	0.3	-1.2	74	$1
ERA Potl 60%	2nd Half	1	0	0	32	24	5.33	1.50	285			3.8	33%	64%	3.59	53	20	27	3.4	6.7	**2.0**	11%	0.8	-3.3	55	$1
LIMA Plan B	07 Proj	**1**	**1**	**0**	**44**	**33**	**4.55**	**1.43**	**264**			**3.1**	**30%**	**70%**	**3.90**	**46**	**21**	**34**	**3.7**	**6.8**	**1.8**	**11%**	**1.0**	**2.5**	**51**	**$2**

High GB% kept the ball in the park. But there was no help from the humidor:
HOME: .325 BA/.886 OPS
ROAD: .193 BA/.615 OPS
Low S%, xERA point to some improvement.

DAVE ADLER

Mastny,Tom

Mastny,Tom	Yr	W	L	Sv	IP	K	ERA	WHIP	OBA	vL	vR	BF/G	H%	S%	xERA	G	L	F	Ctl	Dom	Cmd	hr/f	hr/9	RAR	BPV	R$
RH Reliever	02	0	0	0	0	0	0.00	0.00																		
Age 26	03	0	0	0	0	0	0.00	0.00																		
Growth	04	0	0	0	0	0	0.00	0.00																		
Type Power	05 aa	1	1	0	21	16	3.00	1.19	243			17.3	29%	75%	2.98				2.6	6.9	2.7		0.4	3.4	91	$2
Reliability 0	06 CLE *	2	3	6	78	79	3.33	1.27	229	273	282	6.4	31%	72%	3.20	48	23	29	3.9	9.0	2.3	2%	0.1	11.9	108	$11
DL	1st Half	2	2	1	54	55	2.71	1.19	213			7.7	30%	75%					3.8	9.2	2.4		0.0	12.3	118	$8
ERA Potl 60%	2nd Half	0	1	5	24	23	4.71	1.46	261			4.8	34%	66%	3.47	48	23	29	4.2	8.6	2.1	5%	0.4	-0.4	87	$3
LIMA Plan B+	07 Proj	1	2	10	58	57	3.88	1.33	241			5.6	31%	71%	3.24	48	23	29	3.9	8.8	2.3	9%	0.6	8.9	89	$8

5 Sv, 5.51 ERA in 16 IP at CLE. World-beater in August (4 saves, 0.90 ERA), world-weary in Sept. (2 BS, 13.50 ERA). Some nice skills - high DOM, GB%, BPV - but he's got competition for closer.

Mateo,Juan

Mateo,Juan	Yr	W	L	Sv	IP	K	ERA	WHIP	OBA	vL	vR	BF/G	H%	S%	xERA	G	L	F	Ctl	Dom	Cmd	hr/f	hr/9	RAR	BPV	R$
RH Starter	02	0	0	0	0	0	0.00	0.00																		
Age 24	03	0	0	0	0	0	0.00	0.00																		
Growth	04	0	0	0	0	0	0.00	0.00																		
Type	05	0	0	0	0	0	0.00	0.00																		
Reliability 1	06 CHC *	8	7	0	137	95	5.01	1.55	290	277	295	21.2	33%	69%	4.17	41	26	33	3.6	6.2	1.7	11%	1.1	-8.9	39	$4
DL	1st Half	4	4	0	63	41	4.57	1.47	286			21.3	31%	74%					3.1	5.8	1.9		1.5	-0.6	28	$3
ERA Potl 50%	2nd Half	4	3	0	74	54	5.39	1.62	293			21.1	34%	66%	4.27	41	26	33	4.0	6.6	1.6	8%	0.7	-8.2	48	$1
LIMA Plan C+	07 Proj	4	4	0	73	51	4.47	1.48	276			21.2	31%	72%	4.08	41	26	33	3.6	6.3	1.8	11%	1.0	2.5	45	$3

1-3, 5.32 ERA in 46 IP at CHC. High DOM in minors, but it didn't transfer in first year above Single-A. Another Rule 5 pick takes up a roster spot.

Mateo,Julio

Mateo,Julio	Yr	W	L	Sv	IP	K	ERA	WHIP	OBA	vL	vR	BF/G	H%	S%	xERA	G	L	F	Ctl	Dom	Cmd	hr/f	hr/9	RAR	BPV	R$
RH Reliever	02 SEA *	5	2	6	69	48	3.91	1.45	284			6.9	33%	74%	4.30	40	17	43	3.0	6.3	2.1	6%	0.8	4.6	56	$7
Age 27	03 SEA	4	0	1	85	71	3.18	0.96	224	220	219	6.6	25%	76%	3.49	29	18	53	1.4	7.5	5.5	11%	1.5	14.1	126	$13
Pre-Peak	04 SEA	1	2	1	57	43	4.72	1.26	258	275	238	5.3	28%	69%	4.12	31	18	51	2.5	6.8	2.7	12%	1.7	-2.0	49	$3
Type Finesse	05 SEA	3	6	0	88	52	3.06	1.09	241	199	261	6.4	25%	79%	4.19	33	15	52	1.7	5.3	3.1	8%	1.2	14.2	66	$10
Reliability 9	06 SEA	9	4	0	53	31	4.23	1.58	292	394	246	5.0	32%	76%	5.28	24	25	51	3.7	5.2	1.4	6%	1.0	2.2	27	$6
DL 54	1st Half	4	1	0	27	16	4.67	1.59	283			5.1	31%	73%	5.17	29	26	45	4.3	5.3	1.2	7%	1.0	-0.4	26	$2
ERA Potl 35%	2nd Half	5	3	0	26	15	3.78	1.56	302			4.9	33%	79%	5.36	19	25	56	3.1	5.2	1.7	6%	1.0	2.5	30	$3
LIMA Plan C	07 Proj	6	7	0	73	43	4.59	1.43	281			5.5	30%	72%	4.88	27	21	52	3.0	5.3	1.8	9%	1.4	-3.6	27	$5

Living on the Edge, Defined:
- 4-year declining DOM trend
- 25% line drive rate
- 79% 2nd half strand rate
- 51% FB but only 6% hr/f

You don't want him on your roster when the luck changes.

Matsuzaka,Daisuke

Matsuzaka,Daisuke	Yr	W	L	Sv	IP	K	ERA	WHIP	OBA	vL	vR	BF/G	H%	S%	xERA	G	L	F	Ctl	Dom	Cmd	hr/f	hr/9	RAR	BPV	R$
RH Starter	02 JPN	6	2	0	73	82	4.57	1.13	237			21.2	26%	74%	4.79				2.3	10.1	4.4		2.6	-2.7	81	$9
Age 26	03 JPN	16	7	0	194	227	3.51	1.32	244			28.3	33%	77%	3.83				3.6	10.5	2.9		1.0	21.0	100	$24
Growth	04 JPN	10	6	0	146	134	3.60	1.29	249			26.7	31%	74%	3.60				3.2	8.3	2.6		0.7	13.4	87	$15
Type Power	05 JPN	14	13	0	215	238	2.86	1.14	233			31.2	31%	79%	3.14				2.5	10.0	3.9		0.9	38.3	123	$30
Reliability 70	06 JPN	17	5	0	186	211	2.64	1.02	220			29.4	29%	80%	2.78				2.0	10.2	5.0		1.0	43.2	146	$34
DL	1st Half	9	1	0	92	109	2.55	1.06	225			28.2	31%	80%					2.2	10.6	4.9		0.8	22.3	151	$17
ERA Potl 50%	2nd Half	8	4	0	94	102	2.73	0.98	215			30.7	27%	81%					1.9	9.8	5.1		1.3	20.9	141	$17
LIMA Plan C	07 Proj	15	7	0	185	196	3.46	1.17	241			29.0	30%	76%	3.56				2.5	9.6	3.8		1.2	19.5	110	$25

One of the most talented pitching imports to come over from Japan, he has impressive BPIs and is at a peak age. But will success be immediate? This projection hedges a bit, but still yields a $25 rotation stud.

McBride,Macay

McBride,Macay	Yr	W	L	Sv	IP	K	ERA	WHIP	OBA	vL	vR	BF/G	H%	S%	xERA	G	L	F	Ctl	Dom	Cmd	hr/f	hr/9	RAR	BPV	R$
LH Reliever	02	0	0	0	0	0	0.00	0.00																		
Age 24	03	0	0	0	0	0	0.00	0.00																		
Growth	04 aa	1	7	0	103	88	5.59	1.71	311			12.6	37%	67%	5.70				3.9	7.7	2.0		0.9	-15.8	54	($2)
Type Power	05 ATL *	5	6	3	82	77	5.16	1.71	300			7.0	37%	70%	5.52				4.5	8.5	1.9		0.9	-9.2	59	$2
Reliability 0	06 ATL	4	1	1	56	46	3.68	1.51	251	181	312	3.5	31%	75%	4.14	47	20	33	5.1	7.4	1.4	4%	0.3	5.6	70	$5
DL 37	1st Half	1	1	1	23	12	4.66	1.68	234			3.7	27%	69%	5.68	47	19	34	7.4	4.7	0.6	0%	0.0	-0.5	49	$0
ERA Potl 50%	2nd Half	3	0	0	33	34	3.00	1.39	262			3.4	34%	80%	3.24	47	20	32	3.5	9.3	2.6	7%	0.5	6.1	97	$4
LIMA Plan B	07 Proj	3	2	0	44	38	4.55	1.61	277			4.9	34%	72%	4.01	47	20	33	4.8	7.9	1.7	7%	0.6	1.9	63	$2

Reasons for pessimism: S% and hr/f indicate that ERA is going up; Ctl continues to rise; gets lit up by RHers (.312 BA, .835 OPS). He eats up LHers, so expect him to spot pitch vs individual lefties.

McCarthy,Brandon

McCarthy,Brandon	Yr	W	L	Sv	IP	K	ERA	WHIP	OBA	vL	vR	BF/G	H%	S%	xERA	G	L	F	Ctl	Dom	Cmd	hr/f	hr/9	RAR	BPV	R$
RH Reliever	02	0	0	0	0	0	0.00	0.00											0.0	0.0						
Age 23	03	0	0	0	0	0	0.00	0.00											0.0	0.0						
Growth	04 aa	3	1	0	26	25	4.15	1.31	262			27.5	32%	71%	4.12				2.8	8.7	3.1		1.0	0.6	89	$3
Type Power	05 CHW *	10	9	0	186	165	4.31	1.19	249	182	276	23.9	28%	70%	3.46	35	23	42	2.3	8.0	3.5	14%	1.5	1.5	79	$18
Reliability 10	06 CHW	4	7	0	84	69	4.70	1.31	245	197	270	6.7	26%	71%	4.00	38	15	47	3.5	7.4	2.1	15%	1.8	-1.5	40	$7
DL	1st Half	3	4	0	39	26	4.37	1.30	256			6.6	29%	68%	4.21	41	15	44	3.0	6.0	2.0	7%	0.9	0.9	54	$4
ERA Potl 45%	2nd Half	1	3	0	45	43	4.99	1.31	235			6.8	24%	74%	3.83	36	15	49	4.0	8.6	2.2	21%	2.6	-2.4	27	$3
LIMA Plan C+	07 Proj	8	11	0	166	142	4.55	1.30	252			24.1	29%	70%	3.85	38	17	46	3.1	7.7	2.5	12%	1.5	13.0	59	$13

The devil in the fly ball... His slight tendency towards flies (47% is not horrible) gets exacerbated by exorbitant 15% rate at which they go yard. That rate should regress but hasn't in two years. Bid cautiously.

McClung,Seth

McClung,Seth	Yr	W	L	Sv	IP	K	ERA	WHIP	OBA	vL	vR	BF/G	H%	S%	xERA	G	L	F	Ctl	Dom	Cmd	hr/f	hr/9	RAR	BPV	R$
RH Reliever	02 aa	5	7	0	114	54	6.71	1.88	332			27.3	35%	64%	6.60				4.3	4.3	1.0		1.0	-34.3	4	($7)
Age 26	03 TAM	4	1	0	39	25	5.31	1.49	231			14.3	24%	67%	4.52				5.8	5.8	1.0		1.4	-3.8	23	$2
Growth	04 a/a	3	2	0	27	19	5.00	1.37	240			8.3	26%	67%	4.28				4.3	6.3	1.5		1.3	-2.2	36	$2
Type Power	05 TAM *	9	11	0	127	108	6.23	1.54	265	294	197	14.2	30%	62%	4.36	37	21	42	4.7	7.6	1.6	13%	1.5	-29.1	37	$3
Reliability 17	06 TAM	6	12	6	103	59	6.29	1.83	292	299	289	12.5	31%	67%	5.68	37	20	43	5.9	5.2	0.9	9%	1.2	-22.0	9	($0)
DL	1st Half	2	10	0	80	38	6.85	1.81	302			25.3	31%	63%	5.61	39	20	40	5.3	4.3	0.8	10%	1.3	-22.6	-3	($4)
ERA Potl 50%	2nd Half	4	2	6	23	21	4.34	1.89	255			4.6	32%	78%	5.94	28	18	54	8.3	8.3	1.0	6%	0.8	0.6	51	$4
LIMA Plan D	07 Proj	6	5	8	58	42	5.59	1.69	272			5.0	30%	69%	5.22	34	20	46	5.7	6.5	1.1	9%	1.2	-5.3	26	$4

Fared better as RP (4.43 ERA) than SP (6.81). Unbelievable that a team would give this skill set the ball with a game on the line in the 9th inning... 7 times. And he saved six! Dumb luck may live for him, but not for you.

McGowan,Dustin

McGowan,Dustin	Yr	W	L	Sv	IP	K	ERA	WHIP	OBA	vL	vR	BF/G	H%	S%	xERA	G	L	F	Ctl	Dom	Cmd	hr/f	hr/9	RAR	BPV	R$
RH Reliever	02	0	0	0	0	0	0.00	0.00											0.0	0.0						
Age 25	03 aa	7	0	0	76	63	3.78	1.42	293			23.6	37%	71%	3.96				2.2	7.4	3.3		0.1	5.8	107	$7
Growth	04 aa	2	1	0	31	25	6.10	1.52	255			22.9	28%	63%	5.23				4.9	7.3	1.5		1.7	-6.7	26	$1
Type Power	05 TOR *	1	5	0	80	62	5.91	1.54	297	243	301	18.8	33%	66%	3.85	47	17	36	3.2	7.0	2.2	18%	1.8	-15.2	29	($0)
Reliability 0	06 TOR *	5	7	1	111	96	6.32	1.76	292	327	283	13.3	35%	64%	4.32	43	26	31	5.4	7.8	1.4	10%	0.9	-24.1	47	($0)
DL	1st Half	3	3	0	52	53	6.35	1.81	312			12.4	38%	67%	4.14	28	39	33	4.8	9.1	1.9	15%	1.4	-11.6	46	($0)
ERA Potl 65%	2nd Half	2	4	1	59	43	6.29	1.72	272			14.3	33%	61%	4.67	47	23	31	6.0	6.6	1.1	5%	0.5	-12.5	49	($1)
LIMA Plan C+	07 Proj	4	5	0	94	77	5.49	1.58	277			16.2	32%	67%	4.02	47	20	33	4.5	7.4	1.6	13%	1.2	5.4	44	$2

1-2, 7.24 ERA in 27 IP at TOR. Hurt by S%, H% and LD%, but it's not all bad luck. High Ctl didn't help. Skills are there, but haven't yet appeared in the majors. Consider this a long-term investment.

Meadows,Brian

Meadows,Brian	Yr	W	L	Sv	IP	K	ERA	WHIP	OBA	vL	vR	BF/G	H%	S%	xERA	G	L	F	Ctl	Dom	Cmd	hr/f	hr/9	RAR	BPV	R$
RH Reliever	02 PIT *	10	14	0	188	112	4.88	1.37	291	267	248	23.7	32%	66%	4.03	42	19	38	1.9	5.4	2.8	9%	1.1	-18.0	56	$8
Age 31	03 PIT *	9	1	1	127	70	3.61	1.12	268	276	299	11.9	30%	69%	3.40	51	17	32	0.8	5.0	6.4	7%	0.7	10.4	144	$14
Peak	04 PIT	2	4	1	78	46	3.58	1.22	257	226	275	4.7	28%	73%	3.53	52	19	29	2.2	5.3	2.4	10%	0.8	6.6	62	$6
Type Finesse	05 PIT	3	1	0	74	44	4.61	1.42	286	301	279	4.9	32%	69%	4.03	45	21	34	2.5	5.3	2.1	9%	1.0	-3.3	45	$3
Reliability 33	06 TAM	3	6	8	69	35	5.20	1.52	316	254	361	5.8	32%	71%	4.58	38	18	44	2.0	4.6	2.3	13%	1.8	-5.5	14	$4
DL	1st Half	2	1	3	32	17	4.49	1.46	312			5.9	33%	72%	4.28	38	23	38	1.7	4.8	2.8	9%	1.1	0.3	47	$3
ERA Potl 40%	2nd Half	1	5	0	37	18	5.82	1.56	319			5.7	31%	71%	4.84	38	13	49	2.2	4.4	2.0	15%	2.4	-5.8	-13	$1
LIMA Plan C+	07 Proj	3	4	3	69	37	4.73	1.43	298			5.7	31%	71%	4.25	42	18	39	2.1	4.9	2.3	12%	1.4	2.0	30	$4

The poster boy for good CMD not being enough. The tipping point to success with these BPIs is a 5.6 DOM, and that seems unlikely. GB% and FB% are heading in the wrong direction too. Lots of reasons to avoid.

DAVE ADLER

Meche,Gil

Meche,Gil		W	L	Sv	IP	K	ERA	WHIP	OBA	vL	vR	BF/G	H%	S%	xERA	G	L	F	Ctl	Dom	Cmd	hr/f	hr/9	RAR	BPV	R$
RH Starter	02 aa	4	6	0	65	46	9.14	1.86	319			12.4	36%	49%	6.54				4.8	6.4	1.3		1.2	-39.0	20	($6)
Age 28	03 SEA	15	13	0	186	130	4.60	1.34	263	275	248	24.8	28%	70%	4.16	38	18	43	3.0	6.3	2.1	12%	1.5	-1.7	40	$15
Pre-Peak	04 SEA *	8	10	0	184	140	5.23	1.50	279	269	278	24.7	31%	68%	4.36	37	19	44	3.7	6.8	1.9	11%	1.4	-18.1	37	$6
Type Power	05 SEA	10	8	0	143	83	5.09	1.57	275	266	285	22.2	30%	70%	4.91	40	20	40	4.5	5.2	1.2	9%	1.1	-12.8	22	$4
Reliability 51	06 SEA	11	8	0	186	156	4.50	1.43	258	240	271	25.3	30%	72%	3.96	43	18	38	4.1	7.5	1.9	11%	1.2	1.4	53	$14
DL 27	1st Half	7	4	0	91	75	3.95	1.38	251			26.1	29%	75%	4.05	41	17	42	4.0	7.4	1.9	10%	1.1	6.8	56	$9
ERA Potl 50%	2nd Half	4	4	0	95	81	5.02	1.48	266			24.6	31%	69%	3.88	45	20	35	4.2	7.7	1.8	13%	1.2	-5.4	50	$5
LIMA Plan D+	07 Proj	11	10	0	189	153	4.44	1.44	258			24.9	30%	72%	4.09	41	19	40	4.1	7.3	1.8	11%	1.2	9.3	49	$13

Signs of life:
- Improved DOM
- Declining FB rate
- xERA below 4.00
- 50% PQS dominant starts

Ctl 4.7 on road. If he solves that, he could take the next step.

Medders,Brandon

Medders,Brandon		W	L	Sv	IP	K	ERA	WHIP	OBA	vL	vR	BF/G	H%	S%	xERA	G	L	F	Ctl	Dom	Cmd	hr/f	hr/9	RAR	BPV	R$
RH Reliever	02	0	0	0	0	0	0.00	0.00											0.0	0.0						
Age 27	03 aa	5	3	7	69	61	5.10	1.43	276			5.4	35%	62%	4.02				3.2	8.0	2.5		0.4	-6.0	87	$7
Growth	04 aaa	0	0	0	13	15	4.85	1.69	304			5.5	38%	79%	6.66				4.2	10.4	2.5		2.1	-0.8	47	$0
Type Power	05 ARI *	7	3	8	66	71	2.33	1.25	225	239	161	4.4	30%	84%	3.23	44	19	37	3.8	9.6	2.5	8%	0.7	15.7	100	$13
Reliability 0	06 ARI	5	3	0	71	47	3.67	1.46	275	348	196	5.2	32%	76%	4.33	42	20	38	3.5	5.9	1.7	6%	0.6	7.2	52	$5
DL 23	1st Half	1	2	0	34	22	3.44	1.65	310			5.5	36%	80%	4.33	45	22	33	3.4	5.8	1.7	5%	0.5	4.4	48	$1
ERA Potl 50%	2nd Half	4	1	0	37	25	3.87	1.29	239			4.9	27%	71%	4.32	39	18	43	3.6	6.0	1.7	6%	0.7	2.8	57	$4
LIMA Plan B	07 Proj	5	2	0	58	49	3.41	1.36	255			4.9	31%	76%	3.84	42	20	38	3.6	7.6	2.1	6%	0.6	3.8	76	$6

ERA rose as expected, and xERA says it may not stop there. Large DOM drop suggests his early season sore shoulder never really got better. With his injury history, this raises a red flag for '07.

Meredith,Cla

Meredith,Cla		W	L	Sv	IP	K	ERA	WHIP	OBA	vL	vR	BF/G	H%	S%	xERA	G	L	F	Ctl	Dom	Cmd	hr/f	hr/9	RAR	BPV	R$
RH Reliever	02	0	0	0	0	0	0.00	0.00																		
Age 23	03	0	0	0	0	0	0.00	0.00																		
Growth	04	0	0	0	0	0	0.00	0.00																		
Type	05 a/a	3	5	19	61	46	5.16	1.46	300			5.2	35%	65%	4.89				2.2	6.8	3.1		0.9	-6.4	73	$8
Reliability 0	06 SD *	8	1	2	96	70	1.96	0.96	221	281	107	4.8	26%	83%	2.18	69	16	15	1.4	6.5	4.7	14%	0.6	29.9	131	$18
DL	1st Half	4	0	2	47	34	2.87	1.17	258			5.8	30%	77%					1.7	6.5	3.8		0.6	9.4	105	$7
ERA Potl 45%	2nd Half	4	1	0	49	36	1.10	0.75	183			4.1	21%	91%	1.99	69	16	15	1.1	6.6	6.0	15%	0.5	20.6	168	$11
LIMA Plan A	07 Proj	4	2	0	58	43	3.10	1.14	252			4.9	30%	74%	2.32	69	16	15	1.7	6.7	3.9	15%	0.6	14.6	108	$7

5-1, 1.07 ERA in 50 IP at SD. Low H%, high S% say ERA will rise, but BPV is very real. With extreme GB% and superb Ctl, should find continued success. Not too many Grade-A LIMA picks out there; grab him.

Mesa,Jose

Mesa,Jose		W	L	Sv	IP	K	ERA	WHIP	OBA	vL	vR	BF/G	H%	S%	xERA	G	L	F	Ctl	Dom	Cmd	hr/f	hr/9	RAR	BPV	R$
RH Reliever	02 PHI	4	6	45	75	64	3.00	1.39	235	225	237	4.4	29%	80%	4.13	41	19	40	4.7	7.7	1.6	6%	0.6	10.2	71	$21
Age 40	03 PHI	5	7	24	58	45	6.52	1.76	303	213	349	4.4	35%	63%	4.41	45	21	34	4.8	7.0	1.5	11%	1.1	-16.0	34	$7
Decline	04 PIT	5	2	43	69	37	3.26	1.42	286	331	255	4.3	31%	79%	4.27	46	17	37	2.6	4.8	1.9	7%	0.8	8.6	42	$18
Type	05 PIT	2	8	27	56	37	4.80	1.55	278	309	265	4.6	31%	71%	4.55	43	18	40	4.2	5.9	1.4	10%	1.1	-3.9	31	$10
Reliability 34	06 COL	1	5	1	72	39	3.87	1.51	264	270	271	4.0	28%	78%	4.72	46	17	37	4.5	4.9	1.1	10%	1.1	5.5	20	$2
DL	1st Half	0	2	1	36	24	3.23	1.35	266			3.7	31%	77%	4.02	46	18	37	3.0	6.0	2.0	5%	0.5	5.6	65	$2
ERA Potl 35%	2nd Half	1	3	0	36	15	4.51	1.67	262			4.5	25%	79%	5.51	47	16	37	6.0	3.8	0.6	15%	1.8	-0.1	-14	($0)
LIMA Plan C	07 Proj	2	5	1	58	34	4.81	1.57	278			4.3	30%	71%	4.68	45	17	38	4.3	5.3	1.2	10%	1.1	-2.3	24	$1

Reasons he'll crash in 2007:
- Rising xERA trend
- Declining DOM and CMD
- 2nd half skills debacle
- Age 40

DN: ERA over 5.00

Messenger,Randy

Messenger,Randy		W	L	Sv	IP	K	ERA	WHIP	OBA	vL	vR	BF/G	H%	S%	xERA	G	L	F	Ctl	Dom	Cmd	hr/f	hr/9	RAR	BPV	R$
RH Reliever	02	0	0	0	0	0	0.00	0.00																		
Age 25	03	0	0	0	0	0	0.00	0.00																		
Growth	04 aa	6	3	21	69	62	3.08	1.56	284			5.4	35%	81%	4.61				4.0	8.1	2.0		0.5	10.7	73	$13
Type	05 aaa	4	2	7	48	32	3.73	1.29	253			5.2	29%	72%	3.66				3.0	6.0	2.0		0.7	3.4	60	$7
Reliability 5	06 FLA	2	7	0	60	45	5.69	1.60	298	333	267	4.6	34%	66%	4.44	38	19	43	3.6	6.7	1.9	9%	1.2	-8.9	39	$0
DL	1st Half	1	3	0	28	23	3.19	1.21	253			4.5	31%	75%	3.69	40	16	44	2.2	7.3	3.3	5%	0.6	4.5	98	$3
ERA Potl 55%	2nd Half	1	4	0	32	22	7.90	1.94	333			4.7	36%	61%	5.16	37	21	42	4.8	6.2	1.3	13%	1.7	-13.4	2	($3)
LIMA Plan C+	07 Proj	3	3	0	44	32	4.55	1.43	268			4.8	31%	70%	4.28	38	19	43	3.5	6.6	1.9	9%	1.0	0.5	50	$3

Collapsed in the second half. High H%, low S% and unlucky hr/f had something to do with it, but he also lost sight of home plate. Risky until he shows he can adjust and stay consistent over a full season.

Miceli,Dan

Miceli,Dan		W	L	Sv	IP	K	ERA	WHIP	OBA	vL	vR	BF/G	H%	S%	xERA	G	L	F	Ctl	Dom	Cmd	hr/f	hr/9	RAR	BPV	R$
RH Reliever	02 TEX	0	2	0	8	5	9.00	2.00	366			4.4	41%	53%	3.86	67	9	24	3.4	5.6	1.7	14%	1.1	-4.5	17	($1)
Age 36	03 2TM	2	4	1	70	58	3.21	1.20	230	194	244	5.1	25%	83%	3.72	38	19	43	3.2	7.5	2.3	15%	1.7	10.2	52	$7
Decline	04 HOU	6	6	2	78	83	3.58	1.29	252	307	188	4.4	32%	77%	3.25	44	16	41	3.1	9.6	3.1	12%	1.2	6.6	92	$9
Type Power	05 COL	1	2	0	18	19	6.00	1.78	272	303	243	4.5	36%	65%	4.29	39	27	33	6.5	9.5	1.5	6%	0.5	-3.9	73	($0)
Reliability 0	06 TAM	1	2	4	32	18	3.94	1.41	217	130	295	4.2	23%	76%	5.11	42	13	44	5.6	5.1	0.9	9%	1.1	2.4	27	$3
DL 93	1st Half	0	1	4	12	5	6.64	1.80	242			4.1	19%	72%	6.77	37	15	49	8.1	3.7	0.5	20%	3.0	-3.1	-50	$0
ERA Potl 35%	2nd Half	1	1	0	20	13	2.27	1.16	200			4.3	25%	78%	4.21	47	12	41	4.1	5.9	1.4	0%	0.0	5.6	81	$3
LIMA Plan C+	07 Proj	1	2	0	29	21	4.34	1.55	262			5.0	30%	74%	4.64	41	19	40	5.0	6.5	1.3	8%	0.9	-0.6	41	$1

Got a chance to close, then sore shoulder ruined things. 2nd half is a better indicator of skills. Still, DOM was way down, raising more health concerns. Unless that rebounds, be very cautious.

Miller,Matt

Miller,Matt		W	L	Sv	IP	K	ERA	WHIP	OBA	vL	vR	BF/G	H%	S%	xERA	G	L	F	Ctl	Dom	Cmd	hr/f	hr/9	RAR	BPV	R$
RH Reliever	02 aaa	3	7	6	71	49	4.69	1.69	315			6.1	37%	72%	5.34				3.5	6.2	1.8		0.5	-3.7	51	$3
Age 35	03 aaa	5	0	3	63	68	3.00	1.32	249			4.4	35%	75%	2.96				3.4	9.7	2.8		0.0	10.8	123	$9
Past Peak	04 CLE *	5	3	3	69	69	2.87	1.20	217	255	201	4.1	30%	74%	2.96	53	20	27	3.8	9.0	2.4	2%	0.1	13.4	112	$10
Type Power	05 CLE *	1	0	4	39	35	1.62	0.95	185	194	221	4.8	24%	83%	2.63	60	15	26	2.8	8.1	2.9	4%	0.2	13.4	121	$8
Reliability 0	06 CLE	1	0	0	15	12	3.55	1.32	204	250	188	4.6	23%	78%	3.87	55	12	33	5.3	7.1	1.3	14%	1.2	1.9	49	$2
DL 139 77	1st Half	0	0	0	8	8	5.63	1.50	237			5.9	26%	70%	3.84	50	10	40	5.6	9.0	1.6	23%	2.3	-1.1	28	$0
ERA Potl 45%	2nd Half	1	0	0	7	4	1.25	1.11	165			3.6	20%	88%	3.94	59	14	27	5.0	5.0	1.0	0%	0.0	2.9	73	$2
LIMA Plan A	07 Proj	3	1	0	58	53	3.10	1.22	234			4.6	29%	76%	3.04	57	14	29	3.3	8.2	2.5	9%	0.6	10.3	92	$7

Elbow surgery in April wiped out his season. Seemed healthy in Sept return. Prior three seasons say he's a superb LIMA pick, and will likely be off everyone's radar. $1 bid could net $8-$10 in value.

Miller,Trever

Miller,Trever		W	L	Sv	IP	K	ERA	WHIP	OBA	vL	vR	BF/G	H%	S%	xERA	G	L	F	Ctl	Dom	Cmd	hr/f	hr/9	RAR	BPV	R$
LH Reliever	02 aaa	9	5	0	82	61	3.84	1.38	280			5.4	33%	74%	4.27				2.5	6.7	2.7		0.8	4.3	72	$8
Age 33	03 TOR	2	2	4	52	44	4.67	1.42	239	226	237	2.9	28%	70%	4.18	41	19	40	4.8	7.6	1.6	12%	1.2	-1.0	50	$4
Past Peak	04 TAM	1	1	1	49	43	3.12	1.29	258	214	303	3.4	32%	77%	3.13	53	17	29	2.8	7.9	2.9	7%	0.6	7.9	94	$5
Type Power	05 TAM	2	2	0	44	35	4.08	1.68	266	267	289	3.3	31%	77%	4.69	40	25	35	5.9	7.1	1.2	9%	0.8	1.6	46	$2
Reliability 5	06 HOU	2	3	1	50	56	3.05	1.10	229	224	225	2.9	29%	79%	3.13	33	18	49	2.3	10.0	4.3	11%	1.3	8.9	122	$7
DL 23 15	1st Half	0	2	0	22	25	4.09	1.41	270			3.4	33%	81%	3.56	33	15	52	3.3	10.2	3.1	16%	2.0	1.1	67	$1
ERA Potl 50%	2nd Half	2	1	1	28	31	2.23	0.85	193			2.5	26%	77%	2.81	32	21	47	1.6	9.9	6.2	6%	0.6	7.8	187	$6
LIMA Plan B+	07 Proj	2	2	0	44	42	3.31	1.29	246			3.1	30%	78%	3.55	39	20	41	3.3	8.7	2.6	10%	1.0	4.4	82	$4

April Ctl was 7.4 and resulted in 12.27 ERA. Superb after that. Problem is, these Ctl lapses keep happening. We're left to choose between low reliability and potentially elite BPV. High risk/high reward.

Miller,Wade

Miller,Wade		W	L	Sv	IP	K	ERA	WHIP	OBA	vL	vR	BF/G	H%	S%	xERA	G	L	F	Ctl	Dom	Cmd	hr/f	hr/9	RAR	BPV	R$
RH Starter	02 HOU *	15	4	0	172	152	3.30	1.31	252	254	245	26.0	31%	77%	3.57	43	21	36	3.3	8.0	2.4	8%	0.7	17.2	81	$19
Age 30	03 HOU	14	13	0	187	161	4.14	1.31	242	258	227	24.0	29%	70%	3.64	44	21	35	3.7	7.7	2.1	9%	0.8	3.2	73	$17
Peak	04 HOU	7	7	0	88	74	3.37	1.36	234	212	242	25.2	27%	80%	4.25	38	16	46	4.5	7.6	1.7	10%	1.1	9.7	55	$9
Type Power	05 BOS	4	4	0	91	64	4.95	1.57	272	255	282	25.5	31%	69%	4.35	44	24	32	4.6	6.3	1.4	9%	0.8	-6.4	43	$2
Reliability 0	06 CHC	0	2	0	21	20	4.67	1.75	241	273	184	19.8	27%	79%	5.28	32	18	50	7.6	8.5	1.1	14%	1.7	-0.5	30	($0)
DL 153 90	1st Half	0	0	0	0	0	0.00	0.00																		
ERA Potl 40%	2nd Half	0	2	0	21	20	4.67	1.75	241			19.8	27%	79%	5.28	32	18	50	7.6	8.5	1.1	14%	1.7	-0.5	30	($0)
LIMA Plan D+	07 Proj	6	8	0	116	99	4.34	1.46	246			23.1	29%	73%	4.26	39	20	42	4.8	7.7	1.6	11%	1.2	1.5	50	$7

Showed rust in Sept return from shoulder surgery. However, skills were eroding prior to his injury. Very risky until we see what his post-surgery skill level looks like.

HAROLD NICHOLS

Millwood,Kevin

	Yr	Tm	W	L	Sv	IP	K	ERA	WHIP	OBA	vL	vR	BF/G	H%	S%	xERA	G	L	F	Ctl	Dom	Cmd	hr/f	hr/9	RAR	BPV	R$
RH Starter	02	ATL	18	8	0	217	178	3.24	1.16	233	246	215	25.3	28%	74%	3.47	44	19	37	2.7	7.4	2.7	7%	0.7	23.3	90	$26
Age 32	03	PHI	14	12	0	222	169	4.01	1.25	251	246	253	26.5	29%	69%	3.85	40	19	41	2.8	6.9	2.5	7%	0.8	7.3	75	$19
Peak	04	PHI	9	6	0	141	125	4.85	1.46	280	309	250	24.7	34%	68%	3.74	42	21	37	3.3	8.0	2.5	9%	0.9	-10.2	71	$7
Type	05	CLE	9	11	0	192	146	2.86	1.22	252	269	227	26.5	29%	81%	3.44	46	21	33	2.4	6.8	2.8	10%	0.9	35.8	77	$21
Reliability 85	06	TEX	16	12	0	215	157	4.52	1.31	273	285	258	26.7	31%	67%	3.60	45	21	34	2.2	6.6	3.0	10%	1.0	1.0	73	$20
DL 20	1st Half		8	4	0	106	75	4.49	1.38	294			26.9	34%	69%	3.64	44	23	33	1.9	6.4	3.4	9%	0.8	0.9	80	$9
ERA Potl 60%	2nd Half		8	8	0	109	82	4.55	1.23	251			26.6	29%	65%	3.56	45	19	36	2.6	6.8	2.6	11%	1.1	0.1	69	$11
LIMA Plan C	07	Proj	13	11	0	203	156	4.08	1.29	264			25.9	31%	71%	3.59	44	21	35	2.5	6.9	2.7	10%	0.9	22.5	73	$19

Drastic home/road splits:

	ERA	Dom	Cmd
Home	5.38	5.7	2.0
Road	3.74	7.3	4.4

TEX hurts, but xERA, 59% PQS DOM show upside. If S% drops: UP: sub-3.60 ERA

Milton,Eric

	Yr	Tm	W	L	Sv	IP	K	ERA	WHIP	OBA	vL	vR	BF/G	H%	S%	xERA	G	L	F	Ctl	Dom	Cmd	hr/f	hr/9	RAR	BPV	R$
LH Starter	02	MIN	13	9	0	171	121	4.84	1.19	264	306	249	24.2	29%	62%	4.01	33	16	51	1.6	6.4	4.0	9%	1.3	-8.1	87	$15
Age 31	03	MIN	1	0	0	17	7	2.65	0.94	238	389	174	21.9	24%	79%	4.42	27	15	58	0.5	3.7	7.0	6%	1.1	3.9	145	$3
Peak	04	PHI	14	6	0	201	161	4.75	1.35	257	252	256	25.2	27%	72%	4.30	30	18	52	3.4	7.2	2.1	14%	1.9	-12.0	34	$13
Type	05	CIN	8	15	0	186	123	6.48	1.55	311	284	307	24.5	33%	62%	4.50	33	21	46	2.5	5.9	2.4	14%	1.9	-51.3	20	($2)
Reliability 80	06	CIN	8	8	0	152	90	5.20	1.35	275	216	286	25.0	28%	66%	4.57	31	19	50	2.5	5.3	2.1	11%	1.7	-13.4	25	$7
DL 28	1st Half		4	4	0	68	41	5.15	1.29	275			26.1	28%	65%	4.39	30	20	50	2.0	5.4	2.7	12%	1.7	-5.6	38	$4
ERA Potl 45%	2nd Half		4	4	0	84	49	5.24	1.39	275			24.2	28%	67%	4.72	32	18	50	2.9	5.2	1.8	11%	1.7	-7.8	18	$3
LIMA Plan C	07	Proj	10	10	0	185	120	5.41	1.38	281			24.8	29%	66%	4.47	31	19	50	2.5	5.9	2.3	12%	1.8	-2.5	30	$7

Hr/9 same both home and away, so it's not just the CIN park. Gopheritis remains, and DOM is falling. There's nothing here that suggests his ERA is coming down anytime soon.

Miner,Zach

	Yr	Tm	W	L	Sv	IP	K	ERA	WHIP	OBA	vL	vR	BF/G	H%	S%	xERA	G	L	F	Ctl	Dom	Cmd	hr/f	hr/9	RAR	BPV	R$
RH Reliever	02		0	0	0	0	0	0.00	0.00																		
Age 25	03		0	0	0	0	0	0.00	0.00																		
Growth	04	aa	6	10	0	129	96	6.55	1.61	297			21.7	34%	59%	5.49				3.8	6.7	1.8		1.1	-35.2	40	($1)
Type	05	a/a	5	9	1	140	87	4.88	1.73	305			24.2	34%	72%	5.56				4.5	5.6	1.2		0.8	-10.0	31	($0)
Reliability 1	06	DET *	13	6	0	144	94	4.44	1.42	271	320	245	17.3	31%	70%	3.98	47	21	32	3.3	5.9	1.8	9%	0.8	2.1	49	$12
DL	1st Half		10	1	0	82	53	3.29	1.34	257			25.0	30%	76%	4.11	47	16	38	3.3	5.8	1.8	5%	0.5	12.9	59	$11
ERA Potl 50%	2nd Half		3	5	0	62	41	5.96	1.52	289			12.5	32%	62%	3.94	47	23	29	3.3	6.0	1.8	13%	1.2	-10.7	35	$1
LIMA Plan C+	07	Proj	5	5	0	87	57	4.86	1.48	279			18.2	31%	68%	4.03	47	22	31	3.5	5.9	1.7	10%	0.9	4.9	42	$4

7-6, 4.84 ERA in 93 IP at DET
Starter or reliever? You decide.

	ERA	Dom	hr/9
Start	5.31	5.1	1.1
Rel	2.03	8.8	0.7

Could have real value as skills mature.

Mitre,Sergio

	Yr	Tm	W	L	Sv	IP	K	ERA	WHIP	OBA	vL	vR	BF/G	H%	S%	xERA	G	L	F	Ctl	Dom	Cmd	hr/f	hr/9	RAR	BPV	R$
RH Reliever	02		0	0	0	0	0	0.00	0.00											0.0	0.0						
Age 26	03	aa	7	9	0	145	113	4.34	1.62	318			26.4	38%	72%	5.16				2.7	7.0	2.6		0.4	1.0	74	$5
Growth	04	CHC *	8	7	1	153	122	4.28	1.51	286	408	261	22.6	34%	73%	3.32	59	16	25	3.4	7.2	2.1	12%	0.9	-0.4	59	$8
Type Power	05	CHC *	7	11	0	130	85	5.04	1.42	276	294	235	16.6	31%	66%	3.22	66	11	22	3.1	5.9	1.9	17%	1.1	-12.8	42	$5
Reliability 0	06	FLA	1	5	0	41	31	5.71	1.56	276	344	232	12.2	30%	67%	3.83	52	20	28	4.4	6.8	1.6	20%	1.5	-6.2	27	($0)
DL 88	1st Half		1	4	0	35	28	4.89	1.49	283			22.0	32%	72%	3.48	51	21	28	3.3	7.2	2.2	20%	1.5	-1.7	41	$1
ERA Potl 55%	2nd Half		0	1	0	6	3	10.50	2.00	228			3.7	22%	45%	6.56	56	17	28	10.5	4.5	0.4	19%	1.5	-4.4	0	($1)
LIMA Plan D+	07	Proj	5	8	0	104	80	4.59	1.41	271			21.5	31%	69%	3.36	57	16	26	3.3	6.9	2.1	13%	1.0	12.9	58	$5

Pitched well in seven April starts before sore shoulder derailed him. Complained about 'pen role upon return, which may explain 10.50 relief ERA. Has skills if both health and attitude are positive.

Moehler,Brian

	Yr	Tm	W	L	Sv	IP	K	ERA	WHIP	OBA	vL	vR	BF/G	H%	S%	xERA	G	L	F	Ctl	Dom	Cmd	hr/f	hr/9	RAR	BPV	R$
RH Starter	02	2TM *	5	6	0	87	36	5.38	1.49	317	296	308	22.6	32%	67%	5.79				1.7	3.7	2.3		1.4	-11.9	18	$1
Age 35	03	HOU *	0	0	0	16	8	7.31	1.94	357			19.4	36%	67%	8.33				3.4	4.5	1.3		2.3	-6.0	-29	($2)
Past Peak	04	aa	3	9	0	108	42	5.83	1.63	321			24.6	34%	64%	5.75				2.7	3.5	1.3		0.9	-19.9	12	($3)
Type Finesse	05	FLA	6	12	0	158	95	4.55	1.52	308	320	305	19.0	34%	71%	4.01	44	25	31	2.4	5.4	2.3	9%	0.9	-6.0	46	$4
Reliability 10	06	FLA	7	11	0	122	58	6.57	1.66	323	351	297	19.2	34%	62%	4.51	45	22	33	2.8	4.3	1.5	13%	1.4	-31.3	6	($2)
DL 29	1st Half		5	6	0	77	36	6.43	1.70	326			25.4	34%	63%	4.59	46	22	32	3.0	4.2	1.4	11%	1.2	-18.4	9	($2)
ERA Potl 50%	2nd Half		2	5	0	45	22	6.80	1.58	317			13.5	32%	60%	4.38	43	22	35	2.4	4.4	1.8	16%	1.8	-12.8	2	($1)
LIMA Plan F	07	Proj	3	6	0	73	36	5.83	1.59	317			18.2	34%	65%	4.35	44	23	33	2.5	4.5	1.8	12%	1.2	0.1	19	($1)

DOM/DIS split of 19/52 was actually worse than '05's split of 24/44. Was suspended for scuffing the ball in 1999; even bringing back the sandpaper might not help at this point.

Morris,Matt

	Yr	Tm	W	L	Sv	IP	K	ERA	WHIP	OBA	vL	vR	BF/G	H%	S%	xERA	G	L	F	Ctl	Dom	Cmd	hr/f	hr/9	RAR	BPV	R$
RH Starter	02	STL	17	9	0	210	171	3.43	1.30	262	267	255	27.7	32%	75%	3.38	50	19	31	2.7	7.3	2.7	8%	0.7	17.6	82	$21
Age 32	03	STL	11	8	0	172	120	3.77	1.18	253	255	249	26.1	28%	72%	3.49	47	18	35	2.0	6.3	3.1	11%	1.0	10.8	75	$17
Peak	04	STL	15	10	0	202	131	4.72	1.29	265	259	272	26.6	28%	69%	3.61	51	16	33	2.5	5.8	2.3	17%	1.6	-11.5	39	$14
Type Finesse	05	STL	14	10	0	192	117	4.12	1.28	278	279	273	26.0	31%	71%	3.51	49	21	30	1.7	5.5	3.2	12%	1.0	3.0	68	$15
Reliability 86	06	SF	10	15	0	207	117	5.00	1.36	272	277	261	26.8	30%	64%	4.05	46	21	33	2.7	5.1	1.9	10%	1.0	-13.0	41	$9
DL 15	1st Half		6	7	0	102	59	4.24	1.32	262			27.1	29%	69%	4.16	43	21	36	2.9	5.2	1.8	8%	0.8	3.2	48	$7
ERA Potl 55%	2nd Half		4	8	0	105	58	5.73	1.39	281			26.7	30%	59%	3.94	48	21	31	2.6	5.0	1.9	12%	1.1	-16.1	36	$2
LIMA Plan C	07	Proj	12	12	0	200	113	4.42	1.33	275			26.5	30%	69%	3.87	48	20	32	2.4	5.1	2.1	11%	1.1	12.3	43	$12

DOM continued its 5-year free-fall and has now pushed his CMD below acceptable levels. Bad luck S% pushed his ERA into the stratosphere in '06, but even regressed, he is at best a 4.25-4.50 ERA pitcher now.

Mota,Guillermo

	Yr	Tm	W	L	Sv	IP	K	ERA	WHIP	OBA	vL	vR	BF/G	H%	S%	xERA	G	L	F	Ctl	Dom	Cmd	hr/f	hr/9	RAR	BPV	R$
RH Reliever	02	LA *	2	6	1	96	79	3.75	1.21	230	188	213	6.3	28%	68%	3.85	39	17	43	3.3	7.4	2.3	4%	0.5	4.2	87	$7
Age 33	03	LA	6	3	1	105	99	1.97	0.99	209	181	220	5.4	26%	84%	2.87	46	21	33	2.2	8.5	3.8	8%	0.6	29.9	126	$18
Past Peak	04	2NL	9	8	4	96	85	2.99	1.16	217	196	236	5.0	26%	77%	3.38	47	17	36	3.5	8.0	2.3	9%	0.7	15.0	85	$15
Type Power	05	FLA	2	2	2	67	60	4.70	1.45	256	243	262	5.2	32%	67%	4.03	41	19	41	4.3	8.1	1.9	6%	0.7	-3.8	71	$3
Reliability 24	06	2TM	4	3	0	55	46	4.57	1.43	261	252	261	4.6	29%	75%	4.28	34	18	48	3.9	7.5	1.9	14%	1.8	-0.3	34	$4
DL 32	1st Half		0	3	0	28	22	7.05	1.74	300			5.5	30%	68%	5.12	28	17	55	4.8	7.0	1.5	18%	2.9	-8.8	-18	($2)
ERA Potl 40%	2nd Half		4	0	0	27	24	1.99	1.11	216			3.9	27%	86%	3.41	42	19	39	3.0	8.0	2.7	7%	0.7	8.4	96	$6
LIMA Plan C+	07	Proj	2	1	0	29	23	4.66	1.48	262			4.9	30%	72%	4.34	39	18	43	4.3	7.1	1.6	11%	1.2	0.3	43	$2

Rebounded strongly in 2nd half, but a 50-game suspension to start 2007 likely explains why. If he was a risky play before (and he was), he's doubly so now. Not to mention he's out 50 games.

Moyer,Jamie

	Yr	Tm	W	L	Sv	IP	K	ERA	WHIP	OBA	vL	vR	BF/G	H%	S%	xERA	G	L	F	Ctl	Dom	Cmd	hr/f	hr/9	RAR	BPV	R$
LH Starter	02	SEA	13	8	0	230	147	3.33	1.08	234	276	206	27.0	25%	74%	3.93	38	15	47	2.0	5.8	2.9	9%	1.1	32.1	72	$27
Age 44	03	SEA	21	7	0	215	129	3.27	1.23	247	275	233	27.1	27%	76%	4.30	39	16	45	2.8	5.4	2.0	6%	0.8	33.4	55	$26
Decline	04	SEA	7	13	0	202	125	5.21	1.39	276	293	263	25.6	28%	69%	4.38	39	17	44	2.8	5.6	2.0	15%	2.0	-19.5	16	$7
Type Finesse	05	SEA	13	7	0	200	102	4.28	1.39	285	294	278	26.9	30%	72%	4.48	37	22	41	2.3	4.6	2.0	8%	1.0	2.4	36	$12
Reliability 80	06	2TM	11	14	0	211	108	4.31	1.32	277	251	285	27.1	29%	72%	4.25	40	21	39	2.2	4.6	2.1	12%	1.4	5.6	30	$14
DL	1st Half		5	6	0	105	56	3.51	1.29	273			27.6	29%	76%	4.23	38	22	40	2.1	4.8	2.3	8%	1.0	13.0	47	$9
ERA Potl 40%	2nd Half		6	8	0	106	52	5.09	1.36	281			26.7	28%	68%	4.26	42	19	38	2.3	4.4	1.9	15%	1.8	-7.5	12	$5
LIMA Plan D	07	Proj	8	8	0	145	73	4.84	1.42	289			27.4	30%	70%	4.50	39	20	41	2.5	4.5	1.8	11%	1.4	-1.3	22	$6

Second half shows the razor-thin edge on which a finesse pitcher lives. Jump in hr/f corresponded with trade to PHI. Higher risk than with SEA.
DN: ERA over 5.00.

Mujica,Edward

	Yr	Tm	W	L	Sv	IP	K	ERA	WHIP	OBA	vL	vR	BF/G	H%	S%	xERA	G	L	F	Ctl	Dom	Cmd	hr/f	hr/9	RAR	BPV	R$
RH Reliever	02		0	0	0	0	0	0.00	0.00																		
Age 23	03		0	0	0	0	0	0.00	0.00																		
Growth	04		0	0	0	0	0	0.00	0.00																		
Type	05	aa	2	1	10	34	29	3.43	1.35	299			5.4	37%	75%	4.25				1.3	7.7	5.8		0.5	3.7	147	$6
Reliability 0	06	CLE *	4	2	13	69	53	2.21	1.28	275	324	341	6.6	34%	83%	4.31	26	18	55	1.9	6.9	3.5	2%	0.3	20.1	108	$14
DL	1st Half		4	0	8	40	32	0.00	1.09	219			6.5	28%	100%	3.81	33	22	44	2.7	7.1	2.7	0%	0.0	22.7	110	$12
ERA Potl 40%	2nd Half		0	2	5	29	21	5.29	1.56	340			6.8	40%	65%	4.61	25	18	57	0.9	6.5	7.0	3%	0.6	-2.6	155	$2
LIMA Plan B+	07	Proj	2	2	0	44	34	3.93	1.33	277			6.0	32%	75%	4.37	25	18	57	2.3	7.0	3.1	8%	1.2	0.6	69	$4

0-1, 2.95 ERA in 18 IP with CLE Unlucky H% elevated 2nd half ERA, but look at that BPV. Skills transferred well to majors, and at his age he's only going to get better. Excellent LIMA pick.

HAROLD NICHOLS

Mulder,Mark

Mulder,Mark	Yr	Tm	W	L	Sv	IP	K	ERA	WHIP	OBA	vL	vR	BF/G	H%	S%	xERA	G	L	F	Ctl	Dom	Cmd	hr/f	hr/9	RAR	BPV	R$
LH Starter	02	OAK	19	7	0	207	159	3.48	1.14	238	244	228	28.0	27%	73%	3.29	50	17	33	2.4	6.9	2.9	10%	0.9	25.0	82	$27
Age 29	03	OAK	15	9	0	186	128	3.15	1.18	255	252	260	29.4	29%	76%	3.13	55	18	27	1.9	6.2	3.2	10%	0.7	31.7	86	$24
Peak	04	OAK	17	8	0	225	140	4.44	1.36	260	264	263	29.2	29%	69%	3.67	56	17	27	3.3	5.6	1.7	13%	1.0	-0.1	42	$16
Type Finesse	05	STL	16	8	0	205	111	3.64	1.38	268	201	289	27.5	29%	76%	3.48	61	18	21	3.1	4.9	1.6	13%	0.8	15.2	39	$16
Reliability 48	06	STL	6	7	0	93	50	7.15	1.71	321	241	351	25.3	33%	61%	3.98	55	22	24	3.4	4.8	1.4	24%	1.8	-30.6	-5	($3)
DL 94	1st Half		6	5	0	88	48	6.12	1.55	305			26.3	31%	65%	3.66	56	21	23	2.9	4.9	1.7	26%	1.8	-17.8	4	$1
ERA Potl 50%	2nd Half		0	2	0	5	2	25.71	4.49	520			18.2	54%	38%	11.90	33	33	33	12.9	3.7	0.3	11%	1.8	-12.8	-76	($4)
LIMA Plan D	07	Proj	12	7	0	160	89	4.51	1.45	279			27.9	30%	71%	3.77	56	19	25	3.3	5.0	1.5	14%	1.1	11.6	29	$9

Write this season off to a torn rotator cuff and surgery. But the real question is whether this ailment has been festering for 2 1/2 years. This is not the same pitcher who dominated pre-'04. Wait for post-surgery BPIs.

Mussina,Mike

Mussina,Mike	Yr	Tm	W	L	Sv	IP	K	ERA	WHIP	OBA	vL	vR	BF/G	H%	S%	xERA	G	L	F	Ctl	Dom	Cmd	hr/f	hr/9	RAR	BPV	R$
RH Starter	02	NYY	18	10	0	215	182	4.06	1.19	255	257	248	26.8	30%	69%	3.39	40	21	39	2.0	7.6	3.8	11%	1.1	10.6	95	$25
Age 38	03	NYY	17	8	0	214	195	3.41	1.08	241	229	247	27.6	30%	72%	3.17	38	22	40	1.7	8.2	4.9	9%	0.9	29.5	132	$31
Decline	04	NYY	12	9	0	164	132	4.60	1.33	278	254	299	25.8	32%	68%	3.50	44	21	36	2.2	7.2	3.3	12%	1.2	-3.5	76	$13
Type	05	NYY	13	8	0	179	142	4.42	1.37	283	282	286	25.6	33%	71%	3.62	45	18	37	2.4	7.1	3.0	11%	1.2	-1.1	70	$14
Reliability 60	06	NYY	15	7	0	197	172	3.52	1.11	249	223	258	24.8	30%	72%	3.21	42	17	40	1.6	7.9	4.9	10%	1.0	25.3	125	$28
DL 15	1st Half		9	3	0	112	100	3.29	1.08	238			26.4	28%	75%	3.20	42	16	42	1.8	8.0	4.5	11%	1.1	17.5	117	$17
ERA Potl 55%	2nd Half		6	4	0	85	72	3.81	1.15	262			23.1	31%	69%	3.22	43	19	38	1.4	7.6	5.5	8%	0.8	7.8	139	$11
LIMA Plan C+	07	Proj	14	8	0	189	158	3.87	1.23	263			25.2	31%	72%	3.38	43	19	38	2.0	7.5	3.9	10%	1.1	25.6	97	$21

BPIs said a rebound like this was possible. If he can maintain this CMD level, he could do even better. But at age 38, regression is more likely than a repeat.

Myers,Brett

Myers,Brett	Yr	Tm	W	L	Sv	IP	K	ERA	WHIP	OBA	vL	vR	BF/G	H%	S%	xERA	G	L	F	Ctl	Dom	Cmd	hr/f	hr/9	RAR	BPV	R$
RH Starter	02	PHI	* 13	11	0	200	127	4.19	1.27	266	225	314	27.0	30%	69%	3.56	51	18	31	2.2	5.7	2.6	11%	0.9	-1.9	62	$15
Age 26	03	PHI	14	9	0	193	143	4.43	1.46	274	270	273	26.4	32%	71%	3.74	50	20	30	3.5	6.7	1.9	11%	0.9	-3.6	52	$12
Growth	04	PHI	11	11	0	176	116	5.52	1.47	283	278	293	24.1	30%	66%	3.98	47	19	34	3.2	5.9	1.9	16%	1.6	-27.4	26	$5
Type Power	05	PHI	13	8	0	215	208	3.72	1.21	241	241	233	26.1	29%	75%	3.00	46	23	31	2.8	8.7	3.1	17%	1.3	13.8	84	$22
Reliability 62	06	PHI	12	7	0	198	189	3.91	1.30	258	259	254	26.9	31%	75%	3.27	46	18	36	2.9	8.6	3.0	14%	1.3	14.1	78	$19
DL	1st Half		5	3	0	98	82	3.86	1.43	272			26.6	32%	77%	3.66	47	19	34	3.4	7.5	2.2	13%	1.2	7.6	57	$7
ERA Potl 55%	2nd Half		7	4	0	100	107	3.96	1.17	244			27.3	30%	72%	2.91	44	18	38	2.3	9.6	4.1	16%	1.4	6.5	107	$12
LIMA Plan C+	07	Proj	13	9	0	203	192	3.50	1.22	248			25.5	30%	76%	3.12	46	20	34	2.6	8.5	3.3	14%	1.2	31.2	89	$22

Rough stretches in June and August prevented a full-scale breakout. PQS DOM/DIS of 65/13. Kept skills growth from '05, added more in 2nd half. Potential breakout still looms. UP: 18 wins, 3.00 ERA.

Myers,Mike

Myers,Mike	Yr	Tm	W	L	Sv	IP	K	ERA	WHIP	OBA	vL	vR	BF/G	H%	S%	xERA	G	L	F	Ctl	Dom	Cmd	hr/f	hr/9	RAR	BPV	R$
LH Reliever	02	ARI	4	3	4	37	31	4.38	1.51	272	241	317	2.4	34%	70%	3.35	60	17	23	4.1	7.5	1.8	8%	0.5	-1.2	70	$4
Age 37	03	ARI	0	1	0	36	21	5.75	1.64	272	237	290	2.6	30%	65%	4.33	58	16	26	5.3	5.3	1.0	13%	1.0	-6.5	23	($1)
Decline	04	2AL	5	1	0	42	32	4.69	1.61	274	233	344	2.5	31%	73%	4.22	51	16	33	4.9	6.8	1.4	11%	1.1	-1.4	38	$3
Type	05	BOS	3	1	0	37	21	3.15	1.16	223	158	385	2.3	24%	75%	3.70	50	22	28	3.2	5.1	1.6	10%	0.7	5.6	53	$5
Reliability 3	06	NYY	1	2	0	30	22	3.28	1.29	254	257	224	2.1	29%	78%	3.80	47	14	38	3.0	6.6	2.2	9%	0.9	4.8	63	$3
DL	1st Half		0	0	0	13	11	0.69	1.07	213			1.7	26%	100%	3.23	54	8	38	2.7	7.6	2.8	7%	0.7	6.3	95	$2
ERA Potl 40%	2nd Half		1	2	0	17	11	5.26	1.46	283			2.3	31%	65%	4.25	43	18	38	3.2	5.8	1.8	9%	1.1	-1.5	40	$1
LIMA Plan C+	07	Proj	3	2	0	36	24	4.22	1.38	266			2.4	30%	72%	3.91	49	17	34	3.2	6.0	1.8	10%	1.0	2.6	47	$3

Why his ERA may top 4.00:
- Rising FB%
- Declining 2nd half DOM, CMD, OBA
- Rising BA vs LHers
- Won't repeat 1st half S%

Nathan,Joe

Nathan,Joe	Yr	Tm	W	L	Sv	IP	K	ERA	WHIP	OBA	vL	vR	BF/G	H%	S%	xERA	G	L	F	Ctl	Dom	Cmd	hr/f	hr/9	RAR	BPV	R$
RH Reliever	02	aaa	6	12	0	149	97	6.70	1.83	319			20.2	36%	63%	6.30				4.5	5.9	1.3		1.1	-44.7	21	($7)
Age 32	03	SF	12	4	0	79	83	2.96	1.06	186	276	136	4.0	24%	75%	3.56	28	21	51	3.8	9.5	2.5	7%	0.8	12.8	103	$15
Peak	04	MIN	1	2	44	72	89	1.62	0.98	191	212	160	3.9	28%	85%	2.90	35	16	49	2.9	11.1	3.9	4%	0.4	25.0	153	$28
Type Power	05	MIN	7	4	43	70	94	2.70	0.97	189	160	206	3.9	28%	75%	2.67	37	12	50	2.8	12.1	4.3	7%	0.6	14.4	160	$28
Reliability 74	06	MIN	7	0	36	68	95	1.59	0.79	165	193	130	4.0	27%	82%	2.20	36	22	42	2.1	12.6	5.9	5%	0.4	25.0	210	$29
DL	1st Half		5	0	13	33	47	1.91	0.76	184			4.2	29%	78%	1.98	34	25	41	1.1	12.8	11.8	7%	0.5	10.8	325	$14
ERA Potl 50%	2nd Half		2	0	23	35	48	1.28	0.83	147			3.8	24%	86%	2.42	37	19	44	3.1	12.3	4.0	3%	0.3	14.2	176	$16
LIMA Plan C+	07	Proj	5	2	48	65	85	2.21	0.93	182			4.1	27%	79%	2.63	36	18	46	2.8	11.7	4.3	6%	0.6	14.9	162	$29

Amazing growth trends since 2003. Rising DOM and CMD, improving Ctl, and now falling FB%. 2nd half suggests he may have finally peaked. Limited 1st half save opps, so save total likely to grow.

Nelson,Joe

Nelson,Joe	Yr	Tm	W	L	Sv	IP	K	ERA	WHIP	OBA	vL	vR	BF/G	H%	S%	xERA	G	L	F	Ctl	Dom	Cmd	hr/f	hr/9	RAR	BPV	R$
RH Reliever	02		0	0	0	0	0	0.00	0.00																		
Age 32	03		0	0	0	0	0	0.00	0.00																		
Peak	04	a/a	3	2	13	51	57	4.29	1.71	293			5.8	39%	74%	5.00				4.9	9.9	2.0		0.4	0.3	86	$6
Type Power	05	a/a	0	3	7	59	58	5.14	1.65	273			6.1	32%	74%	5.73				5.3	8.8	1.6		1.7	-6.1	36	$2
Reliability 5	06	KC	* 3	3	16	76	76	3.72	1.27	219	180	252	4.8	27%	75%	3.72	34	23	43	4.3	9.0	2.1	11%	1.1	7.9	76	$13
DL	1st Half		1	2	7	39	37	2.41	1.20	203			5.0	25%	85%	3.90	42	4	54	4.3	8.6	2.0	8%	1.0	10.4	79	$8
ERA Potl 50%	2nd Half		2	1	9	37	39	5.09	1.35	234			4.5	29%	64%	3.65	32	28	40	4.4	9.4	2.2	13%	1.2	-2.5	74	$6
LIMA Plan B	07	Proj	2	2	10	58	59	4.19	1.40	238			5.2	30%	73%	3.86	34	24	42	4.7	9.2	2.0	11%	1.1	4.4	71	$8

9 saves, 4.43 ERA in 44 IP at KC Converted 9 of 10 save opps, but weak Ctl and a history of riding the Triple-A shuttle make him far from a sure thing. Some skills here, but don't overbid.

Neshek,Patrick

Neshek,Patrick	Yr	Tm	W	L	Sv	IP	K	ERA	WHIP	OBA	vL	vR	BF/G	H%	S%	xERA	G	L	F	Ctl	Dom	Cmd	hr/f	hr/9	RAR	BPV	R$
RH Reliever	02		0	0	0	0	0	0.00	0.00																		
Age 26	03		0	0	0	0	0	0.00	0.00																		
Growth	04	aa	2	1	2	35	32	5.40	1.77	298			6.3	37%	68%	5.35				5.1	8.3	1.6		0.5	-4.6	63	$1
Type Power	05	aa	6	4	24	82	75	2.92	1.37	275			6.4	33%	84%	4.47				2.7	8.2	3.1		1.1	14.0	80	$17
Reliability 3	06	MIN	* 10	4	14	97	125	2.65	1.02	219	244	140	5.9	29%	84%	2.80	32	14	54	2.1	11.6	5.5	13%	1.4	22.8	155	$25
DL	1st Half		6	2	13	55	68	2.71	1.18	238			7.3	31%	87%					2.7	11.1	4.1		1.5	12.5	114	$15
ERA Potl 50%	2nd Half		4	2	1	42	57	2.57	0.81	192			4.6	27%	79%	2.37	32	14	54	1.3	12.2	9.5	12%	1.3	10.3	251	$10
LIMA Plan A	07	Proj	5	2	0	58	64	3.41	1.22	248			5.9	32%	78%	3.46	32	14	54	2.6	9.9	3.8	10%	1.2	7.3	107	$8

4-2, 2.19 ERA in 37 IP at MIN Skills transferred well to MLB, with 2nd half growth in DOM and CMD. If he can get high FB% under control, more growth is possible. Great LIMA pick.

Niemann,Jeff

Niemann,Jeff	Yr	Tm	W	L	Sv	IP	K	ERA	WHIP	OBA	vL	vR	BF/G	H%	S%	xERA	G	L	F	Ctl	Dom	Cmd	hr/f	hr/9	RAR	BPV	R$
RH Starter	02		0	0	0	0	0	0.00	0.00																		
Age 24	03		0	0	0	0	0	0.00	0.00																		
Growth	04		0	0	0	0	0	0.00	0.00																		
Type Power	05	aa	0	1	0	10	12	5.40	1.30	199			7.0	30%	54%	2.27				5.4	10.8	2.0		0.0	-1.4	122	$0
Reliability 0	06	aa	5	5	0	77	70	4.09	1.39	252			23.7	31%	73%	4.06				4.0	8.2	2.1		1.0	4.1	68	$7
DL	1st Half		0	2	0	8	11	5.63	1.38	237			17.2	34%	60%					4.5	12.4	2.8		1.1	-1.1	106	$0
ERA Potl 50%	2nd Half		5	3	0	69	59	3.91	1.39	254			24.8	30%	74%					3.9	7.7	2.0		0.9	5.2	63	$6
LIMA Plan C+	07	Proj	2	1	0	29	27	4.66	1.55	275			21.6	34%	71%	4.77				4.3	8.4	1.9		0.9	-1.3	63	$2

Shoulder surgery sidelined him until June. Displayed solid skills upon his return. Needs more time in minors, but could contribute some time in 2007. Sleeper, especially in keeper leagues.

Nieve,Fernando

Nieve,Fernando	Yr	Tm	W	L	Sv	IP	K	ERA	WHIP	OBA	vL	vR	BF/G	H%	S%	xERA	G	L	F	Ctl	Dom	Cmd	hr/f	hr/9	RAR	BPV	R$
RH Reliever	02		0	0	0	0	0	0.00	0.00																		
Age 24	03		0	0	0	0	0	0.00	0.00																		
Growth	04		0	0	0	0	0	0.00	0.00																		
Type Power	05	a/a	8	7	0	167	142	4.58	1.43	273			26.9	32%	70%	4.55				3.3	7.7	2.3		1.0	-5.7	64	$9
Reliability 0	06	HOU	3	3	0	96	70	4.21	1.33	243	262	224	10.2	26%	75%	4.19	41	15	44	3.8	6.6	1.7	14%	1.7	3.2	31	$6
DL 15	1st Half		3	3	0	69	47	4.69	1.30	262			17.2	27%	72%	4.06	40	16	44	2.7	6.1	2.2	16%	2.0	-1.7	28	$4
ERA Potl 40%	2nd Half		0	0	0	27	23	3.00	1.41	191			5.1	22%	83%	4.58	44	13	43	6.7	7.7	1.2	10%	1.0	5.0	57	$2
LIMA Plan C	07	Proj	1	1	0	44	35	4.34	1.40	251			10.4	29%	73%	4.16	42	14	43	4.1	7.2	1.8	11%	1.2	1.1	48	$2

Was a bit stronger after being moved to bullpen in 2nd half, although CMD suffered. Keys to taking next step up: BA vs LH, hr/9, stamina. Keep him on your radar.

HAROLD NICHOLS

Nippert,Dustin		W	L	Sv	IP	K	ERA	WHIP	OBA	vL	vR	BF/G	H%	S%	xERA	G	L	F	Ctl	Dom	Cmd	hr/f	hr/9	RAR	BPV	R$
RH Starter	02	0	0	0	0	0	0.00	0.00																		
Age 26	03	0	0	0	0	0	0.00	0.00																		
Growth	04 aa	2	5	0	71	65	4.30	1.81	306			24.1	40%	74%	5.06				5.1	8.2	1.6		0.0	0.4	77	$0
Type Power	05 aa	8	3	0	117	84	3.07	1.36	258			27.8	31%	77%	3.58				3.4	6.4	1.9		0.4	17.8	70	$11
Reliability 4	06 ARI *	13	10	0	150	123	6.11	1.69	317	333	375	25.7	37%	64%	3.76	56	12	32	3.4	7.4	2.1	11%	1.0	-30.0	50	$2
DL	1st Half	8	4	0	82	65	6.09	1.74	312			25.5	37%	65%	4.76	35	18	47	4.1	7.2	1.8	7%	1.0	-16.2	43	$1
ERA Potl 65%	2nd Half	5	6	0	68	57	6.13	1.64	324			25.9	38%	63%	2.56	76	6	18	2.7	7.6	2.8	20%	1.1	-13.8	64	$1
LIMA Plan B	07 Proj	2	2	0	29	23	4.34	1.52	281			25.7	34%	71%	2.69	81	0	19	3.7	7.1	1.9	12%	0.6	6.0	63	$2

0-2, 11.70 ERA in 10 IP at ARI. High H%, low S% ruined ERA, but there are solid skills here, with 2nd half rebound. Likely must succeed at Triple-A before getting MLB rotation shot, but worth watching.

Nolasco,Ricky		W	L	Sv	IP	K	ERA	WHIP	OBA	vL	vR	BF/G	H%	S%	xERA	G	L	F	Ctl	Dom	Cmd	hr/f	hr/9	RAR	BPV	R$
RH Reliever	02	0	0	0	0	0	0.00	0.00																		
Age 24	03	0	0	0	0	0	0.00	0.00																		
Growth	04 a/a	8	7	0	147	134	5.53	1.57	301			23.6	36%	67%	5.52				3.1	8.2	2.6		1.2	-21.6	62	$4
Type	05 aa	1	3	0	161	152	3.74	1.41	281			25.8	35%	76%	4.53				2.7	8.5	3.1		0.9	11.2	86	$9
Reliability 18	06 FLA	11	11	0	140	99	4.82	1.41	285	338	240	17.3	32%	69%	4.06	39	21	40	2.6	6.4	2.4	11%	1.3	-5.8	48	$9
DL	1st Half	6	4	0	66	48	3.27	1.33	276			14.8	31%	80%	3.81	43	18	39	2.3	6.5	2.8	10%	1.1	9.9	66	$7
ERA Potl 55%	2nd Half	5	7	0	74	51	6.21	1.49	292			20.4	32%	60%	4.28	36	23	41	2.9	6.2	2.1	12%	1.5	-15.7	35	$1
LIMA Plan C+	07 Proj	8	9	0	160	131	4.40	1.38	275			20.8	32%	71%	3.82	38	21	40	2.8	7.4	2.7	11%	1.2	10.8	65	$10

Took a small step back. Strong 1st half partly S% driven; struggled in 2nd half as S% and hr/9 rose, CMD faded. FB ways mean HR issue may linger. Has potential, but 2nd half fade may mean sophomore struggles.

Novoa,Roberto		W	L	Sv	IP	K	ERA	WHIP	OBA	vL	vR	BF/G	H%	S%	xERA	G	L	F	Ctl	Dom	Cmd	hr/f	hr/9	RAR	BPV	R$
RH Reliever	02	0	0	0	0	0	0.00	0.00											0.0	0.0						
Age 27	03	0	0	0	0	0	0.00	0.00											0.0	0.0						
Pre-Peak	04 aa	7	1	4	79	43	3.80	1.22	259			8.0	28%	71%	3.76				2.2	4.9	2.3		0.9	5.3	54	$9
Type Power	05 CHC *	6	7	4	71	63	4.21	1.49	257	221	291	4.6	32%	72%	4.07	38	26	36	4.6	7.9	1.7	7%	0.6	0.3	68	$6
Reliability 23	06 CHC	2	1	0	76	53	4.26	1.43	264	279	255	5.0	28%	78%	4.20	43	18	39	3.8	6.3	1.7	16%	1.8	2.1	21	$3
DL	1st Half	0	0	0	35	26	4.89	1.51	251			6.0	26%	76%	4.65	41	14	45	5.1	6.7	1.3	17%	2.1	-1.7	11	$0
ERA Potl 40%	2nd Half	2	1	0	41	27	3.73	1.37	276			4.4	29%	80%	3.84	44	22	34	2.6	5.9	2.3	15%	1.5	3.8	37	$3
LIMA Plan C+	07 Proj	4	3	0	69	50	4.20	1.43	263			5.1	30%	74%	4.15	41	21	38	3.8	6.6	1.7	11%	1.2	1.8	43	$4

Reigned in problem Ctl in 2nd half, but HR became a problem for the first time. MLEs, hr/f say that issue won't linger, but lucky 2006 S% means it won't show up as a better ERA either. That means expect more of the same.

O'Connor,Mike		W	L	Sv	IP	K	ERA	WHIP	OBA	vL	vR	BF/G	H%	S%	xERA	G	L	F	Ctl	Dom	Cmd	hr/f	hr/9	RAR	BPV	R$
LH Starter	02	0	0	0	0	0	0.00	0.00																		
Age 26	03	0	0	0	0	0	0.00	0.00																		
Growth	04	0	0	0	0	0	0.00	0.00																		
Type	05	0	0	0	0	0	0.00	0.00																		
Reliability 11	06 WAS *	4	8	0	131	83	4.53	1.37	247	253	242	20.8	26%	70%	4.65	36	18	46	4.0	5.7	1.4	10%	1.2	-0.8	33	$6
DL	1st Half	3	4	0	87	63	3.41	1.26	222			22.8	26%	74%	4.36	38	17	45	4.1	6.5	1.6	5%	0.6	11.6	64	$8
ERA Potl 40%	2nd Half	1	4	0	44	20	6.78	1.58	292			17.9	27%	63%	5.24	33	19	48	3.7	4.1	1.1	16%	2.5	-12.4	-29	($2)
LIMA Plan C	07 Proj	3	9	0	121	68	5.23	1.49	274			19.7	28%	69%	4.95	35	18	47	3.9	5.1	1.3	11%	1.6	-8.7	11	$1

3-8, 4.80 ERA in 105 IP at WAS. Evidence that hitters caught on to him (using DOM/DIS):
First 11 starts: 45/0
Next 9 starts: 0/67
2nd half DOM drop also a bad sign. Stay far away.

Ohka,Tomo		W	L	Sv	IP	K	ERA	WHIP	OBA	vL	vR	BF/G	H%	S%	xERA	G	L	F	Ctl	Dom	Cmd	hr/f	hr/9	RAR	BPV	R$
RH Starter	02 MON	13	8	0	192	118	3.19	1.24	264	218	298	25.0	29%	78%	3.78	48	16	36	2.1	5.5	2.6	8%	0.9	21.8	64	$18
Age 31	03 MON	10	12	0	199	118	4.16	1.40	293	311	279	25.3	32%	73%	3.99	45	19	36	2.0	5.3	2.6	10%	1.1	2.9	51	$11
Peak	04 MON	3	7	0	84	38	3.42	1.40	292	278	298	24.3	30%	80%	4.50	42	17	41	2.1	4.1	1.9	9%	1.2	8.7	26	$4
Type Finesse	05 2NL	11	9	0	180	98	4.05	1.35	271	258	277	24.1	29%	73%	4.23	42	22	37	2.7	4.9	1.8	10%	1.1	4.4	35	$11
Reliability 23	06 MIL	4	5	0	97	50	4.82	1.37	264	265	266	23.1	28%	67%	4.56	39	21	40	3.2	4.6	1.4	9%	1.1	-4.0	27	$4
DL 77	1st Half	2	1	0	34	19	3.18	1.35	256			24.2	27%	81%	4.18	44	23	32	3.4	5.0	1.5	11%	1.1	5.5	33	$3
ERA Potl 45%	2nd Half	2	4	0	63	31	5.71	1.38	268			22.6	28%	59%	4.76	36	20	44	3.1	4.4	1.4	9%	1.1	-9.5	23	$1
LIMA Plan C+	07 Proj	6	7	0	131	68	4.41	1.40	278			23.5	30%	71%	4.43	41	20	39	2.8	4.7	1.7	9%	1.1	-1.0	29	$6

Shoulder, hamstring injuries cut into IP, but there are other negative trends, most notably steady CMD and GB% declines. Health may facilitate a rebound, but these are bad signs for a soft-tosser.

Ohman,Will		W	L	Sv	IP	K	ERA	WHIP	OBA	vL	vR	BF/G	H%	S%	xERA	G	L	F	Ctl	Dom	Cmd	hr/f	hr/9	RAR	BPV	R$
LH Reliever	02	0	0	0	0	0	0.00	0.00											0.0	0.0						
Age 29	03	0	0	0	0	0	0.00	0.00											0.0	0.0						
Peak	04 aaa	3	3	0	52	64	4.73	1.70	286			5.3	39%	74%	5.47				5.1	11.0	2.2		1.1	-2.5	76	$2
Type Power	05 CHC *	3	2	1	51	55	3.21	1.22	201	175	231	2.8	24%	81%	3.05	53	15	33	4.6	9.7	2.1	20%	1.4	6.5	74	$6
Reliability 10	06 CHC	1	1	0	65	74	4.15	1.31	217	158	243	3.5	29%	70%	3.59	34	23	44	4.7	10.2	2.2	9%	0.8	2.7	94	$5
DL	1st Half	1	1	0	34	34	4.49	1.29	238			3.8	29%	68%	3.73	33	21	46	3.7	9.0	2.4	9%	1.1	0.0	81	$2
ERA Potl 65%	2nd Half	0	0	0	31	40	3.77	1.32	194			3.3	29%	72%	3.43	35	24	41	5.8	11.6	2.0	7%	0.6	2.7	111	$2
LIMA Plan A	07 Proj	2	1	0	44	50	3.72	1.33	222			3.4	30%	74%	3.41	41	20	39	4.8	10.3	2.2	9%	0.8	5.1	93	$4

Hates Wrigley Field:

	ERA	WHIP	hr/9	Ctl
Home	7.14	1.72	1.2	6.5
Road	1.73	0.97	0.5	3.2

A solid LIMA pick with improving skills, but imagine him in a different home park.

Oliver,Darren		W	L	Sv	IP	K	ERA	WHIP	OBA	vL	vR	BF/G	H%	S%	xERA	G	L	F	Ctl	Dom	Cmd	hr/f	hr/9	RAR	BPV	R$
LH Reliever	02 BOS *	4	7	0	74	40	5.84	1.84	304	462	272	18.5	33%	69%	5.23	47	18	35	5.5	4.9	0.9	9%	1.0	-12.6	13	($2)
Age 36	03 COL	13	11	0	180	88	5.05	1.46	284	256	292	23.9	30%	67%	4.39	48	16	35	3.1	4.4	1.4	10%	1.1	-17.1	23	$7
Decline	04 2NL	3	3	0	72	46	5.98	1.48	297	321	300	11.8	31%	63%	4.30	39	19	42	2.6	5.7	2.2	14%	1.7	-15.3	24	$0
Type Finesse	05 aaa	1	3	0	31	15	10.93	2.50	441			24.1	46%	56%	11.11				2.4	4.4	1.8		1.8	-25.5	-24	($7)
Reliability 0	06 NYM	4	1	0	81	60	3.44	1.12	235	208	244	7.3	25%	77%	3.36	48	17	35	2.3	6.7	2.9	16%	1.4	10.4	65	$9
DL	1st Half	3	0	0	44	31	2.45	1.02	205			7.5	22%	83%	3.35	52	14	34	2.7	6.3	2.4	12%	1.0	11.0	71	$7
ERA Potl 35%	2nd Half	1	1	0	37	29	4.62	1.24	267			7.0	28%	71%	3.37	44	21	36	1.9	7.1	3.6	20%	1.9	-0.6	62	$2
LIMA Plan C	07 Proj	2	2	0	44	28	4.97	1.59	317			10.9	35%	73%	4.16	45	18	37	2.5	5.8	2.3	12%	1.4	1.1	32	$1

Produced his best ERA since 1995, mostly driven by unrepeatable 1st half H% and S%. DOM spike is nice, but with his history and age, note the reliability score, and be very skeptical of a repeat.

Olsen,Scott		W	L	Sv	IP	K	ERA	WHIP	OBA	vL	vR	BF/G	H%	S%	xERA	G	L	F	Ctl	Dom	Cmd	hr/f	hr/9	RAR	BPV	R$
LH Starter	02	0	0	0	0	0	0.00	0.00																		
Age 23	03	0	0	0	0	0	0.00	0.00																		
Growth	04	0	0	0	0	0	0.00	0.00																		
Type Power	05 FLA *	7	5	0	100	106	4.68	1.47	277	333	238	23.1	35%	70%	3.63	41	14	45	3.5	9.5	2.7	9%	1.1	-5.3	82	$6
Reliability 0	06 FLA	12	10	0	180	166	4.05	1.30	239	182	255	24.6	29%	73%	3.54	45	18	37	3.7	8.3	2.2	12%	1.1	9.8	69	$17
DL	1st Half	6	4	0	80	68	4.27	1.26	229			23.9	26%	70%	3.61	44	21	35	3.8	7.6	2.0	14%	1.2	2.2	60	$8
ERA Potl 55%	2nd Half	6	6	0	100	98	3.87	1.34	248			25.1	31%	75%	3.48	45	16	38	3.7	8.8	2.4	11%	1.1	7.7	76	$9
LIMA Plan C	07 Proj	13	8	0	174	170	3.83	1.30	244			23.7	30%	74%	3.43	44	18	38	3.6	8.8	2.5	11%	1.0	20.0	80	$18

Signs of a budding star: 1st half xERA below 4.00, even better in 2nd half with growth in DOM and CMD. 2H DOM/DIS was 60/13. May be last chance to buy him at a reasonable price.
UP: 15 wins, 3.50 ERA.

Ortiz,Ramon		W	L	Sv	IP	K	ERA	WHIP	OBA	vL	vR	BF/G	H%	S%	xERA	G	L	F	Ctl	Dom	Cmd	hr/f	hr/9	RAR	BPV	R$
RH Starter	02 ANA	15	9	0	217	162	3.77	1.18	235	218	243	27.8	25%	76%	3.73	41	18	41	2.8	6.7	2.4	15%	1.7	18.3	49	$24
Age 33	03 ANA	16	13	0	180	94	5.20	1.51	292	291	282	24.9	30%	69%	4.80	39	17	44	3.2	4.7	1.5	10%	1.4	-15.0	14	$9
Past Peak	04 ANA	5	7	0	128	82	4.43	1.38	278	305	253	16.2	30%	72%	4.29	38	18	44	2.7	5.8	2.2	10%	1.3	0.0	41	$6
Type Finesse	05 CIN	9	11	0	171	96	5.37	1.50	299	288	315	25.2	31%	70%	4.30	45	17	38	2.7	5.0	1.9	15%	1.8	-23.6	11	$3
Reliability 80	06 WAS	11	16	0	190	104	5.58	1.55	300	316	278	25.7	32%	67%	4.57	41	20	39	3.0	4.9	1.6	12%	1.5	-25.7	15	$3
DL 21	1st Half	5	6	0	90	50	5.19	1.50	296			26.5	32%	67%	4.45	41	20	39	2.8	5.0	1.8	10%	1.2	-7.9	27	$2
ERA Potl 50%	2nd Half	6	10	0	100	54	5.93	1.59	303			25.1	31%	66%	4.68	41	19	40	3.2	4.9	1.5	13%	1.7	-17.9	4	$0
LIMA Plan C	07 Proj	9	14	0	178	100	5.01	1.51	294			23.9	31%	70%	4.50	41	19	40	3.0	5.1	1.7	11%	1.4	-3.1	21	$5

Highly reliable and incredibly mediocre. DOM/DIS 30/30. CMD decline continues, hr/9 still poor. Skills of '02 are but a distant memory. xERA suggests a bit of give in the ERA, but he's barely roster filler now.

HAROLD NICHOLS

Ortiz,Russ

		Yr	Tm	W	L	Sv	IP	K	ERA	WHIP	OBA	vL	vR	BF/G	H%	S%	xERA	G	L	F	Ctl	Dom	Cmd	hr/f	hr/9	RAR	BPV	R$
RH	Reliever	02	SF	14	10	0	214	137	3.62	1.33	240	247	235	27.6	27%	74%	4.26	45	18	37	4.0	5.8	**1.5**	6%	0.6	12.9	53	$17
Age	32	03	ATL	21	7	0	212	149	3.82	1.32	228	265	187	26.4	26%	72%	4.27	43	17	40	4.3	6.3	**1.5**	7%	0.7	12.0	56	$21
Peak		04	ATL	15	9	0	204	143	4.14	1.51	255	257	262	26.6	29%	75%	4.55	42	21	37	4.9	6.3	**1.3**	10%	1.0	3.0	38	$12
Type		05	ARI	5	11	0	115	46	6.89	1.84	312	329	296	24.9	32%	64%	5.73	37	26	37	5.1	3.6	**0.7**	11%	1.4	-37.5	-13	($8)
Reliability	17	06	2TM *	1	8	0	83	53	6.96	1.89	324	378	299	13.4	34%	67%	5.14	37	24	39	4.9	5.7	**1.2**	17%	2.1	-25.1	-13	($6)
DL	43 56	1st Half		1	5	0	42	30	5.60	1.90	308			20.4	35%	71%	5.20	40	22	37	5.8	6.3	**1.1**	8%	0.9	-5.6	28	($2)
ERA Potl	45%	2nd Half		0	3	0	41	23	8.38	1.89	339			9.8	32%	63%	5.03	35	25	39	4.0	5.1	**1.3**	25%	3.3	-19.4	-55	($5)
LIMA Plan	F	07	Proj	**2**	**5**	**0**	**58**	**34**	**6.36**	**1.78**	**306**			**17.0**	**32%**	**67%**	**5.10**	**38**	**24**	**38**	**4.8**	**5.3**	**1.1**	**14%**	**1.7**	**-4.8**	**-3**	**($2)**

0-8, 8.14 ERA in 63 IP at ARI and BAL. Is this the ultimate in futility? PQS DOM/DIS 0/82. Might do slightly better in relief (4.97 ERA vs 10.27 as a starter), but even then there are long ball issues.

Orvella,Chad

		Yr	Tm	W	L	Sv	IP	K	ERA	WHIP	OBA	vL	vR	BF/G	H%	S%	xERA	G	L	F	Ctl	Dom	Cmd	hr/f	hr/9	RAR	BPV	R$
RH	Reliever	02		0	0	0	0	0	0.00	0.00											0.0	0.0						
Age	26	03		0	0	0	0	0	0.00	0.00											0.0	0.0						
Growth		04	a/a	0	0	4	9	13	2.00	0.56	106			3.9	14%	75%	0.37				2.0	13.0	**6.5**		1.0	2.6	218	$3
Type	Power	05	TAM *	3	3	10	75	66	2.53	1.27	238	218	265	5.9	30%	81%	3.98	34	21	45	3.6	7.9	**2.2**	4%	0.5	17.0	87	$12
Reliability	0	06	TAM *	5	5	1	62	63	4.38	1.68	297	275	391	5.8	37%	77%	4.07	36	22	41	4.4	9.0	**2.1**	10%	1.2	1.4	58	$5
DL		1st Half		3	4	0	33	31	4.89	1.91	296			5.7	36%	78%	4.77	40	22	38	6.5	8.5	**1.3**	13%	1.4	-1.4	33	$1
ERA Potl	50%	2nd Half		2	1	1	29	31	3.79	1.41	298			6.0	39%	76%	3.52	28	24	48	1.9	9.7	**5.1**	7%	0.9	2.7	132	$4
LIMA Plan	B	07	Proj	**4**	**4**	**10**	**69**	**66**	**3.68**	**1.45**	**269**			**5.9**	**33%**	**78%**	**3.80**	**37**	**21**	**41**	**3.7**	**8.7**	**2.4**	**10%**	**1.1**	**5.8**	**71**	**$10**

1-5, 7.40 ERA in 24 IP at TAM. High H% ruined ERA in TAM, and still has problem keeping the ball down. But look at the 2nd half BPV and consider this a buying opportunity. Still an elite relief prospect.

Oswalt,Roy

		Yr	Tm	W	L	Sv	IP	K	ERA	WHIP	OBA	vL	vR	BF/G	H%	S%	xERA	G	L	F	Ctl	Dom	Cmd	hr/f	hr/9	RAR	BPV	R$
RH	Starter	02	HOU	19	9	0	233	208	3.01	1.19	247	251	244	27.4	31%	77%	3.19	46	20	34	2.4	8.0	**3.4**	7%	0.7	31.4	105	$29
Age	29	03	HOU	10	5	0	127	108	2.98	1.14	245	263	234	24.6	29%	79%	3.13	46	21	34	2.1	7.7	**3.7**	12%	1.1	20.4	98	$17
Peak		04	HOU	20	10	0	237	206	3.49	1.24	259	257	264	27.4	32%	73%	3.35	43	23	35	2.4	7.8	**3.3**	7%	0.6	22.5	101	$26
Type		05	HOU	20	12	0	241	184	2.95	1.21	263	279	247	28.4	31%	78%	3.17	49	22	29	1.8	6.9	**3.8**	8%	0.7	38.6	104	$29
Reliability	92	06	HOU	15	8	0	220	166	2.98	1.17	262	264	262	27.3	31%	77%	3.18	49	20	31	1.6	6.8	**4.4**	9%	0.7	40.8	113	$27
DL	15	1st Half		6	3	0	102	69	3.26	1.24	269			28.3	31%	75%	3.39	49	21	30	1.8	6.1	**3.5**	8%	0.7	15.4	89	$11
ERA Potl	55%	2nd Half		9	5	0	118	97	2.74	1.12	255			26.5	31%	79%	3.01	49	19	32	1.4	7.4	**5.4**	9%	0.8	25.5	139	$17
LIMA Plan	C+	07	Proj	**17**	**9**	**0**	**218**	**172**	**3.02**	**1.17**	**257**			**27.0**	**31%**	**77%**	**3.17**	**48**	**21**	**32**	**1.8**	**7.1**	**4.0**	**9%**	**0.7**	**32.0**	**108**	**$27**

He's thrown a lot of IP and that might be reflected in his slowly declining DOM. But his maturity is reflected by how that decline has not stopped the upward trends in other BPIs. He may even have more upside - scary.

Otsuka,Akinori

		Yr	Tm	W	L	Sv	IP	K	ERA	WHIP	OBA	vL	vR	BF/G	H%	S%	xERA	G	L	F	Ctl	Dom	Cmd	hr/f	hr/9	RAR	BPV	R$
RH	Reliever	02	JPN	2	1	22	42	57	1.60	0.65	166			3.7	22%	96%	1.57				0.8	12.2	**15.3**		1.4	13.9	373	$17
Age	35	03	JPN	1	3	17	43	59	2.60	0.92	215			3.2	30%	82%	2.80				1.3	12.4	**9.5**		1.4	9.5	244	$13
Past Peak		04	SD	7	2	2	77	87	1.75	1.06	205	214	183	4.2	28%	88%	2.66	51	16	33	3.0	10.2	**3.3**	10%	0.7	23.9	124	$15
Type		05	SD	2	8	1	62	60	3.62	1.43	239	207	263	4.1	31%	74%	3.52	47	26	27	4.9	8.7	**1.8**	7%	0.4	4.8	83	$4
Reliability	37	06	TEX	2	4	32	59	47	2.13	1.08	241	287	190	3.8	29%	82%	2.93	52	19	28	1.7	7.1	**4.3**	6%	0.5	17.7	126	$19
DL		1st Half		2	3	15	34	28	2.38	0.91	220			3.6	27%	76%	2.82	47	19	33	1.1	7.4	**7.0**	6%	0.5	9.1	187	$11
ERA Potl	45%	2nd Half		0	1	17	25	19	1.79	1.31	268			3.9	32%	88%	3.06	58	19	23	2.5	6.8	**2.7**	6%	0.4	8.6	88	$8
LIMA Plan	C+	07	Proj	**4**	**3**	**40**	**65**	**53**	**2.90**	**1.21**	**243**			**4.0**	**29%**	**78%**	**3.16**	**52**	**20**	**28**	**2.8**	**7.3**	**2.7**	**9%**	**0.7**	**10.7**	**85**	**$21**

It's not often that you'll see a pitcher improve his BPIs moving from an extreme pitchers park to an extreme hitters park, but he essentially reinvented himself in '06. Less power, more precision, and it worked out well.

Padilla,Vicente

		Yr	Tm	W	L	Sv	IP	K	ERA	WHIP	OBA	vL	vR	BF/G	H%	S%	xERA	G	L	F	Ctl	Dom	Cmd	hr/f	hr/9	RAR	BPV	R$
RH	Starter	02	PHI	14	11	0	206	128	3.28	1.22	254	272	236	26.6	29%	75%	3.44	54	18	28	2.3	5.6	**2.4**	9%	0.7	21.1	67	$20
Age	29	03	PHI	14	12	0	208	133	3.63	1.24	250	267	239	27.0	28%	74%	3.78	48	17	35	2.7	5.8	**2.1**	10%	1.0	16.5	56	$19
Peak		04	PHI	7	7	0	115	82	4.54	1.35	268	289	241	24.6	30%	70%	3.87	44	18	38	2.8	6.4	**2.3**	12%	1.3	-3.9	50	$7
Type		05	PHI	9	12	0	147	103	4.71	1.50	260	297	222	24.0	28%	72%	4.19	46	22	32	4.5	6.3	**1.4**	15%	1.3	-8.5	30	$6
Reliability	53	06	TEX	15	10	0	200	156	4.50	1.38	268	305	228	26.1	31%	69%	3.74	44	22	34	3.2	7.0	**2.2**	10%	0.9	1.4	62	$17
DL	25	1st Half		6	5	0	92	75	4.78	1.44	266			25.1	31%	68%	3.89	43	23	35	3.8	7.3	**1.9**	9%	0.9	-2.6	60	$6
ERA Potl	55%	2nd Half		9	5	0	108	81	4.26	1.33	269			26.9	31%	70%	3.62	45	21	34	2.6	6.8	**2.6**	11%	1.0	4.0	67	$11
LIMA Plan	C	07	Proj	**13**	**11**	**0**	**189**	**143**	**3.96**	**1.31**	**259**			**24.9**	**30%**	**72%**	**3.64**	**45**	**21**	**34**	**2.9**	**6.8**	**2.4**	**10%**	**0.9**	**19.6**	**67**	**$18**

Healthy for the first time in three years and the BPI rebound shows it. Solid 2nd half gains. Has pitched in hitters' parks since '04 and could take a step up if he lands in the right spot. UP: 3.50 ERA, maybe better

Papelbon,Jon

		Yr	Tm	W	L	Sv	IP	K	ERA	WHIP	OBA	vL	vR	BF/G	H%	S%	xERA	G	L	F	Ctl	Dom	Cmd	hr/f	hr/9	RAR	BPV	R$
RH	Reliever	02		0	0	0	0	0	0.00	0.00											0.0	0.0						
Age	26	03		0	0	0	0	0	0.00	0.00											0.0	0.0						
Growth		04		0	0	0	0	0	0.00	0.00											0.0	0.0						
Type	Power	05	BOS *	9	5	1	148	125	3.11	1.14	233	190	319	15.9	27%	77%	3.55	35	25	40	2.6	7.6	**2.9**	10%	1.0	23.0	86	$19
Reliability	0	06	BOS	4	2	35	68	75	0.93	0.78	172	203	128	4.3	24%	92%	2.69	37	17	46	1.7	9.9	**5.8**	4%	0.4	30.5	189	$28
DL		1st Half		2	1	23	39	41	0.46	0.72	166			4.1	23%	96%	2.59	40	19	42	1.4	9.4	**6.8**	3%	0.2	19.8	215	$17
ERA Potl	35%	2nd Half		2	1	12	29	34	1.55	0.86	180			4.6	25%	87%	2.84	34	14	51	2.2	10.6	**4.9**	6%	0.6	10.8	166	$11
LIMA Plan	C+	07	Proj	**11**	**6**	**0**	**174**	**156**	**3.47**	**1.14**	**237**			**26.2**	**28%**	**74%**	**3.54**	**36**	**17**	**46**	**2.4**	**8.1**	**3.4**	**9%**	**1.0**	**20.4**	**96**	**$22**

Why he's not yet THIS good:
- Low H%, high S%
- Rising FB rate, low hr/f
- Moving to rotation
- Late season health issues

Outstanding, but will most likely be overpriced in '07.

Park,Chan Ho

		Yr	Tm	W	L	Sv	IP	K	ERA	WHIP	OBA	vL	vR	BF/G	H%	S%	xERA	G	L	F	Ctl	Dom	Cmd	hr/f	hr/9	RAR	BPV	R$
RH	Starter	02	TEX	9	9	0	148	124	6.32	1.66	283	287	254	26.1	33%	63%	4.40	40	22	38	4.9	7.5	**1.5**	11%	1.2	-34.1	39	$1
Age	33	03	TEX *	3	3	0	58	29	7.76	2.22	352	367	235	24.9	37%	67%	6.19	43	16	41	6.2	4.5	**0.7**	12%	1.7	-23.1	-24	($7)
Past Peak		04	TEX *	4	11	0	125	82	6.17	1.56	303	277	284	25.6	31%	66%	4.21	46	14	40	3.0	5.9	**2.0**	18%	2.2	-26.9	6	($1)
Type		05	2TM	12	8	0	155	113	5.74	1.68	292	305	279	23.8	34%	65%	4.20	50	21	29	4.6	6.6	**1.4**	7%	0.6	-27.6	47	$2
Reliability	31	06	SD	7	7	0	136	96	4.82	1.40	275	266	278	24.5	30%	69%	3.96	44	18	38	2.9	6.3	**2.2**	12%	1.3	-5.6	44	$7
DL	51	1st Half		5	4	0	94	70	4.31	1.30	258			24.8	30%	69%	3.84	43	18	39	2.9	6.7	**2.3**	9%	1.0	2.1	64	$7
ERA Potl	50%	2nd Half		2	3	0	42	26	5.97	1.61	312			23.9	32%	69%	4.24	45	20	36	3.0	5.5	**1.9**	19%	2.1	-7.7	1	($0)
LIMA Plan	C	07	Proj	**4**	**6**	**0**	**87**	**59**	**5.17**	**1.44**	**275**			**23.7**	**31%**	**66%**	**4.04**	**46**	**19**	**35**	**3.3**	**6.1**	**1.8**	**11%**	**1.1**	**3.4**	**41**	**$3**

Revived in SD? Actually, only Ctl really improved, and overall BPIs dove in 2nd half. This was just a detour on the road back to another 5.00+ ERA.

Paronto,Chad

		Yr	Tm	W	L	Sv	IP	K	ERA	WHIP	OBA	vL	vR	BF/G	H%	S%	xERA	G	L	F	Ctl	Dom	Cmd	hr/f	hr/9	RAR	BPV	R$
RH	Reliever	02	a/a	0	0	1	13	5	0.69	1.30	289			6.1	32%	94%	3.50				1.4	3.4	**2.5**		0.0	5.8	70	$2
Age	31	03	aaa	3	5	18	56	38	6.22	1.94	344			5.6	40%	66%	6.49				4.1	6.1	**1.5**		0.5	-12.6	38	$4
Peak		04	aaa	5	3	4	55	30	2.34	1.44	258			5.1	29%	86%	3.96				4.1	4.9	**1.2**		0.5	13.6	42	$7
Type		05	aaa	6	2	4	79	51	4.68	1.87	323			7.3	37%	76%	6.18				4.7	5.8	**1.2**		0.8	-3.6	29	$2
Reliability	2	06	ATL *	3	4	4	73	53	2.84	1.33	266	288	234	4.0	31%	81%	3.69	43	25	32	2.7	6.5	**2.4**	8%	0.7	14.9	69	$8
DL		1st Half		1	1	4	39	34	2.78	1.43	275			4.6	34%	83%	3.91	32	29	39	3.2	7.8	**2.4**	7%	0.7	8.3	77	$5
ERA Potl	30%	2nd Half		2	3	0	34	19	2.91	1.21	256			3.5	28%	79%	3.58	49	23	28	2.1	5.0	**2.4**	10%	0.8	6.6	60	$4
LIMA Plan	C+	07	Proj	**3**	**2**	**0**	**44**	**28**	**3.72**	**1.47**	**277**			**4.8**	**31%**	**77%**	**4.09**	**45**	**25**	**31**	**3.5**	**5.8**	**1.6**	**9%**	**0.8**	**1.5**	**44**	**$3**

2-3, 3.18 ERA in 56 IP at ATL. Fine season for career minor leaguer, fueled by CMD that doubled. His pro career level, however, is 1.8, with no growth trend before 2006. Make him repeat before investing.

Patterson,John

		Yr	Tm	W	L	Sv	IP	K	ERA	WHIP	OBA	vL	vR	BF/G	H%	S%	xERA	G	L	F	Ctl	Dom	Cmd	hr/f	hr/9	RAR	BPV	R$
RH	Starter	02	ARI *	12	5	0	142	118	4.44	1.43	279	236	233	23.8	32%	73%	4.33	23	26	51	3.0	7.5	**2.5**	10%	1.3	-5.8	56	$10
Age	29	03	ARI *	11	9	1	164	107	4.12	1.50	275	281	281	21.3	31%	74%	4.75	34	22	44	3.9	5.9	**1.5**	6%	0.8	3.3	44	$9
Pre-Peak		04	MON	4	7	0	98	99	5.05	1.49	266	228	283	22.8	32%	71%	4.01	32	21	47	4.2	9.1	**2.2**	14%	1.7	-9.5	52	$4
Type	Power	05	WAS	9	7	0	198	185	3.13	1.20	235	229	237	26.3	29%	77%	3.69	30	23	46	3.0	8.4	**2.8**	8%	0.9	27.1	92	$21
Reliability	0	06	WAS	1	2	0	40	42	4.48	1.12	241	299	188	20.3	31%	61%	3.41	30	16	54	2.0	9.4	**4.7**	7%	0.9	0.0	134	$4
DL	146 15	1st Half		1	1	0	31	35	3.46	0.90	207			23.8	26%	67%	3.01	28	15	58	1.4	10.1	**7.0**	9%	1.2	3.9	187	$5
ERA Potl	65%	2nd Half		0	1	0	9	7	8.00	1.89	339			14.4	41%	53%	4.98	36	18	45	4.0	7.0	**1.8**	0%	0.0	-3.9	66	($1)
LIMA Plan	B+	07	Proj	**8**	**7**	**0**	**160**	**148**	**3.89**	**1.29**	**253**			**24.0**	**30%**	**74%**	**3.80**	**32**	**19**	**48**	**3.0**	**8.4**	**2.8**	**10%**	**1.2**	**11.1**	**78**	**$14**

Battled forearm woes all year, finally succumbing to surgery. But BPV showed that 2005 was no fluke. Supposed to be ready for spring, and could be a bargain if healthy. UP: Repeat of 2005.

HAROLD NICHOLS

Pavano,Carl

	Yr	Tm	W	L	Sv	IP	K	ERA	WHIP	OBA	vL	vR	BF/G	H%	S%	xERA	G	L	F	Ctl	Dom	Cmd	hr/f	hr/9	RAR	BPV	R$
RH Reliever	02	2NL *	9	10	0	156	100	5.02	1.60	315	357	276	17.6	35%	70%	4.08	48	19	33	2.7	5.8	**2.1**	10%	1.1	-17.6	38	$3
Age 31	03	FLA	12	13	0	201	133	4.30	1.26	265	267	263	25.5	30%	67%	3.94	41	18	41	2.2	6.0	**2.7**	7%	0.9	-0.5	69	$15
Peak	04	FLA	18	8	0	222	139	3.00	1.18	253	267	240	29.3	29%	76%	3.55	48	19	32	2.0	5.6	**2.8**	7%	0.6	34.6	78	$26
Type Finesse	05	NYY	4	6	0	100	56	4.77	1.47	314	335	294	25.8	33%	72%	3.78	50	19	31	1.6	5.0	**3.1**	15%	1.5	-4.9	42	$3
Reliability 0	06	a/a	2	0	0	17	15	1.59	1.12	250			17.2	33%	84%	2.45				1.6	7.9	**5.0**		0.0	6.1	158	$3
DL 182 95	1st Half		1	0	0	7	4	1.84	0.82	224			13.1	27%	75%					0.0	5.4			0.0	2.3	43	$2
ERA Potl 35%	2nd Half		1	0	0	10	11	1.41	1.33	267			21.2	37%	88%					2.7	9.7	**3.6**		0.0	3.8	135	$2
LIMA Plan B	07	Proj	**7**	**5**	**0**	**102**	**63**	**4.26**	**1.35**	**285**			**24.1**	**31%**	**71%**	**3.81**	**47**	**19**	**35**	**2.0**	**5.6**	**2.7**	**10%**	**1.1**	**7.6**	**57**	**$8**

Prior to this lost season, had four years of Ctl and CMD improvement under his belt. Injury history and inflated '05 ERA may let you get him cheap. Given toxic risk level, bargain hunting is the only way to shop.

Peavy,Jake

	Yr	Tm	W	L	Sv	IP	K	ERA	WHIP	OBA	vL	vR	BF/G	H%	S%	xERA	G	L	F	Ctl	Dom	Cmd	hr/f	hr/9	RAR	BPV	R$
RH Starter	02	SD *	10	12	0	177	165	4.02	1.37	264	321	225	24.5	33%	72%	3.52	44	19	37	3.3	8.4	**2.6**	8%	0.8	2.0	84	$13
Age 25	03	SD	12	11	0	194	156	4.13	1.31	240	246	230	25.7	26%	75%	3.96	40	19	41	3.8	7.2	**1.9**	14%	1.5	3.6	44	$15
Growth	04	SD	15	6	0	166	173	2.28	1.20	238	235	238	25.3	31%	84%	3.09	43	20	37	2.9	9.4	**3.3**	8%	0.7	40.7	111	$25
Type Power	05	SD	13	7	0	203	216	2.88	1.04	221	223	212	26.8	29%	77%	2.76	44	20	35	2.2	9.6	**4.3**	10%	0.8	34.2	135	$29
Reliability 56	06	SD	11	14	0	202	215	4.10	1.23	247	242	243	26.2	32%	69%	3.27	38	18	44	2.8	9.6	**3.5**	10%	1.0	9.7	105	$20
DL	1st Half		4	8	0	94	101	4.50	1.17	251			25.6	31%	66%	3.21	34	18	48	2.0	9.7	**4.8**	11%	1.3	-0.1	124	$9
ERA Potl 65%	2nd Half		7	6	0	108	114	3.75	1.29	243			26.7	32%	72%	3.32	42	19	39	3.4	9.5	**2.8**	8%	0.7	9.9	99	$12
LIMA Plan C+	07	Proj	**13**	**11**	**0**	**203**	**211**	**3.29**	**1.20**	**240**			**26.0**	**31%**	**76%**	**3.16**	**41**	**19**	**40**	**2.8**	**9.4**	**3.4**	**10%**	**0.9**	**30.0**	**107**	**$25**

Low S% and giant leap in FB% hurt him in 1st half, loss of Ctl got him in the 2nd. Surface stats will make some owners gun shy; Dom, xERA and BPV show there's little to worry about. Bid with confidence.

Pelfrey,Mike

	Yr	Tm	W	L	Sv	IP	K	ERA	WHIP	OBA	vL	vR	BF/G	H%	S%	xERA	G	L	F	Ctl	Dom	Cmd	hr/f	hr/9	RAR	BPV	R$
RH Starter	02		0	0	0	0	0	0.00	0.00																		
Age 23	03		0	0	0	0	0	0.00	0.00																		
Growth	04		0	0	0	0	0	0.00	0.00																		
Type Power	05		0	0	0	0	0	0.00	0.00																		
Reliability 0	06	NYM *	7	3	0	95	84	4.16	1.57	279	278	326	23.7	35%	73%	3.70	49	23	29	4.3	7.9	**1.9**	6%	0.5	3.9	72	$6
DL	1st Half		3	2	0	59	56	3.96	1.61	299			24.3	38%	74%					3.7	8.5	**2.3**		0.3	3.9	86	$3
ERA Potl 55%	2nd Half		4	1	0	36	28	4.49	1.50	245			22.8	29%	71%	4.06	49	23	29	5.2	7.0	**1.3**	10%	0.7	0.0	53	$3
LIMA Plan C+	07	Proj	**6**	**5**	**0**	**91**	**77**	**4.05**	**1.49**	**268**			**23.6**	**32%**	**74%**	**3.67**	**49**	**23**	**29**	**4.2**	**7.6**	**1.8**	**10%**	**0.8**	**7.8**	**62**	**$6**

2-1, 5.48 ERA in 21 IP at NYM. Went straight from Double-A to majors and looked overmatched (5.1 Ctl, 1.1 Cmd). 1st half DOM and CMD show his potential, but he would probably benefit from some time in Triple-A.

Penny,Brad

	Yr	Tm	W	L	Sv	IP	K	ERA	WHIP	OBA	vL	vR	BF/G	H%	S%	xERA	G	L	F	Ctl	Dom	Cmd	hr/f	hr/9	RAR	BPV	R$
RH Starter	02	FLA	8	7	0	129	93	4.67	1.53	289	294	284	23.9	32%	73%	4.10	45	18	36	3.5	6.5	**1.9**	12%	1.3	-9.0	37	$5
Age 28	03	FLA	14	10	0	196	138	4.13	1.28	261	269	258	25.7	30%	70%	3.75	45	18	36	2.6	6.3	**2.5**	9%	1.0	3.5	64	$16
Pre-Peak	04	2NL	9	10	0	143	111	3.15	1.22	244	242	243	24.7	29%	77%	3.69	43	19	38	2.8	7.0	**2.5**	7%	0.8	19.7	77	$15
Type	05	LA	7	9	0	175	122	3.91	1.29	273	263	276	25.4	31%	72%	3.59	47	20	34	2.1	6.3	**3.0**	9%	0.9	7.3	74	$12
Reliability 68	06	LA	16	9	0	189	148	4.33	1.38	279	275	283	23.9	33%	70%	3.70	44	20	36	2.6	7.0	**2.7**	9%	0.9	3.6	72	$16
DL 22	1st Half		8	2	0	94	70	3.06	1.21	249			24.3	30%	76%	3.72	41	21	38	2.5	6.7	**2.7**	6%	0.6	16.5	85	$12
ERA Potl 50%	2nd Half		8	7	0	95	78	5.59	1.54	306			23.5	36%	65%	3.67	46	19	34	2.7	7.4	**2.8**	12%	1.2	-12.9	60	$4
LIMA Plan C	07	Proj	**13**	**11**	**0**	**193**	**148**	**3.96**	**1.33**	**270**			**24.1**	**31%**	**73%**	**3.64**	**45**	**20**	**36**	**2.6**	**6.9**	**2.7**	**10%**	**1.0**	**17.2**	**70**	**$16**

Surface stats from last three seasons make it look like he's declining, but BPIs have been flat going back four years (check out the xERAs). If he can stay healthy all year... UP: 18 Wins, 3.50 ERA.

Penn,Hayden

	Yr	Tm	W	L	Sv	IP	K	ERA	WHIP	OBA	vL	vR	BF/G	H%	S%	xERA	G	L	F	Ctl	Dom	Cmd	hr/f	hr/9	RAR	BPV	R$
RH Starter	02		0	0	0	0	0	0.00	0.00											0.0	0.0						
Age 22	03		0	0	0	0	0	0.00	0.00											0.0	0.0						
Growth	04	aa	3	0	0	20	19	5.85	1.70	299			23.1	38%	64%	5.09				4.5	8.6	**1.9**		0.5	-3.7	73	$1
Type Power	05	BAL *	10	8	0	148	128	5.40	1.49	282	289	301	23.4	33%	66%	3.57	49	20	32	3.5	7.8	**2.2**	14%	1.2	-18.8	55	$7
Reliability 0	06	BAL *	7	8	0	108	89	5.43	1.53	290	327	467	23.0	33%	67%	4.10	38	21	40	3.5	7.4	**2.1**	11%	1.3	-11.6	47	$5
DL 61	1st Half		2	2	0	30	27	1.99	1.20	226			24.8	29%	84%					3.4	8.2	**2.4**		0.3	9.5	100	$5
ERA Potl 55%	2nd Half		5	6	0	78	62	6.75	1.66	312			22.4	35%	62%	4.28	38	21	40	3.5	7.1	**2.0**	14%	1.7	-21.2	27	$0
LIMA Plan C+	07	Proj	**7**	**9**	**0**	**124**	**100**	**4.79**	**1.48**	**280**			**23.7**	**32%**	**70%**	**3.95**	**42**	**21**	**37**	**3.5**	**7.3**	**2.1**	**11%**	**1.2**	**8.1**	**51**	**$7**

0-4, 15.10 ERA in 20 IP at BAL. H% and S% have undermined his skills in the minors. In the majors, he's undermined himself, with back-to-back cups of coffee featuring more walks than Ks. Potential requires patience.

Peralta,Joel

	Yr	Tm	W	L	Sv	IP	K	ERA	WHIP	OBA	vL	vR	BF/G	H%	S%	xERA	G	L	F	Ctl	Dom	Cmd	hr/f	hr/9	RAR	BPV	R$
RH Reliever	02	aa	0	0	0	17	8	9.42	2.56	405			7.9	39%	70%	12.17				5.8	4.2	**0.7**		3.7	-10.9	-95	($4)
Age 27	03	a/a	5	4	20	52	36	2.98	1.26	256			4.5	30%	78%	3.50				2.6	6.2	**2.4**		0.6	9.1	73	$13
Growth	04	aaa	4	2	1	56	54	5.18	1.56	307			6.4	38%	67%	5.24				2.8	8.7	**3.1**		0.9	-5.8	86	$3
Type	05	ANA *	5	1	10	54	47	3.82	1.16	216	273	178	4.7	25%	70%	3.83	34	20	46	3.5	7.8	**2.2**	9%	1.0	3.7	76	$10
Reliability 13	06	KC	1	3	1	73	57	4.43	1.24	264	338	234	4.8	30%	68%	3.88	32	22	46	2.1	7.0	**3.4**	10%	1.2	1.2	78	$6
DL	1st Half		1	0	0	35	24	4.63	1.31	267			4.9	31%	65%	4.27	34	20	46	2.6	6.2	**2.4**	6%	0.8	-0.3	66	$2
ERA Potl 55%	2nd Half		0	3	1	38	33	4.24	1.18	261			4.6	29%	71%	3.54	30	24	46	1.6	7.8	**4.7**	13%	1.6	1.5	99	$4
LIMA Plan B	07	Proj	**3**	**4**	**0**	**73**	**60**	**4.10**	**1.24**	**258**			**4.9**	**30%**	**71%**	**3.81**	**32**	**22**	**46**	**2.4**	**7.4**	**3.2**	**10%**	**1.2**	**6.0**	**77**	**$7**

Skills have been hinting at something bigger - 2nd half Cmd, BPV and xERA certainly fit that description. Needs to cut down on FBs (and the HR that come with them). The seeds of LIMA worthiness are here.

Perez,Beltran

	Yr	Tm	W	L	Sv	IP	K	ERA	WHIP	OBA	vL	vR	BF/G	H%	S%	xERA	G	L	F	Ctl	Dom	Cmd	hr/f	hr/9	RAR	BPV	R$
RH Reliever	02	aa	3	8	0	97	68	6.03	1.56	307			21.7	35%	61%	5.27				2.8	6.3	**2.3**		0.9	-21.1	51	($1)
Age 25	03	aa	2	11	0	147	78	5.99	1.69	323			23.4	35%	64%	5.85				3.1	4.8	**1.5**		0.9	-29.0	25	($5)
Growth	04	aa	2	6	3	104	71	5.11	1.52	280			12.5	31%	69%	5.18				3.8	6.1	**1.6**		1.3	-9.8	31	$2
Type	05	aa	2	3	3	31	26	2.99	1.26	213			7.6	27%	76%	2.66				4.5	7.6	**1.7**		0.3	5.0	85	$5
Reliability 0	06	WAS *	10	7	1	142	95	3.90	1.57	295	270	171	16.4	34%	76%	4.77	35	19	46	3.6	6.0	**1.7**	5%	0.7	10.3	46	$8
DL	1st Half		5	2	1	66	55	4.29	1.67	311			15.2	37%	76%					3.6	7.5	**2.1**		0.9	1.6	56	$3
ERA Potl 40%	2nd Half		5	5	0	76	40	3.56	1.49	280			17.6	31%	77%	5.01	35	19	46	3.5	4.8	**1.4**	4%	0.6	8.7	38	$5
LIMA Plan C+	07	Proj	**4**	**5**	**0**	**73**	**51**	**4.34**	**1.48**	**274**			**12.7**	**31%**	**73%**	**4.59**	**35**	**19**	**46**	**3.7**	**6.3**	**1.7**	**8%**	**1.0**	**-2.0**	**44**	**$4**

2-1, 3.86 ERA in 21 IP at WAS. Five straight years in Double-A with almost no skill growth to show for it. High S%, excessively low hr/9 rates have propped up his last two years' ERAs. Don't buy into it.

Perez,Odalis

	Yr	Tm	W	L	Sv	IP	K	ERA	WHIP	OBA	vL	vR	BF/G	H%	S%	xERA	G	L	F	Ctl	Dom	Cmd	hr/f	hr/9	RAR	BPV	R$
LH Reliever	02	LA	15	10	0	222	155	3.00	0.99	225	223	226	27.1	25%	73%	3.25	46	19	35	1.5	6.3	**4.1**	9%	0.9	30.3	108	$29
Age 29	03	LA	12	12	0	185	141	4.52	1.28	268	201	284	25.9	30%	69%	3.14	53	20	27	2.2	6.9	**3.1**	18%	1.4	-5.6	66	$14
Peak	04	LA	7	6	0	196	128	3.26	1.14	246	270	241	25.7	27%	77%	3.36	52	16	32	2.0	5.9	**2.9**	14%	1.2	24.3	66	$18
Type Finesse	05	LA	7	8	0	108	74	4.57	1.27	263	256	264	23.8	29%	66%	3.70	44	20	36	2.3	6.2	**2.6**	11%	1.1	-4.4	62	$8
Reliability 38	06	2TM	6	8	0	126	81	6.21	1.59	322	336	316	17.8	35%	62%	4.02	44	23	34	2.2	5.8	**2.6**	12%	1.3	-26.3	42	$0
DL 88	1st Half		4	3	0	52	31	6.90	1.84	361			16.6	40%	63%	4.18	47	23	30	2.2	5.3	**2.4**	12%	1.2	-15.3	29	($2)
ERA Potl 60%	2nd Half		2	5	0	74	50	5.72	1.41	292			18.8	32%	61%	3.90	41	22	37	2.2	6.1	**2.8**	12%	1.3	-11.0	51	$2
LIMA Plan B	07	Proj	**8**	**10**	**0**	**160**	**106**	**4.51**	**1.33**	**278**			**24.2**	**31%**	**69%**	**3.71**	**45**	**21**	**34**	**2.2**	**6.0**	**2.7**	**11%**	**1.1**	**14.1**	**59**	**$10**

CMD, GB%, xERA and BPV are all trending in wrong direction, though bottoming out in 2006 had more to do with H% and S%. Still enough skill here to say don't write him off. As a bonus, should be cheap.

Perez,Oliver

	Yr	Tm	W	L	Sv	IP	K	ERA	WHIP	OBA	vL	vR	BF/G	H%	S%	xERA	G	L	F	Ctl	Dom	Cmd	hr/f	hr/9	RAR	BPV	R$
LH Starter	02	SD *	5	5	0	113	123	3.11	1.30	207	294	191	23.8	26%	81%	3.71	32	26	42	5.1	9.8	**1.9**	12%	1.1	13.9	79	$11
Age 25	03	2NL *	7	13	0	173	183	4.84	1.51	263	292	258	23.9	33%	72%	3.84	33	26	41	4.5	9.5	**2.1**	14%	1.4	-11.9	62	$8
Growth	04	PIT	12	10	0	196	239	2.98	1.15	208	220	204	26.6	28%	79%	3.15	37	15	48	3.7	11.0	**3.0**	10%	1.0	30.9	111	$26
Type Power	05	PIT	7	5	0	103	97	5.85	1.67	260	313	255	23.6	29%	70%	4.75	34	17	49	6.1	8.5	**1.4**	16%	2.0	-20.4	23	$1
Reliability 6	06	2NL *	5	18	0	163	152	7.08	1.71	288	260	300	23.6	33%	61%	4.59	30	23	47	5.1	8.4	**1.7**	14%	1.8	-52.2	29	($5)
DL 73	1st Half		2	10	0	76	61	6.63	1.83	291			24.1	33%	66%	5.31	30	23	47	6.0	7.2	**1.2**	11%	1.5	-20.1	19	($4)
ERA Potl 60%	2nd Half		3	8	0	87	91	7.47	1.60	286			23.2	34%	56%	4.00	30	24	46	4.3	9.4	**2.2**	17%	2.0	-32.1	42	($2)
LIMA Plan C+	07	Proj	**8**	**8**	**0**	**127**	**127**	**4.84**	**1.48**	**250**			**23.2**	**30%**	**71%**	**4.14**	**32**	**20**	**47**	**4.8**	**9.0**	**1.9**	**12%**	**1.4**	**3.5**	**56**	**$7**

3-13, 6.55 ERA in 113 IP at PIT and NYM. Two years of too many walks and HR, but he still has the DOM, he's only 25, in new environs and showed a glimmer of 2nd half life. And he still owns those '04 skills. Speculate.

BRANDON KRUSE

Petit,Yusmeiro

		Yr	Tm	W	L	Sv	IP	K	ERA	WHIP	OBA	vL	vR	BF/G	H%	S%	xERA	G	L	F	Ctl	Dom	Cmd	hr/f	hr/9	RAR	BPV	R$
RH	Reliever	02		0	0	0	0	0	0.00	0.00											0.0	0.0						
Age	22	03		0	0	0	0	0	0.00	0.00											0.0	0.0						
Green		04	aa	1	1	0	12	15	5.25	1.50	262			26.5	37%	65%	4.31				4.5	11.3	2.5		0.8	-1.3	100	$1
Type		05	a/a	9	6	0	132	133	3.65	1.03	234			21.7	28%	70%	3.24				1.5	9.1	6.1		1.3	10.6	152	$18
Reliability	0	06	FLA *	5	7	0	122	88	5.27	1.39	293	381	400	16.5	33%	65%	4.17	29	24	46	2.0	6.5	3.2	10%	1.4	-11.8	62	$5
DL		1st Half		2	4	0	62	43	4.60	1.24	263			16.2	29%	66%	4.08	34	18	47	2.1	6.2	2.9	9%	1.2	-0.8	65	$4
ERA Potl	55%	2nd Half		3	3	0	60	45	5.97	1.55	323			16.8	36%	64%	4.26	26	28	46	1.9	6.8	3.6	11%	1.6	-11.0	60	$1
LIMA Plan	B	07	Proj	4	4	0	73	56	4.34	1.30	268			18.0	30%	70%	4.03	29	25	46	2.4	7.0	2.9	10%	1.2	3.0	68	$5

1-1, 9.57 ERA in 26 IP at FLA. Declining Dom and high FB rate don't exactly ease concerns about the quality of his stuff, but Ctl is strong enough to succeed. FLA ERA ruined by 42 H% and 56 S%. Decent upside here.

Pettitte,Andy

		Yr	Tm	W	L	Sv	IP	K	ERA	WHIP	OBA	vL	vR	BF/G	H%	S%	xERA	G	L	F	Ctl	Dom	Cmd	hr/f	hr/9	RAR	BPV	R$
LH	Starter	02	NYY *	13	5	0	140	100	3.21	1.28	271	255	276	25.6	32%	75%	3.63	45	20	35	2.1	6.4	3.1	4%	0.4	21.5	93	$17
Age	34	03	NYY	21	8	0	208	180	4.02	1.33	279	321	254	26.8	34%	72%	3.12	50	22	29	2.2	7.8	3.6	11%	0.9	12.8	94	$24
Past Peak		04	HOU	6	4	0	83	79	3.90	1.23	233	290	208	23.0	29%	70%	2.92	53	21	26	3.4	8.6	2.5	14%	0.9	3.7	87	$9
Type		05	HOU	17	9	0	222	171	2.39	1.03	231	200	239	26.6	27%	80%	2.89	50	23	27	1.7	6.9	4.2	10%	0.7	50.8	117	$33
Reliability	63	06	HOU	14	13	0	214	178	4.20	1.44	283	259	290	25.9	33%	74%	3.38	50	22	29	2.9	7.5	2.5	14%	1.1	7.5	63	$15
DL		1st Half		6	9	0	108	81	5.58	1.61	309			27.2	35%	69%	3.73	49	22	29	3.2	6.8	2.1	17%	1.5	-14.6	34	$2
ERA Potl	55%	2nd Half		8	4	0	106	97	2.80	1.26	254			24.7	32%	81%	3.03	51	21	28	2.7	8.2	3.0	10%	0.8	22.1	94	$14
LIMA Plan	C+	07	Proj	15	10	0	200	168	3.51	1.27	259			25.4	31%	74%	3.15	50	22	28	2.6	7.6	2.9	10%	0.8	29.9	88	$21

1st half was torpedoed by high H% and hr/f, otherwise this was another great season. Health of his elbow should be monitored, but his BPIs support continued success at this level should he choose not to retire.

Pineiro,Joel

		Yr	Tm	W	L	Sv	IP	K	ERA	WHIP	OBA	vL	vR	BF/G	H%	S%	xERA	G	L	F	Ctl	Dom	Cmd	hr/f	hr/9	RAR	BPV	R$
RH	Starter	02	SEA	14	7	0	194	136	3.25	1.25	257	270	240	21.9	29%	79%	3.72	46	16	38	2.5	6.3	2.5	11%	1.1	29.0	61	$21
Age	28	03	SEA	16	11	0	211	151	3.80	1.27	244	234	251	27.6	28%	72%	3.87	45	17	37	3.2	6.4	2.0	8%	0.8	19.0	62	$22
Pre-Peak		04	SEA	6	11	0	140	111	4.69	1.33	267	209	316	28.4	30%	69%	3.72	43	17	39	2.8	7.1	2.6	13%	1.3	-4.4	58	$8
Type	Finesse	05	SEA	7	11	0	189	107	5.62	1.48	296	295	305	27.7	32%	63%	4.13	45	22	33	2.7	5.1	1.9	11%	1.1	-29.1	34	$3
Reliability	52	06	SEA	8	13	1	165	87	6.37	1.65	310	287	332	18.9	33%	62%	4.38	47	23	29	3.5	4.7	1.4	13%	1.3	-37.0	12	($1)
DL	20	1st Half		6	7	0	95	44	5.39	1.56	300			26.6	31%	68%	4.29	47	25	28	3.1	4.2	1.3	15%	1.3	-9.8	8	$2
ERA Potl	50%	2nd Half		2	6	1	70	43	7.70	1.78	322			13.7	35%	56%	4.50	48	21	31	4.0	5.5	1.4	12%	1.2	-27.2	18	($4)
LIMA Plan	D	07	Proj	7	10	0	148	84	5.25	1.55	296			20.6	32%	68%	4.27	46	21	32	3.2	5.1	1.6	11%	1.1	3.8	27	$3

Sliding DOM rate shows that he's likely not fully over his elbow and shoulder problems. Keep this '06 split in mind:
As starter - 4.3 DOM, 1.2 CMD
As reliever - 7.4 DOM, 2.0 CMD
If he's starting again, be wary.

Ponson,Sidney

		Yr	Tm	W	L	Sv	IP	K	ERA	WHIP	OBA	vL	vR	BF/G	H%	S%	xERA	G	L	F	Ctl	Dom	Cmd	hr/f	hr/9	RAR	BPV	R$
RH	Starter	02	BAL	7	9	0	176	120	4.09	1.34	257	243	273	26.7	28%	74%	3.81	47	20	33	3.2	6.1	1.9	14%	1.3	8.0	40	$12
Age	30	03	2TM	17	12	0	216	134	3.75	1.26	257	271	243	29.1	29%	71%	3.61	53	17	30	2.5	5.6	2.2	8%	0.7	17.1	63	$21
Peak		04	BAL	11	15	0	215	115	5.31	1.55	304	305	298	29.2	33%	67%	4.19	51	18	32	2.9	4.8	1.7	10%	1.0	-23.3	29	$4
Type		05	BAL	7	11	0	130	68	6.23	1.73	325	360	299	26.3	35%	65%	4.27	53	20	27	3.3	4.7	1.4	12%	1.1	-29.8	15	($3)
Reliability	58	06	2TM	4	5	0	85	48	6.25	1.69	311	304	328	20.6	34%	63%	4.42	51	18	31	3.8	5.1	1.3	11%	1.1	-18.1	20	($1)
DL	19	1st Half		4	3	0	60	27	4.95	1.52	296			22.2	31%	68%	4.17	53	20	27	3.0	4.1	1.4	10%	0.9	-3.2	22	$2
ERA Potl	50%	2nd Half		0	2	0	25	21	9.36	2.12	344			18.0	40%	55%	4.96	48	13	40	5.8	7.6	1.3	12%	1.4	-14.9	16	($4)
LIMA Plan	F	07	Proj	1	1	0	15	8	6.21	1.66	306			22.1	33%	64%	4.43	51	17	32	3.7	5.0	1.3	12%	1.2	-0.0	14	($0)

Which of these crimes is worse - punching a judge in Aruba, or meriting 430 IP the past three seasons? Legal scholars may debate the issue for years. Released by two teams in '06; learn from their mistakes.

Prior,Mark

		Yr	Tm	W	L	Sv	IP	K	ERA	WHIP	OBA	vL	vR	BF/G	H%	S%	xERA	G	L	F	Ctl	Dom	Cmd	hr/f	hr/9	RAR	BPV	R$
RH	Starter	02	CHC *	11	8	0	167	217	3.07	1.17	229	204	242	24.4	33%	77%	2.79	32	28	41	3.0	11.7	3.9	9%	0.8	21.3	138	$23
Age	26	03	CHC	18	6	0	211	245	2.43	1.10	235	240	223	27.4	32%	81%	2.74	37	26	37	2.1	10.5	4.9	8%	0.6	48.1	154	$34
Growth		04	CHC	6	4	0	118	139	4.04	1.35	252	258	245	24.1	34%	73%	3.34	37	19	44	3.7	10.6	2.9	10%	1.1	3.3	97	$10
Type	Power	05	CHC	11	7	0	166	188	3.68	1.22	234	216	236	25.5	30%	76%	3.12	37	21	41	3.2	10.2	3.2	14%	1.4	11.5	96	$19
Reliability	0	06	CHC	1	6	0	43	38	7.29	1.71	274	321	226	22.2	31%	60%	4.69	37	21	43	5.8	7.9	1.4	16%	1.9	-14.9	20	($2)
DL	148 47	1st Half		0	2	0	9	6	9.89	1.87	369			21.8	36%	54%	3.94	33	39	28	2.0	5.9	3.0	42%	4.0	-6.1	-39	($1)
ERA Potl	65%	2nd Half		1	4	0	34	32	6.60	1.67	244			22.4	29%	62%	4.91	38	14	48	6.9	8.4	1.2	11%	1.3	-8.9	43	($1)
LIMA Plan	C	07	Proj	8	9	0	145	150	4.10	1.33	241			23.7	30%	73%	3.54	36	24	40	3.9	9.3	2.4	12%	1.1	14.8	79	$12

Low IP total and sharp drop in skills make this year's injuries feel more serious than previous ones. He's now a member of the high-risk, high-reward squad, which means you can no longer build your staff around him.

Proctor,Scott

		Yr	Tm	W	L	Sv	IP	K	ERA	WHIP	OBA	vL	vR	BF/G	H%	S%	xERA	G	L	F	Ctl	Dom	Cmd	hr/f	hr/9	RAR	BPV	R$
RH	Reliever	02	aa	7	9	0	133	103	4.94	1.83	277			24.3	33%	74%	5.39				6.7	7.0	1.0		0.8	-10.9	39	($0)
Age	30	03	a/a	7	4	1	85	66	3.29	1.36	270			7.1	32%	77%	3.93				2.8	6.9	2.5		0.6	11.6	77	$9
Peak		04	aaa	2	3	4	44	33	3.66	1.44	263			5.5	31%	77%	4.30				3.9	6.8	1.8		0.9	3.7	54	$4
Type	Power	05	NYY *	6	1	14	85	77	5.65	1.53	297	300	217	6.0	34%	69%	4.24	30	17	53	3.0	8.1	2.7	13%	2.0	-13.5	41	$8
Reliability	30	06	NYY	6	4	1	102	89	3.53	1.19	236	204	250	5.1	28%	75%	3.84	33	18	49	2.9	7.8	2.7	8%	1.1	13.0	80	$13
DL		1st Half		2	1	0	49	39	4.22	1.31	237			5.4	27%	72%	4.45	29	17	54	3.9	7.2	1.9	9%	1.3	2.0	51	$4
ERA Potl	50%	2nd Half		4	3	1	53	50	2.88	1.09	235			4.7	29%	77%	3.31	37	18	45	2.0	8.5	4.2	8%	0.8	11.0	121	$9
LIMA Plan	C	07	Proj	5	3	0	78	65	4.04	1.38	267			5.7	31%	75%	4.19	33	18	49	3.2	7.5	2.3	9%	1.3	2.9	57	$7

A terrific 2nd half, with growth in every skill area, put him on the LIMA map. But 100 IP is the threshold for warning flags about reliever overuse, and his DOM rate was 6.8 after August 1. Expect some regression.

Putz,J.J.

		Yr	Tm	W	L	Sv	IP	K	ERA	WHIP	OBA	vL	vR	BF/G	H%	S%	xERA	G	L	F	Ctl	Dom	Cmd	hr/f	hr/9	RAR	BPV	R$
RH	Reliever	02	a/a	5	14	0	138	81	4.96	1.59	299			25.9	33%	69%	5.16				3.5	5.3	1.5		0.8	-11.7	34	$1
Age	30	03	aaa	0	3	11	86	52	3.24	1.37	253			9.0	29%	76%	3.58				3.8	5.4	1.4		0.4	12.2	55	$8
Peak		04	SEA	0	3	9	63	47	4.71	1.43	271	234	308	5.1	30%	71%	3.69	52	15	32	3.4	6.7	2.0	16%	1.4	-2.2	39	$5
Type	Power	05	SEA	6	5	1	60	45	3.60	1.35	255	321	197	4.0	29%	78%	3.44	55	17	28	3.5	6.8	2.0	16%	1.2	5.7	50	$7
Reliability	39	06	SEA	4	1	36	78	104	2.30	0.92	211	211	204	4.2	32%	76%	2.02	51	16	33	1.5	12.0	8.0	7%	0.5	21.7	239	$27
DL		1st Half		1	0	13	36	50	2.49	0.89	203			3.9	33%	71%	1.81	55	15	30	1.5	12.5	8.3	4%	0.2	9.2	257	$11
ERA Potl	60%	2nd Half		3	1	23	42	54	2.14	0.95	218			4.4	32%	81%	2.20	47	17	36	1.5	11.6	7.7	9%	0.6	12.5	224	$16
LIMA Plan	C+	07	Proj	4	3	45	83	94	2.95	1.04	226			4.2	31%	75%	2.40	52	17	31	2.0	10.3	5.2	11%	0.8	21.2	158	$28

Added a 2-seam fastball and a curveball to his repertoire, but this was still a huge leap. A 200+ BPV is tough to maintain; chances are he'll come down to earth a little. Even if he does, he's still a top-tier closer.

Qualls,Chad

		Yr	Tm	W	L	Sv	IP	K	ERA	WHIP	OBA	vL	vR	BF/G	H%	S%	xERA	G	L	F	Ctl	Dom	Cmd	hr/f	hr/9	RAR	BPV	R$
RH	Reliever	02	aa	6	13	0	163	116	5.58	1.72	313			26.1	36%	67%	5.53				4.0	6.4	1.6		0.7	-26.3	45	($2)
Age	28	03	aa	8	11	0	175	101	5.24	1.66	310			28.6	34%	69%	5.52				3.5	5.2	1.5		0.8	-18.3	31	$1
Pre-Peak		04	HOU *	7	6	2	139	82	5.95	1.64	326	264	267	11.1	36%	63%	3.77	58	15	27	2.5	5.3	2.2	9%	0.8	-29.0	44	($1)
Type		05	HOU	6	4	0	79	60	3.30	1.21	246	218	275	4.3	29%	75%	2.88	58	21	20	2.6	6.8	2.6	15%	0.8	9.3	78	$9
Reliability	25	06	HOU	7	3	0	88	56	3.78	1.18	234	229	251	4.5	26%	71%	3.26	60	14	26	2.9	5.7	2.0	14%	1.0	7.7	54	$10
DL		1st Half		3	2	0	43	24	4.17	1.16	238			4.6	25%	68%	3.32	61	13	26	2.5	5.0	2.0	17%	1.3	1.7	42	$4
ERA Potl	45%	2nd Half		4	1	0	45	32	3.40	1.20	230			4.3	26%	74%	3.21	59	16	25	3.2	6.4	2.0	12%	0.8	6.0	65	$6
LIMA Plan	C+	07	Proj	6	3	5	83	55	3.90	1.30	259			5.4	30%	71%	3.28	59	17	24	2.8	6.0	2.1	11%	0.8	11.1	61	$9

Seems to be settling into a zone where he'll get you some wins to go with a better-than-average ERA and WHIP. It won't sell a bunch of jerseys with his name on the back, but it'll keep him gainfully employed.

Radke,Brad

		Yr	Tm	W	L	Sv	IP	K	ERA	WHIP	OBA	vL	vR	BF/G	H%	S%	xERA	G	L	F	Ctl	Dom	Cmd	hr/f	hr/9	RAR	BPV	R$
RH	Starter	02	MIN	9	5	0	118	62	4.73	1.22	271	247	300	23.3	29%	62%	4.07	41	17	41	1.5	4.7	3.1	7%	0.9	-3.9	67	$9
Age	34	03	MIN	14	10	0	212	120	4.50	1.27	288	297	278	26.9	31%	69%	3.95	41	18	41	1.2	5.1	4.3	11%	1.4	0.6	77	$16
Past Peak		04	MIN	11	8	0	219	143	3.49	1.16	270	267	281	26.3	30%	73%	3.54	43	19	38	1.1	5.9	5.5	9%	0.9	25.5	123	$21
Type		05	MIN	9	12	0	200	117	4.05	1.18	275	291	252	26.5	29%	72%	3.68	42	19	38	1.0	5.3	5.1	13%	1.5	8.0	94	$16
Reliability	78	06	MIN	12	9	0	162	83	4.33	1.41	301	303	311	25.1	32%	74%	4.23	42	20	38	1.8	4.6	2.6	11%	1.3	4.5	37	$12
DL		1st Half		6	7	0	93	49	5.41	1.65	329			26.6	34%	72%	4.50	42	20	37	2.4	4.7	2.0	13%	1.6	-9.8	9	$2
ERA Potl		2nd Half		6	2	0	69	34	2.87	1.09	259			23.0	28%	78%	3.86	41	19	40	0.9	4.4	4.9	8%	0.9	14.4	104	$10
LIMA Plan		07	Proj	0	0	0	0	0	0.00	0.00																		

Likely retiring after pitching with torn labrum and a stress fracture in his shoulder. A good case study of how the 5.6 DOM benchmark correlates with a sub-4.00 ERA, particularly for these precision soft-tossers.

BRANDON KRUSE

147

Ramirez,Elizardo

		W	L	Sv	IP	K	ERA	WHIP	OBA	vL	vR	BF/G	H%	S%	xERA	G	L	F	Ctl	Dom	Cmd	hr/f	hr/9	RAR	BPV	R$
RH Starter	02	0	0	0	0	0	0.00	0.00																		
Age 24	03	0	0	0	0	0	0.00	0.00																		
Growth	04 PHI *	3	6	0	79	45	5.58	1.70	335			18.2	36%	70%	6.58				2.5	5.1	**2.0**		1.5	-12.9	17	($2)
Type Finesse	05 CIN *	7	10	0	153	81	4.59	1.40	303			24.5	33%	70%	5.07				1.5	4.8	**3.1**		1.1	-6.5	55	$6
Reliability 0	06 CIN *	4	10	0	124	85	5.43	1.46	300	291	294	21.7	34%	65%	3.79	44	23	33	2.3	6.2	**2.8**	12%	1.2	-14.5	53	$3
DL 26	1st Half	3	7	0	83	59	4.01	1.25	271			23.1	30%	72%	3.62	43	20	37	1.8	6.4	**3.5**	11%	1.2	4.9	76	$6
ERA Potl 55%	2nd Half	1	3	0	41	26	8.33	1.89	354			19.7	39%	55%	4.17	46	27	26	3.1	5.8	**1.9**	15%	1.3	-19.4	19	($4)
LIMA Plan C+	07 Proj	**3**	**5**	**0**	**73**	**46**	**4.47**	**1.43**	**294**			**21.0**	**32%**	**72%**	**3.79**	**45**	**25**	**30**	**2.4**	**5.7**	**2.4**	**12%**	**1.1**	**5.1**	**48**	**$3**

4-9, 5.37 ERA in 104 IP at CIN. Could be nicely undervalued thanks to high H% and low S%. Three-year xERA trend is very encouraging. As a soft-tosser, his upside is limited, but he's a good back-of-the-rotation guy.

Ramirez,Horacio

		W	L	Sv	IP	K	ERA	WHIP	OBA	vL	vR	BF/G	H%	S%	xERA	G	L	F	Ctl	Dom	Cmd	hr/f	hr/9	RAR	BPV	R$
LH Starter	02 aa	9	5	0	92	54	3.52	1.37	268			24.7	30%	74%	3.82				3.0	5.3	**1.7**		0.5	8.5	55	$9
Age 27	03 ATL	12	4	0	182	100	4.01	1.39	261	206	278	27.0	28%	74%	4.08	53	16	31	3.6	4.9	**1.4**	11%	1.0	6.1	31	$12
Growth	04 ATL	2	4	0	60	31	2.40	1.35	231	220	227	25.6	24%	88%	4.12	54	20	26	4.5	4.6	**1.0**	14%	1.0	13.8	27	$5
Type Finesse	05 ATL	11	9	0	202	80	4.63	1.39	273	267	286	26.4	27%	71%	4.26	48	23	29	3.0	3.6	**1.2**	15%	1.4	-9.6	5	$8
Reliability 0	06 ATL	5	5	0	76	37	4.49	1.52	284	286	288	24.2	31%	71%	4.18	54	20	26	3.7	4.4	**1.2**	9%	0.7	-0.1	28	$3
DL 99	1st Half	3	2	0	41	20	3.72	1.51	289			26.0	32%	75%	4.25	51	21	28	3.3	4.4	**1.3**	5%	0.4	3.9	38	$3
ERA Potl 45%	2nd Half	2	3	0	35	17	5.40	1.54	278			22.3	29%	66%	4.10	57	20	23	4.1	4.4	**1.1**	14%	1.0	-3.9	17	$0
LIMA Plan C	07 Proj	**7**	**9**	**0**	**131**	**62**	**4.55**	**1.49**	**278**			**25.0**	**30%**	**70%**	**4.21**	**53**	**21**	**26**	**3.7**	**4.3**	**1.2**	**10%**	**0.8**	**2.4**	**25**	**$4**

Another season of stagnant, inferior skills, though this time mercifully cut short by injuries. Hey, you have to give stagnant inferiority some credit... At least there's no danger of missing out on a Cy Young Award candidate.

Ramirez,Ramon

		W	L	Sv	IP	K	ERA	WHIP	OBA	vL	vR	BF/G	H%	S%	xERA	G	L	F	Ctl	Dom	Cmd	hr/f	hr/9	RAR	BPV	R$
RH Reliever	02	0	0	0	0	0	0.00	0.00																		
Age 25	03 a/a	1	2	0	27	22	2.66	1.29	254			19.0	28%	90%	4.55				3.0	7.3	**2.4**		1.7	5.8	50	$3
Growth	04 a/a	4	9	0	133	121	6.02	1.49	296			26.7	36%	60%	5.06				2.7	8.2	**3.0**		1.0	-27.6	78	$2
Type Power	05 a/a	9	9	0	141	107	4.73	1.43	274			20.5	31%	71%	4.91				3.3	6.8	**2.1**		1.4	-7.5	43	$8
Reliability 9	06 COL	4	3	0	67	61	3.48	1.26	234	274	194	4.6	29%	74%	3.81	41	14	45	3.6	8.2	**2.3**	6%	0.7	8.3	85	$7
DL	1st Half	3	1	0	34	35	2.11	0.88	200			4.3	27%	76%	2.74	45	14	41	1.6	9.2	**5.8**	3%	0.3	10.0	185	$7
ERA Potl 50%	2nd Half	1	2	0	33	26	4.89	1.66	267			4.9	31%	73%	5.08	37	14	49	5.7	7.1	**1.2**	8%	1.1	-1.7	37	$0
LIMA Plan C+	07 Proj	**3**	**3**	**0**	**58**	**49**	**4.50**	**1.40**	**262**			**7.8**	**30%**	**71%**	**4.06**	**38**	**17**	**45**	**3.6**	**7.6**	**2.1**	**10%**	**1.2**	**2.1**	**56**	**$3**

Three Scary Things:
1) 2nd half rookie year decline.
2) Stats vs the Dodgers... eight games, 6.2 IP, 15.88 ERA. (vs everyone else: 2.32 ERA.)
3) Coors could revert to old.
Despite BPIs, be a little scared.

Rauch,Jon

		W	L	Sv	IP	K	ERA	WHIP	OBA	vL	vR	BF/G	H%	S%	xERA	G	L	F	Ctl	Dom	Cmd	hr/f	hr/9	RAR	BPV	R$
RH Reliever	02 CHW *	9	9	0	137	109	5.91	1.42	262	258	234	22.0	29%	62%	5.08				3.8	7.2	**1.9**		1.7	-24.6	34	$6
Age 28	03 aaa	7	1	0	124	84	5.43	1.45	291			22.6	31%	66%	5.42				2.6	6.1	**2.3**		1.6	-16.0	34	$4
Pre-Peak	04 2TM *	11	5	0	122	82	3.91	1.29	257	321	203	18.4	28%	74%	4.20	43	11	47	2.9	6.0	**2.1**	10%	1.0	6.6	46	$12
Type Power	05 WAS *	3	5	0	51	43	3.53	1.16	234	255	186	9.5	27%	74%	3.93	26	23	51	2.6	7.6	**2.9**	8%	1.1	4.5	82	$6
Reliability 6	06 WAS	4	5	2	91	86	3.36	1.25	233	254	216	4.5	28%	79%	3.86	30	21	49	3.6	8.5	**2.4**	11%	1.3	12.7	71	$10
DL 103	1st Half	2	1	0	45	42	2.99	1.24	235			4.7	28%	82%	3.75	36	17	47	3.4	8.4	**2.5**	10%	1.2	8.3	74	$5
ERA Potl 45%	2nd Half	2	4	2	46	44	3.72	1.26	231			4.3	27%	76%	3.95	24	26	50	3.7	8.6	**2.3**	11%	1.4	4.4	68	$5
LIMA Plan C+	07 Proj	**5**	**5**	**3**	**83**	**79**	**3.90**	**1.29**	**248**			**5.5**	**30%**	**75%**	**3.85**	**29**	**22**	**49**	**3.3**	**8.6**	**2.6**	**10%**	**1.3**	**5.2**	**73**	**$9**

Seems to have found his niche in bullpen. Walks, FB% are still holding him back, but continued DOM growth could be a cure-all. Career skills say pen is right fit...
As Starter: 5.7 DOM, 1.5 CMD
As Reliever: 8.2 DOM, 2.3 CMD

Ray,Chris

		W	L	Sv	IP	K	ERA	WHIP	OBA	vL	vR	BF/G	H%	S%	xERA	G	L	F	Ctl	Dom	Cmd	hr/f	hr/9	RAR	BPV	R$
RH Reliever	02	0	0	0	0	0	0.00	0.00											0.0	0.0						
Age 25	03	0	0	0	0	0	0.00	0.00											0.0	0.0						
Growth	04	0	0	0	0	0	0.00	0.00											0.0	0.0						
Type Power	05 BAL *	2	5	18	77	77	2.12	1.05	203	284	174	4.3	25%	87%	3.22	35	23	41	2.9	9.0	**3.1**	11%	1.1	21.5	100	$18
Reliability 0	06 BAL	4	4	33	66	51	2.73	1.09	195	184	202	4.3	21%	84%	4.01	35	16	48	3.7	7.0	**1.9**	11%	1.4	14.9	57	$20
DL	1st Half	1	2	20	33	32	3.27	1.09	191			4.1	22%	77%	3.47	42	12	46	3.8	8.7	**2.3**	13%	1.4	5.2	76	$11
ERA Potl 30%	2nd Half	3	2	13	33	19	2.18	1.09	198			4.6	20%	90%	4.55	29	20	51	3.5	5.2	**1.5**	10%	1.4	9.7	36	$10
LIMA Plan D	07 Proj	**3**	**4**	**33**	**65**	**53**	**3.59**	**1.29**	**240**			**4.6**	**28%**	**76%**	**4.12**	**34**	**19**	**47**	**3.6**	**7.3**	**2.0**	**9%**	**1.1**	**3.0**	**61**	**$17**

Four Warning Signs:
- 2nd half "dead arm," DOM slide
- High FB% = Gopheritis
- 57 BPV not closer-worthy
- H% and S% hid the damage
Likely to be overvalued.
DN: 4.50 ERA, loses his job.

Ray,Ken

		W	L	Sv	IP	K	ERA	WHIP	OBA	vL	vR	BF/G	H%	S%	xERA	G	L	F	Ctl	Dom	Cmd	hr/f	hr/9	RAR	BPV	R$
RH Reliever	02	0	0	0	0	0	0.00	0.00																		
Age 32	03 aa	2	1	4	61	33	4.97	2.11	358			9.9	39%	79%	7.91				4.8	4.8	**1.0**		1.3	-4.4	-5	($2)
Peak	04	0	0	0	0	0	0.00	0.00																		
Type Power	05 aaa	2	4	0	67	33	5.09	1.79	306			18.6	33%	73%	5.94				4.9	4.5	**0.9**		1.0	-6.5	10	($2)
Reliability 5	06 ATL	1	1	5	67	50	4.55	1.55	258	282	237	4.4	29%	74%	4.75	37	19	44	5.1	6.7	**1.3**	10%	1.2	-0.5	35	$3
DL	1st Half	0	0	4	35	26	3.07	1.31	214			4.1	23%	83%	4.48	36	19	45	4.9	6.6	**1.4**	11%	1.3	6.2	43	$4
ERA Potl 40%	2nd Half	1	1	1	32	24	6.19	1.81	302			4.6	35%	67%	5.04	38	20	42	5.3	6.7	**1.3**	9%	1.1	-6.7	28	($1)
LIMA Plan C	07 Proj	**1**	**2**	**3**	**58**	**40**	**4.97**	**1.66**	**281**			**6.8**	**31%**	**74%**	**4.95**	**37**	**20**	**43**	**5.0**	**6.2**	**1.3**	**11%**	**1.4**	**-4.2**	**20**	**$0**

It was a Cinderella story, the career minor-leaguer suddenly winning a major-league closer job, but the skills were never there. And now he's just another pumpkin with poor Ctl, no CMD and an ERA pushing 5.00.

Redman,Mark

		W	L	Sv	IP	K	ERA	WHIP	OBA	vL	vR	BF/G	H%	S%	xERA	G	L	F	Ctl	Dom	Cmd	hr/f	hr/9	RAR	BPV	R$
LH Starter	02 DET	8	15	0	203	109	4.21	1.29	269	289	261	28.5	30%	68%	4.33	42	15	43	2.3	4.8	**2.1**	5%	0.7	6.2	55	$13
Age 33	03 FLA	14	9	0	190	151	3.60	1.23	243	200	248	27.2	29%	72%	3.80	40	18	42	2.9	7.2	**2.5**	7%	0.8	15.9	79	$20
Peak	04 OAK	11	12	0	191	102	4.71	1.50	288	286	294	26.4	30%	72%	4.63	40	19	40	3.2	4.8	**1.5**	11%	1.3	-6.6	18	$7
Type Finesse	05 PIT	5	15	0	178	101	4.90	1.37	272	256	283	25.5	30%	65%	3.92	49	21	30	2.8	5.1	**1.8**	10%	0.9	-14.4	42	$5
Reliability 58	06 KC	11	10	0	167	76	5.71	1.59	300	229	326	26.0	32%	65%	4.75	44	20	35	3.4	4.1	**1.2**	9%	1.0	-23.8	14	$3
DL 15	1st Half	5	4	0	69	25	5.35	1.52	278			25.5	28%	66%	5.04	43	21	35	3.9	3.3	**0.8**	9%	1.0	-6.7	5	$2
ERA Potl 50%	2nd Half	6	6	0	98	51	5.97	1.63	315			26.2	34%	64%	4.56	45	19	35	3.0	4.7	**1.5**	9%	1.0	-17.1	22	$1
LIMA Plan C	07 Proj	**7**	**13**	**0**	**164**	**83**	**5.17**	**1.49**	**287**			**25.8**	**31%**	**67%**	**4.49**	**45**	**20**	**36**	**3.2**	**4.6**	**1.4**	**9%**	**1.0**	**-0.0**	**24**	**$4**

The ultimate irony... Six teams in 6 years and the absolute worst performance yields him an All-Star invite. There have been no signs of life since 2003 and the trends are only getting more bleak. Pass. Then pass again.

Reitsma,Chris

		W	L	Sv	IP	K	ERA	WHIP	OBA	vL	vR	BF/G	H%	S%	xERA	G	L	F	Ctl	Dom	Cmd	hr/f	hr/9	RAR	BPV	R$
RH Reliever	02 CIN *	8	12	0	159	95	3.74	1.35	265	265	268	19.4	29%	76%	4.00	49	16	35	2.9	5.4	**1.8**	11%	1.1	7.3	40	$10
Age 29	03 CIN *	10	7	12	102	62	4.50	1.39	291	298	270	7.2	31%	72%	3.49	57	15	28	2.1	5.5	**2.6**	16%	1.3	-2.8	44	$11
Pre-Peak	04 ATL	6	4	2	79	60	4.09	1.38	285	310	262	4.1	33%	73%	3.42	53	16	32	2.3	6.8	**3.0**	11%	1.0	1.7	71	$7
Type Finesse	05 ATL	3	6	15	73	42	3.94	1.27	277	252	298	4.0	32%	68%	3.45	53	21	26	1.7	5.2	**3.0**	5%	0.4	2.8	83	$10
Reliability 7	06 ATL	1	2	8	28	13	8.68	1.93	368	422	302	5.0	37%	57%	4.52	50	20	30	2.6	4.2	**1.6**	21%	2.3	-14.5	-27	($0)
DL 107	1st Half	1	2	8	26	13	9.27	1.98	373			4.9	38%	56%	4.57	49	21	31	2.7	4.5	**1.6**	22%	2.4	-15.5	-31	($1)
ERA Potl 60%	2nd Half	0	0	0	2	0	0.00	1.11	283			7.3	28%	100%	3.43	67	17	17	0.0	0.0		0%	0.0	1.0	-2	$0
LIMA Plan D	07 Proj	**4**	**5**	**0**	**69**	**38**	**4.96**	**1.46**	**299**			**5.0**	**32%**	**68%**	**3.90**	**51**	**19**	**30**	**2.3**	**5.0**	**2.1**	**11%**	**1.0**	**3.9**	**38**	**$2**

Problems with ulnar nerve in his elbow ended his season and caused a skill implosion, though it's worth noting that he also had a paltry 4.4 DOM in the 2nd half of 2005. If the strikeouts don't return, neither will his value.

Reyes,Anthony

		W	L	Sv	IP	K	ERA	WHIP	OBA	vL	vR	BF/G	H%	S%	xERA	G	L	F	Ctl	Dom	Cmd	hr/f	hr/9	RAR	BPV	R$
RH Starter	02	0	0	0	0	0	0.00	0.00											0.0	0.0						
Age 25	03	0	0	0	0	0	0.00	0.00											0.0	0.0						
Growth	04 aa	6	2	0	74	90	3.28	1.09	246			24.8	35%	69%	2.70				1.6	10.9	**6.9**		0.4	9.7	206	$11
Type Power	05 STL *	8	7	0	141	132	3.82	1.10	230	125	148	21.0	28%	67%	3.55	35	13	52	2.3	8.4	**3.7**	7%	0.9	7.4	110	$16
Reliability 9	06 STL *	11	9	0	169	143	4.20	1.25	259	278	249	23.5	30%	72%	3.74	35	20	46	2.4	7.6	**3.2**	12%	1.4	5.9	72	$16
DL	1st Half	5	3	0	96	73	3.47	1.03	239			25.3	27%	71%	3.58	30	23	47	1.3	6.8	**5.2**	9%	1.1	12.1	124	$12
ERA Potl 55%	2nd Half	6	6	0	73	70	5.17	1.55	285			21.8	33%	72%	4.00	36	18	45	3.8	8.6	**2.3**	15%	1.8	-6.2	42	$4
LIMA Plan C+	07 Proj	**12**	**10**	**0**	**185**	**168**	**4.10**	**1.24**	**252**			**22.6**	**30%**	**70%**	**3.64**	**35**	**19**	**46**	**2.6**	**8.2**	**3.2**	**9%**	**1.1**	**16.5**	**87**	**$18**

5-8, 5.06 ERA in 85 IP at STL.
PRO: FB% reduction, 2nd half DOM surge, CMD still strong.
CON: Three-year skill slide.
Though to be fair, he's simply gone from otherworldly to good. Good is good enough for now.

BRANDON KRUSE

Reyes,Dennys	Yr	Tm	W	L	Sv	IP	K	ERA	WHIP	OBA	vL	vR	BF/G	H%	S%	xERA	G	L	F	Ctl	Dom	Cmd	hr/f	hr/9	RAR	BPV	R$
LH Reliever	02	2TM	4	4	0	82	59	5.38	1.74	298	299	299	6.6	34%	71%	5.76				4.9	6.5	**1.3**		1.1	-11.2	29	($0)
Age 30	03	aaa	2	1	2	31	25	3.46	1.60	241			4.3	31%	76%	3.60				6.3	7.2	**1.1**		0.0	3.6	74	$3
Peak	04	KC	4	8	0	108	91	4.75	1.52	272	316	254	12.0	32%	70%	3.74	51	17	32	4.2	7.6	**1.8**	11%	1.0	-4.2	54	$4
Type Power	05	SD	3	2	0	43	35	5.21	2.06	319	208	359	6.0	38%	74%	4.01	65	17	18	6.7	7.3	**1.1**	11%	0.6	-5.1	39	($1)
Reliability 15	06	MIN *	6	0	0	68	59	0.80	1.01	208	148	244	3.8	26%	95%	2.35	69	11	20	2.4	7.8	**3.2**	8%	0.4	31.6	116	$15
DL	1st Half		2	0	0	37	25	1.00	1.05	226			6.1	26%	97%	2.58	70	9	20	2.0	6.1	**3.0**	13%	0.7	16.3	88	$7
ERA Potl 35%	2nd Half		4	0	0	31	34	0.58	0.96	185			2.6	27%	93%	2.07	68	12	20	2.9	9.8	**3.4**	0%	0.0	15.3	148	$8
LIMA Plan B	07	Proj	**5**	**3**	**0**	**73**	**63**	**3.60**	**1.37**	**252**			**4.6**	**31%**	**74%**	**2.94**	**64**	**14**	**22**	**3.7**	**7.8**	**2.1**	**11%**	**0.6**	**13.8**	**77**	**$7**

5-0, 0.89 ERA in 51 IP at MIN. Another convert to MIN "throw strikes" philosophy. Ctl was key to breakout, but can he do it again? History and 3.6 Ctl in Aug/Sept suggest caution. And don't expect encore from S%.

Rheinecker,John	Yr	Tm	W	L	Sv	IP	K	ERA	WHIP	OBA	vL	vR	BF/G	H%	S%	xERA	G	L	F	Ctl	Dom	Cmd	hr/f	hr/9	RAR	BPV	R$
LH Starter	02	aa	7	7	0	128	83	4.08	1.43	304			27.8	35%	71%	4.51				1.8	5.8	**3.3**		0.5	3.0	84	$7
Age 27	03	a/a	11	6	0	180	95	5.15	1.70	340			28.7	37%	70%	6.03				2.2	4.8	**2.1**		0.7	-16.8	39	$1
Pre-Peak	04	aaa	11	9	0	172	108	4.70	1.48	298			27.1	33%	71%	5.23				2.6	5.6	**2.2**		1.2	-7.6	40	$7
Type Finesse	05	aaa	4	0	0	45	20	2.05	1.00	200			25.3	23%	77%	1.61				2.7	4.1	**1.5**		0.0	12.6	71	$7
Reliability 0	06	TEX *	8	11	0	163	84	4.80	1.69	333	197	392	20.9	36%	72%	3.77	59	19	22	2.6	4.6	**1.8**	11%	0.8	-4.9	31	$3
DL	1st Half		5	3	0	88	48	4.83	1.73	343			25.6	38%	72%	3.82	54	24	22	2.3	4.9	**2.1**	10%	0.7	-3.0	39	$1
ERA Potl 50%	2nd Half		3	8	0	75	36	4.76	1.65	320			17.1	34%	72%	3.71	65	14	21	2.9	4.3	**1.5**	12%	0.9	-1.9	22	$1
LIMA Plan C+	07	Proj	**4**	**4**	**0**	**73**	**37**	**4.22**	**1.38**	**279**			**22.3**	**30%**	**70%**	**3.49**	**60**	**18**	**22**	**2.6**	**4.6**	**1.8**	**11%**	**0.7**	**8.9**	**41**	**$5**

4-6, 5.86 ERA in 71 IP at TEX. PRO: Good xERA, extreme GB% helps counter low DOM CON: 3.6 DOM, 1.5 CMD w/TEX, 23%/69% DOM/DIS Late arrival to majors makes him a questionable horse to back.

Rhodes,Arthur	Yr	Tm	W	L	Sv	IP	K	ERA	WHIP	OBA	vL	vR	BF/G	H%	S%	xERA	G	L	F	Ctl	Dom	Cmd	hr/f	hr/9	RAR	BPV	R$
LH Reliever	02	SEA	10	4	2	69	81	2.35	0.84	188	158	215	3.9	27%	74%	2.26	43	26	32	1.7	10.6	**6.2**	8%	0.5	18.0	196	$17
Age 37	03	SEA	3	3	3	54	48	4.17	1.31	258	269	243	3.4	32%	69%	3.50	43	22	35	3.0	8.0	**2.7**	7%	0.7	2.4	87	$6
Decline	04	OAK	3	3	9	38	34	5.18	1.75	299	314	283	4.8	33%	78%	4.44	40	17	43	4.9	8.0	**1.6**	18%	2.1	-3.5	14	$4
Type Power	05	CLE	3	1	0	43	43	2.09	1.04	214	286	155	3.6	28%	81%	3.02	41	23	36	2.5	9.0	**3.6**	5%	0.4	12.1	129	$8
Reliability 0	06	PHI	0	5	4	45	48	5.38	1.70	269	290	246	3.8	36%	67%	4.35	36	22	41	6.0	9.6	**1.6**	4%	0.4	-5.0	80	$1
DL 21	1st Half		0	2	1	25	30	5.00	1.90	304			4.1	43%	71%	4.09	40	25	36	6.1	10.7	**1.8**	0%	0.0	-1.6	96	($0)
ERA Potl 65%	2nd Half		0	3	3	20	18	5.85	1.45	221			3.5	27%	59%	4.63	32	20	48	5.8	8.1	**1.4**	8%	0.9	-3.4	61	$1
LIMA Plan B	07	Proj	**2**	**4**	**0**	**44**	**42**	**4.76**	**1.49**	**251**			**3.8**	**31%**	**70%**	**4.06**	**38**	**21**	**41**	**5.0**	**8.7**	**1.8**	**10%**	**1.0**	**1.6**	**63**	**$2**

Signs that time may be up:
- Loss of Ctl, 2nd half DOM drop
- 2nd half jumps in FB and hr/9
- Late-season elbow problems

Fanalytic value often dies before MLB value for players with LH next to their name.

Rincon,Juan	Yr	Tm	W	L	Sv	IP	K	ERA	WHIP	OBA	vL	vR	BF/G	H%	S%	xERA	G	L	F	Ctl	Dom	Cmd	hr/f	hr/9	RAR	BPV	R$
RH Reliever	02	MIN *	7	6	0	129	85	5.44	1.60	309	283	415	20.1	35%	67%	4.29	45	17	38	3.0	5.9	**2.0**	10%	1.2	-15.6	37	$2
Age 28	03	MIN	5	6	0	85	63	3.71	1.32	236	222	239	6.2	28%	72%	4.21	42	17	41	4.0	6.7	**1.7**	5%	0.5	8.6	67	$8
Pre-Peak	04	MIN	11	6	2	82	106	2.63	1.02	184	148	206	4.2	27%	76%	2.60	45	16	39	3.5	11.6	**3.3**	7%	0.5	18.2	141	$18
Type Power	05	MIN	6	6	0	77	84	2.45	1.21	225	218	228	4.2	31%	79%	2.97	48	20	32	3.5	9.8	**2.8**	3%	0.2	18.2	121	$12
Reliability 28	06	MIN	3	1	1	74	65	2.91	1.35	267	222	303	4.2	34%	78%	3.22	51	22	28	2.9	7.9	**2.7**	3%	0.2	15.0	99	$8
DL	1st Half		2	0	1	39	37	2.07	1.22	240			4.5	32%	81%	3.01	53	18	28	3.0	8.5	**2.8**	0%	0.0	12.0	118	$6
ERA Potl 55%	2nd Half		1	1	0	35	28	3.87	1.49	294			3.9	36%	74%	3.46	49	25	27	2.8	7.2	**2.5**	7%	0.5	3.0	77	$2
LIMA Plan B+	07	Proj	**5**	**3**	**0**	**73**	**67**	**3.21**	**1.27**	**246**			**4.4**	**31%**	**75%**	**3.18**	**50**	**21**	**29**	**3.2**	**8.3**	**2.6**	**7%**	**0.5**	**11.7**	**95**	**$9**

DOM trend is worrisome, and this was the 2nd straight year with a 2nd half drop-off. But with his knack for keeping the ball in the park (thanks to declining FB%) and good CMD, he should remain LIMA-worthy.

Riske,David	Yr	Tm	W	L	Sv	IP	K	ERA	WHIP	OBA	vL	vR	BF/G	H%	S%	xERA	G	L	F	Ctl	Dom	Cmd	hr/f	hr/9	RAR	BPV	R$
RH Reliever	02	CLE *	2	3	4	66	87	5.18	1.56	253	253	259	4.6	34%	71%	3.55	31	26	43	5.5	11.9	**2.2**	17%	1.6	-5.9	72	$4
Age 30	03	CLE	2	2	8	74	82	2.31	0.97	199	145	241	4.2	25%	84%	2.83	37	22	41	2.4	10.0	**4.1**	12%	1.1	20.2	128	$15
Peak	04	CLE	7	3	5	77	78	3.74	1.43	241	224	255	4.7	29%	79%	3.98	36	18	45	4.8	9.1	**1.9**	12%	1.3	6.6	63	$10
Type	05	CLE	3	4	1	72	48	3.12	0.97	213	210	204	4.8	22%	76%	3.44	42	20	38	1.9	6.0	**3.2**	14%	1.4	11.2	74	$10
Reliability 17	06	2AL	1	2	0	44	28	3.89	1.30	244	280	224	4.5	26%	75%	4.33	36	22	42	3.5	5.7	**1.6**	11%	1.2	3.6	38	$3
DL 47	1st Half		0	1	0	14	8	2.57	0.93	202			4.5	20%	82%	4.03	35	14	51	1.9	5.1	**2.7**	9%	1.3	3.4	63	$2
ERA Potl 45%	2nd Half		1	1	0	30	20	4.50	1.47	262			4.5	29%	73%	4.47	36	26	38	4.2	6.0	**1.4**	11%	1.2	0.2	33	$1
LIMA Plan C+	07	Proj	**2**	**2**	**0**	**44**	**29**	**4.14**	**1.40**	**260**			**4.7**	**29%**	**73%**	**4.43**	**38**	**21**	**42**	**3.7**	**6.0**	**1.6**	**9%**	**1.0**	**0.3**	**42**	**$3**

Five-year DOM trend is a symbol of his journey from future closer to just another guy fighting for bullpen innings. Walks and HRs continue to be his twin enemies, and they've finally driven his xERA over 4.00. ERA is next.

Rivera,Mariano	Yr	Tm	W	L	Sv	IP	K	ERA	WHIP	OBA	vL	vR	BF/G	H%	S%	xERA	G	L	F	Ctl	Dom	Cmd	hr/f	hr/9	RAR	BPV	R$
RH Reliever	02	NYY	1	4	28	46	41	2.74	1.00	212	181	225	4.0	27%	74%	2.96	46	22	33	2.2	8.0	**3.7**	7%	0.6	9.8	121	$16
Age 37	03	NYY	5	2	40	70	63	1.67	1.01	236	197	283	4.3	30%	85%	2.54	54	20	26	1.3	8.1	**6.3**	6%	0.4	24.6	177	$27
Decline	04	NYY	4	2	53	78	66	1.96	1.09	228	234	215	4.2	29%	83%	2.84	60	11	29	2.3	7.6	**3.3**	5%	0.3	23.9	114	$30
Type	05	NYY	7	4	43	78	80	1.38	0.87	185	177	176	4.2	25%	85%	2.38	57	14	29	2.1	9.2	**4.4**	4%	0.2	28.8	160	$31
Reliability 60	06	NYY	5	5	34	75	55	1.80	0.96	224	194	248	4.6	27%	83%	2.92	54	16	30	1.3	6.6	**5.0**	5%	0.4	25.5	144	$25
DL	1st Half		4	4	17	43	32	1.88	0.95	214			4.8	27%	78%	2.84	56	17	27	1.7	6.7	**4.0**	0%	0.0	14.2	136	$14
ERA Potl 50%	2nd Half		1	1	17	32	23	1.69	0.97	237			4.4	27%	89%	3.01	51	14	35	0.8	6.5	**7.7**	9%	0.8	11.3	182	$11
LIMA Plan C+	07	Proj	**5**	**4**	**35**	**73**	**56**	**2.59**	**1.07**	**231**			**4.5**	**28%**	**78%**	**3.03**	**55**	**15**	**30**	**2.0**	**6.9**	**3.5**	**8%**	**0.6**	**13.1**	**105**	**$23**

Showed his age with back pain, MRIs and DOM drop. But thanks to improved Ctl, none of it really slowed him down. 2nd half rise in FB, hr/9 bears monitoring. No longer the best closer in baseball, but he's still elite.

Rivera,Saul	Yr	Tm	W	L	Sv	IP	K	ERA	WHIP	OBA	vL	vR	BF/G	H%	S%	xERA	G	L	F	Ctl	Dom	Cmd	hr/f	hr/9	RAR	BPV	R$
RH Reliever	02	aa	2	5	16	57	38	3.93	1.54	254			5.7	30%	73%	3.89				5.2	6.0	**1.2**		0.3	2.4	55	$7
Age 29	03		0	0	0	0	0	0.00	0.00																		
Pre-Peak	04	aa	2	3	4	54	30	7.08	2.23	358			6.3	39%	69%	8.10				5.9	4.9	**0.8**		1.1	-18.2	-4	($5)
Type Power	05	aa	3	3	9	76	50	3.27	1.53	304			8.5	35%	79%	4.72				2.7	5.9	**2.2**		0.4	9.7	62	$7
Reliability 3	06	WAS *	4	1	2	88	61	3.01	1.52	264	194	290	5.9	31%	81%	4.39	46	19	35	4.6	6.2	**1.3**	5%	0.5	16.1	52	$7
DL	1st Half		1	1	1	42	30	2.87	1.52	266			6.7	31%	83%	4.64	40	19	42	4.5	6.3	**1.4**	6%	0.7	8.4	50	$3
ERA Potl 30%	2nd Half		3	0	1	46	31	3.13	1.52	262			5.4	31%	79%	4.36	48	19	33	4.7	6.1	**1.3**	4%	0.4	7.7	54	$4
LIMA Plan C+	07	Proj	**3**	**2**	**0**	**58**	**38**	**4.34**	**1.55**	**275**			**6.3**	**31%**	**74%**	**4.39**	**47**	**19**	**34**	**4.3**	**5.9**	**1.4**	**9%**	**0.9**	**-0.2**	**36**	**$2**

3-0, 3.43 ERA in 60 IP at WAS. Gap between ERA and xERA and history of poor CMD mean you should steer clear. Only the second Saul in MLB history, after Saul Rogovin, so he's got that going for him.

Robertson,Nate	Yr	Tm	W	L	Sv	IP	K	ERA	WHIP	OBA	vL	vR	BF/G	H%	S%	xERA	G	L	F	Ctl	Dom	Cmd	hr/f	hr/9	RAR	BPV	R$
LH Starter	02	aa	10	9	0	163	86	4.20	1.50	291			26.7	32%	73%	4.67				3.1	4.7	**1.5**		0.7	1.5	38	$7
Age 29	03	DET *	10	9	0	199	119	4.48	1.51	292	300	307	27.6	32%	72%	4.18	46	21	32	3.2	5.4	**1.7**	9%	0.9	1.2	38	$9
Peak	04	DET	12	10	1	196	155	4.91	1.41	275	252	279	25.0	31%	69%	3.55	50	17	33	3.0	7.1	**2.3**	15%	1.4	-11.5	51	$12
Type	05	DET	7	16	0	196	122	4.50	1.36	267	244	272	26.2	29%	71%	3.79	49	20	30	3.0	5.6	**1.9**	15%	1.3	-3.0	36	$10
Reliability 97	06	DET	13	13	0	208	137	3.85	1.31	260	181	284	27.5	28%	75%	3.79	47	20	33	2.9	5.9	**2.0**	13%	1.3	18.2	44	$19
DL	1st Half		8	3	0	100	70	3.15	1.30	250			26.4	28%	80%	3.79	47	19	34	3.2	6.3	**1.9**	11%	1.0	17.4	54	$12
ERA Potl 40%	2nd Half		5	10	0	108	67	4.50	1.32	269			28.7	28%	71%	3.79	46	21	33	2.6	5.6	**2.2**	16%	1.5	0.8	35	$8
LIMA Plan D	07	Proj	**14**	**11**	**0**	**214**	**142**	**3.75**	**1.33**	**268**			**26.7**	**30%**	**76%**	**3.73**	**48**	**20**	**32**	**2.7**	**6.0**	**2.2**	**12%**	**1.1**	**20.0**	**49**	**$19**

ERA finally came in line with skills, though we're still waiting for his luck with hr/f to turn around. Reliability gives him value at the back end of a rotation, where you can stick him in and forget about him.

Rodney,Fernando	Yr	Tm	W	L	Sv	IP	K	ERA	WHIP	OBA	vL	vR	BF/G	H%	S%	xERA	G	L	F	Ctl	Dom	Cmd	hr/f	hr/9	RAR	BPV	R$
RH Reliever	02	a/a	2	1	15	42	37	1.28	1.09	212			4.1	27%	89%	2.11				3.0	7.9	**2.6**		0.2	15.6	109	$12
Age 30	03	aaa	1	1	23	40	49	1.85	1.00	191			4.1	30%	79%	1.44				3.0	11.1	**3.7**		0.0	12.6	161	$15
Peak	04	DET	0	0	0	0	0	0.00	0.00											0.0	0.0						
Type Power	05	DET	2	3	9	44	42	2.86	1.27	239	265	219	4.7	29%	82%	3.31	40	28	31	3.5	8.6	**2.5**	13%	1.0	8.2	80	$8
Reliability 0	06	DET	7	4	7	71	65	3.54	1.19	203	202	192	4.6	25%	72%	3.25	57	12	31	4.3	8.2	**1.9**	10%	0.8	8.9	81	$13
DL 73	1st Half		4	2	7	38	39	2.83	1.07	170			4.6	21%	78%	3.27	48	12	40	4.5	9.2	**2.1**	11%	0.9	8.2	91	$9
ERA Potl 50%	2nd Half		3	2	0	33	26	4.36	1.33	238			4.7	29%	67%	3.20	64	12	23	4.1	7.1	**1.7**	9%	0.5	0.8	70	$3
LIMA Plan B	07	Proj	**5**	**4**	**5**	**73**	**65**	**3.35**	**1.26**	**230**			**4.6**	**29%**	**74%**	**3.26**	**53**	**17**	**30**	**3.7**	**8.1**	**2.2**	**8%**	**0.6**	**10.9**	**84**	**$11**

Likely missed his window of opportunity for DET closer job, and dwindling CMD may limit future chances. GB trend is encouraging though, and if Ctl ever improves...
UP: 2.50 ERA.

BRANDON KRUSE

Rodriguez,Francisco

		Yr	Tm	W	L	Sv	IP	K	ERA	WHIP	OBA	vL	vR	BF/G	H%	S%	xERA	G	L	F	Ctl	Dom	Cmd	hr/f	hr/9	RAR	BPV	R$
RH	Reliever	02	a/a	5	6	15	83	113	2.39	1.06	212			6.6	33%	78%	2.09				2.7	12.3	4.5		0.3	19.3	171	$19
Age	25	03	ANA	8	3	2	86	95	3.03	0.99	171	186	156	5.7	20%	77%	2.84	43	22	35	3.7	9.9	2.7	17%	1.3	15.8	100	$17
Growth		04	ANA	4	1	12	84	123	1.82	1.00	177	213	127	4.8	30%	82%	2.29	44	19	37	3.5	13.2	3.7	3%	0.2	27.0	170	$20
Type	Power	05	ANA	2	5	45	67	91	2.68	1.15	192	213	153	4.1	28%	81%	2.66	46	17	38	4.3	12.2	2.8	13%	0.9	14.0	121	$25
Reliability	66	06	ANA	2	3	47	73	98	1.73	1.10	202	215	179	4.2	30%	89%	2.79	39	14	47	3.5	12.1	3.5	8%	0.7	25.5	138	$28
DL	17	1st Half		0	2	19	34	42	3.18	1.09	220			4.4	28%	81%	2.81	40	13	47	2.6	11.1	4.2	16%	1.6	5.8	118	$11
ERA Potl	45%	2nd Half		2	1	28	39	56	0.46	1.10	185			4.1	32%	95%	2.77	37	16	47	4.2	12.9	3.1	0%	0.0	19.7	161	$18
LIMA Plan	C+	07	Proj	**3**	**3**	**48**	**73**	**99**	**2.36**	**1.13**	**203**			**4.5**	**30%**	**84%**	**2.79**	**38**	**16**	**46**	**3.7**	**12.3**	**3.3**	**10%**	**0.9**	**15.2**	**131**	**$28**

Nice step back toward the skills he displayed in 2004, and from R$ standpoint, his best season yet. FB has been over 45% since 2nd half of '05, which could lead to some HR troubles. Otherwise, he's top-shelf.

Rodriguez,Wandy

		Yr	Tm	W	L	Sv	IP	K	ERA	WHIP	OBA	vL	vR	BF/G	H%	S%	xERA	G	L	F	Ctl	Dom	Cmd	hr/f	hr/9	RAR	BPV	R$
LH	Starter	02		0	0	0	0	0	0.00	0.00											0.0	0.0						
Age	28	03		0	0	0	0	0	0.00	0.00											0.0	0.0						
Pre-Peak		04	aa	11	6	0	142	86	5.98	1.85	334			26.1	37%	69%	6.77				3.9	5.5	1.4		1.2	-28.7	14	($2)
Type	Power	05	HOU *	14	12	0	177	118	5.42	1.50	279	275	273	23.1	30%	67%	4.06	46	23	31	3.7	6.0	1.6	16%	1.4	-25.6	26	$6
Reliability	8	06	HOU *	11	12	0	161	110	5.97	1.65	294	262	298	21.0	33%	65%	4.38	45	22	33	4.3	6.1	1.4	11%	1.1	-29.6	30	$1
DL		1st Half		8	5	0	99	63	4.81	1.53	277			26.0	30%	71%	4.36	45	22	34	4.1	5.7	1.4	11%	1.1	-3.9	31	$5
ERA Potl	50%	2nd Half		3	7	0	62	47	7.84	1.84	319			16.4	37%	57%	4.35	46	24	30	4.6	6.8	1.5	13%	1.2	-25.6	28	($4)
LIMA Plan	C+	07	Proj	**5**	**5**	**0**	**73**	**51**	**4.97**	**1.53**	**276**			**20.2**	**31%**	**70%**	**4.13**	**45**	**23**	**32**	**4.1**	**6.3**	**1.5**	**12%**	**1.1**	**2.1**	**37**	**$3**

9-10, 5.64 ERA in 136 IP at HOU. What happened over the last two months?
Apr-Jul21: 5.6 DOM, 1.3 CMD
Aug19-Sep: 10.7 DOM, 2.7 CMD
The gap was a AAA demotion but he struggled there too.

Rogers,Kenny

		Yr	Tm	W	L	Sv	IP	K	ERA	WHIP	OBA	vL	vR	BF/G	H%	S%	xERA	G	L	F	Ctl	Dom	Cmd	hr/f	hr/9	RAR	BPV	R$
LH	Starter	02	TEX	13	8	0	210	107	3.86	1.34	264	193	280	27.1	28%	74%	3.88	56	16	29	3.0	4.6	1.5	10%	0.9	15.6	35	$15
Age	42	03	MIN	13	8	0	195	116	4.57	1.42	292	251	307	25.6	32%	70%	4.19	43	18	39	2.3	5.4	2.3	9%	1.0	-1.1	47	$12
Decline		04	TEX	18	9	0	213	127	5.07	1.52	300	292	292	27.0	33%	69%	4.24	43	21	35	2.8	5.4	1.9	10%	1.1	-16.7	33	$10
Type	Finesse	05	TEX	14	8	0	195	87	3.46	1.32	271	201	291	27.6	29%	75%	4.20	47	20	33	2.4	4.0	1.6	7%	0.7	21.9	39	$16
Reliability	80	06	DET	17	8	0	204	99	3.84	1.26	253	200	268	25.1	27%	73%	3.99	50	18	32	2.7	4.4	1.6	11%	1.0	18.1	34	$21
DL		1st Half		10	3	0	104	59	3.45	1.14	242			26.5	26%	74%	3.65	49	17	33	2.2	5.1	2.4	11%	1.0	14.2	56	$14
ERA Potl	40%	2nd Half		7	5	0	100	40	4.24	1.38	264			23.9	27%	72%	4.36	51	19	30	3.3	3.6	1.1	11%	1.0	3.9	17	$7
LIMA Plan	F	07	Proj	**12**	**9**	**0**	**178**	**82**	**4.25**	**1.43**	**284**			**26.7**	**30%**	**72%**	**4.30**	**48**	**19**	**33**	**2.8**	**4.1**	**1.5**	**9%**	**1.0**	**4.0**	**25**	**$11**

Post-season magic might drive bidding up, but be cautious... Low DOM is subject to the whim of H% and S%. Rising GB helps, but age, luck and the possibility of a pine tar alert add to the risk. DN: 2004 minus 10 wins.

Romero,J.C.

		Yr	Tm	W	L	Sv	IP	K	ERA	WHIP	OBA	vL	vR	BF/G	H%	S%	xERA	G	L	F	Ctl	Dom	Cmd	hr/f	hr/9	RAR	BPV	R$
LH	Reliever	02	MIN	9	2	1	81	76	1.89	1.21	213	216	211	4.1	28%	85%	3.21	50	22	28	4.0	8.4	2.1	5%	0.3	25.7	97	$15
Age	30	03	MIN	2	0	0	63	50	5.00	1.71	271	214	314	4.0	32%	72%	4.39	51	19	30	6.0	7.1	1.2	12%	1.0	-3.7	39	$1
Peak		04	MIN	7	4	1	74	69	3.52	1.34	226	261	199	4.3	29%	74%	3.36	56	15	29	4.6	8.4	1.8	7%	0.5	8.3	84	$9
Type	Power	05	MIN	4	3	0	57	48	3.47	1.56	237	198	268	3.8	28%	81%	4.10	55	14	31	6.2	7.6	1.2	12%	0.9	6.3	50	$4
Reliability	23	06	ANA	1	2	0	48	31	6.74	1.77	296	202	382	3.5	34%	60%	4.38	57	16	27	5.2	5.8	1.1	7%	0.6	-12.9	37	($2)
DL		1st Half		1	2	0	28	23	7.07	1.96	307			4.0	36%	63%	4.28	59	17	24	6.4	7.4	1.2	13%	1.0	-8.7	33	($2)
ERA Potl	70%	2nd Half		0	0	0	20	8	6.27	1.49	280			2.9	31%	53%	4.51	55	15	30	3.6	3.6	1.0	0%	0.0	-4.2	42	($0)
LIMA Plan	D	07	Proj	**2**	**2**	**0**	**44**	**31**	**4.76**	**1.59**	**264**			**3.6**	**30%**	**71%**	**4.13**	**55**	**16**	**29**	**5.2**	**6.4**	**1.2**	**10%**	**0.8**	**1.9**	**42**	**$1**

Lousy Ctl caught up with him, and then bad luck piled on. BA vs. LH hints that he still has value as a lefty specialist, but 4.6 Ctl, 1.0 Cmd vs. LH puts even that into question.

Rusch,Glendon

		Yr	Tm	W	L	Sv	IP	K	ERA	WHIP	OBA	vL	vR	BF/G	H%	S%	xERA	G	L	F	Ctl	Dom	Cmd	hr/f	hr/9	RAR	BPV	R$
LH	Reliever	02	MIL	10	16	0	210	140	4.71	1.44	277	237	292	26.9	30%	71%	3.91	49	19	32	3.3	6.0	1.8	14%	1.3	-15.7	36	$8
Age	32	03	MIL *	2	13	1	144	109	6.31	1.68	322	307	338	18.4	37%	62%	4.19	40	24	36	3.1	6.8	2.2	9%	1.0	-36.1	48	($4)
Peak		04	CHC *	8	3	2	148	103	3.34	1.23	263	225	265	17.1	31%	74%	3.75	40	23	37	2.1	6.3	3.0	6%	0.6	16.8	85	$14
Type		05	CHC	9	8	0	145	111	4.53	1.57	300	333	294	14.2	35%	72%	4.10	38	28	35	3.3	6.9	2.1	8%	0.9	-5.1	54	$6
Reliability	33	06	CHC	3	8	0	66	59	7.49	1.80	316	348	310	12.5	34%	65%	4.41	35	22	43	4.5	8.0	1.8	23%	2.9	-24.5	-8	($3)
DL	33	1st Half		2	7	0	47	43	7.83	1.63	300			14.3	31%	60%	4.17	31	23	46	3.8	8.2	2.2	25%	3.2	-19.4	-8	($2)
ERA Potl		2nd Half		1	1	0	19	16	6.63	2.21	351			9.7	40%	74%	5.01	44	21	35	6.2	7.6	1.2	17%	1.9	-5.0	-1	($2)
LIMA Plan		07	Proj	**0**	**0**	**0**	**0**	**0**	**0.00**	**0.00**																		

Blood clot in lung means he'll likely sit out 2007, and may never pitch again. When pitching in '06, one in every nine batters walked, and one in every four fly balls went over the fence. Not a fun year.

Ryan,B.J.

		Yr	Tm	W	L	Sv	IP	K	ERA	WHIP	OBA	vL	vR	BF/G	H%	S%	xERA	G	L	F	Ctl	Dom	Cmd	hr/f	hr/9	RAR	BPV	R$
LH	Reliever	02	BAL	2	1	1	57	56	4.74	1.47	241	192	283	3.7	30%	70%	3.78	44	22	34	5.2	8.8	1.7	13%	1.1	-2.0	62	$3
Age	31	03	BAL	4	1	0	50	63	3.42	1.38	230	186	273	2.8	34%	74%	2.96	45	27	28	4.9	11.3	2.3	3%	0.2	6.8	121	$7
Peak		04	BAL	4	6	3	87	122	2.28	1.14	207	94	252	4.6	33%	81%	2.55	41	22	38	3.6	12.6	3.5	6%	0.4	23.1	150	$15
Type	Power	05	BAL	1	4	36	70	100	2.44	1.14	215	211	206	4.1	34%	80%	2.35	45	21	34	3.3	12.8	3.8	8%	0.5	16.7	154	$22
Reliability	66	06	TOR	2	2	38	72	86	1.37	0.86	171	120	182	4.2	25%	86%	2.66	37	20	43	2.5	10.7	4.3	4%	0.4	28.3	164	$27
DL		1st Half		1	0	21	38	45	0.47	0.66	137			3.9	21%	92%	2.57	31	21	48	1.9	10.7	5.6	0%	0.0	19.1	210	$16
ERA Potl	40%	2nd Half		1	2	17	34	41	2.38	1.09	206			4.6	29%	82%	2.78	42	20	38	3.2	10.8	3.4	10%	0.8	9.2	127	$11
LIMA Plan	C+	07	Proj	**3**	**3**	**43**	**80**	**97**	**2.48**	**1.12**	**213**			**4.2**	**30%**	**81%**	**2.80**	**41**	**21**	**38**	**3.2**	**10.9**	**3.5**	**8%**	**0.7**	**16.6**	**130**	**$26**

Terrific season, but xERA shows that sub-2.00 ERA may be tough to repeat. Ctl problems returned in 2nd half, and DOM dropped two K/9 from 2005. Little things, but they could lead to a small step backward in '07 value.

Saarloos,Kirk

		Yr	Tm	W	L	Sv	IP	K	ERA	WHIP	OBA	vL	vR	BF/G	H%	S%	xERA	G	L	F	Ctl	Dom	Cmd	hr/f	hr/9	RAR	BPV	R$
RH	Reliever	02	HOU *	18	8	0	184	141	3.86	1.21	248	301	302	22.3	29%	69%	3.28				2.5	6.9	2.8		0.7	5.5	83	$20
Age	27	03	HOU *	7	1	0	110	72	4.66	1.37	282	270	287	9.6	32%	66%	4.25				2.4	5.9	2.5		0.7	-5.1	64	$6
Pre-Peak		04	OAK *	4	3	0	51	32	5.82	1.73	311			18.2	33%	70%	6.53				4.1	5.6	1.4		1.6	-8.8	8	$0
Type	Finesse	05	OAK	10	9	0	159	53	4.18	1.41	275	304	249	23.8	29%	70%	4.11	57	20	23	3.1	3.0	1.0	8%	0.6	3.7	20	$8
Reliability	21	06	OAK	7	7	2	121	52	4.76	1.67	304	319	298	15.9	31%	75%	4.43	54	21	25	3.9	3.9	1.0	17%	1.4	-3.0	-4	$3
DL		1st Half		3	4	1	63	24	4.57	1.57	277			16.6	27%	77%	4.61	54	19	27	4.4	3.4	0.8	20%	1.7	-0.1	-15	$2
ERA Potl	30%	2nd Half		4	3	1	58	28	4.96	1.77	331			15.1	35%	74%	4.23	54	22	23	3.4	4.3	1.3	14%	1.1	-2.9	9	$1
LIMA Plan	C	07	Proj	**4**	**5**	**0**	**83**	**35**	**4.77**	**1.63**	**297**			**15.1**	**31%**	**72%**	**4.38**	**55**	**21**	**24**	**3.9**	**3.8**	**1.0**	**11%**	**0.9**	**1.1**	**13**	**$1**

Had some bad luck with hr/f, but even so, who's in the market for a pitcher with a -4 BPV and more walks than strikeouts? This game is hard enough without taking on that kind of baggage.

Sabathia,C.C.

		Yr	Tm	W	L	Sv	IP	K	ERA	WHIP	OBA	vL	vR	BF/G	H%	S%	xERA	G	L	F	Ctl	Dom	Cmd	hr/f	hr/9	RAR	BPV	R$
LH	Starter	02	CLE	13	11	0	210	149	4.37	1.36	251	240	255	27.2	29%	68%	4.12	44	18	38	3.8	6.4	1.7	7%	0.7	2.3	57	$15
Age	26	03	CLE	13	9	0	197	141	3.61	1.30	255	275	248	27.7	29%	75%	3.93	43	19	39	3.0	6.4	2.1	8%	0.9	22.2	62	$20
Growth		04	CLE	11	10	0	188	139	4.12	1.32	249	265	248	26.6	29%	71%	4.09	39	20	41	3.4	6.7	1.9	9%	1.0	7.3	57	$15
Type		05	CLE	15	10	0	196	161	4.04	1.26	251	248	248	26.4	30%	70%	3.31	49	20	31	2.8	7.4	2.6	11%	0.9	8.1	78	$20
Reliability	60	06	CLE	12	11	0	192	172	3.23	1.18	251	271	242	28.1	31%	75%	3.17	45	19	36	2.1	8.1	3.9	9%	0.8	31.5	111	$25
DL	28 22	1st Half		6	4	0	74	68	3.88	1.20	248			25.5	31%	70%	3.26	45	18	38	2.4	8.2	3.4	9%	0.8	6.2	101	$10
ERA Potl	55%	2nd Half		6	7	0	118	104	2.82	1.16	253			30.1	31%	79%	3.11	45	20	34	1.8	7.9	4.3	9%	0.8	25.3	120	$16
LIMA Plan	C	07	Proj	**14**	**8**	**0**	**189**	**162**	**3.39**	**1.21**	**251**			**26.8**	**30%**	**75%**	**3.31**	**45**	**19**	**36**	**2.4**	**7.7**	**3.2**	**10%**	**0.9**	**27.4**	**92**	**$24**

Career-best skills, but...
- Highest BF/G of career
- 104.9 pitches per start
- Strained oblique in April, knee surgery in September

Could be in line for a huge year, but you can't ignore the risk.

Saito,Takashi

		Yr	Tm	W	L	Sv	IP	K	ERA	WHIP	OBA	vL	vR	BF/G	H%	S%	xERA	G	L	F	Ctl	Dom	Cmd	hr/f	hr/9	RAR	BPV	R$
RH	Reliever	02	JPN	1	2	20	48	48	3.03	1.22	227			5.1	27%	84%	3.85				3.5	9.1	2.6		1.6	7.4	72	$12
Age	37	03	JPN	6	7	0	103	76	5.21	1.34	276			25.8	28%	70%	5.59				2.4	6.6	2.8		2.3	-10.4	29	$6
Decline		04	JPN	2	5	0	44	39	9.65	1.93	356			13.3	36%	58%	10.02				3.3	8.0	2.4		4.1	-28.8	-40	($5)
Type	Power	05	JPN	3	4	0	106	98	4.75	1.46	285			22.1	33%	73%	5.41				3.1	8.3	2.7		1.7	-5.8	54	$4
Reliability	1	06	LA	6	2	24	78	107	2.07	0.91	179	229	129	4.2	28%	78%	2.53	36	16	49	2.7	12.3	4.7	4%	0.3	23.2	181	$24
DL		1st Half		3	2	5	37	49	1.69	0.78	167			4.0	24%	85%	2.28	41	14	45	1.9	11.9	6.1	9%	0.7	12.8	200	$10
ERA Potl	55%	2nd Half		3	0	19	41	58	2.42	1.03	190			4.2	32%	74%	2.76	30	18	52	3.3	12.8	3.9	0%	0.0	10.4	175	$14
LIMA Plan	C	07	Proj	**4**	**3**	**40**	**73**	**78**	**3.48**	**1.30**	**247**			**6.8**	**31%**	**78%**	**3.57**	**35**	**16**	**49**	**3.4**	**9.7**	**2.9**	**9%**	**1.1**	**7.1**	**91**	**$21**

If this was any other player, we'd all scream "Fluke!", but the move from Japan clouds the issue. Still, he's 37, his high FB% puts him at risk for HR, and at least some regression is likely.
UP: LA DN: JPN

BRANDON KRUSE

Sanchez,Anibal	Yr	Tm	W	L	Sv	IP	K	ERA	WHIP	OBA	vL	vR	BF/G	H%	S%	xERA	G	L	F	Ctl	Dom	Cmd	hr/f	hr/9	RAR	BPV	R$
RH Starter	02		0	0	0	0	0	0.00	0.00																		
Age 23	03		0	0	0	0	0	0.00	0.00																		
Growth	04		0	0	0	0	0	0.00	0.00																		
Type Power	05	aa	3	5	0	57	54	4.41	1.38	281			22.3	35%	70%	4.46				2.5	8.5	**3.4**		0.9	-0.8	92	$4
Reliability 0	06	FLA	* 13	9	0	199	155	3.48	1.33	252	229	202	25.7	30%	76%	3.97	45	14	41	3.5	7.0	**2.0**	7%	0.8	24.8	66	$19
DL	1st Half		4	6	0	90	85	4.18	1.52	294			25.1	37%	74%	3.64	41	23	36	3.1	8.5	**2.7**	8%	0.8	3.4	81	$5
ERA Potl 45%	2nd Half		9	3	0	109	70	2.89	1.18	213			26.3	24%	78%	4.18	45	14	41	3.8	5.8	**1.5**	7%	0.7	21.4	57	$14
LIMA Plan C	07	Proj	**11**	**12**	**0**	**189**	**148**	**4.06**	**1.40**	**262**			**24.7**	**30%**	**74%**	**4.03**	**45**	**14**	**41**	**3.6**	**7.1**	**2.0**	**9%**	**1.0**	**7.9**	**56**	**$13**

10-3, 2.83 ERA in 114 IP at FLA. No-hit wonder looked like the real deal in spurts. BPV Jul-Sep: 18, 37, 79; 43/18 DOM/DIS. H%, S%, and sub-6.0 DOM mean he's not there yet.

Sanchez,Duaner	Yr	Tm	W	L	Sv	IP	K	ERA	WHIP	OBA	vL	vR	BF/G	H%	S%	xERA	G	L	F	Ctl	Dom	Cmd	hr/f	hr/9	RAR	BPV	R$
RH Reliever	02	a/a	5	7	20	63	56	4.86	1.48	280			5.0	35%	66%	4.31				3.4	8.0	**2.3**		0.6	-4.6	79	$10
Age 27	03	aaa	4	4	1	61	29	4.87	1.66	304			6.8	33%	69%	5.07				3.8	4.3	**1.1**		0.4	-3.6	30	$1
Pre-Peak	04	LA	3	1	0	80	44	3.38	1.35	264	276	260	5.1	28%	79%	4.00	52	16	33	3.0	5.0	**1.6**	11%	1.0	8.8	36	$5
Type Power	05	LA	4	7	8	82	71	3.73	1.35	245	310	182	4.4	29%	75%	3.71	44	21	35	4.0	7.8	**2.0**	10%	0.9	5.2	68	$9
Reliability 20	06	NYM	5	1	0	55	44	2.61	1.22	217	276	179	4.7	26%	80%	3.60	52	13	34	3.9	7.2	**1.8**	6%	0.5	12.7	79	$8
DL 61	1st Half		4	0	0	41	30	2.62	1.24	216			4.9	26%	80%	3.83	52	14	34	4.2	6.6	**1.6**	5%	0.4	9.5	71	$6
ERA Potl 40%	2nd Half		1	1	0	14	14	2.59	1.15	219			4.0	28%	80%	2.97	54	11	34	3.2	9.1	**2.8**	8%	0.6	3.3	105	$2
LIMA Plan C+	07	Proj	**5**	**3**	**0**	**79**	**61**	**3.67**	**1.39**	**258**			**5.1**	**30%**	**76%**	**3.76**	**50**	**15**	**34**	**3.7**	**7.0**	**1.9**	**10%**	**0.9**	**5.9**	**58**	**$6**

Shoulder separation sidelined him for last two months. Still plagued by bouts of wildness, but good stuff and groundball approach provide room for error. xERA says ERA will go up, but he's worth a bid.

Sanchez,Jonathan	Yr	Tm	W	L	Sv	IP	K	ERA	WHIP	OBA	vL	vR	BF/G	H%	S%	xERA	G	L	F	Ctl	Dom	Cmd	hr/f	hr/9	RAR	BPV	R$
LH Reliever	02		0	0	0	0	0	0.00	0.00																		
Age 24	03		0	0	0	0	0	0.00	0.00																		
Growth	04		0	0	0	0	0	0.00	0.00																		
Type Power	05		0	0	0	0	0	0.00	0.00																		
Reliability 0	06	SF	* 7	4	2	95	96	3.79	1.22	210	256	248	8.6	28%	67%	3.73	36	20	45	4.3	9.1	**2.1**	3%	0.3	8.2	104	$12
DL	1st Half		3	1	2	40	44	1.39	0.89	154			6.7	23%	83%	2.96	50	5	45	3.4	9.8	**2.9**	0%	0.0	15.3	143	$9
ERA Potl 60%	2nd Half		4	3	0	55	52	5.54	1.46	246			10.5	32%	60%	4.25	33	23	45	4.9	8.6	**1.8**	4%	0.5	-7.1	79	$3
LIMA Plan B	07	Proj	**3**	**5**	**0**	**66**	**56**	**4.36**	**1.45**	**247**			**9.0**	**30%**	**71%**	**4.41**	**36**	**20**	**45**	**4.8**	**7.6**	**1.6**	**7%**	**0.8**	**-0.3**	**61**	**$3**

3-1, 4.95 ERA in 40 IP at SF. Start or relieve? Your choice:

	Ctl	Dom	ERA
SP	4.0	7.5	7.36
RP	6.1	7.3	2.91

Fared well as SP in the minors. Nice K upside, but expect bumps

Santana,Ervin	Yr	Tm	W	L	Sv	IP	K	ERA	WHIP	OBA	vL	vR	BF/G	H%	S%	xERA	G	L	F	Ctl	Dom	Cmd	hr/f	hr/9	RAR	BPV	R$
RH Starter	02		0	0	0	0	0	0.00	0.00											0.0	0.0						
Age 24	03	aa	1	1	0	29	21	4.70	1.27	238			20.4	25%	68%	4.11				3.5	6.5	**1.8**		1.5	-1.1	41	$2
Growth	04	aa	2	1	0	43	41	3.75	1.44	270			23.5	34%	75%	4.16				3.5	8.5	**2.4**		0.6	3.2	84	$3
Type	05	ANA	* 18	9	0	191	140	4.14	1.34	264	261	271	24.7	30%	72%	4.16	37	19	44	3.0	6.6	**2.2**	8%	1.0	5.5	59	$18
Reliability 44	06	ANA	16	8	0	204	141	4.28	1.23	239	254	229	25.7	27%	67%	4.13	38	17	44	3.1	6.2	**2.0**	8%	0.9	7.0	59	$21
DL	1st Half		8	3	0	98	70	3.94	1.21	239			25.4	28%	68%	4.13	36	18	46	2.9	6.4	**2.2**	6%	0.7	7.5	70	$12
ERA Potl 55%	2nd Half		8	5	0	106	71	4.59	1.25	240			25.9	26%	66%	4.13	40	17	42	3.2	6.0	**1.9**	10%	1.1	-0.5	49	$10
LIMA Plan D	07	Proj	**13**	**10**	**0**	**189**	**140**	**4.15**	**1.33**	**258**			**25.0**	**29%**	**72%**	**4.11**	**38**	**18**	**44**	**3.1**	**6.7**	**2.2**	**9%**	**1.1**	**8.8**	**54**	**$17**

Looked like a top-flight hurler in June and early July. 2nd half affected by minor knee injury. He's got sub-4.00 ERA upside in '07, but he's unlikely to reach it unless his skills sustain their growth.

Santana,Johan	Yr	Tm	W	L	Sv	IP	K	ERA	WHIP	OBA	vL	vR	BF/G	H%	S%	xERA	G	L	F	Ctl	Dom	Cmd	hr/f	hr/9	RAR	BPV	R$
LH Starter	02	MIN	* 13	8	1	156	201	3.12	1.28	220	195	216	17.2	32%	78%	3.21	29	27	43	4.3	11.6	**2.7**	9%	0.8	25.9	113	$23
Age 28	03	MIN	12	3	0	158	169	3.08	1.10	222	191	227	14.1	28%	76%	3.35	28	23	49	2.7	9.6	**3.6**	9%	1.0	28.2	115	$25
Pre-Peak	04	MIN	20	6	0	228	265	2.61	0.92	195	192	191	25.8	26%	77%	2.65	41	16	43	2.1	10.5	**4.9**	10%	0.9	51.4	153	$42
Type Power	05	MIN	16	7	0	231	238	2.88	0.97	216	256	200	27.3	28%	74%	2.92	40	17	43	1.8	9.3	**5.3**	9%	0.9	42.5	153	$38
Reliability 88	06	MIN	19	6	0	233	245	2.78	1.00	220	254	206	26.9	28%	77%	2.81	41	20	40	1.8	9.5	**5.2**	10%	0.9	51.2	149	$41
DL	1st Half		9	4	0	118	124	2.59	0.97	220			27.0	28%	78%	2.79	39	20	41	1.5	9.4	**6.2**	10%	0.9	28.6	170	$22
ERA Potl 55%	2nd Half		10	2	0	115	121	2.97	1.03	221			26.8	28%	76%	2.83	42	20	38	2.1	9.5	**4.5**	11%	0.9	22.5	134	$20
LIMA Plan C	07	Proj	**18**	**6**	**0**	**230**	**247**	**2.82**	**1.02**	**220**			**25.1**	**29%**	**77%**	**2.88**	**40**	**19**	**41**	**2.0**	**9.7**	**4.8**	**10%**	**0.9**	**45.6**	**142**	**$39**

There's nothing here to suggest his roll is about to end. Perhaps even more impressive: he threw fewer than 110 pitches in all but two starts. Sit back and enjoy the ride.

Santos,Victor	Yr	Tm	W	L	Sv	IP	K	ERA	WHIP	OBA	vL	vR	BF/G	H%	S%	xERA	G	L	F	Ctl	Dom	Cmd	hr/f	hr/9	RAR	BPV	R$
RH Starter	02	COL	* 4	13	0	144	138	7.56	1.90	342			15.4	41%	62%	7.38				3.9	8.6	**2.2**		1.8	-61.4	33	($10)
Age 30	03	aaa	5	4	1	108	54	4.83	1.67	318			24.8	35%	71%	5.52				3.2	4.5	**1.4**		0.7	-5.8	28	$1
Peak	04	MIL	11	12	0	154	115	4.97	1.47	280	244	303	21.8	32%	68%	4.19	41	17	42	3.3	6.7	**2.0**	9%	1.1	-13.4	50	$7
Type	05	MIL	4	13	0	141	89	4.59	1.51	278	259	277	21.6	30%	73%	4.38	42	23	36	3.8	5.7	**1.5**	12%	1.3	-6.0	26	$3
Reliability 60	06	PIT	5	9	0	115	81	5.71	1.67	316	264	361	21.1	35%	68%	4.22	44	22	35	3.3	6.3	**1.9**	12%	1.3	-17.3	33	($0)
DL 26	1st Half		4	7	0	78	55	4.84	1.51	288			23.1	33%	69%	4.14	42	23	35	3.3	6.3	**1.9**	9%	0.9	-3.4	48	$3
ERA Potl 55%	2nd Half		1	2	0	37	26	7.54	2.00	369			18.2	40%	65%	4.38	47	20	34	3.2	6.3	**2.0**	17%	1.9	-13.9	3	($3)
LIMA Plan D	07	Proj	**5**	**10**	**0**	**133**	**92**	**4.74**	**1.53**	**288**			**21.9**	**32%**	**72%**	**4.18**	**44**	**21**	**36**	**3.5**	**6.2**	**1.8**	**11%**	**1.2**	**3.1**	**38**	**$4**

A reverse righty - tough on LHers, but RHers can get the best of him. A H% correction should send his ERA below 5.00, but he's swimming uphill as a SP until he can get RHers out.

Saunders,Joe	Yr	Tm	W	L	Sv	IP	K	ERA	WHIP	OBA	vL	vR	BF/G	H%	S%	xERA	G	L	F	Ctl	Dom	Cmd	hr/f	hr/9	RAR	BPV	R$
LH Starter	02		0	0	0	0	0	0.00	0.00																		
Age 25	03		0	0	0	0	0	0.00	0.00																		
Growth	04	aa	4	3	0	39	20	6.66	1.85	344			23.3	37%	65%	6.94				3.3	4.7	**1.4**		1.2	-11.2	8	($1)
Type	05	a/a	10	7	0	160	88	4.00	1.47	290			26.0	32%	73%	4.55				2.8	5.0	**1.7**		0.6	6.1	44	$9
Reliability 0	06	ANA	* 17	7	0	205	132	3.48	1.27	254	220	274	25.3	29%	75%	3.75	48	20	32	2.8	5.8	**2.1**	8%	0.8	27.2	60	$23
DL	1st Half		9	3	0	107	64	2.46	1.14	243			27.2	27%	81%					2.1	5.4	**2.5**		0.6	27.7	75	$16
ERA Potl 50%	2nd Half		8	4	0	98	68	4.60	1.42	266			23.6	30%	69%	3.93	48	20	32	3.6	6.2	**1.7**	10%	0.9	-0.6	48	$8
LIMA Plan C+	07	Proj	**6**	**5**	**0**	**94**	**62**	**4.24**	**1.37**	**269**			**25.1**	**30%**	**71%**	**3.82**	**48**	**20**	**32**	**3.0**	**6.0**	**2.0**	**10%**	**1.0**	**7.7**	**50**	**$7**

7-3, 4.71 ERA in 70 IP at ANA. Soft-tosser, but all-or-nothing results in '06: 54% DOM%, 31% DIS%. DOM trend suggests MLB sub-4 ERA is possible. Solid GB limits HR risk. End-game pick, with upside depending on role.

Schilling,Curt	Yr	Tm	W	L	Sv	IP	K	ERA	WHIP	OBA	vL	vR	BF/G	H%	S%	xERA	G	L	F	Ctl	Dom	Cmd	hr/f	hr/9	RAR	BPV	R$
RH Starter	02	ARI	23	7	0	259	316	3.23	0.97	230	242	208	28.0	31%	71%	2.31	40	24	36	1.1	11.0	**9.6**	13%	1.0	27.9	246	$42
Age 40	03	ARI	8	9	0	168	194	2.95	1.05	233	255	210	27.8	31%	76%	2.59	39	25	36	1.7	10.4	**6.1**	11%	0.9	27.6	171	$24
Decline	04	BOS	21	6	0	226	203	3.26	1.07	244	238	241	28.2	30%	73%	3.05	42	20	38	1.4	8.1	**5.8**	9%	0.9	32.6	149	$33
Type	05	BOS	* 8	8	9	104	95	5.92	1.57	323	290	343	13.7	39%	63%	3.83	34	23	43	2.0	8.2	**4.1**	10%	1.2	-19.9	89	$7
Reliability 28	06	BOS	15	7	0	204	183	3.97	1.22	277	277	275	27.2	33%	72%	3.23	40	20	40	1.2	8.1	**6.5**	11%	1.2	14.8	148	$24
DL 99	1st Half		9	2	0	107	96	3.61	1.08	254			26.8	30%	72%	3.19	38	19	44	1.1	8.1	**7.4**	10%	1.2	12.5	172	$16
ERA Potl 60%	2nd Half		6	5	0	97	87	4.37	1.36	300			27.7	36%	72%	3.28	42	21	37	1.4	8.1	**5.8**	12%	1.3	2.3	126	$9
LIMA Plan C+	07	Proj	**13**	**8**	**0**	**174**	**155**	**3.83**	**1.22**	**267**			**21.2**	**32%**	**72%**	**3.34**	**39**	**21**	**40**	**1.8**	**8.0**	**4.6**	**10%**	**1.1**	**24.5**	**113**	**$20**

Reversed CMD and BPV declines in a big way. Ignore 2nd half ERA spike; blame aberrant 36% H%. At 40, he'll be more inconsistent going forward, but don't expect a big decline in 2007.

Schmidt,Jason	Yr	Tm	W	L	Sv	IP	K	ERA	WHIP	OBA	vL	vR	BF/G	H%	S%	xERA	G	L	F	Ctl	Dom	Cmd	hr/f	hr/9	RAR	BPV	R$
RH Starter	02	SF	* 15	8	0	197	205	3.47	1.20	225	259	180	26.2	29%	72%	3.48	33	23	44	3.4	9.4	**2.7**	7%	0.7	15.4	103	$23
Age 34	03	SF	17	5	0	207	208	2.35	0.96	207	197	204	27.7	27%	78%	3.04	36	20	44	2.0	9.0	**4.5**	6%	0.6	49.3	145	$36
Past Peak	04	SF	18	7	0	225	251	3.20	1.08	206	191	212	28.1	28%	72%	2.88	46	15	39	3.1	10.0	**3.3**	9%	0.7	29.5	121	$32
Type Power	05	SF	12	7	0	172	165	4.40	1.42	248	264	223	25.8	31%	70%	3.90	38	21	40	4.4	8.6	**1.9**	8%	0.8	-3.2	73	$12
Reliability 72	06	SF	11	9	0	213	180	3.59	1.26	239	262	215	27.9	29%	74%	3.87	37	19	43	3.4	7.6	**2.3**	8%	0.9	23.6	73	$20
DL 16	1st Half		6	3	0	108	94	2.83	1.10	212			29.0	26%	77%	3.78	32	20	48	3.1	7.8	**2.5**	6%	0.7	22.1	90	$15
ERA Potl 55%	2nd Half		5	6	0	105	86	4.37	1.43	265			26.9	31%	72%	3.95	42	19	39	3.7	7.4	**2.0**	10%	0.7	1.5	57	$6
LIMA Plan D+	07	Proj	**12**	**9**	**0**	**203**	**179**	**3.77**	**1.32**	**247**			**27.8**	**30%**	**74%**	**3.80**	**39**	**19**	**41**	**3.5**	**7.9**	**2.2**	**9%**	**1.0**	**14.0**	**71**	**$18**

There is more talent per square inch on this page than any other in the book. That said, his declining DOM and rising FB% are concerns. May fall from elite, but he'll remain solid if healthy.

STEPHEN NICKRAND

Schoeneweis,Scott

		W	L	Sv	IP	K	ERA	WHIP	OBA	vL	vR	BF/G	H%	S%	xERA	G	L	F	Ctl	Dom	Cmd	hr/f	hr/9	RAR	BPV	R$
LH Reliever	02 ANA	9	8	1	118	65	4.88	1.42	263	202	290	9.5	28%	69%	4.44	47	16	37	3.7	5.0	**1.3**	12%	1.3	-6.1	21	$7
Age 33	03 2AL	3	2	0	64	56	4.22	1.30	262	227	275	4.6	33%	66%	3.21	49	21	29	2.7	7.9	**2.9**	5%	0.4	2.4	99	$6
Past Peak	04 CHW	6	9	0	112	69	5.61	1.59	290	244	303	25.3	31%	67%	4.50	44	19	36	3.9	5.5	**1.4**	12%	1.4	-16.4	19	$1
Type	05 TOR	3	4	1	57	43	3.32	1.39	251	188	306	3.1	31%	75%	3.42	59	17	24	3.9	6.8	**1.7**	5%	0.3	7.4	72	$5
Reliability 13	06 2TM	4	2	4	51	29	4.92	1.41	250	236	257	3.1	28%	65%	3.96	58	16	26	4.2	5.1	**1.2**	9%	0.7	-2.5	40	$4
DL	1st Half	2	0	0	25	14	5.76	1.32	254			2.8	27%	57%	3.80	54	18	28	3.2	5.0	**1.6**	13%	1.1	-3.8	35	$1
ERA Potl 55%	2nd Half	2	2	4	26	15	4.12	1.49	245			3.5	28%	71%	4.11	61	15	24	5.2	5.2	**1.0**	5%	0.3	1.3	48	$3
LIMA Plan C+	07 Proj	**3**	**4**	**3**	**58**	**35**	**4.50**	**1.47**	**265**			**3.9**	**30%**	**70%**	**3.99**	**55**	**17**	**28**	**4.0**	**5.4**	**1.3**	**10%**	**0.8**	**3.1**	**40**	**$3**

Lefty specialist keeps ball on ground well, but that's about it. Control became a critical issue in 2nd half which now means, lots of baserunners, lots of ground balls... and DOUBLE PLAYS! That's how he does it!

Seanez,Rudy

		W	L	Sv	IP	K	ERA	WHIP	OBA	vL	vR	BF/G	H%	S%	xERA	G	L	F	Ctl	Dom	Cmd	hr/f	hr/9	RAR	BPV	R$
RH Reliever	02 TEX	1	3	0	37	43	5.59	1.51	235	220	238	4.4	31%	65%	4.46				5.8	10.5	**1.8**		1.2	-5.2	72	$1
Age 38	03 aaa	3	5	5	38	37	5.68	1.74	277			5.1	33%	70%	5.75				5.9	8.8	**1.5**		1.4	-6.1	41	$2
Decline	04 2TM *	5	3	3	80	79	2.81	1.17	218	256	202	5.2	28%	79%	3.21	48	16	37	3.5	8.9	**2.5**	9%	0.8	15.2	95	$12
Type Power	05 SD	7	1	0	60	84	2.70	1.18	224	231	212	4.3	34%	79%	2.61	37	23	39	3.3	12.6	**3.8**	8%	0.6	11.5	148	$11
Reliability 0	06 2TM	3	3	0	53	54	4.92	1.70	280	266	273	5.0	34%	74%	4.43	31	24	45	5.4	9.2	**1.7**	12%	1.4	-2.6	49	$2
DL 35	1st Half	2	0	0	30	35	5.10	1.53	281			4.6	36%	71%	3.71	28	25	47	3.9	10.5	**2.7**	13%	1.5	-2.1	73	$2
ERA Potl 55%	2nd Half	1	3	0	23	19	4.70	1.91	278			5.6	32%	78%	5.54	34	23	42	7.4	7.4	**1.0**	10%	1.2	-0.5	30	($0)
LIMA Plan B+	07 Proj	**3**	**3**	**0**	**44**	**45**	**4.55**	**1.49**	**255**			**4.9**	**32%**	**72%**	**4.01**	**33**	**23**	**44**	**4.8**	**9.3**	**2.0**	**9%**	**1.0**	**2.2**	**70**	**$3**

Career resurgence hit the skids in '06. Why he's a risky bet to rebound to '04-'05 levels:
- 2nd half collapse
- FB% trend
- Age 40's around the corner

End-gamer; don't invest much.

Sele,Aaron

		W	L	Sv	IP	K	ERA	WHIP	OBA	vL	vR	BF/G	H%	S%	xERA	G	L	F	Ctl	Dom	Cmd	hr/f	hr/9	RAR	BPV	R$
RH Reliever	02 ANA	8	9	0	160	82	4.89	1.49	296	315	283	27.2	31%	70%	4.49	43	18	38	2.8	4.6	**1.7**	10%	1.2	-8.6	23	$5
Age 36	03 ANA	7	11	0	121	53	5.80	1.60	283	252	322	21.9	29%	65%	5.30	41	16	43	4.3	3.9	**0.9**	9%	1.3	-19.1	3	$1
Decline	04 ANA	9	4	0	132	51	5.05	1.62	305	296	324	21.4	31%	71%	5.20	44	15	42	3.5	3.5	**1.0**	8%	1.1	-10.0	3	$2
Type Finesse	05 SEA	6	12	0	116	53	5.66	1.62	310	325	302	25.1	32%	68%	4.91	40	20	39	3.2	4.1	**1.3**	11%	1.4	-18.5	3	($0)
Reliability 23	06 LA *	11	6	0	132	80	4.11	1.38	283	280	298	17.2	32%	72%	4.11	46	15	39	2.4	5.4	**2.3**	7%	0.8	6.2	54	$11
DL	1st Half	7	2	0	81	49	2.70	1.22	252			24.1	29%	79%	3.98	46	15	39	2.5	5.4	**2.2**	4%	0.4	17.9	70	$10
ERA Potl 45%	2nd Half	4	4	0	51	31	6.37	1.63	328			12.2	36%	63%	4.31	45	16	39	2.3	5.5	**2.4**	11%	1.4	-11.8	30	$0
LIMA Plan C	07 Proj	**4**	**7**	**0**	**83**	**43**	**5.20**	**1.53**	**301**			**18.5**	**32%**	**68%**	**4.57**	**43**	**17**	**40**	**2.8**	**4.7**	**1.7**	**9%**	**1.2**	**-2.1**	**22**	**$1**

8-6, 4.53 ERA in 103 IP at LA. Decent rebound season, but in retrospect, he really only had two good months as a SP with LA. There's way too much bad history to expect that these newfound skills are sustainable.

Seo,Jae

		W	L	Sv	IP	K	ERA	WHIP	OBA	vL	vR	BF/G	H%	S%	xERA	G	L	F	Ctl	Dom	Cmd	hr/f	hr/9	RAR	BPV	R$
RH Starter	02 a/a	6	9	0	134	76	4.90	1.49	318			21.1	35%	69%	5.37				1.6	5.1	**3.2**		1.0	-10.4	58	$3
Age 29	03 NYM	9	12	0	188	110	3.83	1.27	267	223	291	24.6	29%	72%	4.31	37	17	46	2.2	5.3	**2.4**	6%	0.9	10.4	58	$14
Peak	04 NYM *	5	12	0	139	70	4.66	1.57	288	273	322	22.3	30%	73%	5.01	38	21	41	3.9	4.5	**1.2**	9%	1.2	-6.8	14	$1
Type Finesse	05 NYM *	15	6	0	211	145	4.22	1.35	284	233	272	27.3	32%	71%	3.95	38	23	40	2.1	6.2	**3.0**	9%	1.0	0.6	68	$15
Reliability 35	06 2TM	3	12	0	157	88	5.33	1.61	308	310	313	19.8	32%	72%	4.83	35	21	44	3.2	5.0	**1.6**	13%	1.8	-15.7	3	($0)
DL 15	1st Half	2	4	0	69	50	5.61	1.49	281			15.2	30%	67%	4.32	40	17	44	3.5	6.5	**1.9**	15%	1.8	-9.3	22	$1
ERA Potl 40%	2nd Half	1	8	0	88	38	5.11	1.70	328			25.4	33%	75%	5.24	33	24	44	3.0	3.9	**1.3**	12%	1.7	-6.4	-12	($2)
LIMA Plan F	07 Proj	**6**	**10**	**0**	**160**	**92**	**4.85**	**1.50**	**294**			**22.1**	**31%**	**71%**	**4.63**	**36**	**21**	**43**	**3.0**	**5.2**	**1.7**	**10%**	**1.4**	**-4.2**	**23**	**$4**

His xERA indicated some ERA upside in the 1st half. That all changed after his trade to the AL, where he had just two PQS-4/5 outings in 16 starts. His 2005 line looks like the aberration now.

Sheets,Ben

		W	L	Sv	IP	K	ERA	WHIP	OBA	vL	vR	BF/G	H%	S%	xERA	G	L	F	Ctl	Dom	Cmd	hr/f	hr/9	RAR	BPV	R$
RH Starter	02 MIL	11	16	0	216	170	4.17	1.42	280	318	247	27.6	33%	72%	3.65	46	21	33	2.9	7.1	**2.4**	10%	0.9	-1.6	66	$12
Age 28	03 MIL	11	13	0	220	157	4.46	1.25	272	247	286	27.0	30%	67%	3.65	42	19	39	1.8	6.4	**3.7**	11%	1.2	-4.9	80	$15
Pre-Peak	04 MIL	12	14	0	237	264	2.70	0.98	231	232	220	27.2	30%	78%	2.59	43	17	40	1.2	10.0	**8.3**	10%	0.9	45.8	214	$35
Type Power	05 MIL	10	9	0	156	141	3.34	1.07	244	234	241	28.3	29%	74%	3.19	37	21	42	1.4	8.1	**5.6**	10%	1.1	17.4	141	$20
Reliability 22	06 MIL	6	7	0	106	116	3.82	1.09	260	248	266	25.0	34%	66%	2.74	40	19	40	0.9	9.8	**10.5**	8%	0.8	8.7	261	$13
DL 106 71	1st Half	1	3	0	20	28	6.72	1.39	323			21.7	48%	48%	2.16	44	26	30	0.4	12.5	**28.0**	6%	0.4	-5.5	640	$1
ERA Potl 70%	2nd Half	5	4	0	86	88	3.14	1.02	244			26.1	31%	73%	2.87	40	17	43	1.0	9.2	**8.8**	8%	0.8	14.2	221	$13
LIMA Plan B+	07 Proj	**13**	**8**	**0**	**164**	**172**	**3.19**	**1.04**	**244**			**24.9**	**31%**	**73%**	**2.74**	**41**	**20**	**39**	**1.2**	**9.5**	**8.2**	**10%**	**0.9**	**32.8**	**207**	**$25**

This year, the ailments were shoulder tendinitis and pectoral muscle tightness, but 2006 was his best skilll year yet. High risk, but the only thing standing between him and a Cy Young Award is health.

Sherrill,George

		W	L	Sv	IP	K	ERA	WHIP	OBA	vL	vR	BF/G	H%	S%	xERA	G	L	F	Ctl	Dom	Cmd	hr/f	hr/9	RAR	BPV	R$
LH Reliever	02	0	0	0	0	0	0.00	0.00											0.0	0.0						
Age 30	03 aa	3	0	0	27	24	0.38	1.44	249			7.4	32%	100%	3.64				4.6	8.1	**1.8**		0.4	13.4	79	$5
Peak	04 SEA *	6	3	13	74	70	3.00	1.23	257			5.4	32%	79%	3.78				2.2	8.5	**3.8**		0.9	13.0	108	$14
Type Power	05 SEA *	5	6	7	43	54	3.98	1.14	219	116	273	3.4	31%	67%	2.80	42	16	42	3.1	11.3	**3.6**	9%	0.8	2.1	130	$9
Reliability 8	06 SEA	2	4	1	40	42	4.28	1.43	210	143	297	2.4	30%	67%	4.44	30	19	51	6.1	9.5	**1.6**	0%	0.0	1.4	102	$4
DL	1st Half	2	1	1	21	23	3.84	1.47	201			2.6	29%	71%	4.34	42	10	48	6.8	9.8	**1.4**	0%	0.0	1.9	104	$3
ERA Potl 70%	2nd Half	0	3	0	19	19	4.76	1.38	220			2.2	30%	62%	4.48	18	29	53	5.2	9.0	**1.7**	0%	0.0	-0.5	102	$1
LIMA Plan A	07 Proj	**3**	**5**	**3**	**44**	**48**	**3.93**	**1.31**	**227**			**2.9**	**30%**	**72%**	**3.57**	**42**	**11**	**47**	**4.3**	**9.9**	**2.3**	**8%**	**0.8**	**4.9**	**92**	**$6**

Lefty specialist with a top-flight DOM who amazingly didn't allow a HR, despite high FB. Another 100+ BPV year hidden by lack of IP. Fine LIMA target if he can cut down the walks and keep the ball down.

Shields,Jamie

		W	L	Sv	IP	K	ERA	WHIP	OBA	vL	vR	BF/G	H%	S%	xERA	G	L	F	Ctl	Dom	Cmd	hr/f	hr/9	RAR	BPV	R$
RH Starter	02	0	0	0	0	0	0.00	0.00																		
Age 25	03	0	0	0	0	0	0.00	0.00																		
Growth	04 aa	0	3	0	18	13	8.50	1.94	339			21.9	36%	60%	8.30				4.5	6.5	**1.4**		2.5	-9.2	-18	($2)
Type	05 a/a	8	5	0	115	94	3.13	1.23	253			26.5	31%	74%	3.19				2.5	7.4	**2.9**		0.4	16.7	98	$13
Reliability 0	06 TAM *	9	10	0	185	159	4.37	1.38	289	266	309	25.7	34%	71%	3.41	43	23	34	2.1	7.7	**3.6**	11%	1.0	4.3	89	$15
DL	1st Half	7	3	0	96	89	3.75	1.36	294			25.7	38%	71%	2.76	49	30	21	1.7	8.3	**4.9**	5%	0.3	9.6	142	$11
ERA Potl 60%	2nd Half	2	7	0	89	70	5.04	1.40	282			25.7	31%	70%	3.77	41	21	39	2.6	7.1	**2.7**	17%	1.8	-5.4	43	$4
LIMA Plan C+	07 Proj	**9**	**9**	**0**	**174**	**145**	**3.93**	**1.26**	**263**			**26.0**	**31%**	**71%**	**3.43**	**42**	**23**	**35**	**2.3**	**7.5**	**3.2**	**10%**	**0.9**	**22.7**	**87**	**$17**

6-8, 4.84 ERA in 124 IP at TAM. The makings of an impact SP:
- Ctl and DOM trends
- 48/10 DOM/DIS%
- GB approach
- 100+ BPV in Jun and Aug

Still inconsistent, but tuck away.

Shields,Scot

		W	L	Sv	IP	K	ERA	WHIP	OBA	vL	vR	BF/G	H%	S%	xERA	G	L	F	Ctl	Dom	Cmd	hr/f	hr/9	RAR	BPV	R$
RH Reliever	02 ANA *	7	5	1	96	71	2.81	1.06	217	184	191	6.7	25%	77%	3.13	53	18	29	2.5	6.7	**2.6**	11%	0.8	19.5	81	$14
Age 31	03 ANA	5	6	1	148	111	2.86	1.19	248	229	264	13.8	29%	79%	3.34	49	19	32	2.3	6.8	**2.9**	8%	0.7	30.4	85	$17
Peak	04 ANA	8	2	4	105	109	3.34	1.30	247	235	242	7.4	33%	75%	2.94	56	14	30	3.4	9.3	**2.7**	7%	0.5	14.2	103	$14
Type Power	05 ANA	10	11	7	91	98	2.76	1.13	204	202	203	4.7	28%	77%	2.75	54	17	28	3.7	9.7	**2.6**	8%	0.5	18.1	113	$18
Reliability 51	06 ANA	7	7	2	87	84	2.89	1.08	222	207	227	4.7	28%	77%	2.87	52	15	33	2.5	8.7	**3.5**	10%	0.8	17.9	111	$15
DL	1st Half	4	5	1	42	40	2.35	1.04	212			4.9	28%	79%	2.95	53	11	36	2.6	8.5	**3.3**	5%	0.4	11.5	121	$8
ERA Potl 55%	2nd Half	3	2	1	45	44	3.40	1.11	230			4.5	28%	75%	2.79	51	18	31	2.4	8.8	**3.7**	16%	1.2	6.4	103	$7
LIMA Plan B	07 Proj	**7**	**6**	**3**	**87**	**85**	**3.00**	**1.14**	**224**			**5.3**	**29%**	**76%**	**2.89**	**53**	**16**	**31**	**2.9**	**8.8**	**3.0**	**10%**	**0.7**	**17.1**	**105**	**$14**

Posted a 100+ BPV in first four months before tiring a bit in Aug/Sept. Sub-3.00 ERA the last two years have nearly matched his xERA. Remains ready for a bigger role if the opportunity arises.

Shouse,Brian

		W	L	Sv	IP	K	ERA	WHIP	OBA	vL	vR	BF/G	H%	S%	xERA	G	L	F	Ctl	Dom	Cmd	hr/f	hr/9	RAR	BPV	R$
LH Reliever	02 KC *	1	0	0	37	29	6.32	1.59	306			3.6	35%	62%	3.44	60	11	28	3.2	7.1	**2.2**	17%	1.5	-8.5	39	($0)
Age 38	03 TEX	0	1	1	61	40	3.10	1.25	265	195	364	4.1	32%	73%	3.02	61	17	21	2.1	5.9	**2.9**	2%	0.1	10.7	93	$5
Decline	04 TEX	2	0	0	45	34	2.59	1.31	239	188	277	3.6	28%	84%	3.24	58	20	22	3.8	6.8	**1.8**	14%	0.8	10.2	61	$5
Type	05 TEX	3	2	0	53	35	5.25	1.37	269	209	337	3.6	29%	64%	3.47	54	21	25	3.1	5.9	**1.9**	17%	1.2	-5.8	42	$2
Reliability 2	06 2TM	1	3	2	38	23	4.02	1.52	271	238	309	2.6	30%	76%	4.19	51	20	29	4.3	5.4	**1.3**	11%	0.9	2.4	32	$2
DL 17	1st Half	1	0	1	18	10	2.50	1.50	283			2.9	32%	85%	3.84	52	26	21	3.5	5.0	**1.4**	8%	0.5	4.5	43	$2
ERA Potl 40%	2nd Half	0	3	1	20	13	5.37	1.54	261			2.4	28%	68%	4.48	50	14	36	4.9	5.8	**1.2**	13%	1.3	-2.1	22	$0
LIMA Plan C+	07 Proj	**1**	**2**	**0**	**44**	**26**	**4.55**	**1.47**	**268**			**3.0**	**30%**	**70%**	**3.99**	**53**	**20**	**27**	**3.9**	**5.4**	**1.4**	**10%**	**0.8**	**2.3**	**38**	**$1**

Used to be a lefty-killer but you can see that slowly dwindling along with the rest of his BPIs. Has to be kept at least 2 miles away from all RHed hitters. By law.

STEPHEN NICKRAND

Silva,Carlos

Silva,Carlos	Yr	Tm	W	L	Sv	IP	K	ERA	WHIP	OBA	vL	vR	BF/G	H%	S%	xERA	G	L	F	Ctl	Dom	Cmd	hr/f	hr/9	RAR	BPV	R$
RH Starter	02	PHI	5	0	2	87	42	3.10	1.26	264	292	276	5.2	29%	75%	3.45	58	21	22	2.3	4.3	**1.9**	6%	0.4	10.8	56	$8
Age 28	03	PHI	3	1	1	87	48	4.45	1.48	273	300	266	6.2	30%	70%	4.10	55	17	28	3.8	5.0	**1.3**	9%	0.7	-1.8	36	$3
Pre-Peak	04	MIN	14	8	0	203	76	4.21	1.43	308	328	289	26.8	32%	73%	4.15	51	17	32	1.6	3.4	**2.2**	10%	1.0	5.5	29	$10
Type Finesse	05	MIN	9	8	0	188	71	3.44	1.17	286	302	277	28.5	29%	76%	3.67	49	20	31	0.4	3.4	**7.9**	12%	1.2	21.5	148	$16
Reliability 64	06	MIN	11	15	0	180	70	5.95	1.54	326	329	320	22.3	32%	66%	4.38	44	22	34	1.6	3.5	**2.2**	16%	1.9	-30.9	-0	$2
DL 15	1st Half		4	8	0	84	32	6.43	1.52	331			20.7	33%	62%	4.44	40	23	37	1.2	3.4	**2.9**	15%	1.9	-19.4	13	($0)
ERA Potl 45%	2nd Half		7	7	0	96	38	5.53	1.56	322			23.9	32%	70%	4.32	47	22	32	2.0	3.6	**1.8**	17%	1.9	-11.5	-6	$2
LIMA Plan C	07	Proj	**9**	**13**	**0**	**189**	**75**	**4.58**	**1.42**	**304**			**24.0**	**31%**	**72%**	**4.16**	**47**	**20**	**32**	**1.7**	**3.6**	**2.1**	**13%**	**1.4**	**7.6**	**19**	**$8**

GB and hr/9 trends tell the story here. True, hr/f has been unlucky, but even a correction there only puts him at 2004 levels. With that paltry DOM, he needs a repeat of 2005 Ctl -- and that's not happening.

Sisco,Andy

Sisco,Andy	Yr	Tm	W	L	Sv	IP	K	ERA	WHIP	OBA	vL	vR	BF/G	H%	S%	xERA	G	L	F	Ctl	Dom	Cmd	hr/f	hr/9	RAR	BPV	R$
LH Reliever	02		0	0	0	0	0	0.00	0.00											0.0	0.0						
Age 24	03		0	0	0	0	0	0.00	0.00											0.0	0.0						
Growth	04		0	0	0	0	0	0.00	0.00											0.0	0.0						
Type Power	05	KC	2	5	0	75	76	3.12	1.46	243	216	255	4.9	31%	81%	3.83	42	21	37	5.0	9.1	**1.8**	8%	0.7	11.6	77	$6
Reliability 0	06	KC	1	3	1	58	52	7.13	1.82	287	318	271	4.2	34%	61%	4.90	39	17	44	6.2	8.1	**1.3**	10%	1.2	-18.4	36	($2)
DL	1st Half		0	1	1	33	32	7.59	1.90	294			4.3	35%	61%	5.00	35	18	47	6.5	8.7	**1.3**	13%	1.6	-12.4	27	($2)
ERA Potl 70%	2nd Half		1	2	0	25	20	6.51	1.73	278			4.1	33%	61%	4.75	44	16	39	5.8	7.2	**1.3**	7%	0.7	-6.0	47	($0)
LIMA Plan D+	07	Proj	**1**	**3**	**0**	**44**	**40**	**4.97**	**1.63**	**264**			**4.4**	**32%**	**71%**	**4.40**	**41**	**18**	**41**	**5.6**	**8.3**	**1.5**	**10%**	**1.0**	**0.5**	**52**	**$1**

I like it when the beat goes
Baby make your booty go
Baby I know you wanna show
That thong thong thong thong

What? Not Sisqo?
Oh, never mind.

Smoltz,John

Smoltz,John	Yr	Tm	W	L	Sv	IP	K	ERA	WHIP	OBA	vL	vR	BF/G	H%	S%	xERA	G	L	F	Ctl	Dom	Cmd	hr/f	hr/9	RAR	BPV	R$
RH Starter	02	ATL	3	2	55	80	85	3.26	1.04	207	213	199	4.2	28%	68%	2.86	42	24	35	2.7	9.6	**3.5**	6%	0.5	8.3	132	$28
Age 40	03	ATL	0	2	45	64	73	1.13	0.88	210	189	218	3.9	30%	89%	2.36	42	23	35	1.1	10.3	**9.1**	4%	0.3	24.9	258	$26
Decline	04	ATL	0	1	44	81	85	2.77	1.08	247	255	236	4.5	32%	79%	2.63	48	18	34	1.4	9.4	**6.5**	11%	0.9	14.9	173	$22
Type	05	ATL	14	7	0	229	169	3.06	1.15	245	252	233	28.3	29%	76%	3.26	48	22	30	2.1	6.6	**3.2**	9%	0.7	33.4	92	$26
Reliability 72	06	ATL	16	9	0	232	211	3.49	1.19	253	278	226	27.2	31%	74%	3.08	46	20	33	2.1	8.2	**3.8**	10%	0.9	28.5	107	$27
DL	1st Half		4	5	0	111	93	3.73	1.20	253			26.9	30%	72%	3.27	45	21	34	2.2	7.5	**3.4**	11%	1.0	10.4	93	$10
ERA Potl 60%	2nd Half		12	4	0	121	118	3.27	1.18	252			27.6	32%	75%	2.91	47	20	32	2.1	8.8	**4.2**	10%	0.8	18.1	121	$17
LIMA Plan C	07	Proj	**10**	**6**	**0**	**189**	**157**	**3.63**	**1.22**	**256**			**26.4**	**31%**	**72%**	**3.25**	**47**	**21**	**33**	**2.2**	**7.5**	**3.3**	**9%**	**0.8**	**25.9**	**95**	**$18**

His ERA doesn't reflect it, but this was a better showing than 2005. I've been analyzing baseball for 21 years and I can't ever recall so many 40-year-old arms posting such incredible BPIs without decline. Hmmm.

Snell,Ian

Snell,Ian	Yr	Tm	W	L	Sv	IP	K	ERA	WHIP	OBA	vL	vR	BF/G	H%	S%	xERA	G	L	F	Ctl	Dom	Cmd	hr/f	hr/9	RAR	BPV	R$
RH Starter	02		0	0	0	0	0	0.00	0.00											0.0	0.0						
Age 25	03		0	0	0	0	0	0.00	0.00											0.0	0.0						
Growth	04	aa	11	7	0	151	120	3.75	1.34	280			24.8	33%	75%	4.47				2.2	7.2	**3.2**		1.0	10.9	80	$13
Type Power	05	PIT *	12	5	0	154	122	4.32	1.21	245	304	239	19.3	28%	67%	3.75	37	21	42	2.6	7.1	**2.7**	9%	1.1	-1.5	74	$15
Reliability 39	06	PIT	14	11	0	186	169	4.74	1.46	274	305	251	25.5	32%	72%	3.67	43	21	36	3.6	8.2	**2.3**	15%	1.4	-5.8	55	$13
DL	1st Half		7	5	0	88	70	4.90	1.55	295			24.7	34%	70%	3.99	43	21	36	3.4	7.1	**2.1**	10%	1.0	-4.5	53	$4
ERA Potl 55%	2nd Half		7	6	0	98	99	4.60	1.38	254			26.3	30%	73%	3.39	43	21	36	3.8	9.1	**2.4**	19%	1.7	-1.4	57	$8
LIMA Plan C+	07	Proj	**15**	**10**	**0**	**203**	**187**	**3.99**	**1.28**	**249**			**22.4**	**30%**	**72%**	**3.44**	**42**	**21**	**37**	**3.1**	**8.3**	**2.7**	**11%**	**1.1**	**23.2**	**80**	**$20**

Dialed it up in the 2nd half. Keeps ball on ground, which means hr/f correction could lead to big gains. Finding an out pitch against LHers will stand between moderate improvement and this... UP: 3.50 ERA, 200 K

Snyder,Kyle

Snyder,Kyle	Yr	Tm	W	L	Sv	IP	K	ERA	WHIP	OBA	vL	vR	BF/G	H%	S%	xERA	G	L	F	Ctl	Dom	Cmd	hr/f	hr/9	RAR	BPV	R$
RH Starter	02	aa	2	2	0	25	14	6.48	1.44	284			18.2	28%	60%	5.81				2.9	5.0	**1.8**		2.2	-6.8	0	$0
Age 29	03	KC *	4	6	0	119	52	4.69	1.36	285	273	297	24.3	30%	68%	4.73				2.1	3.9	**1.9**		1.1	-2.4	27	$5
Peak	04		0	0	0	0	0	0.00	0.00																		
Type	05	KC *	4	6	0	107	56	5.24	1.60	311			16.7	34%	66%	5.08				2.9	4.7	**1.6**		0.5	-11.5	38	$0
Reliability 4	06	2AL *	5	10	1	140	97	5.99	1.66	337	349	314	21.4	38%	65%	4.03	40	26	34	2.1	6.2	**3.0**	11%	1.2	-24.9	53	$0
DL	1st Half		1	4	1	73	43	5.86	1.59	336			25.4	37%	64%	3.95	41	28	31	1.5	5.4	**3.6**	10%	1.0	-11.7	65	($0)
ERA Potl 60%	2nd Half		4	6	0	67	54	6.15	1.75	339			18.4	39%	67%	4.01	40	26	34	2.7	7.2	**2.7**	13%	1.4	-13.2	46	$0
LIMA Plan B	07	Proj	**3**	**5**	**0**	**83**	**55**	**4.99**	**1.43**	**291**			**19.0**	**32%**	**67%**	**3.96**	**40**	**26**	**34**	**2.5**	**6.0**	**2.4**	**11%**	**1.1**	**5.4**	**50**	**$3**

4-5, 6.56 ERA in 60 IP at BOS. Former top prospect is finally giving us some BPIs to talk about. Posted 8.3 DOM in 2nd half with BOS. If DOM trend continues and H% corrects, who knows? Decent end-game flyer.

Soriano,Rafael

Soriano,Rafael	Yr	Tm	W	L	Sv	IP	K	ERA	WHIP	OBA	vL	vR	BF/G	H%	S%	xERA	G	L	F	Ctl	Dom	Cmd	hr/f	hr/9	RAR	BPV	R$
RH Reliever	02	SEA *	2	6	1	93	76	3.87	1.25	243	297	179	19.4	27%	75%	4.14				3.1	7.4	**2.4**		1.5	6.7	57	$8
Age 27	03	SEA *	7	3	1	115	125	2.82	0.90	198	191	132	8.6	28%	68%	1.61				1.9	9.8	**5.2**		0.3	24.2	174	$21
Growth	04	SEA *	1	3	0	15	17	4.80	1.47	274			6.0	36%	70%	4.91				3.6	10.2	**2.8**		1.2	-0.7	85	$1
Type Power	05	SEA	0	0	0	7	9	2.54	0.99	231	571	100	4.0	35%	71%	2.76	32	16	53	1.3	11.4	**9.0**	0%	0.0	1.6	266	$1
Reliability 0	06	SEA	1	2	2	60	65	2.25	1.08	206	244	179	4.5	27%	85%	3.49	27	19	54	3.2	9.8	**3.1**	7%	0.9	17.1	110	$10
DL 15 156	1st Half		1	1	2	42	47	1.92	1.02	207			4.7	27%	87%	3.23	25	24	51	2.6	10.0	**3.9**	8%	0.9	13.7	130	$8
ERA Potl 45%	2nd Half		0	1	0	18	18	3.03	1.24	206			4.1	25%	80%	4.15	33	7	61	4.6	9.1	**2.0**	7%	1.0	3.3	80	$2
LIMA Plan A	07	Proj	**4**	**5**	**0**	**123**	**126**	**3.89**	**1.20**	**235**			**22.9**	**29%**	**71%**	**3.75**	**30**	**13**	**57**	**3.0**	**9.3**	**3.1**	**8%**	**1.1**	**11.1**	**95**	**$13**

Liner off his head ended season on Aug 30. Cranky shoulder probably needed the rest anyway. High FB% will be more problematic as a SP. Elite stuff in any role, but temper your expectations if he is a starter.

Sosa,Jorge

Sosa,Jorge	Yr	Tm	W	L	Sv	IP	K	ERA	WHIP	OBA	vL	vR	BF/G	H%	S%	xERA	G	L	F	Ctl	Dom	Cmd	hr/f	hr/9	RAR	BPV	R$
RH Reliever	02	TAM	2	7	0	106	51	5.18	1.41	239	289	183	13.9	24%	67%	5.37	33	16	50	4.7	4.3	**0.9**	10%	1.4	-9.4	9	$2
Age 30	03	TAM *	6	13	0	152	87	5.09	1.61	291	315	241	20.9	32%	70%	5.07	38	17	45	4.1	5.2	**1.3**	7%	1.0	-10.6	24	$2
Peak	04	TAM *	5	9	1	112	112	5.30	1.49	263	286	236	10.7	32%	67%	4.00	38	16	47	4.3	9.0	**2.1**	11%	1.4	-12.0	59	$5
Type	05	ATL	13	3	0	134	85	2.55	1.39	244	247	235	13.1	27%	85%	4.63	35	24	41	4.3	5.7	**1.3**	7%	0.8	28.0	44	$15
Reliability 49	06	2NL	3	11	4	118	75	5.42	1.51	293	326	270	11.6	30%	72%	4.47	35	21	44	3.1	5.7	**1.9**	17%	2.3	-13.5	1	$2
DL	1st Half		2	10	1	76	47	5.45	1.55	303			18.9	31%	73%	4.49	35	22	42	3.0	5.6	**1.9**	17%	2.3	-9.0	-0	$1
ERA Potl 40%	2nd Half		1	1	3	42	28	5.36	1.43	275			6.8	27%	71%	4.43	35	18	47	3.2	6.0	**1.9**	17%	2.4	-4.5	4	$2
LIMA Plan C	07	Proj	**4**	**5**	**0**	**94**	**61**	**4.91**	**1.51**	**279**			**10.9**	**30%**	**72%**	**4.65**	**36**	**20**	**44**	**3.8**	**5.9**	**1.6**	**12%**	**1.5**	**-3.3**	**21**	**$2**

This year's biggest projected reversal of fortune was not unexpected. A hr/f correction will help a bit, and Ctl shows some improvement, but there is still far more downside than upside.

Sowers,Jeremy

Sowers,Jeremy	Yr	Tm	W	L	Sv	IP	K	ERA	WHIP	OBA	vL	vR	BF/G	H%	S%	xERA	G	L	F	Ctl	Dom	Cmd	hr/f	hr/9	RAR	BPV	R$
LH Starter	02		0	0	0	0	0	0.00	0.00																		
Age 24	03		0	0	0	0	0	0.00	0.00																		
Growth	04		0	0	0	0	0	0.00	0.00																		
Type Finesse	05	a/a	6	1	0	88	65	2.25	1.11	262			25.4	31%	84%	3.31				1.0	6.6	**6.5**		0.7	22.3	158	$13
Reliability 0	06	CLE *	16	5	0	185	83	2.62	1.23	253	225	259	26.5	27%	80%	3.99	48	21	30	2.4	4.0	**1.7**	6%	0.5	44.2	47	$24
DL	1st Half		9	2	0	102	51	2.03	1.25	252			26.6	28%	84%	4.00	50	19	31	2.7	4.5	**1.6**	3%	0.3	31.9	58	$15
ERA Potl 35%	2nd Half		7	3	0	83	32	3.36	1.19	254			26.3	26%	75%	3.98	48	22	30	2.1	3.5	**1.7**	9%	0.9	12.3	34	$10
LIMA Plan D+	07	Proj	**8**	**6**	**0**	**139**	**74**	**3.90**	**1.31**	**271**			**25.5**	**30%**	**72%**	**3.85**	**48**	**22**	**30**	**2.3**	**4.8**	**2.1**	**9%**	**0.8**	**10.8**	**49**	**$11**

7-4, 3.57 ERA in 88 IP at CLE. Great debut, but looking closer, he posted a sub-40 BPV each month with CLE. Good control and GB tendency limit his downside, but his DOM trend leaves him no room for error.

Speier,Justin

Speier,Justin	Yr	Tm	W	L	Sv	IP	K	ERA	WHIP	OBA	vL	vR	BF/G	H%	S%	xERA	G	L	F	Ctl	Dom	Cmd	hr/f	hr/9	RAR	BPV	R$
RH Reliever	02	COL *	7	1	3	76	58	4.50	1.28	259	240	197	4.3	29%	69%	4.16	30	19	51	2.6	6.9	**2.6**	10%	1.4	-3.7	57	$8
Age 33	03	COL	3	1	9	73	66	4.07	1.32	262	273	245	4.3	31%	74%	3.80	32	22	46	2.8	8.1	**2.9**	11%	1.4	1.9	71	$8
Past Peak	04	TOR	3	8	7	69	52	3.91	1.25	239	258	220	4.6	27%	76%	4.21	34	17	49	3.3	6.8	**2.1**	8%	1.0	4.4	60	$8
Type Power	05	TOR	3	2	0	66	56	2.58	0.95	205	167	219	3.9	23%	83%	3.44	35	16	49	2.0	7.6	**3.7**	11%	1.4	14.6	97	$10
Reliability 13	06	TOR	2	0	0	51	55	2.99	1.33	246	183	264	3.7	32%	81%	3.75	30	20	50	3.7	9.7	**2.6**	7%	0.9	9.9	93	$6
DL 33	1st Half		1	0	0	29	31	2.47	1.41	241			3.6	31%	87%	4.01	30	20	50	4.6	9.6	**2.1**	8%	0.9	7.5	80	$3
ERA Potl 45%	2nd Half		1	0	0	22	24	3.68	1.23	253			4.0	33%	72%	3.44	30	20	51	2.5	9.8	**4.0**	7%	0.8	2.4	123	$3
LIMA Plan B	07	Proj	**3**	**2**	**3**	**64**	**61**	**3.52**	**1.28**	**253**			**4.1**	**30%**	**78%**	**3.78**	**32**	**18**	**50**	**3.0**	**8.6**	**2.9**	**10%**	**1.3**	**5.6**	**79**	**$8**

Great 2nd half cut short by forearm soreness. Primary worry remains growing inability to keep the ball down. That means more HRs are in his future. Don't bet on another sub-3.00 ERA.

STEPHEN NICKRAND

Springer,Russ

Springer,Russ	Yr	Tm	W	L	Sv	IP	K	ERA	WHIP	OBA	vL	vR	BF/G	H%	S%	xERA	G	L	F	Ctl	Dom	Cmd	hr/f	hr/9	RAR	BPV	R$
RH Reliever	02	ARI	0	0	0	0	0	0.00	0.00											0.0	0.0						
Age 38	03	STL *	1	1	0	23	16	6.65	1.35	245			4.1	20%	64%	6.30				3.9	6.3	1.6		3.5	-6.7	-28	$0
Decline	04	HOU *	1	3	6	45	36	3.80	1.62	291			5.2	35%	78%	5.04				4.2	7.2	1.7		0.8	2.6	52	$3
Type	05	HOU	4	4	0	59	54	4.73	1.19	228	209	231	3.9	26%	64%	3.57	40	16	44	3.2	8.2	2.6	13%	1.4	-3.5	72	$5
Reliability 2	06	HOU	1	1	0	59	46	3.50	1.05	216	253	187	3.3	23%	75%	4.02	27	15	58	2.4	7.0	2.9	10%	1.5	7.2	69	$6
DL	1st Half		1	0	0	27	22	4.00	1.04	216			3.2	23%	70%	3.88	30	12	58	2.3	7.3	3.1	11%	1.7	1.6	72	$3
ERA Potl 35%	2nd Half		0	1	0	32	24	3.07	1.06	216			3.3	23%	79%	4.15	24	18	57	2.5	6.7	2.7	9%	1.4	5.6	66	$3
LIMA Plan C+	07	Proj	2	2	0	58	44	4.19	1.28	252			3.8	28%	72%	4.25	32	16	52	2.9	6.8	2.3	10%	1.4	0.8	52	$4

A career year at age 37? The CMD trend is nice, but his 3.50 ERA in large part was mainly H% induced. His high FB% and the resulting HR risk also make a repeat unlikely.

Stanton,Mike

Stanton,Mike	Yr	Tm	W	L	Sv	IP	K	ERA	WHIP	OBA	vL	vR	BF/G	H%	S%	xERA	G	L	F	Ctl	Dom	Cmd	hr/f	hr/9	RAR	BPV	R$
LH Reliever	02	NYY	7	1	6	78	44	3.00	1.29	249	268	247	4.2	28%	77%	4.52	40	16	44	3.2	5.1	1.6	4%	0.5	14.0	55	$11
Age 39	03	NYM	2	7	5	45	34	4.60	1.24	226	206	226	3.7	25%	66%	4.28	34	17	49	3.8	6.8	1.8	9%	1.2	-1.8	52	$5
Decline	04	NYM	2	6	0	77	58	3.16	1.34	244	269	219	3.9	29%	78%	4.00	44	18	38	3.9	6.8	1.8	7%	0.7	10.5	63	$6
Type	05	2TM	3	3	0	42	27	4.69	1.52	292	235	358	3.2	33%	69%	4.17	41	27	32	3.2	5.8	1.8	7%	0.6	-2.0	50	$2
Reliability 18	06	2NL	7	7	8	67	48	4.02	1.44	270	271	276	3.6	32%	71%	4.27	42	19	39	3.6	6.4	1.8	2%	0.3	3.9	69	$9
DL	1st Half		1	5	0	32	22	5.06	1.75	291			3.5	35%	69%	4.94	42	22	36	5.3	6.2	1.2	3%	0.3	-2.3	50	($0)
ERA Potl 50%	2nd Half		6	2	8	35	26	3.07	1.16	249			3.7	30%	73%	3.72	42	15	42	2.0	6.6	3.3	2%	0.3	6.2	106	$9
LIMA Plan C	07	Proj	5	5	5	58	39	4.50	1.47	268			3.6	31%	70%	4.36	42	20	38	3.9	6.1	1.6	7%	0.8	0.0	47	$5

A tale of two halves...

	1H ERA	2H ERA
2005	7.07	3.51
2006	5.06	3.07

Weakening skills don't support a sub-4.00 ERA over long stretches, so don't hold him long.

Street,Huston

Street,Huston	Yr	Tm	W	L	Sv	IP	K	ERA	WHIP	OBA	vL	vR	BF/G	H%	S%	xERA	G	L	F	Ctl	Dom	Cmd	hr/f	hr/9	RAR	BPV	R$
RH Reliever	02		0	0	0	0	0	0.00	0.00											0.0	0.0						
Age 23	03		0	0	0	0	0	0.00	0.00											0.0	0.0						
Growth	04	a/a	1	0	4	15	13	2.40	1.33	262			5.3	32%	84%	3.78				3.0	7.8	2.6		0.6	3.6	86	$3
Type Power	05	OAK	5	1	23	78	72	1.73	1.01	194	224	172	4.6	25%	84%	3.22	45	17	38	3.0	8.3	2.8	4%	0.3	25.5	114	$21
Reliability 37	06	OAK	4	4	37	70	67	3.33	1.10	244	274	211	4.1	31%	70%	3.19	37	21	42	1.7	8.6	5.2	5%	0.5	10.6	151	$22
DL 19	1st Half		1	3	18	33	29	3.80	0.90	211			3.8	25%	62%	3.22	31	22	47	1.4	7.9	5.8	10%	1.1	3.1	149	$11
ERA Potl 65%	2nd Half		3	1	19	37	38	2.92	1.27	272			4.3	37%	74%	3.13	42	21	37	1.9	9.2	4.8	0%	0.0	7.5	156	$12
LIMA Plan C+	07	Proj	4	3	45	73	71	2.98	1.06	233			4.2	30%	75%	3.04	40	19	40	1.9	8.8	4.7	8%	0.7	12.9	138	$26

He's becoming an elite closer. ERA rose as expected, but he received neither H% nor S% support this time. DOM trend and improved Ctl suggest he hasn't reached his ceiling yet.

Suppan,Jeff

Suppan,Jeff	Yr	Tm	W	L	Sv	IP	K	ERA	WHIP	OBA	vL	vR	BF/G	H%	S%	xERA	G	L	F	Ctl	Dom	Cmd	hr/f	hr/9	RAR	BPV	R$
RH Starter	02	KC	9	16	0	208	109	5.32	1.43	281	276	281	27.4	29%	66%	4.34	47	15	38	2.9	4.7	1.6	12%	1.4	-22.1	19	$6
Age 32	03	2TM	13	11	0	204	110	4.19	1.31	274	310	239	27.0	29%	71%	3.95	49	16	35	2.3	4.9	2.2	10%	1.0	5.1	44	$15
Peak	04	STL	16	9	0	188	110	4.16	1.37	266	272	260	26.0	28%	73%	4.03	48	18	34	3.1	5.3	1.7	12%	1.2	2.2	33	$14
Type Finesse	05	STL	16	10	0	194	114	3.57	1.39	273	271	279	26.1	30%	78%	4.00	46	21	32	2.9	5.3	1.8	12%	1.1	16.2	37	$16
Reliability 95	06	STL	12	7	0	190	104	4.12	1.45	279	302	257	26.0	30%	74%	4.17	47	23	31	3.3	4.9	1.5	11%	1.0	8.6	31	$11
DL	1st Half		6	4	0	86	45	5.12	1.55	289			25.7	30%	70%	4.61	42	23	35	3.7	4.7	1.3	12%	1.4	-6.7	12	$2
ERA Potl 45%	2nd Half		6	3	0	104	59	3.29	1.37	270			26.2	30%	78%	3.80	51	23	27	2.9	5.1	1.7	9%	0.7	15.3	47	$9
LIMA Plan D+	07	Proj	13	8	0	189	106	4.01	1.41	274			26.3	30%	74%	4.08	47	21	32	3.1	5.1	1.7	11%	1.1	6.7	34	$12

As reliable as they come. Even his splits are reliable. Compare his 1H/2H to these from '05...

	Ctl	DOM	ERA
1H	2.8	4.7	4.15
2H	3.1	5.8	3.06

Good mid-season acquisition.

Sweeney,Brian

Sweeney,Brian	Yr	Tm	W	L	Sv	IP	K	ERA	WHIP	OBA	vL	vR	BF/G	H%	S%	xERA	G	L	F	Ctl	Dom	Cmd	hr/f	hr/9	RAR	BPV	R$
RH Reliever	02	aaa	9	5	2	142	90	4.82	1.55	323			21.2	36%	71%	5.66				1.8	5.7	3.1		1.1	-9.6	57	$5
Age 32	03	aaa	11	10	0	141	94	5.82	1.75	345			22.7	39%	68%	6.67				2.3	6.0	2.6		1.2	-24.8	40	$1
Peak	04	aaa	11	4	0	138	84	4.49	1.43	284			25.1	31%	71%	4.75				2.8	5.5	1.9		1.0	-2.4	41	$8
Type Finesse	05	aaa	7	9	0	161	90	4.82	1.61	328			24.4	36%	72%	5.85				2.1	5.0	2.4		1.0	-10.2	40	$2
Reliability 9	06	SD *	4	1	2	86	41	3.73	1.30	267	263	237	8.3	29%	73%	4.44	39	20	40	2.4	4.3	1.8	7%	0.8	8.0	39	$7
DL	1st Half		2	0	1	37	13	2.66	1.21	245			6.1	26%	77%	4.71	39	22	39	2.7	3.1	1.2	2%	0.2	8.4	42	$4
ERA Potl 45%	2nd Half		2	1	1	49	28	4.54	1.37	284			11.1	30%	71%	4.27	41	17	42	2.3	5.1	2.3	10%	1.3	-0.3	38	$3
LIMA Plan C+	07	Proj	1	2	0	44	23	4.34	1.43	294			12.6	31%	73%	4.40	39	20	40	2.3	4.8	2.1	10%	1.2	-0.2	31	$1

2-0, 3.20 ERA in 56 IP at SD. Many owners will buy him based on his low ERA and WHIP with SD, but you'll notice the eroding DOM and 26% hit rate, and let them search for fool's gold.

Tallet,Brian

Tallet,Brian	Yr	Tm	W	L	Sv	IP	K	ERA	WHIP	OBA	vL	vR	BF/G	H%	S%	xERA	G	L	F	Ctl	Dom	Cmd	hr/f	hr/9	RAR	BPV	R$
LH Reliever	02	a/a	12	4	0	146	81	4.25	1.58	301			25.3	33%	75%	5.19				3.3	5.0	1.5		0.9	0.4	30	$7
Age 29	03	aaa	4	4	0	84	55	7.07	1.74	316			26.1	35%	60%	6.39				4.0	5.9	1.5		1.4	-27.7	16	($3)
Peak	04	a/a	1	1	1	32	23	6.45	1.86	314			8.1	38%	62%	5.33				5.2	6.6	1.3		0.0	-8.3	59	($1)
Type Power	05	aaa	6	5	0	97	49	4.48	1.40	288			19.1	30%	73%	5.07				2.4	4.6	1.9		1.4	-2.1	23	$5
Reliability 10	06	TOR *	4	2	3	79	53	5.36	1.65	282	220	246	5.7	31%	70%	4.85	41	18	41	4.9	6.1	1.2	10%	1.2	-7.8	25	$2
DL	1st Half		2	2	3	42	31	7.48	1.98	330			6.3	36%	66%	4.99	40	23	38	5.3	6.7	1.3	17%	2.0	-15.3	-5	($2)
ERA Potl 45%	2nd Half		2	0	0	37	22	2.93	1.27	218			5.0	25%	76%	4.62	41	17	42	4.4	5.4	1.2	2%	0.2	7.4	62	$4
LIMA Plan C	07	Proj	2	3	0	58	36	5.12	1.64	284			8.0	31%	71%	4.92	41	18	41	4.7	5.6	1.2	10%	1.2	-3.1	20	$1

3-0, 3.81 ERA in 54 IP at TOR. Don't let the 2nd half ERA fool you. There's no skill support here for even a sub-4.00 ERA, let alone an outlandish 2.93 mark. Not rosterable.

Tankersley,Taylor

Tankersley,Taylor	Yr	Tm	W	L	Sv	IP	K	ERA	WHIP	OBA	vL	vR	BF/G	H%	S%	xERA	G	L	F	Ctl	Dom	Cmd	hr/f	hr/9	RAR	BPV	R$
LH Reliever	02		0	0	0	0	0	0.00	0.00																		
Age 24	03		0	0	0	0	0	0.00	0.00																		
Growth	04		0	0	0	0	0	0.00	0.00																		
Type Power	05		0	0	0	0	0	0.00	0.00																		
Reliability 0	06	FLA *	6	2	9	69	81	2.23	1.29	192	236	222	4.1	27%	85%	3.46	44	16	40	5.5	10.5	1.9	6%	0.5	19.2	104	$14
DL	1st Half		5	1	8	34	43	1.62	1.14	168			4.2	27%	84%	2.54	64	7	29	5.1	11.3	2.2	0%	0.0	12.1	136	$10
ERA Potl 45%	2nd Half		1	1	1	35	38	2.83	1.43	215			4.0	27%	85%	3.91	41	17	42	5.9	9.8	1.7	11%	1.0	7.2	75	$4
LIMA Plan B+	07	Proj	4	2	10	58	64	3.88	1.41	220			4.2	29%	75%	3.80	41	17	42	5.6	9.9	1.8	10%	0.9	4.1	80	$9

2-1, 2.85 ERA in 41 IP at FLA.
In favor of him becoming closer:
- Excellent DOM
- No LH/RH splits

Not in favor of closing:
- Poor control
- Anti-southpaw bias

Tavarez,Julian

Tavarez,Julian	Yr	Tm	W	L	Sv	IP	K	ERA	WHIP	OBA	vL	vR	BF/G	H%	S%	xERA	G	L	F	Ctl	Dom	Cmd	hr/f	hr/9	RAR	BPV	R$
RH Reliever	02	FLA	10	12	0	153	67	5.41	1.71	303	332	285	24.4	33%	67%	4.76	55	16	29	4.4	3.9	0.9	6%	0.5	-24.6	21	($1)
Age 33	03	PIT	3	3	11	83	39	3.69	1.23	243	292	215	5.4	28%	67%	3.34	67	13	20	2.9	4.2	1.4	2%	0.1	6.1	59	$9
Past Peak	04	STL	7	4	4	64	48	2.39	1.19	240	253	231	3.4	30%	79%	3.36	50	21	29	2.7	6.7	2.5	2%	0.1	14.8	96	$11
Type	05	STL	2	3	4	65	47	3.45	1.33	270	294	271	3.7	31%	77%	3.45	51	21	28	2.6	6.5	2.5	10%	0.8	6.4	67	$6
Reliability 37	06	BOS	5	4	1	98	56	4.49	1.57	284	248	327	7.6	31%	73%	4.03	57	17	26	4.0	5.1	1.3	12%	0.9	0.8	28	$4
DL	1st Half		1	2	1	36	25	5.73	1.55	287			5.0	31%	66%	3.98	49	21	31	3.7	6.2	1.7	17%	1.5	-5.2	25	$1
ERA Potl 50%	2nd Half		4	2	0	62	31	3.77	1.58	283			10.7	31%	77%	4.03	62	16	23	4.2	4.5	1.1	8%	0.6	6.0	30	$4
LIMA Plan C+	07	Proj	7	6	0	131	80	4.07	1.46	273			18.4	31%	73%	3.85	55	19	27	3.6	5.5	1.5	10%	0.8	10.2	43	$8

Showed poor skills as both a SP and RP. Previous two seasons would make a rebound seem plausible, but growing troubles vs. RHers say otherwise. He needs a sub-3.0 Ctl to have any value.

Tejeda,Rob

Tejeda,Rob	Yr	Tm	W	L	Sv	IP	K	ERA	WHIP	OBA	vL	vR	BF/G	H%	S%	xERA	G	L	F	Ctl	Dom	Cmd	hr/f	hr/9	RAR	BPV	R$
RH Starter	02		0	0	0	0	0	0.00	0.00											0.0	0.0						
Age 25	03		0	0	0	0	0	0.00	0.00											0.0	0.0						
Growth	04	aa	8	14	0	150	117	5.52	1.46	273			24.3	30%	66%	5.22				3.6	7.0	2.0		1.6	-21.7	35	$5
Type Power	05	PHI *	6	3	0	113	96	3.34	1.36	220	210	226	15.6	28%	75%	4.37	36	21	43	5.1	7.6	1.5	4%	0.4	12.7	76	$10
Reliability 6	06	TEX *	11	7	0	153	108	4.52	1.56	271	331	250	23.7	30%	74%	4.79	37	18	45	4.6	6.3	1.4	10%	1.2	0.6	31	$9
DL	1st Half		4	5	0	70	54	6.92	1.81	285			22.1	31%	64%	5.20	35	22	43	6.2	6.9	1.1	14%	1.7	-20.5	13	($2)
ERA Potl 50%	2nd Half		7	2	0	83	54	2.49	1.35	259			25.3	29%	86%	4.46	38	16	46	3.3	5.9	1.8	7%	0.9	21.1	50	$11
LIMA Plan C	07	Proj	9	6	0	145	111	4.47	1.50	260			20.7	30%	73%	4.55	37	19	45	4.5	6.9	1.5	10%	1.2	-1.2	41	$9

5-5, 4.28 ERA in 73 IP at TEX. Electric stuff, but still looking for the right mix. Control improved in each month w/TEX, but DOM got worse. LHers hit him for a 116 PX. He's a work in progress, but follow him.

STEPHEN NICKRAND

Thompson,Brad		W	L	Sv	IP	K	ERA	WHIP	OBA	vL	vR	BF/G	H%	S%	xERA	G	L	F	Ctl	Dom	Cmd	hr/f	hr/9	RAR	BPV	R$
RH Reliever	02	0	0	0	0	0	0.00	0.00											0.0	0.0						
Age 25	03	0	0	0	0	0	0.00	0.00											0.0	0.0						
Growth	04 a/a	9	2	0	87	59	3.31	1.13	253			22.0	28%	75%	3.56				1.6	6.1	**3.9**		1.0	11.1	93	$12
Type Finesse	05 STL *	6	1	1	68	39	3.04	1.19	235	224	228	5.7	26%	77%	3.43	58	17	25	2.9	5.1	**1.8**	11%	0.8	10.2	52	$8
Reliability 4	06 STL *	3	2	0	98	61	3.11	1.28	265	284	256	7.3	30%	77%	3.34	55	21	24	2.4	5.6	**2.3**	9%	0.6	16.7	66	$8
DL	1st Half	1	1	0	36	19	4.49	1.61	316			5.4	34%	74%	4.09	50	23	27	2.7	4.7	**1.7**	11%	1.0	0.0	27	$0
ERA Potl 45%	2nd Half	2	1	0	62	42	2.31	1.09	232			9.3	27%	80%	2.49	68	17	15	2.2	6.1	**2.8**	11%	0.4	16.7	91	$8
LIMA Plan B	07 Proj	**3**	**1**	**0**	**44**	**27**	**3.72**	**1.29**	**264**			**7.3**	**30%**	**72%**	**3.37**	**56**	**19**	**24**	**2.5**	**5.6**	**2.3**	**9%**	**0.6**	**5.3**	**64**	**$4**

1-2, 3.34 ERA in 56 IP at STL. Took GB approach to an extreme in 2nd half. Very little DOM upside, which means he needs to keep a sub-2.5 Ctl. If he does, he'll have some LIMA value.

Thompson,Mike		W	L	Sv	IP	K	ERA	WHIP	OBA	vL	vR	BF/G	H%	S%	xERA	G	L	F	Ctl	Dom	Cmd	hr/f	hr/9	RAR	BPV	R$
RH Starter	02	0	0	0	0	0	0.00	0.00																		
Age 26	03	0	0	0	0	0	0.00	0.00																		
Growth	04 aa	10	2	0	121	56	4.14	1.49	304			15.3	32%	75%	5.20				2.3	4.2	**1.8**		1.0	3.1	28	$7
Type Finesse	05 a/a	10	8	0	174	82	3.41	1.31	277			27.3	30%	74%	3.82				2.0	4.3	**2.1**		0.5	19.2	55	$14
Reliability 11	06 SD *	10	6	0	161	71	4.43	1.38	277	283	288	21.7	29%	69%	4.27	49	18	33	2.7	3.9	**1.4**	9%	0.9	1.2	27	$9
DL	1st Half	8	2	0	87	47	3.94	1.21	253			22.5	28%	68%	3.80	50	18	32	2.3	4.8	**2.1**	7%	0.6	5.8	59	$9
ERA Potl 45%	2nd Half	2	4	0	74	24	5.00	1.59	302			20.8	30%	71%	4.86	48	19	33	3.3	2.9	**0.9**	11%	1.2	-4.7	-6	($0)
LIMA Plan C	07 Proj	**6**	**6**	**0**	**116**	**51**	**4.50**	**1.41**	**284**			**21.8**	**30%**	**70%**	**4.25**	**49**	**19**	**33**	**2.6**	**4.0**	**1.5**	**10%**	**1.0**	**1.6**	**24**	**$5**

4-5, 4.99 ERA in 92 IP at SD. Posted a PQS-4/5 just once in 16 MLB starts, and DOM is just horrible. Another arm who lives and dies by the ground ball, and his infield defense. His fate rests in the hands of others, not him.

Thomson,John		W	L	Sv	IP	K	ERA	WHIP	OBA	vL	vR	BF/G	H%	S%	xERA	G	L	F	Ctl	Dom	Cmd	hr/f	hr/9	RAR	BPV	R$
RH Starter	02 2NL	9	14	0	181	107	4.72	1.35	283	285	264	25.8	32%	63%	4.42	38	16	46	2.2	5.3	**2.4**	3%	0.3	-13.8	71	$8
Age 33	03 TEX	13	14	0	217	136	4.85	1.30	277	281	270	26.2	30%	65%	3.68	48	18	34	2.0	5.6	**2.8**	11%	1.1	-8.8	58	$15
Past Peak	04 ATL	14	8	0	198	133	3.73	1.32	273	274	277	25.5	31%	74%	3.69	48	19	33	2.4	6.0	**2.6**	9%	0.9	13.1	63	$16
Type Finesse	05 ATL	4	6	0	98	61	4.49	1.42	286	276	292	25.0	33%	68%	3.85	46	24	30	2.6	5.6	**2.2**	6%	0.5	-3.0	61	$4
Reliability 14	06 ATL	2	7	0	80	46	4.83	1.56	292	276	313	19.9	31%	72%	4.48	44	21	36	3.6	5.2	**1.4**	11%	1.2	-3.4	21	$1
DL 96 88	1st Half	2	6	0	73	42	4.68	1.53	290			21.7	31%	73%	4.38	45	20	35	3.5	5.2	**1.5**	12%	1.2	-1.8	23	$1
ERA Potl 45%	2nd Half	0	1	0	7	4	6.34	1.83	310			11.2	33%	67%	5.56	29	29	42	5.1	5.1	**1.0**	10%	1.3	-1.6	6	($0)
LIMA Plan C+	07 Proj	**6**	**8**	**0**	**120**	**71**	**4.05**	**1.41**	**282**			**24.7**	**31%**	**74%**	**4.06**	**46**	**20**	**34**	**2.7**	**5.3**	**2.0**	**9%**	**1.0**	**4.6**	**43**	**$7**

Shoulder soreness wiped out 2nd half. 47% PQS DIS% suggests it may have affected him all year. '02-'04 xERA keeps giving hope that '03 wasn't the aberration, but his health problems haven't gone away.

Thornton,Matt		W	L	Sv	IP	K	ERA	WHIP	OBA	vL	vR	BF/G	H%	S%	xERA	G	L	F	Ctl	Dom	Cmd	hr/f	hr/9	RAR	BPV	R$
LH Reliever	02 aa	1	5	0	62	33	5.66	1.71	292			23.9	33%	65%	4.98				4.9	4.8	**1.0**		0.4	-10.6	33	($2)
Age 30	03 a/a	3	2	0	34	18	3.43	1.26	232			23.8	26%	73%	3.14				3.7	4.8	**1.3**		0.5	4.0	48	$4
Peak	04 SEA *	8	7	0	115	93	5.63	1.93	286	300	225	16.0	35%	69%	5.43	40	20	40	7.2	7.3	**1.0**	4%	0.5	-17.0	49	($1)
Type Power	05 SEA	0	4	0	57	57	5.21	1.68	251	262	235	4.8	28%	76%	4.40	43	15	42	6.6	9.0	**1.4**	20%	2.1	-5.9	26	($0)
Reliability 8	06 CHW	5	3	2	54	49	3.33	1.24	232	211	240	3.6	28%	76%	3.28	49	19	32	3.5	8.2	**2.3**	10%	0.8	8.2	82	$8
DL	1st Half	3	1	0	26	27	3.79	1.15	214			4.1	26%	73%	2.98	51	13	36	3.4	9.3	**2.7**	17%	1.4	2.5	83	$4
ERA Potl 45%	2nd Half	2	2	2	28	22	2.90	1.33	248			3.2	31%	78%	3.58	48	24	29	3.5	7.1	**2.0**	4%	0.3	5.7	80	$4
LIMA Plan B	07 Proj	**3**	**3**	**4**	**51**	**44**	**3.72**	**1.38**	**251**			**4.7**	**30%**	**75%**	**3.69**	**47**	**18**	**35**	**3.9**	**7.8**	**2.0**	**10%**	**0.9**	**5.0**	**67**	**$6**

3 reasons for profit potential:
- Big Ctl gains without much DOM erosion
- No LH/RH splits
- Keeps ball on ground

Former top prospect finally might be ready for a bigger role.

Timlin,Mike		W	L	Sv	IP	K	ERA	WHIP	OBA	vL	vR	BF/G	H%	S%	xERA	G	L	F	Ctl	Dom	Cmd	hr/f	hr/9	RAR	BPV	R$
RH Reliever	02 2NL	4	6	0	96	50	3.00	0.93	217	208	214	5.1	24%	69%	3.28	55	13	32	1.3	4.7	**3.6**	6%	0.6	13.1	98	$12
Age 41	03 BOS	6	4	2	83	65	3.58	1.04	248	287	198	4.6	28%	71%	2.82	51	18	31	1.0	7.0	**7.2**	15%	1.2	9.7	164	$12
Decline	04 BOS	5	4	1	76	56	4.14	1.24	259	269	247	4.2	30%	69%	3.30	50	21	29	2.2	6.6	**2.9**	12%	0.9	2.7	76	$7
Type Finesse	05 BOS	7	3	13	80	59	2.25	1.32	276	296	257	4.2	33%	83%	3.49	45	27	29	2.2	6.6	**3.0**	3%	0.2	21.0	95	$15
Reliability 14	06 BOS	6	6	9	64	30	4.36	1.47	302	306	303	4.1	32%	72%	4.56	40	21	39	2.3	4.2	**1.9**	8%	1.0	1.6	30	$7
DL 18	1st Half	3	0	1	26	16	1.73	1.23	254			3.9	30%	87%	3.99	41	22	37	2.4	5.5	**2.3**	3%	0.3	9.1	75	$5
ERA Potl 45%	2nd Half	3	6	8	38	14	6.16	1.63	331			4.3	34%	64%	4.96	39	21	40	2.1	3.3	**1.6**	10%	1.4	-7.5	-1	$3
LIMA Plan C	07 Proj	**5**	**4**	**5**	**58**	**32**	**4.50**	**1.40**	**284**			**4.2**	**31%**	**70%**	**4.13**	**43**	**22**	**35**	**2.5**	**5.0**	**2.0**	**10%**	**1.1**	**2.6**	**37**	**$6**

With this DOM trend, his value as a 5-10 save guy is just about over. Increasing troubles against LHers, ominous GB% trend are other reasons to stay away.

Tomko,Brett		W	L	Sv	IP	K	ERA	WHIP	OBA	vL	vR	BF/G	H%	S%	xERA	G	L	F	Ctl	Dom	Cmd	hr/f	hr/9	RAR	BPV	R$
RH Reliever	02 SD	10	10	0	204	126	4.50	1.33	269	270	264	27.1	29%	71%	3.82	49	17	34	2.6	5.6	**2.1**	14%	1.4	-9.9	38	$10
Age 34	03 STL	13	9	0	202	114	5.30	1.53	307	325	292	27.2	32%	69%	4.16	47	18	35	2.5	5.1	**2.0**	14%	1.6	-25.5	19	$5
Past Peak	04 SF	11	7	0	194	108	4.04	1.34	264	294	233	25.8	29%	72%	4.26	42	21	37	3.0	5.0	**1.7**	8%	0.9	5.4	41	$12
Type	05 SF	8	15	1	190	114	4.50	1.38	277	282	264	24.8	30%	69%	4.22	40	22	38	2.7	5.4	**2.0**	8%	0.9	-5.9	46	$9
Reliability 65	06 LA	8	7	0	112	76	4.74	1.36	280	300	258	10.9	31%	69%	4.15	37	18	45	2.3	6.1	**2.6**	10%	1.4	-3.4	50	$8
DL 35	1st Half	6	6	0	82	47	5.15	1.40	291			23.7	30%	67%	4.37	37	19	44	2.2	5.1	**2.4**	11%	1.5	-6.7	31	$4
ERA Potl 55%	2nd Half	2	1	0	30	29	3.61	1.24	249			4.3	31%	74%	3.57	38	14	48	2.7	8.7	**3.2**	8%	0.9	3.2	98	$3
LIMA Plan C+	07 Proj	**4**	**4**	**3**	**69**	**50**	**3.94**	**1.31**	**272**			**7.6**	**31%**	**74%**	**3.88**	**40**	**19**	**41**	**2.4**	**6.6**	**2.8**	**10%**	**1.2**	**4.1**	**63**	**$6**

Starter or reliever? You decide:

	Ctl	Dom	ERA
SP	2.2	5.1	5.12
RP	2.7	8.6	3.64

He wants to close, and his skills support a role change. Possible sleeper.

Torres,Salomon		W	L	Sv	IP	K	ERA	WHIP	OBA	vL	vR	BF/G	H%	S%	xERA	G	L	F	Ctl	Dom	Cmd	hr/f	hr/9	RAR	BPV	R$
RH Reliever	02 PIT *	10	6	0	192	116	4.78	1.55	311	241	273	27.7	35%	69%	3.97	54	14	32	2.5	5.4	**2.1**	7%	0.7	-16.0	50	$4
Age 35	03 PIT	7	5	2	121	84	4.76	1.40	273	307	252	12.8	30%	70%	3.54	53	19	27	3.1	6.2	**2.0**	18%	1.4	-7.2	38	$7
Past Peak	04 PIT	7	7	0	92	62	2.64	1.18	251	254	257	4.5	29%	80%	3.11	59	15	26	2.2	6.1	**2.8**	8%	0.6	18.4	83	$11
Type Power	05 PIT	5	5	3	94	55	2.77	1.19	222	272	189	5.0	25%	79%	3.93	51	16	34	3.4	5.3	**1.5**	7%	0.7	17.1	54	$11
Reliability 39	06 PIT	3	6	12	93	72	3.29	1.46	272	281	269	4.3	33%	78%	3.52	55	19	26	3.7	7.0	**1.9**	8%	0.6	13.8	65	$10
DL	1st Half	2	4	0	51	30	4.76	1.49	298			4.7	33%	70%	3.68	55	20	26	2.6	5.3	**2.0**	13%	1.1	-1.7	37	$1
ERA Potl 45%	2nd Half	1	2	12	42	42	1.50	1.43	238			4.0	33%	88%	3.33	56	16	27	4.9	9.0	**1.8**	0%	0.0	15.5	100	$9
LIMA Plan C	07 Proj	**3**	**4**	**5**	**73**	**55**	**3.60**	**1.35**	**255**			**4.8**	**30%**	**75%**	**3.49**	**55**	**17**	**28**	**3.5**	**6.8**	**2.0**	**10%**	**0.7**	**7.8**	**64**	**$7**

Flashed 159 BPV as fill-in closer in September. Converted 11 saves in 12 chances, aided by a 90% S%. At age 35, and given Sept. was his only high-skill month, it's tough to bet on a repeat.

Towers,Josh		W	L	Sv	IP	K	ERA	WHIP	OBA	vL	vR	BF/G	H%	S%	xERA	G	L	F	Ctl	Dom	Cmd	hr/f	hr/9	RAR	BPV	R$
RH Starter	02 BAL *	0	12	0	96	49	8.72	1.93	380			23.3	38%	59%	5.09	34	19	47	1.8	4.6	**2.6**	15%	2.6	-50.4	-18	($12)
Age 30	03 TOR *	13	8	1	196	106	4.50	1.31	293	281	250	23.7	31%	69%	4.08	40	18	41	1.3	4.9	**3.8**	10%	1.2	0.6	68	$15
Peak	04 TOR *	12	10	0	152	72	4.73	1.46	306	312	308	24.7	32%	71%	4.16	47	19	34	2.0	4.3	**2.2**	12%	1.3	-5.7	26	$7
Type Finesse	05 TOR	13	12	0	208	112	3.72	1.28	288	274	297	26.5	31%	74%	3.86	45	19	36	1.3	4.8	**3.9**	9%	1.0	16.8	77	$17
Reliability 46	06 TOR *	7	15	0	163	95	6.96	1.75	356	325	357	25.4	38%	63%	4.46	39	21	40	1.7	5.2	**3.1**	14%	1.9	-48.3	24	($5)
DL	1st Half	3	11	0	83	43	7.27	1.78	357			24.4	37%	63%	4.74	37	23	40	2.0	4.6	**2.3**	15%	2.1	-27.8	-2	($4)
ERA Potl 60%	2nd Half	4	4	0	80	52	6.64	1.71	356			26.4	39%	64%	3.92	57	4	39	1.3	5.9	**4.4**	13%	1.7	-20.6	60	($1)
LIMA Plan B	07 Proj	**4**	**6**	**0**	**83**	**46**	**4.66**	**1.41**	**306**			**24.0**	**32%**	**71%**	**4.03**	**43**	**19**	**38**	**1.5**	**5.0**	**3.3**	**12%**	**1.4**	**4.7**	**51**	**$4**

2-10, 8.42 ERA in 62 IP at TOR. The blame is threefold: H%, S%, hr/f, all elements largely out of his control. Still, even with a mass regression to all those means, he still profiles out to no more than a 4.50 ERA arm.

Traber,Billy		W	L	Sv	IP	K	ERA	WHIP	OBA	vL	vR	BF/G	H%	S%	xERA	G	L	F	Ctl	Dom	Cmd	hr/f	hr/9	RAR	BPV	R$
LH Starter	02 a/a	17	5	0	162	99	3.89	1.37	292			25.7	33%	73%	4.43				1.9	5.5	**2.9**		0.8	7.6	68	$15
Age 27	03 CLE	6	9	0	111	88	5.27	1.55	297	219	318	15.0	34%	68%	3.68	48	21	30	3.2	7.1	**2.2**	14%	1.2	-10.2	48	$4
Pre-Peak	04 CLE	0	0	0	0	0	0.00	0.00											0.0	0.0						
Type Finesse	05 a/a	6	9	0	110	65	5.90	1.68	321			21.1	36%	64%	5.65				3.2	5.3	**1.7**		0.7	-21.7	36	($1)
Reliability 0	06 WAS *	11	10	0	167	107	5.46	1.59	322	263	312	20.9	37%	65%	4.15	45	19	36	2.3	5.7	**2.5**	6%	0.7	-20.2	56	$4
DL	1st Half	5	6	0	94	63	5.10	1.59	318			25.0	37%	67%	4.19	38	27	35	2.5	6.0	**2.4**	6%	0.6	-7.1	60	$2
ERA Potl 60%	2nd Half	6	4	0	73	44	5.94	1.59	326			17.3	36%	62%	4.16	46	17	36	2.0	5.4	**2.7**	7%	0.9	-13.1	52	$1
LIMA Plan C+	07 Proj	**7**	**7**	**0**	**102**	**65**	**4.70**	**1.49**	**299**			**19.5**	**33%**	**70%**	**3.95**	**47**	**20**	**33**	**2.6**	**5.8**	**2.2**	**10%**	**1.0**	**5.2**	**48**	**$5**

4-3, 6.44 ERA in 43 IP at WAS. Doomed by a high H%, there is a decent BPI foundation here but not much upside. RHers managed a 124 PX against him. Probably destined to be a future lefty specialist.

STEPHEN NICKRAND

Trachsel,Steve		W	L	Sv	IP	K	ERA	WHIP	OBA	vL	vR	BF/G	H%	S%	xERA	G	L	F	Ctl	Dom	Cmd	hr/f	hr/9	RAR	BPV	R$
RH Starter	02 NYM	12	11	0	178	108	3.29	1.39	257	233	281	24.8	29%	79%	4.24	46	19	35	3.7	5.5	**1.5**	8%	0.8	18.0	43	$14
Age 36	03 NYM	16	10	0	204	111	3.79	1.32	262	199	312	26.2	28%	75%	4.45	40	16	43	2.9	4.9	**1.7**	9%	1.1	12.2	33	$17
Decline	04 NYM	12	13	0	202	117	4.01	1.41	263	245	279	26.6	28%	75%	4.46	43	18	39	3.7	5.2	**1.4**	10%	1.1	6.4	30	$12
Type	05 NYM	1	4	0	37	24	4.14	1.32	262	288	243	26.2	28%	74%	3.97	41	23	36	2.9	5.8	**2.0**	14%	1.5	0.5	36	$2
Reliability 16	06 NYM	15	8	0	164	79	4.99	1.60	285	267	306	24.7	30%	72%	5.09	42	18	40	4.3	4.3	**1.0**	10%	1.3	-10.1	7	$6
DL 146	1st Half	6	4	0	84	39	4.82	1.55	284			25.0	29%	72%	5.17	38	17	45	3.9	4.2	**1.1**	9%	1.3	-3.5	7	$3
ERA Potl 40%	2nd Half	9	4	0	80	40	5.16	1.66	287			24.5	30%	71%	4.99	45	19	35	4.7	4.5	**1.0**	11%	1.2	-6.7	8	$3
LIMA Plan D+	07 Proj	**13**	**13**	**0**	**189**	**103**	**4.73**	**1.52**	**279**			**25.4**	**30%**	**72%**	**4.68**	**42**	**19**	**38**	**3.9**	**4.9**	**1.3**	**10%**	**1.2**	**-7.5**	**20**	**$7**

A big skills regression across the board. Balky back may have been to blame, as could his personal issues. But at 36 and with so little upside, let someone else take the risk. DN: 5.00+ ERA

Tsao,Chin Hui		W	L	Sv	IP	K	ERA	WHIP	OBA	vL	vR	BF/G	H%	S%	xERA	G	L	F	Ctl	Dom	Cmd	hr/f	hr/9	RAR	BPV	R$
RH Reliever	02	0	0	0	0	0	0.00	0.00											0.0	0.0						
Age 25	03 aa	11	4	0	113	109	3.58	1.20	256			25.9	32%	73%	3.68				2.1	8.7	**4.2**		1.0	11.3	115	$15
Growth	04 COL *	2	2	1	34	30	6.07	1.67	333	286	143	9.8	37%	71%	3.31	48	24	28	2.4	7.9	**3.3**	28%	2.4	-7.6	35	$0
Type	05 COL	1	0	3	11	4	6.55	1.91	340	462	182	5.3	32%	72%	6.29	26	21	53	4.1	3.3	**0.8**	13%	2.5	-3.1	-50	$0
Reliability 0	06 COL	0	0	0	0	0	0.00	0.00																		
DL 181 159	1st Half	0	0	0	0	0	0.00	0.00																		
ERA Potl	2nd Half	0	0	0	0	0	0.00	0.00																		
LIMA Plan	07 Proj	**2**	**1**	**0**	**29**	**21**	**4.74**	**1.51**	**291**			**5.0**	**32%**	**74%**	**4.60**	**28**	**21**	**51**	**3.2**	**6.6**	**2.1**	**11%**	**1.6**	**-0.8**	**33**	**$1**

Still more shoulder injury setbacks, and at this writing, COL isn't sure if he'll ever pitch again. This projection assumes best case; he should not be on your fanalytic radar for 2007.

Turnbow,Derrick		W	L	Sv	IP	K	ERA	WHIP	OBA	vL	vR	BF/G	H%	S%	xERA	G	L	F	Ctl	Dom	Cmd	hr/f	hr/9	RAR	BPV	R$
RH Reliever	02 ANA	0	0	0	0	0	0.00	0.00											0.0	0.0						
Age 29	03 ANA *	4	2	5	84	82	4.82	1.49	282			7.0	36%	67%	4.52				3.4	8.8	**2.6**		0.7	-3.1	85	$7
Pre-Peak	04 aaa	2	6	6	74	46	5.13	1.60	275			7.3	31%	68%	4.79				4.8	5.5	**1.2**		0.8	-7.2	35	$2
Type Power	05 MIL	7	1	39	67	64	1.74	1.09	206	233	167	3.9	26%	88%	2.91	50	22	28	3.2	8.6	**2.7**	10%	0.7	20.7	101	$25
Reliability 26	06 MIL	4	9	24	56	69	6.90	1.69	261	245	263	4.0	35%	60%	3.66	42	25	33	6.3	11.1	**1.8**	17%	1.3	-16.7	68	$9
DL	1st Half	4	3	22	34	43	3.43	1.26	219			4.0	31%	75%	2.66	49	23	28	4.2	11.3	**2.7**	13%	0.8	4.4	112	$13
ERA Potl 75%	2nd Half	0	6	2	22	26	12.27	2.36	319			4.2	40%	47%	5.46	35	26	39	9.4	10.6	**1.1**	20%	2.0	-21.1	17	($4)
LIMA Plan B	07 Proj	**3**	**6**	**0**	**53**	**55**	**4.75**	**1.49**	**254**			**4.4**	**32%**	**70%**	**3.59**	**43**	**24**	**33**	**4.8**	**9.3**	**2.0**	**12%**	**1.0**	**5.1**	**71**	**$3**

Throwing harder doesn't mean throwing better. Completely lost the plate in the 2nd half. Now out as closer, and with a fat contract, MIL has little choice but to hope he rebounds. xERA is optimistic, but I'd bet against.

Valverde,Jose		W	L	Sv	IP	K	ERA	WHIP	OBA	vL	vR	BF/G	H%	S%	xERA	G	L	F	Ctl	Dom	Cmd	hr/f	hr/9	RAR	BPV	R$
RH Reliever	02 aaa	2	4	5	47	54	6.51	1.49	270			4.2	34%	58%	5.08				4.0	10.3	**2.6**		1.5	-13.0	71	$2
Age 27	03 ARI *	3	2	15	79	94	2.73	1.16	192	169	112	4.2	27%	78%	3.39	28	26	46	4.4	10.7	**2.4**	6%	0.6	15.0	114	$15
Pre-Peak	04 ARI	1	2	8	29	38	4.32	1.37	218	152	258	4.3	27%	79%	3.17	36	25	39	5.2	11.7	**2.2**	27%	2.2	-0.2	64	$5
Type Power	05 ARI	3	4	15	66	75	2.45	1.07	215	168	241	4.3	29%	80%	2.98	38	19	43	2.7	10.2	**3.8**	7%	0.7	14.6	132	$15
Reliability 11	06 ARI	2	3	18	49	69	5.87	1.47	265	323	192	4.9	39%	61%	2.98	35	24	41	4.0	12.6	**3.1**	12%	1.1	-8.3	111	$8
DL 38	1st Half	2	3	14	30	45	8.34	1.82	303			4.8	44%	55%	3.35	32	27	41	5.4	13.4	**2.5**	19%	1.8	-14.4	74	$4
ERA Potl 80%	2nd Half	0	0	4	19	24	1.90	0.90	196			5.2	31%	76%	2.40	42	18	40	1.9	11.4	**6.0**	0%	0.0	6.0	210	$5
LIMA Plan A	07 Proj	**3**	**3**	**38**	**73**	**91**	**3.35**	**1.10**	**218**			**4.5**	**31%**	**73%**	**2.76**	**37**	**22**	**41**	**2.9**	**11.3**	**4.0**	**10%**	**0.9**	**14.3**	**136**	**$22**

Shaky Ctl bothered him early, but he completely turned it around in the 2nd half. Ended the year with a solid grip on the closer role. Closer-worthy BPIs, only spotty health could stop him from keeping the job.

Vargas,Claudio		W	L	Sv	IP	K	ERA	WHIP	OBA	vL	vR	BF/G	H%	S%	xERA	G	L	F	Ctl	Dom	Cmd	hr/f	hr/9	RAR	BPV	R$
RH Starter	02 a/a	6	13	0	109	84	6.28	1.60	300			19.7	34%	62%	5.71				3.5	6.9	**2.0**		1.4	-26.9	36	$0
Age 28	03 MON *	7	8	0	135	82	3.93	1.30	249	270	242	21.1	27%	73%	4.64	34	16	50	3.3	5.5	**1.7**	8%	1.1	5.7	39	$10
Pre-Peak	04 MON	5	5	0	118	89	5.26	1.56	265	301	239	11.8	28%	73%	4.72	33	22	45	4.9	6.8	**1.4**	16%	2.0	-14.5	12	$2
Type	05 2NL *	11	11	0	160	124	5.10	1.44	276	268	288	23.3	31%	69%	4.12	35	23	41	3.3	6.9	**2.1**	14%	1.6	-16.8	38	$7
Reliability 42	06 ARI	12	10	0	167	123	4.84	1.42	282	275	272	23.4	31%	70%	4.06	40	18	42	2.8	6.6	**2.4**	12%	1.5	-7.4	44	$10
DL 56	1st Half	6	4	0	78	54	4.85	1.41	281			22.5	31%	69%	4.20	39	17	44	2.8	6.2	**2.3**	11%	1.4	-3.5	42	$5
ERA Potl 50%	2nd Half	6	6	0	89	69	4.84	1.42	282			24.2	32%	71%	3.93	41	19	41	2.8	7.0	**2.5**	13%	1.5	-3.9	47	$5
LIMA Plan C	07 Proj	**10**	**10**	**0**	**160**	**123**	**4.46**	**1.38**	**272**			**19.6**	**31%**	**72%**	**4.02**	**37**	**20**	**43**	**2.9**	**6.9**	**2.4**	**11%**	**1.4**	**6.8**	**51**	**$11**

Nice CMD growth, but remains limited by hr/9. FB ways mean that will continue to be part of the package. But with a little better hr/f luck, we'd see that ERA drift down toward his xERA. Possible sleeper.

Vargas,Jason		W	L	Sv	IP	K	ERA	WHIP	OBA	vL	vR	BF/G	H%	S%	xERA	G	L	F	Ctl	Dom	Cmd	hr/f	hr/9	RAR	BPV	R$
LH Starter	02	0	0	0	0	0	0.00	0.00											0.0	0.0						
Age 24	03	0	0	0	0	0	0.00	0.00											0.0	0.0						
Growth	04	0	0	0	0	0	0.00	0.00											0.0	0.0						
Type Power	05 FLA *	6	5	0	92	79	3.90	1.36	249	192	269	19.7	30%	73%	4.21	31	21	47	3.8	7.7	**2.0**	6%	0.8	3.9	71	$8
Reliability 0	06 FLA *	4	8	0	112	71	7.55	1.89	328	262	302	21.6	36%	61%	5.61	32	17	51	4.7	5.7	**1.2**	9%	1.5	-42.4	4	($8)
DL	1st Half	3	3	0	65	43	5.79	1.65	289			19.9	31%	68%	5.16	32	19	49	4.5	5.9	**1.3**	10%	1.5	-10.5	15	($0)
ERA Potl 55%	2nd Half	1	5	0	47	28	10.02	2.23	375			24.0	41%	54%	6.37	31	12	57	4.8	5.4	**1.1**	8%	1.5	-31.9	-10	($8)
LIMA Plan C	07 Proj	**3**	**5**	**0**	**69**	**49**	**5.26**	**1.59**	**282**			**20.6**	**31%**	**70%**	**4.93**	**32**	**19**	**50**	**4.3**	**6.4**	**1.5**	**10%**	**1.4**	**-4.7**	**25**	**$1**

1-2, 7.33 ERA in 43 IP at FLA. Given inexperience, this step back is not surprising. Sure, ridiculous H% and S% made 2nd half look worse than it should have, but it was plenty bad already. Needs more time.

Vazquez,Javier		W	L	Sv	IP	K	ERA	WHIP	OBA	vL	vR	BF/G	H%	S%	xERA	G	L	F	Ctl	Dom	Cmd	hr/f	hr/9	RAR	BPV	R$
RH Starter	02 MON	10	13	0	230	179	3.91	1.27	273	282	262	28.3	31%	73%	3.72	39	19	43	1.9	7.0	**3.7**	9%	1.1	5.5	86	$17
Age 30	03 MON	13	12	0	230	241	3.25	1.11	234	233	225	27.3	29%	76%	3.11	34	23	43	2.2	9.4	**4.2**	11%	1.1	29.2	121	$29
Peak	04 NYY	14	10	0	198	150	4.91	1.29	259	253	256	26.0	28%	66%	3.90	39	18	43	2.7	6.8	**2.5**	13%	1.5	-11.6	52	$15
Type Power	05 ARI	11	15	0	215	192	4.43	1.25	269	244	285	27.2	31%	70%	3.14	43	23	34	1.9	8.0	**4.2**	16%	1.5	-5.0	93	$17
Reliability 80	06 CHW	11	12	0	202	184	4.85	1.30	265	256	261	25.8	32%	64%	3.51	40	20	41	2.5	8.2	**3.3**	10%	1.0	-7.3	89	$17
DL	1st Half	8	4	0	95	75	5.02	1.31	274			26.8	32%	62%	3.72	41	18	40	2.3	7.1	**3.1**	8%	0.9	-5.4	83	$8
ERA Potl 70%	2nd Half	3	8	0	107	109	4.71	1.28	258			25.0	32%	66%	3.32	38	21	41	2.7	9.2	**3.4**	11%	1.2	-2.0	95	$9
LIMA Plan B	07 Proj	**14**	**10**	**0**	**214**	**200**	**3.92**	**1.22**	**254**			**26.0**	**31%**	**71%**	**3.33**	**40**	**20**	**40**	**2.4**	**8.4**	**3.6**	**10%**	**1.0**	**30.5**	**99**	**$24**

A real enigma. Skills continue to shout "big winner," and results say ".500 pitcher." Dialed it up in the 2nd half, but S% is still conspiring against him. All it will take is just a little change in luck: UP: 18 Wins, 3.25 ERA

Verlander,Justin		W	L	Sv	IP	K	ERA	WHIP	OBA	vL	vR	BF/G	H%	S%	xERA	G	L	F	Ctl	Dom	Cmd	hr/f	hr/9	RAR	BPV	R$
RH Starter	02	0	0	0	0	0	0.00	0.00																		
Age 24	03	0	0	0	0	0	0.00	0.00																		
Growth	04	0	0	0	0	0	0.00	0.00																		
Type	05 DET *	2	2	0	43	35	2.08	0.88	181			18.2	22%	78%	1.40				2.3	7.3	**3.2**		0.4	12.2	117	$8
Reliability 0	06 DET	17	9	0	186	124	3.63	1.33	263	279	253	26.3	29%	76%	3.94	42	23	35	2.9	6.0	**2.1**	10%	1.0	21.3	51	$21
DL	1st Half	10	4	0	103	65	3.14	1.21	244			26.6	27%	78%	3.92	42	20	37	2.7	5.7	**2.1**	9%	1.0	18.1	55	$14
ERA Potl 45%	2nd Half	7	5	0	83	59	4.24	1.47	285			26.0	32%	74%	3.96	41	27	33	3.2	6.4	**2.0**	11%	1.1	3.3	47	$7
LIMA Plan D+	07 Proj	**13**	**10**	**0**	**174**	**127**	**3.88**	**1.23**	**248**			**22.6**	**29%**	**71%**	**3.66**	**42**	**24**	**35**	**2.7**	**6.6**	**2.4**	**9%**	**0.9**	**17.7**	**70**	**$19**

Terrific debut - with caveats. 2nd half fade more due to luck correction; 1st half xERA wasn't so kind and overall skills were just okay. Any time a kid has some late season arm fatigue, it's something to watch. A risk.

Villanueva,Carlos		W	L	Sv	IP	K	ERA	WHIP	OBA	vL	vR	BF/G	H%	S%	xERA	G	L	F	Ctl	Dom	Cmd	hr/f	hr/9	RAR	BPV	R$
RH Starter	02	0	0	0	0	0	0.00	0.00																		
Age 23	03	0	0	0	0	0	0.00	0.00																		
Growth	04	0	0	0	0	0	0.00	0.00																		
Type	05 aa	1	3	0	21	13	8.14	1.57	280			23.6	29%	48%	5.66				4.3	5.6	**1.3**		1.7	-9.9	8	($1)
Reliability 0	06 MIL *	13	8	0	181	146	4.22	1.22	246	226	204	23.5	28%	69%	3.65	43	16	41	2.7	7.2	**2.7**	11%	1.1	6.0	71	$18
DL	1st Half	4	5	0	79	65	4.89	1.35	281			22.5	33%	66%	3.59	46	15	40	2.3	7.4	**3.3**	10%	1.1	-4.0	77	$5
ERA Potl 55%	2nd Half	9	3	0	102	81	3.69	1.12	217			24.3	24%	72%	3.67	41	17	41	3.1	7.1	**2.3**	11%	1.1	10.0	69	$13
LIMA Plan C+	07 Proj	**10**	**6**	**0**	**131**	**105**	**4.21**	**1.30**	**260**			**23.9**	**30%**	**71%**	**3.73**	**43**	**16**	**41**	**2.8**	**7.2**	**2.6**	**11%**	**1.2**	**10.2**	**66**	**$12**

2-2, 3.69 ERA in 54 IP at MIL. Skills carried well to MIL, and while 2nd half H% was lucky, xERA shows the BPI support. Solid DOM rate for a guy who doesn't throw hard. Should follow up well.

ROD TRUESDELL

Villarreal,Oscar

Villarreal,Oscar		Yr	Tm	W	L	Sv	IP	K	ERA	WHIP	OBA	vL	vR	BF/G	H%	S%	xERA	G	L	F	Ctl	Dom	Cmd	hr/f	hr/9	RAR	BPV	R$
RH Reliever		02	a/a	9	6	0	148	116	4.07	1.22	253			25.5	30%	66%	3.28				2.4	7.1	**2.9**		0.5	3.6	91	$14
Age	25	03	ARI	10	7	0	98	80	2.57	1.29	224	252	204	4.8	27%	82%	3.87	38	28	34	4.2	7.3	**1.7**	6%	0.6	20.6	74	$13
Growth		04	ARI *	0	4	0	29	28	9.93	2.03	365	250	400	6.2	43%	51%	4.26	29	35	35	3.7	8.7	**2.3**	17%	1.9	-20.3	27	($5)
Type		05	ARI *	2	3	0	31	12	5.52	1.35	262	207	278	5.8	27%	59%	4.88	33	29	38	3.2	3.5	**1.1**	7%	0.9	-4.9	20	$1
Reliability	3	06	ATL	9	1	0	92	55	3.62	1.30	264	264	259	6.7	28%	78%	3.88	47	19	34	2.6	5.4	**2.0**	13%	1.3	9.9	39	$10
DL		1st Half		7	1	0	37	19	4.14	1.43	262			4.7	26%	78%	4.57	47	14	39	3.9	4.6	**1.2**	15%	1.7	1.6	4	$5
ERA Potl	40%	2nd Half		2	0	0	55	36	3.27	1.22	265			9.5	30%	77%	3.44	47	23	31	1.8	5.9	**3.3**	11%	1.0	8.3	77	$5
LIMA Plan	C	07	Proj	**4**	**2**	**0**	**44**	**29**	**3.93**	**1.38**	**273**			**6.7**	**30%**	**75%**	**3.97**	**42**	**23**	**35**	**2.9**	**6.0**	**2.1**	**10%**	**1.0**	**2.1**	**49**	**$4**

All things considered, this was a successful return from rotator cuff woes. Got better as the year went on, a good sign. Watch his DOM rate in 2007; if it's back to pre-injury levels, target him.

Villone,Ron

Villone,Ron		Yr	Tm	W	L	Sv	IP	K	ERA	WHIP	OBA	vL	vR	BF/G	H%	S%	xERA	G	L	F	Ctl	Dom	Cmd	hr/f	hr/9	RAR	BPV	R$
LH Reliever		02	PIT	4	6	0	93	55	5.81	1.39	266	233	289	8.9	30%	57%	4.32	45	16	39	3.3	5.3	**1.6**	7%	0.8	-19.5	44	$1
Age	37	03	HOU *	10	8	1	160	123	3.77	1.34	242	267	221	17.5	28%	75%	4.21	37	20	42	4.0	6.9	**1.7**	9%	1.0	10.1	54	$13
Decline		04	SEA	8	6	0	117	86	4.08	1.42	236	203	247	9.1	27%	73%	4.58	38	19	43	4.9	6.6	**1.3**	8%	0.9	5.1	48	$8
Type	Power	05	2TM	5	5	1	64	70	4.08	1.44	240	222	258	3.5	32%	72%	3.52	43	22	35	4.9	9.8	**2.0**	7%	0.6	1.8	91	$6
Reliability	3	06	NYY	3	3	0	80	72	5.06	1.57	249	179	289	5.1	30%	69%	4.77	31	21	48	5.7	8.1	**1.4**	8%	1.0	-4.9	53	$3
DL		1st Half		1	1	0	33	25	2.18	1.24	191			4.3	24%	83%	4.46	37	20	43	5.2	6.8	**1.3**	3%	0.3	9.7	77	$4
ERA Potl	55%	2nd Half		2	2	0	47	47	7.07	1.80	285			5.9	34%	62%	4.97	27	21	52	6.1	9.0	**1.5**	11%	1.5	-14.6	37	($1)
LIMA Plan	B	07	Proj	**3**	**3**	**0**	**58**	**52**	**4.81**	**1.53**	**252**			**5.3**	**30%**	**71%**	**4.43**	**36**	**21**	**44**	**5.3**	**8.1**	**1.5**	**10%**	**1.1**	**0.4**	**53**	**$3**

Two brief brushes with major DOM -- in '05 and the 2nd half of '06. The only difference: in '06, he lost sight of the strike zone and the rest of his stats tanked. At 37, these are signs of desperation, not growth.

Vizcaino,Luis

Vizcaino,Luis		Yr	Tm	W	L	Sv	IP	K	ERA	WHIP	OBA	vL	vR	BF/G	H%	S%	xERA	G	L	F	Ctl	Dom	Cmd	hr/f	hr/9	RAR	BPV	R$
RH Reliever		02	MIL	5	3	5	81	79	3.00	1.05	194	225	170	4.2	25%	73%	3.56	29	23	48	3.3	8.8	**2.6**	6%	0.7	11.1	104	$13
Age	32	03	MIL	4	3	0	62	61	6.39	1.44	268	253	269	3.6	30%	62%	3.79	32	24	45	3.6	8.9	**2.4**	20%	2.3	-16.1	36	$2
Peak		04	MIL	4	4	1	72	63	3.75	1.18	231	163	290	4.0	26%	75%	3.76	35	17	48	3.0	7.9	**2.6**	12%	1.5	4.5	66	$8
Type	Power	05	CHW	6	5	0	70	43	3.73	1.47	273	330	242	4.7	30%	78%	4.38	43	21	36	3.7	5.5	**1.5**	10%	1.0	5.6	34	$5
Reliability	23	06	ARI	4	6	0	65	72	3.59	1.23	217	163	256	3.9	28%	75%	3.11	45	19	36	4.0	10.0	**2.5**	14%	1.1	7.2	90	$8
DL		1st Half		2	3	0	34	38	4.24	1.41	256			3.8	33%	74%	3.46	36	24	40	4.0	10.1	**2.5**	14%	1.3	1.1	78	$3
ERA Potl	50%	2nd Half		2	3	0	31	34	2.89	1.03	170			4.0	22%	76%	2.69	57	13	31	4.1	9.8	**2.4**	14%	0.9	6.1	105	$5
LIMA Plan	B	07	Proj	**6**	**5**	**3**	**73**	**68**	**3.70**	**1.29**	**237**			**4.2**	**29%**	**74%**	**3.57**	**43**	**19**	**38**	**3.7**	**8.4**	**2.3**	**10%**	**1.0**	**7.2**	**76**	**$9**

Rediscovered some long-lost DOM, combined it with an improving GB rate and posted his best season in 4 years. Got better as the season wore on and looks good to follow-up strongly in '07.

Waechter,Doug

Waechter,Doug		Yr	Tm	W	L	Sv	IP	K	ERA	WHIP	OBA	vL	vR	BF/G	H%	S%	xERA	G	L	F	Ctl	Dom	Cmd	hr/f	hr/9	RAR	BPV	R$
RH Starter		02	aa	1	3	0	18	15	11.00	2.44	379			24.1	43%	55%	9.76				6.5	7.5	**1.2**		2.0	-14.9	-12	($4)
Age	26	03	a/a	8	6	0	127	68	5.02	1.43	293			24.1	31%	67%	5.05				2.3	4.8	**2.1**		1.2	-9.9	32	$5
Growth		04	TAM *	5	9	0	99	54	6.63	1.62	279	279	216	20.5	25%	69%	5.58	29	15	56	4.8	4.9	**1.0**	18%	3.0	-26.9	-40	($2)
Type	Finesse	05	TAM *	5	14	0	171	102	5.95	1.48	302	310	283	23.5	32%	64%	4.30	38	21	41	2.3	5.4	**2.3**	14%	1.7	-33.2	23	$1
Reliability	0	06	TAM *	2	16	0	132	63	9.20	2.01	373	284	331	23.3	40%	52%	5.59	33	23	44	3.0	4.3	**1.4**	6%	1.0	-75.6	7	($17)
DL	26	1st Half		2	7	0	75	33	7.71	1.74	335			21.8	36%	54%	5.33	33	23	44	2.9	4.0	**1.4**	6%	1.0	-29.2	12	($5)
ERA Potl	70%	2nd Half		0	9	0	57	30	11.16	2.37	417			25.1	45%	50%					3.2	4.7	**1.5**		1.0	-46.4	2	($13)
LIMA Plan	F	07	Proj	**1**	**3**	**0**	**29**	**15**	**5.90**	**1.66**	**317**			**22.1**	**33%**	**67%**	**5.10**	**34**	**20**	**46**	**3.1**	**4.7**	**1.5**	**10%**	**1.6**	**-2.2**	**4**	**($0)**

1-4, 6.62 ERA in 53 IP at TAM. (which means he went 1-12 in AAA - yeesh!) He was pitching hurt, but with such soft skills, it's hard to tell. Labrum surgery will keep him on the shelf much of '07.

Wagner,Billy

Wagner,Billy		Yr	Tm	W	L	Sv	IP	K	ERA	WHIP	OBA	vL	vR	BF/G	H%	S%	xERA	G	L	F	Ctl	Dom	Cmd	hr/f	hr/9	RAR	BPV	R$
LH Reliever		02	HOU	4	2	35	75	88	2.52	0.97	194	180	201	4.2	26%	79%	2.64	39	25	36	2.6	10.6	**4.0**	11%	0.8	14.7	138	$23
Age	35	03	HOU	1	4	44	86	105	1.78	0.87	177	216	154	4.2	24%	87%	2.45	39	24	37	2.4	11.0	**4.6**	11%	0.8	26.5	156	$29
Decline		04	PHI	4	0	21	48	59	2.43	0.77	186	103	197	3.9	25%	75%	2.19	45	14	41	1.1	11.0	**9.8**	11%	0.9	10.9	262	$16
Type	Power	05	PHI	4	3	38	77	87	1.52	0.84	171	128	173	3.9	23%	88%	2.48	46	19	35	2.3	10.1	**4.4**	10%	0.7	26.0	152	$28
Reliability	50	06	NYM	3	2	40	72	94	2.25	1.11	225	161	234	4.2	32%	85%	2.26	53	16	31	2.6	11.7	**4.5**	13%	0.9	19.9	148	$25
DL		1st Half		3	1	15	36	46	2.49	1.16	197			4.3	28%	82%	2.37	59	15	26	4.2	11.4	**2.7**	14%	0.7	8.9	119	$11
ERA Potl	50%	2nd Half		0	1	25	36	48	2.01	1.06	251			4.0	36%	88%	2.14	47	16	36	1.0	12.0	**12.0**	13%	1.0	11.0	299	$14
LIMA Plan	C+	07	Proj	**3**	**2**	**43**	**73**	**90**	**2.48**	**1.06**	**209**			**4.1**	**30%**	**80%**	**2.50**	**44**	**19**	**37**	**2.9**	**11.2**	**3.9**	**10%**	**0.7**	**16.7**	**140**	**$25**

'17 walks in 36 IP in the 1st half might have been worrisome, but 59% ground ball rate likely helped (though it yielded only 2 DPs). At 35, he might start showing some small cracks, but still a low risk investment.

Wagner,Ryan

Wagner,Ryan		Yr	Tm	W	L	Sv	IP	K	ERA	WHIP	OBA	vL	vR	BF/G	H%	S%	xERA	G	L	F	Ctl	Dom	Cmd	hr/f	hr/9	RAR	BPV	R$
RH Reliever		02		0	0	0	0	0	0.00	0.00											0.0	0.0						
Age	24	03	a/a	1	1	0	9	9	3.00	1.11	240			4.0	33%	70%	2.33				2.0	9.0	**4.5**		0.0	1.5	156	$2
Growth		04	CIN *	4	3	1	67	52	4.42	1.68	284	224	307	4.8	33%	75%	4.09	50	24	26	5.1	7.0	**1.4**	12%	0.9	-1.3	41	$2
Type		05	CIN	3	2	0	45	39	6.17	1.62	305	311	297	4.9	37%	61%	2.86	61	23	15	3.4	7.8	**2.3**	18%	0.8	-10.7	65	$0
Reliability	0	06	WAS *	4	6	1	77	48	6.64	1.85	337	197	387	5.5	38%	63%	3.76	62	18	20	3.7	5.6	**1.5**	12%	0.8	-20.5	28	($3)
DL	85	1st Half		1	2	1	33	20	9.00	2.21	388			5.5	43%	58%					3.8	5.5	**1.4**		1.1	-18.4	7	($5)
ERA Potl	60%	2nd Half		3	4	0	44	28	4.88	1.58	294			5.5	34%	69%	3.52	62	18	20	3.7	5.7	**1.6**	10%	0.6	-2.1	45	$1
LIMA Plan	B	07	Proj	**3**	**4**	**0**	**58**	**42**	**4.34**	**1.50**	**281**			**4.9**	**33%**	**71%**	**3.42**	**57**	**22**	**21**	**3.6**	**6.5**	**1.8**	**10%**	**0.6**	**6.8**	**58**	**$3**

3-3, 4.70 ERA in 31 IP at WAS. Trade to WAS seems to have been a good tonic. But even then, skills fell short of '05, and now save opps are gone. xERA shows why you should still tuck him away.

Wainwright,Adam

Wainwright,Adam		Yr	Tm	W	L	Sv	IP	K	ERA	WHIP	OBA	vL	vR	BF/G	H%	S%	xERA	G	L	F	Ctl	Dom	Cmd	hr/f	hr/9	RAR	BPV	R$
RH Reliever		02		0	0	0	0	0	0.00	0.00																		
Age	25	03	aa	10	8	0	149	108	4.58	1.33	277			23.5	32%	65%	4.04				2.3	6.5	**2.8**		0.7	-3.5	79	$11
Growth		04	aaa	4	4	0	63	56	5.55	1.55	288			23.5	33%	68%	5.60				3.7	8.0	**2.2**		1.6	-9.4	44	$2
Type	Power	05	aaa	9	10	0	176	123	4.86	1.48	301			27.7	35%	68%	4.91				2.4	6.3	**2.6**		0.8	-12.0	63	$7
Reliability	1	06	STL	2	1	3	75	72	3.12	1.15	232	301	182	5.0	29%	75%	3.07	48	17	35	2.6	8.6	**3.3**	8%	0.7	12.7	108	$10
DL		1st Half		2	1	1	38	33	2.59	0.92	200			5.2	24%	77%	3.16	44	12	44	1.9	7.8	**4.1**	9%	0.9	8.9	120	$7
ERA Potl	55%	2nd Half		0	0	2	37	39	3.67	1.39	263			4.8	35%	73%	2.92	52	23	26	3.4	9.5	**2.8**	8%	0.5	3.7	103	$3
LIMA Plan	B+	07	Proj	**3**	**2**	**30**	**73**	**68**	**3.48**	**1.26**	**252**			**5.0**	**31%**	**75%**	**3.15**	**48**	**18**	**33**	**2.7**	**8.4**	**3.1**	**10%**	**0.9**	**10.8**	**94**	**$17**

Went from middling starter to playoff-hero closer in one year. BPIs certainly say closer-worthy. His kind of success in the spotlight can launch a new career path, if given the opportunity.

Wakefield,Tim

Wakefield,Tim		Yr	Tm	W	L	Sv	IP	K	ERA	WHIP	OBA	vL	vR	BF/G	H%	S%	xERA	G	L	F	Ctl	Dom	Cmd	hr/f	hr/9	RAR	BPV	R$
RH Starter		02	BOS	11	5	3	163	134	2.82	1.06	208	195	213	14.4	25%	77%	3.54	39	19	42	2.8	7.4	**2.6**	8%	0.8	33.0	88	$25
Age	40	03	BOS	11	7	1	202	169	4.10	1.31	253	266	228	24.4	30%	71%	3.75	40	20	40	3.2	7.5	**2.4**	10%	1.0	10.6	69	$19
Decline		04	BOS	12	10	0	188	116	4.88	1.38	271	230	298	25.3	29%	68%	4.16	47	14	40	3.0	5.6	**1.8**	12%	1.4	-10.4	31	$10
Type		05	BOS	16	12	0	225	151	4.16	1.24	249	202	278	28.3	27%	72%	3.96	41	17	42	2.7	6.0	**2.2**	12%	1.4	5.9	46	$21
Reliability	49	06	BOS	7	11	0	140	90	4.63	1.33	255	221	265	25.9	28%	68%	4.35	39	16	44	3.3	5.8	**1.8**	10%	1.2	-1.2	39	$10
DL	57	1st Half		5	8	0	105	71	3.86	1.24	241			27.3	27%	71%	4.14	40	15	44	3.1	6.1	**2.0**	8%	0.9	9.1	56	$10
ERA Potl	50%	2nd Half		2	3	0	35	19	6.94	1.60	293			22.6	29%	60%	4.98	37	19	44	3.9	4.9	**1.3**	15%	2.1	-10.3	-9	($0)
LIMA Plan	C	07	Proj	**10**	**10**	**0**	**160**	**102**	**4.40**	**1.36**	**262**			**24.4**	**29%**	**71%**	**4.32**	**40**	**17**	**43**	**3.2**	**5.8**	**1.8**	**10%**	**1.2**	**3.2**	**39**	**$11**

Returned late from a broken rib, so 2nd half numbers are a little skewed. 1st half looked a lot like '05, and should maintain. Knuckleballers live forever, so we're already writing his comment for the 2048 book.

Walker,Jamie

Walker,Jamie		Yr	Tm	W	L	Sv	IP	K	ERA	WHIP	OBA	vL	vR	BF/G	H%	S%	xERA	G	L	F	Ctl	Dom	Cmd	hr/f	hr/9	RAR	BPV	R$
LH Reliever		02	DET *	1	2	2	56	48	3.54	0.93	202	202	194	3.2	21%	73%	3.30	33	20	47	1.9	7.7	**4.0**	16%	1.8	6.4	92	$8
Age	35	03	DET	4	3	3	65	45	3.32	1.20	250	212	276	3.4	27%	78%	4.08	35	17	48	2.4	6.2	**2.6**	9%	1.2	9.6	61	$9
Decline		04	DET	3	4	1	64	53	3.22	1.26	276	200	313	3.8	32%	78%	3.65	36	20	44	1.7	7.4	**4.4**	9%	1.1	9.6	103	$7
Type		05	DET	4	3	0	48	30	3.73	1.29	265	245	271	3.1	29%	74%	4.06	41	19	40	2.4	5.6	**2.3**	8%	0.9	3.8	56	$5
Reliability	16	06	DET	0	1	0	48	37	2.81	1.15	258	238	262	3.5	28%	85%	3.75	31	20	49	1.5	6.9	**4.6**	11%	1.5	10.3	97	$5
DL		1st Half		0	0	0	21	17	1.28	0.85	212			3.1	23%	100%	3.49	27	16	57	0.9	7.3	**8.5**	9%	1.3	8.5	196	$4
ERA Potl	35%	2nd Half		0	1	0	27	20	4.01	1.38	290			3.9	32%	78%	3.94	33	24	43	2.0	6.7	**3.3**	13%	1.7	1.8	57	$2
LIMA Plan	B+	07	Proj	**2**	**2**	**0**	**58**	**43**	**3.26**	**1.21**	**262**			**3.4**	**29%**	**79%**	**3.83**	**35**	**20**	**45**	**1.9**	**6.7**	**3.6**	**10%**	**1.2**	**4.7**	**81**	**$6**

Another small data set tossed about at the whims of H% and S%. Solid skills overall but you can never look too closely at the in-season swings; they're meaningless.

ROD TRUESDELL

Walker,Tyler

Profile	Yr	Tm	W	L	Sv	IP	K	ERA	WHIP	OBA	vL	vR	BF/G	H%	S%	xERA	G	L	F	Ctl	Dom	Cmd	hr/f	hr/9	RAR	BPV	R$
RH Reliever	02	aaa	10	5	1	142	89	4.94	1.54	308			22.6	35%	68%	5.14				2.5	5.6	**2.2**		0.8	-11.8	49	$5
Age 31	03	aaa	2	9	0	131	97	6.04	1.69	319			23.2	37%	64%	5.84				3.3	6.7	**2.0**		1.0	-26.6	45	($3)
Peak	04	SF	* 6	2	1	78	60	3.79	1.44	282	287	288	5.6	33%	77%	3.93	42	20	38	3.0	6.9	**2.3**	10%	1.0	4.6	57	$6
Type: Power	05	SF	6	4	23	61	54	4.26	1.55	283	284	278	4.1	33%	77%	4.04	42	18	41	4.0	7.9	**2.0**	12%	1.3	-0.1	48	$12
Reliability 7	06	2TM	1	4	10	25	19	7.17	1.55	276	333	226	4.3	33%	50%	4.47	35	28	37	4.3	6.8	**1.6**	3%	0.4	-8.2	63	$3
DL 109 18	1st Half		1	4	10	25	19	7.17	1.55	276			4.3	33%	50%	4.47	35	28	37	4.3	6.8	**1.6**	3%	0.4	-8.2	63	$3
ERA Potl 65%	2nd Half		0	0	0	0	0	0.00	0.00																		
LIMA Plan C+	07	Proj	**1**	**1**	**0**	**15**	**11**	**4.97**	**1.66**	**294**			**4.4**	**33%**	**73%**	**4.48**	**39**	**23**	**38**	**4.3**	**6.8**	**1.6**	**11%**	**1.2**	**-0.1**	**33**	**$0**

Out until at least mid-season after Tommy John surgery. BPIs weren't closer-worthy anyway, so the injury just saved his owners future blown saves, and the discomfort of waiting for TAM save opps.

Wang,Chien-Ming

Profile	Yr	Tm	W	L	Sv	IP	K	ERA	WHIP	OBA	vL	vR	BF/G	H%	S%	xERA	G	L	F	Ctl	Dom	Cmd	hr/f	hr/9	RAR	BPV	R$
RH Starter	02		0	0	0	0	0	0.00	0.00											0.0	0.0						
Age 27	03	aa	7	6	0	122	71	5.63	1.63	325			26.4	37%	64%	5.50				2.4	5.2	**2.1**		0.6	-18.6	48	$1
Growth	04	a/a	11	6	0	149	102	4.23	1.34	282			26.5	33%	68%	4.12				2.1	6.1	**2.9**		0.6	2.0	78	$11
Type: Finesse	05	NYY	* 10	6	0	150	65	4.21	1.30	271	258	254	26.4	29%	69%	3.46	64	14	22	2.3	3.9	**1.7**	11%	0.8	3.0	36	$10
Reliability 40	06	NYY	19	6	1	218	76	3.63	1.31	275	275	279	27.1	29%	72%	3.57	63	17	20	2.1	3.1	**1.5**	8%	0.5	24.9	35	$21
DL 59	1st Half		8	3	1	112	38	4.01	1.28	268			26.1	28%	68%	3.56	63	17	20	2.2	3.1	**1.4**	8%	0.5	7.5	35	$10
ERA Potl 45%	2nd Half		11	3	0	106	38	3.23	1.34	281			28.2	30%	76%	3.58	63	17	20	2.1	3.2	**1.5**	8%	0.5	17.4	35	$12
LIMA Plan F	07	Proj	**15**	**9**	**0**	**214**	**90**	**3.96**	**1.34**	**281**			**26.8**	**30%**	**71%**	**3.47**	**63**	**16**	**21**	**2.2**	**3.8**	**1.7**	**10%**	**0.6**	**26.7**	**39**	**$16**

With so many balls in play, his ERA is subject to a lot of luck-driven fluctuation. For two years, they've found a glove. At least very few go over the fence. Needs '04 DOM for any real growth.

Washburn,Jarrod

Profile	Yr	Tm	W	L	Sv	IP	K	ERA	WHIP	OBA	vL	vR	BF/G	H%	S%	xERA	G	L	F	Ctl	Dom	Cmd	hr/f	hr/9	RAR	BPV	R$
LH Starter	02	ANA	18	6	0	206	139	3.15	1.17	240	199	246	26.4	27%	76%	4.34	30	17	53	2.6	6.1	**2.4**	6%	0.8	33.4	68	$26
Age 32	03	ANA	10	15	0	207	118	4.43	1.25	260	230	264	27.0	27%	70%	4.51	32	17	51	2.3	5.1	**2.2**	10%	1.5	2.3	35	$15
Peak	04	ANA	11	8	0	149	86	4.65	1.33	274	225	283	25.4	29%	68%	4.26	38	20	41	2.4	5.2	**2.2**	10%	1.2	-4.0	40	$10
Type: Finesse	05	ANA	8	8	0	177	94	3.20	1.33	269	266	276	25.9	29%	80%	4.35	39	21	40	2.6	4.8	**1.8**	8%	1.0	25.6	40	$14
Reliability 76	06	SEA	8	14	0	187	103	4.67	1.35	273	317	257	25.8	29%	68%	4.40	40	18	42	2.6	5.0	**1.9**	10%	1.2	-2.6	33	$11
DL 15	1st Half		4	8	0	99	55	4.91	1.25	262			25.8	27%	64%	4.13	42	17	41	2.3	5.0	**2.2**	11%	1.4	-4.3	38	$6
ERA Potl 50%	2nd Half		4	6	0	88	48	4.40	1.47	285			25.7	31%	72%	4.70	38	19	43	3.1	4.9	**1.6**	8%	1.0	1.7	30	$4
LIMA Plan D+	07	Proj	**10**	**12**	**0**	**203**	**113**	**4.30**	**1.35**	**274**			**25.5**	**29%**	**72%**	**4.40**	**39**	**19**	**42**	**2.6**	**5.0**	**1.9**	**10%**	**1.2**	**2.1**	**33**	**$13**

As expected, S% regressed and with it his ERA. Was headed toward a return to 200 IP until he strained his calf in Sept. Set your expectations based on that, and an ERA close to xERA, but not on 2005.

Weathers,David

Profile	Yr	Tm	W	L	Sv	IP	K	ERA	WHIP	OBA	vL	vR	BF/G	H%	S%	xERA	G	L	F	Ctl	Dom	Cmd	hr/f	hr/9	RAR	BPV	R$
RH Reliever	02	NYM	6	3	0	77	61	2.92	1.36	241	267	232	4.6	29%	81%	3.84	47	20	33	4.2	7.1	**1.7**	8%	0.7	11.2	64	$8
Age 37	03	NYM	1	6	7	87	75	3.10	1.46	262	239	276	4.9	32%	80%	3.72	47	22	31	4.1	7.8	**1.9**	7%	0.6	12.6	70	$7
Decline	04	2NL	7	7	0	82	61	4.17	1.46	269	241	294	5.5	30%	76%	3.89	49	18	33	3.8	6.7	**1.7**	14%	1.3	1.0	39	$6
Type: Power	05	CIN	7	4	15	77	61	3.96	1.30	246	265	226	4.5	29%	71%	3.42	50	21	28	3.4	7.1	**2.1**	11%	0.8	2.7	68	$12
Reliability 28	06	CIN	4	4	12	73	50	3.57	1.30	228	219	230	4.6	24%	80%	4.14	45	17	38	4.2	6.1	**1.5**	14%	1.5	8.3	33	$11
DL	1st Half		2	2	9	34	22	5.54	1.61	278			4.8	28%	72%	4.47	47	18	35	4.8	5.8	**1.2**	21%	2.1	-4.4	-3	$3
ERA Potl 30%	2nd Half		2	2	3	39	28	1.84	1.02	179			4.4	20%	89%	3.85	42	17	42	3.7	6.4	**1.8**	9%	0.9	12.8	67	$7
LIMA Plan D+	07	Proj	**3**	**4**	**30**	**58**	**40**	**4.03**	**1.41**	**255**			**4.8**	**29%**	**74%**	**4.11**	**47**	**19**	**35**	**4.0**	**6.2**	**1.5**	**10%**	**0.9**	**1.8**	**46**	**$13**

Strong finish more a function of lucky H% and S% than any skills improvement. So he's still 37, still has mediocre control, marginal dominance and is a closer only because he is in the right place at the right time.

Weaver,Jeff

Profile	Yr	Tm	W	L	Sv	IP	K	ERA	WHIP	OBA	vL	vR	BF/G	H%	S%	xERA	G	L	F	Ctl	Dom	Cmd	hr/f	hr/9	RAR	BPV	R$
RH Starter	02	2AL	11	11	2	199	132	3.53	1.21	256	233	268	25.7	30%	71%	3.75	46	16	38	2.2	6.0	**2.8**	5%	0.5	22.9	81	$20
Age 30	03	NYY	7	9	0	159	93	6.00	1.62	320	342	290	22.6	35%	63%	4.52	41	20	39	2.7	5.3	**2.0**	7%	0.9	-28.9	37	($0)
Peak	04	LA	13	13	0	220	153	4.01	1.30	261	291	231	27.3	30%	70%	3.99	40	21	39	2.7	6.3	**2.3**	7%	0.8	6.9	65	$16
Type	05	LA	14	11	0	224	157	4.22	1.17	258	297	208	27.0	28%	69%	3.57	41	21	38	1.7	6.3	**3.7**	13%	1.4	0.7	76	$20
Reliability 80	06	2TM	8	14	0	172	107	5.76	1.51	305	340	267	24.6	32%	66%	4.21	39	23	38	2.5	5.6	**2.3**	15%	1.8	-26.2	22	$3
DL	1st Half		3	10	0	88	62	6.33	1.53	314			24.5	34%	62%	3.98	39	23	38	2.1	6.3	**3.0**	16%	1.8	-19.7	37	$0
ERA Potl 55%	2nd Half		5	4	0	84	45	5.16	1.49	295			24.6	30%	71%	4.47	39	22	39	2.8	4.8	**1.7**	14%	1.7	-6.6	10	$3
LIMA Plan B	07	Proj	**13**	**11**	**0**	**203**	**136**	**4.52**	**1.38**	**285**			**25.7**	**31%**	**71%**	**3.99**	**40**	**21**	**39**	**2.3**	**6.0**	**2.6**	**11%**	**1.2**	**10.7**	**51**	**$13**

BPIs cause for concern, but not why you think. 2nd half DOM dip, problems with LHers are bigger issues than the HR. Assuming DOM rebounds, ERA should too, but he's limited until he can get lefties out.

Weaver,Jered

Profile	Yr	Tm	W	L	Sv	IP	K	ERA	WHIP	OBA	vL	vR	BF/G	H%	S%	xERA	G	L	F	Ctl	Dom	Cmd	hr/f	hr/9	RAR	BPV	R$
RH Starter	02		0	0	0	0	0	0.00	0.00																		
Age 24	03		0	0	0	0	0	0.00	0.00																		
Growth	04		0	0	0	0	0	0.00	0.00																		
Type: Power	05	aa	3	3	0	43	39	4.19	1.49	275			23.7	33%	75%	4.73				3.8	8.2	**2.2**		1.0	0.6	63	$3
Reliability 0	06	ANA	* 17	3	0	200	184	2.43	1.02	222	250	174	25.4	27%	82%	3.48	30	18	52	1.9	8.3	**4.4**	8%	1.0	52.5	123	$36
DL	1st Half		10	1	0	103	101	1.92	0.93	222			24.8	28%	85%	3.37	23	19	59	1.1	8.8	**7.8**	6%	0.8	33.5	203	$22
ERA Potl 40%	2nd Half		7	2	0	97	83	2.97	1.10	222			26.0	25%	80%	3.77	32	18	51	2.7	7.7	**2.9**	10%	1.2	19.0	81	$15
LIMA Plan D+	07	Proj	**13**	**9**	**0**	**189**	**166**	**3.92**	**1.32**	**255**			**25.0**	**30%**	**76%**	**4.08**	**31**	**18**	**52**	**3.2**	**7.9**	**2.5**	**10%**	**1.3**	**9.4**	**63**	**$19**

11-2, 2.56 ERA in 123 IP at ANA. The good part you know: elite skills which translated well to majors. Bad part you didn't: 130 IP spike over 2005 means injury risk. High S% and low H% means his ERA is heading up.

Webb,Brandon

Profile	Yr	Tm	W	L	Sv	IP	K	ERA	WHIP	OBA	vL	vR	BF/G	H%	S%	xERA	G	L	F	Ctl	Dom	Cmd	hr/f	hr/9	RAR	BPV	R$
RH Starter	02	a/a	10	7	0	159	106	3.57	1.38	264			25.3	31%	73%	3.54				3.3	6.0	**1.8**		0.2	13.8	70	$13
Age 28	03	ARI	* 11	10	0	198	187	3.23	1.20	223	257	167	25.5	28%	74%	2.62	61	20	19	3.5	8.5	**2.4**	12%	0.5	25.7	96	$22
Pre-Peak	04	ARI	7	16	0	208	164	3.59	1.50	249	268	223	26.3	30%	78%	3.33	64	17	19	5.1	7.1	**1.4**	15%	0.7	17.2	55	$10
Type	05	ARI	14	12	0	229	172	3.54	1.26	262	298	228	29.0	31%	74%	2.59	65	19	16	2.3	6.8	**2.9**	18%	0.8	20.0	80	$21
Reliability 78	06	ARI	16	8	0	235	178	3.10	1.13	246	261	231	28.9	29%	74%	2.42	66	17	16	1.9	6.8	**3.6**	13%	0.6	40.2	104	$29
DL	1st Half		8	3	0	123	90	2.85	1.18	266			29.7	31%	77%	2.45	66	17	17	1.4	6.6	**4.7**	12%	0.6	24.8	123	$15
ERA Potl 55%	2nd Half		8	5	0	112	88	3.38	1.08	222			28.0	27%	69%	2.38	67	18	15	2.5	7.1	**2.8**	14%	0.6	15.3	96	$15
LIMA Plan C+	07	Proj	**15**	**10**	**0**	**223**	**173**	**2.95**	**1.18**	**248**			**27.7**	**30%**	**76%**	**2.52**	**65**	**18**	**17**	**2.3**	**7.0**	**3.0**	**12%**	**0.5**	**50.7**	**95**	**$26**

A stellar season, with Ctl and CMD improving despite flat DOM, and still rising GB%. If his balky elbow can take the climbing IP, we could see: UP: 20 Wins, 2.50 ERA

Wellemeyer,Todd

Profile	Yr	Tm	W	L	Sv	IP	K	ERA	WHIP	OBA	vL	vR	BF/G	H%	S%	xERA	G	L	F	Ctl	Dom	Cmd	hr/f	hr/9	RAR	BPV	R$
RH Reliever	02	aa	3	3	0	46	31	6.26	1.30	236			24.3	28%	48%	3.13				3.9	6.1	**1.6**		0.4	-11.3	65	$2
Age 28	03	CHC	* 7	7	1	114	105	6.69	1.71	286	219	257	16.5	35%	61%	5.48				5.2	8.3	**1.6**		1.1	-34.0	48	($1)
Pre-Peak	04	CHC	* 3	2	0	46	50	5.48	1.85	286	302	275	6.6	38%	70%	4.77	25	30	45	6.5	9.8	**1.5**	7%	0.8	-6.9	65	$0
Type: Power	05	CHC	* 5	3	1	85	72	4.55	1.56	264	234	284	11.2	31%	73%	4.21	47	15	38	5.0	7.6	**1.5**	9%	1.0	-3.2	52	$4
Reliability 21	06	2TM	1	4	1	78	54	4.15	1.51	236	208	265	7.5	27%	73%	4.64	49	14	37	5.8	6.2	**1.1**	7%	0.7	3.6	47	$3
DL	1st Half		0	2	0	27	23	4.65	1.40	224			5.3	28%	65%	4.12	47	15	37	5.3	7.6	**1.4**	4%	0.3	-0.4	76	$1
ERA Potl 45%	2nd Half		1	2	1	51	31	3.88	1.57	242			9.5	27%	77%	4.92	50	14	37	6.0	5.5	**0.9**	9%	0.9	4.0	32	$2
LIMA Plan C+	07	Proj	**2**	**3**	**3**	**58**	**47**	**4.66**	**1.57**	**252**			**8.4**	**30%**	**72%**	**4.44**	**46**	**16**	**38**	**5.6**	**7.3**	**1.3**	**9%**	**0.9**	**-0.2**	**48**	**$3**

Ctl still awful - it begins and ends right there. Lucked into a decent ERA and some save chances with KC, but eleven different pitchers had save opps on that team, so that's nothing to be crowing about.

Wells,David

Profile	Yr	Tm	W	L	Sv	IP	K	ERA	WHIP	OBA	vL	vR	BF/G	H%	S%	xERA	G	L	F	Ctl	Dom	Cmd	hr/f	hr/9	RAR	BPV	R$
LH Starter	02	NYY	19	7	0	206	137	3.76	1.24	266	213	274	27.6	30%	72%	3.85	43	15	41	2.0	6.0	**3.0**	8%	0.9	17.8	74	$23
Age 44	03	NYY	15	7	0	213	101	4.14	1.23	287	274	290	28.5	30%	69%	3.92	45	16	38	0.8	4.3	**5.1**	8%	1.0	10.1	99	$18
Decline	04	SD	12	8	0	195	101	3.73	1.14	269	275	263	25.6	29%	71%	3.59	49	17	35	0.9	4.7	**5.1**	10%	1.1	12.7	103	$18
Type: Finesse	05	BOS	15	7	0	184	107	4.45	1.31	298	343	282	25.9	33%	68%	3.50	48	22	30	1.0	5.2	**5.1**	11%	1.0	-1.8	103	$15
Reliability 10	06	2TM	3	5	0	75	38	4.43	1.45	314	303	317	25.3	33%	73%	3.94	49	18	33	1.4	4.6	**3.2**	12%	1.3	0.8	46	$3
DL 122 22	1st Half		0	1	0	8	1	8.89	1.98	396			19.8	33%	67%	5.04	51	14	35	1.1	1.1	**1.0**	31%	4.4	-4.4	-130	($1)
ERA Potl 45%	2nd Half		3	4	0	67	37	3.90	1.39	303			26.2	33%	74%	3.82	48	18	33	1.5	5.0	**3.4**	9%	0.9	5.2	67	$4
LIMA Plan C+	07	Proj	**5**	**3**	**0**	**70**	**33**	**4.37**	**1.34**	**288**			**27.1**	**30%**	**70%**	**4.00**	**49**	**18**	**34**	**1.8**	**4.2**	**2.4**	**10%**	**1.0**	**3.6**	**41**	**$5**

Showed flashes of old CMD, but age and injuries (and gout? what player gets gout?) are clear signs the end is near. If he does come back, pick him off the scrap heap for his one good month.

ROD TRUESDELL

Wells,Kip		Yr	Tm	W	L	Sv	IP	K	ERA	WHIP	OBA	vL	vR	BF/G	H%	S%	xERA	G	L	F	Ctl	Dom	Cmd	hr/f	hr/9	RAR	BPV	R$
RH	Starter	02	PIT	12	14	0	198	134	3.59	1.35	261	274	249	25.6	29%	77%	3.60	55	16	29	3.2	6.1	1.9	12%	1.0	12.6	50	$15
Age	30	03	PIT	10	9	0	197	147	3.29	1.25	235	252	219	26.5	26%	78%	3.52	52	18	31	3.5	6.7	1.9	14%	1.1	24.0	56	$18
Peak		04	PIT	5	7	0	138	116	4.56	1.53	271	300	244	25.6	32%	72%	3.88	46	22	32	4.3	7.8	1.8	11%	0.9	-5.1	56	$5
Type		05	PIT	8	18	0	182	132	5.09	1.57	266	288	249	24.7	30%	69%	4.32	47	20	33	4.9	6.5	1.3	12%	1.1	-19.0	35	$3
Reliability	14	06	2TM	2	5	0	44	20	6.53	1.86	329	353	323	23.4	36%	63%	4.92	51	20	29	4.3	4.1	1.0	6%	0.6	-10.9	15	($2)
DL	129	1st Half		0	2	0	8	2	12.22	2.59	380			22.3	40%	48%	6.69	56	24	21	7.8	2.2	0.3	0%	0.0	-7.7	-2	($2)
ERA Potl	60%	2nd Half		2	3	0	36	18	5.25	1.69	316			23.7	35%	69%	4.57	50	19	31	3.5	4.5	1.3	7%	0.7	-3.2	23	$0
LIMA Plan	D	07	Proj	7	10	0	145	99	4.59	1.50	272			24.6	31%	71%	3.97	50	21	29	4.0	6.1	1.5	11%	0.9	8.1	42	$6

Three-year injury roll call:
- carpal tunnel syndrome
- cracked fingernail
- blocked artery & blood clot
- sore shoulder
- ankle ligament surgery
- dislocated fanalytic value

Westbrook,Jake		Yr	Tm	W	L	Sv	IP	K	ERA	WHIP	OBA	vL	vR	BF/G	H%	S%	xERA	G	L	F	Ctl	Dom	Cmd	hr/f	hr/9	RAR	BPV	R$
RH	Starter	02	CLE *	2	4	0	62	29	6.39	1.44	303	292	300	18.0	32%	55%	3.95	53	16	31	1.9	4.2	2.2	10%	1.0	-14.7	36	($0)
Age	29	03	CLE	7	10	0	133	58	4.33	1.49	275	276	287	17.2	30%	71%	3.92	63	15	22	3.8	3.9	1.0	9%	0.6	3.2	27	$6
Peak		04	CLE	14	9	0	215	116	3.39	1.25	255	255	247	27.2	28%	75%	3.33	63	14	23	2.6	4.9	1.9	12%	0.8	27.7	49	$20
Type	Finesse	05	CLE	15	15	0	210	119	4.50	1.30	269	275	255	26.1	30%	66%	3.11	62	19	19	2.4	5.1	2.1	15%	0.8	-3.2	52	$15
Reliability	89	06	CLE	15	10	0	211	109	4.18	1.43	293	290	300	28.7	32%	71%	3.48	61	17	22	2.3	4.6	2.0	9%	0.6	9.9	47	$15
DL		1st Half		6	4	0	103	55	4.37	1.27	266			27.0	29%	66%	3.31	63	13	23	2.3	4.8	2.1	10%	0.7	2.4	54	$8
ERA Potl	50%	2nd Half		9	6	0	108	54	4.00	1.58	318			30.4	35%	75%	3.65	59	21	21	2.4	4.5	1.9	9%	0.6	7.5	40	$7
LIMA Plan	D+	07	Proj	14	11	0	203	106	4.03	1.34	275			26.2	30%	71%	3.38	61	17	21	2.4	4.7	1.9	11%	0.7	27.7	47	$16

Another extreme GB pitcher whose fate often rests in the fickle hands of luck. CLE's shaky infield defense isn't helping. Same skills, more swings in 2007, but xERA shows the upside that's his for the taking.

Wheeler,Dan		Yr	Tm	W	L	Sv	IP	K	ERA	WHIP	OBA	vL	vR	BF/G	H%	S%	xERA	G	L	F	Ctl	Dom	Cmd	hr/f	hr/9	RAR	BPV	R$
RH	Reliever	02	aaa	9	6	0	155	92	5.69	1.48	301			25.2	32%	64%	5.48				2.4	5.3	2.2		1.5	-27.1	30	$3
Age	29	03	NYM *	5	5	6	96	72	4.31	1.45	279	208	279	7.4	32%	72%	4.09	41	18	40	3.2	6.8	2.1	8%	0.9	-0.4	56	$7
Pre-Peak		04	2NL	3	1	0	65	55	4.29	1.48	293	380	226	6.2	34%	76%	3.84	38	22	40	2.8	7.6	2.8	12%	1.4	-0.2	58	$3
Type	Power	05	HOU	2	3	3	73	69	2.22	0.98	205	206	204	4.0	25%	83%	3.21	38	18	44	2.3	8.5	3.6	8%	0.9	18.3	115	$12
Reliability	33	06	HOU	3	5	9	71	68	2.53	1.15	224	273	183	3.9	29%	81%	3.50	37	20	44	3.0	8.6	2.8	6%	0.6	17.2	102	$13
DL		1st Half		1	5	1	33	30	4.07	1.30	255			4.0	32%	68%	3.54	42	19	38	3.0	8.1	2.7	5%	0.5	1.7	94	$3
ERA Potl	45%	2nd Half		2	0	8	38	38	1.19	1.03	196			3.7	25%	94%	3.45	31	20	49	3.1	9.0	2.9	6%	0.7	15.4	110	$10
LIMA Plan	B	07	Proj	3	3	5	73	68	3.10	1.23	244			4.6	30%	79%	3.54	37	20	43	2.9	8.4	3.0	9%	1.0	7.3	89	$9

Not quite as dominant in Sept. closer's audition, but thanks to low H% (18% for a 1.84 Sept. ERA), he's still in the discussion. Entering 2007, he's slated to set up again - watch the spring box scores.

White,Rick		Yr	Tm	W	L	Sv	IP	K	ERA	WHIP	OBA	vL	vR	BF/G	H%	S%	xERA	G	L	F	Ctl	Dom	Cmd	hr/f	hr/9	RAR	BPV	R$
RH	Reliever	02	2NL *	5	8	0	67	46	4.57	1.40	270	295	245	4.4	32%	67%	3.93	48	18	34	3.2	6.2	1.9	6%	0.5	-3.8	62	$4
Age	38	03	2TM	1	2	1	67	54	5.78	1.42	281	223	322	5.9	31%	63%	3.61	45	21	35	2.8	7.3	2.6	18%	1.7	-11.4	44	$1
Decline		04	2TM *	5	5	3	89	55	4.64	1.37	268	243	335	5.9	28%	71%	3.86	50	18	32	3.0	5.5	1.8	16%	1.5	-3.2	28	$6
Type		05	PIT	4	7	2	75	40	3.72	1.59	299	314	305	4.8	34%	76%	3.97	55	23	22	3.5	4.8	1.4	5%	0.4	4.9	42	$3
Reliability	16	06	2NL	4	1	1	64	40	5.19	1.43	285	295	292	4.4	31%	65%	3.35	61	17	22	2.8	5.6	2.0	17%	1.1	-5.5	40	$3
DL		1st Half		1	0	1	29	17	5.88	1.37	299			4.6	32%	60%	3.23	60	15	25	1.5	5.3	3.4	20%	1.5	-5.0	52	$1
ERA Potl	50%	2nd Half		3	1	0	35	23	4.62	1.48	272			4.2	31%	69%	3.44	61	18	20	3.8	5.9	1.5	13%	0.8	-0.6	45	$2
LIMA Plan	C+	07	Proj	3	2	0	44	27	4.34	1.43	277			4.6	31%	71%	3.59	57	19	25	3.1	5.6	1.8	11%	0.8	4.1	46	$3

Crazy hr/f swings have driven his ERA fluctuations. It's easy to just write him off now at 38, but look at the GB% trend, and the xERAs. He's unlikely to be fanalytically relevant, but he can still pitch.

Wickman,Bob		Yr	Tm	W	L	Sv	IP	K	ERA	WHIP	OBA	vL	vR	BF/G	H%	S%	xERA	G	L	F	Ctl	Dom	Cmd	hr/f	hr/9	RAR	BPV	R$
RH	Reliever	02	CLE	1	3	20	34	36	4.50	1.53	305	275	294	4.2	39%	71%	5.09				2.6	9.5	3.6		0.8	-0.2	103	$8
Age	38	03	aa	0	0	0	1	2	37.50	5.00	596			4.8	78%	17%	20.77				7.5	15.0	2.0		0.0	-4.9	68	($1)
Decline		04	CLE *	0	2	13	33	29	5.95	1.59	283	354	192	4.3	34%	63%	3.53	57	15	27	4.3	7.8	1.8	14%	1.1	-6.2	51	$4
Type		05	CLE	0	4	45	62	41	2.47	1.26	246	243	250	4.0	26%	88%	3.60	50	20	30	3.0	6.0	2.0	16%	1.3	14.6	43	$20
Reliability	28	06	2TM	1	6	33	54	42	2.67	1.22	258	267	236	3.9	32%	78%	3.49	42	24	34	2.2	7.0	3.2	4%	0.3	12.3	103	$17
DL		1st Half		1	3	11	23	15	3.12	1.34	261			4.1	31%	74%	4.25	36	27	37	3.1	5.8	1.9	0%	0.0	4.0	77	$6
ERA Potl	50%	2nd Half		0	3	22	31	27	2.33	1.13	256			3.8	32%	82%	2.97	46	22	32	1.5	7.9	5.4	7%	0.6	8.3	147	$11
LIMA Plan	C	07	Proj	3	4	30	73	55	3.48	1.31	263			4.0	31%	76%	3.54	47	22	32	2.7	6.8	2.5	10%	0.9	7.9	70	$16

Just when we thought it was about over, he turns in this gem. Scintillating after trade to ATL (25/2 K/BB in 26 IP). Age, S%, hr/f say ERA will go up some more, but he always seems to get those saves.

Williamson,Scott		Yr	Tm	W	L	Sv	IP	K	ERA	WHIP	OBA	vL	vR	BF/G	H%	S%	xERA	G	L	F	Ctl	Dom	Cmd	hr/f	hr/9	RAR	BPV	R$
RH	Reliever	02	CIN	3	4	8	74	84	2.92	1.11	181	198	170	4.7	25%	75%	3.27	33	27	40	4.4	10.2	2.3	7%	0.6	10.8	111	$12
Age	31	03	2TM	5	4	21	62	74	4.21	1.42	236	200	245	4.1	32%	73%	3.41	38	25	37	4.9	10.7	2.2	12%	1.0	1.4	87	$13
Peak		04	BOS	0	1	1	28	28	1.28	1.03	122	120	109	4.0	18%	86%	3.80	43	11	46	5.7	8.9	1.6	0%	0.0	11.0	117	$5
Type	Power	05	CHC	0	0	0	14	23	5.74	1.49	274	333	250	3.7	42%	67%	2.25	42	26	32	3.8	14.7	3.8	29%	1.9	-2.6	111	$0
Reliability	0	06	2NL	2	4	0	39	42	5.75	1.61	271	200	307	4.2	35%	64%	3.52	50	19	31	5.1	9.7	1.9	12%	0.9	-6.1	71	$1
DL	50 180	1st Half		2	2	0	21	27	4.27	1.47	222			4.0	34%	68%	3.30	44	25	31	6.0	11.5	1.9	0%	0.0	0.6	120	$2
ERA Potl	75%	2nd Half		0	2	0	18	15	7.50	1.78	321			4.5	36%	61%	3.80	55	14	31	4.0	7.5	1.9	22%	2.0	-6.7	15	($1)
LIMA Plan	A	07	Proj	2	3	0	34	37	4.03	1.34	235			4.1	31%	71%	3.20	47	19	33	4.3	9.9	2.3	10%	0.8	4.8	92	$3

More arm trouble, and he now hasn't managed even 40 IP in three seasons. When he's out there, he still has great stuff, as DOM and xERA show. It's the "out there" part that's the problem.

Williams,Dave		Yr	Tm	W	L	Sv	IP	K	ERA	WHIP	OBA	vL	vR	BF/G	H%	S%	xERA	G	L	F	Ctl	Dom	Cmd	hr/f	hr/9	RAR	BPV	R$
LH	Starter	02	PIT	2	5	0	43	33	5.02	1.44	239	86	271	20.8	25%	72%	4.83				5.0	6.9	1.4		1.9	-4.9	21	$1
Age	28	03	aaa	7	4	0	77	48	5.49	1.58	300			21.7	33%	66%	5.28				3.4	5.6	1.7		0.9	-10.4	35	$2
Pre-Peak		04	PIT *	8	5	0	154	119	4.14	1.30	265	282	192	21.0	31%	69%	3.34	54	14	32	2.5	6.9	2.8	9%	0.8	2.3	77	$11
Type	Finesse	05	PIT	10	11	0	138	88	4.43	1.41	260	281	256	23.9	28%	73%	4.48	39	19	42	3.8	5.7	1.5	11%	1.3	-3.1	30	$8
Reliability	20	06	2NL *	9	9	0	145	62	6.46	1.64	317	283	335	22.8	32%	64%	5.11	33	25	41	3.0	3.8	1.3	12%	1.7	-35.2	-9	($2)
DL		1st Half		3	5	0	56	19	7.99	1.86	339			24.4	33%	59%	5.86	32	25	43	3.7	3.0	0.8	12%	1.8	-24.3	-31	($5)
ERA Potl	50%	2nd Half		6	4	0	89	43	5.48	1.50	303			21.8	31%	67%	4.58	35	26	38	2.5	4.4	1.8	13%	1.6	-10.9	9	$2
LIMA Plan	C	07	Proj	6	6	0	94	51	5.10	1.53	292			23.1	31%	70%	4.71	37	22	41	3.3	4.9	1.5	11%	1.4	-4.0	14	$2

7-7, 6.77 ERA in 109 IP at CIN and NYM. A bad year, but some bad luck at play... 64% strand rate, 25% line drive rate should both regress, leaving us with a marginally draftable, mostly forgettable pitcher.

Williams,Todd		Yr	Tm	W	L	Sv	IP	K	ERA	WHIP	OBA	vL	vR	BF/G	H%	S%	xERA	G	L	F	Ctl	Dom	Cmd	hr/f	hr/9	RAR	BPV	R$
RH	Reliever	02	aaa	3	5	24	48	17	5.06	1.75	344			4.9	36%	72%	6.41				2.4	3.2	1.3		0.9	-4.7	5	$7
Age	36	03	aaa	3	2	4	69	29	2.08	1.21	258			5.1	28%	83%	3.13				2.1	3.8	1.8		0.3	19.7	56	$9
Decline		04	BAL *	5	3	11	81	31	3.88	1.48	302	256	217	5.1	32%	74%	3.44	69	12	18	2.3	3.4	1.5	9%	0.6	5.5	30	$8
Type	Finesse	05	BAL	5	5	1	76	38	3.31	1.29	251	263	244	4.4	28%	75%	3.28	66	16	18	3.1	4.5	1.5	11%	0.6	10.0	45	$7
Reliability	11	06	BAL	2	4	1	57	24	4.74	1.67	321	342	314	4.2	33%	75%	4.16	58	18	25	3.0	3.8	1.3	15%	1.3	-1.3	2	$1
DL	36	1st Half		2	3	1	31	14	4.06	1.68	325			5.1	35%	78%	4.04	57	19	23	2.9	4.1	1.4	11%	0.9	1.9	18	$1
ERA Potl	40%	2nd Half		0	1	0	26	10	5.54	1.65	317			3.5	31%	71%	4.29	58	15	27	3.1	3.5	1.1	19%	1.7	-3.1	-16	($1)
LIMA Plan	C	07	Proj	3	4	0	65	29	4.00	1.50	295			4.3	31%	75%	3.82	61	16	23	2.9	4.0	1.4	11%	0.8	5.3	24	$3

Calf injury led to shoulder soreness, which probably led to GB% dip, which finally led to this ERA spike. DOM also dipped back to more typical levels (not a good thing). Needs to get that sinker working again.

Williams,Woody		Yr	Tm	W	L	Sv	IP	K	ERA	WHIP	OBA	vL	vR	BF/G	H%	S%	xERA	G	L	F	Ctl	Dom	Cmd	hr/f	hr/9	RAR	BPV	R$
RH	Starter	02	STL	10	4	0	108	82	2.50	1.03	218	182	256	23.7	25%	80%	3.46	41	20	40	2.2	6.8	3.2	8%	0.8	21.4	94	$17
Age	40	03	STL	18	9	0	220	153	3.89	1.25	262	268	246	27.0	30%	71%	3.97	39	18	43	2.3	6.3	2.8	7%	0.8	10.6	74	$21
Decline		04	STL	11	8	0	189	131	4.19	1.33	266	223	296	25.9	30%	71%	4.11	38	20	42	2.8	6.2	2.3	8%	1.0	1.8	58	$13
Type	Finesse	05	SD	9	12	0	159	106	4.86	1.41	279	259	288	24.6	30%	69%	4.29	35	22	42	2.9	6.0	2.1	11%	1.4	-12.1	38	$7
Reliability	42	06	SD	12	5	0	145	72	3.66	1.29	271	245	287	24.4	28%	77%	4.42	36	21	43	2.2	4.5	2.1	10%	1.3	14.8	32	$14
DL	49 34	1st Half		3	1	0	41	26	3.28	1.19	242			21.1	26%	77%	4.19	34	20	45	2.6	5.7	2.2	9%	1.1	6.1	53	$5
ERA Potl	40%	2nd Half		9	4	0	104	46	3.81	1.33	282			26.0	29%	77%	4.52	36	21	42	2.0	4.0	2.0	10%	1.4	8.7	23	$9
LIMA Plan	D+	07	Proj	9	6	0	131	79	4.28	1.34	274			24.2	30%	72%	4.29	36	21	43	2.5	5.4	2.2	10%	1.2	1.3	42	$9

Nice stats rebound, but lots of bad skills indicators. BPV declined again, with a sharp acceleration of DOM slide. Another muscle strain meant fewer IP. In 2007, the ERA goes up, and innings drop even more.

ROD TRUESDELL

Willis,Dontrelle

Willis,Dontrelle	Yr	Tm	W	L	Sv	IP	K	ERA	WHIP	OBA	vL	vR	BF/G	H%	S%	xERA	G	L	F	Ctl	Dom	Cmd	hr/f	hr/9	RAR	BPV	R$
LH Starter	02		0	0	0	0	0	0.00	0.00											0.0	0.0						
Age 25	03	FLA	* 18	6	0	196	171	3.03	1.23	240	216	250	24.7	30%	78%	3.59	40	21	39	3.1	7.9	**2.6**	7%	0.7	30.2	87	$25
Growth	04	FLA	10	11	0	197	139	4.02	1.38	274	203	287	26.4	31%	73%	3.87	45	19	36	2.8	6.4	**2.3**	9%	0.9	5.9	59	$12
Type	05	FLA	22	10	0	236	170	2.63	1.14	242	222	247	28.2	29%	77%	3.39	45	24	32	2.1	6.5	**3.1**	5%	0.4	47.0	98	$33
Reliability 66	06	FLA	12	12	0	223	160	3.87	1.42	271	231	281	28.5	31%	75%	3.87	48	20	33	3.3	6.5	**1.9**	9%	0.8	16.9	55	$15
DL	1st Half		4	7	0	109	60	4.05	1.39	279			29.4	31%	73%	3.92	49	22	29	2.7	5.0	**1.8**	9%	0.8	5.9	42	$6
ERA Potl 50%	2nd Half		8	5	0	114	100	3.71	1.45	263			27.7	32%	77%	3.82	46	17	37	3.9	7.9	**2.0**	9%	0.9	11.0	66	$10
LIMA Plan D+	07	Proj	**13**	**12**	**0**	**218**	**152**	**3.97**	**1.37**	**266**			**28.3**	**30%**	**73%**	**3.89**	**46**	**20**	**34**	**3.2**	**6.3**	**2.0**	**9%**	**0.9**	**12.8**	**55**	**$15**

Red flags abound. Another 220+ IP season, with BF/G at an all time high. Now witness CMD splits: 1st half DOM way down, then he tried to dial it up in 2H, but Ctl nosedived. Burnout?... DN: 4.25+ ERA, DL time

Wilson,C.J.

Wilson,C.J.	Yr	Tm	W	L	Sv	IP	K	ERA	WHIP	OBA	vL	vR	BF/G	H%	S%	xERA	G	L	F	Ctl	Dom	Cmd	hr/f	hr/9	RAR	BPV	R$
LH Reliever	02	aa	1	0	0	30	15	2.40	1.33	249			25.5	29%	80%	3.02				3.6	4.5	**1.3**		0.0	6.9	59	$3
Age 26	03	aa	6	9	0	123	78	6.73	1.63	318			25.5	35%	59%	5.85				2.9	5.7	**2.0**		1.1	-35.5	35	($2)
Growth	04	TEX	0	0	0	0	0	0.00	0.00											0.0	0.0						
Type Power	05	TEX	* 1	11	1	92	65	6.49	1.72	327	290	339	11.9	36%	64%	3.38	60	20	20	3.2	6.4	**2.0**	23%	1.4	-24.1	27	($3)
Reliability 0	06	TEX	2	4	1	44	43	4.08	1.29	239	155	292	4.2	28%	74%	3.12	49	21	30	3.7	8.8	**2.4**	20%	1.4	2.6	67	$5
DL 21	1st Half		1	2	0	19	19	5.18	1.41	218			5.2	22%	73%	3.75	48	13	38	5.7	9.0	**1.6**	26%	2.4	-1.5	28	$1
ERA Potl 55%	2nd Half		1	2	1	25	24	3.24	1.20	254			3.7	32%	75%	2.66	50	27	23	2.2	8.6	**4.0**	12%	0.7	4.1	118	$4
LIMA Plan B+	07	Proj	**2**	**4**	**0**	**44**	**37**	**3.93**	**1.36**	**268**			**6.6**	**32%**	**73%**	**3.19**	**52**	**21**	**27**	**2.9**	**7.7**	**2.6**	**11%**	**0.8**	**6.9**	**78**	**$4**

Another solid growth season. Impressive DOM spike while maintaining Ctl, with terrific CMD overall in 2nd half. If his hr/f luck holds to 2nd half levels, he's got something. Worth a late flyer as a LIMA sleeper.

Windsor,Jason

Windsor,Jason	Yr	Tm	W	L	Sv	IP	K	ERA	WHIP	OBA	vL	vR	BF/G	H%	S%	xERA	G	L	F	Ctl	Dom	Cmd	hr/f	hr/9	RAR	BPV	R$
RH Starter	02		0	0	0	0	0	0.00	0.00																		
Age 24	03		0	0	0	0	0	0.00	0.00																		
Growth	04		0	0	0	0	0	0.00	0.00																		
Type	05	aa	3	6	0	56	32	6.27	1.76	325			23.9	36%	64%	6.01				3.6	5.1	**1.4**		0.8	-13.7	26	($2)
Reliability 0	06	OAK	* 17	3	0	164	137	4.39	1.48	298	381	371	24.1	36%	70%	3.76	40	23	37	2.5	7.5	**3.0**	6%	0.6	3.4	84	$16
DL	1st Half		11	1	0	90	83	3.91	1.41	285			24.4	36%	72%					2.6	8.3	**3.2**		0.5	7.2	101	$11
ERA Potl 55%	2nd Half		6	2	0	74	54	4.96	1.56	313			23.7	36%	68%	4.06	40	23	37	2.5	6.5	**2.6**	7%	0.7	-3.7	64	$4
LIMA Plan B	07	Proj	**5**	**3**	**0**	**58**	**41**	**4.50**	**1.43**	**281**			**22.9**	**32%**	**70%**	**4.03**	**40**	**23**	**37**	**2.9**	**6.4**	**2.2**	**9%**	**0.9**	**3.2**	**54**	**$4**

0-1, 6.59 ERA in 14 IP at OAK. Didn't carry it to ML debut, but nice skills growth across the board. Continues to be hurt by soaring H%; if that manages to regress to the mean... UP: sub-4.00 ERA, more innings

Wise,Matt

Wise,Matt	Yr	Tm	W	L	Sv	IP	K	ERA	WHIP	OBA	vL	vR	BF/G	H%	S%	xERA	G	L	F	Ctl	Dom	Cmd	hr/f	hr/9	RAR	BPV	R$
RH Reliever	02	aaa	3	4	0	78	63	6.12	1.64	341			22.2	39%	65%	6.58				1.6	7.3	**4.5**		1.5	-17.7	80	($1)
Age 31	03		0	0	0	0	0	0.00	0.00											0.0	0.0						
Peak	04	MIL	* 2	3	0	72	46	3.86	1.18	242	244	259	8.0	27%	69%	3.74	47	16	36	2.5	5.7	**2.3**	9%	0.9	3.5	63	$5
Type	05	MIL	4	4	1	64	62	3.37	0.97	170	130	187	5.1	21%	68%	3.37	41	12	47	3.5	8.7	**2.5**	8%	0.8	6.9	100	$10
Reliability 8	06	MIL	5	6	0	44	27	3.88	1.34	266	206	310	4.7	29%	75%	4.05	45	18	37	2.9	5.5	**1.9**	11%	1.2	3.3	39	$5
DL 48 23	1st Half		4	4	0	26	16	4.50	1.35	262			4.8	27%	73%	4.00	48	15	37	3.1	5.5	**1.8**	16%	1.7	-0.0	21	$3
ERA Potl 40%	2nd Half		1	2	0	18	11	2.98	1.33	271			4.5	31%	78%	4.10	41	22	37	2.5	5.5	**2.2**	5%	0.5	3.4	65	$2
LIMA Plan B	07	Proj	**4**	**5**	**3**	**58**	**42**	**4.03**	**1.34**	**268**			**5.8**	**30%**	**73%**	**3.91**	**43**	**17**	**39**	**2.8**	**6.5**	**2.3**	**10%**	**1.1**	**3.2**	**57**	**$5**

Again battled injuries, with ulnar nerve surgery the season-ender this time. DOM regression suggests the elbow may have bothered him all year. 2005 was probably his peak, but skills should bounce back part-way.

Wolf,Randy

Wolf,Randy	Yr	Tm	W	L	Sv	IP	K	ERA	WHIP	OBA	vL	vR	BF/G	H%	S%	xERA	G	L	F	Ctl	Dom	Cmd	hr/f	hr/9	RAR	BPV	R$
LH Starter	02	PHI	11	9	0	210	172	3.21	1.12	225	258	216	27.4	26%	75%	3.57	39	20	41	2.7	7.4	**2.7**	10%	1.0	23.1	82	$23
Age 30	03	PHI	16	10	0	200	177	4.23	1.27	238	232	234	25.4	28%	70%	3.67	40	20	40	3.5	8.0	**2.3**	12%	1.2	1.2	66	$19
Peak	04	PHI	5	8	0	136	89	4.30	1.33	274	254	276	25.2	30%	72%	4.17	35	21	43	2.4	5.9	**2.5**	10%	1.3	-0.6	48	$7
Type Power	05	PHI	6	4	0	80	61	4.39	1.41	278	238	293	26.7	31%	75%	4.07	35	23	42	2.9	6.9	**2.3**	13%	1.6	-1.4	43	$5
Reliability 6	06	PHI	4	0	0	56	44	5.60	1.71	284	86	323	21.7	30%	73%	4.81	37	19	44	5.3	7.0	**1.3**	17%	2.1	-7.7	6	$1
DL 110	1st Half		0	0	0	0	0	0.00	0.00																		
ERA Potl 45%	2nd Half		4	0	0	56	44	5.61	1.71	284			21.7	30%	73%	4.81	37	19	44	5.3	7.0	**1.3**	17%	2.1	-7.8	6	$1
LIMA Plan C+	07	Proj	**11**	**6**	**0**	**170**	**130**	**4.61**	**1.43**	**269**			**24.6**	**30%**	**72%**	**4.21**	**37**	**21**	**43**	**3.5**	**6.9**	**1.9**	**12%**	**1.4**	**3.2**	**42**	**$10**

Predictably, showed rust upon return from TJ surgery, but seemed healthy for the first time since '03. Still owns those skills, but won't regain that form overnight. Keep him in mind as a potential 2H target.

Woods,Jake

Woods,Jake	Yr	Tm	W	L	Sv	IP	K	ERA	WHIP	OBA	vL	vR	BF/G	H%	S%	xERA	G	L	F	Ctl	Dom	Cmd	hr/f	hr/9	RAR	BPV	R$
LH Reliever	02		0	0	0	0	0	0.00	0.00											0.0	0.0						
Age 25	03		0	0	0	0	0	0.00	0.00											0.0	0.0						
Growth	04	a/a	15	6	0	173	102	4.42	1.50	294			26.4	33%	72%	4.91				3.0	5.3	**1.8**		0.8	-1.7	41	$10
Type	05	ANA	* 3	2	0	58	44	5.24	1.64	310	229	302	6.3	34%	74%	4.33	37	22	41	3.4	6.8	**2.0**	15%	1.8	-6.3	20	$1
Reliability 20	06	SEA	7	4	1	105	66	4.20	1.60	280	291	273	12.8	31%	76%	4.74	42	20	38	4.5	5.7	**1.2**	9%	1.0	4.6	28	$6
DL	1st Half		2	1	1	31	25	4.65	1.52	236			8.1	27%	72%	4.73	40	15	45	5.8	7.3	**1.3**	10%	1.2	-0.3	43	$2
ERA Potl 40%	2nd Half		5	3	0	74	41	4.01	1.64	297			16.9	32%	78%	4.75	43	22	36	4.0	5.0	**1.2**	9%	1.0	5.0	22	$4
LIMA Plan C	07	Proj	**4**	**9**	**0**	**131**	**89**	**4.62**	**1.56**	**283**			**9.6**	**31%**	**73%**	**4.50**	**41**	**20**	**40**	**4.0**	**6.1**	**1.5**	**10%**	**1.2**	**-0.2**	**32**	**$4**

Mediocre skills didn't improve in first full ML season, despite apparent step up. ERA gain was S% driven; xERA is where he is right now. Expect struggles until he can get CMD ratio to a consistent 2.0 or higher.

Wood,Kerry

Wood,Kerry	Yr	Tm	W	L	Sv	IP	K	ERA	WHIP	OBA	vL	vR	BF/G	H%	S%	xERA	G	L	F	Ctl	Dom	Cmd	hr/f	hr/9	RAR	BPV	R$
RH Starter	02	CHC	12	11	0	213	217	3.68	1.25	220	223	219	26.9	28%	73%	3.62	34	24	42	4.1	9.2	**2.2**	10%	0.9	11.3	85	$21
Age 29	03	CHC	14	11	0	211	266	3.20	1.19	203	198	206	27.1	28%	78%	2.89	39	26	35	4.3	11.3	**2.7**	14%	1.0	28.1	108	$28
Peak	04	CHC	8	9	0	140	144	3.73	1.27	243	262	227	26.7	31%	74%	3.16	46	19	35	3.3	9.3	**2.8**	12%	1.0	9.3	90	$14
Type Power	05	CHC	3	4	0	66	77	4.23	1.18	218	220	211	12.9	26%	73%	3.09	34	24	42	3.5	10.5	**3.0**	21%	1.9	0.1	79	$7
Reliability 0	06	CHC	1	2	0	19	13	4.22	1.41	260	206	293	20.8	25%	82%	4.54	39	10	51	3.8	6.1	**1.6**	16%	2.3	0.6	3	$1
DL 167 158	1st Half		1	2	0	19	13	4.22	1.41	260			20.8	25%	82%	4.54	39	10	51	3.8	6.1	**1.6**	16%	2.3	0.6	3	$1
ERA Potl 30%	2nd Half		0	0	0	0	0	0.00	0.00																		
LIMA Plan B+	07	Proj	**3**	**4**	**10**	**58**	**57**	**3.88**	**1.31**	**241**			**5.8**	**29%**	**75%**	**3.62**	**39**	**18**	**43**	**3.7**	**8.8**	**2.4**	**12%**	**1.2**	**5.3**	**72**	**$9**

Opted for rest and rehab for partially torn cuff; only time will tell if that was the right call. Plans to return as a reliever, but can he warm up quickly? Could be an ace closer, but for now - RISKY.

Wood,Mike

Wood,Mike	Yr	Tm	W	L	Sv	IP	K	ERA	WHIP	OBA	vL	vR	BF/G	H%	S%	xERA	G	L	F	Ctl	Dom	Cmd	hr/f	hr/9	RAR	BPV	R$
RH Reliever	02	aa	11	3	0	105	54	3.69	1.36	280			26.4	31%	74%	4.16				2.4	4.6	**1.9**		0.7	7.6	47	$10
Age 27	03	aaa	9	3	0	91	50	3.36	1.27	268			23.9	30%	74%	3.62				2.2	4.9	**2.3**		0.5	11.6	64	$10
Growth	04	KC	* 14	11	0	190	110	4.50	1.32	272	323	234	25.2	29%	69%	3.74	52	16	32	2.4	5.2	**2.2**	12%	1.1	-1.6	43	$13
Type Finesse	05	KC	5	8	2	115	60	4.46	1.57	285	295	279	11.0	30%	76%	4.38	53	17	31	4.1	4.7	**1.2**	15%	1.4	-1.3	8	$4
Reliability 14	06	KC	3	3	0	64	29	5.75	1.70	322	320	309	12.9	33%	69%	4.53	52	16	32	3.2	4.1	**1.3**	13%	1.4	-9.4	-1	($1)
DL 64	1st Half		3	2	0	57	24	4.89	1.65	318			13.0	33%	72%	4.35	55	17	28	3.0	3.8	**1.3**	12%	1.1	-2.3	8	$1
ERA Potl 50%	2nd Half		0	1	0	7	5	12.67	2.11	355			11.9	35%	42%	5.78	32	11	57	5.1	6.3	**1.3**	20%	3.8	-7.1	-66	($2)
LIMA Plan D	07	Proj	**5**	**5**	**0**	**87**	**44**	**4.34**	**1.47**	**290**			**15.9**	**31%**	**73%**	**4.05**	**54**	**17**	**30**	**2.9**	**4.6**	**1.6**	**11%**	**1.0**	**4.7**	**26**	**$4**

Back troubles did him in, but he wasn't helping KC anyway. To be fair, minor league BPIs were solid. But it's tough for finesse types to take that step up. He can have success if he regains that sub-2.5 Ctl.

Worrell,Tim

Worrell,Tim	Yr	Tm	W	L	Sv	IP	K	ERA	WHIP	OBA	vL	vR	BF/G	H%	S%	xERA	G	L	F	Ctl	Dom	Cmd	hr/f	hr/9	RAR	BPV	R$
RH Reliever	02	SF	8	2	0	72	55	2.25	1.18	213	204	218	3.7	26%	82%	4.27	34	16	50	3.8	6.9	**1.8**	3%	0.4	16.5	81	$11
Age 39	03	SF	4	4	38	78	65	2.88	1.31	252	241	250	4.3	31%	79%	3.51	49	18	33	3.2	7.5	**2.3**	7%	0.6	13.4	81	$20
Decline	04	PHI	5	6	19	78	64	3.69	1.23	254	310	211	4.2	29%	74%	3.45	44	18	37	2.4	7.4	**3.0**	12%	1.2	5.5	78	$14
Type	05	2NL	1	2	1	48	39	4.11	1.47	303	295	303	4.2	34%	78%	3.70	42	21	37	2.2	7.3	**3.3**	14%	1.5	0.8	62	$2
Reliability 0	06	SF	3	2	6	20	12	7.61	1.74	331	256	354	4.1	30%	69%	4.86	38	12	50	3.1	5.4	**1.7**	25%	4.0	-7.7	-64	$2
DL 110 58	1st Half		3	2	6	20	12	7.61	1.74	331			4.1	30%	69%	4.86	38	12	50	3.1	5.4	**1.7**	25%	4.0	-7.7	-64	$2
ERA Potl 40%	2nd Half		0	0	0	0	0	0.00	0.00																		
LIMA Plan C+	07	Proj	**4**	**3**	**0**	**44**	**33**	**4.76**	**1.45**	**285**			**4.1**	**31%**	**73%**	**4.03**	**41**	**16**	**42**	**2.9**	**6.8**	**2.4**	**14%**	**1.7**	**1.8**	**39**	**$3**

Herniated disk in his neck scuttled this season. Also had labrum scoped in August. He's expected to be ready by spring, but at 39, he's no sure thing. Be sure DOM is back before taking a flyer.

ROD TRUESDELL

Wright,Jamey

Wright,Jamey	Yr	Tm	W	L	Sv	IP	K	ERA	WHIP	OBA	vL	vR	BF/G	H%	S%	xERA	G	L	F	Ctl	Dom	Cmd	hr/f	hr/9	RAR	BPV	R$
RH Starter	02	2NL *	8	14	0	144	87	5.31	1.60	270	271	267	25.0	29%	68%	4.51	51	18	31	5.0	5.4	1.1	12%	1.1	-21.4	25	$1
Age 32	03	KC *	7	11	0	163	113	6.13	1.79	311	296	175	24.8	34%	68%	4.40	51	18	31	4.7	6.2	1.3	14%	1.4	-32.3	17	($3)
Peak	04	COL *	10	9	0	182	96	5.28	1.69	307	253	281	26.3	32%	72%	4.44	50	22	28	4.0	4.7	1.2	15%	1.3	-22.9	7	($0)
Type	05	COL	8	16	0	171	101	5.47	1.65	294	314	279	23.0	32%	68%	4.23	53	20	27	4.3	5.3	1.2	14%	1.2	-25.9	20	($1)
Reliability 65	06	SF	6	10	0	156	79	5.19	1.48	275	261	300	20.2	29%	66%	3.91	58	18	23	3.7	4.6	1.2	13%	0.9	-13.6	26	$3
DL	1st Half		5	7	0	98	47	4.86	1.39	262			28.2	28%	66%	3.80	59	18	23	3.5	4.3	1.2	13%	0.9	-4.5	27	$4
ERA Potl 45%	2nd Half		1	3	0	58	32	5.75	1.64	297			13.9	32%	65%	4.10	56	19	24	4.0	5.0	1.2	12%	0.9	-9.0	23	($1)
LIMA Plan C+	07	Proj	2	4	0	58	32	5.28	1.59	288			6.9	31%	67%	4.12	55	19	25	4.0	5.0	1.2	12%	0.9	1.8	25	($0)

Routinely underperforms relative to skills, and his skills are no bargain. The result is one of the longest runs of consistently awful pitching in recent memory. Trust us, there's no reason to bid.

Wright,Jaret

Wright,Jaret	Yr	Tm	W	L	Sv	IP	K	ERA	WHIP	OBA	vL	vR	BF/G	H%	S%	xERA	G	L	F	Ctl	Dom	Cmd	hr/f	hr/9	RAR	BPV	R$
RH Starter	02	CLE *	7	6	0	73	48	8.01	2.15	350			20.6	39%	63%	6.16	28	21	51	5.7	5.9	1.0	7%	1.2	-32.0	5	($6)
Age 31	03	2NL *	4	6	2	75	66	5.88	1.76	308	365	313	5.7	37%	67%	4.04	45	25	31	4.6	7.9	1.7	12%	1.1	-14.8	45	($0)
Peak	04	ATL	15	8	0	186	159	3.29	1.28	242	261	225	24.4	30%	75%	3.57	46	19	35	3.4	7.7	2.3	6%	0.5	22.3	84	$20
Type	05	NYY	5	5	0	63	34	6.12	1.79	312	273	358	22.9	34%	67%	4.87	45	23	32	4.6	4.8	1.1	11%	1.1	-13.7	10	($1)
Reliability 28	06	NYY	11	7	0	140	84	4.50	1.53	284	314	255	20.8	32%	71%	4.61	38	24	38	3.7	5.4	1.5	6%	0.6	1.1	42	$9
DL 113	1st Half		4	5	0	64	34	4.21	1.53	290			22.0	32%	72%	4.64	40	24	36	3.4	4.8	1.4	5%	0.6	2.8	38	$4
ERA Potl 45%	2nd Half		7	2	0	76	50	4.74	1.53	279			19.9	32%	69%	4.59	37	23	40	3.9	5.9	1.5	6%	0.7	-1.7	45	$5
LIMA Plan C	07	Proj	12	8	0	145	93	4.66	1.53	284			18.4	31%	72%	4.39	41	23	36	3.7	5.8	1.6	10%	1.1	1.7	34	$8

There's so little good in this skills set, and yet so little that's really bad. He's settled into an exquisite mediocrity. Sure, his DOM rebounded a bit, and he still owns 2004, but that seems so long ago. Don't overbid.

Wuertz,Mike

Wuertz,Mike	Yr	Tm	W	L	Sv	IP	K	ERA	WHIP	OBA	vL	vR	BF/G	H%	S%	xERA	G	L	F	Ctl	Dom	Cmd	hr/f	hr/9	RAR	BPV	R$
RH Reliever	02	aaa	9	5	0	154	115	5.32	1.63	302			25.0	34%	70%	5.66				3.7	6.7	1.8		1.2	-19.9	36	$3
Age 28	03	aaa	3	9	1	124	81	5.23	1.53	307			12.8	34%	68%	5.54				2.5	5.9	2.3		1.2	-12.7	40	$2
Pre-Peak	04	CHC *	2	1	20	73	82	3.20	1.17	207	212	221	4.4	27%	77%	3.63	29	16	55	3.9	10.1	2.6	8%	1.0	9.6	98	$14
Type Power	05	CHC	6	2	0	75	89	3.83	1.33	221	260	197	4.3	30%	72%	3.34	43	17	40	4.8	10.7	2.2	8%	0.7	3.9	100	$8
Reliability 10	06	CHC *	9	1	10	81	98	2.61	1.22	241	184	245	4.7	33%	83%	2.51	54	16	30	2.9	10.8	3.7	13%	0.9	18.9	122	$17
DL	1st Half		4	0	8	36	48	3.51	1.53	279			6.2	40%	80%	1.37	73	20	7	3.9	11.8	3.0	57%	0.9	4.3	106	$7
ERA Potl 45%	2nd Half		5	1	2	45	51	1.88	0.97	207			3.9	27%	88%	2.47	51	16	34	2.1	10.1	4.7	12%	0.9	14.5	146	$10
LIMA Plan B+	07	Proj	7	2	0	79	89	3.21	1.20	232			4.8	31%	77%	2.91	46	17	37	3.1	10.2	3.3	11%	0.9	14.1	111	$11

3-1, 2.66 ERA in 41 IP at CHC. Pitched in terribly bad luck early (H%, hr/f), but skills were as good as ever. Better results, predictably, after recall. Enters '07 much as '06, a top LIMA pick with outside saves chances.

Yates,Tyler

Yates,Tyler	Yr	Tm	W	L	Sv	IP	K	ERA	WHIP	OBA	vL	vR	BF/G	H%	S%	xERA	G	L	F	Ctl	Dom	Cmd	hr/f	hr/9	RAR	BPV	R$
RH Reliever	02	aaa	2	2	6	34	29	1.59	1.35	256			6.1	32%	89%	3.38				3.4	7.7	2.2		0.3	11.3	89	$6
Age 29	03	a/a	2	4	0	59	39	5.48	1.66	293			22.5	33%	67%	5.33				4.4	5.9	1.3		0.9	-7.9	33	($0)
Peak	04	NYM *	8	6	4	85	69	5.48	1.70	285	330	296	7.7	34%	68%	3.89	55	21	25	5.2	7.3	1.4	12%	0.8	-12.8	46	$3
Type Power	05	NYM	0	0	0	0	0	0.00	0.00																		
Reliability 0	06	ATL	2	5	1	50	46	3.96	1.46	230	217	235	3.9	27%	76%	4.11	41	22	37	5.6	8.3	1.5	12%	1.1	3.3	58	$4
DL 180	1st Half		0	1	0	12	9	4.50	1.92	293			4.1	34%	77%	5.49	32	30	38	6.8	6.8	1.0	7%	0.8	-0.0	35	($0)
ERA Potl 45%	2nd Half		2	4	1	38	37	3.79	1.32	207			3.8	25%	76%	3.70	44	19	36	5.2	8.8	1.7	14%	1.2	3.3	66	$4
LIMA Plan B	07	Proj	4	5	0	64	56	3.94	1.55	262			7.1	31%	77%	4.01	44	23	33	4.9	7.9	1.6	11%	1.0	2.8	54	$4

Shoulder seemed to bounce back nicely from rotator cuff surgery. Unfortunately, as wild as ever, although CMD did improve after the rust came off. With better Ctl and health, a power arm to watch.

Young,Chris

Young,Chris	Yr	Tm	W	L	Sv	IP	K	ERA	WHIP	OBA	vL	vR	BF/G	H%	S%	xERA	G	L	F	Ctl	Dom	Cmd	hr/f	hr/9	RAR	BPV	R$
RH Starter	02		0	0	0	0	0	0.00	0.00											0.0	0.0						
Age 27	03	aa	4	4	0	83	50	4.91	1.45	295			24.2	32%	68%	5.05				2.4	5.5	2.3		1.1	-5.3	42	$3
Pre-Peak	04	a/a	9	6	0	118	89	5.05	1.57	299			23.1	34%	70%	5.48				3.3	6.8	2.1		1.2	-10.3	43	$5
Type Power	05	TEX	12	7	0	164	137	4.28	1.26	259	281	220	22.1	30%	69%	3.93	33	18	49	2.5	7.5	3.0	8%	1.0	2.0	81	$16
Reliability 46	06	SD	11	5	0	179	164	3.47	1.13	210	175	234	23.4	24%	77%	3.99	25	18	56	3.5	8.2	2.4	10%	1.4	22.5	70	$22
DL	1st Half		7	3	0	97	88	2.97	1.09	201			24.3	23%	80%	3.94	27	18	56	3.4	8.2	2.4	10%	1.3	18.2	75	$14
ERA Potl 40%	2nd Half		4	2	0	82	76	4.06	1.18	219			22.4	25%	72%	4.04	24	19	57	3.5	8.3	2.4	11%	1.5	4.4	65	$8
LIMA Plan D	07	Proj	13	7	0	203	181	3.90	1.32	257			23.3	30%	76%	4.12	28	18	54	3.1	8.0	2.6	10%	1.4	6.1	65	$18

Another "breakout" that wasn't. Low H% suppressed ERA, and skills were mostly unchanged. That said, DOM climb continues, and those skills are pretty good as-is. Ironically, he could pitch better in '07 with worse stats.

Zambrano,Carlos

Zambrano,Carlos	Yr	Tm	W	L	Sv	IP	K	ERA	WHIP	OBA	vL	vR	BF/G	H%	S%	xERA	G	L	F	Ctl	Dom	Cmd	hr/f	hr/9	RAR	BPV	R$
RH Starter	02	CHC	4	8	0	117	104	3.38	1.40	225	209	253	14.4	28%	77%	3.58	51	23	25	5.2	8.0	1.5	11%	0.7	10.4	69	$8
Age 25	03	CHC	13	11	0	214	168	3.11	1.32	238	245	235	28.3	29%	76%	3.41	56	18	26	4.0	7.1	1.8	6%	0.4	30.8	76	$21
Growth	04	CHC	16	8	0	209	188	2.75	1.22	228	232	218	27.9	28%	79%	3.26	51	18	31	3.5	8.1	2.3	8%	0.6	38.9	89	$26
Type Power	05	CHC	14	6	0	223	202	3.27	1.15	213	212	212	27.5	26%	74%	3.12	50	20	30	3.5	8.1	2.3	12%	0.8	26.9	85	$26
Reliability 65	06	CHC	16	7	0	214	210	3.41	1.29	212	247	174	27.3	27%	76%	3.57	47	17	36	4.8	8.8	1.8	10%	0.8	28.5	79	$24
DL	1st Half		6	3	0	113	112	2.95	1.24	197			27.6	24%	80%	3.52	46	18	36	4.9	8.9	1.8	12%	1.0	21.5	78	$14
ERA Potl 45%	2nd Half		10	4	0	101	98	3.92	1.36	228			27.0	29%	72%	3.62	48	17	36	4.7	8.7	1.8	8%	0.7	7.1	79	$11
LIMA Plan D+	07	Proj	16	8	0	218	203	3.72	1.35	233			28.2	29%	74%	3.54	49	18	33	4.5	8.4	1.9	9%	0.7	22.2	76	$21

All the IP haven't sent him down the Prior/Wood path yet, but there are small warning signs... throwing harder but wilder, rising FB rate could lead to more HRs, rising xERA... DN: 4.50 ERA, in '07 or '08

Zambrano,Victor

Zambrano,Victor	Yr	Tm	W	L	Sv	IP	K	ERA	WHIP	OBA	vL	vR	BF/G	H%	S%	xERA	G	L	F	Ctl	Dom	Cmd	hr/f	hr/9	RAR	BPV	R$
RH Starter	02	TAM *	8	9	2	128	85	5.20	1.59	266	292	266	11.1	29%	69%	4.82	42	18	41	5.1	6.0	1.2	10%	1.2	-11.7	27	$4
Age 32	03	TAM	12	10	0	188	132	4.21	1.44	237	263	206	24.1	27%	73%	4.35	47	17	35	5.1	6.3	1.2	11%	1.0	7.2	41	$13
Peak	04	2TM	11	7	0	142	123	4.37	1.56	229	241	217	24.4	28%	73%	4.44	46	18	36	6.5	7.8	1.2	9%	0.8	-0.5	57	$8
Type Power	05	NYM	7	12	0	166	112	4.17	1.49	266	260	268	23.6	31%	72%	4.05	50	21	29	4.2	6.1	1.5	8%	0.7	1.5	49	$7
Reliability 4	06	NYM	1	2	0	21	15	6.82	1.71	296	344	259	19.5	31%	65%	4.91	30	27	43	4.7	6.4	1.4	17%	2.1	-6.1	-1	($1)
DL 147	1st Half		1	2	0	21	15	6.82	1.71	296			19.5	31%	65%	4.91	30	27	43	4.7	6.4	1.4	17%	2.1	-6.1	-1	($1)
ERA Potl 50%	2nd Half		0	0	0	0	0	0.00	0.00																		
LIMA Plan D	07	Proj	3	4	0	54	40	4.83	1.57	262			20.2	30%	72%	4.55	41	21	37	5.2	6.7	1.3	11%	1.2	-1.2	35	$2

Massive elbow surgery ended 2006 season in May, and 2007 is in jeopardy as well. This projection assumes three things: He comes back late, he pitches as a starter, and he still isn't as good as Scott Kazmir.

Zito,Barry

Zito,Barry	Yr	Tm	W	L	Sv	IP	K	ERA	WHIP	OBA	vL	vR	BF/G	H%	S%	xERA	G	L	F	Ctl	Dom	Cmd	hr/f	hr/9	RAR	BPV	R$
LH Starter	02	OAK	23	5	0	229	182	2.75	1.14	220	275	203	26.5	25%	81%	3.93	34	18	48	3.1	7.2	2.3	8%	0.9	48.2	75	$35
Age 29	03	OAK	14	12	0	231	146	3.31	1.19	222	223	218	27.1	25%	74%	4.29	40	15	45	3.4	5.7	1.7	6%	0.7	34.6	57	$25
Pre-Peak	04	OAK	11	11	0	213	163	4.48	1.39	264	263	248	27.0	30%	71%	4.20	37	19	44	3.4	6.9	2.0	10%	1.2	-1.2	50	$13
Type	05	OAK	14	13	0	228	171	3.87	1.20	223	215	223	26.9	25%	71%	3.81	42	21	37	3.5	6.7	1.9	11%	1.0	14.2	60	$23
Reliability 71	06	OAK	16	10	0	221	151	3.83	1.40	253	260	257	28.1	28%	76%	4.54	38	17	45	4.0	6.1	1.5	9%	1.1	19.9	40	$20
DL	1st Half		8	4	0	109	85	3.46	1.32	232			27.2	27%	76%	4.21	40	17	43	4.2	7.0	1.7	7%	0.8	14.7	61	$12
ERA Potl 40%	2nd Half		8	6	0	112	66	4.18	1.48	272			29.0	29%	77%	4.87	37	16	47	3.9	5.3	1.4	10%	1.4	5.2	20	$8
LIMA Plan D	07	Proj	13	13	0	218	145	4.14	1.42	260			27.7	29%	74%	4.50	39	18	43	3.8	6.0	1.6	9%	1.2	-0.3	37	$15

More delicious innings eaten by the erstwhile Cy Young winner. CMD took a nasty dip, and he again lucked into a high S%. BPIs are just plain dangerous. Someone will pay for an ace, and will get a staff filler.

Zumaya,Joel

Zumaya,Joel	Yr	Tm	W	L	Sv	IP	K	ERA	WHIP	OBA	vL	vR	BF/G	H%	S%	xERA	G	L	F	Ctl	Dom	Cmd	hr/f	hr/9	RAR	BPV	R$
RH Reliever	02		0	0	0	0	0	0.00	0.00																		
Age 22	03		0	0	0	0	0	0.00	0.00																		
Growth	04	aa	2	2	0	20	25	7.20	1.65	271			22.9	31%	65%	7.07				5.4	11.3	2.1		3.2	-7.0	17	$0
Type Power	05	a/a	9	5	0	151	181	3.46	1.25	212			24.2	30%	73%	2.88				4.4	10.8	2.4		0.6	15.7	110	$18
Reliability 0	06	DET	6	3	1	83	97	1.95	1.18	193	183	188	5.5	27%	87%	3.40	34	21	45	4.5	10.5	2.3	7%	0.6	26.7	108	$15
DL	1st Half		4	1	1	38	48	2.37	1.08	170			4.7	22%	86%	3.10	34	19	47	4.5	11.4	2.5	13%	1.2	10.3	107	$8
ERA Potl 45%	2nd Half		2	2	0	45	49	1.60	1.26	211			6.3	30%	88%	3.67	34	22	44	4.6	9.8	2.1	2%	0.2	16.5	110	$7
LIMA Plan B	07	Proj	5	3	3	80	94	3.05	1.28	216			8.2	29%	80%	3.45	34	21	45	4.5	10.6	2.4	9%	0.9	10.1	98	$12

Phenom spent '06 blowing 100-mph heat and malevolent slider by hitters. Ctl and health are his only potential Achilles' heels. Projection assumes he stays in current role. As a starter or closer, value soars.

ROD TRUESDELL

PQS Pitching Logs

We've always approached performance measures on an aggregate basis. Each individual event that our statistics chronicle gets dumped into a huge pool of data. We then use our formulas to try to sort and slice and manipulate the data into more usable information.

Pure Quality Starts (PQS) take a different approach. *(See Glossary for complete definition).* It says that the smallest unit of measure should not be the "event" but instead be the "game." Within that game, we can accumulate all the strikeouts, hits and walks, and evaluate that outing as a whole. After all, when a pitcher takes the mound, he is either "on" or "off" his game; he is either dominant or struggling, or somewhere in between.

PQS captures the array of events and slaps an evaluative label on that outing, on a scale of 0 to 5. It doesn't matter if a few extra balls got through the infield, or the pitcher was given the hook in the 4th or 6th inning, or the bullpen was able to strand their inherited base-runners. When we look at performance in the aggregate, *those events do matter,* and will affect a pitcher's BPIs and ERA. But with PQS, the minutia is less relevant than the overall performance.

In the end, a dominating performance is a dominating performance, whether Chris Carpenter is hurling a 1-hit shutout or giving up 3 runs while striking out 8 in 6 IP. And a disaster is still a disaster, whether Casey Fossum gets a 2nd inning hook after giving up 5 runs, or "takes one for the team" getting shelled for 8 runs in 4 IP.

With Gene McCaffrey's Domination and Disaster percentages, we can sort out the PQS scores even more.

Domination Per Cent (DOM%) measures the portion of a pitcher's starts that scored a 4 or 5 on the PQS scale.

Disaster Per Cent (DIS%) measures the portion of a pitcher's starts that scored a 0 or 1 on the PQS scale.

DOM/DIS percentages open up a new perspective, providing us with two separate scales of performance. In tandem, they measure something completely different — *consistency.* For instance, a pitcher with a 50/20% DOM/DIS split was dominating in half of his starts but was rocked one every five outings. Compare him to a pitcher with a 50/5% split — also dominating half of the time but saw an early shower only once every 20 times out.

This is important because a pitcher might possess incredible skill but be unable to sustain it on a start-by-start basis. For instance, a pitcher who posts PQS scores of 5,0,5,0,5 might have an ERA that is identical to one who posts scores of 3,3,3,3,3 — less skill, but more consistent. ERAs, WHIPs, and even BPIs don't capture that subtle difference. DOM/DIS *does* capture that difference, and in doing so, helps us identify pitchers who might be better or worse than their stats — and sabermetrics — indicate.

The final step is to convert a pitcher's DOM/DIS split back to an expected ERA. By creating a grid of individual DOM and DIS levels, we can determine the average ERA at each cross point. The result is an ERA based purely on PQS, and so we can call it the PQS ERA, or *qERA*.

Some important comparisons:
ERA: The pitcher's actual season earned run average.
xERA: The pitcher's ERA based on the component elements of his skill, essentially stripping away the effects of bullpen and defense.
qERA: The pitcher's ERA based on a comparison of his dominating versus disastrous starts.

Is qERA predictive? We looked at all pitchers with at least 15 starts in the three year period of 2001-2003, then isolated those with a qERA to ERA variance of at least half a run. How often did those variances predict an ERA swing for the following year?

Year	IMPROVEMENT			DECLINE		
	Hit	Miss	%	Hit	Miss	%
2001-2002	11	3	79%	14	9	61%
2002-2003	11	2	85%	32	7	82%

The following pitching logs include:
- Up to three years of data for all pitchers who had at least five starts in 2006.
- Number of starts in that year. (No.)
- Start-by-start listing of PQS scores, separated by half season. These are not time-phased, so any gaps do not necessarily represent gaps of time.
- Average pitch counts for all starts (PC)
- Domination and Disaster percentages (DOM, DIS)
- Earned Run Average (ERA)
- Expected Earned Run Average (xERA)
- PQS Earned Run Average (qERA)

There is much insight that can be gleaned from these charts. A casual scan uncovers a few random tidbits:

Kris Benson's ERA (4.32, 4.14, 4.82) does not reflect the consistent decline he's experienced over the past three years. His DOM/DIS (48/3, 38/25, 23/37) is more telling, and his qERA trend (3.68, 4.82, 5.36) is downright scary.

Dan Haren's ERA dropped from 3.73 to 4.12 in 2006. However, his DOM/DIS improved from 50/18 to 53/6 and his qERA reflects a more positive trend (4.37, 3.85).

Livan Hernandez's workload and performance have been a source of constant intrigue. Dipping back into some history, look at his DOM, ERA and pitch count trends. It appears that the branch breaks each time his PC peaks:

Year	DOM	DIS	PC	ERA	qERA
1999	39%	10%	113	4.64	4.32
2000	48%	6%	116	3.75	3.98
2001	32%	18%	109	5.25	4.60
2002	36%	18%	105	4.38	4.52
2003	64%	9%	108	3.21	3.50
2004	57%	6%	112	3.60	3.68
2005	32%	18%	114	3.99	4.60
2006	26%	9%	103	4.83	4.48

Tim Hudson had managed to keep his ERA in check until 2006 (3.54, 3.52, 4.86). However, DOM/DIS has tracked a slow trend of fading skills (37/11, 34/27, 31/20), and qERA has spelled out it out blatantly (4.41, 4.60, 4.71).

PQS PITCHING LOGS

Pitcher	Year	No.	FIRST HALF	SECOND HALF	PC	DOM	DIS	ERA	xERA	qERA
Acevedo,Jose	2004	27	4 5 5 3 3 0 3 5 4 4 3 0 0 1 4 1 5 3	0 0 0 0 2 5 0 0 3	86	33%	41%	5.95	5.61	5.29
	2005	5		4 0 3 0 1	76	20%	60%	6.47	4.78	7.98
Affeldt,Jeremy	2004	8	1 0 4 3 2 3 1 0		98	13%	50%	4.97	5.12	7.08
	2006	9	0 0 3 4 2 0 3 1 0		90	11%	56%	6.20	4.62	7.77
Armas Jr.,Tony	2004	16	4 3 0 0 5 0 3	2 3 0 4 0 0 4 0 0	83	25%	50%	4.88	4.94	6.56
	2005	19	2 3 2 2 3 3 4 1 0 3 4	0 4 3 3 4 3 0 0	94	21%	26%	4.99	4.88	4.98
	2006	30	4 4 2 5 4 0 5 5 1 3 5 5 3 0 0	4 4 0 0 4 5 1 0 0 3 2 0 3 5 3	92	43%	33%	5.03	4.13	4.92
Arroyo,Bronson	2004	29	3 4 5 5 5 2 0 3 1 4 4 2 4 5	5 3 4 5 4 4 2 5 0 2 5 4 3 4 0	95	59%	14%	4.04	3.63	3.97
	2005	32	5 1 3 3 5 5 3 4 4 0 4 0 5 4 2 4 3	0 4 2 3 0 4 3 4 1 3 4 3 3 3 0	101	41%	22%	4.52	4.40	4.56
	2006	34	4 4 1 5 5 3 2 5 4 5 4 4 4 4 4 5 4 5 0	4 4 3 4 0 3 3 2 3 3 5 5 5 1 5	110	65%	12%	3.29	3.37	3.61
Astacio,Ezequiel	2005	14	3 2 3 0 3	5 4 2 0 3 3 0 2 3	88	14%	21%	5.67	4.09	4.79
Astacio,Pedro	2005	22	5 4 4 0 0 0 5 4 5 4 0 0 0	4 0 4 5 3 3 5 3	89	50%	32%	4.71	3.99	4.71
	2006	17	3 0	1 2 4 3 3 4 4 0 0 1 4 0 2 3 4	85	29%	35%	5.98	4.62	5.27
Backe,Brandon	2004	9		3 0 3 5 3 0 0 3 4	83	22%	33%	4.30	5.16	5.21
	2005	25	3 4 5 3 5 1 3 4 3 4 2 4 0 3 4 0 2 4	4 3 0 0 5 5 0	91	44%	24%	4.77	4.33	4.56
	2006	8	4 0	0 2 3 3 2 3	84	13%	25%	3.77	4.60	5.08
Baek,Cha Seung	2006	6		4 2 4 4 0 5	96	67%	17%	3.67	3.65	3.73
Baker,Scott	2005	9	4	5 5 4 0 3 4 2 3	90	56%	11%	3.38	3.89	3.97
	2006	16	0 4 1 5 1 3 0 2 0	3 3 0 3 1 3 0	90	13%	50%	6.37	3.87	7.08
Bannister,Brian	2006	6	4 4 2 3 1	4	100	50%	17%	4.26	4.86	4.37
Batista,Miguel	2006	33	5 2 3 2 0 2 4 2 3 2 4 4 0 4 1 3 4 0	3 3 5 3 0 2 2 4 3 4 3 5 3 3 0	99	30%	18%	4.58	3.97	4.60
Bautista,Denny	2004	5		2 2 0 3 4	96	20%	20%	8.63	6.99	4.75
	2005	7	5 0 3 3 5 0 0		90	29%	43%	5.88	3.92	5.40
	2006	8	4 3 0 0 4 0 0	0	80	25%	63%	5.62	4.12	7.72
Beckett,Josh	2004	26	5 5 3 3 4 5 3 4 5 4 0 0 0	0 0 4 4 5 2 4 5 5 3 5 4	94	58%	19%	3.80	3.35	4.10
	2005	29	5 5 4 5 4 0 5 4 4 5 4 4 4 1 5 0	5 5 5 2 5 5 0 4 3 5 4 5	97	76%	14%	3.38	3.20	3.41
	2006	33	5 3 5 2 0 2 5 5 2 5 0 0 4 4 5 4 4 3	0 5 5 4 2 5 4 1 3 3 3 4 4 3	98	52%	15%	5.01	3.49	4.37
Bedard,Erik	2004	26	0 0 2 4 3 4 0 2 0 3 3 2 4 4 4	4 4 0 0 4 3 4 0 1 5 0	100	38%	35%	4.60	4.91	5.13
	2005	24	5 2 0 5 5 5 2 2 5	5 4 3 0 0 4 5 0 3 2 4 5 0	103	50%	17%	4.02	3.65	4.37
	2006	33	1 5 4 4 1 2 0 2 3 0 0 0 3 4 5 5 5 5 5	5 5 4 3 4 5 2 4 4 5 5 5 0 2	100	58%	21%	3.76	3.13	4.23
Belisle,Matt	2005	5	4 0 3 5 1		73	40%	40%	4.44	3.65	5.21
Benoit,Joaquin	2004	15	5 4 4 4 2 0 0 0 0 2 5 3	0 0 0	89	33%	47%	5.68	5.18	5.83
	2005	9		2 2 4 2 0 0 2 4 0	95	22%	33%	3.72	3.87	5.21
Benson,Kris	2004	31	2 3 5 2 5 2 2 3 4 2 5 5 5 2 3 3 4	4 4 3 3 5 3 2 3 0 5 5 5 5 4	102	48%	3%	4.32	3.72	3.68
	2005	28	0 2 5 3 5 4 4 4 1 3 3 3 5	5 4 4 2 1 4 3 0 1 3 1 0 3 2 4	98	39%	25%	4.14	4.04	4.82
	2006	30	3 5 1 2 3 3 0 5 3 0 1 1 5 4 4 3 0 2 0	3 2 1 0 4 0 3 2 5 3 0	95	23%	37%	4.82	4.15	5.36
Bergmann,Jason	2006	6		4 3 2 4 0 0	87	33%	33%	6.68	4.01	5.08
Billingsley,Chad	2006	16	1 2 1 3 1	2 4 0 4 5 3 5 3 2 0 2	95	25%	31%	3.80	4.48	5.13
Blanton,Joe	2005	33	2 3 3 4 0 3 0 0 0 3 4 4 4 4 4 2	2 1 4 4 5 3 4 5 5 5 2 3 3 3 4 5	93	45%	18%	3.54	4.02	4.40
	2006	31	5 4 0 3 2 2 2 4 0 3 4 1 4 3 3 0 3 2	4 2 4 2 3 3 3 4 2 3 0 2 2	101	26%	16%	4.82	4.06	4.62
Bonderman,Jeremy	2004	32	4 5 2 2 4 2 3 4 3 0 0 0 5 4 3 3 4	4 3 0 0 2 5 0 5 3 5 5 2 5 4 5	90	47%	19%	4.89	4.01	4.40
	2005	29	5 3 4 3 4 3 5 5 3 4 4 3 4 2 3 5 0 4 4	4 4 5 2 4 5 3 0 0 5 0	98	55%	14%	4.57	3.58	3.97
	2006	34	5 4 0 3 5 5 2 5 0 3 3 5 5 5 5 5 3 4	1 4 3 5 3 4 5 0 4 2 0 3 3 3 4 0	97	50%	18%	4.08	2.93	4.37
Bonser,Boof	2006	18	5 3 4 1 0 4 0	0 3 3 3 3 5 5 4 5 5 2	87	44%	22%	4.22	3.33	4.56
Buchholz,Taylor	2006	19	3 4 3 4 0 0 4 0 2 1 5 5 5 5 4	2 2 0 0	87	42%	32%	5.89	3.57	4.92
Buehrle,Mark	2004	35	2 4 3 0 5 0 5 4 5 4 5 3 4 4 2 5 5 3	2 4 3 4 4 3 4 3 2 3 3 1 4 5	106	51%	9%	3.89	4.29	3.85
	2005	33	4 3 5 4 2 3 3 4 4 3 4 5 4 5 4 2 3	5 2 2 3 1 3 5 4 2 3 4 4	105	48%	3%	3.12	2.63	3.68
	2006	32	0 3 4 5 4 1 3 2 3 3 3 2 3 4 3 4 2 3	0 3 1 4 1 4 2 1 4 3 0 3 2 0	97	25%	25%	4.99	3.99	4.93
Burnett,A.J.	2004	19	0 0 3 5 4 0 5 4	3 3 3 3 5 5 5 3 4 5	94	53%	16%	3.68	2.90	4.37
	2005	32	4 4 5 5 3 5 3 5 5 3 5 5 4 4 5 0 5	1 5 4 5 5 3 2 2 0 4 5 5	103	63%	9%	3.44	2.95	3.50
	2006	21	3 0 5 5 0 3	5 5 0 0 4 5 3 2 2 4 5 5 4 5 5	103	57%	19%	3.98	2.97	4.10
Bush,David	2004	16	4 3	5 3 0 4 4 3 4 5 1 3 4 0 5	92	50%	19%	3.70	3.87	4.37
	2005	24	1 4 0 4 3 4 0 3 0 0	3 4 0 0 4 0 5 5 5 3 0 0 5 3	88	38%	42%	4.50	3.84	5.25
	2006	32	5 2 4 5 3 5 3 4 3 0 3 4 4 0 4 4 4 4	3 0 4 5 1 4 3 4 5 3 0 3 4	93	56%	19%	4.41	2.96	4.10
Byrd,Paul	2004	19	4 3 0 4	5 3 3 3 4 2 3 5 4 4 3 0 3 0	88	37%	16%	3.94	4.43	4.52
	2005	31	3 2 3 0 3 3 3 4 3 4 4 4 4 4 3	3 4 0 3 4 3 3 1 4 4 4 4 0 3	94	39%	13%	3.75	3.98	4.41
	2006	31	3 0 4 0 4 4 2 4 4 5 3 5 3 4 4 0	1 3 0 0 3 2 4 0 3 3 1 2 0 2	92	32%	29%	4.88	4.07	4.90
Cabrera,Daniel	2004	27	3 2 0 2 3 4 2 2 4 3 3 5	4 2 0 2 2 3 0 0 0 3 3 0 0	92	15%	30%	5.01	4.64	5.29
	2005	29	0 2 2 5 5 4 0 5 1 4 0 4 4 3 5 3	5 3 3 4 0 0 5 3 4 3 3	99	41%	24%	4.53	3.53	4.56
	2006	26	0 3 5 3 5 5 3 0 4 5 2 0 3 3	1 5 0 5 5 1 3 3 0 5 4	103	38%	27%	4.74	3.69	4.82
Cain,Matt	2005	7		2 4 5 3 5 4 3	102	57%	0%	2.34	4.15	3.38
	2006	31	3 4 1 4 5 0 1 3 3 3 0 4 5 0 5 0	4 4 3 5 0 3 5 5 5 4 5 2 4 3	106	52%	23%	4.15	3.56	4.50
Capuano,Chris	2004	17	3 1 0 0 4 4 4 5 2 5	4 2 5 3 5 0 0	87	47%	29%	5.01	5.21	4.67
	2005	35	4 2 2 2 3 5 4 4 3 5 0 3 3 3 2 3 2	4 3 4 1 0 5 5 2 5 4 3 3 3 0	104	37%	11%	3.99	3.95	4.41
	2006	34	5 4 5 5 4 3 5 5 3 4 3 4 4 5 5 4 0 4	0 3 2 3 4 4 5 3 4 5 3 2 2 1 0	99	59%	12%	4.03	3.29	3.97
Carmona,Fausto	2006	7	5 0 3	0 2 3 5	87	29%	29%	5.42	3.46	4.93
Carpenter,Chris	2004	28	2 2 5 4 4 4 3 5 4 4 5 5 4 0	3 3 1 5 0 5 5 5 5 3 0	96	50%	14%	3.46	3.53	4.21
	2005	33	4 0 4 4 3 4 4 4 5 4 4 5 5 5 5 5 5	5 3 5 4 4 5 2 4 4 5 5 0 2 3	103	76%	6%	2.84	2.76	3.13
	2006	32	2 5 5 5 3 3 5 4 5 4 3 5 4 3 4 3 5	5 5 3 0 4 4 5 4 5 3 4 5 2 4	102	66%	3%	3.09	2.69	3.14
Carrasco,Hector	2005	5		0 4 4 5 4	86	80%	20%	2.04	3.49	3.55
	2006	3	0 3 3		81	0%	33%	3.41	3.19	5.53
Chacin,Gustavo	2005	34	4 4 3 5 3 3 3 0 2 2 5 4 0 2 2 3 4	1 4 4 4 2 2 4 3 1 3 5 5 3 0 0 4	95	38%	18%	3.72	4.17	4.52
	2006	17	4 2 1 3 5 2 0 2 0 0	0 3 3 3 4 1 0	86	18%	41%	5.05	4.45	5.60
Chacon,Shawn	2005	24	5 5 1 3 2 2 4 0 1 2	5 4 4 4 3 3 4 2 0 3 4 3	102	38%	17%	3.45	4.50	4.52
	2006	20	0 4 3 3 4 0 0 0 0 2 0	3 0 2 0 3 3 3 3 3	86	10%	40%	6.36	5.11	5.70
Chen,Bruce	2004	7		3 2 0 4 4 3 3	102	29%	14%	3.05	3.59	4.50
	2005	32	4 4 3 2 4 4 3 4 2 5 4 4 4 2 0 0 4	4 0 0 3 5 4 3 4 5 4 5 3 3 0 3	95	53%	16%	3.84	3.91	4.37
	2006	12	2 3 0 0 3 0 0 0 5 0	3 3	91	8%	50%	6.93	4.34	7.26
Claussen,Brandon	2004	14		4 0 3 2 0 3 3 4 0 0 4 0 0 3	90	21%	43%	6.14	5.86	5.50
	2005	29	3 2 0 0 0 3 3 3 4 2 2 5 3	0 0 5 4 3 5 4 3 2 5 3 5 5 2 2	98	34%	17%	4.22	4.12	4.60
	2006	14	4 3 5 0 1 4 2 5 3 4 1 3 5 0		95	43%	29%	6.19	4.00	4.74

163

PQS PITCHING LOGS

Pitcher	Year	No.	FIRST HALF	SECOND HALF	PC	DOM	DIS	ERA	xERA	qERA
Clemens,Roger	2004	33	5 3 5 2 4 5 5 5 3 5 5 4 3 0 4 4 4 5	5 2 5 5 4 3 0 5 4 5 5 5 5 5 5	104	76%	6%	2.98	2.67	3.13
	2005	32	5 5 5 4 4 4 5 5 3 4 5 3 4 5 4 5 4 3	3 5 4 5 4 5 5 5 5 2 0 4 3 4	100	78%	3%	1.88	2.97	2.84
	2006	19	3 3 3 4	3 5 4 5 4 5 3 5 4 5 4 3 5 4 5	96	68%	0%	2.30	2.78	3.14
Clement,Matt	2004	30	0 5 4 5 4 4 4 4 5 4 0 4 4 5 5 4 0 4 4	4 3 3 4 2 3 5 3 0 0 0 4 0	100	63%	20%	3.68	3.64	3.95
	2005	32	0 4 5 5 0 4 5 4 1 5 4 4 0 5 5 5 4 3 3	0 4 0 3 5 5 4 3 4 3 5 0 4 1	99	59%	25%	4.57	3.71	4.39
	2006	12	4 0 4 3 4 3 3 4 0 0 5 0		97	42%	33%	6.61	4.44	4.92
Colon,Bartolo	2004	34	5 4 2 2 0 4 3 2 2 3 0 0 1 2 5 0 0 4	3 5 5 4 4 1 3 4 4 0 5 5 4 0 4 5	100	47%	26%	5.02	4.95	4.67
	2005	33	4 4 5 5 0 5 4 2 3 5 4 4 3 3 4 5 3 4 2	2 2 5 4 4 4 4 4 4 4 2 4 2 3	98	67%	3%	3.48	3.52	3.14
	2006	10	3 0 3 3 2 3 4	4 3 0	85	20%	20%	5.11	3.85	4.75
Colon,Roman	2005	7	5 3 4 0	0 2 0	73	29%	43%	5.60	3.78	5.40
Contreras,Jose	2004	31	1 0 0 5 0 5 2 0 4 5 4 5 2 3	5 3 0 4 4 5 4 4 2 5 3 0 0 3 3 1	97	42%	29%	5.50	5.02	4.74
	2005	32	5 3 0 0 5 5 3 2 4 5 4 5 2 4 2 0 2	5 3 2 3 5 4 3 5 4 3 4 3 5 5	99	50%	9%	3.61	3.68	3.85
	2006	30	3 4 5 3 4 3 3 4 2 3 5 4 1 3 4 4	3 3 4 2 4 4 3 1 0 3 5 5 2 0	101	43%	13%	4.27	3.56	4.32
Cook,Aaron	2004	16	3 4 3 3 0 2 2 2 2 1 2	3 3 2 4 0	92	13%	19%	4.30	4.78	4.66
	2005	13		0 3 4 3 3 1 3 3 3 2 3 0 1	91	8%	31%	3.68	3.94	5.45
	2006	32	4 3 4 2 5 2 3 5 1 4 3 3 2 4 4 3 2 3	3 0 3 3 1 2 2 2 4 1 3 4 4 3	97	31%	13%	4.23	3.66	4.49
Corcoran,Tim	2006	16	2 5 3	2 0 0 3 2 3 0 5 3 5 0 5 4	88	31%	25%	4.38	4.23	4.90
Cormier,Lance	2006	9	0 1	0 4 3 4 0 4 0	84	33%	56%	4.89	4.28	6.91
Cruz,Juan	2006	15	4 4 2 0 5 5 3 0 4	2 0 5 3 4 0	84	47%	27%	4.18	3.42	4.67
Davies,Kyle	2005	14	4 4 2 3 3 0 0 1 2 3 2	5 4 3	98	29%	21%	4.95	4.77	4.73
	2006	14	3 0 4 5 3 2 0 0	0 2 0 4 0 0	89	21%	50%	8.38	4.34	6.74
Davis,Doug	2004	34	2 0 3 5 3 3 5 4 3 4 4 3 0 2 5 5 4 0 5	3 3 4 4 4 0 5 5 5 0 4 3 4 5 3	100	53%	15%	3.26	3.27	4.37
	2005	35	5 4 0 3 0 5 1 3 4 4 4 5 4 4 1 0 5 5 3 4	5 0 5 3 0 4 4 5 3 5 5 3 4 5 5 3	106	60%	20%	3.85	3.45	3.95
	2006	34	4 3 5 0 3 3 3 3 3 3 0 5 3 5 0 3 2	3 3 2 3 1 4 4 4 0 3 5 4 5 3 4	103	32%	15%	4.91	3.81	4.60
Davis,Jason	2004	19	2 4 3 2 2 3 0 3 0 4 4 1 3 0 4 2 1 2	3	98	21%	26%	5.52	6.01	4.98
	2005	4	4 0 4 5		91	75%	25%	4.71	3.93	3.87
Day,Zach	2004	19	3 3 5 2 1 4 5 3 3 4 4 4 0 4 2 2 0	3 3	96	37%	16%	3.95	4.24	4.52
	2005	8	3 0 3 2 0	2 1 0	79	0%	50%	6.88	5.53	7.46
	2006	8	3 0 0 1 5 4 0 0		86	25%	63%	6.75	4.57	7.72
de la Rosa,Jorge	2006	13	0 1 0	3 0 5 3 0 2 3 3 2 0	84	8%	46%	6.49	4.30	6.53
Dempster,Ryan	2005	6	0 5 4 4 2 4		99	67%	17%	3.13	3.30	3.73
Dessens,Elmer	2004	10	3 0 3 3 0 0 0 0	0 0	83	0%	70%	4.46	5.11	10.58
	2005	7	2 0 5 0 1	0 0	70	14%	71%	3.59	3.82	9.84
Dinardo,Lenny	2006	6	1 0 0 3 0	0	73	0%	83%	7.85	4.55	12.14
Downs,Scott	2004	12	0 0 2 5	0 2 2 4 0 0 4 5	87	33%	42%	5.14	5.72	5.29
	2005	13	0	4 0 4 6 3 5 5 5 0 ? ? 4 3	90	46%	23%	4.31	3.36	4.53
	2006	5	3 0 0	2 0	59	0%	60%	4.09	3.20	9.02
Drese,Ryan	2004	33	2 1 3 4 3 4 3 0 4 3 4 2 3 4 2 0 4	3 3 3 0 4 3 3 5 0 2 3 5 3 3 0 0	93	27%	21%	4.21	4.40	4.73
	2005	23	3 1 4 1 3 0 3 0 1 2 3 0 3 0 4 4 2	0 3 0 4 1 0	89	17%	48%	5.79	4.55	6.25
Duckworth,Brandon	2006	8	3 2 1 0 3	0 5 2	97	13%	38%	6.11	4.52	5.54
Duke,Zach	2005	14	5 5	4 3 0 4 4 0 5 0 0 3 5 3	91	50%	29%	1.82	3.35	4.61
	2006	34	4 0 5 3 2 4 3 4 4 3 3 3 1 1 2 3 3 1	1 4 0 3 2 5 3 3 3 2 4 5 5 3 3	96	32%	18%	4.47	3.76	4.60
Eaton,Adam	2004	33	4 5 4 3 3 4 0 2 5 3 4 5 3 3 5 4 5 3	1 3 0 2 3 4 4 4 2 3 5 4 4 3	99	52%	9%	4.61	4.24	3.85
	2005	22	0 4 2 2 5 4 3 4 4 3 5 3 5 0	2 3 5 4 2 2 0 5	100	45%	14%	4.28	3.81	4.28
	2006	13		0 4 0 3 5 1 0 4 3 4 3 2 2	87	31%	31%	5.12	4.03	5.08
Elarton,Scott	2004	21	3 0 0 4 5 0	0 5 4 3 5 4 2 3 4 4 2 2 3 3	96	38%	19%	5.92	5.32	4.52
	2005	31	2 0 0 3 4 3 1 3 4 3 4 3 3 2 4 3	2 3 4 4 2 0 5 0 0 0 5 3 4 4 0 0	92	32%	26%	4.62	4.30	4.90
	2006	20	0 4 3 0 3 0 4 3 3 2 3 3 1 0 5 3 2 2 0	2	95	15%	30%	5.34	5.04	5.29
Escobar,Kelvim	2004	33	3 4 3 3 0 2 4 2 5 5 4 2 5 5 3 3 4	4 5 3 5 5 0 5 5 5 2 5 5 5 5 3 4 3	104	52%	6%	3.94	3.73	3.85
	2005	7	5 3 4 3 4 5 0		91	57%	14%	3.04	2.99	3.97
	2006	30	4 0 4 3 4 5 3 4 4 3 2 3 5 4 0 4 2	2 5 4 5 2 5 4 5 5 4 0 5 0	97	60%	13%	3.61	3.28	3.71
Estes,Shawn	2004	34	3 3 0 4 0 3 0 5 5 1 3 4 2 3 3 5 2 1 4	3 5 1 3 1 3 1 1 1 3 3 2 5 5 0	99	26%	32%	5.84	5.38	5.13
	2005	21	3 5 2 3 4 1 4 5 3 3 3 1 4 3 3 0 3	3 0 2 0	92	24%	24%	4.82	4.11	4.75
Eveland,Dana	2006	5	2 2 0 3 0		97	0%	40%	8.13	3.38	5.90
Floyd,Gavin	2006	11	0 5 2 0 3 1 2 2 1 0 0		91	9%	55%	7.29	4.77	7.99
Fogg,Josh	2004	32	1 0 0 3 2 3 3 2 5 0 2 0 4 3 1 3	1 0 2 3 2 5 2 4 4 2 2 2 2 5	87	19%	25%	4.65	4.46	5.03
	2005	28	5 4 2 0 4 3 3 1 3 0 4 3 4 4 4	0 2 1 2 2 4 2 3 2 1 3	93	32%	21%	5.06	4.45	4.71
	2006	31	4 3 3 3 3 3 2 3 2 0 4 1 2 3 3	5 2 0 4 0 2 2 0 0 3 1 0 4 4	89	23%	29%	5.49	4.18	4.98
Fossum,Casey	2004	27	3 0 1 3 0 5 0 5 0 2 1 0	5 3 0 2 0 0 5 0 5 4 0	89	30%	44%	6.65	6.28	5.29
	2005	25	3 3 4 0 0 4 4 4 3 2	4 0 4 4 2 0 4 1 2 3 4 5 3 4 0	98	44%	24%	4.94	3.90	4.56
	2006	25	0 3 3 0 3 3 3 2 0 0 2 1 4 2 4 5	2 3 0 5 5 0 4 4 0	88	28%	32%	5.33	3.98	5.13
Francis,Jeff	2004	7		2 0 3 1 3 4 3	93	14%	29%	5.22	5.86	5.08
	2005	33	0 2 3 3 4 3 4 3 1 4 2 3 4 5 5 3 0	2 3 4 5 0 0 2 3 4 0 0 4 4 1	95	33%	27%	5.70	4.26	4.90
	2006	32	0 3 5 4 5 3 4 3 1 4 4 3 3 1 3 2	4 4 5 2 3 3 4 2 2 2 2 0 4 1 3	99	34%	16%	4.16	3.79	4.60
Franklin,Ryan	2004	32	2 3 3 0 4 4 3 4 3 4 2 3 1 2 2	4 4 3 2 4 4 2 4 1 0 1 4 2 5 5	100	38%	16%	4.90	5.17	4.52
	2005	30	3 3 3 0 2 4 4 4 2 0 3 2 3 2 3 4 3	2 4 4 0 4 1 3 2 2 3 0 5 4	96	30%	17%	5.11	4.58	4.60
Garcia,Freddy	2004	31	5 4 5 3 4 4 1 5 4 4 3 5 5	5 5 3 4 0 4 2 5 3 5	106	65%	6%	3.81	3.57	3.38
	2005	33	5 4 1 4 4 3 3 4 4 1 5 3 5 5 5 3 2	3 1 4 2 3 3 0 5 2 1 1 3 4	103	39%	18%	3.87	3.60	4.52
	2006	33	0 5 3 3 4 4 5 3 4 2 4 0 4 4 1 2 3	2 4 4 2 4 3 2 5 3 5 4 4 3 4	101	52%	9%	4.53	3.68	3.85
Garland,Jon	2004	33	3 1 4 4 1 3 5 2 3 4 0 5 2 3 3	3 4 3 5 2 4 2 0 2 2 3 3 2 2 4	103	30%	12%	4.89	4.74	4.49
	2005	32	3 3 4 4 4 3 3 3 4 3 3 3 4 4 3 2	2 3 4 3 3 3 3 4 0 5 1 5 3 1 5	104	41%	6%	3.50	3.71	4.11
	2006	32	3 1 4 3 3 0 4 3 3 4 3 4 1 4 4	5 4 2 3 3 4 4 3 4 5 1 3 2 5	104	44%	13%	4.51	3.80	4.32
Garza,Matt	2006	9		0 4 3 5 0 0 3 1 0	89	22%	56%	5.76	4.20	7.36
Glavine,Tom	2004	33	3 3 4 3 5 3 3 3 3 3 4 3 4 3 2 2	3 5 2 1 2 1 4 2 1 3 1 3 2 4	103	27%	12%	3.61	3.72	4.50
	2005	33	3 3 5 5 0 0 2 4 2 2 4 3 5 2 0 2 1 1	3 4 3 4 2 3 3 3 4 4 3 3 5 5	99	36%	18%	3.54	4.03	4.52
	2006	32	4 5 5 3 4 3 5 2 3 5 3 3 0 0 4 3 2 3	3 2 1 0 3 3 4 3 3 5 5 3 4 4	102	38%	13%	3.82	3.52	4.41
Gobble,Jimmy	2004	24	3 1 2 4 3 0 4 3 0 4 3 3 3 0 0 3	4 0 0 3 4 3 4 1	92	25%	33%	5.35	4.83	5.13
	2005	4		0 0 0 1	70	0%	100%	5.75	4.84	15.00
	2006	6	0 2 0	3 0 4	79	17%	50%	5.14	3.37	6.90
Gonzalez,Edgar	2006	5	4 4	4 4 3	94	80%	0%	4.17	3.54	2.69
Gonzalez,Enrique	2006	18	5 5 4 1 0 4 0	3 4 3 2 4 4 3 0 2 4 2	91	44%	22%	5.67	3.80	4.56

164

PQS PITCHING LOGS

Pitcher	Year	No.	FIRST HALF	SECOND HALF	PC	DOM	DIS	ERA	xERA	qERA
Gonzalez,Geremi	2004	8	0 1 0 3 5 0 0 3		89	13%	63%	7.01	7.19	8.46
	2005	3	3 4 0		92	33%	33%	6.11	4.44	5.08
	2006	4	3 0 1 3		85	0%	50%	5.79	4.12	7.46
Gorzelanny,Tom	2006	11	3 0	0 4 5 5 4 5 0 2 3	92	45%	27%	3.79	3.83	4.67
Greinke,Zack	2004	24	2 4 4 5 3 4 3 4 3	4 0 3 3 5 1 4 5 2 5 2 5 4 5 3	95	54%	8%	3.97	4.27	3.85
	2005	33	0 4 2 5 0 4 3 4 3 2 2 0 0 3 3 3 1 1	2 4 0 5 2 0 5 4 2 0 1 3 3 4 5 0	94	27%	33%	5.80	4.22	5.13
Guzman,Angel	2006	10	2 3 0 0	0 5 0 0 0 0	87	10%	70%	7.39	3.95	9.84
Halladay,Roy	2004	21	3 4 4 4 3 3 3 2 5 2 5 4 3 5 1 5 3	0 0 0 4	98	43%	19%	4.20	4.21	4.44
	2005	19	4 3 5 2 3 5 2 4 5 4 3 5 5 5 4 4 5 5 5 0		101	68%	5%	2.42	2.64	3.38
	2006	32	3 3 2 2 2 4 4 4 5 3 4 3 4 4 3 4 4 5	2 3 4 3 4 3 4 4 4 4 5 0 4 0	95	56%	9%	3.19	2.88	3.68
Halsey,Brad	2004	7	3 0 4 0	0 0 2	85	14%	57%	6.47	5.98	7.77
	2005	26	5 3 3 3 3 2 0 4 3 5 2 4 0 2 3 1 3	4 3 4 3 1 3 0 2 2	90	23%	19%	4.61	4.21	4.63
	2006	7	2 1 0 3 1 0	3	89	0%	57%	4.67	4.48	8.24
Hamels,Cole	2006	23	3 4 2 3 0 5 1 0 3	2 2 5 5 5 5 4 0 3 4 0 5 5 4	95	48%	22%	4.08	2.98	4.53
Hammel,Jason	2006	9	0 3	2 1 4 0 0 0 3	89	11%	56%	7.77	4.30	7.77
Hampton,Mike	2004	29	0 0 3 2 4 2 4 3 2 3 0 3 1 3 1 2 4	4 3 5 0 1 3 0 3 3 0 4 4	94	24%	31%	4.29	4.75	5.21
	2005	12	2 4 3 3 4 3 4 0 0	0 1 0	85	25%	42%	3.52	4.12	5.40
Harang,Aaron	2004	28	5 2 3 4 0 3 4 5 2 0 3 4 5 5	3 2 2 4 4 3 4 4 2 0 0 4 3 3	97	43%	14%	4.86	4.97	4.32
	2005	32	4 2 5 4 3 4 5 3 5 5 3 5 0 3 4 3 5	5 3 2 4 3 2 3 2 4 5 3 4 4 3 2 3	107	50%	3%	3.84	3.56	3.47
	2006	34	2 4 4 0 4 5 5 3 0 5 4 5 2 3 4 4 4 2 4	5 0 5 4 3 3 3 5 2 4 4 3 3 2 4	106	56%	9%	3.76	3.06	3.68
Harden,Rich	2004	31	0 5 3 5 4 5 3 4 3 5 3 5 0 3 1	4 5 3 5 3 2 4 2 4 5 0 4 5 5 4	102	55%	13%	4.00	3.65	3.97
	2005	19	4 5 5 3 5 4 0 4 4 4 3	5 5 3 3 5 4 5 5	99	74%	5%	2.53	3.01	3.25
	2006	9	2 5 4 3 0 0	0 4 0	89	33%	44%	4.24	3.05	5.29
Haren,Dan	2004	5	0	3 3 4 3	89	20%	20%	4.50	3.82	4.75
	2005	34	5 3 4 0 5 0 0 1 2 4 4 4 4 5 5 3 3 4 2	4 1 3 3 5 4 2 3 3 4 0 5 5 3 5	99	50%	18%	3.73	3.35	4.37
	2006	34	3 3 4 3 4 2 5 4 3 5 4 5 3 4 5 1 3 5 3	3 4 4 4 5 5 4 4 2 5 3 2 5 0 3 3	103	53%	6%	4.12	3.12	3.85
Heilman,Aaron	2004	5		0 4 4 3 4	89	60%	20%	5.46	4.45	3.95
	2005	7	2 5 0 5 4 4 2		90	57%	14%	3.17	2.98	3.97
Hendrickson,Mark	2004	30	3 2 0 4 5 2 2 3 0 3 3 4 3 0 0 4 0	4 4 4 0 3 0 0 0 3 4 3 5 5	94	33%	30%	4.82	4.79	5.08
	2005	31	3 2 3 2 2 2 1 2 0 2 2 2 0 3 0	1 0 0 4 2 1 2 5 4 5 3 2 2 4 3	91	16%	26%	5.91	4.25	5.03
	2006	25	4 5 2 3 4 2 2 1 3 3 5 2 4 1 3	4 1 3 3 5 2 0 5 0 0	98	32%	24%	4.21	3.93	4.71
Hennessey,Brad	2004	7		0 2 5 0 0 3 0	90	14%	57%	5.01	5.07	7.77
	2005	21	4 4 2 0 0 4	3 0 5 3 0 0 3 2 4 2 2 0 4 3 3	94	29%	29%	4.65	4.40	4.93
	2006	12	3 2 3 1 2 4	3 0 2 2 0 0	80	8%	33%	4.26	4.35	5.45
Hensley,Clay	2006	29	0 2 3 3 1 4 3 4 2 0 3 1 0 4 4 2	3 3 4 4 3 3 5 1 4 5 2 4 5	94	38%	21%	3.71	3.57	4.64
Hernandez,Felix	2005	12		4 5 5 5 3 5 4 0 5 4 4	102	83%	8%	2.68	2.54	3.00
	2006	31	3 0 2 5 1 3 5 0 3 5 4 5 5 3 3 4 5	2 5 4 3 4 3 4 0 4 3 3 3 4 5	99	48%	13%	4.52	2.80	4.28
Hernandez,Livan	2004	35	5 4 2 5 5 2 5 5 5 4 3 4 2 3 3 4 4 0	0 5 4 4 3 5 4 4 2 3 2 3 4 4 5	112	57%	6%	3.60	3.52	3.68
	2005	34	0 4 3 1 2 3 3 3 3 5 4 5 3 3 4 2 3 3 1 2	4 4 4 3 1 3 3 0 3 2 4 2 1 4 5	114	32%	18%	3.99	3.22	4.60
	2006	34	4 4 2 3 3 3 2 2 2 3 5 2 3 2 3 0 3 3 0	3 3 5 4 5 3 3 4 3 4 1 3 3	103	26%	9%	4.83	4.24	4.48
Hernandez,Orlando	2004	15	3	3 5 0 2 5 4 3 5 5 4 0 4 0	95	53%	20%	3.31	3.64	4.50
	2005	22	5 1 3 3 4 3 3 0 4 4 0	3 3 5 4 5 4 2 5 0 0	100	41%	23%	5.13	4.14	4.56
	2006	29	3 0 3 4 5 0 1 0 5 4 3 3 0 4 0 4 5	0 4 5 4 4 0 5 3 5 5 5 3	98	52%	28%	4.66	3.32	4.61
Hernandez,Runelvys	2005	29	3 2 2 3 4 3 2 3 0 5 3 4 3 4 2 5 2 4 3	3 3 2 3 0 4 0 0 0 3 1	88	21%	21%	5.54	4.76	4.75
	2006	21	4 3 0 1 0 2 0	5 1 0 0 2 0 4 3 2 1 0 0 0	90	14%	57%	6.48	4.77	7.77
Hill,Rich	2006	16	0 3 3 0	0 5 5 0 4 4 5 5 3 5 3 5	101	50%	25%	4.17	3.58	4.61
Hill,Shawn	2006	6	3 2 3 2 1 2		96	0%	17%	4.66	4.08	4.69
Hirsh,Jason	2006	9		0 3 0 3 5 4 5 0 0	86	33%	44%	6.04	4.68	5.29
Howell,J.P.	2005	15	4 3 1 0 2 0	0 4 3 5 4 0 0 4 5	86	40%	40%	6.23	3.93	5.21
	2006	8		0 0 5 3 0 1 3 3	89	13%	50%	5.10	3.42	7.08
Hudson,Luke	2004	9		2 4 5 0 4 5 0 4 3	93	56%	22%	2.43	2.80	4.23
	2005	16	2 3 2 0 0 0	0 4 3 5 2 0 4 4 0 0	82	25%	44%	6.41	4.84	5.40
	2006	15	2	3 4 4 3 2 0 3 2 5 4 3 2 4 4	95	40%	7%	5.12	3.65	4.11
Hudson,Tim	2004	27	2 4 5 4 3 3 4 3 3 0 4 5 2 1	3 3 4 3 4 0 3 4 3 3 5	102	37%	11%	3.54	3.50	4.41
	2005	29	1 5 5 3 2 4 0 4 1 3 3 3 0 0	4 3 4 5 3 4 3 3 4 2 2 3 3 5	100	34%	17%	3.52	3.58	4.60
	2006	35	0 0 2 4 3 3 2 5 4 3 3 5 2 3 5 3 0 0 4	0 2 2 1 5 5 2 3 4 2 3 5 1 5 2 3	98	31%	20%	4.86	3.46	4.71
Jackson,Edwin	2004	5	3 0 3	0 0	71	0%	60%	7.44	7.32	9.02
	2005	6		0 3 2 0 2 2	88	0%	33%	6.38	5.65	5.53
Jackson,Zach	2006	7	3 3 0 2 1 2	2	92	0%	29%	5.40	4.12	5.18
James,Chuck	2006	18	5 3 1	3 4 0 2 5 4 4 3 5 3 5 5 0 1 5	99	50%	22%	3.78	3.95	4.50
Janssen,Casey	2006	17	0 3 4 4 4 3 1 3 5 0 0 2 3 0	0 3 0	87	24%	41%	5.07	3.71	5.50
Jennings,Jason	2004	33	0 3 4 2 1 1 3 2 4 4 2 3 3 5 3 0 4	2 1 5 2 2 0 5 2 4 3 2 4 4 5	101	39%	18%	5.51	5.70	4.52
	2005	20	0 4 3 3 4 2 0 3 0 3 3 2 2 4 5 5 3 3	5 4	99	35%	15%	5.02	4.31	4.52
	2006	32	5 3 2 2 2 3 5 2 2 4 5 2 2 5 4 4 5 5	4 2 4 4 5 4 3 4 2 3 5 1 1 1	103	50%	9%	3.78	3.81	3.85
Johnson,Jason	2004	33	3 0 0 1 3 4 0 1 4 5 0 3 5 0 5 4 3 4 5	5 3 3 2 1 3 0 3 2 0 2 0 4 3	95	30%	33%	5.14	4.78	5.08
	2005	33	4 0 4 3 0 4 1 3 5 3 5 3 0 2 1 4 0 3	3 0 2 3 4 2 3 1 1 3 3 3 3 3 5	91	24%	21%	4.54	4.02	4.75
	2006	20	4 3 4 3 2 0 3 3 0 4 3 3 0 1 0 0	1 4 3 0	87	20%	40%	6.10	3.89	5.50
Johnson,Josh	2006	24	3 5 3 4 5 5 4 4 2 4 3 3	2 5 4 5 0 5 3 5 4 5 0 4	99	63%	8%	3.10	3.37	3.50
Johnson,Randy	2004	35	5 3 5 5 5 5 5 5 5 4 4 4 5 5 5 5 3	5 5 5 5 5 5 5 4 5 4 5 3 5 4	104	91%	0%	2.61	1.86	2.39
	2005	34	5 4 4 4 5 5 5 5 4 4 5 5 0 5 1 5 4	3 5 4 0 5 3 5 5 4 5 0 5 4 4	101	74%	12%	3.80	3.05	3.51
	2006	33	4 5 4 0 4 1 3 0 3 1 2 4 5 0 5 5 4 4	5 5 4 0 5 4 3 3 4 4 3 3	99	58%	18%	5.00	3.34	4.10
Karstens,Jeff	2006	6		0 3 3 2 2 4	86	17%	17%	3.80	4.51	4.65
Kazmir,Scott	2004	7		3 0 3 5 0 0 4	83	29%	43%	5.71	4.93	5.40
	2005	32	2 0 2 4 4 4 4 0 2 4 3 4 0 0 4 4 5 0	4 5 5 4 5 5 0 1 5 5 4 1 4	103	59%	25%	3.77	3.87	4.39
	2006	24	0 3 4 4 1 5 3 5 5 5 3 0 4 3 5 2 5 3	4 5 4 4 5	101	58%	13%	3.24	2.84	3.97
Kennedy,Joe	2004	27	4 5 5 4 2 5 3 3 5 2 4 0 3 2 4 2 4	2 0 3 5 4 2 4 4 4 3	93	52%	7%	3.66	4.22	3.85
	2005	24	1 0 2 2 3 2 1 4 2 2 1 1 2 5 2 2	4 2 5 2 4 0 0 4	95	25%	29%	6.03	4.37	4.93
Keppel,Bobby	2006	6	3 3 1 0 0 0		78	0%	67%	5.50	4.27	9.80
Kim,Byung-Hyun	2005	22	3 1 5 5 0 3 3 5	2 5 4 3 1 0 4 5 5 4 0 2 0	97	41%	27%	4.86	4.19	4.74
	2006	27	5 5 0 4 3 2 1 3 0 4 5 0 0	5 0 5 4 1 4 0 3 0 2 4 4 4 0	94	44%	37%	5.57	3.57	5.07

PQS PITCHING LOGS

Pitcher	Year	No.	FIRST HALF	SECOND HALF	PC	DOM	DIS	ERA	xERA	qERA
Kim,Sun-Woo	2004	17	4 3 0 0 4 0 0	0 0 2 4 0 2 4 0 5 0	81	29%	53%	4.88	4.90	6.56
	2005	10	3 0	0 4 2 5 4 2 4 0	86	40%	30%	4.93	3.81	4.92
Koronka,John	2006	23	2 5 3 4 1 4 2 0 3 3 3 0 3 0 2 3 4 2 3	0 3 3 0 0	88	17%	30%	5.69	4.37	5.29
Kuo,Hong-Chih	2006	5		5 4 3 5 3	92	60%	0%	4.22	2.98	3.29
Lackey,John	2004	32	0 2 2 3 5 4 3 3 1 0 4 5 4 4 2 5 3	3 3 5 2 3 2 3 3 0 0 3 2 5 4 3 0	100	31%	16%	4.68	4.52	4.60
	2005	33	0 3 3 3 2 5 3 2 5 5 2 4 2 5 5 3 3 4	5 4 5 4 5 4 3 4 4 3 4 3 2 5 4	106	55%	3%	3.44	3.26	3.38
	2006	33	0 5 4 3 4 3 4 4 3 4 5 3 0 5 3 4 5 5	5 0 5 4 0 4 2 0 4 3 4 5 0 5 5	106	61%	18%	3.56	3.25	3.83
Lawrence,Brian	2004	34	2 3 2 1 0 2 5 4 4 1 5 4 4 4 3 5 4 3 3 0	2 4 3 4 0 2 4 4 0 3 3 4 5 0 0	89	41%	24%	4.12	4.63	4.56
	2005	33	5 0 4 0 5 2 3 3 2 4 0 4 4 4 5 3 4 3	3 4 5 1 3 0 2 4 4 0 4 0 0 0 4	89	45%	27%	4.84	4.01	4.67
Ledezma,Wil	2004	8		0 3 4 4 2 0 2 4	79	38%	25%	4.41	3.91	4.82
	2005	10	3 2 2 1 1 3 3 0 0 0		94	0%	50%	7.13	4.85	7.46
	2006	7		3 3 3 0 0 3 3	78	0%	29%	3.58	4.11	5.18
Lee,Cliff	2004	33	0 3 3 4 4 5 5 3 5 4 3 2 0 5 4 3 5 4	5 0 0 0 3 5 0 4 1 0 3 0 3 5 4	96	45%	27%	5.43	5.18	4.67
	2005	32	0 4 5 5 1 1 5 3 4 4 3 5 4 2 4 2 1 5	4 3 4 4 2 4 4 5 5 4 4 4 3 4 4	97	66%	13%	3.79	3.84	3.61
	2006	33	2 5 5 3 4 3 2 3 4 1 0 4 4 3 3 4 3 2	3 2 0 4 3 4 3 5 1 4 3 0 1 4 4	102	39%	18%	4.40	4.13	4.52
Lester,Jon	2006	15	0 4 5 3 2 3	3 3 3 3 3 2 2 0 1	101	13%	20%	4.76	4.15	4.79
Lidle,Cory	2004	34	3 4 3 3 1 5 5 4 0 4 3 5 0 1 5 4 3 3 4	5 0 1 1 4 3 0 2 5 4 1 3 4 4 2	92	44%	26%	4.90	4.40	4.74
	2005	31	2 2 3 3 3 5 5 4 5 1 0 4 3 3 4 5 5	0 0 1 2 5 3 2 0 3 3 3 3 5	90	32%	19%	4.54	3.45	4.60
	2006	30	3 4 4 5 5 4 0 5 4 3 3 3 3 5 0 3 3 5	1 3 4 5 0 3 4 0 5 0 0 4	92	47%	23%	4.85	3.43	4.53
Lieber,Jon	2004	27	4 3 5 4 4 0 2 3 3 0 3 5 4	4 2 4 0 4 4 3 4 4 3 3	94	52%	11%	4.34	4.77	4.23
	2005	35	2 3 4 3 2 5 5 1 0 4 3 3 4 3 4 3 3 2 0 0 4	3 5 4 0 5 5 5 3 5 5 4 4 3 5 4 5	89	51%	14%	4.21	3.43	4.23
	2006	27	3 0 3 5 3 4 2 4 2 1 0 4	1 2 3 0 5 4 4 1 4 2 2 0 5 2	92	37%	26%	4.93	3.48	4.82
Lilly,Ted	2004	32	2 3 2 5 2 3 3 4 4 3 5 5 5 0 3 3 4	3 5 3 4 3 4 5 3 3 3 5 3 0	103	38%	6%	4.06	3.93	4.29
	2005	25	3 3 0 3 3 0 0 5 3 0 3 1 5 5 0 2 5	5 1 0 0 2 5 0 3	86	24%	40%	5.57	4.31	5.50
	2006	32	0 5 2 2 4 5 2 0 0 3 0 4 4 5 5 5 5 3	3 5 3 1 3 2 0 3 4 4 5 4 4 4	100	50%	19%	4.31	3.68	4.37
Lima,Jose	2004	24	1 0 2 5 4 4 3 0 1 5 5	2 3 3 4 4 3 5 0 4 4 4 2 0 2	89	42%	25%	4.07	4.67	4.74
	2005	32	0 0 3 0 3 1 1 2 0 3 0 0 3 5 0 0 2 3	2 3 4 2 0 4 1 2 1 2 0 0 0 4	90	13%	50%	7.01	4.90	7.08
	2006	4	2 0 0 0		92	0%	75%	9.87	4.58	11.36
Liriano,Francisco	2006	16	3 4 4 2 5 5 5 4 5 5	3 5 4 5 0 0	89	69%	13%	2.16	2.03	3.61
Loaiza,Esteban	2004	27	3 1 4 4 1 1 2 4 2 5 3 2 3 4 0 3 2 1	4 2 3 3 1 0 0 3	105	22%	30%	5.70	5.80	5.21
	2005	34	3 4 4 4 5 2 3 4 4 3 3 5 3 0 5 4 5 4	4 3 4 3 3 3 2 4 4 0 5 4 5 5 5 4	98	59%	6%	3.77	3.43	3.68
	2006	26	0 0 4 0 5 3 0 4 3 1	2 3 0 1 3 3 4 5 5 4 4 3 5 4 2 0	92	38%	31%	4.89	3.76	5.00
Loewen,Adam	2006	19	2 2 2 0 3	3 2 4 4 0 3 5 1 3 5 1 3 4 3	97	26%	21%	5.37	3.60	4.73
Loe,Kameron	2005	8		4 4 3 2 1 0 3 1	91	25%	38%	3.42	3.81	5.27
	2006	15	3 3 4 0 2 4 2 4 1 3 1 3 0 3 0		86	20%	33%	5.86	4.14	5.21
Lohse,Kyle	2004	34	0 2 3 1 2 2 0 3 3 2 5 4 4 2 2 2 5	1 2 2 0 3 3 1 4 2 0 0 2 4 2 2 0	98	18%	26%	5.34	5.82	5.03
	2005	30	1 4 2 0 4 2 3 4 2 2 4 0 3 5 2	2 2 0 1 3 5 1 3 1 4 0 3 2 4 2	95	27%	27%	4.19	4.18	4.93
	2006	19	0 3 0 4 1 0 4 0	4 5 5 3 2 3 5 0 3 0 4	89	37%	37%	5.83	3.68	5.13
Lopez,Rodrigo	2004	23	0 1 4 3 2 5 5 2 2	2 2 0 5 5 1 2 4 5 2 3 4 5 4	98	43%	17%	3.60	4.03	4.44
	2005	35	3 5 3 5 0 2 0 3 2 4 4 0 2 5 2 4 3 0 5	2 4 4 0 4 1 3 0 5 0 3 3 1 4 0 3	94	34%	29%	4.91	4.15	4.90
	2006	29	3 1 4 0 4 2 3 3 0 1 4 2 2 5 0 5 3 0 3	3 0 3 4 3 4 3 4 3 4	97	31%	24%	5.90	3.70	4.71
Lowe,Derek	2004	33	2 0 3 3 1 2 2 0 3 1 4 4 3 5 0 0 4	0 1 3 2 2 3 5 1 5 5 3 5 0 3 0 0	93	21%	36%	5.23	5.15	5.36
	2005	35	4 0 4 3 4 4 5 4 2 4 4 2 3 4 3 3 0 2	0 5 4 2 5 2 3 0 4 5 5 4 4 0 4 3	95	49%	14%	3.61	3.22	4.28
	2006	34	1 3 4 5 4 3 5 3 3 5 4 4 3 3 1 3 3 1 1 0	4 0 4 3 5 4 3 5 0 1 3 2 5 3 4	96	38%	24%	3.63	3.06	4.64
Lowry,Noah	2004	14	0 3 5	5 4 0 5 3 2 2 4 3 5 3	95	43%	14%	3.82	3.89	4.32
	2005	33	3 2 4 3 0 4 4 0 4 5 0 3 3 1 4 4 4 4	5 5 4 5 5 5 4 5 3 3 2 2 5	107	58%	12%	3.79	3.69	3.97
	2006	27	0 3 1 3 2 5 2 3 0 2 4 3 2	0 4 4 1 4 4 3 4 3 0 0 0 3 4	97	30%	30%	4.74	4.30	5.08
Maddux,Greg	2004	33	2 0 3 5 2 5 5 4 4 1 2 5 5 4 3 0 3 3	4 3 5 2 4 5 4 5 4 3 4 2 3	89	52%	9%	4.03	4.20	3.85
	2005	35	2 0 4 4 3 5 2 3 4 4 4 0 2 4 2 4 4	5 2 3 0 5 3 5 2 4 4 3 3 4 4 3 2	89	46%	9%	4.24	3.35	3.98
	2006	34	3 5 5 4 4 3 0 4 1 4 2 1 2 3 4 4 2 4	4 4 4 5 3 3 4 5 1 3 1 3 3 3 3 4	82	47%	15%	4.20	3.28	4.40
Madson,Ryan	2006	17	3 2 0 2 2 2 3 2 3 2 3 0 5 2	2 0 4	90	12%	18%	5.69	3.85	4.66
Maholm,Paul	2005	6		3 3 4 5 1 4	102	50%	17%	2.19	3.62	4.37
	2006	30	3 1 4 0 4 2 1 5 4 2 3 3 3 2 0 0 4 2 0	3 5 4 4 4 2 3 2 2 3 5 3	97	33%	17%	4.76	3.78	4.60
Maine,John	2005	8		3 0 3 3 2 0 0 0	79	0%	50%	6.30	4.77	7.46
	2006	15	3 0 3	4 5 4 3 4 2 3 3 1 5 3 3	100	33%	13%	3.60	3.56	4.49
Marcum,Shaun	2006	14		4 3 0 0 3 1 0 4 3 3 0 0 5 0	88	21%	50%	5.06	4.12	6.74
Marmol,Carlos	2006	13	5 4 1 5 0 4	4 0 3 1 1 2 0	95	38%	46%	6.08	5.03	5.75
Maroth,Mike	2004	33	2 4 4 2 3 4 0 2 2 4 5 2 3 3 1 2 3	5 3 3 3 1 2 3 5 2 4 3 2 4	101	30%	12%	4.31	4.70	4.49
	2005	34	0 3 4 4 4 3 4 1 1 0 2 3 4 1 3 2 4 3	2 3 0 3 1 3 4 0 5 5 3 1 3 3 3	96	29%	26%	4.74	3.98	4.93
	2006	9	1 5 3 2 4 2 3 4 0		85	33%	22%	4.19	4.34	4.71
Marquis,Jason	2004	32	3 2 4 3 4 3 3 1 0 4 3 4 4 3 5 2	2 3 5 1 5 2 5 3 3 3 3 4 0	104	34%	13%	3.71	4.60	4.49
	2005	32	4 5 4 3 3 3 3 0 2 4 2 3 1 0 3 5 5	3 0 3 2 1 2 2 0 4 4 4 3 3 3	100	28%	19%	4.13	4.10	4.62
	2006	33	3 4 4 1 1 1 1 3 2 4 2 3 2 3 2 3 4 4	4 2 4 0 2 0 4 3 3 1 4 3 0 1 0	93	27%	30%	6.02	4.40	5.13
Marshall,Sean	2006	24	0 3 3 5 4 5 0 4 0 2 3 4 0 0 0 4 3	2 0 1 0 0 0 3	86	25%	46%	5.59	4.14	5.98
Martinez,Pedro	2004	33	4 5 1 5 5 0 5 5 5 5 3 3 5 5 5 3 4 5	5 4 4 5 5 3 5 5 5 5 1 3 3	106	73%	9%	3.90	3.49	3.25
	2005	31	5 5 5 5 5 5 5 5 4 4 4 3 3 4 5	5 3 5 4 2 4 5 4 3 5 5 1	98	77%	3%	2.82	3.02	2.84
	2006	23	4 4 5 5 5 5 5 4 5 5 5 2 4 4 4 0	3 5 2 0 0 4 0	92	70%	17%	4.48	2.92	3.63
Mateo,Juan	2006	10		1 3 3 2 0 0 5 0 3 0	78	10%	50%	5.32	3.91	7.08
Mathieson,Scott	2006	8	4 0 4	2 0 0 0 0	75	25%	63%	7.47	4.17	7.72
Mays,Joe	2005	26	3 4 2 1 3 3 4 2 3 3 1 0 0 4 3 0	5 0 2 5 0 1 2 0 0 3	86	19%	38%	5.65	4.45	5.45
	2006	10	0 0 2 0 0 0 4 1 2	0	80	10%	70%	8.70	4.94	9.84
McCarthy,Brandon	2005	10	4 1 0 5 0	4 5 4 2 3	95	50%	30%	4.03	3.72	4.71
McClung,Seth	2005	17	4 5 3	5 3 4 1 0 3 5 4 0 5 0 1 0 4	94	47%	35%	6.60	4.38	4.98
	2006	15	0 2 2 0 3 3 2 5 3 2 1 1 0 0 0		98	7%	47%	6.29	5.18	6.53
McGowan,Dustin	2005	7		4 2 3 0 0 2 0	89	14%	43%	6.39	3.92	5.70
	2006	3		0 0 0	62	0%	100%	7.24	5.18	15.00
Meche,Gil	2004	23	4 2 2 0 4 3 0 4 0 0	3 4 4 4 3 2 4 4 2 1 3 3	101	39%	22%	5.02	5.18	4.64
	2005	26	0 0 4 2 4 4 3 2 4 0 3 2 4 2 0 0 5	3 3 0 0 2 0 3 0	98	23%	35%	5.09	4.79	5.36
	2006	32	4 0 6 2 3 5 2 5 2 5 5 1 5 2 5 4 4 3 5	4 5 0 2 1 0 1 5 5 2 4 2 0 4	103	50%	22%	4.48	3.63	4.50
Michalak,Chris	2006	6		0 3 0 0 0 0	72	0%	83%	4.89	4.83	12.14

PQS PITCHING LOGS

Pitcher	Year	No.	FIRST HALF	SECOND HALF	PC	DOM	DIS	ERA	xERA	qERA
Miller, Wade	2004	15	5 3 4 5 4 5 2 2 2 0 0 5 5 3 2		104	47%	13%	3.37	3.85	4.28
	2005	16	4 3 5 0 3 2 3 4 2 2 4 3	2 3 3 0	105	25%	13%	4.95	4.31	4.50
	2006	5		0 3 0 2 0	86	0%	60%	4.57	4.76	9.02
Millwood, Kevin	2004	25	4 4 5 4 4 5 3 2 4 0 5 0 3 4 5 4 4 1	4 5 4 5 0 0 0 0	94	64%	24%	4.85	4.52	3.95
	2005	30	3 4 3 3 5 3 5 0 5 0 4 3 5 3 3	5 2 4 3 4 3 4 5 2 2 3 4 3 5	99	47%	7%	2.86	3.43	3.98
	2006	34	3 4 5 3 3 4 3 0 5 5 2 4 5 4 4 3 4 0	3 5 2 1 4 3 4 4 3 5 5 5 5 4 0 4	97	59%	12%	4.52	3.33	3.97
Milton, Eric	2004	34	3 5 4 1 4 2 1 2 5 5 5 2 0 5 3 0 4 3	5 3 5 2 2 5 2 5 4 2 0 2 5 4 4 4	101	50%	15%	4.75	4.88	4.37
	2005	34	1 0 5 2 1 5 2 0 1 4 0 1 2 1 2 3 5 4 5	3 0 4 5 0 4 2 5 5 0 0 3 0 4 5	93	38%	38%	6.48	4.43	5.13
	2006	26	4 5 0 1 5 4 4 4 5 2 0 0 5 3	5 2 4 3 4 3 3 0 2 0 4 3 0	91	42%	27%	5.19	4.20	4.74
Miner, Zach	2006	16	0 5 3 4 3 3 4	0 0 5 2 3 2 3 0 0	89	25%	31%	4.84	3.69	5.13
Mitre, Sergio	2004	9	4 2 5 0 0 3 3 2 0		85	22%	33%	6.68	6.24	5.21
	2005	7	5 0 0 5 4 1 0		97	43%	57%	5.39	3.72	6.59
	2006	7	5 1 4 3 5 0 0		81	43%	43%	5.71	3.67	5.21
Moehler, Brian	2005	25	0 3 5 5 3 2 5 1 3 3 4 1 3 1 1	3 4 0 0 3 5 0 3 0 0	86	24%	40%	4.55	3.94	5.50
	2006	21	0 3 0 4 0 1 2 4 3 4 0 3 4 0 0	3 1 0 3 0 0	81	19%	52%	6.57	4.21	6.90
Morris, Matt	2004	32	2 3 2 4 2 4 2 4 2 3 5 3 1 4 4 5 4 3	4 0 3 0 3 3 5 4 3 5 0 3 4 0	96	41%	16%	4.72	4.51	4.44
	2005	31	5 4 5 5 1 5 3 5 2 3 4 5 0 4 5 4	3 3 3 2 4 1 5 3 3 0 2 2 4 4 0	93	48%	16%	4.12	3.55	4.40
	2006	33	3 4 2 0 1 4 1 2 3 2 5 4 5 4 3 5 5 2	5 3 0 3 5 1 4 4 3 2 4 3 2 2 0 4	99	45%	18%	4.98	3.76	4.40
Moyer, Jamie	2004	33	0 2 4 0 3 3 4 2 4 5 3 3 5 5 3 0 0 4	3 1 5 2 3 0 1 1 2 3 3 5 1 3	102	27%	27%	5.21	5.39	4.93
	2005	32	4 2 3 4 4 0 0 0 1 3 3 4 4 3 3 0 4 2	3 2 4 3 2 5 1 4 1 4 2 5 2 4	102	38%	22%	4.28	4.36	4.64
	2006	33	3 3 4 2 5 2 4 4 4 3 3 2 4 1 4 4 3 3 3	2 0 3 3 0 1 2 5 4 2 4 3 4 1 3	99	33%	15%	4.30	3.93	4.60
Mulder, Mark	2004	33	4 5 5 4 4 2 2 4 5 5 3 4 3 2 4	4 4 3 1 3 3 3 3 2 4 2 3 0 0 0	100	45%	12%	4.44	4.20	4.28
	2005	32	3 3 3 4 4 5 2 1 4 3 0 3 2 0 3 1 3	3 3 1 2 3 0 4 3 5 3 3 2 0 0	94	19%	25%	3.64	3.72	5.03
	2006	17	4 4 2 4 3 3 3 5 4 3 0 1 0 2 0	0 0	87	29%	35%	7.14	3.90	5.27
Mussina, Mike	2004	27	1 0 4 1 2 4 3 5 2 5 2 3 5 0 3 3 2 3	0 4 4 5 5 5 5 4 2	96	44%	19%	4.60	4.55	4.44
	2005	30	2 2 2 3 2 3 3 5 3 5 0 1 5 4 5 4 4 4	4 5 3 3 0 4 4 5 0 0 5 0	99	47%	20%	4.42	3.59	4.53
	2006	32	4 5 5 5 4 5 3 5 4 4 4 5 3 1 5 0 4	4 5 5 5 4 5 0 3 5 4 0 5	95	75%	3%	3.51	2.97	3.41
Myers, Brett	2004	31	0 4 0 3 5 2 4 2 0 4 3 5 0 2 0 0	0 2 2 5 5 0 3 5 3 3 0 4 0 3 3	90	29%	32%	5.52	5.24	5.13
	2005	34	4 4 4 4 5 4 5 4 3 2 3 5 3 0 0 5 3	3 2 5 5 3 3 4 4 0 5 5 0 4 3 5 5	102	59%	12%	3.72	3.04	3.97
	2006	31	1 3 4 4 5 4 5 4 5 4 2 0 0 4 2	4 5 5 4 2 2 0 5 4 5 4 2 5 5 5	104	65%	13%	3.91	3.02	3.61
Nieve, Fernando	2006	11	0 0 4 1 2 0 4 4 2 5 2		90	36%	36%	4.20	3.87	5.13
Nolasco, Ricky	2006	22	0 3 0 5 5 5 3 3 0 0	4 5 3 0 3 3 2 0 0 4 0 3	87	27%	36%	4.82	3.71	5.27
O'Connor, Mike	2006	20	2 5 3 3 4 4 4 3 3 2 4 3 1 0	0 0 2 0 0 3	83	25%	30%	4.80	4.32	5.13
Ohka, Tomo	2004	15	2 0 0 2 3 5 3 5 4 2 2 0	0 1 2	83	20%	33%	3.42	4.84	5.21
	2005	29	3 3 1 0 4 0 4 3 0 4 2 2 2 1 4	5 2 3 0 5 3 2 3 5 0 5 2 3 2	94	28%	24%	4.05	4.16	4.73
	2006	18	4 0 5 0 4 4	3 5 3 2 0 2 4 1 2 3 0 0	86	33%	33%	4.82	4.15	5.08
Olsen, Scott	2006	31	3 2 2 0 0 5 0 2 4 4 5 5 4 4 4 3	2 5 5 5 4 2 0 4 4 5 3 3 5 0 4	93	55%	16%	4.04	3.25	4.10
Ortiz, Ramon	2004	14	0 2 0 4 1 5 4	3 4 2 3 0 5 1	90	36%	36%	4.43	4.76	5.13
	2005	30	4 0 2 1 4 2 3 5 0 2 2 4 0 3 2	3 5 3 0 3 3 3 5 4 4 4 4 1 2 2	88	33%	20%	5.37	4.28	4.71
	2006	33	2 2 1 4 2 1 2 2 5 5 4 5 5 4 0 3 4 2	1 4 3 1 2 4 0 0 3 3 3 2 1 0 4 0	95	30%	30%	5.57	4.23	5.08
Ortiz, Russ	2004	34	0 4 5 4 0 5 5 0 0 4 5 4 4 4 4 4 5 3 1	4 3 3 3 1 1 2 2 0 3 0 0 2 0 3	102	44%	29%	4.14	4.42	4.74
	2005	22	3 1 5 3 3 0 0 3 1 2 0 3 3 1	2 0 0 1 4 0 1 0	94	9%	55%	6.89	5.59	7.99
	2006	11	3 0 0 0 3 0 0 0	0 0 0	74	0%	82%	8.14	4.84	12.14
Oswalt, Roy	2004	35	3 4 5 4 5 4 2 4 5 2 4 5 0 4 3 5 3 5 4	0 5 5 4 5 3 5 0 3 4 5 4 4 1 4 5	102	69%	11%	3.49	3.43	3.61
	2005	35	2 3 5 5 5 1 3 4 5 3 4 4 4 4 4 3 5 4	4 5 5 3 3 2 4 3 0 4 3 4 4 4	103	66%	6%	2.95	3.19	3.38
	2006	32	5 2 3 5 3 3 3 0 2 5 4 3 4 5 3 4	4 2 2 5 4 5 4 5 5 5 3 4 3 5	101	56%	3%	2.98	2.95	3.38
Padilla, Vicente	2004	20	3 3 5 3 1 5 2 3 4 4	4 4 3 5 1 5 5 1 0 3	89	45%	20%	4.54	4.41	4.53
	2005	27	0 0 2 0 3 3 3 4 2 0 0 0 3	5 4 5 3 4 4 5 4 0 3 1 5 0 3	95	33%	33%	4.71	4.19	5.08
	2006	33	5 2 2 5 1 0 4 5 5 2 4 0 4 5 3 3 4 5	3 4 5 0 5 5 0 3 5 2 3 3 3 2 2	100	45%	15%	4.50	3.45	4.40
Park, Chan Ho	2004	16	5 4 3 0 0 1 4 2	4 3 2 0 1 2 0 3	95	25%	38%	5.48	5.74	5.27
	2005	29	2 5 0 4 4 0 3 5 4 4 2 0 5 0 5 3	1 3 0 0 3 0 3 2 4 2 0 3	97	31%	31%	5.74	4.21	5.08
	2006	21	3 3 3 2 3 4 5 0 3 5 4 3 2 3 4	0 5 3 2 1	101	29%	14%	4.81	3.69	4.50
Patterson, John	2004	19	5 0 4 3	0 0 0 3 3 5 0 5 0 0 3 5 4 4 0	95	37%	42%	5.05	4.67	5.25
	2005	31	5 5 5 4 4 0 2 3 4 5 3 2 3 5 5	4 5 5 5 5 0 3 4 4 0 5 0 4 3 3 1	103	58%	16%	3.13	3.52	4.10
	2006	8	0 4 5 5 4 0 4 0		82	63%	38%	4.43	3.10	4.53
Pauley, David	2006	3	0 2 3		98	0%	33%	7.88	4.24	5.53
Pavano, Carl	2004	31	4 4 1 3 3 4 4 4 4 5 5 4 5 4 3 4	3 0 3 4 3 3 4 4 4 4 4 4	102	61%	6%	3.00	3.21	3.50
	2005	17	4 0 0 4 3 2 2 0 5 3 0 1 3 4 2 4 2		91	29%	29%	4.77	3.85	4.93
Peavy, Jake	2004	27	2 4 3 4 3 4 3 4 5 4 0	2 4 3 5 5 4 5 3 5 3 5 4 5 5 5	99	63%	4%	2.28	3.08	3.29
	2005	30	5 5 5 5 5 5 3 5 5 4 0 3 5 4 2 5 3	5 2 5 5 5 5 4 3 3 4 3 4	105	70%	3%	2.88	2.74	2.99
	2006	32	5 0 5 3 4 3 5 2 5 2 0 3 4 5 4 0	2 0 5 4 3 5 5 5 0 5 2 4 2 5 4	105	59%	13%	4.09	2.96	3.97
Penny, Brad	2004	24	4 5 3 4 2 4 5 5 5 4 2 3 5 4 5 1 2 4	2 3 4 4 0 0	95	58%	13%	3.15	3.29	3.97
	2005	29	3 5 4 0 1 4 4 4 2 3 4 5 3 5 3	0 4 3 1 4 4 4 0 2 5 5 3 0	96	52%	21%	3.91	3.57	4.50
	2006	33	4 5 5 4 3 2 2 5 3 4 0 4 4 5 2 3 5 5	3 3 3 4 3 4 2 0 3 2 2 5 3 3 0	98	42%	9%	4.33	3.39	4.11
Penn, Hayden	2005	8	0 2 2 0 4 0 0	3	84	13%	50%	6.38	5.05	7.08
	2006	6		0 0 0 3 0 0	69	0%	83%	15.10	6.40	12.14
Perez, Odalis	2004	31	2 4 5 2 4 2 4 4 5 5 2 5 5 3 4	2 3 0 4 5 3 3 0 4 3 0 3 3 5	91	48%	10%	3.26	3.53	4.28
	2005	19	1 5 3 1 5 3 3 4 2 3	2 5 3 3 4 5 0 0 0	86	32%	26%	4.57	3.65	4.90
	2006	20	0 1 3 5 0 0 0 0	0 1 5 4 4 0 4 5 3 4 2 0	87	35%	50%	6.20	3.74	6.25
Perez, Oliver	2004	30	2 5 5 3 4 5 0 3 3 4 4 4 5 5 3	5 5 5 4 4 5 5 5 2 5 1 5 4 5	104	73%	7%	2.98	2.87	3.25
	2005	20	4 0 2 0 5 0 0 4 3 3 5 5 2 4 1	0 0 0 4 3	94	35%	40%	5.85	4.59	5.25
	2006	22	4 0 0 3 3 0 0 4 4 5 0 0 4 4 0	3 0 4 4 4 1 0	96	41%	45%	6.55	4.30	5.67
Pettitte, Andy	2004	15	1 4 4 4 5 4 0 4 2 4	3 5 3 3 3	90	53%	13%	3.90	3.25	4.23
	2005	33	4 3 2 5 4 3 3 5 5 5 4 5 4 4 4	4 5 5 5 4 4 5 5 5 4 4 4 3 5	97	82%	0%	2.39	2.93	2.69
	2006	35	0 1 2 5 4 3 2 2 5 3 0 3 2 4 5 4 0 2 2 5	5 1 3 5 4 5 5 3 3 5 3 0 2 2 5	100	40%	17%	4.20	3.18	4.44
Pineiro, Joel	2004	21	0 0 4 3 4 2 4 5 5 4 5 3 4 5 3 3	4 0 5	107	57%	14%	4.69	4.55	3.97
	2005	30	1 2 3 4 3 0 2 0 5 3 4 4 2 1 3	3 3 1 1 2 4 4 2 2 5 3 4 1 4 0	98	30%	27%	5.62	4.10	4.90
	2006	25	2 4 5 2 0 4 5 0 2 0 2 4 1 0 3 4 0 2	4 3 3 0 2 0 0	96	28%	36%	6.36	4.12	5.27
Ponson, Sidney	2004	33	1 3 0 4 3 0 2 4 4 3 0 0 4 0 3 2 2 4	2 3 4 3 5 2 2 4 2 4 2 2 2 2	100	30%	15%	5.31	5.30	4.60
	2005	23	3 0 4 4 2 5 3 0 3 2 2 4 2 4 1 1 0 1	1 3 0 0 0	90	22%	43%	6.23	4.37	5.50
	2006	16	2 4 1 4 2 0 3 3 2 0 3 0 4	4 0 0	82	25%	38%	6.25	4.14	5.27

PQS PITCHING LOGS

Pitcher	Year	No.	FIRST HALF	SECOND HALF	PC	DOM	DIS	ERA	xERA	qERA
Prior,Mark	2004	21	5 0 4 3 4 3 0	0 5 0 5 0 3 4 4 2 4 2 5 4 5	98	52%	24%	4.04	3.98	4.50
	2005	27	5 5 5 2 5 5 4 4 0 4 3 0	5 4 2 5 0 3 3 5 4 3 5 5 3 5 2	105	59%	11%	3.68	3.07	3.97
	2006	9	0 3 3 4	0 2 1 3 0	93	11%	44%	7.21	4.29	5.70
Radke,Brad	2004	34	2 3 4 0 3 4 4 3 4 5 4 3 5 5 4 2 4 4	0 4 4 3 5 5 5 4 2 5 4 4 0 5 1	98	65%	12%	3.49	3.80	3.61
	2005	31	4 3 4 3 2 4 5 2 4 4 4 4 3 3 3 2 2 4 2	4 5 3 3 5 3 2 3 3 3 3 0 4 0	95	42%	6%	4.05	3.68	4.11
	2006	28	2 4 2 2 0 5 1 1 3 1 3 2 1 3 2 5 4 2	5 3 2 0 5 3 4 3 0 2	89	25%	25%	4.32	3.90	4.93
Ramirez,Elizardo	2006	19	4 4 0 4 3 3 5 4 5 3 3 3 3	4 2 5 0 0 0	88	42%	21%	5.37	3.62	4.56
Ramirez,Horacio	2004	9	4 3 3 4 0 3 3 4 1		101	33%	22%	2.40	3.74	4.71
	2005	32	0 1 3 1 3 4 0 2 0 2 3 3 2 1 3 3 0 4	2 3 2 4 1 3 3 5 3 4 2 0 3 2 4	93	19%	28%	4.63	4.29	5.03
	2006	14	4 0 3 4 0 3 4 4 0	2 4 0 3 0	87	36%	36%	4.48	3.99	5.13
Redman,Mark	2004	32	3 4 4 2 3 1 3 2 2 4 3 2 5 5 0 2 0	2 3 2 4 4 0 4 4 0 4 1 0 2 3 2	97	31%	22%	4.71	5.26	4.71
	2005	30	4 5 3 4 2 2 3 4 4 5 0 5 4 3 3 3 0 3 4	0 2 4 2 0 3 3 2 3 2 0 4	91	33%	17%	4.90	3.91	4.60
	2006	29	1 5 0 2 5 3 0 1 3 3 1 3 2 3	2 5 2 0 2 0 0 3 2 4 4 0 3 0 3	95	17%	34%	5.71	4.36	5.29
Reyes,Anthony	2006	17	2 5 5 3 1 3	3 1 3 4 4 0 5 0 4 4 0	85	41%	29%	5.06	3.71	4.74
Rheinecker,John	2006	13	0 4 4 1 0 1 0 4 3	0 0 0 0	82	23%	69%	5.86	3.98	8.60
Robertson,Nate	2004	32	4 5 3 0 0 5 3 3 3 5 4 3 5 2 5 0 4	4 2 3 3 0 0 4 5 5 4 0 3 4 4 3	93	47%	19%	4.91	4.87	4.40
	2005	32	4 2 0 3 2 4 0 4 3 3 3 2 4 5 4 0	3 4 3 2 2 3 3 5 2 3 3 0 3 4 3	92	31%	13%	4.50	3.86	4.49
	2006	32	3 5 0 4 5 5 0 1 4 3 4 3 3 4 3 3 3	3 3 3 4 3 5 3 3 3 3 5 4 4 0	97	38%	13%	3.84	3.55	4.41
Rodriguez,Wandy	2005	22	2 4 0 3 2 3 2 3 0	4 4 3 1 0 2 2 4 5 3 3 0 3	92	23%	23%	5.55	4.12	4.75
	2006	24	1 4 5 5 5 3 2 2 4 0 4 2 0 3 2 4 3 3 1 1	0 3 0 4 2	92	33%	29%	5.64	3.90	4.90
Rogers,Kenny	2004	35	3 4 3 2 2 4 4 3 3 4 1 0 4 5 4 4 3 1 0	4 2 3 1 0 1 3 0 5 3 3 3 0 2 4 3	100	31%	26%	5.07	5.30	4.90
	2005	30	3 2 3 3 3 4 3 4 2 3 3 5 3 4 2 0 4 3	3 4 2 3 5 2 4 3 1 4 3 3 2	100	30%	7%	3.46	4.17	4.48
	2006	33	5 3 3 3 3 4 1 3 4 1 0 5 5 5 3 1 0 2	0 3 0 2 2 4 2 4 3 3 2 2 3 4 0	93	27%	24%	3.84	3.76	4.73
Rusch,Glendon	2004	16	0 5 4 2 2 3 5 4 2 5	3 3 0 5 5 4	100	50%	13%	3.48	3.48	4.23
	2005	19	0 1 4 5 3 5 3 2 3 1	0 4 0 0 4 3 3 3 5	99	32%	32%	4.53	3.98	5.08
	2006	9	0 3 5 0 0 4 0 0 4		84	33%	56%	7.46	4.05	6.91
Saarloos,Kirk	2005	27	4 0 1 2 2 4 2 1 2 2 5 4 2	1 0 4 0 4 3 0 2 4 3 0 2	87	26%	30%	4.18	4.27	5.13
	2006	16	3 0 3 0 3 3 2 2 1 0	3 3 3 0 1 3	93	0%	38%	4.75	4.29	5.72
Sabathia,C.C.	2004	30	5 3 4 4 3 2 5 2 3 5 5 2 4 4 0 0 3	4 5 3 3 5 5 2 1 5 2 5 3 2	104	47%	10%	4.12	3.91	4.28
	2005	31	4 5 4 0 3 2 4 3 4 3 4 5 0 0 3 4 0	3 3 0 3 4 4 4 5 5 5 4 5 2 5	102	55%	16%	4.04	3.34	4.10
	2006	28	0 2 4 5 5 5 4 1 5 4 0 4 3 5	4 0 2 4 5 5 5 4 4 4 5 2 5 1	105	68%	14%	3.22	2.93	3.61
Sanchez,Anibal	2006	17	2 1	4 4 4 0 5 3 3 3 4 5 3 4 4 5 1	99	53%	18%	2.83	3.83	4.37
Santana,Ervin	2005	23	0 5 4 0 4 0 3 0	5 0 5 5 3 4 0 4 0 2 5 3 4 4	98	52%	30%	4.66	4.11	4.71
	2006	33	2 3 2 5 3 0 5 4 0 3 3 5 4 5 2 4 4 4	5 0 4 3 3 0 1 4 3 0 0 3 5 1 3 3	97	39%	21%	4.28	3.75	4.64
Santana,Johan	2004	34	0 4 4 4 4 5 0 5 3 0 5 4 5 5 5 5 5 5 5	5 5 5 4 4 5 5 5 5 5 5 5 5 5 4	101	88%	9%	2.61	2.19	2.88
	2005	33	4 5 4 5 4 5 4 3 0 4 4 4 5 5 5 3 2 1 2	4 3 5 5 3 5 5 5 5 1 5 4 5 5	101	79%	3%	2.88	2.85	2.84
	2006	34	2 3 3 5 5 5 5 5 5 4 4 5 3 5 5 5 5 3 4	5 4 4 1 5 5 5 5 3 5 5 5 5 2 4	102	76%	3%	2.77	2.57	2.84
Santos,Victor	2004	28	4 3 5 2 0 4 3 2 5 0 5 3 3 3	5 4 3 3 0 0 5 3 0 4 0 0 5 0	90	36%	29%	4.97	4.69	4.82
	2005	24	3 4 4 5 4 0 4 0 4 5 3 4 4 2 2 1 2 0	0 2 3 1 0 3 0	94	33%	33%	4.59	4.35	5.08
	2006	19	0 4 0 4 2 5 3 3 2 4 5 3 4 0	2 2 3 3 0	95	32%	21%	5.70	3.88	4.71
Saunders,Joe	2006	13		4 3 5 5 0 2 0 4 4 0 5 4 0	89	54%	31%	4.71	3.61	4.71
Schilling,Curt	2004	32	5 5 5 4 5 5 5 2 5 4 4 4 3 5 3 5 3	5 1 3 5 1 2 5 4 3 4 5 4	107	72%	6%	3.26	3.14	3.25
	2005	11	2 3 4	3 4 2 5 2 5 4 3	105	45%	0%	5.70	3.66	3.68
	2006	31	5 4 5 4 5 4 2 1 5 4 4 3 4 4 4 5 3 5	5 4 4 2 2 4 3 5 4 2 3 5	105	71%	3%	3.97	2.96	2.99
Schmidt,Jason	2004	32	3 0 2 5 5 2 5 5 5 5 4 5 2 3 5 5	5 2 4 4 5 5 0 0 4 5 5 5 2 5	113	69%	9%	3.20	2.39	3.38
	2005	29	5 5 2 5 2 2 0 4 0 0 3 4 5 4 0 3	4 5 5 5 3 4 0 3 3 5 0 3 0	105	45%	24%	4.40	3.79	4.53
	2006	32	3 5 4 3 5 5 4 3 4 5 4 5 4 3 4 5 3 3	3 4 5 5 2 5 3 2 0 4 3 0 2 5	108	56%	6%	3.59	3.50	3.68
Sele,Aaron	2004	24	3 2 4 3 3 5 2 3 0 4 1	0 3 2 3 0 3 0 0 2 0 4	85	17%	33%	5.05	5.62	5.29
	2005	21	1 3 0 5 2 0 0 4 4 4 3 3 2 3 0 0 2	3 0 2 0	93	19%	38%	5.66	5.72	5.45
	2006	15	4 3 4 5 2 5 0 0 5 4 5	3 0 2 0	90	47%	27%	4.53	4.01	4.67
Seo,Jae	2004	21	0 2 3 0 2 3 3 5 0 0 0 3 1 1	5 2 0 4 1 3 0	84	14%	48%	4.91	5.29	6.39
	2005	14	5 2 5	4 5 4 4 2 5 4 3 3 1 5	98	64%	7%	2.60	3.56	3.50
	2006	26	2 4 0 4 4 0 3 4 0 0 1 4	2 0 1 0 3 5 3 0 3 0 2 3 0 2	87	23%	42%	5.33	4.43	5.50
Sheets,Ben	2004	34	0 5 4 5 5 5 4 5 2 5 4 4 5 5 4 5 5	4 3 4 5 4 4 4 5 3 5 5 4 4 5	105	88%	3%	2.70	2.68	2.54
	2005	22	4 4 5 3 4 2 4 4 3 5 5 3	3 4 5 5 5 4 5 5	104	73%	0%	3.34	3.12	2.99
	2006	17	3 5 5 0	5 5 0 5 3 5 4 4 5 4 5 4	92	76%	12%	3.82	2.49	3.41
Shields,Jamie	2006	21	2 4 5 5 4 3 3 2	2 0 4 3 4 5 5 4 3 5 0 3 3	95	48%	10%	4.84	3.31	4.28
Silva,Carlos	2004	33	4 1 3 3 3 4 3 0 0 3 3 3 4 0 1 2 3 1	3 3 2 2 0 3 3 3 3 4 2 3 2 2	88	12%	21%	4.21	5.12	4.79
	2005	27	3 5 3 3 3 3 4 4 1 2 3 4 2 3 4	4 3 4 4 4 4 4 4 2 3 0	85	48%	7%	3.44	3.70	3.98
	2006	31	2 2 2 1 0 3 2 0 3 3 3 5 4 0 0	5 0 3 4 2 2 4 0 1 0 4 3 4 1 0 2	84	23%	35%	5.94	4.15	5.36
Smoltz,John	2005	33	0 4 3 5 2 2 3 4 4 0 3 3 3 4 4 5 5	5 5 4 4 4 5 0 4 4 5 4 5 4	100	64%	6%	3.06	3.26	3.50
	2006	35	2 4 4 2 4 5 5 5 5 5 2 3 3 5 4 0 5 4 5	5 4 3 5 5 5 3 5 5 1 4 0 5 4 5 4	101	74%	9%	3.49	2.86	3.25
Snell,Ian	2006	32	2 0 1 5 5 3 5 0 3 2 3 5 4 5 1 1 2 5	2 5 5 3 4 5 4 3 3 2 2 5 5 2	95	44%	16%	4.74	3.36	4.44
Snyder,Kyle	2006	11	0 3	0 2 1 3 0 5 0 3 0	80	9%	55%	6.56	3.46	7.99
Soler,Alay	2006	8	4 0 5 3 5 3 0 0		98	38%	38%	6.00	4.63	5.13
Sosa,Jorge	2004	8		3 5 3 3 1 5 0 5	98	38%	25%	5.54	5.22	4.82
	2005	20	4 0 2 3 3 2	4 3 3 2 5 1 3 2 3 4 1 4 1 0	85	25%	25%	2.55	4.45	4.93
	2006	13	0 0 0 4 3 2 5 3 4 3 0 2 2		91	23%	31%	5.42	4.15	5.21
Sowers,Jeremy	2006	14	3 4 0	2 4 4 4 2 4 3 5 1 4 1	91	50%	21%	3.57	3.72	4.50
Suppan,Jeff	2004	31	0 4 3 3 0 0 4 4 4 2 2 2 5 5 4	3 2 0 3 4 4 3 2 3 0 0 2 2	98	32%	16%	4.16	4.39	4.60
	2005	32	0 3 2 3 4 2 0 4 2 0 3 3 2 4 0 3 2	4 3 4 3 4 3 1 5 3 5	95	31%	19%	3.57	3.99	4.60
	2006	32	1 3 0 4 3 3 3 3 2 1 2 2 0 3 1 1 0	5 3 3 1 5 2 0 3 4 4 1 4 4 0 3	96	22%	34%	4.12	3.89	5.21
Taubenheim,Ty	2006	7	3 0 4 0 2 4 0		77	29%	43%	4.89	4.16	5.40
Tejeda,Rob	2005	13	4 2 5 0 4 0	4 3 5 4 5 0 3	88	54%	23%	3.59	4.25	4.73
	2006	14	2 0 3 0 0	4 3 0 2 5 4 1 3 1	90	21%	43%	4.28	4.60	5.50
Thompson,Mike	2006	16	3 4 2 0 3 3 2 3 3	2 3 3 1 0 2 0	84	6%	25%	4.99	4.22	5.13
Thomson,John	2004	33	3 5 3 4 2 4 0 5 3 4 3 0 3 2 0 3 2 2	3 3 5 4 0 5 4 3 4 4 5 4 0	89	45%	15%	3.73	4.10	4.40
	2005	17	4 3 3 5 4 4 0 0	4 0 0 2 4 2 5 4 1	92	47%	29%	4.49	4.23	4.67
	2006	15	3 5 3 4 1 3 2 1 3 0 0 0 3 0 0		82	13%	47%	4.82	4.15	6.39
Tomko,Brett	2004	31	0 4 0 2 2 1 4 3 2 3 0 1 3 4 2 4	2 4 1 2 3 3 1 4 4 5 5 5 2 0 4	101	35%	26%	4.04	3.99	4.82
	2005	30	3 0 2 2 5 3 4 3 4 4 0 3 0 3	5 2 5 3 3 2 0 4 5 4 3 0 4	100	40%	17%	4.50	4.12	4.44
	2006	15	3 2 3 4 4 5 3 4 4 0 0 0 0 1 3		95	33%	33%	4.73	3.82	5.08

PQS PITCHING LOGS

Pitcher	Year	No.	FIRST HALF	SECOND HALF	PC	DOM	DIS	ERA	xERA	qERA
Towers,Josh	2004	21	0 0 3 0 4 4 0 3	4 4 4 0 4 4 2 0 2 0 0 0 3	79	33%	43%	5.12	5.55	5.29
	2005	33	5 5 0 3 5 4 4 2 0 3 0 2 2 2 4 5 0 4	0 4 4 4 4 2 4 3 4 4 3 1 4 4	90	55%	18%	3.72	3.82	4.10
	2006	12	0 3 0 1 0 1 0 4 1 0 3 0		73	8%	75%	8.42	4.36	10.91
Traber,Billy	2006	8	2 0	4 2 5 0 0 0 0	74	25%	50%	6.44	4.03	6.56
Trachsel,Steve	2004	33	0 3 4 4 2 3 4 3 4 4 0 1 3 4 4 2 4 3	4 1 4 2 2 3 4 0 3 2 2 2 3 5 4	101	39%	15%	4.01	4.38	4.52
	2005	6		5 2 1 3 5 0	94	33%	33%	4.14	3.93	5.08
	2006	30	5 3 3 3 0 4 0 3 1 3 4 0 2 3 0 2 2	3 0 0 0 2 4 5 0 4 0 0 0 4 1	94	23%	40%	4.97	4.67	5.50
Vargas,Claudio	2004	14	4 4 0 0 2 4 3 3 5 0 2 0 0	0	88	29%	43%	5.26	5.58	5.40
	2005	23	4 0 0 0 2 2 5 2 5	2 5 5 5 3 5 5 3 1 2 4 4 2 2	96	43%	17%	5.25	4.15	4.44
	2006	30	5 0 0 4 3 5 0 5 1 2 3 3 5 5 4 0	0 5 5 5 0 5 5 5 0 2 5 4 3 3 5	95	50%	27%	4.83	3.76	4.61
Vargas,Jason	2005	13		3 4 4 3 5 1 1 3 0 3 4 4 0	89	38%	31%	4.06	4.20	5.00
	2006	5	2 3 0 3 0		94	0%	40%	7.33	5.56	5.90
Vazquez,Javier	2004	32	4 2 5 5 4 2 3 5 5 2 4 5 5 3 2 3 2 2	0 4 3 2 4 1 3 0 5 0 4 2 0 2	100	41%	16%	4.91	4.46	4.44
	2005	33	0 4 4 4 4 5 5 5 5 5 3 0 2 4 3 4 4 5	4 0 4 4 3 2 0 5 5 2 3 4 5 5 3	101	61%	12%	4.43	3.14	3.71
	2006	32	5 4 5 3 5 5 2 2 3 4 4 3 2 1 4 3	4 3 1 5 2 1 4 3 2 5 5 5 5 5 0	103	50%	13%	4.84	3.22	4.23
Verlander,Justin	2006	30	5 0 4 3 4 2 2 4 5 5 2 3 3 2 3 5 4	5 4 5 3 2 3 3 0 4 4 0 0 2	99	43%	13%	3.63	3.61	4.32
Villanueva,Carlos	2006	6	5 1 3	5 3 3	98	33%	17%	3.69	3.19	4.60
Volquez,Edinson	2006	8		4 3 0 0 0 2 0 0	81	13%	63%	7.29	5.14	8.46
Waechter,Doug	2004	14	5 3 1 4 0 2 0 3 0	0 0 3 0 3	85	14%	50%	6.03	5.84	7.08
	2005	25	2 1 3 1 3 0 2 3 2 4 0 2	4 1 3 3 4 3 4 2 4 0 2 3 0	87	20%	28%	5.62	4.30	4.98
	2006	10	0 4 0 2 0 2 3 1 2 4		82	20%	40%	6.62	4.71	5.50
Wakefield,Tim	2004	30	3 3 4 4 2 4 3 4 2 2 0 0 3 5 3	0 3 3 1 3 4 3 5 3 0 1 0 3 5	98	27%	23%	4.88	4.78	4.73
	2005	33	3 5 4 2 2 3 2 2 3 0 1 4 4 5 2 4 2	2 1 3 4 5 3 0 1 3 5 5 4 5 5 1	103	45%	18%	4.16	3.92	4.40
	2006	23	0 5 4 3 2 3 2 5 4 3 4 4 5 4 5 5 4 2	0 1 0 2 3	98	48%	17%	4.63	4.02	4.40
Wang,Chien-Ming	2005	17	3 2 3 4 4 3 0 4 1 3 4 2	1 3 4 4 3	90	35%	18%	4.03	3.79	4.52
	2006	33	0 2 5 1 3 1 3 3 4 2 4 0 2 4 3 3 4 1 3	3 2 3 3 1 1 2 5 3 2 3 3 4 4	92	24%	21%	3.63	3.58	4.75
Washburn,Jarrod	2004	25	3 3 3 3 4 4 0 2 3 0 3 5 0 4 0 4	3 0 4 5 4 3 5 0	97	40%	20%	4.65	4.54	4.56
	2005	29	4 0 5 3 3 3 0 1 3 1 2 4 3 4 4 4 1	3 4 4 3 3 3 5 3 2 3 0	93	31%	21%	3.20	4.21	4.71
	2006	31	5 0 4 4 4 4 3 1 3 0 5 0 5 1 4 4 3 2	2 3 5 4 0 2 5 3 3 5 0 0	99	42%	26%	4.67	4.06	4.74
Weaver,Jeff	2004	34	4 0 1 4 5 4 5 2 5 5 4 3 2 4 5 3 3 4	2 2 5 5 5 5 4 3 3 5 2 5 0 4 4	101	62%	9%	4.01	3.74	3.50
	2005	34	4 0 5 0 4 4 5 4 5 1 0 4 5 5 4 3 5 4	4 3 3 5 4 2 3 4 5 2 4 5 4 3	99	65%	12%	4.22	3.53	3.61
	2006	31	2 3 4 5 0 4 1 0 0 5 3 2 3 4 5 0	0 1 1 0 5 1 4 3 2 4 3 1 5 4 2	93	35%	35%	5.76	3.92	5.13
Weaver,Jered	2006	19	5 5 4 5 5 5	3 3 1 5 5 5 0 5 3 5 3 3	102	58%	11%	2.56	3.36	3.97
Webb,Brandon	2004	35	5 2 4 3 4 2 3 2 0 4 2 2 5 4 2 4 3	4 3 3 2 1 1 4 4 5 5 0 3 0 2 4	98	40%	14%	3.59	4.05	4.32
	2005	33	2 4 5 4 2 4 3 4 5 3 5 3 4 5 4 2 4 2	2 0 3 4 5 5 2 3 4 4 4 4 5 4	102	64%	3%	3.54	2.94	3.29
	2006	33	3 4 4 2 4 4 4 3 4 5 4 5 5 3 3 4 5 5	5 4 3 3 3 2 3 5 4 5 4 5 0	101	64%	3%	3.10	2.54	3.29
Wells,David	2004	31	3 0 1 3 4 5 2 3 2 4 4 3 2 5 4	2 1 3 4 1 4 4 3 2 5 4 1 4 2	91	42%	16%	3.73	3.75	4.44
	2005	30	0 2 4 4 0 0 3 3 3 4 5 3 2 4 3	5 4 4 4 4 0 4 4 4 1 3 0 3 5	93	50%	20%	4.45	3.53	4.50
	2006	13	0 0	0 4 3 2 4 3 4 2 2 4 4	85	38%	23%	4.42	3.72	4.64
Wells,Kip	2004	24	5 3 5 2 5 2 0 2 5 5 2 2 0 0 5 2 4 3	5 4 2 4 0 0	101	42%	21%	4.56	4.58	4.56
	2005	33	1 2 4 3 4 4 4 5 5 0 5 4 0 0 3 0 5 1	0 5 3 0 5 0 4 1 0 2 0 2 3	94	39%	36%	5.09	4.31	5.13
	2006	9	0 1 0 3	4 1 3 1 0	86	11%	67%	6.50	4.59	9.15
Westbrook,Jake	2004	30	3 3 3 3 1 2 4 4 2 5 3 2	5 3 1 2 2 4 5 4 5 2 4 3 3	99	30%	7%	3.39	3.68	4.48
	2005	34	4 0 3 4 0 3 0 0 5 3 3 3 3 4 4 4 3 4 4	3 4 4 1 5 0 2 2 3 4 3 3 2 5 3	94	38%	18%	4.50	3.43	4.52
	2006	32	4 4 3 0 1 5 4 2 4 1 4 2 4 4 5 3 4	0 3 3 2 5 3 3 3 1 5	102	44%	16%	4.17	3.45	4.44
Williams,David	2004	6		0 5 5 5 2 0	85	50%	33%	4.48	3.02	4.71
	2005	25	2 5 4 3 3 3 3 5 4 3 0 4 5 0 0 4	3 3 2 1 3 5 2 3 0	89	32%	20%	4.43	4.35	4.71
	2006	13	3 0 0 0 2 1 4 0	2 3 4 5 0	87	23%	46%	6.52	4.50	6.12
Williams,Woody	2004	31	0 5 0 4 3 1 4 4 2 2 5 2 4 4 4 5 3	3 5 3 5 4 4 3 5 5 4 3 4 3 0	101	48%	13%	4.19	4.04	4.28
	2005	28	0 5 2 3 4 2 2 3 4 4 4 3 3	1 3 2 2 0 5 4 3 5 3 2 0 1 4	96	32%	18%	4.86	4.19	4.60
	2006	24	3 5 3 2 3 4 0 4 1	3 2 1 2 3 3 4 4 0 1 4 5 3 1 3	95	29%	25%	3.65	4.07	4.93
Willis,Dontrelle	2004	32	5 3 4 2 0 1 3 0 3 5 4 3 5 0 0 0 3 5	4 5 5 3 5 5 3 4 1 4 3 4 3	98	44%	22%	4.02	4.25	4.56
	2005	34	4 5 5 1 5 4 4 0 4 5 4 4 4 4 4 3 3	5 0 5 3 3 4 5 4 2 4 5 4 5 5 0 4	105	68%	9%	2.63	3.33	3.38
	2006	34	3 4 1 4 5 4 0 0 2 3 3 3 2 3 5 5 0	5 3 4 0 3 2 3 4 5 4 3 4 1 0	106	38%	18%	3.87	3.57	4.52
Wolf,Randy	2004	23	3 2 4 4 5 3 1 4 5 4 0 5 0 2	2 0 4 2 5 4 3 4 0	92	48%	22%	4.30	4.52	4.53
	2005	13	4 3 3 0 2 3 4 5 4 3 4 3 2		100	38%	8%	4.39	3.94	4.29
	2006	12		0 0 4 2 2 3 3 4 0 3 3 0	88	17%	33%	5.56	4.40	5.29
Woods,Jake	2006	8		3 3 1 0 2 4 0 4	90	25%	38%	4.20	4.35	5.27
Wood,Kerry	2004	22	4 5 4 5 5 5 0 4	5 4 3 5 2 5 0 0 5 4 5 5 5 2	101	73%	14%	3.73	3.64	3.51
	2005	10	3 3 3 4 0 5 3 4	5 0	88	40%	20%	4.23	3.06	4.56
	2006	4	3 3 5 0		79	25%	25%	4.12	4.20	4.93
Wood,Mike	2004	17	3 2 0	3 3 2 4 3 2 0 0 5 3 4 3 2	92	18%	18%	5.94	5.07	4.65
	2005	10		3 1 4 1 2 3 0 3 1 0	88	10%	50%	4.46	4.48	7.08
	2006	7	0 2 0 3 1 0 0		83	0%	71%	5.71	4.33	10.58
Wright,Jamey	2004	14		2 3 3 4 0 3 2 3 0 1 4 3 0	98	14%	29%	4.14	4.85	5.08
	2005	27	3 0 4 2 4 1 3 3 0 3 4 4 4 2 2 4 1	3 4 0 3 3 2 3 3 4 3	95	30%	19%	5.47	4.33	4.60
	2006	21	3 4 3 2 1 3 4 5 4 0 3 0 3 2 2 2 4	4 1 2 2	98	29%	19%	5.19	3.81	4.62
Wright,Jaret	2004	32	4 5 0 2 4 2 5 0 5 3 2 5 3 5 3 5 3	4 4 4 5 2 4 0 5 4 4 4 2 4 5 0	93	59%	13%	3.29	3.20	3.97
	2005	13	0 1 2 1	4 4 3 2 2 3 0 0 0	86	15%	46%	6.12	4.85	6.25
	2006	27	0 1 3 3 4 3 2 1 2 3 5 0 5	1 0 3 4 3 2 0 0 0 5 3 2 4 3	84	22%	30%	4.49	4.17	5.21
Young,Chris	2004	7		2 0 4 0 5 0 4	95	43%	43%	4.74	4.69	5.21
	2005	31	0 0 3 4 4 1 2 4 4 5 4 5 3 3 3 0 0	3 0 0 0 4 5 4 5 3 0 2 4	92	42%	32%	4.28	3.80	4.92
	2006	31	3 5 4 0 5 3 2 3 4 0 5 4 3 4 4 5 4	0 3 1 0 3 5 0 5 2 4 4 4 5	98	55%	19%	3.46	3.58	4.10
Zambrano,Carlos	2004	31	5 5 4 0 5 4 5 4 1 4 5 4 4 5 2 3 2	4 3 5 4 5 5 5 2 4 4 4 5 5 3	112	74%	6%	2.75	2.92	3.25
	2005	33	0 5 4 4 0 5 3 0 5 4 5 3 2 5 0 5 5 4	3 5 4 5 5 5 5 2 2 4 4 4 5 5 3	108	64%	5%	3.27	3.15	3.83
	2006	33	0 4 4 3 5 0 4 5 4 4 5 5 3 5 3 5 3 5	4 5 3 4 4 0 3 5 5 5 0 4 5 5	110	70%	12%	3.41	3.28	3.51
Zambrano,Victor	2004	25	5 2 4 4 4 5 4 1 0 0 5 5 0 4 0 3 2 4	0 4 2 3 5 0	105	52%	24%	4.37	4.00	4.50
	2005	27	3 3 3 2 2 0 4 3 3 3 4 4 3 4	4 0 4 0 3 4 4 3 3 0 3	100	30%	15%	4.17	4.07	4.60
	2006	5	2 2 0 5 0		73	20%	40%	6.75	4.46	5.50
Zito,Barry	2004	34	3 1 5 0 3 4 4 3 5 4 4 2 2 1 2 4 0 4	4 1 2 2 3 5 5 3 4 2 5 5 2 3 4	108	47%	15%	4.48	4.51	4.40
	2005	35	3 0 5 4 3 0 4 3 4 5 5 3 5 3 3 3	4 5 1 5 4 5 5 4 5 0 5 2 5 4 1	109	66%	11%	3.87	3.75	3.61
	2006	34	0 5 5 3 3 4 4 2 4 4 5 3 5 3 2 3 3	2 4 2 3 1 2 5 3 4 0 1 3 5 4	108	41%	12%	3.83	4.09	4.32

Bullpen Indicators

2006 Volatility Report

After three years of elevated closer volatility, 2006 saw the lowest failure rate since 2002. Two of the 10 failures were pitchers who had been given the role but were unproven (Orvella, Reitsma), while another pair narrowly exceeded the 50% ROI cut-off though might have been considered failures anyway (Lidge, F.Cordero).

Of the 10 failures in 2006, five were due to injury and five to ineffectiveness. Of the 12 new sources, only three can legitimately be considered front-line closer candidates for 2007. Those three do not include Jon Papelbon, who is targeted for the Red Sox rotation in 2007.

From a Draft Day investment perspective, the cost of saves dropped to an all-time low of just under $18. This extreme risk aversion netted quite a few large-scale profits. Drafted closers that returned at least 30% profit were led by Joe Borowski ($22 return on $11 draft price), Chris Ray ($20 on $13), Hoffman ($30 on $21), Bobby Jenks ($21 on $15) and Brian Fuentes ($21 on $16).

The frequent phenomenon of each year's draft prices being influenced by the previous year's closer failure rate continued in 2006. This was observed in each of the past three years, as well as 1999 (as a result of 1998) and 1998 (as a result of 1997). If we are to use this as a guide for 2007, we can probably expect average closer prices to rise slightly again.

The volatility of closers is further reflected in how often some pitchers appear on one or both of the accompanying lists. Both Mike MacDougal and Tom Gordon have twice appeared on *both* the Failure List *and* the New Sources List (Gordon's first Failure was in 1999). Matt Mantei and Keith Foulke have been drafted as closers *three times* only to fail. Even current and former established names like Billy Wagner, Todd Jones, Eric Gagne and Armando Benitez have burned their unlucky owners more than once.

Buyer beware. Despite the slightly lower availability of new closer options in 2006, we continue to advise that you should not invest in closers at the draft table. Instead, work the free agent pool for saves during the season (particularly in 5x5 leagues).

The Closer Volatility Chart summarizes all this.

A bit of explanation... CLOSERS DRAFTED refers to the number of saves sources purchased in both AL and NL LABR Leagues each year. These only include relievers drafted for at least $10 specifically for saves. AVG $ refers to the average purchase price of these pitchers. FAILED is the number (and percentage) of CLOSERS DRAFTED that did not return at least 50% of their value that year. The Failures include those that lost their value due to ineffectiveness, injury or managerial decision. NEW SOURCES are arms that were drafted for less than $10 (if they were drafted at all) but finished with at least double-digit saves and/or double-digit value. The body of the chart lists the pitchers who make up the study.

Tools for Speculation

The structured analysis provided in the following Bullpen Indicator Charts (which are compiled by HQ analyst Matt Dodge) can offer some insight for the speculating process.

To aid in this process, these charts help focus on many of the statistical and situational factors that might go into a manager's decision to grant any individual pitcher a save opportunity. It's not all-encompassing, but it's a good start. In the following pages, we provide a three-year scan of indicators for all pitchers who posted at least 1 save and/or three holds in 2006.

Some of the tidbits worthy of analysis...

Saves Percentage: What it says is simple... "Who is getting it done?" Intuitively, this percentage should be a major factor in determining which closers might be in danger of losing their jobs. However, Doug Dennis' study showed little correlation between saves success rate alone and future opportunity. Better to prospect for pitchers who have *both* a high saves percentage (80% or better) *and* high skills, as measured by base performance value.

Base Performance Value: The components of BPV are evaluated in many ways. Big league managers tend to look for a pitcher who can strike out eight or nine batters per 9 IP, sometimes even if he's also walking that many. In using BPV, we set a benchmark of 75 as the minimum necessary for success. BPV's over 100 are much better, however.

Situational Performance: is the last piece of the puzzle. Our chart includes the opposition batting averages for each pitcher versus RH and LH hitters, with runners on base, in his first 15 pitches, etc. which are all good indicators. We'll set a benchmark of a .250 BA; anything over and the risk level increases.

There are other variables that come into play as well. Left-handed relievers rarely move into a closer's role unless the team's bullpen has sufficient southpaw depth. Some managers do see the value of having a high-skills arm available for the middle innings, so those pitchers don't get promoted into a closer's role either.

The tools are here. Whether or not a major league manager will make a decision reflective of this information remains to be seen. But I do think the data can help us increase our odds of uncovering those elusive saves and minimizing at least some of the risk.

Closer Volatility Analysis

FAILURES

2000	2001	2002	2003	2004	2005	2006
Howry	Jones,T	Alfonseca	Alfonseca	Biddle	Adams	Benitez
Jackson	Kohlmeier	Anderson,M	Anderson,M	Borowski	Affeldt	Dempster
Mantei	Leskanic	Foulke	Benitez	Guardado	Benitez	Foulke
Rocker	Lowe	Fox	Dejean	Koch	Dotel	Gagne
Shuey	Mantei	Gordon	Embree	Lopez,Aq	Foulke	Guardado
Timlin	Rocker	Strickland	Escobar	MacDougal	Gagne	MacDougal
Trombley	Veres	Wickman	Hoffman	Mantei	Graves	Orvella
Urbina		Zimmerman	Isringhausen	Nen	Kolb	Reitsma
Wagner			Jimenez	Rhodes	Mota	Turnbow
Williamson			Koch	Riske	Percival	Valverde
			Mesa	Wagner	Speier	
			Nen		Takatsu	
			Sasaki			
			Stewart			
			Urbina			
			Williams,M			
			Williamson			

NEW SOURCES

2000	2001	2002	2003	2004	2005	2006
Dotel	Fassero	Acevedo	Beck	Affeldt	Brazoban	Burgos
Isringhausen	Gordon	Baez	Biddle	Aquino	Bruney	Duchscherer
Jimenez	Kim	Cordero	Borowski	Chacon	Dempster	Julio,J
Kohlmeir	Mesa	DeJean	Carter,L	Cordero	Farnsworth	Nelson,J
Leskanic	Prinz	Gagne	Cordero,F	Frasor	Fuentes	Otsuka
Sasaki	Yan	Irabu	Gordon	Herges	Hermanson	Papelbon
Strickland	Zimmerman	Julio	Hasegawa	Hermanson	Jones,T	Putz
Wells,B		Looper	Kolb,D	Hawkins	Lyon	Saito,T
Williams,M		Marte	Lopez,Aq	Lidge	MacDougal	Timlin
		Nunez,V	MacDougal	Putz	Reitsma	Torres,S
		Osuna	Marte	Rodriguez,Fr	Rodney	Walker,T
		Williamson	Polite	Takatsu	Street	Wheeler
			Tavarez	Wickman	Turnbow	
			Worrell	Worrell	Walker,T	
				Yan	Weathers	

SUMMARY

YEAR	Drafted	Avg R$	Failed	Failure %	New Sources
1996	24	$30	3	13%	2
1997	26	$30	5	19%	8
1998	25	$32	11	44%	9
1999	23	$25	5	22%	7
2000	27	$25	10	37%	9
2001	25	$26	7	28%	7
2002	28	$22	8	29%	12
2003	29	$22	17	59%	14
2004	29	$20	11	38%	15
2005	28	$21	12	43%	15
2006	30	$18	10	33%	12

(NUMBER OF CLOSERS)

Pitcher			Tm	IP/g (BPIs)	bpv (BPIs)	S% (BPIs)	Sv% (Results)	Eff% (Results)	Emp (Runners)	On (Runners)	1-15 (Pitch Ct)	16-30 (Pitch Ct)	vLH (Platoon)	vRH (Platoon)
Aardsma,David	R	06	CHC	1.2	41	75%	0%	100%	189	247	219	197	190	225
Accardo,Jeremy	R	05	SF	1.0	48	67%	0%	45%	239	222	203	313	182	265
		06	TOR	1.1	72	62%	38%	62%	226	364	286	276	241	307
Adkins,Jon	R	06	SD	1.0	46	71%	0%	91%	278	263	300	158	287	259
Affeldt,Jeremy	L	04	KC	2.0	43	69%	76%	67%	233	305	253	320	259	272
		05	KC	1.0	55	68%	0%	86%	300	259	293	268	263	283
		06	COL	1.8	9	62%	33%	58%	165	315	260	180	213	240
Ayala,Luis	R	04	MON	1.1	119	79%	29%	63%	249	292	272	291	244	284
		05	WAS	1.0	64	83%	33%	78%	308	261	275	328	352	229
Baez,Danys	R	04	TAM	1.1	62	75%	91%	83%	279	198	260	148	250	225
		05	TAM	1.1	48	82%	84%	79%	256	234	234	280	268	215
		06	ATL	1.1	70	65%	53%	65%	252	287	249	327	295	244
Bauer,Rick	R	06	TEX	1.2	41	75%	40%	75%	254	294	279	292	234	299
Beimel,Joe	L	06	LA	1.1	26	79%	100%	93%	258	267	286	185	232	279
Benitez,Armando	R	04	FLA	1.1	112	92%	92%	89%	154	148	140	204	167	141
		05	SF	1.0	27	72%	83%	75%	269	167	233	182	212	246
		06	SF	0.9	32	83%	68%	69%	301	222	268	290	270	265
Benoit,Joaquin	R	05	TEX	2.7	64	72%	0%	69%	143	133	172	106	119	156
		06	TEX	1.4	88	62%	0%	73%	240	210	231	178	191	245
Betancourt,Raf	R	04	CLE	1.0	128	73%	36%	62%	253	290	282	235	261	275
		05	CLE	1.2	129	77%	33%	75%	215	238	233	200	264	204
		06	CLE	1.1	104	71%	50%	65%	214	278	248	236	221	254
Birkins,Kurt	L	06	BAL	0.9	48	65%	0%	75%	246	196	250	194	212	230
Borowski,Joe	R	04	CHC	1.0	17	59%	82%	65%	263	333	333	182	343	278
		05	TAM	1.1	32	64%	0%	70%	159	328	240	184	198	244
		06	FLA	1.0	63	75%	84%	80%	237	233	239	230	167	291
Bowie,Micah	L	06	WAS	1.3	49	88%	0%	83%	208	53	116	190	273	111
Bradford,Chad	R	04	OAK	0.9	46	66%	25%	67%	198	283	220	289	293	213
		05	BOS	0.8	64	72%	0%	83%	308	315	297	389	409	282
		06	NYM	0.9	108	73%	67%	84%	284	224	238	333	262	251
Bray,Bill	L	06	CIN	1.1	63	74%	67%	73%	302	267	259	283	329	254
Brazoban,Yhency	R	04	LA	1.0	76	82%	0%	85%	246	189	225	185	224	215
		05	LA	1.0	45	65%	78%	67%	233	296	260	269	267	250
Breslow,Craig	L	06	BOS	0.9	96	72%	0%	60%	316	222	242	364	316	222
Britton,Chris	R	06	BAL	1.0	72	73%	33%	64%	191	272	226	235	301	186
Broxton,Jonathar	R	06	LA	1.1	106	83%	43%	79%	253	172	234	192	244	196
Bruney,Brian	R	04	ARI	1.0	69	71%	0%	55%	220	149	185	216	214	172
		05	ARI	1.0	55	62%	75%	71%	227	364	277	339	280	314
		06	NYY	1.1	87	96%	0%	83%	195	182	184	200	115	229
Burgos,Ambiorix	R	05	KC	1.1	74	74%	33%	64%	258	243	251	266	300	216
		06	KC	1.1	35	72%	60%	61%	268	298	290	256	339	242
Burres,Brian	L	06	BAL	0.7	133	83%	0%	100%	158	273	200	200	71	313
Byrdak,Tim	L	05	BAL	0.6	85	77%	100%	92%	250	260	247	261	214	300
		06	BAL	0.4	-56	60%	0%	100%	412	467	444	400	381	545
Cabrera,Fernand	R	06	CLE	1.2	56	68%	0%	56%	225	270	275	172	235	248
Calero,Kiko	R	04	STL	1.1	150	72%	67%	89%	167	196	196	132	186	170
		05	OAK	1.0	82	75%	50%	89%	205	233	204	271	319	162
		06	OAK	0.8	102	74%	40%	85%	213	258	230	238	278	208
Camp,Shawn	R	06	TAM	1.0	64	71%	67%	79%	316	310	300	365	370	284
Capellan,Jose	R	05	MIL	0.9	91	81%	0%	80%	310	276	261	417	235	317
		06	MIL	1.2	42	72%	0%	83%	253	233	257	231	248	242
Capps,Matt	R	06	PIT	1.0	95	72%	10%	70%	265	268	266	288	250	275
Carmona,Fausto	R	06	CLE	2.0	49	67%	0%	46%	319	295	289	359	273	333
Carrara,Giovanni	R	04	LA	1.3	103	82%	67%	81%	248	202	256	196	179	258
		05	LA	1.0	50	72%	0%	75%	211	284	229	290	234	248
		06	LA	1.1	75	69%	50%	60%	274	217	205	429	157	333
Carrasco,Hector	R	05	WAS	1.4	69	85%	50%	71%	223	175	195	232	202	198
		06	ANA	1.8	68	75%	50%	69%	280	194	295	149	257	230
Cassidy,Scott	R	06	SD	1.0	66	90%	0%	62%	289	210	280	239	237	255
Castro,Fabio	L	06	PHI	1.6	51	77%	50%	33%	190	140	180	167	71	205
Choate,Randy	L	06	ARI	0.5	124	71%	0%	83%	344	270	303	333	294	314
Chulk,Vinnie	R	04	TOR	1.2	48	71%	40%	73%	282	261	257	314	305	230
		05	TOR	1.2	27	74%	0%	87%	276	230	245	273	283	231
		06	SF	1.0	60	66%	0%	58%	217	295	303	157	206	282
Coffey,Todd	R	05	CIN	1.0	51	73%	50%	80%	413	289	322	433	337	348
		06	CIN	1.0	64	77%	67%	72%	269	280	278	288	344	243
Colon,Roman	R	06	DET	1.9	31	72%	100%	100%	362	203	359	171	220	318
Cordero,Chad	R	04	MON	1.2	75	82%	78%	81%	229	212	231	243	237	209
		05	WAS	1.0	87	90%	87%	82%	194	204	242	74	192	205
		06	WAS	1.1	69	81%	88%	82%	236	183	239	113	219	212
Cordero,Francisc	R	04	TEX	1.1	116	82%	91%	85%	258	197	281	110	233	217
		05	TEX	1.0	98	76%	82%	82%	231	236	249	194	250	214
		06	MIL	1.0	90	74%	67%	75%	229	266	260	231	286	219
Corey,Bryan	R	06	BOS	1.2	71	69%	0%	83%	224	261	235	231	225	257
Cormier,Rheal	L	04	PHI	1.0	56	72%	0%	73%	206	280	250	194	250	230
		05	PHI	0.8	32	65%	0%	84%	303	288	300	308	260	321
		06	CIN	0.8	17	87%	0%	70%	298	240	268	261	286	250
Corpas,Manuel	R	06	COL	0.9	91	76%	0%	67%	282	291	311	150	281	290
Correia,Kevin	R	06	SF	1.5	79	73%	0%	92%	215	273	266	241	275	218

Bullpen Indicators

Pitcher			Tm	IP/g (BPIs)	bpv (BPIs)	S% (BPIs)	Sv% (Results)	Eff% (Results)	Emp (Runners)	On (Runners)	1-15 (Pitch Ct)	16-30 (Pitch Ct)	vLH (Platoon)	vRH (Platoon)
Cortes,David	R	05	COL	1.0	66	71%	67%	89%	238	273	264	220	278	229
		06	COL	1.0	47	71%	0%	75%	308	311	315	286	279	329
Cotts,Neal	L	04	CHW	1.2	39	64%	0%	57%	248	224	226	269	250	228
		05	CHW	0.9	90	82%	0%	89%	171	188	196	114	206	155
		06	CHW	0.8	21	75%	25%	76%	295	287	285	309	263	314
Crain,Jesse	R	05	MIN	1.1	15	79%	25%	75%	218	219	228	185	209	225
		06	MIN	1.1	91	74%	25%	65%	243	289	250	256	259	263
Davis,Jason	R	06	CLE	1.4	87	72%	33%	71%	288	317	281	342	316	294
Delcarmen,Mann	R	06	BOS	1.1	91	66%	0%	80%	273	345	283	371	319	302
Dempster,Ryan	R	04	CHC	0.9	67	71%	100%	86%	190	229	213	200	222	200
		05	CHC	1.5	79	78%	94%	88%	204	233	196	313	245	197
		06	CHC	1.0	69	68%	73%	60%	269	254	268	265	307	228
Dessens,Elmer	R	06	LA	1.2	58	69%	29%	66%	275	290	284	298	264	293
Dohmann,Scott	R	04	COL	1.1	72	75%	0%	36%	214	263	235	239	211	255
		05	COL	1.0	47	67%	0%	69%	250	279	321	86	328	212
		06	KC	1.0	27	67%	33%	60%	330	295	287	415	357	293
Donnelly,Brendar	R	04	ANA	1.1	130	80%	0%	83%	200	258	222	263	211	237
		05	ANA	1.0	65	74%	0%	76%	258	228	260	194	213	274
		06	ANA	1.0	51	74%	0%	94%	234	246	256	194	290	204
Dotel,Octavio	R	04	OAK	1.1	125	75%	80%	74%	240	190	232	184	245	188
		05	OAK	1.0	52	79%	64%	57%	143	212	175	273	269	107
Downs,Scott	L	06	TOR	1.3	54	72%	25%	72%	246	134	199	203	177	208
Duchscherer,Just	R	04	OAK	1.8	45	79%	0%	62%	262	209	266	257	246	236
		05	OAK	1.3	126	82%	71%	79%	179	273	211	235	230	203
		06	OAK	1.1	149	75%	82%	90%	276	190	265	182	248	241
Embree,Alan	L	04	BOS	0.8	85	69%	0%	88%	216	276	250	200	231	258
		05	NYY	0.8	45	48%	33%	65%	268	330	303	265	317	278
		06	SD	0.7	108	75%	0%	87%	212	289	256	208	240	258
Eveland,Dana	L	05	MIL	1.2	49	66%	50%	82%	292	344	301	340	324	315
Eyre,Scott	L	04	SF	0.6	53	74%	20%	81%	236	198	205	255	204	235
		05	SF	0.8	92	76%	0%	89%	233	167	188	239	182	213
		06	CHC	0.8	67	85%	0%	76%	280	248	298	179	281	255
Farnsworth,Kyle	R	04	CHC	0.9	73	72%	0%	71%	273	246	257	275	276	248
		05	ATL	1.0	116	82%	89%	92%	180	181	168	200	197	165
		06	NYY	0.9	85	70%	60%	73%	209	294	234	292	215	264
Feldman,Scott	R	06	TEX	1.2	76	71%	0%	70%	213	333	257	311	280	259
Feliciano,Pedro	L	06	NYM	0.9	87	86%	0%	77%	255	242	270	173	231	266
Flores,Randy	L	05	STL	0.8	93	76%	33%	83%	280	194	228	310	176	300
		06	STL	0.6	58	68%	0%	90%	286	293	306	182	258	329
Flores,Ron	L	06	OAK	1.2	51	77%	100%	60%	209	326	267	257	323	228
Foulke,Keith	R	04	BOS	1.2	156	83%	82%	79%	206	205	221	167	187	229
		05	BOS	1.1	32	65%	79%	70%	247	333	252	400	255	333
		06	BOS	1.1	98	70%	0%	94%	286	250	295	227	301	236
Frasor,Jason	R	04	TOR	1.1	61	72%	89%	78%	244	257	254	240	232	274
		05	TOR	1.1	63	78%	33%	73%	248	246	250	244	236	257
		06	TOR	1.0	75	71%	0%	83%	207	293	248	235	211	262
Fruto,Emiliano	R	06	SEA	1.6	51	67%	50%	57%	179	310	206	265	267	237
Fuentes,Brian	L	04	COL	0.9	83	62%	0%	75%	234	312	301	190	222	296
		05	COL	1.0	101	79%	91%	83%	261	171	235	182	164	237
		06	COL	1.0	86	75%	83%	77%	240	173	216	184	183	218
Fultz,Aaron	L	04	MIN	1.1	49	66%	0%	87%	267	313	315	238	218	345
		05	PHI	1.3	85	81%	0%	0%	148	267	192	182	286	171
		06	PHI	1.1	67	71%	0%	80%	304	265	262	342	263	291
Gagne,Eric	R	04	LA	1.2	189	79%	96%	91%	174	191	187	178	233	129
		05	LA	0.9	203	82%	100%	100%	200	200	238	0	217	185
		06	LA	1.0	144	0%	100%	0%	0	0	0	0	0	0
Gaudin,Chad	R	06	OAK	1.2	36	79%	67%	85%	271	170	210	234	261	196
Geary,Geoff	R	05	PHI	1.5	58	73%	0%	71%	222	277	212	313	192	294
		06	PHI	1.1	81	79%	25%	85%	337	234	303	253	348	249
Gobble,Jimmy	L	05	KC	1.9	19	71%	0%	83%	219	371	277	174	304	287
		06	KC	1.4	71	68%	50%	68%	285	243	273	233	289	250
Gonzalez,Mike	L	04	PIT	0.9	271	89%	25%	81%	204	197	198	212	227	183
		05	PIT	1.0	91	80%	100%	86%	225	169	207	173	152	223
		06	PIT	1.0	102	83%	100%	88%	168	267	223	184	163	227
Gordon,Tom	R	04	NYY	1.1	153	77%	40%	83%	193	162	187	154	185	174
		05	NYY	1.0	70	81%	22%	78%	210	194	227	103	187	217
		06	PHI	1.0	86	80%	87%	80%	218	250	247	200	185	277
Grabow,John	L	04	PIT	0.9	62	73%	14%	56%	367	285	331	328	316	331
		05	PIT	0.8	48	66%	0%	80%	217	257	242	237	219	250
		06	PIT	1.0	70	73%	0%	79%	223	307	259	214	275	251
Green,Sean	R	06	SEA	1.3	33	69%	0%	75%	273	286	250	294	190	325
Grilli,Jason	R	06	DET	1.2	27	71%	0%	79%	239	290	223	319	292	249
Guardado,Eddie	L	04	SEA	1.1	92	84%	72%	69%	175	228	192	216	96	241
		05	SEA	1.0	80	83%	88%	83%	234	244	240	239	231	242
		06	CIN	0.9	47	87%	72%	67%	303	288	308	250	234	327
Guerrier,Matt	R	06	MIN	1.8	31	81%	100%	100%	304	273	276	318	337	258
Haeger,Charles	R	06	CHW	2.6	87	72%	100%	67%	111	190	167	133	83	167
Halsey,Brad	L	06	OAK	1.8	23	73%	0%	76%	282	279	292	246	304	270
Hamulack,Tim	L	06	LA	1.0	31	67%	0%	57%	175	342	259	271	295	250

Bullpen Indicators

Pitcher		Yr	Tm	BPIs IP/g	bpv	S%	Results Sv%	Eff%	Runners Emp	On	Pitch Ct 1-15	16-30	Platoon vLH	vRH
Hancock,Josh	R	06	STL	1.2	49	69%	33%	64%	203	283	253	221	239	241
Hansen,Craig	R	06	BOS	1.0	49	61%	0%	71%	304	306	287	325	344	276
Harper,Travis	R	04	TAM	1.5	79	69%	0%	83%	219	250	200	260	222	242
		05	TAM	1.4	13	58%	0%	63%	271	343	299	321	292	313
		06	TAM	1.4	54	75%	0%	78%	313	392	343	298	400	322
Hawkins,Latroy	R	04	CHC	1.1	132	82%	74%	72%	259	194	233	246	237	229
		05	SF	0.9	45	77%	40%	58%	203	370	236	345	228	297
		06	BAL	1.0	44	69%	0%	76%	313	287	314	278	323	285
Heilman,Aaron	R	05	NYM	2.0	98	73%	83%	79%	198	216	207	213	185	225
		06	NYM	1.2	85	69%	0%	76%	205	267	228	239	231	231
Hennessey,Brad	R	06	SF	2.9	11	71%	100%	57%	192	232	159	255	132	258
Herges,Matt	R	04	SF	0.9	33	71%	74%	71%	291	392	341	352	368	315
		05	ARI	1.0	-23	59%	0%	80%	317	288	346	154	256	333
		06	FLA	1.1	35	75%	0%	61%	318	323	296	386	300	340
Hermanson,Dust	R	04	SF	2.8	63	69%	85%	67%	222	227	259	59	186	255
		05	CHW	1.0	53	85%	87%	82%	254	183	224	226	240	206
Hernandez,Rob	R	04	PHI	0.9	27	76%	0%	57%	311	284	295	289	278	311
		05	NYM	1.0	74	81%	40%	71%	211	244	225	258	244	213
		06	NYM	0.9	51	81%	40%	70%	287	205	258	219	293	218
Hoey,James	R	06	BAL	0.8	31	44%	0%	67%	316	400	321	375	375	348
Hoffman,Trevor	R	04	SD	1.0	188	80%	91%	86%	244	158	199	273	250	165
		05	SD	1.0	131	74%	93%	83%	240	230	235	235	298	179
		06	SD	1.0	98	84%	90%	87%	257	122	212	133	194	214
Howry,Bob	R	04	CLE	1.1	98	82%	0%	75%	278	167	243	196	291	169
		05	CLE	0.9	84	74%	60%	87%	181	212	201	148	180	198
		06	CHC	0.9	110	76%	56%	77%	240	250	253	224	247	244
Huber,Jon	R	06	SEA	1.0	74	88%	0%	89%	143	217	133	308	67	209
Isringhausen,Jas	R	04	STL	1.0	114	74%	87%	85%	204	194	201	200	207	194
		05	STL	0.9	68	85%	91%	87%	200	205	208	175	168	229
		06	STL	1.0	31	83%	77%	67%	239	202	237	204	270	187
Jenks,Bobby	R	05	CHW	1.2	118	80%	75%	77%	224	227	221	268	105	298
		06	CHW	1.0	97	72%	91%	85%	241	266	254	261	227	268
Johnson,Tyler	L	06	STL	0.7	52	71%	0%	68%	167	296	237	235	221	276
Jones,Todd	R	04	PHI	1.1	57	72%	25%	78%	284	261	284	226	250	291
		05	FLA	1.1	131	79%	89%	81%	236	222	220	280	231	229
		06	DET	1.0	60	69%	86%	76%	236	340	249	409	264	284
Julio,Jorge	R	04	BAL	1.1	53	72%	85%	74%	229	226	225	236	222	234
		05	BAL	1.1	42	62%	0%	68%	274	261	240	354	281	257
		06	ARI	1.1	84	73%	80%	70%	223	195	190	259	185	234
Kensing,Logan	R	06	FLA	1.0	71	70%	14%	64%	203	246	204	212	218	222
King,Ray	L	04	STL	0.7	80	74%	0%	92%	197	198	187	258	153	250
		05	STL	0.5	34	81%	0%	67%	236	341	282	400	244	352
		06	COL	0.7	16	77%	50%	77%	364	298	325	350	299	351
Kline,Steve	L	04	STL	0.8	80	86%	75%	87%	196	225	188	350	141	272
		05	BAL	0.9	8	77%	0%	61%	270	241	281	160	317	209
		06	SF	0.7	45	76%	100%	88%	295	255	258	367	269	280
Kolb,Danny	R	04	MIL	0.9	48	74%	89%	82%	197	280	181	486	250	220
		05	ATL	0.9	41	68%	61%	57%	346	316	316	375	336	323
		06	MIL	0.9	34	68%	33%	69%	221	333	262	364	323	260
League,Brandon	R	06	TOR	1.3	85	78%	25%	74%	211	219	230	180	276	178
Lidge,Brad	R	04	HOU	1.2	198	85%	88%	85%	197	141	167	208	185	161
		05	HOU	1.0	154	83%	91%	85%	239	205	235	186	244	202
		06	HOU	1.0	100	64%	84%	78%	224	256	242	236	286	201
Linebrink,Scott	R	04	SD	1.2	111	85%	0%	81%	241	177	221	179	182	232
		05	SD	1.0	101	85%	17%	85%	227	186	208	200	197	221
		06	SD	1.0	81	75%	18%	78%	258	224	248	230	204	294
Liriano,Francisco	L	06	MIN	4.3	139	82%	100%	0%	311	277	300	242	222	323
Littleton,Wes	R	06	TEX	1.1	38	85%	100%	91%	205	163	176	250	256	157
Logan,Boone	L	06	CHW	0.8	37	59%	50%	75%	194	378	302	176	357	244
Looper,Braden	R	04	NYM	1.2	111	79%	85%	76%	239	301	291	186	307	229
		05	NYM	1.0	18	76%	78%	68%	283	257	251	328	336	210
		06	STL	1.1	62	72%	0%	83%	253	310	277	308	284	274
Lopez,Javier	L	04	COL	0.6	30	53%	0%	81%	317	266	252	455	208	363
		05	ARI	0.5	30	49%	50%	75%	231	417	354	333	278	421
		06	BOS	0.6	45	81%	100%	100%	222	237	204	1000	250	208
Lowe,Mark	R	06	SEA	1.2	90	85%	0%	100%	182	200	189	182	167	205
Lugo,Ruddy	R	06	TAM	1.3	45	70%	0%	71%	240	239	276	218	213	264
Lyon,Brandon		05	ARI	0.9	12	69%	93%	83%	382	311	356	320	317	364
		06	ARI	1.0	52	72%	0%	69%	290	226	294	143	244	270
Macdougal,Mike	R	04	KC	0.9	34	78%	33%	40%	320	308	351	214	304	321
		05	KC	1.0	95	77%	84%	72%	231	281	266	238	240	270
		06	CHW	1.0	103	85%	50%	87%	180	244	195	250	281	171
Madson,Ryan	R	04	PHI	1.5	92	83%	50%	81%	241	200	229	189	231	217
		05	PHI	1.1	81	70%	0%	76%	247	273	304	160	292	233
		06	PHI	2.7	41	68%	50%	63%	344	256	342	235	296	311
Mahay,Ron	L	04	TEX	1.1	69	83%	0%	89%	250	220	229	273	236	234
		05	TEX	1.2	24	65%	100%	78%	314	313	326	370	302	322
		06	TEX	0.9	62	76%	0%	71%	248	252	245	254	240	258

Bullpen Indicators

Pitcher		Yr	Tm	BPIs IP/g	bpv	S%	Results Sv%	Eff%	Runners Emp	On	Pitch Ct 1-15	16-30	Platoon vLH	vRH
Majewski,Gary	R	04	MON	1.3	55	77%	50%	33%	333	318	340	276	419	273
		05	WAS	1.1	54	77%	20%	78%	275	221	223	298	236	259
		06	CIN	1.1	45	70%	0%	52%	303	265	316	203	287	281
Marte,Damaso	L	04	CHW	1.0	65	78%	50%	75%	227	202	216	219	144	261
		05	CHW	0.7	69	81%	50%	78%	222	291	269	222	267	244
		06	PIT	0.8	78	75%	0%	56%	257	230	238	206	225	258
Martinez,Carlos	R	06	FLA	0.9	96	87%	0%	83%	222	278	280	125	250	250
Martin,Tom	L	06	COL	0.9	62	64%	0%	93%	243	283	275	265	276	255
Mastny,Tom	R	06	CLE	1.1	67	62%	67%	57%	300	258	349	63	273	282
Mateo,Julio	R	04	SEA	1.3	54	69%	25%	62%	252	250	238	219	275	238
		05	SEA	1.6	59	79%	0%	58%	257	185	250	204	194	257
		06	SEA	1.1	31	76%	0%	70%	232	371	322	263	394	246
Mcbride,Macay	L	05	ATL	0.6	151	64%	100%	100%	474	225	209	500	172	433
		06	ATL	0.8	64	75%	50%	88%	269	226	225	359	187	308
McCarthy,Brand	R	06	CHW	1.6	34	71%	0%	65%	263	224	241	258	204	272
McClung,Seth	R	06	TAM	2.6	12	67%	86%	48%	263	250	281	154	231	277
Meadows,Brian	R	04	PIT	1.2	69	73%	50%	76%	263	254	282	206	226	275
		05	PIT	1.1	47	69%	0%	77%	261	320	319	229	301	279
		06	TAM	1.3	22	74%	80%	65%	329	295	307	333	254	361
Medders,Brandor	R	06	ARI	1.2	52	76%	0%	79%	252	288	269	274	348	196
Mercker,Kent	L	04	CHC	0.8	80	82%	0%	83%	216	193	216	129	240	167
		05	CIN	0.8	54	77%	57%	87%	242	299	289	152	225	304
		06	CIN	0.8	8	76%	33%	73%	245	273	272	200	260	259
Meredith,Cla	R	06	SD	1.1	153	91%	0%	88%	216	114	161	200	281	107
Mesa,Jose	R	04	PIT	1.0	48	79%	90%	87%	322	254	272	346	331	255
		05	PIT	1.0	32	71%	79%	67%	317	257	291	229	309	265
		06	COL	0.9	18	78%	12%	64%	254	289	274	262	270	271
Messenger,Rand	R	06	FLA	1.0	44	66%	0%	58%	299	293	265	338	333	267
Miceli,Dan	R	04	HOU	1.0	95	77%	25%	73%	269	219	273	188	316	177
		05	COL	1.0	72	65%	0%	60%	242	297	304	227	303	243
		06	TAM	1.0	16	76%	57%	69%	193	241	218	222	130	295
Miller,Matt	R	04	CLE	1.0	111	72%	50%	86%	226	208	230	158	259	200
		05	CLE	1.3	82	84%	50%	86%	226	196	254	143	194	221
Miller,Trever	L	04	TAM	0.8	99	77%	33%	79%	256	257	257	200	211	304
		05	TAM	0.7	44	77%	0%	72%	239	308	282	257	267	289
		06	HOU	0.7	113	79%	33%	75%	271	176	234	161	221	228
Mota,Guillermo	R	04	FLA	1.2	85	77%	50%	78%	242	187	215	248	195	237
		05	FLA	1.2	68	67%	50%	82%	231	279	283	211	243	262
		06	NYM	1.1	32	75%	0%	81%	261	253	237	300	252	261
Munter,Scott	R	05	SF	0.9	28	80%	0%	82%	284	276	294	176	360	237
	R	06	SF	0.8	13	55%	0%	83%	344	380	343	500	405	333
Myers,Mike	L	04	BOS	0.6	36	73%	0%	94%	315	242	274	333	229	356
		05	BOS	0.6	43	75%	0%	86%	266	186	226	200	158	385
		06	NYY	0.5	59	78%	0%	86%	176	294	267	67	254	229
Nathan,Joe	R	04	MIN	1.0	155	85%	94%	90%	207	159	176	231	211	161
		05	MIN	1.0	143	75%	90%	85%	165	215	171	224	158	206
		06	MIN	1.1	188	82%	95%	96%	168	141	176	63	193	130
Nelson,Joe	R	06	KC	1.0	61	70%	90%	88%	226	225	212	225	180	252
Neshek,Patrick	R	06	MIN	1.2	219	87%	0%	78%	202	128	157	225	244	140
Novoa,Roberto	R	04	DET	1.3	41	67%	0%	67%	213	441	245	423	333	292
		05	CHC	0.9	72	74%	0%	64%	286	241	272	263	221	291
		06	CHC	1.2	19	78%	0%	86%	299	219	261	256	279	255
Ohman,Will	L	05	CHC	0.6	58	84%	0%	75%	202	200	194	286	173	231
		06	CHC	0.8	82	70%	0%	91%	190	227	215	224	157	245
Oliver,Darren	L	06	NYM	1.8	57	77%	0%	88%	215	259	259	161	208	244
Orvella,Chad	R	05	TAM	1.4	64	76%	50%	82%	208	289	257	209	218	265
		06	TAM	1.1	58	77%	0%	20%	472	279	375	353	275	391
Otsuka,Akinori	R	04	SD	1.1	126	88%	29%	86%	190	210	194	205	202	196
		05	SD	0.9	76	74%	14%	64%	277	190	230	220	207	263
		06	TEX	1.0	119	82%	89%	84%	250	229	242	233	287	190
Papelbon,Jon	R	05	BOS	2.0	64	87%	0%	78%	262	259	262	292	200	308
		06	BOS	1.2	169	92%	85%	83%	199	112	180	132	203	128
Paronto,Chad	R	06	ATL	0.9	61	78%	0%	67%	245	259	273	147	288	234
Pena,Tony	R	06	ARI	1.2	39	66%	100%	60%	253	356	309	289	382	179
Peralta,Joel	R	06	KC	1.2	76	68%	33%	79%	276	250	271	259	338	234
Pineiro,Joel	R	06	SEA	4.1	19	62%	50%	0%	145	324	133	381	167	245
Pinto,Renyel	L	06	FLA	1.1	66	84%	100%	100%	156	217	207	222	150	215
Proctor,Scott	R	06	NYY	1.2	71	75%	12%	74%	216	251	236	210	204	250
Putz,J.J.	R	04	SEA	1.2	42	71%	69%	63%	276	271	287	275	232	310
		05	SEA	0.9	46	78%	25%	78%	236	276	225	364	321	197
		06	SEA	1.1	226	76%	84%	85%	176	257	200	229	211	204
Qualls,Chad	R	04	HOU	1.3	86	74%	50%	93%	259	277	288	233	264	267
		05	HOU	1.0	72	75%	0%	88%	263	234	251	242	218	275
		06	HOU	1.1	46	71%	0%	77%	242	242	258	181	227	253
Ramirez,Ramon	R	06	COL	1.1	76	74%	0%	74%	241	218	265	141	274	194
Rauch,Jon	R	06	WAS	1.1	63	79%	40%	75%	215	252	257	180	254	216
Ray,Chris	R	05	BAL	1.0	74	85%	0%	56%	208	237	218	261	284	174
		06	BAL	1.1	41	84%	87%	80%	188	202	221	119	184	202

Bullpen Indicators

Pitcher	Th	Yr	Tm	BPIs			Results		Runners		Pitch Ct		Platoon	
				IP/g	bpv	S%	Sv%	Eff%	Emp	On	1-15	16-30	vLH	vRH
Ray,Ken	R	06	ATL	1.0	32	74%	62%	76%	213	324	238	328	282	237
Reitsma,Chris	R	04	ATL	0.9	78	73%	22%	78%	292	274	286	288	311	261
		05	ATL	1.0	83	68%	63%	67%	259	288	266	311	252	298
		06	ATL	1.0	-8	57%	67%	67%	338	390	337	429	422	302
Reyes,Dennys	L	04	KC	2.7	54	70%	0%	50%	313	233	313	202	319	254
		05	SD	1.4	39	74%	0%	100%	192	237	219	190	136	262
		06	MIN	0.8	105	96%	0%	95%	229	151	205	143	148	244
Rhodes,Arthur	L	04	OAK	1.0	12	78%	64%	65%	365	229	308	256	321	279
		05	CLE	0.9	117	81%	0%	83%	220	188	200	235	286	155
		06	PHI	0.8	79	67%	57%	77%	224	305	243	333	286	248
Rincon,Juan	R	04	MIN	1.1	140	76%	33%	74%	161	206	169	200	149	205
		05	MIN	1.0	111	79%	0%	74%	229	219	207	278	218	228
		06	MIN	1.0	97	77%	33%	91%	273	266	260	313	222	303
Riske,David	R	04	CLE	1.1	59	79%	42%	68%	229	252	254	205	225	253
		05	CLE	1.2	62	76%	100%	50%	201	220	212	187	213	204
		06	CHW	1.1	38	75%	0%	50%	236	247	254	233	280	224
Rivera,Mariano	R	04	NYY	1.1	119	83%	93%	90%	269	181	230	227	233	215
		05	NYY	1.1	142	85%	91%	86%	166	194	166	179	177	176
		06	NYY	1.2	132	83%	92%	83%	258	174	237	194	192	250
Rivera,Saul	R	06	WAS	1.1	46	78%	33%	87%	232	263	275	209	194	290
Rleal,Sendy	R	06	BAL	1.1	-19	79%	0%	67%	309	235	309	213	242	310
Rodney,Fernandc	R	05	DET	1.1	73	82%	60%	61%	273	207	283	130	265	219
		06	DET	1.1	67	72%	64%	80%	185	208	176	214	202	192
Rodriguez,Francs	R	04	ANA	1.2	169	82%	63%	84%	178	164	200	112	213	127
		05	ANA	1.0	105	81%	90%	82%	190	173	184	154	213	153
		06	ANA	1.1	124	89%	92%	88%	201	191	202	176	215	179
Romero,J.C.	L	04	MIN	1.0	80	74%	13%	69%	173	287	254	153	266	196
		05	MIN	0.8	43	81%	0%	79%	248	223	244	214	198	268
		06	ANA	0.7	41	60%	0%	73%	225	363	300	333	202	382
Ryan,B.J.	L	04	BAL	1.1	149	81%	43%	74%	191	208	187	215	109	248
		05	BAL	1.0	142	80%	88%	80%	229	181	193	246	211	206
		06	TOR	1.1	150	86%	90%	87%	190	142	196	85	120	182
Saarloos,Kirk	R	06	OAK	3.5	1	75%	67%	0%	266	278	259	371	347	217
Saito,Takashi	R	06	LA	1.1	161	78%	92%	90%	159	206	170	164	227	129
Sanchez,Duaner	R	04	LA	1.2	39	79%	0%	78%	297	233	269	304	280	257
		05	LA	1.0	62	75%	67%	69%	250	245	252	241	310	182
		06	NYM	1.1	67	79%	0%	90%	225	220	223	246	276	179
Sanchez,Jonatha	L	06	SF	1.5	61	67%	0%	89%	243	209	196	278	241	216
Sauerbeck,Scott	L	05	CLE	0.6	69	74%	0%	88%	236	286	256	286	162	377
		06	OAK	0.6	24	70%	0%	62%	196	279	247	167	234	234
Schoeneweis,Scc	L	05	TOR	0.7	67	75%	25%	78%	238	252	246	240	188	306
		06	CIN	0.7	35	65%	67%	87%	200	310	233	364	236	257
Seanez,Rudy	R	04	FLA	1.2	96	75%	0%	64%	193	265	202	293	253	205
		05	SD	1.1	138	79%	0%	86%	220	223	255	138	231	212
		06	SD	1.1	50	74%	0%	55%	263	277	259	250	266	273
Sherrill,George	L	04	SEA	1.1	43	77%	0%	83%	255	261	281	194	255	261
		05	SEA	0.7	98	53%	0%	81%	188	200	204	182	156	273
		06	SEA	0.6	89	67%	100%	83%	194	232	217	158	143	297
Shields,Scot	R	04	ANA	1.8	105	75%	57%	85%	243	233	235	235	226	250
		05	ANA	1.2	99	77%	54%	75%	186	220	205	202	199	203
		06	ANA	1.2	101	77%	25%	75%	217	218	232	174	207	227
Shouse,Brian	L	04	TEX	0.9	61	84%	0%	100%	282	193	235	167	177	324
		05	TEX	0.8	41	64%	0%	78%	200	340	247	342	209	337
		06	MIL	0.6	31	76%	40%	75%	200	333	244	429	238	309
Sisco,Andy	L	05	KC	1.1	71	81%	0%	62%	273	217	301	175	216	255
		06	KC	0.9	38	61%	20%	50%	286	292	297	262	318	271
Smith,Matt	L	06	PHI	0.8	92	89%	0%	86%	105	111	82	231	167	85
Soriano,Rafael	R	06	SEA	1.1	97	85%	33%	78%	214	192	232	121	244	179
Sosa,Jorge	R	04	TAM	2.3	41	68%	100%	61%	250	257	242	246	315	205
		05	ATL	3.1	38	85%	0%	85%	220	260	266	207	342	177
		06	STL	2.6	5	73%	57%	33%	271	256	224	260	260	268
Speier,Justin	R	04	TOR	1.1	62	72%	64%	59%	234	244	243	242	263	213
		05	TOR	1.0	83	83%	0%	70%	191	211	210	137	167	219
		06	TOR	0.9	87	81%	0%	90%	235	235	254	143	183	264
Springer,Russ	R	04	HOU	0.8	46	85%	0%	83%	308	250	349	0	240	310
		05	HOU	1.0	62	64%	0%	67%	205	247	206	286	209	231
		06	HOU	0.8	57	75%	0%	91%	220	198	221	156	253	187
Stanton,Mike	L	04	NYM	0.9	63	78%	0%	69%	243	231	254	192	269	220
		05	BOS	0.7	53	69%	0%	75%	307	286	318	250	235	358
		06	SF	0.8	68	70%	57%	70%	289	261	272	298	271	276
Street,Huston	R	05	OAK	1.2	98	84%	85%	85%	192	197	194	195	224	172
		06	OAK	1.0	144	70%	77%	74%	205	276	238	242	274	211
Sturtze,Tanyon	R	04	NYY	2.8	48	62%	100%	80%	209	317	157	295	280	229
		05	NYY	1.2	32	67%	17%	73%	259	259	262	230	230	278
		06	NYY	0.6	-25	70%	0%	100%	400	321	368	250	333	361
Sweeney,Brian	R	06	SD	1.5	23	78%	67%	80%	270	220	270	250	263	237
Switzer,Jon	L	06	TAM	0.8	9	77%	0%	58%	328	243	274	320	220	321
Tallet,Brian	L	06	TOR	1.2	37	75%	0%	100%	271	218	264	231	220	258
Tankersley,Taylo	L	06	FLA	0.8	71	84%	43%	84%	246	214	231	182	232	225

Bullpen Indicators

Pitcher	Th	Yr	Tm	BPIs			Results		Runners		Pitch Ct		Platoon	
				IP/g	bpv	S%	Sv%	Eff%	Emp	On	1-15	16-30	vLH	vRH
Taschner,Jack	L	05	SF	0.9	77	86%	0%	83%	238	128	193	182	265	128
		06	SF	0.8	31	59%	0%	60%	316	365	359	318	275	400
Tavarez,Julian	R	04	STL	0.8	101	79%	67%	83%	188	302	225	289	262	226
		05	STL	0.9	66	77%	67%	88%	299	254	286	229	294	271
		06	BOS	1.7	30	73%	33%	57%	320	278	311	286	262	326
Thompson,Brad	R	05	STL	1.4	45	77%	100%	100%	256	179	194	259	224	228
		06	STL	1.3	45	77%	0%	67%	262	260	237	323	268	256
Thornton,Matt	L	05	SEA	1.0	21	76%	0%	50%	292	213	262	167	262	235
		06	CHW	0.9	73	76%	40%	81%	223	235	213	316	211	240
Timlin,Mike	R	04	BOS	1.0	83	69%	25%	79%	236	278	248	284	259	255
		05	BOS	1.0	95	83%	65%	81%	281	271	275	299	299	257
		06	BOS	0.9	35	72%	53%	72%	306	303	301	328	306	303
Tomko,Brett	R	06	LA	2.6	51	69%	0%	57%	250	240	238	250	261	235
Torres,Salomon	R	04	PIT	1.1	89	80%	0%	77%	271	239	259	231	252	258
		05	PIT	1.2	44	79%	100%	76%	233	208	212	221	272	189
		06	PIT	1.0	64	78%	80%	80%	294	255	265	298	281	269
Tsao,Chin-Hui	R	04	COL	0.9	260	67%	50%	67%	185	250	214	143	286	143
		05	COL	1.1	-37	72%	75%	80%	455	231	389	167	462	182
Turnbow,Derrick	R	05	MIL	1.0	87	88%	91%	91%	226	165	205	150	235	165
		06	MIL	0.9	65	60%	75%	65%	239	270	240	313	245	263
Valverde,Jose	R	04	ARI	1.0	58	79%	80%	78%	200	233	203	258	170	246
		05	ARI	1.1	120	80%	88%	81%	222	200	236	172	168	241
		06	ARI	1.1	109	61%	82%	75%	245	268	270	246	323	192
Veras,Enger	R	06	NYY	1.2	55	78%	100%	100%	211	211	231	182	188	227
Villone,Ron	L	04	SEA	2.1	44	73%	0%	68%	185	204	145	219	191	196
		05	FLA	0.8	84	72%	11%	68%	181	298	263	170	222	258
		06	NYY	1.1	47	70%	0%	67%	239	259	237	240	185	286
Vizcaino,Luis	R	04	MIL	1.0	69	75%	20%	76%	254	202	197	364	162	292
		05	CHW	1.1	33	78%	0%	65%	282	268	276	257	321	242
		06	ARI	0.9	79	75%	0%	78%	229	194	216	196	163	256
Wagner,Billy	L	04	PHI	1.1	272	75%	84%	87%	162	222	194	146	88	204
		05	PHI	1.0	131	88%	93%	88%	176	147	174	143	128	173
		06	NYM	1.0	138	85%	89%	86%	248	171	250	136	161	234
Wagner,Ryan	R	04	CIN	1.0	27	75%	0%	69%	239	333	315	214	220	309
		05	CIN	1.1	71	61%	0%	83%	294	313	285	360	311	297
		06	WAS	1.2	37	73%	0%	55%	273	309	299	229	197	387
Wainwright,Adam	R	06	STL	1.2	99	75%	60%	88%	231	229	233	235	301	182
Walker,Jamie	L	04	DET	0.9	112	79%	14%	69%	254	273	288	192	202	311
		05	DET	0.7	54	74%	0%	78%	250	264	268	185	245	271
		06	DET	0.9	94	85%	0%	92%	252	250	257	225	238	262
Walker,Pete	R	05	TOR	2.1	23	78%	40%	57%	264	234	252	267	255	246
		06	TOR	1.3	47	71%	100%	83%	292	302	312	263	318	284
Walker,Tyler	R	04	SF	1.2	51	74%	100%	92%	302	270	333	219	311	269
		05	SF	0.9	50	77%	82%	78%	231	343	292	241	287	276
		06	TAM	1.0	63	50%	71%	60%	350	224	253	364	333	226
Weathers,David	R	04	FLA	1.2	40	76%	0%	63%	273	294	326	190	245	308
		05	CIN	1.1	62	71%	79%	79%	229	258	244	222	265	226
		06	CIN	1.1	24	80%	63%	69%	234	216	230	239	219	230
Wellemeyer,Todc	R	05	CHC	1.5	26	68%	100%	86%	232	292	321	271	234	284
		06	KC	1.7	39	73%	100%	56%	236	246	267	256	208	265
Wheeler,Dan	R	04	HOU	1.4	64	76%	0%	89%	267	307	309	238	363	231
		05	HOU	1.0	101	83%	60%	81%	205	202	225	145	204	204
		06	HOU	1.0	92	81%	75%	82%	204	245	232	200	273	183
White,Rick	R	04	CLE	1.3	12	70%	33%	53%	286	302	300	269	244	333
		05	PIT	1.1	47	76%	67%	69%	286	329	273	375	314	305
		06	PHI	1.0	42	65%	50%	86%	261	330	283	340	299	290
Wickman,Bob	R	04	CLE	1.0	68	74%	93%	85%	258	309	278	300	359	189
		05	CLE	1.0	38	88%	90%	83%	306	149	279	98	243	250
		06	ATL	1.0	100	78%	89%	77%	274	223	267	158	267	236
Williamson,Scott	R	04	BOS	1.0	103	86%	50%	67%	170	61	153	0	118	111
		05	CHC	0.8	111	67%	0%	100%	300	240	289	125	333	250
		06	SD	0.9	70	64%	0%	56%	299	243	280	194	200	307
Williams,Todd	R	04	BAL	1.1	49	76%	0%	100%	220	245	213	304	238	229
		05	BAL	1.1	40	75%	33%	77%	275	230	259	188	263	244
		06	BAL	0.9	11	75%	20%	67%	324	323	321	347	342	314
Wilson,Brian	R	06	SF	1.0	55	67%	50%	64%	404	177	280	294	348	235
Wilson,C.J.	L	05	TEX	2.0	41	58%	100%	46%	140	270	213	286	178	204
		06	TEX	1.0	60	74%	50%	67%	218	247	241	238	155	292
Wise,Matt	R	04	MIL	1.7	66	63%	0%	67%	212	310	220	245	234	258
		05	MIL	1.3	79	68%	33%	71%	153	170	125	193	130	187
		06	MIL	1.1	37	75%	0%	66%	275	258	283	217	206	310
Woods,Jake	L	06	SEA	2.8	29	76%	100%	71%	277	232	278	295	271	248
Worrell,Tim	R	04	PHI	1.0	83	74%	70%	76%	274	229	254	283	307	214
		05	ARI	1.0	67	78%	25%	74%	288	314	289	310	295	303
		06	SF	0.9	-52	69%	75%	71%	295	319	297	353	256	354
Wuertz,Mike	R	04	CHC	0.9	62	71%	100%	100%	229	208	200	192	207	222
		05	CHC	1.0	89	72%	0%	83%	208	232	218	231	260	197
		06	CHC	1.0	78	85%	0%	82%	200	253	207	231	184	245
Yates,Tyler	R	06	ATL	0.9	48	76%	17%	60%	196	268	240	188	217	235
Zumaya,Joel	R	06	DET	1.3	92	87%	17%	82%	162	207	174	228	183	188

Health Conditions

Off-Season Injury Report
By Rick Wilton

Brandon Backe (RHP, HOU) underwent Tommy John surgery in September 2006 for a torn ulnar collateral ligament in his pitching elbow. He'll miss the 2007 season.

Armando Benitez (RHP, SF) struggled with arthritis and inflammation in both knees this past season. His right knee is more of a concern but he did not have surgery in the off-season. The Giants medical staff elected to rehab his knees instead. His knees are close to becoming a chronic problem and they will reduce his effectiveness the rest of his career.

Matt Clement (RHP, BOS) needed surgery in September to repair damage to both his labrum and rotator cuff. He'll pitch late in 2007 but won't be productive due to the extent of the surgery.

For the second off-season in a row, **Bartolo Colon (RHP, ANA)** elected not to have surgery to repair damage to his pitching shoulder. He decided to skip surgery last fall and rehab the shoulder, and struggled to get healthy for 2006. A long rehab is expected to get him game ready by the season's opener. A risky investment in 2007.

Coco Crisp (OF, BOS) had a second surgery in September on his fractured left index finger. He played most of the season with the fracture and it clearly had an impact on his production. Crisp should be close to 100% by the season's opener.

Bobby Crosby's (SS, OAK) season ended with a lower back strain. He is focusing on strengthening his back and improving his flexibility during the off-season to avoid more back woes in 2007.

Morgan Ensberg (3B, HOU) suffered a huge drop-off in offensive production last season. A nagging contusion to his right shoulder landed him on the disabled list and reduced strength in the shoulder. An extended rest and rehab program is supposed to eliminate the shoulder problems heading into spring training.

Darin Erstad (1B, ANA) underwent arthroscopic surgery on his arthritic right ankle last October. He's likely to struggle with the ankle the rest of his pro career.

With all the injury reports on **Cliff Floyd (OF, NYM)** this past season, its amazing he managed to get to the plate for 332 at-bats. A strained left Achilles tendon was the major issue. He underwent surgery in mid-October to repair the damage and will need a long rehab to get game-ready. He's likely to start the year on the DL.

Eric Gagne (RHP, LA) had one long roller coaster season regarding his health. Early in the year, it looked like he'd have a second Tommy John surgery. Instead, he had nerve damage in his pitching elbow repaired. In the end, a herniated disc in his lower back was repaired via surgery during the summer. He's expected to be healthy by spring training with the only question being, how effective can he be after being hurt the past two seasons?

Jonny Gomes (OF, TAM) needed surgery in September on his left shoulder. Early off-season reports point to a solid recovery and he should be ready for the season's opener.

Off and on tendinitis in his pitching elbow cost **Mike Gonzalez (LHP, PIT)** both innings and effectiveness last season. He didn't have surgery over the winter and expected a rest and a rehab program to clear up his elbow woes.

Eddie Guardado (LHP, CIN) needed reconstructive surgery on his pitching elbow late in the 2006 season and isn't expected to pitch in 2007.

Jose Guillen (OF, WAS) underwent Tommy John surgery on his throwing elbow in July. By early November, he was already starting to swing a bat. He should be close to game-ready by the end of spring training.

Rich Harden (RHP, OAK) struggled with a sore pitching elbow most of the 2006 season. At issue was a sprained ulnar collateral ligament. The A's will be cautious with him in 2007 and there is a slight risk drafting him this season.

J.J. Hardy (SS, MIL) suffered a serious high right ankle sprain early in the season and finally underwent surgery in July to repair the ligament damage. He's expected to be 100% by spring training.

A strained right hip flexor curtailed **Jeremy Hermida's (OF, FLA)** effectiveness early in the year, then he battled a torn tendon in his right ankle that ended his season in September.

An arthritic left hip caused pain most of the season for **Jason Isringhausen (RHP, STL)**. He underwent surgery to repair some of the damage and talk resumed that he might come back in 2007. Considering how painful the hip was, it will never be close to 100% again and the future of his career is in doubt.

Nick Johnson (1B, WAS) needed surgery on a fractured right femur in September. He needed additional surgery in early November to remove some scar tissue that was causing pain and impeding his recovery. He's a good candidate to start the year on the disabled list.

Randy Johnson (LHP, NYY) underwent back surgery to repair a herniated disc in his lower back in October. The fact he'll be 44 years old during the 2007 season and coming off of back surgery makes him a risky investment in 2007. He'll start spring training behind the other pitchers but should be ready to pitch close to Opening Day.

Oblique and foot injuries curtailed **Chipper Jones' (3B, ATL)** playing time last season. He is no longer able to play through injuries as he did earlier in his career.

Scott Kazmir (LHP, TAM) was shut down several times late in the year with a sore pitching shoulder. The Devil Rays didn't believe surgery was needed, and they opted instead for rest and rehab to clear up his problem. If he suffers any kind of shoulder woes in the spring, surgery may become an option.

Corey Koskie (3B, MIL) struggled with the symptoms of post concussion syndrome the second half of the season and didn't play after July 5. He is expected to be ready for spring training and won't have any restrictions.

Brian Lawrence (RHP, WAS) needed extensive surgery in February 2006 to repair damage to both his rotator cuff and labrum. His near future is in doubt due to the extent of the surgery done on his shoulder.

Derrek Lee's (1B, CHC) season ended due to his daughter's serious illness. He's likely to benefit from the extra rest and rehab of his surgically repaired right wrist. He should be ready for spring training though his power could be limited very early in the season.

John Lester (LHP, BOS) was diagnosed with a treatable form of lymphoma in early September. He underwent chemotherapy during the off-season with the prognosis for a full recovery. However, he may need time during the 2007 season to regain his strength and stamina.

Francisco Liriano (LHP, MIN) underwent elbow reconstruction surgery in October. He'll miss the 2007 but should be ready for the 2008 season.

Pedro Martinez (RHP, NYM) struggled with an injury to his big toe and hip most of the season. However, a torn tendon in his rotator cuff ended his season in September. The surgery is expected to keep him off the mound until the second half of 2007.

Though **Mike Matheny (C, SF)** does not have a long history of concussions, he played in only 47 games before missing the rest of the year due to post concussion syndrome. His struggles were serious; his future is in doubt.

Hideki Matsui (OF, NYY) suffered a fractured left wrist last May and missed most of the 2006 season. He returned late in the season but wasn't 100%. He should be all the way back by Opening Day.

Doug Mientkiewicz (1B, KC) had surgery to repair nerve damage in his lower back in August. This free agent is expected to be game-ready by the opener.

Matt Morris (RHP, SF) pitched poorly down the stretch. After the season, he revealed he pitched with a fractured rib and two more with a stress reaction. He's expected to be healed by spring training.

Mark Mulder (LHP, STL) had surgery on the rotator cuff in his pitching shoulder in September. Look for him to miss the early part of the 2007 season as he recovers.

Jonathan Papelbon (RHP, BOS) struggled with a fatigued shoulder late in the year and was shut down in September. He's being moved back to the starting rotation in 2007 but he'll need to be watched closely with the demands on his pitching arm.

John Patterson (RHP, WAS) underwent surgery on his right forearm in late July. He had some nerve damage and soft tissue repaired. The ligament was intact in his elbow. He was throwing near the end of the season and expects to be close to 100% by the start of the 2007 campaign.

Carl Pavano (RHP, NYY) never pitched in 2006 due to various ailments, including a sore elbow. He's a high-risk investment and a sure bet to open 2007 on the DL.

A fractured left thumb and the follow-up surgery cost **Jeremy Reed (OF, SEA)** the second half of the season. If he doesn't have any setbacks during the off-season, he's expected to be ready by spring training.

Aaron Rowand (OF, PHI) suffered a fractured left ankle in August and needed surgery to insert two screws to hold the bone in place. Barring a setback over the winter, he should be ready for spring training.

A partial tear in his left patellar tendon cost **Reggie Sanders (OF, KC)** the last six weeks of the season. The Royals believe the surgery to repair the damage to his knee should get him close to game ready for spring training.

Shannon Stewart (OF, MIN) battled plantar fasciitis in his left foot most of the season. The Twins hope the high frequency treatment he'll undergo during the off-season will have the same positive effects on his foot as it did for Albert Pujols a couple of years ago.

A tendon injury to his right wrist cost **Rickie Weeks (2B, MIL)** about two months of the 2006 season. The surgery was a success and an extensive rehab should have him game ready by the end of spring training.

Kip Wells (RHP, TEX) underwent surgery to repair ligament damage in his left foot in early September. It's not out of the question he might need extra time to recover and could open the season in extended spring training.

Brad Wilkerson (OF, TEX) needed surgery in August to repair damage to his rotator cuff. He's expected to be close to 100% by the time pitchers and catchers report.

Kerry Wood (RHP, CHC) elected to skip surgery to repair his partially torn rotator cuff; rather, he began a rehab program and believes he'll be ready to pitch next spring.

Tim Worrell (RHP, SF) needed surgery to clean up a frayed labrum in his pitching shoulder in August. Worrell also battled a herniated disc in his neck. His career may be over due to the injuries and his age.

Major League Disabled List Days 2002-2006 BATTERS

NAME	02	03	04	05	06	Tot
Alomar Jr.,Sandy	0	0	16	0	0	**16**
Alou,Moises	0	0	0	31	49	**80**
Anderson,Garret	0	0	49	0	0	**49**
Ardoin,Danny	0	0	0	0	64	**64**
Atkins,Garrett	0	0	0	23	0	**23**
Aurilia,Rich	0	0	0	18	15	**33**
Aybar,Willy	0	0	0	0	20	**20**
Bako,Paul	0	0	0	127	25	**152**
Baldelli,Rocco	0	0	18	180	74	**272**
Barajas,Rod	0	38	0	0	0	**38**
Barmes,Clint	0	0	0	88	0	**88**
Barrett,Michael	0	43	0	0	28	**71**
Bay,Jason	0	0	42	0	0	**42**
Bellhorn,Mark	0	22	18	33	0	**73**
Belliard,Ron	0	20	0	0	0	**20**
Bell,David	0	72	0	0	0	**72**
Beltran,Carlos	0	22	0	0	0	**22**
Bennett,Gary	0	36	0	0	0	**36**
Berkman,Lance	0	0	0	37	0	**37**
Berroa,Angel	0	0	14	0	0	**14**
Blake,Casey	0	0	0	0	47	**47**
Bloomquist,Willie	0	0	19	32	0	**51**
Blum,Geoff	0	0	0	16	0	**16**
Bonds,Barry	0	0	0	171	0	**171**
Boone,Aaron	0	0	180	0	0	**180**
Bradley,Milton	49	13	0	87	69	**218**
Branyan,Russ	0	87	0	31	0	**118**
Broussard,Ben	0	13	0	0	0	**13**
Burke,Chris	0	0	0	0	15	**15**
Burnitz,Jeromy	0	30	0	0	0	**30**
Burrell,Pat	0	0	30	0	0	**30**
Bynum,Freddie	0	0	0	0	57	**57**
Byrd,Marlon	0	15	0	26	0	**41**
Cabrera,Orlando	0	0	0	15	0	**15**
Cairo,Miguel	0	0	0	17	34	**51**
Cameron,Mike	0	0	0	78	23	**101**
Cano,Robinson	0	0	0	0	42	**42**
Cantu,Jorge	0	0	0	0	41	**41**
Casey,Sean	39	0	17	0	44	**100**
Castillo,Jose	0	0	0	68	0	**68**
Castro,Juan	64	20	21	22	0	**127**
Castro,Ramon	23	0	121	18	62	**224**
Catalanotto,Franl	143	0	83	0	0	**226**
Chavez,Eric	0	0	37	0	0	**37**
Church,Ryan	0	0	0	35	0	**35**
Cirillo,Jeff	0	25	38	69	0	**132**
Clark,Brady	0	19	0	15	0	**34**
Clark,Tony	0	0	0	0	39	**39**
Costa,Shane	0	0	0	0	20	**20**
Cota,Humberto	0	0	66	17	0	**83**
Counsell,Craig	0	61	0	0	38	**99**
Crede,Joe	0	0	0	15	0	**15**
Crisp,Coco	0	0	0	15	47	**62**
Crosby,Bobby	0	0	0	73	58	**131**
Cruz,Jose	36	0	0	29	0	**65**
Cuddyer,Michael	0	0	0	15	0	**15**
DaVanon,Jeff	0	0	17	0	50	**67**
DeJesus,David	0	0	0	0	38	**38**
Delgado,Carlos	16	0	37	19	0	**72**
Dellucci,David	0	42	0	0	0	**42**
DeRosa,Mark	60	0	0	0	15	**75**
Diaz,Matt	0	0	0	37	0	**37**
Doumit,Ryan	0	0	0	0	100	**100**
Drew,J.D.	13	39	0	89	0	**141**
Duffy,Chris	0	0	0	36	0	**36**
Durham,Ray	0	40	38	0	15	**93**
Dye,Jermaine	27	91	0	0	0	**118**
Eckstein,David	0	20	0	0	23	**43**
Ellis,Mark	0	0	180	0	29	**209**
Encarnacion,Edw	0	0	0	0	29	**29**
Encarnacion,Jua	0	0	15	0	0	**15**
Ensberg,Morgan	0	0	0	0	22	**22**
Erstad,Darin	0	105	35	0	112	**252**
Escobar,Alex	180	0	45	0	83	**308**
Estrada,Johnny	0	0	0	16	0	**16**
Everett,Adam	0	0	55	0	0	**55**
Everett,Carl	16	0	50	0	0	**66**
Fasano,Sal	0	180	0	0	17	**197**
Fick,Robert	0	0	0	0	75	**75**
Finley,Steve	0	0	0	23	0	**23**
Floyd,Cliff	0	43	32	0	48	**123**
Ford,Lew	0	43	0	0	28	**71**
Franco,Julio	0	14	0	0	0	**14**
Frandsen,Kevin	0	0	0	0	15	**15**
Freel,Ryan	0	37	0	51	0	**88**
Garciaparra,Nom	0	0	75	106	33	**214**
German,Esteban	0	0	27	0	0	**27**
Giambi,Jason	0	0	61	0	0	**61**
Gibbons,Jay	0	0	61	0	61	**122**

NAME	02	03	04	05	06	Tot
Giles,Brian	0	25	0	0	0	**25**
Giles,Marcus	48	0	58	0	0	**106**
Glaus,Troy	0	71	103	0	0	**174**
Gomes,Jonny	0	0	0	0	34	**34**
Gomez,Chris	0	25	0	0	60	**85**
Gonzalez,Alex	135	0	0	0	15	**150**
Gonzalez,Luis	0	0	102	0	18	**120**
Graffanino,Tony	37	0	86	0	0	**123**
Greene,Khalil	0	0	0	68	15	**83**
Greene,Todd	0	0	24	71	0	**95**
Griffey Jr.,Ken	75	110	73	26	28	**312**
Grudzielanek,Mark	0	30	70	0	0	**100**
Guerrero,Vladimir	0	46	0	20	0	**66**
Guiel,Aaron	0	0	62	0	0	**62**
Guillen,Carlos	0	26	0	61	0	**87**
Guillen,Jose	0	0	0	0	88	**88**
Guzman,Cristian	0	0	0	0	183	**183**
Guzman,Freddy	0	0	0	180	0	**180**
Hafner,Travis	0	0	0	18	0	**18**
Hairston Jr.,Jerry	0	106	90	15	0	**211**
Hairston,Scott	0	0	0	62	43	**105**
Hardy,J.J.	0	0	0	0	138	**138**
Hawpe,Brad	0	0	0	54	0	**54**
Helms,Wes	32	16	38	0	0	**86**
Helton,Todd	0	0	0	15	15	**30**
Hermida,Jeremy	0	0	0	0	39	**39**
Hernandez,Anders	0	0	0	0	35	**35**
Hernandez,Ramor	0	0	35	54	0	**89**
Hillenbrand,Shea	0	10	0	0	0	**10**
Hinske,Eric	0	31	0	0	0	**31**
Hollandsworth,Tod	14	12	95	0	0	**121**
Holliday,Matt	0	0	0	40	0	**40**
Hudson,Orlando	0	0	19	0	0	**19**
Huff,Aubrey	0	0	0	0	24	**24**
Hunter,Torii	0	0	16	64	15	**95**
Ibanez,Raul	0	0	37	0	0	**37**
Inge,Brandon	0	0	18	0	0	**18**
Izturis,Cesar	0	0	0	54	103	**157**
Izturis,Maicer	0	0	0	52	46	**98**
Jackson,Damian	0	0	0	0	17	**17**
Jenkins,Geoff	105	48	0	0	0	**153**
Jeter,Derek	0	43	0	0	0	**43**
Johnson,Ben	0	0	0	0	27	**27**
Johnson,Kelly	0	0	0	0	183	**183**
Johnson,Nick	24	72	96	29	6	**227**
Jones,Chipper	0	0	19	42	45	**106**
Jones,Jacque	0	12	0	0	0	**12**
Jordan,Brian	15	0	83	57	75	**230**
Kapler,Gabe	22	0	0	15	0	**37**
Kearns,Austin	36	76	104	0	0	**216**
Kennedy,Adam	0	13	0	37	0	**50**
Kent,Jeff	16	27	0	0	36	**79**
Kinsler,Ian	0	0	0	0	43	**43**
Klesko,Ryan	0	0	20	0	172	**192**
Koskie,Corey	16	22	13	68	87	**206**
Kotchman,Casey	0	0	0	0	145	**145**
Kotsay,Mark	0	13	0	0	0	**13**
Kubel,Jason	0	0	0	180	0	**180**
Laird,Gerald	0	0	69	0	0	**69**
LaRoche,Adam	0	0	35	0	0	**35**
LaRue,Jason	9	0	15	0	23	**47**
LeCroy,Matt	0	0	33	0	0	**33**
Lee,Derrek	0	0	0	0	100	**100**
Lee,Travis	0	15	172	18	0	**205**
Lieberthal,Mike	0	0	0	0	62	**62**
Lofton,Kenny	0	0	30	17	15	**62**
Lopez,Javy	15	0	0	61	15	**91**
Loretta,Mark	0	0	0	60	0	**60**
Lowell,Mike	0	28	0	0	0	**28**
Lugo,Julio	51	0	0	0	31	**82**
Mabry,John	0	23	0	0	0	**23**
Marrero,Eli	0	111	40	66	0	**217**
Martinez,Ramon	12	0	15	19	0	**46**
Martinez,Victor	0	24	0	0	0	**24**
Matheny,Mike	0	0	15	0	122	**137**
Matos,Luis	0	0	71	39	18	**128**
Matsui,Hideki	0	0	0	0	124	**124**
Matsui,Kazuo	0	0	46	51	24	**121**
Matthews Jr.,Gary	0	0	0	0	19	**19**
Mauer,Joe	0	0	133	0	0	**133**
McCann,Brian	0	0	0	0	16	**16**
McDonald,John	0	16	0	0	15	**31**
McLouth,Nate	0	0	0	0	47	**47**
McPherson,Dallas	0	0	0	85	69	**154**
Mench,Kevin	0	107	18	0	0	**125**
Michaels,Jason	0	0	0	0	18	**18**
Mientkiewicz,Doug	0	0	15	41	67	**123**
Miles,Aaron	0	0	0	33	0	**33**
Mirabelli,Doug	0	0	0	24	0	**24**

NAME	02	03	04	05	06	Tot
Molina,Ben	15	26	29	25	0	**95**
Molina,Yadier	0	0	0	41	0	**41**
Monroe,Craig	0	0	17	0	0	**17**
Mora,Melvin	0	28	15	0	0	**43**
Morneau,Justin	0	0	0	15	0	**15**
Mueller,Bill	39	0	43	0	142	**224**
Munson,Eric	0	48	0	0	0	**48**
Nady,Xavier	0	0	0	0	19	**19**
Navarro,Dioner	0	0	0	0	43	**43**
Nevin,Phil	54	114	16	27	0	**211**
Newhan,David	0	0	0	0	133	**133**
Niekro,Lance	0	0	0	0	31	**31**
Nixon,Trot	0	0	126	27	34	**187**
Nix,Laynce	0	0	26	78	0	**104**
Norton,Greg	17	0	38	0	0	**55**
Olivo,Miguel	0	0	15	0	0	**15**
Ordonez,Magglio	0	0	105	77	0	**182**
Pagan,Angel	0	0	0	0	75	**75**
Patterson,Corey	0	86	0	0	0	**86**
Paul,Josh	0	0	0	24	0	**24**
Pena,Wily Mo	0	25	0	35	51	**111**
Perez,Antonio	0	0	0	38	0	**38**
Perez,Eduardo	0	0	143	0	0	**143**
Phillips,Andy	0	0	0	0	15	**15**
Piazza,Mike	0	89	19	23	0	**131**
Podsednik,Scott	0	0	0	16	0	**16**
Polanco,Placido	0	16	29	15	38	**98**
Pujols,Albert	0	0	0	0	18	**18**
Punto,Nick	0	0	116	30	0	**146**
Quinlan,Robb	0	0	45	53	0	**98**
Quintanilla,Omar	0	0	0	0	19	**19**
Ramirez,Aramis	0	0	0	37	0	**37**
Randa,Joe	0	15	26	0	37	**78**
Reed,Jeremy	0	0	0	0	90	**90**
Repko,Jason	0	0	0	0	75	**75**
Reyes,Jose	0	11	120	0	0	**131**
Rios,Alexis	0	0	0	0	27	**27**
Rivera,Juan	84	0	0	0	16	**100**
Roberts,Brian	0	0	0	12	24	**36**
Roberts,Dave	0	36	23	20	17	**96**
Rolen,Scott	0	0	0	109	0	**109**
Ross,Cody	0	0	0	0	21	**21**
Ross,David	0	0	0	0	18	**18**
Rowand,Aaron	0	0	0	0	56	**56**
Salmon,Tim	10	0	72	180	0	**262**
Sanchez,Freddy	0	0	106	0	0	**106**
Sanders,Reggie	0	0	0	56	52	**108**
Schneider,Brian	0	0	0	0	15	**15**
Sexson,Richie	0	0	152	0	0	**152**
Shealy,Ryan	0	0	0	0	44	**44**
Sheffield,Gary	0	0	0	0	127	**127**
Sledge,Terrmel	0	0	0	151	0	**151**
Snelling,Chris	118	72	180	49	60	**479**
Spiezio,Scott	0	0	15	0	0	**15**
Stairs,Matt	18	0	15	0	0	**33**
Stewart,Shannon	15	25	52	0	118	**210**
Sullivan,Cory	0	0	180	0	0	**180**
Sweeney,Mike	29	50	38	15	98	**230**
Swisher,Nick	0	0	0	23	0	**23**
Teahen,Mark	0	0	0	20	0	**20**
Teixeira,Mark	0	0	13	0	0	**13**
Thomas,Frank	0	0	89	138	15	**242**
Thome,Jim	0	0	0	110	0	**110**
Torrealba,Yorvit	0	0	0	0	91	**91**
Treanor,Matt	0	0	0	0	15	**15**
Uribe,Juan	0	77	0	0	0	**77**
Valentin,Jose	0	0	18	88	0	**106**
Varitek,Jason	0	0	0	0	33	**33**
Vidro,Jose	0	0	40	61	24	**125**
Vizcaino,Jose	0	57	0	0	0	**57**
Vizquel,Omar	0	100	0	0	0	**100**
Walker,Todd	0	0	0	44	0	**44**
Ward,Daryle	0	0	49	0	0	**49**
Weeks,Rickie	0	0	0	0	64	**64**
Wells,Vernon	0	0	30	0	0	**30**
White,Rondell	0	0	0	47	31	**78**
Wigginton,Ty	0	0	15	0	33	**48**
Wilkerson,Brad	0	0	0	0	47	**47**
Williams,Bernie	0	44	0	0	0	**44**
Willingham,Josh	0	0	0	0	16	**16**
Wilson,Craig	0	0	0	104	0	**104**
Wilson,Preston	0	0	112	0	0	**112**
Wilson,Vance	0	0	38	0	0	**38**
Woodward,Chris	21	0	27	0	0	**48**
Youkilis,Kevin	0	0	16	0	0	**16**
Young,Dmitri	0	0	55	0	80	**135**
Young,Eric	0	0	0	85	0	**85**
Zaun,Gregg	0	0	0	16	15	**31**

Major League Disabled List Days 2002-2006 — PITCHERS

NAME	02	03	04	05	06	Tot
Affeldt,Jeremy	44	16	55	67	0	182
Aquino,Greg	0	0	0	64	19	83
Armas Jr.,Tony	23	160	57	57	27	324
Astacio,Pedro	0	150	0	31	91	272
Ayala,Luis	0	26	0	0	183	209
Backe,Brandon	0	0	0	40	141	181
Baek,Cha Seung	0	0	0	0	15	15
Baez,Danys	0	0	0	0	38	38
Bannister,Brian	0	0	0	0	130	130
Bauer,Rick	0	0	14	0	0	14
Bautista,Denny	0	0	0	140	25	165
Beckett,Josh	74	53	57	30	0	214
Bedard,Erik	0	180	0	53	0	233
Belisle,Matt	0	0	0	0	65	65
Benitez,Armando	0	0	21	110	36	167
Benoit,Joaquin	0	21	13	53	0	87
Benson,Kris	44	75	0	31	17	167
Betancourt,Rafael	0	0	15	17	25	57
Borowski,Joe	0	0	117	51	0	168
Bradford,Chad	0	0	14	107	0	121
Brazoban,Yhency	0	0	0	0	170	170
Bruney,Brian	0	0	39	0	0	39
Burgos,Ambiorix	0	0	0	24	0	24
Burnett,A.J.	26	177	69	0	83	355
Byrd,Paul	0	170	76	0	0	246
Cabrera,Daniel	0	0	0	20	21	41
Cabrera,Fernand	0	0	0	0	15	15
Calero,Kiko	0	94	27	27	0	148
Capellan,Jose	0	0	0	0	15	15
Capuano,Chris	0	0	85	0	0	85
Carpenter,Chris	0	0	0	0	17	17
Chacin,Gustavo	0	0	0	0	94	94
Chacon,Shawn	0	63	0	33	25	121
Claussen,Brandon	0	0	0	0	106	106
Clemens,Roger	25	0	0	0	0	25
Clement,Matt	0	0	0	0	107	107
Colon,Bartolo	0	0	0	0	125	125
Colon,Roman	0	0	0	0	41	41
Contreras,Jose	0	77	0	0	16	93
Cook,Aaron	0	0	54	127	0	181
Cordero,Francisco	32	0	0	0	0	32
Cormier,Rheal	0	0	0	0	15	15
Cruz,Juan	36	0	0	0	26	62
Davies,Kyle	0	0	0	0	108	108
De La Rosa,Jorge	0	0	0	0	45	45
Dempster,Ryan	0	77	0	0	0	77
Dessens,Elmer	25	0	0	56	15	96
Dohmann,Scott	0	0	0	0	19	19
Donnelly,Brendan	0	0	83	0	0	83
Dotel,Octavio	0	0	0	137	145	282
Duchscherer,Justin	0	0	0	0	47	47
Duckworth,Brandon	0	0	0	0	62	62
Duke,Zach	0	0	0	20	0	20
Eaton,Adam	157	15	0	66	117	355
Elarton,Scott	180	31	0	0	75	286
Embree,Alan	14	20	0	0	15	49
Escobar,Kelvim	0	0	0	127	15	142
Eyre,Scott	0	0	26	0	16	42
Farnsworth,Kyle	55	0	0	0	0	55
Flores,Randy	0	0	0	15	0	15
Fogg,Josh	0	35	0	0	0	35
Fossum,Casey	0	39	41	0	15	95
Foulke,Keith	0	0	0	57	67	124
Francisco,Frank	0	0	0	180	88	268
Franklin,Ryan	8	0	0	0	0	8
Fuentes,Brian	0	0	69	0	0	69
Fultz,Aaron	0	16	0	0	0	16
Gagne,Eric	0	0	0	150	175	325
Geary,Geoff	0	0	0	15	0	15
Gonzalez,Mike	0	0	0	54	34	88
Gordon,Tom	96	0	0	0	15	111
Gorzelanny,Tom	0	0	0	0	19	19
Grilli,Jason	180	0	0	0	0	180
Guardado,Eddie	0	0	61	0	42	103
Halladay,Roy	0	0	78	84	0	162
Hamels,Cole	0	0	0	0	15	15
Hampton,Mike	0	21	0	107	183	311
Harang,Aaron	0	0	22	0	0	22
Harden,Rich	0	0	0	38	141	179
Hawkins,LaTroy	0	0	0	24	0	24
Hendrickson,Mark	0	0	0	16	18	34
Hermanson,Dustin	136	16	11	0	157	320
Hernandez,Orland	0	180	104	52	0	336
Hernandez,Robert	33	32	16	0	0	81
Hernandez,Runelvys	0	0	180	15	115	310
Hoffman,Trevor	0	165	0	0	0	165
Hudson,Luke	0	0	0	68	0	68
Hudson,Tim	0	0	42	30	0	72
Isringhausen,Jason	0	74	0	16	22	112
James,Chuck	0	0	0	0	32	32
Jennings,Jason	0	0	0	70	0	70
Johnson,Jason	74	0	0	0	0	74
Johnson,Randy	0	94	0	0	0	94
Jones,Todd	0	0	0	0	19	19
Kazmir,Scott	0	0	0	0	52	52
Kennedy,Joe	0	38	33	0	86	157
Kim,Byung-Hyun	0	26	34	0	31	91
King,Ray	15	0	0	0	0	15
Kline,Steve	29	0	33	0	0	62
Lawrence,Brian	0	0	0	0	183	183
Lee,Cliff	0	62	0	0	0	62
Lester,Jon	0	0	0	0	38	38
Lidle,Cory	12	16	0	15	0	43
Lieber,Jon	0	180	30	0	38	248
Lilly,Ted	51	0	0	59	0	110
Linebrink,Scott	23	0	0	0	0	23
Liriano,Francisco	0	0	0	0	35	35
Loaiza,Esteban	52	0	0	0	45	97
Loe,Kameron	0	0	0	0	44	44
Lopez,Rodrigo	0	43	0	0	0	43
Lowe,Mark	0	0	0	0	42	42
Lowry,Noah	0	0	0	0	31	31
Lugo,Ruddy	0	0	0	0	23	23
Lyon,Brandon	0	38	180	92	0	310
MacDougal,Mike	0	0	24	0	110	134
Maddux,Greg	7	0	0	0	0	7
Madson,Ryan	0	0	38	0	0	38
Mahay,Ron	20	0	0	16	0	36
Maine,John	0	0	0	0	40	40
Majewski,Gary	0	0	0	0	25	25
Marmol,Carlos	0	0	0	0	15	15
Maroth,Mike	0	0	0	0	103	103
Marquis,Jason	26	0	0	0	0	26
Marshall,Sean	0	0	0	0	40	40
Marte,Damaso	0	0	0	17	0	17
Martinez,Carlos	0	0	0	0	146	146
Martinez,Pedro	0	26	0	0	52	78
Martin,Tom	120	0	0	0	0	120
Mateo,Julio	0	0	19	0	54	73
McBride,Macay	0	0	0	0	37	37
McGowan,Dustin	0	0	138	0	0	138
Meche,Gil	0	0	0	27	0	27
Medders,Brandon	0	0	0	0	23	23
Miceli,Dan	0	0	19	0	93	112
Miller,Matt	0	0	0	77	139	216
Miller,Trever	0	0	0	15	23	38
Miller,Wade	47	0	97	90	153	387
Millwood,Kevin	0	0	37	20	0	57
Milton,Eric	26	180	0	0	28	234
Mitre,Sergio	0	0	0	0	88	88
Moehler,Brian	0	167	0	0	29	196
Morris,Matt	0	32	0	15	0	47
Mota,Guillermo	0	0	0	32	0	32
Mulder,Mark	18	41	0	0	94	153
Mussina,Mike	0	0	40	0	15	55
Nieve,Fernando	0	0	0	0	15	15
Ohka,Tomo	0	0	95	0	77	172
Ohman,Will	180	180	0	0	0	360
Oliver,Darren	0	0	28	0	0	28
Ortiz,Ramon	0	0	0	21	0	21
Ortiz,Russ	0	0	0	56	43	99
Oswalt,Roy	0	41	0	0	15	56
Padilla,Vicente	0	0	73	25	0	98
Park,Chan Ho	38	156	98	0	51	343
Patterson,John	0	0	78	15	146	239
Pavano,Carl	0	0	0	95	182	277
Peavy,Jake	0	0	43	0	0	43
Penny,Brad	44	0	47	22	0	113
Penn,Hayden	0	0	0	0	61	61
Perez,Odalis	0	0	14	88	0	102
Perez,Oliver	26	0	0	73	0	99
Pettitte,Andy	59	0	97	0	0	156
Pineiro,Joel	0	0	66	20	0	86
Ponson,Sidney	23	0	0	0	19	42
Prior,Mark	0	14	61	47	148	270
Radke,Brad	80	0	0	0	0	80
Ramirez,Elizardo	0	0	0	0	26	26
Ramirez,Horacio	0	0	119	0	99	218
Rauch,Jon	0	0	0	103	0	103
Redman,Mark	0	30	0	0	15	45
Reitsma,Chris	0	0	0	0	107	107
Rhodes,Arthur	0	0	54	21	0	75
Riske,David	28	0	0	0	47	75
Rivera,Mariano	67	32	0	0	0	99
Rodney,Fernando	0	0	180	73	0	253
Rodriguez,Francisco	0	0	0	17	0	17
Rusch,Glendon	0	23	0	0	33	56
Sabathia,C.C.	0	0	0	22	28	50
Sanchez,Duaner	0	0	0	0	61	61
Santos,Victor	0	0	0	0	26	26
Schilling,Curt	0	52	0	99	0	151
Schmidt,Jason	34	0	21	16	0	71
Schoeneweis,Scott	0	0	71	0	0	71
Seanez,Rudy	0	0	0	35	0	35
Sele,Aaron	39	43	15	0	0	97
Seo,Jae	0	0	0	0	15	15
Sheets,Ben	0	0	0	71	106	177
Shouse,Brian	11	0	0	0	17	28
Silva,Carlos	12	0	0	15	0	27
Smoltz,John	0	27	0	0	0	27
Soriano,Rafael	0	0	144	156	15	315
Sosa,Jorge	30	0	0	0	0	30
Speier,Justin	36	0	28	0	33	97
Springer,Russ	180	120	0	0	0	300
Stanton,Mike	0	43	0	0	0	43
Street,Huston	0	0	0	0	19	19
Tavarez,Julian	24	0	0	0	0	24
Thomson,John	0	0	0	88	96	184
Timlin,Mike	0	0	0	0	18	18
Tomko,Brett	0	0	13	0	35	48
Traber,Billy	0	0	180	0	0	180
Trachsel,Steve	20	0	0	146	0	166
Tsao,Chin Hui	0	0	0	159	181	340
Turnbow,Derrick	180	0	0	0	0	180
Valverde,Jose	0	0	105	38	0	143
Vargas,Claudio	0	38	0	56	0	94
Waechter,Doug	0	0	83	26	0	109
Wagner,Billy	0	0	69	0	0	69
Wagner,Ryan	0	0	0	85	0	85
Wakefield,Tim	0	0	0	0	57	57
Walker,Pete	0	0	0	18	109	127
Wang,Chien-Ming	0	0	0	59	0	59
Washburn,Jarrod	0	0	42	15	0	57
Webb,Brandon	0	15	0	0	0	15
Wells,David	0	0	19	22	122	163
Wells,Kip	0	0	22	0	129	151
Westbrook,Jake	139	0	0	0	0	139
Wickman,Bob	0	170	95	0	0	265
Williams,Scott	0	0	94	180	50	324
Williams,Dave	0	0	17	0	0	17
Williams,Todd	0	0	0	0	36	36
Williams,Woody	86	0	0	34	49	169
Wilson,C.J.	0	41	180	0	21	242
Wise,Matt	0	180	0	23	48	251
Wolf,Randy	18	0	53	110	0	181
Wood,Kerry	0	0	52	158	167	377
Wood,Mike	0	0	0	0	64	64
Worrell,Tim	0	0	0	58	110	168
Wright,Jaret	112	0	0	113	0	225
Yates,Tyler	0	0	0	180	0	180
Zambrano,Victor	0	0	43	0	147	190

Hidden injuries: 2006 Speculations
by Ray Murphy

One reality of our fantasy game is that we are forced to make decisions and conduct evaluations based on incomplete information. We're not in MLB clubhouses to see who is icing down after every game, who is injecting who with what, or who can't be bothered to watch film or look at scouting reports. Sometimes, these things become a little more obvious after the fact. In this space, we take a look back at some anomalous performances from 2006, and try to attribute some injury-related root causes.

Andruw Jones took an erratic path to 41 HR and a 158 PX in 2006: PXs by month of 193-122-111-200-170-179. Jones reportedly struggled with back problems at various times throughout the year. His PX in his 50-HR 2005 campaign was 180; the back troubles may be all that kept him from returning to that level. He could get back there in 2007.

Hank Blalock had shoulder surgery right after the season. Although the problem was first reported in September, could the issue have existed all year and thus explain his disappointing production? Quite possibly. Remember that Blalock is entering his power prime and still owns terrific skills, so better health could be all that is needed to spark a breakout.

Todd Helton's career-worst power output (15 HR) likely confirms that his ongoing back problems are here to stay. Helton's career path is starting to resemble that of Don Mattingly in the late 1980's: slugging first basemen crushes the ball through their 20's, but back problems suddenly rob them of their power as they cross over into their 30's.

Late in the season, **Alex Rodriguez** claimed that his underwhelming season was partially due to an injury. The report seemed odd at the time, since the nature of the injury was never disclosed. A-Rod did back up the claim, in a way, by posting his highest OPS of the season in September. Skeptical Yankee fans might point out that September was the only month where the Yankees held a comfortable lead in the AL East, reducing the pressure on Rodriguez. But could this much-scrutinized decline have been caused by a simple nagging injury? If Rodriguez posts a monster season again in 2007, for NYY or anyone else, we'll have our answer. Don't bet against it.

Ramon Hernandez's season should be filed under "catcher abuse" — on June 28, he inexplicably caught both ends of a doubleheader on an 88-degree day. Through that day, his OPS was in the upper 800's. He then collapsed to a sub-.600 OPS over July and August. Then, after finally resting four straight games in late August/early September, he rebounded with a 1.100 OPS in the final month.

Coco Crisp missed time at the beginning and end of the season with the same finger injury that he admits never fully healed. Give him a mulligan on his disappointing 2006 and consider him a buy-low target for 2007.

Josh Beckett's up-and-down season was driven by his HR/9. After getting devastated by home runs over the first two thirds of the season, Beckett reversed the trend and allowed only 5 HR in his last 10 starts. It was an achievement for the usually-fragile Beckett to stay healthy all season, but did he trade off durability for dominance? Whether Beckett was actually hiding an injury that affected his stuff earlier in the year, or was just being overly cautious in trying to stay in the rotation, it appears that the problem was solved in August and September. If he carries that trend into 2007, he may finally reach ace status.

Chris Shelton was the hottest hitter in the game in April, then quickly collapsed. Obviously his 286 PX from April was unsustainable. His monthly PX levels that followed (61-108-61 before being sent to Triple-A) were far below even his 2005 PX, but his other BPI's remained mostly steady. Was an injury to blame for the sudden power outage? If so, Shelton might exhibit further growth next year.

Oscar Villarreal might be an example of WBC-related fatigue. He accumulated most of his roto value very early in the year thanks to vulture wins, but his monthly BPV trend (18, 4, -10, 64, 90, 69) shows that he was far more effective in the second half. Perhaps the March tournament work set him back early in the year. There may yet be a future closer here.

Danys Baez does not own truly closer-worthy skills, still his meltdown this summer was startling. Sudden and dramatic ineffectiveness forced him out of the LA closer role, and eventually all the way to Atlanta. An appendectomy ended his season before he could steady himself. If his collapse was related to health issues, we would be more optimistic about his chances for success in 2006, perhaps in a closer role.

Randy Winn never hit the DL in 2006, but did have to deal with a series of leg injuries that may have affected his production. His speed has been declining over several years, so we can't just blame some nagging 2006 injuries for that. But we might be able to relate those injuries to his power outage. If he's healthy in 2007, that might be enough to get Winn back to the 20 HR level.

Geoff Jenkins suffered through a disappointing season, salvaged only by a 7-HR September. Jenkins has long been a streaky hitter, but could the cause of his awful summer have been a concussion he suffered in early June? If so, Jenkins may surprise us by returning to the 25-HR level in 2007.

Doug Davis suffered a dip in command and his ERA skyrocketed as a result. Davis is young for an age-related decline, and his BPI's had been very stable entering 2006. What if a hidden injury was what drove up his walk rate? After 440 IP in 2004-05, perhaps burnout was a factor. If Davis was hurt and gets back to 100% in 2007, his ERA could dive right back below 4.00.

As good as **Derrick Turnbow** was in seizing the MIL closer role in 2005, he was every bit as bad in giving it up in 2006. A sudden loss of control was his primary problem, to a degree not seen anywhere in his MLE history. Whether the problem was mechanical or injury-related, the root cause may be correctable, and could lead to Turnbow quickly regaining his 2005 form.

IV.
MINOR
LEAGUES

Top Prospects for 2007

by Deric McKamey

Albers, Matt (RHP, HOU) gained more consistency to his stuff and had little trouble overpowering hitters with his power sinker and curveball. Between Triple and Double-A, he went 12-3 with a 2.49 ERA, a 2.1 Cmd, 7.7 K/9, and a .228 oppBA. He pitched in relief (6.00 ERA in 15 IP) in the Majors, but will compete for a fifth starter role.

Aybar, Erick (SS, ANA) doesn't really have a clear path to the Majors, but has nothing to prove in Triple-A either. Wiry strong and fast, his power output has dropped, but can still hit for BA and steal bases. He hit .283/.327/.413 with 32 SB and a 0.58 Eye.

Bailey, Homer (RHP, CIN) went 10-6 with a 2.47 ERA, a 3.0 Cmd, 10.1 K/9, and a .198 oppBA between Double and high Class-A. His power curveball can be a plus pitch and he maintains velocity into mid-90's. He needs to be more efficient, but could be Cincinnati's top starter in 2007.

Baker, Jeff (RF, COL) finally stayed healthy for the entire season and his offensive production in Triple-A (.305/.369/.508 with 20 HR) and the Majors (.368 BA) puts him in the outfield mix. His plate discipline is not great (0.36 Eye) and can be gotten out by good pitching.

Bannister, Brian (RHP, NYM) made the Opening Day rotation, but a hamstring injury kept him out most of the year. Not an overpowering pitcher, but he sports good command (3.7 Cmd) and offers hitters five pitches. Between Triple and high Class-A, he posted a 3.19 ERA with 7.0 K/9; that figures to drop at the Major League level.

Barton, Brian (RF, CLE) improved his prospect status more than any player, showing five tools and is now in contention for an outfield spot. He has the ability to impact the game with his power (19 HR/.511 SLG) and speed (41 SB), and hit .323 between Double and high Class-A.

Barton, Daric (1B, OAK) missed time with elbow and hamstring injuries, but will compete for the starting 1B role in 2007. A pure hitter with contact ability and plate discipline, he lacks over-the-fence power, but Oakland is used to that (Hatteberg and Johnson). In Triple-A, he hit .259/.389/.395 with a 1.23 Eye.

Braun, Ryan (3B, MIL) hit much better with a mid-season promotion to Double-A (.303 vs .274) and though the Brewers' infield is crowded, he might force their hand. He makes hard contact and shows good power (22 HR/.514 SLG). He runs well despite average speed (26 SB), but defense is below average and may hold him back.

Braun, Ryan (RHP, KC) has the skills to possibly wrestle away the closer role. He can ramp his fastball up to 97 MPH and has two breaking pitches to offer hitters from both sides. Between Triple and Double-A, he saved 13 games with a 2.19 ERA, a 2.8 Cmd, 11.0 K/9, and a .221 oppBA, and only needs to cut-down his walks (4.0 BB/9).

Butler, Billy (LF/DH, KC) wasn't able to duplicate his HR production from the California League, but he hit .331/.388/.499 with 15 HR in Double-A. He has good bat speed and rarely swings at pitches out of the zone. His lackluster defense in LF will likely relegate him to the DH role.

Callaspo, Alberto (2B/SS, ARI) is an extreme contact hitter who has always hit for BA (.337); he doesn't walk or strike out much, leaving him with a 2.07 Eye. He showed surprising power in the PCL (7 HR/.478 SLG), but didn't utilize speed on the bases.

Carrillo, Cesar (RHP, SD) missed the second half with a forearm injury. He throws three pitches for strikes with the same arm speed, which keeps hitters off-balance, but he isn't going to be a strikeout pitcher. He went 1-3 with a 3.21 ERA, a 2.3 Cmd, 7.3 K/9, and a .239 oppBA between Triple and Double-A.

Danks, John (LHP, TEX) is one of the top LH pitchers in the minors, with a plus curveball and solid fastball velocity (87-93 MPH). He is equally adept at getting strikeouts (9.9 K/9) and groundball outs, and gets good downward plane with his high ¾ slot. Between Triple and Double-A, he went 9-9 with a 4.24 ERA, a 2.8 Cmd, and a .261 oppBA.

Devine, Joey (RHP, ATL) missed most of 2006 with a degenerative back condition, but returned strong in August. At three levels, he posted a 4.30 ERA with a 3.0 Cmd and was very difficult to hit (14.7 K/9, and a .167 oppBA). He attacks hitters with high velocity (95 MPH) and a slider that is tough on RH batters, but will have to overcome a max-effort delivery.

Fields, Josh (3B/LF, CHW) put together his first productive season by being more confident and patient at the plate. A strong athlete, he generates good bat speed through the strike zone, which enabled him to hit .305/.379/.515 with 19 HR and 28 SB in Triple-A. A former quarterback, he possesses good arm strength and range, but stiff hands leave him an average fielder.

Gallardo, Yovanni (RHP, MIL) was one of the minors' hottest pitchers in the second half. He repeats his ¾ delivery well and can throw all four pitches for strikes (3.7 Cmd), disrupting hitters' timing. Between Double and high Class-A he went 11-5 with a 1.86 ERA and got plenty of swings and misses (10.9 K/9, and a .192 oppBA).

Gordon, Alex (3B, KC) was the consensus Minor League Player of the Year after hitting .325/.427/.588 with 29 HR, 22 SB, and a 0.64 Eye in Double-A. He possesses great bat speed and plate coverage, giving him power to all fields. He draws walks and steals bases, and his defense at 3B is very good.

Guzman, Freddy (CF, TEX) is one of the fastest players in the minors, but also possesses hitting skills that makes him better than the average speedster. At Triple-A, he hit .282 and was able to get on base (.375 OBP) by hitting the ball on the ground and drawing walks (1.00 Eye), which allowed him to use his speed (31 SB).

Guzman, Joel (1B/RF/3B, TAM) hit .274/.327/.447 with 15 HR and nine SB, but has unlimited power potential. He could use more Triple-A time and might be best utilized as a multi-position reserve.

Hirsh, Jason (RHP, HOU) was named PCL Pitcher of the Year, leading the league with 13 wins and a 2.10 ERA. His slider is a plus pitch and gets strikeouts with both two and four-seam fastballs. A strong frame and good arm strength helps him maintain velocity (88-94 MPH) and show stamina. His strong skill set (2.3 Cmd, 7.7 K/9, and a .193) were outstanding in league context.

Hughes, Phil (RHP, NYY) dominated all season, going 12-6 with a 2.16 ERA, a 4.9 Cmd, 10.4 K/9, and a .179 oppBA between Triple and Double-A. His fastball and curve move very well and knows how to change speeds.

Iannetta, Chris (C, COL) emerged as one of the top catching prospects in the minors. Between the Triple and Double-A levels, he hit .336/.433/.567 with 14 HR, showing power to all fields and improved strike zone judgment (0.87 Eye). His arm strength and quick release offsets mediocre receiving skills.

Jimenez, Ubaldo (RHP, COL) has two plus pitches with his 90-96 MPH fastball and drop-dead curveball from a high ¾ slot. His command (1.8 Cmd) has been inconsistent throughout his career, but he has always been able to miss bats (8.9 K/9 and a .225 oppBA). He won 14 games with a 3.80 ERA in two hitter friendly leagues.

Jones, Adam (CF, SEA) struggled when thrust into the CF role in August (.216 BA), but made adjustments and should come back strong. His power emerged in Triple-A (16 HR/.484 SLG), but poor plate discipline (0.36 Eye) will keep BA/OBP suppressed. He possesses one of the best outfield arms in the minors and has solid range.

Kouzmanoff, Kevin (3B, SD) has as much pure power as any hitter in the minors, generating good bat speed with his strong wrists. Between Triple and Double-A, he hit .379/.437/.656 with 22 HR, and improved his plate discipline (0.72 Eye).

LaRoche, Andy (3B, LAD) played through a shoulder injury in the second half, attesting to his toughness. The ball jumps off his bat, showing power to all fields and ability to hit for BA. Between Triple and Double-A, he hit .315/.410/.514 with 19 HR and a 1.03 Eye.

Lincecum, Tim (RHP, SF) possesses the most electric arm of any 2006 Draftee. At two levels, he posted a 1.71 ERA and a 4.8 Cmd, and was untouchable (16.5 K/9 and a .127 oppBA). His curveball is lethal and his power sinker from an unconventional delivery is incredibly heavy.

Lind, Adam (LF, TOR) is one of the better pure hitters in the minors with a fluid stroke and bat speed. He hit .330/.394/.556 with 24 HR between Triple and Double-A, and followed up by hitting .367 in 60 AB for Toronto. His range and arm strength are below average, but his bat is strong enough to DH.

Loney, James (1B, LA) led the minors with a .380 BA in Triple-A and proved he was more than a BA hitter with a .546 SLG. His swing mechanics are very fluid and has good bat speed, but doesn't generate much loft and likely won't hit more than 20 HR at his peak. He hit well in 102 AB for the Dodgers (.284 BA) and is an excellent defender.

Mastny, Tom (RHP, CLE) pitched well enough to grasp a brief hold on the closer role (five saves/5.51 ERA), but is better suited for setup relief. He keeps the ball low with his sinker and uses his two breaking pitches to notch strikeouts. He posted a 2.01 ERA, a 3.2 Cmd, 10.9 K/9, and a .178 oppBA between Triple and Double-A.

Miller, Adam (RHP, CLE) showed the type of skills that makes him a future ace, going 15-6 with a 2.84 ERA, a 3.5 Cmd, 9.2 K/9, and a .227 oppBA between Triple and Double-A. His fastball is overpowering and hitters are rendered helpless when his 84-88 MPH slider is on. He has had elbow problems in the past, but managed to toss 158 pain-free innings.

Montero, Miguel (C, ARI) maintained his hitting stroke and was able to improve his defensive shortcomings. With a compact swing and good bat speed, he hit .286/.373/.461 with 17 HR and a 0.82 Eye between Triple and Double-A. His receiving skills are excellent and can halt running game despite average arm strength.

Niemann, Jeff (RHP, TAM) returned strong from off-season shoulder surgery, posting a 2.68 ERA, a 2.9 Cmd, 9.8 K/9, and a .202 oppBA at Double-A. His tall/large frame gives him downward plane, and coupled with an overpowering fastball and two solid breaking pitches, he has excellent upside.

Nippert, Dustin (RHP, ARI) was more hittable in 2006 (.290 oppBA in Triple-A) and struggled in his spot starts in Arizona (11.70 ERA), but has the solid base skills (2.5 Cmd and 8.3 K/9) to succeed. He can overpower hitters with a 91-96 MPH fastball and spike curveball, though he needs to change speeds better.

Owens, Jerry (CF, CHW): Athletic with plus speed, his BA has been sporadic and he doesn't have much power, but knows how to get on and steal bases. He hit .262 with a .330 OBP, 40 SB, and a 0.74 Eye in Triple-A. He has good range and an average throwing arm, so at worst, can be a solid fourth outfielder.

Owings, Micah (RHP, ARI) pitched better in Double-A than in Triple-A, but won all 10 decisions at the upper level. His sinker/slider combination is more conducive to groundball outs, but did manage to strike out 7.2 per 9 IP. Overall, he went 16-2 with a 2.91 ERA and a 2.5 Cmd. He has the versatility to either start or relieve.

Pedroia, Dustin (2B, BOS): With good hand-eye coordination, he makes solid contact and draws walks, giving him an above average BA/OBP. He doesn't hit for power and is a below average runner, so doesn't have a lot of upside. He hit .305/.384/.426 with a 1.78 Eye at Triple-A, but hit just .191 for the Red Sox.

Pelfrey, Mike (RHP, NYM) destroyed hitters at three levels (7-3 with a 2.43 ERA, a 3.3 Cmd, 10.2 K/9, and a .232 oppBA) and features two plus pitches; an electric fastball and power curveball that are difficult to hit. His change-up is solid and he learned from his mediocre performance in New York (5.48 ERA).

Pence, Hunter (RF, HOU): With his short stroke and physical strength, he could find the Crawford Boxes to his liking. At Double-A, he hit .283/.357/.533 with 28 HR and a 0.55 Eye. He runs well for his size (17 SB) and shows range in the outfield, but his arm strength is average at best.

Pereira, Nick (RHP, SF) rarely pushes 90 MPH, but shows exquisite command (2.1 Cmd) and the ability to keep ball low (0.6 HR/9). His slider is tough on RH batters and has made improvements to change-up. Between Triple and high Class-A, he went 11-4 with a 4.00 ERA and 7.8 K/9.

Perkins, Glen (LHP, MIN) will offer a sharp contrast to the two hard-throwing LH pitchers in the Twins' rotation with his modest fastball, but changes speeds very well and provides deception with his delivery. Between Triple and Double-A, he went just 4-12 with a 3.85 ERA, but his base skills were solid (2.7 Cmd, 9.9 K/9, and a .247 oppBA).

Petit, Yusmeiro (RHP, FLA) settled into the pitcher he is likely to become, showing solid command (3.4 Cmd) and a deceptive delivery. He posted a 4.28 ERA in a high offensive league, but failed to miss bats (6.3 K/9 and a .268 oppBA) for the first time in his career. His change-up remains his best pitch and his fastball is deceptively quick.

Pie, Felix (CF, CHC): A tremendous athlete with a power/speed combination, he hit .283/.341/.451 with 15 HR and 17 SB in Triple-A, but needs work on his plate discipline (0.37 Eye). Make-up questions surrounded him in the minors and likely cost him a late-season promotion.

Sanchez, Humberto (RHP, NYY), acquired for Gary Sheffield, he could work his way into the Yankees' rotation through a period of middle relief. Always regarded as having good stuff with four quality pitches, but never seems to stay healthy through an entire season. He went 10-6 with a 2.63 ERA, a 2.7 Cmd, 9.4 K/9, and a .220 oppBA between Triple and Double-A.

Tata, Jordan (RHP, DET) earned a roster spot with a strong spring training, but was demoted to get innings as a starter. He went 10-6 with a 3.84 ERA in Triple-A, but his base skills were on the soft side (1.8 Cmd, 6.3 K/9, and a .252 oppBA). Easing him into the rotation as a middle reliever might be a viable option.

Tulowitzki, Troy (SS, COL) could become one of the top NL shortstops. He has a line-drive stroke that is excellent for hitting for BA and doubles, and will draw walks. He hit .291/.370/.473 with 13 HR and a 0.65 Eye in Double-A, and hit .240 for the Rockies.

Volquez, Edinson (RHP, TEX) will get another chance to earn a rotation spot despite a wretched 7.29 ERA in the Majors. He works with a plus change-up which makes his 89-95 MPH fastball look even quicker. His slider really took shape and repeats his delivery. He went 6-6 with a 3.21 ERA and 9.7 K/9 in Triple-A, but his walk rate (5.4 BB/9) and command (1.8 Cmd) need to improve.

Windsor, Jason (RHP, OAK) is one of the more cerebral pitchers in the minors and succeeds through plus command (3.8 Cmd) and changing speeds. Between Triple and Double-A, he went 17-2 with a 3.63 ERA, 9.4 K/9, and a .263 oppBA. His ability to miss bats was even more impressive due to his low velocity.

Young, Chris (CF, ARI) will help usher in youth to the ARI outfield with his power/speed combination and defensive prowess. At Triple-A, he hit .276/.363/.532 with 21 HR, 17 SB, and a 0.73 Eye. His offense improves every year and has the ability to be a 30/30 player at his peak.

Young, Delmon (RF, TAM) gave a glimpse into his enormous potential by hitting .317 for the Devil Rays in September. A classic run producer with excellent power and ability to hit for BA, he doesn't draw many walks (0.24 Eye). He hit .316/.341/.474 with eight HR in Triple-A and showed base-running instincts by stealing 22 bases.

Top Ranked Prospects for 2007

TOP 10
Delmon Young (OF, TAM)
Troy Tulowitzki (SS, COL)
Alex Gordon (3B, KC)
Mike Pelfrey (RHP, NYM)
Homer Bailey (RHP, CIN)
Chris Young (OF, ARI)
Adam Lind (OF, TOR)
James Loney (1B, LAD)
Dustin Pedroia (2B, BOS)
Tim Lincecum (RHP, SF)

11-20
Jason Hirsh (RHP, HOU)
Kevin Kouzmanoff (3B, SD)
Jeff Baker (OF, COL)
Phil Hughes (RHP, NYY)
Jeff Niemann (RHP, TAM)
Andy LaRoche (3B, LAD)
Billy Butler (OF, KC)
Ryan Braun (RHP, KC)
Jason Windsor (RHP, OAK)
Chris Iannetta (C, COL)

21-30
Glen Perkins (LHP, MIN)
Hunter Pence (OF, HOU)
Alberto Callaspo (2B/SS, ARI)
Dustin Nippert (RHP, ARI)
Brian Bannister (RHP, NYM)
Tom Mastny (RHP, CLE)
Matt Albers (RHP, HOU)
Miguel Montero (C, ARI)
Adam Miller (RHP, CLE)
Yovanni Gallardo (RHP, MIL)

31-40
Ryan Braun (3B, MIL)
John Danks (LHP, TEX)
Jerry Owens (OF, CHW)
Yusmeiro Petit (RHP, FLA)
Edinson Volquez (RHP, TEX)
Ubaldo Jimenez (RHP, COL)
Josh Fields (3B, CHW)
Erick Aybar (SS, LAA)
Brian Barton (OF, CLE)
Freddy Guzman (OF, TEX)

41-50
Joey Devine (RHP, ATL)
Humberto Sanchez (RHP, NYY)
Micah Owings (RHP, ARI)
Daric Barton (1B, OAK)
Joel Guzman (1B/OF, TAM)
Nick Pereira (RHP, SF)
Cesar Carillo (RHP, SD)
Felix Pie (OF, CHC)
Jordan Tata (RHP, DET)
Adam Jones (OF, SEA)

Major League Equivalents

In his 1985 *Baseball Abstract*, Bill James introduced the concept of major league equivalencies. His assertion was that, with the proper adjustments, a minor leaguer's statistics could be converted to an equivalent major league level performance with a great deal of accuracy.

Because of wide variations in the level of play among different minor leagues, it is difficult to get a true reading on a player's potential. For instance, a .300 AVG achieved in the high-offense Pacific Coast League is not nearly as much of an accomplishment as a similar level in the Eastern League. MLEs normalize these type of variances, for all statistical categories.

The actual MLEs are not projections. They represent how a player's previous performance might look at the major league level. However, that MLE stat line can be used in forecasting future performance in just the same way as a major league stat line would.

The model we use contains a few variations to James' version and updates all of the minor league and ballpark factors. In addition, we designed a module to convert pitching statistics, which is something James did not do.

Another of the enhancements we made is to include an adjustment for each player's age and relative level reached at that age. This serves to truly separate the prospects from the suspects. In other words, it might seem that Jon Knott's 32 HR, .280 season may look worthy of a shot in the majors, but a 28-year-old facing young Triple-A pitching is bound to put up good numbers. His MLE of 20 HRs, .217 shows the appropriate — albeit radical — adjustment facing potential big league pitchers, and diffuses any thought of him being able to help a major league club.

Do MLEs really work?

Used correctly, MLEs are excellent indicators of potential. But, just like we cannot take traditional major league statistics at face value, the same goes for MLEs. The underlying measures of base skill — batting eye ratios, pitching command ratios, etc. — are far more accurate in evaluating future talent than raw home runs, batting averages or ERAs.

The charts we present here also provide the unique perspective of looking at two year's worth of data. These are only short-term trends, for sure. But even here we can find small indications of players improving their skills, or struggling, as they rise through more difficult levels of competition. Since players — especially those with any modicum of talent — are promoted rapidly through major league systems, a two-year scan is often all we get to spot any trends. Five-year trends will appear in the new *Minor League Baseball Analyst*.

Here are some things to look for as you scan these charts:

Target players who...
- spent a full season in Double-A and then a full season at Triple-A
- had consistent playing time from one year to the next
- maintained or improved their base skills levels as they were promoted.

Raise the warning flag for players who...
- were stuck at the same level both years, or regressed
- displayed marked changes in playing time from one year to the next.
- showed large drops in BPIs from one year to the next.

Also be sure to keep an eye on each player's age. While minor leaguers over 26 have officially lost their "prospect" status, there are still some who will make it to the majors. Don't discount them completely or you might end up missing out on a player like Emil Brown.

Players are listed on the charts if they spent at least part of 2005 or 2006 in Triple-A or Double-A and had at least 100 at bats or 30 innings pitched within those two levels. Each is listed with the organization they finished the season with.

Only statistics accumulated in Triple-A and Double-A ball are included (players who split a season are indicated as a/a); major league and Single-A stats are excluded.

Each player's actual AB and IP totals are used as the base for the conversion. However, it is more useful to compare performances using common levels, so rely on the ratios and sabermetric gauges. Complete explanations of these formulas appear in the glossary.

Major League Equivalent Statistics

BATTER	Yr	Age	Pos	Lev	Org	ab	r	h	d	t	hr	rbi	bb	k	sb	cs	ba	ob	slg	ops	bb%	ct%	eye	px	sx	rc/g	bpv
Abad,Andy	05	33	8	aaa	CLE	418	45	95	24	1	12	58	30	52	2	5	226	277	372	650	7%	88%	0.57	97	48	3.42	27
	06	34	8	aaa	CIN	266	32	62	11	0	8	28	22	32	0	1	233	291	365	656	8%	88%	0.67	83	33	3.69	25
Abercrombie,Regg	05	25	8	aa	FLA	178	23	37	5	2	7	18	9	41	5	5	207	245	379	625	5%	77%	0.22	98	129	2.74	14
Abernathy,Brent	05	28	4	aaa	MIN	215	28	60	12	0	5	20	17	19	6	3	281	333	402	735	7%	91%	0.86	83	70	4.88	45
	06	29	4	aaa	MIL	439	52	107	15	0	5	35	34	59	15	10	245	298	309	607	7%	86%	0.57	45	79	3.14	12
Abreu,Michel	06	27	3	aa	NYM	398	52	111	23	1	13	59	37	95	0	0	280	342	439	781	9%	76%	0.39	103	36	5.61	44
Abreu,Tony	06	22	4	aa	LA	457	64	123	22	2	6	53	31	69	8	4	269	316	365	681	6%	85%	0.45	67	93	4.16	26
Abruzzo,Jared	05	24	3	aa	TEX	153	14	29	4	0	4	10	15	41	0	1	190	261	292	552	9%	73%	0.35	62	27	2.52	-4
Aceves,Jonathan	05	28	2	a/a	CHW	271	28	55	14	1	6	25	22	60	0	1	202	262	327	589	7%	78%	0.36	83	46	2.87	9
	06	29	2	a/a	FLA	255	27	47	16	0	4	23	17	69	0	1	183	234	297	531	6%	73%	0.24	82	44	2.26	-0
Acuna,Ron	05	26	8	aa	TOR	400	41	86	25	2	1	26	22	100	10	3	215	256	294	549	5%	75%	0.22	63	108	2.59	2
	06	27	8	aa	MIL	400	37	85	15	2	1	41	22	94	2	5	212	253	264	517	5%	77%	0.24	40	66	2.17	-8
Adams,Russ	06	26	6	aaa	TOR	161	18	48	9	2	0	14	15	22	3	2	295	354	374	727	8%	87%	0.67	59	100	4.95	36
Aguila,Chris	05	27	8	aaa	FLA	138	18	40	11	2	5	17	10	16	6	3	288	335	499	834	7%	88%	0.59	135	131	5.91	64
	06	28	8	aaa	FLA	302	40	80	12	2	8	46	21	48	6	4	264	312	393	705	6%	84%	0.43	81	93	4.31	30
Airoso,Kurt	05	31	0	aa	DET	381	39	66	17	1	12	41	22	119	1	1	173	217	314	531	5%	69%	0.18	89	61	2.17	-2
	06	32	8	aa	DET	430	43	68	11	1	11	42	54	163	1	1	158	252	260	512	11%	62%	0.33	62	43	2.21	-15
Aldridge,Cory	05	26	8	a/a	KC	470	50	93	19	3	18	58	24	101	9	5	197	237	364	601	5%	78%	0.24	100	101	2.77	12
	06	27	8	a/a	NYM	376	29	79	17	2	3	29	24	120	8	5	211	259	285	543	6%	68%	0.20	54	84	2.43	-4
Alexander,Manny	05	35	6	aaa	SD	433	45	103	20	5	7	48	29	62	19	11	237	285	353	638	6%	86%	0.46	75	123	3.32	19
	06	36	6	aaa	SD	430	54	86	16	0	5	25	24	52	10	5	201	244	270	514	5%	88%	0.47	50	95	2.18	-3
Alfaro,Jason	05	28	5	aaa	TOR	381	32	83	23	1	8	34	14	54	0	1	217	245	342	587	4%	86%	0.27	86	38	2.77	13
	06	29	5	aaa	PIT	374	33	86	22	1	9	47	20	48	2	4	229	269	368	637	5%	87%	0.42	94	46	3.26	23
Alfonzo,Edgardo	06	33	4	aaa	NYM	141	9	30	5	0	3	16	14	16	0	1	211	280	306	586	9%	89%	0.87	64	16	2.91	14
Alfonzo,Eliezer	05	27	2	a/a	SF	186	23	45	8	0	5	23	5	34	1	0	242	263	373	636	3%	81%	0.16	83	56	3.39	18
	06	28	2	a/a	SF	139	10	26	3	1	2	10	8	33	1	0	188	231	257	488	5%	76%	0.23	42	66	1.99	-16
Allegra,Matthew	05	24	8	aa	OAK	203	13	31	7	0	5	17	8	61	0	0	154	185	257	442	4%	70%	0.12	65	22	1.49	-19
	06	25	8	aa	OAK	355	40	77	23	1	11	47	29	107	3	3	215	274	378	652	8%	70%	0.27	108	63	3.47	22
Allen,Chad	05	31	8	aaa	STL	285	32	76	15	0	7	33	13	41	7	5	265	296	395	691	4%	86%	0.31	87	71	4.01	30
	06	32	8	aaa	KC	417	32	111	23	3	10	63	26	58	1	4	265	309	406	714	6%	86%	0.45	92	42	4.36	36
Allen,Luke	05	27	8	aaa	ANA	455	58	105	16	4	15	63	36	67	9	4	232	288	384	672	7%	85%	0.54	91	106	3.82	25
	06	28	8	aaa	SD	305	28	68	14	1	7	42	25	68	1	1	223	282	338	620	8%	78%	0.37	76	47	3.29	13
Alvarez,Gerardo	06	27	4	aa	BAL	326	34	57	10	0	3	25	21	74	8	5	176	226	238	463	6%	77%	0.28	43	84	1.71	-18
Alvarez,Nick	05	29	8	aa	LA	237	18	48	7	0	2	22	16	33	2	0	203	253	253	506	6%	86%	0.49	37	45	2.22	-7
	06	30	8	a/a	LA	202	23	39	6	1	2	12	9	39	3	2	195	229	268	497	4%	81%	0.23	48	97	2.00	-11
Alvarez,Rafael	06	30	8	aa	PIT	244	21	44	5	2	3	18	16	85	0	0	178	228	252	480	6%	65%	0.18	44	76	1.90	-19
Alvarez,Tony	06	28	8	a/a	BAL	334	34	72	12	1	6	31	18	73	12	9	216	256	310	567	5%	78%	0.24	61	91	2.47	2
Amador,Christoph	06	24	6	aa	CHW	231	24	47	9	1	2	15	13	71	12	3	202	243	273	516	5%	69%	0.18	50	123	2.28	-9
Ambres,Chip	05	26	8	aaa	BOS	279	36	74	20	2	7	39	36	49	15	6	266	349	426	775	11%	82%	0.72	108	111	5.43	47
	06	27	8	aaa	KC	187	16	34	8	1	2	13	19	36	2	4	182	258	265	523	9%	81%	0.54	57	68	2.16	-5
Amezaga,Alfredo	05	28	6	aaa	PIT	185	20	54	10	1	1	9	12	21	10	9	293	337	375	712	6%	89%	0.59	62	96	4.19	35
Anderson,Brian	05	24	8	aaa	CHW	440	58	118	21	2	15	45	36	93	3	2	268	324	427	751	8%	79%	0.39	99	70	5.00	38
Anderson,Bryan	05	27	3	aa	CIN	257	17	33	13	0	2	13	17	65	1	2	129	182	210	392	6%	75%	0.26	61	47	1.17	-27
Anderson,Dennis	05	28	2	aa	FLA	177	17	45	9	0	1	19	17	25	1	2	253	320	319	639	9%	86%	0.69	53	36	3.65	20
Anderson,Drew	06	25	4	aa	CIN	148	16	35	8	2	2	13	12	26	2	2	237	293	353	646	7%	83%	0.46	78	102	3.52	20
	06	25	8	a/a	MIL	465	67	124	28	4	7	46	37	93	18	10	268	322	386	708	7%	80%	0.40	82	123	4.38	31
Anderson,Josh	05	23	8	aa	HOU	524	61	140	16	9	1	23	25	75	46	19	267	300	335	635	5%	86%	0.34	44	171	3.44	14
	06	24	8	aa	HOU	561	67	152	22	4	3	41	22	65	35	14	271	298	339	637	4%	88%	0.33	48	128	3.53	17
Andino,Robert	05	21	6	aa	FLA	516	56	127	28	0	4	42	34	103	19	8	246	293	324	616	6%	80%	0.33	60	86	3.32	13
	06	22	6	aaa	FLA	498	57	116	16	5	6	38	28	79	11	14	232	273	323	596	5%	84%	0.36	57	109	2.76	8
Ankiel,Rick	05	26	8	aa	STL	136	11	24	5	0	6	19	6	25	0	0	179	214	352	566	4%	81%	0.24	103	17	2.42	7
Ardoin,Danny	05	31	2	aaa	COL	142	15	38	10	1	5	14	12	26	2	1	266	322	444	766	8%	82%	0.46	116	72	5.14	46
Arias,Joaquin	05	21	6	aa	TEX	499	52	147	22	6	5	45	14	36	16	12	295	314	393	707	3%	93%	0.39	65	114	4.23	33
	06	22	6	aaa	TEX	493	56	139	15	12	4	48	19	56	26	11	281	308	383	691	4%	89%	0.34	60	178	4.17	25
Arlis,Patrick	06	26	2	aa	FLA	205	18	41	12	0	2	12	32	54	2	1	202	311	285	596	14%	73%	0.60	64	40	3.23	6
Arnold,Eric	06	26	5	aa	TOR	141	11	31	9	0	4	22	8	53	0	3	222	263	376	639	5%	63%	0.15	102	26	3.07	19
Arteaga,Josh	05	26	0	a/a	ATL	144	9	31	8	0	0	11	8	33	0	2	218	257	270	527	5%	77%	0.23	47	26	2.23	-4
	06	27	6	aa	ATL	328	24	61	10	0	6	23	23	75	2	0	186	240	271	511	7%	77%	0.31	55	42	2.19	-9
Asadoorian,Rick	05	25	8	a/a	CIN	395	39	83	20	2	6	33	13	91	12	5	209	235	313	548	3%	77%	0.15	71	113	2.40	2
	06	26	8	aa	CIN	300	30	66	10	2	3	23	15	82	4	5	220	257	302	559	5%	73%	0.18	54	88	2.48	-1
Ashby,Chris	05	31	2	a/a	FLA	252	17	42	6	0	2	14	13	35	0	2	168	208	213	421	5%	86%	0.37	32	31	1.39	-23
	06	32	2	aaa	FLA	198	19	48	9	0	3	27	12	27	2	1	241	283	327	611	6%	87%	0.44	61	50	3.24	14
Ash,Jonathan	06	24	4	aa	HOU	392	32	108	19	5	1	23	20	33	4	9	276	311	356	668	5%	92%	0.61	57	80	3.72	28
Aspito,Jason	05	27	8	aa	ANA	157	17	32	6	0	5	22	8	25	1	2	205	243	344	586	5%	84%	0.31	86	50	2.64	10
	06	28	8	a/a	ANA	386	36	74	10	1	11	37	20	71	3	8	192	231	311	542	5%	82%	0.28	71	53	2.14	-1
Athas,Jamie	05	26	6	a/a	SF	217	19	44	6	2	3	13	11	41	5	2	201	241	285	526	5%	81%	0.28	51	105	2.28	-6
	06	27	6	aa	FLA	159	14	28	3	1	3	9	12	39	3	0	175	234	257	491	7%	75%	0.31	50	87	2.06	-15
Aubrey,Michael	05	23	3	aa	CLE	106	15	26	5	1	3	16	6	16	1	0	247	286	393	680	5%	84%	0.35	91	97	4.00	27
Aviles,Mike	05	25	6	aa	KC	521	56	119	28	5	9	57	22	49	8	8	228	259	348	607	4%	91%	0.44	80	100	2.91	18
	06	26	6	aaa	KC	469	46	115	21	3	6	42	25	41	12	5	245	283	340	623	5%	91%	0.60	64	97	3.33	20
Avlas,Phil	05	23	2	aa	ARI	113	12	25	5	0	2	14	15	16	4	2	221	313	319	631	12%	86%	0.94	67	65	3.53	20
	06	24	2	aa	ARI	278	39	70	17	0	7	26	42	46	3	5	251	349	387	736	13%	83%	0.90	93	47	4.80	40
Aybar,Erick	05	22	6	aa	ANA	535	78	142	26	6	7	42	22	40	38	28	265	294	376	670	4%	93%	0.55	73	151	3.35	30
	06	23	6	aaa	ANA	339	51	88	19	2	5	37	17	27	26	23	260	295	375	670	5%	92%	0.63	79	135	3.11	32
Aybar,Willy	05	23	5	aaa	LA	401	32	98	20	2	3	41	26	35	1	9	244	290	327	617	6%	91%	0.74	61	41	3.03	21
	06	24	5	aaa	ATL	207	25	57	11	1	7	32	19	21	1	4	275	336	440	776	8%	90%	0.90	104	52	5.09	53
Bacani,David	05	26	5	a/a	NYM	281	26	62	14	1	4	33	23	53	3	6	221	279	317	596	7%	81%	0.42	68	57	2.81	10
	06	27	4	aa	BOS	406	45	76	17	1	3	33	39	70	8	4	186	257	258	515	9%	83%	0.56	52	86	2.25	-5
Bacon,Dwaine	05	26	8	a/a	CHC	342	49	69	9	5	2	14	39	98	32	14	203	284	271	555	10%	71%	0.40	43	177	2.61	-7
	06	28	8	aa	ANA	339	26	51	11	2	3	17	22	71	22	12	152	204	223	427	6%	79%	0.32	48	122	1.36	-23
Badeaux,Brooks	05	29	4	aaa	TAM	229	19	42	10	1	2	13	7	32	1	0	183	208	260	468	3%	86%	0.23	56	68	1.76	-11
	06	30	4	a/a	BAL	272	22	47	7	0	5	24	16	57	1	3	172	219	253	472	6%	79%	0.29	52	39	1.70	-16

Major League Equivalent Statistics

BATTERS

BATTER	Yr	Age	Pos	Lev	Org	ab	r	h	d	t	hr	rbi	bb	k	sb	cs	ba	ob	slg	ops	bb%	ct%	eye	px	sx	rc/g	bpv
Bailey,Jeff	05	27	3	a/a	BOS	219	26	48	11	0	9	28	21	51	3	1	218	285	390	676	9%	77%	0.41	107	57	3.85	25
	06	28	3	aaa	BOS	458	57	118	23	4	19	72	67	111	1	2	257	351	448	799	13%	76%	0.60	116	63	5.78	45
Bailie,Stefan	05	25	0	aa	BOS	129	7	16	5	0	4	8	5	44	1	0	126	161	244	405	4%	66%	0.12	74	40	1.21	-25
Baker,Casey	05	25	4	aa	SD	268	29	46	7	1	1	11	23	60	6	2	171	238	215	453	8%	78%	0.39	32	100	1.77	-22
Baker,Jeff	05	24	5	aaa	COL	228	25	60	14	1	8	26	10	26	2	1	263	294	439	733	4%	89%	0.38	113	66	4.53	42
	06	25	8	aaa	COL	482	52	137	28	3	17	80	34	78	5	1	283	330	458	788	7%	84%	0.43	110	78	5.61	49
Baker,John	05	25	2	aaa	OAK	346	33	70	22	2	4	32	23	70	1	0	202	252	312	564	6%	80%	0.33	79	70	2.67	7
	06	26	2	aaa	OAK	293	39	70	18	1	3	30	31	61	5	0	240	312	338	650	9%	79%	0.51	73	91	3.91	20
Baker,Steve	05	25	8	aa	SD	256	20	59	11	2	4	25	8	64	3	2	232	256	330	586	3%	75%	0.13	65	80	2.82	7
	06	26	8	aa	SD	128	12	24	4	1	1	10	13	48	1	0	190	265	258	524	9%	62%	0.27	47	82	2.41	-12
Baldiris,Aarom	05	23	4	aa	NYM	493	52	118	30	1	9	49	32	64	5	1	239	286	359	645	6%	87%	0.50	84	71	3.62	24
	06	24	4	a/a	TEX	352	30	81	17	1	4	30	13	47	3	5	230	258	318	576	4%	87%	0.28	63	58	2.63	8
Balentien,Wladimir	06	22	8	aa	SEA	444	72	96	22	1	21	77	69	139	13	7	216	322	412	734	13%	69%	0.50	119	91	4.60	31
Ball,Jarred	05	22	8	aa	ARI	396	54	92	19	2	6	27	60	89	30	20	232	333	336	669	13%	78%	0.67	70	112	3.74	20
Bankston,Wes	05	22	3	aa	TAM	298	35	78	15	2	9	39	25	54	2	4	262	319	416	735	8%	82%	0.46	97	67	4.59	37
	06	23	3	a/a	TAM	362	41	98	19	1	9	47	21	77	4	2	271	311	403	714	5%	79%	0.27	87	67	4.50	32
Bannon,Jeff	05	26	6	a/a	CIN	529	50	113	29	1	14	56	20	100	12	1	213	241	347	588	4%	81%	0.20	89	95	2.85	12
	06	27	6	a/a	CIN	350	26	73	20	1	6	37	12	68	4	3	209	235	323	559	3%	81%	0.18	80	66	2.47	6
Barden,Brian	05	25	5	aaa	ARI	514	54	140	34	4	11	59	28	76	10	6	272	310	418	728	5%	85%	0.37	99	94	4.56	39
	06	26	5	aaa	ARI	494	61	134	34	2	13	73	35	71	1	4	271	318	425	743	7%	86%	0.49	104	49	4.77	43
Barfield,Josh	05	23	4	aaa	SD	512	61	142	22	1	11	60	45	82	17	6	277	335	386	721	8%	84%	0.55	72	85	4.78	33
Barker,Kevin	05	30	3	a/a	TOR	528	52	115	29	2	21	78	48	144	2	2	218	283	397	680	8%	73%	0.33	112	46	3.85	26
	06	31	3	aaa	TOR	473	59	114	36	2	15	62	66	122	5	3	242	334	422	757	12%	74%	0.54	121	67	5.09	41
Barker,Sean	05	25	8	aa	COL	468	51	106	21	6	12	54	26	109	11	7	227	268	373	641	5%	77%	0.24	90	132	3.27	17
	06	26	8	aaa	COL	330	39	90	13	8	11	40	21	74	13	8	273	317	456	773	6%	78%	0.29	105	174	4.94	40
Barkett,Andy	05	31	3	aaa	ATL	118	7	20	5	0	1	10	14	24	0	0	168	258	236	495	11%	79%	0.59	52	14	2.12	-11
Barnes,John	05	29	8	a/a	ATL	328	23	70	14	0	2	21	16	27	1	1	213	248	278	526	5%	92%	0.58	49	34	2.31	3
Barnes,Larry	05	31	8	aaa	FLA	218	19	41	6	1	5	16	7	37	1	3	186	212	285	497	3%	83%	0.20	61	64	1.82	-9
Barnwell,Chris	05	27	5	a/a	MIL	292	25	58	14	1	3	16	14	47	4	4	197	233	277	510	4%	84%	0.29	58	73	2.04	-5
	06	28	6	aaa	MIL	383	39	103	17	2	4	31	33	59	13	7	268	326	352	679	8%	85%	0.56	59	90	4.15	25
Barthelemy,Ryan	05	25	3	aa	PHI	354	30	70	20	2	10	27	12	83	1	1	198	224	348	572	3%	76%	0.14	97	61	2.52	9
Bartlett,Jason	05	26	6	aaa	MIN	229	35	69	10	2	4	28	25	30	2	2	303	371	415	786	10%	87%	0.82	73	83	5.87	47
	06	27	6	aaa	MIN	235	41	69	22	3	1	19	10	30	6	3	293	321	425	746	4%	87%	0.32	101	141	4.92	46
Barton,Brian	06	24	8	aa	CLE	151	29	47	5	0	5	23	11	26	13	5	308	357	434	791	7%	83%	0.43	77	112	5.77	43
Barton,Daric	05	20	3	aa	OAK	212	32	62	19	1	4	30	28	23	1	1	292	376	451	826	12%	89%	1.24	114	62	6.48	69
	06	21	3	aaa	OAK	147	22	36	7	2	2	19	28	18	1	0	247	366	367	732	16%	88%	1.51	76	103	5.19	44
Basak,Chris	05	27	6	aaa	NYM	276	43	67	16	2	7	34	24	46	14	3	243	304	387	690	8%	83%	0.52	94	134	4.25	30
	06	28	6	aaa	NYM	371	49	91	21	2	7	33	36	77	16	3	246	313	366	679	9%	79%	0.47	82	118	4.24	25
Bass,Bryan	06	24	5	aa	BAL	212	29	41	10	2	3	22	37	80	9	3	193	313	296	609	15%	62%	0.46	68	129	3.39	2
Bass,Chris	05	24	5	aa	FLA	313	31	70	22	0	4	31	31	71	1	4	223	293	332	625	9%	77%	0.44	82	34	3.27	17
Batista,Wilson	06	26	6	aa	NYM	468	55	98	17	1	9	36	36	88	5	7	210	266	308	574	7%	81%	0.41	64	68	2.66	4
Bautista,Jose	05	25	5	a/a	PIT	487	50	118	26	1	16	68	38	84	6	5	243	298	402	700	7%	83%	0.45	102	58	4.11	32
	06	26	5	aaa	PIT	101	12	28	9	0	2	9	13	18	2	1	274	356	421	778	11%	82%	0.71	108	52	5.61	50
Bautista,Rayner	06	28	6	aa	BAL	424	35	85	19	1	6	30	5	131	3	2	200	209	289	498	1%	69%	0.04	62	71	1.90	-7
Bear,Ryan	06	26	3	aa	FLA	477	32	100	18	1	6	52	56	104	4	5	209	292	291	583	10%	78%	0.53	56	39	2.94	3
Beattie,Andrew	05	28	4	a/a	OAK	520	63	118	33	2	8	49	50	109	8	6	228	295	343	638	9%	79%	0.45	83	79	3.47	19
	06	29	4	aaa	OAK	276	36	64	11	1	7	42	33	57	6	3	233	316	361	676	11%	79%	0.59	81	80	4.05	22
Bellorin,Edwin	06	25	2	aaa	LA	321	24	63	11	0	6	37	10	46	1	2	196	221	287	507	3%	86%	0.22	59	38	2.00	-6
Bell,Rick	05	27	5	a/a	CIN	307	23	52	12	0	2	23	14	59	0	0	170	207	226	433	4%	81%	0.24	43	30	1.51	-21
	06	28	5	aaa	KC	364	24	68	11	2	3	27	14	60	2	1	188	219	253	472	4%	84%	0.24	44	64	1.80	-14
Benavidez,Julian	05	23	3	aa	SF	103	7	13	3	0	4	11	3	30	0	1	122	147	264	410	3%	71%	0.10	83	40	1.07	-23
Benjamin,Casey	06	26	6	aa	TEX	329	35	77	17	2	6	34	25	53	3	3	233	287	352	639	7%	84%	0.48	80	70	3.46	20
Bergeron,Peter	05	28	8	aa	BAL	348	43	82	11	1	4	27	27	93	11	5	236	292	308	600	7%	73%	0.30	48	94	3.14	4
	06	29	8	a/a	PHI	446	51	93	19	3	8	35	42	91	9	9	208	275	313	588	9%	80%	0.46	69	89	2.79	7
Berger,Brandon	05	31	8	aaa	STL	296	34	55	11	0	13	41	22	51	2	2	185	241	350	591	7%	83%	0.42	98	54	2.72	11
Bergolla,William	05	23	4	aaa	CIN	391	48	104	22	2	2	33	16	30	14	4	266	294	349	643	4%	92%	0.53	63	113	3.67	25
	06	24	4	aaa	CIN	416	44	112	21	1	2	32	21	45	14	8	269	304	339	643	5%	89%	0.47	54	87	3.59	21
Berg,Dave	05	35	5	aaa	BOS	420	50	107	25	1	1	39	43	57	1	0	255	324	326	650	9%	87%	0.76	58	52	3.93	24
Bernier,Douglas	05	25	6	aa	COL	369	23	65	13	2	3	28	32	84	1	5	176	242	241	484	8%	77%	0.38	46	45	1.87	-15
	06	26	6	aa	COL	246	30	57	13	3	1	18	20	38	3	1	230	288	315	603	8%	85%	0.53	62	105	3.20	13
Betancourt,Yunies	05	24	6	a/a	SEA	410	33	103	17	6	6	43	14	29	16	14	251	276	366	642	3%	93%	0.48	72	121	3.13	23
Bibbs,Kennard	05	26	8	aa	MIL	358	32	81	15	4	1	18	25	43	17	8	226	277	297	574	7%	88%	0.58	51	122	2.79	8
	06	27	8	a/a	MIL	164	23	50	8	1	1	17	27	44	14	5	302	401	379	779	14%	73%	0.61	57	114	6.19	36
Bikowski,Scott	05	29	8	aaa	CHW	290	26	58	15	1	2	20	21	57	2	6	199	254	276	530	7%	80%	0.38	58	58	2.19	-2
Bixler,Brian	06	24	6	aa	PIT	226	32	64	13	1	3	16	14	53	6	2	283	324	386	710	6%	77%	0.26	73	99	4.61	30
Blakely,Darren	05	29	8	aa	CHW	456	45	92	22	2	13	55	29	123	3	4	202	249	340	590	6%	73%	0.24	88	65	2.74	8
	06	30	8	a/a	CHW	321	24	48	10	1	5	17	12	82	3	2	151	182	232	415	4%	75%	0.15	53	77	1.31	-25
Blalock,Jake	06	23	8	aa	TEX	376	30	91	17	0	7	34	33	72	7	3	243	304	343	647	8%	81%	0.46	69	53	3.71	18
Blanco,Andres	05	21	6	a/a	KC	146	15	33	3	2	1	12	11	20	2	0	223	275	295	570	7%	86%	0.53	43	114	2.90	3
	06	22	6	aaa	KC	283	28	66	9	3	2	19	20	33	5	4	234	284	312	596	7%	88%	0.60	51	102	3.00	11
Blanco,Gregor	05	22	8	aa	ATL	401	56	92	10	8	5	32	64	108	24	13	229	335	332	667	14%	73%	0.59	59	176	3.95	13
	06	23	8	a/a	ATL	520	84	146	27	3	0	27	93	107	30	16	281	390	344	734	15%	79%	0.87	51	110	5.20	32
Blue,Vincent	06	24	8	aa	DET	409	43	88	13	1	0	19	46	102	22	15	216	294	251	546	10%	75%	0.45	29	94	2.52	-7
Bocachica,Hiram	06	31	8	aaa	OAK	291	44	77	13	2	14	43	31	48	13	4	263	333	458	791	10%	84%	0.64	116	112	5.56	48
Boeve,Adam	05	25	8	aa	PIT	158	17	38	8	1	4	16	15	43	4	2	239	306	370	677	9%	73%	0.35	86	86	3.98	22
	06	26	8	a/a	PIT	454	50	115	25	2	7	52	39	119	23	6	254	312	365	677	8%	74%	0.33	77	108	4.16	23
Bohn Jr.,T.J.	05	26	8	a/a	SEA	515	67	135	28	1	10	51	32	113	26	10	262	305	380	685	6%	78%	0.29	80	106	4.10	26
	06	27	8	aaa	SEA	378	44	93	17	1	8	36	28	75	13	3	246	299	359	658	7%	80%	0.37	75	95	3.86	21
Bolivar,Luis	06	26	4	aa	CIN	318	38	75	12	1	4	24	18	54	10	4	235	276	311	587	5%	83%	0.33	53	99	2.98	7
Bolivar,Papo	05	27	8	aa	STL	425	38	85	17	2	6	40	23	69	11	9	201	241	293	534	5%	84%	0.33	62	91	2.21	-1
Bonifay,Josh	05	27	3	aa	PIT	372	35	79	17	2	16	51	22	100	0	1	212	255	395	650	5%	73%	0.22	111	42	3.35	21
	06	28	4	aa	HOU	394	42	75	18	2	14	51	25	103	3	4	191	239	347	586	6%	74%	0.24	97	73	2.62	8

Major League Equivalent Statistics

BATTER	Yr	Age	Pos	Lev	Org	ab	r	h	d	t	hr	rbi	bb	k	sb	cs	ba	ob	slg	ops	bb%	ct%	eye	px	sx	rc/g	bpv
Bonvechio,Brett	06	24	3	aa	SD	263	28	56	13	3	6	31	40	92	0	1	214	317	350	668	13%	65%	0.43	86	79	3.95	16
Borchard,Joe	05	27	8	aaa	CHW	486	52	114	16	0	25	51	39	118	5	5	236	292	425	717	7%	76%	0.33	110	42	4.20	31
Borowiak,Zach	06	25	6	aa	BOS	306	29	58	13	0	3	26	12	57	4	3	188	218	256	474	4%	81%	0.21	50	71	1.77	-12
Boscan,Jean	05	26	2	aaa	ATL	212	15	43	6	0	3	18	22	53	1	2	201	275	271	546	9%	75%	0.41	46	28	2.52	-6
	06	27	2	a/a	MIL	132	5	22	7	0	0	13	9	43	0	1	164	217	218	435	6%	67%	0.21	48	22	1.50	-21
Botts,Jason	05	25	8	aaa	TEX	506	63	128	28	5	20	70	47	103	1	5	252	315	444	759	8%	80%	0.45	118	70	4.84	42
	06	26	8	a/a	TEX	236	37	61	17	1	12	32	27	62	5	0	259	335	488	823	10%	74%	0.43	144	91	6.09	55
Boucher,Sebastier	06	25	8	aa	SEA	416	54	91	9	4	1	26	61	96	24	10	219	319	265	584	13%	77%	0.63	30	130	3.15	-2
Bourgeois,Jason	05	24	4	aaa	ATL	383	29	84	18	1	2	14	28	49	7	6	219	273	287	560	7%	87%	0.57	52	65	2.61	6
	06	25	4	aa	SEA	411	59	102	20	5	4	34	35	69	21	7	247	307	347	653	8%	83%	0.51	67	148	3.83	20
Bourn,Michael	05	23	8	aa	PHI	539	68	134	16	6	6	37	52	103	32	14	249	315	334	649	9%	81%	0.50	53	139	3.72	15
	06	24	8	a/a	PHI	470	91	129	10	12	5	39	51	91	42	5	274	345	379	724	10%	81%	0.56	58	232	5.28	27
Bowen,Rob	05	25	2	aaa	MIN	258	32	63	13	2	5	20	32	58	0	2	244	328	368	696	11%	78%	0.55	81	62	4.29	26
Bowers,Jason	05	28	6	aaa	WAS	328	19	61	9	1	1	25	27	42	7	4	185	246	226	472	8%	87%	0.63	30	66	1.87	-13
	06	29	6	aaa	BAL	174	15	36	7	1	0	7	14	30	5	1	208	267	257	524	7%	83%	0.46	38	91	2.44	-6
Boyd,Shaun	05	24	8	aa	STL	502	58	112	19	1	5	42	32	76	10	10	223	270	293	564	6%	85%	0.43	50	79	2.59	4
	06	25	8	a/a	STL	320	40	69	13	1	2	23	29	44	10	4	217	283	282	565	8%	86%	0.67	49	98	2.80	6
Bozied,Tagg	06	27	3	aaa	NYM	160	17	38	11	0	7	21	19	44	0	1	238	318	433	752	11%	72%	0.43	127	22	4.82	40
Braun,Ryan	06	23	5	aa	MIL	231	40	68	19	1	15	38	21	45	11	0	294	353	580	933	8%	81%	0.47	177	118	8.02	81
Brazell,Craig	05	25	8	aaa	NYM	173	18	39	10	1	5	24	11	28	2	0	223	269	378	647	6%	84%	0.39	100	79	3.53	23
	06	26	3	aa	LA	421	47	85	21	1	18	76	16	107	1	0	203	231	386	618	4%	75%	0.15	113	58	2.94	17
Brewer,Jace	05	26	6	a/a	TEX	334	33	78	16	1	2	21	14	42	6	8	234	266	304	571	4%	87%	0.34	54	76	2.55	7
	06	27	6	a/a	TEX	213	11	44	8	2	2	14	10	40	2	4	208	245	286	531	5%	81%	0.26	52	65	2.15	-4
Brignac,Reid	06	21	6	aa	TAM	110	20	35	6	2	3	18	7	31	3	0	315	358	496	854	6%	71%	0.23	112	172	7.04	56
Brito,Juan	05	28	2	aaa	ARI	232	20	49	9	0	4	20	14	40	0	0	213	258	299	557	6%	83%	0.36	58	24	2.64	2
	06	27	2	aaa	ARI	247	26	65	14	0	7	32	18	42	0	1	263	314	401	715	7%	83%	0.44	91	26	4.49	34
Broadway,Larry	05	25	3	a/a	WAS	239	24	49	15	0	9	21	17	41	2	0	207	261	377	638	7%	83%	0.42	110	51	3.36	23
	06	26	3	aaa	WAS	444	53	114	23	2	13	69	40	109	4	1	256	317	404	721	8%	75%	0.36	94	76	4.65	32
Brown,Adrian	05	32	8	aaa	KC	549	73	119	23	5	5	33	51	61	21	8	216	283	307	590	9%	89%	0.84	60	133	3.02	14
	06	33	8	aaa	TEX	122	13	32	4	1	1	9	14	19	9	1	266	343	332	675	11%	85%	0.76	44	113	4.64	22
Brown,Dee	05	28	8	a/a	WAS	272	16	41	10	0	6	25	12	55	2	6	150	187	253	439	4%	80%	0.22	66	38	1.29	-18
	06	29	8	a/a	KC	437	42	97	19	0	10	57	20	71	2	0	222	256	335	591	4%	84%	0.29	74	48	2.93	10
Brown,Dustin	06	24	2	aa	BOS	295	28	62	17	0	4	34	21	59	2	1	209	262	306	568	7%	80%	0.35	71	50	2.72	6
Brown,Hunter	05	26	5	aaa	SEA	333	43	83	27	1	6	43	29	61	7	5	250	309	389	699	8%	82%	0.47	101	83	4.16	34
	06	27	5	aaa	SEA	385	52	87	26	1	6	40	48	82	10	6	227	312	345	657	11%	79%	0.58	86	87	3.77	23
Brown,Jason	05	31	2	aa	NYY	151	12	23	4	1	3	11	9	59	0	1	153	201	241	442	6%	61%	0.16	53	61	1.51	-24
Brown,Jeremy	05	26	2	aa	OAK	394	45	81	22	1	14	50	36	76	0	0	206	272	375	647	8%	81%	0.48	107	37	3.48	22
	06	27	2	aaa	OAK	275	31	60	13	0	10	31	17	48	0	0	219	265	370	636	6%	82%	0.36	95	30	3.35	19
Brown,Matthew	06	24	5	aa	ANA	515	54	124	34	2	13	56	32	84	5	8	240	285	391	676	6%	84%	0.38	102	62	3.67	30
Brown,Neb	05	26	4	a/a	ARI	172	14	40	9	1	1	14	11	23	7	4	232	280	309	589	6%	87%	0.49	57	92	2.90	11
Brown,Roosevelt	05	30	8	aaa	CHW	380	44	95	24	1	10	37	31	52	2	2	251	307	398	705	7%	86%	0.59	99	53	4.31	36
Bubela,Jaime	05	27	8	aa	SEA	520	62	114	15	3	7	42	27	134	30	6	219	257	298	555	5%	74%	0.20	51	144	2.70	-2
Buchanan,Brian	05	32	0	aaa	COL	365	47	95	20	2	12	40	23	69	3	2	261	306	422	728	6%	81%	0.34	102	74	4.57	36
Buckley,Jim	05	26	2	a/a	BOS	167	14	26	8	0	2	12	18	64	1	0	156	238	237	476	10%	61%	0.28	60	46	1.93	-18
Buck,Travis	06	23	8	aa	OAK	212	27	58	21	1	3	19	18	32	8	1	274	330	425	755	8%	85%	0.56	114	105	5.30	49
Budde,Ryan	05	26	2	aaa	ANA	191	17	36	8	2	3	16	6	30	2	1	188	212	295	506	3%	84%	0.19	69	105	1.99	-5
	06	27	2	aaa	ANA	215	24	42	12	0	6	25	16	45	1	1	194	251	331	582	7%	79%	0.36	92	51	2.74	10
Budzinski,Mark	05	32	8	aaa	PHI	467	50	101	20	5	4	30	29	92	6	5	216	261	304	566	6%	80%	0.31	60	115	2.65	3
Burgamy,Brian	05	24	8	aa	SD	172	11	29	5	2	1	11	23	39	2	0	166	263	232	495	12%	77%	0.59	43	88	2.19	-15
Burke,Jamie	05	34	2	aaa	CHW	351	37	77	18	1	8	38	25	47	1	3	218	270	344	614	7%	87%	0.54	83	48	3.09	18
	06	35	2	aaa	TEX	370	39	93	19	1	9	41	19	42	0	0	251	287	379	666	5%	89%	0.45	85	35	3.83	28
Burnham,Gary	06	32	3	a/a	PHI	336	46	92	19	0	14	51	24	44	2	1	274	322	460	782	7%	87%	0.55	117	47	5.38	50
Burroughs,Sean	05	25	5	aaa	SD	124	16	31	7	0	2	11	7	12	0	0	248	287	351	639	5%	90%	0.57	74	39	3.56	25
	06	26	5	aaa	TAM	131	7	25	2	0	1	10	8	28	1	3	193	238	230	467	6%	79%	0.28	25	32	1.66	-20
Burrus,Josh	05	22	8	a/a	ATL	184	19	38	6	1	4	18	21	51	10	4	207	288	315	603	10%	72%	0.41	67	106	3.13	5
	06	23	8	aa	ATL	291	33	58	12	0	3	26	13	69	5	4	200	233	270	503	4%	76%	0.18	51	81	2.00	-9
Buscher,Brian	05	24	5	aa	SF	215	15	43	7	1	1	18	16	32	4	3	199	255	252	507	7%	85%	0.51	38	70	2.13	-8
	06	25	5	aa	SF	467	40	109	21	3	6	45	36	83	5	4	233	288	330	618	7%	82%	0.43	65	69	3.28	13
Butler,Billy	05	19	8	aa	KC	112	12	33	9	0	3	15	6	12	0	0	295	328	462	789	5%	89%	0.47	115	22	5.62	55
	06	20	8	aa	KC	477	67	147	33	1	11	79	34	48	1	0	308	354	447	801	7%	90%	0.71	96	54	6.08	57
Butler,Brent	05	28	6	aa	TAM	121	15	23	5	1	4	14	10	14	2	0	192	254	350	603	8%	88%	0.69	96	92	3.03	17
	06	29	4	aaa	TAM	439	33	103	22	3	2	33	20	46	3	5	235	268	311	579	4%	89%	0.42	57	63	2.76	10
Buttler,Vic	06	26	8	a/a	PIT	490	55	127	22	11	5	48	34	63	23	6	259	307	375	682	7%	87%	0.54	73	175	4.17	27
Bynum,Freddie	05	26	8	aaa	OAK	378	44	90	15	5	2	31	29	66	18	9	238	292	320	612	7%	83%	0.44	54	141	3.19	11
Bynum,Seth	06	26	6	aa	WAS	203	15	38	8	0	0	9	23	48	4	2	186	270	226	496	10%	76%	0.49	35	55	2.16	-14
Byrd,Marlon	05	28	8	aaa	WAS	100	18	33	7	0	6	12	7	9	3	1	335	375	567	943	6%	91%	0.76	144	72	8.30	86
	06	29	8	aaa	WAS	155	16	35	7	0	5	24	13	32	3	1	223	282	376	658	8%	79%	0.40	96	57	3.66	22
Cabrera,Asdrubal	06	21	6	aaa	SEA	393	58	106	25	1	5	39	37	78	13	12	269	332	375	706	9%	80%	0.47	78	90	4.25	31
Cabrera,Melky	05	21	8	a/a	NYY	523	63	133	22	2	12	68	32	72	12	2	255	297	371	669	6%	86%	0.44	75	98	3.98	25
	06	22	8	aaa	NYY	122	18	46	5	1	4	23	9	8	3	1	379	423	542	966	7%	94%	1.24	99	87	9.68	92
Caligiuri,Jay	05	26	5	aa	NYM	373	34	68	15	2	11	34	25	81	1	1	183	235	321	556	6%	78%	0.31	85	59	2.46	3
	06	27	5	aa	NYM	410	43	79	14	1	14	54	49	98	1	1	193	279	333	612	11%	76%	0.50	84	42	3.19	9
Callaspo,Alberto	05	22	4	a/a	ANA	557	60	147	26	1	8	59	28	22	8	16	264	299	357	656	5%	96%	1.27	65	57	3.42	40
	06	23	4	aaa	ARI	490	72	152	24	10	6	53	44	21	6	6	310	367	437	804	8%	96%	2.10	80	126	6.03	78
Calloway,Ron	05	29	8	aaa	NYM	392	43	86	21	0	8	34	31	77	11	6	218	275	334	610	7%	80%	0.40	80	77	3.07	14
	06	30	8	aaa	BOS	406	41	104	27	2	4	41	34	77	7	5	257	315	359	674	8%	81%	0.45	76	76	3.98	26
Calzado,Napoleon	05	29	5	aaa	BAL	443	44	117	19	1	9	49	18	42	8	7	265	293	374	666	4%	91%	0.42	72	68	3.73	26
	06	30	8	aaa	BAL	246	27	63	14	1	3	25	5	31	5	0	255	271	351	623	2%	87%	0.18	70	94	3.41	17
Camacaro,Armanc	05	27	2	aa	CLE	103	9	22	3	0	2	9	3	25	3	2	211	237	287	524	3%	75%	0.14	49	67	2.16	-7
Campusano,Jose	06	23	8	aa	FLA	337	41	92	13	1	1	15	16	82	37	12	273	306	326	632	5%	76%	0.20	41	130	3.60	12
Cancel,Robinson	05	29	2	a/a	STL	325	27	64	12	1	7	25	24	51	2	2	197	252	300	552	7%	84%	0.46	67	55	2.52	3

Major League Equivalent Statistics

BATTERS

BATTER	Yr	Age	Pos	Lev	Org	ab	r	h	d	t	hr	rbi	bb	k	sb	cs	ba	ob	slg	ops	bb%	ct%	eye	px	sx	rc/g	bpv
Canizares,Barbaro	06	27	8	aa	ATL	279	28	70	15	1	3	28	24	49	0	0	253	313	349	662	8%	82%	0.49	69	36	3.97	23
Cannizaro,Andy	05	27	6	a/a	NYY	372	38	75	17	1	1	29	21	29	5	1	201	243	259	502	5%	92%	0.72	47	84	2.14	0
	06	28	6	aaa	NYY	416	60	102	28	1	3	28	42	58	5	5	244	313	336	649	9%	86%	0.72	71	74	3.70	25
Cannon,Chip	05	24	3	aa	TOR	166	15	42	14	1	7	21	10	58	2	0	251	293	467	760	6%	65%	0.17	141	73	4.87	45
	06	25	3	aa	TOR	475	70	111	25	1	26	62	46	160	0	2	234	301	452	753	9%	66%	0.29	131	44	4.70	38
Cano,Robinson	05	23	4	aaa	NYY	108	17	34	7	2	3	21	5	10	0	0	311	343	506	849	5%	90%	0.50	123	108	6.58	64
Cardona,Javier	05	30	2	a/a	STL	165	10	30	6	0	3	18	8	26	0	0	179	217	276	494	5%	84%	0.30	64	14	1.95	-8
Carlin,Luke	05	25	2	aa	SD	230	19	49	7	1	1	20	29	41	3	3	215	304	264	568	11%	82%	0.72	36	59	2.85	1
	06	26	2	aaa	SD	249	21	54	12	1	3	22	38	44	0	0	219	321	310	631	13%	82%	0.85	64	31	3.66	16
Carroll,Brett	06	24	8	aa	FLA	251	28	52	13	3	8	29	18	68	4	1	208	261	375	636	7%	73%	0.26	104	119	3.32	17
Carroll,Wesley	05	27	4	aaa	WAS	128	7	24	4	0	1	7	4	18	1	1	189	213	243	456	3%	86%	0.22	39	39	1.63	-17
Carter,Chris	05	27	3	aa	ARI	125	14	30	3	0	7	21	14	10	0	3	244	319	438	758	10%	92%	1.35	111	22	4.47	54
	06	24	3	aaa	ARI	509	67	140	29	2	16	75	62	52	8	5	275	354	434	788	11%	90%	1.19	103	72	5.68	58
Casanova,Raul	05	33	2	aaa	CHW	233	18	51	11	0	11	31	14	27	0	0	220	266	406	671	6%	89%	0.54	113	7	3.66	31
Cash,Kevin	05	28	2	aaa	TAM	143	16	32	7	0	6	18	9	33	0	0	226	270	392	662	6%	77%	0.26	103	28	3.62	23
	06	29	2	aaa	TAM	240	15	38	8	1	2	18	20	75	1	2	159	225	225	450	8%	69%	0.27	46	51	1.63	-23
Casilla,Alexi	06	22	4	aa	MIN	170	26	48	10	1	1	12	17	20	18	4	282	348	371	718	9%	88%	0.85	66	136	5.07	38
Castellano,John	05	28	0	a/a	PHI	319	31	67	13	0	4	33	20	42	2	2	211	258	290	548	6%	87%	0.48	56	49	2.51	3
	06	29	8	a/a	PHI	188	12	46	7	0	3	21	5	27	0	0	244	264	331	595	3%	86%	0.18	58	14	3.01	9
Castillo,Alberto	06	37	2	aaa	WAS	254	26	55	14	0	0	24	28	43	1	2	216	294	273	567	10%	83%	0.64	50	41	2.81	6
Casto,Kory	06	25	5	aa	WAS	489	72	114	21	5	16	68	67	102	5	6	233	326	394	720	12%	79%	0.66	98	94	4.50	31
Castro,Bernie	05	26	4	aaa	BAL	502	69	141	18	3	1	31	36	43	35	7	280	328	334	662	7%	91%	0.83	41	131	4.27	27
	06	27	4	aaa	WAS	268	30	65	5	2	2	21	15	34	19	2	241	282	294	576	5%	87%	0.45	33	136	3.17	3
Castro,Ismael	05	22	4	aa	SEA	421	37	100	22	1	8	45	11	40	5	10	238	257	352	608	3%	90%	0.28	78	58	2.76	17
	06	23	4	a/a	SEA	287	33	73	21	2	5	27	9	41	6	3	254	277	394	671	3%	86%	0.22	98	104	3.72	30
Castro,Nelson	05	32	5	aa	MIL	116	9	16	4	0	0	8	4	34	1	0	139	169	175	344	3%	70%	0.12	32	66	0.94	-38
Castro,Ramon	05	30	6	aa	WAS	130	17	25	7	1	5	18	8	24	1	1	190	239	375	614	6%	82%	0.34	114	85	2.88	17
Cates Jr.,Gary	06	25	4	aa	CHC	237	33	58	11	1	2	24	25	38	7	3	243	316	319	635	10%	84%	0.67	55	98	3.67	17
Cedeno,Ronny	05	23	6	aaa	CHC	245	35	81	13	1	7	29	17	24	9	4	330	373	480	853	6%	90%	0.71	96	91	6.86	64
Cepicky,Matt	05	28	8	aaa	WAS	342	36	73	19	2	10	47	29	65	1	4	214	276	364	640	8%	81%	0.45	97	57	3.30	20
	06	29	8	aaa	FLA	320	28	68	15	2	5	25	33	59	2	1	212	287	314	601	9%	82%	0.57	69	63	3.15	10
Cervenak,Mike	05	29	3	aaa	SF	494	44	118	23	2	11	66	24	47	4	0	239	274	359	633	5%	90%	0.50	78	67	3.45	22
	06	30	5	aaa	SF	269	25	60	14	1	5	37	9	31	0	0	224	249	341	591	3%	88%	0.29	78	41	2.87	13
Chaves,Brandon	05	26	6	aa	PIT	172	14	29	5	1	0	5	10	32	2	2	167	215	207	422	6%	81%	0.32	31	80	1.42	-25
	06	27	6	aa	PIT	377	32	69	12	2	3	40	37	82	7	1	183	256	251	507	9%	78%	0.46	47	87	2.26	-11
Chavez,Angel	05	24	6	aaa	SF	334	32	79	15	2	7	45	12	41	4	1	237	263	356	619	3%	88%	0.29	77	84	3.22	17
	06	25	5	a/a	PHI	464	55	114	30	2	10	54	26	85	13	3	246	285	387	672	5%	82%	0.30	96	106	3.90	28
Chavez,Ozzie	06	23	6	a/a	MIL	398	35	95	16	4	2	36	34	61	6	5	239	299	314	613	8%	85%	0.56	52	90	3.25	12
Chavez,Raul	05	33	2	aaa	HOU	119	6	23	6	0	0	10	4	20	0	0	197	220	250	470	3%	83%	0.18	47	20	1.80	-12
	06	34	2	aa	BAL	196	12	34	7	0	1	14	8	26	0	0	171	203	229	431	4%	87%	0.30	43	23	1.49	-19
Chen,Chin-Feng	05	28	8	aaa	LA	312	35	65	13	1	10	38	23	55	2	4	207	261	347	608	7%	82%	0.42	88	61	2.92	13
Chen,Yung Chi	06	23	4	aa	SEA	149	20	40	9	1	3	20	17	24	5	3	267	344	397	741	10%	84%	0.74	88	95	4.91	40
Chiaffredo,Paul	05	29	2	a/a	PIT	161	14	26	9	0	5	17	3	48	2	0	163	180	311	490	2%	70%	0.07	97	70	1.76	-4
	06	30	2	aaa	PIT	129	7	14	5	0	1	7	5	48	1	1	112	147	174	322	4%	63%	0.11	48	60	0.76	-41
Chiaravalloti,Vito	05	25	3	aa	TOR	148	15	33	9	0	3	17	14	33	1	0	225	293	340	633	9%	78%	0.44	81	43	3.55	17
	06	26	3	aa	TOR	137	14	23	3	0	5	15	12	48	0	0	171	236	309	545	8%	65%	0.24	78	28	2.40	-6
Choi,Hee Seop	06	28	3	aaa	BOS	227	31	44	10	1	7	24	42	54	0	0	193	318	331	649	16%	76%	0.78	86	47	3.80	15
Choo,Shin-Soo	05	23	8	aaa	SEA	426	60	105	19	3	9	44	59	84	16	12	246	338	369	707	12%	80%	0.70	78	104	4.34	29
	06	24	8	aaa	SEA	375	61	109	19	2	11	41	40	66	22	5	291	359	440	799	10%	82%	0.61	95	122	6.10	48
Christianson,Ryan	05	24	2	aaa	SEA	286	29	61	11	0	7	33	30	82	2	1	213	288	325	613	9%	71%	0.37	72	45	3.27	8
	06	25	2	aa	TAM	328	36	57	8	0	13	36	29	130	8	1	173	240	313	552	8%	60%	0.22	81	84	2.54	-4
Christian,Justin	06	26	8	aa	NYY	467	64	108	16	6	5	37	35	84	57	11	231	284	324	608	7%	82%	0.41	59	186	3.43	9
Church,Ryan	06	28	8	a/a	WAS	194	25	37	5	0	7	25	22	49	4	1	188	270	323	593	10%	75%	0.44	79	76	3.02	4
Ciriaco,Juan	06	23	6	aa	SD	442	44	88	18	3	2	29	31	102	9	3	200	252	268	520	7%	77%	0.30	50	107	2.30	-7
Clark,Doug	05	30	8	aaa	SF	468	51	113	23	4	7	38	22	66	18	15	241	275	352	627	4%	86%	0.33	74	113	3.04	18
	06	31	8	aaa	OAK	494	67	113	18	1	11	48	41	90	18	9	230	288	335	623	8%	82%	0.45	68	98	3.29	13
Clark,Howie	05	32	0	aa	PIT	106	8	25	1	1	1	7	11	4	1	1	238	306	304	610	9%	96%	2.45	38	59	3.35	44
	06	33	8	aaa	BAL	308	37	71	14	1	3	24	33	30	2	2	231	306	310	616	10%	90%	1.11	58	60	3.37	23
Clark,Jermaine	05	29	4	aaa	OAK	254	23	50	11	2	4	20	27	29	10	7	197	275	297	572	10%	89%	0.96	67	97	2.64	12
	06	30	4	aaa	MIL	375	46	74	12	2	5	30	40	73	27	6	197	274	274	547	10%	80%	0.54	50	131	2.72	-3
Clements,Jason	05	28	4	aa	SD	225	23	42	6	2	2	20	15	64	2	1	184	235	255	490	6%	72%	0.23	44	111	1.99	-16
Clements,Zachary	05	25	2	aa	NYM	178	8	32	6	0	0	7	4	42	0	2	177	193	212	406	2%	76%	0.09	31	28	1.22	-26
Clement,Jeff	06	23	2	aaa	SEA	304	26	72	15	1	5	36	20	55	0	2	237	284	342	626	6%	82%	0.36	72	36	3.31	16
Clendenin,Morgan	05	24	0	aa	BAL	150	17	34	7	0	7	14	2	48	0	0	228	238	405	643	1%	68%	0.04	108	35	3.21	21
Cleveland,Brian	06	25	4	aa	FLA	134	15	27	4	1	1	7	8	31	1	0	199	242	262	504	5%	77%	0.25	42	93	2.16	-11
Cleveland,Jeremy	05	24	8	aa	TEX	198	24	44	9	0	0	10	24	37	2	1	221	304	264	568	11%	81%	0.64	38	57	2.93	2
Clevlen,Brent	06	23	8	aa	DET	395	44	86	15	0	10	43	44	128	6	2	218	296	332	628	10%	68%	0.34	73	63	3.48	9
Cliffords,Woody	05	25	8	a/a	BAL	336	35	72	17	1	1	29	51	67	7	8	214	318	280	598	13%	80%	0.77	53	66	3.10	8
Closser,JD	06	27	2	aaa	COL	225	23	61	14	1	7	22	22	28	6	2	272	337	431	768	9%	88%	0.80	104	75	5.36	49
Coats,Buck	05	23	6	aa	CHC	435	41	110	29	4	1	42	34	76	15	6	252	306	343	650	7%	82%	0.45	71	111	3.75	22
	06	24	8	aaa	CHC	450	55	120	20	0	7	47	36	81	16	4	267	321	358	679	7%	82%	0.44	63	86	4.27	24
Colamarino,Brant	05	25	3	a/a	OAK	463	51	109	24	4	16	69	27	88	0	0	235	277	411	688	6%	81%	0.31	109	61	3.93	29
	06	26	3	aa	OAK	495	52	115	30	5	13	69	45	100	2	2	233	297	387	684	8%	80%	0.45	101	76	4.01	28
Colangelo,Mike	05	29	8	aaa	FLA	331	38	75	14	1	9	36	20	58	1	3	228	273	360	632	6%	82%	0.35	83	53	3.26	17
	06	30	8	aaa	FLA	176	23	45	13	0	4	15	15	33	0	2	253	314	388	701	8%	81%	0.47	96	38	4.21	33
Coleman,Michael	05	30	0	aa	NYY	151	12	25	5	1	6	20	11	53	0	0	167	221	320	541	7%	65%	0.20	90	40	2.29	-3
	06	31	8	aa	TAM	435	37	71	18	2	12	45	29	141	4	0	164	217	296	513	6%	67%	0.21	82	84	2.10	-7
Colina,Alvin	05	24	2	aa	COL	207	17	49	5	0	9	27	16	32	0	2	239	292	389	681	7%	85%	0.49	86	14	3.83	25
	06	25	2	aa	COL	323	33	73	12	1	10	33	16	58	2	2	226	263	359	622	5%	82%	0.28	82	59	3.16	15
Colina,Javier	06	28	6	aa	CIN	358	32	61	19	1	6	32	24	90	4	2	172	224	278	502	6%	75%	0.27	74	77	2.03	-7
Collaro,Thomas	06	24	8	aa	CHW	389	34	80	16	2	13	48	18	129	1	4	204	240	352	592	5%	67%	0.14	90	56	2.67	8

Major League Equivalent Statistics

BATTERS

BATTER	Yr	Age	Pos	Lev	Org	ab	r	h	d	t	hr	rbi	bb	k	sb	cs	ba	ob	slg	ops	bb%	ct%	eye	px	sx	rc/g	bpv
Colonel,Christian	06	25	8	aa	COL	387	34	94	22	0	9	31	26	48	8	6	243	290	366	656	6%	87%	0.53	84	56	3.59	26
Concepcion Jr.,Alb	05	24	2	aa	BOS	326	34	74	19	1	5	37	27	76	3	3	227	286	335	621	8%	77%	0.35	77	64	3.27	14
	06	25	2	a/a	BOS	268	25	55	14	0	4	25	26	72	1	2	206	275	301	576	9%	73%	0.36	69	37	2.80	4
Concepcion,Ambic	06	25	8	aa	NYM	218	22	52	10	1	3	27	7	57	10	2	240	262	336	598	3%	74%	0.12	67	116	3.10	10
Conrad,Brooks	05	26	4	a/a	HOU	491	77	110	24	3	17	53	52	103	16	3	224	299	389	688	10%	79%	0.51	102	125	4.16	27
	06	27	4	aaa	HOU	532	81	126	34	13	19	76	43	114	12	7	237	294	458	751	7%	78%	0.37	134	185	4.54	42
Conti,Jason	05	31	8	aaa	TEX	462	50	95	21	2	11	46	25	88	3	1	205	246	327	573	5%	81%	0.29	79	77	2.69	7
	06	32	8	aaa	STL	171	17	38	7	0	2	10	13	37	2	1	221	275	295	569	7%	79%	0.34	54	55	2.80	3
Conway,Dan	05	26	2	a/a	COL	304	24	62	15	2	5	30	24	56	1	0	203	261	313	573	7%	82%	0.43	74	60	2.79	7
	06	27	2	aaa	COL	128	9	25	6	0	2	7	7	22	0	1	197	237	288	525	5%	83%	0.31	64	28	2.19	-2
Coolbaugh,Mike	05	33	5	aaa	HOU	488	60	108	23	1	19	69	31	93	7	0	221	267	389	656	6%	81%	0.33	104	90	3.62	23
	06	34	5	aaa	KC	197	15	37	8	0	5	20	25	46	1	1	187	279	311	590	11%	77%	0.55	79	27	2.98	6
Cooper,Jason	05	25	8	a/a	CLE	449	65	97	18	2	17	74	42	125	3	7	216	283	382	665	8%	72%	0.33	100	74	3.52	20
	06	26	8	aaa	CLE	412	52	87	23	3	11	57	40	123	5	2	211	281	360	641	9%	70%	0.32	96	103	3.48	17
Coquillette,Trace	05	31	4	aaa	CHW	103	7	23	4	0	4	14	5	27	0	1	227	266	367	633	5%	74%	0.20	85	18	3.20	15
Cordido,Julio	05	25	5	aa	SF	269	27	46	7	0	4	22	13	48	3	2	171	208	238	445	4%	82%	0.26	44	72	1.57	-20
Cornejo,Eduardo	06	25	6	aa	OAK	157	13	29	6	0	0	7	12	12	0	0	182	241	218	459	7%	93%	1.07	32	31	1.79	-5
Cortes,Jorge	05	25	8	aa	PIT	362	37	81	16	1	5	37	34	63	2	1	223	290	312	602	9%	83%	0.54	62	56	3.20	11
	06	26	8	aa	HOU	457	45	111	25	3	6	40	38	60	3	7	242	300	351	651	8%	87%	0.63	75	58	3.53	24
Cortez,Fernando	05	24	4	a/a	TAM	447	47	105	16	4	1	37	17	61	18	5	234	263	293	556	4%	86%	0.29	42	131	2.69	1
	06	25	4	aaa	TAM	461	45	99	15	3	0	18	20	62	12	10	215	247	260	507	4%	87%	0.32	34	102	2.04	-8
Cosby,Rob	05	25	5	aa	TOR	425	52	126	35	0	16	63	22	78	2	1	297	332	494	826	5%	82%	0.28	132	44	6.08	59
	06	26	3	aaa	TOR	453	49	110	25	1	17	59	19	91	1	3	243	273	413	686	4%	80%	0.21	108	44	3.78	29
Cosme,Caonabo	05	27	4	aaa	NYY	203	19	46	10	1	5	19	17	35	4	1	225	286	354	640	8%	83%	0.50	84	78	3.55	19
	06	28	6	a/a	NYY	211	23	37	8	0	5	17	14	66	1	2	177	228	289	517	6%	69%	0.21	71	56	2.08	-7
Costa,Shane	05	24	8	a/a	KC	289	28	69	17	2	5	34	18	18	4	1	239	283	363	647	6%	94%	1.00	85	85	3.61	35
	06	25	8	a/a	KC	207	28	63	12	3	7	24	11	22	3	0	305	339	487	826	5%	90%	0.49	113	115	6.31	58
Coste,Chris	05	33	5	aaa	PHI	499	50	116	20	1	15	59	28	72	2	5	233	273	368	641	5%	86%	0.39	84	41	3.34	20
	06	34	3	aaa	PHI	147	11	23	7	0	2	13	8	30	1	1	159	203	245	448	5%	80%	0.27	62	50	1.56	-16
Cota,Carlo	05	25	4	aa	TOR	144	19	32	8	2	2	15	8	49	1	0	225	266	344	610	5%	66%	0.17	80	125	3.17	11
	06	26	4	aa	TOR	202	25	34	9	1	1	10	28	74	3	0	168	269	233	501	12%	64%	0.38	49	99	2.28	-16
Cota,Jesus	05	24	3	a/a	ARI	472	41	108	17	1	13	62	26	49	1	2	229	269	352	621	5%	90%	0.53	76	36	3.20	18
	06	25	3	aa	ARI	446	42	97	19	0	14	48	27	73	2	1	217	261	356	617	6%	84%	0.37	87	41	3.15	16
Coughlan,Cameroı	05	24	8	aa	TEX	252	28	59	10	2	3	20	32	40	13	11	234	321	324	645	11%	84%	0.81	61	103	3.40	19
Crabbe,Callix	05	23	4	aa	MIL	385	33	81	14	3	1	26	51	53	14	7	210	303	270	573	12%	86%	0.96	43	98	2.93	7
	06	24	4	aa	MIL	472	54	117	17	2	5	43	68	63	30	14	249	343	325	668	13%	87%	1.08	52	99	4.11	26
Craig,Matthew	05	24	3	aa	CHC	325	43	79	21	0	11	48	27	60	6	4	243	300	412	712	8%	82%	0.44	111	68	4.24	36
Creighton,Matt	05	27	8	aa	CHC	101	9	20	5	0	2	9	4	20	0	1	198	231	301	533	4%	81%	0.22	72	40	2.19	0
Crespo,Cesar	05	26	4	aaa	PIT	394	52	88	19	2	6	37	35	49	21	11	224	287	327	615	8%	87%	0.71	71	119	3.15	18
	06	27	4	aaa	ATL	423	47	92	13	2	5	26	50	85	13	6	218	301	292	593	11%	80%	0.59	49	94	3.14	5
Cresse,Brad	05	27	2	a/a	STL	148	8	23	10	0	2	12	10	32	0	0	153	209	253	461	7%	78%	0.32	75	15	1.70	-11
	06	28	2	aa	LA	162	14	32	6	0	6	22	18	58	0	0	198	276	336	612	10%	65%	0.31	84	15	3.19	7
Crosby,Bubba	05	29	8	aaa	NYY	160	14	30	5	1	3	16	9	26	2	1	188	231	284	516	5%	84%	0.35	62	78	2.15	-5
Crowe,Trevor	06	23	8	aa	CLE	154	18	33	7	1	1	12	19	22	15	6	214	301	292	593	11%	86%	0.86	56	127	3.08	12
Crozier,Eric	05	27	3	a/a	NYY	335	26	54	22	1	7	30	22	128	3	4	161	212	293	506	6%	62%	0.17	92	64	1.88	-5
Cruz,Enrique	05	24	0	aa	MIL	497	53	132	32	2	12	48	30	91	3	5	265	307	408	715	6%	82%	0.33	97	56	4.36	35
	06	25	6	a/a	TEX	350	35	90	21	1	4	39	23	101	10	8	258	304	358	662	6%	71%	0.23	74	79	3.68	21
Cruz,Jacob	06	34	8	aaa	NYM	157	16	40	14	0	1	17	19	34	0	0	252	333	361	694	11%	78%	0.55	90	24	4.45	32
Cruz,Luis	05	22	6	aa	SD	151	12	21	2	1	2	5	8	26	0	1	139	182	205	388	5%	83%	0.31	38	71	1.13	-32
	06	23	6	aa	SD	499	63	121	33	3	10	63	29	63	8	4	242	284	381	665	5%	87%	0.46	95	99	3.72	29
Cruz,Nelson	05	25	8	a/a	MIL	455	57	111	29	0	20	60	46	109	14	9	244	313	438	752	9%	76%	0.42	123	72	4.69	41
	06	25	8	aaa	MIL	371	60	104	21	1	19	65	39	94	15	7	280	348	494	842	9%	75%	0.41	130	97	6.19	55
Cuevas,Aneudi	06	25	5	aa	TAM	111	9	23	5	0	1	7	6	53	1	0	203	246	276	521	5%	52%	0.12	56	47	2.31	-7
Cummings,Midre	05	34	8	aaa	BAL	262	31	62	12	0	10	32	27	63	0	1	237	308	395	703	9%	76%	0.43	98	26	4.28	28
Curry,Christopher	05	28	2	aa	SF	224	22	37	9	0	6	18	7	55	1	1	163	187	282	469	3%	75%	0.12	76	62	1.62	-12
Curry,Michael	05	29	8	a/a	TAM	240	29	43	8	1	1	11	14	52	12	6	181	227	230	457	6%	78%	0.28	37	127	1.67	-19
Cust,Jack	05	27	8	aaa	OAK	476	71	105	24	1	15	56	98	123	2	5	220	353	367	720	17%	74%	0.80	94	44	4.70	28
	06	28	8	aaa	SD	441	71	103	19	0	19	57	108	106	0	4	233	384	405	789	20%	76%	1.02	105	20	5.81	41
Czarniecki,Jordan	05	25	8	aa	COL	145	13	32	6	0	4	10	10	23	3	3	217	267	335	602	6%	84%	0.42	77	53	2.88	13
	06	26	8	aa	COL	408	41	92	23	3	8	38	30	71	13	4	226	280	356	636	7%	83%	0.43	86	114	3.44	19
D'Antona,James	05	23	5	aa	ARI	407	44	91	24	2	8	37	35	54	4	7	224	285	350	636	8%	87%	0.65	86	66	3.28	23
	06	24	5	aa	ARI	461	64	134	29	0	16	59	48	84	2	1	291	358	460	818	10%	82%	0.58	111	43	6.24	54
Daigle,Leo	06	27	3	aa	BAL	421	42	78	14	1	12	51	38	137	2	4	185	253	311	565	8%	67%	0.28	77	48	2.54	-1
Dallimore,Brian	05	32	5	aaa	SF	397	42	92	20	2	5	29	20	32	5	3	231	268	324	592	5%	92%	0.61	66	81	2.95	16
Darula,Bobby	05	31	8	aaa	BAL	393	50	100	21	3	2	32	23	34	11	5	254	295	334	629	5%	91%	0.65	60	111	3.47	22
Daubach,Brian	05	34	3	aaa	NYM	338	48	93	24	1	13	48	45	64	1	2	274	360	463	823	12%	81%	0.70	124	45	6.18	56
	06	35	3	aaa	STL	226	23	53	11	0	8	31	30	48	0	1	235	324	390	714	12%	79%	0.62	98	20	4.51	31
Davenport,Ron	05	24	8	aa	TOR	355	32	95	23	1	10	36	20	67	2	2	268	308	421	728	5%	81%	0.30	103	46	4.58	38
	06	25	8	aa	TOR	138	8	24	4	0	3	13	8	25	0	1	172	215	262	477	5%	82%	0.30	56	20	1.76	-13
Davidson,Kevin	06	26	2	aa	HOU	172	17	28	2	1	3	10	23	32	2	1	162	259	228	487	12%	81%	0.70	37	72	2.06	-17
Davis,Ben	06	30	2	aaa	NYY	162	8	31	5	0	4	16	5	37	1	1	191	217	286	504	3%	77%	0.15	60	27	1.98	-9
Davis,J.J.	05	27	8	aaa	COL	242	28	54	11	0	11	28	16	44	3	7	224	271	401	672	6%	82%	0.35	107	52	3.29	26
Davis,Rajai	05	25	8	aa	PIT	499	62	121	20	3	3	26	31	60	34	10	242	287	310	597	6%	88%	0.52	49	132	3.16	11
	06	26	8	aaa	PIT	385	50	107	18	1	2	20	26	57	44	13	278	323	345	668	6%	85%	0.46	51	128	4.14	23
Dawkins,Gookie	05	26	6	aaa	DET	349	47	76	16	6	8	32	25	64	8	8	217	270	364	634	7%	82%	0.39	91	146	3.11	18
	06	27	6	aaa	PIT	203	20	50	14	1	5	24	11	55	3	6	248	288	398	686	5%	73%	0.21	102	71	3.59	29
Day,Devin	06	26	5	aa	ANA	173	13	21	6	0	1	9	6	44	1	3	121	151	171	322	3%	75%	0.14	39	73	0.68	-41
De Aza,Alejandro	06	22	8	aa	FLA	230	40	61	11	2	2	16	22	49	27	10	265	329	357	686	9%	79%	0.45	63	162	4.20	24
de Caster,Yurende	06	27	5	aaa	PIT	421	44	107	22	2	10	48	31	100	7	7	255	307	384	690	7%	76%	0.31	85	73	4.02	26
	05	26	8	aaa	PIT	409	44	98	27	2	8	44	26	75	5	6	240	285	372	658	6%	82%	0.35	92	74	3.54	25
De La Rosa,Toma:	06	29	6	aaa	SF	300	31	73	18	1	6	31	16	37	6	6	242	280	363	642	5%	88%	0.43	84	74	3.32	24

Major League Equivalent Statistics

BATTERS

BATTER	Yr	Age	Pos	Lev	Org	ab	r	h	d	t	hr	rbi	bb	k	sb	cs	ba	ob	slg	ops	bb%	ct%	eye	px	sx	rc/g	bpv
De Renne,Keoni	05	26	4	aaa	ARI	228	29	58	10	2	2	17	16	16	3	0	255	303	340	643	6%	93%	0.94	58	99	3.78	28
	06	27	6	a/a	BOS	283	27	53	6	0	1	17	20	29	3	1	188	241	218	459	7%	90%	0.70	24	63	1.80	-14
Deardorff,Jeff	05	27	8	aaa	TAM	336	34	67	10	2	10	28	29	62	2	3	198	261	325	586	8%	82%	0.46	76	66	2.78	7
	06	28	3	aaa	CHC	320	34	67	19	1	10	36	28	84	7	1	209	273	369	642	8%	74%	0.33	104	86	3.49	19
Deeds,Doug	05	23	8	aa	MIN	490	64	133	32	2	13	68	47	107	2	5	271	334	422	756	9%	78%	0.43	101	54	5.04	41
	06	24	8	aa	MIN	440	64	113	32	3	12	65	62	112	4	3	257	348	428	776	12%	75%	0.55	114	81	5.46	44
Del Chiaro,Brent	05	26	2	a/a	ANA	120	9	15	5	1	4	11	6	42	0	0	128	171	278	449	5%	65%	0.15	93	66	1.46	-16
	06	27	2	aa	ANA	180	10	20	2	0	3	11	7	65	1	0	111	142	180	322	4%	64%	0.10	41	46	0.78	-44
Delarosa,Tomas	05	28	6	aaa	COL	307	27	74	14	1	5	29	17	23	6	5	241	281	340	622	5%	92%	0.74	68	67	3.20	23
Delgado,Mario	06	27	3	aa	BAL	208	14	43	8	1	4	14	10	42	0	0	208	244	315	559	5%	80%	0.24	70	32	2.57	3
Delgado,Wilson	05	33	4	aaa	FLA	351	32	75	16	4	4	23	19	44	2	5	213	253	310	563	5%	87%	0.43	66	82	2.51	7
Delucchi,Dustin	05	28	8	a/a	SD	382	50	83	17	2	2	20	55	61	11	5	216	315	285	599	13%	84%	0.90	51	97	3.27	11
	06	29	8	a/a	SD	197	14	35	5	0	0	9	21	38	3	2	177	257	203	460	10%	81%	0.56	23	50	1.82	-20
Dement,Dan	05	27	8	a/a	WAS	376	43	92	23	3	9	35	23	85	3	0	245	290	391	681	6%	77%	0.28	97	93	4.03	27
	06	28	4	a/a	WAS	476	52	81	14	2	14	47	38	148	4	9	170	231	296	528	7%	69%	0.26	75	73	2.08	-7
Denorfia,Chris	05	25	8	a/a	CIN	511	68	135	25	4	16	67	43	79	10	7	264	321	422	743	8%	85%	0.54	98	95	4.77	39
	06	26	8	aaa	CIN	312	43	103	18	1	7	42	31	40	14	1	330	390	460	850	9%	87%	0.77	89	97	7.46	62
DePastino,Joe	05	32	2	aaa	TOR	175	16	41	10	0	3	16	11	32	0	0	231	276	334	610	6%	82%	0.34	74	25	3.21	14
Deschaine,Jim	05	28	8	aa	PHI	386	32	69	15	1	12	42	23	70	2	2	178	225	315	540	6%	82%	0.33	85	48	2.27	1
Desmond,Ian	06	21	6	aa	WAS	121	7	20	4	1	0	3	4	32	4	1	165	192	215	407	3%	74%	0.13	37	114	1.34	-27
DeVore,Doug	05	28	8	aaa	SF	345	40	80	17	2	10	45	22	62	3	3	231	277	383	660	6%	82%	0.35	96	76	3.57	24
Dewitt,Blake	06	21	5	aa	LA	104	6	18	1	0	1	6	7	21	0	1	173	225	212	437	6%	80%	0.33	23	26	1.51	-26
Diaz,Einar	06	34	2	aaa	LA	227	18	42	13	0	3	25	12	26	0	1	186	226	278	504	5%	89%	0.46	68	34	2.02	-1
Diaz,Frank	06	23	8	aa	WAS	402	39	90	16	1	8	44	16	57	4	6	224	255	326	581	4%	86%	0.29	66	61	2.66	8
Diaz,Juan	05	32	3	aa	STL	198	14	36	8	0	6	20	9	46	0	0	184	220	322	541	4%	77%	0.20	87	15	2.29	1
Diaz,Matt	05	28	8	a/a	KC	285	37	78	17	3	9	42	10	47	8	3	275	300	446	746	4%	83%	0.22	109	117	4.68	41
Diaz,Victor	05	24	3	aaa	NYM	170	25	47	10	0	9	29	11	41	5	2	276	320	494	815	6%	76%	0.27	134	76	5.65	53
	06	25	8	aaa	TEX	392	31	92	16	0	9	40	26	103	5	5	235	282	344	627	6%	74%	0.25	72	43	3.26	13
Dickerson,Christor	06	25	8	aa	CIN	389	58	85	20	4	11	43	56	126	19	6	217	316	376	692	13%	68%	0.44	99	144	4.26	22
DiFelice,Mike	05	36	2	aaa	NYM	300	23	60	14	0	11	40	26	69	1	2	201	265	354	619	8%	77%	0.38	96	23	3.11	14
	06	37	2	a/a	NYM	114	8	24	6	0	1	14	12	29	0	0	211	286	281	566	10%	75%	0.42	54	16	2.84	1
Dillon,Joe	05	30	5	aaa	FLA	350	51	95	16	1	14	46	39	49	7	1	273	345	447	792	10%	86%	0.79	107	83	5.83	51
Dobbs,Greg	05	27	3	aaa	SEA	190	21	51	8	0	2	17	11	20	4	2	270	311	340	651	6%	89%	0.57	51	63	3.81	22
	06	28	5	aaa	SEA	379	47	100	16	2	7	44	31	56	11	6	263	318	373	691	7%	85%	0.55	72	95	4.22	28
Dominique,Andy	05	30	2	aaa	TOR	117	13	24	5	0	3	7	11	18	0	0	202	270	319	589	9%	85%	0.62	77	30	2.97	12
Donovan,Todd	05	27	8	a/a	LA	504	60	101	11	4	5	26	29	82	40	18	200	243	271	514	5%	84%	0.35	44	153	2.09	-8
	06	28	8	a/a	BAL	334	35	69	8	2	3	18	26	56	29	11	206	264	262	526	7%	83%	0.47	37	128	2.36	-7
Dopirak,Brian	06	23	3	aa	CHC	179	17	47	12	0	1	25	18	45	0	0	263	330	346	676	9%	75%	0.40	68	22	4.25	24
Dorta,Melvin	05	24	8	aa	WAS	404	44	87	15	0	9	39	27	38	17	15	216	265	317	582	6%	91%	0.71	65	84	2.57	13
	06	25	6	a/a	WAS	434	52	102	15	2	5	29	26	35	31	13	235	278	311	589	6%	92%	0.75	51	124	2.93	14
Doumit,Ryan	05	25	8	aaa	PIT	165	31	51	10	0	9	27	12	26	1	4	309	356	533	889	7%	84%	0.46	138	56	6.60	69
Dowdy,Brett	06	25	4	a/a	SD	262	31	57	9	2	1	15	26	43	9	6	218	289	278	567	9%	83%	0.60	42	108	2.74	2
Draper,John	05	25	2	aa	KC	182	20	35	8	1	1	9	20	31	6	4	193	272	262	534	10%	83%	0.64	51	99	2.42	-2
Drew,Stephen	06	24	6	aaa	ARI	342	42	88	16	2	11	39	26	38	2	4	257	310	412	722	7%	89%	0.68	96	64	4.40	39
Dubois,Jason	06	28	8	aaa	CLE	455	59	111	29	1	17	79	42	135	4	1	244	308	426	734	8%	70%	0.31	117	69	4.68	36
Duenas,Yobal	05	33	0	aaa	NYY	261	19	50	11	2	2	19	7	53	0	5	193	215	276	491	3%	80%	0.14	58	59	1.72	-9
Duffy,Chris	05	25	8	aaa	PIT	308	42	83	12	4	5	24	12	41	13	11	270	297	383	680	4%	87%	0.29	70	138	3.63	25
	06	26	8	aaa	PIT	106	17	36	7	2	2	17	10	12	13	3	339	394	494	888	8%	88%	0.78	101	175	7.92	70
Dukes,Elijah	05	21	8	aa	TAM	443	61	114	19	4	14	61	37	69	16	11	257	315	413	728	8%	84%	0.54	95	116	4.40	36
	06	22	8	aaa	TAM	283	57	82	15	4	9	49	43	43	8	4	289	383	471	854	13%	85%	1.00	111	139	6.85	62
Duncan,Chris	05	24	3	aaa	STL	430	45	100	20	1	16	58	51	84	1	4	233	314	395	709	11%	80%	0.61	101	32	4.29	31
	06	25	8	aaa	STL	181	21	46	11	0	6	28	23	47	1	2	252	335	410	745	11%	74%	0.48	104	34	4.87	36
Duncan,Eric	05	21	5	aa	NYY	448	55	101	14	2	18	56	51	114	8	3	225	305	384	689	10%	74%	0.45	93	86	4.13	22
	06	22	5	a/a	NYY	316	39	74	18	2	11	35	39	57	0	1	233	317	402	719	11%	82%	0.68	107	54	4.50	35
Duncan,Jeff	05	27	8	a/a	NYM	347	34	71	10	3	5	23	32	76	9	5	205	273	296	568	9%	78%	0.43	56	101	2.71	0
	06	28	8	aaa	LA	278	39	67	8	1	5	19	23	46	15	9	243	300	328	628	8%	83%	0.49	54	109	3.32	13
Duncan,Shelley	05	26	3	aa	NYY	533	64	101	21	1	26	69	41	143	3	2	189	247	379	626	7%	73%	0.29	112	61	3.07	15
	06	27	8	a/a	NYY	394	39	81	20	0	17	53	30	97	3	1	205	262	382	644	7%	75%	0.32	110	46	3.38	20
Dunwoody,Todd	05	30	8	aaa	MIN	293	23	59	15	2	4	30	13	66	5	6	203	236	304	540	4%	78%	0.19	71	82	2.16	1
Duran,Carlos	05	23	8	a/a	ATL	173	12	42	7	4	3	13	4	30	0	2	243	260	382	641	2%	83%	0.13	83	114	3.20	18
	06	24	8	a/a	ATL	123	15	33	4	0	2	10	6	26	4	4	268	302	350	652	5%	79%	0.23	54	73	3.43	16
Durazo,Erubiel	06	32	0	aaa	MIN	192	19	48	12	0	5	22	27	42	0	0	248	341	380	721	12%	78%	0.64	90	16	4.82	33
Durbin,Chris	05	24	8	aa	BOS	394	45	102	30	1	10	47	29	60	3	4	258	308	412	720	7%	85%	0.48	108	55	4.41	40
	06	25	8	aa	BOS	341	42	75	27	1	4	27	32	62	3	5	219	285	335	620	8%	82%	0.51	89	67	3.19	20
Durrington,Trent	05	30	5	aaa	MIL	313	41	73	13	1	4	21	28	53	20	14	233	296	313	609	8%	83%	0.52	56	109	2.98	11
	06	31	5	aaa	BOS	391	41	81	14	2	3	25	28	88	27	6	207	260	272	532	7%	78%	0.32	45	129	2.52	-6
Eckelman,Alex	05	31	6	a/a	HOU	247	14	47	7	0	2	14	7	29	2	2	191	214	249	463	3%	88%	0.25	41	45	1.67	-14
Edwards,Mike	05	29	5	aaa	LA	118	11	24	4	0	3	12	7	15	2	1	205	246	307	554	5%	87%	0.43	65	59	2.50	4
	06	30	5	aaa	PIT	325	35	76	20	2	3	25	24	51	5	4	232	284	330	615	7%	84%	0.47	72	84	3.20	17
Eldred,Brad	05	25	3	a/a	PIT	279	39	70	17	1	20	55	16	64	4	1	252	293	535	827	5%	77%	0.25	168	79	5.47	58
Eldridge,Rashad	05	24	8	a/a	TEX	338	52	91	31	3	4	32	49	63	4	4	269	362	414	776	13%	81%	0.78	107	93	5.53	50
	06	25	8	a/a	TEX	329	30	80	14	3	4	33	27	90	4	7	242	300	336	636	8%	73%	0.30	63	82	3.34	12
Ellison,Jason	06	29	8	aaa	SF	192	30	66	16	2	1	13	10	16	5	5	344	377	460	837	5%	92%	0.63	89	104	6.46	64
Ellis,A.J.	06	26	2	aa	LA	252	30	53	7	1	0	18	45	59	2	0	211	330	246	577	15%	77%	0.76	28	65	3.16	-3
Ellsbury,Jacoby	06	23	8	aa	BOS	198	25	57	11	2	3	16	21	23	14	9	289	358	407	765	10%	89%	0.94	79	119	5.06	48
Emmerick,Joshua	05	25	2	aa	WAS	133	7	21	5	0	0	6	13	43	1	0	157	234	193	427	9%	68%	0.31	32	34	1.57	-28
	06	26	2	aa	WAS	143	5	20	4	0	1	6	9	46	0	0	138	189	183	372	6%	68%	0.20	32	11	1.12	-37
Encarnacion,Edwir	05	23	5	aaa	CIN	290	38	85	22	0	14	46	27	41	6	2	293	354	511	865	9%	86%	0.67	140	62	6.78	69
Erickson,Matt	06	31	4	aaa	ARI	293	29	64	11	0	2	17	20	40	3	2	218	268	273	541	6%	86%	0.50	42	56	2.51	-0
Escalona,Felix	05	27	6	aaa	NYY	299	34	70	11	0	6	34	21	49	4	0	234	285	328	612	7%	83%	0.43	62	68	3.34	12
	06	28	6	a/a	NYY	357	35	70	18	0	10	44	16	74	1	0	197	231	329	560	4%	79%	0.21	87	47	2.51	6

Major League Equivalent Statistics

BATTERS

BATTER	Yr	Age	Pos	Lev	Org	ab	r	h	d	t	hr	rbi	bb	k	sb	cs	ba	ob	slg	ops	bb%	ct%	eye	px	sx	rc/g	bpv
Escobar,Alex	06	28	8	aa	WAS	122	15	27	8	0	3	19	14	28	2	2	223	305	367	672	11%	77%	0.52	99	55	3.83	25
Escobar,Gustavo	05	26	5	aa	COL	125	13	24	3	0	0	6	4	26	7	2	194	217	216	433	3%	80%	0.14	19	110	1.60	-24
Escobar,Yunel	06	24	6	aa	ATL	428	51	107	19	3	2	43	56	77	7	9	249	337	322	658	12%	82%	0.73	53	79	3.84	20
Espinosa,David	05	24	8	a/a	DET	468	62	112	18	11	7	35	62	96	13	8	239	328	370	698	12%	79%	0.65	78	168	4.30	25
	06	25	8	aaa	DET	293	46	76	12	8	8	25	40	63	11	6	259	348	437	785	12%	78%	0.63	103	194	5.44	42
Espino,Damaso	06	23	2	aa	KC	182	14	38	2	0	0	14	16	12	0	2	208	270	219	489	8%	93%	1.25	9	27	1.99	-2
Esposito,Brian	05	27	2	a/a	TEX	159	12	32	6	0	0	5	5	31	1	0	204	230	243	473	3%	80%	0.17	35	48	1.88	-14
	06	28	2	aaa	STL	175	11	37	9	0	2	10	3	31	0	1	212	224	293	517	2%	83%	0.09	60	29	2.09	-3
Espy,Nathan	05	27	0	aa	SEA	440	51	90	21	3	10	45	51	113	8	6	206	289	336	625	10%	74%	0.45	83	99	3.29	12
	06	28	3	aaa	OAK	357	33	81	21	0	7	35	37	68	2	0	227	300	349	649	9%	81%	0.55	85	41	3.74	22
Esquivel,Matt	06	24	8	aa	ATL	253	24	61	16	1	5	36	17	72	4	5	242	291	368	659	6%	71%	0.24	87	69	3.52	21
Estrada,Kevin	05	25	6	aa	STL	292	26	67	15	1	3	13	18	42	12	8	228	273	314	587	6%	86%	0.43	63	89	2.76	11
	06	26	6	a/a	STL	242	27	45	6	1	2	13	23	46	9	3	186	258	242	499	9%	81%	0.51	38	105	2.19	-12
Ethier,Andre	05	23	8	a/a	OAK	516	81	145	28	2	14	64	39	75	1	5	281	332	424	756	7%	85%	0.52	93	57	5.02	43
Eure,Jeffrey	06	26	5	aa	MIL	332	37	70	16	1	10	45	18	99	3	3	212	253	359	612	5%	70%	0.18	93	72	2.95	13
Evans,Terry	06	25	8	aa	STL	263	42	66	11	1	11	29	14	58	10	9	249	288	430	718	5%	78%	0.25	109	112	3.89	33
Evans,Tom	05	31	3	aa	PIT	335	34	60	16	1	8	31	27	96	4	3	178	240	303	543	8%	71%	0.29	82	84	2.35	-1
Eylward,Mike	05	26	3	aa	ANA	418	42	91	20	1	9	48	24	52	2	5	219	262	333	595	6%	88%	0.47	76	48	2.81	14
	06	27	3	a/a	ANA	509	49	126	26	1	9	58	32	64	2	9	248	293	354	646	6%	87%	0.50	73	35	3.41	23
Ezi,Travis	06	25	8	aa	MIL	168	23	32	4	2	2	15	17	61	7	4	193	267	268	535	9%	64%	0.28	45	151	2.42	-12
Fagan,John	05	26	8	aa	HOU	173	15	37	3	1	3	12	17	53	3	0	211	283	287	570	9%	69%	0.33	46	82	2.96	-4
	06	27	8	aa	HOU	127	7	23	6	1	2	12	10	35	2	2	183	242	301	543	7%	72%	0.29	77	75	2.26	-2
Fahey,Brandon	05	25	6	aa	BAL	500	58	133	19	3	3	43	40	71	15	8	266	320	333	653	7%	86%	0.57	47	98	3.85	20
Faison,Vince	06	26	8	aa	NYY	408	60	92	19	5	13	58	42	101	1	5	225	298	390	688	9%	75%	0.42	101	102	3.91	25
Fasano,Jim	06	23	3	aa	TEX	365	39	81	25	0	7	45	25	79	2	0	223	273	348	622	6%	78%	0.32	90	54	3.31	18
Feliciano,Jesus	05	26	8	aa	WAS	322	35	69	10	1	2	17	10	32	7	6	213	236	267	504	3%	90%	0.30	39	93	1.97	-7
	06	27	8	aa	WAS	178	11	31	2	0	1	10	7	17	2	5	173	206	201	406	4%	91%	0.44	20	52	1.17	-26
Fernandez,Alex	05	24	8	a/a	CIN	270	25	69	11	0	5	31	12	34	4	2	255	286	348	634	4%	87%	0.34	63	56	3.47	18
Fernando,Osvaldo	06	26	3	aa	HOU	180	14	32	5	0	0	5	6	27	6	5	175	203	200	403	3%	85%	0.24	22	84	1.18	-28
Fielder,Prince	05	21	3	aaa	MIL	378	56	106	21	0	23	70	45	65	7	7	279	356	518	874	11%	83%	0.70	144	52	6.57	66
Fields,Josh	05	26	5	aa	CHW	474	55	98	22	0	14	57	39	127	5	6	207	267	338	605	8%	73%	0.31	84	59	2.94	10
	06	24	5	aaa	CHW	462	78	137	30	3	20	64	49	125	26	5	297	364	504	868	10%	73%	0.39	130	132	7.10	60
Figueroa,Luis	05	29	6	aaa	BOS	402	42	99	20	1	5	34	20	23	2	7	245	282	335	617	5%	94%	0.91	65	49	3.09	27
	06	30	6	aaa	TOR	377	32	92	21	2	5	32	20	35	9	9	244	282	352	634	5%	91%	0.57	76	77	3.21	24
Fiorentino,Jeff	06	23	8	aa	BAL	385	59	99	13	0	13	58	51	56	9	3	257	345	388	733	12%	86%	0.92	80	74	4.99	37
Fleming,Ryan	05	30	8	a/a	PHI	437	36	91	13	2	9	39	31	61	9	11	208	261	308	569	7%	86%	0.51	62	68	2.51	5
	06	31	8	aaa	PHI	232	24	49	10	3	1	18	17	40	4	5	209	264	287	551	7%	83%	0.43	54	109	2.43	1
Flores,Jose	05	32	6	aaa	LA	322	38	77	7	2	3	24	31	24	1	8	238	304	296	600	9%	92%	1.25	38	55	2.93	20
	06	33	6	aaa	SF	183	20	40	8	0	2	21	20	23	1	1	216	293	290	583	10%	87%	0.85	54	45	2.99	12
Fontenot,Mike	05	25	4	aaa	CHC	375	45	87	19	5	5	30	46	62	2	2	232	315	348	664	11%	84%	0.74	77	96	3.92	24
	06	26	4	aaa	CHC	362	49	98	26	2	8	32	43	61	5	4	271	348	418	766	11%	83%	0.70	102	77	5.31	46
Foster,Quincy	06	32	8	aa	SF	148	17	29	2	1	1	6	9	34	5	1	194	241	241	482	6%	77%	0.27	28	132	2.04	-18
Fox,Adam	05	24	5	aa	TEX	149	17	35	5	1	4	20	15	24	2	0	234	302	358	661	9%	84%	0.61	75	81	3.93	21
Fox,Jacob	06	24	2	aa	CHC	193	21	50	16	0	6	26	10	51	0	0	261	296	433	729	5%	74%	0.19	120	25	4.55	40
Francia,Juan	05	24	4	aa	DET	295	30	74	7	7	2	20	14	34	12	8	250	283	339	622	4%	88%	0.40	51	163	3.14	12
	06	25	4	aa	DET	190	19	29	4	2	0	8	7	26	10	4	150	179	190	369	3%	86%	0.25	27	161	1.05	-34
Francisco,Ben	05	24	8	a/a	CLE	330	39	91	18	4	5	39	21	51	12	5	276	319	400	719	6%	85%	0.41	82	127	4.58	34
	06	25	8	aaa	CLE	515	76	134	32	3	14	56	44	70	24	5	260	318	416	734	8%	86%	0.63	102	125	4.86	41
Francoeur,Jeff	05	22	8	aa	ATL	335	35	84	26	1	11	54	18	66	11	4	251	289	433	722	5%	80%	0.27	122	91	4.31	39
Franco,Iker	05	24	2	a/a	ATL	211	12	54	7	0	3	20	9	36	0	3	257	287	331	618	4%	83%	0.24	50	13	3.15	11
	06	25	2	aa	STL	340	34	64	14	1	7	33	18	71	0	1	188	229	296	525	5%	79%	0.25	70	50	2.20	-3
Frandsen,Kevin	05	23	4	a/a	SF	218	31	61	16	0	3	26	5	15	6	5	280	296	394	690	2%	93%	0.33	86	88	3.89	36
	06	24	4	aaa	SF	293	35	79	23	2	2	23	9	23	5	5	270	291	382	674	3%	92%	0.39	86	95	3.74	33
Frazier,Alex	06	26	8	aa	ARI	313	30	65	15	0	8	36	14	86	1	2	207	240	334	573	4%	73%	0.16	83	42	2.59	7
Freeman,Choo	05	26	8	aa	COL	354	29	86	9	4	8	37	18	46	3	4	243	280	358	638	5%	87%	0.38	67	79	3.35	16
Freire,Alejandro	05	31	0	a/a	BAL	404	42	92	18	1	14	52	30	65	1	0	228	280	382	663	7%	84%	0.46	95	42	3.72	24
	06	32	3	aaa	BAL	177	19	35	6	0	3	12	14	44	0	2	198	259	280	538	8%	75%	0.32	55	40	2.35	-5
French,Anton	05	30	8	aaa	TOR	350	40	77	12	6	7	29	18	76	11	3	219	257	350	607	5%	78%	0.24	77	166	3.06	10
Frese,Nate	05	28	5	a/a	CHC	232	20	48	9	0	5	24	14	48	0	0	205	249	311	561	6%	79%	0.28	70	23	2.61	3
Fulse,Sheldon	05	24	8	aa	BOS	166	17	27	9	1	2	13	14	43	12	8	164	227	263	490	8%	74%	0.31	70	136	1.70	-10
Furmaniak,J.J.	05	26	6	aaa	PIT	519	49	121	19	4	12	50	23	87	11	8	234	267	353	620	4%	83%	0.27	74	94	3.09	14
	06	27	6	aaa	PIT	371	40	74	11	2	6	25	23	85	14	5	200	246	287	533	6%	77%	0.27	56	117	2.37	-5
Gaetti,Joe	06	25	8	aa	COL	392	49	105	21	4	13	46	28	75	4	2	267	315	441	756	7%	81%	0.37	108	96	4.98	41
Gall,John	05	28	8	aaa	STL	369	46	85	19	0	10	48	34	35	7	2	229	295	358	652	8%	91%	0.98	85	73	3.73	31
	06	29	8	aaa	STL	289	26	73	12	1	5	29	23	34	3	4	251	307	348	654	7%	88%	0.68	65	52	3.69	24
Garabito,Eddy	05	29	6	aaa	COL	254	33	64	13	2	6	23	17	22	5	5	253	299	384	683	6%	92%	0.78	86	93	3.86	35
	06	30	4	aaa	BAL	474	50	108	21	1	5	42	45	57	17	7	228	295	305	600	9%	88%	0.78	56	88	3.17	15
Garciaparra,Micha	06	24	4	a/a	SEA	241	35	69	8	1	2	23	28	45	4	4	286	361	353	713	10%	81%	0.62	46	75	4.73	27
Garcia,Danny	06	26	4	aaa	NYY	392	41	85	22	1	3	34	29	64	18	8	218	272	302	574	7%	84%	0.46	64	103	2.78	8
Garcia,Jesse	05	32	6	a/a	SD	241	14	33	6	2	2	18	4	39	5	2	136	150	206	356	2%	84%	0.10	45	110	0.93	-34
	06	33	6	aaa	HOU	255	24	54	11	1	5	20	5	43	4	1	212	228	314	542	2%	83%	0.12	68	87	2.37	1
Garcia,Luis	05	27	8	aaa	NYM	151	18	29	5	0	8	19	11	33	2	0	193	246	379	625	7%	78%	0.32	108	64	3.14	15
Garcia,Sergio	05	26	6	aa	LA	229	21	43	6	0	3	27	18	38	1	1	189	248	252	499	7%	84%	0.48	43	44	2.09	-10
	06	27	4	a/a	LA	385	56	89	20	0	6	40	32	48	5	2	231	291	332	623	8%	88%	0.68	71	80	3.42	20
Garcia,Yunir	06	24	2	a/a	NYM	156	16	18	5	0	1	6	23	71	0	0	118	233	168	401	13%	54%	0.33	37	35	1.39	-39
Gardner,Brett	06	23	8	aa	NYY	217	39	55	4	2	0	13	24	40	26	5	255	330	291	620	10%	81%	0.60	24	166	3.93	7
Garko,Ryan	05	25	3	aaa	CLE	452	58	119	23	2	13	59	34	74	1	4	263	315	409	724	7%	84%	0.46	93	53	4.51	36
	06	26	3	aaa	CLE	364	41	83	18	0	13	55	44	66	4	5	228	311	383	694	11%	82%	0.66	98	43	4.08	30
Garrabrants,Steve	06	25	8	aa	ARI	241	25	49	8	0	3	23	27	56	4	4	205	284	272	556	10%	77%	0.48	46	56	2.62	-3
Garrett,Shawn	05	27	8	aaa	OAK	504	51	126	23	1	14	62	21	90	10	5	250	281	381	662	4%	82%	0.24	84	75	3.66	23
	06	28	8	aaa	STL	385	38	79	20	5	6	48	19	98	2	1	205	242	326	568	5%	75%	0.19	80	108	2.62	5

Major League Equivalent Statistics

BATTERS

BATTER	Yr	Age	Pos	Lev	Org	ab	r	h	d	t	hr	rbi	bb	k	sb	cs	ba	ob	slg	ops	bb%	ct%	eye	px	sx	rc/g	bpv
Gates,David	05	25	8	aa	ANA	381	41	73	17	2	11	40	23	83	1	0	191	238	331	569	6%	78%	0.28	88	68	2.61	6
	06	26	8	aa	ANA	121	10	18	4	1	3	10	9	39	1	0	151	208	288	496	7%	68%	0.22	83	84	1.94	-11
Gathright,Joey	05	24	8	aaa	TAM	226	33	58	8	3	1	13	21	34	22	10	257	320	332	652	9%	85%	0.62	50	161	3.68	18
Gautreau,Jake	05	26	4	aaa	CLE	421	55	91	28	1	12	43	29	69	2	2	216	266	372	638	6%	84%	0.42	104	68	3.32	23
	06	27	4	aaa	CLE	248	25	45	12	0	6	26	23	63	1	1	180	250	297	548	9%	75%	0.37	78	45	2.47	-1
Geiger,Kyle	06	24	2	aa	MIN	102	5	12	1	0	2	5	6	34	1	0	121	168	186	354	5%	67%	0.17	37	37	1.00	-41
Gemoll,Brandon	05	25	3	aa	MIL	428	38	105	23	3	5	43	22	94	2	4	246	282	351	633	5%	78%	0.23	73	62	3.36	17
	06	26	3	aa	PHI	283	17	56	18	2	3	21	15	60	1	2	197	237	301	538	5%	79%	0.25	77	55	2.30	2
Gemoll,Justin	05	28	4	aaa	KC	448	43	97	18	1	5	37	29	81	5	1	216	263	293	556	6%	82%	0.35	54	73	2.67	1
Gerber,Joe	05	27	3	a/a	SD	313	29	57	11	0	9	31	31	97	0	1	183	258	303	561	9%	69%	0.32	75	25	2.61	-1
German,Esteban	05	28	5	aaa	TEX	489	68	128	23	4	4	46	44	54	29	8	262	323	348	671	8%	89%	0.81	60	132	4.19	29
Gettis,Byron	05	26	8	a/a	DET	358	46	76	11	1	9	42	27	98	3	5	212	267	321	588	7%	73%	0.27	68	70	2.79	4
Getz,Christopher	06	23	4	aa	CHW	508	63	124	15	5	2	34	49	47	17	6	244	310	304	614	9%	91%	1.02	40	121	3.45	18
Giarratano,Tony	05	23	6	aa	DET	346	33	82	18	3	2	26	26	59	10	6	237	290	324	614	7%	83%	0.44	63	104	3.21	14
	06	24	6	aa	DET	269	32	72	16	6	0	17	20	43	15	4	267	318	371	690	7%	84%	0.47	73	177	4.36	29
Gil,Benji	05	33	6	aaa	NYM	229	21	49	7	0	5	21	10	61	3	6	212	245	314	559	4%	73%	0.16	64	51	2.27	1
Gil,Jerry	05	23	6	aa	ARI	199	22	47	7	3	8	23	7	40	8	8	236	262	422	684	3%	80%	0.18	107	143	3.20	26
	06	24	6	a/a	ARI	493	64	120	28	5	24	74	15	103	6	7	243	266	467	732	3%	79%	0.15	135	109	4.01	40
Gimenez,Hector	05	23	2	aa	HOU	454	43	115	17	1	11	53	28	85	2	3	254	298	367	665	6%	81%	0.33	72	42	3.82	21
	06	24	2	aaa	HOU	275	26	68	7	0	7	31	20	35	2	3	247	298	349	647	7%	87%	0.57	62	37	3.58	19
Ginter,Keith	06	30	4	aaa	OAK	422	50	90	24	0	9	49	41	64	2	0	213	284	335	618	9%	85%	0.64	84	54	3.33	19
Gipson,Charles	05	33	8	aaa	HOU	393	40	95	20	2	2	17	16	63	13	10	240	271	314	584	4%	84%	0.26	56	97	2.73	8
Gload,Ross	05	30	3	aaa	CHW	236	34	73	18	1	13	34	16	33	0	1	308	353	555	909	6%	86%	0.50	155	44	7.35	77
Godwin,Tyrell	05	26	8	aaa	WAS	494	58	130	19	3	6	34	36	58	16	16	263	313	350	663	7%	88%	0.62	58	92	3.62	24
	06	27	8	aaa	WAS	411	50	86	19	5	6	38	27	66	16	7	210	258	321	580	6%	84%	0.40	73	145	2.76	8
Gold,Nate	06	26	3	aa	TEX	452	54	110	23	1	28	76	40	80	3	3	243	304	481	785	8%	82%	0.50	141	43	5.02	49
Goleski,Ryan	06	25	8	aa	CLE	324	42	85	23	0	13	55	32	86	4	2	261	328	454	782	9%	73%	0.37	126	54	5.37	46
Gomes,Jonny	05	25	8	aaa	TAM	162	25	43	11	0	9	33	22	33	5	1	265	353	500	853	12%	80%	0.67	146	71	6.60	62
Gomez,Alexis	05	27	8	aaa	DET	421	43	115	23	8	6	46	22	80	18	7	273	309	404	713	5%	81%	0.27	85	155	4.44	31
	06	28	8	aaa	DET	226	32	58	15	4	9	32	16	47	7	4	255	304	477	781	7%	79%	0.33	137	149	4.93	48
Gomez,Carlos	06	21	8	aa	NYM	430	54	122	25	5	6	48	27	88	42	9	283	326	410	736	6%	80%	0.31	85	163	5.03	36
Gomez,Francis	05	25	5	a/a	OAK	236	24	48	12	2	3	16	7	53	2	5	201	224	304	528	3%	78%	0.13	70	99	2.00	-1
Gomez,Rudy	05	31	4	a/a	KC	175	12	30	5	0	1	9	10	20	2	1	174	217	215	432	5%	89%	0.48	31	51	1.52	-20
Gonzalez,Adrian	05	23	3	aaa	TEX	328	43	99	15	1	14	46	23	30	0	0	302	348	482	829	7%	91%	0.77	109	35	6.35	61
Gonzalez,Alberto	06	23	6	a/a	ARI	449	58	122	20	3	5	43	33	35	4	1	272	322	363	685	7%	92%	0.94	63	87	4.31	35
Gonzalez,Angel	05	24	6	aa	CHW	430	39	103	16	1	4	49	48	75	5	6	239	315	309	624	10%	82%	0.63	50	51	3.42	13
	06	25	4	aaa	CHW	402	44	105	25	0	6	47	42	71	15	9	261	331	368	699	9%	82%	0.59	78	72	4.32	31
Gonzalez,Daniel	05	24	6	aa	PHI	179	11	35	4	1	2	14	15	35	0	0	195	256	260	516	8%	80%	0.42	41	35	2.28	-10
Gonzalez,Edgar	05	27	5	a/a	WAS	384	35	82	23	2	5	36	29	75	3	8	213	268	322	589	7%	81%	0.38	77	63	2.72	11
	06	24	4	a/a	FLA	353	42	108	18	3	9	54	41	65	9	7	306	378	450	829	10%	82%	0.63	92	89	6.36	53
Gonzalez,Raul	05	32	8	aaa	STL	347	45	86	18	2	9	36	28	42	2	5	246	302	386	689	7%	88%	0.66	91	64	3.92	33
	06	33	8	aaa	PIT	399	43	94	22	2	6	49	46	62	4	5	235	314	345	659	10%	84%	0.74	76	62	3.78	24
Gonzalez,Wiki	05	31	2	aaa	SEA	176	19	43	8	1	4	21	13	12	0	0	245	296	363	659	7%	93%	1.03	77	45	3.82	34
Gordon,Alex	06	23	5	aa	KC	486	87	139	37	1	20	79	57	85	17	4	286	361	490	851	10%	83%	0.67	133	103	6.72	64
Gordon,Brian	05	27	8	aaa	ANA	339	33	74	20	2	11	38	17	79	5	6	219	256	390	646	5%	77%	0.22	109	80	3.14	22
	06	28	8	aaa	HOU	303	37	61	17	3	13	46	21	97	1	3	203	255	405	660	7%	68%	0.22	124	92	3.31	23
Gorecki,Reid	05	25	8	aa	STL	159	9	23	5	0	2	11	12	29	1	4	143	205	209	414	7%	81%	0.42	45	35	1.23	-25
	06	26	8	a/a	STL	401	51	82	23	1	13	48	42	91	16	12	204	279	365	644	9%	77%	0.46	104	96	3.20	20
Gorneault,Nick	05	26	8	aaa	ANA	484	74	116	21	6	17	76	39	89	5	8	240	297	417	714	7%	82%	0.44	106	111	4.11	32
	06	27	8	aaa	ANA	407	49	96	21	5	10	58	28	87	5	5	236	284	387	672	6%	79%	0.32	96	109	3.69	24
Gotay,Ruben	05	23	4	aa	KC	110	16	23	7	0	2	11	9	9	0	2	209	269	327	596	8%	92%	1.00	84	60	2.77	25
	06	24	4	aaa	NYM	491	55	119	27	2	10	55	31	81	9	7	242	287	367	654	6%	84%	0.38	84	83	3.55	23
Grabowski,Jason	05	29	8	aaa	LA	181	22	40	11	0	4	19	17	19	0	0	221	289	342	631	9%	90%	0.93	85	33	3.47	27
Gradoville,Tim	05	26	2	a/a	PHI	244	14	44	5	1	2	14	11	66	1	1	179	216	230	445	4%	73%	0.17	33	52	1.60	-23
	06	27	2	a/a	PHI	119	10	26	6	0	1	11	5	38	0	0	219	253	295	548	4%	68%	0.14	59	27	2.54	0
Granderson,Curtis	05	25	8	aaa	DET	445	69	123	25	16	12	57	42	109	19	7	276	339	485	824	9%	76%	0.39	123	249	5.95	51
Grayson,Luke	06	24	8	aa	TEX	176	19	37	10	0	4	16	11	37	6	4	211	259	329	588	6%	79%	0.31	81	80	2.72	10
Gray,Antoin	05	24	4	aa	CHW	230	29	48	11	1	6	23	20	55	1	1	207	270	339	609	8%	76%	0.36	86	70	3.09	12
Greenberg,Adam	05	25	8	aa	CHC	302	42	70	10	6	4	29	48	64	12	4	233	337	343	680	14%	79%	0.74	67	161	4.32	20
	06	26	8	a/a	LA	320	44	60	10	2	1	17	56	111	11	6	187	308	238	546	15%	65%	0.51	36	111	2.71	-13
Green,Andy	05	28	4	aaa	ARI	530	81	152	40	9	13	52	47	61	6	7	286	344	470	814	8%	88%	0.76	120	122	5.77	60
Gregorio,Tom	06	29	2	a/a	TEX	118	6	21	2	0	2	11	7	28	0	0	174	222	229	452	6%	76%	0.26	34	10	1.69	-23
Grieve,Ben	05	29	8	aaa	CHC	289	29	59	14	1	11	35	35	52	0	0	205	290	372	661	11%	82%	0.67	103	30	3.74	24
Griffin,John-Ford	05	26	8	aaa	TOR	504	63	117	20	1	25	79	49	112	1	2	232	299	422	722	9%	78%	0.43	113	42	4.38	32
	06	27	8	aaa	TOR	227	26	49	18	0	6	19	16	56	2	0	214	267	372	639	7%	75%	0.30	112	61	3.42	23
Grindell,Nate	05	28	8	a/a	PHI	361	21	66	14	0	3	26	20	60	2	5	184	227	252	479	5%	83%	0.34	50	31	1.77	-11
Gross,Gabe	05	26	8	aaa	TOR	390	51	107	29	3	5	37	43	68	11	2	274	346	401	747	10%	83%	0.63	92	111	5.28	42
Groves,Brett	05	27	4	aa	KC	273	27	46	7	0	1	16	18	43	1	2	167	219	201	420	6%	84%	0.42	26	54	1.43	-25
	06	28	6	aa	KC	166	11	24	2	0	0	11	16	26	1	2	145	220	159	379	9%	84%	0.61	13	41	1.16	-34
Guance,Luis	05	24	4	aa	COL	216	20	45	16	0	5	17	23	45	3	3	207	284	346	630	10%	79%	0.51	98	49	3.27	20
Guerrero,Cristian	05	25	8	a/a	WAS	340	35	74	10	1	11	42	19	87	10	9	218	259	355	614	5%	74%	0.22	82	85	2.87	11
	06	26	8	aa	WAS	140	11	28	3	3	3	16	8	48	3	3	199	241	336	577	5%	66%	0.16	77	154	2.53	1
Guerrero,Wilton	05	31	4	aaa	CHW	151	14	34	9	1	3	14	8	16	2	3	226	266	352	618	5%	90%	0.52	86	72	2.98	21
Guiel,Aaron	05	33	8	aaa	KC	496	66	106	26	3	18	67	45	88	5	4	214	279	386	666	8%	82%	0.51	108	83	3.64	26
	06	34	8	aaa	NYY	227	34	48	13	1	11	32	33	57	0	0	210	311	416	727	13%	75%	0.59	126	50	4.57	34
Guillen,Rodolfo	05	22	8	aa	NYY	106	10	26	2	0	2	7	4	17	0	1	245	273	321	593	4%	84%	0.24	46	35	2.91	5
Gutierrez,Franklin	05	23	8	a/a	CLE	450	65	104	29	2	8	40	29	76	13	7	231	278	358	635	6%	83%	0.38	88	114	3.33	21
	06	24	8	aaa	CLE	349	60	92	27	0	8	36	48	82	12	8	264	353	410	762	12%	77%	0.59	104	83	5.17	42
Gutierrez,Jesse	05	27	3	aa	CIN	100	7	22	6	0	2	17	5	19	0	0	224	261	357	618	5%	81%	0.26	90	15	3.17	17
	06	28	3	aaa	CIN	397	41	101	25	1	9	55	43	76	0	0	255	328	394	721	10%	81%	0.56	94	29	4.73	35
Gutierrez,Ricky	05	35	5	aaa	CHW	118	11	18	3	0	0	5	11	20	1	0	153	224	175	399	8%	83%	0.54	20	57	1.37	-30

Major League Equivalent Statistics

BATTER	Yr	Age	Pos	Lev	Org	ab	r	h	d	t	hr	rbi	bb	k	sb	cs	ba	ob	slg	ops	bb%	ct%	eye	px	sx	rc/g	bpv
Guzman,Freddy	06	26	8	aaa	TEX	376	47	96	15	4	3	22	39	42	33	14	255	325	340	664	9%	89%	0.91	56	139	3.91	27
Guzman,Garrett	06	24	8	aa	MIN	222	31	56	15	1	7	23	16	28	4	3	253	305	419	725	7%	87%	0.59	109	86	4.40	41
Guzman,Javier	05	21	6	aa	PIT	260	21	56	9	1	2	19	8	34	6	6	215	239	281	520	3%	87%	0.24	46	81	2.06	-5
	06	22	6	aa	PIT	485	52	125	23	4	6	37	23	58	11	9	258	291	359	650	5%	88%	0.40	68	99	3.51	22
Guzman,Jesus	05	21	5	aa	SEA	453	54	105	16	6	8	47	43	95	5	12	232	298	347	645	9%	79%	0.45	70	103	3.32	15
	06	22	5	aa	SEA	408	54	98	17	2	9	52	45	74	7	3	240	316	358	674	10%	82%	0.61	75	89	4.06	23
Guzman,Joel	05	21	6	aa	LA	439	54	112	26	1	14	63	34	99	6	4	256	309	414	723	7%	77%	0.34	103	71	4.48	35
	06	22	5	aaa	TAM	405	44	107	20	2	12	56	26	70	8	7	263	309	413	721	6%	83%	0.38	94	79	4.37	34
Gwynn,Anthony	05	23	8	aa	MIL	505	65	117	18	3	1	32	59	63	24	17	232	313	286	599	10%	88%	0.94	40	107	3.06	13
	06	24	8	aaa	MIL	447	66	125	20	4	4	38	39	78	27	12	280	337	369	707	8%	83%	0.50	61	134	4.52	29
Haad,Yamid	05	28	2	aaa	SF	216	15	47	10	1	6	22	6	24	1	0	220	239	353	592	3%	89%	0.24	86	49	2.83	13
	06	29	2	aaa	SF	115	9	16	5	0	2	7	2	16	0	0	142	156	237	393	2%	86%	0.11	67	46	1.12	-23
Haerther,Cody	05	22	8	aa	STL	208	22	53	9	1	7	27	7	33	0	1	255	279	409	688	3%	84%	0.21	95	50	3.89	28
	06	23	8	aa	STL	412	45	100	25	2	9	42	29	49	2	5	243	292	377	669	7%	88%	0.59	91	57	3.71	30
Haggerty,Cory	05	24	6	aa	CHW	111	10	21	3	1	2	10	12	22	2	1	188	270	282	552	10%	80%	0.56	57	85	2.61	-3
Hairston,Scott	05	25	8	aaa	ARI	209	31	57	8	2	12	28	15	28	2	0	275	323	502	825	7%	86%	0.53	130	93	5.97	56
	06	26	8	aaa	ARI	381	62	110	21	1	20	61	40	61	2	0	288	355	509	864	9%	84%	0.65	135	63	6.85	64
Haley,Adam	05	25	6	aa	ARI	374	40	90	14	2	3	20	23	61	9	8	241	285	310	596	6%	84%	0.38	50	87	2.93	8
	06	26	4	aa	DET	290	22	51	9	2	2	15	29	70	3	3	177	251	237	488	9%	76%	0.41	41	75	2.00	-16
Hall,Noah	06	29	8	aa	BAL	431	49	86	18	3	9	42	38	80	13	6	198	264	317	580	8%	81%	0.48	75	111	2.79	7
Hall,Victor	05	25	8	aa	NYM	179	14	29	5	1	4	14	5	44	5	1	161	185	256	442	3%	75%	0.12	58	103	1.51	-20
Hammock,Robby	06	29	2	aaa	ARI	369	40	89	18	1	15	46	17	49	2	2	242	276	414	690	4%	87%	0.35	107	53	3.88	32
Hammond,Joey	05	28	4	aa	BAL	420	42	93	14	2	7	39	30	88	4	2	221	273	316	589	7%	79%	0.34	61	73	2.98	6
	06	29	4	aa	PHI	469	41	96	11	2	6	39	39	76	2	3	205	266	280	546	8%	84%	0.51	47	59	2.51	-2
Hanigan,Ryan	05	25	3	aa	CIN	330	31	84	11	0	3	21	34	37	3	1	254	324	311	635	9%	89%	0.93	42	45	3.74	20
	06	26	2	a/a	CIN	139	16	29	2	0	0	13	21	27	0	0	207	310	220	530	13%	81%	0.78	11	31	2.58	-11
Hankins,Ryan	05	29	5	aaa	NYY	269	22	56	15	1	4	20	19	51	1	0	206	259	308	567	7%	81%	0.38	72	51	2.73	6
Hannahan,Buzz	05	29	5	aaa	PHI	285	25	56	9	3	1	15	19	68	3	5	195	245	255	501	6%	76%	0.28	42	93	1.99	-12
Hannahan,Jack	05	26	5	a/a	DET	257	25	56	11	0	3	24	23	57	5	3	218	282	296	578	8%	78%	0.40	56	61	2.87	4
	06	27	5	aaa	DET	415	53	107	23	0	8	56	55	108	8	6	257	344	369	714	12%	74%	0.51	79	60	4.63	28
Hansen,Jed	05	33	5	aaa	SF	290	42	55	16	2	5	25	20	73	7	2	189	241	313	555	6%	75%	0.27	84	134	2.53	3
	06	34	4	aaa	SF	365	32	71	14	1	6	30	22	60	7	4	195	240	288	528	6%	84%	0.36	62	80	2.27	-2
Hanson,Travis	05	25	5	aa	STL	546	58	126	25	2	13	68	39	78	1	3	231	283	357	639	7%	86%	0.50	81	46	3.44	20
	06	26	5	a/a	STL	475	34	92	21	1	2	30	29	84	1	1	194	241	254	495	6%	82%	0.35	47	43	2.05	-9
Harper,Brandon	05	29	2	aaa	DET	248	26	51	10	1	5	25	23	34	4	0	205	272	308	580	8%	86%	0.67	67	81	2.97	10
	06	30	2	aaa	WAS	120	14	28	8	0	2	9	12	22	3	1	233	301	345	646	9%	81%	0.53	83	68	3.69	22
Harper,Brett	05	24	3	aa	NYM	224	27	52	10	0	12	30	18	71	0	0	233	290	441	732	7%	69%	0.26	123	21	4.46	34
Harrison,Ben	06	25	8	aa	TEX	163	21	40	7	1	6	21	7	29	5	1	243	275	414	689	4%	82%	0.25	104	104	3.97	29
Harris,Brendan	05	25	4	aaa	WAS	470	49	106	19	2	9	58	29	57	7	6	225	270	331	601	6%	88%	0.51	68	77	2.96	14
	06	26	4	aaa	CIN	367	50	100	26	1	10	51	33	76	4	2	272	332	428	760	8%	79%	0.43	106	71	5.21	43
Harris,Gary	05	26	8	aa	SEA	457	53	101	17	1	4	33	18	78	11	15	221	251	289	540	4%	83%	0.23	48	88	2.16	-2
	06	27	8	aa	SEA	224	17	40	9	1	0	18	10	51	7	2	178	213	226	439	4%	77%	0.20	39	100	1.57	-21
Harris,Willie	05	27	4	aaa	CHW	109	16	25	10	1	1	8	12	23	8	2	227	305	357	663	10%	79%	0.53	98	143	3.95	27
	06	28	8	aaa	BOS	218	28	44	7	1	7	15	25	55	9	3	201	283	328	612	10%	75%	0.46	76	107	3.25	8
Hart,Bo	05	29	4	aaa	STL	464	56	102	29	1	6	34	34	65	8	4	220	272	328	600	7%	86%	0.52	79	87	3.05	16
	06	30	4	aaa	COL	261	26	50	11	2	3	11	17	43	4	1	193	243	279	522	6%	83%	0.39	59	97	2.29	-4
Hart,Corey	05	24	8	aaa	MIL	429	64	115	27	6	13	52	36	67	23	9	268	325	450	775	8%	84%	0.54	115	154	5.17	48
	06	31	8	aaa	MIL	100	15	27	9	1	4	17	10	26	9	2	270	336	486	822	9%	74%	0.39	143	147	6.08	57
Hart,Jason	05	28	3	aa	TEX	480	38	89	22	1	15	50	26	101	0	1	185	226	328	555	5%	79%	0.25	90	28	2.40	4
	06	29	3	aaa	TEX	387	46	89	21	1	18	47	25	93	1	2	230	278	430	708	6%	76%	0.27	123	47	4.04	33
Harvey,Ken	05	28	3	aaa	KC	104	8	30	4	1	2	13	4	15	0	0	292	317	402	719	4%	86%	0.26	69	46	4.70	31
Hassey,Brad	05	26	6	aa	TOR	302	26	59	13	2	0	14	20	60	1	4	197	246	250	496	6%	80%	0.33	42	65	1.98	-10
	06	27	6	aa	TOR	331	27	56	14	0	2	18	16	49	1	2	168	206	226	432	5%	85%	0.32	45	49	1.47	-19
Hattig,John	06	27	5	aaa	TOR	373	43	97	30	1	4	32	31	103	0	0	260	317	377	694	8%	72%	0.30	90	41	4.35	30
Haynes,Dee	05	28	8	a/a	WAS	415	48	84	17	2	15	46	16	53	1	1	203	232	358	591	4%	87%	0.30	94	67	2.72	13
Haynes,Nathan	06	27	8	a/a	ANA	264	30	53	11	3	2	20	17	56	14	13	201	248	283	532	6%	79%	0.29	57	139	1.98	-4
Heether,Adam	06	25	5	aa	MIL	244	19	48	6	0	1	16	25	53	1	1	195	269	230	498	9%	78%	0.47	27	36	2.16	-15
Heintz,Chris	05	31	0	aaa	MIN	329	30	83	15	2	5	45	17	60	0	0	252	289	358	647	5%	82%	0.29	71	44	3.66	19
	06	32	2	aaa	MIN	374	41	95	20	0	3	35	21	73	0	4	253	292	327	619	5%	80%	0.28	58	33	3.25	14
Hermida,Jeremy	05	22	8	aa	FLA	386	68	103	27	2	15	56	10	83	20	2	267	285	464	749	3%	78%	0.12	127	156	4.82	44
Hernandez,Anders	05	23	4	a/a	NYM	526	65	151	18	3	7	44	28	85	28	21	287	323	373	696	5%	84%	0.33	56	107	4.00	25
	06	24	6	aaa	NYM	414	43	100	11	3	0	22	20	67	15	5	242	276	283	559	5%	84%	0.30	30	117	2.75	-1
Hernandez,Luis	05	21	6	aa	ATL	415	41	92	11	4	2	28	36	49	4	6	222	284	282	566	8%	88%	0.73	39	83	2.69	5
	06	22	6	a/a	ATL	453	40	112	15	3	2	33	20	52	4	5	247	279	307	586	4%	89%	0.38	42	72	2.89	7
Hernandez,Michel	05	27	2	aaa	SD	264	14	62	8	1	2	23	29	28	0	0	234	311	291	602	10%	89%	1.04	40	20	3.32	15
	06	28	2	aaa	STL	285	20	69	9	1	2	23	22	28	3	1	241	297	300	597	7%	90%	0.80	42	54	3.20	14
Herrera,Javier	05	20	8	a/a	OAK	339	44	77	21	0	7	34	17	58	3	4	227	263	347	610	5%	83%	0.28	85	69	2.97	16
Herrera,Javi	06	26	2	aa	CLE	150	13	26	6	0	2	9	7	34	3	0	174	212	252	464	5%	77%	0.21	56	73	1.79	-15
Herr,Aaron	05	25	4	aa	STL	426	40	104	17	1	13	57	10	85	1	4	243	261	381	643	2%	80%	0.12	86	40	3.27	19
	06	26	5	a/a	CIN	389	49	103	26	0	12	52	27	101	4	5	264	311	425	736	6%	74%	0.26	108	53	4.57	38
Hessman,Mike	05	28	5	aaa	DET	469	58	86	15	1	22	62	48	135	4	4	184	261	361	621	9%	71%	0.36	103	63	3.07	11
	06	29	3	aaa	DET	345	39	49	9	0	20	42	39	126	3	1	143	230	340	570	10%	64%	0.31	112	55	2.52	-0
Hietpas,Joe	05	26	2	a/a	NYM	274	16	46	8	0	4	22	23	64	1	1	168	231	236	467	8%	76%	0.35	47	29	1.80	-18
	06	27	2	a/a	NYM	237	14	34	5	0	3	14	10	69	0	1	143	179	198	378	4%	71%	0.15	37	30	1.09	-34
Hill,Aaron	05	24	6	aaa	TOR	156	18	44	11	0	4	15	3	14	2	0	282	296	429	725	2%	91%	0.21	102	62	4.63	40
Hill,Bobby	05	28	4	aaa	PIT	108	10	24	4	0	0	4	9	20	2	0	220	277	255	532	7%	81%	0.43	31	61	2.58	-5
	06	29	5	aaa	SD	309	40	68	19	0	3	24	35	58	0	1	220	300	307	607	10%	81%	0.61	67	39	3.26	13
Hill,Jason	05	29	2	a/a	FLA	419	33	91	25	1	11	50	22	64	2	1	217	256	359	615	5%	85%	0.35	95	45	3.10	18
	06	30	2	a/a	SD	241	14	41	8	0	2	24	16	44	0	0	170	223	225	448	6%	82%	0.37	41	18	1.66	-19
Hill,Koyie	05	27	2	aaa	ARI	168	15	35	8	1	4	17	16	26	2	0	208	279	335	614	9%	85%	0.64	82	69	3.29	16
Hinch,A.J.	05	31	2	aaa	PHI	269	21	59	12	1	3	31	15	39	0	0	221	263	301	564	5%	86%	0.39	57	34	2.72	5

Major League Equivalent Statistics

BATTER	Yr	Age	Pos	Lev	Org	ab	r	h	d	t	hr	rbi	bb	k	sb	cs	ba	ob	slg	ops	bb%	ct%	eye	px	sx	rc/g	bpv
Hitchcox,Brian	05	27	4	aa	PHI	368	26	65	11	1	5	29	22	82	2	2	176	223	250	474	6%	78%	0.27	49	53	1.80	-16
Hocking,Denny	05	36	4	aaa	KC	230	26	52	11	2	0	17	18	37	1	0	227	283	290	573	7%	84%	0.49	48	81	2.91	5
Hoffpauir,Jarrett	06	23	4	aa	STL	393	44	85	18	1	5	36	43	34	7	7	217	294	306	600	10%	91%	1.25	63	69	3.04	23
Hoffpauir,Micah	05	26	3	a/a	CHC	413	38	90	11	2	4	37	30	58	2	0	219	272	283	555	7%	86%	0.53	43	66	2.70	1
	06	27	3	a/a	CHC	393	55	94	18	2	21	71	48	98	1	2	238	321	451	772	11%	75%	0.49	126	55	5.10	41
Holbert,Aaron	05	33	4	aaa	CIN	230	24	56	12	1	5	17	8	28	9	5	243	268	360	628	3%	88%	0.29	79	99	3.13	19
Hooper,Kevin	05	29	4	aaa	DET	305	33	63	8	2	1	21	17	32	13	4	207	249	256	505	5%	89%	0.52	34	123	2.20	-6
	06	30	4	aaa	DET	504	56	121	12	5	1	25	19	71	20	12	240	268	287	555	4%	86%	0.27	32	125	2.54	-2
Hoorelbeke,Jesse	05	28	3	aa	SEA	450	46	84	19	0	17	60	37	176	2	0	186	247	339	587	8%	61%	0.21	95	46	2.81	5
Hoover,Paul	05	29	4	aaa	TAM	248	21	43	13	1	3	15	16	44	4	1	172	224	264	488	6%	82%	0.37	66	83	1.95	-8
	06	30	2	aaa	FLA	302	27	66	16	1	4	29	24	67	2	2	218	276	313	589	7%	78%	0.36	69	55	2.95	8
Hopper,Norris	05	27	8	aa	CIN	447	47	104	11	1	1	24	17	36	17	8	234	262	269	531	4%	92%	0.49	27	99	2.39	-1
	06	28	8	a/a	CIN	429	45	122	11	2	0	30	21	31	23	6	284	317	318	636	5%	93%	0.67	27	107	3.81	19
Horwitz,Brian	06	24	8	a/a	SF	285	21	74	10	1	2	26	29	32	3	3	260	328	323	651	9%	89%	0.91	45	48	3.84	23
House,J.R.	06	27	2	a/a	HOU	493	64	140	31	2	12	81	31	56	2	2	285	327	425	752	6%	89%	0.55	95	59	5.08	45
Howard,Kevin	05	24	4	aa	CIN	475	47	115	19	1	10	51	24	54	10	10	242	278	346	624	5%	89%	0.44	68	68	3.14	18
	06	25	4	aa	NYY	376	39	83	16	3	7	37	22	74	1	5	220	263	335	598	5%	80%	0.29	74	66	2.81	10
Howard,Ryan	05	26	3	aaa	PHI	210	30	70	16	0	14	43	30	53	0	0	335	417	608	1025	12%	75%	0.57	169	13	10.31	93
Hubbard,Thomas	06	24	3	aa	SEA	242	27	63	13	1	5	29	29	61	0	2	259	337	381	718	11%	75%	0.47	82	41	4.63	30
Hubbard,Trenidad	05	39	8	aaa	CHC	386	34	81	16	1	3	21	29	31	14	16	210	265	277	542	7%	92%	0.93	50	80	2.19	9
Hubele,Ryan	05	25	2	a/a	BAL	116	15	27	3	1	6	14	9	27	2	1	229	282	418	700	7%	76%	0.31	105	97	4.00	26
	06	26	2	aa	BAL	312	34	64	13	1	8	29	17	82	3	3	206	248	329	577	5%	74%	0.21	78	76	2.67	5
Huber,Justin	05	23	3	a/a	KC	448	67	127	26	3	15	75	52	78	8	4	283	358	455	813	10%	83%	0.67	109	93	6.09	53
	06	24	3	aaa	KC	352	42	91	22	2	12	39	36	81	2	2	259	327	435	762	9%	77%	0.44	113	65	5.10	42
Huckaby,Ken	06	36	2	aaa	BOS	288	15	56	10	0	2	19	7	72	4	0	194	213	247	460	2%	75%	0.10	40	56	1.75	-17
Huffman,Royce	05	29	3	aaa	HOU	390	40	90	26	2	5	32	37	44	6	4	231	298	343	642	9%	89%	0.84	82	76	3.56	28
	06	30	3	aaa	HOU	351	47	86	20	2	8	45	37	66	3	2	246	319	384	702	10%	81%	0.57	91	76	4.38	31
Huggins,Michael	05	25	3	aa	BAL	394	30	72	13	1	4	31	38	104	0	1	183	254	247	501	9%	73%	0.36	44	33	2.13	-14
Hulett,Timothy	06	24	4	aa	TEX	185	29	52	8	4	0	13	25	31	8	2	283	369	367	736	12%	83%	0.82	56	165	5.35	34
Hummel,Tim	05	27	5	aaa	BOS	413	45	100	30	1	8	41	31	48	1	2	242	295	376	671	7%	88%	0.64	96	46	3.85	33
Hunt,Kelly	06	25	3	aa	DET	382	32	74	13	1	18	44	8	127	0	1	193	210	372	582	2%	67%	0.06	104	35	2.47	9
Hutting,Tim	05	24	6	aa	SF	317	44	72	15	2	1	21	33	58	8	2	226	299	294	593	9%	82%	0.57	51	111	3.20	8
Hu,Chin-lung	06	23	6	aa	LA	488	68	116	19	1	5	33	46	62	11	5	238	303	311	615	9%	87%	0.74	52	90	3.37	16
Hyzdu,Adam	05	34	8	aaa	BOS	317	39	70	14	1	10	41	46	80	2	6	221	320	366	686	13%	75%	0.57	91	47	3.93	23
	06	35	8	aaa	TEX	439	54	107	23	4	18	68	63	104	6	4	244	339	435	773	13%	76%	0.60	116	88	5.31	41
Iannetta,Chris	06	24	2	a/a	COL	307	47	98	20	3	12	37	36	39	1	0	319	391	521	912	10%	87%	0.92	127	77	8.10	77
Inglett,Joe	05	27	4	aaa	CLE	322	41	86	17	5	1	29	12	35	10	7	268	295	360	655	4%	89%	0.36	65	137	3.60	23
	06	28	4	a/a	CLE	221	33	65	14	1	3	18	20	32	8	4	292	350	396	746	8%	86%	0.62	76	95	5.09	41
Inglin,Jeff	05	30	8	aa	BAL	149	13	21	5	0	2	14	17	31	1	2	141	230	206	436	10%	79%	0.56	47	45	1.55	-22
Isenia,Chairon	05	27	2	aa	TAM	390	32	73	17	1	6	49	12	61	2	1	187	212	283	495	3%	84%	0.20	66	61	1.93	-6
	06	28	2	aa	TAM	288	22	56	11	0	2	22	15	64	2	0	193	233	256	489	5%	78%	0.23	47	49	2.01	-12
Ishikawa,Travis	06	23	3	aa	SF	298	33	67	13	4	10	42	35	91	0	0	225	306	391	697	10%	70%	0.38	99	83	4.24	24
Jackson,Conor	05	23	3	aaa	ARI	333	46	106	36	2	6	51	51	22	2	3	318	409	492	901	13%	93%	2.32	129	58	7.93	106
Jackson,Nic	06	27	8	aa	CHC	256	31	64	15	3	4	35	26	66	14	4	250	318	383	701	9%	74%	0.39	88	147	4.41	27
Jackson,Steve	05	28	2	a/a	OAK	138	12	22	5	2	3	12	7	34	0	0	158	198	296	494	5%	75%	0.20	84	88	1.86	-9
Jacobs,Mike	05	25	3	aa	NYM	433	48	117	31	1	19	68	25	79	1	2	270	309	478	788	5%	82%	0.31	134	39	5.24	51
Jaramillo,Jason	06	24	2	a/a	PHI	328	32	77	23	1	6	37	28	53	0	1	234	294	364	658	8%	84%	0.54	93	38	3.73	27
Jaramillo,Milko	05	26	6	a/a	STL	210	15	45	12	0	1	7	9	34	1	2	213	243	285	528	4%	84%	0.25	59	41	2.24	0
Jennings,Todd	06	25	2	aa	SF	138	9	31	4	0	1	16	4	24	1	0	227	248	275	523	3%	82%	0.16	35	38	2.34	-7
Jimenez,D'Angelo	05	28	6	aa	CIN	322	36	66	15	0	7	28	44	31	11	4	204	299	312	611	12%	90%	1.40	73	75	3.31	26
	06	29	6	aaa	OAK	125	22	32	7	1	3	17	18	12	2	5	253	345	387	732	12%	91%	1.49	87	91	4.39	50
Jimenez,Luis Anto	05	23	3	aa	MIN	427	50	107	27	1	13	57	38	93	3	2	250	311	407	718	8%	78%	0.41	104	58	4.49	34
	06	24	3	aa	BOS	395	63	101	23	1	14	60	49	82	8	2	255	338	426	763	11%	79%	0.60	109	87	5.31	42
Jimerson,Charlton	05	26	8	a/a	HOU	444	50	95	21	3	12	34	21	139	22	10	213	248	351	599	4%	69%	0.15	87	132	2.77	10
	06	27	8	aaa	HOU	470	44	100	23	5	14	35	18	158	22	9	212	241	372	613	4%	66%	0.11	99	145	2.88	14
Johnson,Ben	05	24	8	aaa	SD	414	62	109	24	0	16	66	43	71	5	1	263	333	437	770	9%	83%	0.61	111	68	5.36	46
	06	25	8	aaa	SD	198	27	44	9	1	5	17	18	44	5	1	220	284	350	634	8%	78%	0.40	83	104	3.51	16
Johnson,Dan	05	26	3	aaa	OAK	182	27	50	16	0	6	31	24	20	0	1	277	362	458	820	12%	89%	1.24	125	34	6.17	69
	06	27	3	aaa	OAK	172	26	46	11	1	5	33	24	22	0	1	265	354	425	780	12%	87%	1.07	106	56	5.55	54
Johnson,Elliot	05	22	4	aa	TAM	260	26	62	8	5	2	17	11	56	12	6	238	269	331	600	4%	78%	0.20	56	167	2.94	7
	06	23	4	aa	TAM	494	72	138	21	10	15	52	40	130	21	18	279	333	453	787	7%	74%	0.31	103	172	5.01	42
Johnson,Gabe	05	26	3	aa	STL	183	10	34	4	0	4	20	12	45	0	0	185	236	280	517	6%	76%	0.27	58	6	2.20	-9
	06	27	2	a/a	STL	212	22	31	9	1	6	25	17	67	0	1	148	212	283	496	8%	69%	0.26	84	63	1.89	-11
Johnson,Kelly	05	24	8	aaa	ATL	155	31	44	11	2	7	19	30	19	6	1	284	400	516	916	16%	88%	1.58	144	131	8.17	86
Johnson,Mark	05	30	2	aaa	CHC	177	14	37	8	1	3	18	24	22	0	1	208	304	310	614	12%	87%	1.09	69	37	3.32	20
	06	31	2	aaa	MIL	143	12	24	6	0	2	8	12	32	1	0	170	233	252	484	8%	77%	0.36	58	46	1.98	-12
Johnson,Michael	06	26	3	aa	SD	183	18	34	7	0	7	32	26	57	0	0	185	287	338	625	12%	69%	0.45	93	17	3.37	9
Johnson,Rob	06	23	2	aaa	SEA	337	24	69	8	2	3	28	11	66	12	8	205	230	267	497	3%	80%	0.17	40	99	1.89	-12
Johnson,Russ	05	33	5	aaa	NYY	281	32	66	21	0	7	30	28	48	4	5	234	303	384	687	9%	83%	0.58	105	52	3.86	33
	06	34	5	aaa	NYY	375	48	86	14	1	12	32	51	54	2	3	230	323	367	690	12%	85%	0.94	84	48	4.21	30
Johnson,Tripper	05	23	5	aa	BAL	503	58	116	26	3	11	55	39	103	7	5	231	286	359	645	7%	80%	0.38	84	87	3.51	19
	06	24	5	aa	BAL	131	10	24	4	0	2	6	7	23	1	1	181	221	254	475	5%	82%	0.29	48	45	1.79	-14
Johnston,Clint	05	28	3	aa	TOR	279	24	55	10	2	5	22	26	105	0	1	198	265	298	563	8%	62%	0.24	65	55	2.68	-2
Jones,Adam	05	20	6	aa	SEA	228	32	65	9	2	6	19	22	43	8	4	286	349	428	777	9%	81%	0.51	88	112	5.45	42
	06	21	8	aaa	SEA	380	65	108	19	2	15	58	28	64	12	6	284	332	466	798	7%	83%	0.43	111	113	5.57	49
Jones,Brandon	06	23	8	aa	ATL	176	17	46	9	3	7	24	15	37	4	2	261	319	466	785	8%	79%	0.41	122	123	5.25	46
Jones,Garrett	05	24	3	aaa	MIN	481	59	107	21	2	18	58	30	95	4	1	222	268	387	655	6%	80%	0.32	100	82	3.55	22
	06	25	3	aaa	MIN	525	71	121	32	3	21	91	48	128	3	4	230	294	421	714	8%	76%	0.37	120	76	4.21	33
Jones,Jaime	05	29	8	aaa	KC	191	26	41	6	1	3	15	12	38	0	2	214	260	300	560	6%	80%	0.31	56	74	2.55	1
Jones,Kennard	05	24	8	a/a	SD	518	50	121	20	3	1	49	60	103	18	17	234	314	290	604	10%	80%	0.58	43	88	3.06	7
	06	25	8	a/a	SD	332	33	63	7	2	0	19	46	78	7	7	189	287	220	507	12%	77%	0.59	23	83	2.20	-16

Major League Equivalent Statistics

BATTERS

BATTER	Yr	Age	Pos	Lev	Org	ab	r	h	d	t	hr	rbi	bb	k	sb	cs	ba	ob	slg	ops	bb%	ct%	eye	px	sx	rc/g	bpv
Jones,Mitch	05	28	3	aaa	NYY	484	64	109	24	2	22	61	40	154	2	6	226	285	418	703	8%	68%	0.26	117	61	3.92	29
	06	29	8	aaa	NYY	441	47	89	22	1	18	66	41	145	4	3	202	270	377	648	8%	67%	0.28	109	60	3.40	18
Jorgensen,Ryan	05	26	2	aaa	FLA	135	13	20	3	0	1	8	15	33	1	0	151	234	194	428	10%	76%	0.44	30	53	1.58	-28
	06	27	2	aaa	CIN	230	23	46	9	0	8	28	28	57	1	0	198	284	335	619	11%	75%	0.48	84	35	3.32	10
Joseph,Onil	05	24	8	aa	ATL	426	38	94	18	4	3	45	24	108	16	9	221	263	303	566	5%	75%	0.22	57	120	2.61	2
	06	25	8	aa	ATL	338	30	83	10	3	3	29	12	93	7	7	245	271	315	586	4%	73%	0.13	45	98	2.78	3
Jova,Maikel	05	25	8	aa	TOR	387	36	96	21	2	3	29	10	72	2	6	248	266	334	600	2%	82%	0.13	64	63	2.87	12
	06	26	8	a/a	TOR	150	10	28	9	0	0	12	3	27	0	0	184	199	241	440	2%	82%	0.10	50	33	1.53	-16
Jurries,J.J.	05	26	8	aaa	ATL	363	46	92	20	2	18	62	36	98	1	1	254	321	473	794	9%	73%	0.37	133	58	5.42	47
	06	27	3	aaa	ATL	307	27	57	11	0	7	25	31	106	2	0	186	261	288	549	9%	65%	0.29	66	45	2.60	-5
Kaaihue,Kila	06	23	3	aa	KC	327	31	56	14	0	4	35	38	54	0	1	171	258	251	508	10%	83%	0.70	57	31	2.19	-5
Kata,Matt	05	28	4	aaa	PHI	296	24	74	11	3	2	22	7	28	5	3	250	267	327	594	2%	90%	0.23	53	93	2.95	10
	06	29	4	aaa	CIN	331	40	78	19	2	8	31	16	49	4	4	236	271	379	650	5%	85%	0.32	94	86	3.40	24
Kearns,Austin	05	25	8	aaa	CIN	111	19	34	14	0	6	17	9	25	0	0	303	355	589	944	7%	77%	0.35	193	34	7.92	88
Keim,Adam	06	26	4	aa	KC	228	14	43	8	1	1	21	5	20	2	4	189	208	245	453	2%	91%	0.27	41	59	1.52	-15
Kelly,Don	05	26	6	a/a	DET	483	61	131	25	4	8	53	39	49	14	3	271	326	386	711	7%	90%	0.79	77	113	4.69	38
	06	27	6	a/a	DET	444	45	95	20	5	0	36	43	56	20	10	215	284	280	564	9%	87%	0.78	48	123	2.74	7
Kelly,Kenny	05	27	8	a/a	WAS	362	42	83	13	4	4	21	24	66	16	7	229	277	313	591	6%	82%	0.37	55	133	2.95	6
	06	28	8	aaa	WAS	351	40	74	11	2	1	29	36	74	16	9	211	285	263	547	9%	79%	0.49	38	110	2.58	-4
Kelton,David	05	26	8	aaa	CHC	456	45	110	24	1	9	50	24	63	11	6	241	279	356	635	5%	86%	0.38	78	79	3.36	20
	06	27	8	aaa	ATL	153	12	31	6	1	1	9	14	53	2	0	203	268	273	540	8%	66%	0.26	49	80	2.59	-7
Kemp,Matt	06	22	8	a/a	LA	381	63	118	26	4	9	61	31	57	22	6	310	362	470	831	8%	85%	0.54	106	143	6.53	58
Kendrick,Howie	05	22	4	aa	ANA	190	27	57	18	1	5	33	5	16	9	5	300	318	484	802	3%	92%	0.31	129	115	5.29	60
	06	23	4	aaa	ANA	290	45	95	23	3	10	49	9	38	9	4	328	348	531	879	3%	87%	0.24	133	124	6.90	69
Kennedy,Bryan	05	27	2	aa	MIN	230	17	42	7	0	1	18	13	46	0	0	180	225	224	449	5%	80%	0.29	34	27	1.67	-20
Keppinger,Jeff	05	25	4	aaa	NYM	255	34	78	14	2	3	25	13	11	4	1	307	340	412	752	5%	96%	1.16	73	94	5.32	56
	06	26	4	aaa	KC	450	56	136	19	1	4	42	40	30	0	4	302	358	375	734	8%	93%	1.33	53	32	5.03	49
Keylor,Cory	05	26	8	aa	BAL	160	14	29	5	0	3	14	14	40	0	0	179	245	277	522	8%	75%	0.35	63	24	2.28	-7
	06	27	8	aa	BAL	446	46	105	16	1	8	55	40	104	5	4	234	297	329	627	8%	77%	0.38	62	60	3.41	11
Kiger,Mark	05	25	4	aa	OAK	460	48	97	25	0	4	32	47	81	6	5	211	284	290	574	9%	82%	0.58	61	61	2.84	7
	06	26	6	a/a	OAK	427	57	95	17	2	6	25	44	93	8	4	223	296	316	612	9%	78%	0.47	62	94	3.31	10
Kingsale,Gene	05	29	8	a/a	BAL	239	23	48	10	2	1	13	20	41	4	3	199	260	264	524	8%	83%	0.47	48	91	2.28	-4
King,Brennan	05	25	5	aa	KC	435	41	102	23	2	6	40	21	53	4	1	234	269	334	603	5%	88%	0.40	71	75	3.11	15
	06	26	5	aaa	PHI	364	40	95	25	2	13	48	19	67	5	0	261	297	446	743	5%	82%	0.28	120	87	4.79	42
Kinkade,Mike	05	32	5	aaa	CLE	464	55	103	27	2	10	50	26	72	5	5	221	263	351	614	5%	84%	0.36	88	82	3.02	17
	06	33	5	aaa	FLA	381	42	98	20	2	3	35	22	52	5	5	257	297	340	637	5%	86%	0.41	61	74	3.45	19
Kinsler,Ian	05	23	4	aaa	TEX	526	71	127	25	1	18	64	37	61	13	6	241	291	395	687	7%	88%	0.61	97	90	3.96	33
Kirkland,Kody	06	23	5	a/a	DET	445	58	91	24	6	20	62	24	153	8	11	204	245	420	665	5%	66%	0.16	129	147	3.06	25
Klassen,Danny	05	30	6	aaa	HOU	342	42	86	18	2	10	37	18	68	5	1	253	290	403	693	5%	80%	0.27	96	91	4.14	29
Klosterman,Ryan	06	24	6	aa	TOR	137	20	32	5	0	4	14	15	38	7	3	236	312	354	666	10%	72%	0.40	74	87	3.89	17
Knoedler,Justin	05	25	2	a/a	SF	297	27	67	16	1	3	24	20	48	5	7	227	276	317	592	6%	84%	0.41	66	66	2.80	11
	06	26	2	a/a	SF	304	31	62	16	3	4	27	20	78	4	1	204	253	311	564	6%	74%	0.25	73	106	2.67	3
Knott,Jon	05	27	8	aaa	SD	500	59	99	28	3	15	57	43	93	1	0	198	261	355	616	8%	81%	0.46	101	70	3.14	17
	06	28	8	aaa	SD	479	58	104	25	5	20	82	38	90	2	4	217	275	412	687	7%	81%	0.42	118	82	3.76	30
Knox,Ryan	05	28	8	aaa	MIL	297	21	54	9	0	4	18	16	57	14	9	182	223	251	473	5%	81%	0.28	47	83	1.67	-14
	06	29	8	a/a	TAM	190	12	25	8	0	2	9	11	68	4	2	129	179	211	391	6%	64%	0.17	58	74	1.18	-29
Koonce,Graham	05	30	3	aaa	PIT	416	41	88	18	1	15	52	37	83	0	1	212	276	370	646	8%	80%	0.44	97	30	3.48	20
	06	31	3	aaa	MIL	297	35	64	14	1	16	42	42	81	2	1	215	313	430	743	12%	73%	0.52	127	51	4.73	35
Kopitzke,Casey	05	27	2	aa	CHC	177	9	30	2	1	0	7	10	31	1	1	169	213	192	405	5%	82%	0.32	17	53	1.33	-31
Koshansky,Joseph	06	24	3	aa	COL	500	62	127	26	0	26	80	47	101	2	2	255	318	460	778	9%	80%	0.46	125	36	5.20	46
Kotchman,Casey	05	23	3	aaa	ANA	363	47	93	21	1	7	44	32	28	0	3	257	317	382	699	8%	92%	1.14	85	42	4.24	44
Kottaras,George	06	23	2	a/a	SD	376	46	84	26	2	7	43	54	88	0	1	223	321	359	680	13%	77%	0.61	95	51	4.13	26
Kouzmanoff,Kevin	06	25	5	a/a	CLE	346	61	117	27	1	17	67	30	46	4	4	338	391	568	960	8%	87%	0.66	147	66	8.62	86
Kratz,Erik	05	25	2	aa	TOR	289	23	54	10	0	10	30	24	93	2	0	187	250	324	574	8%	68%	0.26	83	39	2.74	2
	06	26	2	a/a	TOR	298	39	60	11	0	6	28	17	61	1	0	202	246	302	548	5%	79%	0.28	65	63	2.50	-0
Kroeger,Josh	05	23	8	aaa	ARI	468	50	107	26	2	10	43	26	74	12	5	229	269	357	626	5%	84%	0.35	86	97	3.25	19
	06	24	8	aaa	PHI	441	41	103	26	4	10	41	22	100	6	3	234	270	379	649	5%	77%	0.22	95	98	3.46	22
Krynzel,Dave	05	24	8	aaa	MIL	450	53	98	23	4	8	38	32	104	18	10	218	270	340	610	7%	77%	0.31	81	129	2.99	12
	06	25	8	aaa	MIL	359	44	77	16	3	6	36	39	99	21	4	214	291	326	617	10%	72%	0.39	73	140	3.46	9
Kubel,Jason	06	24	8	aaa	MIN	120	18	33	7	2	4	22	12	24	2	0	275	341	467	808	9%	80%	0.50	118	132	6.01	50
Kuzmic,Craig	05	28	2	a/a	WAS	289	23	51	10	2	8	34	32	80	2	3	176	259	303	562	10%	72%	0.40	77	58	2.54	-1
Labandeira,Josh	05	27	6	a/a	WAS	239	24	50	14	0	1	15	23	38	5	5	207	278	275	553	9%	84%	0.62	56	62	2.49	4
	06	28	6	aaa	WAS	395	42	93	15	2	3	37	30	51	10	14	236	290	305	596	7%	87%	0.60	49	80	2.77	11
Labarbera,Anthony	05	26	4	aa	SF	468	35	101	16	0	2	43	35	60	11	10	215	270	262	532	7%	87%	0.59	37	58	2.32	-1
Laforest,Pete	05	28	2	aaa	TAM	270	28	57	14	1	13	35	11	76	1	0	211	243	419	662	4%	72%	0.15	126	57	3.39	25
LaHair,Bryan	06	24	3	a/a	SEA	424	52	121	21	0	15	67	44	95	3	0	285	353	441	794	9%	78%	0.46	99	49	5.93	45
Laird,Gerald	05	26	2	aaa	TEX	281	36	77	11	3	13	38	20	42	8	3	275	323	472	795	7%	85%	0.47	115	112	5.47	48
Laker,Tim	05	36	2	aaa	TAM	319	30	52	14	0	6	25	23	63	0	0	164	221	268	489	7%	80%	0.37	71	33	1.93	-9
	06	37	2	aaa	CLE	188	21	33	13	0	0	10	12	53	0	0	177	225	244	469	6%	72%	0.22	59	48	1.82	-12
Lambin,Chase	05	26	4	a/a	NYM	389	43	96	26	1	18	45	28	79	3	4	248	298	458	756	7%	80%	0.35	133	50	4.65	44
	06	27	6	a/a	NYM	403	48	80	19	2	7	43	47	99	4	3	199	282	307	589	10%	75%	0.48	73	78	2.96	6
Lane,Richard	05	26	3	aa	WAS	125	13	22	5	1	1	6	16	21	0	2	173	268	245	513	11%	83%	0.77	49	66	2.15	-7
	06	27	3	aa	WAS	228	14	36	9	2	2	21	9	53	1	1	156	187	233	420	4%	77%	0.16	52	75	1.35	-23
Langaigne,Selwyn	05	30	0	aa	MIN	110	6	20	5	0	2	8	5	36	2	0	177	210	259	469	4%	67%	0.13	57	46	1.80	-15
Larkin,Shaun	05	26	3	aa	CLE	327	36	65	19	2	8	41	29	49	0	2	200	264	341	605	8%	85%	0.58	94	54	2.98	17
	06	27	4	aa	CLE	391	30	76	19	0	4	36	26	53	1	3	195	245	276	521	6%	86%	0.49	60	31	2.19	-1
LaRoche,Andy	05	22	5	aa	LA	223	33	53	10	0	7	34	24	44	2	2	238	312	377	688	10%	80%	0.55	88	58	4.11	27
	06	23	5	a/a	LA	432	66	122	24	1	17	69	55	57	8	6	282	363	461	824	11%	87%	0.96	112	70	6.16	60
Larson,Brandon	05	29	0	aa	TEX	135	12	28	8	0	5	20	5	35	0	0	206	235	361	596	4%	74%	0.15	101	23	2.80	13
	06	30	5	aaa	WAS	380	47	82	14	1	15	61	30	104	4	3	216	272	379	651	7%	73%	0.28	98	69	3.46	18
Lauderdale,Matt	06	25	2	aa	SD	116	11	23	6	1	2	14	17	29	0	0	194	298	310	608	13%	75%	0.59	79	53	3.28	9

Major League Equivalent Statistics

BATTERS

BATTER	Yr	Age	Pos	Lev	Org	ab	r	h	d	t	hr	rbi	bb	k	sb	cs	ba	ob	slg	ops	bb%	ct%	eye	px	sx	rc/g	bpv
Leahy,Ryan	05	24	6	aa	ANA	121	9	23	3	1	1	8	4	14	0	2	188	213	251	464	3%	89%	0.28	40	67	1.58	-15
Leandro,Francisco	06	26	8	aa	TAM	218	18	41	10	0	1	13	23	47	3	1	188	267	247	514	10%	78%	0.50	49	54	2.31	-7
Lee,Taber	06	26	4	a/a	PIT	226	23	46	9	2	3	14	9	51	8	1	202	231	294	525	4%	78%	0.17	60	131	2.32	-4
Leone,Justin	05	28	5	aaa	SEA	309	38	60	15	1	6	28	41	84	4	2	196	290	304	594	12%	73%	0.49	73	75	3.08	5
	06	30	5	aaa	SD	453	46	89	15	0	12	51	44	95	3	5	197	267	309	577	9%	79%	0.46	71	42	2.73	4
Leon,Carlos	05	26	6	a/a	PHI	239	24	54	10	1	1	9	15	34	3	10	226	273	286	559	6%	86%	0.44	46	67	2.25	3
	06	27	4	a/a	PHI	372	53	93	12	2	3	35	37	48	7	5	250	319	313	632	9%	87%	0.77	44	89	3.57	17
Leon,Jose	05	29	5	aaa	CIN	305	23	63	12	1	8	39	18	72	0	0	207	251	335	586	5%	76%	0.25	80	29	2.83	7
Lewis,Fred	05	25	8	aa	SF	508	62	121	25	7	5	38	54	109	24	14	238	311	340	651	10%	78%	0.49	69	139	3.61	18
	06	26	8	aaa	SF	439	64	106	18	8	9	43	50	79	14	10	241	320	379	698	10%	82%	0.64	83	151	4.15	28
Lewis,Richard	05	25	4	a/a	CHC	328	29	62	10	2	3	24	25	73	5	3	188	245	255	500	7%	78%	0.34	44	86	2.08	-12
	06	26	4	aa	CHC	345	39	77	16	2	2	28	28	80	16	4	222	280	293	573	7%	77%	0.35	52	117	2.92	3
Liefer,Jeff	05	31	0	aaa	CLE	321	41	81	23	1	12	47	24	56	2	1	252	305	437	742	7%	83%	0.44	121	61	4.73	43
Linden,Todd	05	25	8	aaa	SF	340	57	91	22	3	19	56	43	69	4	3	268	349	515	865	11%	80%	0.62	150	96	6.51	64
	06	26	8	aaa	SF	187	23	45	10	2	4	17	21	34	4	0	239	317	373	690	10%	82%	0.63	87	110	4.39	28
Lind,Adam	06	23	8	a/a	TOR	457	58	149	32	0	24	83	44	99	3	1	326	385	554	939	9%	78%	0.44	143	39	8.41	77
Little,Mark	05	33	8	aaa	FLA	312	39	64	10	4	11	32	21	69	10	8	205	254	363	618	6%	78%	0.30	92	134	2.84	12
	06	34	8	aaa	FLA	251	28	57	13	2	2	22	23	66	5	6	226	292	312	604	9%	74%	0.36	62	95	2.98	8
Lockwood,Mike	05	29	8	aaa	BOS	321	27	63	12	2	7	35	17	35	4	1	197	237	307	544	5%	89%	0.47	70	81	2.42	4
Logan,Nook	06	27	8	a/a	DET	142	19	27	4	2	0	5	17	41	10	5	190	277	241	518	11%	71%	0.42	34	161	2.33	-14
Lomasney,Steve	05	28	2	aaa	CIN	141	8	18	4	0	1	7	7	53	0	0	125	169	171	341	5%	63%	0.14	34	29	0.91	-42
	06	29	2	a/a	MIN	151	7	24	4	0	2	12	6	63	0	2	157	188	234	422	4%	58%	0.09	49	25	1.25	-25
Lombard,George	05	30	8	aaa	BOS	488	63	103	25	5	14	44	46	133	14	5	210	278	363	641	9%	73%	0.34	97	130	3.44	17
	06	31	8	aaa	WAS	189	28	46	8	1	7	20	18	51	14	2	243	309	410	718	9%	73%	0.35	101	131	4.73	30
Loney,James	05	21	3	aa	LA	500	59	121	25	1	9	51	46	71	0	5	242	306	350	656	8%	86%	0.65	74	33	3.68	24
	06	22	3	aaa	LA	366	53	127	30	1	6	56	26	26	7	6	347	391	488	879	7%	93%	1.02	103	71	7.37	79
Longoria,Evan	06	21	6	aa	TAM	105	15	27	5	0	6	20	1	21	2	1	257	264	476	740	1%	80%	0.05	131	79	4.22	41
Long,Terrence	06	31	8	aaa	NYY	308	28	73	14	1	9	40	18	72	0	0	237	279	374	653	6%	77%	0.25	87	32	3.63	20
Lopez,Gabe	05	26	4	a/a	NYY	459	60	105	15	1	7	46	50	46	7	6	230	306	310	616	10%	90%	1.09	54	71	3.33	20
	06	27	4	aa	NYY	479	57	105	19	2	3	40	58	69	2	1	220	304	289	593	11%	86%	0.85	50	61	3.18	11
Lopez,Jose	05	22	4	aaa	SEA	182	26	56	19	0	4	29	8	20	2	4	308	336	484	820	4%	89%	0.39	128	61	5.59	63
Lopez,Mickey	05	32	4	aaa	SF	419	41	93	18	6	4	26	20	49	11	11	221	256	320	576	5%	88%	0.41	65	128	2.54	9
Lopez,Pedro	05	21	6	a/a	CHW	423	34	89	12	1	6	35	17	40	1	3	211	241	288	529	4%	91%	0.42	49	42	2.24	-1
	06	22	6	a/a	CHW	466	58	137	26	2	11	55	25	57	7	6	294	330	429	759	5%	88%	0.44	90	75	5.08	44
Lubanski,Chris	06	22	8	aa	KC	524	72	131	32	8	10	54	56	84	9	8	250	322	399	721	10%	84%	0.67	97	125	4.48	37
Ludwick,Ryan	05	27	8	aaa	CLE	188	19	29	9	1	3	11	12	40	0	1	157	209	258	466	6%	79%	0.31	68	70	1.68	-13
	06	28	8	aaa	DET	508	71	118	29	2	23	70	42	165	2	6	233	291	434	725	8%	68%	0.25	124	62	4.20	34
Luna,Hector	05	24	4	aaa	STL	223	19	44	12	1	2	17	16	30	9	5	197	251	287	538	7%	87%	0.53	65	97	2.32	3
Lunetta,Anthony	05	25	6	aa	CLE	102	14	20	3	0	1	9	5	24	1	1	196	231	251	483	4%	76%	0.20	39	83	1.87	-15
Lunsford,Trey	05	26	2	aa	SF	111	6	15	1	0	1	8	7	20	0	1	133	184	165	349	6%	82%	0.36	19	32	0.93	-41
Lydon,Wayne	05	24	8	aa	NYM	487	51	98	12	7	2	31	32	83	30	16	201	251	265	516	6%	83%	0.39	41	156	2.12	-9
	06	25	8	aaa	TOR	513	72	130	16	10	9	42	48	112	24	11	253	316	374	691	8%	78%	0.42	71	173	4.16	22
Machado,Alejandro	05	23	4	aaa	BOS	383	47	106	17	1	2	33	25	36	16	5	277	321	342	663	6%	91%	0.69	50	99	4.07	27
	06	24	6	aaa	BOS	373	43	96	13	3	4	30	49	46	20	6	257	344	340	684	12%	88%	1.07	55	113	4.46	30
Machado,Anderson	05	25	6	aaa	COL	139	12	20	5	2	0	10	22	28	1	3	144	261	209	470	14%	80%	0.79	45	100	1.78	-18
	06	26	6	aa	CIN	396	41	81	18	1	6	33	43	108	5	5	205	283	302	585	10%	73%	0.40	67	61	2.87	4
Macias,Drew	06	24	8	aa	SD	430	41	100	18	3	6	44	43	99	4	13	232	302	329	631	9%	77%	0.43	65	64	3.17	13
Macri,Matthew	06	24	5	aa	COL	288	26	60	10	2	7	26	16	49	2	5	208	250	327	576	5%	83%	0.33	74	68	2.55	6
Mahar,Kevin	06	25	8	aa	TEX	505	62	115	32	2	17	62	25	101	10	7	228	265	401	666	5%	80%	0.25	112	92	3.46	27
Mahoney,Mike	05	33	2	aaa	STL	230	22	49	16	1	4	19	10	36	2	0	211	244	337	580	4%	85%	0.28	90	73	2.77	13
	06	34	2	aaa	TOR	225	14	39	7	0	1	14	10	54	0	2	172	207	216	423	4%	76%	0.18	35	30	1.38	-25
Maier,Mitch	05	23	8	aa	KC	322	40	68	17	4	5	35	11	35	7	4	211	236	334	571	3%	89%	0.30	82	137	2.53	10
	06	24	8	aa	KC	543	70	140	31	5	10	68	30	76	10	14	257	297	385	681	5%	86%	0.40	86	99	3.68	29
Majewski,Dustin	06	25	8	aa	TOR	236	37	50	7	1	12	28	43	60	1	1	210	332	397	729	15%	75%	0.72	107	59	4.71	29
Majewski,Val	06	25	8	aaa	BAL	323	44	80	15	4	4	39	39	71	7	8	248	329	356	684	11%	78%	0.55	71	114	4.01	23
Maldonado,Carlos	05	27	2	aa	PIT	274	18	53	10	0	4	22	23	54	0	1	194	257	279	537	8%	80%	0.43	58	18	2.42	-3
	06	28	2	a/a	PIT	354	31	85	18	0	4	38	29	78	2	0	241	298	329	627	8%	78%	0.37	65	42	3.53	14
Malek,Bobby	05	24	8	aa	NYM	390	33	88	18	2	3	28	23	66	1	6	227	269	304	574	6%	83%	0.34	57	50	2.65	6
	06	25	8	a/a	NYM	277	30	58	10	2	5	28	19	53	3	3	209	260	312	572	6%	81%	0.36	66	87	2.67	4
Maniscalco,Matthe	05	25	6	aa	TAM	240	25	57	9	0	0	10	21	43	4	4	238	299	273	572	8%	82%	0.48	32	57	2.83	2
	06	26	6	a/a	TAM	387	29	81	10	4	0	30	41	82	9	6	209	284	253	537	10%	79%	0.50	30	96	2.50	-8
Manriquez,Salomo	06	24	2	aa	WAS	339	33	74	16	0	8	38	27	84	0	0	219	275	333	609	7%	75%	0.32	77	25	3.18	11
Maples,Christophe	05	26	5	aa	DET	333	30	59	18	0	8	40	14	86	2	1	176	210	303	513	4%	74%	0.17	85	56	2.02	-3
	06	27	5	a/a	DET	376	47	87	23	1	18	65	22	103	4	4	232	274	440	714	5%	73%	0.21	129	68	4.00	35
Markakis,Nick	05	22	8	aa	BAL	120	19	39	14	1	3	28	18	26	0	1	325	413	533	946	13%	78%	0.69	149	68	8.67	84
Marsters,Brandon	05	31	2	aa	BAL	361	29	53	12	0	4	15	14	97	2	1	145	177	207	385	4%	73%	0.14	44	66	1.15	-30
	06	32	2	aaa	BAL	190	17	36	4	0	7	24	6	70	0	0	189	215	322	538	3%	63%	0.09	75	26	2.24	-4
Marte,Andy	05	22	5	aaa	ATL	389	50	109	26	1	20	72	63	66	0	3	280	380	506	886	14%	83%	0.94	141	24	7.15	71
	06	23	5	aaa	CLE	357	49	91	24	0	14	46	35	75	1	0	256	322	438	760	9%	79%	0.46	119	45	5.13	44
Martinez,Felix	05	31	4	aaa	CHW	346	26	71	18	0	3	20	17	51	2	3	205	243	281	524	5%	85%	0.33	58	42	2.22	-1
Martinez,Gabriel	05	32	3	aa	TAM	288	18	41	8	1	4	26	17	91	0	1	143	191	221	412	6%	68%	0.18	51	39	1.32	-28
	06	23	3	aa	TAM	425	60	108	24	1	10	47	65	139	5	1	253	352	383	736	13%	67%	0.47	88	73	5.12	30
Martinez,Octavio	05	26	2	a/a	BAL	160	13	34	5	2	1	16	5	19	0	3	214	239	287	526	3%	88%	0.29	49	77	2.09	-3
Martinez,Sandy	05	35	2	aaa	DET	269	23	58	14	0	4	28	16	54	2	2	214	259	304	563	6%	80%	0.30	65	46	2.63	4
	06	36	2	aaa	NYM	272	27	53	9	0	9	34	24	69	1	0	195	261	328	589	8%	75%	0.35	81	39	2.92	5
Martin,Brian	06	26	8	a/a	STL	284	24	61	14	0	5	30	20	78	0	1	215	267	323	590	7%	73%	0.25	74	25	2.91	8
Martin,Russell	05	23	2	aa	LA	405	67	108	14	1	7	48	60	57	12	8	267	361	358	719	13%	86%	1.05	60	85	4.80	35
Marti,Amaury	06	32	8	aa	STL	132	10	19	3	0	4	8	8	47	1	1	143	190	244	434	6%	64%	0.16	60	44	1.44	-24
Mateo,Henry	05	29	4	a/a	WAS	153	9	21	3	1	0	6	12	31	9	6	139	201	172	373	7%	80%	0.39	25	112	1.05	-36
	06	30	4	aaa	WAS	433	45	90	17	5	2	28	30	79	26	11	208	259	282	541	6%	82%	0.38	51	144	2.44	-2
Mateo,Luis	05	24	8	aa	TAM	266	19	52	7	2	3	22	6	80	2	3	196	213	268	481	2%	70%	0.07	45	81	1.76	-15

Major League Equivalent Statistics

BATTER	Yr	Age	Pos	Lev	Org	ab	r	h	d	t	hr	rbi	bb	k	sb	cs	ba	ob	slg	ops	bb%	ct%	eye	px	sx	rc/g	bpv
Mathis,Jeff	05	23	2	aaa	ANA	427	59	105	23	2	16	56	30	59	3	4	246	296	420	717	7%	86%	0.52	109	74	4.24	37
	06	24	2	aaa	ANA	384	48	98	30	2	4	35	20	59	2	1	255	292	375	667	5%	85%	0.34	90	79	3.87	29
Matienzo,Daniel	05	25	3	aa	MIN	527	62	123	32	2	16	68	32	109	1	1	234	277	393	670	6%	79%	0.29	104	57	3.75	26
	06	26	3	aa	MIN	472	47	99	20	1	14	62	20	132	2	2	210	242	345	587	4%	72%	0.15	85	55	2.74	8
Matos,Julius	05	31	6	aaa	TOR	412	35	91	21	1	5	27	12	51	2	3	221	242	308	550	3%	88%	0.23	63	53	2.43	4
	06	32	4	a/a	SD	104	7	21	1	0	0	4	7	28	0	0	200	252	208	459	6%	74%	0.26	7	23	1.81	-25
Matos,Pascual	05	31	2	aaa	COL	174	14	38	10	0	3	14	4	28	1	1	217	233	321	554	2%	84%	0.13	74	45	2.43	6
	06	32	2	aaa	CHW	177	13	27	9	0	2	15	3	37	2	0	153	165	234	399	2%	79%	0.07	61	72	1.21	-23
Matranga,Dave	05	29	6	a/a	ANA	202	22	34	10	1	3	14	20	40	3	4	168	242	265	507	9%	80%	0.49	68	87	1.99	-6
	06	30	4	aaa	SD	302	27	49	8	0	6	22	15	70	3	1	163	204	253	457	5%	77%	0.22	57	66	1.65	-18
Matsui,Kazuo	06	31	4	aaa	COL	127	24	33	5	0	3	14	7	21	3	1	262	302	369	670	5%	83%	0.34	71	97	3.98	23
Mayorson,Manuel	06	24	6	aa	TOR	477	44	126	19	1	2	50	19	43	11	11	264	293	321	614	4%	91%	0.45	44	69	3.14	15
Maza,Luis	05	25	5	a/a	MIN	468	58	112	21	2	13	53	19	63	2	2	240	269	378	647	4%	87%	0.30	87	70	3.45	22
	06	26	4	aaa	MIN	305	28	60	10	5	3	34	15	62	2	2	197	234	289	523	5%	80%	0.24	57	119	2.19	-6
McAnulty,Paul	05	25	3	a/a	SD	449	52	113	27	2	11	54	42	81	4	2	253	316	393	709	8%	82%	0.51	94	70	4.47	33
	06	26	3	aaa	SD	478	58	124	29	4	12	60	49	66	1	3	259	327	410	737	9%	86%	0.74	99	64	4.80	42
McCann,Brian	05	22	2	aa	ATL	166	23	40	12	1	5	23	22	23	2	3	241	330	416	745	12%	86%	0.96	116	75	4.70	47
McCarthy,Bill	05	26	8	aaa	ATL	239	23	50	9	1	4	20	15	52	1	4	207	253	302	556	6%	78%	0.29	62	59	2.40	1
	06	27	8	aaa	ATL	345	28	76	16	1	6	29	20	69	2	0	219	263	321	583	6%	80%	0.29	68	56	2.91	7
McClain,Scott	05	33	5	aaa	CHC	422	52	97	21	1	23	65	32	73	1	1	230	284	444	727	7%	83%	0.43	128	46	4.32	38
	06	34	3	aaa	OAK	547	59	110	28	0	20	77	34	101	5	5	201	248	360	608	6%	82%	0.34	101	60	2.89	15
McCoy,Mike	06	26	4	aa	STL	474	47	95	12	1	2	27	46	88	22	9	201	272	241	513	9%	81%	0.52	29	96	2.30	-10
McCracken,Quinto	06	36	8	aaa	MIN	109	9	27	4	0	1	10	8	20	2	1	248	300	306	605	7%	82%	0.41	42	48	3.26	8
McDonald,Darnell	05	27	8	aaa	TAM	355	38	81	16	1	9	26	17	61	5	1	227	263	352	616	5%	83%	0.29	82	80	3.19	15
	06	28	8	aaa	TAM	538	71	140	29	1	12	50	41	115	27	12	260	312	387	699	7%	79%	0.36	86	101	4.19	29
McDonald,Keith	05	33	2	aaa	TEX	233	17	44	12	1	2	21	15	41	0	0	189	239	270	510	6%	82%	0.37	60	38	2.16	-5
McDougall,Marsha	05	27	5	aaa	TEX	223	27	66	14	1	9	44	20	32	4	0	296	355	483	838	8%	86%	0.64	118	75	6.62	60
McEwing,Joe	06	34	4	aaa	HOU	422	49	109	17	1	8	34	17	60	12	7	258	287	360	647	4%	86%	0.29	67	86	3.50	20
McGehee,Casey	05	23	5	aa	CHC	451	60	123	28	1	8	62	39	59	2	2	273	331	392	723	8%	87%	0.66	84	56	4.75	39
	06	24	5	aaa	CHC	497	51	132	27	1	11	62	38	65	0	3	266	318	390	708	7%	87%	0.58	84	27	4.41	35
McLouth,Nate	05	24	8	aaa	PIT	397	48	105	19	2	4	30	29	42	26	10	264	315	353	667	7%	89%	0.69	62	116	3.96	28
McMains,Derin	06	27	4	a/a	SF	372	35	69	11	2	2	17	38	37	14	6	186	261	240	501	9%	90%	1.03	37	100	2.16	-2
McPherson,Dallas	06	26	5	aaa	ANA	208	26	44	10	3	13	34	11	70	2	1	210	248	466	715	5%	66%	0.15	148	133	3.79	34
Meadows,Tydus	05	28	8	aa	LA	325	38	61	18	0	10	42	50	99	2	1	187	295	330	625	13%	70%	0.50	94	43	3.40	11
	06	29	8	a/a	LA	249	30	55	7	1	8	31	44	67	1	2	221	338	356	694	15%	73%	0.66	80	45	4.36	20
Medrano,Anthony	05	31	4	aaa	PHI	360	31	62	12	0	3	31	19	39	5	1	173	214	228	441	5%	89%	0.49	40	73	1.61	-16
Mejia,Gilberto	05	23	6	aa	DET	211	24	35	2	2	2	14	15	44	2	1	165	219	221	440	6%	79%	0.33	31	111	1.59	-26
Melian,Jackson	06	27	8	a/a	DET	377	45	84	19	5	13	50	21	79	4	1	222	263	396	659	5%	79%	0.26	107	117	3.53	23
Melillo,Kevin	05	23	4	aa	OAK	131	25	32	9	0	6	25	11	19	7	2	244	301	444	746	8%	86%	0.57	128	115	4.69	46
	06	24	4	aa	OAK	500	59	121	29	2	10	59	54	85	11	8	241	315	363	678	10%	83%	0.64	83	82	4.01	27
Melo,Juan	05	29	6	aaa	WAS	311	30	79	14	2	7	38	14	30	1	5	254	286	374	660	4%	90%	0.46	77	54	3.53	26
	06	30	5	aaa	SF	384	30	80	10	1	5	34	16	58	2	2	209	241	281	522	4%	85%	0.28	47	50	2.23	-6
Menchaca,Eriberto	05	25	6	aa	SEA	226	19	44	5	0	0	8	12	46	4	4	193	235	214	450	5%	80%	0.27	19	64	1.61	-23
Mendez,Carlos	05	31	3	aaa	ATL	179	10	36	6	0	3	14	8	21	0	0	201	236	282	517	4%	88%	0.38	54	12	2.21	-3
	06	32	2	aaa	ATL	366	24	92	12	0	5	46	5	38	1	2	251	260	320	580	1%	90%	0.12	47	28	2.80	6
Mendez,Victor	05	25	8	aa	DET	325	33	59	11	2	6	29	23	71	5	5	183	238	285	523	7%	78%	0.33	64	91	2.12	-6
	06	26	8	a/a	DET	101	14	20	4	0	3	7	8	27	0	0	196	256	312	568	7%	74%	0.30	73	48	2.70	2
Mercedes,Victor	05	26	4	aa	WAS	111	9	22	4	1	2	5	4	20	2	0	196	226	298	524	4%	82%	0.22	66	89	2.27	-3
Merchan,Jesus	05	25	6	aa	PHI	148	13	33	6	1	0	10	4	14	2	2	225	244	276	520	3%	91%	0.28	40	85	2.17	-3
	06	26	6	aa	PHI	317	35	76	13	4	1	31	10	16	5	4	238	262	309	571	3%	95%	0.64	50	114	2.70	13
Merloni,Lou	06	36	5	aaa	CLE	330	28	80	20	0	5	32	25	53	0	2	243	296	352	648	7%	84%	0.47	78	20	3.62	23
Merrill,Ronnie	05	27	6	a/a	SD	502	52	96	21	4	5	43	45	82	5	5	192	258	274	533	8%	84%	0.55	57	89	2.37	-2
	06	28	6	aa	OAK	446	32	82	23	1	3	32	27	94	7	12	184	231	262	494	6%	79%	0.29	59	61	1.79	-8
Metcalf,Travis	06	24	5	aa	TEX	425	41	85	14	2	7	29	36	97	8	8	199	262	288	550	8%	77%	0.37	58	79	2.44	-2
Meyer,Drew	05	24	6	a/a	TEX	494	53	129	22	6	3	46	29	72	13	5	261	302	348	650	6%	85%	0.40	60	122	3.75	20
	06	25	6	aaa	TEX	364	35	82	14	4	2	26	25	85	8	11	226	275	302	577	6%	77%	0.29	52	107	2.59	2
Michaelis,Derek	05	27	8	a/a	LA	146	10	23	5	0	1	10	11	41	1	3	160	218	210	428	7%	72%	0.26	37	43	1.38	-26
Milledge,Lastings	05	20	8	aa	NYM	193	27	61	16	0	3	20	12	36	9	6	316	354	446	800	6%	81%	0.32	97	85	5.60	52
	06	22	8	aaa	NYM	307	56	90	23	3	7	39	46	58	14	11	294	386	455	841	13%	81%	0.79	109	127	6.33	59
Miller,Corky	05	30	2	aaa	MIN	166	25	30	6	0	7	18	21	27	0	2	181	273	351	623	11%	83%	0.76	102	49	3.10	18
	06	31	2	aaa	SEA	204	25	45	9	0	12	31	21	49	0	0	221	292	437	729	9%	76%	0.42	128	22	4.43	35
Miller,Matthew	06	24	8	a/a	COL	107	12	25	1	1	1	8	11	13	1	2	234	305	290	595	9%	88%	0.85	31	82	3.01	8
Miller,Tony	05	25	8	aa	COL	460	73	113	15	5	15	41	61	96	19	14	245	333	397	730	12%	79%	0.64	90	123	4.49	31
	06	26	8	a/a	COL	208	22	40	7	0	0	7	35	70	5	5	190	307	225	532	14%	66%	0.50	31	61	2.50	-14
Minges,Tyler	05	26	8	aa	STL	429	66	108	28	3	12	41	32	51	4	5	252	304	411	715	7%	88%	0.63	105	87	4.31	40
	06	27	8	a/a	BOS	439	49	108	33	1	5	45	25	87	5	2	246	287	357	644	5%	80%	0.29	85	73	3.59	23
Mitchell,Lee	06	24	5	aa	FLA	462	52	105	33	1	10	52	46	155	2	6	228	298	366	664	9%	67%	0.29	97	48	3.67	22
Moeller,Chad	06	32	2	aaa	MIL	132	8	24	5	0	2	14	13	29	0	2	184	255	266	521	9%	78%	0.44	57	22	2.17	-6
Mohr,Dustan	06	30	8	aaa	DET	252	26	52	11	5	5	26	36	94	1	4	207	306	350	656	13%	63%	0.38	87	124	3.61	13
Molina,Angel	06	25	8	aa	FLA	189	14	40	10	0	3	20	24	48	3	2	211	299	312	611	11%	74%	0.49	72	43	3.26	10
Molina,Felix	05	22	5	aa	MIN	122	15	32	10	0	2	15	7	24	0	2	262	302	393	696	5%	80%	0.29	98	44	3.96	34
	06	23	4	aa	MIN	385	36	96	15	3	9	46	25	66	8	10	249	296	370	666	6%	83%	0.38	75	82	3.56	22
Molina,Gustavo	06	25	2	a/a	CHW	374	23	79	13	0	8	31	23	68	5	6	210	256	306	562	6%	82%	0.34	62	38	2.52	2
Montanez,Luis	05	24	8	aa	CHC	153	17	37	8	1	2	13	11	20	0	2	241	290	342	633	7%	87%	0.54	70	63	3.32	20
	06	25	8	a/a	CHC	386	46	102	22	0	11	53	31	72	5	4	264	319	405	723	7%	81%	0.43	94	54	4.57	35
Montero,Miguel	05	23	2	aa	ARI	108	10	24	1	2	2	10	6	21	1	0	225	264	323	588	5%	81%	0.28	52	117	2.97	2
	06	23	2	a/a	ARI	423	38	114	23	0	15	63	45	54	1	5	270	340	430	770	10%	87%	0.83	103	14	5.19	49
Monzon,Erick	06	25	6	a/a	SEA	274	29	59	16	1	3	26	23	49	8	0	216	277	312	589	8%	82%	0.47	70	100	3.14	10
Moon,Brian	05	28	2	aa	SEA	161	9	26	4	0	2	10	10	31	0	1	164	211	219	430	6%	81%	0.31	37	24	1.46	-24
Moore,Frank	05	27	4	aa	FLA	245	28	51	8	4	2	17	17	71	4	2	207	257	305	562	6%	71%	0.23	61	152	2.65	-1
	06	28	4	aa	FLA	157	11	26	4	1	2	10	12	45	3	2	163	222	229	452	7%	71%	0.27	43	83	1.62	-23

Major League Equivalent Statistics

BATTERS

BATTER	Yr	Age	Pos	Lev	Org	ab	r	h	d	t	hr	rbi	bb	k	sb	cs	ba	ob	slg	ops	bb%	ct%	eye	px	sx	rc/g	bpv
Moore,Scott	06	23	5	a/a	CHC	467	52	127	28	0	23	74	56	127	12	7	272	350	480	830	11%	73%	0.44	129	55	6.05	53
Morales,Jose	06	24	2	a/a	MIN	258	22	52	14	1	3	25	18	57	2	1	202	254	298	552	7%	78%	0.32	69	66	2.55	2
Morales,Kendry	05	22	3	aa	ANA	281	36	75	11	0	13	42	13	34	2	0	267	299	445	744	4%	88%	0.38	106	54	4.80	40
	06	23	3	aaa	ANA	256	32	73	12	1	9	41	11	31	0	4	285	315	445	760	4%	88%	0.35	99	46	4.77	43
Moran,Javon	06	24	8	aa	CIN	250	30	72	10	2	1	10	10	25	14	7	289	315	357	672	4%	90%	0.38	50	121	3.97	24
Morban,Jose	05	26	8	a/a	CLE	379	39	77	14	1	8	37	25	110	12	8	202	252	309	560	6%	71%	0.23	69	90	2.46	0
Morgan,Matthew	05	24	2	aa	ARI	270	14	65	12	1	3	26	13	32	0	5	239	275	324	599	5%	88%	0.42	60	24	2.85	13
Morgan,Nyjer	06	26	8	aa	PIT	219	31	56	5	3	1	8	12	29	17	10	254	294	322	615	5%	87%	0.42	41	168	3.00	10
Moriarty,Mike	05	32	6	aaa	CHC	248	20	41	16	1	5	18	21	63	4	2	167	231	294	525	8%	74%	0.33	89	76	2.20	-1
Morrissey,Adam	05	24	5	a/a	OAK	309	34	64	9	1	5	27	23	90	2	2	207	263	289	552	7%	71%	0.26	52	68	2.55	-4
	06	25	4	a/a	TEX	352	29	91	20	2	6	37	30	78	4	5	259	318	375	693	8%	78%	0.39	80	61	4.16	27
Morris,Chris	05	26	8	aa	ANA	128	9	26	3	2	0	8	11	25	7	6	204	269	251	520	8%	80%	0.45	30	124	2.06	-11
Morris,Jed	06	27	2	aa	OAK	170	20	41	5	0	4	12	16	24	1	1	241	305	348	653	8%	86%	0.65	67	43	3.75	21
Morris,Warren	05	32	4	a/a	MIL	251	24	44	6	1	4	18	14	35	6	2	175	220	252	472	5%	86%	0.41	47	97	1.84	-14
Morse,Mike	05	24	6	aaa	SEA	182	16	40	11	1	3	19	14	31	1	0	220	276	341	616	7%	83%	0.45	84	62	3.27	17
	06	25	5	aaa	SEA	206	20	46	14	1	4	29	12	41	0	1	223	266	359	625	6%	80%	0.29	94	53	3.19	19
Morton,Colt	06	25	2	aa	SD	139	14	32	9	0	5	20	10	47	0	0	232	286	396	682	7%	66%	0.22	107	22	3.95	26
Moses,Matthew	05	21	5	aa	MIN	182	22	38	9	1	5	26	13	42	3	2	208	259	358	617	6%	77%	0.30	96	96	3.03	15
	06	22	6	aa	MIN	474	44	113	15	2	14	68	32	111	2	2	238	287	367	654	6%	77%	0.29	77	53	3.64	17
Mosquera,Julio	05	34	2	aaa	MIL	240	22	49	14	0	3	20	6	29	3	1	203	223	296	519	3%	88%	0.22	71	69	2.16	1
Moss,Brandon	05	22	8	aa	BOS	500	74	127	31	3	13	53	44	109	5	3	254	314	406	720	8%	78%	0.40	100	92	4.55	34
	06	23	8	aa	BOS	508	66	138	38	2	11	72	49	97	7	5	271	336	416	752	9%	81%	0.51	102	75	5.07	43
Moss,Steve	06	23	8	aa	MIL	484	65	112	27	1	7	41	70	134	7	13	231	329	335	663	13%	72%	0.52	74	61	3.71	18
Moss,Timothy	06	25	4	aa	PHI	206	19	34	5	5	7	19	13	74	5	2	166	217	332	549	6%	64%	0.18	91	193	2.27	-4
Mottola,Chad	05	34	8	aaa	TOR	468	48	101	24	2	15	50	26	86	2	5	215	257	373	630	5%	82%	0.31	100	54	3.07	19
	06	35	8	aaa	TOR	431	40	100	25	2	14	53	24	106	6	0	232	273	399	672	5%	76%	0.23	107	84	3.81	26
Moylan,Dan	05	26	2	a/a	STL	212	20	32	6	1	1	13	25	30	1	4	153	243	204	447	11%	86%	0.84	37	60	1.59	-17
Mulhern,Ryan	05	25	3	aa	CLE	242	33	66	17	2	11	37	23	61	3	2	271	334	499	832	9%	75%	0.37	142	88	5.98	57
	06	26	3	aa	CLE	452	54	101	23	2	11	58	34	129	1	0	223	278	354	632	7%	71%	0.27	86	65	3.42	15
Munhall,Brian	06	26	2	aa	SF	140	9	30	4	1	2	11	8	34	2	0	218	259	298	557	5%	75%	0.23	52	69	2.69	-1
Muniz,J.C.	05	30	8	aa	FLA	304	23	59	14	1	5	29	16	96	3	5	192	232	294	526	5%	68%	0.16	68	59	2.08	-4
	06	31	8	aa	FLA	206	20	34	10	1	6	19	15	84	1	1	163	221	309	531	7%	59%	0.18	92	64	2.19	-4
Munson,Eric	05	28	3	aaa	TAM	378	44	84	17	0	16	47	24	63	1	1	221	268	391	659	6%	83%	0.38	104	41	3.55	24
Murillo,Agustin	06	24	5	aa	ARI	362	39	79	9	0	8	33	32	56	3	1	218	282	304	586	8%	85%	0.58	53	54	3.01	6
Murphy,David	05	24	8	aa	BOS	480	59	123	25	3	12	63	38	72	11	7	257	311	394	705	7%	85%	0.52	89	93	4.27	33
	06	25	8	a/a	BOS	490	59	127	43	4	10	61	49	74	6	5	259	327	422	749	9%	85%	0.67	115	86	4.91	47
Murphy,Donnie	05	23	4	aa	KC	214	25	58	11	1	7	24	10	24	1	1	271	304	430	733	4%	89%	0.42	100	60	4.62	40
	06	24	4	aa	KC	366	43	77	22	1	9	34	15	49	5	4	209	240	347	587	4%	86%	0.29	93	86	2.66	14
Murphy,Tommy	05	26	8	aa	ANA	500	57	109	18	5	11	51	28	87	17	13	218	259	343	602	5%	83%	0.32	77	128	2.77	10
	06	27	8	aaa	ANA	285	32	72	13	2	5	27	14	51	5	15	253	289	363	652	5%	82%	0.28	73	83	2.92	20
Murray,Calvin	05	34	8	aaa	CHC	494	54	115	20	4	4	35	41	63	13	8	233	292	310	602	8%	87%	0.65	53	100	3.11	13
Murton,Matt	05	24	8	a/a	CHC	347	41	105	16	3	8	40	27	44	15	6	302	353	433	786	7%	87%	0.61	84	107	5.72	48
Myers,Casey	05	27	2	aa	OAK	203	21	53	9	0	5	29	10	10	0	0	261	295	381	676	5%	95%	0.93	78	24	4.01	38
Myers,Corey	05	25	3	aaa	ARI	260	21	53	9	2	3	25	18	38	0	1	206	257	289	546	6%	85%	0.46	55	55	2.48	0
	06	26	2	aaa	ANA	156	17	35	4	0	2	9	14	24	1	1	224	286	286	572	8%	85%	0.57	41	49	2.85	3
Myers,Michael	06	27	6	aa	CHW	414	45	93	19	2	4	19	43	89	17	9	225	297	311	608	9%	79%	0.48	61	98	3.19	10
Myrow,Brian	05	29	3	aaa	LA	390	47	77	19	2	13	43	42	59	3	3	198	276	355	631	10%	85%	0.71	98	70	3.28	21
Nakamura,Norihirc	05	32	5	aaa	LA	354	31	61	11	0	13	38	23	50	0	0	173	224	310	534	6%	86%	0.47	82	22	2.26	1
Nanita,Ricardo	06	25	8	aa	CHW	364	42	93	13	2	8	37	44	61	10	5	255	335	366	701	11%	83%	0.72	69	84	4.45	28
Napoli,Mike	05	24	2	aa	ANA	439	71	87	18	1	22	74	63	111	9	5	199	299	398	697	13%	75%	0.57	118	87	4.05	26
Navarrete,Ray	05	27	4	aa	HOU	194	18	36	9	0	4	12	5	34	1	2	184	204	295	500	3%	83%	0.15	75	58	1.80	-5
	06	28	5	a/a	NYM	165	18	27	6	0	3	12	8	27	1	1	165	202	263	465	4%	84%	0.28	64	68	1.66	-13
Navarro,Dioner	05	22	2	aaa	LA	241	22	55	10	0	4	21	26	15	1	3	228	304	324	628	10%	94%	1.82	65	30	3.37	39
Navarro,Oswaldo	06	22	6	a/a	SEA	449	38	106	21	1	3	40	54	85	7	9	236	318	307	625	11%	81%	0.64	54	52	3.39	14
Negron,Miguel	05	23	8	aa	TOR	485	66	123	22	3	12	44	31	101	22	12	254	299	384	683	6%	79%	0.31	83	120	3.89	25
	06	24	8	aa	TOR	395	38	105	26	4	4	38	36	81	11	9	267	328	380	708	8%	79%	0.45	81	101	4.37	31
Nelson,Brad	05	23	8	a/a	MIL	486	59	116	22	2	10	59	55	91	4	9	239	316	354	670	10%	81%	0.60	76	59	3.80	23
	06	24	3	a/a	MIL	395	64	93	24	1	9	52	77	93	9	6	235	360	370	730	16%	76%	0.83	91	79	4.91	33
Nelson,Bryant	05	32	4	aaa	TOR	532	48	110	17	1	5	43	35	44	5	5	206	256	272	528	6%	92%	0.79	46	58	2.31	3
Nelson,John	05	27	6	aaa	STL	426	43	88	24	1	10	38	39	116	2	4	207	273	337	610	8%	73%	0.33	88	49	3.06	12
	06	28	6	aaa	STL	423	48	81	15	1	17	41	36	144	10	2	191	255	353	607	8%	66%	0.25	96	94	3.04	8
Nelson,Jon	05	26	8	aa	SEA	375	35	71	10	5	12	50	13	133	8	9	190	216	334	550	3%	64%	0.09	82	134	2.08	-1
	06	27	8	a/a	SEA	434	53	96	21	3	15	51	15	143	5	4	222	248	388	636	3%	67%	0.11	102	101	3.14	18
Neuberger,Scott	05	28	8	a/a	TAM	143	10	26	4	0	3	14	4	33	1	1	178	202	279	481	3%	77%	0.13	63	44	1.75	-12
Nicholson,Derek	06	30	8	a/a	HOU	162	10	28	8	1	3	16	17	34	1	0	173	251	291	542	9%	79%	0.50	79	49	2.48	0
Nicholson,Tommy	05	26	4	a/a	COL	149	12	35	7	0	0	9	9	19	1	0	236	279	284	563	6%	87%	0.48	43	41	2.82	6
Nichols,Kyle	05	28	3	aa	CIN	115	7	16	3	0	2	12	7	35	0	0	137	184	231	415	5%	70%	0.19	59	22	1.34	-26
Nickeas,Mike	05	23	2	aa	TEX	242	18	46	7	1	4	19	16	34	1	1	190	240	277	517	6%	86%	0.47	55	52	2.19	-5
	06	24	2	aa	TEX	125	16	29	7	0	2	17	21	26	1	1	233	345	334	678	15%	79%	0.83	72	42	4.25	24
Niekro,Lance	06	28	3	aaa	SF	144	20	39	6	0	10	25	5	18	0	0	270	294	508	802	3%	88%	0.27	137	29	5.30	52
Nieves,Melvin	05	34	8	a/a	WAS	152	19	26	5	0	6	20	22	54	1	3	168	272	311	582	12%	65%	0.40	85	46	2.65	-1
Nieves,Raul	05	27	5	a/a	BOS	243	22	42	8	1	1	8	20	37	5	1	174	236	226	462	8%	85%	0.54	39	87	1.84	-15
Nieves,Wil	05	28	2	aaa	NYY	380	34	91	18	2	3	29	9	34	1	1	240	258	318	576	2%	91%	0.27	57	60	2.78	9
	06	29	2	aaa	NYY	321	24	71	11	0	5	28	15	30	2	1	221	255	298	553	4%	91%	0.49	52	41	2.57	5
Niles,Drew	05	29	5	a/a	FLA	334	30	67	14	1	3	26	38	78	3	3	201	283	270	553	10%	77%	0.49	50	57	2.63	-2
	06	30	6	aaa	FLA	152	5	28	4	1	1	8	13	35	1	2	186	249	239	488	8%	77%	0.36	36	46	1.94	-16
Nivar,Ramon	05	26	8	a/a	BAL	257	29	50	10	0	1	14	13	28	17	10	196	235	244	479	5%	89%	0.47	38	114	1.73	-9
Nixon,Mike	05	22	2	a/a	LA	140	8	25	5	0	1	12	5	22	0	0	179	207	236	443	3%	84%	0.23	43	21	1.57	-18
Nix,Jayson	05	23	4	aa	COL	501	52	110	25	0	10	36	22	70	8	7	219	252	327	579	4%	86%	0.32	75	69	2.66	10
	06	24	4	aaa	COL	358	29	84	13	1	2	19	24	43	11	4	235	283	293	576	6%	88%	0.56	43	82	2.92	7
Nix,Laynce	06	26	8	aaa	MIL	354	50	99	19	2	16	62	21	91	4	1	280	320	478	798	6%	74%	0.23	121	90	5.58	48

Major League Equivalent Statistics

BATTERS

BATTER	Yr	Age	Pos	Lev	Org	ab	r	h	d	t	hr	rbi	bb	k	sb	cs	ba	ob	slg	ops	bb%	ct%	eye	px	sx	rc/g	bpv
Norris,Dax	05	33	2	aa	HOU	355	18	53	11	0	8	33	17	56	0	1	150	188	250	439	5%	84%	0.30	63	15	1.47	-18
	06	35	2	a/a	ATL	233	14	42	7	0	2	22	6	43	0	1	182	201	244	445	2%	82%	0.13	43	29	1.54	-19
Norris,Shawn	05	25	5	aa	WAS	283	22	52	8	0	4	20	19	61	0	5	184	236	251	487	6%	78%	0.31	45	27	1.82	-14
Norton,Greg	05	33	5	aaa	CHW	323	41	77	15	1	14	41	32	59	0	2	240	309	426	735	9%	82%	0.55	113	39	4.58	38
Nunez,Abraham	05	30	8	aaa	SEA	481	61	105	21	2	13	65	56	103	9	11	218	300	348	648	10%	79%	0.55	83	77	3.44	18
	06	30	8	aaa	SF	283	31	64	15	2	8	40	28	54	4	4	225	295	379	675	9%	81%	0.52	99	77	3.78	26
Nunnally,Jon	05	34	8	aaa	PIT	205	18	34	5	2	5	19	17	42	4	1	167	231	272	503	8%	79%	0.41	61	100	2.09	-11
Nye,Rodney	05	29	5	aaa	NYM	367	37	91	16	2	7	43	27	56	4	6	248	300	355	655	7%	85%	0.48	70	65	3.60	21
	06	30	5	aaa	TAM	298	25	62	15	1	4	26	25	74	1	0	208	270	302	572	8%	75%	0.35	68	49	2.83	4
O'Riordan,Christop	06	27	4	aa	SD	113	8	16	3	0	1	9	15	28	0	1	139	238	192	431	12%	76%	0.54	39	28	1.54	-27
Ochoa,Ivan	05	23	6	aa	CLE	419	39	100	12	4	2	26	26	73	14	14	239	283	301	584	6%	83%	0.36	41	106	2.70	4
	06	24	6	a/a	CLE	374	53	86	12	2	1	28	39	65	22	4	230	303	281	583	9%	83%	0.60	37	131	3.24	4
Oeltjen,Trent	06	24	8	aa	MIN	401	55	112	16	8	3	40	32	59	21	12	278	332	377	709	7%	85%	0.54	63	164	4.41	29
Offerman,Jose	06	38	4	aaa	NYM	344	37	71	11	1	6	38	47	63	8	0	207	302	298	600	12%	82%	0.74	58	86	3.35	8
Ojeda,Augie	05	31	6	aaa	MIN	310	32	58	14	0	2	25	25	32	3	2	186	247	247	494	8%	90%	0.78	48	61	2.05	-3
	06	32	6	aaa	CHC	306	33	65	9	1	3	21	39	39	4	1	212	300	274	574	11%	87%	1.00	42	69	3.00	8
Oliveros,Luis	05	22	2	aa	SEA	144	13	37	7	1	2	21	2	19	0	0	257	267	361	628	1%	87%	0.11	71	53	3.34	17
	06	23	2	aa	SEA	153	8	24	3	0	0	5	2	19	0	0	158	169	178	347	1%	88%	0.10	17	27	0.93	-38
Olmedo,Ray	06	25	6	aaa	CIN	383	45	103	20	2	3	28	32	69	16	6	269	325	354	679	8%	82%	0.46	62	104	4.21	25
Olson,Tim	05	27	5	aaa	COL	322	32	80	22	1	9	30	17	43	6	10	248	286	401	687	5%	87%	0.40	104	66	3.57	33
	06	28	6	a/a	TEX	207	16	42	9	0	5	15	14	55	5	2	201	250	320	571	6%	73%	0.25	78	63	2.69	4
Ordaz,Luis	05	30	4	aaa	TAM	115	9	24	5	0	1	12	4	10	0	0	211	235	282	517	3%	91%	0.36	54	28	2.20	-0
Orie,Kevin	05	33	3	aaa	WAS	349	45	95	28	1	13	59	38	36	3	1	271	342	464	806	10%	90%	1.06	129	59	5.88	65
Ortiz,Hector	05	36	2	aaa	WAS	254	8	48	5	0	1	18	8	27	0	1	188	213	216	429	3%	90%	0.30	21	11	1.47	-23
Ortmeier,Dan	05	24	8	aa	SF	503	68	120	20	6	14	64	38	102	29	13	238	291	385	677	7%	80%	0.37	89	148	3.75	23
	06	25	8	a/a	SF	429	45	94	21	3	7	36	27	71	12	10	219	265	328	593	6%	84%	0.38	73	102	2.75	11
Osborn,Pat	05	25	5	aa	CLE	474	52	117	17	1	7	51	30	63	11	5	247	292	329	621	6%	87%	0.48	55	84	3.38	15
	06	26	5	aa	CLE	408	39	86	13	1	1	31	28	66	12	10	210	260	251	512	6%	84%	0.43	33	82	2.11	-8
Owens,Jeremy	06	30	8	aa	TAM	414	47	73	11	3	11	32	25	201	19	5	176	222	293	516	6%	51%	0.12	70	159	2.15	-10
Owens,Jerry	05	25	8	aa	CHW	518	75	148	18	4	2	40	39	61	29	22	286	336	347	683	7%	88%	0.64	43	118	3.95	26
	06	26	8	aaa	CHW	439	68	109	14	4	4	44	41	57	37	13	248	312	325	636	8%	87%	0.72	50	150	3.65	18
Padgett,Matt	05	28	8	aaa	FLA	459	47	104	21	2	10	47	30	104	2	1	227	274	348	622	6%	77%	0.29	79	63	3.29	14
	06	29	8	a/a	CHC	196	21	41	10	2	4	21	21	66	0	0	209	284	339	623	9%	66%	0.31	84	67	3.35	11
Padilla,Jorge	05	26	8	aaa	PHI	197	17	47	5	1	1	13	11	32	2	6	236	276	286	561	5%	84%	0.33	34	64	2.43	-1
	06	27	8	aa	NYM	482	53	115	22	1	7	43	33	99	7	4	238	287	332	619	6%	80%	0.34	65	71	3.29	13
Pagan,Angel	05	24	8	aaa	NYM	509	57	124	18	6	6	32	39	96	23	15	244	297	338	635	7%	81%	0.41	60	130	3.34	14
Pali,Matthew	06	26	3	aa	ANA	345	26	61	10	0	5	30	13	57	5	4	177	206	253	459	4%	84%	0.22	50	62	1.62	-16
Palmisano,Lou	06	24	2	aa	MIL	332	35	73	16	1	4	33	45	67	2	0	220	313	309	622	12%	80%	0.66	63	58	3.55	13
Panther,Nathan	06	25	8	aa	CLE	221	25	42	7	3	0	19	18	49	3	4	191	252	248	501	8%	78%	0.37	40	117	2.02	-12
Parrish,David	05	26	2	aaa	NYY	276	26	58	9	0	7	28	18	68	0	0	211	260	316	577	6%	75%	0.27	66	25	2.81	3
	06	27	2	a/a	NYY	252	26	64	13	1	3	30	25	48	0	0	252	320	352	672	9%	81%	0.52	70	37	4.13	23
Patchett,Gary	05	27	6	a/a	CIN	129	7	21	5	0	0	6	4	30	0	0	162	189	202	392	3%	77%	0.15	36	25	1.22	-28
Pattee,Ben	05	24	4	aa	MIN	146	18	27	10	0	0	10	12	18	0	1	182	246	254	500	8%	88%	0.69	63	56	2.05	1
Patterson,Eric	06	24	4	a/a	CHC	508	79	137	23	8	11	59	53	98	46	12	270	339	411	750	9%	81%	0.54	88	178	5.21	37
Patterson,Ryan	06	23	8	aa	TOR	187	17	47	15	1	6	18	12	49	2	0	249	293	431	724	6%	74%	0.24	122	70	4.50	38
Paulino,Ronny	05	24	2	a/a	PIT	436	54	115	21	1	14	46	30	59	5	0	265	312	412	724	6%	87%	0.51	94	76	4.71	37
Pavkovich,Adam	05	24	5	a/a	ANA	365	38	87	19	3	6	39	19	51	4	9	238	276	356	632	5%	86%	0.37	79	82	3.08	19
	06	25	6	aaa	ANA	317	31	68	14	1	8	36	27	51	5	7	215	276	341	617	8%	84%	0.53	81	64	3.00	15
Pedroia,Dustin	05	22	4	a/a	BOS	453	63	125	29	2	10	52	46	34	7	3	276	343	415	758	9%	92%	1.35	95	83	5.28	58
	06	23	4	aaa	BOS	423	51	128	33	2	5	46	45	24	1	4	303	370	426	795	10%	94%	1.88	92	45	5.92	76
Peel,Aaron	06	24	8	aa	ANA	495	49	117	31	2	12	48	19	80	10	14	237	266	378	644	4%	84%	0.24	95	77	3.08	23
Pelaez,Alex	05	30	5	aaa	CIN	307	15	58	14	0	2	17	9	27	0	0	190	213	252	465	3%	91%	0.33	49	16	1.74	-10
Pena,Brayan	05	24	2	aaa	ATL	282	24	85	20	1	0	22	25	17	3	1	301	358	379	738	8%	94%	1.47	66	56	5.26	57
	06	25	2	aaa	ATL	325	30	94	17	1	1	31	20	27	6	6	289	330	357	687	6%	92%	0.74	54	63	4.19	33
Pena,Carlos	05	27	3	aaa	DET	257	36	70	14	1	10	38	38	59	3	4	274	367	447	814	13%	77%	0.64	110	60	5.99	49
	06	28	3	aaa	NYY	418	63	103	17	0	20	65	58	98	4	0	247	338	434	772	12%	77%	0.59	111	61	5.43	40
Pena,Elvis	05	31	4	aaa	COL	255	20	58	13	1	0	15	18	29	3	6	226	277	282	559	7%	89%	0.62	47	55	2.48	7
Pena,Ramiro	05	20	6	aa	NYY	233	25	56	4	1	0	11	8	41	3	1	239	265	266	531	3%	82%	0.21	20	88	2.45	-8
Pena,Tony	05	25	6	aaa	ATL	485	41	109	23	3	4	35	17	100	15	16	225	251	309	560	3%	79%	0.17	60	98	2.31	3
	06	25	6	aaa	ATL	298	36	81	12	3	1	22	12	54	11	3	272	300	342	642	4%	82%	0.22	50	131	3.73	16
Pence,Hunter	06	23	8	aa	HOU	523	81	133	27	7	24	79	49	95	15	5	254	317	471	788	8%	82%	0.51	129	140	5.32	48
Perez,Kenny	05	24	6	a/a	BOS	295	36	72	11	1	4	26	19	35	6	3	243	290	326	616	6%	88%	0.55	55	86	3.30	15
	06	25	6	aaa	ARI	284	27	64	9	2	2	22	20	31	5	4	227	277	293	570	7%	89%	0.63	45	85	2.74	7
Perez,Miguel	06	23	2	aa	CIN	394	30	88	16	0	3	30	16	85	5	1	224	255	286	541	4%	79%	0.20	46	61	2.51	-2
Perez,Santiago	05	30	8	a/a	CIN	369	39	78	23	2	4	19	29	96	12	5	211	268	316	584	7%	74%	0.30	76	106	2.87	8
Perez,Timo	06	32	8	aaa	STL	268	34	67	14	1	10	33	17	27	4	2	249	294	420	713	6%	90%	0.64	108	76	4.28	40
Perry,Jason	05	25	8	aa	OAK	435	47	88	17	2	15	53	31	109	1	5	203	255	356	611	7%	75%	0.28	93	53	2.91	12
	06	26	8	a/a	OAK	425	47	99	20	2	9	47	25	96	4	4	233	276	352	627	6%	78%	0.26	78	72	3.27	15
Petagine,Roberto	05	34	3	aaa	BOS	266	38	72	16	1	14	49	44	39	0	1	271	374	491	865	14%	85%	1.13	135	36	6.90	69
Peterson,Brian	05	27	2	aa	CIN	348	25	70	19	1	4	28	16	52	0	0	203	237	300	537	4%	85%	0.30	70	32	2.36	3
	06	28	2	a/a	DET	193	18	45	7	2	5	15	9	46	2	2	234	267	370	637	4%	76%	0.19	82	86	3.29	16
Phelps,Josh	05	27	0	aaa	TAM	222	24	48	11	2	9	23	10	41	0	1	214	249	398	647	4%	82%	0.25	113	70	3.25	23
	06	28	3	aaa	DET	464	52	126	21	4	20	78	33	123	6	1	273	322	467	789	7%	74%	0.27	116	93	5.50	44
Phillips,Andy	05	29	5	aaa	NYY	300	47	75	11	1	17	42	27	56	2	0	251	313	462	775	8%	81%	0.48	122	70	5.20	44
Phillips,Brandon	05	24	6	aaa	CLE	459	60	102	22	1	10	35	30	71	5	6	222	270	340	610	6%	85%	0.42	78	75	3.01	15
Phillips,Jason	06	33	2	aaa	TOR	249	25	59	10	0	6	32	18	44	1	1	239	290	354	644	7%	82%	0.41	74	37	3.58	18
Phillips,J.R.	05	35	3	a/a	HOU	173	15	37	4	0	6	14	15	48	2	2	213	276	333	609	8%	73%	0.32	71	38	3.09	6
Phillips,Paul	05	28	2	aaa	KC	332	33	72	18	1	5	31	15	35	1	5	216	249	317	566	4%	89%	0.42	71	53	2.48	10
	06	29	2	aaa	KC	345	35	71	10	1	6	32	18	35	0	0	206	246	295	541	5%	90%	0.52	57	42	2.44	2
Pickering,Calvin	05	29	0	aaa	KC	331	39	71	13	0	15	47	40	108	1	0	214	299	385	684	11%	67%	0.37	102	36	4.06	21
Pickler,Jeff	05	30	8	aaa	COL	418	41	111	21	4	4	29	24	29	9	7	266	305	359	664	5%	93%	0.83	65	92	3.77	32

Major League Equivalent Statistics

BATTERS

BATTER	Yr	Age	Pos	Lev	Org	ab	r	h	d	t	hr	rbi	bb	k	sb	cs	ba	ob	slg	ops	bb%	ct%	eye	px	sx	rc/g	bpv
Piedra,Jorge	05	26	8	aaa	COL	186	21	49	17	1	5	28	11	14	3	3	266	306	448	754	5%	92%	0.74	128	77	4.67	56
	06	27	8	aaa	COL	138	10	29	7	0	5	12	10	23	0	2	213	269	365	634	7%	83%	0.45	96	20	3.14	20
Pie,Felix	05	21	8	aa	CHC	240	39	71	17	3	12	23	16	47	13	11	298	341	538	879	6%	81%	0.34	148	145	5.97	67
	06	22	8	aaa	CHC	559	78	165	34	7	17	57	47	106	18	13	295	350	468	818	8%	81%	0.44	110	120	5.82	53
Plumley,Grant	06	25	6	aa	NYY	105	11	26	7	0	2	14	7	20	0	0	244	289	362	651	6%	81%	0.33	84	29	3.69	23
Pond,Simon	05	29	8	a/a	BOS	406	39	91	23	1	14	59	33	120	6	3	224	283	385	668	8%	70%	0.28	104	66	3.74	23
	06	30	3	aa	PIT	461	44	83	24	2	8	54	40	145	2	2	181	246	293	538	8%	68%	0.27	77	64	2.37	-3
Porter,Colin	05	30	8	a/a	ARI	312	24	43	11	1	2	12	24	100	1	4	137	198	192	390	7%	68%	0.24	41	56	1.15	-33
Porter,Gregory	05	25	5	aa	ANA	448	44	101	19	2	7	39	14	72	2	6	225	249	323	573	3%	84%	0.20	66	59	2.54	6
	06	26	3	aa	ANA	440	47	98	22	0	13	46	17	89	3	3	223	252	362	613	4%	80%	0.19	90	52	2.97	15
Prado,Martin	05	22	4	aa	ATL	143	15	37	6	1	1	10	15	15	3	3	259	329	336	665	9%	90%	1.00	54	79	3.88	29
	06	23	4	a/a	ATL	417	45	113	17	2	3	36	25	61	4	4	271	312	343	655	6%	85%	0.41	51	70	3.80	20
Pratt,Scott	05	29	8	aaa	ATL	339	32	75	20	4	7	32	30	89	4	6	222	285	368	653	8%	74%	0.33	95	93	3.43	20
Pratt,Trent	05	26	2	aa	PHI	219	20	34	6	1	2	13	19	41	0	1	155	223	215	437	8%	81%	0.46	40	56	1.56	-22
Pressley,Josh	05	26	3	aa	KC	440	50	105	20	0	13	59	41	59	0	3	239	305	370	675	9%	87%	0.70	84	25	3.93	29
	06	27	3	a/a	FLA	177	11	32	5	1	2	16	28	36	1	0	178	290	244	534	14%	80%	0.78	43	46	2.59	-7
Price,Jared	06	25	2	aaa	KC	139	11	20	6	0	3	11	8	43	1	0	144	190	252	442	5%	69%	0.19	72	54	1.53	-19
Pride,Curtis	05	37	8	aaa	ANA	280	29	61	14	3	5	37	31	52	6	5	219	296	344	639	10%	81%	0.59	81	98	3.40	18
	06	38	8	aaa	ANA	273	38	68	14	0	5	31	37	66	14	6	247	337	359	696	12%	76%	0.56	77	87	4.39	26
Pridie,Jason	06	23	8	aa	TAM	460	40	102	11	4	5	35	31	102	16	5	221	271	293	564	6%	78%	0.30	44	116	2.77	-2
Prieto,Alex	05	29	6	a/a	KC	207	16	41	10	1	2	21	16	44	3	2	198	254	289	543	7%	79%	0.35	64	70	2.46	-0
	06	30	6	aaa	KC	221	19	42	7	0	2	14	18	41	2	2	191	252	248	501	8%	81%	0.44	41	48	2.09	-10
Prieto,Chris	05	33	8	aaa	ANA	363	47	88	14	5	2	30	38	33	17	12	243	314	327	642	9%	91%	1.13	56	138	3.49	27
Putnam,Danny	06	24	8	aa	OAK	225	27	48	11	1	7	29	18	32	2	1	211	270	359	629	7%	86%	0.57	94	73	3.28	21
Quentin,Carlos	05	23	8	aaa	ARI	452	68	121	26	3	16	62	53	49	6	1	268	345	445	789	10%	89%	1.08	112	94	5.73	57
	06	24	8	aaa	ARI	318	51	85	29	2	7	40	35	35	4	0	267	340	437	777	10%	89%	1.00	120	98	5.59	59
Quinn,Mark	06	32	8	a/a	CHW	243	21	49	11	0	10	30	18	50	1	1	201	255	365	620	7%	79%	0.35	102	30	3.09	16
Quintanilla,Omar	05	24	6	a/a	COL	346	43	95	16	3	4	23	18	32	1	4	275	310	373	683	5%	91%	0.56	66	73	4.02	30
	06	25	6	aaa	COL	308	36	79	22	2	3	22	21	38	3	1	256	304	370	674	6%	88%	0.55	84	85	4.04	31
Quintero,Humberto	05	26	2	a/a	HOU	200	17	46	12	0	5	23	7	30	1	1	230	256	369	625	3%	85%	0.24	94	38	3.16	20
	06	27	2	aaa	HOU	292	31	75	18	2	3	29	15	42	3	0	257	294	361	655	5%	86%	0.36	76	86	3.83	24
Quiroz,Guillermo	06	25	2	a/a	SEA	202	17	49	10	0	5	32	13	42	0	0	240	285	360	645	6%	79%	0.30	80	18	3.60	19
Rabelo,Mike	05	26	2	aa	DET	282	24	61	14	1	2	19	14	37	0	1	217	253	290	543	5%	87%	0.37	55	44	2.45	2
	06	27	2	a/a	DET	350	42	82	21	1	7	42	25	73	3	2	234	285	360	645	7%	79%	0.34	86	69	3.55	21
Rabe,Josh	05	27	8	aaa	MIN	277	42	60	16	0	9	41	24	51	4	2	217	280	368	648	8%	82%	0.48	98	78	3.51	23
	06	28	8	aaa	MIN	355	48	99	19	1	6	45	32	41	7	4	278	338	385	724	8%	88%	0.79	75	78	4.79	39
Raburn,John	05	27	4	aa	TAM	400	44	88	12	1	1	23	28	63	19	1	220	270	261	531	7%	84%	0.44	32	117	2.66	-5
	06	28	6	a/a	TAM	394	45	91	14	4	0	28	49	70	23	9	232	316	289	606	11%	82%	0.69	41	133	3.36	8
Raburn,Ryan	05	24	4	aaa	DET	466	53	109	19	5	16	57	40	90	7	3	234	294	399	694	8%	81%	0.44	99	106	4.09	28
	06	25	4	aaa	DET	451	62	116	26	5	18	73	48	111	15	4	257	328	454	782	10%	75%	0.43	121	132	5.41	44
Raglani,John	06	24	8	aa	LA	336	46	75	22	0	9	37	40	90	6	2	222	305	367	671	11%	73%	0.44	99	73	3.96	24
Ragsdale,Corey	05	23	6	aa	NYM	215	24	42	4	2	6	23	15	59	3	4	195	248	316	564	7%	73%	0.25	68	104	2.44	-2
	06	24	6	aa	NYM	437	44	82	18	2	9	35	37	177	12	9	189	252	300	551	8%	59%	0.21	72	99	2.40	-3
Raines Jr.,Tim	05	26	8	aaa	BAL	457	58	102	24	3	6	36	25	101	22	15	223	264	327	590	5%	78%	0.25	72	130	2.70	9
	06	27	8	a/a	WAS	306	37	66	12	0	5	22	20	72	23	5	216	264	307	571	6%	76%	0.28	62	118	2.88	3
Ramirez,Hanley	05	22	6	aa	BOS	461	57	119	22	5	5	45	33	51	22	13	258	308	360	668	7%	89%	0.65	69	128	3.76	27
Ramirez,Julio	05	28	8	aaa	SF	386	37	72	10	1	13	39	14	84	14	9	186	214	318	532	3%	78%	0.17	78	99	2.01	-3
	06	29	8	aaa	NYM	154	14	25	5	0	2	14	8	56	4	3	165	208	230	438	5%	64%	0.15	44	78	1.46	-24
Ramos,Peeter	05	24	4	aa	SD	100	7	14	0	0	1	6	5	18	2	0	136	176	165	341	5%	82%	0.28	15	68	0.97	-43
	06	25	4	a/a	PHI	238	35	61	9	2	4	25	16	34	4	6	257	305	359	664	6%	86%	0.48	65	100	3.61	22
Randel,Kevin	06	25	6	aa	FLA	325	48	78	22	2	10	50	44	102	3	3	241	332	410	741	12%	69%	0.43	111	79	4.84	35
Ransom,Cody	05	30	6	aaa	CHC	262	25	50	8	1	5	23	15	76	5	1	191	236	292	528	6%	71%	0.20	63	87	2.31	-6
	06	31	6	aaa	HOU	380	48	77	18	1	16	46	40	93	2	1	201	277	381	658	9%	75%	0.42	110	60	3.59	21
Redman,Prentice	05	26	8	a/a	NYM	409	46	99	29	1	6	43	28	80	8	5	242	290	363	654	6%	80%	0.35	88	80	3.63	24
	06	27	8	a/a	STL	353	35	80	21	1	9	40	31	76	7	8	227	290	365	655	8%	79%	0.41	93	66	3.44	22
Redman,Tike	06	30	8	a/a	DET	403	36	84	13	2	2	15	22	46	12	5	210	251	262	513	5%	89%	0.48	39	97	2.22	-5
Reed,Eric	05	25	8	a/a	FLA	437	41	102	12	3	1	25	16	76	29	17	233	259	280	539	3%	83%	0.20	33	124	2.26	-5
	06	26	8	aaa	FLA	390	52	102	17	7	4	31	20	80	16	11	261	297	371	668	5%	80%	0.25	70	164	3.65	21
Reed,Keith	05	27	8	aaa	BAL	262	30	67	15	1	7	31	9	47	1	3	255	279	396	676	3%	82%	0.18	93	60	3.69	27
	06	28	8	aaa	BAL	426	53	108	32	1	9	61	19	66	13	10	253	284	397	682	4%	85%	0.28	101	93	3.67	32
Reese,Kevin	05	28	8	aaa	NYY	531	71	124	31	4	11	52	48	76	12	6	234	298	372	671	8%	86%	0.64	92	109	3.87	29
	06	29	8	aaa	NYY	212	25	52	7	1	5	18	12	38	4	7	246	286	351	637	5%	82%	0.32	65	78	3.13	15
Restovich,Michael	06	28	8	aaa	CHC	443	66	118	26	3	25	74	47	118	2	1	266	336	504	840	10%	73%	0.39	143	75	6.17	56
Reyes,Guillermo	05	24	6	a/a	CHW	346	40	82	13	3	2	24	22	39	7	6	237	283	309	592	6%	89%	0.56	50	103	2.93	11
Reyes,Jose	05	22	2	aa	CHC	315	24	74	9	0	3	44	25	43	5	3	235	291	292	583	7%	86%	0.58	40	50	2.98	6
	06	23	2	a/a	CHC	252	25	59	9	0	0	22	23	36	0	2	234	298	270	568	8%	86%	0.64	32	31	2.81	4
Reyes,Milver	06	24	2	aa	PIT	166	8	29	4	0	0	10	5	18	0	0	177	200	200	401	3%	89%	0.27	20	18	1.29	-27
Reynolds,Mark	06	23	6	aa	ARI	114	20	30	7	0	8	18	10	34	0	1	264	322	528	849	8%	70%	0.29	158	48	5.90	59
Richardson,Juan	05	27	5	aa	PHI	381	37	77	11	1	11	36	24	105	0	4	201	249	324	573	6%	73%	0.23	74	36	2.56	2
	06	28	5	aa	STL	444	48	104	25	1	11	53	32	112	0	7	234	284	366	651	7%	75%	0.28	89	34	3.40	20
Richardson,Kevin	06	26	2	aa	TEX	303	39	68	10	3	14	34	24	90	3	1	224	282	411	692	7%	70%	0.27	107	99	3.98	24
Richardson,Mike	05	26	8	aa	SD	139	14	17	3	0	1	9	19	51	0	1	125	231	163	394	12%	64%	0.38	26	43	1.30	-40
Richard,Chris	05	31	3	aaa	TEX	359	41	86	16	2	10	41	25	57	3	3	238	288	376	664	7%	84%	0.44	87	70	3.71	24
	06	32	3	aaa	PIT	337	47	72	15	3	14	59	50	86	5	5	214	314	403	718	13%	75%	0.58	113	94	4.34	30
Richar,Danny	06	23	4	aa	ARI	480	71	134	25	5	8	38	48	72	14	5	279	344	400	744	9%	85%	0.66	80	122	5.14	39
Richie,Anthony	06	25	2	aa	CHC	222	13	49	14	0	0	11	6	52	1	0	223	242	287	529	3%	77%	0.11	57	38	2.35	-0
Rifkin,Aaron	05	27	3	aaa	SEA	380	44	82	25	2	11	43	40	76	3	2	217	291	378	669	9%	80%	0.52	107	72	3.79	27
Riggans,Shawn	05	25	2	aa	TAM	310	30	77	16	0	5	40	19	66	1	2	250	293	354	647	6%	79%	0.29	73	35	3.60	19
	06	26	2	aaa	TAM	417	39	111	23	2	10	49	24	87	2	2	265	306	400	706	5%	79%	0.28	90	55	4.34	31
Riggs,Eric	05	29	4	aa	HOU	452	29	85	20	2	5	41	35	96	4	5	188	246	275	522	7%	79%	0.37	61	57	2.19	-5
	06	30	6	aaa	LA	303	23	70	11	1	6	32	20	52	2	0	232	279	336	614	6%	83%	0.38	66	49	3.29	12

Major League Equivalent Statistics

BATTER	Yr	Age	Pos	Lev	Org	ab	r	h	d	t	hr	rbi	bb	k	sb	cs	ba	ob	slg	ops	bb%	ct%	eye	px	sx	rc/g	bpv
Rios,Kevin	06	25	5	aa	NYM	139	10	27	6	0	1	17	5	38	1	0	194	220	259	479	3%	73%	0.12	50	47	1.88	-12
Risinger,Benjamin	05	28	5	aaa	SD	128	12	21	6	0	2	10	15	23	0	1	163	252	252	504	11%	82%	0.66	62	36	2.10	-7
Rivas,Luis	05	26	4	aaa	MIN	138	14	31	13	0	2	16	7	15	3	2	225	261	358	620	5%	89%	0.44	103	71	3.06	26
	06	27	4	aaa	TAM	229	18	45	7	1	2	21	9	34	2	1	195	224	257	481	4%	85%	0.25	42	70	1.88	-13
Rivera,Carlos	05	27	3	aaa	HOU	451	46	118	29	1	12	49	21	51	0	0	261	294	413	707	4%	89%	0.41	102	31	4.31	37
	06	28	3	aaa	COL	421	38	119	22	1	7	49	12	39	2	2	283	303	393	696	3%	91%	0.31	76	45	4.25	32
Rivera,Mike	05	29	2	aaa	MIL	213	23	47	10	1	11	29	6	31	2	1	222	245	432	676	3%	86%	0.21	125	69	3.48	30
	06	30	2	aaa	MIL	213	24	53	10	0	8	37	11	41	3	3	249	286	410	695	5%	81%	0.26	100	54	3.92	30
Rivera,Rene	05	22	2	a/a	SEA	257	19	60	15	1	2	21	8	42	1	1	233	257	323	580	3%	84%	0.19	67	53	2.79	9
Rivera,Ruben	06	33	8	aaa	CHW	331	42	69	15	1	15	34	26	92	4	1	209	267	400	667	7%	72%	0.28	115	79	3.62	23
Roberson,Chris	05	26	8	aa	PHI	550	67	139	18	5	12	51	29	108	25	14	253	290	372	662	5%	80%	0.27	72	129	3.60	19
	06	27	8	aaa	PHI	284	42	79	13	2	1	16	21	58	24	9	278	327	348	675	7%	80%	0.36	53	138	4.16	21
Roberts,Ryan	05	25	4	aa	TOR	338	48	84	18	3	14	39	50	102	5	1	248	344	437	780	13%	70%	0.48	116	98	5.55	40
	06	26	4	aaa	TOR	362	39	94	28	1	10	43	26	82	5	3	260	310	423	733	7%	77%	0.32	113	67	4.63	39
Robinson,Kerry	05	32	8	aaa	ATL	457	49	111	11	2	2	21	16	42	27	14	242	268	286	554	3%	91%	0.38	30	113	2.50	1
	06	33	8	aaa	KC	396	55	104	22	3	2	32	27	34	14	14	264	311	345	656	6%	91%	0.78	61	107	3.51	29
Robinson,Wade	05	25	6	aa	HOU	219	17	48	4	0	1	14	17	49	8	10	221	278	252	529	7%	77%	0.35	22	60	2.09	-10
	06	26	6	a/a	HOU	169	9	42	2	1	1	11	6	26	0	5	247	272	287	559	3%	84%	0.22	24	38	2.36	-3
Robles,Oscar	06	31	4	aaa	LA	275	20	60	7	0	0	20	24	18	0	1	219	283	245	528	8%	94%	1.37	23	22	2.44	10
Rodland,Eric	06	27	4	aa	ANA	397	42	90	17	1	5	33	37	46	1	5	226	291	311	602	8%	88%	0.79	59	40	3.04	16
Rodriguez,Carlos	05	22	8	aa	HOU	318	28	75	11	1	8	39	7	66	3	4	236	252	352	605	2%	79%	0.11	72	61	2.86	11
Rodriguez,Guilder	05	22	4	aa	MIL	133	14	36	3	1	0	6	16	23	2	0	271	349	308	657	11%	83%	0.70	27	80	4.24	15
	06	23	6	aa	MIL	160	19	32	3	1	0	7	21	31	2	1	200	294	230	525	12%	81%	0.69	21	84	2.48	-11
Rodriguez,Guillern	06	28	2	aaa	SF	127	14	22	7	1	6	11	8	20	0	1	176	227	373	600	6%	84%	0.41	120	72	2.63	16
Rodriguez,John	05	28	8	aaa	STL	290	33	67	15	2	14	48	19	52	4	1	229	277	442	719	6%	82%	0.37	128	86	4.20	37
Rodriguez,Luis	05	32	4	aaa	MIN	130	13	32	7	0	1	14	13	13	0	1	249	316	325	641	9%	90%	0.95	60	30	3.65	27
Rodriguez,Mike	05	25	8	aa	HOU	392	46	102	14	9	5	45	40	48	22	7	259	328	376	703	9%	88%	0.82	70	169	4.53	32
	06	26	8	aaa	HOU	439	57	109	14	6	5	32	41	45	23	7	248	312	341	652	8%	90%	0.89	57	146	3.87	24
Rogers,Ed	05	27	4	aaa	BAL	422	43	94	18	2	6	38	14	59	11	7	223	248	315	563	3%	86%	0.24	63	100	2.53	5
	06	28	6	aaa	BAL	339	37	92	17	1	5	28	13	55	11	7	272	299	368	666	4%	84%	0.24	67	89	3.77	23
Rogers,Omar	05	26	6	aa	BAL	239	20	42	12	0	3	27	17	29	1	1	177	232	260	492	7%	88%	0.59	61	44	1.98	-4
Rogowski,Casey	05	24	3	aa	CHW	501	62	125	29	4	8	58	44	94	15	13	250	310	370	680	8%	81%	0.47	82	104	3.84	27
	06	25	3	aaa	CHW	459	62	120	30	2	14	68	48	90	24	10	261	330	425	755	9%	80%	0.53	108	108	4.99	42
Rohan,Jimmy	06	22	6	aa	LA	182	13	42	8	0	0	19	20	21	0	3	231	307	275	582	10%	88%	0.95	39	21	2.88	12
Rojas,Carlos	06	23	6	aa	CHC	353	29	73	8	0	0	17	31	59	3	0	207	271	229	500	8%	83%	0.53	20	55	2.24	-12
Romano,Jason	05	26	8	aaa	FLA	225	26	59	15	2	3	25	13	32	4	1	263	302	384	686	5%	86%	0.39	85	101	4.17	31
Romero,Alexander	05	22	8	aa	MIN	509	56	141	30	2	12	66	31	61	10	12	277	319	415	733	6%	88%	0.51	92	71	4.46	41
	06	23	8	a/a	MIN	403	47	102	19	3	5	41	39	42	20	9	253	319	352	671	9%	90%	0.93	68	112	3.99	31
Roneberg,Brett	06	28	8	aa	PIT	400	48	97	16	1	7	56	38	63	7	1	243	309	342	651	9%	84%	0.61	66	80	3.87	20
Rosamond Jr.,Micl	05	27	3	a/a	ATL	302	32	54	10	1	8	25	22	86	4	2	179	234	297	531	7%	71%	0.25	73	85	2.27	-5
	06	28	8	aa	ATL	338	37	63	14	2	11	37	16	144	4	2	187	224	343	567	5%	57%	0.11	95	115	2.47	4
Rosa,Wally	06	25	2	a/a	CHW	129	8	19	1	0	0	4	12	28	1	0	150	221	158	379	8%	78%	0.42	7	41	1.23	-39
Rose,Mike	05	29	2	aaa	LA	205	18	36	14	0	3	21	15	36	1	0	178	232	284	516	7%	82%	0.40	80	49	2.19	0
	06	30	2	aaa	TAM	338	36	66	17	0	14	35	38	111	2	1	194	275	365	640	10%	67%	0.34	107	42	3.42	16
Ross,Cody	05	25	8	aaa	LA	388	49	78	15	1	14	40	30	66	3	3	201	258	353	611	7%	83%	0.45	92	70	3.00	14
Rottino,Vinny	05	25	5	a/a	MIL	494	49	124	19	4	6	40	32	62	2	2	250	296	338	634	6%	87%	0.52	59	69	3.54	18
	06	27	5	aaa	MIL	398	49	113	23	2	7	37	36	71	11	8	285	344	405	749	8%	82%	0.50	82	85	5.01	39
Rouse,Mike	05	25	6	aaa	OAK	469	52	109	27	2	6	55	45	91	2	5	232	299	336	634	9%	81%	0.49	74	57	3.43	18
	06	26	6	aaa	OAK	345	46	77	18	1	5	36	32	54	3	1	222	288	323	611	8%	84%	0.60	72	77	3.28	15
Rozema,Mike	06	25	6	aa	ATL	271	23	55	8	2	0	18	14	59	4	3	203	243	246	489	5%	78%	0.24	32	87	1.96	-14
Ruan,Wilkin	05	27	8	aa	KC	244	19	45	2	2	0	12	8	17	11	7	184	211	208	418	3%	93%	0.49	15	113	1.30	-23
	06	28	8	a/a	LA	340	32	69	14	1	1	15	11	34	10	4	203	228	258	485	3%	90%	0.32	44	101	1.91	-8
Ruchti,Justin	06	26	2	aa	SEA	144	11	27	5	0	3	14	5	37	0	0	188	217	275	492	4%	75%	0.15	57	24	1.94	-11
Ruggiano,Justin	05	23	8	aa	LA	156	18	46	7	1	5	22	13	46	7	4	292	345	441	787	7%	70%	0.27	92	98	5.44	41
	06	24	8	aa	TAM	400	72	103	30	6	11	68	61	111	13	9	257	355	447	801	13%	72%	0.55	124	149	5.64	48
Ruiz,Carlos	05	27	2	aaa	PHI	339	37	89	21	7	4	30	21	38	3	6	263	307	401	707	6%	89%	0.56	91	119	4.14	37
	06	28	2	aaa	PHI	368	53	108	24	0	17	66	39	57	4	3	294	362	498	860	10%	85%	0.69	129	50	6.74	65
Ruiz,Junior	05	25	8	aa	CIN	266	25	58	7	0	1	14	20	24	10	6	217	271	254	525	7%	91%	0.81	29	77	2.30	0
Ruiz,Randy	05	28	3	aa	PHI	344	42	93	22	0	22	63	21	89	0	2	270	312	521	833	6%	74%	0.23	153	20	5.72	58
	06	29	3	aa	NYY	491	46	98	25	1	18	56	28	140	2	0	199	242	360	602	5%	71%	0.20	102	52	2.90	12
Rundgren,Rex	05	25	4	aa	FLA	363	22	73	6	3	1	17	25	73	1	1	202	252	241	493	6%	80%	0.34	25	60	2.07	-16
	06	26	6	a/a	FLA	397	28	78	10	0	0	25	29	83	1	4	196	252	220	472	7%	79%	0.35	21	29	1.83	-19
Rushford,Jim	05	32	3	aaa	PHI	404	42	102	22	1	8	43	23	33	4	1	252	293	370	663	5%	92%	0.70	80	65	3.85	31
	06	33	8	a/a	PHI	444	35	94	18	0	4	40	34	49	3	1	211	268	277	545	7%	89%	0.71	49	49	2.58	5
Ryan,Brendan	05	24	6	aa	STL	154	20	35	7	1	1	7	11	14	4	0	227	277	302	579	6%	91%	0.74	54	110	3.04	13
Ryan,Michael	05	28	8	aaa	MIN	152	13	36	7	1	5	20	12	32	0	3	239	295	385	680	7%	79%	0.37	91	47	3.69	24
	06	29	8	aaa	ATL	363	30	76	15	1	5	34	26	79	2	3	211	264	303	567	7%	78%	0.33	63	48	2.67	3
Saccomanno,Mark	05	25	5	aa	HOU	514	56	123	31	1	10	43	22	112	5	3	240	271	361	631	4%	78%	0.19	84	69	3.33	18
	06	26	5	aa	HOU	298	31	58	11	3	16	47	17	82	2	1	196	238	409	647	5%	73%	0.20	123	88	3.16	20
Sadler,Donnie	06	31	4	aaa	ARI	190	25	44	12	3	1	9	18	33	5	2	232	299	336	635	9%	82%	0.54	74	134	3.55	19
Sadler,Ray	05	25	8	a/a	PIT	451	37	97	22	2	10	38	23	84	9	11	215	253	341	594	5%	81%	0.27	82	72	2.62	11
	06	26	8	a/a	PIT	400	42	77	12	4	14	44	40	131	8	5	191	264	340	604	9%	67%	0.30	86	109	2.94	5
Sain,Greg	05	26	3	a/a	SD	396	37	84	20	0	8	48	29	66	1	4	211	264	319	583	7%	83%	0.43	74	33	2.76	10
	06	27	3	aa	MIL	129	14	18	3	0	7	21	13	55	3	0	142	220	324	544	9%	57%	0.24	101	66	2.36	-6
Salazar,Jeff	05	25	8	a/a	COL	497	59	117	27	4	8	40	51	72	11	13	236	308	353	661	9%	85%	0.71	79	92	3.60	26
	06	26	8	aaa	COL	328	46	81	13	6	7	29	34	45	9	6	248	318	386	704	9%	86%	0.74	83	143	4.26	32
Saltalamacchia,Jai	06	21	2	aa	ATL	313	29	69	17	1	8	38	54	69	0	1	220	335	358	693	15%	78%	0.78	90	28	4.36	26
Sanchez,Alex	06	30	8	a/a	CIN	203	13	39	2	1	2	11	5	29	5	2	193	212	236	448	2%	86%	0.17	26	82	1.63	-22
Sanchez,Angel	06	23	6	aa	KC	542	80	131	21	1	3	43	34	48	6	11	242	286	301	587	6%	91%	0.70	45	75	2.83	13
Sanchez,Danilo	06	26	2	aa	DET	237	16	37	5	0	5	21	21	49	1	0	156	224	247	470	8%	79%	0.42	55	33	1.83	-17
Sanchez,Tino	05	27	2	aa	COL	200	15	39	12	1	2	17	17	31	0	3	196	257	291	549	8%	84%	0.53	71	43	2.39	5

Major League Equivalent Statistics

BATTERS

BATTER	Yr	Age	Pos	Lev	Org	ab	r	h	d	t	hr	rbi	bb	k	sb	cs	ba	ob	slg	ops	bb%	ct%	eye	px	sx	rc/g	bpv
Sandberg,Jared	05	28	5	aa	BOS	459	46	85	25	0	12	51	44	133	2	2	186	257	322	579	9%	71%	0.33	90	45	2.75	6
	06	29	5	aa	HOU	265	23	40	17	0	5	25	17	86	3	1	151	202	269	470	6%	67%	0.19	84	72	1.73	-11
Sandoval,Danny	05	26	6	aaa	PHI	390	41	112	16	0	6	37	23	39	9	13	286	326	373	699	6%	90%	0.59	61	54	4.04	32
	06	28	6	a/a	PHI	376	26	83	15	1	2	34	12	56	3	1	220	244	278	522	3%	85%	0.22	44	57	2.29	-4
Santiago,Ramon	05	26	4	aaa	SEA	441	54	93	18	2	8	40	32	55	15	8	211	265	315	579	7%	88%	0.59	68	107	2.75	10
Santos,Chad	05	24	3	aaa	KC	429	39	96	23	0	11	49	30	100	2	1	224	275	354	629	7%	77%	0.30	87	41	3.34	17
	06	25	3	aaa	SF	353	30	80	16	1	10	52	18	65	0	0	227	264	362	626	5%	82%	0.28	86	30	3.27	17
Santos,Omir	05	24	2	aa	NYY	401	36	87	14	0	9	40	9	71	0	1	218	234	317	552	2%	82%	0.12	64	33	2.44	2
	06	25	2	aa	NYY	324	27	76	15	0	4	33	16	72	1	0	233	270	314	584	5%	78%	0.22	59	38	2.95	7
Santos,Sergio	05	22	6	aaa	ARI	487	40	107	21	2	9	49	26	70	1	3	220	260	330	590	5%	86%	0.37	72	45	2.84	10
	06	23	6	aaa	TOR	481	44	100	25	1	5	34	22	89	1	3	208	243	295	538	4%	81%	0.25	64	49	2.33	1
Sardinha,Bronson	05	22	8	aa	NYY	500	55	117	27	1	11	59	45	103	10	6	234	297	358	655	8%	79%	0.44	84	74	3.68	21
	06	24	8	a/a	NYY	519	69	131	18	4	15	63	51	110	3	4	252	319	389	709	9%	79%	0.46	82	78	4.40	27
Sardinha,Dane	05	26	2	aaa	CIN	299	28	57	9	0	9	28	16	60	1	0	191	234	308	542	5%	80%	0.28	71	44	2.39	-1
	06	28	2	aaa	CIN	229	17	37	7	0	2	10	13	64	0	0	162	208	216	424	5%	72%	0.21	39	30	1.46	-26
Sasser,Rob	06	32	5	aa	CHW	120	7	20	4	0	2	11	13	44	1	0	163	247	245	492	10%	63%	0.30	53	27	2.08	-18
Scales,Bobby	05	28	8	aaa	SD	372	36	81	15	2	8	45	41	84	7	5	218	295	335	630	10%	77%	0.49	75	76	3.39	13
	06	29	5	aaa	PHI	357	42	96	20	6	7	40	39	105	3	3	268	340	421	761	10%	70%	0.37	97	126	5.20	37
Scarborough,Steve	05	28	6	aaa	MIL	401	35	84	23	1	8	41	28	74	4	6	208	259	327	586	6%	82%	0.37	82	56	2.72	11
Schierholtz,Nate	06	23	8	aa	SF	470	56	127	26	7	14	55	27	81	8	3	270	310	445	755	5%	83%	0.33	108	127	4.93	41
Schnurstein,Micah	06	22	5	aa	CHW	480	47	104	24	2	10	45	23	98	8	6	217	252	338	590	5%	80%	0.23	80	84	2.76	10
Schrager,Tony	05	28	6	aaa	BOS	294	31	54	14	1	6	21	30	45	2	4	183	259	294	553	9%	85%	0.66	74	59	2.46	5
	06	29	4	a/a	FLA	109	15	25	7	2	1	8	10	27	0	2	233	297	346	643	8%	75%	0.37	78	114	3.41	17
Schuerholz,Jonath	05	25	4	a/a	ATL	441	40	94	12	2	4	27	36	73	8	3	213	273	276	549	8%	84%	0.50	42	82	2.62	-2
	06	26	4	aaa	ATL	375	30	64	11	2	2	23	30	93	5	2	171	232	225	457	7%	75%	0.32	38	85	1.76	-21
Schumaker,Skip	05	26	8	aaa	STL	440	51	111	23	2	4	26	24	43	10	4	252	290	340	630	5%	90%	0.55	64	96	3.47	21
	06	27	8	aaa	STL	369	42	104	13	2	3	23	20	44	10	4	281	319	350	668	5%	88%	0.46	47	94	4.08	22
Schutzenhofer,Anc	05	25	3	aa	STL	193	17	43	8	0	1	12	10	22	1	1	222	261	276	537	5%	89%	0.47	42	45	2.44	1
Scott,Luke	05	27	8	aaa	HOU	398	50	95	21	3	23	63	29	76	2	2	239	291	477	769	7%	81%	0.39	142	72	4.76	46
	06	28	8	aaa	HOU	318	48	81	12	1	16	48	39	58	5	1	254	336	447	783	11%	82%	0.67	113	77	5.53	45
Seabol,Scott	05	30	5	aaa	STL	203	24	43	15	1	6	23	14	36	1	0	213	265	390	655	7%	82%	0.41	119	52	3.51	28
	06	31	5	aaa	FLA	242	28	59	14	1	12	32	22	51	0	4	245	307	454	761	8%	79%	0.42	128	39	4.64	43
Sears,Todd	05	30	3	a/a	FLA	412	40	96	16	2	10	53	33	96	0	1	233	289	352	642	7%	77%	0.34	76	41	3.56	16
	06	31	3	aaa	FLA	181	18	38	7	1	4	19	11	38	2	0	209	253	318	572	6%	79%	0.29	70	78	2.77	4
Self,Todd	05	27	8	aaa	HOU	326	31	82	21	2	6	35	41	71	3	1	253	336	384	720	11%	78%	0.57	91	68	4.77	33
Sellier,Brian	06	29	8	aa	PHI	125	12	27	6	1	5	10	10	15	0	0	218	273	397	670	7%	88%	0.64	110	42	3.71	31
Senreiso,Juan	05	24	8	aa	TEX	497	41	125	23	4	4	27	34	103	12	9	252	300	336	637	6%	79%	0.33	59	91	3.48	15
Serrano,Ray	06	26	2	aa	ATL	227	20	48	13	0	3	19	3	39	1	1	210	219	301	521	1%	83%	0.07	68	53	2.12	-1
Sevilla,Walter	06	25	4	aa	KC	163	13	25	3	3	1	10	13	32	2	0	155	215	221	436	7%	80%	0.39	38	124	1.60	-25
Shabala,Adam	05	28	8	aaa	SF	369	38	81	20	1	9	29	22	54	7	3	219	263	348	610	6%	85%	0.41	86	81	3.07	17
	06	29	8	aaa	SF	289	32	66	17	1	4	29	33	54	5	4	228	309	331	640	10%	81%	0.62	74	70	3.57	19
Shanks,James	05	27	8	a/a	FLA	442	47	102	17	6	5	40	31	108	12	12	230	280	334	614	6%	76%	0.28	66	130	2.99	10
	06	28	8	aaa	FLA	231	23	57	12	2	4	22	11	45	7	7	247	282	366	648	5%	80%	0.25	80	101	3.27	20
Shealy,Ryan	05	26	3	aaa	COL	407	51	113	25	1	19	53	24	49	3	0	276	317	486	803	6%	88%	0.49	131	63	5.65	56
	06	27	3	aaa	COL	222	27	56	14	1	12	39	14	25	0	0	252	298	492	790	6%	89%	0.56	147	37	5.16	56
Shelton,Chris	05	25	3	aaa	DET	181	31	54	17	0	7	35	22	28	0	2	301	376	509	885	11%	84%	0.77	142	38	7.10	74
	06	26	3	aaa	DET	109	18	27	5	2	3	13	16	35	1	0	249	348	409	757	13%	68%	0.47	96	142	5.36	32
Sherrod,Justin	05	28	8	aaa	BOS	431	47	97	28	1	11	48	32	112	2	2	225	279	373	651	7%	74%	0.29	99	55	3.54	22
Shier,Pete	06	26	5	aa	BAL	224	22	55	14	1	0	21	11	41	3	7	245	280	317	597	5%	82%	0.26	60	69	2.71	12
Shoppach,Kelly	05	25	2	aaa	BOS	370	46	84	16	0	19	57	35	88	0	0	227	294	423	716	9%	76%	0.39	117	24	4.33	32
Short,Rick	05	33	3	aaa	WAS	376	49	112	29	1	7	47	31	22	4	5	297	350	436	785	8%	94%	1.38	100	57	5.58	68
Singleton,Justin	05	26	8	a/a	TOR	389	44	84	22	2	9	34	21	121	5	2	215	255	349	604	5%	69%	0.17	89	97	3.00	12
	06	28	8	a/a	TOR	231	23	40	10	1	5	17	20	97	2	0	173	239	290	529	8%	58%	0.21	75	79	2.33	-7
Sing,Brandon	05	25	3	aa	CHC	408	63	101	26	0	24	60	79	106	2	5	247	369	484	853	16%	74%	0.74	146	31	6.43	57
	06	26	3	a/a	CHC	337	34	62	12	0	12	47	59	115	1	1	183	305	330	635	15%	66%	0.51	89	27	3.54	8
Sinisi,Vince	05	24	8	aa	TEX	248	21	58	9	0	4	22	12	32	3	5	235	269	317	586	4%	87%	0.36	55	47	2.73	8
	06	25	8	a/a	TEX	497	56	125	37	2	7	54	52	80	8	4	252	323	375	698	10%	84%	0.65	90	77	4.37	34
Sisk,Aaron	05	27	4	aa	CHC	137	13	26	4	1	5	14	14	35	1	1	188	264	339	603	9%	74%	0.40	88	65	2.97	7
	06	28	5	aa	SF	237	23	38	7	0	8	23	18	78	6	1	159	219	290	510	7%	67%	0.24	79	80	2.11	-10
Slack,Jonathan	06	25	8	aa	NYM	157	12	25	4	1	0	9	10	41	5	3	157	210	194	404	6%	74%	0.25	27	106	1.30	-31
Slavik,Corey	05	26	3	aa	COL	458	42	94	18	5	8	50	43	76	3	2	204	273	316	589	9%	84%	0.57	71	83	2.95	9
Sledge,Terrmel	06	30	8	aaa	SD	367	49	87	14	4	15	52	43	67	4	4	238	318	414	732	10%	82%	0.64	103	91	4.58	35
Smitherman,Steph	05	27	8	a/a	CIN	450	37	91	29	0	9	50	36	103	3	1	203	262	325	586	7%	77%	0.34	86	45	2.89	10
	06	28	8	aa	SD	287	29	50	14	0	13	46	26	124	0	0	173	243	354	597	8%	57%	0.21	111	22	2.83	8
Smith,Bobby	05	31	5	aaa	OAK	405	45	93	15	1	9	45	25	63	6	0	229	274	338	612	6%	84%	0.40	70	86	3.28	13
	06	32	5	aaa	CHW	193	16	43	14	0	5	21	11	61	3	0	224	265	382	647	5%	68%	0.18	109	54	3.52	23
Smith,Casey	05	27	6	aaa	ANA	268	25	48	5	1	0	12	16	29	4	4	177	225	203	428	6%	89%	0.57	19	82	1.46	-22
	06	28	6	a/a	ANA	425	43	88	22	2	3	38	16	52	4	9	207	235	291	526	4%	88%	0.30	62	77	2.06	0
Smith,Corey	05	23	5	aa	SD	512	52	109	25	2	13	59	40	127	3	4	212	269	343	612	7%	75%	0.31	85	61	3.07	12
	06	24	5	aa	CHW	425	43	95	17	2	13	48	56	116	5	1	224	314	367	681	12%	73%	0.48	88	71	4.16	20
Smith,David	06	26	8	aa	TOR	483	57	109	31	1	17	63	34	126	6	4	225	277	399	675	7%	74%	0.27	113	73	3.73	27
Smith,Jason	05	28	3	aaa	DET	180	19	34	8	2	5	20	9	47	7	3	191	231	336	567	5%	74%	0.20	90	136	2.46	5
	06	29	4	aaa	COL	141	17	35	7	4	3	15	10	32	2	1	252	301	413	714	7%	77%	0.31	99	167	4.37	31
Smith,Seth	06	23	8	aa	COL	524	61	146	44	4	13	55	39	53	3	5	279	329	452	781	7%	90%	0.74	119	68	5.29	57
Smith,Will	05	24	8	a/a	TEX	319	35	83	19	3	11	42	22	47	0	0	260	308	442	750	6%	85%	0.47	114	58	4.88	43
	06	25	8	aaa	TEX	132	13	37	7	0	3	14	14	24	0	0	280	349	402	751	10%	82%	0.58	82	16	5.31	39
Snead,Esix	05	29	8	aaa	ATL	347	39	70	9	4	1	8	39	60	36	15	202	283	257	540	10%	83%	0.65	37	152	2.54	-5
	06	30	8	aaa	BAL	127	10	24	3	0	1	13	18	21	14	4	191	292	234	526	12%	83%	0.85	30	91	2.65	-7
Snelling,Chris	05	24	8	aaa	SEA	246	42	81	15	1	7	38	32	38	2	4	329	406	484	890	12%	85%	0.84	102	61	7.59	69
	06	25	8	aaa	SEA	241	30	46	12	1	4	33	27	53	3	2	191	272	299	571	10%	78%	0.51	73	83	2.76	4

Major League Equivalent Statistics

BATTER	Yr	Age	Pos	Lev	Org	ab	r	h	d	t	hr	rbi	bb	k	sb	cs	ba	ob	slg	ops	bb%	ct%	eye	px	sx	rc/g	bpv
Snyder,Brad	05	23	8	aa	CLE	301	46	73	19	2	12	46	21	88	4	3	242	292	435	727	7%	71%	0.24	123	103	4.32	36
	06	24	8	aa	CLE	523	75	124	27	3	14	63	56	157	17	2	236	310	380	690	10%	70%	0.36	92	123	4.33	24
Snyder,Brian	06	25	5	aa	OAK	151	19	27	6	1	4	20	30	39	1	1	176	314	302	616	17%	74%	0.78	78	69	3.39	6
Snyder,Earl	05	29	5	aaa	TAM	498	52	96	25	1	17	57	26	79	1	1	194	234	351	585	5%	84%	0.33	99	51	2.68	12
	06	30	3	aaa	CIN	463	50	104	23	1	16	67	36	104	1	0	225	281	383	664	7%	77%	0.34	99	46	3.74	23
Solano,Danny	05	30	4	aaa	TOR	165	18	33	5	1	2	14	11	33	1	2	199	248	276	524	6%	80%	0.33	51	78	2.21	-6
	06	31	6	a/a	TOR	134	8	20	6	0	1	6	10	43	1	0	149	206	209	415	7%	68%	0.23	46	41	1.43	-27
Sorensen,Zach	05	29	6	aaa	ANA	287	32	69	8	2	1	28	22	43	14	11	240	295	292	586	7%	85%	0.52	37	107	2.78	5
	06	30	4	aaa	MIL	202	17	45	6	1	2	18	22	45	4	4	221	297	288	585	10%	78%	0.48	46	68	2.92	2
Sosa,Juan	05	30	5	a/a	PHI	318	22	60	9	2	4	22	8	48	2	0	189	209	264	473	2%	85%	0.17	48	68	1.79	-14
	06	31	6	a/a	PHI	149	10	22	4	0	0	7	8	33	1	1	150	194	177	371	5%	78%	0.25	24	49	1.09	-35
Soto,Geovany	05	23	2	aaa	CHC	288	24	66	13	0	3	32	40	58	0	1	230	323	306	630	12%	80%	0.69	56	18	3.61	13
	06	24	2	aaa	CHC	342	31	88	20	0	6	35	38	68	0	1	257	332	368	700	10%	80%	0.56	79	18	4.47	29
Spann,Chad	06	23	5	aa	BOS	360	47	104	30	2	9	45	26	74	3	3	289	337	458	795	7%	79%	0.35	117	74	5.61	52
Spanos,Vasili	05	25	5	aa	OAK	149	14	29	5	0	5	20	9	33	1	0	191	235	319	554	5%	78%	0.26	78	47	2.50	1
	06	26	5	aa	OAK	439	53	111	25	1	6	51	40	67	0	1	252	314	357	671	8%	85%	0.59	75	40	4.04	27
Span,Denard	05	22	8	aa	MIN	263	40	71	6	4	0	22	19	36	9	9	270	319	323	642	7%	86%	0.53	34	140	3.45	14
	06	23	8	aa	MIN	536	75	146	16	5	2	42	37	77	23	12	272	319	332	651	6%	86%	0.48	40	127	3.78	17
Specht,Brian	05	25	4	aaa	ANA	259	28	65	15	3	5	25	17	34	9	9	251	297	390	687	6%	87%	0.50	91	115	3.66	31
Spidale,Mike	05	24	8	aaa	CHW	161	14	33	4	0	1	6	8	18	4	3	205	243	248	491	5%	89%	0.44	32	70	1.93	-10
Spilborghs,Ryan	05	26	8	a/a	COL	478	63	134	39	5	7	51	41	73	11	7	281	337	429	766	8%	85%	0.55	105	114	5.19	48
	06	27	8	aaa	COL	269	36	81	18	1	4	25	21	36	6	2	300	351	417	767	7%	87%	0.58	84	83	5.56	47
Spivey,Junior	06	32	4	aaa	STL	285	30	48	11	1	7	23	47	64	11	5	167	285	287	572	14%	77%	0.73	75	87	2.85	1
Sprout,Brian	05	25	5	aa	LA	205	22	40	8	0	4	16	12	29	2	0	193	237	285	522	5%	86%	0.41	62	64	2.28	-2
Stanley,Henri	05	28	8	aaa	LA	337	31	63	10	2	10	28	21	49	4	10	186	234	313	546	6%	85%	0.42	76	72	2.10	2
Stanley,Steve	05	26	8	aa	OAK	514	60	117	22	2	5	32	42	54	5	9	228	286	303	589	8%	89%	0.78	54	68	2.88	14
Stansberry,Craig	05	24	4	aa	PIT	418	46	84	20	7	12	49	33	88	10	6	202	260	367	627	7%	79%	0.38	101	142	3.10	16
	06	25	4	a/a	PIT	457	70	105	28	4	12	50	59	93	16	6	229	318	384	702	11%	80%	0.64	101	127	4.35	31
Stavinoha,Nick	06	24	8	aa	STL	417	43	106	24	2	9	57	22	69	2	1	255	292	383	675	5%	83%	0.31	86	63	3.95	27
Stavisky,Brian	05	25	0	aa	OAK	510	59	128	30	4	8	62	48	73	0	5	251	315	371	685	9%	86%	0.65	82	50	4.04	31
	06	26	8	a/a	OAK	438	56	105	23	1	5	42	59	68	2	1	240	330	335	665	12%	85%	0.86	68	55	4.08	26
Stern,Adam	06	27	8	aaa	BOS	392	53	97	22	2	7	31	21	72	20	7	247	286	366	653	5%	82%	0.30	82	127	3.64	22
Stewart,Chris	05	24	2	aa	CHW	308	30	79	18	0	10	40	17	30	2	4	255	295	409	704	5%	90%	0.58	102	36	4.07	39
	06	25	2	aaa	CHW	272	37	69	16	2	4	26	14	32	3	0	254	290	371	662	5%	88%	0.44	81	102	3.87	27
Stewart,Ian	06	22	5	aa	COL	462	58	118	39	6	9	55	38	74	2	9	255	312	424	736	8%	84%	0.51	116	90	4.39	43
Stocker,Mel	05	25	8	aa	KC	277	23	53	5	7	1	18	18	33	11	6	192	241	270	511	6%	88%	0.54	42	176	2.07	-8
Stokes,Jason	06	25	3	aaa	FLA	237	30	53	11	2	5	27	29	71	2	1	224	308	350	658	11%	70%	0.41	81	92	3.84	16
Stotts,J.T.	05	26	4	aa	NYY	346	40	63	8	1	2	23	24	51	7	2	182	236	226	462	7%	85%	0.48	31	101	1.83	-17
	06	27	6	a/a	NYY	321	33	63	5	0	0	21	35	63	8	3	196	275	210	486	10%	80%	0.55	12	77	2.12	-18
Stratton,Robert	06	29	8	aaa	NYY	207	21	45	7	0	12	34	13	85	0	1	215	261	422	683	6%	59%	0.15	120	21	3.63	24
Strong,Jamal	05	27	8	aaa	SEA	382	45	93	13	3	3	29	36	61	20	7	244	309	316	625	9%	84%	0.59	49	120	3.55	13
	06	28	8	aaa	CHC	357	38	76	12	2	1	23	38	72	15	2	214	289	266	555	10%	80%	0.53	39	114	2.89	-2
St. Pierre,Max	05	25	2	aa	DET	356	34	80	14	0	4	34	17	48	1	1	225	261	293	554	5%	87%	0.36	49	43	2.60	2
	06	26	2	aaa	DET	247	22	46	13	1	3	28	15	34	0	0	185	230	279	509	6%	86%	0.43	67	47	2.12	-2
Suzuki,Kurt	06	23	2	aa	OAK	376	52	94	24	1	6	45	47	42	4	3	250	333	366	699	11%	89%	1.10	83	68	4.43	40
Swann,Pedro	05	35	0	aaa	CIN	447	46	99	23	2	14	59	25	91	4	0	221	263	372	636	5%	80%	0.28	97	77	3.37	19
	06	36	8	a/a	PHI	213	30	54	12	1	5	30	15	53	7	1	252	301	383	685	7%	75%	0.29	88	108	4.24	26
Sweeney,Ryan	05	21	8	aa	CHW	426	54	120	21	2	1	39	29	41	4	7	281	327	348	675	6%	90%	0.72	52	69	4.00	29
	06	22	8	aaa	CHW	449	64	142	26	2	15	70	35	61	7	8	316	366	488	853	7%	86%	0.58	109	72	6.56	62
Tablado,Raul	05	24	6	aa	TOR	360	31	71	14	1	5	33	21	128	6	1	197	242	280	522	6%	64%	0.17	57	84	2.30	-8
Tatis,Fernando	06	32	5	aaa	BAL	326	40	86	14	1	6	33	33	60	7	2	262	331	367	698	9%	82%	0.56	69	81	4.53	27
Taylor,J.R.	05	23	6	aa	MIN	102	12	27	4	0	1	8	10	11	1	6	265	330	333	664	9%	89%	0.91	50	48	3.23	27
	06	24	6	aa	MIN	203	18	39	10	0	1	12	31	37	5	4	191	298	253	552	13%	82%	0.84	50	57	2.65	1
Taylor,Reggie	05	29	8	aaa	TAM	363	38	77	13	4	6	37	22	71	10	16	213	258	315	573	6%	80%	0.31	65	113	2.31	4
Taylor,Seth	05	28	5	aa	TEX	414	26	80	16	1	10	42	14	64	2	5	193	219	305	524	3%	85%	0.21	72	36	2.04	-2
Tejeda,Juan	05	24	3	aa	DET	466	50	118	22	2	11	65	33	67	2	5	254	303	379	682	7%	86%	0.49	82	52	3.95	28
	06	25	3	aaa	NYM	152	10	32	3	1	2	16	10	33	0	1	211	259	283	542	6%	78%	0.30	44	49	2.43	-6
Tena,Hector	05	23	6	a/a	COL	118	6	24	4	0	2	5	3	23	1	1	203	223	288	511	2%	81%	0.13	56	34	2.04	-6
Terrero,Luis	06	26	8	aaa	BAL	302	50	91	19	1	16	43	16	61	17	9	302	338	527	865	5%	80%	0.27	139	113	6.22	64
Thames,Marcus	05	29	8	aaa	DET	257	43	74	14	4	17	47	34	54	4	1	289	373	568	942	12%	79%	0.64	162	121	8.07	76
Theodorou,Nick	05	30	8	aaa	LA	258	23	46	6	1	1	14	16	30	4	1	178	226	220	446	6%	88%	0.54	30	82	1.68	-17
Theriot,Ryan	05	26	4	aa	CHC	445	41	113	23	3	1	43	36	39	19	10	253	309	324	632	7%	91%	0.93	55	99	3.50	25
	06	27	4	aaa	CHC	280	37	78	10	4	0	19	24	33	13	3	277	335	340	674	8%	88%	0.74	43	141	4.36	25
Thigpen,Curtis	05	22	2	aa	TOR	138	18	38	8	0	4	15	8	19	0	0	275	315	420	735	5%	86%	0.42	96	32	4.83	40
	06	23	2	a/a	TOR	362	48	92	29	4	6	42	50	66	5	2	254	345	406	751	12%	82%	0.76	106	105	5.18	44
Thigpen,Jud	05	25	8	a/a	COL	248	24	59	11	2	9	24	13	35	2	2	238	276	402	679	5%	86%	0.38	101	71	3.74	28
	06	26	8	aa	COL	310	24	59	13	1	3	23	10	49	4	2	191	215	272	487	3%	84%	0.19	57	79	1.89	-9
Thissen,Greg	06	25	4	a/a	WAS	132	10	23	5	0	2	10	15	20	2	2	173	258	252	510	10%	85%	0.76	54	47	2.15	-5
Thomas,Charles	05	27	8	aaa	OAK	277	32	53	14	2	4	24	26	45	12	5	193	262	298	560	9%	84%	0.58	71	120	2.62	5
	06	28	8	aaa	OAK	383	44	87	7	1	7	32	29	63	6	10	228	282	303	584	7%	84%	0.45	44	65	2.70	3
Thompson,Kevin	05	26	8	a/a	NYY	514	66	122	36	3	11	50	57	109	33	11	238	314	382	696	10%	79%	0.52	99	122	4.27	31
	06	27	8	aaa	NYY	362	60	85	19	3	8	38	36	62	14	8	234	303	365	668	9%	83%	0.58	86	130	3.78	25
Thompson,Rich	05	26	8	a/a	PIT	433	47	86	10	4	3	23	26	59	41	9	200	245	258	503	6%	86%	0.44	37	156	2.25	-9
	06	27	8	a/a	PIT	282	44	70	13	4	2	23	31	53	14	10	247	322	342	665	10%	81%	0.59	64	155	3.75	21
Thorman,Scott	05	24	3	a/a	ATL	550	63	149	28	4	19	81	33	102	2	2	271	312	440	752	6%	81%	0.32	105	68	4.92	40
	06	25	3	aaa	ATL	309	36	88	15	2	14	46	30	46	4	2	285	348	482	830	9%	85%	0.65	119	72	6.22	57
Thrower,Jake	05	30	4	aaa	CLE	119	8	25	7	0	0	6	2	14	2	2	206	218	268	486	2%	88%	0.13	54	63	1.79	-6
Thurston,Joe	05	26	4	aaa	NYY	357	27	77	10	2	6	27	13	39	4	9	215	241	302	543	3%	89%	0.32	54	64	2.17	0
	06	27	4	aaa	PHI	479	70	129	28	9	10	52	40	65	19	10	270	326	422	748	8%	86%	0.61	97	158	4.86	42
Tiffee,Terry	05	26	5	aaa	MIN	229	27	54	11	1	8	32	13	22	0	1	237	277	394	671	5%	91%	0.58	97	52	3.71	31
	06	27	5	aaa	MIN	308	35	78	19	0	4	36	19	55	1	0	253	296	352	648	6%	82%	0.35	74	47	3.73	22

Major League Equivalent Statistics

BATTER	Yr	Age	Pos	Lev	Org	ab	r	h	d	t	hr	rbi	bb	k	sb	cs	ba	ob	slg	ops	bb%	ct%	eye	px	sx	rc/g	bpv
Timmons,Wes	05	26	5	a/a	ATL	438	59	98	26	1	5	29	50	44	4	7	224	304	325	629	10%	90%	1.13	74	60	3.34	28
	06	27	6	aaa	ATL	250	26	64	13	0	6	24	35	19	5	4	255	346	376	723	12%	92%	1.86	82	48	4.72	56
Timpner,Clay	06	23	8	a/a	SF	499	51	118	18	4	5	28	20	53	14	14	236	266	319	585	4%	89%	0.38	55	104	2.64	9
Toca,Jorge	05	31	3	aaa	CHW	446	41	113	19	1	21	56	17	78	0	1	252	280	438	718	4%	83%	0.22	111	25	4.23	34
Tolbert,Matt	06	24	6	aa	MIN	248	29	58	14	1	3	31	27	44	5	1	234	308	333	641	10%	82%	0.60	72	85	3.74	20
Tomlin,James	05	24	8	aa	MIN	340	41	82	18	1	4	28	21	46	9	6	240	284	333	617	6%	86%	0.45	67	89	3.19	17
Torcato,Tony	05	26	3	aaa	SF	371	28	84	13	4	6	40	14	29	2	5	227	255	331	586	4%	92%	0.47	65	71	2.69	12
	06	27	8	aaa	CHW	225	19	52	10	1	2	19	15	33	1	1	233	279	310	590	6%	85%	0.44	55	55	3.00	9
Toregas,Wyatt	06	24	2	aa	CLE	163	18	38	10	0	3	26	13	32	1	3	232	287	345	632	7%	80%	0.39	80	48	3.24	18
Torres,Andres	06	29	8	aaa	MIN	348	43	74	16	7	2	28	45	98	18	7	214	303	318	621	11%	72%	0.46	67	187	3.43	8
Torres,Eider	05	23	4	aa	CLE	448	62	117	26	3	4	48	14	59	29	10	261	284	359	643	3%	87%	0.24	71	144	3.52	21
	06	24	6	a/a	CLE	472	51	118	12	1	2	41	33	55	41	14	250	299	292	591	7%	88%	0.60	31	113	3.16	8
Torres,Gabby	05	28	2	aa	MIN	178	11	32	7	0	2	14	12	24	1	1	182	232	247	479	6%	86%	0.48	47	34	1.88	-10
Tousa,Scott	05	26	5	aa	DET	208	21	39	3	2	3	22	17	30	0	3	188	248	255	503	7%	86%	0.55	38	69	2.02	-11
	06	27	4	aa	DET	114	3	17	2	0	0	6	9	29	1	1	146	209	160	369	7%	75%	0.32	13	27	1.11	-40
Tracy,Andy	06	33	3	aaa	BAL	455	58	95	25	1	18	66	65	116	6	5	208	306	386	692	12%	75%	0.56	112	64	4.04	27
Tremie,Chris	05	36	2	aaa	HOU	190	12	31	4	0	2	15	9	31	0	0	161	199	208	407	5%	84%	0.29	31	23	1.34	-28
Truby,Chris	05	32	5	aaa	KC	393	39	74	15	2	12	46	24	69	1	4	188	235	325	560	6%	82%	0.35	85	57	2.41	5
	06	33	5	aaa	LA	333	29	62	16	1	6	39	27	97	7	2	186	248	297	545	8%	71%	0.28	75	84	2.49	-1
Trzesniak,Nick	05	25	2	a/a	SD	312	39	74	17	1	4	29	22	66	6	1	236	287	336	623	7%	79%	0.34	72	93	3.44	15
	06	26	2	aaa	TEX	210	22	50	9	1	4	21	18	30	3	2	240	300	349	649	8%	86%	0.59	71	71	3.65	21
Tucker,Michael	05	26	3	aa	FLA	180	15	34	9	0	2	15	17	62	1	0	190	260	270	530	9%	65%	0.27	60	42	2.44	-7
	06	35	8	aaa	NYM	275	39	64	16	1	5	29	42	48	9	3	232	335	347	682	13%	83%	0.89	80	93	4.32	28
Tuiasosopo,Matt	06	20	6	aa	SEA	216	16	39	4	0	1	9	21	60	2	1	180	253	214	466	9%	72%	0.35	25	46	1.87	-23
Tulowitzki,Troy	06	22	6	aa	COL	423	58	116	32	2	11	47	35	51	5	6	274	330	437	767	8%	88%	0.69	111	74	5.07	51
Tupman,Matt	05	26	2	aa	KC	365	40	75	13	2	1	22	32	50	1	2	205	268	256	524	8%	86%	0.63	39	64	2.35	-3
	06	27	2	a/a	KC	293	33	70	7	1	1	26	42	29	1	1	240	336	280	615	13%	90%	1.46	29	48	3.54	21
Turner,Lloyd	05	25	4	aa	OAK	148	11	29	5	0	2	13	13	21	5	4	195	258	261	519	8%	86%	0.60	46	60	2.17	-4
	06	27	4	aa	OAK	318	27	51	4	3	6	30	22	66	9	5	161	215	254	470	6%	79%	0.33	51	121	1.71	-18
Tyner,Jason	05	28	8	aaa	MIN	524	64	128	16	2	1	29	38	54	14	7	245	296	288	584	7%	90%	0.71	33	96	3.03	9
	06	29	8	aaa	MIN	316	47	93	13	4	0	20	22	45	7	2	294	339	357	696	6%	86%	0.48	46	127	4.63	27
Uggla,Dan	05	26	4	aa	ARI	495	62	124	30	3	16	61	39	89	11	8	251	305	420	725	7%	82%	0.44	109	91	4.36	37
Ugueto,Luis	05	27	6	aaa	KC	265	29	47	7	5	5	21	24	57	8	2	176	245	293	538	8%	79%	0.43	67	163	2.42	-5
Upton,B.J.	05	21	6	aaa	TAM	536	75	147	32	4	13	56	61	85	35	19	275	349	425	773	10%	84%	0.72	98	123	5.20	46
	06	22	6	aaa	TAM	398	70	105	18	4	7	40	63	80	45	19	264	364	385	750	14%	80%	0.79	78	155	5.11	36
Ust,Brant	06	28	5	aa	PIT	166	10	26	2	0	3	13	10	43	0	1	154	200	227	427	5%	74%	0.23	43	26	1.42	-26
Valderrama,Carlos	05	28	8	aa	SF	489	43	110	26	2	5	41	23	86	21	7	226	261	319	580	5%	83%	0.27	67	110	2.84	8
Valdez,Wilson	05	27	6	aaa	SD	159	10	30	4	2	1	11	11	23	6	0	191	245	257	502	7%	85%	0.49	41	118	2.28	-10
	06	28	6	aaa	LA	528	67	125	19	0	5	38	39	44	19	20	236	289	298	586	7%	92%	0.89	45	82	2.71	15
Valent,Eric	05	29	8	aaa	NYM	269	33	58	11	1	7	30	40	53	1	1	214	316	346	662	13%	80%	0.76	83	53	3.91	21
Valido,Robert	06	21	6	aa	CHW	168	15	34	9	2	1	11	13	24	8	3	202	260	298	557	7%	86%	0.54	67	130	2.60	6
Van Der Bosch,Ma	06	24	8	a/a	BOS	168	22	31	3	1	4	16	19	32	12	2	185	269	283	552	10%	81%	0.61	56	131	2.79	-3
Van Every,Jonatha	05	26	8	aa	CLE	385	54	76	13	1	18	49	52	156	13	6	196	292	374	666	12%	60%	0.34	103	94	3.68	15
	06	27	8	a/a	CLE	387	49	84	23	5	11	48	37	139	8	3	216	285	381	666	9%	64%	0.27	105	138	3.74	21
Van Iderstine,Ben	05	28	8	aa	MIL	229	16	44	6	2	2	23	10	35	2	3	192	226	254	479	4%	85%	0.29	40	71	1.77	-14
Vanden Berg,John	05	26	2	aa	MIL	211	16	41	13	1	2	16	24	57	1	0	196	279	290	569	10%	73%	0.43	70	53	2.85	3
Varner,Noochie	05	25	8	aa	ARI	418	48	104	29	2	3	30	41	65	14	8	248	315	345	660	9%	84%	0.63	75	95	3.83	26
	06	26	8	aa	CIN	460	53	113	30	1	9	62	27	93	2	0	247	288	374	662	6%	80%	0.29	89	61	3.81	25
Velandia,Jorge	05	31	6	aaa	PIT	324	32	72	18	1	2	26	22	37	2	4	222	271	300	571	6%	89%	0.59	60	56	2.70	11
	06	32	6	aaa	CHW	475	57	120	22	1	10	46	23	87	13	2	252	286	364	650	5%	82%	0.26	74	98	3.73	20
Velazquez,Gilbert	05	26	6	a/a	MIN	317	31	66	12	1	1	25	18	56	3	3	207	250	261	510	5%	82%	0.32	42	71	2.15	-7
	06	27	6	a/a	MIN	180	23	41	5	1	1	17	12	40	2	2	225	272	280	552	6%	78%	0.29	39	88	2.58	-3
Velazquez,Juan	05	27	5	aa	ATL	154	13	30	6	0	0	9	15	30	2	2	194	265	232	497	9%	80%	0.50	33	57	2.12	-12
Vento,Mike	05	27	8	aaa	NYY	494	48	123	30	1	10	67	36	85	1	5	248	299	371	670	7%	83%	0.42	86	34	3.80	27
	06	28	8	aaa	WAS	217	29	62	12	0	6	28	17	35	3	5	287	338	420	758	7%	84%	0.47	89	52	4.94	42
Victorino,Shane	05	25	8	aaa	PHI	494	73	138	21	12	16	55	39	57	13	11	279	332	468	800	7%	88%	0.68	109	163	5.36	52
Von Schell,Tyler	05	26	3	aa	SF	508	38	96	19	1	9	55	21	124	3	4	188	220	281	501	4%	76%	0.17	61	54	1.95	-9
	06	27	3	aa	SF	369	29	70	20	1	7	30	20	123	0	1	189	230	308	539	5%	67%	0.16	81	38	2.31	-0
Votto,Joey	06	23	3	aa	CIN	508	78	152	45	1	21	71	69	105	22	7	300	383	517	901	12%	79%	0.65	144	92	7.64	73
Wald,Jake	06	26	6	aa	SF	435	39	79	17	3	4	28	32	124	6	6	182	237	259	496	7%	71%	0.25	53	91	1.95	-12
Walker,Christophe	06	26	8	aa	CHC	513	66	132	19	9	2	33	38	128	47	19	258	309	339	648	7%	75%	0.30	53	183	3.65	14
Wallace,David	06	27	2	aa	CLE	155	20	29	7	0	4	17	14	36	3	1	185	252	314	567	8%	77%	0.39	83	76	2.66	4
Walter,Randy	05	24	8	aa	SF	225	29	56	11	2	4	25	14	51	8	7	249	294	367	661	6%	78%	0.28	78	117	3.49	21
	06	25	8	aa	SF	251	23	47	12	3	5	21	14	72	10	5	186	228	308	536	5%	71%	0.19	79	139	2.22	-2
Walter,Scott	05	27	2	aaa	KC	145	16	33	8	0	5	22	3	26	0	0	227	243	381	624	2%	82%	0.11	99	33	3.10	19
Washington,Rico	05	27	5	aa	TAM	452	58	100	22	2	12	53	43	64	4	5	222	290	362	652	9%	86%	0.68	90	70	3.54	25
	06	28	6	a/a	STL	451	56	100	27	3	13	55	56	86	6	3	222	308	379	687	11%	81%	0.65	102	85	4.13	29
Wathan,Derek	05	29	4	aaa	FLA	250	21	45	11	1	3	23	13	31	7	4	179	219	264	483	5%	88%	0.42	60	93	1.82	-7
	06	30	4	aaa	STL	258	22	58	15	5	4	16	8	42	7	3	226	250	360	609	3%	84%	0.20	87	145	2.98	15
Wathan,Dusty	05	32	2	aaa	CLE	248	28	51	7	0	9	33	16	43	2	2	207	255	345	600	6%	83%	0.37	82	52	2.90	10
	06	33	2	aaa	PHI	238	23	51	9	0	5	24	18	50	1	0	216	271	321	592	7%	79%	0.36	69	39	3.02	7
Watkins,Tommy	05	25	6	aa	MIN	319	39	60	16	0	3	18	24	63	9	7	189	246	265	512	7%	80%	0.38	58	90	2.07	-5
	06	26	5	a/a	MIN	275	30	61	11	1	4	27	24	58	9	3	223	286	308	593	8%	79%	0.42	58	94	3.11	6
Watson,Brandon	05	24	8	a/a	WAS	518	61	141	15	2	1	23	26	43	28	21	272	307	313	619	5%	92%	0.60	31	102	3.14	15
	06	25	8	aaa	CIN	219	24	56	6	1	0	19	12	19	7	3	258	296	294	590	5%	91%	0.62	28	94	3.10	10
Watson,Matt	05	27	8	aaa	OAK	419	62	113	24	2	14	61	50	46	9	1	271	349	435	784	11%	89%	1.09	105	95	5.78	56
	06	28	8	aaa	OAK	126	16	33	7	1	4	20	14	13	0	1	266	339	421	760	10%	90%	1.08	98	58	5.14	51
Weber,Jon	05	28	8	aa	LA	450	54	96	18	2	7	46	29	77	7	6	214	262	315	577	6%	83%	0.38	67	93	2.71	6
	06	29	8	aaa	LA	428	47	97	29	0	6	43	30	54	7	5	226	276	332	609	7%	87%	0.55	80	71	3.11	19
Webster,Anthony	06	24	8	a/a	TEX	458	60	129	24	6	8	34	28	53	17	10	282	323	413	736	6%	88%	0.53	85	131	4.67	40
Weeks,Rickie	05	23	4	aaa	MIL	203	32	57	13	6	9	36	21	39	8	1	281	348	537	885	9%	81%	0.54	151	209	7.07	67

Major League Equivalent Statistics

BATTERS

BATTER	Yr	Age	Pos	Lev	Org	ab	r	h	d	t	hr	rbi	bb	k	sb	cs	ba	ob	slg	ops	bb%	ct%	eye	px	sx	rc/g	bpv
Wesson,Barry	05	29	8	aaa	HOU	399	28	89	15	2	7	31	13	67	5	2	224	248	319	568	3%	83%	0.20	62	70	2.66	4
West,Jeremy	05	24	3	aa	BOS	468	40	115	33	2	8	42	34	65	1	0	247	298	375	673	7%	86%	0.52	92	48	3.98	30
	06	25	3	aa	BOS	450	54	113	33	1	10	56	35	58	1	3	251	305	399	704	7%	87%	0.61	103	45	4.25	38
West,Kevin	05	26	8	aaa	MIN	419	50	103	25	1	15	53	37	83	2	2	246	306	416	722	8%	80%	0.44	109	52	4.48	36
	06	27	8	aaa	MIN	256	33	60	9	1	11	40	19	74	0	2	235	289	402	690	7%	71%	0.26	98	52	3.92	24
Whiteman,Tommy	05	26	6	a/a	HOU	385	27	69	12	0	5	32	32	98	3	5	180	244	245	489	8%	75%	0.33	45	37	1.93	-15
	06	27	6	aaa	COL	147	8	21	3	1	2	7	5	39	1	1	142	169	213	382	3%	74%	0.12	43	72	1.08	-32
Whitesell,Josh	06	24	3	aa	WAS	402	40	90	10	0	15	48	45	123	2	7	225	302	362	664	10%	69%	0.36	79	25	3.63	15
Whiteside,Eli	05	26	2	aa	BAL	309	23	64	20	1	4	23	18	54	1	3	208	251	317	569	5%	83%	0.33	79	45	2.57	9
	06	27	2	aaa	BAL	315	36	73	17	1	11	46	10	73	1	3	231	254	394	648	3%	77%	0.13	104	60	3.24	23
Whitrock,Scott	06	26	8	aa	MIN	222	26	40	11	2	3	14	15	87	13	1	178	231	280	511	6%	61%	0.18	69	164	2.30	-9
Wigginton,Ty	05	28	5	aaa	PIT	280	38	69	16	0	10	37	31	42	6	6	248	323	407	731	10%	85%	0.74	104	62	4.50	40
Wilken,Kris	05	26	3	aaa	BAL	185	12	37	7	0	2	15	13	38	0	0	199	250	267	518	6%	79%	0.33	49	16	2.27	-7
Williams,Gerald	05	39	8	aaa	NYM	139	18	26	8	1	3	12	6	20	1	2	188	223	317	540	4%	86%	0.32	87	102	2.16	5
Williams,Glenn	05	28	5	aaa	MIN	175	17	46	11	1	4	18	6	33	2	0	260	283	399	682	3%	81%	0.17	94	74	4.03	29
	06	29	5	aaa	MIN	370	34	85	18	4	6	33	32	97	3	1	229	290	349	639	8%	74%	0.33	79	89	3.56	15
Williams,Marland	05	24	8	aaa	ARI	381	41	79	12	6	6	34	29	87	29	8	207	262	314	576	7%	77%	0.33	65	173	2.85	2
Willingham,Josh	05	27	2	aaa	FLA	219	39	57	12	2	12	37	34	41	4	1	261	360	492	852	13%	81%	0.82	137	104	6.62	60
Willits,Reggie	05	24	8	aa	ANA	487	55	124	19	3	1	34	38	64	29	16	254	308	310	618	7%	87%	0.59	43	113	3.28	14
	06	25	8	aaa	ANA	352	66	101	16	2	2	31	58	39	24	18	287	388	360	748	14%	89%	1.48	54	113	5.05	47
Wilson,Andy	06	31	2	aa	NYM	319	21	49	12	0	4	19	21	117	0	1	154	206	224	430	6%	63%	0.18	50	28	1.46	-25
Wilson,Bobby	06	24	2	aa	ANA	374	32	89	22	0	7	38	23	36	1	8	239	283	353	636	6%	90%	0.65	81	26	3.18	26
Wilson,Enrique	06	33	4	aaa	BOS	203	14	41	9	1	3	15	20	16	3	3	200	271	293	563	9%	92%	1.27	64	56	2.63	18
Wilson,John	05	27	2	a/a	WAS	302	25	58	11	0	3	23	18	28	1	5	193	239	265	504	6%	91%	0.66	51	37	1.95	-1
Wilson,Josh	05	25	6	aa	FLA	521	61	111	26	4	11	57	35	82	12	9	213	263	342	604	6%	84%	0.43	84	109	2.90	14
	06	26	6	aaa	COL	335	46	96	17	3	8	34	28	29	11	5	287	341	426	767	8%	91%	0.95	89	109	5.32	51
Wilson,Michael	06	23	8	aa	SEA	249	29	55	11	1	12	40	27	87	1	1	222	299	413	711	10%	65%	0.31	114	56	4.27	27
Wilson,Tom	05	35	2	aaa	COL	210	23	56	14	1	7	28	19	28	0	0	266	326	446	772	8%	87%	0.68	118	35	5.32	51
	06	36	2	aaa	FLA	278	35	65	18	0	7	32	23	63	1	2	233	293	376	668	8%	77%	0.37	97	46	3.77	25
Winchester,Jeff	05	26	2	aa	MIL	265	20	56	13	0	0	21	14	37	0	2	211	251	258	509	5%	86%	0.39	42	29	2.13	-5
Wise,Dewayne	05	28	8	aaa	DET	375	35	80	10	6	6	37	19	66	18	8	213	251	314	565	5%	82%	0.29	59	151	2.58	1
	06	29	8	a/a	CIN	204	31	51	14	2	6	23	13	42	6	2	250	294	425	719	6%	79%	0.30	115	127	4.39	37
Witt,Kevin	06	31	3	aaa	TAM	485	69	119	24	1	29	83	41	140	0	0	245	304	477	781	8%	71%	0.30	138	38	5.13	44
Woods,Michael	05	25	8	aaa	DET	448	38	85	14	6	5	34	36	102	4	5	189	249	283	532	7%	77%	0.35	58	104	2.27	-6
Wood,Brandon	06	22	6	aa	ANA	453	55	107	37	2	18	61	39	110	14	4	236	297	446	743	8%	76%	0.35	138	103	4.61	43
Wood,Jason	05	36	5	aaa	FLA	447	47	101	14	2	13	49	32	67	4	4	226	276	348	625	7%	85%	0.47	74	64	3.25	15
	06	37	5	aaa	FLA	441	45	99	17	2	7	54	32	86	1	1	224	276	320	597	7%	81%	0.37	63	56	3.06	8
Wooten,Shawn	05	33	2	aaa	BOS	419	32	91	18	0	12	41	24	60	0	0	217	260	344	604	5%	86%	0.41	81	14	3.04	14
	06	34	2	aaa	MIN	352	22	78	18	0	5	37	20	90	1	0	222	264	320	583	5%	74%	0.22	69	27	2.90	7
Yan,Ruddy	05	25	8	a/a	TEX	498	56	131	14	4	3	33	35	30	30	13	263	311	323	635	7%	94%	1.17	40	120	3.59	28
	06	25	8	a/a	TEX	252	36	59	8	2	0	16	22	26	13	5	235	297	281	578	8%	90%	0.87	34	128	3.00	10
Youkilis,Kevin	05	27	5	aaa	BOS	152	22	44	15	1	6	20	26	23	1	2	287	392	511	902	15%	85%	1.15	150	62	7.48	81
Youngbauer,Scott	05	27	4	aa	BOS	314	31	70	17	3	7	30	16	76	6	3	222	259	363	622	5%	76%	0.21	91	19	3.14	15
	06	28	4	a/a	SEA	361	39	71	14	3	9	31	25	89	3	5	198	250	323	573	7%	75%	0.29	78	88	2.56	4
Young,Chris	05	22	8	aa	CHW	462	78	115	35	2	24	61	56	103	25	7	249	330	489	819	11%	78%	0.54	151	122	5.78	56
	06	27	8	aaa	ARI	402	57	97	29	3	16	56	39	56	12	6	241	308	449	757	9%	86%	0.70	133	111	4.77	49
Young,Delmon	05	20	8	aa	TAM	548	75	163	22	6	21	81	24	69	28	17	297	327	472	799	4%	87%	0.35	103	126	5.28	49
	06	21	8	aaa	TAM	342	52	112	23	4	8	61	15	56	23	4	328	357	489	846	4%	84%	0.27	106	157	6.88	59
Young,Delwyn	05	23	4	a/a	LA	526	54	133	29	0	15	55	24	86	1	4	253	285	394	679	4%	84%	0.28	93	30	3.82	28
	06	24	8	aa	LA	532	58	124	35	0	14	75	32	82	2	5	233	277	378	654	6%	85%	0.39	99	40	3.48	26
Young,Ernie	05	36	0	aaa	CLE	385	52	84	11	0	13	54	44	100	5	4	217	298	344	641	10%	74%	0.44	75	60	3.54	12
	06	37	3	aaa	CHW	350	42	92	23	0	13	56	45	87	2	2	262	346	435	781	11%	75%	0.52	113	36	5.52	44
Young,Walter	05	26	3	aaa	BAL	466	42	122	26	1	12	70	26	78	1	1	261	300	397	697	5%	83%	0.33	90	37	4.23	31
	06	27	3	aaa	SD	381	28	81	14	0	8	50	12	49	3	6	213	236	312	548	3%	87%	0.24	64	38	2.26	2
Yount,Dustin	06	24	3	aa	BAL	167	19	36	5	0	5	18	24	51	0	2	215	314	331	645	13%	70%	0.48	71	28	3.59	10
Zamora,Junior	05	29	5	aa	HOU	126	7	18	5	0	0	3	4	39	0	0	143	168	185	352	3%	69%	0.10	37	29	0.96	-35
Zapp,A.J.	05	27	3	aaa	CIN	391	24	77	22	0	5	29	28	95	0	0	197	250	289	539	7%	76%	0.29	68	14	2.44	-0
	06	28	3	aa	LA	269	22	45	12	0	6	26	31	123	0	1	167	253	283	536	10%	54%	0.25	76	23	2.39	-8
Zeringue,Jon	05	23	8	aaa	ARI	433	36	97	18	3	5	40	16	66	9	9	224	252	314	566	4%	85%	0.24	61	90	2.48	5
	06	24	8	aa	ARI	203	14	42	5	1	4	17	17	40	1	2	205	268	296	565	8%	80%	0.43	55	46	2.64	-0
Zimmerman,Ryan	05	21	5	aa	WAS	233	33	67	19	0	7	26	12	28	1	6	288	322	459	782	5%	88%	0.43	119	47	4.89	53
Zinter,Alan	05	37	0	aaa	ARI	111	5	19	4	1	9	8	22	0	0	170	227	243	470	7%	80%	0.36	48	44	1.83	-16	
	06	38	5	aaa	HOU	212	31	45	9	2	9	32	25	58	1	0	212	296	399	695	11%	73%	0.44	111	89	4.14	25
Zobrist,Ben	06	25	6	a/a	TAM	384	58	109	25	6	3	30	54	53	10	7	285	373	401	774	12%	86%	1.03	82	76	5.62	49
Zoccolillo,Peter	05	29	8	a/a	STL	311	26	60	9	2	8	28	19	42	0	2	194	240	298	538	6%	86%	0.44	65	25	2.31	0
Zuniga,Tony	05	31	5	a/a	MIL	425	32	88	16	0	6	44	22	55	3	1	207	245	290	535	5%	87%	0.39	57	50	2.40	0

Major League Equivalent Statistics

PITCHER	Yr	Age	Lev	Org	Actual				Major League Equivalents																
					w	l	g	sv	ip	h	er	hr	bb	k	era	br/ip	bf/g	oob	ctl	dom	cmd	hr/9	h%	s%	bpv
Aardsma,David	05	24	aa	CHC	10	3	42	2	96	109	46	5	37	62	4.34	1.52	10.2	280	3.5	5.8	1.7	0.5	33%	71%	54
	06	25	aaa	CHC	2	3	29	8	36	38	18	1	16	32	4.49	1.50	5.5	265	4.0	8.0	2.0	0.2	35%	68%	84
Abbott,Jim	05	26	a/a	MIN	7	6	30	0	109	155	91	13	37	67	7.46	1.75	17.0	327	3.0	5.6	1.8	1.0	37%	56%	30
Abraham,Paul	05	26	aa	SD	2	1	30	0	40	56	21	2	13	20	4.73	1.71	6.2	321	3.0	4.4	1.5	0.5	36%	72%	34
	06	27	aa	SD	3	4	43	1	65	80	33	6	39	42	4.62	1.84	7.2	298	5.4	5.8	1.1	0.8	35%	76%	29
Abreu,Winston	05	28	aaa	ARI	2	3	27	2	33	43	28	6	15	35	7.60	1.75	5.7	308	4.1	9.6	2.3	1.8	39%	58%	48
	06	29	aaa	BAL	9	4	46	1	65	72	28	5	23	65	3.87	1.45	6.2	275	3.1	9.0	2.9	0.7	36%	75%	92
Accardo,Jeremy	05	24	a/a	SF	3	0	33	7	42	35	8	0	10	38	1.71	1.07	5.1	222	2.1	8.1	3.8	0.0	30%	82%	139
Acevedo,Jose	06	29	aaa	COL	6	8	15	0	87	135	73	14	19	42	7.56	1.78	27.3	348	2.0	4.3	2.2	1.4	37%	58%	13
Acosta,Manny	06	25	a/a	ATL	1	6	51	21	60	58	33	6	54	48	4.89	1.86	5.6	248	8.1	7.1	0.9	0.9	30%	75%	38
Adams,Mike	05	27	aaa	MIL	3	4	26	2	36	39	25	3	12	37	6.32	1.40	6.0	270	2.9	9.3	3.2	0.8	36%	53%	100
	06	28	aaa	SD	1	3	48	2	60	76	32	3	25	39	4.84	1.68	5.8	304	3.7	5.9	1.6	0.5	36%	70%	48
Adams,Terry	06	34	aaa	PIT	5	3	48	1	63	85	44	9	24	34	6.31	1.73	6.1	316	3.5	4.9	1.4	1.4	35%	65%	10
Adkins,Jon	05	28	aaa	CHW	4	9	22	0	124	180	97	27	46	71	7.01	1.82	26.7	331	3.4	5.1	1.5	1.9	35%	65%	-7
Aguilar,Ray	05	26	aa	FLA	5	2	13	0	84	90	41	7	20	40	4.40	1.31	27.4	268	2.1	4.2	2.0	0.7	30%	67%	47
	06	27	aa	OAK	12	7	28	0	158	245	107	15	46	75	6.08	1.84	26.9	346	2.6	4.3	1.6	0.9	38%	67%	20
Akin,Brian	06	25	aa	LA	2	1	20	6	36	32	17	2	25	37	4.19	1.57	8.1	230	6.3	9.2	1.5	0.5	31%	73%	79
Albaladejo,Jonathan	06	24	aa	PIT	1	2	18	1	36	51	22	5	5	22	5.41	1.55	8.9	325	1.3	5.6	4.3	1.3	36%	67%	76
Albers,Matt	06	24	a/a	HOU	12	3	23	0	141	136	46	7	56	102	2.94	1.36	26.2	248	3.6	6.5	1.8	0.4	30%	79%	69
Alexander,Mark	06	26	a/a	LA	5	3	52	27	61	43	12	2	24	68	1.71	1.10	4.7	195	3.6	10.1	2.8	0.3	28%	85%	127
Allen,Blake	05	24	aa	HOU	1	3	16	0	42	57	37	5	20	25	7.89	1.83	12.5	317	4.3	5.3	1.2	1.1	35%	56%	16
Almanza,Armando	05	33	a/a	STL	2	1	33	2	35	46	21	7	16	30	5.40	1.74	5.0	307	4.0	7.6	1.9	1.7	36%	73%	28
Almonte,Edwin	05	29	aa	DET	1	5	52	33	50	78	39	11	16	34	6.95	1.87	4.6	346	2.9	6.2	2.1	2.0	38%	67%	7
Alvarado,Carlos	06	29	a/a	CIN	5	2	33	0	51	58	31	4	31	42	5.38	1.72	7.2	278	5.4	7.3	1.4	0.6	35%	68%	53
Alvarez,Abe	05	23	aaa	BOS	11	6	26	0	144	151	85	16	28	98	5.29	1.24	23.1	265	1.7	6.1	3.5	1.0	30%	58%	83
	06	24	aaa	BOS	6	9	22	0	118	168	105	28	42	62	8.01	1.78	25.2	328	3.2	4.7	1.5	2.1	34%	58%	-15
Alvarez,Carlos	05	20	aa	LA	4	0	25	0	38	38	17	4	14	27	4.05	1.37	6.5	255	3.4	6.4	1.9	0.9	30%	73%	56
	06	22	aa	LA	4	1	33	1	55	58	23	9	15	47	3.76	1.32	7.1	265	2.5	7.7	3.1	1.5	31%	78%	70
Alvarez,Oscar	05	25	aa	STL	6	2	29	0	106	129	44	10	41	47	3.77	1.60	16.5	294	3.5	4.0	1.1	0.8	32%	78%	18
	06	26	aa	WAS	8	8	30	0	133	193	108	18	45	65	7.30	1.79	20.9	332	3.0	4.4	1.5	1.2	36%	59%	8
Anderson,Craig	06	26	a/a	BAL	3	4	17	0	90	126	59	9	17	50	5.89	1.59	23.9	325	1.7	5.0	3.0	0.9	36%	63%	55
Anderson,Jason	05	26	aaa	NYY	4	1	55	10	67	49	23	4	19	49	3.04	1.01	4.8	201	2.5	6.5	2.6	0.6	24%	71%	92
	06	27	aaa	SD	5	2	60	4	79	79	29	6	28	52	3.35	1.36	5.6	255	3.2	5.9	1.8	0.7	30%	77%	57
Anderson,Jimmy	05	30	aaa	HOU	8	10	27	0	144	166	57	7	64	57	3.57	1.59	24.1	283	4.0	3.6	0.9	0.4	31%	77%	26
	06	31	aaa	FLA	2	3	22	0	43	68	32	7	21	29	6.71	2.06	9.8	350	4.4	6.0	1.4	1.4	40%	69%	8
Anderson,Matt	05	29	aaa	COL	3	3	45	8	46	40	23	7	18	35	4.52	1.24	4.3	228	3.4	6.8	2.0	1.3	26%	67%	53
	06	30	aaa	SF	1	2	26	0	34	58	42	8	30	25	11.14	2.57	7.2	367	7.9	6.7	0.8	2.1	41%	57%	-22
Andrade,Steve	05	28	aa	TOR	3	2	35	3	50	35	20	5	22	52	3.68	1.13	5.8	193	3.9	9.4	2.4	0.9	25%	70%	97
	06	29	aaa	SD	3	2	38	0	67	63	29	4	32	55	3.89	1.42	7.7	244	4.3	7.3	1.7	0.6	31%	73%	69
Andrews,Clayton	05	27	a/a	ANA	9	8	30	1	132	201	99	16	55	47	6.73	1.94	21.4	343	3.8	3.2	0.9	1.1	36%	66%	-9
Andrew,Jason	05	26	aa	CIN	3	4	48	0	80	93	38	4	30	48	4.24	1.54	7.4	285	3.4	5.4	1.6	0.5	33%	72%	49
Appier,Kevin	06	39	aaa	SEA	1	2	10	0	35	46	22	0	26	22	5.65	2.06	17.5	311	6.7	5.6	0.8	0.0	37%	70%	44
Arakawa,Yusuke	05	27	aa	COL	4	4	41	0	53	83	49	16	25	28	8.39	2.05	6.4	349	4.3	4.8	1.1	2.7	36%	64%	-43
Arias,Alberto	06	23	aa	COL	8	6	49	0	111	121	70	20	43	71	5.67	1.47	10.0	271	3.5	5.7	1.7	1.6	29%	65%	21
Armitage,Barry	05	26	aa	KC	4	3	41	7	79	83	39	5	41	47	4.45	1.57	8.7	264	4.7	5.4	1.1	0.5	31%	71%	42
Arnold,Jason	05	26	aaa	TOR	0	4	47	5	62	70	55	16	28	46	7.93	1.58	5.9	279	4.0	6.6	1.6	2.4	29%	53%	1
Arredondo,Jose	06	23	aa	ANA	2	3	11	0	60	83	44	7	20	41	6.58	1.71	25.3	321	3.0	6.1	2.1	1.0	37%	61%	39
Artiles,Carlos	05	25	a/a	NYY	3	2	33	0	46	59	22	4	31	30	4.22	1.94	6.8	303	6.0	5.9	1.0	0.8	35%	80%	26
Asahina,Jonathan	05	25	aa	COL	12	10	26	0	169	241	114	25	36	76	6.05	1.64	29.7	328	1.9	4.0	2.1	1.3	35%	65%	18
	06	26	a/a	COL	4	10	29	0	147	239	136	32	44	54	8.31	1.92	24.6	357	2.7	3.3	1.2	1.9	37%	59%	-29
Ascanio,Jose	06	21	aa	ATL	4	2	24	0	38	46	25	2	19	33	5.92	1.71	7.3	293	4.5	7.8	1.7	0.5	37%	63%	66
Asencio,Miguel	06	26	aaa	COL	8	7	38	1	111	153	80	18	40	59	6.52	1.74	13.6	320	3.3	4.8	1.5	1.4	35%	64%	8
Astacio,Ezequiel	05	25	aaa	HOU	4	4	13	1	65	58	24	6	11	47	3.31	1.06	20.0	234	1.5	6.5	4.3	0.8	28%	71%	112
	06	27	aaa	HOU	8	4	21	0	92	110	60	16	43	62	5.84	1.67	20.1	291	4.2	6.1	1.4	1.6	32%	68%	15
Atchison,Scott	06	31	aaa	SEA	4	0	30	1	50	61	17	2	17	32	3.00	1.56	7.5	295	3.0	5.7	1.9	0.4	35%	81%	58
Atlee,Thomas	05	26	aa	CHC	3	1	29	3	34	53	21	5	13	16	5.44	1.92	5.7	346	3.3	4.1	1.2	1.2	37%	74%	0
	06	27	a/a	CHC	3	6	56	6	83	98	48	10	51	44	5.23	1.79	7.0	287	5.5	4.8	0.9	1.1	32%	73%	11
Austen,David	05	24	aa	ANA	4	3	27	0	46	48	23	4	12	24	4.51	1.30	7.2	264	2.3	4.6	2.1	0.8	29%	66%	48
Autrey,Scott	05	25	aa	TAM	3	11	21	0	108	174	83	24	34	53	6.92	1.92	24.9	355	2.8	4.4	1.6	2.0	37%	68%	-17
Axelson,Josh	05	27	aa	STL	1	2	28	0	49	74	53	8	31	36	9.71	2.13	8.8	340	5.7	6.6	1.1	1.5	39%	54%	6
Aybar,Manny	05	33	aaa	NYM	3	0	24	4	32	31	6	1	8	22	1.78	1.22	5.5	246	2.4	6.1	2.6	0.3	30%	86%	88
Bacsik,Mike	05	28	aaa	PHI	7	10	30	0	160	217	99	28	42	90	5.56	1.62	24.2	317	2.4	5.1	2.1	1.6	34%	69%	19
	06	29	aaa	ARI	11	0	28	0	87	98	33	10	19	47	3.45	1.35	13.3	278	2.0	4.8	2.4	1.0	31%	78%	49
Baek,Cha Seung	05	25	aaa	SEA	8	8	24	0	112	159	88	19	35	65	7.05	1.73	21.7	326	2.8	5.2	1.8	1.5	36%	61%	14
	06	26	aaa	SEA	12	4	24	0	147	154	59	19	39	90	3.60	1.31	25.9	264	2.4	5.5	2.3	1.1	29%	77%	50
Baerlocher,Ryan	05	28	a/a	KC	7	6	18	0	98	106	48	6	38	54	4.43	1.46	23.9	270	3.5	4.9	1.4	0.5	31%	69%	44
	06	29	aaa	KC	5	4	20	1	80	100	49	10	32	46	5.56	1.65	18.3	300	3.6	5.2	1.5	1.1	33%	68%	24
Baez,Federico	05	24	a/a	CHC	4	3	45	2	59	86	39	5	35	35	5.97	2.04	6.5	331	5.3	5.3	1.0	0.8	38%	71%	18
	06	25	a/a	CHC	2	5	34	1	88	103	47	17	36	54	4.84	1.58	11.6	286	3.7	5.5	1.5	1.7	31%	75%	11
Bailey,Homer	06	20	aa	CIN	7	1	13	0	68	57	15	1	28	68	2.02	1.25	21.8	223	3.7	9.0	2.5	0.1	31%	83%	113
Bajenaru,Jeff	05	28	aaa	CHW	4	6	61	19	70	54	14	5	31	67	1.76	1.20	4.7	208	3.9	8.7	2.2	0.7	27%	89%	92
	06	29	aaa	ARI	4	3	52	7	80	95	51	8	41	59	5.69	1.69	7.1	288	4.6	6.6	1.4	0.8	34%	66%	42
Baker,Brad	05	25	aaa	SD	4	5	59	27	66	71	35	7	30	69	4.77	1.53	5.0	269	4.1	9.4	2.3	1.0	35%	70%	77
	06	26	a/a	BOS	3	4	41	3	63	102	56	9	22	42	7.96	1.97	7.5	357	3.2	6.0	1.9	1.4	40%	60%	19
Baker,Chris	05	28	aaa	TOR	7	7	30	0	122	191	96	16	32	68	7.05	1.83	19.3	349	2.4	5.0	2.1	1.2	39%	62%	24
	06	29	aaa	TEX	9	4	27	1	86	103	37	7	33	32	3.91	1.58	14.3	291	3.5	3.3	1.0	0.7	31%	76%	16
Baker,Ryan	05	28	aa	FLA	3	2	25	0	39	59	29	5	31	22	6.64	2.31	8.2	340	7.2	5.0	0.7	1.1	38%	72%	-2
Baker,Scott	05	24	aaa	MIN	5	8	22	0	134	141	55	16	27	93	3.69	1.25	25.4	265	1.8	6.2	3.4	1.1	30%	74%	80
	06	25	aaa	MIN	5	4	12	0	84	98	37	5	29	57	4.00	1.51	31.1	285	3.1	6.1	2.0	0.5	34%	74%	60
Baldwin,James	05	34	aaa	BAL	3	2	8	0	47	63	32	7	4	21	6.05	1.43	25.6	315	0.8	4.0	5.0	1.4	33%	60%	78

Major League Equivalent Statistics

PITCHERS

PITCHER	Yr	Age	Lev	Org	w	l	g	sv	ip	h	er	hr	bb	k	era	br/ip	bf/g	oob	ctl	dom	cmd	hr/9	h%	s%	bpv
Ballouli,Khalid	05	26	aa	MIL	4	7	24	2	74	116	51	6	26	48	6.20	1.90	14.9	348	3.1	5.8	1.9	0.7	41%	66%	39
	06	27	aa	MIL	2	4	23	1	56	84	43	6	25	40	6.82	1.95	11.9	339	4.1	6.4	1.6	0.9	40%	64%	31
Banks,Josh	05	23	aa	TOR	8	12	27	0	162	209	107	27	12	124	5.95	1.37	25.7	307	0.7	6.9	10.0	1.5	35%	59%	201
	06	24	aaa	TOR	10	11	29	0	170	224	135	47	30	109	7.14	1.49	25.9	311	1.6	5.8	3.6	2.5	32%	57%	29
Bannister,Brian	05	25	a/a	NYM	13	5	26	0	154	158	55	11	41	115	3.19	1.29	25.0	260	2.4	6.7	2.8	0.7	31%	77%	82
	06	26	aaa	NYM	3	3	6	0	30	42	18	5	5	21	5.44	1.58	22.6	326	1.5	6.2	4.1	1.5	37%	69%	68
Barrett,Ricky	05	25	a/a	MIN	5	4	49	6	78	91	58	10	58	70	6.66	1.90	7.7	285	6.7	8.1	1.2	1.2	35%	66%	36
	06	26	aaa	MIN	5	1	27	1	47	39	26	0	30	41	5.02	1.48	7.7	223	5.8	7.8	1.3	0.0	30%	62%	85
Barry,Kevin	05	27	a/a	ATL	5	3	35	1	86	84	37	10	57	61	3.84	1.64	11.2	250	6.0	6.4	1.1	1.1	29%	80%	33
	06	28	aaa	ATL	4	5	18	0	95	114	52	6	42	60	4.88	1.64	24.1	291	4.0	5.6	1.4	0.6	34%	70%	42
Bartlett,Richard	05	24	aa	LA	3	3	35	3	59	69	34	3	42	24	5.19	1.89	8.1	286	6.4	3.7	0.6	0.5	32%	71%	18
Barzilla,Philip	05	27	a/a	HOU	7	7	42	5	113	161	52	8	33	65	4.16	1.72	12.5	328	2.7	5.2	1.9	0.6	38%	76%	43
	06	28	aaa	HOU	8	5	25	1	112	135	59	5	49	65	4.73	1.64	20.5	292	4.0	5.2	1.3	0.4	34%	70%	43
Basham,Bobby	05	26	aa	CIN	5	3	10	0	51	62	20	6	10	35	3.52	1.41	22.1	294	1.8	6.2	3.5	1.0	34%	78%	78
Basner,Ryan	05	24	a/a	ATL	2	10	37	1	97	136	72	9	27	54	6.68	1.68	12.4	324	2.5	5.0	2.0	0.9	37%	59%	37
	06	25	a/a	ATL	4	5	41	1	82	111	53	11	32	60	5.76	1.73	9.3	315	3.5	6.6	1.9	1.2	37%	68%	36
Bass,Adam	05	24	aa	ARI	5	10	26	0	154	191	91	18	42	102	5.28	1.51	26.3	297	2.5	5.9	2.4	1.0	34%	66%	50
	06	25	a/a	ARI	11	7	29	0	170	226	120	22	60	92	6.35	1.68	27.0	313	3.2	4.9	1.5	1.2	34%	63%	19
Bass,Brian	05	24	aa	KC	12	8	27	0	165	199	99	11	48	86	5.40	1.50	27.0	292	2.6	4.7	1.8	0.6	33%	63%	44
	06	25	a/a	KC	5	6	13	0	59	90	46	8	20	24	7.08	1.85	21.7	342	3.0	3.7	1.2	1.3	36%	62%	-3
Bateman,Joe	06	26	aa	SF	4	6	53	10	72	95	53	5	29	57	6.61	1.72	6.3	312	3.6	7.2	2.0	0.6	38%	60%	60
Bauer,Peter	05	27	a/a	FLA	6	10	27	1	128	180	102	23	50	68	7.18	1.80	22.4	325	3.5	4.8	1.4	1.6	35%	62%	-2
Bauer,Rick	05	29	aaa	BAL	3	8	29	0	73	104	44	15	37	34	5.43	1.93	12.2	328	4.5	4.2	0.9	1.9	34%	77%	-21
Baugh,Kenny	05	27	aaa	DET	12	8	28	0	165	188	78	13	60	89	4.27	1.50	26.1	280	3.3	4.9	1.5	0.7	32%	72%	38
Bausher,Tim	05	26	aaa	BOS	3	2	44	5	71	75	32	9	35	54	4.05	1.55	7.2	266	4.4	6.9	1.5	1.2	31%	78%	40
	06	27	aaa	CIN	4	4	39	0	73	105	59	7	42	33	7.27	2.02	9.2	331	5.2	4.1	0.8	0.9	36%	63%	3
Bautista,Denny	06	26	aaa	COL	3	9	16	0	80	126	80	6	51	52	9.05	2.20	25.6	350	5.7	5.9	1.0	0.7	41%	56%	21
Bayliss,Jonah	05	25	aa	KC	1	2	30	8	57	50	20	4	26	50	3.16	1.33	8.1	231	4.0	7.8	1.9	0.7	29%	78%	75
	06	26	aaa	PIT	3	3	46	23	58	47	21	5	31	55	3.20	1.35	5.4	219	4.8	8.6	1.8	0.8	28%	79%	76
Bay,Ronald	05	22	aa	CLE	3	3	8	0	45	51	28	5	13	35	5.59	1.42	24.5	279	2.6	7.0	2.7	1.0	33%	61%	68
	06	23	a/a	CLE	8	8	28	0	138	147	80	24	56	107	5.22	1.47	21.6	267	3.7	7.0	1.9	1.6	30%	69%	37
Bazardo,Yorman	05	21	aa	SEA	11	8	25	0	142	172	82	17	51	91	5.20	1.57	25.5	293	3.2	5.8	1.8	1.1	33%	68%	36
	06	22	aa	SEA	6	5	25	0	138	171	73	12	49	72	4.76	1.59	24.9	298	3.2	4.7	1.5	0.8	33%	71%	31
Bazzell,Shane	05	27	a/a	TEX	4	6	36	2	100	160	86	17	34	49	7.69	1.94	13.5	354	3.1	4.4	1.4	1.5	38%	61%	-5
Beam,Randy	05	23	aa	BOS	2	3	33	2	45	41	18	3	20	40	3.50	1.35	5.8	238	3.9	7.9	2.0	0.6	30%	75%	79
	06	24	aa	BOS	3	3	35	1	51	61	37	13	13	34	6.49	1.44	6.4	290	2.2	6.0	2.7	2.2	31%	60%	23
Beam,T.J.	06	26	a/a	NYY	6	0	37	4	73	56	14	2	30	53	1.78	1.17	8.1	206	3.7	6.5	1.8	0.3	26%	85%	82
Bean,Colter	05	29	aaa	NYY	4	7	65	7	71	71	29	5	42	64	3.67	1.59	4.9	254	5.3	8.1	1.5	0.7	32%	78%	65
	06	30	aaa	NYY	9	2	47	0	88	78	36	2	62	87	3.70	1.58	8.4	233	6.3	8.9	1.4	0.2	32%	75%	85
Beckstead,Jentry	05	25	aa	COL	5	3	51	3	68	107	47	7	17	34	6.18	1.81	6.3	349	2.2	4.5	2.1	0.9	39%	66%	29
	06	26	a/a	COL	6	3	48	0	72	83	31	11	27	52	3.88	1.53	6.7	284	3.3	6.5	2.0	1.4	32%	80%	37
Beech,Matt	05	34	aa	DET	2	3	6	0	32	44	22	5	20	17	6.25	1.97	26.3	316	5.6	4.8	0.9	1.3	34%	70%	-1
Begg,Chris	05	26	aa	SF	8	7	23	0	138	185	64	9	26	64	4.20	1.53	26.7	315	1.7	4.1	2.4	0.6	35%	73%	49
	06	27	aa	SF	13	10	26	0	174	246	122	12	41	69	6.29	1.65	30.6	326	2.1	3.6	1.7	0.6	36%	60%	28
Beimel,Joe	05	28	aaa	TAM	1	2	48	0	52	63	24	2	20	29	4.08	1.61	4.9	294	3.5	5.0	1.4	0.4	34%	74%	45
Bell,Heath	06	29	aaa	NYM	3	3	30	12	35	36	8	1	9	44	1.98	1.29	4.9	262	2.3	11.2	5.0	0.3	39%	85%	166
Bell,Rob	05	29	aaa	TAM	1	3	22	0	44	70	40	11	19	20	8.12	2.02	9.9	352	3.9	4.2	1.1	2.2	36%	63%	-34
	06	30	aaa	CLE	9	10	30	1	142	187	95	22	41	79	5.99	1.60	21.4	311	2.6	5.0	1.9	1.4	34%	65%	22
Benes,Alan	06	35	aaa	STL	5	6	30	0	66	83	47	18	25	37	6.45	1.64	10.0	301	3.4	5.0	1.5	2.4	30%	67%	-17
Bennett,Jeff	05	25	aaa	MIL	2	3	49	12	62	47	22	6	24	49	3.22	1.15	5.2	207	3.5	7.0	2.0	0.9	25%	75%	71
Bentz,Chad	05	25	a/a	FLA	1	1	38	1	40	47	18	4	19	32	4.01	1.65	4.8	288	4.2	7.2	1.7	0.9	35%	78%	48
	06	26	a/a	CHW	6	4	39	0	50	56	49	22	42	24	8.78	1.95	6.3	275	7.6	4.4	0.6	4.0	22%	65%	-82
Bergmann,Jason	05	24	a/a	WAS	5	2	41	7	74	56	19	7	27	66	2.31	1.12	7.3	206	3.3	8.0	2.4	0.9	26%	84%	88
	06	25	aaa	WAS	8	2	26	4	60	62	26	5	21	51	3.93	1.38	9.9	260	3.2	7.7	2.4	0.8	32%	73%	78
Bergman,Dusty	05	28	aaa	SF	8	5	47	8	74	91	32	8	19	48	3.84	1.48	6.9	295	2.3	5.8	2.5	1.0	34%	77%	53
	06	29	aaa	SF	0	5	49	1	46	83	42	2	24	28	8.17	2.30	4.9	380	4.6	5.4	1.2	0.4	44%	62%	24
Bernero,Adam	05	29	aaa	ATL	5	5	10	0	53	71	27	8	16	33	4.56	1.64	24.2	314	2.7	5.7	2.1	1.3	35%	76%	31
	06	30	aaa	KC	6	4	21	1	104	105	49	12	32	51	4.28	1.32	21.0	258	2.8	4.4	1.6	1.0	28%	70%	32
Bevis,P.J.	05	25	a/a	COL	2	6	54	21	59	85	56	13	28	26	8.51	1.93	5.3	331	4.3	3.9	0.9	1.9	34%	57%	-27
Billingsley,Chad	05	21	aa	LA	13	6	28	0	146	122	59	12	47	136	3.64	1.16	21.3	222	2.9	8.4	2.9	0.7	29%	70%	99
	06	22	aaa	LA	6	3	13	0	70	56	30	7	29	69	3.79	1.21	22.3	215	3.7	8.9	2.4	0.9	28%	71%	91
Birkins,Kurt	05	25	aa	BAL	7	11	26	0	129	182	87	12	49	89	6.05	1.79	23.4	326	3.4	6.2	1.8	0.9	38%	66%	40
Birtwell,John	05	26	aa	DET	0	2	29	0	40	51	25	7	17	17	5.68	1.69	6.4	302	3.9	3.9	1.0	1.5	31%	70%	-7
Bittner,Tim	05	25	aa	ANA	1	7	14	0	58	89	48	6	34	31	7.40	2.12	20.9	344	5.3	4.7	0.9	0.9	38%	64%	8
	06	26	aaa	ANA	3	2	35	0	43	86	47	7	38	18	9.86	2.89	7.1	407	7.9	3.8	0.5	1.4	44%	66%	-37
Blackburn,Nick	05	24	a/a	MIN	2	4	10	0	63	63	22	3	13	30	3.14	1.21	26.0	255	1.9	4.3	2.3	0.4	29%	74%	65
	06	25	a/a	MIN	7	8	30	0	132	181	94	15	43	66	6.38	1.70	20.3	319	2.9	4.5	1.5	1.0	35%	62%	20
Blackley,Travis	06	24	a/a	SEA	9	12	27	0	155	172	86	23	53	94	4.99	1.45	25.1	275	3.1	5.5	1.8	1.3	30%	69%	30
Blair,Buddy	05	24	aa	STL	1	6	8	0	36	60	36	6	19	17	8.95	2.19	23.0	363	4.7	4.3	0.9	1.6	39%	59%	-20
Bland,Nate	06	32	aaa	ANA	7	6	32	0	108	151	74	14	26	66	6.13	1.64	14.9	323	2.2	5.5	2.5	1.2	36%	63%	41
Blank,Matt	05	29	aaa	FLA	3	0	13	0	34	38	11	1	10	15	2.91	1.42	11.4	279	2.6	4.1	1.6	0.3	32%	79%	48
	06	31	a/a	SD	4	3	28	0	80	124	63	14	49	34	7.01	2.15	14.5	346	5.5	3.9	0.7	1.5	36%	69%	-22
Boehringer,Brian	06	37	aaa	KC	5	5	18	0	71	108	40	7	13	27	5.07	1.70	18.2	343	1.6	3.4	2.1	0.9	37%	71%	23
Bondurant,Steven	06	26	aa	OAK	12	9	28	0	165	203	99	22	62	98	5.39	1.61	26.7	297	3.4	5.4	1.6	1.2	33%	68%	24
Bonilla,Henry	05	27	aa	MIN	6	7	35	2	118	166	86	16	48	52	6.58	1.82	16.0	326	3.7	4.0	1.1	1.2	35%	65%	0
	06	28	aaa	MIN	3	7	35	1	95	120	71	9	40	49	6.72	1.69	12.5	303	3.8	4.7	1.2	0.8	34%	59%	24
Bonser,Boof	05	24	aaa	MIN	11	9	28	0	160	176	87	23	59	147	4.89	1.47	25.1	274	3.3	8.3	2.5	1.3	33%	70%	63
	06	25	aaa	MIN	6	4	14	0	86	86	40	5	41	70	4.18	1.48	27.0	255	4.3	7.3	1.7	0.5	32%	71%	68

					Actual				Major League Equivalents																
PITCHER	Yr	Age	Lev	Org	w	l	g	sv	ip	h	er	hr	bb	k	era	br/ip	bf/g	oob	ctl	dom	cmd	hr/9	h%	s%	bpv
Booker,Chris	05	29	aaa	CIN	8	4	59	20	65	53	22	2	29	71	2.98	1.26	4.6	217	4.0	9.8	2.4	0.3	31%	76%	112
	06	30	a/a	WAS	2	2	29	0	32	39	18	4	23	33	5.14	1.94	5.4	295	6.5	9.2	1.4	1.0	38%	75%	50
Bootcheck,Chris	05	27	aaa	ANA	7	4	21	0	116	152	69	11	46	73	5.35	1.70	25.6	309	3.6	5.6	1.6	0.9	36%	69%	34
	06	28	aaa	ANA	4	3	40	1	65	94	54	9	34	34	7.41	1.95	7.9	330	4.6	4.7	1.0	1.3	36%	63%	-1
Borkowski,Dave	05	29	aaa	BAL	10	10	29	0	182	269	116	23	40	85	5.74	1.69	29.0	336	2.0	4.2	2.1	1.1	36%	67%	24
Borner,Brady	05	26	aa	PIT	6	1	48	0	90	99	28	9	14	66	2.75	1.25	7.8	273	1.4	6.6	4.8	0.9	32%	82%	113
Borrell,Danny	05	27	aa	NYY	1	1	10	0	38	63	37	10	18	23	8.69	2.14	19.3	362	4.3	5.5	1.3	2.4	39%	63%	-31
	06	28	aa	NYY	3	5	15	0	81	111	67	16	33	48	7.49	1.77	25.3	319	3.6	5.3	1.5	1.7	35%	59%	2
Bostick II,Adam	05	23	aa	FLA	4	3	9	0	44	49	29	3	27	35	5.92	1.72	22.8	276	5.5	7.1	1.3	0.6	34%	64%	52
	06	24	a/a	FLA	9	9	27	0	142	157	70	11	85	126	4.44	1.70	24.3	275	5.4	8.0	1.5	0.7	35%	74%	58
Bott,Glenn	05	24	aa	LA	2	4	25	1	38	38	24	6	25	33	5.70	1.65	7.0	254	6.0	7.8	1.3	1.5	30%	69%	34
Bouknight,Kip	05	27	a/a	WAS	6	6	28	0	137	159	67	19	51	72	4.38	1.53	21.8	284	3.4	4.7	1.4	1.2	31%	75%	19
	06	28	a/a	WAS	9	8	27	0	157	205	110	17	62	84	6.32	1.70	26.9	308	3.6	4.8	1.4	1.0	34%	63%	21
Bowie,Micah	06	32	aaa	WAS	2	0	31	1	42	39	22	0	26	46	4.73	1.55	6.1	241	5.6	9.7	1.7	0.0	35%	66%	102
Bowles,Brian	06	30	aaa	BAL	10	10	30	0	156	216	89	18	62	63	5.13	1.78	24.4	321	3.6	3.6	1.0	1.0	34%	73%	3
Bowyer,Travis	05	24	aaa	MIN	4	2	59	23	74	59	28	4	41	84	3.40	1.35	5.4	214	5.0	10.2	2.0	0.5	31%	75%	102
Boyer,Blaine	05	24	aa	ATL	2	4	14	0	48	75	35	4	19	33	6.50	1.95	16.7	347	3.5	6.2	1.8	0.8	41%	66%	36
Braden,Dallas	05	22	aa	OAK	9	5	16	0	97	111	44	5	30	61	4.08	1.45	26.5	282	2.8	5.7	2.0	0.5	33%	71%	61
Bradley,David	05	28	aa	MIL	6	5	35	0	104	138	55	13	40	58	4.75	1.70	13.8	311	3.5	5.0	1.4	1.1	35%	74%	20
	06	29	aa	OAK	6	11	31	0	131	232	123	15	75	52	8.42	2.34	22.2	377	5.1	3.6	0.7	1.0	41%	63%	-15
Brandenburg,Adam	06	25	aa	FLA	1	2	21	0	34	62	41	4	24	16	10.82	2.53	8.9	384	6.4	4.3	0.7	1.2	42%	55%	-17
Brannon,Nick	05	27	aa	OAK	1	1	26	0	36	41	22	4	37	22	5.41	2.17	7.1	280	9.3	5.6	0.6	0.9	32%	76%	18
Braun,Ryan	06	23	a/a	KC	1	8	43	13	65	59	19	2	27	70	2.62	1.32	6.4	237	3.7	9.7	2.6	0.3	33%	80%	112
Bray,Bill	06	23	aaa	WAS	4	1	21	5	31	29	17	5	9	38	4.90	1.22	6.1	241	2.6	11.0	4.2	1.4	32%	64%	118
Bray,Steve	05	25	a/a	KC	1	1	21	0	32	43	16	2	11	37	4.61	1.70	7.1	315	3.2	10.3	3.3	0.6	43%	73%	105
	06	26	a/a	MIL	7	4	50	1	85	86	32	9	13	64	3.34	1.16	6.9	258	1.3	6.7	5.0	1.0	30%	75%	120
Brazelton,Dewon	05	25	a/a	TAM	2	2	6	0	32	35	14	3	14	26	3.85	1.51	23.6	271	3.8	7.2	1.9	0.9	33%	77%	57
	06	26	aaa	SD	5	7	17	0	91	105	45	11	24	46	4.48	1.41	23.2	283	2.3	4.5	1.9	1.1	31%	71%	32
Breslow,Craig	05	25	a/a	SD	2	2	47	0	61	55	22	3	18	48	3.26	1.19	5.3	235	2.6	7.1	2.7	0.5	29%	73%	94
	06	26	aaa	BOS	7	1	39	7	67	63	29	4	26	65	3.88	1.32	7.3	243	3.5	8.7	2.5	0.6	32%	71%	95
Bridges,Donnie	05	27	a/a	WAS	3	9	18	0	89	124	60	10	51	54	6.07	1.97	24.2	324	5.2	5.5	1.1	1.0	37%	70%	15
Brito,Eude	05	24	aaa	PHI	6	2	28	0	98	108	61	15	38	64	5.60	1.49	15.4	274	3.5	5.9	1.7	1.4	30%	65%	30
	06	28	aaa	PHI	10	8	26	1	147	161	87	18	65	80	5.33	1.53	25.2	273	3.9	4.9	1.2	1.1	30%	67%	22
Broadway,Lance	06	23	a/a	CHW	8	8	26	0	160	202	68	15	44	100	3.82	1.54	27.4	302	2.5	5.6	2.3	0.8	35%	77%	51
Brock,Chris	05	36	aaa	TAM	2	5	15	1	36	57	23	5	12	22	5.76	1.89	11.6	350	2.9	5.4	1.9	1.3	39%	72%	18
Brooks,Conor	05	27	aa	BOS	4	2	51	2	67	105	55	5	22	30	7.42	1.88	6.3	348	2.9	4.0	1.4	0.6	39%	58%	19
Brooks,Frank	05	27	aaa	ATL	3	4	55	0	57	48	16	3	22	41	2.48	1.23	4.3	225	3.5	6.4	1.8	0.5	27%	81%	73
	06	28	a/a	KC	2	8	34	0	104	141	76	24	53	69	6.61	1.86	14.6	317	4.6	6.0	1.3	2.0	34%	69%	-6
Broshuis,Garrett	06	25	aa	SF	7	10	27	0	152	216	135	17	47	85	7.98	1.73	26.2	327	2.8	5.0	1.8	1.0	37%	52%	27
Brower,Jim	06	34	aaa	SD	5	3	39	1	52	62	28	7	21	34	4.90	1.59	6.0	289	3.6	5.9	1.6	1.3	33%	72%	28
Brownlie,Robert	05	25	aaa	CHC	6	7	27	0	104	106	60	12	41	64	5.19	1.41	16.7	259	3.5	5.5	1.6	1.0	29%	64%	38
	06	26	a/a	CHC	3	14	41	0	86	178	101	18	50	52	10.56	2.64	11.7	414	5.2	5.5	1.0	1.9	46%	60%	-29
Brown,Andrew	05	25	aaa	CLE	4	2	49	4	69	55	27	6	18	71	3.51	1.05	5.6	214	2.3	9.2	3.9	0.8	28%	69%	127
	06	26	aaa	CLE	5	4	39	5	62	62	23	5	38	47	3.37	1.61	7.2	254	5.6	6.7	1.2	0.7	31%	81%	48
Broxton,Jonathan	05	21	aa	LA	5	3	33	5	96	83	35	4	29	90	3.27	1.16	11.9	228	2.7	8.4	3.1	0.4	30%	71%	114
Bruback,Matt	05	27	a/a	BAL	5	7	30	0	128	182	96	21	36	74	6.72	1.70	19.7	328	2.5	5.2	2.1	1.5	36%	62%	20
	06	28	aa	BAL	1	4	18	0	43	77	39	5	11	32	8.07	2.05	11.9	380	2.3	6.8	3.0	1.0	45%	59%	52
Bruksch,Jeffrey	05	25	a/a	CIN	4	9	28	0	95	100	55	13	66	67	5.17	1.75	15.9	265	6.3	6.4	1.0	1.2	30%	73%	26
Brunet,Michael	05	29	a/a	ANA	7	4	33	0	47	78	44	5	21	31	8.30	2.09	7.2	360	4.0	6.0	1.5	0.9	42%	59%	23
Buchholz,Taylor	05	24	aaa	HOU	6	0	19	0	74	84	45	14	24	36	5.46	1.46	17.1	279	2.9	4.4	1.5	1.7	29%	67%	6
	06	25	aaa	HOU	1	3	7	0	44	53	28	2	17	31	5.73	1.59	28.4	292	3.5	6.3	1.8	0.4	35%	62%	61
Buckner,Billy	06	23	aa	KC	5	3	13	0	75	87	43	6	36	53	5.18	1.63	26.3	283	4.3	6.4	1.5	0.7	34%	68%	46
Bucktrot,Keith	05	25	aa	PHI	3	4	11	0	62	94	52	14	27	28	7.49	1.95	27.5	341	4.0	4.0	1.0	2.0	35%	65%	-28
Bueno,Francisley	06	26	aa	ATL	1	7	17	0	80	106	50	13	23	67	5.62	1.61	21.3	311	2.6	7.5	2.9	1.5	37%	68%	53
Buglovsky,Chris	05	26	aaa	SEA	3	5	34	0	105	129	57	7	39	63	4.84	1.61	14.0	296	3.4	5.4	1.6	0.6	34%	69%	44
Bukvich,Ryan	06	28	aaa	TEX	3	2	31	0	35	60	39	13	26	30	9.93	2.45	6.1	370	6.6	7.6	1.2	3.3	41%	65%	-48
Bulger,Jason	05	27	aaa	ARI	3	6	56	4	56	56	24	3	26	49	3.81	1.45	4.4	254	4.1	7.8	1.9	0.5	32%	74%	76
	06	28	aaa	ANA	2	2	27	4	34	34	20	0	15	35	5.28	1.42	5.5	253	3.9	9.3	2.4	0.0	36%	59%	110
Bullard,Jim	05	26	a/a	CHW	5	5	23	0	77	103	64	18	42	48	7.49	1.88	16.1	314	4.9	5.5	1.1	2.1	33%	64%	-13
	06	27	aa	TOR	3	2	42	2	39	59	24	6	24	33	5.54	2.11	4.7	339	5.5	7.6	1.4	1.3	41%	76%	22
Bullinger,Kirk	05	36	aaa	PIT	2	7	55	4	69	82	29	7	15	32	3.84	1.40	5.4	290	1.9	4.2	2.2	1.0	32%	75%	40
Bullington,Bryan	05	25	aaa	PIT	9	5	18	0	109	113	45	10	23	69	3.71	1.25	25.3	262	1.9	5.7	3.0	0.8	30%	72%	75
Bumatay,Mike	05	26	a/a	DET	2	4	53	2	68	71	36	8	38	64	4.73	1.59	5.8	262	5.0	8.4	1.7	1.1	33%	73%	55
	06	27	a/a	BOS	2	4	53	3	56	87	54	7	44	38	8.67	2.34	5.6	348	7.0	6.1	0.9	1.1	40%	62%	7
Bumstead,Michael	05	28	a/a	SEA	2	6	34	0	81	126	64	5	48	32	7.05	2.15	12.1	347	5.4	3.6	0.7	0.5	38%	65%	5
	06	29	a/a	TEX	1	2	34	5	56	60	20	0	26	39	3.12	1.52	7.3	267	4.1	6.3	1.5	0.0	33%	77%	72
Bumstead,Nathan	06	24	aa	DET	7	14	27	0	158	216	120	17	85	105	6.84	1.91	28.2	319	4.9	6.0	1.2	1.0	37%	64%	24
Burba,Dave	05	39	aaa	HOU	4	3	18	0	35	53	21	1	9	17	5.40	1.77	9.1	339	2.4	4.4	1.8	0.3	39%	67%	43
Burch,Jason	06	24	aa	COL	3	4	45	0	63	75	46	7	28	43	6.61	1.63	6.4	290	4.0	6.1	1.5	1.0	33%	59%	35
Burke,Erick	05	28	a/a	PHI	6	2	57	3	72	81	35	5	40	56	4.41	1.68	5.8	278	5.0	7.0	1.4	0.6	34%	74%	53
	06	29	aaa	SD	3	3	49	0	80	88	40	8	46	64	4.44	1.67	7.5	273	5.2	7.2	1.4	0.9	33%	75%	46
Burnett,Sean	06	24	aaa	PIT	8	11	25	0	120	168	97	16	49	39	7.27	1.81	22.7	324	3.7	2.9	0.8	1.2	34%	60%	-11
Burnside,Adrian	05	29	aaa	TOR	4	4	50	0	57	63	25	5	17	37	3.90	1.41	4.9	276	2.7	5.9	2.2	0.8	32%	74%	55
	06	30	aaa	TOR	3	0	33	0	33	35	20	5	15	25	5.36	1.52	4.5	266	4.2	6.9	1.7	1.5	30%	68%	33
Burns,Mike	05	27	aaa	HOU	2	1	25	13	30	25	8	4	4	27	2.53	0.98	4.7	224	1.3	8.0	6.3	1.3	27%	83%	153
	06	28	aaa	CIN	6	1	40	0	56	61	16	4	14	41	2.58	1.34	6.0	272	2.2	6.6	2.9	0.7	33%	83%	81
Burres,Brian	05	24	aa	SF	9	6	26	0	128	155	75	13	59	85	5.25	1.67	22.6	292	4.1	5.9	1.4	0.9	34%	69%	36
	06	26	aaa	BAL	10	6	26	0	139	167	84	19	61	98	5.43	1.64	24.4	291	3.9	6.3	1.6	1.2	33%	69%	32
Burton,Jared	06	25	aa	OAK	6	5	53	1	74	88	43	8	29	50	5.27	1.58	6.3	289	3.5	6.1	1.7	0.9	34%	67%	42

PITCHER	Yr	Age	Lev	Org	Actual				Major League Equivalents																
					w	l	g	sv	ip	h	er	hr	bb	k	era	br/ip	bf/g	oob	ctl	dom	cmd	hr/9	h%	s%	bpv
Bush,David	05	26	aaa	TOR	2	2	9	0	55	75	33	7	9	35	5.45	1.52	27.2	318	1.5	5.7	3.8	1.2	36%	66%	71
Bush,Paul	05	26	aa	ATL	2	0	19	1	52	37	19	2	24	41	3.26	1.17	11.2	194	4.2	7.0	1.7	0.4	24%	72%	81
	06	27	a/a	ATL	5	9	37	0	98	129	77	16	48	74	7.06	1.80	12.5	310	4.4	6.8	1.5	1.5	36%	62%	22
Butto,Francisco	05	23	aa	PHI	2	5	36	3	56	69	30	12	22	46	4.79	1.61	7.1	296	3.5	7.3	2.1	2.0	33%	78%	24
	06	26	a/a	NYY	3	2	32	0	78	98	39	6	36	47	4.48	1.71	11.3	300	4.1	5.4	1.3	0.6	35%	74%	36
Buzachero,Edward	05	24	aa	TOR	4	4	45	0	77	104	54	18	35	66	6.26	1.80	8.1	316	4.0	7.6	1.9	2.1	36%	70%	15
	06	25	aa	CLE	8	3	49	4	79	94	32	2	29	57	3.67	1.56	7.2	290	3.3	6.5	2.0	0.3	36%	75%	69
Bynum,Mike	05	28	a/a	DET	5	1	13	0	50	61	32	8	24	35	5.77	1.69	17.8	294	4.3	6.2	1.4	1.4	33%	69%	21
Byrdak,Tim	05	32	aaa	BAL	3	2	37	11	38	28	12	5	16	36	2.73	1.16	4.2	203	3.7	8.5	2.3	1.2	24%	84%	76
Cabrera,Fernando	05	24	aaa	CLE	6	1	30	3	51	38	7	3	11	59	1.23	0.96	6.6	203	1.9	10.4	5.4	0.5	29%	91%	174
Cain,Matt	05	21	aaa	SF	10	5	26	0	145	104	59	15	56	171	3.67	1.10	22.5	198	3.4	10.6	3.1	0.9	27%	69%	116
Cali,Carmen	05	27	aaa	STL	4	5	49	2	58	82	39	5	27	39	6.08	1.88	5.7	327	4.2	6.0	1.4	0.8	38%	67%	32
	06	28	a/a	STL	1	6	50	1	66	103	41	6	39	41	5.63	2.16	6.7	349	5.3	5.6	1.0	0.8	40%	74%	17
Camacho,Eddie	06	24	aa	NYM	3	4	53	1	79	92	46	7	27	49	5.27	1.50	6.6	284	3.1	5.6	1.8	0.8	33%	65%	45
Cameron,Kevin	05	26	aa	MIN	6	2	43	6	79	97	32	9	31	47	3.67	1.62	8.3	295	3.5	5.3	1.5	1.0	33%	80%	29
	06	27	aaa	MIN	6	4	40	9	66	69	33	3	31	53	4.49	1.51	7.3	264	4.2	7.3	1.7	0.4	33%	69%	69
Cameron,Ryan	05	28	aa	PHI	6	5	57	18	88	103	40	18	40	66	4.09	1.62	7.0	285	4.1	6.8	1.7	1.8	32%	82%	20
	06	29	aaa	PHI	6	2	45	7	59	68	36	7	37	35	5.52	1.79	6.2	283	5.7	5.3	0.9	1.0	32%	70%	19
Campbell,Brett	06	25	a/a	WAS	0	4	28	8	35	35	18	1	24	32	4.51	1.68	5.7	255	6.1	8.2	1.3	0.3	34%	71%	74
Campillo,Jorge	05	27	aaa	SEA	4	1	12	0	66	72	23	5	19	37	3.15	1.37	23.6	271	2.6	5.0	2.0	0.7	31%	79%	51
Camp,Shawn	05	30	aaa	KC	3	6	21	1	67	85	33	8	22	34	4.42	1.59	14.4	301	2.9	4.5	1.5	1.0	33%	74%	23
Candelario,Eddie	05	28	aa	PIT	3	4	13	0	75	102	36	6	17	42	4.34	1.59	26.0	319	2.0	5.0	2.5	0.7	36%	73%	51
Cannon,Jon	05	31	aaa	ARI	3	5	15	0	73	86	40	12	44	36	4.92	1.78	22.9	286	5.5	4.4	0.8	1.5	30%	76%	-4
Capellan,Jose	05	25	aaa	MIL	5	3	36	6	90	93	41	4	40	66	4.09	1.47	11.0	261	4.0	6.6	1.7	0.4	32%	71%	65
Caraccioli,Lance	05	28	aa	CIN	5	5	15	0	68	84	39	7	35	42	5.10	1.75	21.2	298	4.6	5.6	1.2	1.0	34%	72%	26
Carlson,Jesse	05	25	a/a	TOR	4	3	60	5	57	66	25	8	13	50	3.91	1.39	4.1	284	2.1	8.0	3.8	1.3	34%	77%	86
	06	26	a/a	TEX	6	5	53	3	69	93	44	11	24	41	5.77	1.69	6.0	315	3.2	5.3	1.7	1.4	35%	68%	18
Carlyle,Buddy	05	28	aaa	LA	1	2	20	2	48	49	22	5	18	42	4.14	1.40	10.4	261	3.4	7.8	2.3	1.0	32%	73%	69
Carmona,Fausto	05	22	a/a	CLE	13	9	27	0	173	183	74	14	33	97	3.86	1.25	26.7	266	1.7	5.0	2.9	0.7	30%	70%	71
Carnes,Matt	05	30	aaa	TAM	5	1	37	0	54	61	29	3	16	30	4.80	1.41	6.3	279	2.6	4.9	1.9	0.6	32%	65%	52
Carrara,Giovanni	06	39	aaa	PIT	3	2	30	4	40	35	20	4	17	27	4.49	1.29	5.6	229	3.8	6.0	1.6	0.9	26%	67%	50
Carrillo,Cesar	05	21	aa	SD	4	0	5	0	30	25	12	2	7	32	3.58	1.06	24.0	221	2.1	9.5	4.6	0.6	30%	67%	146
	06	22	a/a	SD	1	3	10	0	53	51	21	4	18	39	3.56	1.30	22.4	248	3.1	6.6	2.2	0.7	30%	74%	70
Carter,Lance	05	31	aaa	TAM	1	5	8	0	35	46	21	8	12	23	5.43	1.65	20.0	308	3.1	6.0	1.9	2.0	33%	73%	10
	06	32	aaa	LA	2	4	45	13	57	63	26	7	16	41	4.15	1.38	5.5	275	2.5	6.4	2.6	1.2	32%	74%	58
Carvajal,Marcos	06	22	aa	TAM	2	2	39	0	72	84	46	9	44	59	5.74	1.78	8.7	285	5.5	7.4	1.3	1.1	34%	69%	37
Casadiego,Gerardo	06	26	aa	NYY	2	3	22	1	34	33	12	1	17	24	3.24	1.47	6.8	251	4.4	6.4	1.5	0.3	31%	77%	65
Casilla,Santiago	05	23	a/a	OAK	3	6	54	26	65	58	28	7	27	88	3.88	1.31	5.1	234	3.7	12.2	3.3	1.0	35%	73%	121
	06	24	aaa	OAK	2	0	25	4	33	27	13	2	9	27	3.55	1.09	5.3	219	2.5	7.4	3.0	0.5	27%	68%	102
Cassel,Jack	05	25	a/a	SD	6	5	47	1	82	109	39	2	33	44	4.27	1.73	8.1	314	3.6	4.8	1.3	0.2	36%	74%	42
	06	26	a/a	SD	9	8	30	0	155	196	91	14	51	95	5.29	1.59	23.3	302	3.0	5.5	1.8	0.8	35%	67%	41
Cassidy,Scott	05	30	aaa	BOS	6	4	43	11	79	80	41	7	32	66	4.63	1.42	8.0	258	3.6	7.6	2.1	0.8	32%	68%	70
Castellanos,Jonathan	06	25	a/a	ARI	3	1	25	0	38	42	25	6	15	20	5.98	1.50	6.7	275	3.5	4.7	1.4	1.5	29%	63%	12
Castillo,Frank	05	36	aaa	FLA	9	11	27	0	143	172	87	17	57	69	5.49	1.60	23.9	291	3.6	4.4	1.2	1.1	32%	67%	17
Cavazos,Andy	06	26	aaa	STL	1	5	44	4	56	56	28	2	16	48	4.54	1.28	5.4	253	2.6	7.6	2.9	0.3	33%	62%	102
Cave,Kevin	05	25	aa	FLA	5	3	37	1	42	41	27	1	29	29	5.70	1.66	5.2	251	6.2	6.2	1.0	0.2	31%	63%	56
	06	26	aa	FLA	3	2	43	5	51	77	38	8	45	34	6.68	2.38	6.3	340	7.9	6.0	0.8	1.4	38%	74%	-4
Cedeno,Juan	06	23	aa	KC	2	9	37	2	90	102	64	7	72	55	6.38	1.93	11.8	280	7.2	5.5	0.8	0.7	32%	66%	27
Cerda,Jaime	05	27	aaa	KC	4	1	35	2	49	53	31	5	20	40	5.66	1.47	6.2	268	3.6	7.3	2.0	0.9	32%	62%	59
	06	28	aaa	COL	3	3	36	1	45	59	39	11	26	33	7.76	1.89	6.0	309	5.2	6.6	1.3	2.1	34%	62%	-3
Chantres,Carlos	05	29	a/a	PHI	5	12	27	0	147	229	111	29	71	55	6.79	2.04	27.0	348	4.3	3.4	0.8	1.8	36%	70%	-32
Chavez,Jesse	05	22	aa	TEX	4	3	31	1	57	84	47	13	25	23	7.42	1.91	8.9	335	3.9	3.6	0.9	2.1	34%	65%	-33
	06	23	a/a	PIT	4	6	51	4	78	86	47	6	37	74	5.42	1.58	6.9	274	4.3	8.5	2.0	0.7	35%	65%	73
Chavez,Wilton	05	24	aaa	COL	4	7	27	0	106	133	60	7	36	64	5.09	1.59	17.7	301	3.1	5.4	1.8	0.6	35%	67%	47
	06	25	aaa	MIL	6	4	40	0	85	108	62	14	45	53	6.60	1.79	10.0	302	4.8	5.6	1.2	1.5	33%	65%	9
Chenard,Kenneth	05	27	a/a	NYM	8	8	23	0	110	139	77	17	55	72	6.30	1.76	22.4	302	4.5	5.9	1.3	1.4	34%	66%	15
Cherry,Rocky	06	27	a/a	CHC	5	1	33	2	51	67	25	5	20	40	4.45	1.69	7.1	309	3.4	7.0	2.0	0.8	37%	75%	54
Chiasson,Scott	05	28	a/a	COL	0	2	26	0	35	55	42	8	21	31	10.89	2.18	6.9	351	5.4	8.1	1.5	2.1	41%	50%	1
	06	29	aaa	CIN	3	2	60	29	61	54	20	4	34	37	2.91	1.44	4.4	232	5.0	5.5	1.1	0.6	27%	82%	45
Chiavacci,Ron	06	29	a/a	PIT	5	7	27	0	99	144	72	16	38	57	6.53	1.83	17.5	332	3.4	5.2	1.5	1.4	37%	66%	9
Chick,Travis	05	21	aa	CIN	3	11	26	0	137	159	85	18	61	90	5.58	1.60	23.9	284	4.0	5.9	1.5	1.2	32%	67%	29
	06	22	aa	CIN	8	7	27	0	151	161	87	18	75	101	5.18	1.56	25.1	267	4.5	6.0	1.3	1.1	31%	68%	34
Chico,Matt	05	22	aa	ARI	1	7	10	0	52	86	43	10	15	32	7.41	1.93	25.3	361	2.6	5.5	2.1	1.7	40%	64%	9
	06	23	aa	WAS	9	2	17	0	103	108	37	11	32	62	3.24	1.36	25.9	265	2.8	5.4	1.9	1.0	30%	80%	46
Childers,Jason	05	31	aaa	ATL	1	2	37	15	37	40	12	2	22	24	2.96	1.67	4.6	269	5.4	5.9	1.1	0.5	32%	83%	43
	06	32	aaa	TAM	2	3	39	2	52	73	40	9	24	31	6.91	1.86	6.4	323	4.2	5.4	1.3	1.6	35%	65%	1
Childers,Matt	05	27	aaa	ATL	4	2	50	2	71	82	41	5	22	50	5.22	1.46	6.2	284	2.7	6.4	2.3	0.7	34%	64%	66
	06	28	a/a	NYY	4	7	36	0	111	162	90	20	37	57	7.26	1.79	14.5	333	3.0	4.6	1.5	1.6	36%	61%	1
Childress,Daylan	05	27	a/a	MIN	3	5	45	2	91	116	84	11	48	57	8.30	1.81	9.6	304	4.8	5.6	1.2	1.1	34%	53%	18
Choate,Randy	05	30	aaa	ARI	1	1	47	3	40	52	18	4	22	16	4.00	1.86	4.1	309	5.0	3.6	0.7	1.0	33%	81%	0
	06	31	aaa	ARI	6	0	43	8	45	46	14	0	11	37	2.72	1.26	4.4	260	2.1	7.4	3.5	0.0	34%	76%	121
Choi,Hyang-Nam	06	36	aaa	CLE	8	5	34	0	106	117	38	5	39	87	3.21	1.47	13.7	274	3.3	7.4	2.2	0.4	35%	78%	78
Chulk,Vinnie	06	28	aaa	TOR	3	2	19	1	32	25	12	5	16	35	3.26	1.28	7.1	213	4.4	9.9	2.2	1.5	27%	82%	74
Clippard,Tyler	06	22	aa	NYY	12	10	28	0	166	144	85	18	60	145	4.61	1.23	24.6	229	3.3	7.9	2.4	1.0	28%	64%	78
Clontz,Brad	06	35	aaa	FLA	6	5	57	23	58	64	25	4	27	47	3.92	1.58	4.6	275	4.2	7.2	1.7	0.7	34%	76%	59
Coenen,Matt	05	26	aa	ATL	3	9	19	0	95	142	76	10	48	41	7.14	2.00	24.6	338	4.5	3.8	0.8	0.9	37%	64%	-0
Collazo,Willie	05	26	a/a	ANA	1	6	37	0	95	124	78	21	37	56	7.38	1.70	11.9	309	3.5	5.3	1.5	2.0	33%	59%	-3
	06	27	a/a	NYM	10	9	25	0	160	203	98	14	34	81	5.50	1.49	28.2	303	1.9	4.6	2.4	0.8	34%	63%	47
Colome,Jesus	06	29	a/a	NYY	3	1	28	0	38	52	24	6	22	19	5.57	1.95	6.6	318	5.3	4.4	0.8	1.4	34%	74%	-6

Major League Equivalent Statistics

PITCHER	Yr	Age	Lev	Org	Actual				Major League Equivalents																
					w	l	g	sv	ip	h	er	hr	bb	k	era	br/ip	bf/g	oob	ctl	dom	cmd	hr/9	h%	s%	bpv
Colyer,Steve	06	28	a/a	COL	2	3	54	1	63	83	62	14	56	42	8.85	2.20	6.0	310	8.0	6.0	0.7	2.0	34%	61%	-15
Condrey,Clay	05	30	aaa	PHI	7	8	25	0	132	196	78	16	31	57	5.32	1.71	24.5	336	2.1	3.9	1.9	1.1	36%	71%	17
	06	31	aaa	PHI	4	2	39	6	51	59	19	2	18	21	3.33	1.50	5.8	283	3.1	3.6	1.2	0.4	31%	78%	33
Connolly,Jonathan	06	23	a/a	DET	3	4	11	0	63	97	57	7	17	33	8.12	1.80	27.1	345	2.4	4.7	1.9	1.0	38%	53%	25
Connolly,Michael	05	23	a/a	PIT	7	10	28	0	155	180	74	13	48	88	4.29	1.47	24.3	284	2.8	5.1	1.8	0.8	32%	72%	45
	06	24	a/a	PIT	8	10	29	0	136	171	109	24	63	81	7.22	1.72	21.8	301	4.2	5.3	1.3	1.6	33%	59%	7
Cook,Jeremy	05	27	aa	STL	3	8	37	0	103	175	76	12	29	40	6.63	1.97	13.6	367	2.5	3.5	1.4	1.1	39%	67%	-0
Cooper,Brian	05	31	aaa	SF	7	8	29	0	137	148	69	18	51	66	4.56	1.45	20.7	271	3.3	4.3	1.3	1.2	29%	72%	19
	06	32	aaa	SF	4	9	27	0	123	164	76	22	41	58	5.54	1.67	20.9	314	3.0	4.2	1.4	1.6	33%	71%	-1
Cooper,Chris	05	27	a/a	CLE	4	1	55	8	72	84	28	8	23	59	3.47	1.50	5.8	287	2.9	7.3	2.5	1.0	35%	80%	65
Corcoran,Roy	05	25	aaa	WAS	4	4	51	3	67	70	36	6	32	47	4.87	1.52	5.8	262	4.3	6.2	1.4	0.8	31%	68%	46
	06	26	a/a	WAS	2	6	49	27	59	46	13	1	40	59	2.03	1.45	5.3	209	6.1	8.9	1.5	0.2	29%	86%	92
Corcoran,Tim	05	27	aaa	TAM	5	1	29	0	56	53	18	2	21	40	2.88	1.32	8.2	243	3.4	6.4	1.9	0.3	30%	78%	74
	06	28	aaa	TAM	5	1	19	1	37	38	11	2	11	25	2.60	1.30	8.3	257	2.6	6.1	2.3	0.5	31%	81%	73
Corey,Bryan	05	32	aaa	FLA	3	6	44	0	60	83	51	9	20	38	7.58	1.72	6.3	322	3.0	5.7	1.9	1.4	36%	56%	22
	06	33	a/a	BOS	1	0	28	15	37	41	13	3	11	31	3.23	1.41	5.7	275	2.7	7.4	2.8	0.8	34%	80%	78
Corey,Mark	05	31	aaa	PIT	5	5	61	28	65	74	36	7	23	46	4.92	1.50	4.7	282	3.2	6.4	2.0	0.9	33%	68%	50
	06	32	aaa	NYY	7	4	53	8	81	97	53	5	31	53	5.85	1.57	6.9	291	3.4	5.9	1.7	0.6	34%	61%	51
Cormier,Lance	06	26	aaa	ATL	4	3	9	0	54	81	34	5	15	23	5.65	1.79	28.4	340	2.6	3.9	1.5	0.9	37%	69%	16
Cornejo,Nate	05	26	aa	DET	4	12	19	0	102	153	64	16	18	37	5.69	1.68	24.7	340	1.6	3.3	2.1	1.4	35%	69%	9
Corpas,Manuel	06	24	a/a	COL	2	1	42	19	45	32	6	1	6	36	1.20	0.84	4.0	195	1.2	7.2	6.0	0.2	25%	86%	179
Correia,Kevin	05	25	aaa	SF	3	2	31	7	46	52	30	5	20	30	5.93	1.56	6.6	277	4.0	5.8	1.5	1.0	32%	62%	36
Cortez,Renee	05	23	aa	SEA	5	3	44	10	63	69	33	4	24	57	4.70	1.47	6.3	272	3.4	8.1	2.4	0.6	35%	67%	82
	06	24	aaa	SEA	5	3	31	5	51	68	28	3	29	45	4.92	1.89	8.0	313	5.1	7.9	1.6	0.5	40%	73%	57
Costello,Ryan	05	26	aa	MIL	0	5	9	0	32	69	47	6	16	15	13.25	2.66	19.8	425	4.5	4.2	0.9	1.6	46%	48%	-34
Coutlangus,Jonathan	06	26	a/a	CIN	1	3	51	9	65	54	28	0	37	47	3.92	1.39	5.5	220	5.1	6.4	1.3	0.0	28%	69%	76
Cox,J.B.	06	22	aa	NYY	6	2	41	3	77	66	21	3	26	50	2.45	1.19	7.7	227	3.0	5.8	1.9	0.4	27%	80%	75
Crawford,Tristan	06	24	aa	MIN	6	5	46	2	98	114	58	11	39	78	5.31	1.56	9.5	284	3.6	7.1	2.0	1.0	34%	67%	54
Cressend,Jack	05	30	aaa	BOS	5	5	40	0	69	98	49	17	24	52	6.37	1.77	8.1	326	3.2	6.8	2.1	2.2	36%	69%	10
Crockett,Ben	05	26	a/a	COL	0	0	19	0	39	60	24	1	12	18	5.56	1.83	9.8	344	2.7	4.1	1.6	0.2	39%	67%	37
Cromer,Jason	05	25	aa	TAM	5	7	21	0	118	149	73	15	35	55	5.54	1.56	25.2	302	2.6	4.2	1.6	1.1	33%	66%	19
	06	26	a/a	TAM	4	6	32	0	106	132	51	6	52	64	4.29	1.73	15.4	298	4.4	5.4	1.2	0.5	35%	75%	38
Crowder,Justin	06	27	aa	OAK	1	2	41	2	47	67	35	8	22	31	6.69	1.90	5.5	330	4.2	5.9	1.4	1.6	37%	67%	6
Crowell,Jim	05	31	aaa	FLA	2	4	55	12	60	58	18	5	14	38	2.68	1.19	4.5	248	2.0	5.7	2.8	0.8	29%	81%	74
	06	32	aaa	PHI	2	3	40	2	73	112	49	8	25	34	6.08	1.87	8.8	343	3.1	4.2	1.4	1.0	37%	68%	9
Crowell,Kyle	05	26	aa	OAK	3	1	39	0	65	78	30	8	23	37	4.13	1.55	7.5	291	3.2	5.1	1.6	1.1	32%	77%	27
Cruceta,Francisco	05	24	aaa	SEA	7	5	32	0	111	139	64	16	33	93	5.18	1.55	15.5	300	2.7	7.5	2.8	1.3	36%	69%	61
	06	25	aaa	SEA	13	9	28	0	160	170	91	27	79	164	5.11	1.55	25.6	266	4.4	9.2	2.1	1.5	33%	71%	55
Cruz,Juan	05	25	aaa	OAK	5	1	13	0	75	55	21	4	26	77	2.52	1.08	23.1	201	3.1	9.2	3.0	0.5	27%	78%	118
Cruz,Nelson	05	33	aaa	DET	5	4	14	0	64	83	39	8	17	46	5.47	1.56	20.5	308	2.4	6.4	2.7	1.2	36%	67%	53
Cullen,Ryan	06	27	a/a	NYM	5	4	39	1	68	74	39	7	21	45	5.15	1.41	7.5	273	2.8	6.0	2.1	0.9	32%	64%	54
Cummings,Jeremy	05	29	a/a	STL	12	4	26	0	122	131	62	15	42	72	4.60	1.42	20.4	268	3.1	5.3	1.7	1.1	30%	70%	35
	06	30	aaa	PHI	8	6	25	0	138	169	104	31	58	77	6.80	1.65	25.2	296	3.8	5.0	1.3	2.0	31%	63%	-6
Cunnane,Will	05	31	aaa	HOU	1	5	51	8	65	91	41	11	26	43	5.67	1.79	6.0	322	3.6	5.9	1.6	1.5	36%	71%	16
Curtis,Dan	05	26	a/a	ATL	5	10	27	0	118	160	78	6	48	54	5.93	1.76	20.5	317	3.7	4.1	1.1	0.5	36%	65%	25
	06	27	a/a	ATL	5	10	28	0	153	218	119	13	80	83	6.99	1.94	26.6	328	4.7	4.9	1.0	0.8	37%	63%	17
Cyr,Eric	05	27	aaa	ANA	5	5	38	1	99	137	62	12	26	49	5.62	1.65	11.9	322	2.3	4.5	1.9	1.1	35%	67%	24
Daigle,Casey	05	24	aa	ARI	9	3	57	18	63	91	24	4	19	42	3.45	1.73	5.2	329	2.7	6.0	2.2	0.6	39%	81%	53
	06	26	aaa	ARI	3	5	42	4	48	68	29	7	16	36	5.49	1.75	5.3	326	3.0	6.7	2.2	1.3	38%	71%	37
Danks,John	05	20	aa	TEX	4	10	18	0	98	131	74	15	32	77	6.82	1.67	25.0	315	3.0	7.0	2.4	1.4	37%	60%	42
	06	21	a/a	TEX	9	9	27	0	140	166	89	30	56	140	5.69	1.59	23.4	288	3.6	9.0	2.5	1.9	35%	69%	46
Dannemiller,Beau	05	26	a/a	LA	1	3	56	6	80	77	48	9	49	55	5.45	1.58	6.4	248	5.6	6.2	1.1	1.1	28%	67%	34
Darensbourg,Vic	05	35	aaa	DET	2	0	44	7	30	20	1	0	12	25	0.31	1.05	2.7	185	3.5	7.4	2.1	0.0	25%	97%	107
	06	36	aaa	CLE	1	5	33	0	41	51	24	2	17	33	5.30	1.64	5.7	296	3.7	7.3	2.0	0.5	37%	66%	67
Davidson,Daniel	05	25	aa	ANA	13	5	28	0	154	199	88	21	44	87	5.16	1.58	24.8	307	2.6	5.1	2.0	1.2	34%	70%	29
	06	26	a/a	ANA	3	10	33	0	136	197	93	16	47	64	6.12	1.79	19.5	331	3.1	4.2	1.3	1.0	36%	66%	11
Davies,Kyle	05	22	aaa	ATL	5	2	13	0	73	72	33	7	32	57	4.10	1.43	24.5	253	4.0	7.0	1.8	0.8	31%	73%	58
Davis,Allen	05	30	a/a	PHI	14	10	29	0	187	291	112	30	26	69	5.39	1.69	29.8	348	1.2	3.3	2.7	1.5	36%	71%	18
	06	31	a/a	PHI	8	8	26	0	140	214	118	39	48	65	7.57	1.87	25.8	344	3.1	4.2	1.4	2.5	35%	65%	-35
Davis,Jason	05	25	aaa	CLE	8	5	16	0	95	112	51	8	26	66	4.77	1.45	26.0	287	2.5	6.3	2.5	0.8	34%	67%	65
Davis,Kane	05	30	aaa	MIL	4	2	45	1	62	58	20	6	24	64	2.89	1.32	5.9	241	3.5	9.2	2.6	0.8	32%	81%	93
Davis,Lance	06	30	a/a	DET	3	3	30	1	69	115	54	10	16	26	7.00	1.90	11.1	363	2.1	3.3	1.6	1.3	38%	64%	-4
Day,Zach	05	27	a/a	COL	3	3	10	0	49	80	40	7	17	20	7.36	1.99	24.1	359	3.2	3.7	1.2	1.3	38%	63%	-8
De Jong,Jordan	05	26	aa	TOR	1	4	44	2	64	113	72	8	25	45	10.17	2.15	7.4	376	3.6	6.4	1.8	1.1	44%	50%	22
	06	28	a/a	TOR	6	0	45	0	76	91	39	8	34	53	4.62	1.64	7.7	290	4.1	6.3	1.5	1.0	34%	74%	38
De La Cruz,Sandy	06	19	a/a	DET	5	6	39	2	107	110	50	4	42	90	4.17	1.42	11.9	261	3.5	7.5	2.1	0.4	33%	69%	82
De La Rosa,Jorge	06	26	aa	MIL	3	1	6	0	30	42	12	1	3	18	3.67	1.52	22.2	325	1.0	5.4	5.4	0.3	38%	75%	126
De Los Santos,Valeri	06	34	aaa	CHW	1	1	19	0	56	59	26	9	26	38	4.21	1.52	13.1	264	4.2	6.1	1.4	1.5	29%	78%	23
De Paula,Jorge	05	27	aaa	NYY	4	2	21	0	116	124	68	24	42	73	5.28	1.43	24.0	268	3.3	5.6	1.7	1.8	28%	69%	16
	06	28	a/a	NYY	4	14	24	0	132	215	100	24	39	57	6.82	1.92	26.6	358	2.7	3.9	1.4	1.6	38%	67%	-12
Deago,Roger	06	29	a/a	SD	10	8	28	0	124	159	83	16	65	61	6.01	1.80	20.9	304	4.7	4.4	0.9	1.1	33%	68%	6
Deaton,Kevin	05	24	aa	NYM	3	4	11	0	53	63	28	7	14	44	4.81	1.44	21.1	289	2.3	7.4	3.2	1.2	34%	70%	71
Dehart,James	05	28	a/a	ATL	4	3	40	0	63	95	61	14	37	30	8.69	2.09	7.9	341	5.2	4.3	0.8	2.0	36%	60%	-29
DeHoyos,Gabe	06	26	aa	KC	2	1	22	7	33	24	7	1	20	21	1.88	1.32	6.4	200	5.3	5.7	1.1	0.3	24%	86%	62
Delcarmen,Manny	05	24	a/a	BOS	7	5	45	5	59	55	21	3	30	62	3.20	1.44	5.7	242	4.6	9.5	2.1	0.5	33%	78%	93
Demaria,Chris	06	26	aaa	MIL	4	0	38	1	51	59	23	5	19	43	3.99	1.51	6.0	282	3.3	7.5	2.3	0.9	35%	76%	65
Denham,Dan	05	23	a/a	CLE	9	9	24	0	150	143	67	8	38	99	4.02	1.21	25.8	246	2.3	5.9	2.6	0.5	29%	66%	82
	06	24	a/a	CLE	7	4	32	0	91	124	74	6	52	48	7.31	1.93	13.8	318	5.1	4.7	0.9	0.6	36%	60%	21
Denney,Kyle	05	28	aaa	CLE	1	1	9	0	38	59	25	9	11	18	5.83	1.83	20.2	346	2.5	4.2	1.6	2.0	36%	74%	-16

					Actual				Major League Equivalents																
PITCHER	Yr	Age	Lev	Org	w	l	g	sv	ip	h	er	hr	bb	k	era	br/ip	bf/g	oob	ctl	dom	cmd	hr/9	h%	s%	bpv
DePaula,Julio	06	24	aa	MIN	2	2	43	7	66	73	27	1	31	35	3.64	1.57	6.9	275	4.2	4.7	1.1	0.1	32%	75%	48
DePriest,Derrick	06	30	aa	KC	0	4	24	1	34	63	39	4	21	15	10.18	2.46	7.7	386	5.6	3.9	0.7	1.1	42%	57%	-15
Desalvo,Matt	05	25	aa	NYY	9	5	25	0	149	133	66	10	76	113	3.96	1.40	25.8	235	4.6	6.8	1.5	0.6	29%	72%	63
	06	26	a/a	NYY	6	10	27	0	116	168	121	14	111	61	9.38	2.40	22.9	331	8.6	4.7	0.6	1.1	37%	60%	-5
Deschenes,Marc	05	33	a/a	BOS	6	5	50	8	77	81	39	10	31	63	4.55	1.46	6.7	265	3.6	7.4	2.0	1.2	32%	72%	54
	06	34	aaa	BOS	8	5	29	0	117	149	88	11	41	61	6.80	1.63	18.4	304	3.2	4.7	1.5	0.8	34%	57%	29
Devaney,Michael	06	24	aa	NYM	4	2	11	0	53	51	26	6	39	35	4.47	1.69	22.2	246	6.6	6.0	0.9	1.1	28%	76%	28
Devey,Philip	05	28	aa	PHI	2	7	38	0	51	81	45	9	26	33	7.91	2.10	6.8	352	4.6	5.8	1.2	1.5	39%	63%	-1
DeWitt,Matt	05	28	aa	MIL	1	3	26	5	31	64	23	3	14	22	6.53	2.50	6.5	413	4.0	6.3	1.6	0.7	48%	73%	21
Diamond,Thomas	05	22	aa	TEX	5	4	14	0	69	78	53	11	39	59	6.91	1.70	22.7	279	5.1	7.7	1.5	1.4	33%	60%	34
	06	24	aa	TEX	12	5	27	0	129	128	84	20	82	121	5.82	1.63	21.8	253	5.7	8.5	1.5	1.4	31%	66%	45
Diaz,Felix	05	25	aaa	CHW	6	8	21	0	122	171	82	19	33	91	6.03	1.67	26.7	324	2.5	6.7	2.7	1.4	37%	66%	45
Diaz,Jose	05	22	a/a	CLE	3	4	45	3	73	53	38	5	45	77	4.70	1.34	6.9	200	5.5	9.5	1.7	0.6	27%	64%	90
	06	23	a/a	KC	4	3	49	4	82	68	36	6	56	79	3.95	1.51	7.4	221	6.1	8.7	1.4	0.7	29%	75%	73
Dickey,R.A.	05	31	aaa	TEX	10	6	19	0	121	184	100	14	40	63	7.43	1.85	30.4	343	3.0	4.7	1.6	1.1	38%	59%	15
	06	32	aaa	TEX	9	8	22	1	131	180	115	27	53	50	7.87	1.77	28.0	320	3.6	3.5	1.0	1.9	32%	57%	-24
Dickinson,Drew	05	26	aa	OAK	6	10	27	0	120	198	92	12	57	41	6.91	2.12	22.4	361	4.2	3.0	0.7	0.9	38%	67%	-11
DiFelice,Mark	05	29	aaa	WAS	1	2	14	0	30	44	30	9	13	16	8.90	1.90	10.3	334	4.0	4.9	1.2	2.6	34%	57%	-35
Dillard,Tim	06	23	aa	MIL	10	7	29	0	163	212	84	13	41	93	4.61	1.56	25.2	309	2.3	5.1	2.3	0.7	35%	71%	49
DiNardo,Lenny	05	26	aaa	BOS	6	3	23	0	108	125	44	7	34	78	3.69	1.47	20.6	283	2.8	6.5	2.3	0.6	34%	76%	67
Dingman,Craig	05	32	aaa	DET	2	1	35	4	48	51	19	3	14	55	3.55	1.34	5.8	265	2.6	10.3	4.0	0.6	37%	74%	131
Dittler,Jake	05	23	aa	CLE	9	9	27	0	168	206	82	12	60	88	4.39	1.58	28.0	296	3.2	4.7	1.5	0.6	33%	72%	36
	06	24	aaa	CLE	5	12	25	0	130	178	87	6	52	48	6.02	1.77	24.4	319	3.6	3.3	0.9	0.4	35%	64%	18
Dobies,Andrew	06	23	aa	BOS	1	2	6	0	34	47	21	7	7	14	5.44	1.60	25.7	323	1.9	3.6	1.9	1.9	33%	72%	-6
Dohmann,Scott	05	28	aaa	COL	2	1	34	1	39	46	21	6	15	43	4.86	1.57	5.1	289	3.4	9.9	2.9	1.5	37%	73%	74
Dominguez,Juan	05	25	a/a	TEX	4	1	22	2	73	81	35	13	19	46	4.27	1.37	14.3	275	2.3	5.6	2.4	1.6	30%	75%	38
	06	26	aaa	OAK	5	10	17	0	87	116	64	10	37	40	6.60	1.76	24.0	314	3.8	4.1	1.1	1.1	34%	63%	7
Dorman,Rich	05	27	a/a	SEA	7	4	13	0	58	49	36	7	43	38	5.50	1.58	20.2	223	6.7	5.8	0.9	1.0	25%	66%	33
	06	28	aaa	SEA	7	7	31	1	118	122	75	15	74	95	5.73	1.66	17.4	260	5.6	7.2	1.3	1.1	31%	67%	39
Douglass,Chance	06	23	aa	HOU	7	8	28	0	161	165	76	15	56	86	4.25	1.37	24.7	260	3.1	4.8	1.5	0.8	29%	70%	39
Douglass,Sean	05	26	aaa	DET	9	1	14	0	81	72	33	5	27	64	3.66	1.22	24.0	233	3.0	7.1	2.4	0.6	29%	70%	84
Downs,Scott	05	28	aaa	TOR	2	3	7	0	39	54	26	6	3	29	6.06	1.45	24.4	320	0.7	6.8	9.3	1.5	37%	60%	184
Doyne,Cory	05	24	aa	STL	2	1	48	19	55	40	13	4	35	45	2.06	1.36	4.9	199	5.7	7.3	1.3	0.7	24%	88%	65
	06	25	a/a	STL	1	7	56	6	71	61	32	1	47	67	4.00	1.52	5.6	227	6.0	8.4	1.4	0.1	31%	72%	86
Drew,Tim	05	27	aaa	COL	4	3	11	0	56	79	52	13	20	46	8.29	1.77	23.9	326	3.2	7.3	2.3	2.0	37%	55%	21
Driskill,Travis	05	34	aaa	HOU	9	5	47	4	101	113	57	17	32	67	5.07	1.43	9.3	276	2.8	5.9	2.1	1.5	30%	69%	34
	06	35	aaa	HOU	4	8	52	15	64	67	28	9	14	47	3.98	1.26	5.2	264	1.9	6.5	3.4	1.3	30%	74%	73
DuBose,Eric	05	29	a/a	BAL	8	11	23	0	130	188	88	23	37	87	6.07	1.72	26.3	331	2.5	6.0	2.4	1.6	37%	68%	27
	06	30	a/a	BAL	10	5	28	0	123	175	93	16	74	70	6.77	2.02	21.7	328	5.4	5.1	0.9	1.2	36%	67%	4
Duckworth,Brandon	05	30	aaa	HOU	8	6	20	0	115	165	70	19	38	67	5.50	1.77	27.0	329	3.0	5.3	1.8	1.5	36%	72%	14
	06	31	aaa	PIT	8	3	12	0	74	92	31	6	27	43	3.78	1.60	27.9	299	3.2	5.2	1.6	0.7	34%	77%	40
Duensing,Brian	06	24	aa	MIN	1	2	10	0	49	64	28	8	21	24	5.10	1.72	22.8	308	3.8	4.4	1.2	1.5	33%	74%	-1
Duke,Zach	05	22	aaa	PIT	12	3	16	0	108	111	36	8	20	59	3.02	1.22	27.9	261	1.7	4.9	2.9	0.6	30%	77%	75
Dumatrait,Phil	05	24	aa	CIN	4	12	24	0	127	129	51	4	69	81	3.57	1.56	23.8	258	4.9	5.7	1.2	0.3	31%	76%	53
	06	25	a/a	CIN	8	11	26	0	137	183	95	20	64	82	6.22	1.80	24.9	314	4.2	5.4	1.3	1.3	35%	67%	12
Dunn,Scott	05	27	aaa	ANA	5	7	47	9	92	89	40	6	39	78	3.91	1.40	8.4	250	3.8	7.6	2.0	0.6	31%	72%	74
	06	28	aaa	TAM	4	2	38	0	66	72	28	2	32	56	3.81	1.58	7.8	272	4.4	7.6	1.7	0.3	35%	75%	74
Durbin,Chad	05	28	aaa	WAS	4	5	26	0	115	131	76	21	45	82	5.93	1.53	19.7	280	3.5	6.4	1.8	1.6	31%	65%	26
	06	29	aaa	DET	11	8	28	0	185	215	89	20	51	120	4.34	1.44	28.8	285	2.5	5.8	2.4	1.0	33%	72%	53
Durbin,J.D.	05	24	aaa	MIN	5	5	22	0	104	111	61	8	53	79	5.28	1.58	21.3	268	4.6	6.8	1.5	0.7	32%	66%	53
	06	25	aaa	MIN	4	3	16	0	89	84	34	4	58	69	3.44	1.60	25.1	244	5.9	7.0	1.2	0.4	31%	78%	61
Ebert,Derrin	05	29	a/a	KC	7	3	29	1	108	165	78	10	43	39	6.49	1.92	18.0	343	3.6	3.3	0.9	0.8	37%	65%	1
Echols,Justin	05	25	aa	WAS	9	7	31	0	116	158	77	21	40	99	5.96	1.71	17.3	318	3.1	7.7	2.5	1.6	37%	68%	40
	06	26	a/a	WAS	6	8	25	0	124	148	81	16	93	92	5.88	1.94	24.2	290	6.8	6.7	1.0	1.1	34%	71%	24
Eckenstahler,Eric	05	29	aa	CIN	0	0	35	0	37	71	50	5	49	19	12.16	3.24	6.5	397	11.9	4.7	0.4	1.2	44%	61%	-25
Eckert,Harold	05	28	aaa	LA	5	10	33	1	135	159	83	18	56	94	5.52	1.59	18.5	287	3.7	6.3	1.7	1.2	33%	67%	34
	06	29	aaa	LA	5	10	29	1	119	186	109	26	69	67	8.23	2.14	20.8	348	5.2	5.1	1.0	2.0	37%	64%	-24
Edens,Kyle	06	27	aa	ANA	3	3	25	1	47	82	39	6	31	23	7.47	2.39	10.0	372	5.9	4.5	0.8	1.1	41%	69%	-10
Edwards,Bill	06	26	aa	ANA	8	7	52	4	80	108	57	4	39	34	6.37	1.83	7.3	315	4.4	3.8	0.9	0.5	35%	63%	18
Edwards,Bryan	05	26	aa	NYM	6	6	35	1	118	153	59	9	51	62	4.47	1.72	15.7	307	3.9	4.7	1.2	0.7	35%	75%	26
	06	27	aa	NYM	4	8	21	0	87	125	77	10	46	38	7.96	1.96	20.3	330	4.7	3.9	0.8	1.0	36%	58%	0
Ekstrom,Michael	06	23	aa	SD	3	7	14	0	84	104	46	2	21	42	4.96	1.48	26.5	298	2.2	4.5	2.0	0.2	34%	64%	58
Elbert,Scott	06	21	aa	LA	6	4	11	0	62	47	33	13	47	64	4.78	1.51	25.0	206	6.8	9.3	1.4	1.9	23%	75%	42
Elder,Dave	06	31	aaa	KC	1	0	20	1	38	53	15	1	19	23	3.49	1.88	9.1	322	4.5	5.4	1.2	0.2	38%	81%	41
Emanuel,Brandon	05	29	aaa	SD	2	3	37	0	64	73	42	10	25	55	5.85	1.52	7.7	279	3.5	7.7	2.2	1.4	33%	64%	49
	06	31	aaa	CHC	1	2	54	1	75	107	46	14	31	50	5.45	1.83	6.6	327	3.7	5.9	1.6	1.7	36%	75%	7
Ennis,John	05	26	aaa	DET	3	5	50	1	72	89	48	7	29	55	6.05	1.64	6.6	297	3.7	6.9	1.9	0.9	36%	63%	50
	06	27	a/a	DET	2	4	46	13	63	76	28	3	28	44	3.97	1.64	6.2	291	4.0	6.3	1.6	0.5	35%	76%	54
Enochs,Chris	05	30	aaa	PIT	4	4	33	0	102	138	70	9	42	45	6.19	1.76	14.5	317	3.7	3.9	1.1	0.8	35%	64%	14
Erickson,Scott	05	38	aaa	LA	2	4	7	0	40	46	27	4	18	21	6.16	1.61	25.9	284	4.0	4.7	1.2	0.9	31%	61%	23
Espineli,Eugene	06	24	aa	SF	8	7	35	2	107	158	79	8	34	53	6.63	1.79	14.4	335	2.8	4.5	1.6	0.7	38%	61%	27
Esposito,Mike	05	24	aaa	COL	8	9	27	0	155	209	99	23	35	80	5.74	1.57	25.8	316	2.0	4.6	2.3	1.3	34%	66%	28
	06	25	aaa	COL	6	13	27	0	140	220	132	25	43	77	8.50	1.88	24.9	350	2.8	5.0	1.8	1.6	38%	55%	3
Estrada,Paul	06	24	aa	HOU	8	5	56	15	88	74	38	12	39	107	3.87	1.28	6.6	222	4.0	11.0	2.8	1.2	31%	74%	99
Etherton,Seth	05	29	aaa	OAK	7	6	19	0	109	104	39	12	30	76	3.20	1.23	23.8	247	2.5	6.3	2.5	1.0	29%	78%	67
	06	30	aaa	SD	3	6	19	0	84	109	59	19	30	63	6.36	1.65	20.2	307	3.2	6.7	2.1	2.0	34%	66%	18
Evangelista,Nicholas	06	25	aa	PHI	3	0	22	1	43	43	20	4	11	18	4.19	1.25	8.1	256	2.2	3.8	1.7	0.9	27%	68%	36
Eveland,Dana	05	22	aa	MIL	10	4	18	0	109	106	38	4	38	85	3.14	1.32	25.7	250	3.1	7.0	2.2	0.3	31%	76%	84
	06	23	aaa	MIL	6	5	20	0	105	81	40	5	42	103	3.43	1.17	21.5	209	3.6	8.8	2.5	0.4	28%	70%	105

					Actual				Major League Equivalents																
PITCHER	Yr	Age	Lev	Org	w	l	g	sv	ip	h	er	hr	bb	k	era	br/ip	bf/g	oob	ctl	dom	cmd	hr/9	h%	s%	bpv
Evert,Brett	05	25	a/a	MIL	2	1	36	1	69	84	37	8	27	59	4.83	1.59	8.7	292	3.5	7.7	2.2	1.1	36%	72%	57
	06	26	a/a	BOS	1	6	37	0	54	72	45	15	34	40	7.53	1.95	7.1	312	5.6	6.6	1.2	2.5	34%	66%	-16
Eyre,Willie	05	27	aaa	MIN	1	3	56	7	82	96	33	3	31	62	3.57	1.54	6.5	285	3.3	6.8	2.0	0.3	35%	76%	71
Fahrner,Evan	05	28	aa	OAK	7	2	45	3	76	92	27	5	31	48	3.13	1.61	7.7	292	3.7	5.7	1.5	0.6	34%	82%	46
	06	29	aa	TOR	1	4	36	3	51	69	38	5	39	38	6.62	2.11	7.1	316	6.8	6.8	1.0	0.9	38%	68%	27
Falkenborg,Brian	05	28	aaa	STL	4	4	40	5	50	48	26	3	25	32	4.73	1.47	5.5	249	4.5	5.8	1.3	0.6	29%	67%	50
	06	29	aaa	STL	4	5	47	16	51	65	33	8	16	43	5.86	1.58	4.9	301	2.8	7.5	2.7	1.3	36%	65%	56
Farnsworth,Jeff	06	31	aaa	CHW	7	3	48	14	49	72	37	12	11	32	6.74	1.67	4.7	333	1.9	5.9	3.1	2.1	36%	64%	25
Feierabend,Ryan	06	21	aa	SEA	9	12	28	0	153	185	96	19	60	114	5.64	1.60	24.7	293	3.5	6.7	1.9	1.1	34%	66%	43
Feldman,Scott	05	23	aa	TEX	1	2	46	14	61	51	21	4	23	35	3.10	1.21	5.5	223	3.4	5.2	1.5	0.6	26%	76%	56
Fernandez,Jared	05	34	aaa	PHI	9	7	20	0	125	148	64	15	41	66	4.62	1.52	27.7	289	3.0	4.7	1.6	1.1	32%	72%	27
	06	35	aaa	MIL	6	4	24	3	129	177	65	12	26	65	4.55	1.57	24.2	319	1.8	4.5	2.5	0.8	36%	72%	45
Fesh,Sean	05	33	a/a	PHI	4	0	47	0	42	56	21	4	22	20	4.50	1.84	4.3	311	4.7	4.2	0.9	0.9	34%	77%	8
Fields,Joshua	05	26	aaa	CHW	4	5	55	0	68	70	25	7	21	44	3.33	1.33	5.3	259	2.8	5.7	2.1	0.9	30%	78%	53
Field,Nate	06	31	aaa	COL	3	3	49	25	49	82	37	10	10	42	6.72	1.88	4.8	364	1.8	7.8	4.2	1.8	43%	68%	62
Figueroa,Nelson	06	32	aaa	WAS	3	5	16	0	76	91	46	13	23	35	5.48	1.50	21.0	290	2.7	4.2	1.5	1.5	30%	67%	9
Fikac,Jeremy	05	30	aaa	SF	4	10	50	1	99	127	52	14	34	66	4.74	1.62	9.0	304	3.1	6.0	1.9	1.3	34%	74%	31
Fillinger,Chad	06	24	aa	SEA	7	1	32	0	68	77	35	7	26	48	4.64	1.52	9.4	280	3.4	6.3	1.8	1.0	33%	71%	47
Finch,Brian	06	25	aa	BAL	6	12	27	0	145	198	90	26	79	68	5.58	1.91	26.0	318	4.9	4.2	0.9	1.6	33%	74%	-13
Fiore,Tony	05	34	aaa	BAL	9	5	30	0	166	204	87	18	51	81	4.73	1.53	24.7	296	2.7	4.4	1.6	1.0	32%	71%	26
Flanagan,Jeremy	06	25	aa	TAM	6	1	32	1	56	72	38	3	27	30	6.05	1.76	8.2	306	4.3	4.8	1.1	0.5	35%	64%	30
Flannery,Mike	05	26	a/a	SEA	2	3	56	16	65	73	34	6	28	50	4.76	1.55	5.2	278	3.8	7.0	1.8	0.8	34%	70%	56
	06	27	a/a	SEA	0	7	36	1	60	89	49	3	48	35	7.39	2.27	8.7	335	7.2	5.2	0.7	0.5	39%	66%	19
Flinn,Chris	05	25	aa	TAM	5	6	36	2	77	110	54	3	27	47	6.36	1.77	10.0	328	3.1	5.5	1.8	0.4	38%	62%	47
	06	26	a/a	TAM	1	6	24	0	74	127	67	9	38	40	8.11	2.22	15.9	370	4.6	4.8	1.0	1.1	41%	63%	-0
Flores,Ron	05	26	aaa	OAK	5	3	52	3	60	51	18	5	29	54	2.62	1.32	4.9	224	4.3	8.1	1.9	0.8	28%	83%	75
Floyd,Gavin	05	23	aaa	PHI	6	9	24	0	137	165	104	12	61	86	6.81	1.65	26.1	292	4.0	5.7	1.4	0.8	34%	57%	36
	06	24	aaa	PHI	7	4	17	0	115	151	84	14	41	71	6.57	1.67	31.0	310	3.2	5.6	1.7	1.1	35%	61%	30
Floyd,Jesse	06	26	aa	SF	4	14	25	0	135	178	101	13	47	77	6.74	1.66	24.7	311	3.1	5.2	1.7	0.9	35%	58%	32
Flury,Pat	05	33	a/a	FLA	2	1	25	0	30	33	20	4	23	20	5.98	1.88	5.8	275	7.0	5.9	0.8	1.3	31%	70%	13
Foley,Travis	05	23	aa	CLE	6	2	36	1	53	60	27	5	27	35	4.57	1.64	6.7	279	4.6	5.9	1.3	0.8	32%	73%	37
	06	24	a/a	CLE	4	5	43	3	85	99	45	7	33	78	4.75	1.55	8.9	285	3.5	8.2	2.4	0.7	36%	70%	75
Foli,Daniel	06	26	a/a	WAS	5	1	24	3	47	60	32	2	27	39	6.05	1.86	9.4	304	5.2	7.5	1.4	0.4	38%	65%	57
Foppert,Jesse	05	25	aaa	SEA	3	2	16	0	58	58	28	5	35	49	4.39	1.60	16.4	254	5.5	7.5	1.4	0.8	31%	74%	55
Ford,Matt	05	24	a/a	KC	1	4	26	0	32	47	19	3	20	20	5.22	2.09	6.2	337	5.5	5.7	1.0	0.9	39%	76%	18
	06	26	aaa	MIN	1	2	33	0	58	78	43	9	29	28	6.74	1.85	8.4	315	4.5	4.3	0.9	1.4	34%	65%	-5
Forystek,Brian	05	27	aa	BAL	2	5	14	0	70	114	53	14	28	50	6.79	2.02	24.7	357	3.5	6.5	1.8	1.8	40%	69%	8
	06	28	aa	BAL	6	3	43	2	70	77	46	12	40	47	5.87	1.66	7.5	273	5.1	6.1	1.2	1.5	30%	68%	15
Franco,Martire	05	24	aaa	PHI	5	6	43	2	96	131	63	8	35	58	5.91	1.73	10.4	318	3.3	5.4	1.7	0.8	37%	65%	36
Franklin,Wayne	05	32	aaa	NYY	2	3	46	1	42	42	20	4	12	40	4.28	1.28	3.8	255	2.5	8.5	3.4	0.9	32%	68%	101
	06	33	aaa	ATL	2	3	35	4	53	51	20	2	19	44	3.39	1.31	6.4	246	3.2	7.4	2.3	0.4	31%	73%	88
Freed,Mark	05	27	aaa	ARI	8	6	34	0	129	168	79	16	38	71	5.50	1.60	17.2	309	2.6	5.0	1.9	1.1	34%	67%	30
Fritz,Benjamin	06	26	a/a	OAK	7	10	29	0	168	201	105	20	65	88	5.64	1.58	26.1	291	3.5	4.7	1.4	1.1	32%	65%	22
Fruto,Emiliano	05	21	a/a	SEA	3	5	48	12	76	70	38	7	31	71	4.50	1.34	6.8	241	3.7	8.4	2.3	0.8	31%	67%	82
	06	22	aaa	SEA	1	3	28	10	45	35	18	1	21	51	3.61	1.25	6.7	211	4.2	10.3	2.5	0.2	31%	69%	120
Fuell,Jerrod	05	25	a/a	FLA	4	3	46	4	59	62	26	4	25	42	3.92	1.46	5.6	264	3.8	6.3	1.7	0.6	32%	74%	57
Fulchino,Jeff	05	26	aaa	FLA	11	7	29	0	153	183	82	17	63	91	4.81	1.60	23.9	290	3.7	5.4	1.5	1.0	33%	72%	29
	06	27	aaa	FLA	6	10	25	0	140	158	75	11	58	96	4.84	1.54	25.0	278	3.7	6.2	1.7	0.7	33%	69%	49
Fussell,Chris	05	29	aaa	HOU	1	6	20	0	54	68	49	10	52	23	8.24	2.22	13.9	302	8.6	3.8	0.4	1.6	31%	64%	-23
Gabbard,Kason	05	23	aa	BOS	9	11	27	0	132	156	91	11	68	80	6.18	1.69	22.6	287	4.6	5.4	1.2	0.8	33%	63%	31
	06	25	a/a	BOS	10	9	22	0	125	129	73	15	55	98	5.27	1.47	24.9	261	3.9	7.0	1.8	1.1	31%	66%	49
Galarraga,Armando	05	24	aa	WAS	3	3	12	0	71	86	48	10	19	47	6.13	1.46	26.0	292	2.3	5.9	2.5	1.3	33%	59%	46
	06	25	aa	TEX	1	6	9	0	41	71	35	7	14	31	7.63	2.05	22.7	371	3.0	6.9	2.3	1.6	43%	64%	22
Gallagher,Sean	06	21	aa	CHC	7	5	15	0	86	94	41	6	62	84	4.28	1.81	27.2	273	6.5	8.8	1.4	0.6	36%	77%	64
Gallardo,Yovani	06	21	aa	MIL	5	2	13	0	77	59	19	3	30	80	2.22	1.15	24.1	208	3.4	9.3	2.7	0.3	29%	81%	116
Gallo,Mike	05	28	aaa	HOU	4	2	37	0	54	66	26	2	20	25	4.29	1.59	6.6	293	3.4	4.2	1.2	0.4	33%	72%	36
	06	30	aaa	HOU	2	0	33	0	40	57	32	4	18	19	7.17	1.87	5.8	329	4.0	4.3	1.1	1.0	36%	61%	8
Gamble,Jerome	05	25	aa	MIL	4	1	30	5	40	60	38	2	13	36	8.46	1.82	6.4	338	3.0	8.1	2.7	0.5	43%	50%	77
Garcia,Anderson	05	25	aa	NYM	4	2	29	5	49	65	32	8	20	32	5.78	1.73	7.9	312	3.7	5.9	1.6	1.5	35%	70%	16
	06	26	a/a	BAL	4	6	40	1	67	86	44	5	25	39	5.93	1.66	7.7	306	3.4	5.2	1.5	0.7	35%	63%	36
Garcia,James	05	26	aa	SF	6	7	32	0	95	141	69	21	38	57	6.53	1.88	14.3	337	3.6	5.4	1.5	2.0	36%	70%	-9
	06	27	a/a	SF	8	11	27	0	140	173	103	17	76	86	6.63	1.78	24.4	297	4.9	5.5	1.1	1.1	34%	63%	21
Garcia,Jose	06	22	a/a	FLA	6	8	15	0	88	90	42	10	30	87	4.28	1.35	25.1	258	3.0	8.9	3.0	1.0	33%	70%	90
	06	22	aa	FLA	6	7	14	0	84	94	44	12	28	79	4.70	1.45	26.3	277	3.0	8.4	2.8	1.3	34%	71%	71
Gardner,Lee	05	31	aaa	TAM	4	3	48	15	52	63	20	8	16	27	3.46	1.52	4.8	294	2.7	4.7	1.7	1.3	32%	83%	20
	06	32	aaa	DET	5	5	58	30	61	58	27	3	18	37	4.02	1.24	4.4	245	2.6	5.4	2.1	0.5	29%	67%	68
Gardner,Richard	05	24	aa	CIN	3	6	13	0	66	89	46	6	24	38	6.33	1.70	23.5	315	3.2	5.2	1.6	0.8	36%	62%	31
Garza,Justin	06	24	aa	STL	2	3	25	0	39	42	16	1	25	22	3.63	1.72	7.3	269	5.8	5.0	0.9	0.2	32%	78%	42
Garza,Matt	06	23	a/a	MIN	9	3	15	0	91	74	33	4	24	85	3.26	1.08	24.3	218	2.4	8.4	3.5	0.4	29%	69%	124
Gassner,Dave	05	27	aaa	MIN	8	8	22	0	116	163	80	20	35	54	6.23	1.70	24.4	325	2.7	4.2	1.5	1.5	34%	66%	2
Gaudin,Chad	05	22	aaa	TOR	9	8	23	0	150	152	65	13	33	105	3.88	1.24	27.1	258	2.0	6.3	3.2	0.8	30%	70%	83
George,Chris	05	26	aaa	KC	8	7	31	0	142	179	93	23	47	84	5.88	1.60	20.7	302	3.0	5.3	1.8	1.4	33%	66%	21
	06	27	aaa	FLA	5	6	22	0	107	147	74	5	55	69	6.19	1.89	23.4	320	4.6	5.8	1.3	0.4	38%	65%	39
Germano,Justin	05	23	aaa	CIN	10	8	27	0	161	184	71	16	35	116	3.97	1.36	25.5	281	2.0	6.5	3.3	0.9	33%	73%	80
	06	24	aaa	PHI	10	6	25	0	155	207	88	19	25	77	5.11	1.50	27.4	314	1.5	4.5	3.1	1.1	34%	68%	51
Giese,Dan	05	28	aaa	PHI	3	4	26	2	38	61	30	12	1	22	7.13	1.64	6.7	356	0.3	5.3	20.8	2.8	37%	64%	367
	06	29	a/a	PHI	3	4	48	1	72	111	39	15	23	41	4.88	1.86	7.2	345	2.9	5.1	1.8	1.8	37%	80%	-1
Gil,David	05	27	a/a	WAS	2	4	29	1	70	72	30	6	21	45	3.85	1.33	10.3	261	2.7	5.8	2.1	0.7	30%	72%	61
	06	28	a/a	WAS	3	4	20	0	71	101	45	9	20	36	5.67	1.71	16.4	328	2.5	4.5	1.8	1.2	36%	68%	18

					Actual				Major League Equivalents																
PITCHER	Yr	Age	Lev	Org	w	l	g	sv	ip	h	er	hr	bb	k	era	br/ip	bf/g	oob	ctl	dom	cmd	hr/9	h%	s%	bpv
Ginter,Matt	05	28	aaa	DET	4	3	17	0	68	87	42	9	11	40	5.56	1.44	17.5	305	1.4	5.3	3.8	1.3	34%	63%	68
	06	29	aaa	BOS	5	14	24	1	141	204	113	22	30	69	7.20	1.66	26.9	331	1.9	4.4	2.3	1.4	36%	57%	22
Giron,Roberto	05	30	a/a	HOU	6	6	43	1	95	128	59	11	38	57	5.54	1.74	10.3	316	3.6	5.4	1.5	1.0	36%	69%	25
	06	31	aaa	HOU	2	5	47	13	86	116	60	13	34	50	6.26	1.74	8.5	315	3.6	5.3	1.5	1.4	35%	66%	13
Gissell,Chris	05	28	aaa	STL	8	8	23	0	137	153	61	16	36	103	4.01	1.37	25.6	276	2.3	6.7	2.9	1.0	33%	74%	69
Glant,Dustin	06	25	aa	ARI	4	6	51	1	62	96	52	11	26	39	7.58	1.95	5.9	345	3.7	5.6	1.5	1.6	38%	63%	3
Glover,Gary	05	29	aaa	MIL	6	4	17	1	92	104	34	10	29	60	3.37	1.45	23.6	280	2.8	5.9	2.1	0.9	32%	80%	50
Glynn,Ryan	05	31	aaa	TOR	5	5	20	0	92	107	54	12	37	61	5.32	1.56	20.6	284	3.6	6.0	1.7	1.2	32%	68%	33
Gobble,Jimmy	05	24	aaa	KC	2	7	12	0	58	81	45	7	19	39	6.97	1.72	22.5	323	2.9	6.0	2.1	1.1	37%	59%	37
Gomez,Mariano	05	23	aa	CLE	4	3	18	0	40	53	34	4	22	23	7.65	1.86	10.6	310	4.9	5.2	1.1	0.9	35%	57%	19
Gonzalez,Alfredo	05	26	a/a	LA	4	3	50	3	71	81	39	9	37	39	4.92	1.65	6.5	281	4.6	4.9	1.1	1.1	31%	72%	17
Gonzalez,Edgar	05	23	aaa	ARI	11	5	27	0	160	184	80	18	33	100	4.50	1.36	25.3	282	1.9	5.6	3.0	1.0	32%	69%	65
	06	24	aaa	ARI	3	8	24	0	138	159	70	12	26	94	4.56	1.34	24.5	283	1.7	6.1	3.6	0.8	33%	66%	88
Gonzalez,Enrique	05	23	aa	ARI	11	8	27	0	161	190	78	10	54	128	4.38	1.51	26.4	287	3.0	7.2	2.4	0.6	35%	71%	73
	06	24	aaa	ARI	4	3	10	0	60	68	17	2	13	31	2.55	1.35	25.6	279	1.9	4.6	2.4	0.3	32%	81%	68
Gonzalez,Gio	06	21	aa	PHI	7	12	27	0	154	170	109	33	83	139	6.36	1.64	26.0	274	4.8	8.1	1.7	1.9	32%	65%	26
Gonzalez,Geremi	05	31	aaa	BOS	5	2	11	0	69	78	26	9	14	48	3.33	1.34	26.7	279	1.9	6.2	3.3	1.2	32%	80%	71
	06	32	aaa	NYM	1	2	6	0	35	40	18	1	9	25	4.58	1.41	25.4	280	2.4	6.3	2.6	0.3	34%	65%	84
Gonzalez,Luis	05	23	a/a	LA	7	3	50	7	69	47	23	3	40	47	3.00	1.26	5.8	189	5.2	6.1	1.2	0.4	23%	76%	67
	06	39	aaa	LA	2	4	35	1	44	52	28	4	40	31	5.81	2.08	6.3	286	8.2	6.4	0.8	0.9	34%	72%	27
Gonzalez,Miguel	06	22	aa	ANA	0	2	31	4	53	42	23	7	15	32	3.90	1.07	6.8	213	2.5	5.4	2.1	1.2	23%	68%	54
Goocher,Clint	05	23	aa	ARI	8	11	26	0	135	215	106	25	38	66	7.07	1.88	24.9	353	2.5	4.4	1.7	1.6	38%	64%	-2
	06	24	aa	ARI	7	7	42	0	85	115	49	12	34	44	5.24	1.75	9.4	316	3.6	4.6	1.3	1.2	34%	72%	10
Good,Andrew	05	26	aaa	DET	9	5	23	0	134	153	69	19	41	75	4.64	1.45	25.5	280	2.8	5.0	1.8	1.2	31%	71%	30
	06	27	aaa	WAS	9	9	28	0	147	209	99	23	38	75	6.05	1.68	24.2	328	2.3	4.6	2.0	1.4	35%	66%	16
Gorzelanny,Tom	05	23	aa	PIT	8	5	23	0	129	131	56	6	44	102	3.88	1.36	24.0	258	3.1	7.1	2.3	0.4	32%	71%	81
	06	24	aaa	PIT	6	5	16	0	99	83	37	5	29	80	3.36	1.13	25.1	223	2.6	7.3	2.8	0.5	28%	70%	98
Gosling,Mike	05	25	aaa	ARI	4	6	18	0	92	138	65	11	28	69	6.35	1.80	24.2	339	2.7	6.7	2.5	1.1	40%	65%	47
	06	26	aaa	CIN	6	8	23	0	118	148	86	16	58	81	6.53	1.75	23.9	301	4.4	6.2	1.4	1.3	34%	64%	24
Gothreaux,Jared	05	26	aaa	HOU	3	8	15	0	86	95	45	8	27	39	4.76	1.42	24.9	274	2.9	4.0	1.4	0.8	30%	67%	29
	06	27	aaa	HOU	9	9	29	0	143	190	84	22	40	73	5.26	1.61	22.3	312	2.5	4.6	1.8	1.4	34%	70%	17
Gracesqui,Franklyn	06	27	aaa	BAL	0	2	29	0	36	45	28	1	22	29	7.11	1.87	5.9	301	5.5	7.4	1.3	0.3	38%	59%	59
Graman,Alex	05	28	aaa	CIN	7	7	27	1	114	129	48	16	48	88	3.82	1.56	18.9	280	3.8	7.0	1.8	1.2	33%	80%	42
Graves,Danny	06	33	aaa	CLE	1	1	33	1	51	68	31	5	15	23	5.37	1.62	7.1	314	2.6	4.0	1.5	0.9	34%	68%	21
Green,Nick	06	28	aa	ANA	8	5	17	0	112	149	69	25	24	52	5.52	1.54	29.4	312	1.9	4.2	2.2	2.0	32%	70%	3
Green,Sean	05	26	a/a	SEA	4	3	54	15	73	70	36	2	42	51	4.37	1.53	6.0	247	5.2	6.3	1.2	0.3	30%	70%	61
Green,Steve	05	28	a/a	DET	4	4	50	3	76	98	46	6	45	64	5.43	1.87	7.3	305	5.3	7.6	1.4	0.7	38%	71%	49
	06	29	aaa	DET	5	5	32	2	54	67	31	2	32	28	5.18	1.83	8.0	296	5.4	4.6	0.9	0.4	34%	70%	31
Gregg,Kevin	05	27	aaa	ANA	3	1	7	0	34	39	15	2	9	29	3.88	1.42	21.2	281	2.5	7.5	3.0	0.6	35%	73%	90
Greinke,Zack	06	23	aa	KC	8	3	18	0	105	103	55	10	24	82	4.71	1.21	24.1	251	2.1	7.0	3.4	0.9	30%	62%	93
Greisinger,Seth	05	30	aaa	ATL	4	7	16	0	98	97	46	6	31	44	4.18	1.30	25.9	252	2.9	4.0	1.4	0.5	28%	67%	43
Griffin,Colt	05	23	aa	KC	1	1	37	1	56	47	25	3	38	31	4.02	1.52	6.7	223	6.1	5.0	0.8	0.5	26%	73%	43
Grilli,Jason	05	29	aaa	DET	12	9	27	0	160	201	96	22	59	86	5.38	1.63	27.0	301	3.3	4.9	1.5	1.2	33%	69%	18
Gronkiewicz,Lee	05	27	a/a	TOR	2	1	66	30	66	62	20	7	28	55	2.66	1.35	4.3	243	3.8	7.5	2.0	0.9	29%	85%	65
	06	28	aaa	TOR	2	3	41	17	44	61	24	5	10	27	4.84	1.61	4.9	323	2.0	5.5	2.8	1.1	37%	72%	49
Gryboski,Kevin	06	33	aaa	WAS	4	6	52	7	60	80	32	3	28	34	4.72	1.80	5.5	313	4.2	5.1	1.2	0.5	36%	73%	34
Guevara,Carlos	06	25	aa	CIN	2	3	49	1	77	94	45	8	29	71	5.28	1.60	7.1	294	3.4	8.3	2.4	1.0	37%	68%	67
Guthrie,Jeremy	05	26	aaa	CLE	12	10	25	0	136	165	81	13	48	84	5.39	1.57	24.4	293	3.2	5.6	1.7	0.9	34%	66%	40
	06	28	aaa	CLE	9	5	21	0	123	128	58	6	53	74	4.23	1.47	25.7	263	3.8	5.4	1.4	0.5	31%	70%	51
Gutierrez,Juan	06	23	aa	HOU	8	4	20	0	103	111	43	11	35	87	3.78	1.42	22.4	270	3.1	7.6	2.5	1.0	33%	76%	69
Guzman,Angel	06	25	aaa	CHC	4	4	15	0	75	87	46	7	26	68	5.51	1.50	22.2	284	3.1	8.1	2.6	0.8	36%	63%	77
Gwyn,Marcus	05	28	a/a	OAK	2	3	53	3	69	79	43	2	59	44	5.53	1.99	6.4	282	7.6	5.7	0.7	0.3	34%	70%	39
	06	29	a/a	ANA	3	1	51	7	67	82	33	6	33	41	4.41	1.72	6.1	296	4.4	5.5	1.2	0.8	34%	75%	31
Habel,Josh	05	25	aa	MIL	3	7	20	0	64	101	44	13	28	37	6.23	2.01	15.8	350	3.9	5.2	1.3	1.9	38%	73%	-12
Haberer,Eric	06	24	aa	STL	3	3	11	0	61	76	45	11	35	30	6.67	1.81	26.3	298	5.1	4.5	0.9	1.6	32%	65%	-6
Haeger,Charles	05	22	aa	CHW	6	3	13	0	85	94	42	1	44	41	4.44	1.62	29.8	274	4.6	4.3	0.9	0.1	32%	70%	43
	06	23	aaa	CHW	14	6	26	0	170	172	78	13	83	111	4.13	1.50	28.9	257	4.4	5.9	1.3	0.7	30%	73%	46
Haigwood,Daniel	05	22	aa	CHW	6	1	11	0	67	44	15	0	30	65	2.01	1.10	24.5	183	4.0	8.7	2.2	0.0	26%	80%	116
	06	23	aa	TEX	3	7	27	0	146	174	86	16	93	123	5.30	1.83	25.7	290	5.7	7.6	1.3	1.0	35%	72%	41
Haines,Talley	05	29	a/a	CHC	6	4	50	13	62	72	16	4	12	43	2.39	1.35	5.3	284	1.7	6.2	3.6	0.5	34%	84%	96
	06	30	a/a	PHI	5	3	38	0	67	93	46	9	23	33	6.22	1.73	8.2	321	3.1	4.4	1.4	1.1	35%	65%	13
Hale,Beau	06	28	aa	BAL	4	6	19	0	95	124	57	12	25	48	5.36	1.57	22.5	309	2.4	4.6	1.9	1.1	34%	68%	26
Hall,Josh	05	25	aa	CIN	5	6	18	0	112	129	49	7	35	73	3.97	1.46	27.3	283	2.8	5.9	2.1	0.6	33%	73%	60
	06	26	a/a	CIN	10	9	26	0	151	209	86	20	54	72	5.14	1.74	27.1	322	3.2	4.3	1.3	1.2	35%	73%	9
Hamman,Corey	05	25	aa	DET	3	5	45	3	92	132	54	8	18	47	5.32	1.63	9.3	330	1.7	4.6	2.6	0.8	37%	67%	49
	06	27	aaa	DET	2	8	37	0	103	126	62	18	28	47	5.40	1.49	12.3	295	2.4	4.1	1.7	1.5	31%	67%	10
Hammel,Jason	05	23	a/a	TAM	11	4	22	0	136	135	51	11	44	106	3.38	1.32	26.2	254	2.9	7.0	2.4	0.7	31%	76%	75
	06	24	aaa	TAM	5	9	24	0	127	157	78	12	38	100	5.52	1.53	23.6	297	2.7	7.1	2.6	0.8	36%	64%	68
Hammond,Steve	06	24	aa	MIL	5	6	13	0	73	82	36	9	29	49	4.40	1.52	25.0	278	3.6	6.1	1.7	1.2	32%	74%	36
Hampson,Justin	05	25	aaa	COL	5	13	27	0	144	179	102	20	62	79	6.37	1.67	24.5	298	3.8	4.9	1.3	1.3	33%	63%	14
	06	26	aaa	COL	8	4	31	0	121	145	59	13	38	79	4.36	1.51	17.3	291	2.8	5.8	2.1	1.0	33%	73%	45
Hamulack,Tim	05	29	a/a	NYM	5	3	49	12	64	52	11	1	18	43	1.49	1.08	5.2	217	2.5	6.1	2.5	0.2	27%	86%	95
	06	30	aaa	LA	0	1	28	3	38	34	7	1	26	34	1.56	1.59	6.1	235	6.2	8.0	1.3	0.3	31%	91%	75
Hancock,Josh	05	27	aaa	CIN	1	2	11	0	44	67	34	5	17	30	6.89	1.91	19.3	344	3.4	6.2	1.8	1.1	40%	64%	29
Hanrahan,Joel	05	24	aa	LA	9	8	23	0	111	129	65	16	54	82	5.26	1.64	22.1	284	4.3	6.7	1.5	1.3	33%	71%	30
	06	25	a/a	LA	11	5	26	0	140	139	67	13	81	91	4.32	1.57	24.2	253	5.2	5.9	1.1	0.8	29%	74%	39
Hansack,Devern	06	29	aa	BOS	8	7	31	1	132	184	81	21	46	86	5.54	1.74	19.9	323	3.2	5.9	1.9	1.4	36%	71%	22
Hansen,Craig	06	23	a/a	BOS	2	2	19	0	47	43	17	0	24	33	3.26	1.43	10.7	239	4.6	6.3	1.4	0.0	30%	75%	74
Happ,James	06	24	a/a	PHI	7	2	13	0	80	76	33	4	32	71	3.70	1.35	26.3	245	3.6	8.0	2.2	0.4	32%	72%	87

PITCHER	Yr	Age	Lev	Org	w	l	g	sv	ip	h	er	hr	bb	k	era	br/ip	bf/g	oob	ctl	dom	cmd	hr/9	h%	s%	bpv
					Actual				Major League Equivalents																
Harben,Adam	06	23	aa	MIN	4	9	29	1	122	148	76	6	77	61	5.62	1.85	20.1	294	5.7	4.5	0.8	0.5	33%	68%	26
Harrison,Matt	06	21	aa	ATL	3	4	13	0	77	102	44	7	19	48	5.14	1.57	26.6	312	2.2	5.6	2.5	0.8	36%	68%	55
Harris,Jeff	05	31	a/a	SEA	10	2	27	1	102	92	37	13	28	72	3.23	1.18	15.5	236	2.4	6.3	2.6	1.2	27%	78%	65
	06	32	aaa	SEA	0	3	15	0	31	51	23	6	7	11	6.72	1.87	9.9	358	2.1	3.3	1.5	1.8	37%	67%	-19
Harts,Jeremy	05	25	aa	PIT	1	2	29	0	39	41	44	4	54	35	10.26	2.45	7.2	265	12.6	8.1	0.6	1.0	33%	56%	33
Hawksworth,Blake	06	24	aa	STL	4	2	13	0	79	82	35	8	31	55	3.98	1.43	26.5	263	3.5	6.3	1.8	0.9	31%	75%	50
Hayhurst,Dirk	06	26	a/a	SD	4	7	16	0	72	99	49	8	28	51	6.18	1.77	21.1	320	3.5	6.4	1.8	1.1	37%	65%	36
Heaverlo,Jeff	05	28	aaa	SEA	6	3	46	4	82	105	48	3	46	62	5.31	1.85	8.5	305	5.1	6.8	1.3	0.3	38%	70%	52
	06	29	a/a	ANA	2	5	25	0	60	86	51	9	41	29	7.58	2.11	12.1	329	6.2	4.3	0.7	1.4	35%	65%	-12
Helling,Rick	05	35	aaa	MIL	9	3	21	0	130	143	66	13	49	87	4.58	1.48	27.3	274	3.4	6.0	1.8	0.9	32%	70%	47
Henderson,Brian	05	23	aa	TAM	5	1	48	1	55	71	26	3	22	41	4.22	1.69	5.3	307	3.5	6.7	1.9	0.5	37%	75%	58
	06	24	aa	TAM	2	2	41	5	50	62	19	3	13	23	3.41	1.49	5.4	298	2.3	4.1	1.8	0.6	33%	78%	41
Hendrickson,Ben	05	25	aaa	MIL	6	12	28	0	155	187	90	17	55	106	5.22	1.56	24.8	292	3.2	6.1	1.9	1.0	34%	68%	44
	06	26	aaa	MIL	9	8	23	0	139	145	69	11	49	85	4.44	1.40	26.1	264	3.2	5.5	1.7	0.7	30%	69%	50
Henkel,Rob	05	27	a/a	DET	7	8	28	0	91	152	82	18	45	47	8.05	2.16	16.5	363	4.4	4.6	1.0	1.8	39%	65%	-22
Hennessey,Brad	05	26	aaa	SF	4	2	11	0	67	77	37	5	19	39	5.01	1.43	26.6	281	2.6	5.2	2.0	0.7	32%	64%	52
Henn,Sean	05	24	a/a	NYY	7	6	20	0	111	109	39	6	37	69	3.17	1.32	23.6	252	3.0	5.6	1.9	0.5	30%	76%	62
	06	25	aaa	NYY	3	1	18	0	42	52	24	1	21	27	5.17	1.72	10.9	295	4.5	5.7	1.3	0.2	35%	68%	50
Hensley,Clay	05	26	aaa	SD	2	2	15	0	90	67	31	6	21	63	3.09	0.97	23.4	203	2.1	6.3	3.1	0.6	24%	70%	98
Hensley,Matt	06	28	aaa	ANA	2	1	20	2	33	47	23	3	11	21	6.14	1.75	7.7	329	2.9	5.8	2.0	0.9	38%	65%	40
Hernandez,Carlos	05	25	aaa	HOU	5	8	21	0	89	108	61	17	52	54	6.13	1.79	20.0	294	5.2	5.5	1.1	1.7	32%	70%	-1
Hernandez,Chris	06	26	aa	PIT	5	3	42	2	66	79	41	3	25	52	5.63	1.58	7.1	291	3.4	7.1	2.1	0.5	36%	63%	69
Hernandez,Felix	05	19	aaa	SEA	9	4	19	0	88	56	20	3	40	110	2.05	1.09	18.6	178	4.1	11.3	2.8	0.3	28%	81%	137
Hernandez,Runelvys	06	28	aaa	KC	5	6	12	0	64	82	44	6	28	35	6.18	1.71	24.8	304	3.9	5.0	1.3	0.9	34%	64%	23
Hernandez,Yoel	05	23	a/a	PHI	8	4	49	3	69	74	28	6	30	57	3.65	1.51	6.2	268	3.9	7.4	1.9	0.8	33%	78%	62
Herndon,Junior	06	28	aa	KC	12	6	27	0	160	265	126	23	43	61	7.10	1.92	28.7	362	2.4	3.4	1.4	1.3	38%	64%	-5
Hertzler,Barry	06	26	a/a	BOS	4	2	50	7	77	97	37	1	54	38	4.30	1.95	7.5	301	6.3	4.4	0.7	0.1	35%	76%	33
Hill,Danny	06	25	aa	TOR	3	7	44	0	74	118	69	15	35	51	8.43	2.06	8.4	352	4.2	6.2	1.5	1.8	40%	60%	-1
Hill,Rich	05	26	a/a	CHC	10	4	21	0	122	113	59	24	38	152	4.34	1.23	24.2	240	2.8	11.2	4.0	1.8	31%	73%	105
	06	27	aaa	CHC	7	1	15	0	100	77	28	4	24	115	2.51	1.01	26.2	209	2.1	10.4	4.9	0.4	31%	76%	167
Hill,Shawn	06	25	a/a	WAS	3	3	11	0	55	62	21	2	7	28	3.44	1.26	20.9	279	1.2	4.5	3.7	0.3	32%	72%	95
Hines,Carlos	05	25	a/a	TAM	3	3	48	6	69	73	29	2	32	38	3.75	1.52	6.4	266	4.2	4.9	1.2	0.3	31%	74%	48
	06	32	aaa	TAM	3	6	52	2	65	88	38	7	28	41	5.24	1.79	5.9	317	3.9	5.6	1.4	1.0	36%	72%	25
Hirsh,Jason	05	24	aa	HOU	13	8	29	0	172	173	79	15	46	133	4.15	1.28	24.9	256	2.4	6.9	2.9	0.8	31%	69%	81
	06	25	aaa	HOU	13	2	23	0	137	106	37	5	50	100	2.43	1.14	24.2	209	3.3	6.6	2.0	0.3	26%	79%	85
Hodges,Trey	05	27	aaa	ATL	0	3	15	0	32	53	33	5	20	17	9.12	2.26	11.1	359	5.6	4.8	0.9	1.5	39%	59%	-14
Hodge,Kevin	05	29	a/a	PHI	4	6	40	5	58	78	51	12	20	40	7.82	1.68	6.7	314	3.1	6.2	2.0	1.8	35%	55%	17
Hoelscher,Nate	05	26	aa	KC	3	2	51	4	54	72	38	3	24	32	6.28	1.79	5.0	314	4.1	5.2	1.3	0.6	36%	63%	34
	06	27	aa	KC	0	5	44	3	46	56	34	6	15	31	6.72	1.54	4.7	295	2.9	6.1	2.1	1.1	34%	56%	43
Holcomb,James	06	26	aa	ANA	0	7	13	0	62	87	42	6	20	32	6.11	1.71	22.2	323	2.9	4.7	1.6	0.8	36%	64%	28
Holdzkom,Lincoln	06	25	aa	CHC	2	3	18	0	32	35	13	0	13	23	3.54	1.48	7.8	270	3.5	6.4	1.8	0.0	34%	73%	77
Homer,Chris	06	26	aa	DET	1	4	42	13	48	80	58	13	16	32	10.81	1.99	5.6	363	2.9	6.1	2.1	2.5	39%	46%	-12
Honel,Kris	05	23	aa	CHW	5	7	21	0	93	113	71	12	63	60	6.86	1.89	21.3	294	6.1	5.8	1.0	1.2	33%	64%	16
Hoorelbeke,Casey	06	27	aa	LA	2	2	52	7	72	57	31	6	37	44	3.88	1.31	5.9	215	4.6	5.5	1.2	0.7	25%	71%	49
Horgan,Joe	05	28	aaa	WAS	4	3	46	3	63	75	30	9	29	38	4.29	1.65	6.3	290	4.1	5.4	1.3	1.2	32%	78%	20
	06	29	aaa	FLA	5	6	45	3	43	42	22	5	19	26	4.60	1.41	4.1	250	3.9	5.5	1.4	1.2	28%	70%	33
Hottovy,Thomas	06	25	aa	BOS	2	4	7	0	41	38	29	1	17	24	6.34	1.33	24.9	240	3.7	5.3	1.5	0.2	29%	48%	62
Houlton,D.J.	06	27	aaa	LA	9	11	29	0	162	197	106	25	59	106	5.90	1.58	25.1	294	3.3	5.9	1.8	1.4	33%	65%	28
Housman,Jeff	05	24	aaa	MIL	5	12	28	0	130	165	99	26	68	96	6.84	1.79	21.9	303	4.7	6.6	1.4	1.8	34%	65%	10
	06	25	aa	MIL	1	4	12	0	56	77	37	1	23	35	5.88	1.78	22.0	319	3.7	5.6	1.5	0.2	38%	64%	51
Houston,Ryan	05	26	aa	TOR	3	2	33	7	40	38	21	5	16	38	4.64	1.35	5.2	245	3.6	8.6	2.4	1.0	31%	67%	77
	06	27	a/a	TOR	3	4	51	2	72	105	47	5	51	59	5.87	2.15	7.2	332	6.3	7.4	1.2	0.6	41%	72%	40
Howard,Ben	05	27	aaa	FLA	6	3	54	2	83	89	42	10	29	77	4.57	1.41	6.7	267	3.1	8.3	2.7	1.1	33%	70%	74
	06	28	aaa	TOR	3	2	45	11	57	77	51	8	24	24	7.98	1.77	5.9	316	3.8	3.8	1.0	1.3	33%	55%	-5
Howell,J.P.	05	22	a/a	KC	5	1	10	0	55	55	23	2	22	45	3.75	1.39	23.8	254	3.6	7.3	2.0	0.3	32%	72%	81
	06	23	aaa	TAM	8	5	18	0	91	107	44	5	30	70	4.35	1.51	22.4	287	3.0	6.9	2.3	0.5	35%	70%	73
Huber,Jon	05	24	aa	SEA	7	8	26	0	148	189	98	13	54	98	5.95	1.64	26.0	305	3.3	6.0	1.8	0.8	36%	63%	45
	06	25	aa	SEA	3	4	50	23	65	93	33	3	16	48	4.51	1.67	6.0	328	2.2	6.7	3.1	0.4	40%	72%	81
Hudgins,John	05	24	a/a	TEX	4	9	22	0	120	166	93	16	45	74	6.96	1.76	25.5	321	3.4	5.5	1.6	1.2	36%	61%	21
	06	25	a/a	TEX	6	5	18	0	76	89	45	6	26	64	5.35	1.52	18.8	287	3.1	7.5	2.4	0.7	35%	64%	71
Hudson,Luke	06	29	aaa	KC	2	0	13	1	35	38	15	0	8	16	3.94	1.31	11.4	273	2.0	4.2	2.1	0.0	32%	67%	70
Hughes,Philip	06	20	aa	NYY	10	3	21	0	116	85	38	6	33	120	2.96	1.02	21.8	200	2.6	9.3	3.6	0.4	28%	71%	133
Hughes,Travis	05	27	aaa	WAS	2	5	52	13	59	51	20	3	23	60	3.04	1.24	4.7	226	3.5	9.1	2.6	0.5	31%	76%	104
	06	28	aaa	WAS	2	6	51	4	73	61	25	3	45	69	3.04	1.45	6.3	223	5.6	8.5	1.5	0.4	30%	79%	81
Huisman,Justin	05	26	aaa	KC	8	2	42	1	78	98	37	10	38	49	4.28	1.74	8.7	301	4.4	5.6	1.3	1.2	34%	79%	19
	06	27	aaa	SEA	2	0	22	0	40	61	46	8	22	28	10.42	2.08	9.1	343	5.0	6.2	1.2	1.9	38%	49%	-7
Hull,Eric	05	26	a/a	LA	7	8	29	3	125	119	48	8	48	99	3.49	1.34	18.4	246	3.5	7.1	2.0	0.6	30%	75%	73
	06	27	aaa	LA	2	4	44	2	73	58	35	6	41	64	4.32	1.36	7.1	213	5.1	7.9	1.6	0.8	27%	69%	69
Humber,Philip	06	24	aa	NYM	2	2	6	0	34	32	15	5	10	30	4.08	1.24	23.6	243	2.7	7.9	2.9	1.4	29%	72%	74
Hunter,Christopher	06	26	aa	ANA	4	14	25	0	125	193	114	21	69	37	8.23	2.09	25.1	346	5.0	2.7	0.5	1.5	35%	61%	-33
Hurley,Eric	06	21	aa	TEX	3	1	6	0	37	25	11	5	11	27	2.68	0.97	24.0	188	2.7	6.6	2.5	1.2	21%	81%	72
Iriki,Yusaku	06	34	aaa	NYM	4	8	19	0	76	119	59	9	36	50	6.96	2.03	19.9	348	4.2	5.9	1.4	1.1	40%	66%	17
Isaacson,Charlie	05	25	a/a	NYY	6	4	29	0	101	142	49	9	45	75	4.40	1.85	16.7	325	4.0	6.7	1.7	0.8	39%	78%	40
Isenberg,Kurt	06	25	aa	TOR	3	9	20	0	87	159	83	7	25	46	8.59	2.11	21.9	385	2.6	4.7	1.8	0.8	43%	57%	21
Izquierdo,Hansel	05	29	a/a	PIT	8	6	31	0	133	193	94	11	55	77	6.37	1.87	20.5	332	3.7	5.2	1.4	0.7	38%	65%	28
Jackson,Edwin	05	22	a/a	LA	9	11	23	0	117	126	70	17	48	65	5.38	1.49	22.4	269	3.7	5.0	1.4	1.3	29%	66%	20
	06	23	aaa	TAM	3	7	22	5	73	99	58	8	37	56	7.15	1.86	15.9	317	4.6	6.9	1.5	1.0	38%	61%	35
Jackson,Kyle	06	24	aa	BOS	3	1	22	1	36	40	14	2	27	30	3.59	1.85	7.9	276	6.7	7.5	1.1	0.5	35%	81%	53
Jackson,Steven	06	25	aa	ARI	8	11	24	0	149	172	66	8	51	105	4.00	1.49	27.4	283	3.0	6.3	2.1	0.5	34%	73%	65

Major League Equivalent Statistics

PITCHERS

PITCHER	Yr	Age	Lev	Org	w	l	g	sv	ip	h	er	hr	bb	k	era	br/ip	bf/g	oob	ctl	dom	cmd	hr/9	h%	s%	bpv
Jackson,Zach	05	22	a/a	TOR	8	7	17	0	101	142	68	8	35	67	6.05	1.75	27.8	325	3.1	6.0	1.9	0.7	38%	64%	45
	06	23	aaa	MIL	4	6	18	0	107	126	65	14	47	52	5.47	1.62	27.0	287	4.0	4.4	1.1	1.2	31%	68%	12
Jacobsen,Landon	06	27	aaa	PIT	14	10	28	0	164	223	105	13	70	61	5.74	1.79	27.6	318	3.8	3.3	0.9	0.7	34%	67%	9
James,Chuck	05	24	a/a	ATL	10	4	22	0	119	96	41	9	28	117	3.10	1.04	21.5	216	2.1	8.8	4.2	0.7	28%	72%	132
	06	25	aaa	ATL	1	0	7	0	33	37	14	4	6	22	3.80	1.30	20.0	276	1.6	6.0	3.7	1.1	32%	74%	80
James,Craig	06	24	aa	SEA	4	3	43	1	62	66	25	4	37	49	3.59	1.66	6.6	267	5.4	7.0	1.3	0.6	33%	79%	53
James,Delvin	05	28	aa	ANA	3	4	17	0	59	98	46	6	28	21	6.96	2.12	17.5	361	4.2	3.2	0.7	0.9	39%	67%	-10
James,Justin	06	25	aa	TOR	2	0	24	0	41	58	18	3	12	30	3.88	1.70	7.9	324	2.7	6.5	2.4	0.7	39%	78%	58
Janssen,Casey	05	24	aa	TOR	3	3	9	0	43	65	22	4	4	39	4.63	1.62	21.7	342	0.9	8.2	9.3	0.9	43%	73%	203
	06	25	aaa	TOR	1	5	9	0	42	58	32	4	9	28	6.89	1.58	21.1	318	1.9	5.9	3.0	0.9	37%	55%	65
Jan,Carlos	06	27	aa	CHC	1	2	31	1	53	61	38	7	44	46	6.44	1.97	8.4	282	7.4	7.8	1.1	1.2	34%	68%	33
Jarvis,Kevin	05	36	aaa	STL	11	6	26	0	157	186	67	18	39	94	3.86	1.43	26.3	289	2.2	5.4	2.4	1.0	33%	76%	49
	06	37	aaa	ARI	3	6	15	0	83	89	39	8	22	48	4.21	1.34	23.6	269	2.4	5.2	2.2	0.9	30%	70%	51
Jenks,Bobby	05	25	aa	CHW	1	2	35	19	41	40	16	1	21	39	3.47	1.49	5.2	250	4.6	8.6	1.9	0.2	34%	75%	88
Jensen,Ryan	05	30	aaa	KC	2	11	18	0	90	146	84	11	39	43	8.44	2.05	24.8	356	3.9	4.3	1.1	1.1	39%	58%	-0
	06	31	aa	TEX	2	4	11	0	50	87	52	9	15	27	9.32	2.05	22.6	374	2.8	4.9	1.8	1.7	41%	54%	-4
Jimenez,Cesar	05	21	a/a	SEA	3	5	49	4	76	74	29	7	23	64	3.44	1.27	6.5	249	2.7	7.5	2.8	0.9	31%	76%	84
	06	22	aa	SEA	5	12	27	3	123	129	67	9	60	71	4.87	1.53	20.3	263	4.4	5.2	1.2	0.6	30%	68%	40
Jimenez,Kelvin	05	25	a/a	TEX	4	6	42	5	88	103	43	7	38	58	4.42	1.60	9.5	286	3.9	5.9	1.5	0.7	34%	73%	43
	06	26	aaa	TEX	4	2	26	1	38	52	33	6	26	35	7.89	2.05	7.3	317	6.2	8.2	1.3	1.4	39%	62%	25
Jimenez,Ubaldo	05	22	aa	COL	2	5	12	0	63	70	52	18	31	45	7.43	1.60	23.7	276	4.4	6.4	1.5	2.6	28%	59%	-8
	06	23	aa	COL	14	4	26	0	151	145	82	12	79	128	4.88	1.48	25.6	247	4.7	7.6	1.6	0.7	31%	67%	64
Johnson,James	05	29	aa	PIT	5	4	31	1	51	75	29	5	20	35	5.17	1.85	7.9	334	3.5	6.1	1.7	0.9	39%	73%	33
	06	23	aa	BAL	13	6	27	0	156	207	109	18	61	108	6.30	1.72	26.8	313	3.5	6.2	1.8	1.0	36%	63%	37
Johnson,Jeremy	05	27	aa	DET	9	8	24	0	132	212	96	25	47	59	6.57	1.96	26.9	355	3.2	4.0	1.3	1.7	37%	70%	-17
	06	24	aa	DET	2	4	8	0	38	72	38	7	12	20	8.98	2.19	24.3	392	2.7	4.7	1.7	1.7	40%	60%	-11
Johnson,Jonathan	06	32	aaa	ATL	2	3	23	0	51	58	29	2	19	39	5.18	1.50	9.8	279	3.3	6.8	2.1	0.4	35%	63%	72
Johnson,Josh	05	23	aa	FLA	12	4	26	0	139	161	74	4	53	102	4.78	1.54	23.9	284	3.4	6.6	1.9	0.3	35%	67%	70
Johnson,Mark	05	30	a/a	DET	4	3	38	0	94	154	89	16	25	43	8.50	1.90	11.9	359	2.4	4.1	1.7	1.6	38%	55%	-2
Johnson,Tyler	05	24	aaa	STL	2	1	57	7	59	55	30	5	25	68	4.58	1.36	4.4	242	3.8	10.4	2.7	0.8	34%	67%	103
Johnston,Mike	05	26	aaa	PIT	2	1	52	0	57	48	22	5	28	43	3.41	1.33	4.7	225	4.4	6.7	1.5	0.8	27%	77%	58
	06	28	aaa	PIT	1	3	28	0	42	63	40	7	22	29	8.55	2.03	7.4	339	4.7	6.1	1.3	1.6	38%	58%	3
Jones,Bobby	06	35	aa	DET	3	4	28	0	80	114	54	15	49	50	6.08	2.04	14.2	328	5.6	5.6	1.0	1.7	36%	74%	-7
Jones,Geoffrey	05	26	aa	SD	3	5	55	0	70	93	40	2	36	48	5.17	1.84	6.1	313	4.6	6.2	1.3	0.3	38%	70%	49
	06	27	aa	SD	1	1	53	1	61	92	43	4	31	44	6.39	2.01	5.7	339	4.6	6.5	1.4	0.5	41%	67%	40
Jones,Greg	06	30	aaa	ANA	5	6	47	17	55	60	30	8	20	35	4.86	1.46	5.1	273	3.2	5.7	1.7	1.3	30%	70%	33
Jones,Jason	06	30	aa	NYY	4	3	10	0	50	105	49	19	27	17	8.86	2.63	27.8	419	4.8	3.1	0.6	3.4	43%	73%	-97
Journell,Jimmy	05	28	aaa	STL	1	4	34	1	42	44	25	5	38	41	5.40	1.95	6.0	265	8.1	8.7	1.1	1.1	33%	74%	43
Juarez,William	05	24	aa	LA	6	5	38	0	104	128	58	12	47	60	5.01	1.69	12.6	297	4.1	5.2	1.3	1.0	33%	72%	23
	06	25	aa	LA	4	5	11	0	57	53	26	7	36	24	4.14	1.56	23.2	240	5.7	3.7	0.7	1.1	25%	77%	10
Julianel,Ben	05	26	aa	NYY	5	3	46	1	87	115	52	9	59	77	5.34	1.99	9.3	311	6.1	8.0	1.3	0.9	39%	74%	40
	06	27	aa	FLA	1	3	7	0	34	35	14	0	11	17	3.83	1.35	20.7	260	2.9	4.4	1.5	0.0	31%	68%	61
Junge,Eric	05	29	a/a	NYM	11	8	29	2	148	180	82	22	62	91	5.01	1.64	23.3	294	3.8	5.5	1.4	1.4	33%	73%	19
	06	30	aaa	SD	4	5	21	0	71	97	44	5	26	49	5.56	1.73	15.8	317	3.3	6.2	1.9	0.7	38%	67%	47
Jurrjens,Jair	06	21	aa	DET	4	3	12	0	67	81	31	8	21	48	4.22	1.52	24.8	293	2.8	6.5	2.3	1.0	34%	75%	53
Kahn,Stephen	06	23	aa	SEA	1	3	31	0	39	59	35	4	34	30	8.08	2.38	6.7	341	7.8	6.9	0.9	0.9	41%	65%	19
Kaiser,Marc	06	24	aa	COL	10	10	25	0	164	217	104	21	41	59	5.71	1.57	29.5	311	2.3	3.2	1.4	1.2	33%	65%	8
Karnuth,Jason	05	29	aaa	DET	7	2	63	23	67	82	22	1	18	28	2.94	1.49	4.7	296	2.4	3.8	1.6	0.1	34%	79%	48
	06	30	aaa	OAK	2	7	62	17	71	92	49	8	28	32	6.19	1.69	5.3	308	3.5	4.0	1.1	1.0	33%	63%	12
Karp,Josh	05	26	a/a	WAS	5	6	32	0	93	110	61	14	38	54	5.90	1.59	13.1	288	3.6	5.2	1.4	1.4	31%	65%	17
Karsay,Steve	05	34	aaa	TEX	1	3	23	0	33	50	23	2	8	27	6.33	1.74	6.7	340	2.1	7.3	3.5	0.6	42%	62%	86
Karstens,Jeff	05	23	aa	NYY	12	11	28	0	169	217	93	18	43	123	4.95	1.54	26.9	305	2.3	6.6	2.9	1.0	36%	69%	65
	06	24	a/a	NYY	11	5	25	0	147	165	73	16	48	92	4.48	1.45	25.7	277	3.0	5.6	1.9	1.0	31%	71%	43
Kaye,Justin	05	29	aa	PIT	3	3	53	22	61	93	43	5	36	35	6.27	2.11	5.8	343	5.3	5.1	1.0	0.8	39%	70%	13
Keefer,Ryan	05	24	aa	BAL	7	3	54	1	84	82	44	9	35	76	4.73	1.39	6.7	251	3.7	8.1	2.2	1.0	31%	68%	69
Keisler,Randy	05	30	aaa	CIN	5	2	12	2	56	65	22	7	13	35	3.53	1.39	20.2	284	2.1	5.7	2.7	1.1	32%	78%	57
	06	31	aaa	OAK	9	5	25	0	103	129	53	2	49	63	4.66	1.72	19.2	300	4.3	5.5	1.3	0.2	36%	71%	49
Kelly,Steven	05	26	aaa	CIN	5	5	19	0	104	118	62	11	39	55	5.32	1.51	24.3	280	3.4	4.8	1.4	1.0	31%	66%	29
	06	27	a/a	CIN	13	11	27	0	151	218	78	17	64	79	4.66	1.87	26.8	331	3.8	4.7	1.2	1.0	37%	77%	12
Kemp,Bo	05	25	aaa	MIN	4	5	61	5	77	84	37	1	33	59	4.31	1.52	5.6	271	3.8	6.9	1.8	0.1	34%	69%	76
	06	26	aaa	MIN	7	4	49	3	89	117	34	3	30	30	3.47	1.66	8.3	311	3.1	3.0	1.0	0.3	34%	78%	22
Kennard,Jeff	06	25	aa	NYY	3	6	27	1	54	69	30	7	26	43	4.98	1.74	9.4	303	4.2	7.2	1.7	1.1	36%	73%	40
Kensing,Logan	05	23	aa	FLA	4	1	7	0	39	41	18	4	15	29	4.02	1.45	24.5	265	3.6	6.7	1.9	0.9	31%	75%	53
Kent,Steve	05	27	a/a	COL	3	5	39	3	48	86	61	4	31	24	11.43	2.43	6.6	379	5.8	4.5	0.8	0.8	42%	50%	-2
	06	28	a/a	HOU	1	0	38	2	41	60	27	7	36	15	5.94	2.35	5.7	334	8.0	3.4	0.4	1.5	35%	78%	-29
Keppel,Bob	06	24	aaa	KC	6	7	25	1	98	147	78	12	27	38	7.16	1.77	18.4	339	2.5	3.5	1.4	1.1	36%	59%	5
Kershner,Jason	05	29	aaa	SD	5	4	61	3	79	80	33	6	16	46	3.80	1.21	5.4	256	1.8	5.2	2.8	0.7	29%	70%	72
	06	30	aaa	MIL	3	2	23	2	33	54	19	1	11	20	5.06	1.95	7.0	357	3.0	5.4	1.8	0.3	42%	72%	45
Kester,Tim	05	34	aaa	BOS	11	8	29	0	159	224	105	18	28	82	5.95	1.59	24.7	326	1.6	4.6	2.9	1.0	36%	63%	48
	06	35	a/a	BAL	8	5	19	0	107	172	74	14	19	39	6.26	1.79	26.5	355	1.6	3.3	2.0	1.2	37%	66%	10
Key,Chris	05	28	a/a	SEA	4	1	26	3	62	83	23	8	10	24	3.34	1.50	10.5	314	1.5	3.5	2.4	1.2	33%	82%	28
	06	29	aa	PHI	3	2	37	20	49	91	24	4	16	14	4.35	2.19	6.8	389	3.0	2.5	0.8	0.7	41%	81%	-11
Kida,Masao	05	37	aaa	SEA	3	6	53	22	79	82	41	6	28	57	4.67	1.40	6.4	262	3.2	6.5	2.0	0.7	31%	67%	62
Kieschnick,Brooks	05	33	a/a	HOU	2	4	50	1	65	111	50	16	31	29	6.92	2.19	6.6	369	4.3	4.0	0.9	2.2	38%	73%	-40
Kim,Sunny	05	28	aaa	WAS	4	2	9	0	49	51	16	3	14	31	2.96	1.32	23.1	261	2.6	5.6	2.2	0.6	31%	79%	65
	06	29	aaa	COL	8	6	21	0	124	191	97	20	37	56	7.01	1.84	28.2	345	2.7	4.0	1.5	1.4	37%	63%	-2
Kinney,Josh	05	26	a/a	STL	6	4	58	11	67	80	31	6	32	53	4.17	1.67	5.3	290	4.3	7.1	1.6	0.7	35%	76%	52
	06	28	aaa	STL	2	2	51	3	71	57	16	2	32	63	2.00	1.25	5.8	215	4.0	7.9	2.0	0.3	28%	84%	93

215

PITCHER	Yr	Age	Lev	Org	Actual				Major League Equivalents																
					w	l	g	sv	ip	h	er	hr	bb	k	era	br/ip	bf/g	oob	ctl	dom	cmd	hr/9	h%	s%	bpv
Kinney,Matt	05	29	aaa	SF	7	8	19	0	114	128	68	15	43	86	5.35	1.50	26.5	278	3.4	6.8	2.0	1.2	32%	66%	47
	06	30	aaa	SF	8	7	28	0	153	188	98	23	54	99	5.75	1.58	24.6	296	3.2	5.8	1.8	1.4	33%	66%	29
Kinsey,Chris	06	24	a/a	ARI	2	2	48	3	58	66	35	9	28	39	5.43	1.62	5.5	280	4.3	6.1	1.4	1.4	31%	69%	23
Kleine,Victor	05	26	a/a	CLE	1	6	33	0	72	87	40	8	34	34	4.99	1.68	10.0	292	4.3	4.3	1.0	1.0	32%	72%	14
Knight,Brandon	06	31	aa	PIT	2	7	51	27	64	72	25	8	24	62	3.47	1.49	5.5	277	3.3	8.7	2.6	1.2	35%	81%	72
Knox,Brad	06	24	aa	OAK	12	5	27	0	161	181	81	11	62	82	4.53	1.51	26.4	278	3.5	4.6	1.3	0.6	31%	70%	37
Kohn,Shawn	05	26	aa	OAK	4	3	55	8	84	76	32	6	21	71	3.45	1.15	6.2	235	2.3	7.6	3.4	0.6	30%	71%	106
	06	27	a/a	OAK	3	2	52	4	68	63	32	7	18	52	4.26	1.19	5.4	242	2.3	6.9	2.9	0.9	29%	66%	83
Kolb,Dan	06	26	aa	WAS	4	2	40	8	78	78	44	7	39	60	5.03	1.50	8.6	255	4.5	6.9	1.5	0.8	31%	67%	54
Kometani,Paul	06	24	aa	TEX	8	5	17	0	88	116	63	5	35	65	6.42	1.72	24.0	312	3.6	6.6	1.9	0.5	38%	61%	56
Komine,Shane	05	25	aa	OAK	2	1	5	0	31	31	13	5	7	27	3.66	1.22	25.7	252	2.1	7.7	3.6	1.5	29%	77%	81
	06	26	aaa	OAK	11	8	24	0	140	159	69	13	35	98	4.42	1.39	25.1	280	2.3	6.3	2.8	0.8	33%	69%	70
Koplove,Mike	06	30	aaa	ARI	5	0	48	0	65	79	33	6	26	39	4.62	1.61	6.1	294	3.5	5.4	1.5	0.8	34%	72%	37
Korecky,Robert	06	27	a/a	MIN	6	5	50	13	76	116	46	8	38	31	5.44	2.02	7.5	343	4.5	3.7	0.8	1.0	37%	74%	-3
Koronka,John	05	25	aaa	CHC	9	11	23	0	136	148	71	13	47	84	4.68	1.44	25.8	272	3.1	5.6	1.8	0.9	31%	69%	45
Kozlowski,Ben	05	25	a/a	CIN	6	7	28	0	156	205	83	15	49	89	4.80	1.63	25.4	311	2.9	5.2	1.8	0.9	35%	71%	36
	06	26	a/a	LA	3	6	41	1	97	138	59	14	48	59	5.46	1.91	11.4	327	4.4	5.5	1.2	1.3	37%	74%	9
Kranawetter,Josh	06	26	aa	TAM	2	0	28	3	31	44	32	7	17	15	9.31	1.96	5.4	325	5.0	4.3	0.9	2.0	34%	53%	-26
Kuo,Hong-Chih	06	25	aaa	LA	4	3	23	1	53	55	18	5	21	52	3.09	1.43	10.0	261	3.6	8.9	2.5	0.9	34%	81%	83
Laffey,Aaron	06	21	aa	CLE	8	3	19	0	112	139	54	9	34	54	4.34	1.54	26.3	298	2.7	4.3	1.6	0.7	33%	73%	33
Lambert,Chris	05	23	aa	STL	3	8	18	0	85	100	59	8	44	61	6.25	1.69	21.8	287	4.7	6.5	1.4	0.8	34%	63%	40
	06	24	a/a	STL	10	10	24	0	124	150	90	21	63	99	6.52	1.71	24.0	293	4.6	7.2	1.6	1.5	34%	64%	27
Lamura,William	05	25	aa	CHW	5	2	55	1	71	86	46	6	59	65	5.86	2.04	6.4	294	7.5	8.2	1.1	0.8	37%	71%	44
	06	26	aa	LA	6	1	48	4	76	61	21	8	56	70	2.50	1.53	7.1	216	6.6	8.3	1.3	0.9	27%	88%	61
Landeros,Leonard	05	25	aa	OAK	2	2	18	0	31	49	22	3	11	16	6.38	1.92	8.4	352	3.0	4.7	1.5	0.9	39%	67%	17
Lara,Juan	06	26	a/a	CLE	5	3	53	8	61	60	25	3	26	53	3.72	1.41	5.0	251	3.9	7.8	2.0	0.5	32%	73%	80
Larrison,Preston	05	25	aa	DET	4	3	7	0	32	44	22	3	8	10	6.18	1.63	21.0	320	2.4	2.7	1.1	0.9	34%	62%	4
Lavigne,Tim	05	27	a/a	NYM	1	3	52	6	76	92	37	6	41	34	4.34	1.75	6.8	292	4.9	4.0	0.8	0.7	32%	76%	17
	06	28	aaa	NYM	3	2	45	4	82	97	37	9	28	39	4.01	1.52	8.1	288	3.1	4.3	1.4	0.9	31%	76%	24
League,Brandon	05	23	aaa	TOR	4	4	19	0	63	85	46	8	17	33	6.53	1.62	15.0	315	2.4	4.7	1.9	1.1	35%	60%	27
	06	24	aaa	TOR	3	2	31	8	54	69	18	0	16	37	2.99	1.57	7.8	304	2.7	6.1	2.3	0.0	37%	79%	80
Ledezma,Wil	05	25	aaa	DET	4	3	10	0	50	58	37	3	26	36	6.66	1.68	23.0	284	4.7	6.5	1.4	0.5	34%	58%	50
	06	26	aaa	DET	4	3	12	0	71	72	26	7	23	56	3.32	1.34	25.2	257	2.9	7.1	2.4	0.9	31%	78%	71
Leek,Randy	05	28	a/a	STL	15	8	29	0	191	244	98	29	32	78	4.60	1.44	28.7	304	1.5	3.7	2.5	1.4	32%	72%	27
	06	29	aaa	STL	3	7	17	0	101	164	74	22	26	40	6.55	1.88	28.6	357	2.3	3.6	1.5	2.0	37%	69%	-22
Lee,Corey	05	31	aaa	ANA	6	2	14	0	79	70	26	4	40	59	2.91	1.39	24.4	233	4.6	6.7	1.5	0.5	28%	80%	64
Lee,David	05	33	aaa	STL	2	5	40	5	47	64	35	7	21	28	6.62	1.81	5.6	318	4.0	5.3	1.3	1.4	35%	65%	8
	06	34	aaa	BOS	1	2	36	1	50	58	29	6	32	43	5.29	1.79	6.5	284	5.7	7.7	1.4	1.1	34%	72%	39
Lee,Derek	05	31	aaa	TEX	5	2	14	0	88	104	44	8	20	40	4.51	1.41	27.3	288	2.0	4.1	2.0	0.9	31%	69%	38
	06	32	aaa	TEX	6	12	29	0	143	209	108	24	61	75	6.81	1.89	23.7	334	3.8	4.7	1.2	1.5	36%	66%	-3
Lee,Seung Hak	05	26	a/a	PHI	3	2	15	0	66	80	29	6	30	39	3.93	1.66	20.2	293	4.1	5.3	1.3	0.8	33%	78%	32
	06	27	aaa	PHI	8	9	31	2	93	121	74	17	38	49	7.13	1.71	13.9	308	3.7	4.8	1.3	1.6	33%	60%	0
Lehr,Justin	05	28	aaa	MIL	7	7	27	1	88	116	44	9	32	55	4.51	1.69	15.0	311	3.3	5.6	1.7	0.9	36%	75%	36
	06	29	aaa	MIL	4	7	19	0	112	157	71	21	36	73	5.74	1.73	27.4	325	2.9	5.9	2.0	1.7	36%	71%	17
Leicester,Jon	05	27	aaa	CHC	3	8	24	1	98	129	68	19	42	62	6.25	1.75	19.1	311	3.9	5.7	1.5	1.7	34%	68%	7
Lerew,Anthony	05	23	a/a	ATL	10	6	27	0	148	153	75	17	55	102	4.56	1.41	23.7	261	3.3	6.2	1.9	1.0	30%	70%	48
	06	24	a/a	ATL	7	7	25	0	119	166	98	16	53	93	7.40	1.84	22.7	323	4.0	7.0	1.8	1.2	38%	60%	33
Lester,Jon	05	22	aa	BOS	11	6	26	0	148	135	56	11	58	139	3.40	1.30	24.1	238	3.5	8.4	2.4	0.7	31%	75%	88
	06	23	aaa	BOS	3	4	11	0	46	50	19	6	25	40	3.71	1.63	19.1	272	4.8	7.8	1.6	1.1	33%	81%	48
Lewis,Colby	06	27	aaa	DET	6	7	24	0	147	193	89	16	39	86	5.47	1.57	27.6	309	2.4	5.2	2.2	1.0	35%	66%	42
Lewis,Jensen	06	22	aa	CLE	1	2	7	0	39	47	21	4	12	39	4.83	1.51	24.7	292	2.8	9.0	3.3	0.9	38%	69%	91
Ligtenberg,Kerry	05	34	aaa	ARI	4	3	38	1	50	58	20	4	7	43	3.60	1.31	5.6	284	1.3	7.7	5.8	0.8	35%	74%	143
	06	35	aaa	CHC	4	4	53	18	58	82	33	12	6	37	5.06	1.52	4.9	327	1.0	5.7	5.9	1.8	36%	73%	93
Lima,Jose	06	34	aaa	NYM	7	8	25	0	140	181	91	19	22	71	5.82	1.45	24.5	307	1.4	4.6	3.2	1.2	33%	61%	52
Lindstrom,Matt	05	26	aa	NYM	2	5	35	0	73	107	52	12	59	44	6.43	2.26	10.8	333	7.3	5.4	0.7	1.5	37%	74%	-8
	06	27	aa	NYM	2	4	35	11	40	59	28	2	17	40	6.18	1.89	5.5	333	3.9	9.0	2.3	0.5	43%	66%	75
Liotta,Ray	06	24	aa	CHW	3	8	18	0	96	140	78	5	53	43	7.33	2.00	26.3	333	4.9	4.0	0.8	0.5	37%	61%	15
Liriano,Francisco	05	22	a/a	MIN	12	7	27	0	167	138	57	10	50	187	3.08	1.12	25.0	220	2.7	10.1	3.8	0.5	31%	73%	135
Liriano,Pedro	05	25	aaa	PHI	4	9	22	0	99	101	50	13	47	67	4.54	1.49	19.9	259	4.3	6.1	1.4	1.2	29%	73%	34
	06	26	aaa	SF	1	6	24	0	67	92	43	5	27	32	5.83	1.78	13.1	320	3.7	4.3	1.2	0.7	36%	66%	21
Litsch,Jesse	06	22	aa	TOR	3	4	12	0	69	106	56	8	14	47	7.29	1.74	26.8	344	1.8	6.1	3.4	1.0	40%	57%	62
Littleton,Wes	05	23	aa	TEX	2	3	48	3	81	113	48	12	25	59	5.37	1.70	7.8	324	2.7	6.6	2.4	1.4	37%	71%	39
	06	24	a/a	TEX	7	1	30	5	44	34	8	6	13	34	1.69	1.08	5.9	209	2.7	6.9	2.5	1.3	24%	95%	70
Livingston,Bobby	05	23	a/a	SEA	14	6	28	0	168	173	73	9	43	109	3.91	1.29	25.2	261	2.3	5.8	2.5	0.5	31%	69%	77
	06	24	aaa	SEA	8	11	23	0	135	184	80	19	37	62	5.33	1.64	26.8	318	2.5	4.1	1.7	1.3	34%	70%	13
Lizarraga,Sergio	05	24	a/a	ARI	0	2	17	0	30	56	28	6	10	23	8.32	2.19	9.1	388	3.1	7.0	2.3	1.8	45%	64%	11
Liz,Radhames	06	23	aa	BAL	3	1	10	0	50	69	42	12	33	48	7.59	2.04	24.8	321	5.9	8.5	1.4	2.2	38%	67%	6
Lockwood,Brian	05	25	aa	TAM	3	6	24	0	77	131	75	14	28	59	8.71	2.06	16.0	367	3.3	6.9	2.1	1.6	42%	58%	19
Lockwood,Luke	05	24	aa	FLA	2	8	34	1	114	134	54	6	25	68	4.24	1.39	14.5	287	2.0	5.4	2.7	0.5	33%	69%	72
Loewen,Adam	06	23	a/a	BAL	6	2	12	0	71	69	25	4	30	68	3.17	1.39	25.5	250	3.8	8.6	2.3	0.5	33%	78%	89
Logan,Boone	06	22	aaa	CHW	3	1	38	11	42	40	20	1	12	51	4.27	1.24	4.6	245	2.6	11.0	4.2	0.2	37%	63%	153
Looper,Aaron	06	30	aaa	SEA	0	2	41	0	64	110	56	11	26	29	7.79	2.11	7.9	370	3.6	4.0	1.1	1.6	39%	64%	-18
Lopez,Aquilino	05	30	aaa	COL	5	4	45	5	65	71	40	15	11	57	5.59	1.26	6.0	271	1.5	7.9	5.2	2.1	31%	62%	94
	06	31	aaa	SD	3	4	41	2	62	71	39	13	24	60	5.65	1.53	6.7	280	3.5	8.7	2.5	1.8	33%	68%	48
Lopez,Javier	06	29	aaa	BOS	2	1	39	16	49	64	16	3	15	30	3.02	1.61	5.7	307	2.8	5.5	2.0	0.6	36%	83%	49
Lopez,Rafael	05	27	aa	NYM	2	10	32	0	84	134	69	10	39	43	7.38	2.06	13.1	354	4.2	4.6	1.1	1.1	39%	64%	1
Lorenzo,Matt	05	23	aa	TEX	3	5	10	0	46	87	49	12	23	23	9.64	2.37	24.4	391	4.4	4.5	1.0	2.4	41%	62%	-47
Lorraine,Andrew	05	33	aaa	SEA	9	8	33	0	141	184	85	12	55	67	5.44	1.69	19.7	309	3.5	4.3	1.2	0.7	34%	68%	23
Loux,Shane	06	27	aaa	KC	2	5	31	2	54	91	52	2	16	19	8.58	1.97	8.5	364	2.6	3.2	1.2	0.4	40%	53%	16

					Actual				Major League Equivalents																
PITCHER	Yr	Age	Lev	Org	w	l	g	sv	ip	h	er	hr	bb	k	era	br/ip	bf/g	oob	ctl	dom	cmd	hr/9	h%	s%	bpv
Lowery,Devon	06	24	aa	KC	5	1	24	4	33	32	23	4	18	26	6.17	1.50	6.1	248	4.8	7.1	1.5	1.1	29%	59%	46
Lubisich,Nik	05	26	aa	CHW	8	4	20	1	99	131	44	11	23	31	3.97	1.56	22.2	312	2.1	2.8	1.4	1.0	33%	77%	7
Lugo,Ruddy	05	25	aa	TAM	1	1	26	2	40	31	7	1	26	37	1.50	1.41	6.7	210	5.7	8.3	1.4	0.2	28%	90%	86
Lumsden,Tyler	06	23	aa	CHW	11	5	27	0	159	168	56	10	60	80	3.15	1.43	25.6	266	3.4	4.5	1.3	0.6	30%	79%	39
Lundberg,Spike	05	28	aaa	TOR	8	6	50	1	86	124	49	6	27	53	5.16	1.75	8.0	329	2.8	5.5	2.0	0.7	38%	70%	44
	06	29	a/a	LA	15	6	28	0	172	218	76	7	57	86	3.96	1.60	27.8	303	3.0	4.5	1.5	0.4	35%	75%	41
Lynch,Matt	05	25	aa	OAK	7	7	35	1	110	141	60	7	38	53	4.90	1.63	14.3	305	3.1	4.3	1.4	0.6	34%	69%	32
Mabeus,Chris	05	27	aaa	OAK	9	2	42	1	62	67	32	4	24	60	4.64	1.46	6.5	270	3.4	8.7	2.5	0.6	35%	68%	89
	06	28	a/a	OAK	2	3	36	0	48	61	45	5	41	30	8.39	2.13	6.7	303	7.7	5.7	0.7	0.9	35%	59%	18
MacDonald,Michael	06	25	aa	TOR	13	9	28	0	171	236	114	14	43	85	5.98	1.63	27.8	321	2.3	4.4	2.0	0.7	36%	62%	37
Machi,Jean	06	24	aa	TAM	6	1	49	16	71	89	32	3	43	56	4.04	1.85	6.9	299	5.5	7.1	1.3	0.4	37%	78%	53
Mackintosh,Jason	06	26	aa	SEA	4	5	36	0	98	132	55	11	43	46	5.06	1.78	12.8	316	3.9	4.2	1.1	1.1	34%	73%	8
MacLane,Evan	05	23	aa	NYM	3	2	9	0	58	67	29	7	9	40	4.48	1.31	27.3	283	1.4	6.2	4.4	1.1	33%	68%	96
	06	24	a/a	ARI	13	9	28	0	162	228	108	20	41	85	6.00	1.66	26.5	325	2.3	4.7	2.1	1.1	36%	65%	28
MacRae,Scott	05	31	a/a	HOU	6	3	32	1	88	112	40	8	27	37	4.08	1.57	12.4	303	2.7	3.8	1.4	0.8	33%	75%	22
Maduro,Calvin	05	31	a/a	NYY	3	2	12	0	41	60	24	2	14	20	5.34	1.81	16.2	333	3.2	4.3	1.4	0.5	37%	69%	29
	06	32	aa	BAL	1	5	24	0	38	46	31	1	20	36	7.24	1.73	7.4	293	4.7	8.5	1.8	0.3	38%	55%	76
Magrane,Jim	05	27	a/a	TAM	3	10	35	0	112	193	91	14	31	48	7.30	2.00	15.7	371	2.5	3.8	1.5	1.1	40%	63%	3
	06	28	a/a	TAM	12	12	28	0	172	233	114	15	66	88	5.97	1.74	28.6	317	3.4	4.6	1.3	0.8	35%	65%	23
Maholm,Paul	05	23	a/a	PIT	7	3	22	0	117	124	48	7	35	81	3.69	1.36	22.8	266	2.7	6.2	2.3	0.5	32%	73%	72
Mahomes,Pat	05	35	aaa	LA	9	9	40	1	133	155	66	18	59	75	4.49	1.61	15.1	285	4.0	5.1	1.3	1.2	31%	75%	19
	06	36	aaa	KC	1	1	7	0	35	45	29	3	16	23	7.56	1.74	23.4	306	4.0	5.8	1.4	0.8	36%	55%	35
Maine,John	05	24	aaa	BAL	6	11	23	0	128	148	80	15	41	97	5.62	1.48	24.5	283	2.9	6.8	2.4	1.1	33%	63%	57
	06	25	aaa	NYM	3	5	10	0	56	69	31	2	21	41	5.01	1.60	25.4	295	3.4	6.5	1.9	0.3	36%	67%	65
Malaska,Mark	05	28	aaa	BOS	5	3	39	1	87	86	48	2	39	70	5.01	1.44	9.7	254	4.0	7.3	1.8	0.2	32%	62%	79
Maldonado,Ivan	06	26	aa	NYM	2	3	48	3	61	87	28	8	32	43	4.07	1.96	6.2	329	4.7	6.3	1.3	1.2	38%	82%	19
Mallette,Brian	05	31	aaa	PIT	2	1	24	0	37	46	23	7	21	23	5.66	1.80	7.3	296	5.1	5.5	1.1	1.6	32%	72%	2
Malone,Corwin	05	25	aa	CHW	5	5	33	1	97	124	63	8	60	62	5.87	1.90	14.2	305	5.6	5.8	1.0	0.7	36%	69%	29
	06	26	aa	CHW	9	11	27	0	154	201	125	23	118	90	7.32	2.07	28.5	309	6.9	5.2	0.8	1.3	34%	66%	0
Manning,Charlie	05	26	a/a	NYY	5	4	52	2	82	89	42	7	51	55	4.62	1.70	7.3	270	5.6	6.0	1.1	0.7	32%	73%	38
	06	28	a/a	NYY	8	3	49	1	84	86	38	7	34	59	4.06	1.44	7.5	260	3.7	6.3	1.7	0.7	31%	73%	55
Manon,Julio	06	33	aaa	BAL	0	2	47	30	50	45	18	5	22	52	3.21	1.34	4.6	236	4.0	9.4	2.4	0.9	31%	80%	85
Mansfield,Monte	05	25	aa	HOU	3	2	43	0	75	84	47	9	37	62	5.68	1.61	7.9	277	4.4	7.4	1.7	1.1	33%	66%	45
	06	26	aa	HOU	2	1	30	0	52	68	30	3	37	37	5.17	2.00	8.6	308	6.3	6.4	1.0	0.6	37%	74%	36
Marcum,Shaun	05	24	a/a	TOR	13	5	27	0	157	188	96	28	29	115	5.50	1.38	25.0	291	1.7	6.6	4.0	1.6	33%	64%	72
	06	25	aaa	TOR	4	0	18	0	52	58	27	8	10	52	4.66	1.30	12.2	276	1.7	9.0	5.2	1.4	34%	68%	121
Markray,Thad	05	26	aa	KC	4	7	22	1	65	75	44	9	21	33	6.05	1.47	13.0	282	2.9	4.6	1.6	1.3	30%	60%	21
	06	27	aa	KC	5	0	35	1	64	76	25	10	27	32	3.55	1.60	8.3	288	3.7	4.5	1.2	1.4	31%	83%	10
Marmol,Carlos	05	23	aa	CHC	3	4	14	0	81	83	43	13	43	62	4.77	1.55	25.9	260	4.8	6.9	1.4	1.4	30%	73%	31
	06	24	a/a	CHC	3	2	13	0	61	60	28	1	30	58	4.11	1.47	20.6	251	4.4	8.6	1.9	0.2	34%	70%	93
Marsonek,Sam	05	27	aaa	NYY	3	7	49	7	77	107	67	8	37	48	7.85	1.87	7.5	323	4.3	5.6	1.3	1.0	37%	57%	23
Martinez,Anastacio	05	25	aaa	BOS	3	4	35	1	58	82	44	4	26	39	6.80	1.86	7.9	325	4.0	6.0	1.5	0.6	38%	62%	39
	06	28	a/a	WAS	7	11	26	0	141	171	94	16	72	93	6.02	1.73	25.2	294	4.6	5.9	1.3	1.0	34%	66%	28
Martinez,Edgar	06	25	aa	BOS	5	3	49	12	69	65	28	12	19	48	3.71	1.22	5.8	245	2.5	6.3	2.6	1.5	27%	77%	52
Martinez,Ronnie	06	23	aa	HOU	3	1	10	0	49	66	37	7	19	37	6.82	1.73	22.8	316	3.4	6.8	2.0	1.3	37%	61%	34
Martin,J.D.	05	23	aa	CLE	3	1	10	0	56	47	18	3	8	55	2.88	0.98	21.9	223	1.3	8.8	6.9	0.5	30%	71%	193
Masset,Nick	05	23	aa	TEX	7	12	29	0	157	240	144	26	64	88	8.27	1.94	26.3	344	3.7	5.1	1.4	1.5	38%	57%	1
	06	24	a/a	TEX	6	7	32	3	115	148	68	6	53	88	5.32	1.75	16.8	306	4.1	6.9	1.7	0.5	38%	68%	56
Mastny,Tom	06	26	a/a	CLE	2	2	36	1	62	48	19	0	26	65	2.74	1.20	7.1	210	3.8	9.3	2.5	0.0	30%	75%	121
Mateo,Juan	06	24	aa	CHC	7	4	18	0	92	107	49	10	32	60	4.83	1.51	22.7	285	3.1	5.9	1.9	1.0	33%	70%	43
Mateo,Nathaniel	05	25	aa	SEA	3	8	62	1	69	92	38	5	27	52	4.94	1.72	5.2	312	3.6	6.8	1.9	0.7	38%	71%	53
	06	26	aa	SEA	3	7	26	0	68	103	64	13	37	49	8.52	2.06	13.0	342	4.8	6.4	1.3	1.8	39%	60%	0
Mathes,JR	06	25	aa	CHC	10	8	27	0	159	232	101	17	39	95	5.71	1.70	27.2	333	2.2	5.4	2.4	1.0	38%	67%	43
Mathieson,Scott	06	23	a/a	PHI	10	3	19	0	127	124	70	15	41	113	4.96	1.30	28.2	251	2.9	8.0	2.8	1.1	31%	63%	79
Matos,Josue	05	28	a/a	TOR	8	4	30	0	103	143	71	28	18	61	6.21	1.56	15.4	321	1.6	5.3	3.3	2.4	33%	67%	20
Mattioni,Nick	05	27	a/a	OAK	2	5	49	4	78	82	37	11	29	57	4.23	1.42	6.9	265	3.3	6.5	2.0	1.3	30%	74%	44
	06	28	a/a	PHI	5	5	40	5	71	95	47	17	21	39	5.97	1.63	8.1	315	2.6	5.0	1.9	2.2	33%	70%	-4
Maust,David	05	27	aa	WAS	5	4	26	0	100	99	32	8	15	58	2.89	1.14	15.6	253	1.3	5.2	3.9	0.7	29%	77%	96
	06	28	aa	WAS	6	10	23	0	121	171	94	19	47	44	6.98	1.80	24.9	326	3.5	3.3	0.9	1.4	34%	62%	-14
Mays,Joe	06	31	aaa	CIN	6	3	10	0	67	92	36	6	16	31	4.77	1.61	30.4	320	2.1	4.1	2.0	0.7	35%	71%	35
May,Darrell	05	33	aaa	NYY	6	2	10	0	58	78	32	6	5	31	4.89	1.43	25.3	315	0.8	4.9	6.0	1.0	35%	67%	117
	06	34	aaa	CIN	3	3	8	0	46	53	29	8	15	29	5.74	1.46	25.3	281	2.9	5.7	2.0	1.6	30%	64%	26
Mazone,Brian	05	29	aa	SF	11	8	29	1	121	180	69	11	43	56	5.15	1.84	19.9	337	3.2	4.1	1.3	0.8	37%	72%	16
	06	30	a/a	PHI	14	6	26	0	166	219	71	16	56	74	3.86	1.66	29.2	311	3.0	4.0	1.3	0.9	34%	79%	18
McBeth,Marcus	06	26	a/a	OAK	3	3	51	25	61	61	30	8	28	56	4.41	1.45	5.2	255	4.1	8.2	2.0	1.1	31%	73%	61
McBride,Macay	05	23	a/a	ATL	4	6	31	2	68	81	38	8	34	55	5.02	1.69	10.1	289	4.5	7.3	1.6	1.1	35%	72%	43
McCarthy,Brandon	05	22	aaa	CHW	7	7	20	0	119	112	59	19	30	117	4.46	1.20	24.5	244	2.3	8.8	3.8	1.4	30%	68%	96
McClaskey,Tim	05	30	a/a	HOU	8	12	29	0	170	217	105	24	33	77	5.55	1.47	25.7	304	1.7	4.1	2.3	1.3	32%	64%	29
	06	31	aa	PHI	4	8	32	0	128	241	139	23	30	48	9.73	2.12	20.2	392	2.1	3.3	1.6	1.6	41%	53%	-18
McClellan,Zach	05	27	aaa	COL	3	3	44	0	71	100	51	11	23	55	6.40	1.73	7.5	325	2.9	7.0	2.4	1.4	38%	65%	40
	06	28	aaa	COL	4	3	54	3	64	95	40	4	29	40	5.61	1.93	5.8	336	4.1	5.6	1.4	0.6	39%	70%	32
McConnell,Sam	05	30	aaa	ATL	4	9	20	0	92	165	76	23	24	35	7.42	2.05	22.9	380	2.4	3.4	1.4	2.3	39%	68%	-38
McCurdy,Nick	05	26	aa	BAL	5	5	30	2	64	96	47	14	18	38	6.56	1.77	10.0	338	2.5	5.3	2.1	2.0	36%	67%	3
	06	27	a/a	BAL	5	2	52	3	79	121	40	8	24	49	4.56	1.84	7.2	344	2.8	5.5	2.0	0.9	39%	77%	35
McGill III,Trae	05	28	aa	KC	3	4	29	2	46	66	33	4	30	28	6.33	2.08	8.0	329	5.8	5.5	0.9	0.7	38%	69%	20
McGinley,Blake	05	27	a/a	NYM	5	4	45	2	87	102	43	18	23	51	4.40	1.44	8.4	287	2.4	5.3	2.2	1.9	30%	77%	19
	06	28	aaa	NYM	2	2	22	1	58	78	29	8	16	29	4.51	1.63	12.0	317	2.5	4.5	1.8	1.2	35%	75%	21
McGlinchy,Kevin	05	28	a/a	CHC	0	2	27	3	37	59	31	7	18	19	7.40	2.06	6.9	351	4.3	4.5	1.1	1.7	38%	66%	-17

					Actual				Major League Equivalents																
PITCHER	Yr	Age	Lev	Org	w	l	g	sv	ip	h	er	hr	bb	k	era	br/ip	bf/g	oob	ctl	dom	cmd	hr/9	h%	s%	bpv
McGowan,Dustin	05	23	aa	TOR	0	2	6	0	35	46	21	9	11	28	5.30	1.65	26.7	312	2.9	7.2	2.5	2.4	34%	77%	16
	06	25	aaa	TOR	4	5	23	1	84	94	56	9	42	74	6.00	1.62	16.6	277	4.5	7.9	1.8	1.0	34%	63%	55
McLeary,Marty	05	31	aaa	SD	5	8	41	0	110	140	63	8	52	86	5.18	1.75	12.5	304	4.3	7.0	1.6	0.6	37%	70%	52
	06	32	aaa	PIT	3	4	35	2	104	124	46	7	37	92	4.01	1.55	13.3	290	3.2	8.0	2.5	0.6	37%	75%	78
McLemore,Mark	05	25	aa	HOU	5	6	15	0	73	76	34	6	38	51	4.14	1.55	21.8	262	4.7	6.3	1.4	0.8	31%	75%	46
	06	26	aaa	HOU	2	3	21	0	57	56	22	5	38	43	3.41	1.64	12.4	250	6.0	6.7	1.1	0.8	30%	81%	44
McNab,Timothy	05	25	aa	NYM	1	4	41	1	79	122	62	7	21	45	7.09	1.81	9.1	346	2.4	5.1	2.1	0.8	39%	59%	38
	06	26	a/a	NYM	3	2	16	1	42	71	28	4	2	20	5.95	1.75	12.2	367	0.5	4.2	8.9	1.0	40%	66%	166
McNichol,Brian	05	31	aaa	BAL	6	7	36	0	83	109	52	12	28	41	5.59	1.66	10.6	311	3.1	4.4	1.4	1.3	34%	68%	12
McNutt,Michael	05	26	aa	FLA	3	2	31	1	54	59	32	10	29	31	5.37	1.63	7.9	272	4.8	5.1	1.1	1.7	29%	71%	3
Mears,Chris	05	28	a/a	ATL	3	5	44	3	57	72	40	5	30	14	6.35	1.79	6.1	303	4.7	2.2	0.5	0.7	32%	64%	-4
Meaux,Ryan	05	27	aa	SD	7	2	53	3	84	115	34	3	22	61	3.69	1.63	7.2	319	2.3	6.5	2.8	0.4	39%	77%	78
	06	28	a/a	SD	3	4	48	1	86	135	66	9	40	51	6.89	2.04	8.9	350	4.2	5.3	1.3	1.0	40%	66%	14
Medders,Brandon	05	26	aaa	ARI	3	2	36	8	36	33	11	3	17	40	2.77	1.40	4.3	240	4.3	9.9	2.3	0.8	33%	83%	92
Medlock,Calvin	06	24	aa	CIN	7	2	42	2	63	67	29	5	30	57	4.11	1.53	6.7	266	4.3	8.1	1.9	0.7	34%	74%	69
Mendoza,Luis	06	23	aa	TEX	3	9	16	0	86	158	95	8	27	43	9.93	2.15	27.3	386	2.8	4.5	1.6	0.8	43%	51%	13
Mendoza,Ramiro	06	34	aaa	NYY	2	5	24	0	63	109	65	14	16	29	9.31	1.99	12.9	373	2.3	4.2	1.9	2.0	39%	54%	-14
Mercado,Hector	05	31	aaa	TEX	3	0	21	1	30	35	7	1	19	24	2.21	1.79	6.7	284	5.7	7.1	1.3	0.3	36%	88%	58
	06	32	aaa	DET	3	2	26	1	32	45	19	1	19	21	5.33	2.01	6.1	326	5.3	5.9	1.1	0.3	39%	72%	39
Merchant,Jamie	05	25	aa	HOU	3	3	24	2	50	56	35	9	23	36	6.23	1.57	9.4	276	4.2	6.5	1.6	1.7	31%	64%	20
Meredith,Cla	05	22	a/a	BOS	3	5	51	19	61	74	35	6	15	46	5.16	1.46	5.2	293	2.2	6.8	3.1	0.9	35%	65%	75
	06	23	aaa	SD	3	0	32	2	46	47	15	3	9	33	2.93	1.22	5.9	259	1.8	6.5	3.7	0.6	31%	77%	101
Messenger,Randy	05	24	aaa	FLA	4	2	39	7	48	46	20	4	16	32	3.73	1.29	5.2	246	3.0	6.0	2.0	0.7	29%	72%	61
Meyers,Mike	05	28	a/a	MIL	7	4	44	1	100	134	64	18	49	69	5.78	1.84	10.8	315	4.4	6.2	1.4	1.7	35%	72%	9
	06	29	a/a	MIL	5	6	32	0	72	89	48	7	35	54	6.02	1.73	10.5	298	4.4	6.7	1.5	0.9	35%	65%	41
Meyer,Dan	05	24	aaa	OAK	2	8	19	0	89	108	56	15	41	54	5.66	1.67	21.5	294	4.1	5.5	1.3	1.5	32%	69%	11
	06	25	aaa	OAK	3	3	10	0	49	69	30	10	19	25	5.54	1.79	23.2	323	3.5	4.5	1.3	1.8	34%	74%	-11
Miadich,Bart	05	30	aaa	FLA	3	2	29	11	32	25	9	2	21	49	2.46	1.43	4.8	212	5.8	13.7	2.4	0.6	36%	85%	126
	06	31	aaa	TAM	3	8	61	10	67	48	36	6	58	66	4.78	1.58	4.9	196	7.8	8.8	1.1	0.7	26%	70%	70
Michalak,Chris	05	35	aaa	ARI	9	13	26	0	165	197	92	29	41	64	5.00	1.44	27.7	290	2.2	3.5	1.6	1.6	29%	70%	2
	06	36	aaa	CIN	9	5	23	0	132	183	64	24	32	48	4.37	1.63	26.1	322	2.2	3.3	1.5	1.6	33%	79%	-7
Middleton,Kyle	05	25	aa	KC	10	9	28	0	171	252	112	19	37	86	5.90	1.69	28.2	335	1.9	4.5	2.3	1.0	37%	65%	34
	06	26	a/a	KC	5	11	29	1	159	252	107	20	56	77	6.04	1.94	26.6	352	3.1	4.3	1.4	1.1	38%	70%	6
Mildren,Paul	06	22	aa	FLA	10	10	28	0	167	195	105	22	61	136	5.66	1.53	26.6	286	3.3	7.3	2.2	1.2	34%	65%	53
Miller,Adam	06	22	a/a	CLE	15	6	27	0	158	147	60	9	46	150	3.42	1.22	24.2	241	2.6	8.5	3.3	0.5	32%	72%	112
Miller,Colby	05	24	aa	MIN	2	7	12	0	70	82	35	7	21	35	4.51	1.47	25.6	287	2.7	4.5	1.7	0.9	32%	71%	32
Miller,Greg	06	22	a/a	LA	4	0	44	1	59	48	22	1	44	49	3.33	1.54	6.0	216	6.7	7.5	1.1	0.1	28%	77%	76
Miller,Jason	05	23	a/a	MIN	3	2	39	4	75	71	32	9	40	72	3.83	1.48	8.5	244	4.8	8.6	1.8	1.1	31%	77%	63
	06	24	aaa	MIN	3	8	32	1	99	127	62	14	42	74	5.63	1.71	14.3	305	3.8	6.7	1.8	1.3	35%	69%	33
Miller,Jeff	05	26	aaa	PIT	5	7	57	0	80	86	35	12	24	51	3.97	1.37	6.0	268	2.7	5.8	2.1	1.4	30%	76%	40
Miller,Jim	06	24	aa	COL	0	3	45	12	44	62	26	14	14	33	5.37	1.72	4.5	325	2.8	6.8	2.4	2.8	35%	80%	-2
Miller,Joshua	06	28	aa	HOU	11	10	33	0	152	224	102	19	49	72	6.06	1.80	21.7	336	2.9	4.3	1.5	1.1	36%	67%	10
Miller,Justin	05	28	aaa	TOR	3	1	28	2	50	48	17	3	15	46	3.09	1.27	7.5	249	2.7	8.2	3.0	0.6	32%	77%	101
Miner,Zach	05	24	a/a	DET	5	9	27	1	140	173	76	12	70	87	4.88	1.73	24.2	297	4.5	5.6	1.2	0.8	34%	72%	32
	06	25	aaa	DET	6	0	9	0	51	51	21	2	21	35	3.71	1.41	24.5	255	3.7	6.2	1.7	0.4	31%	73%	65
Minix,Travis	05	28	a/a	PHI	2	1	53	8	76	72	21	7	21	49	2.50	1.22	5.9	244	2.5	5.8	2.3	0.8	28%	84%	65
	06	29	aaa	PHI	1	3	40	3	48	63	22	7	14	21	4.10	1.60	5.4	308	2.7	3.9	1.5	1.2	33%	78%	11
Misch,Patrick	05	24	a/a	SF	7	11	28	0	163	219	105	22	45	92	5.80	1.62	26.4	315	2.5	5.1	2.0	1.2	35%	66%	29
	06	25	a/a	SF	9	6	28	0	168	208	74	16	37	110	3.94	1.46	26.3	298	2.0	5.9	3.0	0.8	35%	75%	68
Mitchell,Andy	05	27	aaa	BAL	8	0	47	0	77	101	55	7	32	31	6.38	1.72	7.6	310	3.7	3.7	1.0	0.9	33%	62%	10
	06	28	aaa	BAL	1	1	50	0	67	96	26	4	30	41	3.46	1.87	6.4	328	4.0	5.5	1.4	0.6	38%	82%	34
Mitre,Sergio	05	25	aaa	CHC	5	6	13	0	70	78	37	5	22	48	4.74	1.42	23.5	276	2.8	6.2	2.2	0.6	33%	66%	63
Mobley,Chris	06	23	aa	FLA	1	4	52	4	58	72	36	6	35	45	5.58	1.84	5.3	298	5.4	6.9	1.3	1.0	36%	70%	35
Mock,Garrett	06	23	aa	WAS	4	12	27	0	147	209	120	21	61	104	7.31	1.83	25.9	327	3.7	6.3	1.7	1.3	38%	60%	26
Montero,Agustin	05	28	a/a	TEX	2	4	44	2	66	93	56	13	41	54	7.70	2.03	7.4	325	5.6	7.3	1.3	1.8	38%	64%	8
	06	29	aaa	CHW	2	3	39	1	59	71	47	12	23	43	7.20	1.60	6.8	293	3.5	6.5	1.9	1.8	32%	57%	19
Montero,Oscar	05	27	aa	SF	5	4	35	0	50	61	31	8	31	43	5.64	1.86	6.8	296	5.6	7.8	1.4	1.5	35%	73%	26
	06	28	aa	SF	2	1	32	1	46	73	43	6	28	43	8.32	2.17	7.3	351	5.4	8.5	1.6	1.2	43%	61%	32
Montes,Alberto	05	26	aa	SF	0	2	23	0	36	68	40	7	10	20	9.94	2.15	8.0	391	2.5	4.9	2.0	1.7	43%	53%	-2
Moorhead,Brandon	06	27	aa	SEA	2	3	9	0	40	70	40	5	22	19	9.03	2.29	23.2	375	4.9	4.3	0.9	1.0	41%	59%	-7
Moreno,Anthony	05	21	aa	SF	2	4	18	0	50	67	33	4	22	28	5.93	1.78	13.1	314	4.0	5.0	1.3	0.7	36%	66%	28
Moreno,Victor	05	25	aaa	OAK	4	2	48	2	73	78	39	4	43	59	4.85	1.66	7.0	267	5.3	7.3	1.4	0.5	33%	70%	59
	06	27	aaa	OAK	5	4	34	4	100	134	68	7	40	55	6.15	1.74	13.7	314	3.6	5.0	1.4	0.7	36%	63%	31
Morillo,Juan	06	23	aa	COL	12	8	27	0	140	151	93	17	77	113	5.97	1.63	23.6	270	4.9	7.3	1.5	1.1	32%	64%	43
Morris,Cory	05	26	aa	BAL	8	5	29	0	142	163	77	17	93	121	4.87	1.80	23.2	282	5.9	7.7	1.3	1.1	34%	75%	39
	06	27	a/a	BAL	2	9	18	0	78	107	57	9	72	56	6.61	2.29	22.6	319	8.3	6.4	0.8	1.1	37%	72%	14
Moseley,Dustin	05	24	aaa	ANA	4	6	17	0	82	104	44	9	27	32	4.82	1.60	21.8	303	3.0	3.5	1.2	1.0	32%	71%	11
	06	25	aaa	ANA	13	8	26	0	149	175	82	17	48	96	4.95	1.49	25.3	287	2.9	5.8	2.0	1.0	33%	68%	44
Moss,Damian	05	29	aaa	SEA	9	7	25	0	137	145	67	10	81	79	4.37	1.65	25.1	266	5.3	5.2	1.0	0.6	31%	74%	34
Moylan,Peter	06	28	aaa	ATL	1	7	35	1	56	78	58	5	43	46	9.27	2.15	8.1	322	6.9	7.3	1.1	0.8	39%	55%	31
Muecke,Joshua	06	25	aa	HOU	0	7	25	0	62	111	65	9	28	34	9.47	2.24	12.8	379	4.1	5.0	1.2	1.4	42%	57%	-7
Muegge,Danny	06	26	aa	LA	9	9	25	0	141	190	88	26	44	64	5.59	1.66	25.9	315	2.8	4.1	1.4	1.6	33%	70%	-2
Mujica,Edward	05	21	aa	CLE	2	1	27	10	34	41	13	2	5	29	3.43	1.35	5.4	292	1.3	7.7	5.8	0.5	37%	75%	149
	06	22	a/a	CLE	4	1	34	13	51	49	11	1	15	41	1.93	1.25	6.3	247	2.6	7.2	2.7	0.2	32%	84%	101
Munoz,Arnie	05	23	aaa	CHW	8	13	39	1	126	156	69	20	58	91	4.92	1.70	14.9	297	4.1	6.5	1.6	1.4	34%	75%	25
	06	24	a/a	CHW	2	5	33	2	52	61	41	7	24	44	7.12	1.62	7.2	286	4.1	7.5	1.8	1.2	34%	56%	44
Munro,Pete	05	30	aaa	NYY	10	7	43	0	116	161	73	16	41	60	5.68	1.74	12.6	322	3.2	4.7	1.5	1.2	35%	69%	13
	06	31	aaa	MIN	8	12	30	0	162	249	121	20	57	78	6.72	1.89	26.0	345	3.2	4.3	1.4	1.1	38%	65%	7
Munter,Scott	06	27	aa	SF	1	4	28	1	40	67	37	1	20	17	8.28	2.16	7.3	363	4.4	3.7	0.8	0.3	40%	58%	15

PITCHER	Yr	Age	Lev	Org	Actual				Major League Equivalents																
					w	l	g	sv	ip	h	er	hr	bb	k	era	br/ip	bf/g	oob	ctl	dom	cmd	hr/9	h%	s%	bpv
Murphy,Bill	05	24	aaa	ARI	6	8	23	0	121	145	81	15	72	79	6.02	1.79	24.8	291	5.4	5.9	1.1	1.1	33%	67%	22
	06	25	a/a	ARI	5	5	42	0	101	134	85	9	49	82	7.58	1.81	11.4	311	4.4	7.3	1.7	0.8	38%	56%	46
Murray,A.J.	05	24	a/a	TEX	5	4	13	0	68	83	33	8	17	52	4.37	1.47	23.0	295	2.3	6.9	3.1	1.1	35%	73%	70
Musser,Neal	05	25	aaa	NYM	6	11	24	0	123	160	82	13	54	74	5.98	1.73	23.9	307	3.9	5.4	1.4	1.0	35%	66%	26
	06	26	a/a	ARI	8	6	28	2	129	166	93	19	81	72	6.50	1.91	22.3	305	5.7	5.0	0.9	1.3	33%	67%	3
Nageotte,Clint	05	25	aaa	SEA	2	1	19	2	34	23	11	2	22	32	2.91	1.32	7.6	188	5.8	8.5	1.5	0.5	25%	79%	83
	06	26	aaa	SEA	7	7	19	0	89	115	67	6	55	46	6.73	1.90	22.6	307	5.5	4.6	0.8	0.6	35%	63%	20
Nall,T.J.	05	25	aaa	LA	6	7	29	0	108	143	69	15	39	80	5.75	1.69	17.2	312	3.3	6.7	2.1	1.3	36%	68%	38
	06	26	a/a	LA	10	7	31	2	143	144	56	12	33	125	3.51	1.23	19.2	256	2.1	7.9	3.8	0.7	32%	73%	110
Nance,Shane	05	28	aaa	KC	3	4	45	2	59	65	39	8	28	46	5.89	1.56	5.9	272	4.3	6.9	1.6	1.1	32%	63%	42
Nannini,Mike	05	25	a/a	TOR	10	4	32	1	110	122	82	16	35	56	6.71	1.42	15.0	275	2.8	4.6	1.6	1.3	29%	53%	23
	06	26	a/a	DET	1	2	39	2	61	77	43	19	31	43	6.39	1.77	7.3	301	4.6	6.4	1.4	2.8	31%	73%	-21
Narveson,Chris	05	24	aaa	STL	4	6	23	0	118	124	67	15	48	65	5.11	1.46	22.5	265	3.7	5.0	1.4	1.1	29%	67%	26
	06	25	aaa	STL	8	5	15	0	80	83	32	10	34	50	3.60	1.46	23.4	262	3.8	5.6	1.5	1.1	29%	79%	33
Neal,Blaine	06	29	aa	PIT	2	0	29	2	40	51	15	3	13	31	3.36	1.59	6.2	304	2.8	7.0	2.5	0.6	37%	80%	72
Nelson,Bubba	05	24	aa	CIN	2	4	42	12	68	76	39	5	27	56	5.15	1.51	7.2	276	3.6	7.4	2.0	0.7	34%	66%	66
	06	25	aa	SD	5	7	52	2	83	87	49	8	52	65	5.30	1.67	7.3	263	5.7	7.0	1.2	0.8	32%	69%	45
Nelson,Joe	05	31	a/a	TAM	0	3	44	7	59	63	34	11	35	58	5.14	1.65	6.1	266	5.3	8.8	1.6	1.7	32%	74%	38
	06	32	aaa	KC	2	2	24	7	32	23	9	4	13	32	2.66	1.12	5.4	199	3.6	9.1	2.6	1.2	25%	83%	88
Neshek,Patrick	05	25	aa	MIN	6	4	55	24	82	88	27	10	24	75	2.92	1.37	6.4	268	2.7	8.2	3.1	1.1	33%	84%	82
	06	26	aaa	MIN	6	2	33	14	60	54	20	9	16	72	2.94	1.17	7.4	234	2.5	10.8	4.4	1.4	31%	83%	122
Neu,Mike	05	28	aaa	LA	2	2	34	1	81	86	40	7	53	40	4.44	1.71	11.1	267	5.8	4.4	0.8	0.8	29%	75%	20
Newman,Joshua	06	24	aa	COL	9	5	62	2	77	69	37	11	24	63	4.31	1.22	5.1	236	2.8	7.3	2.6	1.2	28%	68%	69
Niemann,Jeff	06	24	aa	TAM	5	5	14	0	77	73	35	8	34	70	4.09	1.39	23.7	245	4.0	8.2	2.1	1.0	31%	73%	69
Nieve,Fernando	05	23	a/a	HOU	8	7	27	0	167	177	85	19	62	142	4.58	1.43	26.9	266	3.3	7.7	2.3	1.0	32%	70%	65
Nin,Sandy	05	25	aa	COL	10	6	20	0	129	147	70	24	18	61	4.88	1.27	27.1	280	1.2	4.3	3.4	1.7	29%	67%	46
	06	26	aaa	COL	1	3	6	0	31	38	21	4	8	21	5.95	1.49	22.9	295	2.4	6.2	2.6	1.2	34%	61%	52
Nippert,Dustin	05	24	aa	ARI	8	3	18	0	117	115	40	5	44	84	3.07	1.36	27.8	251	3.4	6.4	1.9	0.4	31%	77%	71
	06	25	aaa	ARI	13	8	25	0	140	182	89	12	51	114	5.71	1.66	25.7	308	3.2	7.3	2.3	0.8	38%	65%	61
Nitkowski,C.J.	05	33	a/a	WAS	4	2	45	6	54	50	18	3	17	32	2.96	1.23	5.0	241	2.8	5.4	1.9	0.6	28%	77%	63
	06	34	aaa	PIT	5	1	58	4	60	74	29	5	32	46	4.41	1.75	4.8	295	4.7	6.8	1.4	0.8	36%	76%	44
Nolasco,Ricky	05	23	aa	CHC	14	3	27	0	161	178	67	17	49	152	3.74	1.41	25.8	274	2.7	8.5	3.1	0.9	35%	76%	88
Nomo,Hideo	05	37	aaa	NYY	2	3	7	0	37	35	18	1	23	32	4.34	1.56	23.7	243	5.6	7.8	1.4	0.3	32%	70%	75
Norderum,Jason	05	24	aa	WAS	3	3	25	2	47	55	27	3	25	28	5.13	1.69	8.7	285	4.7	5.4	1.1	0.6	33%	69%	36
	06	25	a/a	WAS	1	0	19	0	48	58	27	3	29	20	5.02	1.80	11.9	291	5.4	3.8	0.7	0.6	32%	72%	17
Norton,Phil	05	30	aaa	CHC	3	5	33	0	63	74	51	13	36	37	7.21	1.74	8.9	286	5.2	5.3	1.0	1.9	30%	61%	-5
Nunez,Franklin	05	29	aaa	TAM	5	1	27	3	32	35	24	1	20	27	6.61	1.74	5.6	274	5.7	7.5	1.3	0.3	35%	59%	64
	06	30	aaa	ATL	1	6	30	2	44	74	45	5	31	28	9.19	2.37	7.8	364	6.3	5.8	0.9	1.1	41%	60%	2
Nunez,Leo	06	23	a/a	KC	3	4	38	8	59	61	22	7	23	48	3.36	1.42	6.7	261	3.5	7.3	2.1	1.1	31%	81%	58
Nunez,Vladimir	05	31	aaa	ARI	4	4	56	12	67	74	33	7	28	55	4.47	1.52	5.3	275	3.7	7.4	2.0	0.9	34%	72%	59
Nussbeck,Mark	05	31	a/a	STL	6	6	25	2	85	98	37	9	14	58	3.87	1.32	14.4	282	1.5	6.1	4.0	0.9	33%	73%	91
O'Connor,Brian	05	28	a/a	ATL	9	7	31	0	134	173	78	9	76	72	5.22	1.86	20.7	307	5.1	4.9	0.9	0.6	35%	72%	24
	06	29	aaa	ATL	8	10	28	0	148	214	104	11	87	62	6.34	2.03	26.2	331	5.3	3.8	0.7	0.7	36%	68%	6
O'Flaherty,Eric	06	22	a/a	SEA	3	2	27	7	43	52	6	0	16	38	1.20	1.59	7.2	294	3.4	7.9	2.3	0.0	39%	92%	93
O'Malley,Ryan	05	25	a/a	CHC	6	5	37	0	104	139	65	16	37	67	5.64	1.69	13.0	314	3.2	5.7	1.8	1.4	35%	69%	24
	06	27	aaa	CHC	7	7	26	0	123	169	78	12	33	61	5.72	1.64	21.6	320	2.4	4.5	1.9	0.9	35%	65%	30
O'Sullivan,Mark	05	27	aa	ANA	1	4	45	0	76	111	62	10	41	33	7.35	2.01	8.3	334	4.9	3.9	0.8	1.2	36%	64%	-8
Obenchain,Stephen	05	24	aa	OAK	4	3	11	0	51	76	38	4	28	30	6.66	2.04	23.1	336	5.0	5.3	1.1	0.7	39%	66%	20
Obermueller,Wes	05	29	aaa	MIL	3	1	9	1	42	44	14	1	14	32	2.99	1.38	20.1	264	3.0	6.8	2.3	0.2	33%	77%	83
Ohlendorf,Ross	06	24	a/a	ARI	10	8	28	0	182	226	88	16	30	111	4.33	1.40	28.1	298	1.5	5.5	3.7	0.8	34%	70%	81
Ojeda,Alvis	06	23	aa	LA	7	3	30	1	85	100	37	6	39	51	3.93	1.64	12.9	287	4.1	5.4	1.3	0.7	33%	77%	38
Oldham,Thomas	05	23	aa	SEA	13	7	27	0	154	209	77	16	48	102	4.51	1.67	26.2	317	2.8	5.9	2.1	1.0	37%	75%	42
Olenberger,Kasey	05	28	aa	ANA	9	7	32	0	123	172	64	16	42	48	4.66	1.74	17.9	324	3.1	3.5	1.1	1.1	34%	76%	1
	06	29	aaa	ANA	7	5	25	0	121	149	78	16	48	57	5.83	1.63	22.1	297	3.6	4.2	1.2	1.2	32%	66%	10
Olivera,Manuel	06	29	aa	FLA	5	9	25	0	108	181	81	6	55	47	6.76	2.19	22.1	365	4.6	3.9	0.9	0.5	40%	67%	8
Oliver,Darren	05	35	aaa	CHC	1	3	7	0	31	69	38	6	8	15	10.93	2.50	24.1	433	2.4	4.4	1.8	1.8	46%	56%	-22
Olsen,Kevin	06	30	aa	OAK	6	1	13	0	84	123	56	10	27	29	5.96	1.78	30.5	333	2.9	3.1	1.1	1.1	35%	67%	-2
Olsen,Scott	05	22	aa	FLA	6	4	14	0	80	87	43	7	29	85	4.83	1.45	25.0	271	3.3	9.6	2.9	0.8	36%	67%	96
Olson,Garrett	06	23	aa	BAL	6	5	14	0	84	95	44	6	32	76	4.71	1.51	26.6	279	3.4	8.1	2.4	0.6	36%	69%	79
Olson,Jason	05	27	a/a	ANA	1	3	43	6	75	97	57	10	45	47	6.90	1.89	8.4	306	5.4	5.6	1.0	1.2	34%	64%	12
Olson,Justin	05	25	aa	MIN	9	8	31	0	109	120	79	20	57	81	6.51	1.62	16.0	274	4.7	6.7	1.4	1.7	31%	62%	21
	06	27	aa	MIN	7	7	32	1	88	134	79	15	52	75	8.10	2.11	13.9	343	5.3	7.6	1.4	1.5	41%	62%	17
Ool,Kevin	06	26	aa	STL	3	3	45	0	83	104	49	11	21	33	5.29	1.51	8.2	301	2.3	3.6	1.6	1.2	32%	67%	13
Orenduff,Justin	05	22	aa	LA	5	1	13	0	61	54	27	6	21	53	3.98	1.23	19.5	232	3.1	7.8	2.5	0.9	29%	70%	82
	06	23	aa	LA	4	2	10	0	50	48	26	5	21	45	4.63	1.38	21.5	249	3.7	8.0	2.2	0.9	31%	68%	71
Ormond,Rodney	05	28	aaa	BAL	4	1	40	0	69	70	37	9	33	43	4.76	1.49	7.6	257	4.3	5.6	1.3	1.1	29%	70%	30
	06	29	a/a	TOR	6	6	55	6	79	90	41	17	24	41	4.72	1.45	6.3	281	2.8	4.7	1.7	1.9	29%	75%	4
Orvella,Chad	06	26	aaa	TAM	4	0	27	1	38	38	10	2	10	46	2.43	1.27	5.9	255	2.4	10.7	4.4	0.5	37%	82%	147
Osborne,Donovan	05	36	aaa	FLA	5	3	14	0	81	97	44	11	26	46	4.91	1.52	25.7	290	2.9	5.1	1.7	1.2	32%	70%	29
	06	37	aaa	KC	0	6	17	0	52	105	52	9	15	25	8.89	2.30	16.0	408	2.5	4.3	1.7	1.6	44%	62%	-15
Osoria,Franquelis	05	24	aaa	LA	6	4	40	9	55	59	13	2	11	29	2.13	1.27	5.8	269	1.8	4.7	2.6	0.3	31%	84%	75
	06	25	aaa	LA	2	2	44	2	51	85	25	2	20	24	4.44	2.05	5.8	362	3.6	4.2	1.2	0.4	41%	77%	22
Ostlund,Ian	06	28	aa	DET	9	5	53	0	65	96	52	8	30	50	7.17	1.95	6.0	337	4.2	6.9	1.7	1.2	40%	63%	29
Owens,Henry	06	27	aa	NYM	2	2	37	20	40	28	12	1	12	52	2.71	0.99	4.2	192	2.7	11.8	4.3	0.3	30%	72%	170
Owings,Micah	06	24	a/a	ARI	16	2	27	0	162	197	79	10	53	112	4.41	1.54	26.8	294	2.9	6.2	2.1	0.6	35%	71%	61
Oxspring,Chris	05	28	aaa	SD	12	6	26	0	160	165	76	12	42	106	4.29	1.29	25.9	260	2.4	6.0	2.5	0.7	31%	67%	72
Oyervidez,Jose	05	24	aa	SD	7	9	27	0	153	143	72	13	81	115	4.24	1.47	24.9	243	4.8	6.8	1.4	0.8	29%	72%	53
	06	25	aa	SD	6	12	28	0	149	179	86	12	84	109	5.21	1.76	24.9	291	5.1	6.6	1.3	0.7	35%	70%	43
Padilla,Juan	05	29	aaa	NYM	3	2	37	11	63	55	13	4	10	46	1.84	1.02	6.7	229	1.4	6.5	4.7	0.6	28%	86%	129

PITCHER	Yr	Age	Lev	Org	Actual				Major League Equivalents																
					w	l	g	sv	ip	h	er	hr	bb	k	era	br/ip	bf/g	oob	ctl	dom	cmd	hr/9	h%	s%	bpv
Palmer,Matt	06	28	a/a	SF	11	7	30	0	153	190	72	14	46	85	4.26	1.54	22.8	298	2.7	5.0	1.9	0.8	34%	74%	40
Pals,Jordan	05	25	aa	STL	7	11	27	0	159	176	71	14	39	86	3.99	1.35	25.2	274	2.2	4.8	2.2	0.8	31%	72%	52
	06	26	aa	STL	8	7	27	0	160	249	112	27	43	69	6.31	1.83	28.1	347	2.4	3.9	1.6	1.5	37%	68%	-2
Pannone,Anthony	05	24	aa	SF	1	2	24	1	36	48	28	2	24	13	7.09	2.01	7.4	315	6.0	3.3	0.5	0.5	34%	63%	8
Papelbon,Jonathan	05	25	a/a	BOS	6	4	21	1	114	94	41	12	26	91	3.25	1.05	21.6	220	2.0	7.2	3.5	1.0	26%	73%	99
Parisi,Mike	06	23	aa	STL	9	8	27	0	150	193	91	13	63	89	5.44	1.70	25.7	305	3.8	5.3	1.4	0.8	35%	68%	32
Parker,Christian	05	30	a/a	COL	6	6	24	0	135	210	94	13	50	50	6.25	1.92	27.3	347	3.3	3.4	1.0	0.8	37%	67%	2
Parker,Josh	05	25	aa	TAM	2	8	43	4	58	69	37	6	17	26	5.70	1.48	6.0	290	2.6	4.0	1.5	1.0	31%	62%	23
Parker,Zach	05	24	aa	COL	12	10	27	0	161	218	98	23	37	70	5.47	1.58	26.9	316	2.1	3.9	1.9	1.3	34%	68%	17
	06	25	a/a	COL	4	8	25	0	86	125	101	17	73	52	10.58	2.30	18.0	333	7.6	5.5	0.7	1.8	36%	53%	-17
Paronto,Chad	05	30	aaa	MIL	6	2	52	4	79	107	41	7	41	51	4.68	1.87	7.3	316	4.7	5.8	1.2	0.8	37%	76%	30
Parra,Manuel	05	23	aa	MIL	5	6	16	0	91	123	46	4	21	75	4.55	1.58	25.6	316	2.1	7.4	3.6	0.4	40%	70%	99
	06	24	aa	MIL	3	0	6	0	31	33	14	0	9	25	4.18	1.36	22.2	266	2.7	7.3	2.7	0.0	35%	66%	103
Patterson,Scott	06	27	aa	NYY	0	1	26	1	38	39	17	10	11	30	3.97	1.29	6.2	257	2.6	7.0	2.8	2.3	27%	82%	36
Patton,Troy	06	21	aa	HOU	2	5	8	0	45	55	27	7	13	31	5.39	1.51	25.0	295	2.6	6.2	2.4	1.4	33%	67%	41
Pauley,David	05	22	aa	BOS	9	7	27	0	156	199	85	20	34	89	4.90	1.49	25.5	304	2.0	5.1	2.6	1.2	34%	69%	45
	06	23	a/a	BOS	3	6	19	0	110	139	65	20	36	63	5.31	1.59	26.1	302	2.9	5.1	1.8	1.6	32%	71%	13
Paulk,Robert	06	26	a/a	NYM	6	2	28	0	56	67	23	1	19	26	3.72	1.54	8.9	292	3.0	4.1	1.4	0.2	33%	74%	45
Pavlik,Isaac	06	26	aa	CHC	2	1	9	0	40	66	29	6	20	27	6.47	2.13	22.4	359	4.4	6.1	1.4	1.3	41%	71%	10
Pearce,Josh	05	28	a/a	STL	2	3	31	0	57	74	29	12	9	34	4.63	1.46	8.1	307	1.5	5.3	3.6	1.9	33%	75%	46
Pearson,Jason	06	31	aa	BAL	3	6	50	2	65	96	43	11	21	39	5.92	1.80	6.2	335	3.0	5.3	1.8	1.6	37%	70%	10
Peguero,Jailen	05	25	aa	HOU	2	2	50	12	64	80	31	4	28	49	4.29	1.69	5.9	299	4.0	6.9	1.7	0.6	37%	75%	55
	06	24	a/a	HOU	3	2	48	15	75	59	20	3	33	66	2.40	1.23	6.5	212	4.0	7.9	2.0	0.4	28%	81%	91
Peguero,Tony	05	25	aa	TAM	5	1	9	0	51	68	27	4	16	30	4.81	1.64	26.0	314	2.8	5.3	1.9	0.7	36%	71%	42
	06	26	aa	TAM	10	12	31	1	151	186	82	14	49	72	4.89	1.55	21.8	296	2.9	4.3	1.5	0.9	33%	69%	27
Pelfrey,Michael	06	23	a/a	NYM	5	2	14	0	74	79	31	4	33	71	3.77	1.51	23.5	267	4.0	8.6	2.2	0.5	35%	75%	84
Pelland,Tyler	06	23	aa	CIN	9	5	28	0	142	179	88	15	96	87	5.55	1.94	24.6	302	6.1	5.5	0.9	1.0	34%	72%	18
Pena,Tony	05	24	aa	ARI	7	13	25	0	148	195	92	21	41	83	5.58	1.59	26.7	311	2.5	5.1	2.0	1.3	34%	67%	28
	06	25	a/a	ARI	5	1	41	13	46	42	9	1	7	32	1.81	1.07	4.5	239	1.4	6.2	4.4	0.2	30%	83%	132
Penn,Hayden	05	21	aa	BAL	7	6	20	0	110	118	62	14	36	110	5.06	1.40	23.8	269	3.0	9.0	3.0	1.2	34%	66%	84
	06	22	a/a	BAL	7	4	15	0	89	87	32	8	29	81	3.27	1.29	25.0	250	2.9	8.2	2.8	0.8	32%	77%	90
Pereira,Nick	06	24	aaa	SF	4	3	15	0	79	94	57	9	45	51	6.49	1.76	24.6	290	5.1	5.8	1.1	1.0	33%	63%	25
Perez,Beltran	05	24	aa	LA	2	3	17	3	31	24	10	1	15	26	2.99	1.26	7.6	208	4.5	7.6	1.7	0.3	27%	76%	86
	06	25	a/a	WAS	8	6	31	1	121	152	53	8	43	86	3.91	1.61	17.7	300	3.2	6.4	2.0	0.6	36%	76%	57
Perez,Franklin	05	30	aaa	PHI	1	7	57	23	64	74	47	14	37	32	6.55	1.73	5.2	285	5.1	4.4	0.9	2.0	29%	67%	-18
	06	28	a/a	PIT	2	5	33	3	49	59	32	7	22	26	5.81	1.65	6.8	291	4.1	4.8	1.2	1.3	32%	67%	12
Perez,Juan	05	25	aaa	BOS	4	5	40	1	62	68	35	7	28	63	5.08	1.55	6.9	273	4.1	9.1	2.3	1.0	35%	69%	72
	06	28	aaa	PIT	0	1	47	0	70	90	30	5	42	48	3.87	1.89	7.2	306	5.4	6.2	1.2	0.7	36%	81%	34
Perez,Miguel	06	23	a/a	NYM	6	9	24	0	130	177	95	13	56	76	6.58	1.79	25.5	318	3.9	5.3	1.4	0.9	36%	63%	24
Perez,Oliver	06	25	aaa	NYM	2	5	10	0	51	58	46	12	24	50	8.18	1.60	23.1	278	4.3	8.9	2.1	2.1	33%	51%	32
Perez,Rafael	05	23	aa	CLE	4	3	15	1	66	62	15	5	12	39	2.10	1.12	17.8	242	1.7	5.3	3.1	0.7	28%	85%	83
	06	25	a/a	CLE	4	8	25	0	94	88	37	3	32	75	3.55	1.27	15.8	242	3.1	7.1	2.3	0.3	31%	71%	90
Perisho,Matt	06	31	aaa	STL	2	4	47	1	46	66	37	4	23	39	7.21	1.95	4.8	331	4.5	7.6	1.7	0.8	41%	62%	45
Perkins,Glen	05	23	aa	MIN	4	4	14	0	79	92	53	4	36	58	6.04	1.62	25.6	285	4.1	6.6	1.6	0.5	35%	60%	58
	06	24	a/a	MIN	4	12	24	0	121	142	74	14	57	113	5.50	1.64	23.0	286	4.2	8.4	2.0	1.0	36%	68%	59
Perkins,Vince	05	24	aa	TOR	7	7	26	0	131	163	92	13	59	95	6.29	1.69	23.3	298	4.0	6.5	1.6	0.9	35%	62%	41
Perrin,Devin	06	25	a/a	WAS	3	4	37	3	58	72	39	6	49	39	6.02	2.08	7.9	296	7.7	6.0	0.8	1.0	34%	72%	19
Person,Robert	05	36	aaa	CHW	2	3	7	0	36	40	35	15	26	20	8.68	1.84	24.5	276	6.6	5.0	0.8	3.7	24%	61%	-65
Pesco,Nick	06	23	aa	CLE	6	8	18	0	88	119	72	13	42	55	7.37	1.83	23.2	315	4.3	5.6	1.3	1.4	35%	60%	12
Petersen,Jeff	06	25	a/a	SF	3	6	35	0	63	95	64	5	33	25	9.13	2.03	8.9	340	4.7	3.6	0.8	0.7	37%	52%	3
Peterson,Adam	05	26	a/a	ARI	4	3	49	0	66	102	67	9	46	48	9.08	2.24	7.0	346	6.2	6.5	1.0	1.2	40%	58%	10
Peterson,Matt	05	24	aa	PIT	11	9	27	0	143	179	104	20	70	72	6.54	1.74	24.7	300	4.4	4.5	1.0	1.2	32%	63%	7
	06	25	aa	PIT	6	6	31	0	112	144	87	13	51	67	7.01	1.74	16.9	306	4.1	5.3	1.3	1.0	34%	59%	23
Petit,Yusmeiro	05	21	a/a	NYM	9	6	24	0	132	114	54	19	22	133	3.65	1.03	21.7	228	1.5	9.1	6.1	1.3	28%	70%	153
	06	22	aaa	FLA	4	6	17	0	96	97	44	12	18	68	4.08	1.20	23.3	257	1.7	6.4	3.8	1.1	30%	69%	87
Pettyjohn,Adam	06	29	a/a	OAK	5	6	28	2	115	161	67	13	40	62	5.24	1.75	19.2	324	3.1	4.8	1.5	1.0	36%	71%	20
Phelps,Tommy	06	33	aaa	NYY	7	4	17	0	95	137	62	13	33	47	5.88	1.78	26.3	330	3.1	4.4	1.4	1.2	36%	68%	9
Phelps,Travis	05	28	a/a	CHC	4	2	47	1	67	108	71	22	46	45	9.48	2.30	7.4	356	6.2	6.1	1.0	3.0	37%	63%	-49
	06	29	aa	MIL	5	8	31	5	86	124	64	12	60	53	6.69	2.14	14.0	330	6.3	5.5	0.9	1.3	37%	70%	3
Phillips,Heath	05	23	a/a	CHW	9	8	26	0	154	211	94	27	42	80	5.49	1.64	27.0	319	2.5	4.7	1.9	1.6	34%	70%	12
	06	25	aaa	CHW	13	5	25	0	155	183	68	17	41	87	3.95	1.45	27.1	288	2.4	5.1	2.1	1.0	32%	75%	43
Phillips,Jason	05	32	a/a	TAM	4	5	31	1	106	167	78	10	31	57	6.60	1.87	16.4	350	2.6	4.8	1.8	0.8	39%	64%	27
Piersoll,Chris	05	28	a/a	BAL	6	1	36	2	63	51	21	7	18	57	2.95	1.09	7.0	215	2.6	8.1	3.1	1.0	26%	78%	95
	06	29	aaa	BAL	6	2	42	0	67	89	45	9	31	46	6.05	1.79	7.5	313	4.1	6.2	1.5	1.2	36%	67%	26
Pignatiello,Carmen	05	23	a/a	CHC	6	9	37	0	126	128	58	11	49	104	4.14	1.40	14.7	258	3.5	7.4	2.1	0.8	32%	72%	69
	06	24	a/a	CHC	3	1	46	0	67	77	31	4	25	67	4.15	1.52	6.5	283	3.3	9.0	2.7	0.6	37%	73%	92
Pinango,Miguel	06	24	aa	NYM	10	7	28	0	152	201	107	24	44	66	6.35	1.61	24.6	312	2.6	3.9	1.5	1.4	33%	62%	5
Pinto,Renyel	05	23	a/a	CHC	11	5	28	0	152	149	76	7	84	129	4.50	1.53	24.2	251	5.0	7.6	1.5	0.4	32%	69%	70
	06	24	aaa	FLA	8	2	18	0	95	87	37	7	47	87	3.50	1.41	22.9	239	4.4	8.2	1.9	0.7	31%	76%	76
Plexico,Gerald	06	27	aa	WAS	4	3	34	3	65	85	40	6	29	35	5.56	1.75	8.9	309	4.0	4.8	1.2	0.8	35%	68%	24
Pollok,Dwayne	05	25	aa	CHW	4	5	56	11	87	104	37	9	20	48	3.80	1.42	6.8	290	2.1	4.9	2.4	1.0	32%	76%	47
	06	26	aa	CHW	4	5	54	3	82	121	47	13	24	41	5.11	1.77	7.1	335	2.7	4.5	1.7	1.5	36%	75%	7
Pomeranz,Stuart	05	21	aa	STL	5	6	18	0	98	109	54	10	35	61	4.98	1.46	23.9	275	3.2	5.6	1.7	0.9	31%	67%	44
	06	22	aa	STL	7	4	18	0	98	119	55	13	29	55	5.05	1.51	24.1	293	2.7	5.0	1.9	1.2	32%	69%	31
Pope,Justin	05	26	aa	NYY	6	4	57	29	77	82	32	2	22	41	3.77	1.36	5.8	268	2.6	4.8	1.9	0.3	31%	71%	62
	06	27	a/a	NYY	2	3	46	23	63	79	36	7	32	41	5.07	1.76	6.4	300	4.6	5.9	1.3	1.0	35%	72%	29
Portobanco,Luz	05	26	aa	NYM	2	12	40	2	75	124	77	10	53	36	9.24	2.36	9.9	362	6.3	4.3	0.7	1.2	39%	60%	-15
Porzio,Mike	05	33	a/a	ATL	2	4	16	0	37	52	26	6	18	17	6.22	1.89	11.1	326	4.3	4.2	1.0	1.4	35%	69%	-6

					Actual				Major League Equivalents																
PITCHER	Yr	Age	Lev	Org	w	l	g	sv	ip	h	er	hr	bb	k	era	br/ip	bf/g	oob	ctl	dom	cmd	hr/9	h%	s%	bpv
Pote,Lou	05	34	aaa	TEX	2	1	14	1	42	52	19	2	26	29	4.04	1.85	14.4	295	5.6	6.1	1.1	0.4	35%	78%	42
	06	35	aa	TEX	3	2	17	0	30	46	26	5	18	18	7.74	2.11	8.9	343	5.3	5.3	1.0	1.4	38%	64%	-3
Powell,Brian	05	32	aaa	WAS	7	13	29	0	157	220	104	16	40	64	5.97	1.65	24.8	324	2.3	3.6	1.6	0.9	35%	64%	18
Pratt,Andy	05	26	a/a	MIL	4	5	43	2	77	104	68	16	69	65	7.90	2.25	9.3	317	8.0	7.6	0.9	1.8	37%	67%	2
Prieto,Ariel	05	36	aaa	FLA	9	5	25	0	133	154	56	11	36	85	3.77	1.42	23.1	283	2.4	5.7	2.4	0.7	33%	75%	61
Prochaska,Mike	06	26	a/a	TAM	5	7	24	0	104	140	83	14	53	48	7.20	1.86	20.7	315	4.6	4.1	0.9	1.2	34%	61%	-2
Proctor,Scott	05	29	aaa	NYY	5	1	34	14	41	56	24	9	12	41	5.17	1.64	5.5	317	2.6	8.9	3.5	1.9	39%	75%	61
Puffer,Brandon	05	30	aaa	SF	6	5	53	0	71	93	46	7	21	35	5.84	1.61	6.1	310	2.6	4.4	1.7	0.8	34%	63%	29
	06	31	aaa	OAK	5	1	50	4	69	80	45	12	20	42	5.90	1.45	6.0	284	2.6	5.4	2.1	1.5	31%	62%	30
Pullin,Aaron	05	25	aa	ANA	5	6	51	5	77	89	47	13	34	42	5.54	1.60	6.8	285	3.9	4.9	1.2	1.5	30%	69%	9
	06	26	aa	ANA	2	0	28	1	46	53	27	4	27	22	5.22	1.74	7.7	284	5.2	4.2	0.8	0.9	31%	71%	14
Pulsipher,Bill	05	32	a/a	STL	7	7	26	0	131	188	73	19	31	82	5.04	1.67	23.1	329	2.1	5.6	2.6	1.3	37%	73%	39
Purcey,David	05	23	aa	TOR	4	3	8	0	43	42	22	3	29	39	4.53	1.65	24.6	252	6.0	8.1	1.3	0.6	32%	73%	62
	06	24	a/a	TOR	6	12	28	0	140	191	125	23	93	106	8.02	2.03	24.7	318	6.0	6.8	1.1	1.5	37%	61%	12
Raggio,Brady	05	33	aa	PHI	1	2	8	0	30	53	27	4	7	14	8.09	1.99	18.5	376	2.1	4.1	1.9	1.1	41%	58%	13
Rakers,Aaron	05	29	aaa	BAL	6	5	57	7	77	86	29	12	23	74	3.39	1.41	5.8	277	2.6	8.7	3.3	1.4	34%	82%	80
Rall,Tim	05	26	a/a	SEA	2	3	44	0	64	61	36	6	40	55	5.03	1.58	6.5	246	5.6	7.7	1.4	0.9	30%	69%	55
Ramirez,Elizardo	05	23	aaa	CIN	7	7	21	0	131	155	57	14	16	72	3.92	1.31	26.4	289	1.1	5.0	4.5	1.0	32%	73%	92
Ramirez,Erasmo	06	30	aaa	TEX	6	3	54	9	67	98	46	9	9	37	6.10	1.59	5.6	333	1.2	4.9	4.2	1.2	37%	63%	70
Ramirez,Ismael	05	25	aa	TOR	8	13	27	0	150	207	109	28	38	105	6.56	1.63	25.3	321	2.3	6.3	2.8	1.7	36%	63%	35
	06	26	a/a	TOR	9	5	23	0	126	131	51	19	40	68	3.61	1.35	23.4	262	2.9	4.9	1.7	1.4	28%	79%	27
Ramirez,Ramon	05	24	a/a	NYY	9	9	30	0	141	151	74	22	52	107	4.73	1.43	20.5	268	3.3	6.8	2.1	1.4	31%	71%	44
Ramirez,Santiago	05	27	aaa	KC	5	5	50	17	67	91	43	9	19	44	5.79	1.63	6.1	316	2.5	5.9	2.3	1.3	36%	66%	37
Ramos,Mario	05	28	aaa	OAK	4	6	49	0	86	120	56	14	37	64	5.83	1.82	8.3	323	3.9	6.7	1.7	1.4	37%	71%	24
	06	29	a/a	SD	0	3	15	0	35	59	36	6	19	20	9.32	2.21	12.0	364	4.8	5.0	1.0	1.5	40%	57%	-11
Ramos,Victor	06	25	aa	BOS	3	1	29	1	35	49	34	10	14	23	8.86	1.81	5.7	324	3.7	6.0	1.6	2.6	34%	54%	-17
Ramsey,Keith	05	26	aa	COL	1	3	10	0	41	78	53	13	21	18	11.71	2.41	21.9	394	4.6	4.0	0.9	2.9	40%	53%	-70
Randall,Scott	05	30	a/a	COL	4	5	19	0	63	95	55	6	38	36	7.83	2.11	16.7	340	5.4	5.1	1.0	0.9	39%	62%	12
Randolph,Stephen	05	31	aaa	SF	3	3	36	0	68	53	46	9	61	67	6.11	1.67	8.7	209	8.1	8.9	1.1	1.3	26%	65%	52
	06	32	aaa	CHW	9	9	28	0	154	164	88	28	127	117	5.16	1.89	26.5	267	7.4	6.8	0.9	1.7	30%	77%	12
Rapada,Clay	06	26	a/a	CHC	6	4	61	21	67	76	19	1	29	55	2.54	1.57	4.9	279	4.0	7.4	1.9	0.1	36%	83%	79
Rasner,Darrell	05	25	aa	WAS	6	7	27	0	150	172	69	11	29	79	4.17	1.34	23.7	281	1.8	4.7	2.7	0.6	32%	69%	64
	06	26	aaa	NYY	4	0	10	0	58	71	23	5	12	39	3.59	1.42	25.3	294	1.9	6.0	3.2	0.8	34%	77%	76
Rawson,Anthony	05	25	aa	STL	4	3	38	1	41	52	22	7	21	30	4.87	1.78	5.1	303	4.6	6.5	1.4	1.5	35%	77%	19
	06	26	aa	OAK	1	2	31	0	35	59	31	2	29	24	7.96	2.49	6.1	364	7.4	6.2	0.8	0.6	43%	66%	20
Rayborn,Kenny	05	31	aaa	CLE	2	0	17	2	38	53	24	3	13	25	5.76	1.75	10.5	323	3.1	5.9	1.9	0.8	38%	67%	42
Ray,Chris	05	24	aa	BAL	1	2	31	18	37	22	6	4	7	34	1.50	0.78	4.4	167	1.8	8.2	4.7	1.0	20%	92%	140
Ray,Ken	05	32	aaa	ATL	2	4	17	0	67	83	38	7	37	33	5.09	1.79	18.6	298	4.9	4.5	0.9	1.0	33%	73%	11
Reames,Britt	05	32	aaa	OAK	6	6	42	8	92	102	38	3	35	70	3.70	1.49	9.7	275	3.4	6.9	2.0	0.3	34%	74%	74
	06	33	aaa	PIT	4	2	14	0	64	80	29	4	16	34	4.14	1.49	20.2	299	2.2	4.8	2.2	0.6	34%	72%	52
Redding,Tim	05	28	aaa	NYY	3	4	12	0	61	80	36	4	16	42	5.27	1.57	22.9	310	2.3	6.2	2.6	0.6	37%	66%	67
	06	29	aaa	CHW	12	10	29	0	187	217	102	32	63	118	4.91	1.50	28.5	284	3.1	5.7	1.9	1.6	31%	72%	25
Register,Steven	06	23	aa	COL	4	10	27	0	155	231	129	34	53	64	7.48	1.83	27.3	338	3.1	3.7	1.2	2.0	35%	62%	-24
Reid,Justin	05	28	aaa	PIT	7	5	24	0	94	139	72	20	42	47	6.90	1.92	19.0	336	4.0	4.5	1.1	2.0	35%	68%	-21
	06	29	aaa	LA	2	7	43	3	107	134	71	15	48	67	6.00	1.70	11.5	300	4.1	5.7	1.4	1.3	34%	66%	19
Reimers,Cameron	05	27	a/a	TOR	6	7	20	0	110	194	86	11	26	44	7.05	2.00	27.1	377	2.2	3.6	1.6	0.9	41%	64%	7
Reineke,Chad	06	25	aa	HOU	1	3	15	0	44	40	19	3	27	36	3.87	1.53	13.1	237	5.6	7.4	1.3	0.6	29%	75%	60
Reith,Brian	05	28	aaa	PIT	2	2	24	1	31	40	20	4	12	15	5.81	1.66	5.9	306	3.4	4.4	1.3	1.2	33%	67%	11
Resop,Chris	05	23	aa	FLA	3	2	43	24	49	54	17	2	17	51	3.12	1.45	5.0	274	3.1	9.4	3.0	0.4	37%	78%	108
	06	24	aaa	FLA	4	0	40	2	49	52	22	4	15	39	4.02	1.36	5.3	266	2.7	7.1	2.6	0.7	32%	71%	77
Reyes,Anthony	05	24	aaa	STL	7	6	23	0	128	113	56	12	32	120	3.93	1.13	22.6	232	2.2	8.4	3.8	0.8	29%	67%	113
	06	25	aaa	STL	6	1	13	0	84	83	31	10	11	71	3.32	1.12	26.1	253	1.2	7.6	6.5	1.1	31%	75%	153
Reynoso,Paulino	05	25	aa	CHW	4	4	54	8	57	79	32	8	44	35	5.08	2.16	5.4	321	7.0	5.5	0.8	1.2	36%	79%	4
	06	26	aaa	CHW	3	3	47	0	59	60	40	4	49	49	6.11	1.85	6.0	257	7.5	7.4	1.0	0.6	32%	66%	50
Rheinecker,John	05	26	aaa	OAK	4	0	7	0	45	32	10	0	13	20	2.05	1.00	25.3	195	2.7	4.1	1.5	0.0	23%	77%	72
	06	27	aaa	TEX	4	5	15	0	93	125	41	8	27	56	3.97	1.64	28.3	316	2.6	5.4	2.0	0.8	36%	77%	43
Rice,Scott	05	24	aa	BAL	4	1	56	1	73	87	39	5	35	34	4.80	1.67	6.0	290	4.3	4.2	1.0	0.6	32%	71%	23
	06	25	aaa	BAL	3	4	52	1	65	82	40	5	30	34	5.59	1.72	5.8	301	4.2	4.7	1.1	0.7	34%	67%	25
Richardson,Jason	05	25	aa	ATL	0	2	17	0	30	43	19	3	12	23	5.63	1.84	8.5	329	3.6	6.7	1.8	1.0	39%	70%	38
Ridgway,Jeff	06	26	a/a	TAM	2	4	50	2	58	61	28	6	24	51	4.31	1.48	5.1	265	3.8	8.0	2.1	0.9	33%	72%	68
Rijo,Fernando	05	28	aa	HOU	3	2	34	1	61	86	51	17	43	30	7.45	2.11	9.0	324	6.4	4.4	0.7	2.5	33%	70%	-43
Ring,Royce	05	25	aaa	NYM	3	0	33	2	38	38	16	2	13	22	3.77	1.34	4.9	254	3.1	5.2	1.7	0.5	30%	71%	57
	06	26	aaa	NYM	2	2	36	11	39	37	18	2	16	34	4.19	1.37	4.7	247	3.7	7.7	2.1	0.5	32%	69%	82
Rivera,Saul	05	28	aa	WAS	3	3	40	9	76	94	28	4	23	50	3.27	1.53	8.5	297	2.7	5.9	2.2	0.4	35%	79%	64
Rleal,Sendy	05	25	aa	BAL	4	4	56	16	70	62	24	6	21	59	3.13	1.19	5.1	233	2.7	7.5	2.8	0.7	29%	76%	90
Roach,Jason	05	29	a/a	TAM	6	8	32	2	121	218	98	21	44	34	7.25	2.17	19.2	382	3.3	2.6	0.8	1.5	39%	68%	-36
	06	30	a/a	PIT	8	9	27	0	149	238	103	25	51	49	6.18	1.94	26.8	353	3.1	2.9	1.0	1.5	36%	71%	-23
Robbins,Jake	05	29	aaa	CLE	3	5	49	23	52	59	20	2	26	22	3.41	1.64	4.9	280	4.5	3.8	0.8	0.4	31%	79%	28
	06	30	aaa	CIN	2	3	51	4	53	73	28	6	38	40	4.70	2.09	5.2	321	6.4	6.7	1.0	0.9	38%	79%	25
Robertson,Connor	06	25	aa	OAK	7	2	55	6	83	91	33	1	23	75	3.61	1.38	6.5	273	2.5	8.1	3.2	0.1	36%	72%	113
Robertson,Jeriome	05	28	aaa	CIN	5	11	27	0	119	186	84	20	30	63	6.34	1.81	20.9	348	2.3	4.8	2.1	1.5	38%	68%	12
	06	30	aaa	NYM	1	6	11	0	38	78	51	8	21	16	11.91	2.59	19.1	412	4.9	3.9	0.8	1.8	44%	53%	-42
Rodney,Lee	05	28	a/a	DET	5	3	45	3	82	122	48	6	34	40	5.29	1.90	8.8	337	3.8	4.4	1.2	0.6	38%	72%	19
Rodriguez,Eddy	05	24	aaa	BAL	2	3	49	3	61	63	30	1	35	43	4.43	1.61	5.6	261	5.2	6.3	1.2	0.1	32%	70%	62
	06	25	aaa	BAL	3	1	42	12	47	41	13	0	19	49	2.51	1.29	4.7	231	3.7	9.3	2.5	0.0	33%	78%	117
Rodriguez,Jose	05	31	aa	NYM	3	5	33	2	61	96	41	4	41	34	6.10	2.24	9.6	349	6.1	5.1	0.8	0.6	40%	72%	14
	06	25	a/a	TAM	4	2	54	2	80	93	33	6	34	56	3.70	1.58	6.7	284	3.8	6.3	1.7	0.7	34%	78%	50
Rodriguez,Nerio	06	36	a/a	PIT	1	4	12	0	61	80	54	12	20	41	8.01	1.63	23.2	309	2.9	6.1	2.1	1.8	34%	52%	19
Rodriguez,Rafael	06	22	aa	ANA	5	10	24	0	133	181	97	25	50	70	6.56	1.74	25.8	318	3.4	4.7	1.4	1.7	34%	65%	-2

					Actual				Major League Equivalents																
PITCHER	Yr	Age	Lev	Org	w	l	g	sv	ip	h	er	hr	bb	k	era	br/ip	bf/g	oob	ctl	dom	cmd	hr/9	h%	s%	bpv
Rodriguez,Ricardo	05	24	aaa	TEX	7	3	13	0	80	70	29	9	22	41	3.26	1.15	25.1	230	2.5	4.6	1.9	1.0	25%	76%	45
	06	28	aaa	STL	8	12	27	0	162	252	141	31	57	67	7.83	1.90	28.9	347	3.2	3.7	1.2	1.7	36%	60%	-19
Rodriguez,Ryan	06	22	aa	CHW	4	10	21	0	116	178	102	6	56	53	7.91	2.02	27.3	344	4.3	4.1	0.9	0.5	39%	58%	17
Rodriguez,Wandy	05	27	a/a	HOU	4	2	9	0	49	59	28	9	20	38	5.08	1.60	24.7	291	3.7	6.9	1.9	1.6	33%	73%	29
Rodriguez,Wilfredo	05	27	a/a	TEX	4	5	14	0	75	81	40	8	36	56	4.80	1.56	24.0	270	4.3	6.7	1.6	0.9	32%	70%	46
Rogers,Brian	06	24	a/a	PIT	4	3	46	3	76	64	24	9	18	67	2.80	1.07	6.6	223	2.1	7.9	3.8	1.1	27%	80%	105
Rohlicek,Russ	05	26	aaa	CHC	3	1	55	3	62	53	33	5	44	48	4.83	1.56	5.1	225	6.4	6.9	1.1	0.7	27%	69%	52
	06	27	aa	MIL	0	2	24	0	34	46	28	5	21	25	7.30	1.96	6.9	317	5.5	6.7	1.2	1.2	37%	63%	21
Rohrbaugh,Robert	06	23	aa	SEA	5	5	14	0	85	103	47	11	29	57	4.96	1.55	27.2	293	3.1	6.0	2.0	1.2	33%	70%	39
Rojas,Chris	05	28	a/a	PHI	12	7	23	0	138	178	86	26	45	80	5.60	1.61	27.2	306	2.9	5.2	1.8	1.7	33%	69%	12
Rollandini,David	06	28	aa	HOU	4	4	47	2	76	96	55	14	34	35	6.56	1.71	7.5	303	4.0	4.1	1.0	1.7	31%	65%	-10
Roman,Orlando	05	27	aa	NYM	4	4	31	0	120	152	80	21	64	99	6.03	1.80	18.3	302	4.8	7.4	1.5	1.6	35%	69%	25
	06	28	a/a	NYM	4	3	39	2	68	92	46	6	41	40	6.09	1.96	8.5	317	5.5	5.3	1.0	0.8	36%	68%	21
Romero,Davis	06	24	a/a	TOR	10	9	30	1	118	127	60	8	29	92	4.57	1.32	16.7	269	2.2	7.0	3.2	0.6	33%	65%	92
Romero,Ricardo	06	22	aa	TOR	2	7	12	0	67	81	55	10	29	35	7.38	1.64	25.5	292	3.9	4.7	1.2	1.3	32%	55%	10
Roney,Matt	05	26	a/a	TEX	5	3	48	5	81	87	24	5	27	67	2.68	1.41	7.3	269	3.0	7.5	2.5	0.6	34%	83%	80
	06	27	aaa	OAK	4	3	47	6	58	65	22	4	19	54	3.36	1.44	5.4	277	2.9	8.4	2.9	0.6	36%	78%	92
Rosales,Leonel	06	25	aa	SD	5	6	53	0	61	69	31	7	21	43	4.58	1.47	5.1	278	3.1	6.4	2.0	1.0	32%	71%	51
Rosario,Francisco	05	25	aaa	TOR	2	7	30	2	116	128	63	18	42	69	4.85	1.47	17.0	275	3.3	5.4	1.6	1.4	30%	71%	24
	06	26	aaa	TOR	0	3	14	1	42	36	19	3	14	42	3.98	1.20	12.4	227	3.1	8.9	2.9	0.7	30%	67%	104
Rose,Brian	05	30	aaa	CIN	5	6	17	0	67	108	63	13	24	25	8.39	1.96	19.3	354	3.2	3.3	1.0	1.8	36%	58%	-28
Rouwenhorst,Jonathc	05	26	a/a	ANA	7	4	47	3	65	80	31	4	26	40	4.22	1.63	6.3	296	3.6	5.5	1.5	0.6	35%	74%	43
	06	27	aaa	ANA	6	7	50	1	89	107	47	12	37	52	4.78	1.62	8.1	292	3.7	5.3	1.4	1.2	32%	73%	23
Rowe,Steven	05	25	a/a	TEX	2	2	25	1	40	59	32	6	7	21	7.09	1.65	7.3	335	1.7	4.7	2.8	1.4	36%	58%	33
	06	26	aa	TEX	5	5	45	0	83	130	77	22	39	50	8.35	2.04	9.1	349	4.2	5.5	1.3	2.4	37%	63%	-26
Rowland-Smith,Ryan	05	23	aa	SEA	6	7	33	0	122	151	70	8	53	93	5.16	1.67	17.0	298	3.9	6.9	1.8	0.6	36%	68%	56
	06	24	aa	SEA	1	3	23	4	41	46	18	2	21	42	3.84	1.63	8.1	279	4.5	9.1	2.0	0.5	37%	76%	83
Rueckel,Danny	05	26	aa	WAS	9	6	53	7	80	103	44	8	22	56	5.00	1.57	6.8	307	2.5	6.3	2.5	0.9	36%	69%	58
	06	27	a/a	WAS	7	5	41	1	66	86	40	7	28	41	5.48	1.72	7.5	309	3.8	5.6	1.5	0.9	35%	69%	30
Rundles,Rich	05	24	aa	WAS	6	13	27	0	159	202	85	14	49	75	4.82	1.58	26.5	303	2.8	4.2	1.5	0.8	34%	70%	28
	06	25	aa	STL	6	9	27	0	129	208	102	17	60	54	7.13	2.07	23.9	355	4.2	3.8	0.9	1.2	38%	66%	-9
Rupe,Josh	05	23	a/a	TEX	10	10	28	0	158	204	109	23	62	101	6.20	1.68	26.0	306	3.5	5.7	1.6	1.3	34%	65%	23
Rupe,Ryan	05	30	aaa	LA	4	6	23	0	75	97	48	11	22	56	5.72	1.58	14.7	306	2.7	6.7	2.5	1.3	35%	66%	47
Russell,Adam	06	23	aa	CHW	3	3	10	0	55	75	43	8	22	39	7.09	1.76	25.8	319	3.5	6.3	1.8	1.3	37%	60%	26
Russ,Chris	06	28	aa	STL	4	4	55	0	73	104	47	4	29	36	5.79	1.81	6.3	327	3.6	4.4	1.2	0.4	37%	66%	29
Russ,James	06	26	aa	FLA	6	10	28	0	156	208	100	21	79	102	5.77	1.84	26.5	313	4.5	5.9	1.3	1.2	36%	70%	18
Rust,Evan	05	27	a/a	STL	3	1	30	4	34	45	23	2	20	21	6.05	1.88	5.5	310	5.1	5.5	1.1	0.6	36%	67%	30
Ryu,Jae-kuk	05	22	aa	CHC	11	8	26	0	162	174	80	14	51	112	4.44	1.39	26.9	269	2.8	6.2	2.2	0.8	32%	69%	61
	06	23	aaa	CHC	8	8	24	0	139	149	68	16	55	100	4.40	1.47	25.4	268	3.6	6.5	1.8	1.0	31%	72%	47
Sadler,William	05	24	aa	SF	6	5	46	5	82	76	39	4	33	63	4.27	1.32	7.6	240	3.6	6.9	1.9	0.5	30%	67%	75
	06	25	a/a	SF	6	3	51	21	55	35	20	2	33	65	3.26	1.22	4.5	177	5.3	10.5	2.0	0.3	26%	73%	114
Saipe,Mike	05	32	aaa	OAK	4	2	27	0	61	65	21	4	17	42	3.11	1.35	9.6	268	2.5	6.2	2.5	0.6	32%	78%	72
Saladin,Miguel	05	30	a/a	CIN	0	2	32	1	48	89	46	5	19	30	8.67	2.24	7.7	388	3.5	5.6	1.6	0.9	44%	60%	16
Salas,Juan	06	28	a/a	TAM	4	1	50	17	63	39	8	5	31	64	1.15	1.11	5.1	175	4.4	9.1	2.0	0.7	23%	95%	98
Salas,Marino	06	26	aa	BAL	2	6	44	19	49	52	24	4	19	37	4.48	1.45	4.9	267	3.5	6.8	2.0	0.8	32%	70%	59
Salmon,Brad	05	26	a/a	CIN	3	8	47	4	89	91	38	5	36	63	3.83	1.42	8.2	258	3.6	6.3	1.8	0.5	31%	73%	62
	06	27	a/a	CIN	7	2	55	5	81	73	33	4	50	72	3.70	1.52	6.5	237	5.6	8.0	1.4	0.5	31%	76%	71
Sampson,Chris	05	27	aa	HOU	4	12	32	4	150	217	88	17	24	63	5.28	1.61	21.2	331	1.4	3.8	2.6	1.0	36%	68%	36
	06	28	aaa	HOU	12	3	27	4	125	133	44	14	15	54	3.17	1.19	19.0	267	1.1	3.9	3.6	1.0	29%	78%	70
Sanches,Brian	05	27	aaa	PHI	4	3	50	1	80	96	41	12	27	57	4.62	1.54	7.1	291	3.1	6.4	2.1	1.3	33%	74%	40
	06	28	aaa	PHI	3	2	36	19	43	33	15	3	15	41	3.14	1.12	4.8	209	3.1	8.5	2.7	0.7	27%	74%	101
Sanchez,Anibal	05	22	aa	BOS	3	5	11	0	57	63	28	6	16	54	4.41	1.38	22.3	274	2.5	8.5	3.4	0.9	35%	70%	94
	06	23	aa	FLA	3	6	15	0	85	99	41	8	31	83	4.33	1.53	25.3	285	3.3	8.8	2.7	0.8	37%	73%	82
Sanchez,Humberto	05	22	aa	DET	3	5	14	0	62	75	43	9	24	53	6.24	1.60	20.0	293	3.5	7.7	2.2	1.3	35%	62%	50
	06	23	a/a	DET	10	6	20	0	123	116	47	5	48	111	3.44	1.33	26.2	244	3.5	8.1	2.3	0.4	32%	74%	92
Sanchez,Jonathan	06	24	a/a	SF	4	3	19	2	55	32	18	1	22	63	2.95	0.98	11.3	166	3.6	10.3	2.9	0.2	25%	68%	139
Sanders,David	05	26	aaa	CHW	4	2	57	1	65	79	27	12	33	39	3.70	1.72	5.3	294	4.6	5.4	1.2	1.7	32%	86%	2
Sandoval,Juan	05	25	aa	SEA	9	11	28	0	160	234	91	7	51	86	5.09	1.77	26.9	333	2.8	4.9	1.7	0.4	38%	70%	41
Santana,Ervin	05	23	a/a	ANA	6	1	10	0	58	55	19	4	16	41	2.94	1.22	24.1	245	2.5	6.4	2.6	0.6	29%	78%	79
Santiago,Jose	05	31	aaa	NYM	7	5	28	0	116	164	73	12	44	43	5.68	1.80	19.6	326	3.4	3.3	1.0	0.9	35%	69%	2
Santos,Alex	05	28	a/a	OAK	2	3	40	19	47	41	18	2	16	33	3.38	1.23	4.9	231	3.2	6.3	2.0	0.5	28%	72%	76
	06	29	a/a	OAK	1	2	23	4	32	51	22	5	13	16	6.17	2.02	6.9	354	3.8	4.4	1.2	1.4	38%	71%	-6
Santos,Arthur	06	25	aa	ATL	2	3	26	3	40	39	12	4	9	22	2.60	1.21	6.4	250	2.1	4.9	2.3	0.9	28%	83%	55
Sarfate,Dennis	05	24	a/a	MIL	9	10	26	0	142	141	66	14	63	102	4.18	1.44	23.8	254	4.0	6.5	1.6	0.9	30%	73%	49
	06	26	aaa	MIL	10	7	34	0	125	151	68	9	85	103	4.87	1.88	17.7	292	6.1	7.4	1.2	0.7	36%	74%	47
Saunders,Joe	05	24	a/a	ANA	10	7	27	0	160	185	71	11	51	88	4.00	1.47	26.0	283	2.8	5.0	1.7	0.6	32%	73%	46
	06	25	aaa	ANA	10	4	21	0	135	126	42	11	35	81	2.83	1.20	26.5	243	2.4	5.4	2.3	0.7	28%	79%	65
Sawatski,Jay	06	24	aa	MIN	4	2	44	0	75	88	35	4	26	55	4.16	1.53	7.6	287	3.2	6.6	2.1	0.5	35%	72%	66
Scalamandre,Rich	06	26	a/a	STL	8	0	55	2	63	81	46	7	29	45	6.49	1.74	5.4	305	4.1	6.4	1.6	0.9	36%	62%	37
Schappert,Paul	06	25	aa	CHC	5	0	24	0	46	64	32	6	25	17	6.15	1.94	9.3	322	4.9	3.3	0.7	1.2	34%	70%	-12
Schmidt,Jeremy	05	26	aa	CIN	3	5	46	0	64	77	37	7	24	42	5.16	1.58	6.3	291	3.4	5.9	1.7	0.9	34%	68%	41
Schmitt,Eric	05	27	a/a	NYY	5	4	39	0	101	140	74	20	28	47	6.54	1.66	11.9	322	2.5	4.2	1.7	1.7	34%	64%	-1
	06	28	a/a	ATL	0	4	33	1	63	124	80	20	20	28	11.39	2.27	9.9	401	2.8	4.0	1.4	2.8	41%	51%	-57
Schmoll,Steve	06	27	aaa	NYM	5	4	42	0	55	71	42	5	21	35	6.89	1.66	6.0	306	3.4	5.7	1.7	0.8	35%	57%	38
Schneider,Scott	05	27	aaa	ANA	2	2	36	0	73	109	71	11	37	37	8.68	2.00	10.0	339	4.5	4.6	1.0	1.3	37%	56%	-3
Schoening,Brent	05	27	aaa	MIN	2	4	35	0	64	95	56	9	32	42	7.85	1.97	8.9	336	4.4	5.9	1.3	1.3	38%	60%	11
Schreiber,Zach	06	24	aa	ATL	1	2	35	21	39	34	17	4	33	38	3.87	1.69	5.2	227	7.5	8.7	1.2	1.0	29%	80%	57
Schroder,Chris	05	27	a/a	WAS	4	3	35	4	46	49	38	10	28	43	7.42	1.67	6.0	269	5.4	8.3	1.5	2.0	31%	59%	23
	06	28	a/a	WAS	4	1	37	2	61	58	22	5	27	53	3.29	1.38	7.1	244	4.0	7.8	1.9	0.7	31%	78%	73

					Actual				Major League Equivalents																
PITCHER	Yr	Age	Lev	Org	w	l	g	sv	ip	h	er	hr	bb	k	era	br/ip	bf/g	oob	ctl	dom	cmd	hr/9	h%	s%	bpv
Schultz,Mike	05	85	aa	ARI	4	6	63	6	65	96	38	5	48	53	5.20	2.22	5.3	337	6.7	7.3	1.1	0.7	41%	76%	35
	06	27	a/a	ARI	3	4	58	7	65	81	33	1	26	38	4.61	1.64	5.1	299	3.5	5.2	1.5	0.2	35%	69%	53
Scobie,Jason	05	27	aaa	NYM	15	7	27	0	167	194	77	15	59	76	4.14	1.51	27.4	284	3.2	4.1	1.3	0.8	31%	74%	26
	06	27	a/a	NYM	4	18	29	1	139	251	145	28	54	64	9.36	2.19	24.5	381	3.5	4.1	1.2	1.8	40%	58%	-25
Searles,Jonathan	05	25	aa	CHC	6	3	58	1	80	94	42	6	35	60	4.73	1.60	6.3	286	3.9	6.7	1.7	0.7	34%	71%	53
	06	26	aa	BOS	7	4	53	1	77	97	54	10	43	44	6.36	1.82	6.9	300	5.1	5.1	1.0	1.2	33%	66%	12
Seddon,Chris	05	22	a/a	TAM	10	10	29	0	148	173	86	12	57	104	5.21	1.56	22.8	286	3.5	6.3	1.8	0.8	34%	66%	51
	06	23	aaa	TAM	9	9	28	0	154	190	100	22	47	97	5.84	1.53	24.5	296	2.7	5.6	2.1	1.3	33%	64%	35
Segovia,Zach	06	24	aa	PHI	11	5	17	0	107	112	52	11	25	61	4.34	1.28	26.4	265	2.1	5.1	2.5	1.0	30%	68%	56
Seibel,Phil	06	28	a/a	BOS	4	3	18	0	60	43	13	8	18	49	1.90	1.02	13.1	195	2.8	7.3	2.6	1.2	22%	91%	79
Seo,Jae	05	28	aaa	NYM	7	4	19	0	121	153	73	15	32	86	5.43	1.53	28.4	301	2.4	6.4	2.7	1.1	35%	66%	56
Sequea,Jacobo	05	24	a/a	BAL	1	2	38	7	52	91	48	12	23	22	8.35	2.17	7.0	373	3.9	3.8	1.0	2.1	39%	64%	-40
Serrano,Alex	05	25	a/a	COL	6	6	56	15	72	76	32	8	16	39	3.98	1.29	5.4	266	2.1	4.8	2.4	1.0	29%	72%	49
Serrano,Jimmy	05	29	aaa	OAK	12	7	28	0	161	191	90	22	77	124	5.03	1.66	26.4	289	4.3	6.9	1.6	1.2	34%	72%	36
	06	30	aaa	BOS	4	5	13	0	72	99	31	3	30	48	3.89	1.79	26.1	320	3.8	6.0	1.6	0.4	38%	78%	48
Sessions,Doug	05	29	aaa	ANA	0	4	8	0	40	58	34	9	15	13	7.70	1.82	23.8	331	3.4	2.9	0.9	1.9	33%	60%	-33
Shackelford,Brian	05	29	aaa	CIN	1	6	31	1	32	42	23	1	11	16	6.45	1.64	4.7	308	3.1	4.6	1.5	0.3	35%	57%	43
Shafer,David	05	24	aa	CIN	1	6	34	6	39	34	20	3	24	33	4.50	1.47	5.1	229	5.4	7.6	1.4	0.7	29%	70%	63
	06	25	aa	CIN	1	2	44	26	49	47	19	3	18	42	3.47	1.33	4.7	248	3.3	7.6	2.3	0.6	31%	75%	83
Shaffar,Ben	05	28	aa	PIT	2	3	44	9	73	98	39	7	29	48	4.75	1.73	7.7	314	3.6	5.9	1.7	0.9	36%	74%	36
Sharpless,Josh	06	26	a/a	PIT	3	1	37	9	54	52	16	1	26	48	2.63	1.44	6.4	246	4.4	8.1	1.8	0.2	33%	81%	88
Shaver,Chris	06	25	aa	CHC	7	10	26	0	150	217	91	12	73	95	5.46	1.93	28.0	331	4.4	5.7	1.3	0.7	38%	72%	28
Shearn,Tom	05	28	aaa	CIN	4	4	43	1	92	96	51	13	45	73	4.94	1.53	9.5	263	4.4	7.1	1.6	1.3	31%	71%	41
	06	29	a/a	CIN	9	4	33	0	98	129	49	16	55	57	4.47	1.88	14.3	311	5.0	5.3	1.0	1.5	34%	80%	3
Shell,Steven	05	23	aa	ANA	10	8	27	0	159	185	84	16	54	106	4.75	1.50	26.1	285	3.1	6.0	2.0	0.9	33%	70%	48
	06	24	a/a	ANA	6	11	27	0	140	185	94	15	33	78	6.03	1.55	23.2	311	2.1	5.0	2.4	1.0	35%	61%	44
Shields,Jamie	05	24	a/a	TAM	8	5	18	0	115	110	40	5	32	94	3.13	1.23	26.6	247	2.5	7.4	2.9	0.4	31%	74%	100
	06	25	aaa	TAM	3	2	10	0	61	71	23	3	6	55	3.39	1.26	25.5	285	0.9	8.1	9.2	0.4	37%	73%	226
Shiell,Jason	06	30	aaa	ATL	2	4	9	0	52	68	40	4	19	27	6.85	1.67	26.5	310	3.2	4.7	1.5	0.8	35%	57%	29
Shipman,Andy	05	24	aa	CHC	3	6	58	15	64	71	29	1	30	58	4.05	1.58	5.0	275	4.2	8.2	1.9	0.1	36%	72%	85
	06	25	a/a	CHC	3	4	57	2	72	99	41	1	34	48	5.15	1.85	6.0	320	4.3	5.9	1.4	0.1	39%	70%	52
Shortslef,Josh	06	25	aa	PIT	6	2	12	0	60	78	42	5	14	40	6.29	1.52	22.3	307	2.0	6.0	2.9	0.8	36%	57%	67
Sierra,Edwardo	05	23	aa	NYY	3	4	46	2	72	70	46	9	54	47	5.78	1.71	7.3	250	6.7	5.8	0.9	1.2	28%	68%	23
	06	24	a/a	COL	2	1	31	0	50	68	49	3	39	39	8.91	2.14	8.2	318	7.1	7.0	1.0	0.6	39%	55%	37
Sikaras,Pete	05	26	aa	ARI	2	3	44	2	64	101	62	9	37	30	8.70	2.15	7.4	350	5.2	4.1	0.8	1.3	38%	59%	-12
Simard,Michel	06	25	aa	ANA	0	1	16	0	33	53	27	4	17	18	7.23	2.11	10.4	355	4.5	4.9	1.1	1.2	39%	66%	-0
Simmons,Justin	06	25	a/a	LA	1	3	31	1	53	55	34	12	34	28	5.72	1.67	7.8	261	5.7	4.7	0.8	2.0	26%	71%	-11
Simonitsch,Errol	05	23	aa	MIN	6	4	13	0	72	100	41	6	28	41	5.15	1.77	26.0	322	3.5	5.1	1.5	0.8	37%	71%	29
	06	24	aa	MIN	8	14	27	0	148	238	107	25	46	71	6.52	1.92	26.6	355	2.8	4.3	1.5	1.5	38%	68%	-4
Simon,Alfredo	05	24	aa	SF	3	8	43	19	91	124	64	6	25	48	6.34	1.64	9.7	318	2.5	4.8	1.9	0.6	36%	60%	42
	06	25	aaa	SF	0	6	10	0	52	83	42	7	18	30	7.34	1.94	25.3	353	3.1	5.1	1.6	1.2	39%	62%	13
Simpson,Allan	05	28	aaa	CIN	4	4	50	1	64	59	34	5	39	70	4.83	1.53	5.7	240	5.4	9.8	1.8	0.8	33%	69%	81
	06	29	aaa	MIL	2	4	42	10	56	59	31	10	32	43	4.93	1.62	6.1	266	5.1	6.8	1.3	1.6	30%	74%	24
Simpson,Gerrit	05	26	aa	COL	4	0	40	5	62	87	34	4	28	36	5.00	1.85	7.4	324	4.0	5.2	1.3	0.6	37%	73%	29
	06	27	aa	MIL	3	3	51	0	76	89	36	10	31	45	4.22	1.57	6.7	285	3.7	5.4	1.5	1.2	32%	77%	24
Sipp,Tony	06	23	aa	CLE	4	2	29	3	60	53	27	2	23	69	4.01	1.25	8.6	231	3.4	10.3	3.0	0.3	33%	66%	125
Skaggs,Jon	05	27	aa	NYY	2	7	22	1	80	135	78	18	47	33	8.80	2.27	18.9	366	5.3	3.7	0.7	2.0	38%	63%	-42
	06	29	aa	HOU	0	0	14	1	30	43	30	6	26	19	8.97	2.28	11.2	326	7.8	5.7	0.7	1.9	36%	62%	-16
Slaten,Doug	05	26	aa	ARI	2	2	58	1	61	78	39	2	29	59	5.73	1.75	4.9	304	4.3	8.6	2.0	0.3	40%	65%	79
	06	27	a/a	ARI	4	4	58	10	63	53	14	1	24	63	2.06	1.23	4.5	225	3.5	9.0	2.6	0.2	31%	83%	113
Slocum,Brian	05	24	aa	CLE	7	5	21	0	102	117	62	9	39	79	5.47	1.53	21.6	282	3.4	7.0	2.0	0.8	34%	64%	58
	06	26	aaa	CLE	6	3	27	1	94	93	45	5	39	80	4.35	1.41	15.1	253	3.8	7.7	2.0	0.5	32%	68%	79
Slowey,Kevin	06	22	aa	MIN	4	3	9	0	59	61	29	8	15	44	4.42	1.29	27.6	261	2.3	6.7	2.9	1.2	30%	69%	68
Small,Aaron	05	34	a/a	NYY	2	4	12	0	54	86	37	7	10	18	6.11	1.77	21.1	352	1.7	3.0	1.8	1.1	37%	66%	7
	06	35	aaa	NYY	2	4	11	0	41	79	35	5	14	13	7.59	2.25	19.4	396	3.0	2.9	1.0	1.1	42%	66%	-21
Smith,Cameron	05	32	a/a	TAM	5	4	46	7	58	47	27	6	53	50	4.14	1.72	5.9	216	8.3	7.8	0.9	0.9	27%	78%	53
Smith,Chris	05	26	aa	BOS	4	3	14	0	72	119	60	13	16	38	7.48	1.86	24.7	361	1.9	4.7	2.4	1.7	39%	61%	12
	06	26	a/a	BOS	10	7	27	0	149	189	94	15	41	84	5.65	1.55	24.7	303	2.5	5.0	2.0	0.9	34%	63%	41
Smith,Chuck	05	36	aaa	BAL	1	7	10	0	61	82	49	6	26	35	7.30	1.78	28.7	316	3.9	5.2	1.3	0.9	36%	58%	23
Smith,Cody	06	24	aa	KC	9	0	46	4	86	99	29	4	22	48	3.08	1.41	8.1	282	2.3	5.1	2.2	0.4	33%	78%	62
Smith,Dan	06	31	aa	ATL	3	6	28	0	60	60	35	5	41	65	5.29	1.68	9.9	255	6.2	9.7	1.6	0.7	35%	68%	74
Smith,Gregory	06	23	aa	ARI	5	4	11	0	60	81	37	6	25	33	5.55	1.77	25.6	316	3.8	5.0	1.3	0.9	36%	69%	22
Smith,Jesse	06	26	a/a	ANA	8	13	29	0	167	237	106	24	66	76	5.69	1.81	27.2	327	3.5	4.1	1.2	1.3	35%	71%	-1
Smith,Matt	05	26	aaa	CHW	1	6	65	4	83	113	45	16	34	46	4.90	1.76	6.0	317	3.6	4.9	1.4	1.7	34%	77%	-2
	06	27	a/a	MIL	1	7	20	1	43	84	51	6	22	17	10.54	2.45	11.6	399	4.5	3.6	0.8	1.2	43%	55%	-22
Smith,Matt	05	27	a/a	NYY	5	4	47	3	82	90	33	6	41	67	3.65	1.60	7.9	272	4.5	7.3	1.6	0.6	34%	78%	60
	06	28	aaa	PHI	0	1	33	4	35	40	11	5	15	22	2.71	1.56	4.8	281	3.8	5.6	1.5	1.4	31%	89%	23
Smith,Mike	05	28	a/a	PHI	5	14	29	0	174	225	127	28	99	82	6.57	1.86	28.7	307	5.1	4.3	0.8	1.5	32%	67%	-7
	06	29	aaa	MIN	11	5	28	0	150	210	105	18	73	85	6.32	1.88	25.8	324	4.3	5.1	1.2	1.1	36%	67%	14
Smith,Sean	06	23	aa	CLE	10	5	25	0	144	161	76	10	46	84	4.75	1.44	25.1	277	2.9	5.3	1.8	0.6	32%	66%	51
Smith,Travis	05	33	aaa	FLA	7	7	17	0	97	109	44	9	27	60	4.09	1.41	24.7	278	2.5	5.5	2.2	0.9	32%	73%	52
	06	34	aaa	STL	8	7	23	0	135	192	102	14	46	76	6.80	1.76	27.5	327	3.1	5.1	1.6	0.9	37%	61%	27
Snare,Ryan	05	27	a/a	SD	6	10	34	2	115	151	73	18	46	63	5.73	1.71	15.7	310	3.6	4.9	1.4	1.4	34%	69%	10
	06	28	aa	KC	2	2	7	0	35	63	34	4	22	19	8.65	2.40	26.7	379	5.6	4.9	0.9	0.9	42%	63%	-1
Snell,Ian	05	24	aaa	PIT	11	3	18	0	112	98	50	13	21	88	4.02	1.06	24.8	231	1.7	7.1	4.2	1.0	27%	65%	108
Snyder,Kyle	05	28	a/a	KC	3	3	16	0	71	81	35	4	25	37	4.47	1.49	19.6	281	3.1	4.6	1.5	0.4	32%	69%	44
	06	29	aaa	KC	1	5	13	1	80	114	49	7	12	40	5.55	1.58	27.7	328	1.4	4.5	3.3	0.7	37%	64%	64
Songster,Judd	05	26	a/a	COL	3	2	51	0	71	66	21	6	21	54	2.67	1.23	5.8	242	2.7	6.9	2.6	0.8	29%	82%	78
	06	27	aa	COL	2	1	47	2	65	62	34	14	32	54	4.77	1.45	6.0	246	4.5	7.5	1.7	1.9	27%	74%	28

					Actual				Major League Equivalents																
PITCHER	Yr	Age	Lev	Org	w	l	g	sv	ip	h	er	hr	bb	k	era	br/ip	bf/g	oob	ctl	dom	cmd	hr/9	h%	s%	bpv
Song,Seung	05	25	a/a	SF	5	6	16	0	91	95	41	8	42	53	4.06	1.50	25.2	263	4.2	5.3	1.3	0.8	30%	75%	36
	06	26	aa	KC	5	10	27	0	130	170	97	16	72	75	6.67	1.86	23.1	309	5.0	5.2	1.0	1.1	35%	64%	13
Sonnanstine,Andrew	06	24	aa	TAM	15	8	28	0	185	197	85	20	39	127	4.11	1.27	27.7	267	1.9	6.2	3.2	1.0	31%	70%	78
Sonnier,Shawn	05	29	a/a	KC	6	0	37	6	66	77	33	7	28	59	4.48	1.58	8.1	284	3.8	8.0	2.1	1.0	35%	74%	61
Sowers,Jeremy	05	22	a/a	CLE	6	1	14	0	88	88	22	7	10	65	2.25	1.11	25.4	255	1.0	6.6	6.5	0.7	31%	84%	159
	06	23	aaa	CLE	9	1	15	0	97	92	19	1	30	48	1.76	1.26	27.0	245	2.8	4.4	1.6	0.1	29%	85%	64
Sparks,Steve	05	30	aaa	OAK	7	5	15	0	83	121	64	12	33	31	6.97	1.86	26.5	333	3.6	3.3	0.9	1.3	35%	63%	-12
Speier,Ryan	05	26	aaa	COL	2	2	44	6	51	75	31	2	16	36	5.45	1.80	5.5	335	2.9	6.3	2.2	0.4	40%	68%	61
Speigner,Levale	05	25	a/a	MIN	6	11	25	0	151	193	91	15	31	83	5.41	1.48	26.6	304	1.8	5.0	2.7	0.9	34%	64%	53
	06	26	a/a	MIN	4	3	49	14	70	106	44	9	24	34	5.70	1.85	6.8	340	3.1	4.4	1.4	1.1	37%	71%	9
Spiehs,R.D.	05	26	a/a	SF	3	3	49	4	71	82	45	12	28	37	5.74	1.56	6.5	284	3.6	4.7	1.3	1.5	30%	66%	10
	06	27	aa	SF	4	1	41	2	64	114	47	3	26	20	6.61	2.18	8.0	378	3.7	2.8	0.8	0.5	41%	68%	-2
Spurling,Chris	06	29	aaa	DET	1	4	49	5	66	79	22	5	11	26	3.00	1.37	5.8	291	1.5	3.6	2.4	0.7	32%	81%	46
Stahl,Richard	05	24	aa	BAL	3	6	18	0	89	107	59	7	63	43	5.96	1.92	23.9	292	6.4	4.3	0.7	0.7	32%	68%	14
	06	26	a/a	CIN	3	10	28	0	80	119	84	9	72	48	9.46	2.38	15.2	337	8.0	5.4	0.7	1.1	38%	59%	3
Stamler,Keith	05	26	a/a	OAK	3	2	45	6	75	117	53	8	36	36	6.38	2.02	8.3	347	4.3	4.3	1.0	0.9	38%	68%	5
Standridge,Jason	05	27	aaa	TEX	5	3	17	0	77	107	58	4	40	43	6.73	1.91	21.9	322	4.7	5.0	1.1	0.5	37%	63%	28
	06	28	aaa	CIN	2	2	37	0	46	52	22	3	17	34	4.32	1.49	5.5	277	3.3	6.7	2.0	0.6	34%	71%	64
Stanford,Jason	06	30	aaa	CLE	6	6	22	0	112	132	70	12	44	66	5.65	1.57	22.9	287	3.5	5.3	1.5	1.0	32%	64%	31
Stark,Denny	05	31	aaa	COL	2	6	14	0	58	82	59	6	40	34	9.11	2.10	20.9	326	6.2	5.3	0.9	0.9	37%	54%	14
Starling,Wardell	06	24	aa	PIT	6	5	15	0	86	100	37	7	29	35	3.87	1.49	25.4	284	3.0	3.6	1.2	0.8	31%	75%	23
Startup,Will	06	22	a/a	ATL	8	2	46	4	67	77	25	4	18	59	3.36	1.42	6.3	282	2.4	7.9	3.3	0.5	36%	77%	99
Stauffer,Tim	05	23	aaa	SD	2	5	12	0	66	90	43	4	16	50	5.85	1.60	24.9	318	2.2	6.8	3.1	0.5	39%	62%	82
	06	24	aaa	SD	7	12	28	0	153	203	91	15	49	78	5.35	1.65	25.0	312	2.9	4.6	1.6	0.9	35%	68%	27
Stephens,John	05	26	aaa	BAL	4	5	23	0	84	107	53	11	17	50	5.62	1.48	16.1	304	1.8	5.4	2.9	1.2	34%	63%	53
	06	27	a/a	BAL	2	7	20	0	86	132	79	10	41	48	8.25	2.01	21.2	345	4.3	5.0	1.2	1.0	39%	58%	9
Stertzbach,Von	05	24	aa	ANA	3	5	44	10	51	66	33	7	24	33	5.74	1.77	5.5	307	4.3	5.8	1.4	1.3	35%	70%	19
Stetter,Mitch	05	25	a/a	MIL	3	4	59	8	77	77	30	8	22	59	3.49	1.29	5.5	256	2.5	6.9	2.7	1.0	30%	76%	74
	06	26	aaa	MIL	2	5	51	0	38	45	25	4	17	32	5.97	1.64	3.4	290	4.1	7.5	1.8	1.0	35%	64%	52
Stevenson,Jason	05	24	aa	WAS	1	9	13	0	53	92	73	15	32	30	12.29	2.31	21.4	371	5.3	5.1	1.0	2.5	39%	47%	-43
Stewart,Cory	05	26	aaa	PIT	7	10	24	0	132	158	89	17	61	64	6.06	1.65	25.2	290	4.1	4.4	1.1	1.2	31%	64%	10
Stewart,Josh	05	27	aaa	CHW	4	4	14	0	65	76	38	7	16	34	5.27	1.42	20.2	286	2.3	4.7	2.1	1.0	32%	64%	39
	06	28	aaa	FLA	1	3	13	0	35	46	27	5	16	18	7.02	1.77	12.7	311	4.0	4.6	1.1	1.3	34%	61%	4
Stewart,Paul	05	27	a/a	PIT	8	10	29	0	131	189	86	21	47	64	5.92	1.80	21.3	330	3.2	4.4	1.3	1.4	35%	70%	1
Stewart,Scott	05	30	aaa	NYM	2	7	37	0	45	61	36	3	17	24	7.08	1.72	5.7	316	3.3	4.8	1.5	0.7	36%	57%	31
Stockman,Phil	05	26	a/a	ARI	2	4	64	1	67	77	42	7	52	40	5.64	1.91	5.1	281	6.9	5.3	0.8	1.0	32%	71%	17
	06	27	a/a	ATL	0	0	21	2	40	19	4	0	14	42	1.00	0.83	7.2	139	3.2	9.5	2.9	0.0	21%	87%	146
Stodolka,Mike	05	24	aa	KC	4	11	25	0	124	164	85	9	33	56	6.13	1.59	22.4	311	2.4	4.1	1.7	0.7	34%	60%	33
Stokes,Brian	05	26	aa	TAM	4	5	15	0	85	101	46	8	30	50	4.86	1.54	25.3	289	3.2	5.2	1.7	0.9	33%	69%	38
	06	27	aaa	TAM	7	7	29	0	133	166	83	9	55	84	5.62	1.66	21.0	300	3.7	5.6	1.5	0.6	35%	65%	42
Stone,Ricky	05	31	aaa	STL	3	2	23	9	30	27	9	0	6	24	2.66	1.07	5.2	233	1.7	7.3	4.4	0.0	31%	72%	144
Strickland,Scott	05	29	aaa	HOU	2	3	28	10	30	32	16	3	10	22	4.91	1.38	4.6	265	2.9	6.5	2.2	1.0	31%	66%	58
	06	30	aaa	PIT	5	2	53	5	73	87	27	6	18	53	3.28	1.43	6.0	289	2.2	6.5	3.0	0.7	35%	79%	79
Stults,Eric	05	26	a/a	LA	7	10	27	0	146	187	78	19	35	94	4.80	1.52	24.0	305	2.1	5.8	2.7	1.2	35%	71%	51
	06	27	aaa	LA	10	11	26	0	153	164	74	9	66	105	4.36	1.50	26.0	268	3.9	6.2	1.6	0.5	32%	71%	55
Sturge,Justin	05	24	aa	BOS	2	1	33	0	48	64	36	3	17	27	6.71	1.69	6.7	314	3.2	5.0	1.6	0.6	36%	58%	37
Sweeney,Brian	05	31	aaa	TAM	7	9	30	0	161	222	86	18	38	90	4.82	1.61	24.4	321	2.1	5.0	2.4	1.0	36%	72%	41
	06	32	aaa	SD	2	1	7	0	30	36	16	2	7	18	4.71	1.43	18.8	289	2.2	5.4	2.4	0.6	33%	67%	62
Switzer,Jon	05	26	a/a	TAM	3	6	23	0	75	114	54	8	29	37	6.52	1.91	15.8	343	3.5	4.4	1.3	0.9	38%	66%	12
	06	27	aaa	TAM	3	0	26	3	31	27	4	1	15	24	1.22	1.36	5.1	232	4.3	6.9	1.6	0.3	29%	92%	75
Sylvester,Billy	05	29	a/a	OAK	2	4	38	0	55	74	51	11	56	48	8.26	2.37	7.7	315	9.2	7.8	0.8	1.7	37%	67%	4
Tadano,Kazuhito	05	25	aaa	CLE	5	5	32	5	96	111	48	13	21	74	4.54	1.38	12.9	284	2.0	7.0	3.5	1.2	33%	70%	77
	06	26	aaa	OAK	2	4	34	3	56	76	36	9	19	49	5.78	1.69	7.6	317	3.0	7.9	2.7	1.5	38%	69%	50
Talbot,Mitch	06	23	aa	TAM	10	7	28	1	156	168	59	7	48	133	3.40	1.38	24.0	269	2.8	7.7	2.8	0.4	34%	75%	93
Tallet,Brian	05	28	aaa	CLE	6	5	22	0	97	111	48	15	26	49	4.48	1.40	19.1	281	2.4	4.6	1.9	1.4	30%	73%	25
Tamayo,Danny	05	26	aaa	KC	9	8	30	0	160	210	102	23	47	87	5.74	1.61	24.2	310	2.7	4.9	1.8	1.3	34%	66%	23
Tankersley,Dennis	05	27	aaa	KC	9	8	32	0	136	162	69	12	56	88	4.57	1.60	19.2	290	3.7	5.8	1.6	0.8	34%	72%	41
	06	28	aaa	STL	4	15	29	0	167	215	109	23	64	101	5.89	1.67	26.5	305	3.5	5.4	1.6	1.2	34%	66%	22
Taschner,Jack	05	27	aaa	SF	3	0	44	10	49	32	9	2	22	49	1.74	1.09	4.5	181	4.1	9.1	2.2	0.4	25%	86%	109
	06	28	aaa	SF	6	7	45	14	49	57	24	5	17	54	4.34	1.51	4.8	284	3.2	9.9	3.1	1.0	38%	73%	94
Tata,Jordan	06	25	aaa	DET	10	6	21	0	122	140	69	13	51	73	5.07	1.56	26.1	283	3.7	5.4	1.5	1.0	32%	69%	32
Taubenheim,Ty	05	23	aa	MIL	2	6	11	0	64	71	35	7	24	38	4.92	1.48	25.6	275	3.4	5.3	1.6	1.0	31%	68%	36
	06	24	aaa	TOR	2	4	18	0	75	91	33	12	20	41	3.95	1.48	18.4	293	2.4	4.9	2.1	1.4	32%	79%	26
Tejeda,Rob	06	25	aaa	TEX	6	2	15	0	80	78	42	11	46	68	4.73	1.55	23.8	250	5.2	7.7	1.5	1.2	30%	73%	45
Tejera,Michael	05	29	aaa	TEX	3	2	43	2	59	61	30	6	29	42	4.58	1.53	6.1	262	4.4	6.4	1.4	1.0	31%	72%	42
	06	30	aaa	SF	8	5	35	0	111	134	56	12	43	63	4.54	1.59	14.3	292	3.5	5.1	1.5	1.0	33%	73%	28
Thayer,Dale	05	25	aa	SD	3	5	55	27	56	67	17	4	26	50	2.70	1.67	4.7	291	4.2	8.1	1.9	0.7	37%	86%	65
	06	26	a/a	SD	7	4	59	27	68	69	22	3	24	51	2.92	1.38	5.0	259	3.2	6.8	2.1	0.4	32%	79%	76
Thomas,Adam	06	27	a/a	LA	2	5	12	1	35	51	28	0	24	20	7.07	2.13	14.8	330	6.2	5.1	0.8	0.0	39%	63%	37
Thomas,Evan	05	31	aaa	ANA	7	5	20	0	92	141	69	15	28	38	6.79	1.84	21.9	344	2.8	3.7	1.3	1.4	36%	65%	-7
Thomas,Jared	05	25	a/a	SEA	3	3	38	0	66	98	44	14	58	60	6.01	2.35	9.2	336	7.9	8.1	1.0	1.9	40%	79%	2
Thomas,John	05	24	aa	MIN	5	4	39	0	79	138	79	16	40	43	8.98	2.25	10.5	374	4.6	4.9	1.1	1.8	40%	61%	-22
	06	25	aa	MIN	1	2	14	0	36	62	38	4	24	23	9.44	2.41	13.7	372	6.1	5.6	0.9	1.1	42%	59%	0
Thompson,Brad	06	25	aaa	STL	2	0	14	0	42	42	13	3	6	29	2.77	1.14	12.2	254	1.3	6.2	4.8	0.6	30%	78%	124
Thompson,Derek	05	25	a/a	LA	1	4	12	0	62	67	24	3	27	49	3.43	1.51	23.0	270	3.9	7.0	1.8	0.4	33%	77%	68
Thompson,Justin	05	33	a/a	TEX	4	2	37	2	56	77	36	6	10	32	5.69	1.54	6.8	318	1.6	5.0	3.2	0.9	36%	63%	61
	06	34	aaa	MIL	2	3	8	0	35	55	34	9	8	19	8.64	1.80	20.7	348	2.2	4.9	2.3	2.4	36%	55%	-11
Thompson,Mike	05	25	a/a	SD	10	8	27	0	174	189	66	9	39	82	3.41	1.31	27.3	271	2.0	4.3	2.1	0.5	30%	74%	56
	06	26	aaa	SD	6	1	13	0	69	71	28	3	19	36	3.68	1.30	22.4	259	2.5	4.6	1.9	0.4	30%	71%	58

PITCHER	Yr	Age	Lev	Org	w	l	g	sv	ip	h	er	hr	bb	k	era	br/ip	bf/g	oob	ctl	dom	cmd	hr/9	h%	s%	bpv
					Actual				Major League Equivalents																
Thompson,Richard	06	22	a/a	ANA	3	5	46	11	71	64	45	13	28	53	5.70	1.30	6.5	236	3.5	6.7	1.9	1.6	26%	59%	38
Thompson,Sean	05	25	aa	SD	4	5	20	0	113	144	66	8	56	82	5.27	1.77	26.5	304	4.4	6.5	1.5	0.7	36%	70%	44
	06	24	aa	SD	6	10	27	0	154	177	86	18	51	114	5.00	1.48	25.1	283	3.0	6.7	2.3	1.0	33%	68%	55
Thompson,Travis	05	31	aa	PHI	4	1	26	1	43	59	20	1	16	15	4.19	1.73	7.7	318	3.3	3.2	1.0	0.3	35%	75%	22
Thorpe,Tracy	05	25	aa	TOR	2	2	26	1	37	40	25	14	20	30	6.15	1.62	6.5	270	4.9	7.4	1.5	3.3	26%	75%	-23
	06	26	aa	TOR	3	1	54	18	55	46	29	7	36	49	4.71	1.47	4.5	220	5.8	7.9	1.4	1.1	27%	70%	55
Threets,Erick	05	24	aa	SF	1	2	30	2	42	51	30	2	31	29	6.38	1.93	6.8	291	6.6	6.2	0.9	0.4	35%	65%	41
	06	25	aaa	SF	2	1	49	0	62	55	22	4	41	44	3.18	1.54	5.7	232	5.9	6.4	1.1	0.6	28%	80%	52
Thurman,Corey	06	28	a/a	MIL	6	10	26	0	148	201	91	15	56	102	5.52	1.74	26.5	318	3.4	6.2	1.8	0.9	37%	69%	39
Till,Brock	06	26	aa	CIN	6	1	40	6	62	69	23	1	36	30	3.33	1.68	7.1	276	5.2	4.3	0.8	0.2	32%	79%	38
Tolar,Kevin	05	35	aaa	ARI	7	2	44	2	47	64	35	7	27	38	6.62	1.94	5.2	318	5.2	7.2	1.4	1.4	37%	68%	22
Tollberg,Brian	05	33	aaa	HOU	4	3	10	0	63	81	38	12	12	32	5.40	1.47	27.7	305	1.6	4.6	2.8	1.6	32%	68%	31
Tomori,Denney	05	38	a/a	BOS	2	8	34	1	86	130	52	10	22	48	5.45	1.77	11.9	341	2.3	5.0	2.1	1.0	38%	70%	31
Totten,Heath	05	27	aaa	LA	7	9	20	0	103	143	68	13	24	57	5.93	1.62	23.4	322	2.1	5.0	2.4	1.2	36%	64%	36
	06	28	aa	LA	8	5	21	0	126	183	75	13	36	55	5.36	1.74	27.9	332	2.6	3.9	1.5	0.9	36%	70%	18
Touchet,Danny	06	25	aa	TEX	3	4	34	2	65	98	52	8	19	37	7.12	1.79	9.0	340	2.6	5.1	2.0	1.2	38%	60%	24
Tovar,Angel	05	27	a/a	SD	4	4	24	0	34	61	30	6	24	17	7.91	2.50	7.7	380	6.4	4.4	0.7	1.5	41%	70%	-26
Towers,Josh	06	30	aaa	TOR	5	5	15	0	101	162	68	18	13	60	6.07	1.73	31.3	354	1.2	5.3	4.6	1.6	39%	68%	65
Traber,Billy	05	26	a/a	CLE	6	9	24	0	110	147	72	9	39	65	5.90	1.68	21.1	313	3.2	5.3	1.7	0.7	36%	64%	37
	06	27	aaa	WAS	7	7	21	0	124	171	71	8	28	82	5.11	1.60	26.7	320	2.1	5.9	2.9	0.6	38%	67%	69
Tracey,Sean	05	25	aa	CHW	14	6	28	0	163	182	91	17	79	86	4.99	1.60	26.3	276	4.4	4.8	1.1	0.9	31%	70%	23
	06	26	aaa	CHW	8	9	29	0	129	134	84	24	82	86	5.84	1.67	20.5	263	5.7	6.0	1.1	1.7	28%	69%	10
Tucker,Glenn	05	24	a/a	ATL	4	2	51	5	65	77	28	5	24	37	3.85	1.55	5.7	289	3.3	5.1	1.6	0.7	33%	76%	39
	06	26	aa	ATL	2	4	50	0	66	98	44	8	21	30	6.04	1.80	6.2	336	2.9	4.0	1.4	1.1	36%	67%	10
Tucker,Rusty	05	25	aa	SD	3	2	51	0	61	79	44	3	51	56	6.54	2.12	6.1	306	7.5	8.2	1.1	0.5	39%	68%	51
	06	26	aa	CHW	1	4	45	2	58	91	59	6	54	33	9.10	2.50	7.0	349	8.4	5.1	0.6	0.9	39%	62%	2
Tyler,Scott	06	24	aa	FLA	1	2	48	3	61	72	36	6	53	45	5.27	2.03	6.3	286	7.8	6.6	0.8	0.9	34%	75%	27
Ulacia,Dennis	05	24	a/a	CHW	4	7	23	0	100	138	85	27	40	50	7.60	1.78	20.5	321	3.6	4.5	1.3	2.4	32%	62%	-28
Ulloa,Enmanuel	05	27	aa	COL	8	3	18	0	103	123	53	15	28	75	4.62	1.46	25.1	290	2.4	6.5	2.7	1.3	33%	72%	54
	06	28	a/a	COL	8	6	24	0	132	172	84	21	40	84	5.71	1.61	24.9	309	2.7	5.7	2.1	1.4	34%	67%	30
Ungs,Nick	05	26	aa	FLA	7	5	22	0	120	163	70	9	41	63	5.26	1.70	25.2	318	3.1	4.7	1.5	0.7	36%	69%	31
	06	27	aaa	FLA	9	9	26	0	144	184	71	14	47	69	4.40	1.61	25.1	304	3.0	4.3	1.5	0.9	34%	74%	25
Valdes,Raul	05	28	a/a	CHC	8	7	30	1	121	211	106	10	49	70	7.85	2.15	20.5	374	3.7	5.2	1.4	0.8	42%	62%	18
	06	29	aaa	CHC	1	3	7	0	32	57	40	8	13	17	11.19	2.18	23.3	379	3.6	4.7	1.3	2.1	40%	48%	-29
Valdez,Edward	05	26	aa	CIN	1	3	12	0	58	101	53	11	26	35	8.26	2.18	24.7	373	4.0	5.4	1.4	1.7	41%	63%	-10
	06	27	aa	CIN	7	10	29	0	136	186	92	14	46	81	6.08	1.70	21.7	319	3.0	5.3	1.8	0.9	36%	64%	33
Valdez,Merkin	05	24	aa	SF	5	6	24	0	107	115	52	7	45	79	4.34	1.50	19.7	270	3.8	6.6	1.7	0.6	33%	71%	59
	06	25	aaa	SF	0	4	46	5	49	56	35	6	36	41	6.40	1.87	5.1	280	6.6	7.5	1.1	1.1	34%	66%	35
Valentine,Joe	05	26	aaa	CIN	0	7	49	3	53	62	37	4	37	37	6.32	1.86	5.2	284	6.3	6.2	1.0	0.7	34%	65%	35
	06	27	a/a	MIL	3	2	42	13	61	77	36	7	33	32	5.25	1.80	6.9	301	4.9	4.8	1.0	1.0	33%	72%	14
Van Buren,Jermaine	05	25	aaa	CHC	2	3	52	25	54	36	13	5	22	56	2.18	1.08	4.2	187	3.7	9.4	2.5	0.8	25%	85%	102
	06	26	aaa	BOS	4	0	33	16	45	47	22	3	20	39	4.32	1.49	6.0	265	3.9	7.7	2.0	0.6	33%	71%	72
Van Hekken,Andy	05	26	a/a	CIN	3	3	37	0	88	122	61	13	36	40	6.24	1.79	11.2	322	3.6	4.0	1.1	1.4	34%	67%	-3
	06	27	aaa	KC	3	5	9	0	53	74	35	7	12	28	5.88	1.60	26.7	322	2.0	4.7	2.4	1.2	35%	65%	31
Vaquedano,Jose	06	25	aa	BOS	9	8	24	0	105	176	114	12	78	68	9.79	2.41	23.4	364	6.7	5.8	0.9	1.0	42%	58%	4
Vargas,Jason	06	24	aaa	FLA	3	6	13	0	69	104	59	10	28	46	7.70	1.91	25.7	340	3.7	6.0	1.6	1.3	39%	60%	18
Vasquez,Carlos	06	24	aa	CHC	3	5	36	3	50	57	34	3	39	51	6.10	1.91	6.7	279	7.0	9.2	1.3	0.6	37%	67%	65
Vasquez,Jorge	05	24	a/a	ATL	2	2	43	12	54	45	28	2	21	55	4.63	1.22	5.2	223	3.4	9.2	2.7	0.3	31%	60%	112
	06	28	aa	PIT	3	3	47	5	65	68	26	3	36	59	3.63	1.60	6.2	262	5.0	8.2	1.6	0.3	34%	77%	76
Vasquez,Virgil	05	23	aa	DET	2	8	15	0	83	105	56	9	13	45	6.02	1.42	24.1	302	1.4	4.8	3.3	1.0	34%	58%	63
	06	24	aa	DET	7	12	27	0	173	219	101	25	54	105	5.25	1.57	28.8	302	2.8	5.5	2.0	1.3	34%	69%	29
Vazquez,Camilo	06	23	aa	CIN	3	5	11	0	60	82	40	8	27	46	6.02	1.82	25.9	320	4.0	6.8	1.7	1.2	37%	68%	31
Venafro,Mike	05	32	aaa	LA	0	1	53	1	44	59	28	3	31	19	5.79	2.02	4.1	314	6.2	3.9	0.6	0.6	35%	71%	9
	06	33	aaa	COL	3	1	56	2	38	41	17	2	15	23	3.98	1.46	3.0	270	3.5	5.4	1.5	0.5	32%	73%	51
Veras,Jose	05	25	aaa	TEX	3	5	57	24	61	69	29	4	31	62	4.26	1.63	4.9	279	4.6	9.1	2.0	0.6	37%	74%	78
	06	26	aaa	NYY	5	3	50	21	59	58	20	4	20	55	3.07	1.31	5.0	250	3.1	8.4	2.7	0.6	32%	78%	95
Verlander,Justin	05	23	aa	DET	2	0	7	0	32	12	1	1	6	28	0.28	0.56	16.0	113	1.7	7.8	4.7	0.3	15%	100%	169
Vermilyea,James	05	24	a/a	TOR	6	3	42	1	100	137	54	14	28	66	4.86	1.65	10.9	319	2.5	5.9	2.4	1.3	36%	74%	38
	06	25	a/a	TOR	6	7	30	2	131	182	75	12	32	59	5.17	1.64	19.9	323	2.2	4.1	1.9	0.8	35%	69%	28
Villacis,Eduardo	05	26	a/a	CHW	3	7	18	1	69	127	80	26	34	47	10.43	2.33	20.1	386	4.5	6.1	1.4	3.3	41%	60%	-57
Villafuerte,Brandon	05	30	aaa	SF	6	3	57	3	76	92	35	4	31	44	4.16	1.62	6.1	294	3.6	5.2	1.4	0.5	34%	74%	41
	06	31	aaa	SF	2	5	49	2	66	72	41	2	19	46	5.59	1.38	5.8	272	2.6	6.2	2.4	0.3	33%	56%	80
Villanueva,Carlos	06	23	a/a	MIL	11	6	22	0	128	124	63	15	44	107	4.42	1.31	24.7	249	3.1	7.5	2.4	1.1	30%	69%	70
Villegas,Felix	05	27	aa	PHI	2	2	26	0	33	57	33	5	18	17	8.85	2.26	6.6	369	4.9	4.7	1.0	1.3	41%	60%	-10
Vogelsong,Ryan	06	29	aaa	PIT	4	5	11	0	67	74	31	7	14	33	4.12	1.31	25.8	273	1.9	4.4	2.3	0.9	30%	70%	48
Volquez,Edinson	05	22	aa	TEX	1	5	10	0	58	69	35	8	17	42	5.41	1.48	25.6	289	2.6	6.5	2.5	1.2	33%	65%	51
	06	23	aaa	TEX	6	6	21	0	120	110	65	14	79	112	4.87	1.57	25.7	239	5.9	8.4	1.4	1.0	30%	71%	56
Voyles,Brad	05	29	aaa	NYY	6	5	19	1	88	104	59	17	33	57	6.03	1.56	20.8	288	3.4	5.8	1.7	1.8	31%	65%	15
Waddell,Jason	06	25	aa	SF	1	3	38	1	48	91	33	6	19	38	6.22	2.28	6.6	393	3.5	7.1	2.0	1.0	47%	73%	30
Waechter,Doug	06	26	aaa	TAM	1	12	17	0	79	155	96	8	25	38	10.93	2.28	24.1	401	2.9	4.3	1.5	0.9	44%	49%	4
Wagner,Ryan	06	24	aaa	WAS	1	3	41	1	47	75	41	4	17	28	7.83	1.95	5.6	353	3.2	5.4	1.6	0.8	40%	58%	28
Wainwright,Adam	05	24	aaa	STL	9	10	28	0	176	214	95	16	47	123	4.86	1.48	27.7	294	2.4	6.3	2.6	0.8	35%	68%	64
Walker,Andy	06	23	aa	TEX	4	4	20	0	93	146	81	29	23	44	7.88	1.82	22.0	350	2.2	4.2	1.9	2.8	35%	63%	-33
Walker,Kevin	05	29	aaa	CHW	1	2	51	5	46	60	35	10	23	40	6.88	1.82	4.3	310	4.5	7.8	1.7	1.9	36%	66%	18
	06	30	aaa	TEX	6	5	46	2	68	109	59	9	39	46	7.79	2.17	7.5	354	5.1	6.1	1.2	1.2	41%	64%	10
Walrond,Les	05	29	aaa	FLA	4	5	15	0	86	105	45	11	37	51	4.72	1.65	26.2	295	3.8	5.3	1.4	1.1	33%	74%	24
	06	30	aaa	CHC	10	5	31	0	133	178	88	16	69	84	5.94	1.86	20.5	314	4.7	5.7	1.2	1.1	36%	69%	18
Wang,Chien-Ming	05	25	aaa	NYY	2	1	6	0	34	44	18	4	6	18	4.81	1.49	25.0	309	1.6	4.7	2.9	1.1	34%	70%	51

Major League Equivalent Statistics

					Actual				Major League Equivalents																
PITCHER	Yr	Age	Lev	Org	w	l	g	sv	ip	h	er	hr	bb	k	era	br/ip	bf/g	oob	ctl	dom	cmd	hr/9	h%	s%	bpv
Warden,Jim Ed	06	27	aa	CLE	5	2	55	11	59	48	28	4	36	35	4.23	1.43	4.7	219	5.5	5.3	1.0	0.6	25%	70%	47
Ward,Jeremy	05	28	a/a	ATL	3	6	43	2	69	89	38	10	23	37	4.95	1.62	7.3	305	3.0	4.8	1.6	1.3	33%	73%	15
	06	29	a/a	TEX	3	2	34	2	58	93	48	8	22	37	7.48	1.99	8.4	354	3.5	5.7	1.6	1.3	40%	63%	14
Wasdin,John	05	33	aaa	TEX	9	2	13	0	73	97	46	13	23	47	5.71	1.64	25.6	312	2.9	5.7	2.0	1.6	35%	69%	22
	06	34	aaa	TEX	3	3	13	0	63	69	22	3	20	51	3.16	1.42	21.0	274	2.9	7.3	2.6	0.5	34%	78%	84
Wassermann,Ehren	06	26	aa	CHW	4	8	61	22	63	83	29	6	30	36	4.12	1.80	4.9	311	4.3	5.1	1.2	0.8	35%	78%	25
Waters,Chris	06	26	aa	ATL	8	14	27	0	155	216	134	34	99	90	7.81	2.03	28.4	323	5.7	5.2	0.9	2.0	34%	64%	-19
Watkins,Steve	05	27	aaa	CLE	9	2	31	0	129	157	65	12	35	71	4.55	1.48	18.3	294	2.4	5.0	2.1	0.8	33%	70%	45
	06	28	aaa	WAS	7	7	21	0	112	128	61	11	45	61	4.92	1.54	23.8	281	3.6	4.9	1.4	0.9	32%	69%	31
Watson,Mark	06	33	aaa	OAK	4	3	49	2	43	53	21	1	24	27	4.41	1.79	4.1	295	5.1	5.6	1.1	0.2	35%	74%	46
Weaver,Jered	05	23	aa	ANA	3	3	8	0	43	46	20	5	18	39	4.19	1.49	23.7	268	3.8	8.2	2.2	1.0	33%	75%	64
	06	24	aaa	ANA	6	1	12	0	77	67	19	7	9	79	2.22	0.99	25.1	230	1.1	9.2	8.8	0.8	30%	83%	224
Webb,John	05	26	aaa	TAM	9	6	27	0	154	175	85	19	57	67	4.94	1.51	25.3	280	3.3	3.9	1.2	1.1	30%	69%	15
	06	27	aaa	STL	6	11	29	0	176	249	112	15	59	92	5.70	1.75	28.4	327	3.0	4.7	1.6	0.8	37%	67%	28
Weber,Ben	06	37	aaa	TOR	1	1	28	1	43	61	31	7	12	34	6.36	1.68	7.1	326	2.4	7.1	3.0	1.5	38%	65%	48
Wellemeyer,Todd	05	27	aaa	CHC	3	2	12	0	53	54	21	2	25	40	3.56	1.48	19.5	257	4.3	6.8	1.6	0.4	32%	75%	67
Wells,Jared	05	24	aa	SD	2	5	7	0	43	57	24	2	15	19	4.96	1.68	28.2	311	3.2	4.1	1.3	0.4	35%	69%	31
	06	25	a/a	SD	6	12	27	0	134	157	87	10	75	89	5.81	1.73	23.1	286	5.1	6.0	1.2	0.7	34%	66%	38
Wells,Randy	06	24	a/a	CHC	9	7	25	0	131	172	75	13	41	97	5.17	1.63	23.8	310	2.8	6.7	2.4	0.9	37%	69%	55
West,Brian	06	26	aa	CHW	2	6	52	4	69	107	76	14	36	30	9.90	2.07	6.6	347	4.6	4.0	0.9	1.8	36%	52%	-27
Whisler,Wesley	06	24	aa	CHW	2	3	7	0	44	64	33	8	16	23	6.72	1.82	29.9	331	3.4	4.7	1.4	1.7	35%	66%	-4
Whitaker,Brian	05	26	a/a	SD	8	12	26	0	147	203	78	4	49	89	4.76	1.72	26.2	321	3.0	5.5	1.8	0.3	38%	70%	54
White,Bill	05	27	aa	ARI	0	2	60	0	42	53	30	1	30	26	6.40	1.97	3.4	301	6.4	5.6	0.9	0.2	36%	65%	39
	06	28	aa	ARI	0	1	54	12	63	88	43	10	42	56	6.18	2.06	5.8	323	6.0	7.9	1.3	1.4	39%	72%	24
White,Matt	05	28	aaa	WAS	8	6	35	0	125	134	55	6	43	82	3.94	1.42	15.5	269	3.1	5.9	1.9	0.5	32%	72%	63
	06	29	aaa	PHI	7	9	38	1	110	158	75	13	43	53	6.10	1.82	13.8	330	3.5	4.3	1.2	1.1	36%	67%	8
White,Sean	05	24	aa	ATL	2	5	8	0	50	52	29	2	19	28	5.29	1.41	27.1	261	3.4	4.9	1.5	0.4	30%	60%	52
	06	25	aa	ATL	5	6	21	1	102	170	79	4	52	58	6.95	2.18	24.8	363	4.6	5.1	1.1	0.4	42%	66%	24
White,Steven	05	24	aa	NYY	2	7	11	0	50	73	45	11	28	43	8.13	2.02	22.5	332	5.1	7.7	1.5	1.9	39%	62%	10
	06	25	a/a	NYY	8	10	28	0	175	191	100	11	79	105	5.14	1.54	27.9	271	4.1	5.4	1.3	0.5	32%	65%	44
Wilhite,Matt	05	24	aa	ANA	1	2	56	2	59	75	29	5	15	26	4.48	1.51	4.7	302	2.2	3.9	1.7	0.8	33%	71%	31
	06	25	aaa	ANA	7	2	54	1	80	85	33	7	20	30	3.75	1.31	6.3	266	2.3	3.3	1.5	0.8	28%	73%	29
Wilkerson,Wes	05	29	a/a	KC	3	7	50	3	78	128	59	7	20	32	6.75	1.89	7.5	360	2.2	3.7	1.6	0.8	39%	63%	14
	06	30	aaa	FLA	0	0	38	0	40	46	23	2	19	28	5.24	1.61	4.8	280	4.2	6.3	1.5	0.5	34%	66%	53
Wilkinson,Matthew	06	29	a/a	ARI	4	6	48	2	58	106	49	10	34	42	7.56	2.41	6.4	386	5.2	6.5	1.2	1.6	44%	70%	-4
Williams,Aaron	05	25	aa	HOU	2	1	22	0	30	35	14	3	17	15	4.08	1.71	6.4	283	5.0	4.5	0.9	0.9	31%	78%	16
	06	26	a/a	HOU	7	6	51	4	67	97	51	12	21	34	6.85	1.75	6.2	330	2.8	4.6	1.6	1.6	35%	63%	1
Williams,Dave	06	28	aaa	NYM	2	2	7	0	36	43	22	4	12	14	5.50	1.51	22.9	290	2.9	3.5	1.2	1.0	31%	65%	13
Williams,Jerome	05	24	aaa	CHC	2	5	10	0	55	80	42	5	23	28	6.87	1.87	26.4	333	3.8	4.6	1.2	0.8	37%	62%	17
	06	25	aaa	CHC	5	7	29	0	111	176	80	23	38	46	6.47	1.92	18.6	352	3.1	3.7	1.2	1.9	36%	70%	-23
Williams,Randy	05	30	aaa	COL	3	3	38	4	41	37	23	2	18	33	5.12	1.33	4.6	234	3.9	7.3	1.9	0.5	29%	60%	77
	06	31	aaa	COL	1	2	47	0	59	87	56	8	29	37	8.51	1.98	6.2	336	4.5	5.7	1.3	1.3	38%	56%	9
Wilson,C.J.	05	25	aa	TEX	0	4	12	0	44	63	29	9	15	35	6.00	1.76	17.2	329	3.0	7.2	2.4	1.9	37%	71%	24
Wilson,Kris	05	29	aaa	NYY	4	1	29	0	67	95	40	9	19	40	5.31	1.69	10.7	325	2.5	5.4	2.1	1.2	36%	71%	32
	06	30	a/a	NYY	9	8	23	0	141	198	98	16	35	70	6.22	1.65	28.0	324	2.2	4.4	2.0	1.0	36%	62%	27
Windsor,Jason	05	23	aa	OAK	3	6	11	0	56	76	39	5	23	32	6.27	1.76	23.9	317	3.6	5.1	1.4	0.8	36%	64%	27
	06	24	a/a	OAK	17	2	26	0	151	175	70	9	41	131	4.18	1.43	25.3	284	2.5	7.8	3.2	0.6	36%	71%	95
Wolfe,Brian	05	25	a/a	MIN	4	3	24	0	38	60	26	2	18	23	6.10	2.03	7.8	350	4.2	5.5	1.3	0.5	41%	68%	31
	06	26	a/a	TOR	1	3	24	0	42	74	43	8	19	26	9.26	2.22	9.0	377	4.0	5.6	1.4	1.7	42%	58%	-8
Wolf,Ross	05	23	aa	FLA	5	4	54	1	78	123	53	6	33	54	6.12	2.00	7.1	351	3.8	6.2	1.6	0.7	41%	69%	36
	06	24	a/a	FLA	5	3	60	0	66	87	35	1	18	37	4.76	1.59	5.0	310	2.4	5.0	2.1	0.1	36%	67%	62
Woods,Jake	05	24	aaa	ANA	2	1	14	0	31	44	20	5	14	24	5.77	1.86	10.7	326	4.0	6.9	1.7	1.4	38%	72%	24
Woodyard,Mark	05	27	aaa	DET	5	2	45	1	70	79	38	7	32	52	4.90	1.59	7.0	279	4.1	6.7	1.6	0.9	33%	70%	46
	06	28	aaa	DET	2	6	39	1	58	98	66	11	41	43	10.15	2.39	7.9	365	6.4	6.6	1.0	1.8	42%	58%	-10
Woolard,Glenn	05	24	aa	MIL	7	11	29	0	146	186	96	17	66	94	5.90	1.73	23.4	304	4.1	5.8	1.4	1.0	35%	67%	28
Worrell,Mark	06	24	aa	STL	3	7	57	27	61	60	37	10	20	63	5.46	1.30	4.5	251	2.9	9.3	3.2	1.5	31%	61%	83
Wright,Matt	05	24	aa	ATL	6	8	17	1	84	120	71	8	38	53	7.62	1.88	23.7	328	4.1	5.7	1.4	0.9	38%	58%	27
	06	25	aa	ATL	10	8	25	0	137	166	76	11	64	101	5.01	1.68	25.2	293	4.2	6.6	1.6	0.7	35%	70%	47
Wuertz,Mike	06	28	aaa	CHC	6	0	30	10	41	38	12	3	11	56	2.53	1.18	5.6	240	2.3	12.2	5.3	0.7	37%	81%	172
Wylie,Mitch	05	29	aaa	SF	3	4	21	2	60	62	27	3	13	42	4.03	1.25	11.9	263	1.9	6.3	3.2	0.5	32%	67%	94
	06	25	aaa	NYM	2	4	27	1	48	59	22	0	12	45	4.15	1.47	7.8	294	2.3	8.3	3.7	0.0	39%	69%	123
Yarnall,Ed	05	30	aaa	WAS	4	6	19	0	77	98	52	11	33	64	6.03	1.70	18.7	303	3.8	7.4	1.9	1.3	36%	66%	41
	06	31	aaa	KC	2	3	29	1	62	73	31	9	17	46	4.52	1.45	9.3	288	2.4	6.7	2.8	1.3	33%	73%	56
Yates,Kyle	06	24	aa	TOR	6	9	28	1	127	152	78	14	43	85	5.55	1.53	20.2	290	3.1	6.0	2.0	1.0	33%	65%	44
Yeatman,Matt	05	23	aa	MIN	5	7	28	0	103	118	60	5	41	63	5.21	1.54	16.4	281	3.6	5.5	1.5	0.4	33%	64%	50
	06	24	aa	MIL	5	2	40	1	70	113	54	13	43	48	6.90	2.23	9.0	355	5.5	6.2	1.1	1.6	40%	71%	-4
Youman,Shane	05	26	aa	PIT	7	6	43	2	93	121	53	10	49	57	5.16	1.83	10.3	308	4.7	5.5	1.2	1.0	35%	73%	22
	06	27	a/a	PIT	11	2	31	1	137	156	55	8	36	61	3.62	1.40	19.1	281	2.3	4.0	1.7	0.5	31%	74%	43
Young,Christopher	05	24	aa	COL	3	2	35	1	53	67	40	9	18	29	6.79	1.61	6.9	303	3.0	4.8	1.6	1.6	32%	60%	9
	06	25	a/a	FLA	5	4	49	12	76	85	34	2	25	54	3.98	1.45	6.8	277	3.0	6.4	2.1	0.2	34%	71%	76
Young,Jason	05	26	aaa	CLE	9	7	27	0	142	204	78	13	37	71	4.92	1.70	24.3	329	2.4	4.5	1.9	0.8	37%	72%	31
Yourkin,Matt	06	25	a/a	FLA	1	4	56	3	66	80	34	5	32	58	4.58	1.69	5.4	293	4.3	7.9	1.8	0.7	37%	73%	61
Ziegler,Brad	06	27	a/a	OAK	9	7	27	0	162	231	86	23	46	74	4.78	1.71	27.8	328	2.6	4.1	1.6	1.3	35%	75%	10
Ziegler,Mike	05	26	a/a	OAK	10	6	33	0	115	141	81	14	64	58	6.34	1.78	16.4	296	5.0	4.5	0.9	1.1	32%	65%	8
Zimmermann,Bob	06	25	aa	ANA	2	3	34	5	45	48	33	4	34	21	6.50	1.82	6.3	268	6.7	4.2	0.6	0.8	29%	64%	14
Zink,Charlie	05	26	a/a	BOS	9	5	26	0	151	128	62	12	83	153	3.71	1.40	25.1	225	5.0	9.1	1.8	0.7	30%	75%	81
	06	27	a/a	BOS	10	4	25	0	116	149	79	11	77	50	6.14	1.95	22.6	306	6.0	3.8	0.6	0.9	33%	68%	4
Zumaya,Joel	05	21	a/a	DET	9	5	26	0	151	114	58	10	74	181	3.46	1.25	24.2	206	4.4	10.8	2.4	0.6	30%	73%	111
Zumwalt,Alec	05	25	a/a	MIL	2	2	37	4	65	67	35	6	30	41	4.84	1.49	7.8	260	4.1	5.6	1.4	0.9	30%	68%	40
	06	26	a/a	MIL	1	3	50	20	54	65	31	11	23	49	5.08	1.63	4.9	292	3.9	8.2	2.1	1.8	35%	74%	38

VI. RATINGS, RANKINGS, CHEAT SHEETS

Ratings, Rankings, Cheat Sheets

Here is what you will find in this section:

Skills Rankings

We start by looking at some important component skills. For batters, we've ranked the top players in terms of pure power, speed, and batting average skill, breaking each down in a number of different ways to provide more insight this year. For pitchers, we rank some of the key base skills, differentiating between starters and relievers, and provide a few interesting cuts that might uncover some late round sleepers.

These are clearly not exhaustive lists of sorts and filters. If there is another cut you'd like to see, drop me a note and I'll consider it for next year's book. Also note that the database at Baseball HQ allows you to construct your own custom sorts and filters. Finally, remember that these are just tools. Some players will appear on multiple lists — even mutually exclusive lists — so you have to assess what makes most sense and make decisions for your specific application.

POWER
Top PX, 400+ AB: Top power skills from among projected full-time players.
Top PX, -300 AB: Top power skills from among projected part-time players. You might find some end-game options here.
Position Scarcity: A quick scan to see which positions have deeper power options than others.
Top PX, Ct% over 85%: Top power skills from among the top contact hitters. Best pure power options here.
Top PX, Ct% under 75%: Top power skills from among the worst contact hitters. These are free-swingers who might be prone to streakiness or lower batting averages.
Top PX, FB% over 40%: Top power skills from among the most extreme fly ball hitters. Most likely to convert their power into home runs.
Top PX, FB% under 35%: Top power skills from among those with lesser fly ball tendencies. There may be more downside to their home run potential.

SPEED
Top SX, 400+ AB: Top speed skills from among projected full-time players.
Top SX, -300 AB: Top speed skills from among projected part-time players. You might find some end-game options here.
Position Scarcity: A quick scan to see which positions have deeper speed options than others.
Top SX, OB% over .350: Top speed skills from among those who get on base most often. Best opportunities for stolen bases here.
Top SX, OB% under .310: Top speed skills from among those who have trouble getting on base. While "you can't steal 1B," these names may bear watching if they can improve their on base ability.
Top SX, SBO% over 20%: Top speed skills from among those who get the green light most often. Most likely to convert their speed into stolen bases.
Top SX, SBO% under 15%: Top speed skills from among those who are currently not getting the green light. There may be sleeper SB's here if given more opps to run.

BATTING AVERAGE
Top Ct%, 400+ AB: Top contact skills from among projected full-time players. Contact does not necessarily convert directly to higher batting averages, but BA and Ct% is still strongly correlated.
Top Ct%, -300 AB: Top contact skills from among projected part-time players. You might find some end-game options here.
Low Ct%, 400+ AB: The poorest contact skills from among projected full-time players. These are potential batting average killers.
Top Ct%, bb% over 10%: Top contact skills from among the most patient hitters. Best pure batting eye and batting average upside here.
Top Ct%, bb% under 6%: Top contact skills from among the least patient hitters. These are free-swingers who might be prone to streakiness or lower batting averages.
Top Ct%, GB% over 50%: Top contact skills from among the most extreme ground ball hitters. A ground ball has a higher chance of becoming a hit than a non-HR fly ball so there may be some batting average upside here.
Top Ct%, GB% under 40%: Top contact skills from among those with lesser ground ball tendencies. These players are making contact but hitting more fly balls, which tend to convert to hits at a lower rate than GB.

PITCHING SKILLS
Top Command: Leaders in projected K/BB rates.
Top Control: Leaders in fewest projected walks allowed.
Top Dominance: Leaders in projected strikeout rate.
Top Ground Ball Rate: GB pitchers tend to have lower ERA's (and higher WHIP) than fly ball pitchers.
Top Fly Ball Rate: FB pitchers tend to have higher ERA's (and lower WHIP) than ground ball pitchers.
High GB, Low Dom: GB pitchers tend to have lower K rates, but these are the most extreme examples. In a year when Chien-Ming Wang had success, we should look at others that have similar profiles.
High GB, High Dom: The best at dominating hitters and keeping the ball down. These are the pitchers who keep runners off the bases and batted balls in the park.
Lowest xERA: Leaders in projected skills-based ERA.
Top BPV: Two lists of top skilled pitchers here. For starters, those projected to be rotation regulars (180+ IP) and fringe starters with skill (-150 IP). For relievers, those projected to be frontline closers (15+ saves) and high-skilled bullpen fillers (5– saves).

Risk Management

Our focus on integrating skills analysis with risk presents us with a few important lists to consider. On these pages are the players who've accumulated the most days on the disabled list over the past three years, and the most reliable batters and pitchers, broken out by position and skill. As a reminder, a high reliability score has nothing to do with skill; it is a gauge of which players manage to accumulate playing time and post consistent output from year to year.

LIMA/RIMA Plan

Here, the players are sorted and ranked based on how well they fit into the LIMA and RIMA Plans. Players are grouped according to the criteria in the description of RIMA in section III.

Position Scarcity Chart

There has been much discussion about position scarcity, its importance and how to leverage it in your draft. This chart provides a visual representation of the depth of talent for the top 45 players at each position and shows you why, in a straight draft league, it might make sense to draft a Marcus Giles before you draft a Manny Ramirez.

Rotisserie Auction Draft

This list is presented with both AL and NL players, mostly because we don't know who is going to end up on what team yet. The values are mostly representative of standard 75%-plus depth leagues.

For those who play in sub-50% depth mixed leagues, these values will seem high, especially for players typically drafted in the end-game. For you, it's best to rely more on the rankings than the actual dollar values, and stick to the players on the first page.

Actually, *all* the values are slightly inflated because our focus is still on performance and we don't know how playing time will shake out yet. Consider these values as what each player could be worth if they were to get optimal playing time.

The free projections update in March will provide better estimates of playing time, and as such, better information for drafting purposes. The custom draft guides on Baseball HQ are available to those who wish to produce accurate valuations for their particular league configuration.

But in the interim, you can still use the information here to plan out the core of your draft. For those who subscribe to Baseball HQ, full projections begin appearing online in mid-December.

Rotisserie Snake Draft

This ranking takes the previous auction list, re-sets it into rounds and adjusts the rankings based on position scarcity. Given the growing popularity of 15-team mixed leagues, like the National Fantasy Baseball Championship, we've set this list up for that type of format.

In the first eight rounds, your target players should be those that are shaded (though your first round pick may depend upon your seed). These are the position scarcity picks. Also pay attention to the bolded players; these are categorical scarcity picks (primarily steals and saves).

If you reach a point where there are still undrafted players from earlier rounds, you can judiciously target those. To build the best foundation, you should come out of the first 10 rounds with all your middle infielders, all your corner infielders, one outfielder, at least one catcher and two pitchers (at least one closer).

The reason we target scarce positions first is that there will be plenty of solid outfielders and starting pitchers later on. The Position Scarcity Chart shows you why. The 25th best catcher on the list is Miguel Olivo; the 25th best starting pitcher is Mike Mussina. Which one would you rather have on your team?

Simulation League Draft

Using Runs Above Replacement creates a more real-world ranking of player value, which serves simulation gamers well. Batters and pitchers are integrated, and value break-points are delineated.

The Missing Piece of Information

For all these lists, equally important to how the players are ranked is how the other owners in your league perceive each player's positioning. For instance, if you see Jimmy Rollins as a first round pick but you know the other owners see him as a third-rounder, you can probably wait to pick him up in round 2.

The Universal Disclaimer

This section is intended solely as a preliminary look based on current factors. Do not treat this guide as the Draft Day gospel. Use the ratings and rankings as a rough guide to get a general sense of where a player falls. For Draft Day, you will need to make your own adjustments based upon about 7,341 different criteria that can impact the world between now and then. Updates will appear next spring online at BaseballHQ.com. And don't forget the free projections update at BaseballForecaster.com.

BATTER SKILLS RANKINGS - POWER

TOP PX, 400+ AB

NAME	POS	PX
Howard,Ryan	3	223
Hafner,Travis	0	219
Ortiz,David	0	197
Thome,Jim	0	194
Dunn,Adam	7	184
Ramirez,Manny	7	178
Delgado,Carlos	3	175
Teixeira,Mark	3	175
Pujols,Albert	3	171
Sexson,Richie	3	171
Beltran,Carlos	8	168
Glaus,Troy	5	166
Jones,Andruw	8	165
Hall,Bill	6	165
LaRoche,Adam	3	165
Giambi,Jason	03	163
Lee,Derrek	3	162
Soriano,Alfonso	7	161
Gomes,Jonny	0	160
Holliday,Matt	7	159
Bay,Jason	7	158
Sizemore,Grady	8	156
Dye,Jermaine	9	155
Swisher,Nick	37	153
Thomas,Frank	0	153
Berkman,Lance	39	153
Pena,Wily Mo	98	151
Burrell,Pat	7	150
Wilkerson,Brad	7	150
Rodriguez,Alex	5	149
Ramirez,Aramis	5	147
Cameron,Mike	8	145
Cabrera,Miguel	5	145
Morneau,Justin	3	144
Duncan,Chris	79	143
Monroe,Craig	70	142
Jacobs,Mike	3	142
Teahen,Mark	5	141

TOP PX, -300 AB

NAME	POS	PX
Saenz,Olmedo	3	163
McPherson,Dallas	5	155
Clark,Tony	3	149
Napoli,Mike	2	142
Lane,Jason	9	142
Marrero,Eli	7	138
Gross,Gabe	87	136
Shoppach,Kelly	2	133
Pena,Carlos	3	131
Hinske,Eric	90	125
Fields,Josh	5	123
Cruz,Nelson	9	123
Hairston,Scott	7	121
Mirabelli,Doug	2	121
Ward,Daryle	9	120
Botts,Jason	0	120
Nix,Laynce	8	120
Bellhorn,Mark	5	118
Norton,Greg	93	118
Guiel,Aaron	9	117
Clevlen,Brent	8	116
Perez,Eduardo	3	116
Rodriguez,John	7	116
Stairs,Matt	0	116
Cruz,Jose	79	115

POSITIONAL SCARCITY

NAME	POS	PX
Hafner,Travis	DH	219
Ortiz,David	2	197
Thome,Jim	3	194
Giambi,Jason	4	163
Gomes,Jonny	5	160
Thomas,Frank	6	153
Ross,David	CA	160
Napoli,Mike	2	142
McCann,Brian	3	137
Shoppach,Kelly	4	133
Posada,Jorge	5	128
Varitek,Jason	6	127
Barrett,Michael	7	126
Mirabelli,Doug	8	121
Howard,Ryan	1B	223
Delgado,Carlos	2	175
Teixeira,Mark	3	175
Pujols,Albert	4	171
Sexson,Richie	5	171
LaRoche,Adam	6	165
Saenz,Olmedo	7	163
Lee,Derrek	8	162
Swisher,Nick	9	153
Berkman,Lance	10	153
Utley,Chase	2B	130
Kent,Jeff	2	124
Valentin,Jose	3	121
Cantu,Jorge	4	117
Cano,Robinson	5	116
Biggio,Craig	6	111
Durham,Ray	7	110
Smith,Jason	8	103
Glaus,Troy	3B	166
McPherson,Dallas	2	155
Rodriguez,Alex	3	149
Ramirez,Aramis	4	147
Cabrera,Miguel	5	145
Jones,Chipper	6	144
Teahen,Mark	7	141
Atkins,Garrett	8	140
Gordon,Alex	9	140
Ensberg,Morgan	10	139
Hall,Bill	SS	165
Uribe,Juan	2	117
Greene,Khalil	3	113
Peralta,Jhonny	4	106
Drew,Stephen	5	106
Guillen,Carlos	6	105
Gonzalez,Alex	7	105
Easley,Damion	8	104
Branyan,Russ	OF	189
Dunn,Adam	2	184
Ramirez,Manny	3	178
Edmonds,Jim	4	172
Beltran,Carlos	5	168
Thames,Marcus	6	166
Jones,Andruw	7	165
Soriano,Alfonso	8	161
Holliday,Matt	9	159
Bay,Jason	10	158
Bonds,Barry	11	157
Sizemore,Grady	12	156
Dye,Jermaine	13	155
Pena,Wily Mo	14	151
Burrell,Pat	15	150
Wilkerson,Brad	16	150

TOP PX, Ct% over 85%

NAME	Ct%	PX
Pujols,Albert	90	171
Ramirez,Aramis	88	147
Atkins,Garrett	88	140
McCann,Brian	87	137
Quentin,Carlos	87	130
Rolen,Scott	85	129
Lee,Carlos	88	128
Crede,Joe	87	127
Barrett,Michael	87	126
Helton,Todd	87	124
Guerrero,Vladimir	89	124
Wells,Vernon	86	124
Baker,Jeff	85	120
Alou,Moises	90	118
Cano,Robinson	89	116
Huff,Aubrey	86	114
Gibbons,Jay	86	111
Kouzmanoff,Kevin	85	110
Durham,Ray	87	110
Lowell,Mike	88	110
Rivera,Juan	87	110
Niekro,Lance	86	108
Hernandez,Ramon	86	107
Mench,Kevin	87	106
Matsui,Hideki	85	106
Guillen,Carlos	85	105
Garciaparra,Nomar	92	105
Sheffield,Gary	87	104
Lieberthal,Mike	90	104
Aurilia,Rich	86	103
Iannetta,Chris	85	102
Gonzalez,Luis	88	102
Tejada,Miguel	88	102
Damon,Johnny	87	101
Rollins,Jimmy	88	101
Crawford,Carl	86	100
Kinsler,Ian	86	100
Loney,James	88	100

TOP PX, Ct% under 75%

NAME	Ct%	PX
Howard,Ryan	69	223
Thome,Jim	70	194
Branyan,Russ	62	189
Dunn,Adam	66	184
Edmonds,Jim	70	172
Sexson,Richie	74	171
Hall,Bill	73	165
Ross,David	71	160
Gomes,Jonny	71	160
Bay,Jason	73	158
McPherson,Dallas	70	155
Pena,Wily Mo	67	151
Burrell,Pat	72	150
Wilkerson,Brad	69	150
Clark,Tony	71	149
Dellucci,David	74	146
Cameron,Mike	73	145
Napoli,Mike	69	142
Wilson,Craig	67	137
Shoppach,Kelly	69	133
Pena,Carlos	73	131
Kearns,Austin	74	128
Varitek,Jason	74	127
Fields,Josh	73	123
Mirabelli,Doug	69	121

TOP PX, FB% over 40%

NAME	FB%	PX
Ortiz,David	46	197
Thome,Jim	41	194
Branyan,Russ	50	189
Dunn,Adam	48	184
Ramirez,Manny	41	178
Edmonds,Jim	45	172
Pujols,Albert	42	171
Beltran,Carlos	43	168
Glaus,Troy	47	166
Thames,Marcus	58	166
Jones,Andruw	41	165
Hall,Bill	42	165
Giambi,Jason	51	163
Saenz,Olmedo	43	163
Soriano,Alfonso	49	161
Ross,David	50	160
Gomes,Jonny	54	160
Bay,Jason	42	158
Bonds,Barry	51	157
Sizemore,Grady	41	156
Dye,Jermaine	41	155
McPherson,Dallas	42	155
Swisher,Nick	46	153
Thomas,Frank	56	153
Burrell,Pat	46	150
Wilkerson,Brad	47	150
Ramirez,Aramis	45	147
Dellucci,David	42	146
Cameron,Mike	44	145
Morneau,Justin	41	144
Monroe,Craig	43	142
Napoli,Mike	54	142
Lane,Jason	55	142
Gordon,Alex	47	140
Ensberg,Morgan	45	139
Marrero,Eli	46	138
McCann,Brian	41	137
Konerko,Paul	41	137

TOP PX, FB% under 35%

NAME	FB%	PX
Howard,Ryan	34	223
Holliday,Matt	33	159
Hawpe,Brad	34	141
Overbay,Lyle	30	131
Cuddyer,Michael	34	129
Abreu,Bobby	30	127
Barrett,Michael	34	126
Fields,Josh	33	123
Markakis,Nick	29	120
Baker,Jeff	28	120
Zimmerman,Ryan	34	119
Jones,Jacque	26	119
Clevlen,Brent	25	116
Cano,Robinson	29	116
Rodriguez,John	32	116
Borchard,Joe	34	115
Hollandsworth,Tod	34	114
Melhuse,Adam	34	113
Wilson,Preston	29	113
Baldelli,Rocco	34	113
Johnson,Kelly	30	110
Rivera,Juan	34	110
Linden,Todd	32	108
DeRosa,Mark	33	107
Young,Dmitri	33	107

BATTER SKILLS RANKINGS - SPEED

TOP SX, 400+ AB

NAME	POS	SX
Reyes,Jose	6	179
Roberts,Dave	7	170
Crawford,Carl	7	166
Figgins,Chone	85	157
Patterson,Corey	8	156
Rollins,Jimmy	6	155
Duffy,Chris	8	154
Pierre,Juan	8	154
Ramirez,Hanley	6	154
Furcal,Rafael	6	152
Weeks,Rickie	4	149
Suzuki,Ichiro	98	145
Gathright,Joey	8	140
Taveras,Willy	8	139
Cameron,Mike	8	135
Podsednik,Scott	7	134
Sizemore,Grady	8	131
Young,Delmon	9	130
Freel,Ryan	89	129
Damon,Johnny	8	127
Roberts,Brian	4	126
Soriano,Alfonso	7	126
Vizquel,Omar	6	126
Rios,Alexis	9	126
Byrnes,Eric	8	126
Burke,Chris	48	124
Jeter,Derek	6	124
Baldelli,Rocco	8	122
Lopez,Felipe	6	122
Upton,B.J.	5	122
Choo,Shin-Soo	9	120
Lugo,Julio	64	120
Beltran,Carlos	8	119
Utley,Chase	4	119
Crisp,Coco	8	118
Granderson,Curtis	8	115
Castillo,Luis	4	115
Kennedy,Adam	4	115

TOP SX, -300 AB

NAME	POS	SX
Lofton,Kenny	8	155
Guzman,Freddy	8	151
Bynum,Freddie	7	144
Logan,Nook	8	144
McLouth,Nate	89	142
Castro,Bernie	4	137
Orr,Pete	4	137
Bloomquist,Willie	8	137
Abercrombie,Reggie	8	136
Pagan,Angel	79	132
DaVanon,Jeff	8	129
Aybar,Erick	6	128
Lewis,Fred	8	127
Cairo,Miguel	4	124
Gwynn Jr.,Tony	8	123
Gomez,Alexis	79	122
Infante,Omar	4	121
Repko,Jason	8	120
Ozuna,Pablo	7	119
Finley,Steve	8	119
Counsell,Craig	6	117
German,Esteban	4057	117
Reed,Jeremy	8	115
Hairston Jr.,Jerry	74	113
Smith,Jason	4	112

POSITIONAL SCARCITY

NAME	POS	SX
Gomes,Jonny	DH	75
Rabe,Josh	2	69
Kouzmanoff,Kevin	3	59
Young,Dmitri	4	58
Ortiz,David	5	50
Botts,Jason	6	48
Laird,Gerald	CA	101
Martin,Russell	2	94
Rodriguez,Ivan	3	94
Torrealba,Yorvit	4	89
Mauer,Joe	5	84
Mathis,Jeff	6	80
Johjima,Kenji	7	80
Olivo,Miguel	8	77
Kendrick,Howie	1B	113
Loney,James	2	92
Gload,Ross	3	91
Lee,Derrek	4	90
Phillips,Andy	5	86
Pujols,Albert	6	86
Lamb,Mike	7	85
Wilson,Craig	8	79
Helton,Todd	9	77
Garciaparra,Nomar	10	74
Weeks,Rickie	2B	149
Castro,Bernie	2	137
Orr,Pete	3	137
Matsui,Kazuo	4	132
Theriot,Ryan	5	129
Roberts,Brian	6	126
Burke,Chris	7	124
Cairo,Miguel	8	124
Punto,Nick	3B	123
Upton,B.J.	2	122
Teahen,Mark	3	114
Perez,Antonio	4	108
Izturis,Maicer	5	108
Wright,David	6	106
Gordon,Alex	7	98
McPherson,Dallas	8	97
Iwamura,Akinori	9	97
Rodriguez,Alex	10	93
Reyes,Jose	SS	179
Rollins,Jimmy	2	155
Ramirez,Hanley	3	154
Furcal,Rafael	4	152
Aybar,Erick	5	128
Vizquel,Omar	6	126
Jeter,Derek	7	124
Lopez,Felipe	8	122
Roberts,Dave	OF	170
Crawford,Carl	2	166
Figgins,Chone	3	157
Patterson,Corey	4	156
Lofton,Kenny	5	155
Duffy,Chris	6	154
Pierre,Juan	7	154
Guzman,Freddy	8	151
Kemp,Matt	9	148
Suzuki,Ichiro	10	145
Bynum,Freddie	11	144
Logan,Nook	12	144
McLouth,Nate	13	142
Gathright,Joey	14	140
Taveras,Willy	15	139
Bloomquist,Willie	16	137

TOP SX, OB% over .350

NAME	OB%	SX
Roberts,Dave	352	170
Lofton,Kenny	354	155
Furcal,Rafael	361	152
Suzuki,Ichiro	352	145
Sizemore,Grady	350	131
Freel,Ryan	350	129
DaVanon,Jeff	368	129
Damon,Johnny	362	127
Roberts,Brian	356	126
Jeter,Derek	374	124
Choo,Shin-Soo	350	120
Beltran,Carlos	382	119
Utley,Chase	358	119
German,Esteban	366	117
Castillo,Luis	371	115
Teahen,Mark	363	114
Guillen,Carlos	384	112
Holliday,Matt	365	111
Giles,Marcus	360	107
Wright,David	372	106
DeJesus,David	362	105
Dellucci,David	355	105
Bay,Jason	384	104
Abreu,Bobby	418	104
Durham,Ray	358	103
Renteria,Edgar	350	102
Hermida,Jeremy	370	101
Matthews Jr.,Gary	351	100
Carroll,Jamey	355	100
Gordon,Alex	369	98
Bradley,Milton	357	95
Martin,Russell	364	94
Rodriguez,Alex	386	93
Young,Michael	360	92
Lee,Derrek	383	90
Jones,Chipper	396	87
Lee,Carlos	361	86
Drew,J.D.	400	86

TOP SX, OB% under .310

NAME	OB%	SX
Patterson,Corey	296	156
Bynum,Freddie	307	144
Logan,Nook	295	144
McLouth,Nate	301	142
Castro,Bernie	297	137
Orr,Pete	297	137
Bloomquist,Willie	303	137
Abercrombie,Reggie	239	136
Aybar,Erick	292	128
Byrnes,Eric	307	126
Cairo,Miguel	298	124
Infante,Omar	300	121
Repko,Jason	309	120
Smith,Jason	276	112
Freeman,Choo	296	111
Cintron,Alex	308	111
Everett,Adam	289	110
Perez,Antonio	301	108
McDonald,John	282	106
Guzman,Cristian	305	106
Matos,Luis	308	105
Hernandez,Anderson	255	105
Jackson,Damian	305	105
Betancourt,Yuniesky	298	104
Clayton,Royce	303	104

TOP SX, SBO% over 20%

NAME	SBO	SX
Reyes,Jose	44%	179
Roberts,Dave	34%	170
Crawford,Carl	37%	166
Figgins,Chone	35%	157
Patterson,Corey	43%	156
Rollins,Jimmy	22%	155
Lofton,Kenny	22%	155
Duffy,Chris	33%	154
Pierre,Juan	40%	154
Ramirez,Hanley	36%	154
Furcal,Rafael	25%	152
Guzman,Freddy	51%	151
Weeks,Rickie	21%	149
Kemp,Matt	26%	148
Bynum,Freddie	31%	144
Logan,Nook	31%	144
McLouth,Nate	25%	142
Gathright,Joey	36%	140
Taveras,Willy	29%	139
Castro,Bernie	32%	137
Bloomquist,Willie	26%	137
Abercrombie,Reggie	28%	136
Cameron,Mike	21%	135
Podsednik,Scott	39%	134
Pagan,Angel	22%	132
Young,Delmon	28%	130
Theriot,Ryan	24%	129
Freel,Ryan	32%	129
DaVanon,Jeff	21%	129
Aybar,Erick	56%	128
Lewis,Fred	22%	127
Roberts,Brian	24%	126
Soriano,Alfonso	31%	126
Burke,Chris	21%	124
Cairo,Miguel	21%	124
Gwynn Jr.,Tony	28%	123
Upton,B.J.	33%	122
Choo,Shin-Soo	22%	120

TOP SX, SBO% under 15%

NAME	SBO	SX
Infante,Omar	13%	121
Finley,Steve	9%	119
Utley,Chase	10%	119
Granderson,Curtis	10%	115
Teahen,Mark	7%	114
Bartlett,Jason	11%	114
Rowand,Aaron	14%	114
Guillen,Carlos	11%	112
Holliday,Matt	11%	111
Hudson,Orlando	8%	108
Spilborghs,Ryan	13%	107
Giles,Marcus	10%	107
Guzman,Cristian	11%	106
DeJesus,David	11%	105
Dellucci,David	8%	105
Bay,Jason	10%	104
Linden,Todd	7%	104
Cora,Alex	12%	104
Inglett,Joe	13%	104
Johnson,Reed	9%	104
Durham,Ray	8%	103
Tyner,Jason	13%	103
Renteria,Edgar	13%	102
Zobrist,Ben	14%	102
Ford,Lew	10%	102

BATTER SKILLS RANKINGS - BATTING AVERAGE

TOP Ct%, 400+ AB

NAME	Ct%	BA
Polanco,Placido	94	305
Pierre,Juan	94	302
Pedroia,Dustin	93	285
LoDuca,Paul	92	298
Kendall,Jason	92	281
Garciaparra,Nomar	92	308
Eckstein,David	92	272
Johjima,Kenji	92	283
Betancourt,Yuniesk	91	274
Sanchez,Freddy	91	307
Loretta,Mark	91	284
Vizquel,Omar	91	276
Cabrera,Orlando	90	270
Casey,Sean	90	301
Castillo,Luis	90	299
Pujols,Albert	90	339
Suzuki,Ichiro	90	306
Hatteberg,Scott	90	267
Vidro,Jose	90	281
Molina,Yadier	90	250
Molina,Ben	90	290
Payton,Jay	89	284
Catalanotto,Frank	89	297
Estrada,Johnny	89	289
Guerrero,Vladimir	89	321
Kotsay,Mark	89	279
Giles,Brian	89	286
Mauer,Joe	89	321
Cano,Robinson	89	316
Wilson,Jack	88	273
Loney,James	88	291
Atkins,Garrett	88	315
Hill,Aaron	88	275
Rollins,Jimmy	88	296
Lowell,Mike	88	290
Ramirez,Aramis	88	297
Lopez,Jose	88	277
Jackson,Conor	88	279

TOP Ct%, -300 AB

NAME	Ct%	BA
Callaspo,Alberto	95	268
Keppinger,Jeff	94	282
Pena,Brayan	92	280
Aybar,Erick	92	263
Frandsen,Kevin	92	264
Young,Eric	91	246
Gomez,Chris	91	282
Hall,Toby	91	268
Ozuna,Pablo	90	290
Lofton,Kenny	90	290
Costa,Shane	90	284
Miles,Aaron	90	273
Redmond,Mike	90	289
Tyner,Jason	89	282
Kotchman,Casey	89	276
Alomar Jr.,Sandy	89	264
Castro,Bernie	89	249
Quintanilla,Omar	88	275
Gload,Ross	88	311
Cora,Alex	88	244
Reed,Jeremy	88	268
Barmes,Clint	88	251
Martinez,Ramon	88	254
Cirillo,Jeff	88	285
Counsell,Craig	87	249

LOW Ct%, 400+ AB

NAME	Ct%	BA
Dunn,Adam	66	242
Pena,Wily Mo	67	258
Wilkerson,Brad	69	255
Howard,Ryan	69	303
Thome,Jim	70	276
Gomes,Jonny	71	256
Burrell,Pat	72	263
Cameron,Mike	73	263
Hall,Bill	73	261
Bay,Jason	73	289
Varitek,Jason	74	268
Sexson,Richie	74	270
Granderson,Curtis	74	256
Kearns,Austin	74	270
Shelton,Chris	75	254
Olivo,Miguel	75	241
Glaus,Troy	75	253
Swisher,Nick	75	258
Jenkins,Geoff	75	277
Iwamura,Akinori	75	284
Hafner,Travis	75	313
Weeks,Rickie	75	264
Betemit,Wilson	75	273
Giambi,Jason	76	252
Peralta,Jhonny	76	266
Abreu,Bobby	77	297
LaRoche,Adam	77	288
Delgado,Carlos	77	291
Patterson,Corey	77	261
Rodriguez,Alex	77	294
Hawpe,Brad	77	278
Broussard,Ben	77	273
Hermida,Jeremy	77	269
Cuddyer,Michael	77	274
Inge,Brandon	77	258
Soriano,Alfonso	77	280
Bautista,Jose	77	240
Duncan,Chris	78	271
Jones,Andruw	78	273
Lee,Derrek	78	295
Jones,Jacque	78	282
Teahen,Mark	79	294
Lopez,Felipe	79	271
Dye,Jermaine	79	296
Drew,J.D.	79	286
Ramirez,Manny	79	315
Ortiz,David	79	311
Willingham,Josh	79	273
Posada,Jorge	79	271
Choo,Shin-Soo	79	272
Sizemore,Grady	79	283
Thomas,Frank	79	273
Ensberg,Morgan	79	274
Crosby,Bobby	79	265
Drew,Stephen	79	272
Johnson,Nick	79	288
Greene,Khalil	79	266
Francoeur,Jeff	79	265
Jacobs,Mike	79	281
Marte,Andy	80	254
Hart,Corey	80	268
Cabrera,Miguel	80	324
Chavez,Eric	80	266
Teixeira,Mark	80	295
Upton,B.J.	80	262
Laird,Gerald	80	267

TOP Ct%, bb% over 10%

NAME	bb%	Ct%
Pujols,Albert	14	90
Hatteberg,Scott	12	90
Giles,Brian	16	89
Mauer,Joe	12	89
Jackson,Conor	11	88
Gonzalez,Luis	12	88
Counsell,Craig	11	87
Sheffield,Gary	12	87
Helton,Todd	16	87
Jimenez,D'Angelo	13	86
Martin,Russell	11	86
Martinez,Victor	11	86
Johnson,Dan	12	86
Mientkiewicz,Doug	11	86
Carroll,Jamey	11	86
Matsui,Hideki	13	85
Iannetta,Chris	11	85
Rolen,Scott	11	85
Zaun,Gregg	12	84
Jones,Chipper	14	84
Kent,Jeff	11	83
Nixon,Trot	12	83
Millar,Kevin	11	83
Bonds,Barry	23	83
Beltran,Carlos	13	82
Klesko,Ryan	14	82
Freel,Ryan	11	81
Berkman,Lance	16	81
Youkilis,Kevin	14	81
Bradley,Milton	11	81
DaVanon,Jeff	13	80
Perez,Eduardo	11	80
Upton,B.J.	11	80
Teixeira,Mark	11	80
Chavez,Eric	13	80
Cabrera,Miguel	11	80
Marte,Andy	11	80
Johnson,Nick	16	79

TOP Ct%, bb% under 6%

NAME	bb%	Ct%
Polanco,Placido	5	94
Pierre,Juan	5	94
Aybar,Erick	4	92
Frandsen,Kevin	3	92
Johjima,Kenji	5	92
Perez,Neifi	3	91
Hall,Toby	4	91
Betancourt,Yuniesk	3	91
Ozuna,Pablo	3	90
Costa,Shane	5	90
Redmond,Mike	4	90
Molina,Ben	5	90
Payton,Jay	5	89
Estrada,Johnny	5	89
Cintron,Alex	4	89
Cano,Robinson	4	89
Alomar Jr.,Sandy	4	89
Wilson,Jack	5	88
Gload,Ross	5	88
Barmes,Clint	4	88
Lopez,Jose	4	88
Kendrick,Howie	3	88
Cairo,Miguel	5	87
Morales,Kendry	5	87
Pierzynski,A.J.	4	87

TOP Ct%, GB% over 50%

NAME	GB%	Ct%
Pierre,Juan	55	94
Keppinger,Jeff	58	94
Pena,Brayan	61	92
Aybar,Erick	72	92
Kendall,Jason	51	92
Izturis,Cesar	51	91
Ozuna,Pablo	57	90
Castillo,Luis	62	90
Suzuki,Ichiro	53	90
Miles,Aaron	55	90
Tyner,Jason	52	89
Chavez,Endy	56	89
Kotchman,Casey	54	89
Castro,Bernie	63	89
Cora,Alex	51	88
Reed,Jeremy	51	88
Kendrick,Howie	52	88
Morales,Kendry	51	87
Vizcaino,Jose	53	87
Roberts,Dave	53	87
Murton,Matt	58	87
Quinlan,Robb	51	86
Guzman,Cristian	54	86
German,Esteban	59	86
Iannetta,Chris	52	85
Ausmus,Brad	53	85
Spilborghs,Ryan	51	85
Bard,Josh	52	85
Ford,Lew	52	84
Denorfia,Chris	60	84
Fahey,Brandon	58	84
Erstad,Darin	52	84
Orr,Pete	54	84
Taveras,Willy	55	83
Green,Shawn	53	83
Jeter,Derek	58	83
Nunez,Abraham O	60	83
Markakis,Nick	51	82

TOP Ct%, GB% under 40%

NAME	GB%	Ct%
Garciaparra,Noma	38	92
Loretta,Mark	37	91
Walker,Todd	39	90
Lieberthal,Mike	37	90
Estrada,Johnny	39	89
Giles,Brian	38	89
Atkins,Garrett	39	88
Lowell,Mike	35	88
Ramirez,Aramis	36	88
Barmes,Clint	34	88
Jackson,Conor	39	88
Lee,Carlos	37	88
Gonzalez,Luis	39	88
McCann,Brian	37	87
Crede,Joe	33	87
Helton,Todd	35	87
Randa,Joe	38	86
Kinsler,Ian	35	86
Navarro,Dioner	37	86
Aurilia,Rich	39	86
Gibbons,Jay	39	86
Rolen,Scott	33	85
Salazar,Jeff	32	85
Montero,Miguel	38	84
Everett,Adam	38	84

PITCHER SKILLS RANKINGS - Starting Pitchers

Top Command (k/bb)

NAME	Cmd
Sheets,Ben	8.2
Santana,Johan	4.8
Schilling,Curt	4.6
Lieber,Jon	4.3
Oswalt,Roy	4.0
Halladay,Roy	3.9
Mussina,Mike	3.9
Matsuzaka,Daisuke	3.8
Carpenter,Chris	3.8
Bush,David	3.7
Haren,Danny	3.6
Vazquez,Javier	3.6
Hamels,Cole	3.6
Martinez,Pedro	3.5
Hill,Rich	3.4
Peavy,Jake	3.4
Papelbon,Jon	3.4
Smoltz,John	3.3
Towers,Josh	3.3
Myers,Brett	3.3
Gonzalez,Edgar	3.3
Sabathia,C.C.	3.2
Shields,Jamie	3.2
Clemens,Roger	3.2
Harang,Aaron	3.2
Reyes,Anthony	3.2
Bonderman,Jeremy	3.1
Soriano,Rafael	3.1
Webb,Brandon	3.0
Burnett,A.J.	3.0
Escobar,Kelvim	3.0

Top Control (bb/9)

NAME	Ctl
Sheets,Ben	1.2
Lieber,Jon	1.3
Towers,Josh	1.5
Halladay,Roy	1.6
Silva,Carlos	1.7
Byrd,Paul	1.7
Maddux,Greg	1.7
Bush,David	1.7
Schilling,Curt	1.8
Gonzalez,Edgar	1.8
Oswalt,Roy	1.8
Wells,David	1.8
Buehrle,Mark	1.9
Carpenter,Chris	1.9
Mussina,Mike	2.0
Haren,Danny	2.0
Colon,Bartolo	2.0
Santana,Johan	2.0
Pavano,Carl	2.0
Garland,Jon	2.2
Wang,Chien-Ming	2.2
Perez,Odalis	2.2
Baker,Scott	2.2
Smoltz,John	2.2
Garcia,Freddy	2.3
Greinke,Zack	2.3
Webb,Brandon	2.3
Duke,Zach	2.3
Shields,Jamie	2.3
Sowers,Jeremy	2.3
Cook,Aaron	2.3

Top Dominance (k/9)

NAME	Dom
Bailey,Homer	10.2
Hamels,Cole	10.2
Kazmir,Scott	9.8
Kuo,Hong-Chih	9.8
Santana,Johan	9.7
Matsuzaka,Daisuke	9.6
Hill,Rich	9.5
Sheets,Ben	9.5
Peavy,Jake	9.4
Prior,Mark	9.3
Soriano,Rafael	9.3
Perez,Oliver	9.0
Hernandez,Felix	9.0
Cabrera,Daniel	8.9
Martinez,Pedro	8.9
Olsen,Scott	8.8
Cain,Matt	8.6
Igawa,Kei	8.6
Clemens,Roger	8.6
Harden,Rich	8.5
Myers,Brett	8.5
Vazquez,Javier	8.4
Zambrano,Carlos	8.4
Niemann,Jeff	8.4
Hughes,Phil	8.4
Patterson,John	8.4
Guzman,Angel	8.3
Burnett,A.J.	8.3
Snell,Ian	8.3
Bonderman,Jeremy	8.2
Reyes,Anthony	8.2

Top Ground Ball Rate

NAME	GB
Webb,Brandon	65
Lowe,Derek	65
Wang,Chien-Ming	63
Westbrook,Jake	61
Rheinecker,John	60
Hernandez,Felix	60
Cook,Aaron	59
Halladay,Roy	59
Hudson,Tim	58
Bautista,Denny	58
Mitre,Sergio	57
Mulder,Mark	56
Hensley,Clay	55
Saarloos,Kirk	55
Tavarez,Julian	55
Loe,Kameron	54
Johnson,Jason	54
Maholm,Paul	54
Carpenter,Chris	54
Wood,Mike	54
Burnett,A.J.	53
Ramirez,Horacio	53
Hampton,Mike	52
Maddux,Greg	52
Lawrence,Brian	51
Janssen,Casey	51
Batista,Miguel	51
Duke,Zach	51
Howell,J.P.	51
Ponson,Sidney	51
Pettitte,Andy	50

Top Fly Ball Rate

NAME	FB
Soriano,Rafael	57
Young,Chris	54
James,Chuck	53
Marmol,Carlos	53
Hirsh,Jason	52
Weaver,Jered	52
Hill,Rich	52
Karstens,Jeff	51
Milton,Eric	50
Vargas,Jason	50
Cain,Matt	49
Patterson,John	48
Perez,Oliver	47
O'Connor,Mike	47
Lee,Cliff	47
Chacon,Shawn	46
Waechter,Doug	46
Marcum,Shaun	46
Petit,Yusmeiro	46
Papelbon,Jon	46
Reyes,Anthony	46
Gonzalez,Edgar	46
Astacio,Ezequiel	46
McCarthy,Brandon	46
Maine,John	45
Elarton,Scott	45
Bannister,Brian	45
Baker,Scott	45
Tejeda,Rob	45
Ledezma,Wil	44
Santana,Ervin	44

High GB, Low Dom

NAME	GB	Dom
Lowe,Derek	65	5.4
Wang,Chien-M	63	3.8
Westbrook,J	61	4.7
Rheinecker,J	60	4.6
Cook,Aaron	59	3.5
Mulder,Mark	56	5.0
Saarloos,Kirk	55	3.8
Tavarez,Julian	55	5.5
Loe,Kameron	54	4.8
Johnson,J	54	4.8
Wood,Mike	54	4.6
Ramirez,H	53	4.3
Hampton,Mike	52	4.3
Maddux,Greg	52	5.1
Lawrence,B	51	5.3
Janssen,C	51	5.0
Batista,Miguel	51	5.3
Duke,Zach	51	5.1
Ponson,S	51	5.0
Thompson,M	49	4.0
Wells,David	49	4.2
Rogers,K	48	4.1
Sowers,J	48	4.8
Morris,Matt	48	5.1
Silva,Carlos	47	3.6
Marquis,J	47	4.9
Hendricksn,M	47	5.0
Suppan,Jeff	47	5.1
Pineiro,Joel	46	5.1
Glavine,Tom	46	5.2
Thomson,J	46	5.3

High GB, High Dom

NAME	GB	Dom
Webb,B	65	7.0
Hernandez,F	60	9.0
Halladay,Roy	59	6.1
Bautista,D	58	6.3
Mitre,Sergio	57	6.9
Hensley,Clay	55	6.0
Maholm,Paul	54	6.1
Carpenter,C	54	7.4
Burnett,A.J.	53	8.3
Howell,J.P.	51	6.9
Pettitte,Andy	50	7.6
Wells,Kip	50	6.1
Clemens,R	49	8.6
Gorzelanny,T	49	6.8
Zambrano,C	49	8.4
Pelfrey,Mike	49	7.6
Robertson,N	48	6.0
Loewen,Adam	48	8.1
Saunders,Joe	48	6.0
Oswalt,Roy	48	7.1
Billingsley,C	48	7.8
Bonderman,J	48	8.2
Miner,Zach	47	5.9
McGowan,D	47	7.4
Smoltz,John	47	7.5
Bush,David	46	6.4
Myers,Brett	46	8.5
Haren,Danny	46	7.2
Willis,D	46	6.3
Park,Chan Ho	46	6.1
Marshall,Sean	46	5.9

Lowest xERA

NAME	xERA
Webb,Brandon	2.52
Hernandez,Felix	2.59
Nippert,Dustin	2.69
Sheets,Ben	2.74
Halladay,Roy	2.84
Santana,Johan	2.88
Carpenter,Chris	2.91
Burnett,A.J.	2.93
Clemens,Roger	2.97
Lowe,Derek	3.03
Hamels,Cole	3.05
Myers,Brett	3.12
Pettitte,Andy	3.15
Bonderman,Jeremy	3.16
Peavy,Jake	3.16
Oswalt,Roy	3.17
Martinez,Pedro	3.25
Smoltz,John	3.25
Kazmir,Scott	3.26
Sabathia,C.C.	3.31
Vazquez,Javier	3.33
Haren,Danny	3.33
Schilling,Curt	3.34
Mitre,Sergio	3.36
Escobar,Kelvim	3.37
Westbrook,Jake	3.38
Mussina,Mike	3.38
Shields,Jamie	3.43
Olsen,Scott	3.43
Snell,Ian	3.44
Bush,David	3.45

Top BPV, 180+ IP

NAME	BPV
Santana,Johan	142
Hamels,Cole	113
Matsuzaka,Daisuke	110
Oswalt,Roy	108
Peavy,Jake	107
Hernandez,Felix	103
Halladay,Roy	101
Carpenter,Chris	101
Vazquez,Javier	99
Mussina,Mike	97
Webb,Brandon	95
Smoltz,John	95
Burnett,A.J.	94
Escobar,Kelvim	94
Sabathia,C.C.	92
Bonderman,Jeremy	91
Haren,Danny	89
Myers,Brett	89
Pettitte,Andy	88
Reyes,Anthony	87
Bedard,Erik	86
Bush,David	86
Lackey,John	86
Cain,Matt	85
Harang,Aaron	82
Lieber,Jon	81
Snell,Ian	80
Arroyo,Bronson	78
Zambrano,Carlos	76
Cabrera,Daniel	75
Millwood,Kevin	73

Top BPV, -150 IP

NAME	BPV
Bailey,Homer	110
Clemens,Roger	107
Martinez,Pedro	101
Soriano,Rafael	95
Garza,Matt	89
Kuo,Hong-Chih	84
Hughes,Phil	81
Prior,Mark	79
Gonzalez,Edgar	75
Billingsley,Chad	70
Hernandez,Orlando	69
Petit,Yusmeiro	68
Albers,Matt	67
Villanueva,Carlos	66
Gorzelanny,Tom	64
Guzman,Angel	63
Nippert,Dustin	63
Niemann,Jeff	63
Pelfrey,Mike	62
Bonser,Boof	60
Greinke,Zack	60
Mitre,Sergio	58
Hirsh,Jason	58
Pavano,Carl	57
Lester,Jon	56
Kim,Byung-Hyun	56
Perez,Oliver	56
Windsor,Jason	54
Gonzalez,Enrique	54
Marcum,Shaun	52
Penn,Hayden	51

PITCHER SKILLS RANKINGS - Relief Pitchers

Top Command (k/bb)

NAME	Cmd
Putz,J.J.	5.2
Street,Huston	4.7
Gagne,Eric	4.6
Capps,Matt	4.4
Corpas,Manuel	4.4
Nathan,Joe	4.3
Duchscherer,Justin	4.2
Betancourt,Rafael	4.1
Valverde,Jose	4.0
Wagner,Billy	3.9
Meredith,Cla	3.9
Neshek,Patrick	3.8
Walker,Jamie	3.6
Hoffman,Trevor	3.5
Howry,Bob	3.5
Rivera,Mariano	3.5
Ryan,B.J.	3.5
Lidge,Brad	3.4
Foulke,Keith	3.4
Rodriguez,Francisco	3.3
Wuertz,Mike	3.3
Embree,Alan	3.3
Peralta,Joel	3.2
Broxton,Jonathan	3.1
Mujica,Edward	3.1
Wainwright,Adam	3.1
Shields,Scot	3.0
Cordero,Chad	3.0
Wheeler,Dan	3.0
Gordon,Tom	2.9
Calero,Kiko	2.9

Top Control (bb/9)

NAME	Ctl
Capps,Matt	1.4
Corpas,Manuel	1.7
Meredith,Cla	1.7
Street,Huston	1.9
Duchscherer,Justin	1.9
Walker,Jamie	1.9
Jones,Todd	1.9
Putz,J.J.	2.0
Rivera,Mariano	2.0
Hoffman,Trevor	2.0
Foulke,Keith	2.1
Ayala,Luis	2.1
Meadows,Brian	2.1
Howry,Bob	2.1
Betancourt,Rafael	2.2
Sweeney,Brian	2.3
Mujica,Edward	2.3
Coffey,Todd	2.3
Reitsma,Chris	2.3
Peralta,Joel	2.4
Tomko,Brett	2.4
Camp,Shawn	2.5
Borkowski,Dave	2.5
Oliver,Darren	2.5
Timlin,Mike	2.5
Thompson,Brad	2.5
Hawkins,LaTroy	2.5
Guerrier,Matt	2.5
Embree,Alan	2.5
Maroth,Mike	2.5
League,Brandon	2.6

Top Dominance (k/9)

NAME	Dom
Gagne,Eric	13.2
Lidge,Brad	12.7
Rodriguez,Francisco	12.3
Nathan,Joe	11.7
Valverde,Jose	11.3
Wagner,Billy	11.2
Ryan,B.J.	10.9
Devine,Joey	10.8
Gonzalez,Mike	10.7
Zumaya,Joel	10.6
Farnsworth,Kyle	10.6
Broxton,Jonathan	10.4
Ohman,Will	10.3
Putz,J.J.	10.3
Wuertz,Mike	10.2
Cordero,Francisco	10.2
Fuentes,Brian	10.2
Jenks,Bobby	10.2
Cabrera,Fernando	10.1
Francisco,Frank	10.1
Williamson,Scott	9.9
Julio,Jorge	9.9
Bruney,Brian	9.9
Neshek,Patrick	9.9
Tankersley,Taylor	9.9
Sherrill,George	9.9
Eyre,Scott	9.8
Saito,Takashi	9.7
Calero,Kiko	9.7
Marte,Damaso	9.6
Gordon,Tom	9.4

Top Ground Ball Rate

NAME	GB
Littleton,Wes	71
League,Brandon	70
Meredith,Cla	69
Reyes,Dennys	64
Bradford,Chad	63
Williams,Todd	61
Feldman,Scott	61
Qualls,Chad	59
Carmona,Fausto	59
MacDougal,Mike	59
Lopez,Javier	59
Camp,Shawn	57
Jenks,Bobby	57
Wagner,Ryan	57
Miller,Matt	57
White,Rick	57
Thompson,Brad	56
Kolb,Danny	56
Romero,J.C.	55
Schoeneweis,Scott	55
Wright,Jamey	55
Rivera,Mariano	55
Torres,Salomon	55
Downs,Scott	55
Shouse,Brian	53
Bauer,Rick	53
Shields,Scot	53
Dempster,Ryan	53
Rodney,Fernando	53
Crain,Jesse	52
Putz,J.J.	52

Top Fly Ball Rate

NAME	FB
Mujica,Edward	57
Neshek,Patrick	54
Springer,Russ	52
Mateo,Julio	52
Foulke,Keith	51
Guardado,Eddie	51
Cordero,Chad	51
Tsao,Chin Hui	51
Britton,Chris	50
Speier,Justin	50
Proctor,Scott	49
Rauch,Jon	49
Saito,Takashi	49
Betancourt,Rafael	49
Benitez,Armando	48
Ray,Chris	47
Sherrill,George	47
Rodriguez,Francisco	46
McClung,Seth	46
Nathan,Joe	46
Peralta,Joel	46
Perez,Beltran	46
Benoit,Joaquin	46
Walker,Jamie	45
Dotel,Octavio	45
Ramirez,Ramon	45
Zumaya,Joel	45
Fuentes,Brian	45
Borowski,Joe	45
Sanchez,Jonathan	45
Gaudin,Chad	45

High GB, Low Dom

NAME	GB	Dom
Williams,Todd	61	4.0
White,Rick	57	5.6
Thompson,B	56	5.6
Schoeneweis	55	5.4
Wright,Jamey	55	5.0
Shouse,Brian	53	5.4
Bauer,Rick	53	4.5
Looper,B	52	5.1
Reitsma,Chris	51	5.0
King,Ray	51	4.8
Jones,Todd	50	4.4
Cormier,Lance	50	5.4
Beimel,Joe	48	4.7
Cormier,Rheal	47	5.0
Grilli,Jason	46	4.7
Borkowski,D	46	5.4
Maroth,Mike	46	4.4
Eyre,Willie	45	5.0
Guerrier,Matt	45	5.3
Mesa,Jose	45	5.3
Herges,Matt	45	5.0

High GB, High Dom

NAME	GB	Dom
Reyes,D	64	7.8
MacDougall,M	59	7.0
Jenks,Bobby	57	10.2
Miller,Matt	57	8.2
Shields,Scot	53	8.8
Dempster,R	53	7.9
Rodney,F	53	8.1
Putz,J.J.	52	10.3
Wilson,C.J.	52	7.7
Otsuka,A	52	7.3
Sanchez,D	50	7.0
Rincon,Juan	50	8.3
Feliciano,P	50	7.8
Lowe,Mark	49	8.9
Wainwright,A	48	8.4
Grabow,John	48	8.1
Carrasco,H	48	7.1
Wagner,Billy	48	11.2
Mastny,Tom	48	8.8
Williamson,S	47	9.9
McBride,M	47	7.9
Thornton,Matt	47	7.8
Aquino,Greg	47	8.9
Frasor,Jason	47	9.2
Wuertz,Mike	46	10.2
Gordon,Tom	46	9.4
Burgos,A	46	9.2
Hernandez,R	46	7.1
Isringhausen,J	46	7.4
Madson,Ryan	46	7.1
Wellemeyer,T	46	7.3

Lowest xERA

NAME	xERA
Gagne,Eric	2.09
Meredith,Cla	2.32
Putz,J.J.	2.40
Wagner,Billy	2.50
Lidge,Brad	2.52
Nathan,Joe	2.63
League,Brandon	2.68
Valverde,Jose	2.76
Jenks,Bobby	2.78
Rodriguez,Francisco	2.79
Ryan,B.J.	2.80
Devine,Joey	2.80
Littleton,Wes	2.85
Bradford,Chad	2.88
Shields,Scot	2.89
Wuertz,Mike	2.91
Reyes,Dennys	2.94
Feldman,Scott	2.99
MacDougal,Mike	3.00
Rivera,Mariano	3.03
Miller,Matt	3.04
Street,Huston	3.04
Gordon,Tom	3.05
Broxton,Jonathan	3.07
Wainwright,Adam	3.15
Otsuka,Akinori	3.16
Farnsworth,Kyle	3.17
Corpas,Manuel	3.17
Gonzalez,Mike	3.17
Rincon,Juan	3.18
Wilson,C.J.	3.19

Top BPV, 15+ Saves

NAME	BPV
Gagne,Eric	182
Nathan,Joe	162
Putz,J.J.	158
Wagner,Billy	140
Street,Huston	138
Valverde,Jose	136
Rodriguez,Francisco	131
Ryan,B.J.	130
Lidge,Brad	127
Broxton,Jonathan	121
Gonzalez,Mike	116
Rivera,Mariano	105
Cordero,Francisco	103
Jenks,Bobby	101
Fuentes,Brian	96
Hoffman,Trevor	96
Wainwright,Adam	94
Gordon,Tom	92
Saito,Takashi	91
Cordero,Chad	86
Otsuka,Akinori	85
Foulke,Keith	73
Borowski,Joe	72
Dempster,Ryan	71
Wickman,Bob	70
Ray,Chris	61
Burgos,Ambiorix	50
Jones,Todd	50
Weathers,David	46

Top BPV, 5- Saves

NAME	BPV
Corpas,Manuel	130
Duchscherer,Justin	118
Betancourt,Rafael	116
Wuertz,Mike	111
Meredith,Cla	108
Neshek,Patrick	107
Shields,Scot	105
Calero,Kiko	103
Delcarmen,Manny	99
Zumaya,Joel	98
Francisco,Frank	96
Rincon,Juan	95
Casilla,Santiago	95
Ohman,Will	93
Sherrill,George	92
Williamson,Scott	92
Miller,Matt	92
Braun,Ryan	91
Britton,Chris	91
Linebrink,Scott	89
Wheeler,Dan	89
Bruney,Brian	89
Embree,Alan	87
Lowe,Mark	86
Accardo,Jeremy	86
Heilman,Aaron	85
Cabrera,Fernando	85
Rodney,Fernando	84
Crain,Jesse	84
Miller,Trever	82
Benoit,Joaquin	82

RISK MANAGEMENT

Most DL Days, 2004-2006

NAME	DL
Wood,Kerry	377
Miller,Wade	340
Tsao,Chin Hui	340
Gagne,Eric	325
Williamson,Scott	324
Soriano,Rafael	315
Hernandez,Runelvy	310
Hampton,Mike	290
Snelling,Chris	289
Dotel,Octavio	282
Pavano,Carl	277
Baldelli,Rocco	272
Lyon,Brandon	272
Francisco,Frank	268
Prior,Mark	256
Rodney,Fernando	253
Salmon,Tim	252
Thomas,Frank	242
Patterson,John	239
Ramirez,Horacio	218
Miller,Matt	216
Jordan,Brian	215
Garciaparra,Nomar	214
Ellis,Mark	209
Castro,Ramon	201
Wilson,C.J.	201
Klesko,Ryan	192
Lee,Travis	190
Zambrano,Victor	190
Nixon,Trot	187
Mueller,Bill	185
Thomson,John	184
Eaton,Adam	183
Ayala,Luis	183
Lawrence,Brian	183
Guzman,Cristian	183
Johnson,Kelly	183
Ordonez,Magglio	182
Backe,Brandon	181
Cook,Aaron	181
Kubel,Jason	180
Sullivan,Cory	180
Traber,Billy	180
Boone,Aaron	180
Yates,Tyler	180
Guzman,Freddy	180
Harden,Rich	179
Sheets,Ben	177
Ohka,Tomo	172
Bonds,Barry	171
Brazoban,Yhency	170
Stewart,Shannon	170
Borowski,Joe	168
Koskie,Corey	168
Worrell,Tim	168
Hermanson,Dustin	168
Benitez,Armando	167
Bautista,Denny	165
Wells,David	163
Wolf,Randy	163
Halladay,Roy	162
Izturis,Cesar	157
Hernandez,Orlando	156
Bradley,Milton	156
McPherson,Dallas	154
Sexson,Richie	152

Highest Reliability Scores

1B/DH	POS	Rel
Konerko,Paul	3	99
Hillenbrand,Shea	305	97
Ortiz,David	0	97
Pujols,Albert	3	95
Teixeira,Mark	3	95
Overbay,Lyle	3	87
Hafner,Travis	0	72
Pena,Carlos	3	63
Delgado,Carlos	3	61
Millar,Kevin	30	59
Wigginton,Ty	345	59
Broussard,Ben	30	59
Conine,Jeff	379	50
Helton,Todd	3	48
Gonzalez,Adrian	3	47
Wilson,Craig	39	46
Fielder,Prince	3	42
Swisher,Nick	37	39
LaRoche,Adam	3	37
Johnson,Dan	3	37
Gibbons,Jay	09	35
Stairs,Matt	0	34
Sweeney,Mike	0	33
Everett,Carl	0	32
Sexson,Richie	3	31
Johnson,Nick	3	30
Mientkiewicz,Doug	3	30
Berkman,Lance	39	29
Garko,Ryan	3	27
Young,Dmitri	0	27
Youkilis,Kevin	3	27
Hatteberg,Scott	3	27

Highest Reliability Scores

2B	POS	Rel
Belliard,Ron	4	96
Iguchi,Tadahito	4	92
Castillo,Luis	4	81
Kennedy,Adam	4	77
Biggio,Craig	4	74
Kent,Jeff	4	74
Giles,Marcus	4	69
Hudson,Orlando	4	66
Perez,Neifi	46	60
Grudzielanek,Mark	4	58
Walker,Todd	435	56
Lopez,Jose	4	53
Hill,Aaron	46	53
Castillo,Jose	4	52
Adams,Russ	46	49
Cantu,Jorge	4	45
Vidro,Jose	4	45
Barfield,Josh	4	41
Cairo,Miguel	4	35
Miles,Aaron	46	34
Graffanino,Tony	45	34
Roberts,Brian	4	31
Luna,Hector	46	31
Burke,Chris	48	30
Cano,Robinson	4	30
Jimenez,D'Angelo	4	29
Utley,Chase	4	26
Weeks,Rickie	4	25
Orr,Pete	4	22
Matsui,Kazuo	4	22
Inglett,Joe	4	21

Highest Reliability Scores

3B	POS	Rel
Inge,Brandon	5	96
Feliz,Pedro	5	91
Ramirez,Aramis	5	86
Wright,David	5	86
Blalock,Hank	50	75
Crede,Joe	5	74
Chavez,Eric	5	72
Cabrera,Miguel	5	70
Glaus,Troy	5	59
Batista,Tony	5	55
Bell,David	5	50
Randa,Joe	5	42
Rodriguez,Alex	5	42
Jones,Chipper	5	41
Betemit,Wilson	5	39
Izturis,Cesar	56	39
Encarnacion,Edwin	5	36
Mora,Melvin	5	35
Ensberg,Morgan	5	33
Keppinger,Jeff	5	30
Huff,Aubrey	59	29
Nunez,Abraham O.	5	28
Lowell,Mike	5	28
Atkins,Garrett	5	24
Mueller,Bill	5	24
Tracy,Chad	5	24
Aybar,Willy	5	23
Punto,Nick	56	23
Bellhorn,Mark	5	23
Beltre,Adrian	5	22
Perez,Tomas	564	21
Rodriguez,Luis	5	21

Highest Reliability Scores

SS	POS	Rel
Furcal,Rafael	6	99
Rollins,Jimmy	6	99
Tejada,Miguel	6	98
Renteria,Edgar	6	97
Gonzalez,Alex	6	85
Jeter,Derek	6	85
Lugo,Julio	64	84
Cabrera,Orlando	6	83
Wilson,Jack	6	77
Young,Michael	6	76
Everett,Adam	6	73
Clayton,Royce	6	69
Cintron,Alex	64	68
Vizquel,Omar	6	65
Berroa,Angel	6	65
Uribe,Juan	6	63
Scutaro,Marco	64	61
Greene,Khalil	6	55
Blum,Geoff	65	46
Cora,Alex	6	39
Castro,Juan	65	38
Hall,Bill	6	37
Lopez,Felipe	6	35
Barmes,Clint	6	32
Guillen,Carlos	6	31
Easley,Damion	65	28
Eckstein,David	6	27
Bartlett,Jason	6	26
Callaspo,Alberto	6	22
Crosby,Bobby	6	21
Reyes,Jose	6	21

Highest Reliability Scores

CA	POS	Rel
Martinez,Victor	23	99
Pierzynski,A.J.	2	80
Johjima,Kenji	2	80
LoDuca,Paul	2	80
Kendall,Jason	2	74
Hall,Toby	2	68
Schneider,Brian	2	68
Barrett,Michael	2	67
Barajas,Rod	2	54
Miller,Damian	2	53
Hernandez,Ramon	2	50
Buck,John	2	49
Lieberthal,Mike	2	49
Molina,Ben	2	48
Zaun,Gregg	2	46
Rodriguez,Ivan	2	44

Highest Reliability Scores

OF	POS	Rel
Crawford,Carl	7	99
Figgins,Chone	85	99
Jones,Andruw	8	98
Suzuki,Ichiro	98	95
Podsednik,Scott	7	94
Guerrero,Vladimir	90	93
Pierre,Juan	8	88
Payton,Jay	789	88
Monroe,Craig	70	88
Jones,Jacque	9	85
Damon,Johnny	8	84
Green,Shawn	9	83
Kotsay,Mark	8	83
Freel,Ryan	89	80
Burrell,Pat	7	78
Anderson,Garret	70	78
Hunter,Torii	8	77
Lee,Carlos	7	76
Dunn,Adam	7	76
Soriano,Alfonso	7	75
Bay,Jason	7	74
Abreu,Bobby	9	73
Wells,Vernon	8	73
Ibanez,Raul	7	73
DeJesus,David	78	72
Mackowiak,Rob	879	71
Holliday,Matt	7	67
Encarnacion,Juan	98	66
Clark,Brady	8	63
Mench,Kevin	97	63
Taveras,Willy	8	61
Wilkerson,Brad	7	60
Cuddyer,Michael	9	59
Granderson,Curtis	8	59
Cameron,Mike	8	58
Crisp,Coco	8	57
Kielty,Bobby	79	53
Roberts,Dave	7	51
Dye,Jermaine	9	51
Drew,J.D.	9	50
Alou,Moises	9	49
Lane,Jason	9	49
Bradley,Milton	9	48
Thames,Marcus	70	48
Nady,Xavier	93	47
Dellucci,David	79	46
Matsui,Hideki	7	45

RISK MANAGEMENT

Highest Reliability

SP	Rel
Garcia,Freddy	99
Robertson,Nate	97
Carpenter,Chris	97
Suppan,Jeff	95
Oswalt,Roy	92
Hernandez,Livan	90
Davis,Doug	90
Harang,Aaron	90
Westbrook,Jake	89
Contreras,Jose	88
Santana,Johan	88
Lowe,Derek	88
Hudson,Tim	88
Morris,Matt	86
Lopez,Rodrigo	86
Millwood,Kevin	85
Lee,Cliff	83
Fogg,Josh	82
Haren,Danny	82
Lackey,John	82
Milton,Eric	80
Moyer,Jamie	80
Glavine,Tom	80
Vazquez,Javier	80
Maddux,Greg	80
Rogers,Kenny	80
Weaver,Jeff	80
Ortiz,Ramon	80
Batista,Miguel	78
Hendrickson,Mark	78
Radke,Brad	78
Webb,Brandon	78
Washburn,Jarrod	76
Marquis,Jason	75
Buehrle,Mark	75
Benson,Kris	73
Schmidt,Jason	72
Smoltz,John	72
Zito,Barry	71
Jennings,Jason	70
Martinez,Pedro	70
Lieber,Jon	69
Capuano,Chris	68
Bonderman,Jeremy	68
Penny,Brad	68
Garland,Jon	67
Arroyo,Bronson	67

Highest Reliability

RP	Rel
Cordero,Francisco	75
Nathan,Joe	74
Lidge,Brad	69
Ryan,B.J.	66
Rodriguez,Francisco	66
Hoffman,Trevor	64
Rivera,Mariano	60
Cordero,Chad	56
Shields,Scot	51
Wagner,Billy	50
Isringhausen,Jason	50
Baez,Danys	49
Dempster,Ryan	44
Linebrink,Scott	40
Julio,Jorge	39
Torres,Salomon	39

POWER

PX over 120	PX	Rel
Konerko,Paul	137	99
Jones,Andruw	165	98
Ortiz,David	197	97
Pujols,Albert	171	95
Teixeira,Mark	175	95
Guerrero,Vladimir	124	93
Monroe,Craig	142	88
Overbay,Lyle	131	87
Ramirez,Aramis	147	86
Wright,David	136	86
Burrell,Pat	150	78
Hunter,Torii	125	77
Lee,Carlos	128	76
Dunn,Adam	184	76
Soriano,Alfonso	161	75
Crede,Joe	127	74
Kent,Jeff	124	74
Bay,Jason	158	74
Abreu,Bobby	127	73
Wells,Vernon	124	73
Hafner,Travis	219	72
Chavez,Eric	126	72
Cabrera,Miguel	145	70
Barrett,Michael	126	67
Holliday,Matt	159	67
Pena,Carlos	131	63
Delgado,Carlos	175	61
Wilkerson,Brad	150	60
Glaus,Troy	166	59
Wigginton,Ty	129	59
Broussard,Ben	127	59
Cuddyer,Michael	129	59

COMMAND

CMD over 2.5	CMD	Rel
Garcia,Freddy	2.7	99
Carpenter,Chris	3.8	97
Oswalt,Roy	4.0	92
Harang,Aaron	3.2	90
Santana,Johan	4.8	88
Millwood,Kevin	2.7	85
Haren,Danny	3.6	82
Lackey,John	2.7	82
Vazquez,Javier	3.6	80
Weaver,Jeff	2.6	80
Maddux,Greg	3.0	80
Webb,Brandon	3.0	78
Buehrle,Mark	2.6	75
Cordero,Francisco	2.6	75
Nathan,Joe	4.3	74
Smoltz,John	3.3	72
Martinez,Pedro	3.5	70
Matsuzaka,Daisuke	3.8	70
Lidge,Brad	3.4	69
Lieber,Jon	4.3	69
Capuano,Chris	2.6	68
Bonderman,Jeremy	3.1	68
Penny,Brad	2.7	68
Arroyo,Bronson	3.0	67
Ryan,B.J.	3.5	66
Rodriguez,Francisco	3.3	66
Tomko,Brett	2.8	65
Hoffman,Trevor	3.5	64
Pettitte,Andy	2.9	63
Myers,Brett	3.3	62
Clemens,Roger	3.2	61

SPEED

SX over 120	SX	Rel
Furcal,Rafael	152	99
Crawford,Carl	166	99
Figgins,Chone	157	99
Rollins,Jimmy	155	99
Suzuki,Ichiro	145	95
Podsednik,Scott	134	94
Pierre,Juan	154	88
Jeter,Derek	124	85
Damon,Johnny	127	84
Lugo,Julio	120	84
Freel,Ryan	129	80
Soriano,Alfonso	126	75
Vizquel,Omar	126	65
Taveras,Willy	139	61
Cameron,Mike	135	58
Roberts,Dave	170	51
Logan,Nook	144	40
Sizemore,Grady	131	39
Byrnes,Eric	126	38
Cairo,Miguel	124	35
Lofton,Kenny	155	35
Lopez,Felipe	122	35
Bloomquist,Willie	137	34
Gathright,Joey	140	33
Roberts,Brian	126	31
Burke,Chris	124	30
Gwynn Jr.,Tony	123	30
Duffy,Chris	154	29
Weeks,Rickie	149	25
Patterson,Corey	156	24
McLouth,Nate	142	24
Punto,Nick	123	23

DOMINANCE

DOM over 7.0	DOM	Rel
Carpenter,Chris	7.4	97
Oswalt,Roy	7.1	92
Davis,Doug	7.2	90
Harang,Aaron	7.6	90
Santana,Johan	9.7	88
Haren,Danny	7.2	82
Lackey,John	7.8	82
Vazquez,Javier	8.4	80
Webb,Brandon	7.0	78
Cordero,Francisco	10.2	75
Nathan,Joe	11.7	74
Schmidt,Jason	7.9	72
Smoltz,John	7.5	72
Martinez,Pedro	8.9	70
Matsuzaka,Daisuke	9.6	70
Lidge,Brad	12.7	69
Capuano,Chris	7.0	68
Bonderman,Jeremy	8.2	68
Arroyo,Bronson	7.1	67
Ryan,B.J.	10.9	66
Rodriguez,Francisco	12.3	66
Zambrano,Carlos	8.4	65
Lilly,Ted	7.7	65
Hoffman,Trevor	7.2	64
Pettitte,Andy	7.6	63
Beckett,Josh	7.8	62
Myers,Brett	8.5	62
Clemens,Roger	8.6	61
Mussina,Mike	7.5	60
Johnson,Randy	7.7	60
Sabathia,C.C.	7.7	60

CONTACT

Ct% over 85%	Ct%	Rel
Crawford,Carl	86	99
Rollins,Jimmy	88	99
Furcal,Rafael	86	99
Martinez,Victor	86	99
Tejada,Miguel	88	98
Hillenbrand,Shea	86	97
Renteria,Edgar	86	97
Suzuki,Ichiro	90	95
Pujols,Albert	90	95
Guerrero,Vladimir	89	93
Pierre,Juan	94	88
Payton,Jay	89	88
Ramirez,Aramis	88	86
Damon,Johnny	87	84
Kotsay,Mark	89	83
Cabrera,Orlando	90	83
Castillo,Luis	90	81
Pierzynski,A.J.	87	80
Johjima,Kenji	92	80
LoDuca,Paul	92	80
Wilson,Jack	88	77
Lee,Carlos	88	76
Young,Michael	86	76
Crede,Joe	87	74
Kendall,Jason	92	74
Wells,Vernon	86	73
DeJesus,David	86	72
Hall,Toby	91	68
Cintron,Alex	89	68
Barrett,Michael	87	67
Vizquel,Omar	91	65
Clark,Brady	87	63

OVERALL PITCHING SKILL

BPV over 75	BPV	Rel
Carpenter,Chris	101	97
Oswalt,Roy	108	92
Harang,Aaron	82	90
Santana,Johan	142	88
Haren,Danny	89	82
Lackey,John	86	82
Vazquez,Javier	99	80
Webb,Brandon	95	78
Cordero,Francisco	103	75
Nathan,Joe	162	74
Smoltz,John	95	72
Martinez,Pedro	101	70
Matsuzaka,Daisuke	110	70
Lidge,Brad	127	69
Lieber,Jon	81	69
Bonderman,Jeremy	91	68
Arroyo,Bronson	78	67
Ryan,B.J.	130	66
Rodriguez,Francisco	131	66
Zambrano,Carlos	76	65
Hoffman,Trevor	96	64
Pettitte,Andy	88	63
Myers,Brett	89	62
Clemens,Roger	107	61
Mussina,Mike	97	60
Sabathia,C.C.	92	60
Rivera,Mariano	105	60
Peavy,Jake	107	56
Cordero,Chad	86	56
Bedard,Erik	86	54
Bush,David	86	53

LIMA/RIMA PLAN

BATTERS

TIER A: High LIMA, High Reliability

NAME	POS	Rel	LIMA
Furcal,Rafael	6	99	B+
Damon,Johnny	8	84	B+
Castillo,Luis	4	81	B+
Dunn,Adam	7	76	B+
Bay,Jason	7	74	B+
Abreu,Bobby	9	73	B+
Figgins,Chone	85	99	B
Jones,Andruw	8	98	B
Pierre,Juan	8	88	B
Wright,David	5	86	B
Cabrera,Orlando	6	83	B
Freel,Ryan	89	80	B
Burrell,Pat	7	78	B
Lee,Carlos	7	76	B
DeJesus,David	78	72	B
Chavez,Eric	5	72	B

TIER B: High LIMA, Mod. Reliability

NAME	POS	Rel	LIMA
Helton,Todd	3	48	A
Giles,Brian	9	45	A
Drew,J.D.	9	50	B+
Cameron,Mike	8	58	B+
Roberts,Dave	7	51	B+
Vizquel,Omar	6	65	B+
Hudson,Orlando	4	66	B
Granderson,Curtis	8	59	B
Giles,Marcus	4	69	B
Glaus,Troy	5	59	B
Matsui,Hideki	7	45	B
Jones,Chipper	5	41	B
Cuddyer,Michael	9	59	B

RIMA TIERS

TIER A: LIMA-caliber with high Reliability scores
TIER B: LIMA-caliber with moderate Reliability scores
TIER C: Non-LIMA with high Reliability scores
TIER D: LIMA-caliber with low Reliability scores
TIER E: Non-LIMA with moderate Reliability scores.
TIER F: Non-LIMA with low Reliability scores.

Tier E players with LIMA grades less than C
and all Tier F players are not shown as
they are not draft-worthy anyway.

For complete description of the RIMA Plan,
see page 38.

BATTERS

TIER C: Low LIMA, High Reliability

NAME	POS	Rel	LIMA
Inge,Brandon	5	96	C+
Suzuki,Ichiro	98	95	C+
Iguchi,Tadahito	4	92	C+
Ramirez,Aramis	5	86	C+
Jeter,Derek	6	85	C+
Jones,Jacque	9	85	C+
Lugo,Julio	64	84	C+
Kotsay,Mark	8	83	C+
Johjima,Kenji	2	80	C+
Hunter,Torii	8	77	C+
Kendall,Jason	2	74	C+
Kent,Jeff	4	74	C+
Wells,Vernon	8	73	C+
Konerko,Paul	3	99	C
Martinez,Victor	23	99	C
Renteria,Edgar	6	97	C
Hillenbrand,Shea	305	97	C
Belliard,Ron	4	96	C
Pujols,Albert	3	95	C
Podsednik,Scott	7	94	C
Feliz,Pedro	5	91	C
Monroe,Craig	70	88	C
Overbay,Lyle	3	87	C
Green,Shawn	9	83	C
Anderson,Garret	70	78	C
Kennedy,Adam	4	77	C
Wilson,Jack	6	77	C
Young,Michael	6	76	C
Blalock,Hank	50	75	C
Crede,Joe	5	74	C
Everett,Adam	6	73	C
Ibanez,Raul	7	73	C
Rollins,Jimmy	6	99	D+
Crawford,Carl	7	99	D+
Tejada,Miguel	6	98	D+
Ortiz,David	0	97	D+
Teixeira,Mark	3	95	D+
Guerrero,Vladimir	90	93	D+
Payton,Jay	789	88	D+
Pierzynski,A.J.	2	80	D+
LoDuca,Paul	2	80	D+
Soriano,Alfonso	7	75	D+
Hafner,Travis	0	72	D+
Gonzalez,Alex	6	85	D
Biggio,Craig	4	74	D
Mackowiak,Rob	879	71	D
Cabrera,Miguel	5	70	D

BATTERS

TIER D: High LIMA, Low Reliability

NAME	POS	Rel	LIMA
Sizemore,Grady	8	39	B+
Pedroia,Dustin	4	0	B+
Bonds,Barry	7	0	B+
Swisher,Nick	37	39	B
Byrnes,Eric	8	38	B
Hall,Bill	6	37	B
Kearns,Austin	9	37	B
Encarnacion,Edwin	5	36	B
Ensberg,Morgan	5	33	B
Guillen,Carlos	6	31	B
Roberts,Brian	4	31	B
Johnson,Nick	3	30	B
Hawpe,Brad	9	30	B
Youkilis,Kevin	3	27	B
Ramirez,Manny	7	27	B
Utley,Chase	4	26	B
Weeks,Rickie	4	25	B
Atkins,Garrett	5	24	B
Sheffield,Gary	9	23	B
Quentin,Carlos	9	21	B
Matthews Jr.,Gary	8	21	B
Durham,Ray	4	18	B
Giambi,Jason	03	12	B
Ramirez,Hanley	6	10	B
Rolen,Scott	5	10	B
Jackson,Conor	3	9	B
Mauer,Joe	2	8	B
Teahen,Mark	5	7	B
Young,Chris	8	0	B

TIER E: Low LIMA, Mod. Reliability

NAME	POS	Rel	LIMA
Delgado,Carlos	3	61	C+
Wilkerson,Brad	7	60	C+
Crisp,Coco	8	57	C+
Greene,Khalil	6	55	C+
Hill,Aaron	46	53	C+
Dye,Jermaine	9	51	C+
Alou,Moises	9	49	C+
Dellucci,David	79	46	C+
Barfield,Josh	4	41	C+
Gonzalez,Luis	7	41	C+
Barrett,Michael	2	67	C
Encarnacion,Juan	98	66	C
Uribe,Juan	6	63	C
Taveras,Willy	8	61	C
Wigginton,Ty	345	59	C
Grudzielanek,Mark	4	58	C
Lopez,Jose	4	53	C
Bradley,Milton	9	48	C
Thames,Marcus	70	48	C
Nady,Xavier	93	47	C
Cantu,Jorge	4	45	C
Rodriguez,Ivan	2	44	C
Fielder,Prince	3	42	C
Catalanotto,Frank	70	41	C

LIMA/RIMA PLAN

PITCHERS

A: High LIMA, High Reliability

NAME	Rel	LIMA
Lieber, Jon	69	B+
Lidge, Brad	69	B+
Weaver, Jeff	80	B
Vazquez, Javier	80	B
Cordero, Francisco	75	B
Martinez, Pedro	70	B
Clemens, Roger	61	B

B: High LIMA, Mod. Reliability

NAME	Rel	LIMA
Farnsworth, Kyle	30	A
Howry, Bob	35	B+
Heilman, Aaron	31	B+
Shields, Scot	51	B
Fossum, Casey	48	B
Towers, Josh	46	B
Kim, Byung-Hyun	44	B
Linebrink, Scott	40	B
Burnett, A.J.	38	B
Perez, Odalis	38	B
Fuentes, Brian	38	B
Wheeler, Dan	33	B

C: Low LIMA, High Reliability

NAME	Rel	LIMA
Carpenter, Chris	97	C+
Oswalt, Roy	92	C+
Davis, Doug	90	C+
Lopez, Rodrigo	86	C+
Webb, Brandon	78	C+
Nathan, Joe	74	C+
Ryan, B.J.	66	C+
Rodriguez, Francisco	66	C+
Wright, Jamey	65	C+
Tomko, Brett	65	C+
Hoffman, Trevor	64	C+
Pettitte, Andy	63	C+
Johnson, Jason	63	C+
Myers, Brett	62	C+
Mussina, Mike	60	C+
Rivera, Mariano	60	C+
Hernandez, Livan	90	C
Harang, Aaron	90	C
Santana, Johan	88	C
Morris, Matt	86	C
Millwood, Kevin	85	C
Fogg, Josh	82	C
Haren, Danny	82	C
Lackey, John	82	C
Milton, Eric	80	C
Ortiz, Ramon	80	C
Batista, Miguel	78	C
Hendrickson, Mark	78	C
Marquis, Jason	75	C
Buehrle, Mark	75	C
Smoltz, John	72	C
Matsuzaka, Daisuke	70	C
Bonderman, Jeremy	68	C
Penny, Brad	68	C
Franklin, Ryan	66	C
Silva, Carlos	64	C
Beckett, Josh	62	C
Sabathia, C.C.	60	C

D: High LIMA, Low Reliability

NAME	Rel	LIMA
Gagne, Eric	0	A+
Delcarmen, Manny	0	A+
Betancourt, Rafael	20	A
Calero, Kiko	15	A
Valverde, Jose	11	A
Ohman, Will	10	A
Sherrill, George	8	A
Accardo, Jeremy	7	A
Neshek, Patrick	3	A
Cabrera, Fernando	1	A
Casilla, Santiago	0	A
Corpas, Manuel	0	A
Meredith, Cla	0	A
Francisco, Frank	0	A
Soriano, Rafael	0	A
Williamson, Scott	0	A
Miller, Matt	0	A
Lowe, Mark	0	A
Gregg, Kevin	29	B+
Rincon, Juan	28	B+
Marte, Damaso	28	B+
Cruz, Juan	28	B+
Benoit, Joaquin	23	B+
Duchscherer, Justin	23	B+
Sheets, Ben	22	B+
Walker, Jamie	16	B+
Eyre, Scott	15	B+
Mahay, Ron	14	B+
Davis, Jason	14	B+
Embree, Alan	11	B+
Wuertz, Mike	10	B+
Crain, Jesse	6	B+
Braun, Ryan	6	B+
Miller, Trever	5	B+
Johnson, Tyler	2	B+
Wainwright, Adam	1	B+
Tankersley, Taylor	0	B+
Brown, Andrew	0	B+
Patterson, John	0	B+
Wilson, C.J.	0	B+
Bruney, Brian	0	B+
Bailey, Homer	0	B+
Mujica, Edward	0	B+
Wood, Kerry	0	B+
Mastny, Tom	0	B+
Britton, Chris	0	B+
Hansen, Craig	0	B+
Harden, Rich	0	B+
Kuo, Hong-Chih	0	B+
Seanez, Rudy	0	B+
Devine, Joey	0	B+
Aardsma, David	0	B+
Madson, Ryan	27	B
Frasor, Jason	26	B
Turnbow, Derrick	26	B
Fultz, Aaron	25	B
Coffey, Todd	24	B
Vizcaino, Luis	23	B
Hernandez, Felix	21	B
Cotts, Neal	17	B
Reyes, Dennys	15	B
Gonzalez, Mike	15	B
Peralta, Joel	13	B

D: High LIMA, Low Reliability

NAME	Rel	LIMA
Speier, Justin	13	B
Eaton, Adam	12	B
Thornton, Matt	8	B
Hernandez, Roberto	8	B
Wise, Matt	8	B
Donnelly, Brendan	5	B
Nelson, Joe	5	B
Thompson, Brad	4	B
Lopez, Javier	4	B
Snyder, Kyle	4	B
Nippert, Dustin	4	B
Cabrera, Daniel	3	B
Hermanson, Dustin	3	B
Gonzalez, Edgar	3	B
Villone, Ron	3	B
Albers, Matt	2	B
Guzman, Angel	2	B
Kazmir, Scott	1	B
Bradford, Chad	1	B
Hill, Rich	1	B
Feldman, Scott	0	B
De La Rosa, Jorge	0	B
Capps, Matt	0	B
Foulke, Keith	0	B
Carmona, Fausto	0	B
Garza, Matt	0	B
Lyon, Brandon	0	B
League, Brandon	0	B
Rhodes, Arthur	0	B
Gonzalez, Enrique	0	B
Jackson, Edwin	0	B
Medders, Brandon	0	B
Broxton, Jonathan	0	B
MacDougal, Mike	0	B
McBride, Macay	0	B
Rodney, Fernando	0	B
Yates, Tyler	0	B
Wagner, Ryan	0	B
Sanchez, Jonathan	0	B
Zumaya, Joel	0	B
Martin, Tom	0	B
Gaudin, Chad	0	B
Bray, Bill	0	B
Orvella, Chad	0	R
Jenks, Bobby	0	B
Pavano, Carl	0	B
Petit, Yusmeiro	0	B
Windsor, Jason	0	B

E: Low LIMA, Mod. Reliab.

NAME	Rel	LIMA
Peavy, Jake	56	C+
Bush, David	53	C+
Loaiza, Esteban	51	C+
Wagner, Billy	50	C+
Baez, Danys	49	C+
Dempster, Ryan	44	C+
Halladay, Roy	41	C+
Snell, Ian	39	C+
Escobar, Kelvim	39	C+
Julio, Jorge	39	C+
Putz, J.J.	39	C+
Street, Huston	37	C+
Tavarez, Julian	37	C+
Otsuka, Akinori	37	C+
Kolb, Danny	36	C+
Looper, Braden	36	C+
Halsey, Brad	34	C+
Gordon, Tom	33	C+
Meadows, Brian	33	C+
Cain, Matt	33	C+
Colon, Bartolo	33	C+
Duke, Zach	31	C+
Byrd, Paul	58	C
Redman, Mark	58	C
Blanton, Joe	58	C
Cordero, Chad	56	C
Bedard, Erik	54	C
Lohse, Kyle	54	C
Padilla, Vicente	53	C
Sosa, Jorge	49	C
Wakefield, Tim	49	C
Lowry, Noah	45	C
Vargas, Claudio	42	C
Torres, Salomon	39	C
Elarton, Scott	38	C
Maroth, Mike	37	C
Mesa, Jose	34	C
Park, Chan Ho	31	C
Proctor, Scott	30	C

POSITION SCARCITY CHART

Legend: $30+ players | $20-29 players | $15-19 players | $10-14 players (30 / 29 / 15 / 10)

FIRST BASE

NAME
Pujols, Albert
Howard, Ryan
Teixeira, Mark
Lee, Derrek
Berkman, Lance
Morneau, Justin
Konerko, Paul
Delgado, Carlos
LaRoche, Adam
Helton, Todd
Fielder, Prince
Sexson, Richie
Gonzalez, Adrian
Johnson, Nick
Overbay, Lyle
Swisher, Nick
Shealy, Ryan
Kendrick, Howie
Garciaparra, Nomar
Hillenbrand, Shea
Jacobs, Mike
Casey, Sean
Loney, James
Jackson, Conor
Wigginton, Ty
Youkilis, Kevin
Broussard, Ben
Garko, Ryan
Helms, Wes
Lamb, Mike
Hatteberg, Scott
Shelton, Chris
Millar, Kevin
Johnson, Dan
Morales, Kendry
Wilson, Craig
Quinlan, Robb
Clark, Tony
Kotchman, Casey
Kielsko, Ryan
Pena, Carlos
Phillips, Andy
Conine, Jeff
Niekro, Lance
Saenz, Olmedo

SECOND BASE

NAME
Utley, Chase
Roberts, Brian
Cano, Robinson
Durham, Ray
Giles, Marcus
Kinsler, Ian
Castillo, Luis
Kent, Jeff
Hudson, Orlando
Weeks, Rickie
Iguchi, Tadahito
Barfield, Josh
Cantu, Jorge
Phillips, Brandon
Lopez, Jose
Polanco, Placido
Uggla, Dan
Grudzielanek, Mark
Belliard, Ron
Theriot, Ryan
Matsui, Kazuo
Burke, Chris
Ellis, Mark
Hill, Aaron
Kennedy, Adam
Pedroia, Dustin
Valentin, Jose
Loretta, Mark
Graffanino, Tony
Vidro, Jose
Walker, Todd
Biggio, Craig
German, Esteban
Anderson, Marlon
Cairo, Miguel
Carroll, Jamey
Castro, Bernie
Castillo, Jose
Luna, Hector
Inglett, Joe
Infante, Omar
Miles, Aaron
Perez, Neifi
Adams, Russ
Frandsen, Kevin

THIRD BASE

NAME
Rodriguez, Alex
Cabrera, Miguel
Wright, David
Ramirez, Aramis
Atkins, Garrett
Rolen, Scott
Zimmerman, Ryan
Ensberg, Morgan
Teahen, Mark
Huff, Aubrey
Glaus, Troy
Jones, Chipper
Encarnacion, Edwin
Crede, Joe
Iwamura, Akinori
Beltre, Adrian
Sanchez, Freddy
Chavez, Eric
Mora, Melvin
Tracy, Chad
Lowell, Mike
Gordon, Alex
Ellis, Mark
Betemit, Wilson
Inge, Brandon
Blalock, Hank
Aurilia, Rich
Feliz, Pedro
Izturis, Maicer
Marte, Andy
Bell, David
Koskie, Corey
Punto, Nick
Randa, Joe
Aybar, Willy
McPherson, Dallas
Spiezio, Scott
Cirillo, Jeff
Izturis, Cesar
Boone, Aaron
Batista, Tony
Perez, Antonio
Easley, Damion
McDonald, John
Nunez, Abraham O.
Keppinger, Jeff
Callaspo, Alberto
Quintanilla, Omar
Vizcaino, Jose
Tatis, Fernando

SHORTSTOP

NAME
Reyes, Jose
Rollins, Jimmy
Furcal, Rafael
Jeter, Derek
Ramirez, Hanley
Tejada, Miguel
Young, Michael
Guillen, Carlos
Renteria, Edgar
Hall, Bill
Lugo, Julio
Lopez Felipe
Cabrera, Orlando
Bartlett, Jason
Uribe, Juan
Vizquel, Omar
Greene, Khalil
Peralta, Jhonny
Betancourt, Yun
Drew, Stephen
Crosby, Bobby
Tulowitzki, Troy
Eckstein, David
Wilson, Jack
Everett, Adam
Cintron, Alex
Hardy, J.J.
Gonzalez, Alex
Clayton, Royce
Cedeno, Ronny
Berroa, Angel
Scutaro, Marco
Guzman, Cristian
Counsell, Craig
Aybar, Erick
Zobrist, Ben
Barmes, Clint
Blum, Geoff
Lopez, Javy
Cora, Alex
Castro, Juan
Torrealba, Yorvit
Hall, Toby
Ausmus, Brad
Rivera, Mike
Blanco, Henry
Redmond, Mike
Montero, Miguel

CATCHERS

NAME
Mauer, Joe
McCann, Brian
Martinez, Victor
Barrett, Michael
Johjima, Kenji
Rodriguez, Ivan
Martin, Russell
Hernandez, Ramn
Posada, Jorge
LoDuca, Paul
Pierzynski, A.J.
Molina, Ben
Varitek, Jason
Iannetta, Chris
Estrada, Johnny
Kendall, Jason
Barajas, Rod
Piazza, Mike
Ross, David
Lieberthal, Mike
Ruiz, Carlos
Paulino, Ronny
Olivo, Miguel
Zaun, Gregg
Valentin, Javier
Bard, Josh
Schneider, Brian
Napoli, Mike
Buck, John
Molina, Yadier
Navarro, Dioner
Coste, Chris
LaRue, Jason
Miller, Damian
Alfonzo, Eliezer
Snyder, Chris

OUTFIELDERS

NAME
Soriano, Alfonso
Holliday, Matt
Crawford, Carl
Beltran, Carlos
Guerrero, Vladimir
Lee, Carlos
Pierre, Juan
Ramirez, Manny
Abreu, Bobby
Bay, Jason
Jones, Andruw
Sizemore, Grady
Dye, Jermaine
Matsui, Hideki
Suzuki, Ichiro
Figgins, Chone
Damon, Johnny
Hunter, Torii
Wells, Vernon
Crisp, Coco
Young, Delmon
Rios, Alexis
Patterson, Corey
Dunn, Adam
Cameron, Mike
Willingham, Josh
Monroe, Craig
Baldelli, Rocco
Giles, Brian
Murton, Matt
Roberts, Dave
Sheffield, Gary
Burrell, Pat
Jones, Jacque
Ibanez, Raul
Hawpe, Brad
Ordonez, Magglio
Taveras, Willy
Cuddyer, Michael
DeJesus, David
Rivera, Juan
Markakis, Nick
Byrnes, Eric
Duffy, Chris

STARTERS

NAME
Santana, Johan
Halladay, Roy
Carpenter, Chris
Oswalt, Roy
Webb, Brandon
Hernandez, Felix
Matsuzaka, Dais
Bonderman, Jer
Sheets, Ben
Peavy, Jake
Vazquez, Javier
Hamels, Cole
Kazmir, Scott
Haren, Danny
Sabathia, C.C.
Escobar, Kelvim
Bedard, Erik
Lackey, John
Arroyo, Bronson
Papelbon, Jon
Myers, Brett
Burnett, A.J.
Harang, Aaron
Mussina, Mike
Peitittle, Andy
Zambrano, Carlos
Beckett, Josh
Schilling, Curt
Cain, Matt
Snell, Ian
Bush, David
Weaver, Jered
Robertson, Nate
Harden, Rich
Millwood, Kevin
Verlander, Justin
Contreras, Jose
Garcia, Freddy
Hill, Rich
Smoltz, John
Young, Chris
Padilla, Vicente
Schmidt, Jason
Lowe, Derek
Reyes, Anthony

RELIEVERS

NAME
Nathan, Joe
Putz, J.J.
Rodriguez, Francisc
Ryan, B.J.
Street, Huston
Wagner, Billy
Cordero, Chad
Cordero, Francisco
Rivera, Mariano
Valverde, Jose
Saito, Takashi
Gordon, Tom
Hoffman, Trevor
Jenks, Bobby
Gonzalez, Mike
Lidge, Brad
Fuentes, Brian
Ray, Chris
Wainwright, Adam
Borowski, Joe
Wickman, Bob
Broxton, Jonathan
Jones, Todd
Shields, Scot
Howry, Bob
Weathers, David
Zumaya, Joel
Wuertz, Mike
Linebrink, Scott
Crain, Jesse
Duchscherer, Justin
Rodney, Fernando
Capps, Matt
Carrasco, Hector
Foulke, Keith
Farnsworth, Kyle
Orvella, Chad
Wheeler, Dan
Calero, Kiko
Rincon, Juan
Betancourt, Rafael
Bray, Bill
Qualls, Chad

ROTISSERIE AUCTION DRAFT
Top 560 players ranked for 75% depth leagues

NAME	POS	5x5
Pujols,Albert	3	$42
Santana,Johan	P	$39
Soriano,Alfonso	7	$34
Ortiz,David	0	$34
Rodriguez,Alex	5	$33
Howard,Ryan	3	$33
Reyes,Jose	6	$32
Holliday,Matt	7	$32
Crawford,Carl	7	$32
Cabrera,Miguel	5	$32
Teixeira,Mark	3	$32
Beltran,Carlos	8	$31
Guerrero,Vladimir	90	$31
Rollins,Jimmy	6	$31
Lee,Derrek	3	$31
Hafner,Travis	0	$30
Berkman,Lance	39	$30
Wright,David	5	$30
Furcal,Rafael	6	$30
Lee,Carlos	7	$30
Pierre,Juan	8	$30
Ramirez,Manny	7	$30
Nathan,Joe	P	$29
Abreu,Bobby	9	$29
Jeter,Derek	6	$29
Bay,Jason	7	$29
Jones,Andruw	8	$29
Halladay,Roy	P	$28
Morneau,Justin	3	$28
Ramirez,Aramis	5	$28
Utley,Chase	4	$28
Carpenter,Chris	P	$28
Putz,J.J.	P	$28
Rodriguez,Francisco	P	$28
Sizemore,Grady	8	$28
Atkins,Garrett	5	$27
Dye,Jermaine	9	$27
Oswalt,Roy	P	$27
Ryan,B.J.	P	$26
Webb,Brandon	P	$26
Hernandez,Felix	P	$26
Konerko,Paul	3	$26
Suzuki,Ichiro	98	$26
Ramirez,Hanley	6	$26
Street,Huston	P	$26
Matsui,Hideki	7	$26
Delgado,Carlos	3	$25
Matsuzaka,Daisuke	P	$25
Wagner,Billy	P	$25
Tejada,Miguel	6	$25
Bonderman,Jeremy	P	$25
Figgins,Chone	85	$25
Damon,Johnny	8	$25
Cordero,Chad	P	$25
Sheets,Ben	P	$25
Peavy,Jake	P	$25
Hunter,Torii	8	$24
Wells,Vernon	8	$24
Crisp,Coco	8	$24
Vazquez,Javier	P	$24
Cordero,Francisco	P	$24
Hamels,Cole	P	$24
Kazmir,Scott	P	$24
Haren,Danny	P	$24
Roberts,Brian	4	$24
Young,Michael	6	$24
LaRoche,Adam	3	$24
Sabathia,C.C.	P	$24
Thome,Jim	0	$23
Escobar,Kelvim	P	$23
Helton,Todd	3	$23
Fielder,Prince	3	$23
Guillen,Carlos	6	$23
Rivera,Mariano	P	$23
Bedard,Erik	P	$23
Lackey,John	P	$23
Rolen,Scott	5	$23
Sexson,Richie	3	$22
Arroyo,Bronson	P	$22
Papelbon,Jon	P	$22
Gonzalez,Adrian	3	$22
Myers,Brett	P	$22
Burnett,A.J.	P	$22
Valverde,Jose	P	$22
Young,Delmon	9	$22
Zimmerman,Ryan	5	$22
Harang,Aaron	P	$22
Renteria,Edgar	6	$22
Rios,Alexis	9	$22
Mauer,Joe	2	$22
Otsuka,Akinori	P	$21
Ensberg,Morgan	5	$21
Patterson,Corey	8	$21
Dunn,Adam	7	$21
Mussina,Mike	P	$21
Cameron,Mike	8	$21
Pettitte,Andy	P	$21
Cano,Robinson	4	$21
Young,Chris	8	$21
Saito,Takashi	P	$21
Willingham,Josh	7	$21
Zambrano,Carlos	P	$21
Johnson,Nick	3	$21
Teahen,Mark	5	$21
Overbay,Lyle	3	$21
Hall,Bill	6	$21
Huff,Aubrey	59	$21
Glaus,Troy	5	$21
Beckett,Josh	P	$21
Lugo,Julio	64	$20
Monroe,Craig	70	$20
Schilling,Curt	P	$20
Thomas,Frank	0	$20
Cain,Matt	P	$20
Baldelli,Rocco	8	$20
Durham,Ray	4	$20
Giles,Brian	9	$20
Snell,Ian	P	$20
McCann,Brian	2	$20
Jones,Chipper	5	$20
Murton,Matt	7	$20
Roberts,Dave	7	$20
Burrell,Pat	7	$20
Sheffield,Gary	9	$20
Jones,Jacque	9	$20
Martinez,Victor	23	$20
Gordon,Tom	P	$20
Duffy,Chris	8	$20
Lopez,Felipe	6	$20
Encarnacion,Edwin	5	$19
Ibanez,Raul	7	$19
Giles,Marcus	4	$19
Hawpe,Brad	9	$19
Kinsler,Ian	4	$19
Bush,David	P	$19
Weaver,Jered	P	$19
Robertson,Nate	P	$19
Ordonez,Magglio	9	$19
Harden,Rich	P	$19
Hoffman,Trevor	P	$19
Millwood,Kevin	P	$19
Taveras,Willy	8	$19
Cuddyer,Michael	9	$19
DeJesus,David	78	$19
Upton,B.J.	5	$19
Crede,Joe	5	$19
Verlander,Justin	P	$19
Giambi,Jason	03	$19
Jenks,Bobby	P	$19
Contreras,Jose	P	$19
Gonzalez,Mike	P	$19
Rivera,Juan	798	$19
Markakis,Nick	97	$19
Byrnes,Eric	8	$19
Swisher,Nick	37	$19
Garcia,Freddy	P	$19
Hill,Rich	P	$18
Iwamura,Akinori	5	$18
Kearns,Austin	9	$18
Smoltz,John	P	$18
Beltre,Adrian	5	$18
Lidge,Brad	P	$18
Young,Chris	P	$18
Francoeur,Jeff	9	$18
Padilla,Vicente	P	$18
Castillo,Luis	4	$18
Shealy,Ryan	3	$18
Matthews Jr.,Gary	8	$18
Schmidt,Jason	P	$18
Kent,Jeff	4	$18
Sanchez,Freddy	564	$18
Lowe,Derek	P	$18
Kendrick,Howie	34	$18
Fuentes,Brian	P	$18
Drew,J.D.	9	$18
Garciaparra,Nomar	3	$18
Rowand,Aaron	8	$18
Bonds,Barry	7	$18
Freel,Ryan	89	$18
Reyes,Anthony	P	$18
Hudson,Orlando	4	$18
Olsen,Scott	P	$18
Weeks,Rickie	4	$18
Winn,Randy	987	$18
Barrett,Michael	2	$17
Cabrera,Orlando	6	$17
Chavez,Eric	5	$17
Mora,Melvin	5	$17
Podsednik,Scott	7	$17
Iguchi,Tadahito	4	$17
Hillenbrand,Shea	305	$17
Ray,Chris	P	$17
Kemp,Matt	8	$17
Tracy,Chad	5	$17
Wainwright,Adam	P	$17
Lowell,Mike	5	$17
Quentin,Carlos	9	$17
Lee,Cliff	P	$17
Santana,Ervin	P	$17
Shields,Jamie	P	$17
Barfield,Josh	4	$17
Garland,Jon	P	$17
Edmonds,Jim	8	$17
Alou,Moises	9	$16
Borowski,Joe	P	$16
Johnson,Randy	P	$16
Cantu,Jorge	4	$16
Gordon,Alex	5	$16
Igawa,Kei	P	$16
Ethier,Andre	7	$16
Anderson,Garret	70	$16
Griffey Jr.,Ken	8	$16
Penny,Brad	P	$16
Bartlett,Jason	6	$16
Wickman,Bob	P	$16
Blanton,Joe	P	$16
Johjima,Kenji	2	$16
Phillips,Brandon	4	$16
Betemit,Wilson	5	$16
Westbrook,Jake	P	$16
Wang,Chien-Ming	P	$16
Rodriguez,Ivan	2	$16
Inge,Brandon	5	$16
Lopez,Jose	4	$16
Jacobs,Mike	3	$16
Choo,Shin-Soo	9	$16
Casey,Sean	3	$16
Encarnacion,Juan	98	$16
Broxton,Jonathan	P	$16
Dellucci,David	79	$16
Martin,Russell	2	$16
Duke,Zach	P	$15
Willis,Dontrelle	P	$15
Uribe,Juan	6	$15
Zito,Barry	P	$15
Vizquel,Omar	6	$15
Lilly,Ted	P	$15
Jones,Todd	P	$15
Nady,Xavier	93	$15
Capuano,Chris	P	$15
Blalock,Hank	50	$15
Loney,James	3	$15
Green,Shawn	9	$15
Jenkins,Geoff	9	$15
Cabrera,Daniel	P	$15
Jackson,Conor	3	$15
Gagne,Eric	P	$15
Wigginton,Ty	345	$15
Duncan,Chris	79	$15
Gomes,Jonny	0	$15
Hermida,Jeremy	9	$15
Aurilia,Rich	536	$14
Hernandez,Ramon	2	$14
Eaton,Adam	P	$14
Greene,Khalil	6	$14
Maddux,Greg	P	$14
Loewen,Adam	P	$14
Polanco,Placido	4	$14
Shields,Scot	P	$14
Youkilis,Kevin	3	$14
Posada,Jorge	2	$14
Broussard,Ben	30	$14
Bradley,Milton	9	$14
Uggla,Dan	4	$14
Patterson,John	P	$14
Scott,Luke	7	$14
Davis,Doug	P	$14
Garza,Matt	P	$14
Lieber,Jon	P	$14
Sweeney,Mike	0	$14
Wilkerson,Brad	7	$14
Milledge,Lastings	79	$14
Buehrle,Mark	P	$14
Peralta,Jhonny	6	$14
Francis,Jeff	P	$14
Grudzielanek,Mark	4	$14
Garko,Ryan	3	$14
Howry,Bob	P	$14
Baker,Scott	P	$14
Pena,Wily Mo	98	$14

ROTISSERIE AUCTION DRAFT

Top 560 players ranked for 75% depth leagues

NAME	POS	5x5	NAME	POS	5x5	NAME	POS	5x5	NAME	POS	5x5
James,Chuck	P	$14	Linebrink,Scott	P	$11	Lieberthal,Mike	2	$9	Miller,Matt	P	$7
Gibbons,Jay	09	$14	Kendall,Jason	2	$11	Qualls,Chad	P	$9	Albers,Matt	P	$7
Johnson,Josh	P	$13	Byrd,Paul	P	$11	Vizcaino,Luis	P	$9	Schneider,Brian	2	$7
Weathers,David	P	$13	Eckstein,David	6	$11	Hardy,J.J.	6	$9	Lane,Jason	9	$7
Feliz,Pedro	5	$13	Marte,Andy	5	$11	Mench,Kevin	97	$9	Saunders,Joe	P	$7
McCarthy,Brandon	P	$13	Wilson,Jack	6	$11	Ruiz,Carlos	2	$9	Scutaro,Marco	64	$7
Payton,Jay	789	$13	Crain,Jesse	P	$11	Heilman,Aaron	P	$9	Anderson,Brian	8	$7
Clemens,Roger	P	$13	Rogers,Kenny	P	$11	DaVanon,Jeff	8	$9	Torres,Salomon	P	$7
LoDuca,Paul	2	$13	Duchscherer,Justin	P	$11	Martinez,Pedro	P	$9	Matos,Luis	7	$7
Lind,Adam	0	$13	Rodney,Fernando	P	$11	Cook,Aaron	P	$9	Ross,Cody	798	$7
Betancourt,Yuniesky	6	$13	Vargas,Claudio	P	$11	Rauch,Jon	P	$9	Corpas,Manuel	P	$7
Belliard,Ron	4	$13	Graffanino,Tony	45	$11	Gonzalez,Alex	6	$9	Randa,Joe	5	$7
Hart,Corey	97	$13	Hirsh,Jason	P	$10	Lohse,Kyle	P	$9	Milton,Eric	P	$7
Weaver,Jeff	P	$13	Barajas,Rod	2	$10	Tankersley,Taylor	P	$9	Penn,Hayden	P	$7
Granderson,Curtis	8	$13	Maine,John	P	$10	Cabrera,Fernando	P	$9	White,Rondell	7	$7
Sanchez,Anibal	P	$13	Catalanotto,Frank	70	$10	Mulder,Mark	P	$9	Donnelly,Brendan	P	$7
Gathright,Joey	8	$13	Bautista,Jose	859	$10	Wood,Kerry	P	$9	Correia,Kevin	P	$7
Meche,Gil	P	$13	Capps,Matt	P	$10	Sullivan,Cory	8	$8	Taguchi,So	78	$7
Pierzynski,A.J.	2	$13	Lowry,Noah	P	$10	Kuo,Hong-Chih	P	$8	Kotchman,Casey	3	$7
Glavine,Tom	P	$13	Michaels,Jason	7	$10	Neshek,Patrick	P	$8	Proctor,Scott	P	$7
Church,Ryan	8	$13	Bell,David	5	$10	Wright,Jaret	P	$8	Guzman,Cristian	6	$7
Theriot,Ryan	4	$13	Hatteberg,Scott	3	$10	Burgos,Ambiorix	P	$8	Aybar,Willy	5	$7
Johnson,Reed	79	$13	Everett,Adam	6	$10	Johnson,Kelly	7	$8	Linden,Todd	7	$7
Soriano,Rafael	P	$13	Lofton,Kenny	8	$10	Hernandez,Livan	P	$8	Klesko,Ryan	3	$7
Matsui,Kazuo	4	$13	Marcum,Shaun	P	$10	Amezaga,Alfredo	84	$8	Julio,Jorge	P	$7
Brown,Emil	79	$13	Perez,Odalis	P	$10	German,Esteban	4057	$8	McPherson,Dallas	5	$7
Drew,Stephen	6	$13	Carrasco,Hector	P	$10	Looper,Braden	P	$8	Napoli,Mike	2	$7
Molina,Ben	2	$13	Victorino,Shane	879	$10	Diaz,Matt	7	$8	Thomson,John	P	$7
Washburn,Jarrod	P	$13	Baek,Cha Seung	P	$10	Lopez,Rodrigo	P	$8	Norton,Greg	93	$7
DeRosa,Mark	954	$13	Shelton,Chris	3	$10	Paulino,Ronny	2	$8	Buck,John	2	$7
Burke,Chris	48	$13	Benson,Kris	P	$10	Olivo,Miguel	2	$8	Bailey,Homer	P	$7
Thames,Marcus	70	$13	Greinke,Zack	P	$10	Francisco,Frank	P	$8	Peralta,Joel	P	$7
Chavez,Endy	978	$13	Nolasco,Ricky	P	$10	Fossum,Casey	P	$8	Molina,Yadier	2	$7
Hensley,Clay	P	$13	Blake,Casey	9	$10	Tavarez,Julian	P	$8	Kim,Byung-Hyun	P	$7
Kotsay,Mark	8	$13	Vidro,Jose	4	$10	Mastny,Tom	P	$8	Miller,Wade	P	$7
Prior,Mark	P	$12	Wolf,Randy	P	$10	Batista,Miguel	P	$8	Hairston,Scott	7	$7
Wilson,Preston	79	$12	Foulke,Keith	P	$10	Denorfia,Chris	9	$8	Williams,Bernie	980	$7
Varitek,Jason	2	$12	Hudson,Luke	P	$10	Silva,Carlos	P	$8	Tomko,Brett	P	$6
Suppan,Jeff	P	$12	Farnsworth,Kyle	P	$10	Wilson,Craig	39	$8	Bannister,Brian	P	$6
Crosby,Bobby	6	$12	Koskie,Corey	5	$10	Baez,Danys	P	$8	McLouth,Nate	89	$6
Morris,Matt	P	$12	Piazza,Mike	2	$10	Nelson,Joe	P	$8	Navarro,Dioner	2	$6
Tulowitzki,Troy	6	$12	Millar,Kevin	30	$10	Zaun,Gregg	2	$8	Benitez,Armando	P	$6
Branyan,Russ	95	$12	Gorzelanny,Tom	P	$10	Speier,Justin	P	$8	Sanchez,Duaner	P	$6
Helms,Wes	35	$12	Walker,Todd	435	$10	Valentin,Javier	2	$8	Frasor,Jason	P	$6
Floyd,Cliff	7	$12	Bonser,Boof	P	$10	Gregg,Kevin	P	$8	Pena,Carlos	3	$6
Loaiza,Esteban	P	$12	Hammel,Jason	P	$10	Clayton,Royce	6	$8	Spiezio,Scott	57	$6
Iannetta,Chris	2	$12	Orvella,Chad	P	$10	Jennings,Jason	P	$8	Buchholz,Taylor	P	$6
Ellis,Mark	4	$12	Maholm,Paul	P	$9	Devine,Joey	P	$8	Wells,Kip	P	$6
Billingsley,Chad	P	$12	Nixon,Trot	9	$9	Davis,Jason	P	$8	MacDougal,Mike	P	$6
Lamb,Mike	35	$12	Wheeler,Dan	P	$9	Anderson,Marlon	47	$8	Feliciano,Pedro	P	$6
Hernandez,Orlando	P	$12	Punto,Nick	56	$9	Cedeno,Ronny	6	$8	Gonzalez,Edgar	P	$6
Hill,Aaron	46	$12	Biggio,Craig	4	$9	Kielty,Bobby	79	$8	Chulk,Vinnie	P	$6
Laird,Gerald	2	$12	Cruz,Nelson	9	$9	Marquis,Jason	P	$8	Counsell,Craig	6	$6
Kennedy,Adam	4	$12	Ross,David	2	$9	Bard,Josh	2	$8	Cruz,Jose	79	$6
Zumaya,Joel	P	$12	Gross,Gabe	87	$9	Pavano,Carl	P	$8	Hampton,Mike	P	$6
Izturis,Maicer	5	$12	Colon,Bartolo	P	$9	Dempster,Ryan	P	$8	Walker,Jamie	P	$6
Howell,J.P.	P	$12	Guillen,Jose	9	$9	League,Brandon	P	$7	Medders,Brandon	P	$6
Villanueva,Carlos	P	$12	Cabrera,Melky	7	$9	Reyes,Dennys	P	$7	Thornton,Matt	P	$6
Kubel,Jason	70	$12	Sanders,Reggie	9	$9	Berroa,Angel	6	$7	Moyer,Jamie	P	$6
Wakefield,Tim	P	$11	Williams,Woody	P	$9	Madson,Ryan	P	$7	Erstad,Darin	8	$6
Baker,Jeff	9	$11	Calero,Kiko	P	$9	Young,Dmitri	0	$7	Cruz,Juan	P	$6
Pedroia,Dustin	4	$11	Rincon,Juan	P	$9	Quinlan,Robb	3	$7	Bradford,Chad	P	$6
Wuertz,Mike	P	$11	Betancourt,Rafael	P	$9	Hinske,Eric	90	$7	Clark,Brady	8	$6
Valentin,Jose	4	$11	Bray,Bill	P	$9	Lawrence,Brian	P	$7	Benoit,Joaquin	P	$6
Estrada,Johnny	2	$11	Johnson,Dan	3	$9	Perez,Oliver	P	$7	Phillips,Andy	3	$6
Chacin,Gustavo	P	$11	Reed,Jeremy	8	$9	Meredith,Cla	P	$7	Pelfrey,Mike	P	$6
Loretta,Mark	4	$11	Morales,Kendry	3	$9	Clark,Tony	3	$7	Finley,Steve	8	$6
Sowers,Jeremy	P	$11	Stewart,Shannon	7	$9	Trachsel,Steve	P	$7	Ayala,Luis	P	$6
Gonzalez,Luis	7	$11	Tejeda,Rob	P	$9	Mackowiak,Rob	879	$7	Timlin,Mike	P	$6
Hudson,Tim	P	$11	Cintron,Alex	64	$9	Burnitz,Jeromy	9	$7	Dotel,Octavio	P	$6

ROTISSERIE SNAKE DRAFT — 15 TEAM MIXED LEAGUE

#	Name	POS	#	Name	POS	#	Name	POS	#	Name	POS
1	Pujols,Albert	3	5	Figgins,Chone	85	9	Teahen,Mark	5	13	Beltre,Adrian	5
	Santana,Johan	P		Damon,Johnny	8		Overbay,Lyle	3		Lidge,Brad	P
	Reyes,Jose	6		**Hall,Bill**	6		Barfield,Josh	4		Young,Chris	P
	Rollins,Jimmy	6		**Cordero,Chad**	P		Huff,Aubrey	59		Francoeur,Jeff	9
	Furcal,Rafael	6		Sheets,Ben	P		Glaus,Troy	5		Pierzynski,A.J.	2
	Soriano,Alfonso	7		Peavy,Jake	P		Beckett,Josh	P		Padilla,Vicente	P
	Jeter,Derek	6		**Lugo,Julio**	64		Monroe,Craig	70		Shealy,Ryan	3
	Ortiz,David	0		Hunter,Torii	8		Schilling,Curt	P		Matthews Jr.,Gary	8
	Utley,Chase	4		Wells,Vernon	8		Thomas,Frank	0		Schmidt,Jason	P
	Rodriguez,Alex	5		**Giles,Marcus**	4		Cain,Matt	P		Sanchez,Freddy	564
	Howard,Ryan	3		Crisp,Coco	8		Cabrera,Orlando	6		Lowe,Derek	P
	Holliday,Matt	7		**Kinsler,Ian**	4		Cantu,Jorge	4		Kendrick,Howie	34
	Crawford,Carl	7		Vazquez,Javier	P		Baldelli,Rocco	8		Fuentes,Brian	P
	Cabrera,Miguel	5		**Cordero,Francisco**	P		Giles,Brian	9		Drew,J.D.	9
	Teixeira,Mark	3		Hamels,Cole	P		Snell,Ian	P		Molina,Ben	2
2	Beltran,Carlos	8	6	Kazmir,Scott	P	10	Jones,Chipper	5	14	Garciaparra,Nomar	3
	Guerrero,Vladimir	90		Haren,Danny	P		Phillips,Brandon	4		Rowand,Aaron	8
	Ramirez,Hanley	6		LaRoche,Adam	3		Murton,Matt	7		Bonds,Barry	7
	Lee,Derrek	3		**Lopez,Felipe**	6		Roberts,Dave	7		Freel,Ryan	89
	Hafner,Travis	0		Sabathia,C.C.	P		Burrell,Pat	7		Reyes,Anthony	P
	Berkman,Lance	39		**Barrett,Michael**	2		Sheffield,Gary	9		Olsen,Scott	P
	Wright,David	5		Thome,Jim	0		Jones,Jacque	9		Winn,Randy	987
	Lee,Carlos	7		Escobar,Kelvim	P		Gordon,Tom	P		Chavez,Eric	5
	Pierre,Juan	8		**Castillo,Luis**	4		Lopez,Jose	4		Greene,Khalil	6
	Ramirez,Manny	7		Helton,Todd	3		Duffy,Chris	8		Polanco,Placido	4
	Nathan,Joe	P		Fielder,Prince	3		Encarnacion,Edwin	5		Mora,Melvin	5
	Tejada,Miguel	6		**Kent,Jeff**	4		Hernandez,Ramon	2		Podsednik,Scott	7
	Abreu,Bobby	9		**Rivera,Mariano**	P		Ibanez,Raul	7		Hillenbrand,Shea	305
	Roberts,Brian	4		Bedard,Erik	P		Hawpe,Brad	9		Uggla,Dan	4
	Bay,Jason	7		Lackey,John	P		Bush,David	P		Ray,Chris	P
3	Jones,Andruw	8	7	Rolen,Scott	5	11	Posada,Jorge	2	15	Kemp,Matt	8
	Mauer,Joe	2		Sexson,Richie	3		Bartlett,Jason	6		Tracy,Chad	5
	Halladay,Roy	P		Arroyo,Bronson	P		Weaver,Jered	P		Wainwright,Adam	P
	Morneau,Justin	3		Papelbon,Jon	P		Robertson,Nate	P		Lowell,Mike	5
	Ramirez,Aramis	5		Gonzalez,Adrian	3		Ordonez,Magglio	9		Quentin,Carlos	9
	Carpenter,Chris	P		Myers,Brett	P		Harden,Rich	P		Lee,Cliff	P
	Young,Michael	6		Burnett,A.J.	P		Hoffman,Trevor	P		Santana,Ervin	P
	Putz,J.J.	P		**Johjima,Kenji**	2		Millwood,Kevin	P		Shields,Jamie	P
	Rodriguez,Francisco	P		Valverde,Jose	P		Taveras,Willy	8		Peralta,Jhonny	6
	Sizemore,Grady	8		**Young,Delmon**	9		Cuddyer,Michael	9		Grudzielanek,Mark	4
	Atkins,Garrett	5		Zimmerman,Ryan	5		DeJesus,David	78		Garland,Jon	P
	Dye,Jermaine	0		Harang,Aaron	P		Upton,B.J.	5		Edmonds,Jim	8
	Oswalt,Roy	P		**Rodriguez,Ivan**	2		Crede,Joe	5		Alou,Moises	9
	McCann,Brian	2		**Hudson,Orlando**	4		Verlander,Justin	P		Borowski,Joe	P
	Guillen,Carlos	6		**Weeks,Rickie**	4		Giambi,Jason	03		Johnson,Randy	P
4	**Martinez,Victor**	23	8	Rios,Alexis	9	12	Jenks,Bobby	P	16	Varitek,Jason	2
	Ryan,B.J.	P		**Martin,Russell**	2		Contreras,Jose	P		Gordon,Alex	5
	Webb,Brandon	P		**Otsuka,Akinori**	P		Gonzalez,Mike	P		Igawa,Kei	P
	Hernandez,Felix	P		Ensberg,Morgan	5		Rivera,Juan	798		Ethier,Andre	7
	Konerko,Paul	3		**Patterson,Corey**	8		Markakis,Nick	97		Anderson,Garret	70
	Cano,Robinson	4		Dunn,Adam	7		Byrnes,Eric	8		Belliard,Ron	4
	Suzuki,Ichiro	98		Mussina,Mike	P		Swisher,Nick	37		Iannetta,Chris	2
	Renteria,Edgar	6		Cameron,Mike	8		Garcia,Freddy	P		Griffey Jr.,Ken	8
	Street,Huston	P		Pettitte,Andy	P		Hill,Rich	P		Penny,Brad	P
	Matsui,Hideki	7		**Iguchi,Tadahito**	4		Iwamura,Akinori	5		Wickman,Bob	P
	Delgado,Carlos	3		Young,Chris	8		Uribe,Juan	6		Blanton,Joe	P
	Matsuzaka,Daisuke	P		Saito,Takashi	P		Kearns,Austin	9		Theriot,Ryan	4
	Wagner,Billy	P		Willingham,Josh	7		LoDuca,Paul	2		Matsui,Kazuo	4
	Durham,Ray	4		Zambrano,Carlos	P		Vizquel,Omar	6		Betemit,Wilson	5
	Bonderman,Jeremy	P		Johnson,Nick	3		Smoltz,John	P		Laird,Gerald	2

ROTISSERIE SNAKE DRAFT — 15 TEAM MIXED LEAGUE

#	Name	POS	#	Name	POS	#	Name	POS	#	Name	POS
17	Westbrook,Jake	P	21	Gibbons,Jay	09	25	Vidro,Jose	4	29	Rincon,Juan	P
	Wang,Chien-Ming	P		Barajas,Rod	2		Byrd,Paul	P		Betancourt,Rafael	P
	Burke,Chris	48		Johnson,Josh	P		Ruiz,Carlos	2		Bray,Bill	P
	Inge,Brandon	5		Weathers,David	P		Marte,Andy	5		Johnson,Dan	3
	Jacobs,Mike	3		Feliz,Pedro	5		Walker,Todd	435		Reed,Jeremy	8
	Choo,Shin-Soo	9		McCarthy,Brandon	P		Crain,Jesse	P		Morales,Kendry	3
	Casey,Sean	3		Payton,Jay	789		Rogers,Kenny	P		Stewart,Shannon	7
	Encarnacion,Juan	98		Clemens,Roger	P		Duchscherer,Justin	P		Tejeda,Rob	P
	Broxton,Jonathan	P		Pedroia,Dustin	4		Rodney,Fernando	P		Qualls,Chad	P
	Dellucci,David	79		Valentin,Jose	4		Vargas,Claudio	P		Vizcaino,Luis	P
	Duke,Zach	P		Lind,Adam	0		Hirsh,Jason	P		Mench,Kevin	97
	Willis,Dontrelle	P		Hart,Corey	97		Maine,John	P		Heilman,Aaron	P
	Zito,Barry	P		Weaver,Jeff	P		Biggio,Craig	4		DaVanon,Jeff	8
	Lilly,Ted	P		Granderson,Curtis	8		Catalanotto,Frank	70		Martinez,Pedro	P
	Estrada,Johnny	2		Sanchez,Anibal	P		Bautista,Jose	859		Cook,Aaron	P
18	Jones,Todd	P	22	Gathright,Joey	8	26	Capps,Matt	P	30	Rauch,Jon	P
	Betancourt,Yuniesky	6		Loretta,Mark	4		Lowry,Noah	P		Lohse,Kyle	P
	Ellis,Mark	4		Meche,Gil	P		Michaels,Jason	7		Tankersley,Taylor	P
	Nady,Xavier	93		Glavine,Tom	P		Bell,David	5		Bard,Josh	2
	Capuano,Chris	P		Church,Ryan	8		Hatteberg,Scott	3		Cabrera,Fernando	P
	Blalock,Hank	50		Johnson,Reed	79		Lofton,Kenny	8		Mulder,Mark	P
	Loney,James	3		Soriano,Rafael	P		Paulino,Ronny	2		Wood,Kerry	P
	Drew,Stephen	6		Brown,Emil	79		Marcum,Shaun	P		Sullivan,Cory	8
	Green,Shawn	9		Eckstein,David	6		Olivo,Miguel	2		Kuo,Hong-Chih	P
	Jenkins,Geoff	9		Washburn,Jarrod	P		Perez,Odalis	P		Neshek,Patrick	P
	Cabrera,Daniel	P		DeRosa,Mark	954		Carrasco,Hector	P		Wright,Jaret	P
	Jackson,Conor	3		Thames,Marcus	70		Victorino,Shane	879		Burgos,Ambiorix	P
	Gagne,Eric	P		Chavez,Endy	978		Baek,Cha Seung	P		Schneider,Brian	2
	Wigginton,Ty	345		Hensley,Clay	P		Shelton,Chris	3		Napoli,Mike	2
	Duncan,Chris	79		Piazza,Mike	2		Benson,Kris	P		Buck,John	2
19	Gomes,Jonny	0	23	Wilson,Jack	6	27	Greinke,Zack	P			
	Hermida,Jeremy	9		Kotsay,Mark	8		Nolasco,Ricky	P			
	Aurilia,Rich	536		Graffanino,Tony	45		Blake,Casey	9			
	Eaton,Adam	P		Prior,Mark	P		Wolf,Randy	P			
	Crosby,Bobby	6		Wilson,Preston	79		Cintron,Alex	64			
	Maddux,Greg	P		Suppan,Jeff	P		Foulke,Keith	P			
	Tulowitzki,Troy	6		Ross,David	2		Hudson,Luke	P			
	Loewen,Adam	P		Morris,Matt	P		Hardy,J.J.	6			
	Shields,Scot	P		Branyan,Russ	95		Farnsworth,Kyle	P			
	Youkilis,Kevin	3		Helms,Wes	35		Koskie,Corey	5			
	Broussard,Ben	30		Floyd,Cliff	7		Zaun,Gregg	2			
	Bradley,Milton	9		Loaiza,Esteban	P		Valentin,Javier	2			
	Patterson,John	P		Billingsley,Chad	P		Millar,Kevin	30			
	Scott,Luke	7		Lamb,Mike	35		Gorzelanny,Tom	P			
	Kendall,Jason	2		Hernandez,Orlando	P		Gonzalez,Alex	6			
20	Davis,Doug	P	24	Lieberthal,Mike	2	28	Bonser,Boof	P			
	Garza,Matt	P		Zumaya,Joel	P		Hammel,Jason	P			
	Hill,Aaron	46		Izturis,Maicer	5		Orvella,Chad	P			
	Lieber,Jon	P		Howell,J.P.	P		Maholm,Paul	P			
	Sweeney,Mike	0		Villanueva,Carlos	P		Nixon,Trot	9			
	Wilkerson,Brad	7		Kubel,Jason	70		Wheeler,Dan	P			
	Kennedy,Adam	4		Wakefield,Tim	P		Punto,Nick	56			
	Milledge,Lastings	79		Baker,Jeff	9		Cruz,Nelson	9			
	Buehrle,Mark	P		Everett,Adam	6		Gross,Gabe	87			
	Francis,Jeff	P		Wuertz,Mike	P		Colon,Bartolo	P			
	Garko,Ryan	3		Chacin,Gustavo	P		Guillen,Jose	9			
	Howry,Bob	P		Sowers,Jeremy	P		Cabrera,Melky	7			
	Baker,Scott	P		Gonzalez,Luis	7		Sanders,Reggie	9			
	Pena,Wily Mo	98		Hudson,Tim	P		Williams,Woody	P			
	James,Chuck	P		Linebrink,Scott	P		Calero,Kiko	P			

SIMULATION LEAGUE DRAFT — TOP 500

Name	POS	RAR	Name	POS	RAR	Name	POS	RAR	Name	POS	RAR
Webb,Brandon	P	50.7	Roberts,Brian	4	23.3	Martin,Russell	2	15.7	Crain,Jesse	P	11.1
Ramirez,Manny	7	50.2	Jones,Chipper	5	23.2	Pedroia,Dustin	4	15.4	Qualls,Chad	P	11.1
Pujols,Albert	3	48.0	Giles,Brian	9	23.2	Reyes,Jose	6	15.3	Patterson,John	P	11.1
Hernandez,Felix	P	47.6	Snell,Ian	P	23.2	Jenks,Bobby	P	15.2	Davis,Doug	P	11.0
Howard,Ryan	3	46.9	Helton,Todd	3	23.0	Rodriguez,Francisco	P	15.2	Zaun,Gregg	2	11.0
Santana,Johan	P	45.6	Bush,David	P	22.8	Swisher,Nick	37	15.1	Lugo,Julio	64	11.0
Ortiz,David	0	44.2	Konerko,Paul	3	22.8	Ramirez,Hanley	6	15.0	Rodney,Fernando	P	10.9
Halladay,Roy	P	44.1	Morneau,Justin	3	22.7	Nathan,Joe	P	14.9	Sowers,Jeremy	P	10.8
Hafner,Travis	0	44.0	Ramirez,Aramis	5	22.7	Prior,Mark	P	14.8	Loaiza,Esteban	P	10.8
Beltran,Carlos	8	42.3	Jeter,Derek	6	22.7	Castillo,Luis	4	14.8	Wainwright,Adam	P	10.8
Carpenter,Chris	P	38.9	Shields,Jamie	P	22.7	Meredith,Cla	P	14.6	Church,Ryan	8	10.8
Rodriguez,Alex	5	38.8	Sexson,Richie	3	22.6	Cook,Aaron	P	14.6	Nolasco,Ricky	P	10.8
Jones,Andruw	8	37.6	Millwood,Kevin	P	22.5	Griffey Jr.,Ken	8	14.5	Duchscherer,Justin	P	10.7
Cabrera,Miguel	5	36.9	Lee,Derrek	3	22.4	Matthews Jr.,Gary	8	14.4	Johnson,Josh	P	10.7
Teixeira,Mark	3	36.3	Tejada,Miguel	6	22.3	Valverde,Jose	P	14.3	Weaver,Jeff	P	10.7
Burnett,A.J.	P	36.1	Kent,Jeff	4	22.2	Ross,David	2	14.3	Otsuka,Akinori	P	10.7
Lowe,Derek	P	35.8	Zambrano,Carlos	P	22.2	Gordon,Alex	5	14.3	Gonzalez,Mike	P	10.7
Sizemore,Grady	8	34.8	Harden,Rich	P	22.1	Wuertz,Mike	P	14.1	Bradford,Chad	P	10.6
Mauer,Joe	2	34.0	Harang,Aaron	P	21.8	Perez,Odalis	P	14.1	MacDougal,Mike	P	10.6
Bonderman,Jeremy	P	33.2	Posada,Jorge	2	21.5	Buehrle,Mark	P	14.0	Garland,Jon	P	10.6
Berkman,Lance	39	33.1	Young,Michael	6	21.3	Schmidt,Jason	P	14.0	Fossum,Casey	P	10.5
Abreu,Bobby	9	33.1	Hudson,Tim	P	21.3	Hernandez,Ramon	2	14.0	Miller,Matt	P	10.3
Sheets,Ben	P	32.8	Putz,J.J.	P	21.2	Huff,Aubrey	59	13.9	Tavarez,Julian	P	10.2
Oswalt,Roy	P	32.0	Damon,Johnny	8	20.9	Cantu,Jorge	4	13.8	Iguchi,Tadahito	4	10.2
Thome,Jim	0	31.6	Burrell,Pat	7	20.6	Reyes,Dennys	P	13.8	Villanueva,Carlos	P	10.2
McCann,Brian	2	31.2	Wells,Vernon	8	20.5	Soriano,Alfonso	7	13.7	Martinez,Pedro	P	10.2
Myers,Brett	P	31.2	Papelbon,Jon	P	20.4	Branyan,Russ	95	13.7	Zumaya,Joel	P	10.1
Vazquez,Javier	P	30.5	Olsen,Scott	P	20.0	Markakis,Nick	97	13.4	Carrasco,Hector	P	10.0
Hamels,Cole	P	30.5	Robertson,Nate	P	20.0	Garza,Matt	P	13.4	Hernandez,Orlando	P	10.0
Peavy,Jake	P	30.0	Cameron,Mike	8	19.8	Capuano,Chris	P	13.3	Cordero,Francisco	P	9.8
Pettitte,Andy	P	29.9	Iannetta,Chris	2	19.7	Hammel,Jason	P	13.2	Billingsley,Chad	P	9.8
Bay,Jason	7	29.8	Padilla,Vicente	P	19.6	Willingham,Josh	7	13.1	DeJesus,David	78	9.7
Atkins,Garrett	5	29.5	Matsuzaka,Daisuke	P	19.5	Rivera,Mariano	P	13.1	Lilly,Ted	P	9.7
Bonds,Barry	7	29.3	Howell,J.P.	P	19.5	Hudson,Orlando	4	13.1	Carmona,Fausto	P	9.6
Haren,Danny	P	28.9	Arroyo,Bronson	P	19.3	Maholm,Paul	P	13.1	Blanton,Joe	P	9.6
Ensberg,Morgan	5	28.7	Durham,Ray	4	19.2	Giles,Marcus	4	13.0	Monroe,Craig	70	9.6
Martinez,Victor	23	28.3	Lee,Carlos	7	19.2	McCarthy,Brandon	P	13.0	Francis,Jeff	P	9.5
Barrett,Michael	2	28.3	Hawpe,Brad	9	19.1	Mitre,Sergio	P	12.9	Gorzelanny,Tom	P	9.4
Guillen,Carlos	6	28.0	Maddux,Greg	P	18.9	Alou,Moises	9	12.9	Farnsworth,Kyle	P	9.4
Westbrook,Jake	P	27.7	League,Brandon	P	18.5	Thomas,Frank	0	12.9	Lopez,Rodrigo	P	9.4
Sabathia,C.C.	P	27.4	Loewen,Adam	P	18.4	Street,Huston	P	12.9	Weaver,Jered	P	9.4
Edmonds,Jim	8	27.0	Johnson,Randy	P	18.1	Piazza,Mike	2	12.9	Colon,Bartolo	P	9.3
Utley,Chase	4	27.0	Garcia,Freddy	P	18.1	Willis,Dontrelle	P	12.8	Jenkins,Geoff	9	9.3
Kazmir,Scott	P	26.8	Lieber,Jon	P	17.9	Wilkerson,Brad	7	12.8	Meche,Gil	P	9.3
Rollins,Jimmy	6	26.8	Hill,Rich	P	17.9	Hunter,Torii	8	12.7	Lawrence,Brian	P	9.2
Wang,Chien-Ming	P	26.7	Verlander,Justin	P	17.7	Kuo,Hong-Chih	P	12.6	Greinke,Zack	P	9.2
Furcal,Rafael	6	26.5	Contreras,Jose	P	17.7	Broxton,Jonathan	P	12.5	Camp,Shawn	P	9.2
Holliday,Matt	7	26.2	Clemens,Roger	P	17.4	Cain,Matt	P	12.3	Zimmerman,Ryan	5	9.2
Smoltz,John	P	25.9	Hensley,Clay	P	17.2	Morris,Matt	P	12.3	Calero,Kiko	P	9.1
Escobar,Kelvim	P	25.9	Penny,Brad	P	17.2	Lowell,Mike	5	12.3	Ellis,Mark	4	9.0
Guerrero,Vladimir	90	25.7	Rolen,Scott	5	17.2	Gagne,Eric	P	12.2	Bray,Bill	P	9.0
Mussina,Mike	P	25.6	Shields,Scot	P	17.1	Quentin,Carlos	9	12.2	Mastny,Tom	P	8.9
Dunn,Adam	7	25.4	Chavez,Eric	5	16.9	Kearns,Austin	9	12.2	Rheinecker,John	P	8.9
Hall,Bill	6	25.4	Varitek,Jason	2	16.9	LaRoche,Adam	3	11.9	Loe,Kameron	P	8.9
Drew,J.D.	9	25.2	Johnson,Nick	3	16.9	Crisp,Coco	8	11.8	Bard,Josh	2	8.8
Bedard,Erik	P	25.1	Duke,Zach	P	16.8	Gordon,Tom	P	11.7	Santana,Ervin	P	8.8
Glaus,Troy	5	24.9	Wagner,Billy	P	16.7	Rincon,Juan	P	11.7	Baldelli,Rocco	8	8.8
Matsui,Hideki	7	24.5	Overbay,Lyle	3	16.7	Littleton,Wes	P	11.7	LoDuca,Paul	2	8.7
Schilling,Curt	P	24.5	Ryan,B.J.	P	16.6	Drew,Stephen	6	11.7	Greene,Khalil	6	8.7
Delgado,Carlos	3	24.4	Lidge,Brad	P	16.5	Sheffield,Gary	9	11.7	Francisco,Frank	P	8.6
Cano,Robinson	4	24.2	Reyes,Anthony	P	16.5	Mulder,Mark	P	11.6	Fuentes,Brian	P	8.6
Lackey,John	P	24.1	Kinsler,Ian	4	16.3	Thames,Marcus	70	11.6	Duncan,Chris	79	8.6
Beckett,Josh	P	24.1	Cabrera,Daniel	P	16.0	Gross,Gabe	87	11.5	Devine,Joey	P	8.4
Teahen,Mark	5	23.8	Renteria,Edgar	6	16.0	Eaton,Adam	P	11.4	Penn,Hayden	P	8.1
Dye,Jermaine	9	23.5	Young,Chris	8	15.8	Dellucci,David	79	11.3	Wells,Kip	P	8.1
Wright,David	5	23.4	Giambi,Jason	03	15.8	Soriano,Rafael	P	11.1	Downs,Scott	P	8.1

SIMULATION LEAGUE DRAFT — TOP 500

NAME	POS	RAR
Hermida,Jeremy	9	8.1
Glavine,Tom	P	8.0
Marcum,Shaun	P	8.0
Granderson,Curtis	8	7.9
Rodriguez,Ivan	2	7.9
Wickman,Bob	P	7.9
Gregg,Kevin	P	7.9
Sanchez,Anibal	P	7.9
Torres,Salomon	P	7.8
Howry,Bob	P	7.8
Bonser,Boof	P	7.8
Frasor,Jason	P	7.8
Scott,Luke	7	7.8
Pelfrey,Mike	P	7.8
Saunders,Joe	P	7.7
Freel,Ryan	89	7.7
Rivera,Juan	798	7.7
Baker,Scott	P	7.7
Silva,Carlos	P	7.6
Pavano,Carl	P	7.6
Cabrera,Fernando	P	7.6
Crawford,Carl	7	7.5
Heilman,Aaron	P	7.5
Johjima,Kenji	2	7.5
Lopez,Felipe	6	7.5
Rios,Alexis	9	7.4
German,Esteban	4057	7.4
Tulowitzki,Troy	6	7.4
Hudson,Luke	P	7.4
German,Esteban	4057	7.4
Neshek,Patrick	P	7.3
Wheeler,Dan	P	7.3
Lohse,Kyle	P	7.3
Molina,Ben	2	7.3
Linebrink,Scott	P	7.2
Madson,Ryan	P	7.2
Vizcaino,Luis	P	7.2
Saito,Takashi	P	7.1
Betancourt,Rafael	P	7.0
Valentin,Javier	2	6.9
Wilson,C.J.	P	6.9
Marte,Andy	5	6.9
Feliciano,Pedro	P	6.9
Vargas,Claudio	P	6.8
Albers,Matt	P	6.8
Wagner,Ryan	P	6.8
Cuddyer,Michael	9	6.8
Grabow,John	P	6.7
Feldman,Scott	P	6.7
Encarnacion,Edwin	5	6.7
Suppan,Jeff	P	6.7
Kim,Byung-Hyun	P	6.6
Walker,Todd	435	6.6
Braun,Ryan	P	6.6
Casilla,Santiago	P	6.6
Cordero,Chad	P	6.6
Donnelly,Brendan	P	6.5
Estrada,Johnny	2	6.5
Lieberthal,Mike	2	6.5
Corpas,Manuel	P	6.4
Accardo,Jeremy	P	6.4
DaVanon,Jeff	8	6.4
Valentin,Jose	4	6.4
Coffey,Todd	P	6.3
Aquino,Greg	P	6.3
Baek,Cha Seung	P	6.2
Dempster,Ryan	P	6.2
Batista,Miguel	P	6.2
Ibanez,Raul	7	6.1
Helms,Wes	35	6.1
Eyre,Scott	P	6.1
Young,Chris	P	6.1
Ruiz,Carlos	2	6.1
Youkilis,Kevin	3	6.0
Peralta,Joel	P	6.0
Bailey,Homer	P	6.0
Nippert,Dustin	P	6.0
Benoit,Joaquin	P	6.0
Vidro,Jose	4	5.9
Julio,Jorge	P	5.9
Byrd,Paul	P	5.9
Polanco,Placido	4	5.9
Sanchez,Duaner	P	5.9
Lowe,Mark	P	5.8
Orvella,Chad	P	5.8
Hill,Aaron	46	5.7
Graffanino,Tony	45	5.7
Speier,Justin	P	5.6
Catalanotto,Frank	70	5.6
Laird,Gerald	2	5.6
Crede,Joe	5	5.5
Burgos,Ambiorix	P	5.5
Hansen,Craig	P	5.4
Napoli,Mike	2	5.4
Loretta,Mark	4	5.4
Snyder,Kyle	P	5.4
Cruz,Juan	P	5.4
McGowan,Dustin	P	5.4
Peralta,Jhonny	6	5.4
Johnson,Jason	P	5.4
Jones,Todd	P	5.3
Williams,Todd	P	5.3
Thompson,Brad	P	5.3
Wood,Kerry	P	5.3
Rauch,Jon	P	5.2
Traber,Billy	P	5.2
Davis,Jason	P	5.2
Ohman,Will	P	5.1
Lee,Cliff	P	5.1
Ramirez,Elizardo	P	5.1
Gobble,Jimmy	P	5.1
Embree,Alan	P	5.1
Hoffman,Trevor	P	5.1
Turnbow,Derrick	P	5.1
Wigginton,Ty	345	5.1
Looper,Braden	P	5.0
Guzman,Angel	P	5.0
Thornton,Matt	P	5.0
Capps,Matt	P	5.0
Cotts,Neal	P	5.0
Grudzielanek,Mark	4	4.9
Sherrill,George	P	4.9
Miner,Zach	P	4.9
Williamson,Scott	P	4.8
Dotel,Octavio	P	4.8
Murton,Matt	7	4.7
Ayala,Luis	P	4.7
Walker,Jamie	P	4.7
Towers,Josh	P	4.7
Wood,Mike	P	4.7
Koskie,Corey	5	4.6
Mahay,Ron	P	4.6
Thomson,John	P	4.6
Borowski,Joe	P	4.5
Nelson,Joe	P	4.4
Betemit,Wilson	5	4.4
Miller,Trever	P	4.4
Geary,Geoff	P	4.3
LaRue,Jason	2	4.2
White,Rick	P	4.1
Delcarmen,Manny	P	4.1
Belliard,Ron	4	4.1
Vizquel,Omar	6	4.1
Iwamura,Akinori	5	4.1
Bruney,Brian	P	4.1
Dessens,Elmer	P	4.1
Tankersley,Taylor	P	4.1
Chulk,Vinnie	P	4.1
Tomko,Brett	P	4.1
Rogers,Kenny	P	4.0
Reitsma,Chris	P	3.9
Kolb,Danny	P	3.9
Benson,Kris	P	3.9
Pineiro,Joel	P	3.8
Lester,Jon	P	3.8
Marte,Damaso	P	3.8
Jones,Jacque	9	3.8
Medders,Brandon	P	3.8
Buchholz,Taylor	P	3.8
Majewski,Gary	P	3.7
Jennings,Jason	P	3.6
Wells,David	P	3.6
Kennedy,Joe	P	3.6
McPherson,Dallas	5	3.5
Perez,Oliver	P	3.5
Park,Chan Ho	P	3.4
Lopez,Javier	P	3.4
Windsor,Jason	P	3.2
Snyder,Chris	2	3.2
Wise,Matt	P	3.2
Guerrier,Matt	P	3.2
Lofton,Kenny	8	3.2
Wolf,Randy	P	3.2
Lane,Jason	9	3.2
Wakefield,Tim	P	3.2
Bradley,Milton	9	3.1
Gonzalez,Edgar	P	3.1
Hendrickson,Mark	P	3.1
Santos,Victor	P	3.1
Britton,Chris	P	3.1
Schoeneweis,Scott	P	3.1
Gonzalez,Enrique	P	3.0
Petit,Yusmeiro	P	3.0
James,Chuck	P	3.0
Kielty,Bobby	79	3.0
Bergmann,Jason	P	3.0
Ray,Chris	P	3.0
Jackson,Edwin	P	2.9
Byrnes,Eric	8	2.9
Hughes,Phil	P	2.9
Hardy,J.J.	6	2.9
Proctor,Scott	P	2.9
Maine,John	P	2.9
Beltre,Adrian	5	2.8
Gonzalez,Luis	7	2.8
Yates,Tyler	P	2.8
Kotsay,Mark	8	2.8
Anderson,Marlon	47	2.8
Belisle,Matt	P	2.7
Spilborghs,Ryan	8	2.7
Foulke,Keith	P	2.7
Brown,Andrew	P	2.6
Myers,Mike	P	2.6
Correia,Kevin	P	2.6
Hernandez,Robert	P	2.6
Timlin,Mike	P	2.6
Mateo,Juan	P	2.5
Escobar,Alex	8	2.5
Martin,Tom	P	2.5
Bautista,Denny	P	2.5
Brazoban,Yhency	P	2.5
Lyon,Brandon	P	2.5
Ramirez,Horacio	P	2.4
Flores,Randy	P	2.4
Chen,Bruce	P	2.4
Fultz,Aaron	P	2.3
Shouse,Brian	P	2.3
Janssen,Casey	P	2.2
Uribe,Juan	6	2.2
Maroth,Mike	P	2.2
Seanez,Rudy	P	2.2
Izturis,Maicer	5	2.2
Hawkins,LaTroy	P	2.2
Saenz,Olmedo	3	2.1
Washburn,Jarrod	P	2.1
Ramirez,Ramon	P	2.1
Baez,Danys	P	2.1
Rodriguez,Wandy	P	2.1
Villarreal,Oscar	P	2.1
Scutaro,Marco	64	2.1
De La Rosa,Jorge	P	2.1
Pierzynski,A.J.	2	2.1
Miller,Damian	2	2.1
Gonzalez,Adrian	3	2.0
Lopez,Jose	4	2.0
Kemp,Matt	8	2.0
Johnson,Tyler	P	2.0
Hampton,Mike	P	2.0
Meadows,Brian	P	2.0
Harville,Chad	P	1.9
Romero,J.C.	P	1.9
Crosby,Bobby	6	1.9
McBride,Macay	P	1.9
Theriot,Ryan	4	1.9
Dohmann,Scott	P	1.8
Bauer,Rick	P	1.8
Aurilia,Rich	536	1.8
Weathers,David	P	1.8
Reed,Jeremy	8	1.8
Novoa,Roberto	P	1.8
Worrell,Tim	P	1.8
Wright,Jamey	P	1.8
Ordonez,Magglio	9	1.8
Cormier,Rheal	P	1.7
Wright,Jaret	P	1.7
Rhodes,Arthur	P	1.6
Thompson,Mike	P	1.6
Hart,Corey	97	1.6
Kline,Steve	P	1.6
Closser,J.D.	2	1.6
Green,Shawn	9	1.6
Miller,Wade	P	1.5
Weeks,Rickie	4	1.5
Paronto,Chad	P	1.5

VII. SABERMETRIC TOOLS

One Glossary
Abbreviations and Beginner Concepts

Avg: Batting Average (see also BA)

BA: Batting Average (see also Avg)

BABIP: Batting Average on Balls-in-Play (see Hit rate)

Base Performance Indicator (BPI): A statistical formula that measures an isolated aspect of a player's situation-independent raw skill or a gauge that helps capture the effects that random chance has on skill. Although there are many such formulas, there are only a few that we are referring to when the term is used in this book. For batters, the skills BPIs are linear weighted power index (PX), speed score index (SX), walk rate (bb%), contact rate (ct%), batting eye (Eye), ground ball/line drive/fly ball ratios (G/L/F) and expected batting average (xBA). Random chance is measured with hit rate on balls in play (H%). For pitchers, our BPIs are control (bb/9), dominance (k/9), command (k/bb), opposition on base avg (OOB), ground/line/fly ratios (G/L/F) and expected ERA (xERA). Random chance is measured with hit rate (H%) and strand rate (S%).

Batting Average (BA, or Avg): A grand old nugget that has long outgrown its usefulness. We revere .300 hitting superstars and scoff at .250 hitters, yet the difference between the two is 1 hit every 20 ABs. This 1 hit every five games is not nearly the wide variance that exists in our perceptions of what it means to be a .300 or .250 hitter. BA is a poor evaluator of baseball performance in that it neglects the offensive value of the base on balls and assumes that all hits are created equal.

bb%: Walk rate (hitters)

bb/9: Opposition Walks per 9 IP

BF/Gm: Batters Faced Per Game

BIP: Balls-in-play

BPI: Base Performance Indicator

BPV: Base Performance Value

BPX: Base Performance Index

Ceiling: The highest professional level at which a player maintains acceptable BPIs. Also, the peak performance level that a player will likely reach, given his BPIs.

Cmd: Command ratio

Ct%: Contact rate

Ctl: Control Rate

DIS%: PQS Disaster Rate

Dom: Dominance Rate

DOM%: PQS Domination Rate

Eye: Batting Eye

Fanalytics: The serious, scientific approach to fantasy baseball analysis. A contraction of "fantasy" and "analytics," fanalytic gaming might be considered a mode of play that requires a more strategic and quantitative approach to player analysis and game decisions.

FB%: Fly ball per cent

G/L/F: Ground Balls, Line Drives, and Fly Balls as percentages of total balls in play (hits *and* outs)

GB%: Ground ball per cent

Gopheritis (also, Acute Gopheritis and Chronic Gopheritis): The dreaded malady in which a pitcher is unable to keep the ball in the ballpark. Pitchers with gopheritis have a fly ball rate of at least 40%. More severe cases have a FB% over 45%.

H%: Hit rate (batters) or Hits Allowed per Balls in Play (pitchers)

hr/9: Opposition Home Runs per 9 IP

IP/G: Innings Pitched per Game Appearance

k/9: Dominance rate (opposition strikeouts per 9 IP)

LD%: Line drive per cent

Leading Indicator: A statistical formula that can be used to project likely future performance.

LW: Linear Weights

LWPwr: Linear Weighted Power

Major League Equivalency *(Bill James):* A formula that converts a player's minor or foreign league statistics into a comparable performance in the major leagues. These are not projections, but conversions of current performance. Contains adjustments for the level of play in individual leagues and teams, and the player's age as compared to that level. Works best with Triple-A stats, not quite as well with Double-A stats, and hardly at all with the lower levels. Foreign conversions are still a work in process. James' formula only addressed batting. Our research has devised conversion formulas for pitchers, however, their best use comes when looking at BPI's, not traditional stats.

Mendoza Line: Named for Mario Mendoza, it represents the benchmark for batting futility. Usually refers to a .200 batting average, but can also be used for low levels of other statistical categories. Despite the "Mendoza Line" being used to describe a .200 hitter, Mendoza's lifetime batting average was actually a much more robust .215.

MLE: Major League Equivalency

Noise: Irrelevant or meaningless pieces of information that can distort the results of an analysis. In news, this is opinion or rumor that can invalidate valuable information. In forecasting, these are unimportant elements of statistical data that can artificially inflate or depress a set of numbers.

OB: On Base Average (batters)

OBA: Opposition On Base Average (pitchers)

Opposition Strikeouts per Game: See Dominance Rate.

Opposition Walks per Game: See Control Rate.

OPS: On Base Plus Slugging Average

PQS: Pure Quality Starts

Pw: Linear Weighted Power

PX: Linear Weighted Power Index

R$: Rotisserie value

RAR: Runs Above Replacement

RC: Runs Created

RC/G: Runs Created Per Game

REff%: Relief Efficiency Per Cent

Rotisserie Value (R$ and 5x5): The dollar value placed on a player's performance in a Rotisserie league, and designed to measure the impact that player has on the standings. These values are highly variable depending upon a variety of factors:
- the salary cap limit
- the number of teams in the league
- each team's roster size
- the impact of any protected players
- each team's positional demands at the time of bidding
- the statistical category demands at the time of bidding
- external factors, e.g. media inflation or deflation of value

In other words, **a $30 player is only a $30 player if someone in your draft pays $30 for him.**

There are a variety of methods to calculate value, most involving a delineation of a least valuable performance level (given league size and structure), and then assigning a certain dollar amount for incremental improvement from that base. The method we use is a variation of the Standings Gain Points method described in the book, *How to Value Players for Rotisserie Baseball,* by Art McGee. (2nd edition coming soon!)

People play Rotisserie in any number of variations. The most popular game is the 5x5 format. Mixed league participation is soaring; here, player pool penetration falls short of the standard 75%. Does this invalidate the ratings in this book? No. Since values are driven by playing time, and our playing time forecasts are preliminary anyway, the best use for this data is to get a *general sense of value* no matter how you play the game.

In fact, since we currently have no idea who is going to play 1B for the Devil Rays, or whether Troy Tulowitzki is going to break camp with Colorado, all the projected values are slightly inflated. They are roughly based on a 12-team AL and 13-team NL league. We've attempted to take some contingencies into account, but the values will not total to anywhere near $3120, so don't bother adding them up and save your irate e-mails.

A $25 player in this book might actually be worth $21. Or $28. This level of precision is irrelevant in a process that is going to be driven by market forces anyway. *So, don't obsess over it.*

I wonder how other writers publish perfect Rotisserie values over the winter. Do they make arbitrary decisions as to where free agents are going to sign and who is going to land jobs in the spring? I'm not about to make those massive leaps of faith. Bottom line... Some things you can predict, to other things you have to react. As roles become more defined over the winter, our online updates will provide better approximations of playing time, and projected Roto values that add up to $3120.

S%: Strand Rate

Save: There are six events that need to occur in order for a pitcher to post a single save...
1. The starting pitcher and middle relievers must pitch well.
2. The offense must score enough runs.
3. It must be a reasonably close game.
4. The manager must choose to put the pitcher in for a save opportunity.
5. The pitcher must pitch well and hold the lead.
6. The manager must let him finish the game.

Of these six events, only one is within the control of the relief pitcher. As such, projecting saves for a reliever has little to do with skill and a lot to do with opportunity. However, pitchers with excellent skills sets may create opportunity for themselves.

SBO: Stolen Base Opportunity Per Cent

Situation Independent: Describing a statistical gauge that measures performance apart from the context of team, ballpark, or other outside variables. Home runs, inasmuch as they are unaffected by the performance of a batter's team, are often considered a situation independent stat (they are, however, affected by park dimensions). Strikeouts and Walks are better examples.

Conversely, RBI's are situation dependent because individual performance varies greatly by the performance of other batters on the team (you can't drive in runs if there is nobody on base). Similarly, pitching wins are as much a measure of the success of a pitcher as they are a measure of the success of the offense and defense performing behind that pitcher, and are therefore a poor measure of pitching performance alone.

Situation independent gauges are important for us to be able to separate a player's contribution to his team and isolate his performance so that we may judge it on its own merits.

Slg: Slugging Average

Soft stats (also, Soft Skills): Batting eyes less than 0.50. Command ratios under 2.0. Strikeout rates below 5.0. Etc.

Soft-tosser: Pitcher with a strikeout rate of 5.0 or less.

Spd: Speed Score

Strikeouts per Game: See Opposition Strikeouts per game.

Surface Stats: Traditional statistical gauges that the mainstream uses to measure performance. Stats like batting average, wins, and ERA only touch the surface of a player's skill. Component skills analysis digs beneath the surface to reveal true skill.

Sv%: Saves Conversion Rate

SX: Speed Score Index

Vulture: A pitcher, typically a middle reliever, who accumulates an unusually high number of wins by preying on other pitchers' misfortunes. More accurately, this is a pitcher typically brought into a game after a starting pitcher has put his team behind, and then pitches well enough and long enough to allow his offense to take the lead, thereby "vulturing" a win from the starter.

Walks per Game: See Opposition Walks per Game.

Wasted talent: A player with a high level skill that is negated by a deficiency in another skill. For instance, basepath speed can be negated by poor on base ability. Pitchers with strong arms can be wasted because home plate is an elusive concept to them.

WHIP: Walks + Hits per Innings Pitched

Wins: There are five events that need to occur in order for a pitcher to post a single win...
1. He must pitch well, allowing few runs.
2. The offense must score enough runs.
3. The defense must successfully field all batted balls.
4. The bullpen must hold the lead.
5. The manager must leave the pitcher in for 5 innings, and not remove him if the team is still behind.

Of these five events, only one is within the control of the pitcher. As such, projecting wins can be an exercise in futility.

xBA: Expected Batting Average

xERA: Expected ERA

xHR: Expected Home Runs

The Other Glossary
Sabermetrics, Fanalytics and Advanced Concepts

Balls-in-play (BIP)

BATTERS: *(AB – K)*

PITCHERS: *((IP x 2.82)) + H – K*

The total number of batted balls that are hit fair, both hits and outs. An analysis of how these balls are hit – on the ground, in the air, hits, outs, etc. – can provide analytical insight, from player skill levels to the impact of luck on statistical output.

Base Performance Value (BPV): A single value that describes a player's overall raw skill level. This is more useful than any traditional statistical gauge to track player performance trends and project future statistical output. The actual BPV formula combines and weights several BPIs.

Batting BPV: (Batting Eye x 20) + ((Batting Average - .300) / .003) + (Linear Weighted Power Index x 0.43)

This formula combines the individual raw skills of batting eye, the ability to hit safely, and the ability to hit with power. **BENCHMARKS:** The best hitters will have a BPV of 50 or greater. (Note: Batting BPV does not appear in this edition of the *Forecaster* but does in the free projections update.)

Pitching BPV: (Dominance Rate x 6) + (Command Ratio x 21) - (Expected Opp. HR Rate x 30) - ((Opp. Batting Average - .275) x 200)

This formula combines the individual raw skills of power, command, the ability to keep batters from reaching base, and the ability to prevent long hits, all characteristics that are unaffected by most external team factors. In tandem with a pitcher's strand rate, it provides a complete picture of the elements that contribute to a pitcher's ERA, and therefore serves as an accurate tool to project likely changes in ERA. **BENCHMARKS:** We consider a BPV of 50 to be the minimum level required for long-term success. The elite of the bullpen aces will have BPV's in excess of 100 and it is rare for these stoppers to enjoy long term success with consistent levels under 75.

Batters Faced per Game *(Craig Wright)*

((IP x 2.82) + H + BB) / G

A measure of pitcher usage and one of the leading indicators for potential pitcher burnout. (See Usage Warning Flags in the Forecaster's Toolbox.)

Batting Eye (Eye)

(Walks / Strikeouts)

A measure of a player's strike zone judgment, the raw ability to distinguish between balls and strikes. **BENCHMARKS:** The best hitters have eye ratios over 1.00 (indicating more walks than strikeouts) and are the most likely to be among a league's .300 hitters. Ratios less than 0.50 represent batters who likely also have lower BA's. (See Forecaster's Toolbox for more.)

Command Ratio (Cmd)

(Strikeouts / Walks)

This is a measure of a pitcher's raw ability to get the ball over the plate. There is no more fundamental a skill than this, and so it is used as a leading indicator to project future rises and falls in other gauges, such as ERA. Command is one of the best gauges to use to evaluate minor league performance. **BENCHMARKS:** Baseball's best pitchers will have ratios in excess of 3.0. Pitchers with ratios under 1.0 — indicating that they walk more batters than they strike out — have virtually no potential for long term success. If you make no other changes in your approach to drafting a pitching staff, limiting your focus to only pitchers with a command ratio of 2.0 or better will substantially improve your odds of success. (See the Forecaster's Toolbox for more command ratio research.)

Contact Rate (ct%)

((AB - K) / AB)

Measures a batter's ability to get wood on the ball and hit it into the field of play. **BENCHMARKS:** Those batters with the best contact skill will have levels of 90% or better. The hackers of society will have levels of 75% or less.

Control Rate (bb/9), or Opposition Walks per Game

BB Allowed x 9 / IP

Measures how many walks a pitcher allows per game equivalent. **BENCHMARK:** The best pitchers will have bb/9 levels of 3.0 or less.

Dominance Rate (k/9), or Opposition Strikeouts per Game

(K Allowed x 9 / IP)

Measures how many strikeouts a pitcher allows per game equivalent. **BENCHMARK:** The best pitchers will have k/9 levels of 6.0 or higher.

ERA Variance: The variance between a pitcher's ERA and his xERA, which is a measure of over or underachievement. A positive variance indicates the potential for a pitcher's ERA to rise. A negative variance indicates the potential for ERA improvement. (See Expected ERA) **BENCHMARK:** Discount variances that are under 0.50. Any variance over 1.00 (one run per game) is regarded as a clear indicator of future change.

Expected Batting Average *(John Burnson)*

xCT% * [xH1% + xH2%]

where

xH1% = GB% * [0.0004 PX + 0.062 ln(SX)]

  + LD% * [0.93 - 0.086 ln(SX)]

  + FB% * 0.12

and

xH2% = FB% * [0.0013 PX - 0.0002 SX - 0.057]

  + GB% * [0.0006 PX]

A hitter's batting average as calculated by multiplying the percentage of balls put in play (contact rate) by the chance that a ball in play falls for a hit. The likelihood that a ball in play falls for a hit is a product of the speed of the ball and distance it is hit (PX), the speed of the batter (SX), and distribution of ground balls, fly balls, and line drives. We further split it out by non-homerun hit rate (xH1%) and homerun hit rate (xH2%). **BENCHMARKS:** In general, xBA should approximate batting average fairly closely. Those hitters who have large variances between the two gauges are candidates for further analysis.

Expected Earned Run Average *(Gill and Reeve)*

(.575 x H [per 9 IP]) + (.94 x HR [per 9 IP]) + (.28 x BB [per 9 IP]) - (.01 x K [per 9 IP]) - Normalizing Factor

"xERA represents the expected ERA of the pitcher based on a normal distribution of his statistics. It is not influenced by situation-dependent factors." xERA erases the inequity between starters' and relievers' ERA's, eliminating the effect that a pitcher's success or failure has on another pitcher's ERA.

Similar to other gauges, the accuracy of this formula changes with the level of competition from one season to the next. The normalizing factor allows us to better approximate a pitcher's actual ERA. This value is usually somewhere around 2.77 and varies by league and year.

BENCHMARKS: xERA should approximate a pitcher's ERA fairly closely. Those pitchers who have large variances between the two gauges are candidates for further analysis.

Projected xERA or projected ERA? Projected xERA is more accurate for looking ahead on a purely skills basis. Projected ERA includes situation-*dependent* events — bullpen support, park factors, etc. — which are reflected better by ERA. The optimal approach is to use *both* gauges as a range of the expectation for the coming year.

Expected Earned Run Average2 *(John Burnson)*

*(xER * 9)/IP, where xER is defined as*

*xER% * { FB/10 + (1-xS%) * [(0.3*BIP) + BB] }*

where

*xER% = 0.96 - (0.0284 * (GB/FB))*

and

*xS% = (64.5 + (K/9 * 1.2) - (BB/9 * (BB/9 + 1)) / 20)*
    *+ ((0.0012 * (GB%^2)) - (0.001 * GB%) - 2.4)*

Note: xERA2 is used in the player boxes for years when G/L/F data is available. Other years use the Gill and Reeve formula.

Expected Home Runs *(John Burnson)*

*[(0.8 * xHR%) - (1.6 * (xHR%^2))] * Plate appearances*

where

*xHR% = [0.15 * (2B / (AB—K))] + [0.09 * (3B / (AB—K))]*
    *+ [0.78 * (HR / (AB—K))]*

We typically measure power skill using some combination of extra base hits. For most fantasy games, however, the goal is to project HRs. A measure of HR potential might be achieved by identifying a more optimal distribution of extra base hits; this often yields hints of latent or inflated HR output.

Expected Opposition Home Run Rate *(John Burnson)*

(FB x 0.10) x 9 / IP

Research has shown that opposition HRs regress to a rate of 10% of fly balls.

Ground Ball, Fly Ball, Line Drive Percentages (G/F/L): The percentage of all Balls-in-Play that are hit on the ground, in the air and as line drives. For batters, increased fly ball tendency may foretell a rise in power skills; increased line drive tendency may foretell an improvement in batting average. For a pitcher, the ability to keep the ball on the ground can contribute to his statistical output exceeding his demonstrated skill level.

*BIP Type	Total%	Out%
Ground ball	45%	72%
Fly ball	35%	85%
Line drive	20%	28%
TOTAL	*100%*	*69%*

* Data only includes fieldable balls and is net of home runs.

Hit Rate (H%)

(H—HR) / (AB – HR - K)

The percent of balls hit into the field of play that fall for hits. See Forecaster's Toolbox for benchmarks. Also called Batting Average on Balls-In-Play (BABIP)

Hits Allowed per Balls in Play *(Voros McCracken)*

(H—HR) / ((IP x 2.82) + H - K - HR)

See Forecaster's Toolbox for a complete discussion on this gauge. Also called Batting Average on Balls-In-Play (BABIP). **BENCHMARK:** The league average H% is 30%, which is also the level that individual pitching performances will regress to on a year to year basis. Any +/- variance of 3% or more can affect a pitcher's ERA.

Linear Weights *(Pete Palmer)*

((Singles x .46) + (Doubles x .8) + (Triples x 1.02) + (Home runs x 1.4) + (Walks x .33) + (Stolen Bases x .3) - (Caught Stealing x .6) - ((At bats - Hits) x Normalizing Factor)

(Also referred to as Batting Runs.) Formula whose premise is that all events in baseball are linear, that is, the output (runs) is directly proportional to the input (offensive events). Each of these offensive events is then weighted according to its relative value in producing runs. Positive events — hits, walks, stolen bases — have positive values. Negative events — outs, caught stealing — have negative values.

The normalizing factor, representing the value of an out, is an offset to the particular level of offense in a given year. As such it changes every season, growing larger in high offense years and smaller in low offense years. The value is usually somewhere around .26 and varies by league.

LW is no longer included in the player forecast boxes, but the LW concept is used with the linear weighted power gauge.

Linear Weighted Power (LWPwr)

((Doubles x .8) + (Triples x .8) + (HR x 1.4)) / (At bats- K) x 100

An excerpt of the linear weights formula that only considers events that are measures of a batter's pure power. **BENCHMARKS:** Baseball's top sluggers typically top the 17 mark. Weak hitters will have a LWPwr level of under 10.

Linear Weighted Power Index (PX)

(Batter's LWPwr / League LWPwr) x 100

LWPwr is presented in this book in its normalized form to get a better read on a batter's accomplishment in each year. For instance, a 30-HR season today is not nearly as much of an accomplishment as 30 HRs hit in a lower offense year like 1995. **BENCHMARKS:** A level of 100 equals league average power skills. Any player with a value over 100 has above average power skills, and those over 175 are the Slugging Elite.

On Base Average (OBA)

(H + BB) / (AB + BB)

Addressing one of the two deficiencies in BA, OB gives value to those events that get batters on base, but are not hits. (Hit batsmen are often part of this formula.). An OB of .350 can be read as "this batter gets on base 35% of the time." When a run is scored, there is no distinction made as to how that runner reached base. So, two thirds of the time — about how often a batter comes to the plate with the bases empty — a walk really is as good as a hit. **BENCHMARKS:** We all know what a .300 hitter is, but what represents "good" for OB? That comparable level would likely be .400, with .275 representing the comparable level of futility.

On Base Plus Slugging Average (OPS): A simple sum of the two gauges, it is considered as one of the better evaluators of overall performance. OPS combines the two basic elements of offensive production — the ability to get on base (OB) and the ability to advance baserunners (Slg). **BENCHMARKS**: The game's top batters will have OPS levels over .900. The worst batters will have levels under .600.

Opposition Batting Average (OBA)

(Hits Allowed / ((IP x 2.82) + Hits Allowed))

A close approximation of the batting average achieved by opposing batters against a particular pitcher.

BENCHMARKS: The converse of the benchmark for batters, the best pitchers will have levels under .250; the worst pitchers levels over .300.

Opposition Home Runs per Game (hr/9)

(HR Allowed x 9 / IP)

Measures how many home runs a pitcher allows per game equivalent. **BENCHMARK**: The best pitchers will have hr/9 levels of under 1.0.

Opposition On Base Average (OOB)

(Hits Allowed + BB) / ((IP x 2.82) + H + BB)

A close approximation of the on base average achieved by opposing batters against a particular pitcher. **BENCHMARK**: The best pitchers will have levels under .300; the worst pitchers levels over .375.

Power/Finesse Rating

(BB + K) / IP

Measures the level by which a pitcher allows balls to be put into play and helps tie a pitcher's success to his team's level of defensive ability. In general, extreme power pitchers can be successful even with poor defensive teams. Power pitchers tend to have greater longevity in the game. Finesse pitchers with poor defenses behind them are high risks to have poor W-L records and ERA. **BENCHMARKS**: A level of 1.13 or greater describes the pure throwers. A level of .93 or lower describes the high contact pitcher. Tip... if you have to draft a pitcher from a poor defensive team, going with power over finesse will usually net you more wins in the long run.

PQS Disaster Rate *(Gene McCaffrey):* The percentage of a starting pitcher's outings that rate as a PQS-0 or PQS-1. See the Pitching Logs section for more information on DIS%.

PQS Domination Rate *(Gene McCaffrey):* The percentage of a starting pitcher's outings that rate as a PQS-4 or PQS-5. See the Pitching Logs section for more information on DOM%.

Pure Quality Starts: PQS is the next step in following pitching lines. The old Quality Start method — minimum 6 IP, maximum 3 earned runs — is simplistic and does not measure any real skill. Bill James' "game score" methodology is better, but is not feasible for quick calculation.

In PQS, we give a starting pitcher credit for exhibiting certain skills in each of his starts. Then by tracking his "PQS Score" over time, we can follow his progress. A starter earns one point for each of the following criteria...

1. The pitcher must have gone a minimum of 6 innings. This measures stamina. If he goes less than 5 innings, he automatically gets a total PQS score of zero, no matter what other stats he produces.

2. He must have allowed no more than an equal number of hits to the number of IP. This measures hit prevention.

3. His number of strikeouts must be no fewer than two less than his innings pitched. This measures dominance.

4. He must have struck out at least twice as many batters as he walked. This measures command.

5. He must have allowed no more than one home run. This measures his ability to keep the ball in the park.

A perfect PQS score would be 5. Any pitcher who averages 3 or more over the course of the season is probably performing admirably. The nice thing about PQS is it allows you to approach each start as more than an all-or-nothing event.

Note the absence of earned runs. No matter how many runs a pitcher allows, if he scores high on the PQS scale, he has hurled a good game in terms of his base skills. The number of runs allowed — a function of not only the pitcher's ability but that of his bullpen and defense — will even out over time.

Reliever Efficiency Per Cent (REff%)

(Wins + Saves + Holds) / (Wins + Losses + SaveOpps + Holds)

This is a measure of how often a reliever contribute positively to the outcome of the game. A record of consistent, positive impact on game outcomes breeds managerial confidence, and that confidence could pave the way to save opportunities. For those pitchers that are suddenly thrust into a closer's role, this formula helps gauge their potential to succeed based on past successes in similar roles. **BENCHMARK:** Minimum of 80%.

Runs Above Replacement (RAR): An estimate of the number of runs a player contributes above a "replacement level" player. "Replacement" is defined as the level of performance at which another player can easily be found at little or no cost to a team. What constitutes replacement level is a topic that is hotly debated. There are a variety of formulas and rules of thumb used to determine this level for each position (replacement level for a shortstop will be very different from replacement level for an outfielder). Our estimates appear below.

One of the major values of RAR for fantasy applications is that it can be used to assemble an integrated ranking of batters and pitchers for drafting purposes.

Batters create runs; pitchers save runs. But are batters and pitchers who have comparable RAR levels truly equal in value? In fact, pitchers might be considered to have higher value. Saving an additional run is more important than producing an additional run. A pitcher who throws a shutout is guaranteed to win that game, whereas no matter how many runs a batter produces, his team can still lose given a poor pitching outing.

To calculate RAR for batters:

Start with a batter's runs created per game (RC/G).
Subtract his position's replacement level RC/G.
Multiply by number of games played: (AB - H + CS) / 25.5.
Replacement levels used in this book, for 2006:

POS	AL	NL
C	4.41	4.34
1B	5.42	6.00
2B	4.12	4.60
3B	5.01	5.49
SS	4.41	4.36
LF	5.18	5.25
CF	4.66	4.44
RF	5.66	4.77
DH	6.43	

To calculate RAR for pitchers:

Start with the replacement level league ERA.

Subtract the pitcher's ERA. (To calculate *projected* RAR, use the pitcher's XERA.)

Multiply by number of games played, calculated as plate appearances (IP x 4.34) divided by 38.

Multiply the resulting RAR level by 1.08 to account for the variance between earned runs and total runs.

RAR can also be used to calculate rough projected team won-loss records. *(Roger Miller)* Total the RAR levels for all the players on a team, divide by 10 and add to 53 wins.

Runs Created *(Bill James)*

(H + BB - CS) x (Total bases + (.55 x SB)) / (AB + BB)

A formula that converts all offensive events into a total of runs scored. As calculated for individual teams, the result approximates a club's actual run total with great accuracy.

Runs Created Per Game *(Bill James)*

Runs Created / ((AB - H + CS) / 25.5)

RC expressed on a per-game basis might be considered the hypothetical ERA compiled against a particular batter. Another way to look at it... a batter with a RC/G of 7.00 would be expected to score 7 runs per game if he were cloned nine times and faced an average pitcher in every at bat. Cloning batters is not a practice we recommend. **BENCHMARKS:** Few players surpass the level of a 10.00 RC/G in any given season, but any level over 7.50 can still be considered very good. At the bottom are levels below 3.00.

Runs Created Per Game2 *(Neil Bonner)*

(SS x 37.96) + (ct% x 10.38) + (bb% x 14.81) – 13.04

where SS, or "swing speed" is defined as

((1B x 0.5) + (2B x 0.8) + (3B x 1.1) + (HR x 1.2)) / (AB - K)

This is the version that is currently used in this book.

Saves Conversion Rate (Sv%)

Saves / Save Opportunities

The percentage of save opportunities that are successfully converted. **BENCHMARK:** We look for a minimum 80% for long-term success.

Slugging Average (Slg)

(Singles + (2 x Doubles) + (3 x Triples) + (4 x HR)) / AB

A measure of the total number of bases accumulated (or the minimum number of runners' bases advanced) per at bat. It is a misnomer; it is not a true measure of a batter's slugging ability because it includes singles. Slg also assumes that each type of hit has proportionately increasing value (i.e. a double is twice as valuable as a single, etc.) which is not true. For instance, with the bases loaded, a HR always scores four runs, a triple always scores three, but a double could score two or three and a single could score one, or two, or even three.

BENCHMARKS: The top batters will have levels over .500. The bottom batters will have levels under .300.

Speed Score *(Bill James):* A measure of the various elements that comprise a runner's speed skills. Although this formula (a variation of James' original version) may be used as a leading indicator for stolen base output, SB attempts are controlled by managerial strategy which makes Spd somewhat less valuable.

The speed scores in this book are calculated as the mean value of the following four elements...

1. Stolen base efficiency = *(((SB + 3)/(SB + CS + 7)) - .4) x 20*
2. Stolen base freq. = *Square root of ((SB + CS)/(Singles + BB)) / .07*
3. Triples rating = *(3B / (AB - HR - K))* and the result assigned a value based on the following chart:

< 0.001	0
0.001	1
0.0023	2
0.0039	3
0.0058	4
0.008	5
0.0105	6
0.013	7
0.0158	8
0.0189	9
.0223+	10

4. Runs scored as a percentage of times on base = *(((R - HR)/(H + BB - HR)) - .1) / .04*

Speed Score Index (SX)

(Batter's Spd / League Spd) x 100

Normalized speed scores are presented in this book to get a better read on a runner's accomplishment in context. A level of 100 equals league average speed skill. Values over 100 indicate above average skill, over 200 represent the Fleet of Feet Elite.

Stolen Base Opportunity Per Cent (SBO)

(SB + CS) / (BB + Singles)

A rough approximation of how often a base-runner attempts a stolen base. Provides a comparative measure for players on a given team and, as a team measure, the propensity of a manager to give a "green light" to his runners.

Strand Rate (S%)

(H + BB - ER) / (H + BB - HR)

Measures the percentage of allowed runners a pitcher strands (earned runs only), which incorporates both individual pitcher skill and bullpen effectiveness. **BENCHMARKS:** The most adept at stranding runners will have S% levels over 75%. Once a pitcher's S% starts dropping down below 65%, he's going to have problems with his ERA. Those pitchers with strand rates over 80% will have artificially low ERAs, which will be prone to relapse. (See the Forecaster's Toolbox for more strand rate research.)

Vintage Eck Territory: A pitching base performance value (BPV) level of 200 or over. Over the course of his career, Dennis Eckersely posted levels this high four times:

1989	345
1990	347
1991	226
1992	210

Walks + Hits per Innings Pitched (WHIP): Decreed as a base Rotisserie category. **BENCHMARKS:** Usually, a WHIP of under 1.20 is considered top level and over 1.50 is indicative of poor performance. Levels under 1.00 — allowing fewer runners than IP — represent extraordinary performance and are rarely maintained over time.

Walk rate (bb%)

(BB / (AB + BB))

A measure of a batter's plate patience. **BENCHMARKS:** The best batters will have levels over 10%. Those with poor plate patience will have levels of 5% or less.

2007 CHEATER'S BOOKMARK

BATTING STATISTICS / BENCHMARKS

Abbrv	Term	Formula / Descr.	BAD UNDER	'06 LG AVG AL	'06 LG AVG NL	BEST OVER
Avg	Batting Average	h/ab	250	275	265	300
xBA	Expected Batting Average	See glossary		271	266	
OB	On Base Average	(h+bb)/(ab+bb)	300	339	334	375
Slg	Slugging Average	total bases/ab	350	437	427	500
OPS	On Base plus Slugging	OB+Slg	650	776	761	875
bb%	Walk Rate	bb/(ab+bb)	5%	8%	9%	10%
ct%	Contact Rate	(ab-k) / ab	75%	82%	80%	85%
Eye	Batting Eye	bb/k	0.50	0.51	0.49	1.00
PX	Power Index	Normalized power skills	80	100	100	120
SX	Speed Index	Normalized speed skills	80	100	100	120
SBO	Stolen Base Opportunity %	(sb+cs)/(singles+bb)		8%	9%	
G/F	Groundball/Flyball Ratio	gb / fb		1.19	1.19	
G	Ground Ball Per Cent	gb / balls in play		44%	44%	
L	Line Drive Per Cent	ld / balls in play		20%	19%	
F	Fly Ball Per Cent	fb / balls in play		36%	37%	
RC/G	Runs Created per Game	See glossary	3.00	5.04	4.87	7.50
RAR	Runs Above Replacement	See glossary	-0.0			+25.0

PITCHING STATISTICS / BENCHMARKS

Abbrv	Term	Formula / Descr.	BAD OVER	'06 LG AVG AL	'06 LG AVG NL	BEST UNDER
ERA	Earned Run Average	er*9/ip	5.00	4.56	4.49	4.00
xERA	Expected ERA	See glossary		4.11	4.06	
WHIP	Baserunners per Inning	(h+bb)/ip	1.50	1.41	1.40	1.25
BF/G	Batters Faced per Game	((ip*2.82)+h+bb)/g	28.0			
PC	Pitch Counts per Start		120	92	92	
OBA	Opposition Batting Avg	Opp. h/ab	290	272	267	250
OOB	Opposition On Base Avg	Opp. (h+bb)/(ab+bb)	350	336	337	300
H%	Hits per balls in play	(h-hr)/((ip*2.82)+h-k-hr)		31%	30%	
Ctl	Control Rate	bb*9/ip		3.2	3.4	3.0
hr/9	Homerun Rate	hr*9/ip		1.1	1.1	1.0
hr/f	Homerun per Fly ball	hr/fb		11%	11%	10%
S%	Strand Rate	(h+bb-er)/(h+bb-hr)		70%	71%	
DIS%	PQS Disaster Rate	% GS that are PQS 0/1		25%	24%	20%

Abbrv	Term	Formula / Descr.	BAD UNDER	'06 LG AVG AL	'06 LG AVG NL	BEST OVER
RAR	Runs Above Replacement	See glossary	-0.0			+25.0
Dom	Dominance Rate	k*9/ip		6.4	6.7	6.5
Cmd	Command Ratio	k/bb		2.0	2.0	2.2
G/F	Groundball/Flyball Ratio	gb / fb		1.19	1.19	
BPV	Base Performance Value	See glossary	50	47	50	75
DOM%	PQS Dominance Rate	% GS that are PQS 4/5		38%	40%	50%
Sv%	Saves Conversion Rate	(saves / save opps)		68%	64%	80%
REff%	Relief Effectiveness Rate	See glossary		66%	64%	80%

NOTES

VIII. Blatant Advertisements for Our Other Products

2007 FANTASY BASEBALL WINNERS RESOURCE GUIDE

10 REASONS
why <u>winners</u> rely on
SHANDLER ENTERPRISES
for fantasy baseball information

1 **NO OTHER RESOURCE** provides you with more vital intelligence to help you win. Compare the depth of our offerings in these pages with any other information product or service.

2 **NO OTHER RESOURCE** provides more exclusive information, like cutting-edge component skills analyses, revolutionary strategies like the LIMA Plan, and innovative gaming formats like Quint-Inning. *You won't find these anywhere else on the internet, guaranteed.*

3 **NO OTHER RESOURCE** has as long and as consistent a track record of success in the top national experts competitions... Our writers have achieved 12 first place, 5 second place and 4 third place finishes since 1997. *No other resource comes remotely close.*

4 **NO OTHER RESOURCE** has as consistent a track record in projecting impact performances. In 2006, our readers had surprises like Garrett Atkins, Michael Barrett, Eric Byrnes, Endy Chavez, Jermaine Dye, Gary Matthews Jr., Dave Roberts, Jimmy Rollins, Ty Wigginton, Erik Bedard, Joe Borowski and Nate Robertson on their teams, *and dozens more.*

5 **NO OTHER RESOURCE** is supported by over 50 top writers and analysts — all paid professionals and proven winners, not weekend hobbyists or corporate staffers.

6 **NO OTHER RESOURCE** has a wider scope, providing valuable information not only for Rotisserie, but for alternative formats like simulations, salary cap contests, online games, points, head-to-head, dynasty leagues and others.

7 **NO OTHER RESOURCE** is as highly regarded by its peers in the industry. Baseball HQ is the *only* three-time winner of the Fantasy Sports Trade Association's "Best Fantasy Baseball Online Content" award and Ron Shandler was a key subject in Sam Walker's *Fantasyland*.

8 **NO OTHER RESOURCE** is as highly regarded *outside* of the fantasy industry. Many Major League general managers are regular customers and several of our writers have been advisors to the World Champion St. Louis Cardinals since the 2004 season.

9 **NO OTHER RESOURCE** has been creating fantasy baseball winners for as long as we have. Our 21 years of stability *guarantees your investment*.

10 Year after year, over 90% of our subscribers report that the products and services of Shandler Enterprises have helped them improve their performance in their fantasy leagues. <u>That's the bottom line</u>.

TO ORDER
MAIL check or money order to: Shandler Enterprises LLC, P.O. Box 20303-A, Roanoke, VA 24018
PHONE 1-800-422-7820
FAX: 540-772-1969
ONLINE secure order form: *https://secure.baseballhq.com/subscribe.html*

https://secure.baseballhq.com/subscribe.html

Baseball HQ is the one web site where fantasy leaguers go to gain an unbeatable edge. Not just news and stats, HQ provides the fantasy implications, analysis of what the future may hold, and all the tools you need to take your team to victory!

News & Analysis
- Statistical news analysis
- Injury reports
- Ron Shandler's "Fanalytics"
- Ray Murphy's "Speculator"
- Research & Analysis
- Subscriber Forums

Buyers Guides
BATTERS
- Interactive player database
- Daily projections
- Weekly surgers and faders
- Power analysis
- Speed analysis
- Batting Average analysis

PITCHERS
- Interactive player database
- Daily projections
- Weekly surgers and faders
- Starting pitcher logs
- Bullpen indicator charts

TEAMS
- Depth chart center
- Weekly rotation planner
- Ballpark factors

Minor Leagues
- Organization reports
- Full coverage of winter baseball
- Prospect rankings by position
- In-season call-ups analysis
- In-season news and analysis
- Major league equivalent statistics

Gaming Tools
- Custom fantasy draft guides
- Custom cheat sheets
- Custom Rotisserie grids
- Team stat tracker
- Mock drafts
- Strategy columns
- Personal advisory service

Fantasy league winners don't wait until March to prepare for their next title run. Baseball HQ gives you tons of vital intelligence to keep the Hot Stove burning all winter long...

- In-depth statistical and situational analysis of every off-season player move
- Sleepers, gambles and end-game draft picks to tuck away
- 2007 player projections, updated daily from March through September *(beginning December 15)*
- 2007 depth charts, bullpen indicators and more
- Strategy columns on keeper decisions, position scarcity and more
- Coverage of Rotisserie, Scoresheet and simulation games, salary cap contests, online gaming, points games, head-to-head and dynasty leagues
- Weekly mock drafts and analysis *(beginning January 2007)*
- Draft guides, cheat sheets and Rotisserie grids
- Comprehensive player database — profile and statistical trend data at a glance.
- Organizational reports on 2007's top prospects
- Scouting reports from the Arizona Fall League, Rule 5 draft and all winter leagues
- Our active subscriber forum community — 24/7/365
- Complete access to our sabermetric archives, pitcher logs, major league equivalents and more — going all the way back to 1998!
- *and much more!*

$99.00	One year subscription
$69.00	6 month subscription
$39.00	3 month subscription

Please read the **Terms of Service** *at http://www.baseballhq.com/terms.html*

Not Ready to Commit?

Get a FREE Weekly Sample of All the Baseball HQ Goodies with…

Fantasy baseball's #1 premium information service brings you the industry's #1 analytical weekly e-mail newsletter — **ABSOLUTELY FREE!**

Baseball HQ Friday is your link to exclusive insights from the experts at Baseball HQ. Every Friday afternoon, you'll receive news analyses and strategies from the top analysts in the game — perennial winners of national experts competitions. It's your direct connection to a fantasy baseball title in 2007!

Every Friday, from January 26 through September 8, you'll receive:

- Comprehensive player analyses
- Cutting edge statistical insight
- Innovative game strategies
- Ron Shandler's Master Notes
- Reviews, discounts and more!

And there's no obligation. It's FREE.

GO TO

http://www.baseballhq.com/friday96.shtml

and sign up TODAY!

DAVITT **ANDRES** **KRUSE** **McKAMEY**

Uncover the inner workings of what it takes to win with Baseball HQ's weekly radio podcast. Join host Patrick Davitt, our top analysts and special guests, each week from February through August, for interviews and insights. All shows are FREE 30+ minute mp3 files available for download or subscription through iTunes.

SAMPLE 2006 PROGRAMS (Still available at the URL below)

March 4: Rob Gordon on rookie pitchers who could win jobs in Spring Training. Ray Murphy on the "phased" approach to straight drafting. Ron Shandler offers his Master Notes and we answer some questions from the HQ subscriber forums.

March 11: Harold Nichols on Spring Training battles to watch. Brandon Kruse talks about applying HQ tools to salary-cap points games. John Burnson talks about the importance of "perspective" in considering pitchers.

April 1: Rob Gordon on prospects who made it onto rosters during spring training - and a few who didn't. Ray Murphy talks about his participation in the National Fantasy Baseball Championship. Host Patrick Davitt talks about how to cope with inflation in keeper leagues. Ron Shandler has his Top 10 Draft Day tips in his weekly Master Notes.

April 22: Brandon Kruse analyzes how some players' unusual starts could impact salary-cap games. Deric McKamey talks about some prospects who are changing positions. Andy Andres updates the AL and Harold Nichols updates the NL. Ron Shandler continues his discussion of starting pitchers.

May 27: NEW — Deric McKamey updates players called up to The Show and Brandon Kruse reviews Baseball HQ's Top 10 Hot Lists. Andy Andres and Harold Nichols update the AL and NL. Ron Shandler's Master Notes.

June 10: In a Baseball HQ Roundtable, Ron Shandler and Ray Murphy join host Patrick Davitt for a free-wheeling discussion of trading... How to decide when the time is right, how to approach potential trading partners, and how to trade tactically. Deric McKamey on call-ups. Brandon Kruse reviews the Top 10 Hot Lists. Andy Andres and Harold Nichols update the AL and NL.

June 17: In another Baseball HQ Roundtable, minor-league experts Deric McKamey and Rob Gordon discuss the June Amateur Draft as well as which rookies and prospects to target — and avoid — if you're looking to rebuild for 2007. Rob also updates call-ups. Brandon Kruse reviews the Top 10 Hot Lists. Andy Andres and Harold Nichols update the AL and NL, and Ron Shandler has his regular Master Notes.

July 15: Our All-Star edition features an HQ Radio Round table discussion with analysts John Burnson and Ray Murphy sharing their mid-season all-star fantasy teams for the AL and NL, and their picks for the MVPs and Cy Youngs in both leagues. Brandon Kruse and Harold Nichols discuss the AL and NL, with Harold focusing on players in the big Nationals-Reds trade this week. Deric McKamey has minor-league call-ups. Ron Shandler talks about the importance of patience and the joy of the long season in his regular Master Notes.

August 26: Our last show for the season brings Ray Murphy and Ron Shandler in for a roundtable discussion of the 2006 fantasy season -- surprises, disappointments, big stories and lessons learned. Andy Andres and Harold Nichols update the AL and NL. Rob Gordon updates callups, including Dustin Pedroia and J.R. House. Shandler talks about trading rules in his regular Master Notes.

LISTEN NOW — it's FREE!
http://www.baseballhq.com/radio/

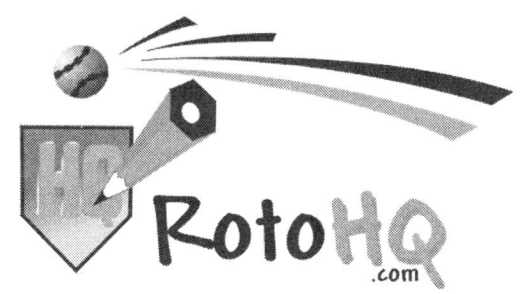

The Industry's Largest Online Library of Rotisserie and Fantasy Tools and Strategies

Other sources give you the news, stats and analysis, but don't tell you **how** to win. RotoHQ.com provides you with a grasp of the economics, an education in the psychology of competition, and a unique perspective on what it takes to win.

RotoHQ.com includes *hundreds* of essays, and *thousands* of tips on league management, draft management, in-season tactical planning, free agent strategies, trading philosophies, and much more. Includes essays, worksheets and checklists.

2007 Season Subscription $12.95
FREE TOPIC PREVIEW at
www.rotohq.com

RotoLab Draft Software

RotoLab is both a draft preparation program and an in-draft management tool. Just make the roster moves and player selections, and the program handles the rest... automatically! All budget calculations, inflation changes, player lists, team stats and standing totals are a single mouse click away. And... **RotoLab comes loaded with industry-leading player projections from BaseballHQ.com!**

... Easy to use interface
... Sort, search and filter data at the click of a mouse
... 5 years of historical and projected stats
... User notes for each player
... Drag-and-drop player moves
... Two-click operation to draft players
... Flexible league setup options
... Customizable valuation process
... User-definable player list
... Roster management from a single screen
... Cheat Sheet and full stat views to draft from

Download the FREE DEMO at
www.rotolab.com
HUGE discount for Baseball HQ subscribers!

OFFICIAL LOGO MERCHANDISE

RULES

1. Draft skills, not stats.
2. Once you display a skill, you own it.
3. This is not a game of precision. It is a game of human beings and tendencies.
4. This is not a game of projections. It is a game of market value versus real value.
4. Exercise excruciating patience.
5. It's easier to be crappy than it is to be good.
6. Chronically injured players never suddenly get healthy.
7. Right brain dominance has a very long shelf life.
8. Poor second halves don't get recognized until it's too late.
10. 100% of winnings must be spent on significant others.

   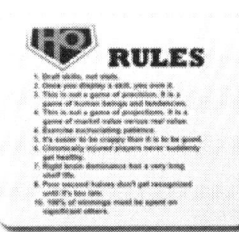

TO ORDER THESE PRODUCTS, and MORE:
http://www.cafepress.com/baseballhq

"The opportunity to interact with experts as well as proven local winners to build strategies and enhance player knowledge is unparalleled... the best roto investment you can make!"
— M.Dodge, Hockessin DE

FIRST PITCH 2007

Get a head start on the 2007 season with a unique opportunity to go one-on-one with some of the top writers and analysts in the fantasy baseball industry. First Pitch Forums bring the experts to some of the top cities in the USA for lively and informative symposium sessions.

Theme for 2007: "20 Lists of Competitive Intelligence"
These 3-hour sessions combine player analysis with fantasy drafting, interactive activities and fun! You've never experienced anything so informational and entertaining! We've selected the top 20 issues, topics and strategies that could make or break your fantasy season...

- Top first-round no-brainers to ignore
- Top players who could start the year on the DL
- Top in-draft strategies to confuse your opponents
- Top speculative minor league end-gamers
- Top bullpens with hidden value
- Top undervalued hitters you should grab early
- Top end-game picks with the most upside
- and 13 more lists!

Ron Shandler and *Baseball Injury Report's* Rick Wilton chair the sessions, bringing a dynamic energy to every event. They are joined by guest experts from Baseball HQ and some of the leading sports media sources. Past panelists have included Jim Callis *(Baseball America)*, Steve Moyer *(Baseball Info Solutions)* and Todd Zola *(FantasyBaseball.com)*. Speakers for 2007 will be announced in December.

What you get for your registration...
- Three hours of baseball talk with some of the industry's top analysts
- The chance to have *your* questions answered, 1-on-1 with the experts
- The opportunity to network with fellow fantasy leaguers from your area
- Freebies and discounts from leading industry vendors

2007 SITES
Dates are tentative. Check the forum website in December for more information.

BOSTON	March 4
CHICAGO	March 10
LOS ANGELES	March 11
MILWAUKEE	March 11
NEW YORK	March 3
PHILADELPHIA	March 2
PHOENIX	Nov. 2-4
SAN FRANCISCO	March 9-10
WASHINGTON DC	March 1

REGISTRATION RATE:
$29 per person in advance
$39 per person at the door

More details coming soon at
www.firstpitchforums.com

Deric McKamey's 2007
MINOR LEAGUE BASEBALL ANALYST

Deric McKamey's **Minor League Baseball Analyst** is the first book to fully integrate sabermetrics and scouting. A long-term Bill James disciple and graduate of Major League Baseball's scout school, Deric provides his unique brand of analysis for over 1000 minor leaguers. For baseball analysts and those who play in fantasy leagues with farm systems, the **Analyst** is the perfect complement to the *Baseball Forecaster* and is designed exactly for your needs:

- *Stats and Sabermetrics...* Over three dozen categories for 1000 minor leaguers, including batter skills ratings, pitch repertoires and more
- *Performance Trends...* spanning each player's last five minor league stops, complete with leading indicators
- *Scouting reports...* for all players, including expected major league debuts, potential major league roles and more
- *Major League Equivalents...* Five year scans for every player
- *Mega-Lists...* The Top 100 of 2007, retrospective looks at the Top 100's of 2003-2006, organizational Top 15's, top prospects by position, power and speed prospects, and more
- *Strategy essays...* on drafting and managing your fantasy team's farm system
- *NEW! Player Potential Ratings...* Deric's exclusive system that evaluates each player's upside potential and chances of achieving that potential.

Available January 2007

Minor League Baseball Analyst
.... $19.95
plus $4.50 Priority Mail shipping and handling

BOOKS from Shandler Enterprises

John Burnson's 2007
GRAPHICAL PLAYER

NOW INCLUDES BATTER CHARTS!

John Burnson's **Graphical Player 2007** is a new way to view statistics. Instead of columns of numbers, it presents its data in the most natural and immediate way -- visually! The new 4th Edition includes more charts and graphs than ever before — complete profiles of over 750 players, each described in several multi-faceted graphs and charts. It includes:

PITCHERS
- Daily pitching logs
- Rolling rates of strikeouts, walks, and ground balls
- Each pitcher's full career workload
- Career trends in fantasy value for 4x4 and 5x5 leagues
- Each pitcher's hit and strand rates over his career
- A three-year snapshot of "Deserved Wins"
- A new probabilistic form of Expected ERA

BATTERS
- Daily hitting logs
- Games played by position, with 3-year playing time snapshot
- Rolling strikeout rates, power index, more
- Batting average scan, OPS, injuries
- OPS versus RH and LH pitchers and compared to peers at position
- Career trends in power and speed, compared to peers at position

Available NOW!

Graphical Player
.... $21.95
plus $4.50 Priority Mail shipping and handling

Art McGee's
HOW TO VALUE PLAYERS FOR ROTISSERIE® BASEBALL Second Edition

Finally... McGee's SGP's are back! Learn how to calculate the best player values for your draft or auction! Art McGee applies concepts from economics, finance, and statistics to develop a pricing method that far surpasses any other published. His method is highly sophisticated, yet McGee explains it in terms that any fantasy baseball owner can understand and apply. In this new Second Edition...

- Discover the power of Standings Gain Points (SGP)
- Learn how to adjust values for position scarcity, injury risk and future potential
- Set up your own pricing spreadsheet, as simple or sophisticated as you want
- Make better decisions on trades, free agents, and long-term contracts
- Apply these methods even if your league uses non-standard categories or has a non-standard number of teams
- PLUS... 10 new essays to expand your knowledge base.

Celebrate the 10th anniversary of a landmark book with this completely revised and updated edition!

Available January 2007

How to Value Players for Rotisserie Baseball
.... **$17.95**
plus $4.50 Priority Mail shipping and handling

BOOKS from Shandler Enterprises

Rick Wilton's
BASEBALL INJURY REPORT 2007 ANNUAL

The **Baseball Injury Report** is fantasy baseball's first and only all-injury web site. Led by Rick Wilton, fantasy baseball's first and most experienced injury analyst, BIR gathers information from a wide range of media, baseball and medical sources to provide you with detailed insight and analysis of current injury situations.

Rick Wilton's NEW! **Baseball Injury Report 2007 Annual** is the first book to chronicle baseball injuries that is designed specifically for fantasy analysis.

- 5-year injury history profiles for hundreds of players.
- In-depth profiles for a group of notable 2006 cases
- 5-year team disabled list tables
- Players to be concerned about in 2007
- Injury Study: Did the New Drug Policy have an impact on DL days in 2006?
- "Steroids: A Scientific Look" by Andy Andres
- Medical primer
- And much more!

http://www.baseball-injury-report.com/

Available February 2007

Baseball Injury Report 2007 Annual
.... **$12.95**
plus $4.50 Priority Mail shipping and handling

Uncommon Stats For Uncommon Fans
www.HeaterMagazine.com

THE WEEKLY BASEBALL MAGAZINE FOR THE 21st CENTURY

HEATER is the magazine that puts baseball front and center. Forget about any other baseball magazine – HEATER does it better: Better statistics... better comparisons... better advice... all of which means a <u>bigger</u> competitive advantage! Leave your leaguemates in the dust!

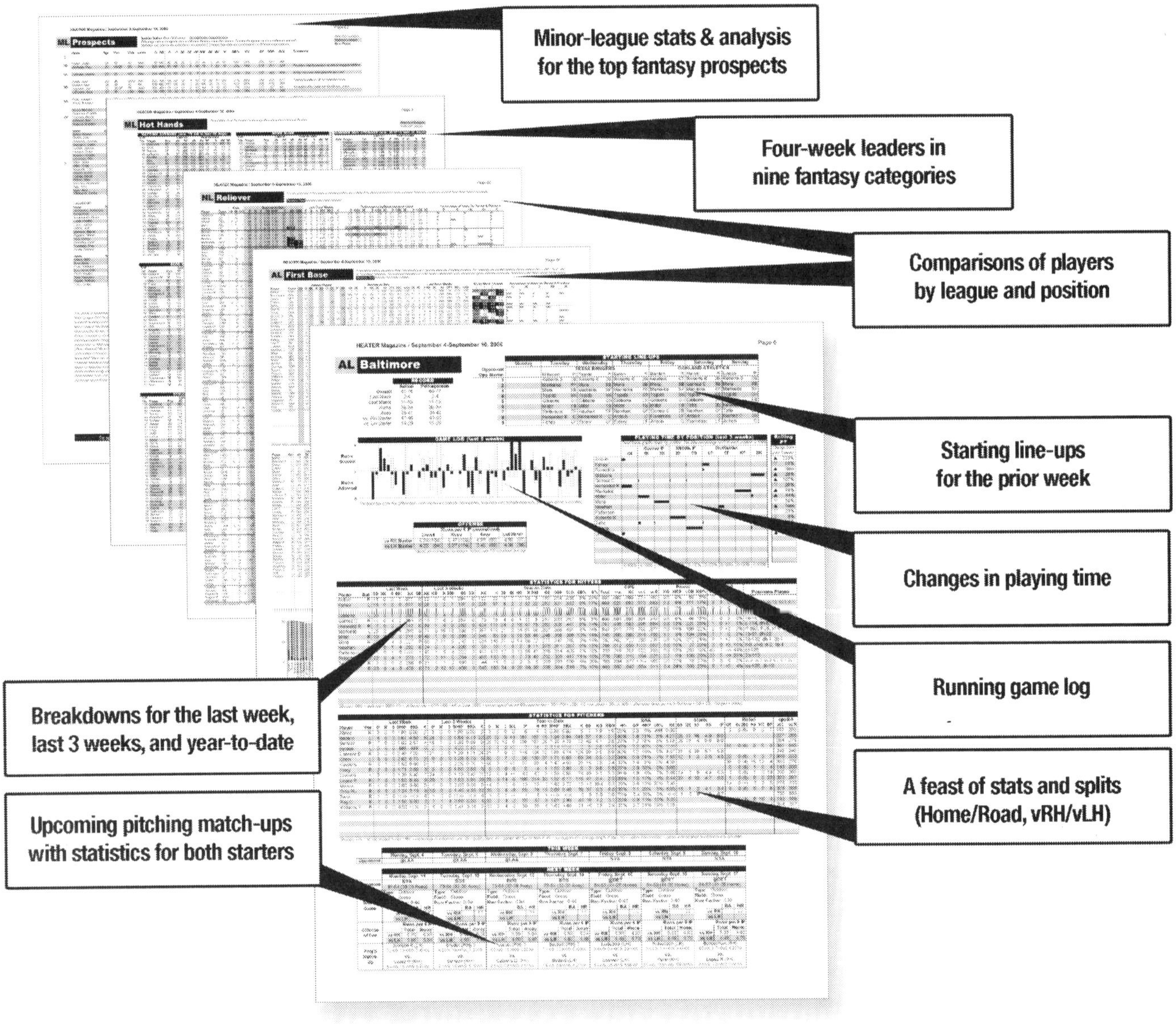

- **Minor-league stats & analysis for the top fantasy prospects**
- **Four-week leaders in nine fantasy categories**
- **Comparisons of players by league and position**
- **Starting line-ups for the prior week**
- **Changes in playing time**
- **Running game log**
- **A feast of stats and splits (Home/Road, vRH/vLH)**
- **Breakdowns for the last week, last 3 weeks, and year-to-date**
- **Upcoming pitching match-ups with statistics for both starters**

HEATER MAGAZINE is published 26 weeks a year during the regular season. We publish as a PDF – there is no special software needed. You can print or read HEATER from any computer! Every Wednesday, subscribers can look forward to 60 pages of cutting-edge stats & analysis.

See our full array of features – go to www.HeaterMagazine.com and download a free full issue.

EIGHT GREAT SITES...
ONE LOW PRICE!!!

Instead of relying on just one fantasy site, subscribe to RotoPass.com and get FULL access to all the best fantasy baseball sites at much less than it would cost to subscribe to them separately!

Ron Shandler's Baseball HQ - 3-time winner of FSTA's "Best Fantasy Baseball Site". 12 expert titles since 1998, including $100,000 NFBC in 2005. Consultant to the St. Louis Cardinals!

Fantasy baseball experts for XM Radio. Up to the second player news and draft kits for MLB, NFL, NBA, NHL, Nascar, PGA, NCAA hoops pools and more.

Fantasy Baseball expert for ESPN2's The Fantasy Show and Cold Pizza, ESPN News and MLB.com. 34 Fantasy Sports Writer Association nominations - more than twice as many as any other website in the industry!

Stats Fantasy Advantage gives you access to every stat you could possibly need!

The first and only site dedicated to fantasy draft preparation - for every sport!

3-time FSTA Award winner for best fantasy magazine. 4 issues a year, mailed right to your home!

JOIN NOW AND ALSO GET ACCESS TO THE AMAZING THEHUDDLE.COM
Voted #1 Fantasy Football site 5 years in a row by Internet Sports Awards!

What's winning worth to you?

When you subscribe to RotoPass.com you get the in-depth, up-to-the minute customizable draft kits, analysis, stats and news that have produced over 45 expert league titles and over 20 FSTA awards the last five years! Easy to use - just login once and now every site is one click away.

Join now and qualify for a discount of at least 10% off. Enter the URL - **www.rotopass.com/?partner=baseballhq** - then click "Join Now". If you are already a member of BBHQ, be sure to enter the email address associated with your current BBHQ membership and have the prorated value of the unused portion of your BBHQ membership applied to your RotoPass purchase. If you are not currently a member of BBHQ, use promo code BBHQ2007 for **10% OFF** of your RotoPass purchase!

www.RotoPass.com

"**The first book to capture the mix of numbers, personalities, and unhealthy love for baseball that makes fantasy baseball so enticing. It's hard not to be charmed.**"
—*The Baltimore Sun*

On sale February 27

"**I** have read many books on baseball, but none of them approach the delight, the zaniness, the lunacy, and the sheer reading pleasure of Sam Walker's *Fantasyland*."
—Buzz Bissinger, author of *Three Nights in August* and *Friday Night Lights*

"**M**r. Walker not only finds the humor in this world of the obsessed, he also finds the drama.... Entertaining and informative."
—Dan Barry, *The New York Times*

"**B**aseball has been so often dissected and analyzed over the years that it's easy to lose sight of the fact that it's a game people love—sometimes with a level of loyalty and commitment that staggers the mind. Sam Walker's *Fantasyland* is a book to remind everyone of that fact."
—Keith Hernandez, former New York Met

"**B**y far the funniest book written about our national pastime in the last decade."
—*Rocky Mountain News*

Penguin Books
A member of Penguin Group (USA) Inc.
www.penguin.com